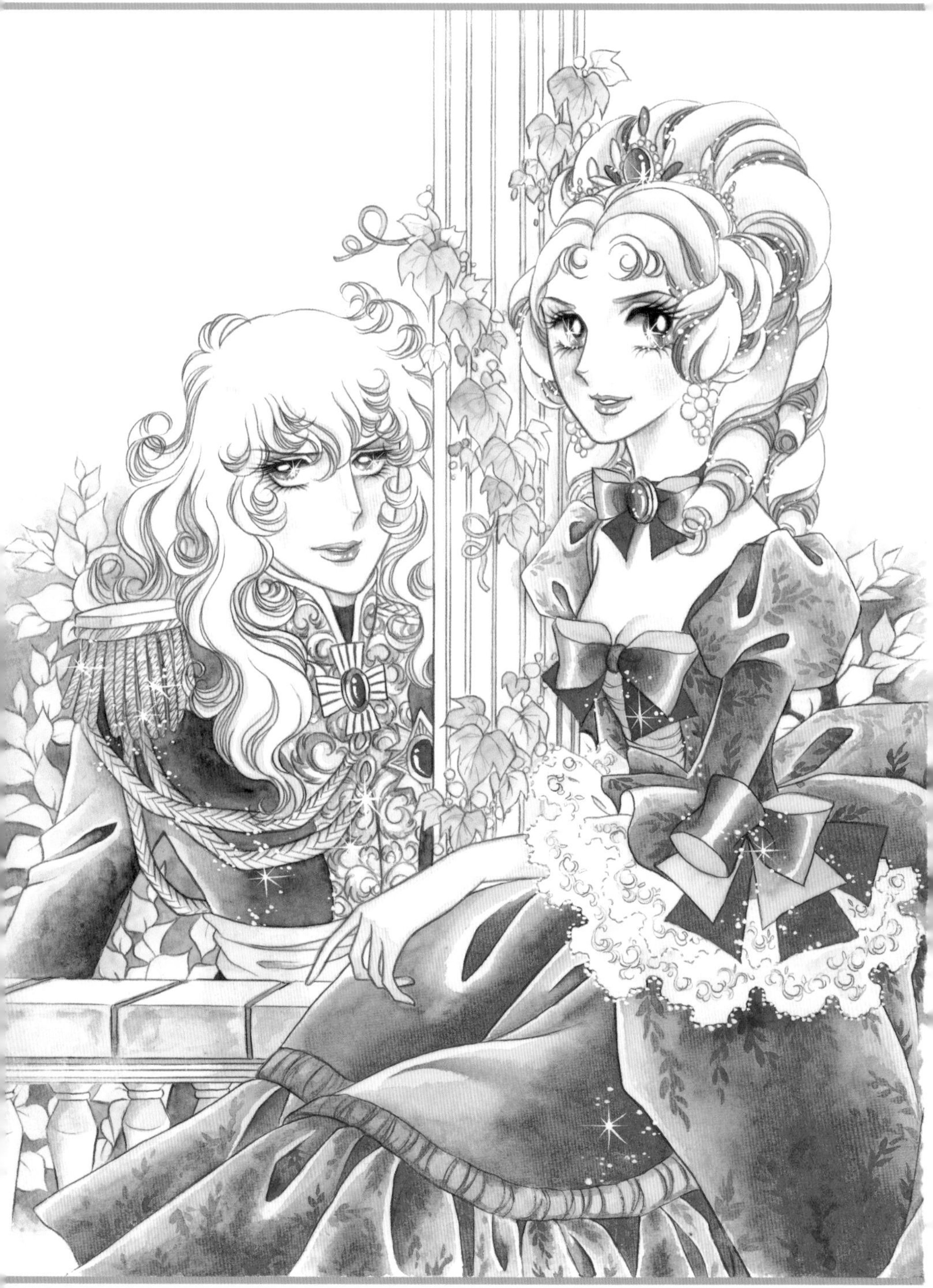

the ROSE of VERSAILLES

ベルサイユのばら

Riyoko Ikeda

the ROSE of VERSAILLES
ベルサイユのばら
Volume 2

English Edition Staff:

Translation: Episode 23-33: Mari Morimoto
Episode 34-44: Jocelyne Allen
Lettering and Touch Up: Jeannie Lee
Editor: Erica Friedman
Cover Design: Andy Tsang

Chief of Operations: Erik Ko
Director of Publishing: Matt Moylan
Associate Editor: M. Chandler
Project Manager: Janice Leung

Special Thanks to: Ms. Yayoi Arima and the staff at Shueisha Inc.
Chigusa Ogino and Alisa Sunago at Tuttle-Mori Agency.

**This English edition was re-edited and revised based on
the Perfect Edition published by SHUEISHA Inc. Tokyo**

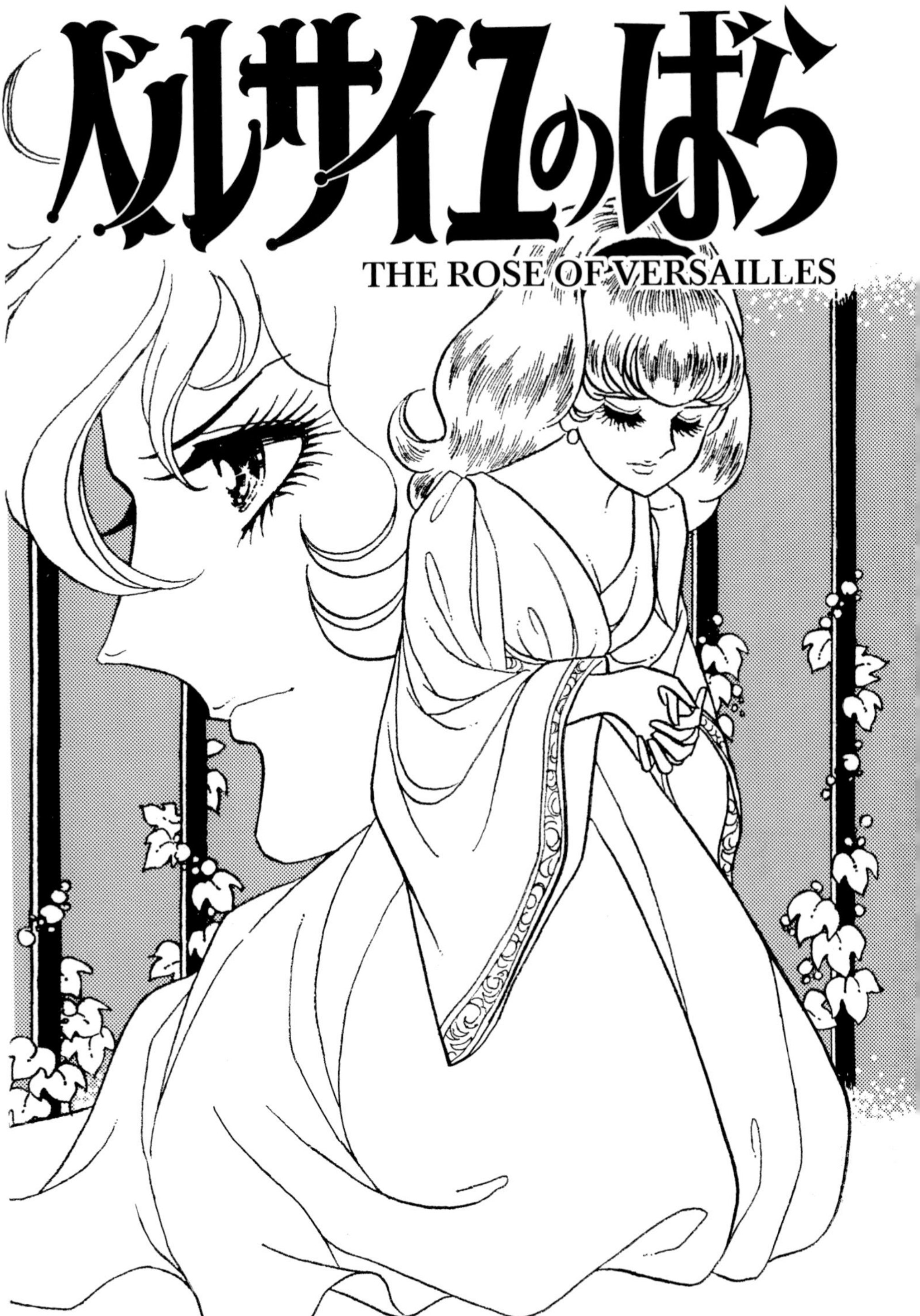
ベルサイユのばら
THE ROSE OF VERSAILLES

1973 WEEKLY MARGARET MAGAZINE
ISSUE 47 SPECIAL ITEM BADGE ART

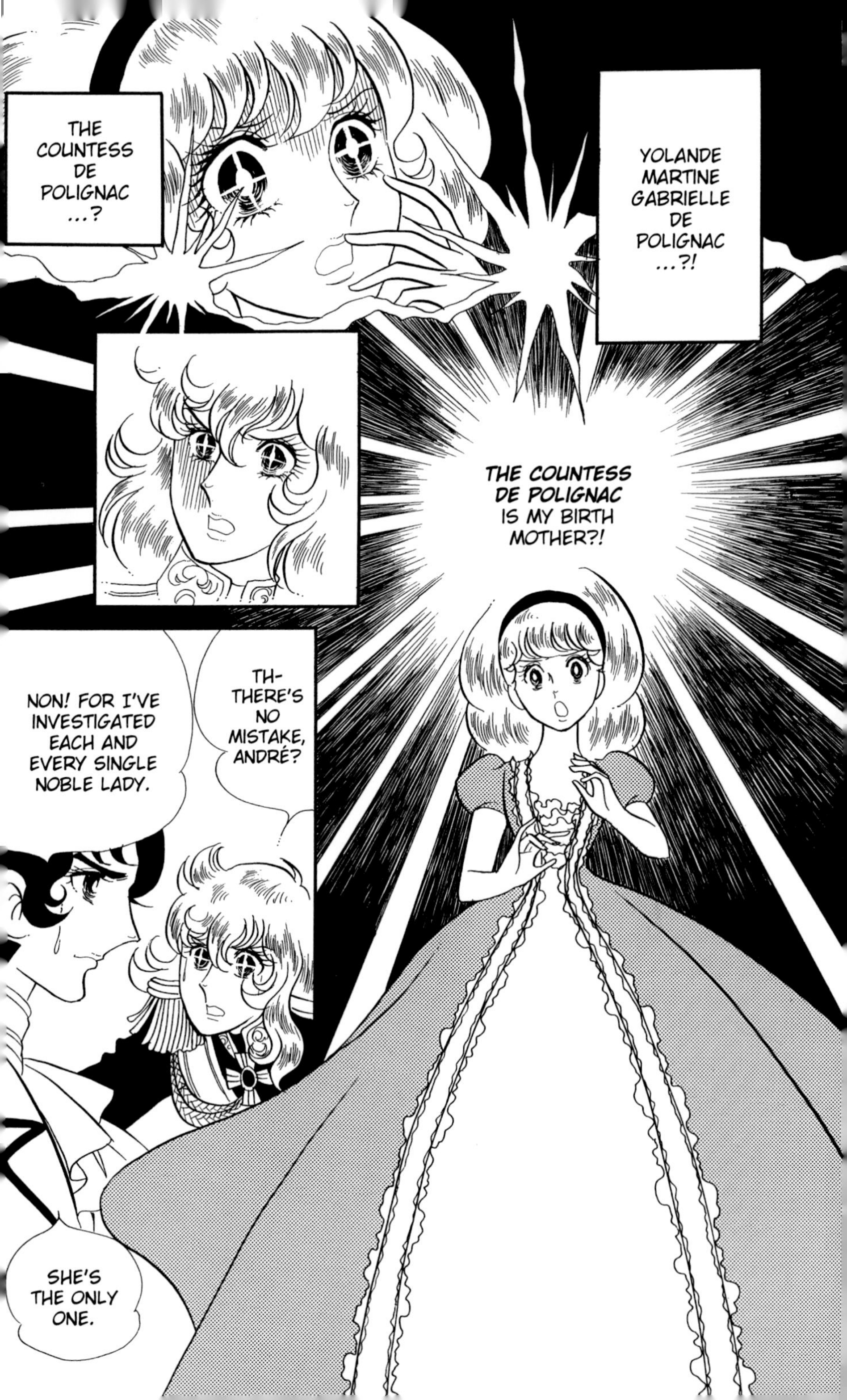
YOLANDE MARTINE GABRIELLE DE POLIGNAC ...?!
THE COUNTESS DE POLIGNAC ...?
THE COUNTESS DE POLIGNAC IS MY BIRTH MOTHER?!
TH-THERE'S NO MISTAKE, ANDRÉ?
NON! FOR I'VE INVESTIGATED EACH AND EVERY SINGLE NOBLE LADY.
SHE'S THE ONLY ONE.

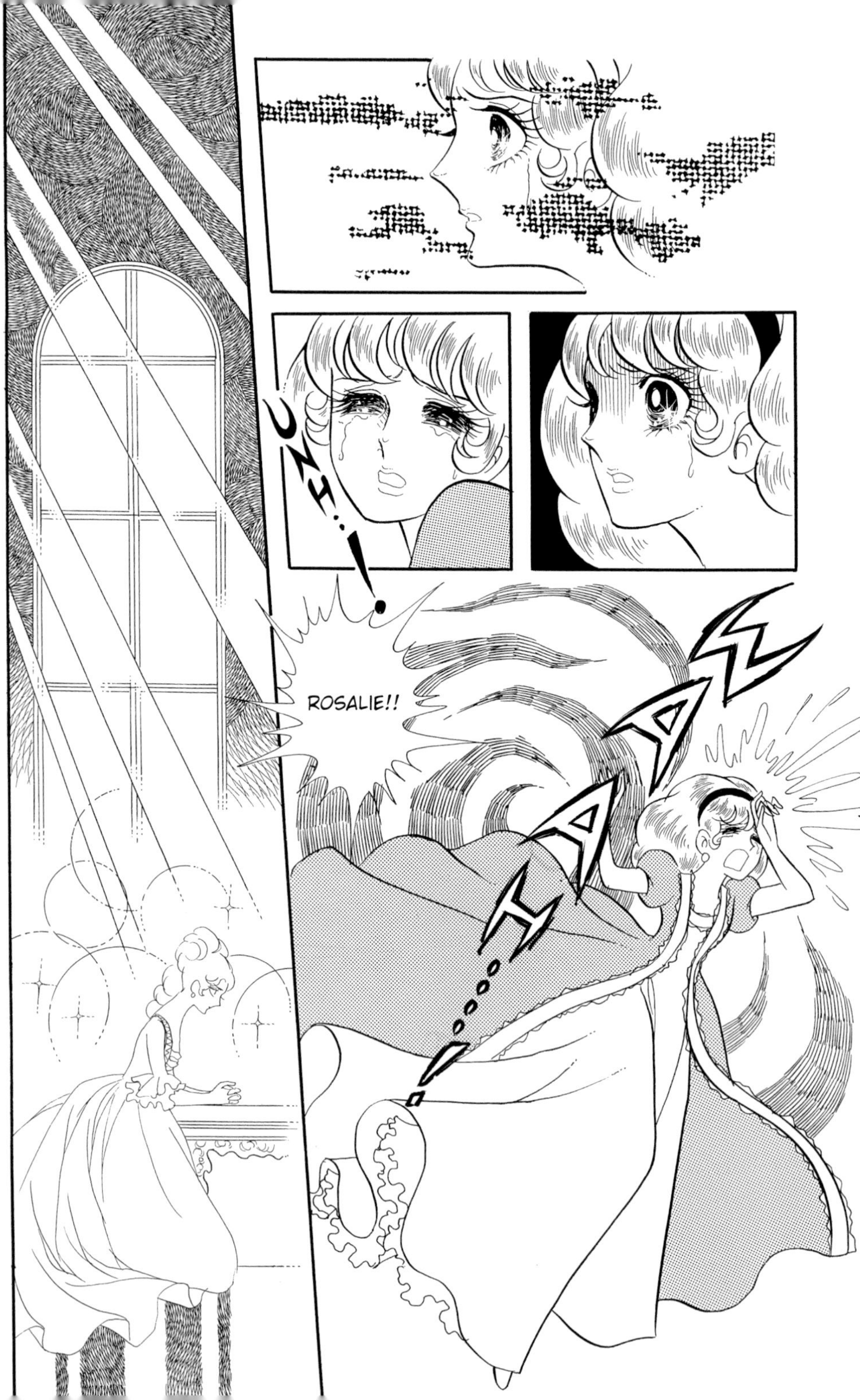

UNH...!
ROSALIE!!
HAAAW

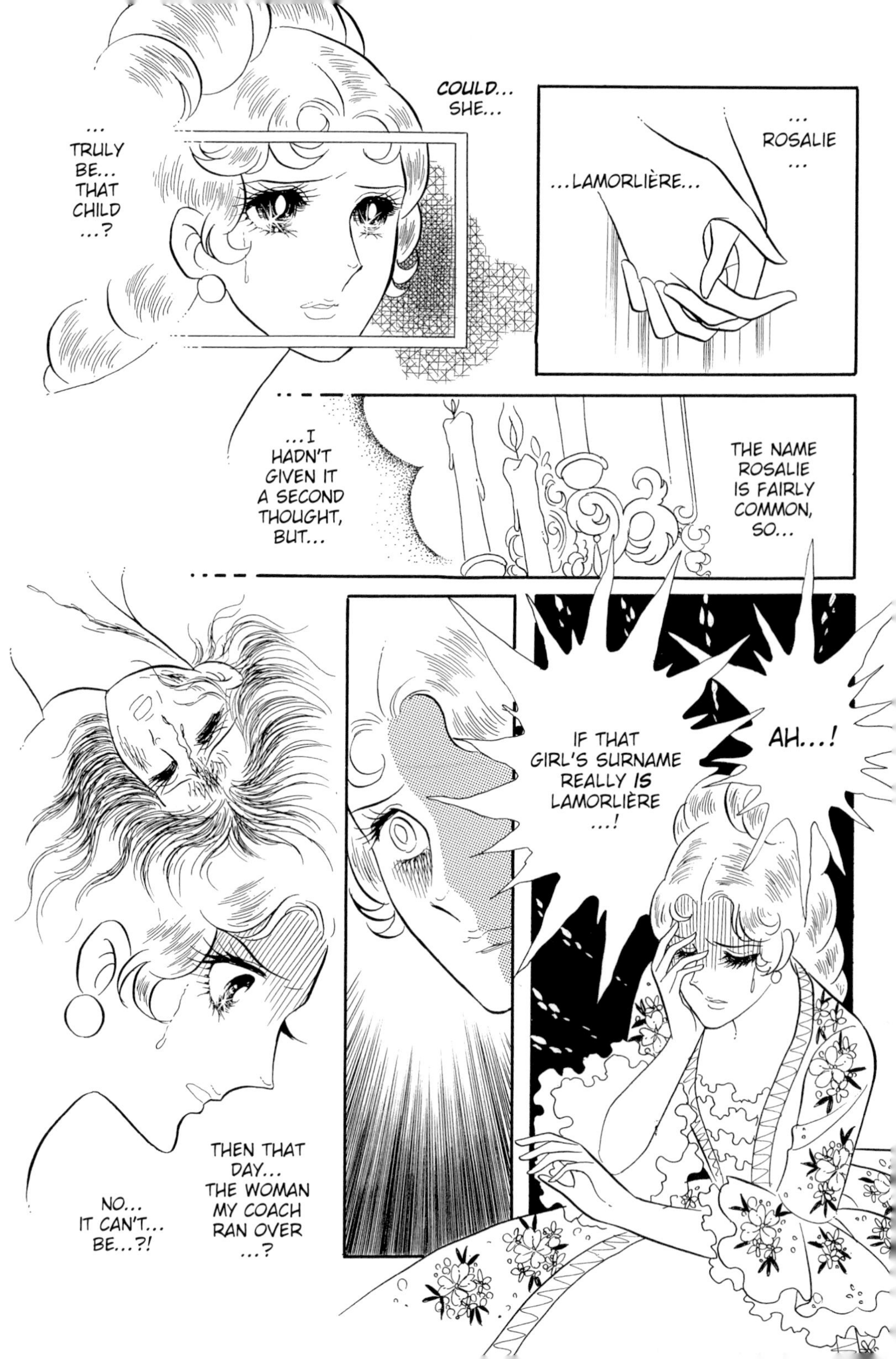
...ROSALIE...
...LAMORLIÈRE...
COULD... SHE...
...TRULY BE... THAT CHILD...?
THE NAME ROSALIE IS FAIRLY COMMON, SO...
...I HADN'T GIVEN IT A SECOND THOUGHT, BUT...
AH...!
IF THAT GIRL'S SURNAME REALLY IS LAMORLIÈRE...!
THEN THAT DAY... THE WOMAN MY COACH RAN OVER...?
NO... IT CAN'T... BE...?!

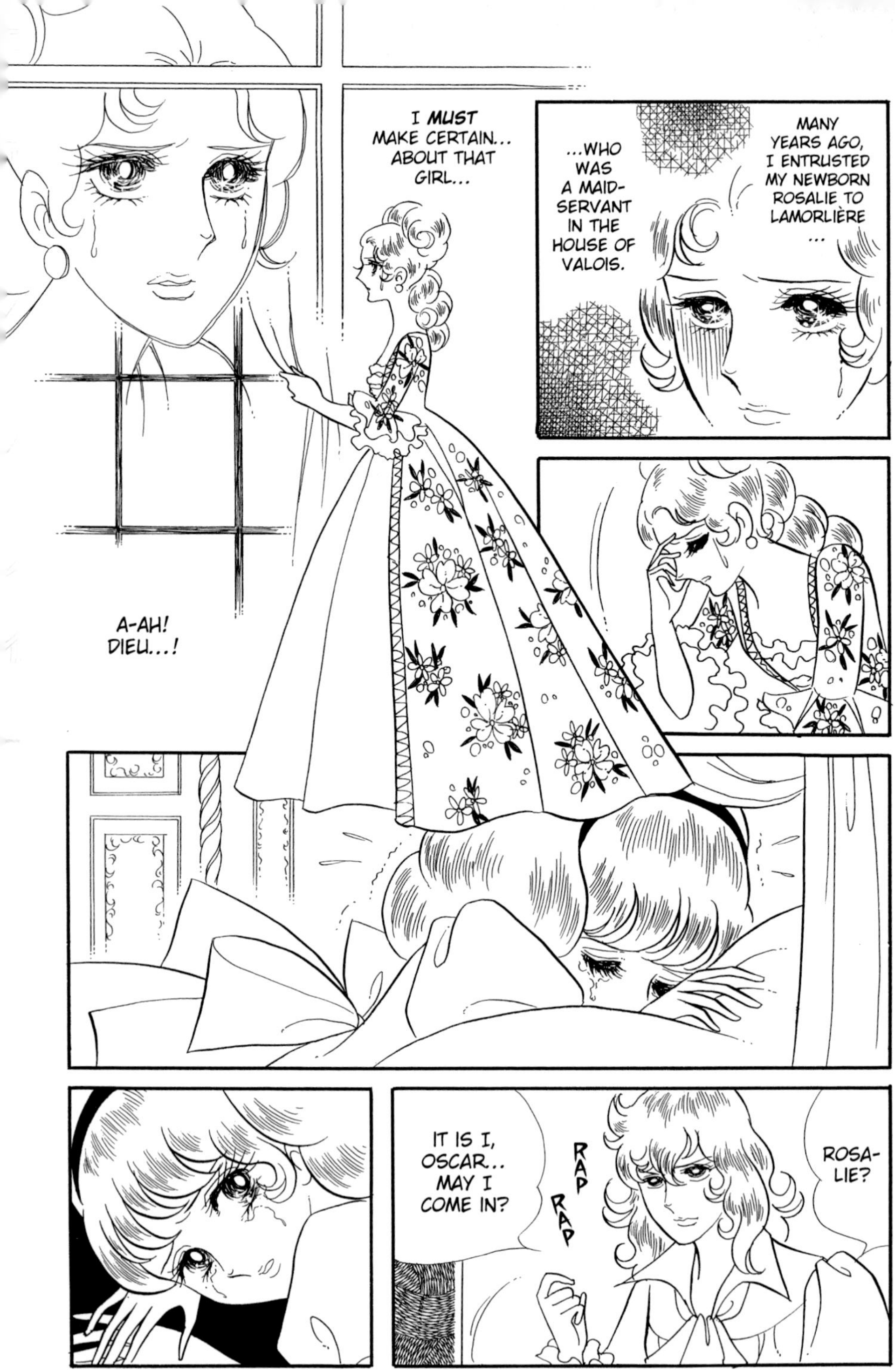
MANY YEARS AGO, I ENTRUSTED MY NEWBORN ROSALIE TO LAMORLIÈRE ...
...WHO WAS A MAID-SERVANT IN THE HOUSE OF VALOIS.
I MUST MAKE CERTAIN... ABOUT THAT GIRL...
A-AH! DIEU...!
ROSA-LIE?
RAP RAP
IT IS I, OSCAR.. MAY I COME IN?

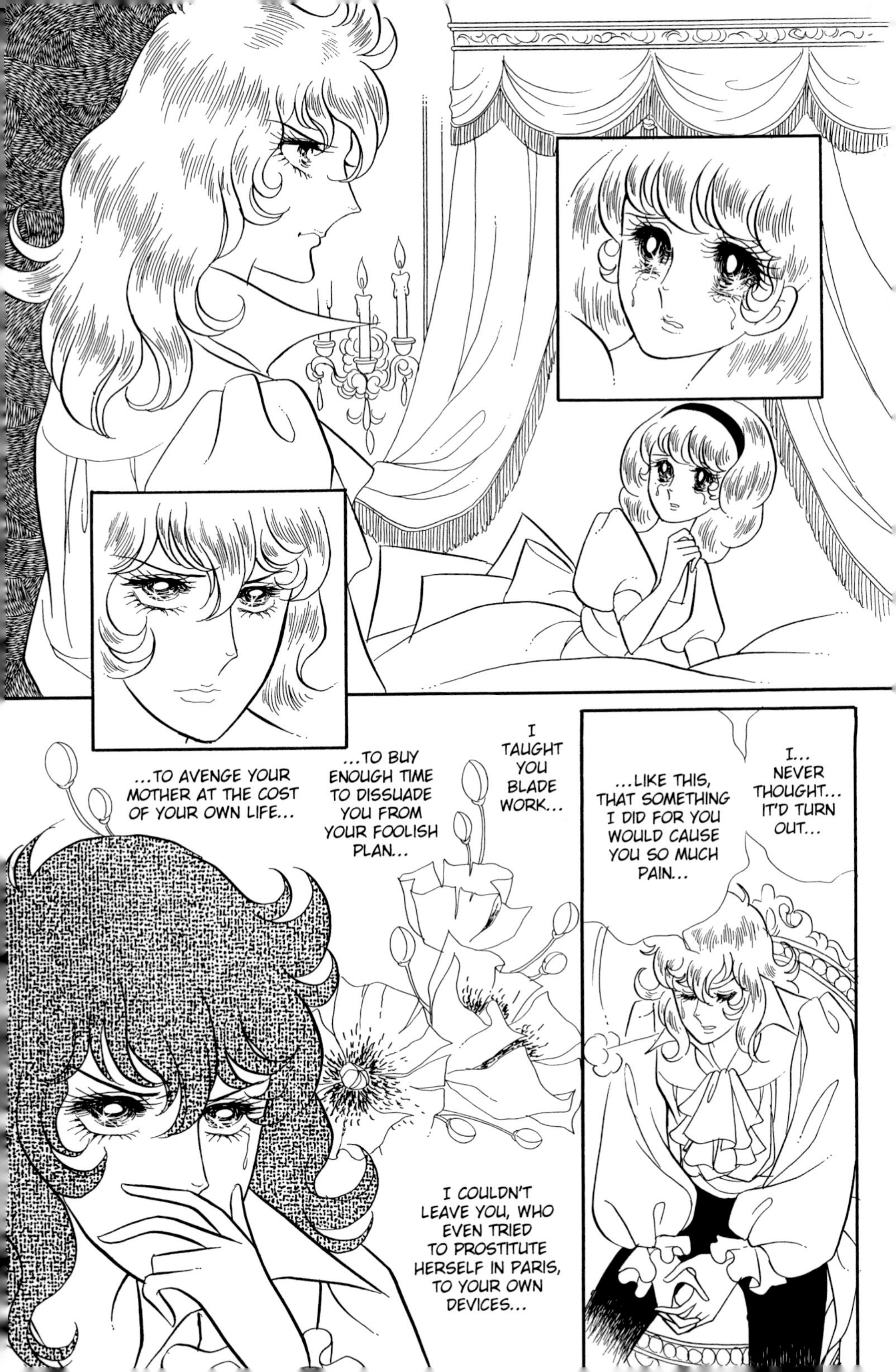
I... NEVER THOUGHT... IT'D TURN OUT...
...LIKE THIS, THAT SOMETHING I DID FOR YOU WOULD CAUSE YOU SO MUCH PAIN...
I TAUGHT YOU BLADE WORK...
...TO BUY ENOUGH TIME TO DISSUADE YOU FROM YOUR FOOLISH PLAN...
...TO AVENGE YOUR MOTHER AT THE COST OF YOUR OWN LIFE...
I COULDN'T LEAVE YOU, WHO EVEN TRIED TO PROSTITUTE HERSELF IN PARIS, TO YOUR OWN DEVICES...

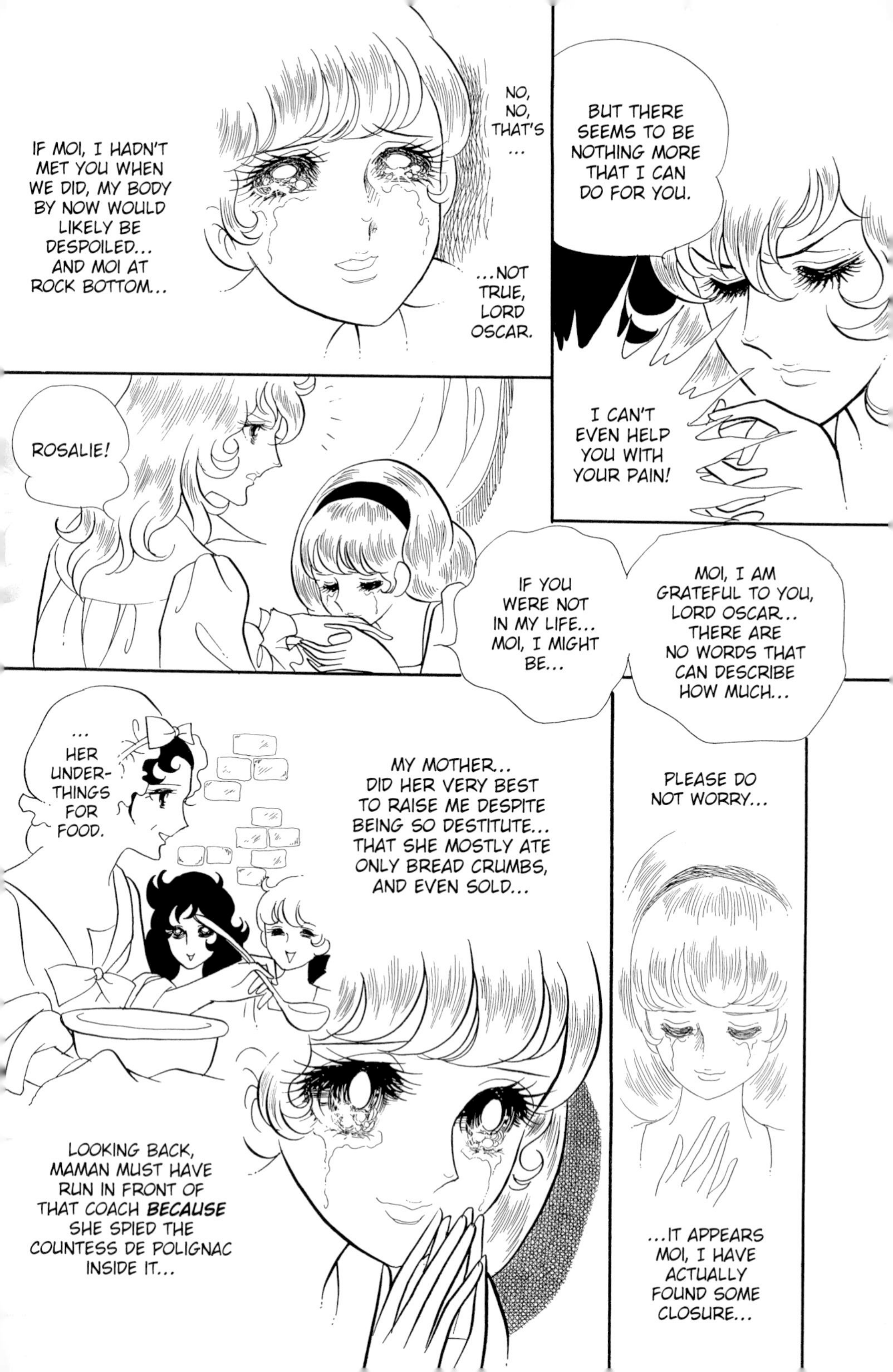

BUT THERE SEEMS TO BE NOTHING MORE THAT I CAN DO FOR YOU.
I CAN'T EVEN HELP YOU WITH YOUR PAIN!
NO, NO, THAT'S ...
...NOT TRUE, LORD OSCAR.
IF MOI, I HADN'T MET YOU WHEN WE DID, MY BODY BY NOW WOULD LIKELY BE DESPOILED... AND MOI AT ROCK BOTTOM...
MOI, I AM GRATEFUL TO YOU, LORD OSCAR.. THERE ARE NO WORDS THAT CAN DESCRIBE HOW MUCH...
IF YOU WERE NOT IN MY LIFE... MOI, I MIGHT BE...
ROSALIE!
PLEASE DO NOT WORRY...
...IT APPEARS MOI, I HAVE ACTUALLY FOUND SOME CLOSURE...
MY MOTHER... DID HER VERY BEST TO RAISE ME DESPITE BEING SO DESTITUTE... THAT SHE MOSTLY ATE ONLY BREAD CRUMBS, AND EVEN SOLD...
... HER UNDER-THINGS FOR FOOD.
LOOKING BACK, MAMAN MUST HAVE RUN IN FRONT OF THAT COACH **BECAUSE** SHE SPIED THE COUNTESS DE POLIGNAC INSIDE IT...

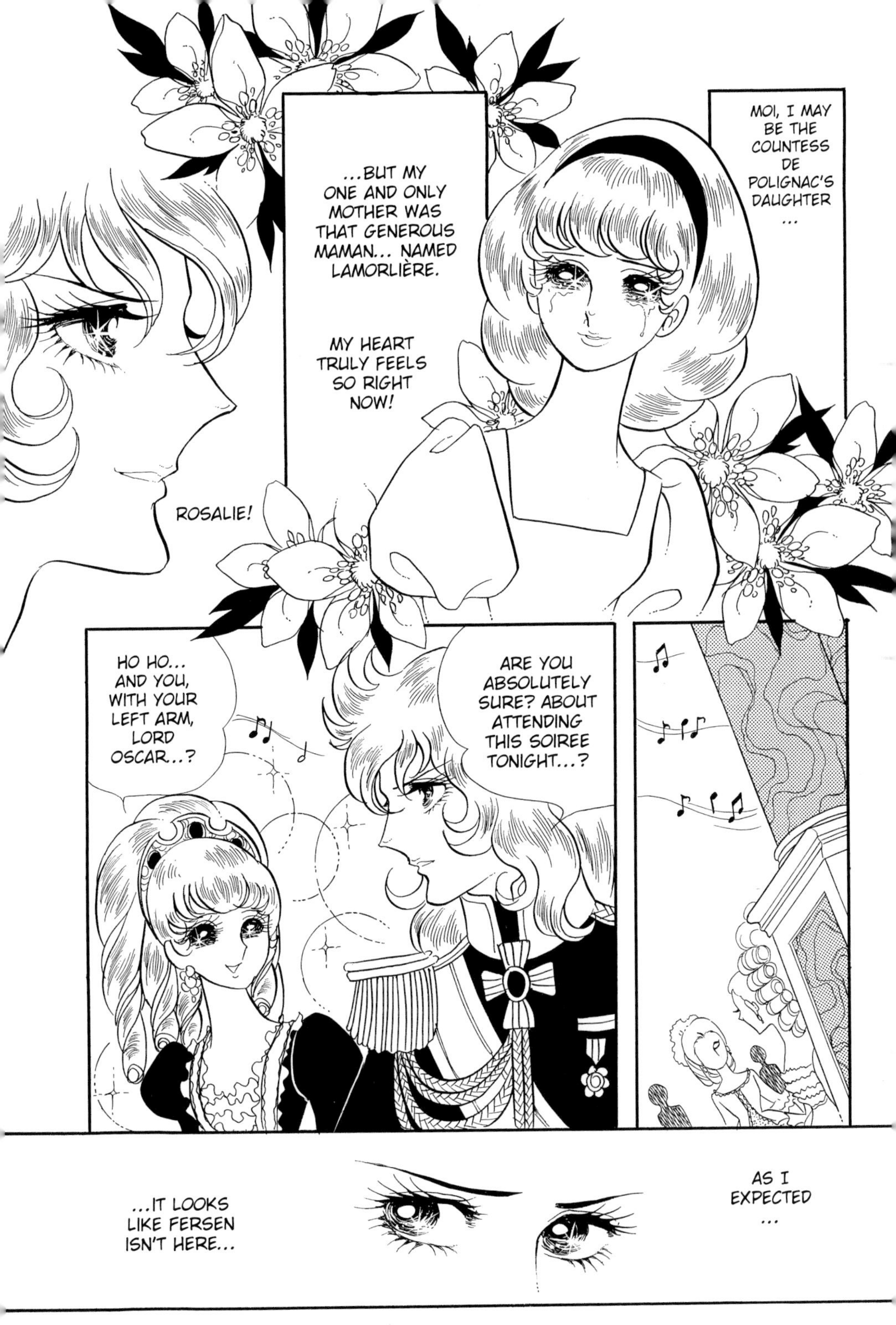
MOI, I MAY BE THE COUNTESS DE POLIGNAC'S DAUGHTER ...
...BUT MY ONE AND ONLY MOTHER WAS THAT GENEROUS MAMAN... NAMED LAMORLIÈRE.
MY HEART TRULY FEELS SO RIGHT NOW!
ROSALIE!
ARE YOU ABSOLUTELY SURE? ABOUT ATTENDING THIS SOIREE TONIGHT...?
HO HO... AND YOU, WITH YOUR LEFT ARM, LORD OSCAR...?
AS I EXPECTED ...
...IT LOOKS LIKE FERSEN ISN'T HERE...

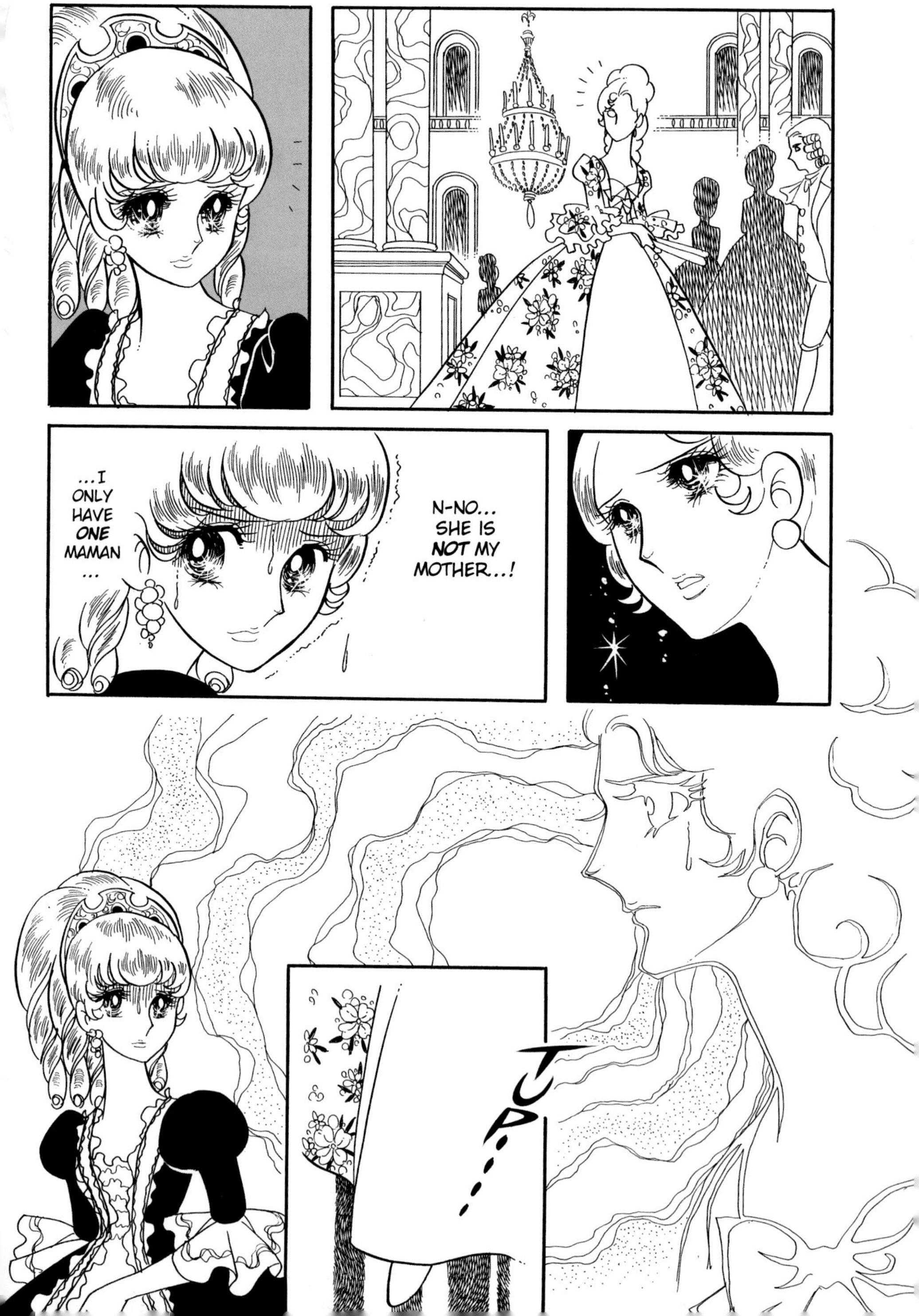

N-NO... SHE IS NOT MY MOTHER...!
...I ONLY HAVE ONE MAMAN...
TUP...

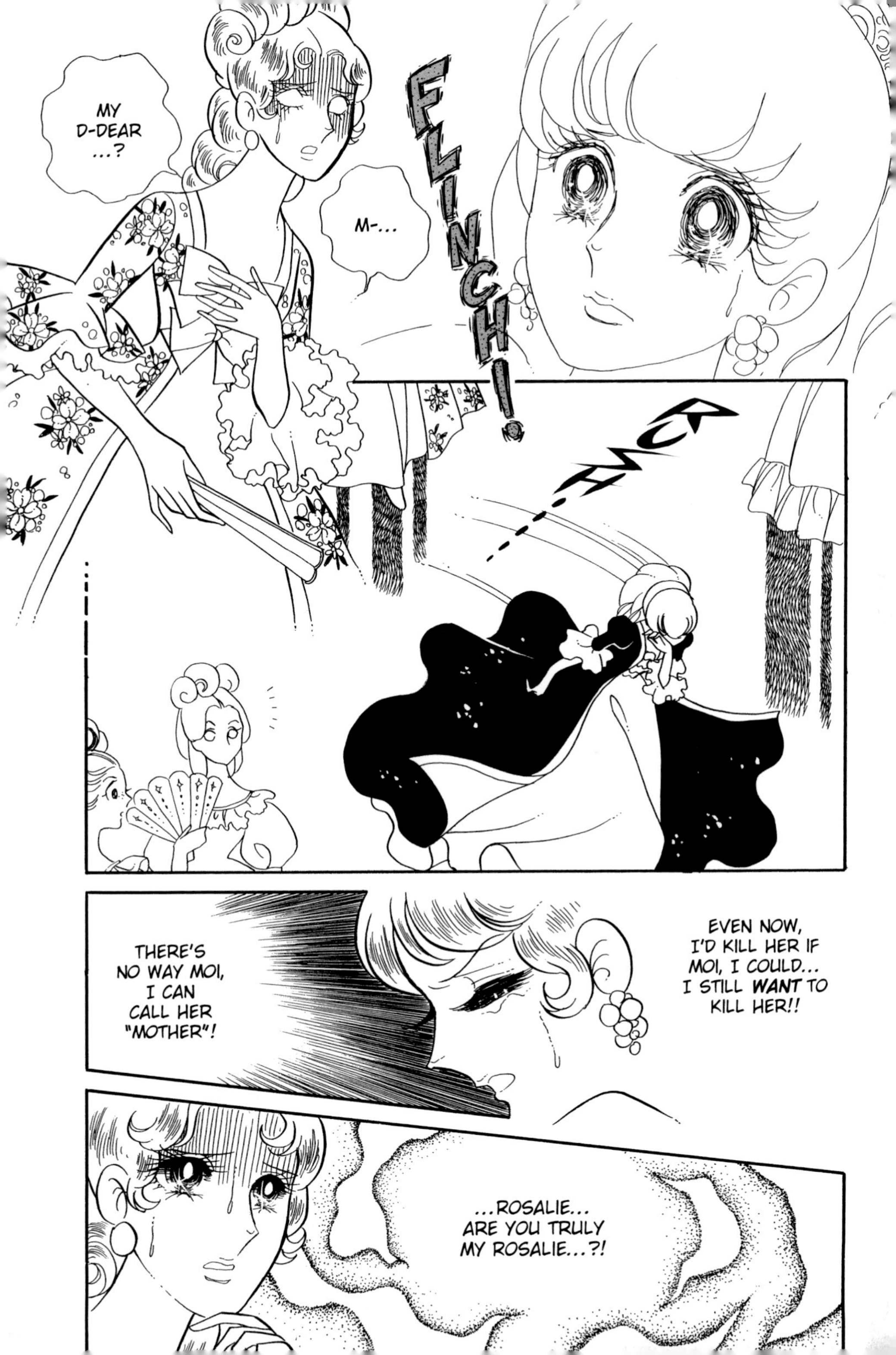
FLINCH!
M-...
MY D-DEAR ...?
EVEN NOW, I'D KILL HER IF MOI, I COULD... I STILL ***WANT*** TO KILL HER!!
THERE'S NO WAY MOI, I CAN CALL HER "MOTHER"!
...ROSALIE... ARE YOU TRULY MY ROSALIE...?!

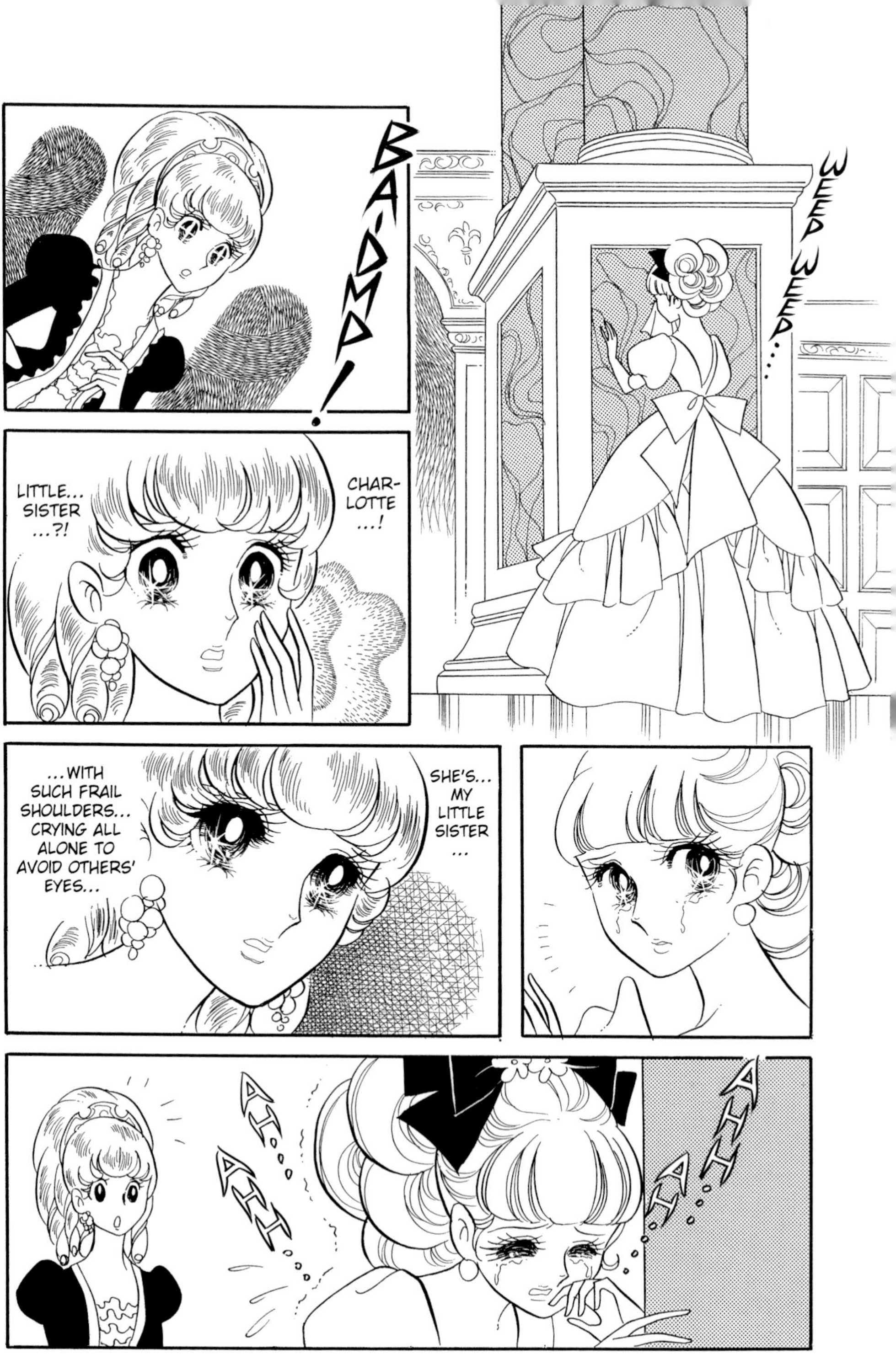
WEEP WEEP...
BA-DUMP!
CHAR-LOTTE...!
LITTLE... SISTER...?!
SHE'S... MY LITTLE SISTER...
...WITH SUCH FRAIL SHOULDERS... CRYING ALL ALONE TO AVOID OTHERS' EYES...
AHH... AHH...
AHH... AHH...

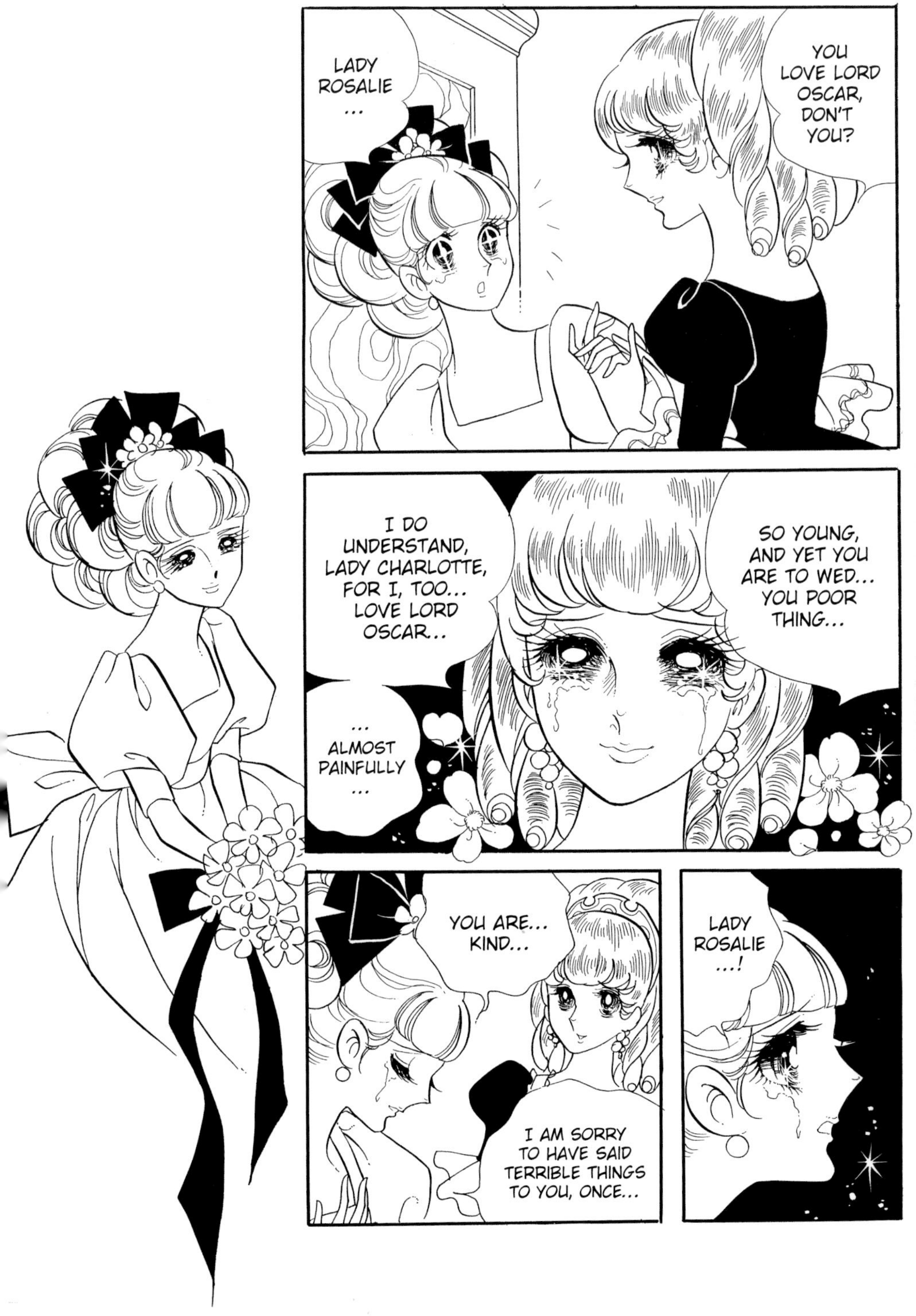
YOU LOVE LORD OSCAR, DON'T YOU?
LADY ROSALIE ...
SO YOUNG, AND YET YOU ARE TO WED... YOU POOR THING...
I DO UNDERSTAND, LADY CHARLOTTE, FOR I, TOO... LOVE LORD OSCAR...
... ALMOST PAINFULLY ...
LADY ROSALIE ...!
YOU ARE... KIND...
I AM SORRY TO HAVE SAID TERRIBLE THINGS TO YOU, ONCE...

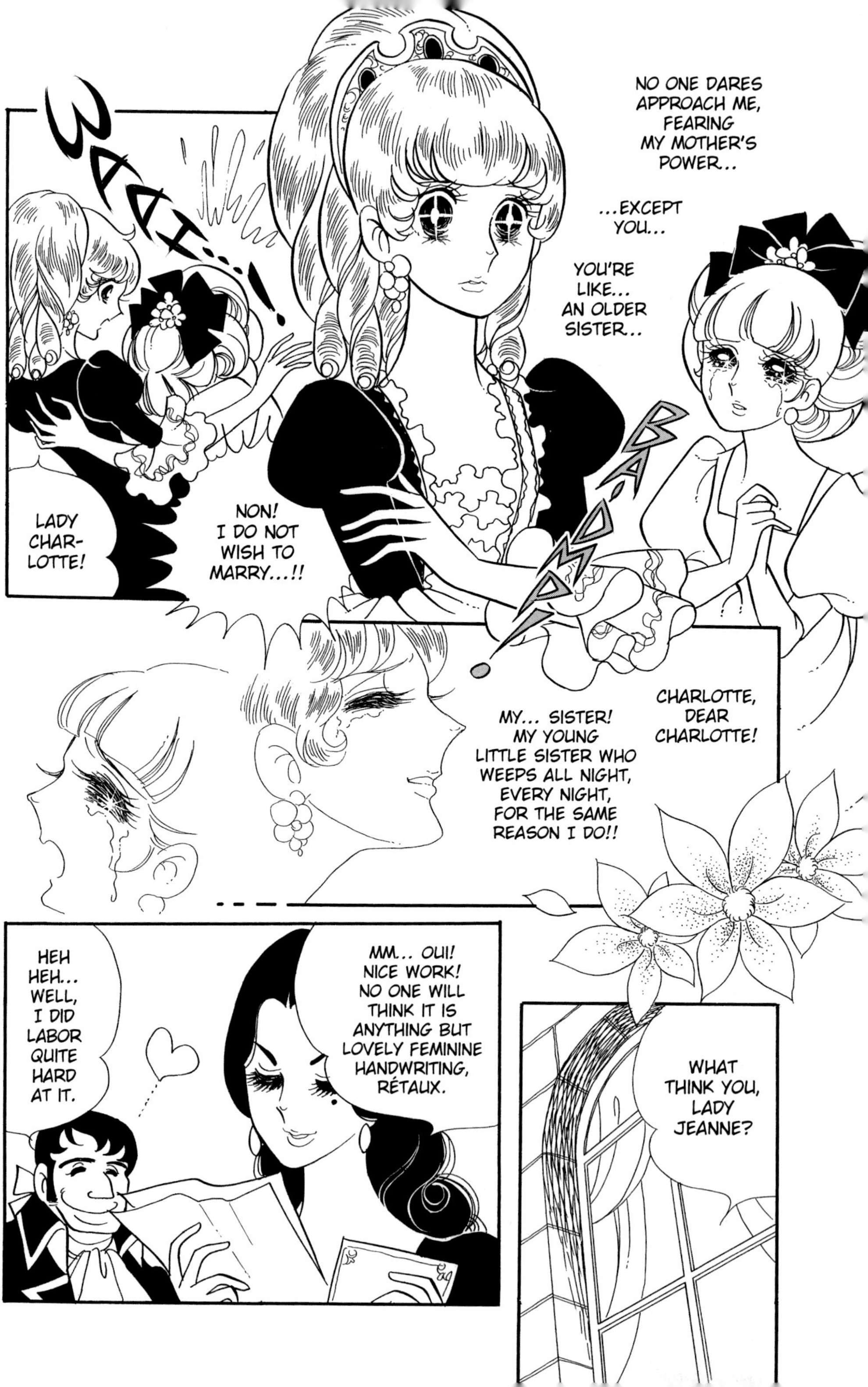
NO ONE DARES APPROACH ME, FEARING MY MOTHER'S POWER...
...EXCEPT YOU...
YOU'RE LIKE... AN OLDER SISTER...
BADAMP
BAAAI...!!
NON! I DO NOT WISH TO MARRY...!!
LADY CHAR-LOTTE!
CHARLOTTE, DEAR CHARLOTTE!
MY... SISTER! MY YOUNG LITTLE SISTER WHO WEEPS ALL NIGHT, EVERY NIGHT, FOR THE SAME REASON I DO!!
WHAT THINK YOU, LADY JEANNE?
MM... OUI! NICE WORK! NO ONE WILL THINK IT IS ANYTHING BUT LOVELY FEMININE HANDWRITING, RÉTAUX.
HEH HEH... WELL, I DID LABOR QUITE HARD AT IT.

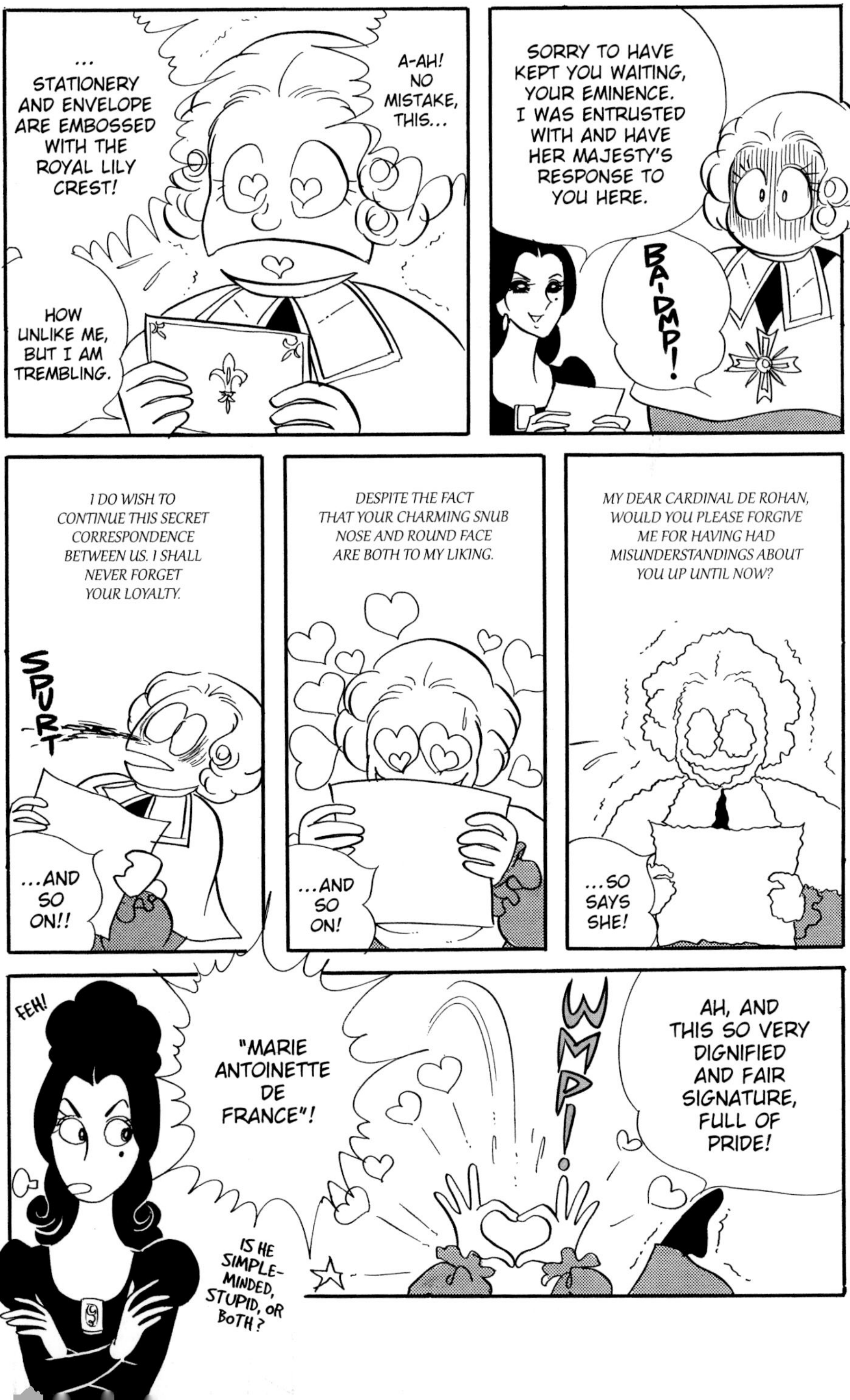
SORRY TO HAVE KEPT YOU WAITING, YOUR EMINENCE. I WAS ENTRUSTED WITH AND HAVE HER MAJESTY'S RESPONSE TO YOU HERE.
BA-DMP!
A-AH! NO MISTAKE, THIS...
... STATIONERY AND ENVELOPE ARE EMBOSSED WITH THE ROYAL LILY CREST!
HOW UNLIKE ME, BUT I AM TREMBLING.
MY DEAR CARDINAL DE ROHAN, WOULD YOU PLEASE FORGIVE ME FOR HAVING HAD MISUNDERSTANDINGS ABOUT YOU UP UNTIL NOW?
...SO SAYS SHE!
DESPITE THE FACT THAT YOUR CHARMING SNUB NOSE AND ROUND FACE ARE BOTH TO MY LIKING.
...AND SO ON!
I DO WISH TO CONTINUE THIS SECRET CORRESPONDENCE BETWEEN US. I SHALL NEVER FORGET YOUR LOYALTY.
SPURT
...AND SO ON!!
AH, AND THIS SO VERY DIGNIFIED AND FAIR SIGNATURE, FULL OF PRIDE!
WMP!
"MARIE ANTOINETTE DE FRANCE"!
FEH!
IS HE SIMPLE-MINDED, STUPID, OR BOTH?

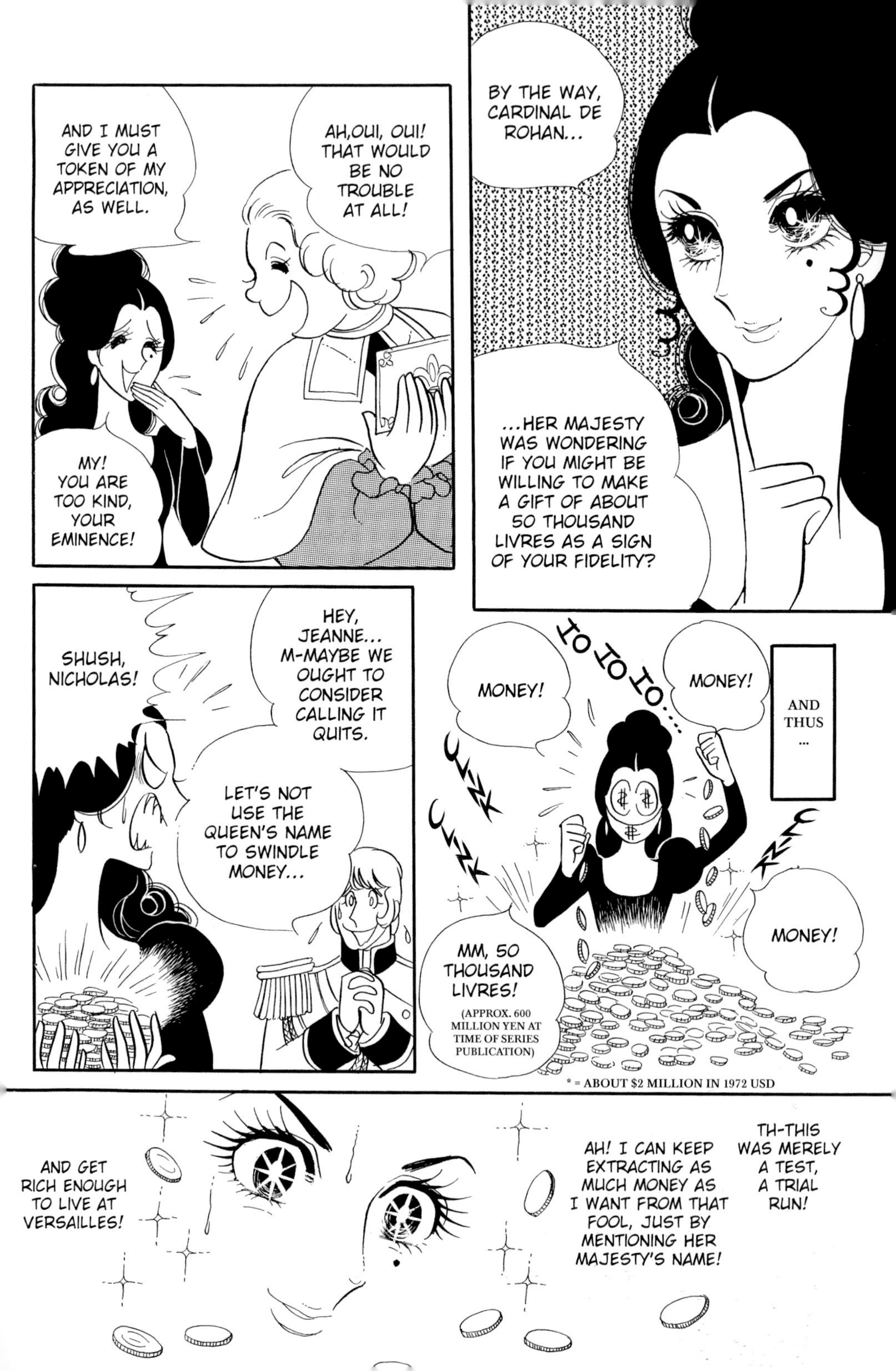
BY THE WAY, CARDINAL DE ROHAN...
...HER MAJESTY WAS WONDERING IF YOU MIGHT BE WILLING TO MAKE A GIFT OF ABOUT 50 THOUSAND LIVRES AS A SIGN OF YOUR FIDELITY?
AH,OUI, OUI! THAT WOULD BE NO TROUBLE AT ALL!
AND I MUST GIVE YOU A TOKEN OF MY APPRECIATION, AS WELL.
MY! YOU ARE TOO KIND, YOUR EMINENCE!
AND THUS ...
MONEY!
TOTOTO....
MONEY!
MONEY!
MM, 50 THOUSAND LIVRES!
(APPROX. 600 MILLION YEN AT TIME OF SERIES PUBLICATION)
HEY, JEANNE... M-MAYBE WE OUGHT TO CONSIDER CALLING IT QUITS.
SHUSH, NICHOLAS!
LET'S NOT USE THE QUEEN'S NAME TO SWINDLE MONEY...
* = ABOUT $2 MILLION IN 1972 USD
TH-THIS WAS MERELY A TEST, A TRIAL RUN!
AH! I CAN KEEP EXTRACTING AS MUCH MONEY AS I WANT FROM THAT FOOL, JUST BY MENTIONING HER MAJESTY'S NAME!
AND GET RICH ENOUGH TO LIVE AT VERSAILLES!

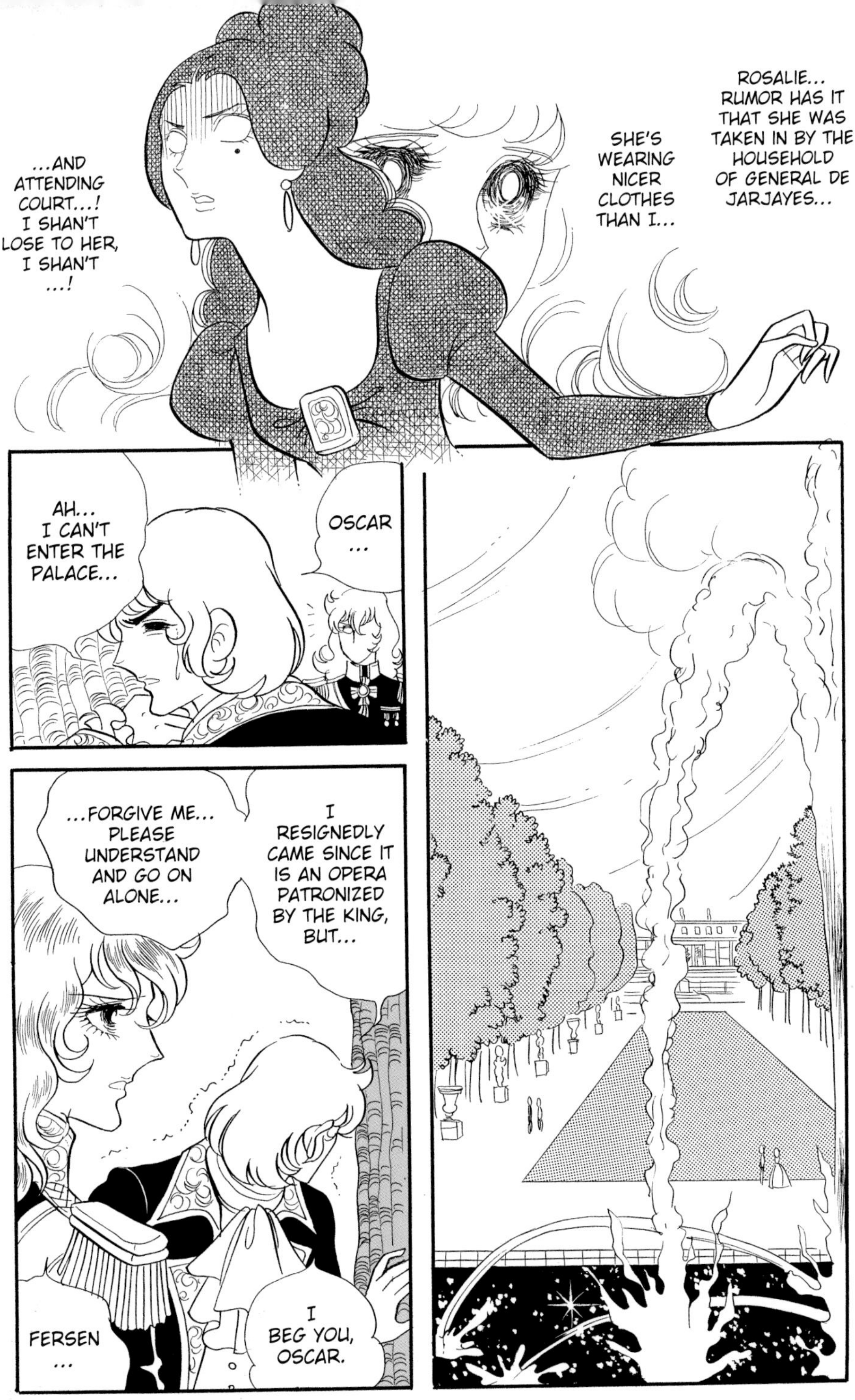
ROSALIE... RUMOR HAS IT THAT SHE WAS TAKEN IN BY THE HOUSEHOLD OF GENERAL DE JARJAYES...
SHE'S WEARING NICER CLOTHES THAN I...
...AND ATTENDING COURT...! I SHAN'T LOSE TO HER, I SHAN'T ...!
OSCAR ...
AH... I CAN'T ENTER THE PALACE...
I RESIGNEDLY CAME SINCE IT IS AN OPERA PATRONIZED BY THE KING, BUT...
...FORGIVE ME... PLEASE UNDERSTAND AND GO ON ALONE...
I BEG YOU, OSCAR.
FERSEN ...

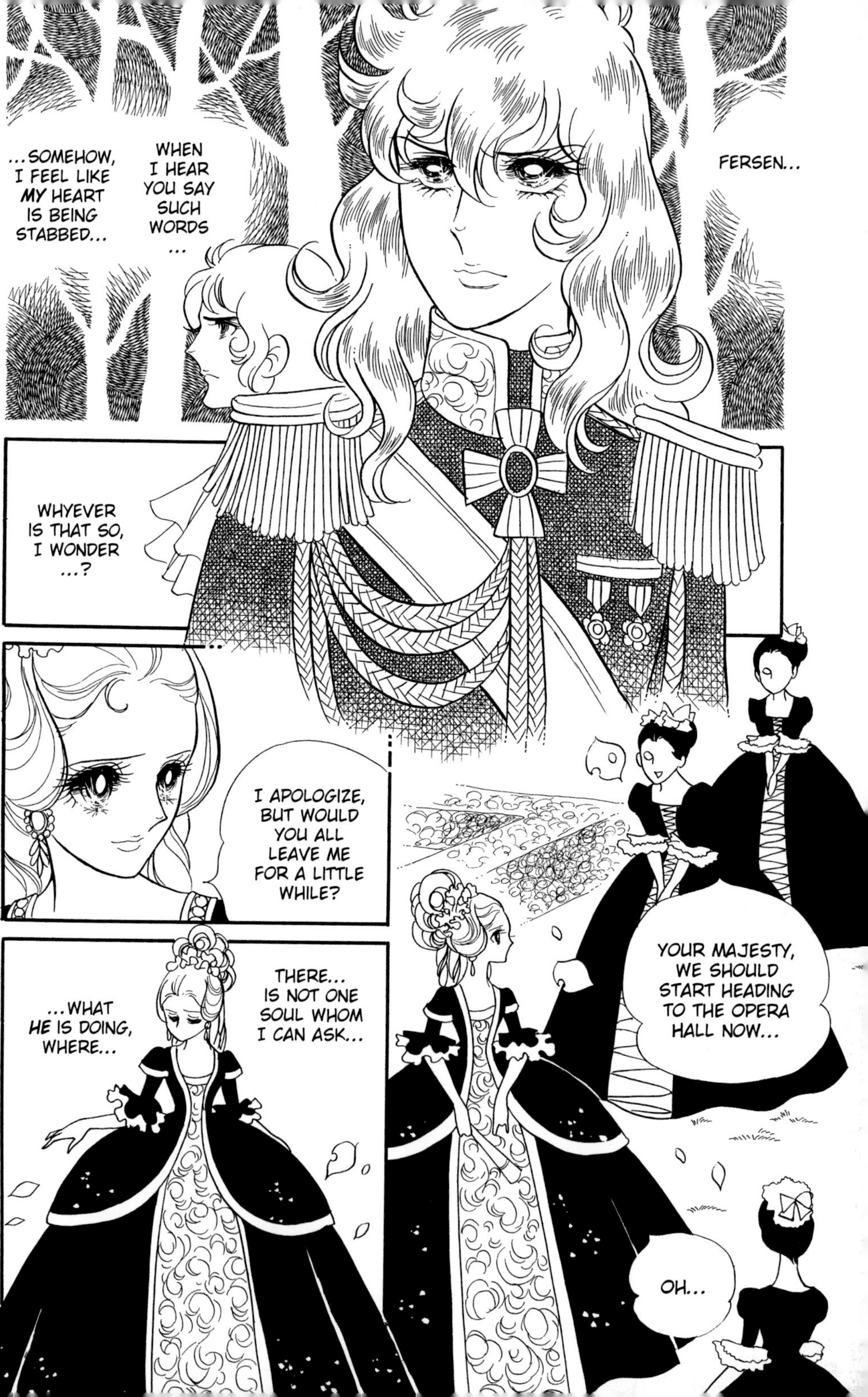
FERSEN...
WHEN I HEAR YOU SAY SUCH WORDS...
...SOMEHOW, I FEEL LIKE MY HEART IS BEING STABBED...
WHYEVER IS THAT SO, I WONDER...?
YOUR MAJESTY, WE SHOULD START HEADING TO THE OPERA HALL NOW...
OH...
I APOLOGIZE, BUT WOULD YOU ALL LEAVE ME FOR A LITTLE WHILE?
THERE... IS NOT ONE SOUL WHOM I CAN ASK...
...WHAT HE IS DOING, WHERE...

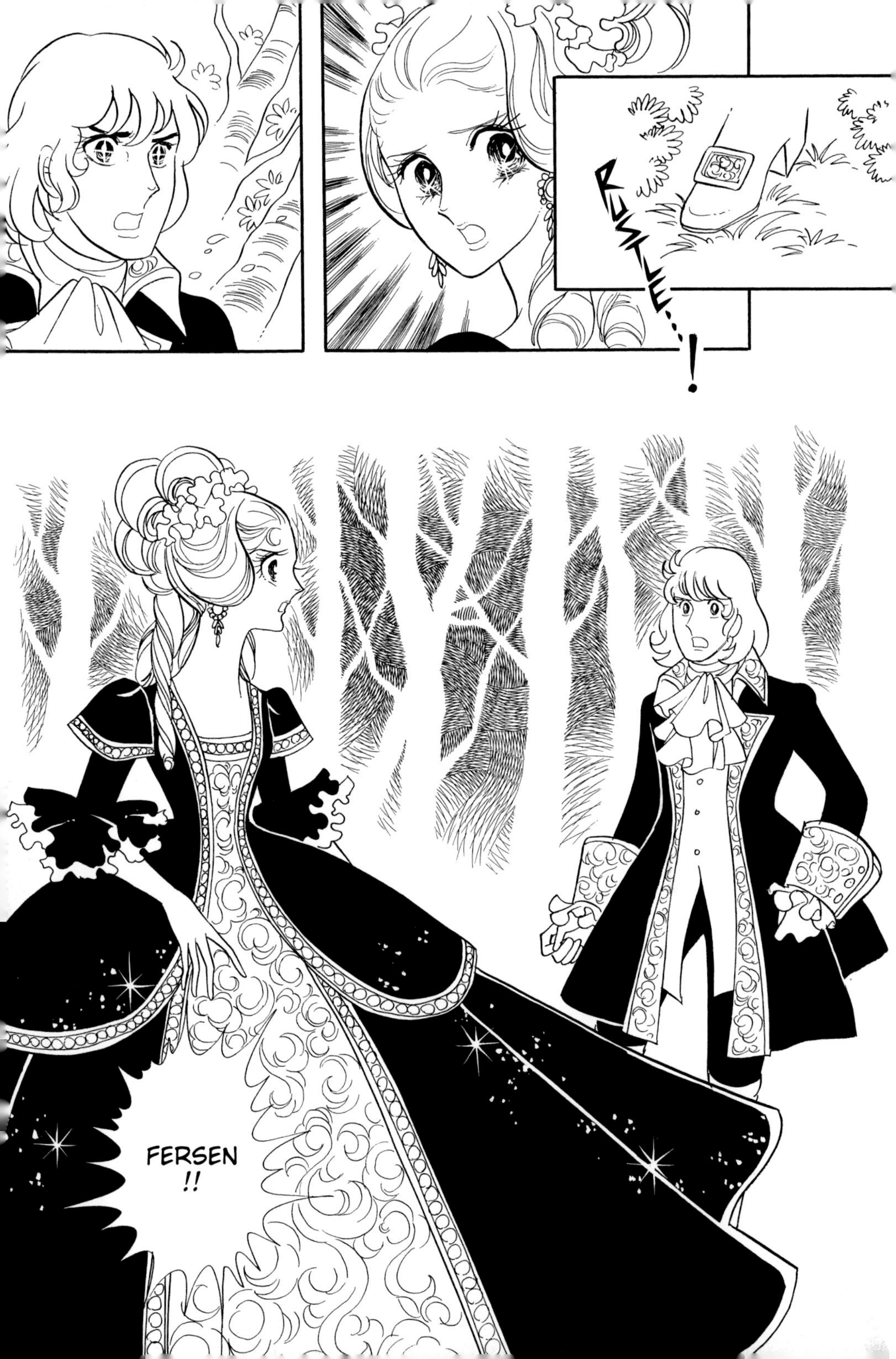
RUSTLE...!
FERSEN !!

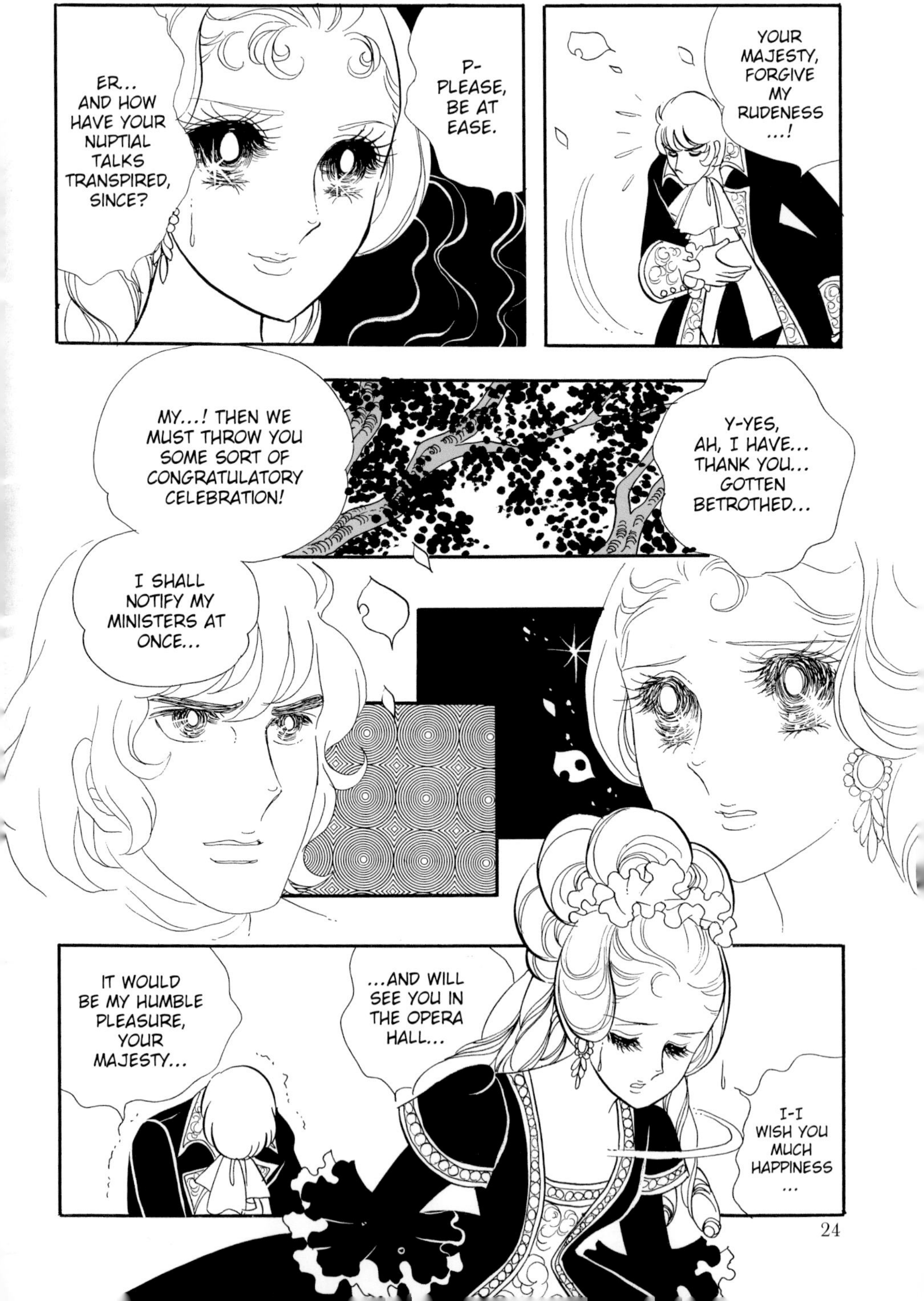
YOUR MAJESTY, FORGIVE MY RUDENESS ...!
P- PLEASE, BE AT EASE.
ER... AND HOW HAVE YOUR NUPTIAL TALKS TRANSPIRED, SINCE?
Y-YES, AH, I HAVE... THANK YOU... GOTTEN BETROTHED...
MY...! THEN WE MUST THROW YOU SOME SORT OF CONGRATULATORY CELEBRATION!
I SHALL NOTIFY MY MINISTERS AT ONCE...
I-I WISH YOU MUCH HAPPINESS ...
...AND WILL SEE YOU IN THE OPERA HALL...
IT WOULD BE MY HUMBLE PLEASURE, YOUR MAJESTY...

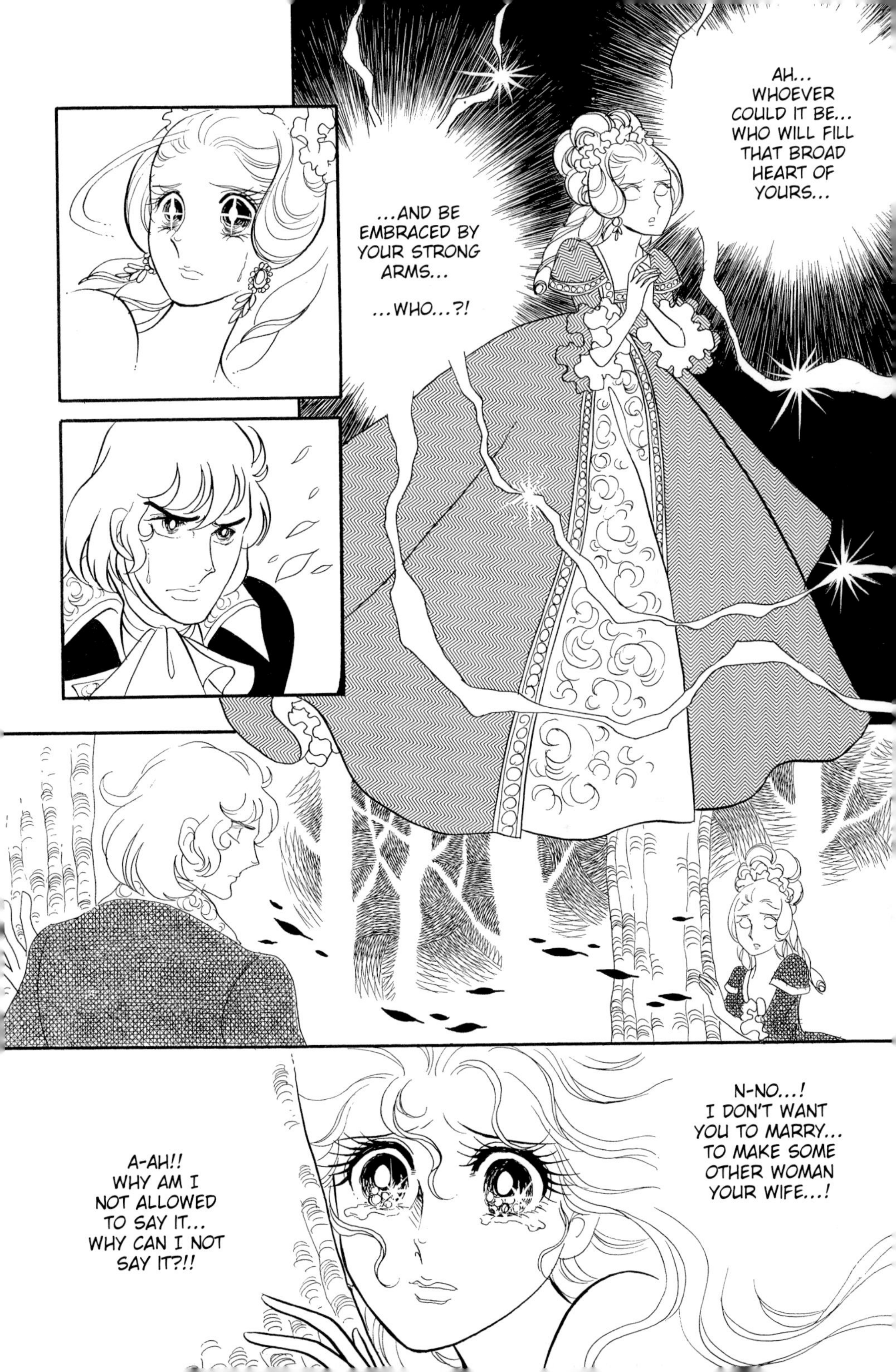
AH... WHOEVER COULD IT BE... WHO WILL FILL THAT BROAD HEART OF YOURS...
...AND BE EMBRACED BY YOUR STRONG ARMS...
...WHO...?!
N-NO...! I DON'T WANT YOU TO MARRY... TO MAKE SOME OTHER WOMAN YOUR WIFE...!
A-AH!! WHY AM I NOT ALLOWED TO SAY IT... WHY CAN I NOT SAY IT?!!

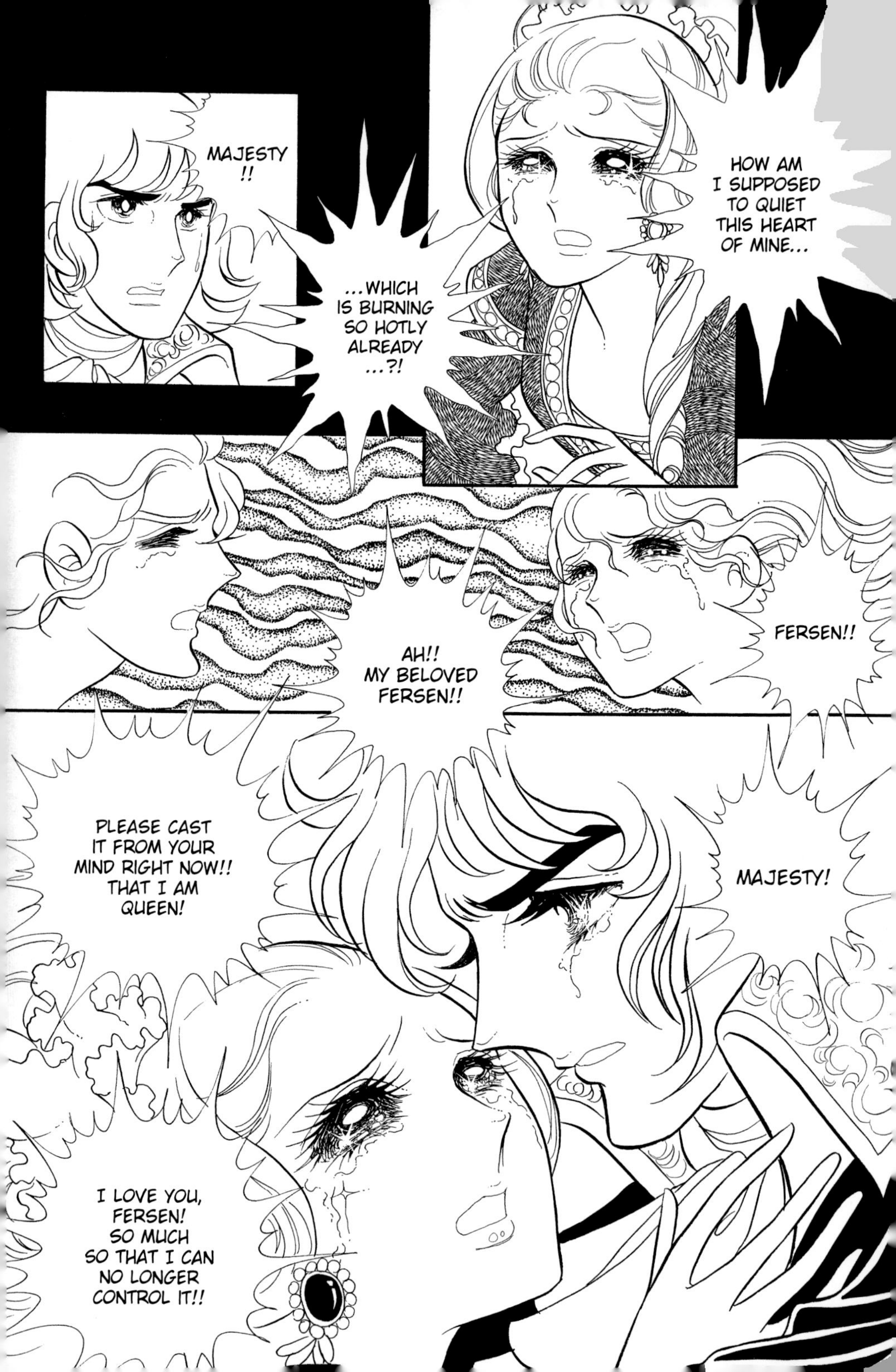
HOW AM I SUPPOSED TO QUIET THIS HEART OF MINE...
...WHICH IS BURNING SO HOTLY ALREADY ...?!
MAJESTY !!
FERSEN!!
AH!! MY BELOVED FERSEN!!
MAJESTY!
PLEASE CAST IT FROM YOUR MIND RIGHT NOW!! THAT I AM QUEEN!
I LOVE YOU, FERSEN! SO MUCH SO THAT I CAN NO LONGER CONTROL IT!!

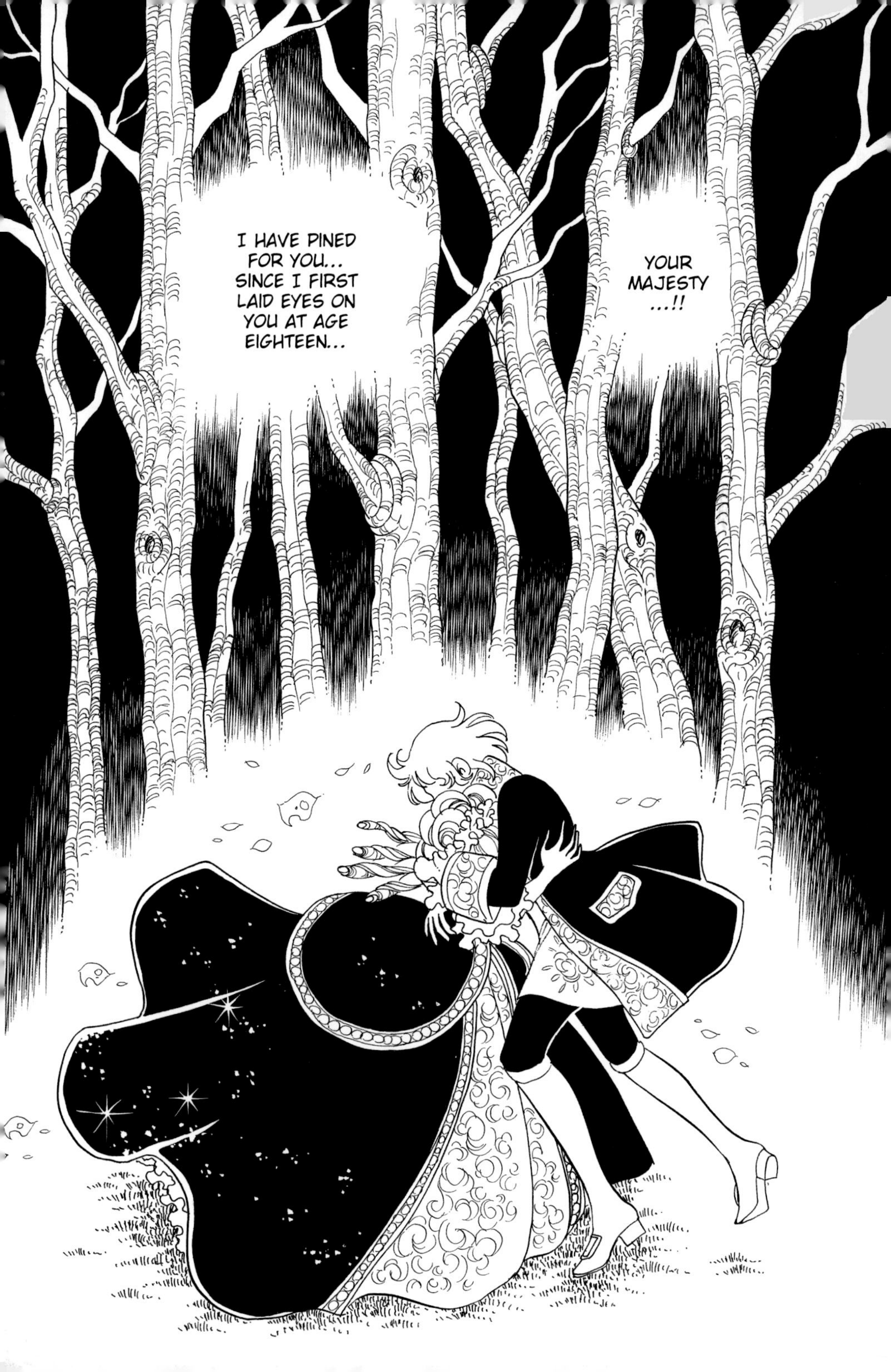
YOUR MAJESTY ...!!
I HAVE PINED FOR YOU... SINCE I FIRST LAID EYES ON YOU AT AGE EIGHTEEN...

1972 WEEKLY MARGARET MAGAZINE
ISSUE 45 COVER INSERT ART

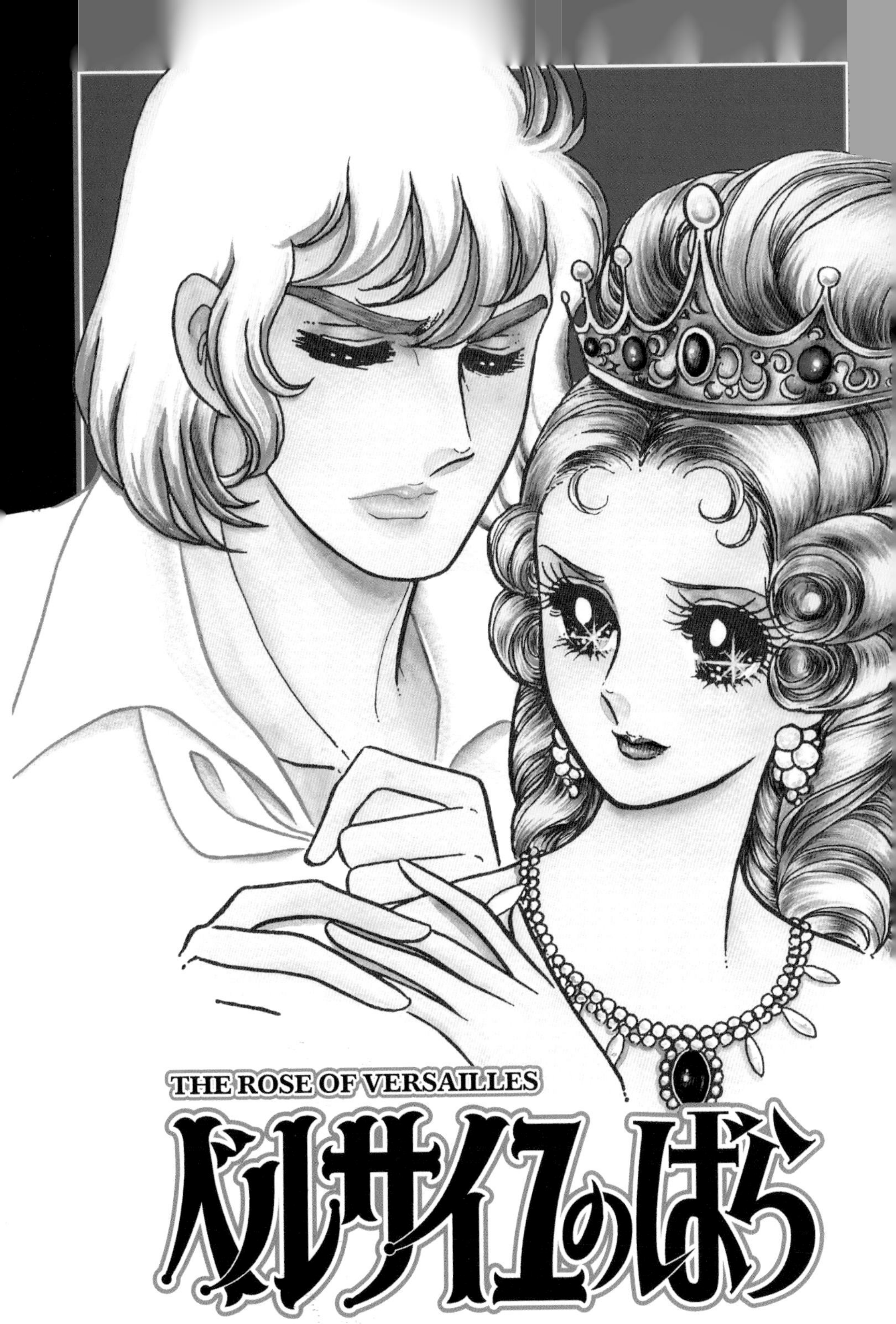

THE ROSE OF VERSAILLES

ベルサイユのばら

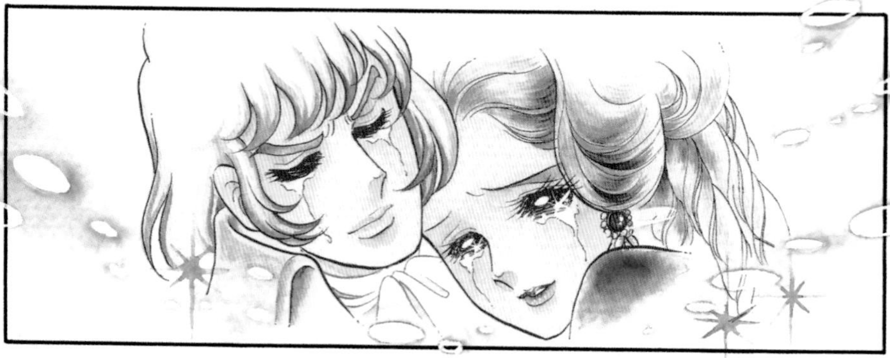

IT...LIKELY BEGAN THAT NIGHT OF THE MASQUERADE, FOUR YEARS EARLIER...

...THAT THESE TWO SOULS QUIETLY STARTED TO SEEK OUT AND CALL TO EACH OTHER, BIT BY BIT...

...VIBRATING IN RESONANCE LIKE SILVER HARP STRINGS, AS THEY PREDICTED...

...THAT THIS DIVINE FORE ORDAINED MOMENT WOULD ONE DAY COME...

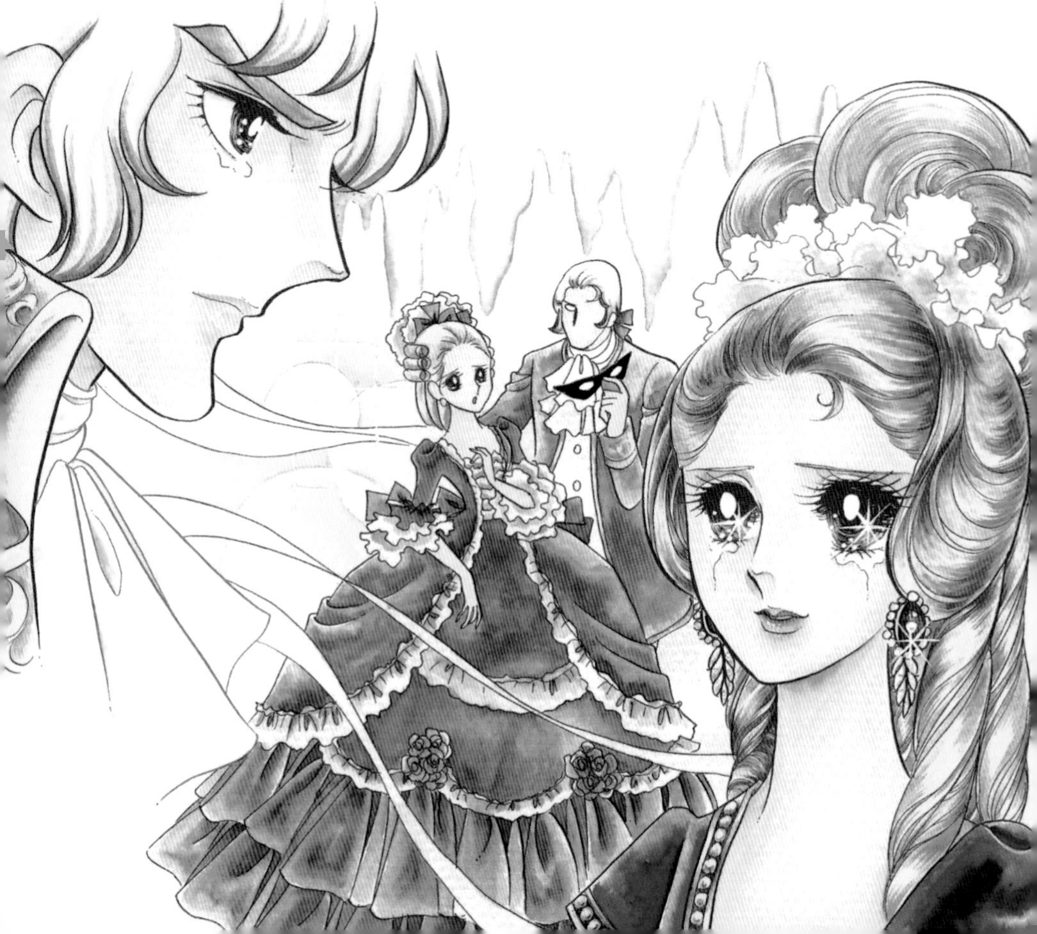

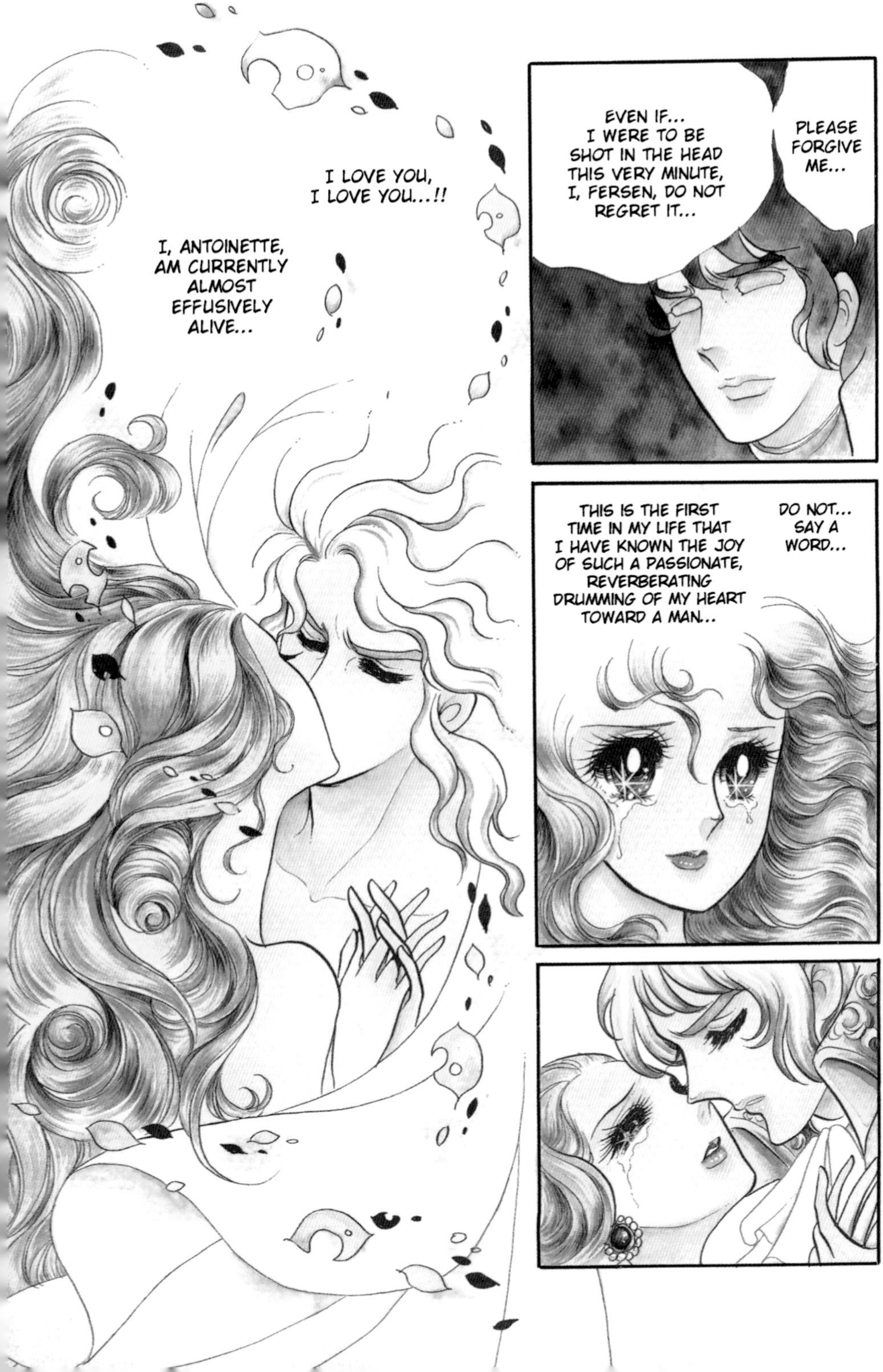
PLEASE FORGIVE ME...
EVEN IF... I WERE TO BE SHOT IN THE HEAD THIS VERY MINUTE, I, FERSEN, DO NOT REGRET IT...
DO NOT... SAY A WORD...
THIS IS THE FIRST TIME IN MY LIFE THAT I HAVE KNOWN THE JOY OF SUCH A PASSIONATE, REVERBERATING DRUMMING OF MY HEART TOWARD A MAN...
I LOVE YOU, I LOVE YOU...!!
I, ANTOINETTE, AM CURRENTLY ALMOST EFFUSIVELY ALIVE...

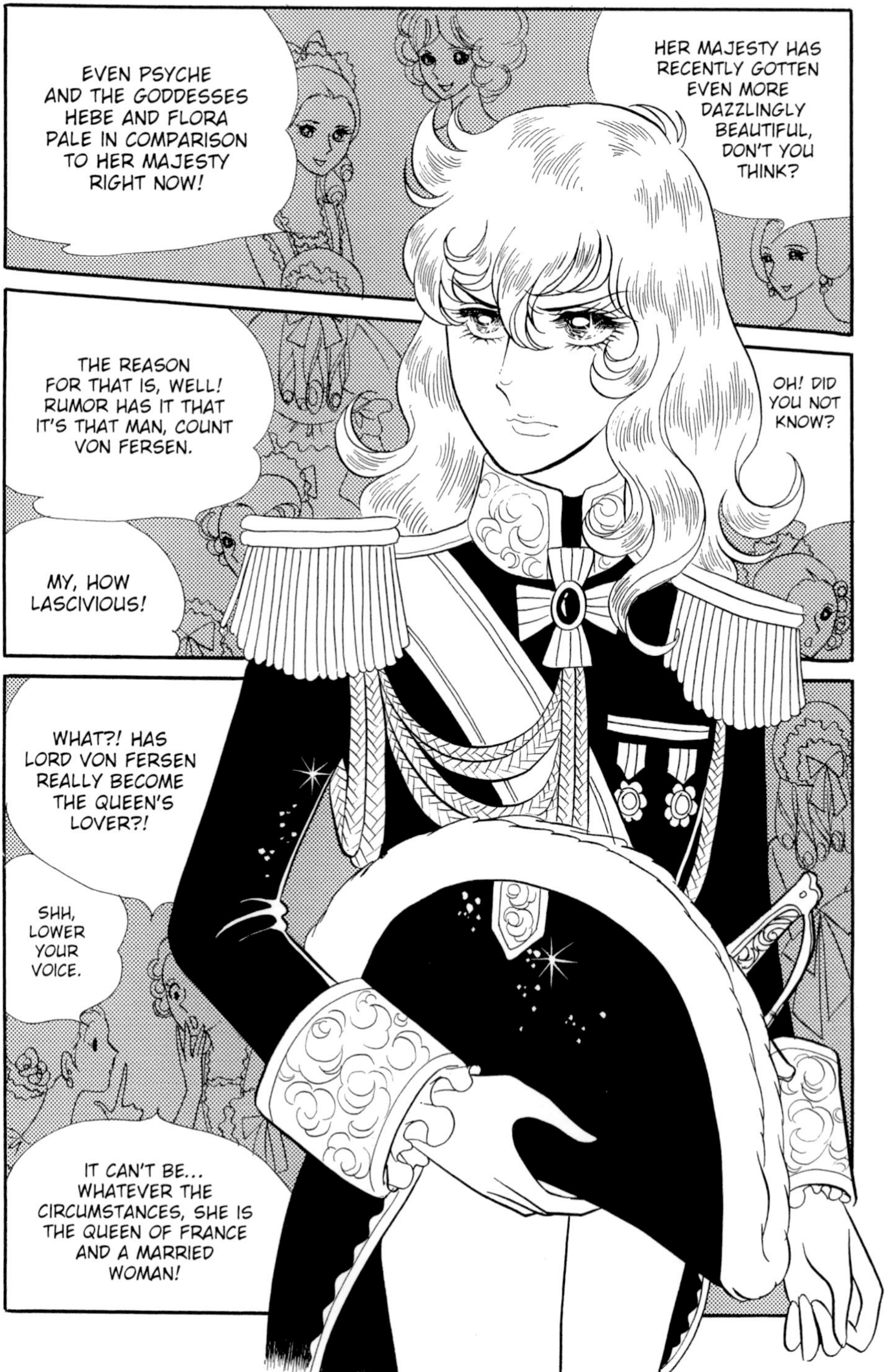
HER MAJESTY HAS RECENTLY GOTTEN EVEN MORE DAZZLINGLY BEAUTIFUL, DON'T YOU THINK?
EVEN PSYCHE AND THE GODDESSES HEBE AND FLORA PALE IN COMPARISON TO HER MAJESTY RIGHT NOW!
OH! DID YOU NOT KNOW?
THE REASON FOR THAT IS, WELL! RUMOR HAS IT THAT IT'S THAT MAN, COUNT VON FERSEN.
MY, HOW LASCIVIOUS!
WHAT?! HAS LORD VON FERSEN REALLY BECOME THE QUEEN'S LOVER?!
SHH, LOWER YOUR VOICE.
IT CAN'T BE... WHATEVER THE CIRCUMSTANCES, SHE IS THE QUEEN OF FRANCE AND A MARRIED WOMAN!

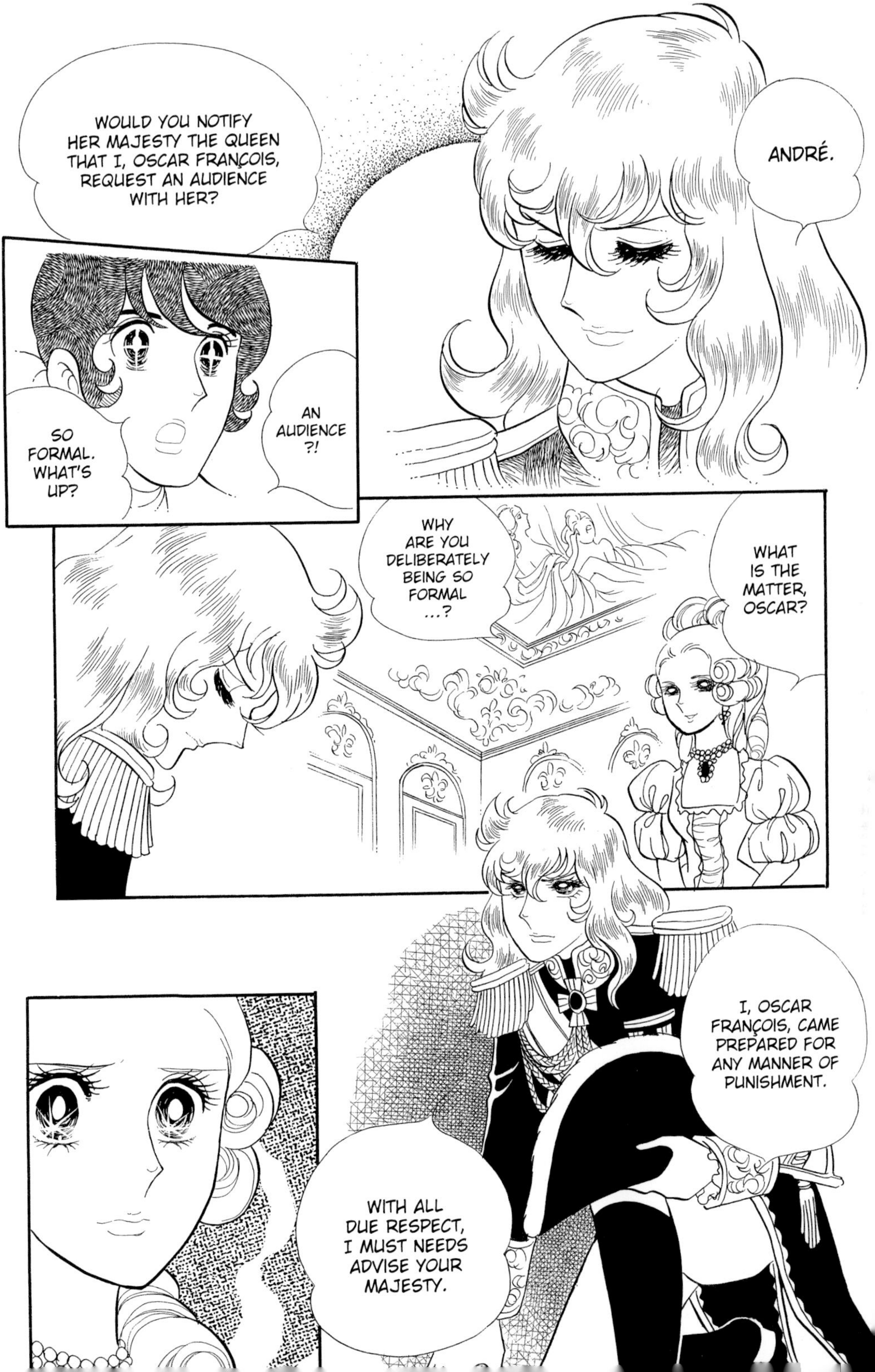
ANDRÉ.
WOULD YOU NOTIFY HER MAJESTY THE QUEEN THAT I, OSCAR FRANÇOIS, REQUEST AN AUDIENCE WITH HER?
AN AUDIENCE ?!
SO FORMAL. WHAT'S UP?
WHAT IS THE MATTER, OSCAR?
WHY ARE YOU DELIBERATELY BEING SO FORMAL ...?
I, OSCAR FRANÇOIS, CAME PREPARED FOR ANY MANNER OF PUNISHMENT.
WITH ALL DUE RESPECT, I MUST NEEDS ADVISE YOUR MAJESTY.

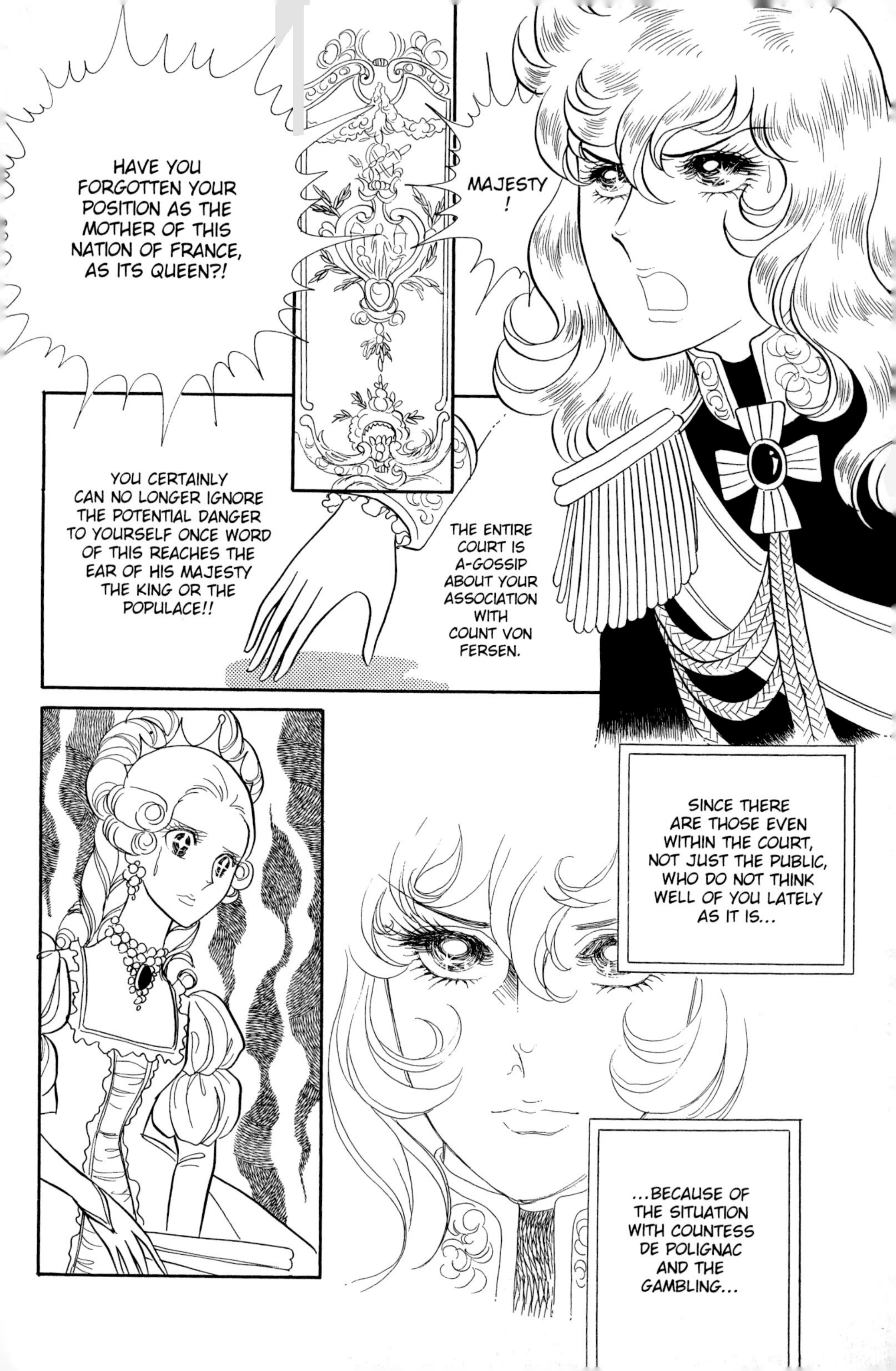
MAJESTY!
HAVE YOU FORGOTTEN YOUR POSITION AS THE MOTHER OF THIS NATION OF FRANCE, AS ITS QUEEN?!
THE ENTIRE COURT IS A-GOSSIP ABOUT YOUR ASSOCIATION WITH COUNT VON FERSEN.
YOU CERTAINLY CAN NO LONGER IGNORE THE POTENTIAL DANGER TO YOURSELF ONCE WORD OF THIS REACHES THE EAR OF HIS MAJESTY THE KING OR THE POPULACE!!
SINCE THERE ARE THOSE EVEN WITHIN THE COURT, NOT JUST THE PUBLIC, WHO DO NOT THINK WELL OF YOU LATELY AS IT IS...
...BECAUSE OF THE SITUATION WITH COUNTESS DE POLIGNAC AND THE GAMBLING...

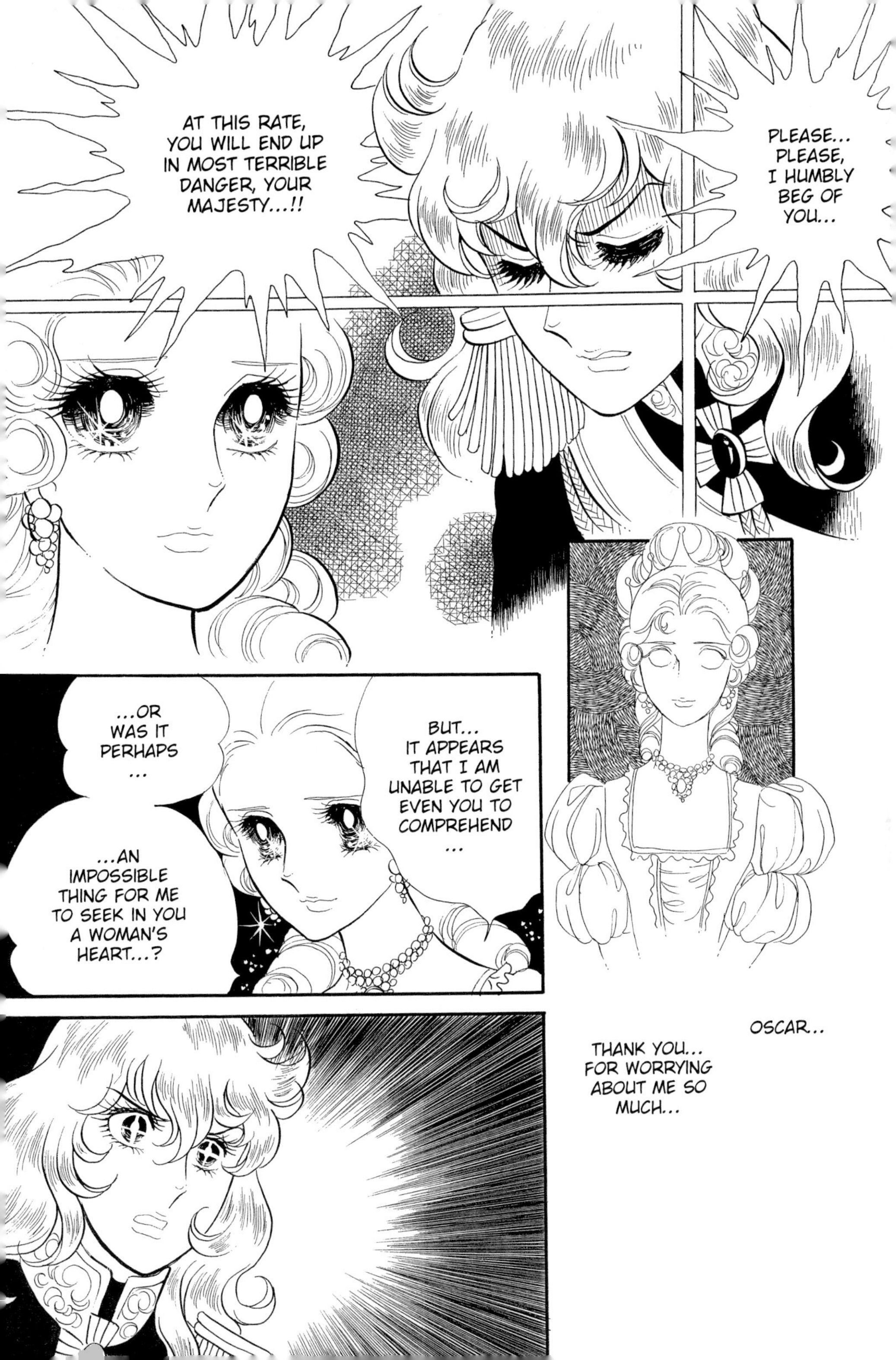

PLEASE... PLEASE, I HUMBLY BEG OF YOU...
AT THIS RATE, YOU WILL END UP IN MOST TERRIBLE DANGER, YOUR MAJESTY...!!
OSCAR...
THANK YOU... FOR WORRYING ABOUT ME SO MUCH...
BUT... IT APPEARS THAT I AM UNABLE TO GET EVEN YOU TO COMPREHEND...
...OR WAS IT PERHAPS...
...AN IMPOSSIBLE THING FOR ME TO SEEK IN YOU A WOMAN'S HEART...?

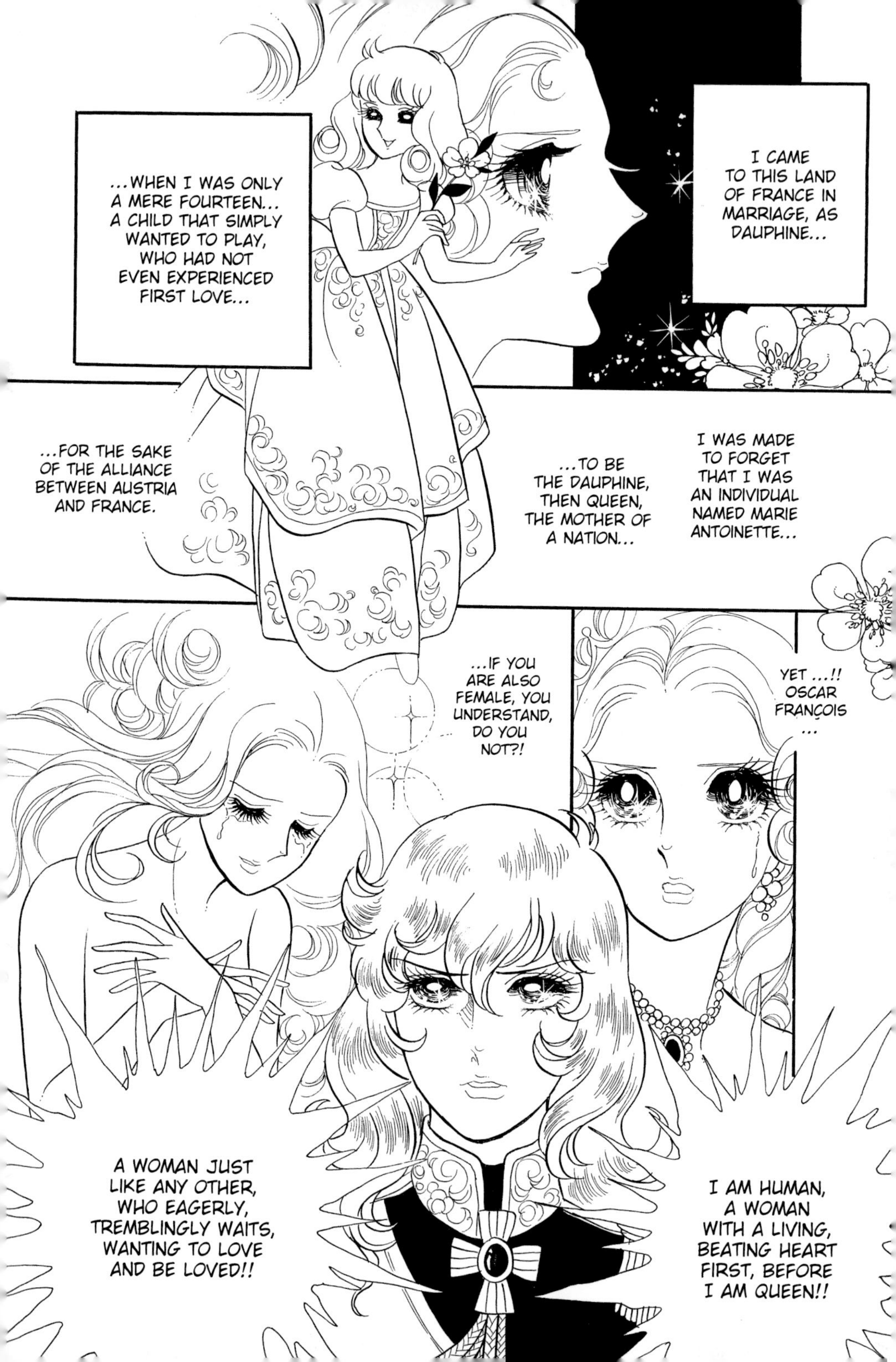
I CAME TO THIS LAND OF FRANCE IN MARRIAGE, AS DAUPHINE...
...WHEN I WAS ONLY A MERE FOURTEEN... A CHILD THAT SIMPLY WANTED TO PLAY, WHO HAD NOT EVEN EXPERIENCED FIRST LOVE...
I WAS MADE TO FORGET THAT I WAS AN INDIVIDUAL NAMED MARIE ANTOINETTE...
...TO BE THE DAUPHINE, THEN QUEEN, THE MOTHER OF A NATION...
...FOR THE SAKE OF THE ALLIANCE BETWEEN AUSTRIA AND FRANCE.
YET ...!! OSCAR FRANÇOIS ...
...IF YOU ARE ALSO FEMALE, YOU UNDERSTAND, DO YOU NOT?!
I AM HUMAN, A WOMAN WITH A LIVING, BEATING HEART FIRST, BEFORE I AM QUEEN!!
A WOMAN JUST LIKE ANY OTHER, WHO EAGERLY, TREMBLINGLY WAITS, WANTING TO LOVE AND BE LOVED!!

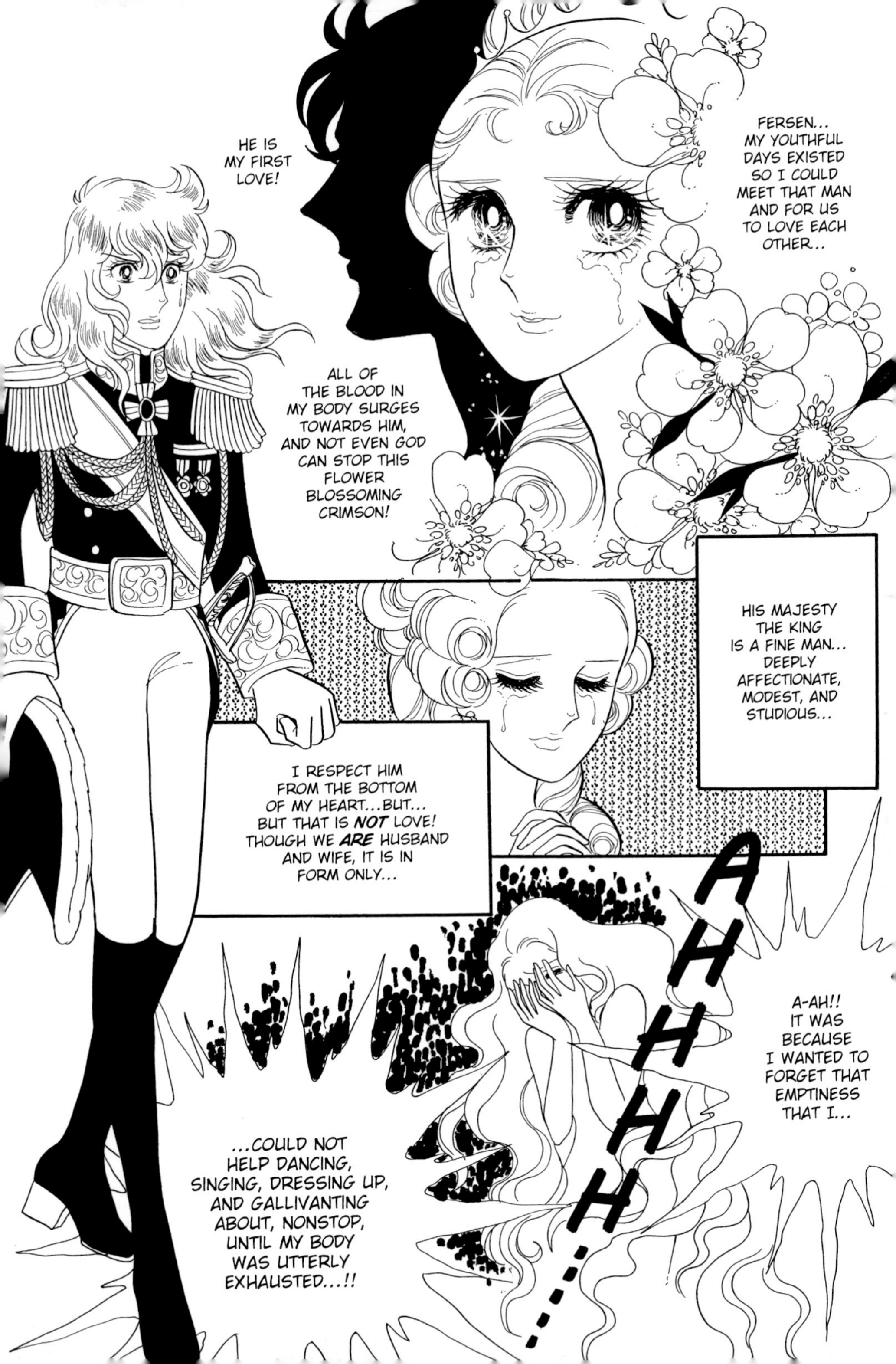

FERSEN... MY YOUTHFUL DAYS EXISTED SO I COULD MEET THAT MAN AND FOR US TO LOVE EACH OTHER...
HE IS MY FIRST LOVE!
ALL OF THE BLOOD IN MY BODY SURGES TOWARDS HIM, AND NOT EVEN GOD CAN STOP THIS FLOWER BLOSSOMING CRIMSON!
HIS MAJESTY THE KING IS A FINE MAN... DEEPLY AFFECTIONATE, MODEST, AND STUDIOUS...
I RESPECT HIM FROM THE BOTTOM OF MY HEART...BUT... BUT THAT IS ***NOT*** LOVE! THOUGH WE ***ARE*** HUSBAND AND WIFE, IT IS IN FORM ONLY...
A-AH!! IT WAS BECAUSE I WANTED TO FORGET THAT EMPTINESS THAT I...
AHHHHH......
...COULD NOT HELP DANCING, SINGING, DRESSING UP, AND GALLIVANTING ABOUT, NONSTOP, UNTIL MY BODY WAS UTTERLY EXHAUSTED...!!

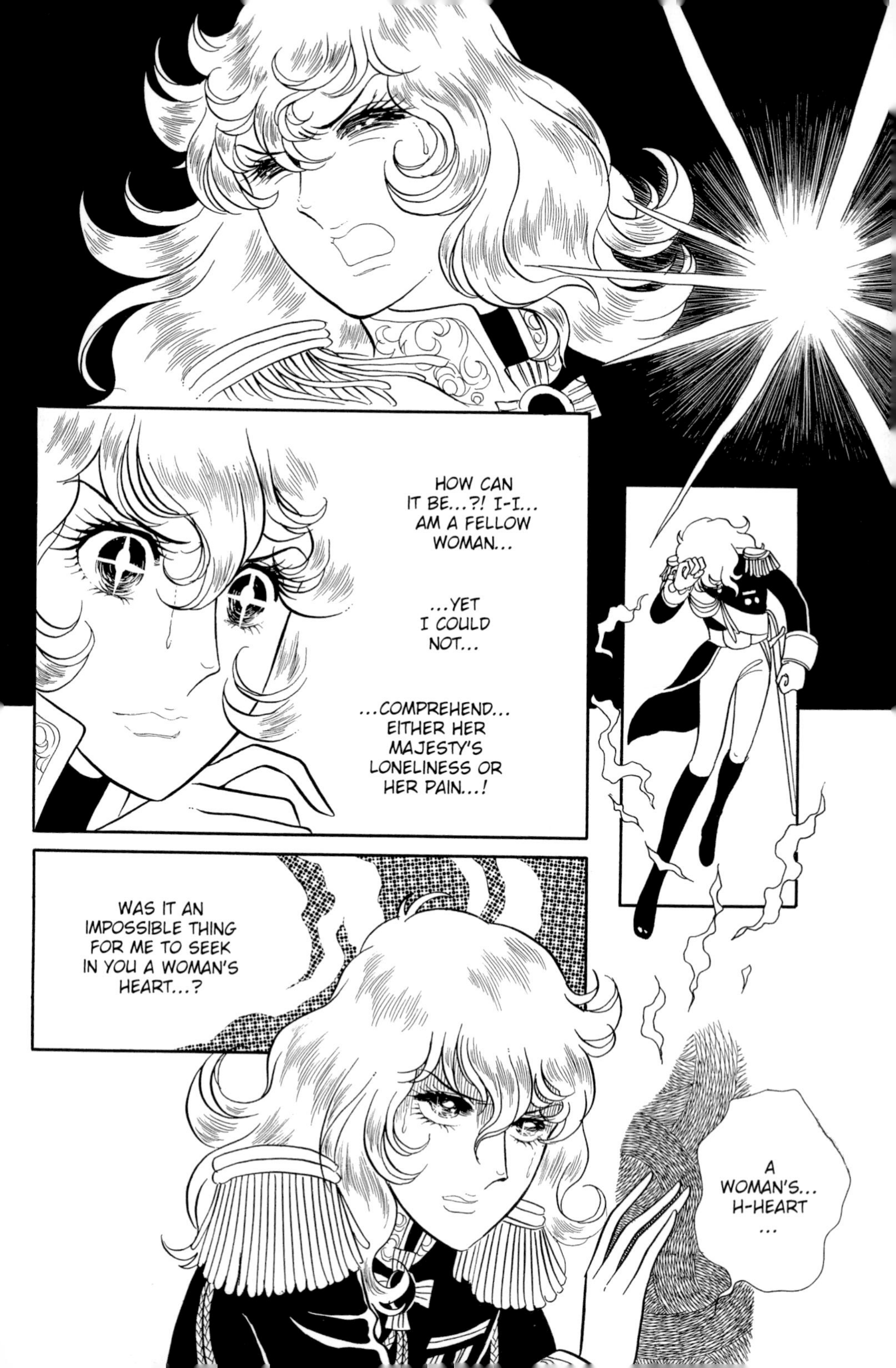
HOW CAN IT BE...?! I-I... AM A FELLOW WOMAN...
...YET I COULD NOT...
...COMPREHEND... EITHER HER MAJESTY'S LONELINESS OR HER PAIN...!
WAS IT AN IMPOSSIBLE THING FOR ME TO SEEK IN YOU A WOMAN'S HEART...?
A WOMAN'S... H-HEART ...

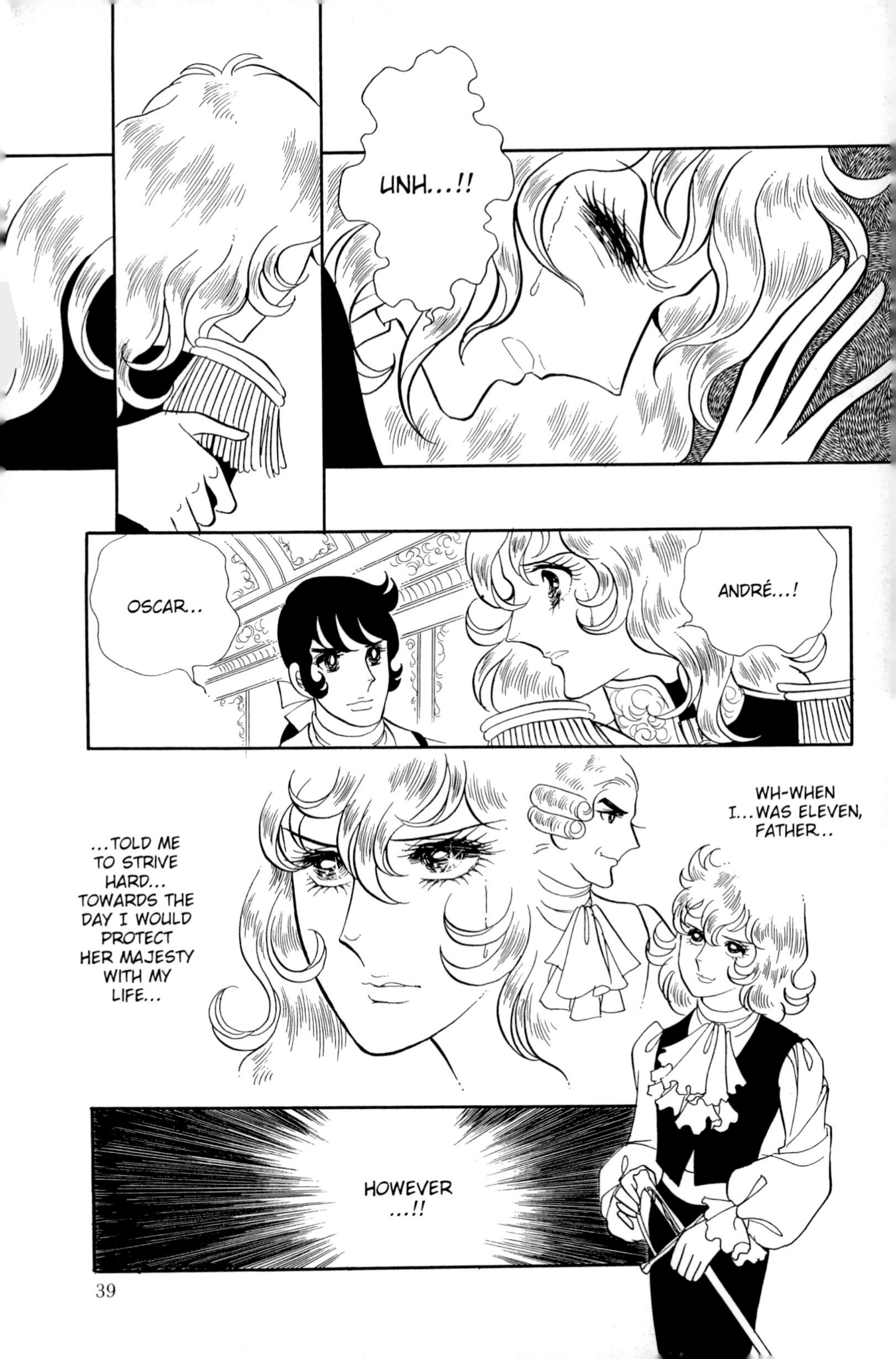
UNH...!!
ANDRÉ...!
OSCAR...
WH-WHEN I...WAS ELEVEN, FATHER...
...TOLD ME TO STRIVE HARD... TOWARDS THE DAY I WOULD PROTECT HER MAJESTY WITH MY LIFE...
HOWEVER ...!!

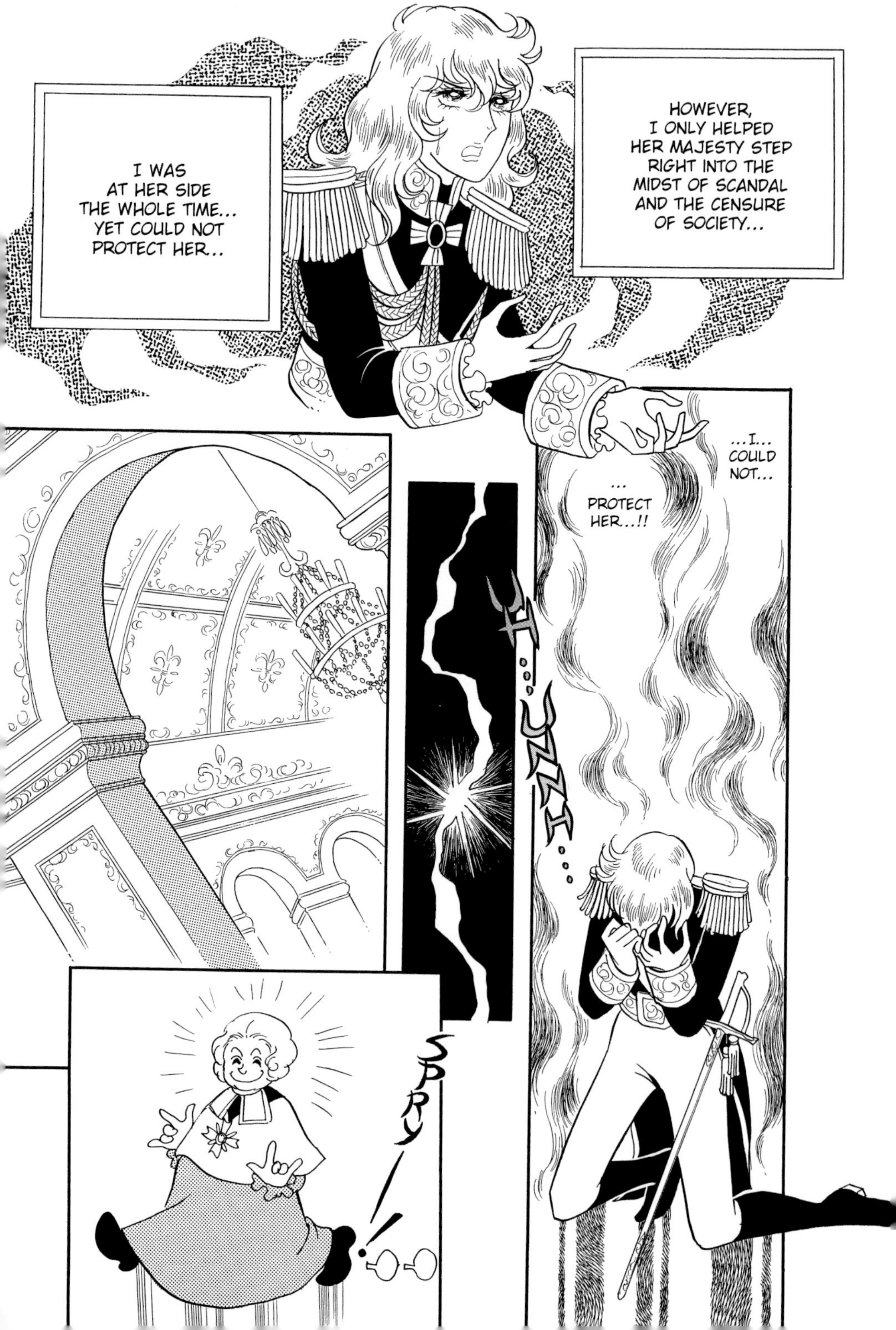
HOWEVER, I ONLY HELPED HER MAJESTY STEP RIGHT INTO THE MIDST OF SCANDAL AND THE CENSURE OF SOCIETY...
I WAS AT HER SIDE THE WHOLE TIME... YET COULD NOT PROTECT HER...
...I... COULD NOT...
... PROTECT HER...!!
SPRY—!!

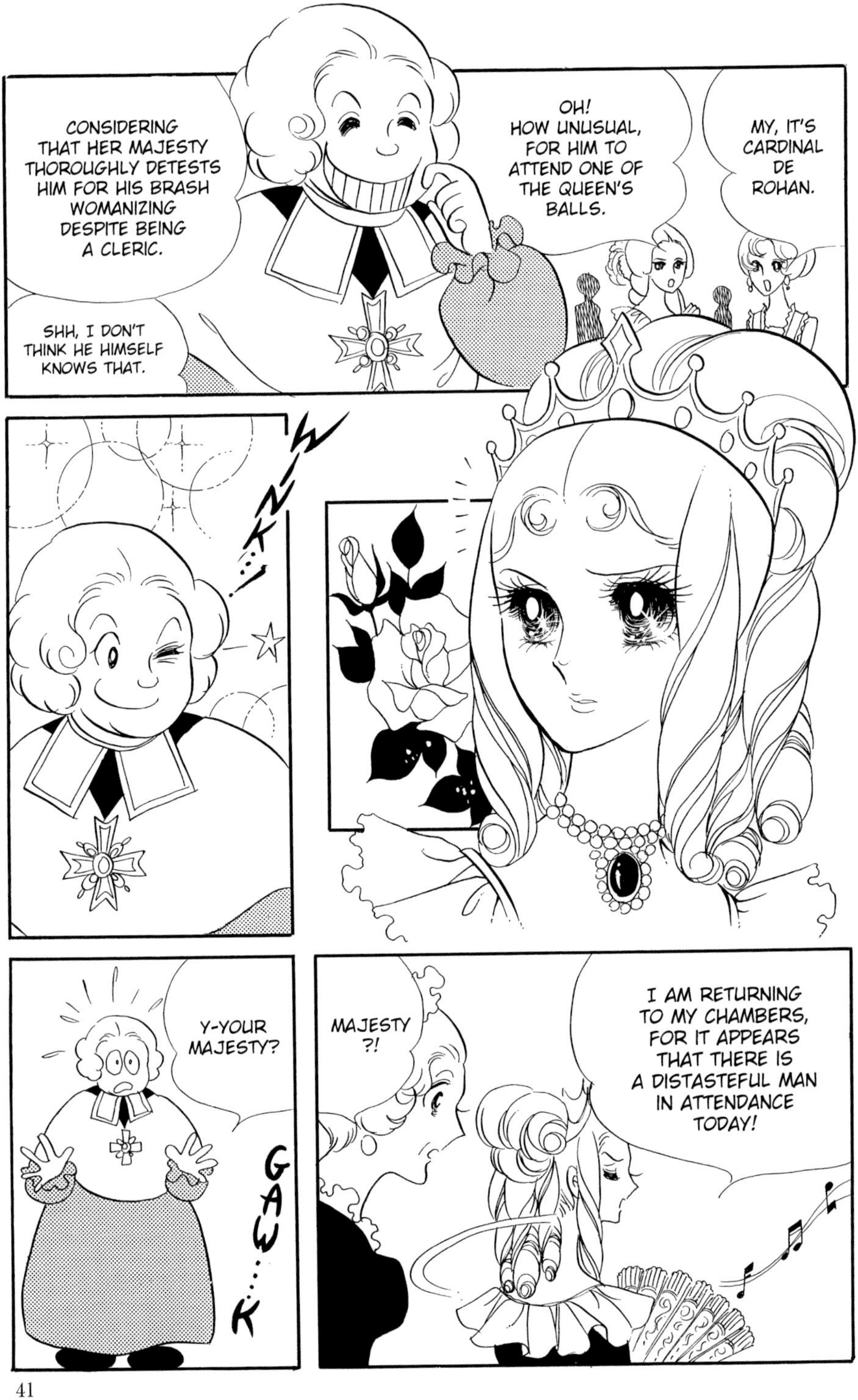
MY, IT'S CARDINAL DE ROHAN.
OH! HOW UNUSUAL, FOR HIM TO ATTEND ONE OF THE QUEEN'S BALLS.
CONSIDERING THAT HER MAJESTY THOROUGHLY DETESTS HIM FOR HIS BRASH WOMANIZING DESPITE BEING A CLERIC.
SHH, I DON'T THINK HE HIMSELF KNOWS THAT.
WINK...!
I AM RETURNING TO MY CHAMBERS, FOR IT APPEARS THAT THERE IS A DISTASTEFUL MAN IN ATTENDANCE TODAY!
MAJESTY ?!
Y-YOUR MAJESTY?
GAWK...K

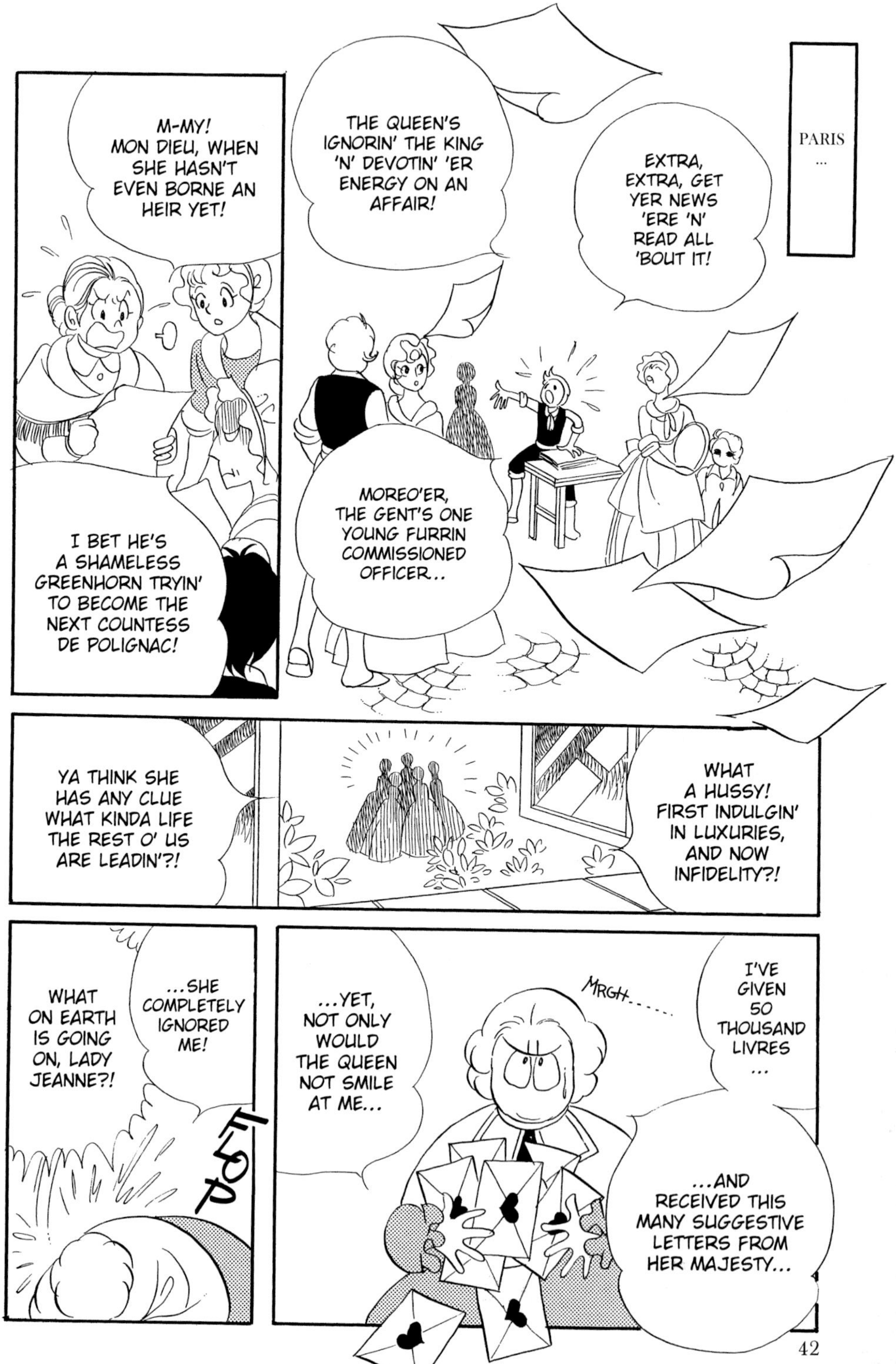
PARIS ...
EXTRA, EXTRA, GET YER NEWS 'ERE 'N' READ ALL 'BOUT IT!
THE QUEEN'S IGNORIN' THE KING 'N' DEVOTIN' 'ER ENERGY ON AN AFFAIR!
MOREO'ER, THE GENT'S ONE YOUNG FURRIN COMMISSIONED OFFICER...
M-MY! MON DIEU, WHEN SHE HASN'T EVEN BORNE AN HEIR YET!
I BET HE'S A SHAMELESS GREENHORN TRYIN' TO BECOME THE NEXT COUNTESS DE POLIGNAC!
WHAT A HUSSY! FIRST INDULGIN' IN LUXURIES, AND NOW INFIDELITY?!
YA THINK SHE HAS ANY CLUE WHAT KINDA LIFE THE REST O' US ARE LEADIN'?!
I'VE GIVEN 50 THOUSAND LIVRES ...
...AND RECEIVED THIS MANY SUGGESTIVE LETTERS FROM HER MAJESTY...
MRGH......
...YET, NOT ONLY WOULD THE QUEEN NOT SMILE AT ME...
...SHE COMPLETELY IGNORED ME!
WHAT ON EARTH IS GOING ON, LADY JEANNE?!
FLOP

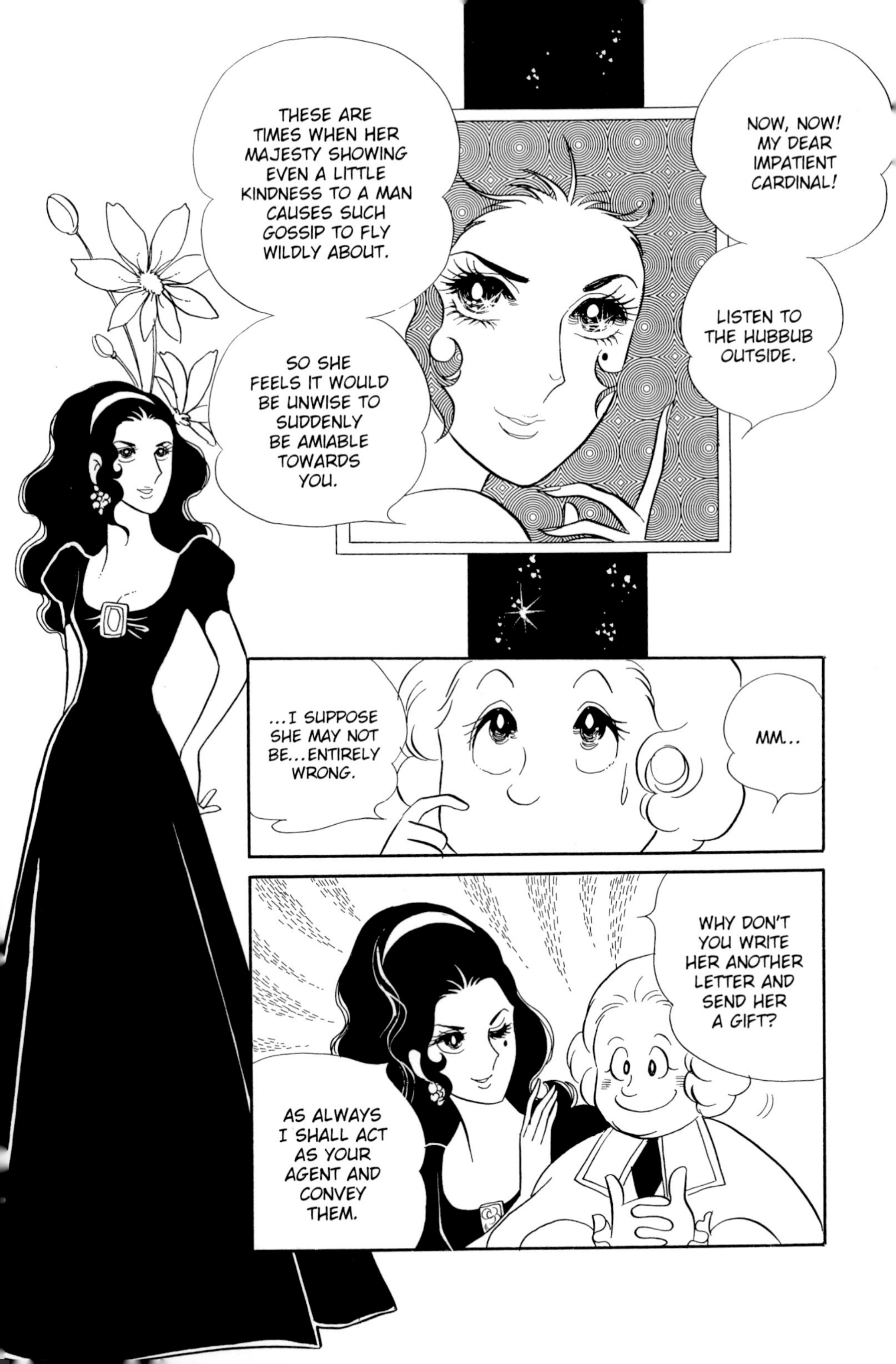
NOW, NOW! MY DEAR IMPATIENT CARDINAL!
LISTEN TO THE HUBBUB OUTSIDE.
THESE ARE TIMES WHEN HER MAJESTY SHOWING EVEN A LITTLE KINDNESS TO A MAN CAUSES SUCH GOSSIP TO FLY WILDLY ABOUT.
SO SHE FEELS IT WOULD BE UNWISE TO SUDDENLY BE AMIABLE TOWARDS YOU.
MM...
...I SUPPOSE SHE MAY NOT BE...ENTIRELY WRONG.
WHY DON'T YOU WRITE HER ANOTHER LETTER AND SEND HER A GIFT?
AS ALWAYS I SHALL ACT AS YOUR AGENT AND CONVEY THEM.

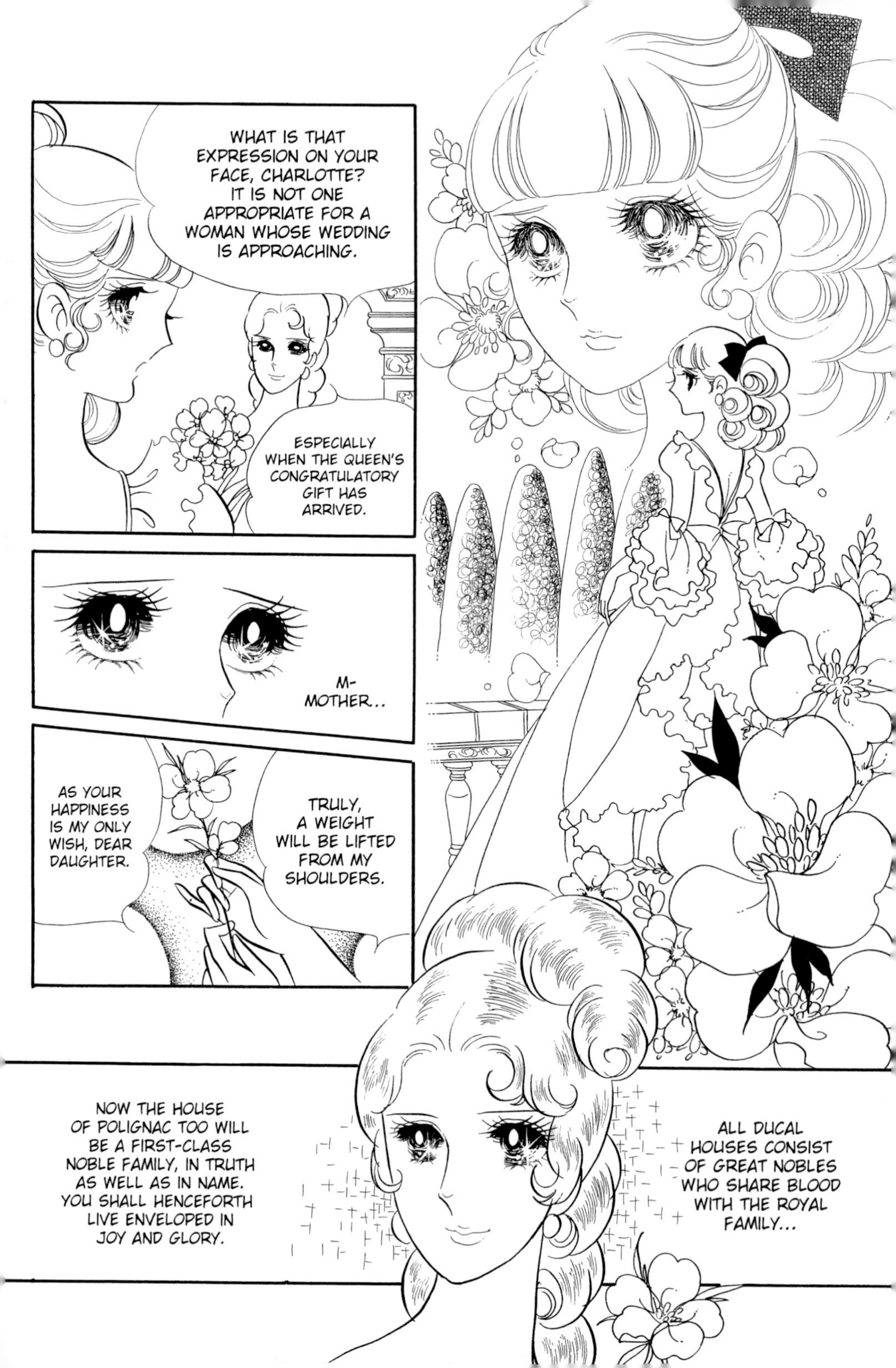
WHAT IS THAT EXPRESSION ON YOUR FACE, CHARLOTTE? IT IS NOT ONE APPROPRIATE FOR A WOMAN WHOSE WEDDING IS APPROACHING.
ESPECIALLY WHEN THE QUEEN'S CONGRATULATORY GIFT HAS ARRIVED.
M- MOTHER...
TRULY, A WEIGHT WILL BE LIFTED FROM MY SHOULDERS.
AS YOUR HAPPINESS IS MY ONLY WISH, DEAR DAUGHTER.
ALL DUCAL HOUSES CONSIST OF GREAT NOBLES WHO SHARE BLOOD WITH THE ROYAL FAMILY...
NOW THE HOUSE OF POLIGNAC TOO WILL BE A FIRST-CLASS NOBLE FAMILY, IN TRUTH AS WELL AS IN NAME. YOU SHALL HENCEFORTH LIVE ENVELOPED IN JOY AND GLORY.

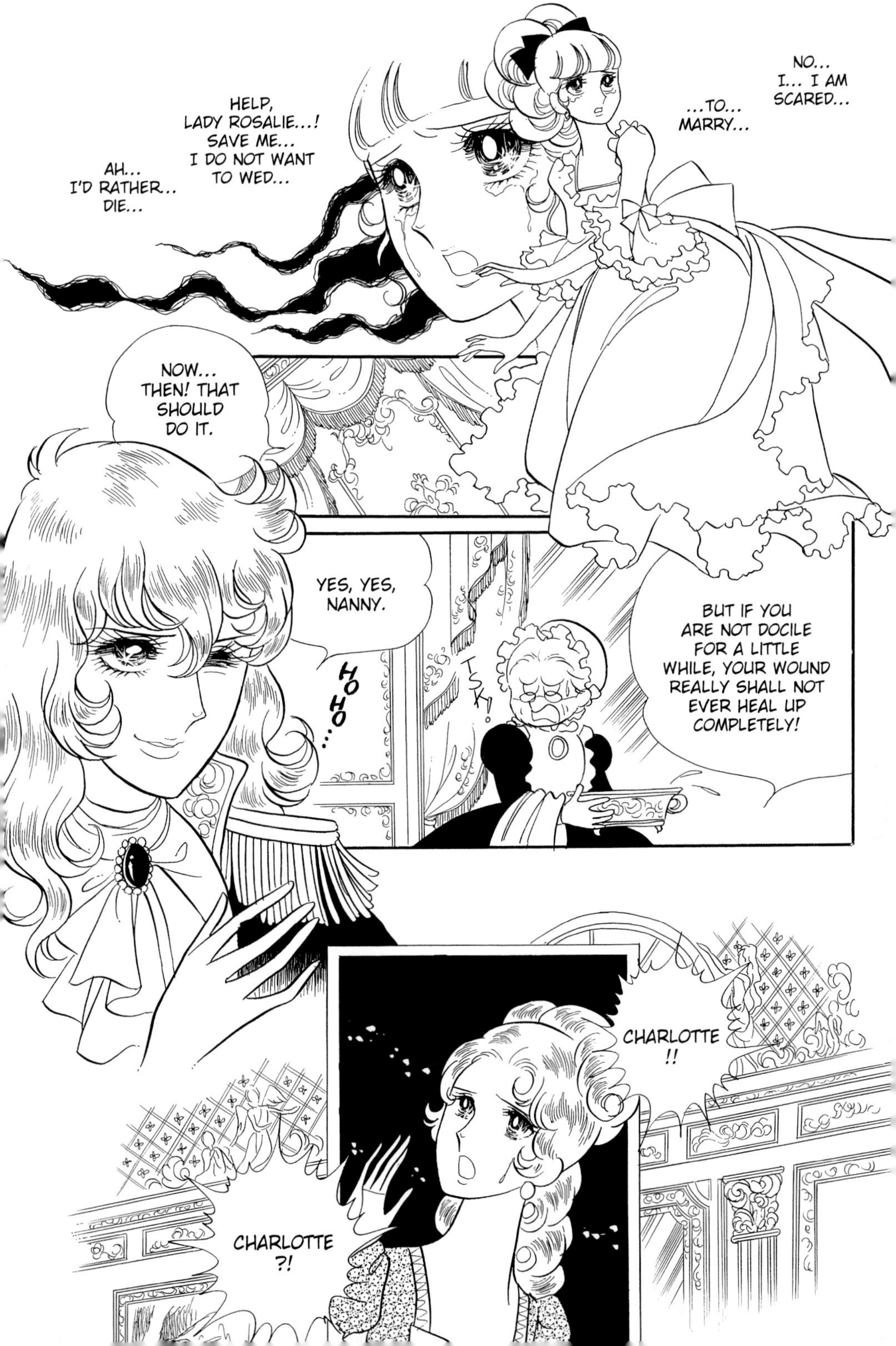
NO... I... I AM SCARED...
...TO... MARRY...
HELP, LADY ROSALIE...! SAVE ME... I DO NOT WANT TO WED...
AH... I'D RATHER.. DIE...
NOW... THEN! THAT SHOULD DO IT.
BUT IF YOU ARE NOT DOCILE FOR A LITTLE WHILE, YOUR WOUND REALLY SHALL NOT EVER HEAL UP COMPLETELY!
TSK!
YES, YES, NANNY.
HO HO HO...
CHARLOTTE !!
CHARLOTTE ?!

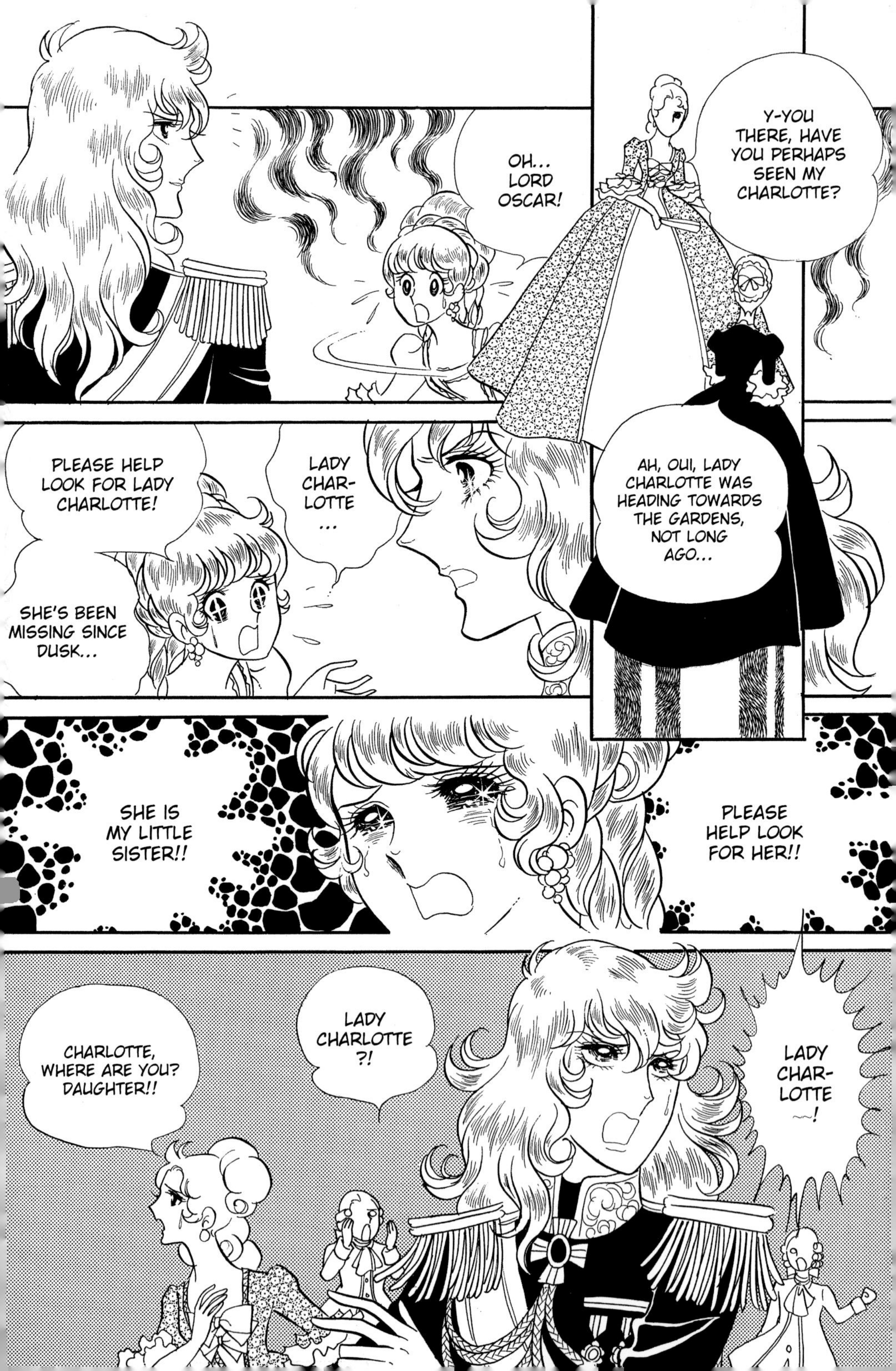
Y-YOU THERE, HAVE YOU PERHAPS SEEN MY CHARLOTTE?
AH, OUI, LADY CHARLOTTE WAS HEADING TOWARDS THE GARDENS, NOT LONG AGO...
OH... LORD OSCAR!
LADY CHAR-LOTTE ...
PLEASE HELP LOOK FOR LADY CHARLOTTE!
SHE'S BEEN MISSING SINCE DUSK...
PLEASE HELP LOOK FOR HER!!
SHE IS MY LITTLE SISTER!!
LADY CHAR-LOTTE ~!
LADY CHARLOTTE ?!
CHARLOTTE, WHERE ARE YOU? DAUGHTER!!

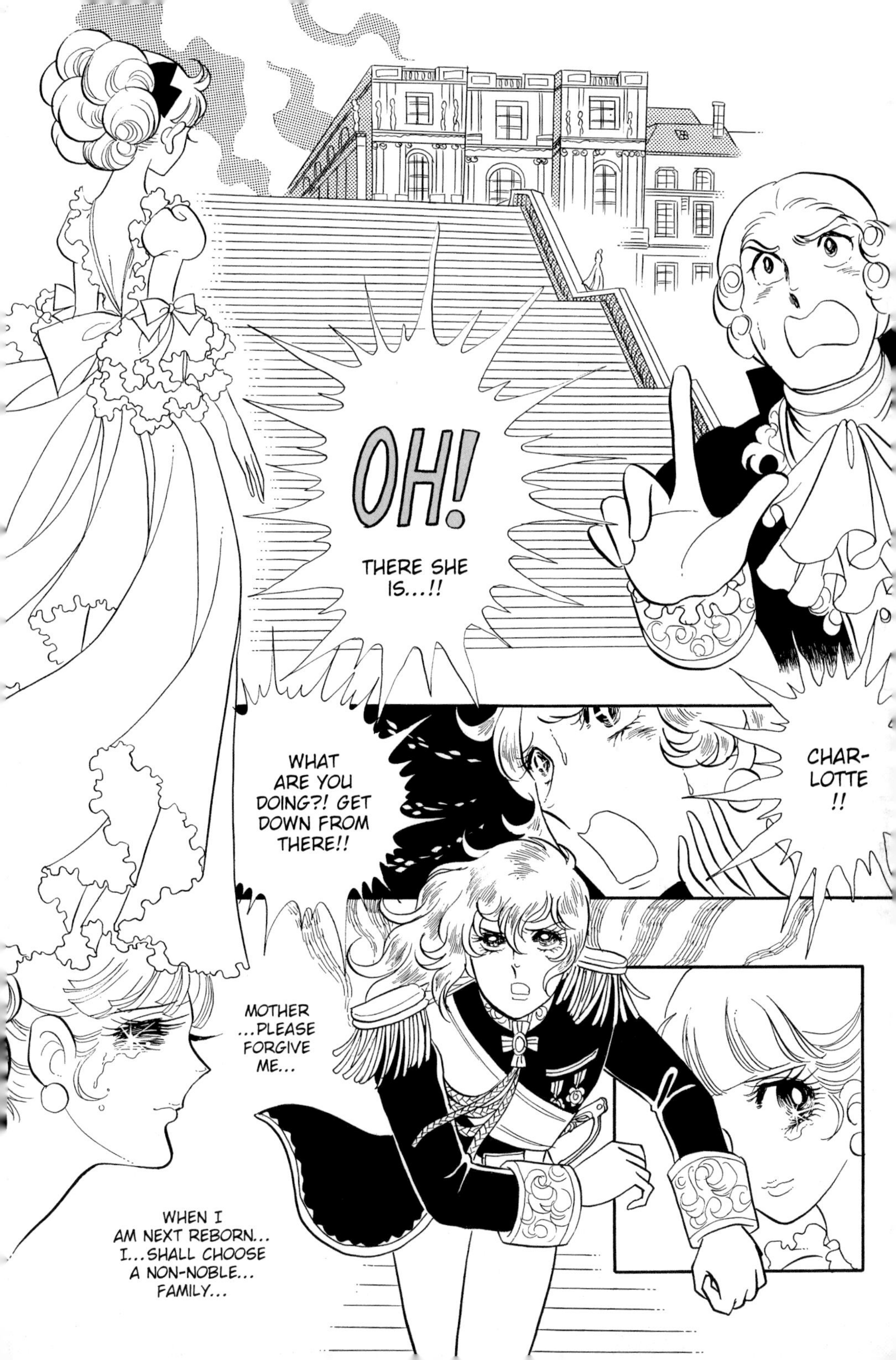
OH!
THERE SHE IS...!!
CHAR-LOTTE !!
WHAT ARE YOU DOING?! GET DOWN FROM THERE!!
MOTHER ...PLEASE FORGIVE ME...
WHEN I AM NEXT REBORN... I...SHALL CHOOSE A NON-NOBLE... FAMILY...

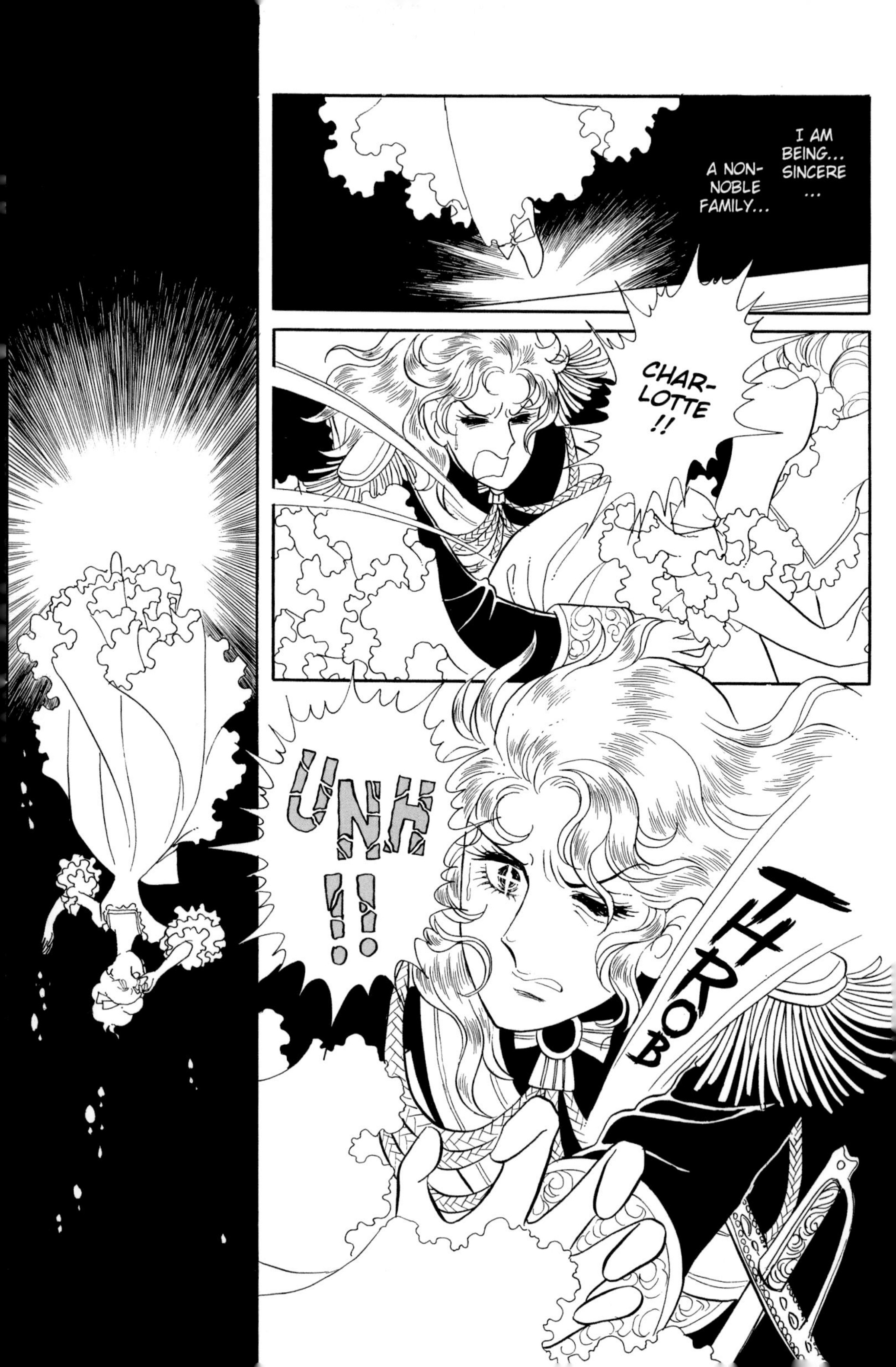
I AM BEING... SINCERE...
A NON-NOBLE FAMILY...
CHAR-LOTTE!!
THROB
UNH!!

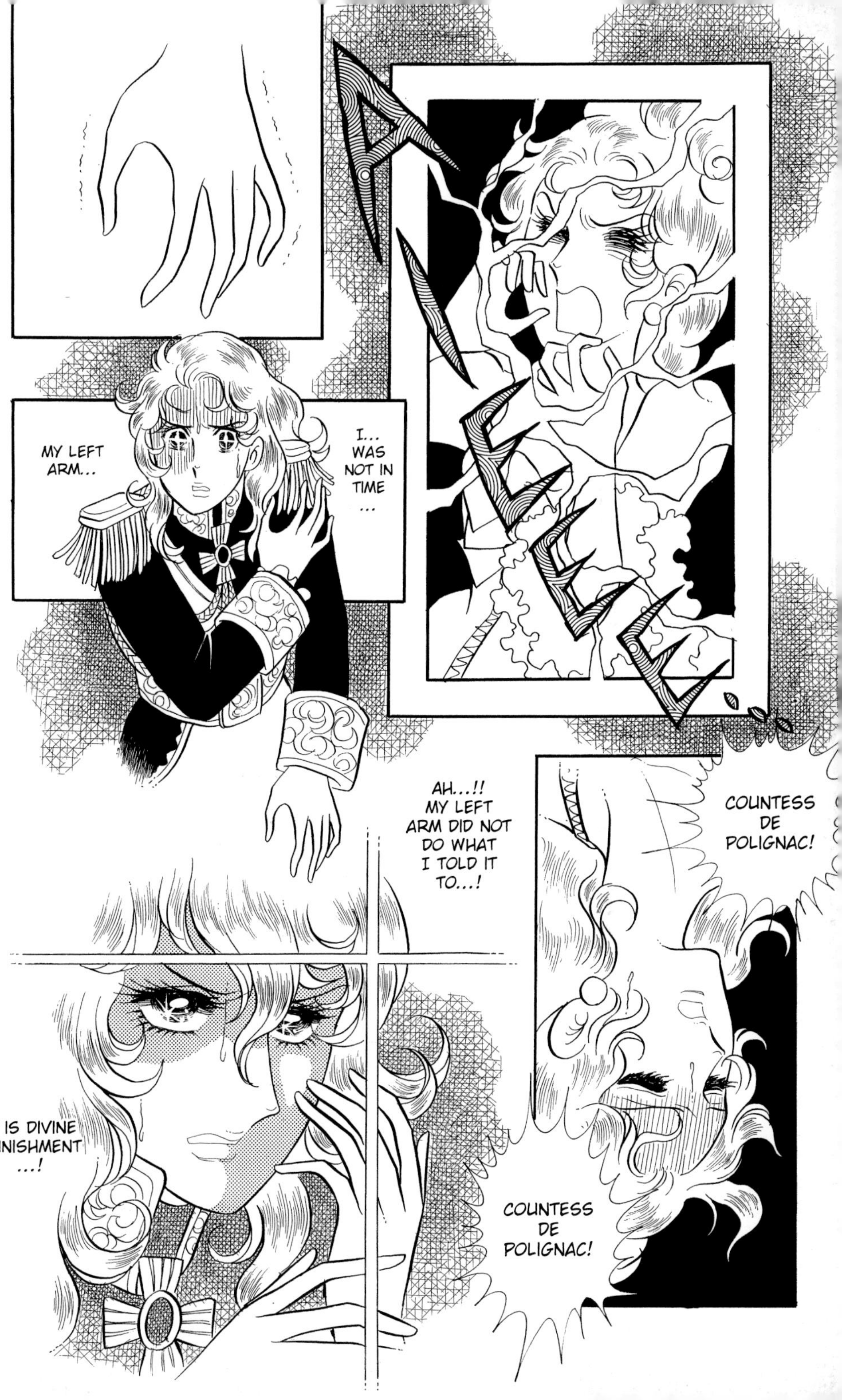
AIEEEE...
I... WAS NOT IN TIME...
MY LEFT ARM...
COUNTESS DE POLIGNAC!
COUNTESS DE POLIGNAC!
AH...!! MY LEFT ARM DID NOT DO WHAT I TOLD IT TO...!
IT IS DIVINE PUNISHMENT...!

This title page is replaced by the special colorized art in this edition.
The original version is presented here for your enjoyment.

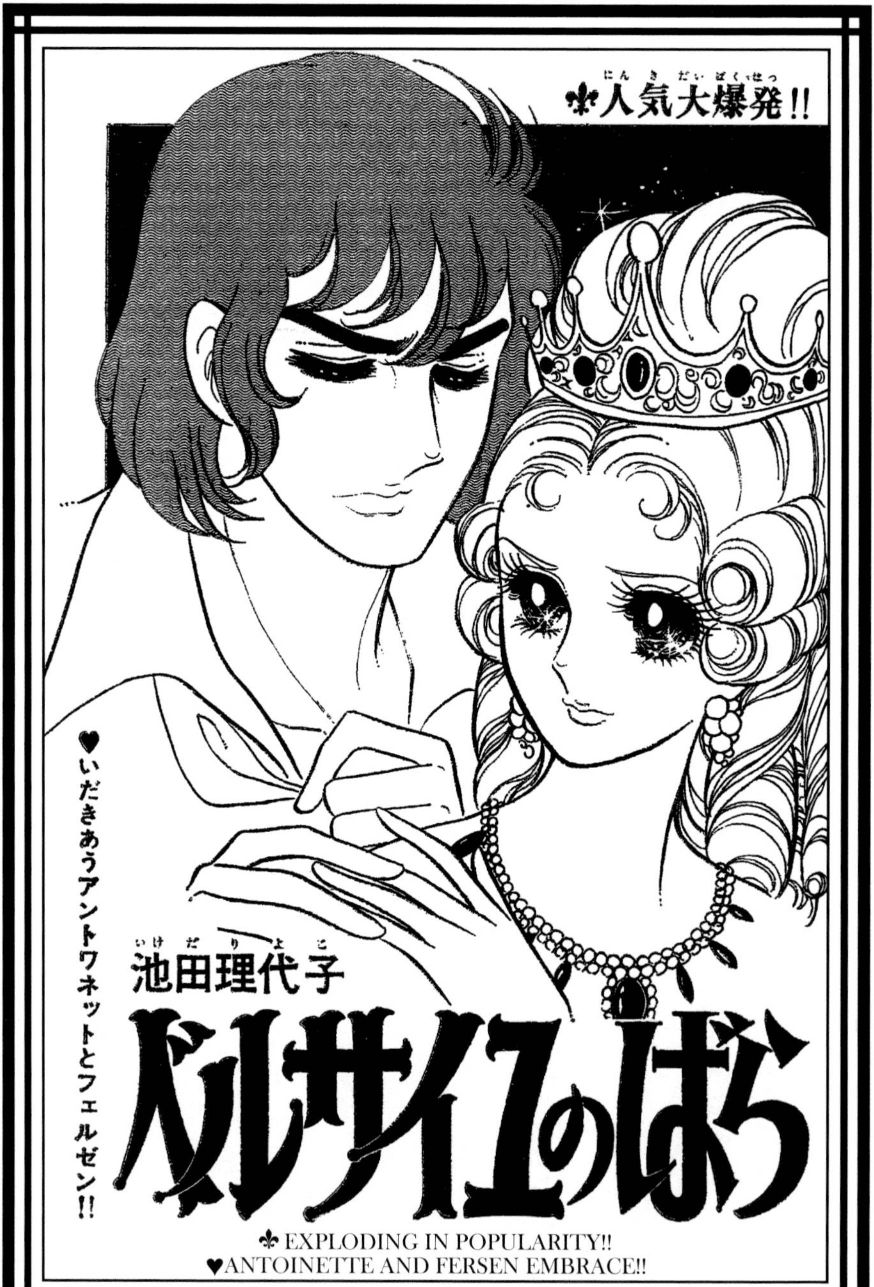
✤人気大爆発!!
♥いだきあうアントワネットとフェルゼン!!
池田理代子
ベルサイユのばら
✤ EXPLODING IN POPULARITY!!
♥ANTOINETTE AND FERSEN EMBRACE!!
EPISODE 24

♦ THE SUPER-GRAND-SCALE DRAMA SMASHING THE MOLD OF SHOJO MANGA
♥ IN EVEN GREATER FROM, EVEN MORE HUGELY POPULAR!! DOES CHARLOTTE LIVE...?!

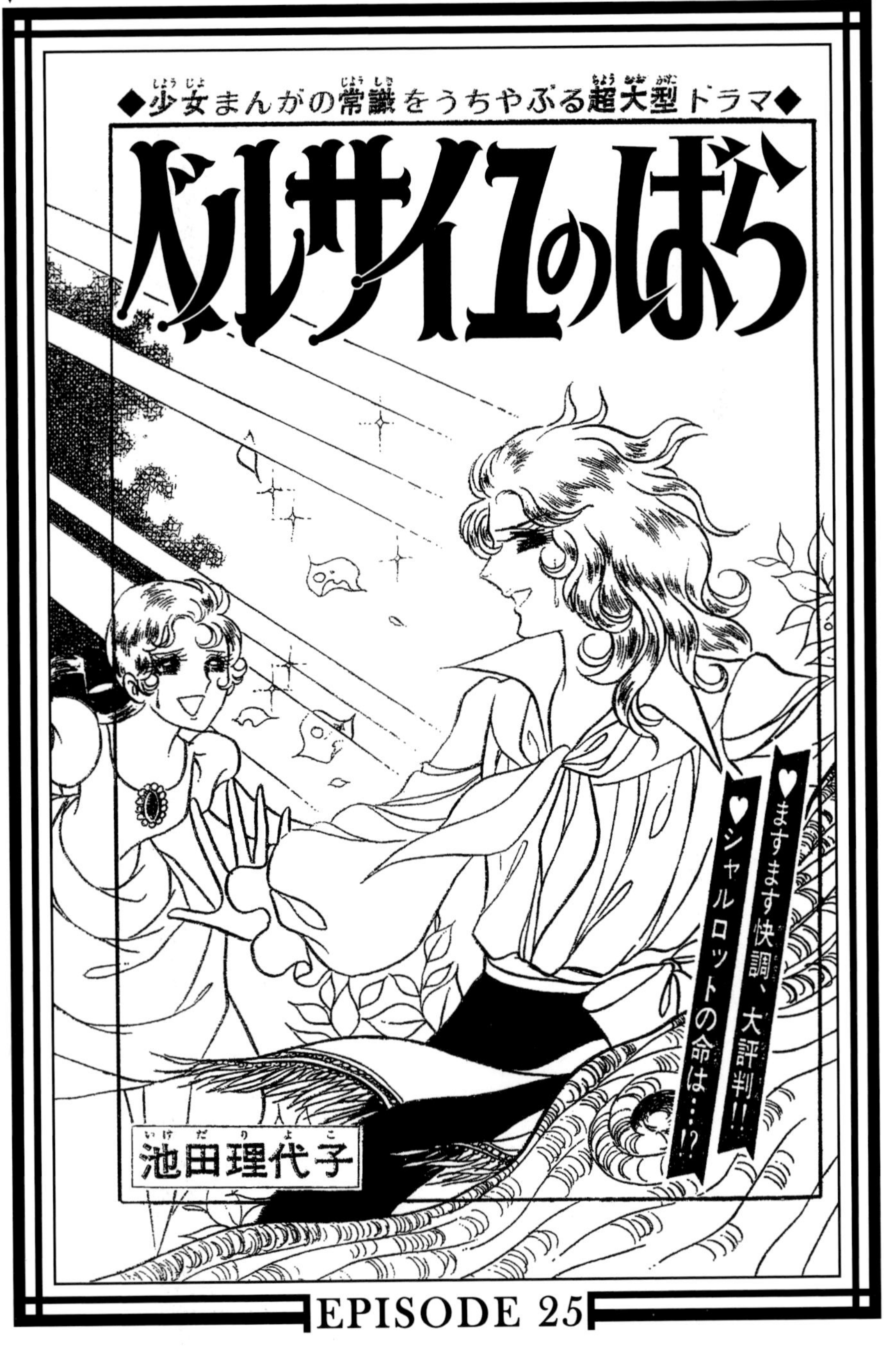
◆少女まんがの常識をうちやぶる超大型ドラマ◆
ベルサイユのばら
♥ますます快調、大評判!!
♥シャルロットの命は…!?
池田理代子
EPISODE 25

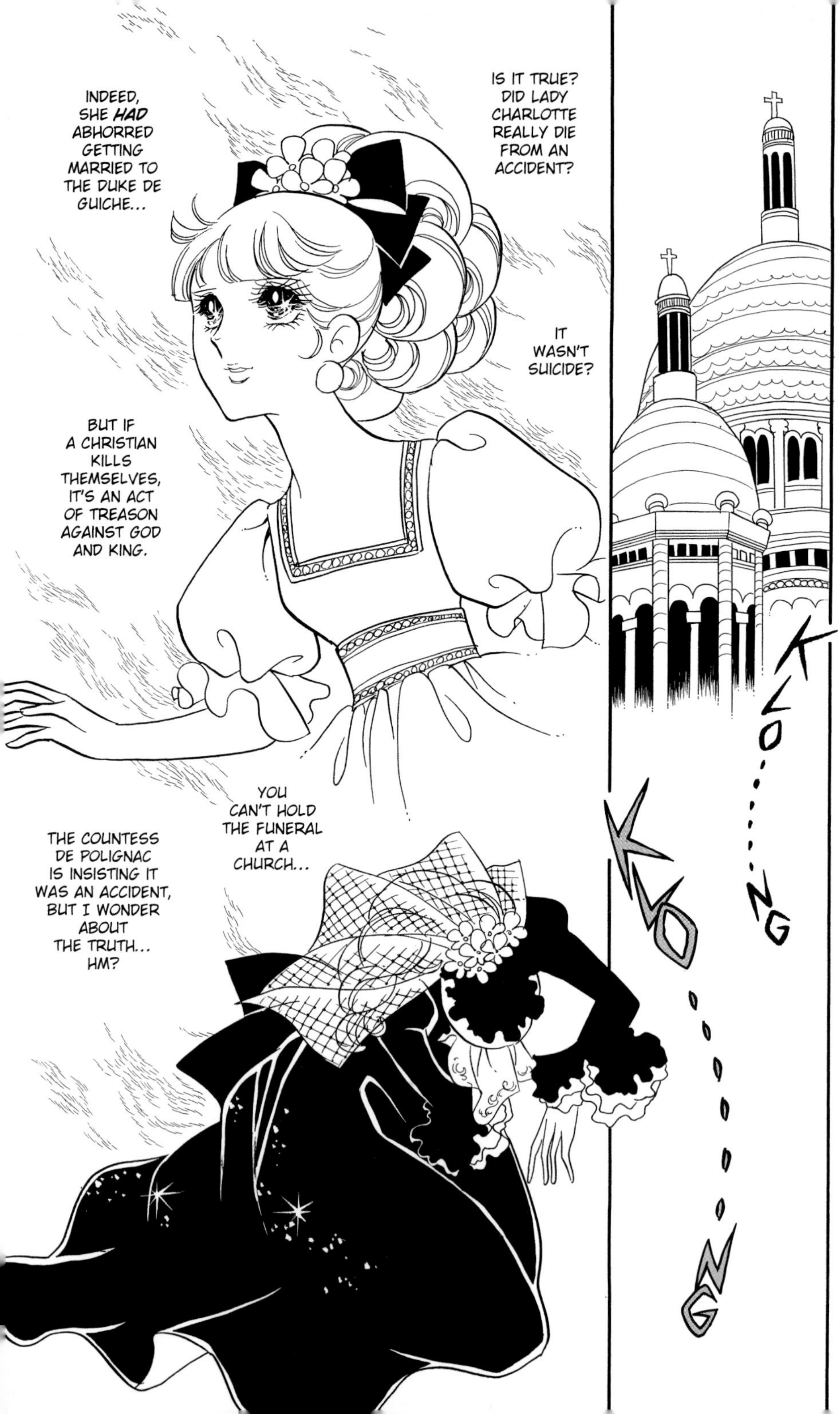
KLO......NG
KLO........NG
IS IT TRUE? DID LADY CHARLOTTE REALLY DIE FROM AN ACCIDENT?
IT WASN'T SUICIDE?
INDEED, SHE *HAD* ABHORRED GETTING MARRIED TO THE DUKE DE GUICHE...
BUT IF A CHRISTIAN KILLS THEMSELVES, IT'S AN ACT OF TREASON AGAINST GOD AND KING.
YOU CAN'T HOLD THE FUNERAL AT A CHURCH...
THE COUNTESS DE POLIGNAC IS INSISTING IT WAS AN ACCIDENT, BUT I WONDER ABOUT THE TRUTH... HM?

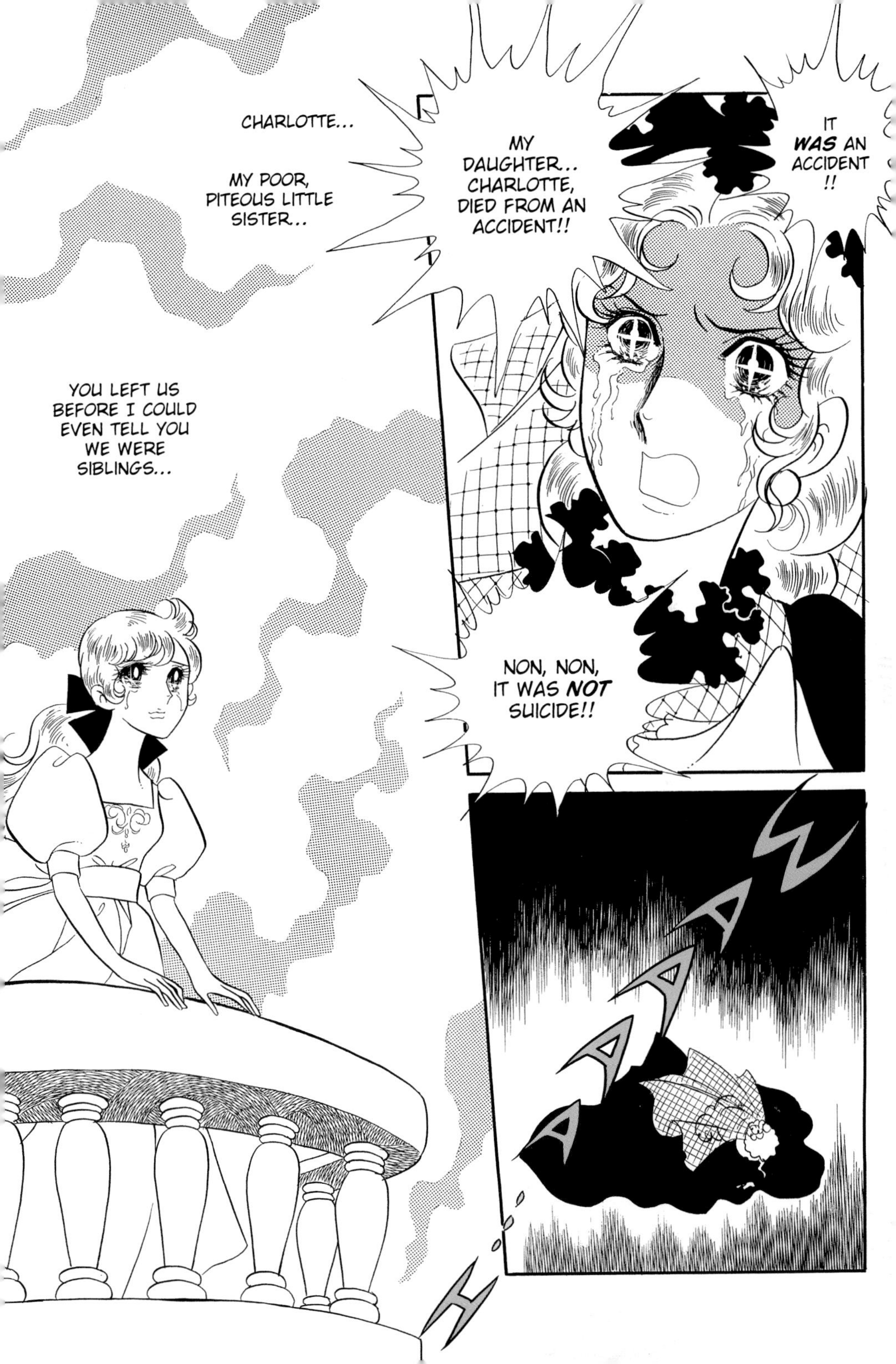
IT WAS AN ACCIDENT!!
MY DAUGHTER... CHARLOTTE, DIED FROM AN ACCIDENT!!
NON, NON, IT WAS NOT SUICIDE!!
CHARLOTTE...
MY POOR, PITEOUS LITTLE SISTER...
YOU LEFT US BEFORE I COULD EVEN TELL YOU WE WERE SIBLINGS...

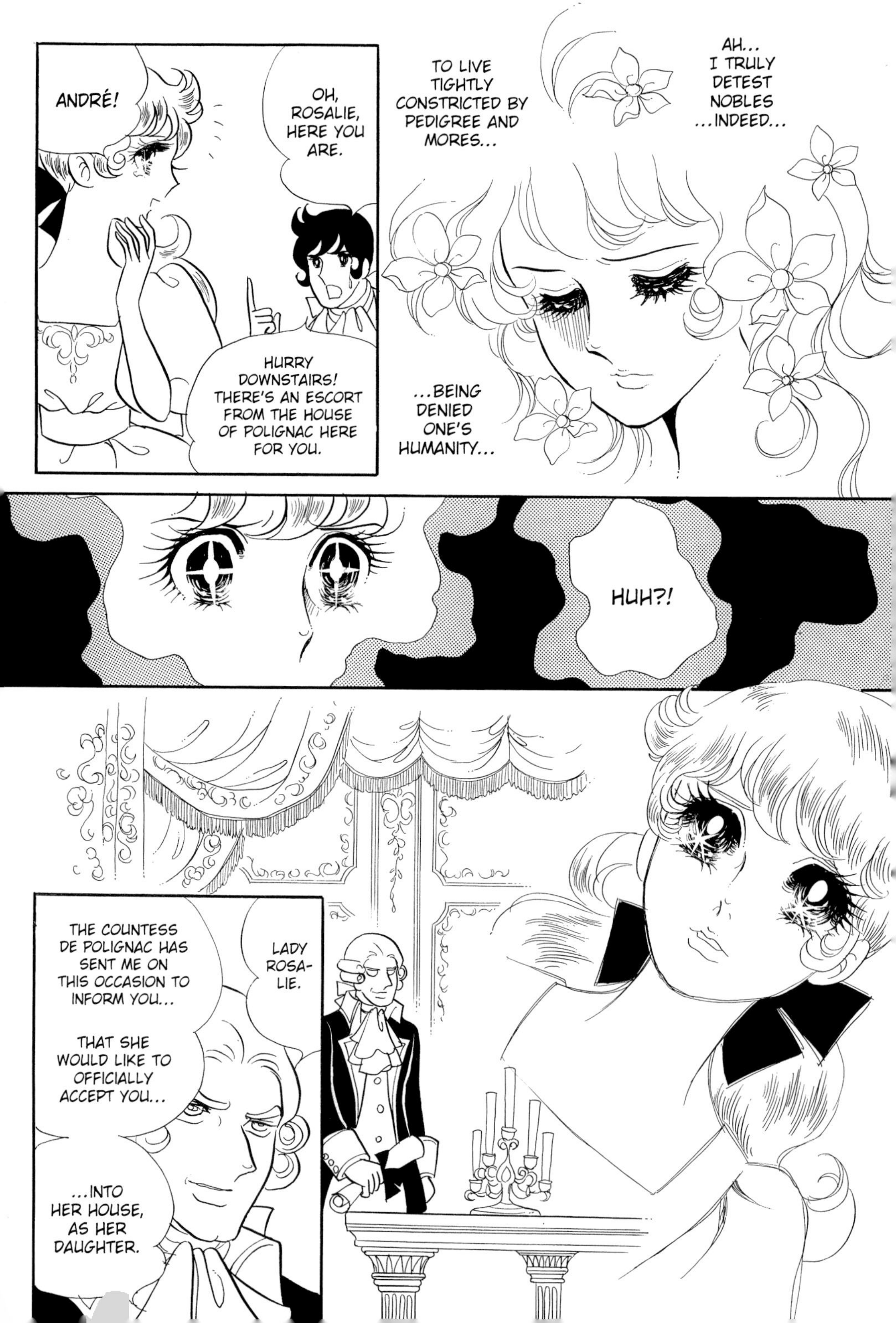
AH... I TRULY DETEST NOBLES ...INDEED...
TO LIVE TIGHTLY CONSTRICTED BY PEDIGREE AND MORES...
...BEING DENIED ONE'S HUMANITY...
OH, ROSALIE, HERE YOU ARE.
ANDRÉ!
HURRY DOWNSTAIRS! THERE'S AN ESCORT FROM THE HOUSE OF POLIGNAC HERE FOR YOU.
HUH?!
LADY ROSA-LIE.
THE COUNTESS DE POLIGNAC HAS SENT ME ON THIS OCCASION TO INFORM YOU...
THAT SHE WOULD LIKE TO OFFICIALLY ACCEPT YOU...
...INTO HER HOUSE, AS HER DAUGHTER.

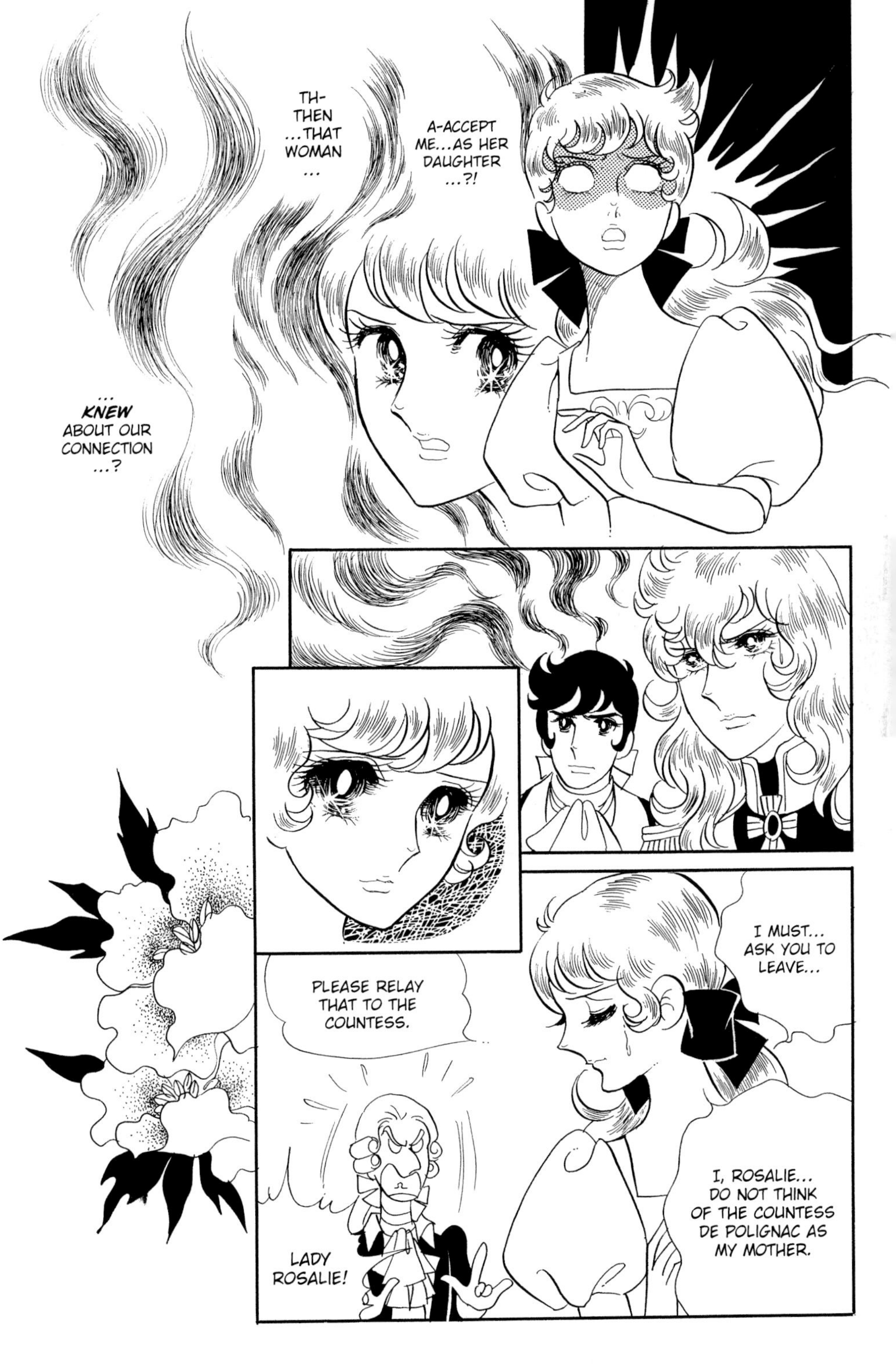
A-ACCEPT ME...AS HER DAUGHTER ...?!
TH- THEN ...THAT WOMAN ...
... KNEW ABOUT OUR CONNECTION ...?
I MUST... ASK YOU TO LEAVE...
I, ROSALIE... DO NOT THINK OF THE COUNTESS DE POLIGNAC AS MY MOTHER.
PLEASE RELAY THAT TO THE COUNTESS.
LADY ROSALIE!

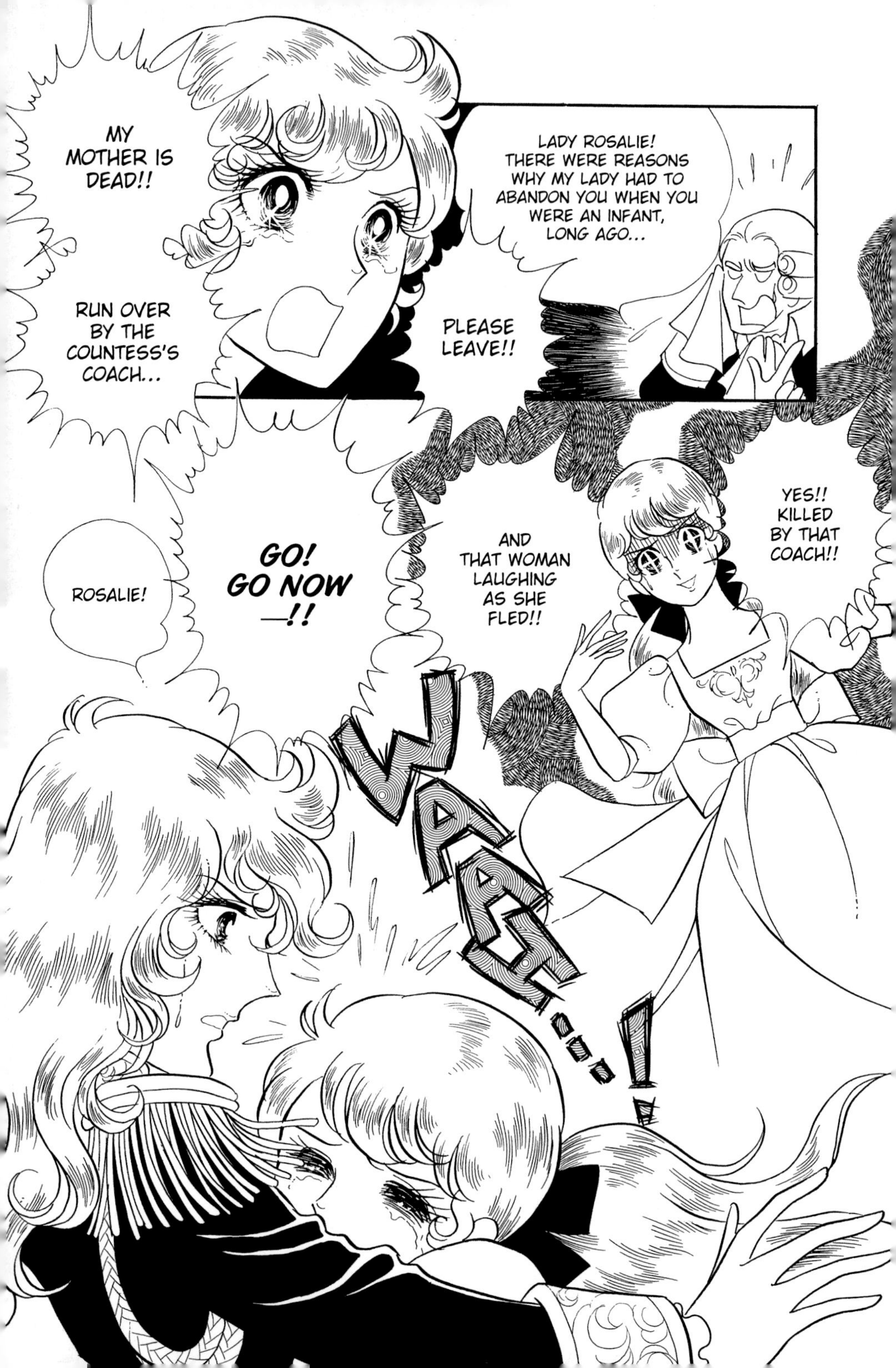
LADY ROSALIE! THERE WERE REASONS WHY MY LADY HAD TO ABANDON YOU WHEN YOU WERE AN INFANT, LONG AGO...
PLEASE LEAVE!!
MY MOTHER IS DEAD!!
RUN OVER BY THE COUNTESS'S COACH...
YES!! KILLED BY THAT COACH!!
AND THAT WOMAN LAUGHING AS SHE FLED!!
GO! GO NOW —!!
ROSALIE!
WAAAH...!!

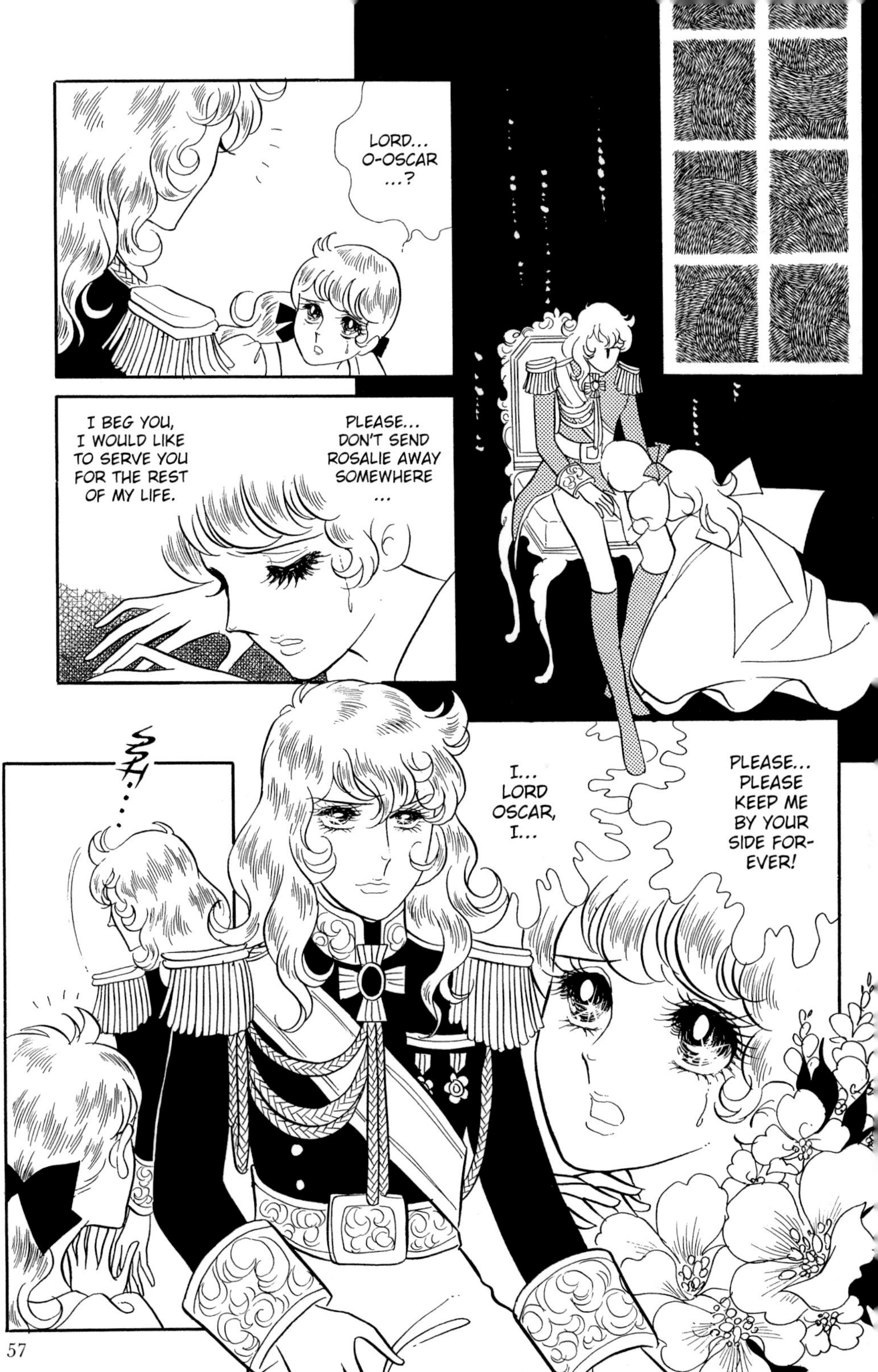
LORD... O-OSCAR ...?
PLEASE... DON'T SEND ROSALIE AWAY SOMEWHERE ...
I BEG YOU, I WOULD LIKE TO SERVE YOU FOR THE REST OF MY LIFE.
PLEASE... PLEASE KEEP ME BY YOUR SIDE FOR-EVER!
I... LORD OSCAR, I...
SSH...

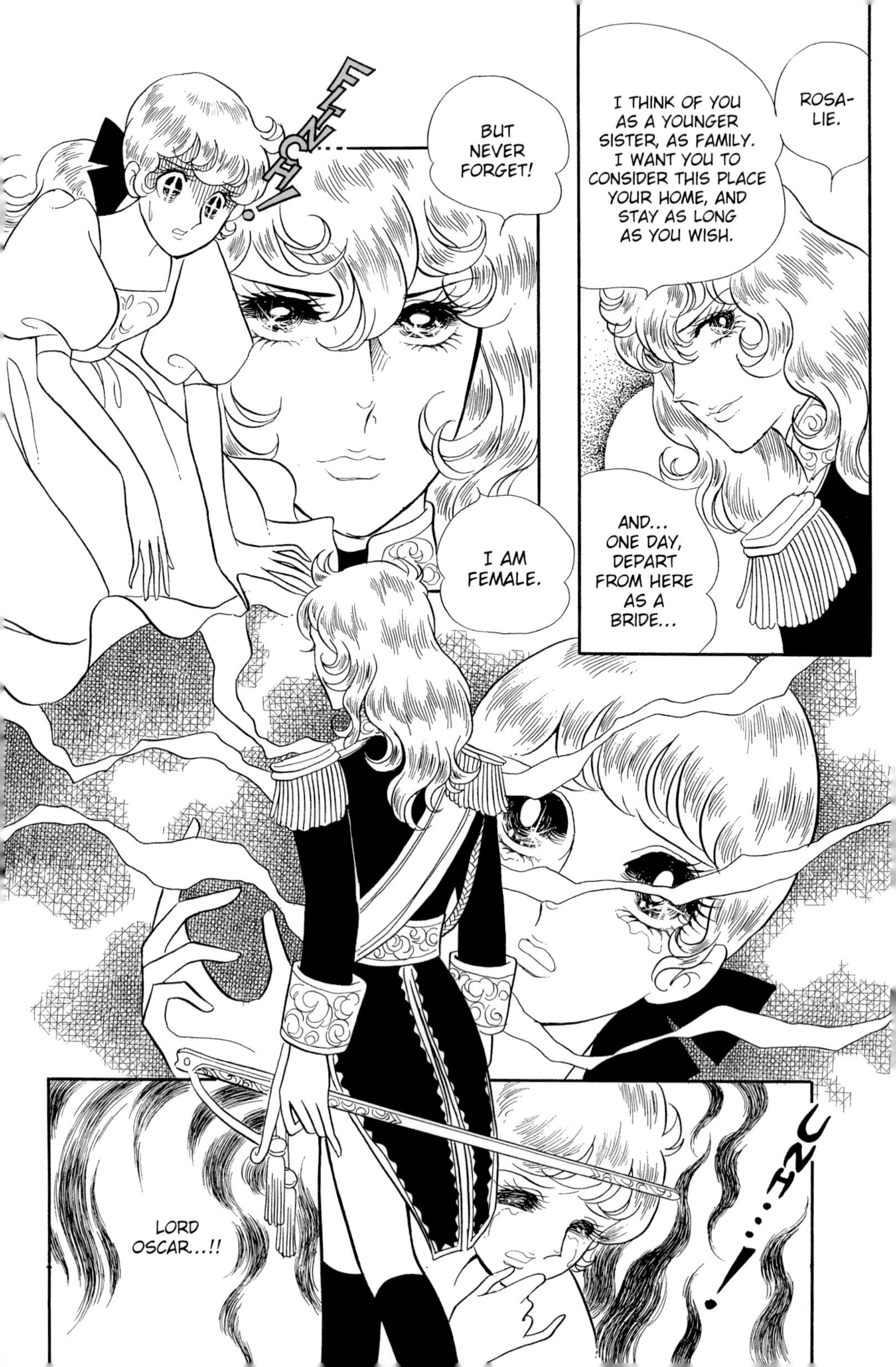
ROSA-LIE.
I THINK OF YOU AS A YOUNGER SISTER, AS FAMILY. I WANT YOU TO CONSIDER THIS PLACE YOUR HOME, AND STAY AS LONG AS YOU WISH.
AND... ONE DAY, DEPART FROM HERE AS A BRIDE...
FLINCH!
BUT NEVER FORGET!
I AM FEMALE.
LORD OSCAR...!!

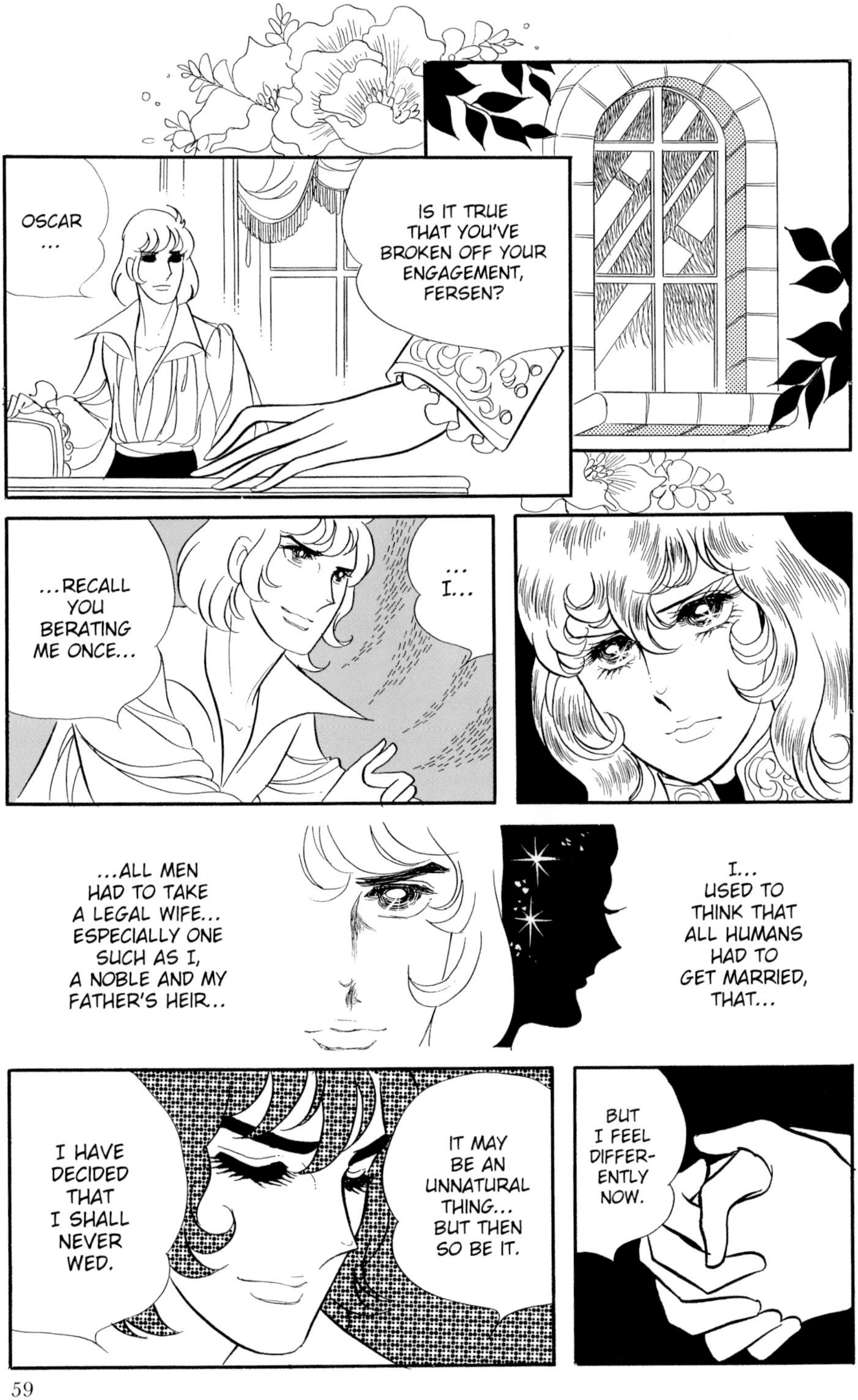
IS IT TRUE THAT YOU'VE BROKEN OFF YOUR ENGAGEMENT, FERSEN?
OSCAR ...
... I...
...RECALL YOU BERATING ME ONCE...
I... USED TO THINK THAT ALL HUMANS HAD TO GET MARRIED, THAT...
...ALL MEN HAD TO TAKE A LEGAL WIFE... ESPECIALLY ONE SUCH AS I, A NOBLE AND MY FATHER'S HEIR...
BUT I FEEL DIFFER-ENTLY NOW.
IT MAY BE AN UNNATURAL THING... BUT THEN SO BE IT.
I HAVE DECIDED THAT I SHALL NEVER WED.

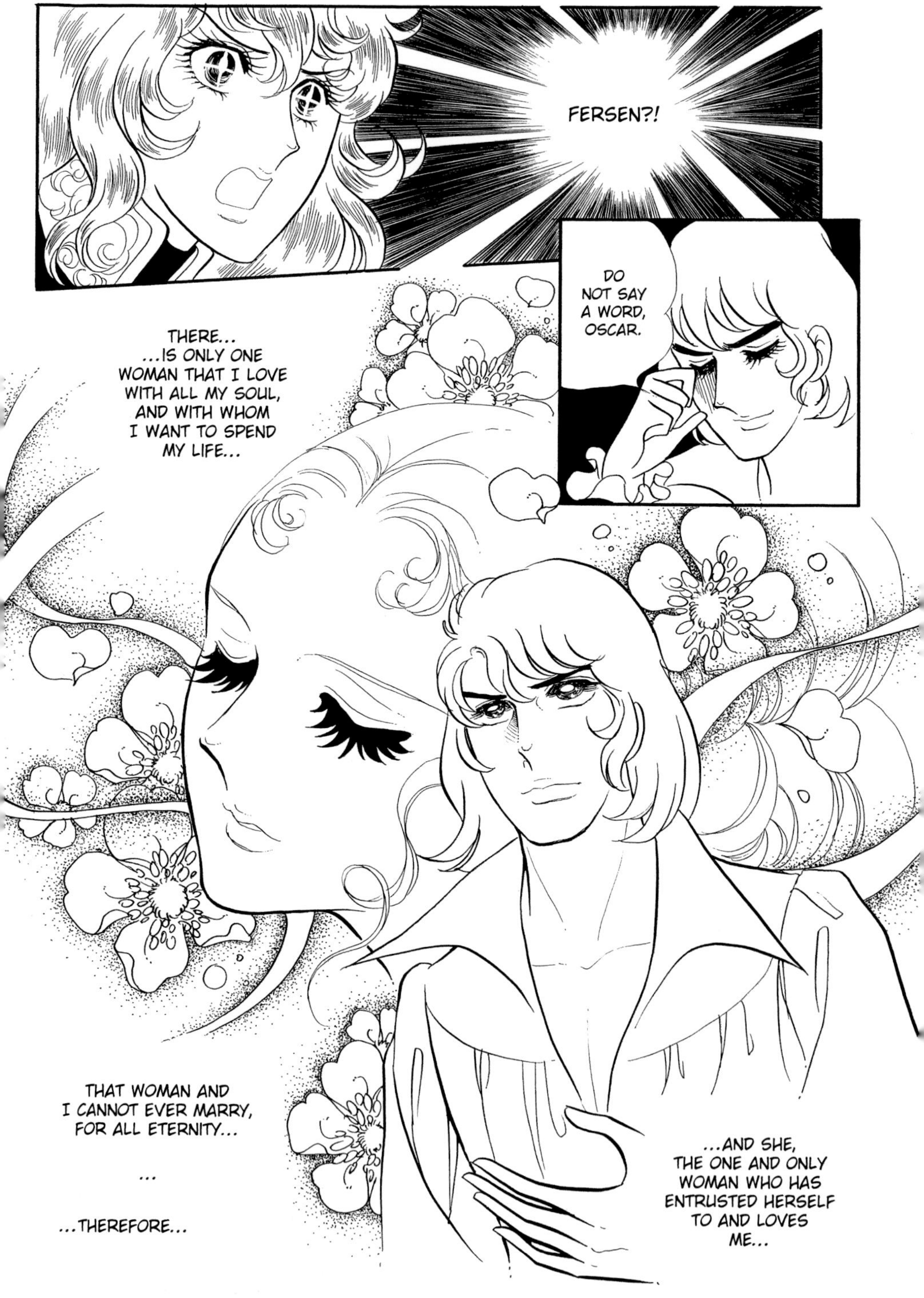
FERSEN?!
DO NOT SAY A WORD, OSCAR.
THERE... ...IS ONLY ONE WOMAN THAT I LOVE WITH ALL MY SOUL, AND WITH WHOM I WANT TO SPEND MY LIFE...
...AND SHE, THE ONE AND ONLY WOMAN WHO HAS ENTRUSTED HERSELF TO AND LOVES ME...
THAT WOMAN AND I CANNOT EVER MARRY, FOR ALL ETERNITY...
...
...THEREFORE...

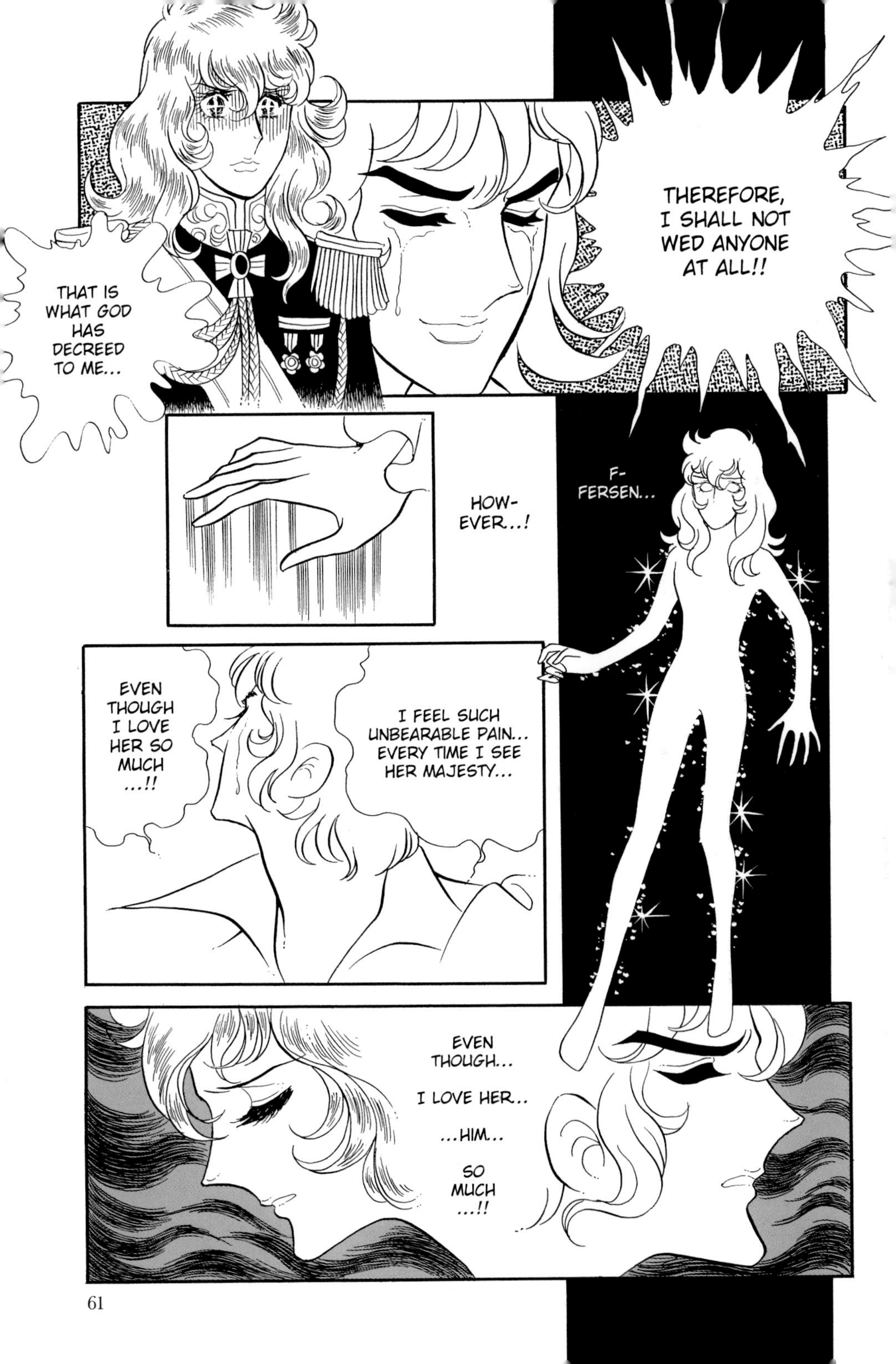
THEREFORE, I SHALL NOT WED ANYONE AT ALL!!
THAT IS WHAT GOD HAS DECREED TO ME...
F- FERSEN...
HOW-EVER...!
I FEEL SUCH UNBEARABLE PAIN... EVERY TIME I SEE HER MAJESTY...
EVEN THOUGH I LOVE HER SO MUCH ...!!
EVEN THOUGH...
I LOVE HER..
...HIM...
SO MUCH ...!!

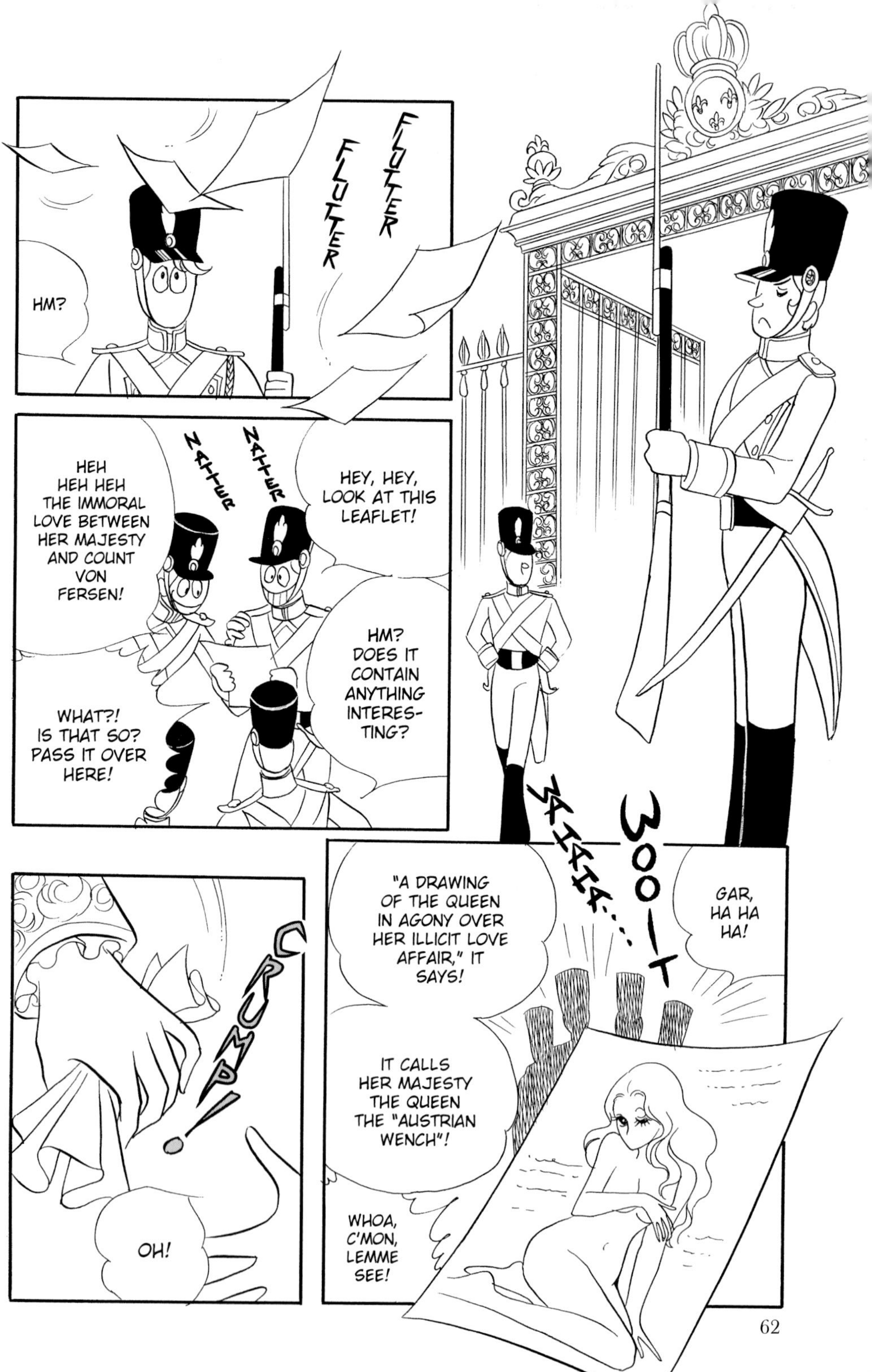
FLUTTER
FLUTTER
HM?
HEY, HEY, LOOK AT THIS LEAFLET!
NATTER
NATTER
HEH HEH HEH THE IMMORAL LOVE BETWEEN HER MAJESTY AND COUNT VON FERSEN!
HM? DOES IT CONTAIN ANYTHING INTERES-TING?
WHAT?! IS THAT SO? PASS IT OVER HERE!
GAR, HA HA HA!
WOO-IT
WAHAHA....
"A DRAWING OF THE QUEEN IN AGONY OVER HER ILLICIT LOVE AFFAIR," IT SAYS!
IT CALLS HER MAJESTY THE QUEEN THE "AUSTRIAN WENCH"!
WHOA, C'MON, LEMME SEE!
CRUMP!
OH!

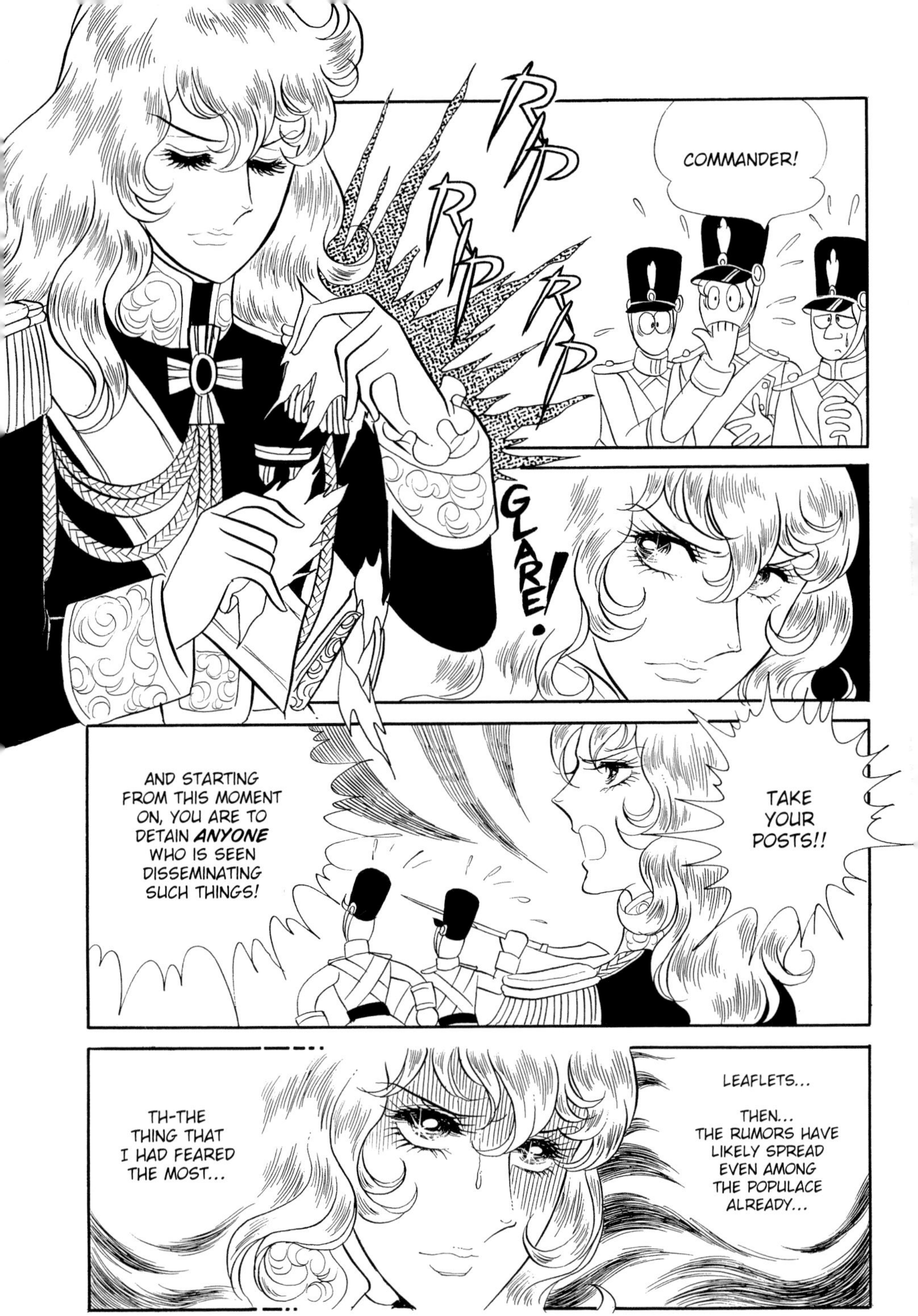
COMMANDER!
GLARE!
RIP RIP RIP RIP
TAKE YOUR POSTS!!
AND STARTING FROM THIS MOMENT ON, YOU ARE TO DETAIN **ANYONE** WHO IS SEEN DISSEMINATING SUCH THINGS!
LEAFLETS...
THEN... THE RUMORS HAVE LIKELY SPREAD EVEN AMONG THE POPULACE ALREADY...
TH-THE THING THAT I HAD FEARED THE MOST...

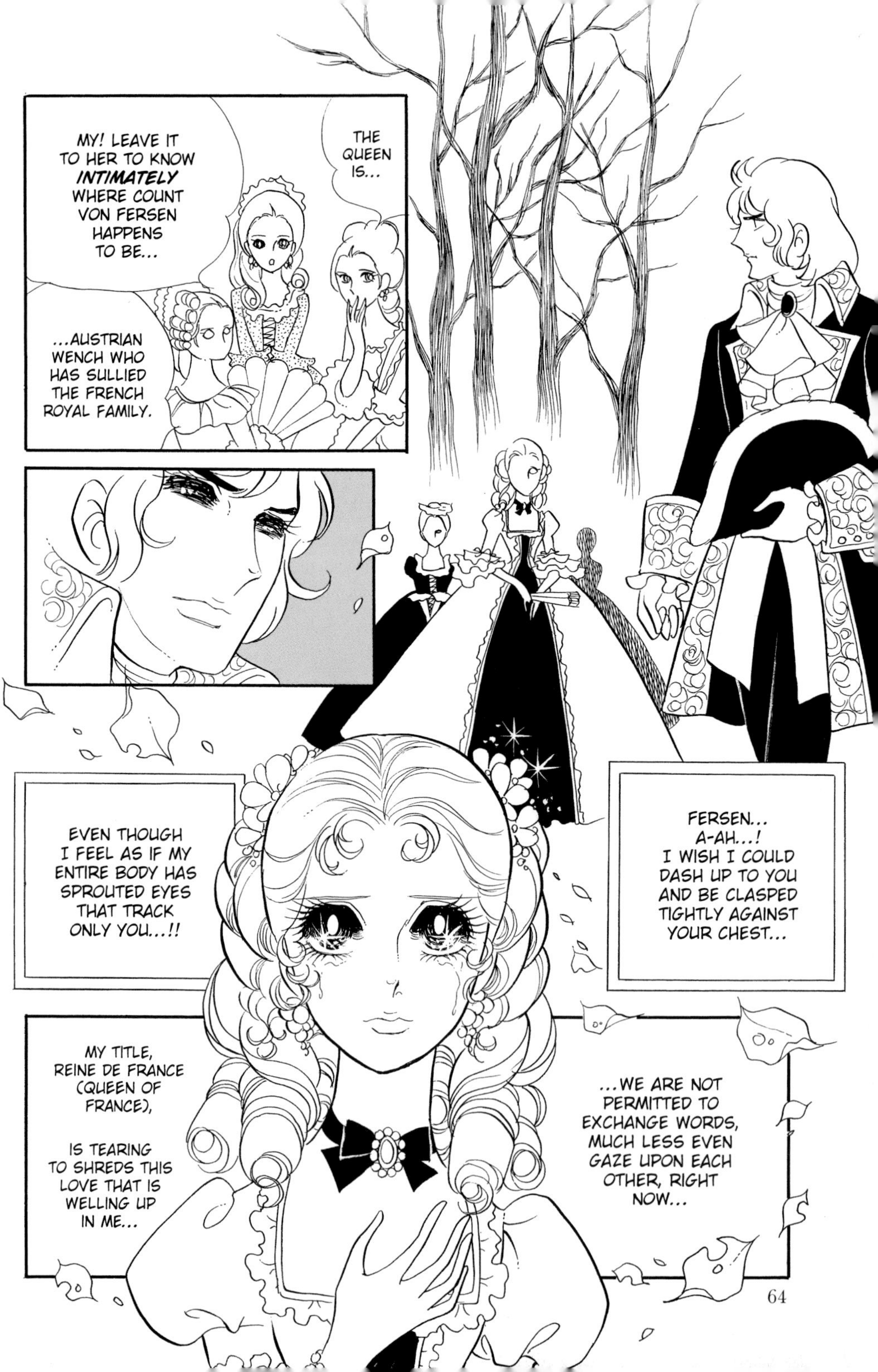
THE QUEEN IS...
MY! LEAVE IT TO HER TO KNOW *INTIMATELY* WHERE COUNT VON FERSEN HAPPENS TO BE...
...AUSTRIAN WENCH WHO HAS SULLIED THE FRENCH ROYAL FAMILY.
FERSEN... A-AH...! I WISH I COULD DASH UP TO YOU AND BE CLASPED TIGHTLY AGAINST YOUR CHEST...
EVEN THOUGH I FEEL AS IF MY ENTIRE BODY HAS SPROUTED EYES THAT TRACK ONLY YOU...!!
...WE ARE NOT PERMITTED TO EXCHANGE WORDS, MUCH LESS EVEN GAZE UPON EACH OTHER, RIGHT NOW...
MY TITLE, REINE DE FRANCE (QUEEN OF FRANCE),
IS TEARING TO SHREDS THIS LOVE THAT IS WELLING UP IN ME...

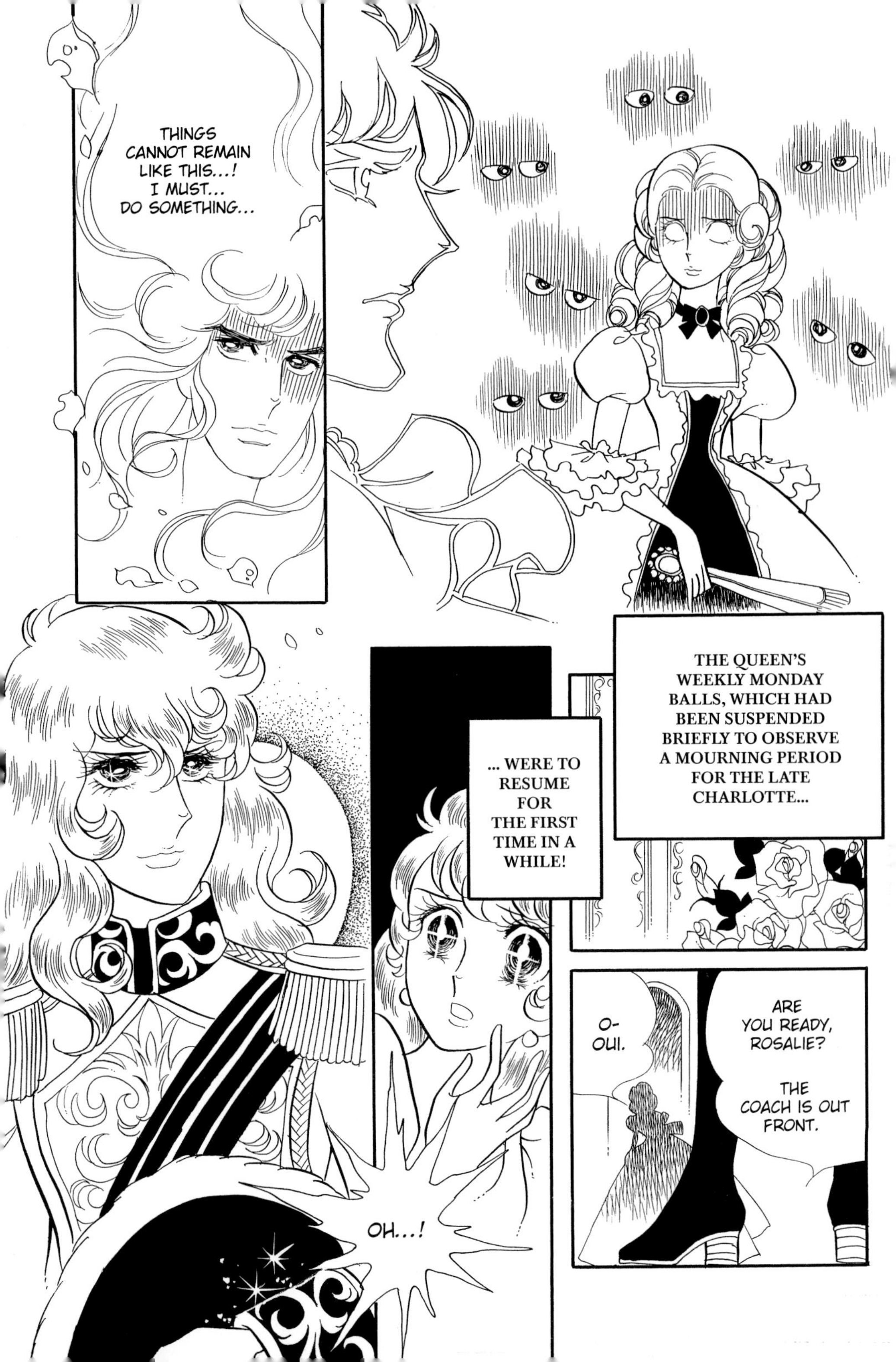
THINGS CANNOT REMAIN LIKE THIS...! I MUST... DO SOMETHING...
THE QUEEN'S WEEKLY MONDAY BALLS, WHICH HAD BEEN SUSPENDED BRIEFLY TO OBSERVE A MOURNING PERIOD FOR THE LATE CHARLOTTE...
... WERE TO RESUME FOR THE FIRST TIME IN A WHILE!
ARE YOU READY, ROSALIE?
THE COACH IS OUT FRONT.
O-OUI.
OH...!

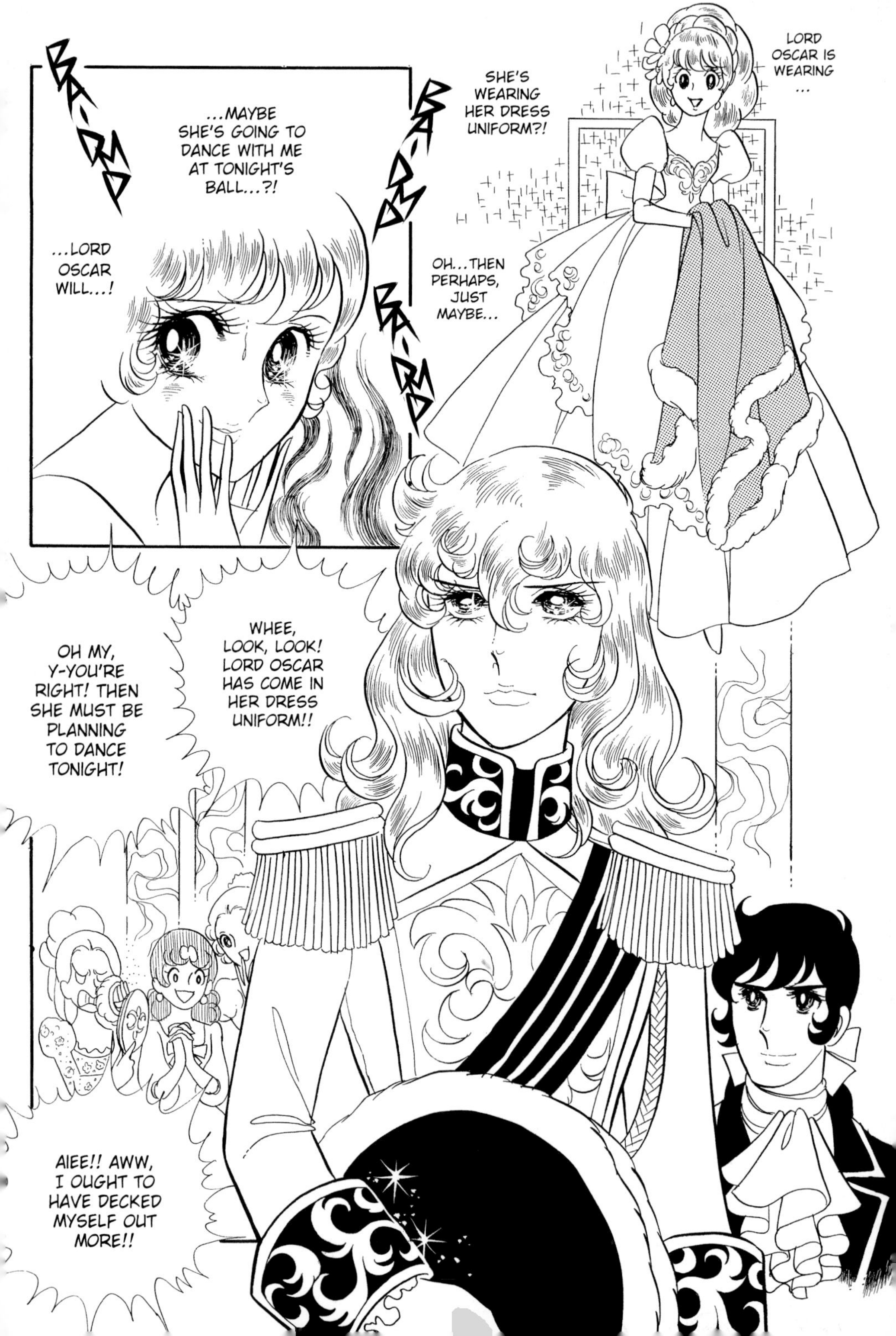
LORD OSCAR IS WEARING ...
SHE'S WEARING HER DRESS UNIFORM?!
OH...THEN PERHAPS, JUST MAYBE...
BA-DMP
BA-DMP
...MAYBE SHE'S GOING TO DANCE WITH ME AT TONIGHT'S BALL...?!
BA-DMP
...LORD OSCAR WILL...!
WHEE, LOOK, LOOK! LORD OSCAR HAS COME IN HER DRESS UNIFORM!!
OH MY, Y-YOU'RE RIGHT! THEN SHE MUST BE PLANNING TO DANCE TONIGHT!
AIEE!! AWW, I OUGHT TO HAVE DECKED MYSELF OUT MORE!!

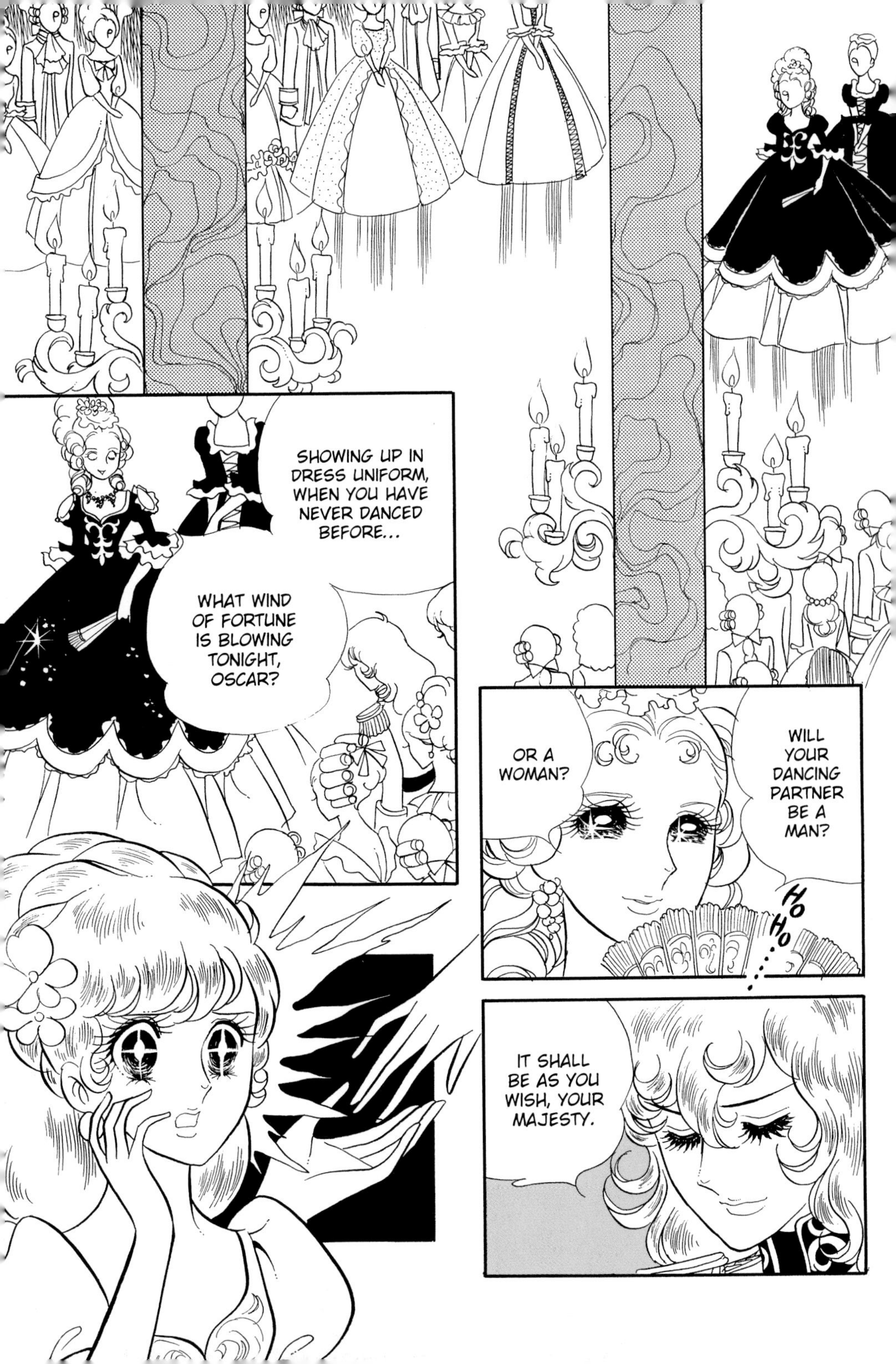
SHOWING UP IN DRESS UNIFORM, WHEN YOU HAVE NEVER DANCED BEFORE...
WHAT WIND OF FORTUNE IS BLOWING TONIGHT, OSCAR?
WILL YOUR DANCING PARTNER BE A MAN?
OR A WOMAN?
HO HO HO...
IT SHALL BE AS YOU WISH, YOUR MAJESTY.

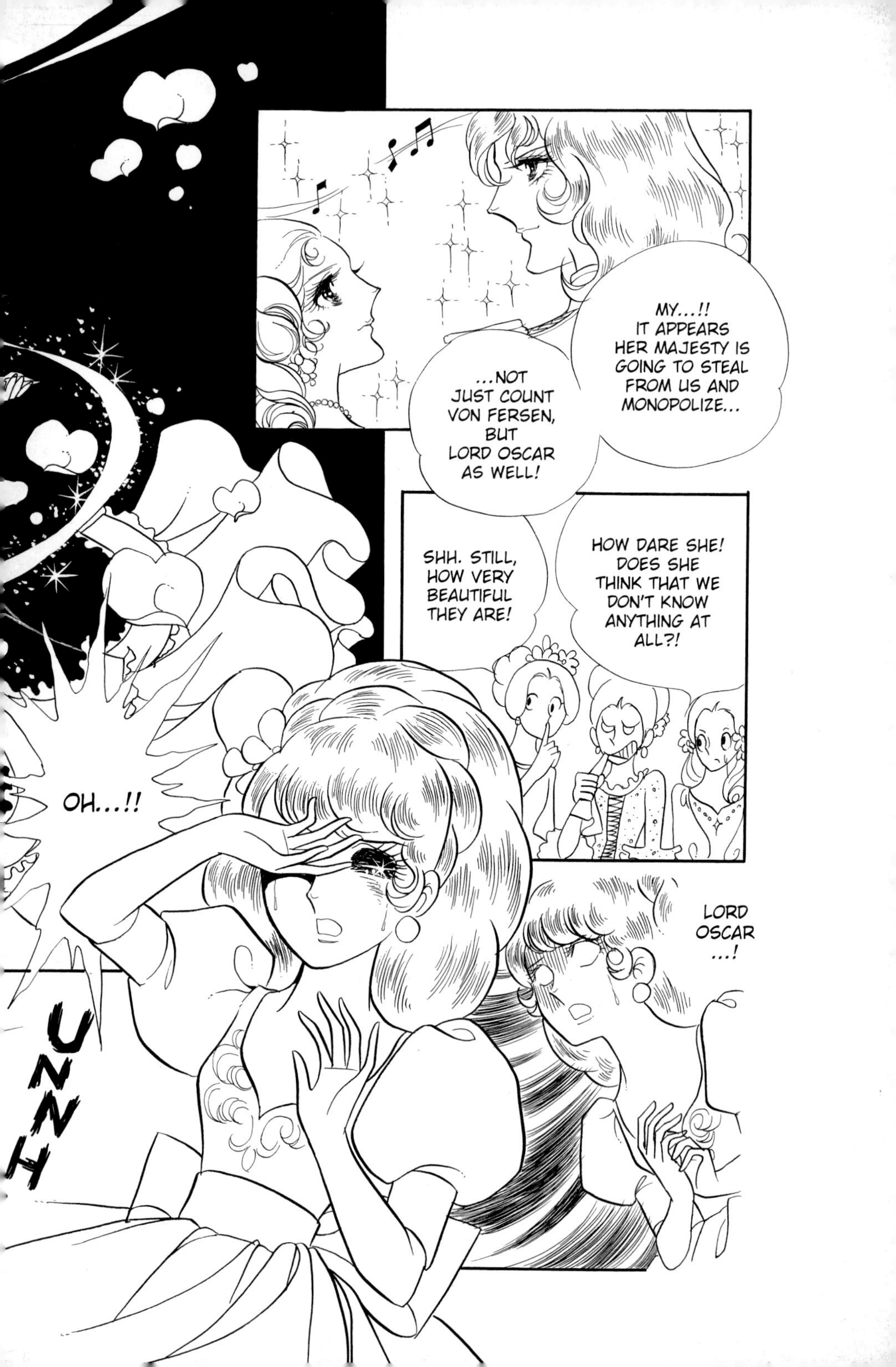
MY...!! IT APPEARS HER MAJESTY IS GOING TO STEAL FROM US AND MONOPOLIZE...
...NOT JUST COUNT VON FERSEN, BUT LORD OSCAR AS WELL!
HOW DARE SHE! DOES SHE THINK THAT WE DON'T KNOW ANYTHING AT ALL?!
SHH. STILL, HOW VERY BEAUTIFUL THEY ARE!
OH...!!
LORD OSCAR ...!
UNNH

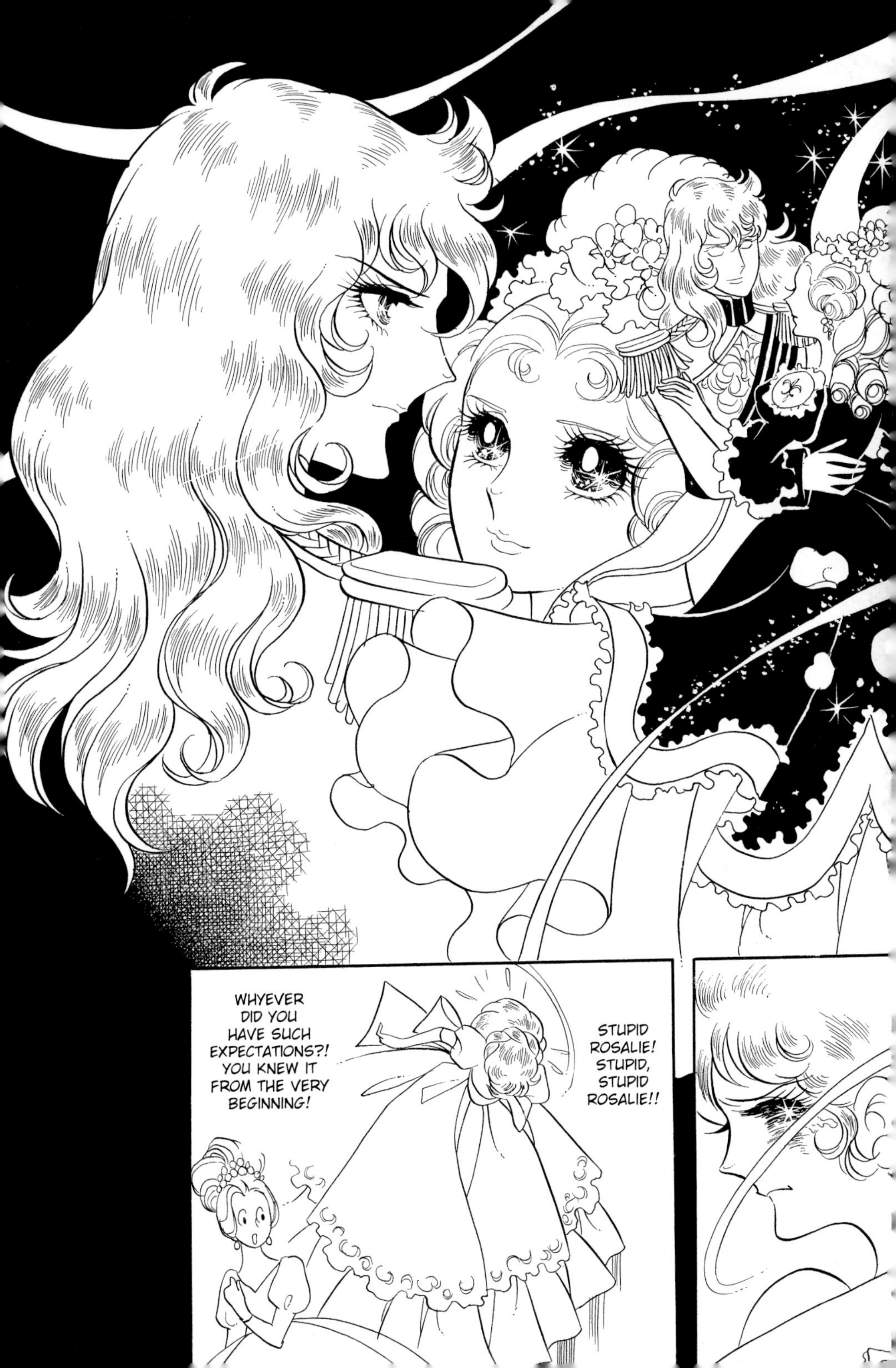
STUPID ROSALIE! STUPID, STUPID ROSALIE!!
WHYEVER DID YOU HAVE SUCH EXPECTATIONS?! YOU KNEW IT FROM THE VERY BEGINNING!

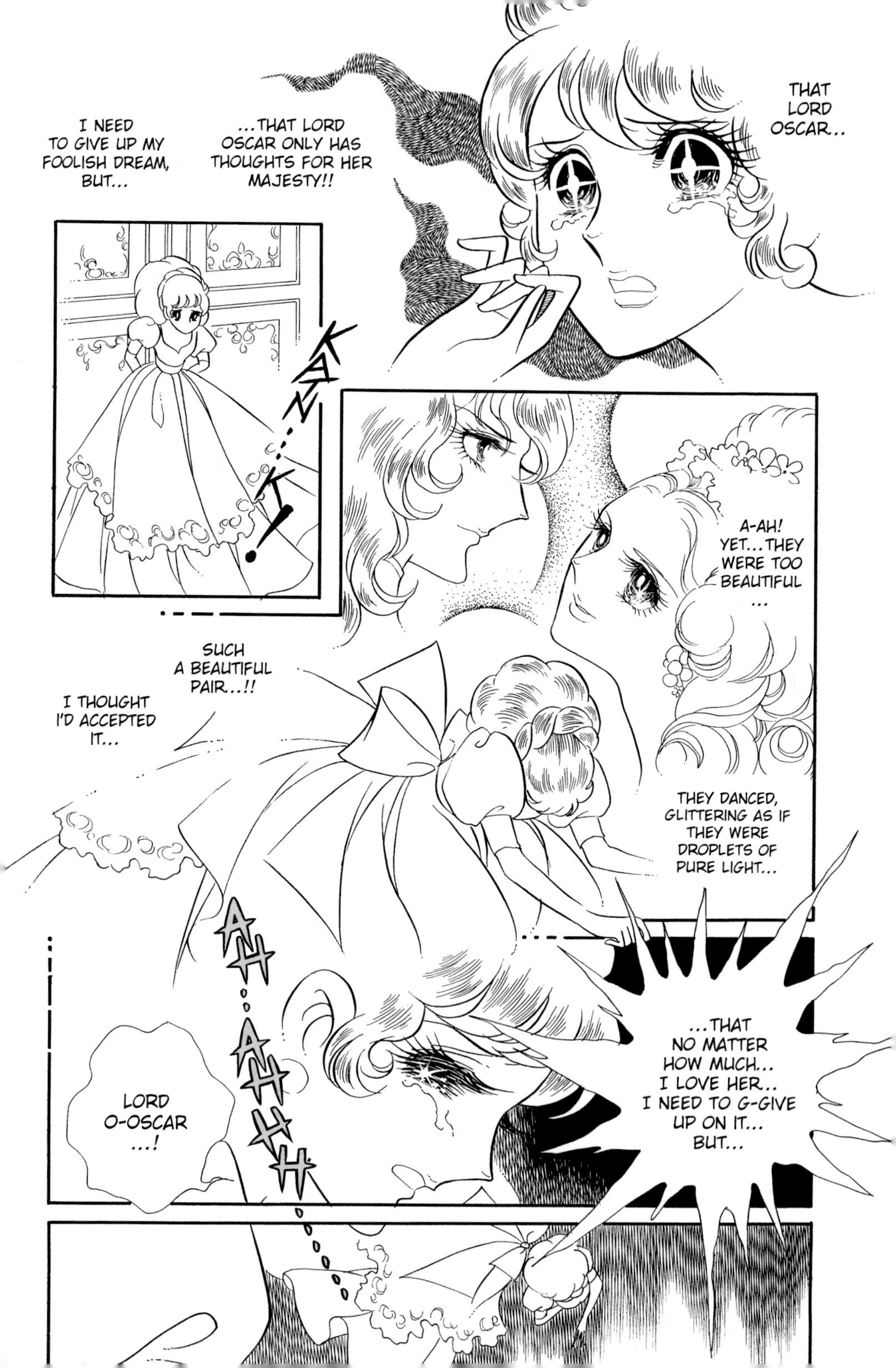
THAT LORD OSCAR...
...THAT LORD OSCAR ONLY HAS THOUGHTS FOR HER MAJESTY!!
I NEED TO GIVE UP MY FOOLISH DREAM, BUT...
A-AH! YET...THEY WERE TOO BEAUTIFUL...
SUCH A BEAUTIFUL PAIR...!!
I THOUGHT I'D ACCEPTED IT...
THEY DANCED, GLITTERING AS IF THEY WERE DROPLETS OF PURE LIGHT...
...THAT NO MATTER HOW MUCH... I LOVE HER.. I NEED TO G-GIVE UP ON IT... BUT...
AH...AHHH
LORD O-OSCAR ...!

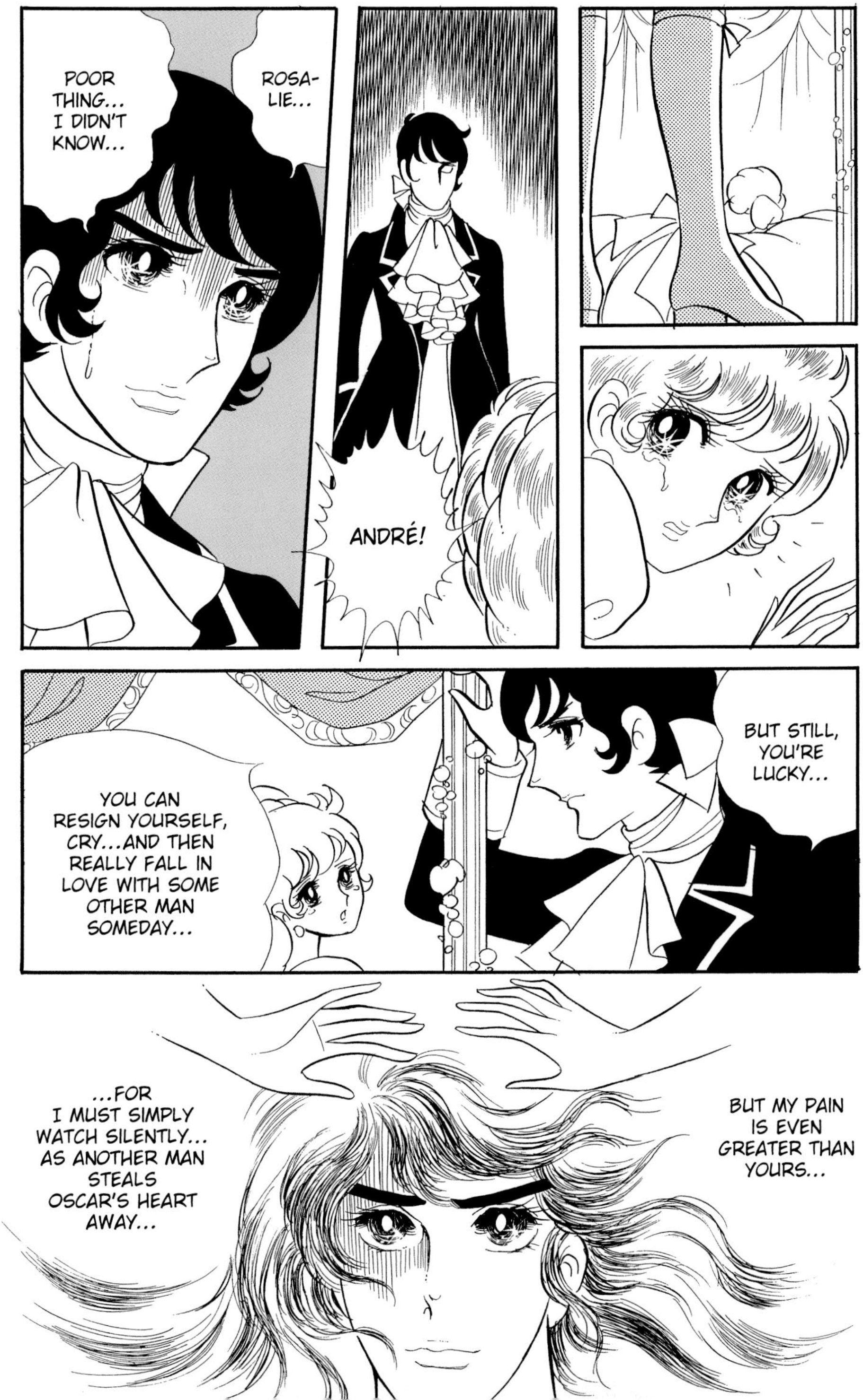
ANDRÉ!
ROSA-LIE...
POOR THING... I DIDN'T KNOW...
BUT STILL, YOU'RE LUCKY...
YOU CAN RESIGN YOURSELF, CRY...AND THEN REALLY FALL IN LOVE WITH SOME OTHER MAN SOMEDAY...
BUT MY PAIN IS EVEN GREATER THAN YOURS...
...FOR I MUST SIMPLY WATCH SILENTLY... AS ANOTHER MAN STEALS OSCAR'S HEART AWAY...

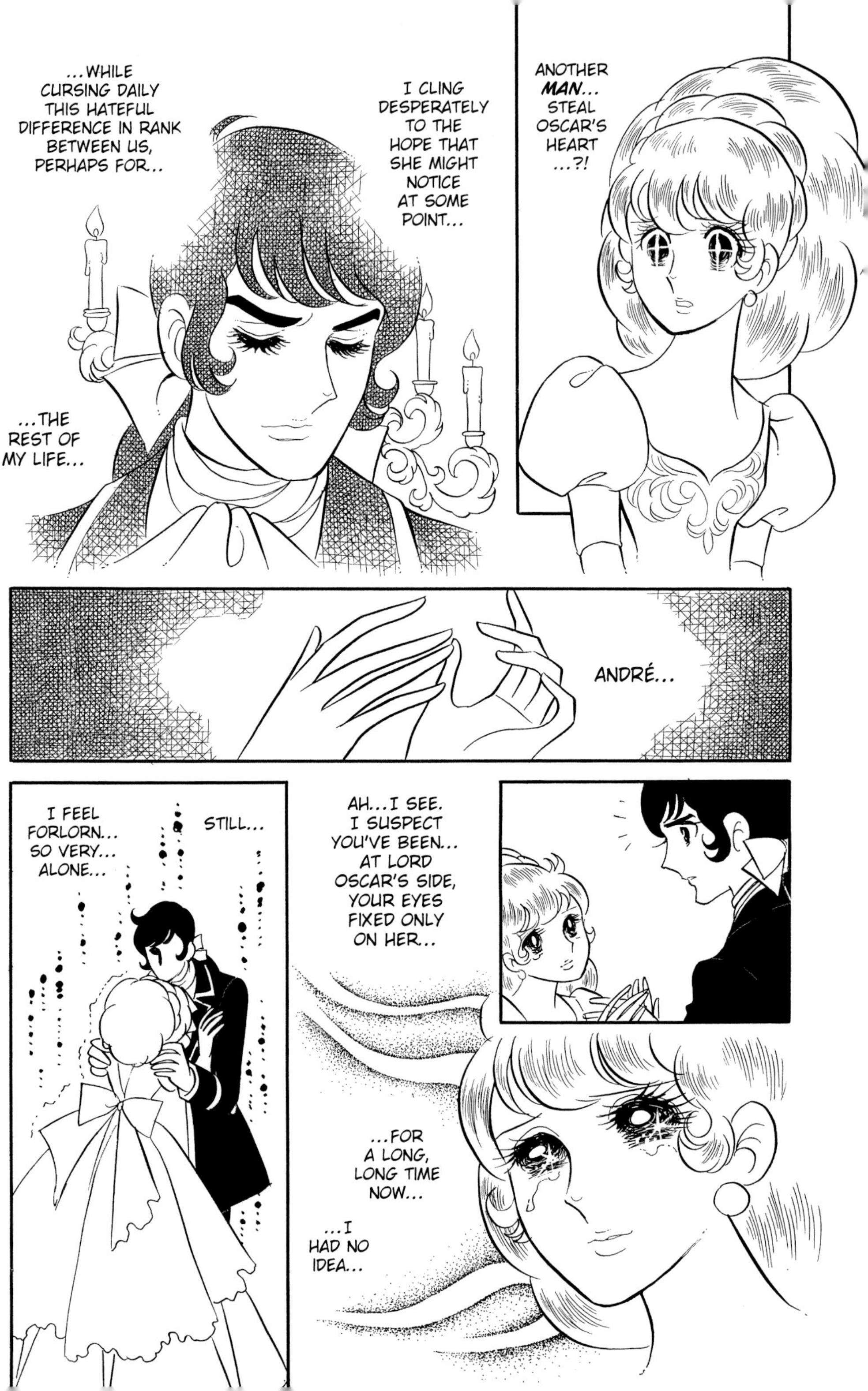
ANOTHER *MAN*... STEAL OSCAR'S HEART ...?!
I CLING DESPERATELY TO THE HOPE THAT SHE MIGHT NOTICE AT SOME POINT...
...WHILE CURSING DAILY THIS HATEFUL DIFFERENCE IN RANK BETWEEN US, PERHAPS FOR...
...THE REST OF MY LIFE...
ANDRÉ...
AH...I SEE. I SUSPECT YOU'VE BEEN... AT LORD OSCAR'S SIDE, YOUR EYES FIXED ONLY ON HER..
...FOR A LONG, LONG TIME NOW...
...I HAD NO IDEA...
STILL...
I FEEL FORLORN... SO VERY... ALONE...

◆ THE SWIRLING EXCITEMENT, THE INCREASINGLY THRILLING GRAND ROMANCE!!
♥ WHAT OF ANTOINETTE AND FERSEN?!

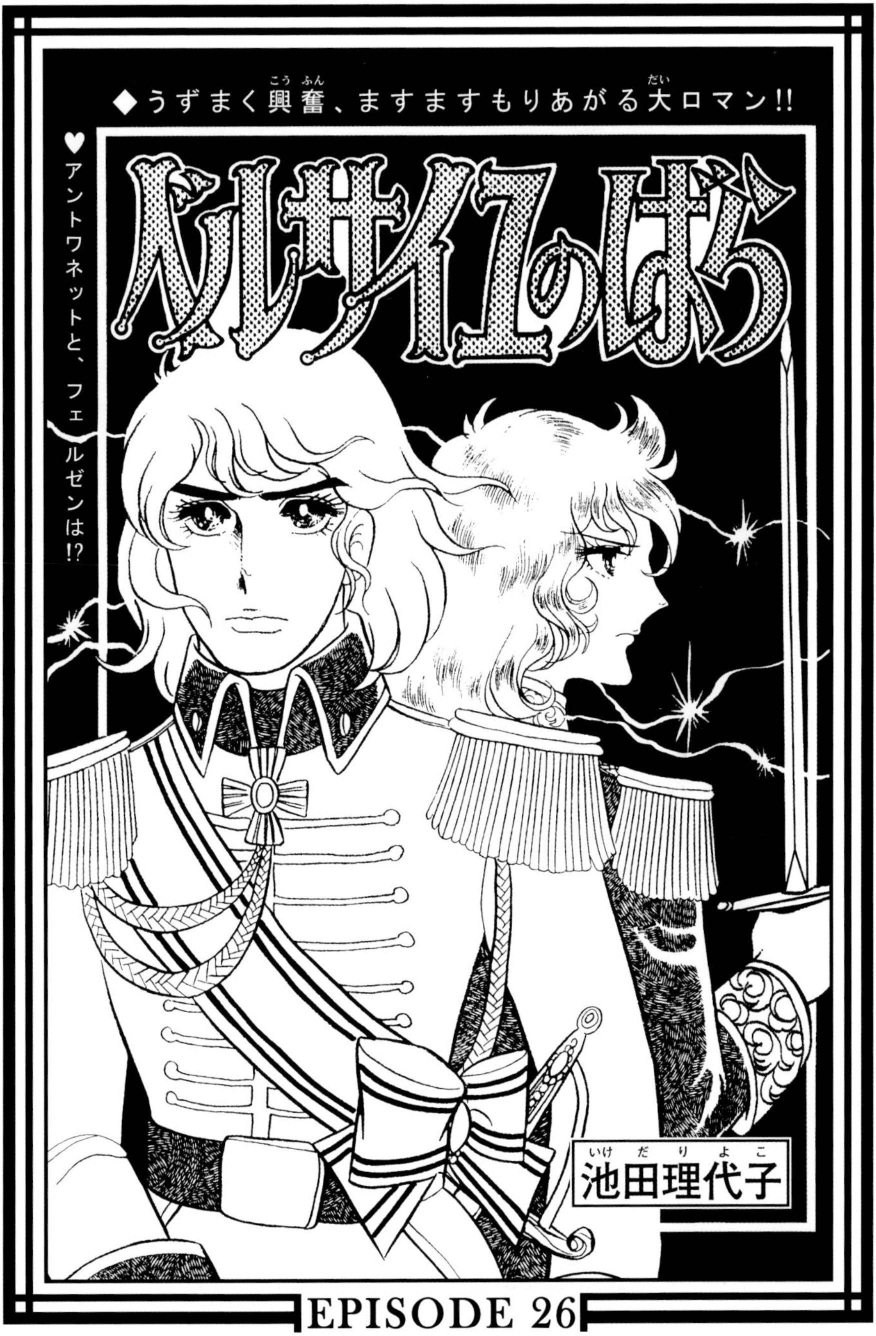

◆うずまく興奮、ますますもりあがる大ロマン!!
♥アントワネットと、フェルゼンは!?
ベルサイユのばら
池田理代子
EPISODE 26

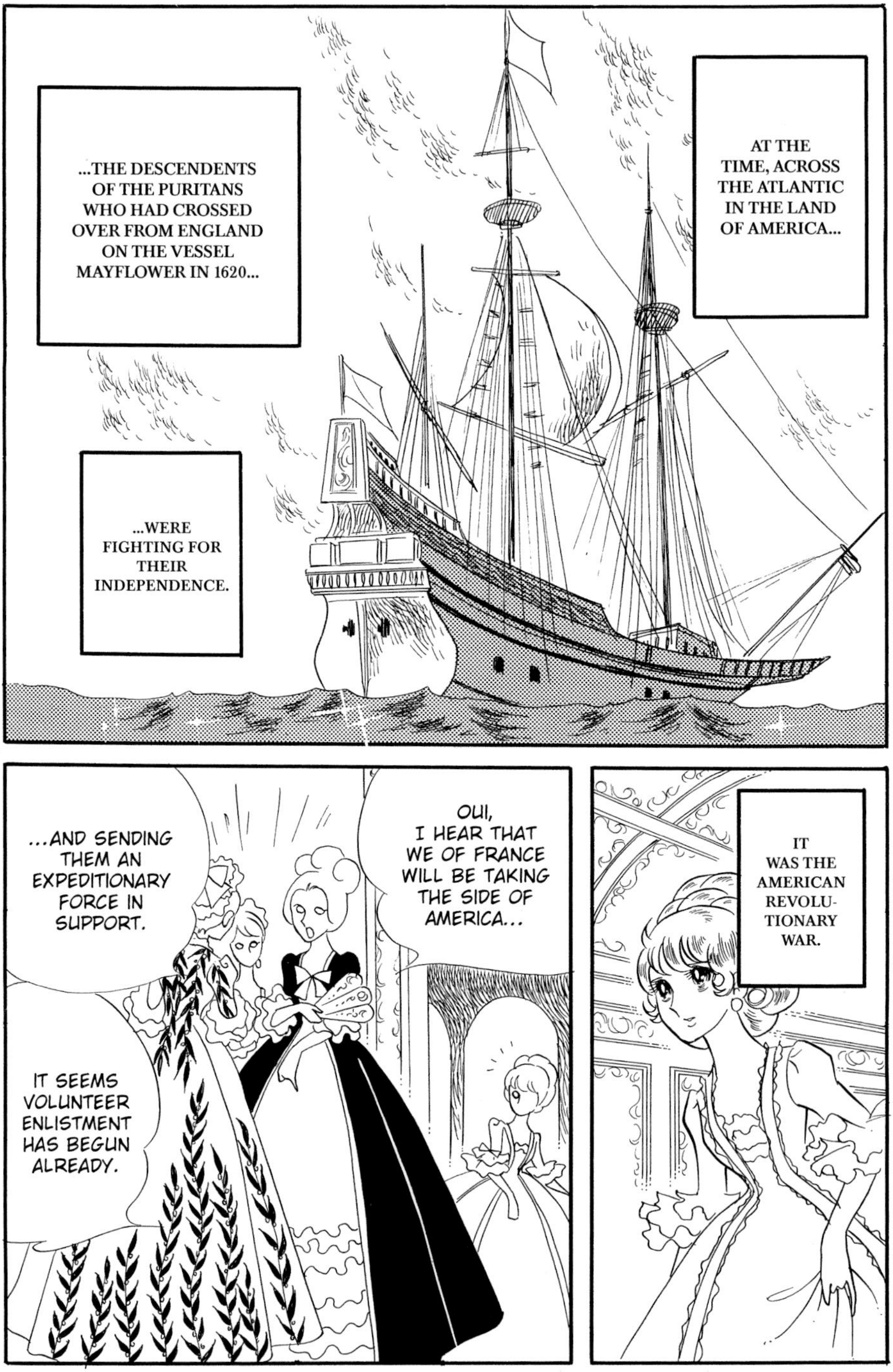
AT THE TIME, ACROSS THE ATLANTIC IN THE LAND OF AMERICA...
...THE DESCENDENTS OF THE PURITANS WHO HAD CROSSED OVER FROM ENGLAND ON THE VESSEL MAYFLOWER IN 1620...
...WERE FIGHTING FOR THEIR INDEPENDENCE.
IT WAS THE AMERICAN REVOLU-TIONARY WAR.
OUI, I HEAR THAT WE OF FRANCE WILL BE TAKING THE SIDE OF AMERICA...
...AND SENDING THEM AN EXPEDITIONARY FORCE IN SUPPORT.
IT SEEMS VOLUNTEER ENLISTMENT HAS BEGUN ALREADY.

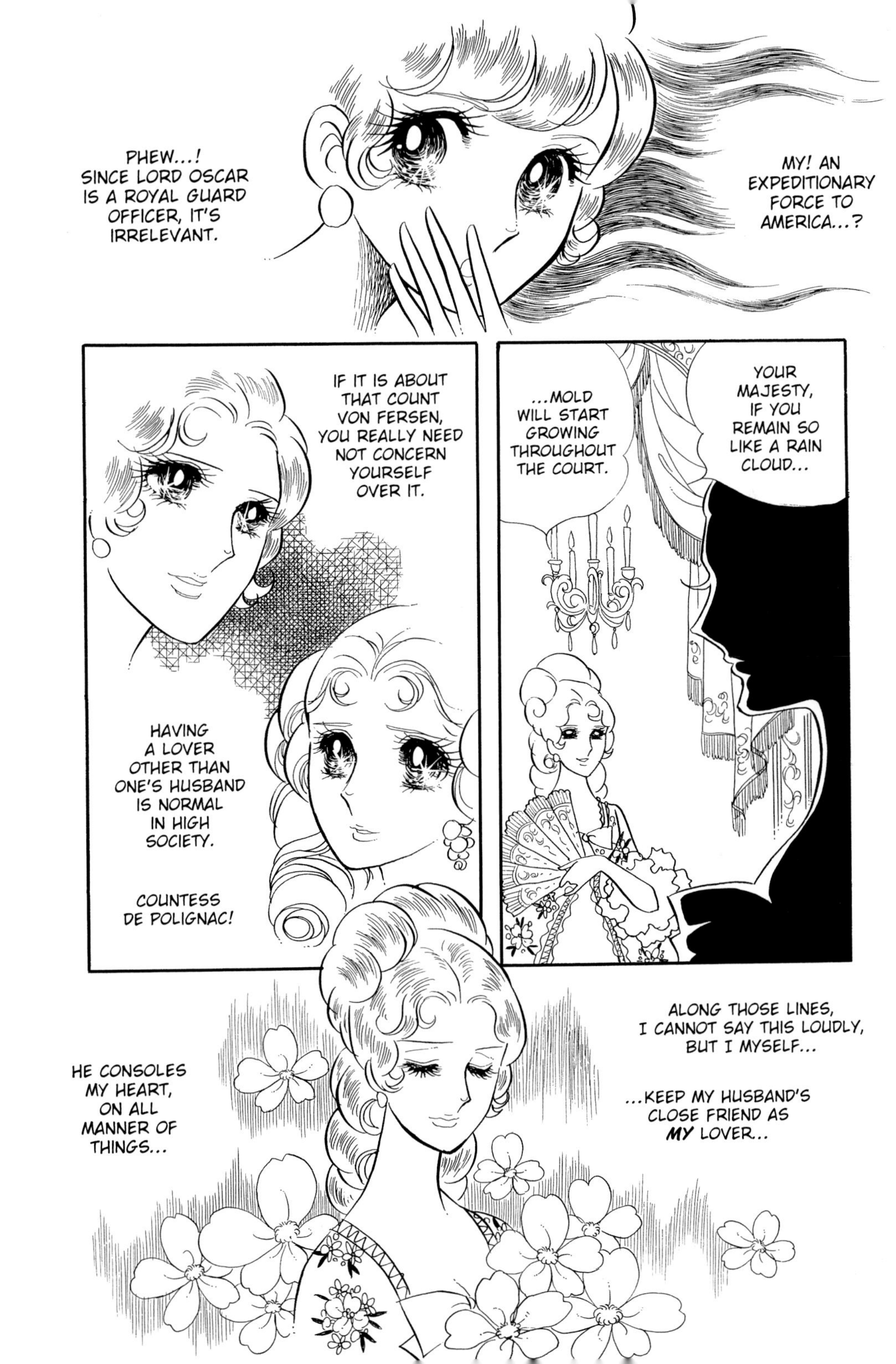
MY! AN EXPEDITIONARY FORCE TO AMERICA...?
PHEW...! SINCE LORD OSCAR IS A ROYAL GUARD OFFICER, IT'S IRRELEVANT.
YOUR MAJESTY, IF YOU REMAIN SO LIKE A RAIN CLOUD...
...MOLD WILL START GROWING THROUGHOUT THE COURT.
IF IT IS ABOUT THAT COUNT VON FERSEN, YOU REALLY NEED NOT CONCERN YOURSELF OVER IT.
HAVING A LOVER OTHER THAN ONE'S HUSBAND IS NORMAL IN HIGH SOCIETY.
COUNTESS DE POLIGNAC!
ALONG THOSE LINES, I CANNOT SAY THIS LOUDLY, BUT I MYSELF...
...KEEP MY HUSBAND'S CLOSE FRIEND AS *MY* LOVER...
HE CONSOLES MY HEART, ON ALL MANNER OF THINGS...

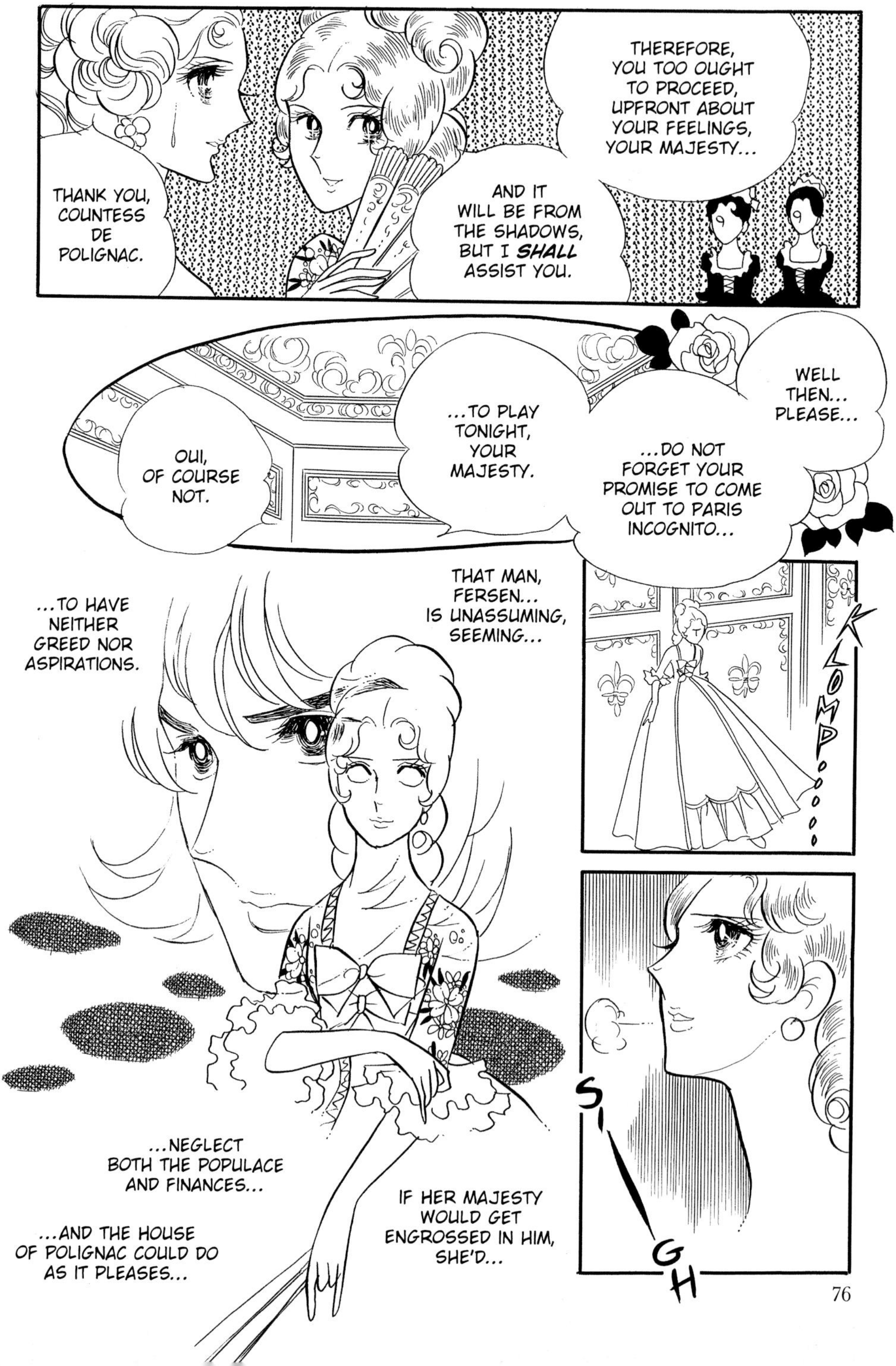
THEREFORE, YOU TOO OUGHT TO PROCEED, UPFRONT ABOUT YOUR FEELINGS, YOUR MAJESTY...
AND IT WILL BE FROM THE SHADOWS, BUT I ***SHALL*** ASSIST YOU.
THANK YOU, COUNTESS DE POLIGNAC.
WELL THEN... PLEASE...
...DO NOT FORGET YOUR PROMISE TO COME OUT TO PARIS INCOGNITO...
...TO PLAY TONIGHT, YOUR MAJESTY.
OUI, OF COURSE NOT.
KLOMPoooo
SIGH
THAT MAN, FERSEN... IS UNASSUMING, SEEMING...
...TO HAVE NEITHER GREED NOR ASPIRATIONS.
IF HER MAJESTY WOULD GET ENGROSSED IN HIM, SHE'D...
...NEGLECT BOTH THE POPULACE AND FINANCES...
...AND THE HOUSE OF POLIGNAC COULD DO AS IT PLEASES...

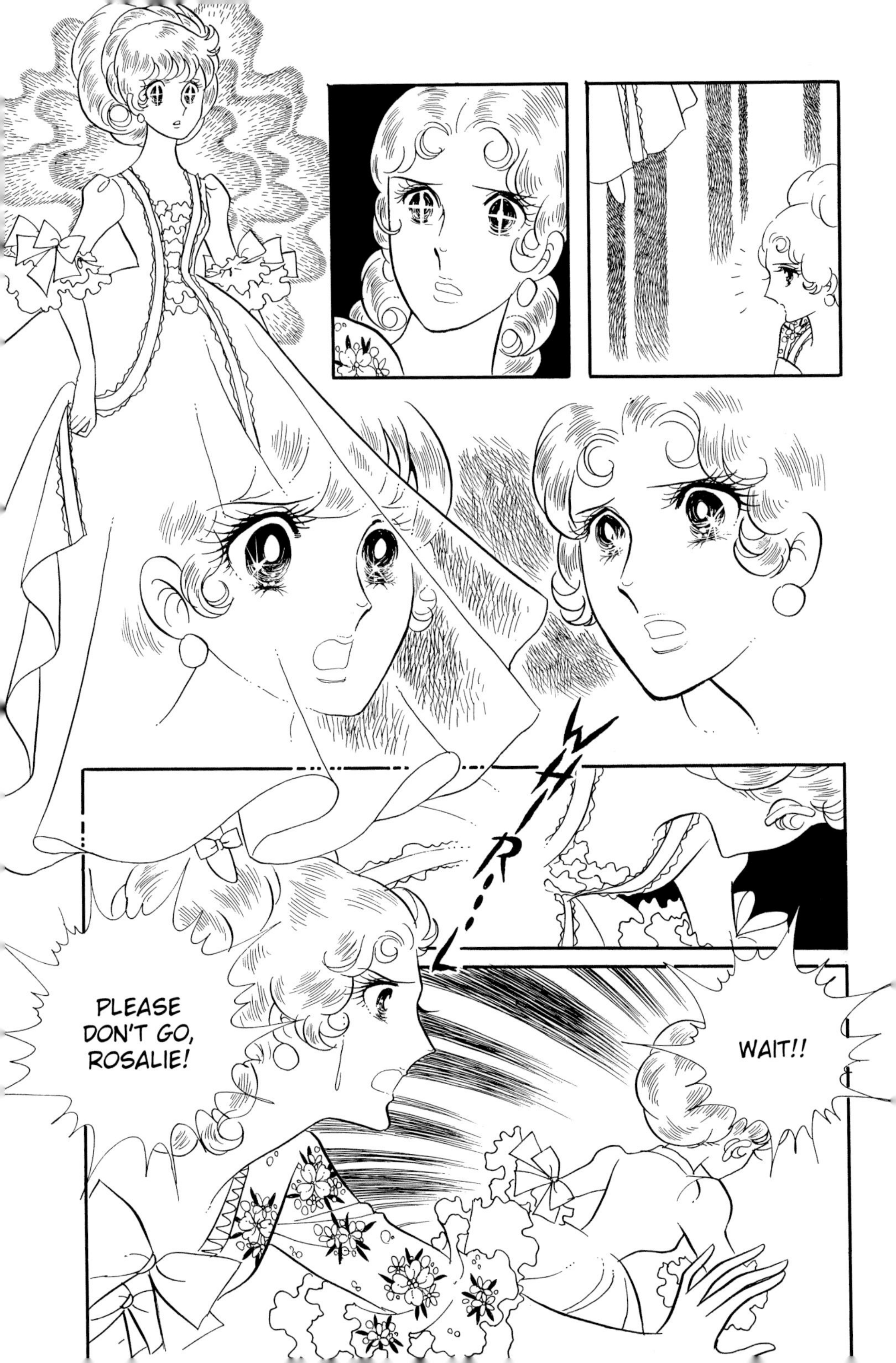
WHIR...L
WAIT!!
PLEASE DON'T GO, ROSALIE!

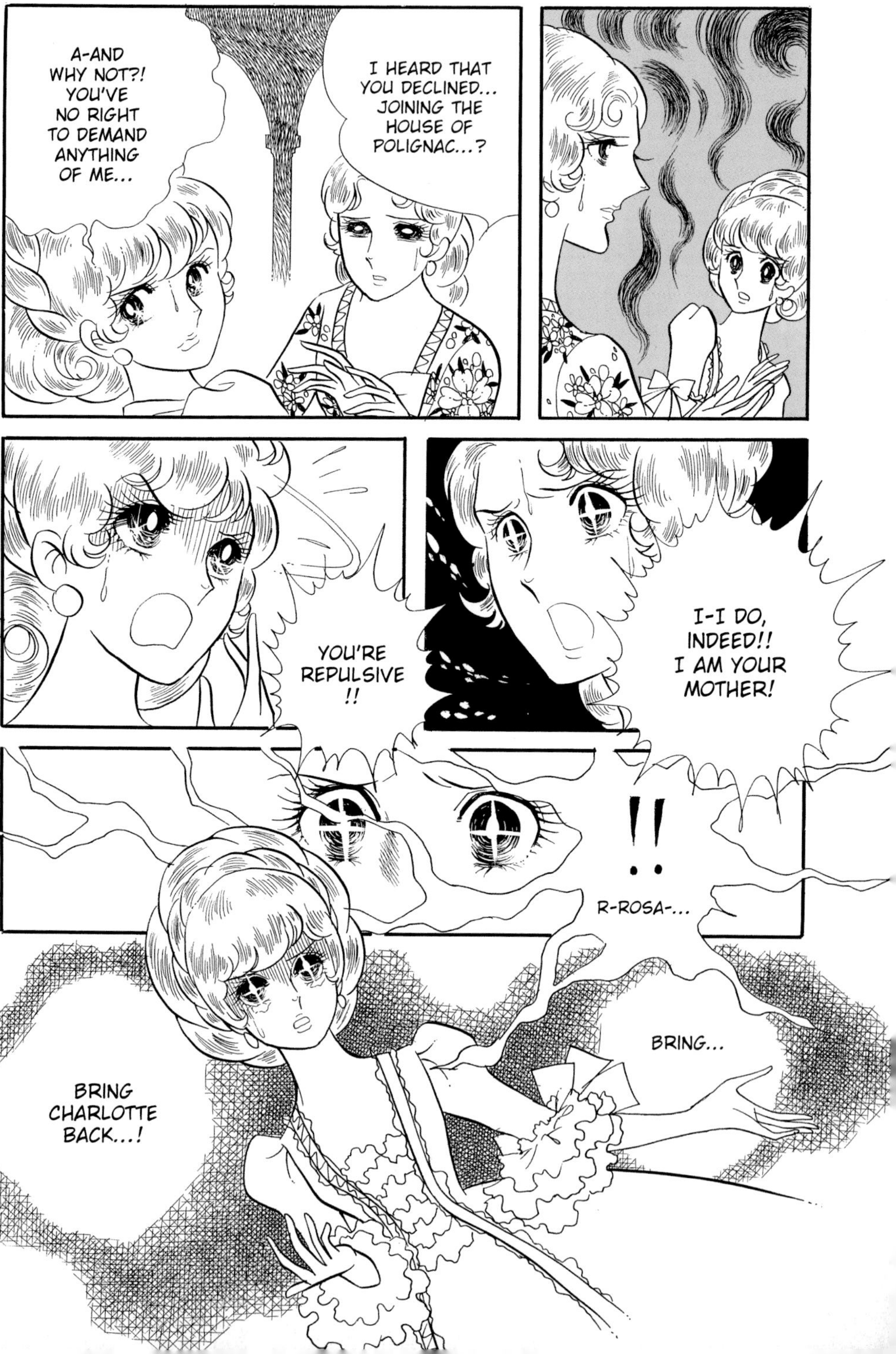
I HEARD THAT YOU DECLINED... JOINING THE HOUSE OF POLIGNAC...?
A-AND WHY NOT?! YOU'VE NO RIGHT TO DEMAND ANYTHING OF ME...
I-I DO, INDEED!! I AM YOUR MOTHER!
YOU'RE REPULSIVE !!
!!
R-ROSA-...
BRING...
BRING CHARLOTTE BACK...!

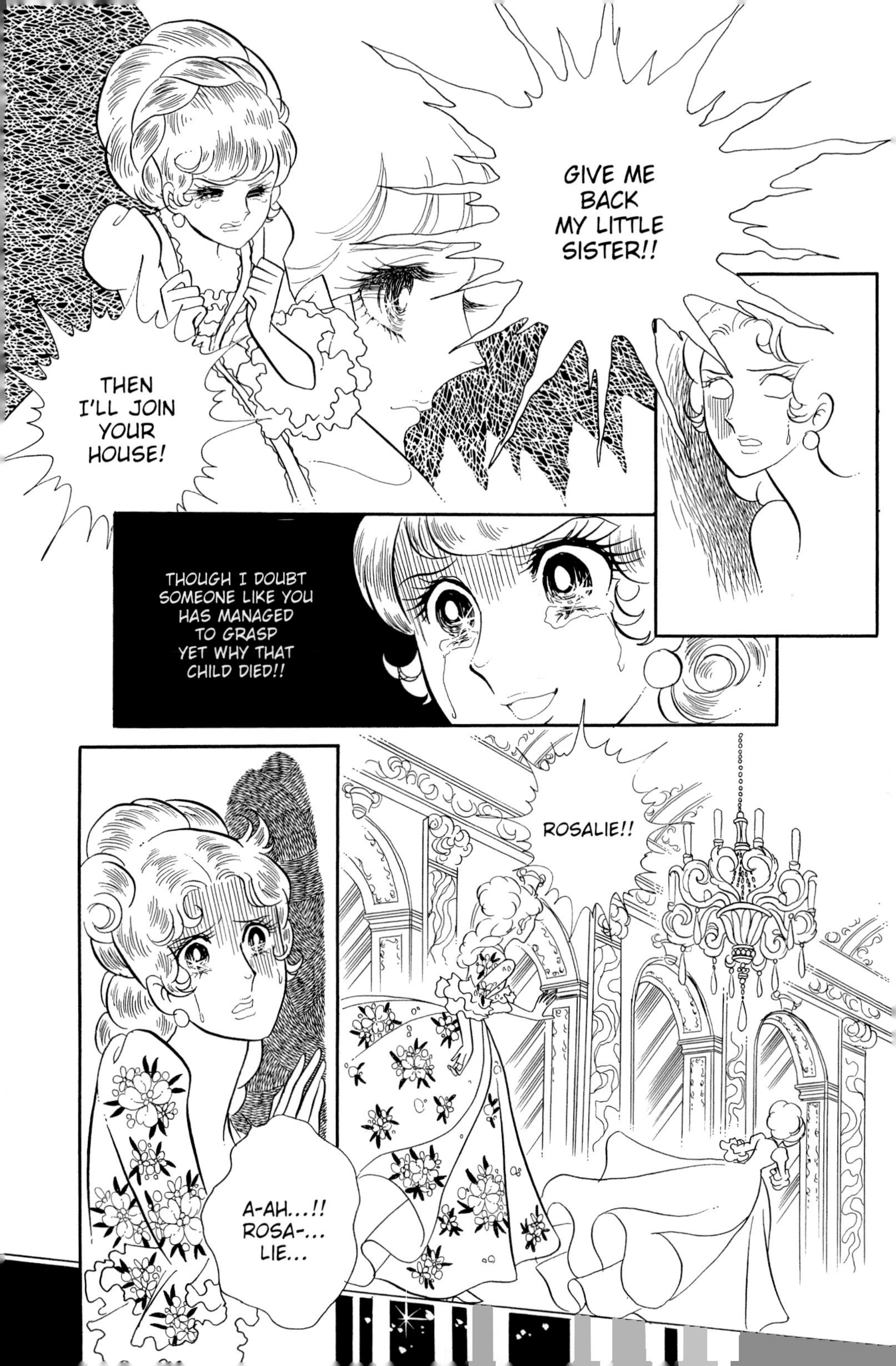
GIVE ME BACK MY LITTLE SISTER!!
THEN I'LL JOIN YOUR HOUSE!
THOUGH I DOUBT SOMEONE LIKE YOU HAS MANAGED TO GRASP YET WHY THAT CHILD DIED!!
ROSALIE!!
A-AH...!! ROSA-... LIE...

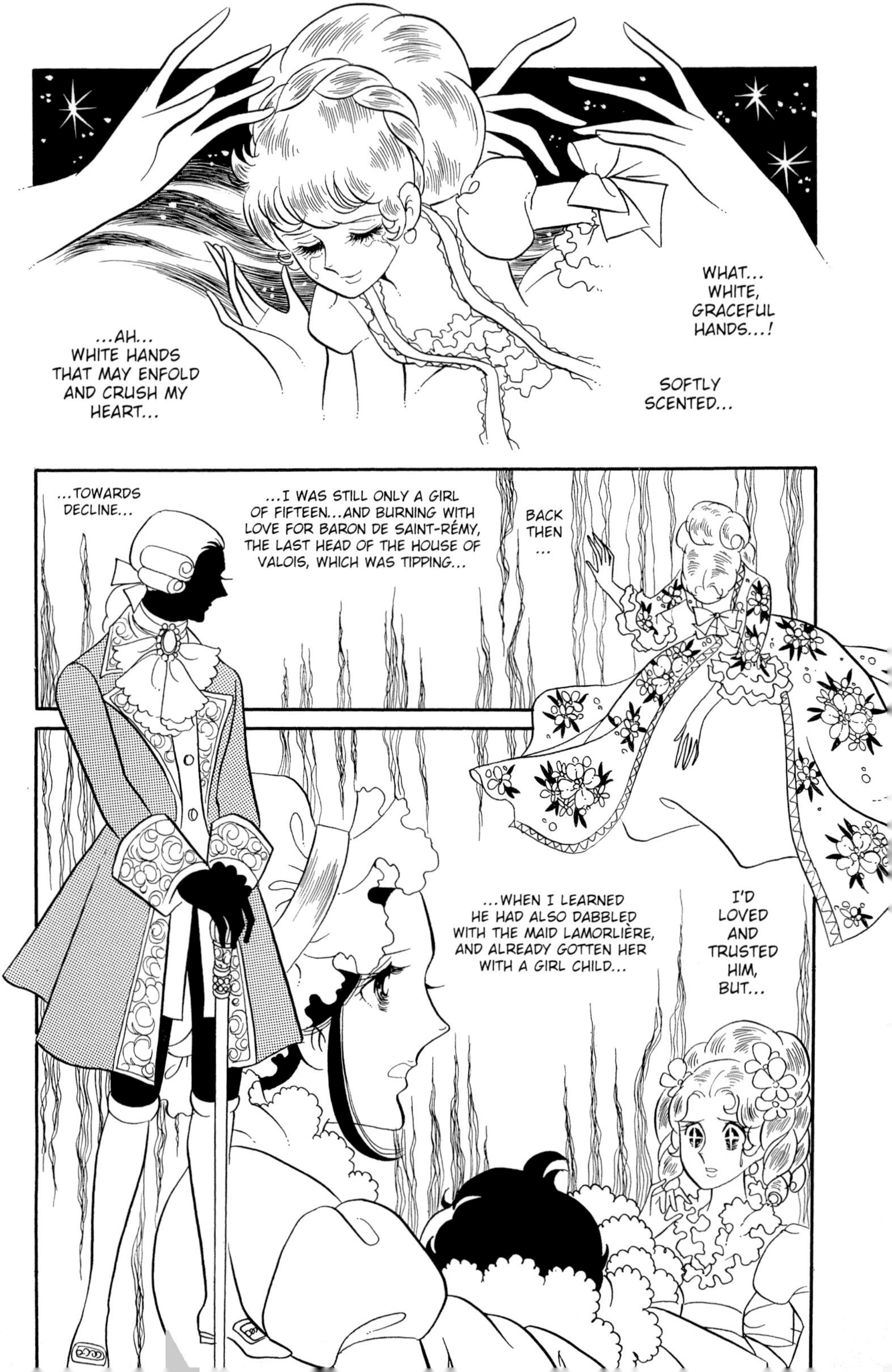
WHAT... WHITE, GRACEFUL HANDS...!
SOFTLY SCENTED...
...AH... WHITE HANDS THAT MAY ENFOLD AND CRUSH MY HEART...
BACK THEN ...
...I WAS STILL ONLY A GIRL OF FIFTEEN...AND BURNING WITH LOVE FOR BARON DE SAINT-RÉMY, THE LAST HEAD OF THE HOUSE OF VALOIS, WHICH WAS TIPPING...
...TOWARDS DECLINE...
I'D LOVED AND TRUSTED HIM, BUT...
...WHEN I LEARNED HE HAD ALSO DABBLED WITH THE MAID LAMORLIÈRE, AND ALREADY GOTTEN HER WITH A GIRL CHILD...

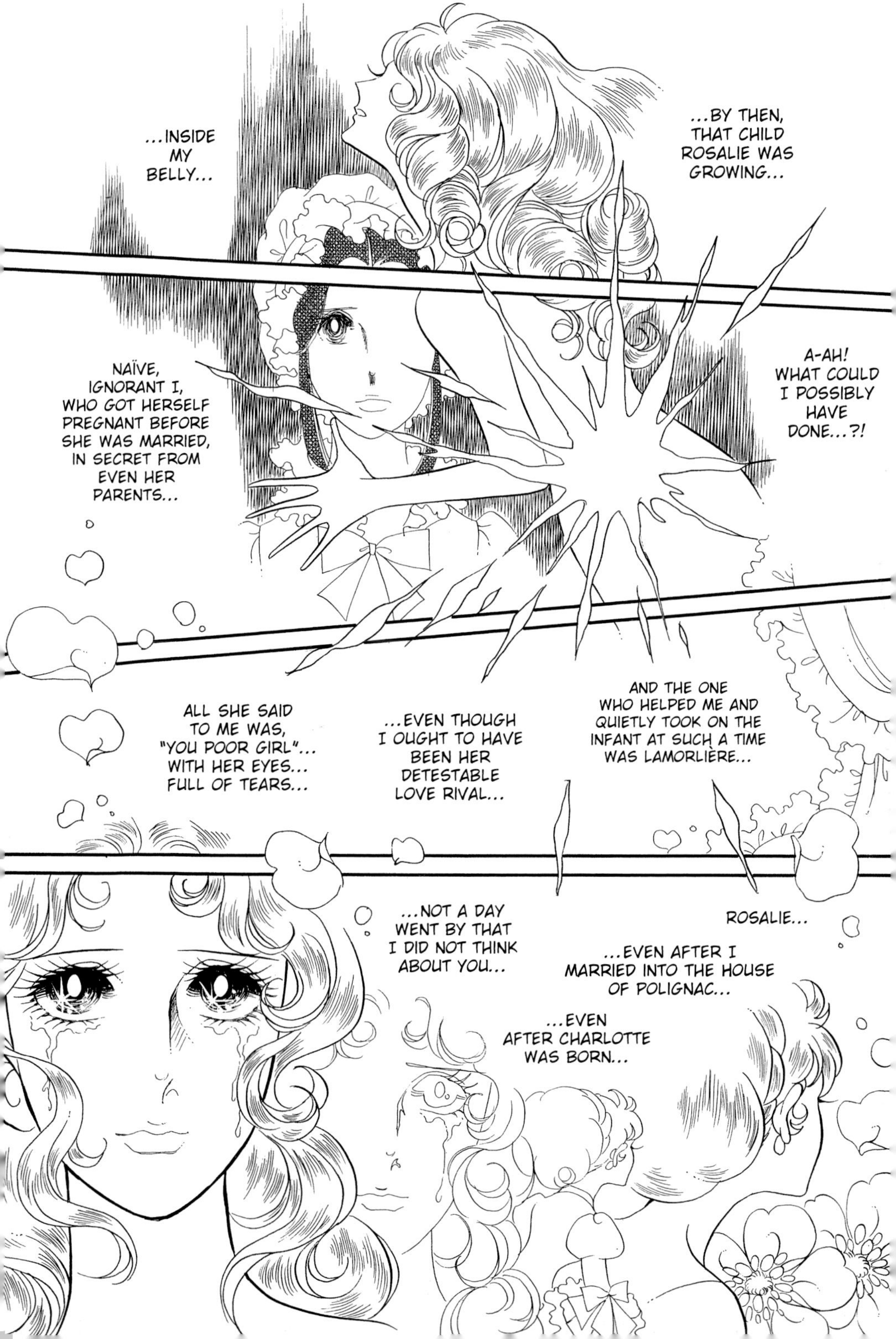
...BY THEN, THAT CHILD ROSALIE WAS GROWING...
...INSIDE MY BELLY...
A-AH! WHAT COULD I POSSIBLY HAVE DONE...?!
NAÏVE, IGNORANT I, WHO GOT HERSELF PREGNANT BEFORE SHE WAS MARRIED, IN SECRET FROM EVEN HER PARENTS...
AND THE ONE WHO HELPED ME AND QUIETLY TOOK ON THE INFANT AT SUCH A TIME WAS LAMORLIÈRE...
...EVEN THOUGH I OUGHT TO HAVE BEEN HER DETESTABLE LOVE RIVAL...
ALL SHE SAID TO ME WAS, "YOU POOR GIRL"... WITH HER EYES... FULL OF TEARS...
ROSALIE...
...EVEN AFTER I MARRIED INTO THE HOUSE OF POLIGNAC...
...EVEN AFTER CHARLOTTE WAS BORN...
...NOT A DAY WENT BY THAT I DID NOT THINK ABOUT YOU...

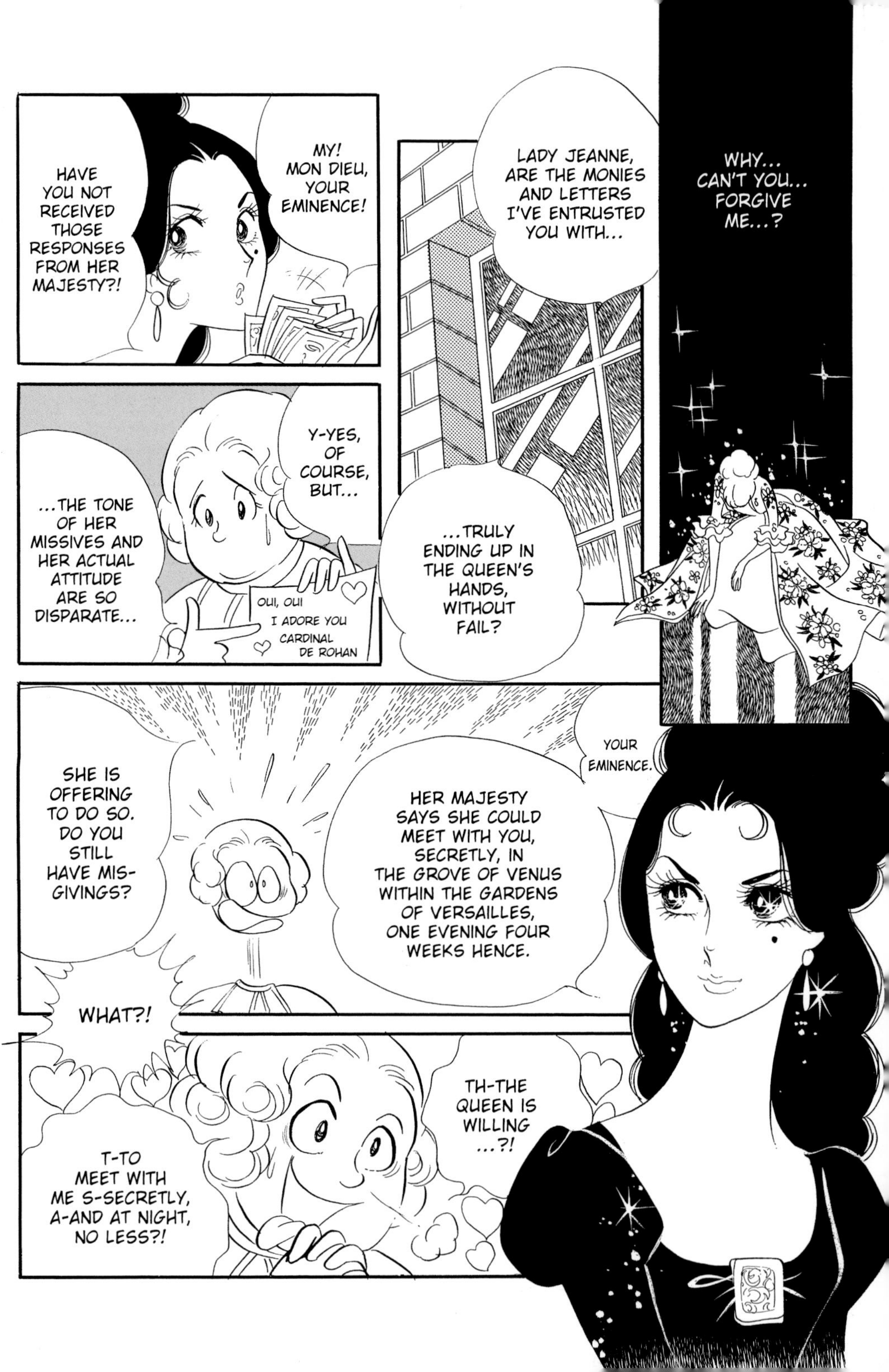
WHY... CAN'T YOU... FORGIVE ME...?
LADY JEANNE, ARE THE MONIES AND LETTERS I'VE ENTRUSTED YOU WITH...
...TRULY ENDING UP IN THE QUEEN'S HANDS, WITHOUT FAIL?
MY! MON DIEU, YOUR EMINENCE!
HAVE YOU NOT RECEIVED THOSE RESPONSES FROM HER MAJESTY?!
Y-YES, OF COURSE, BUT...
...THE TONE OF HER MISSIVES AND HER ACTUAL ATTITUDE ARE SO DISPARATE...
OUI, OUI
I ADORE YOU
CARDINAL DE ROHAN
YOUR EMINENCE.
HER MAJESTY SAYS SHE COULD MEET WITH YOU, SECRETLY, IN THE GROVE OF VENUS WITHIN THE GARDENS OF VERSAILLES, ONE EVENING FOUR WEEKS HENCE.
SHE IS OFFERING TO DO SO. DO YOU STILL HAVE MIS-GIVINGS?
WHAT?!
TH-THE QUEEN IS WILLING ...?!
T-TO MEET WITH ME S-SECRETLY, A-AND AT NIGHT, NO LESS?!

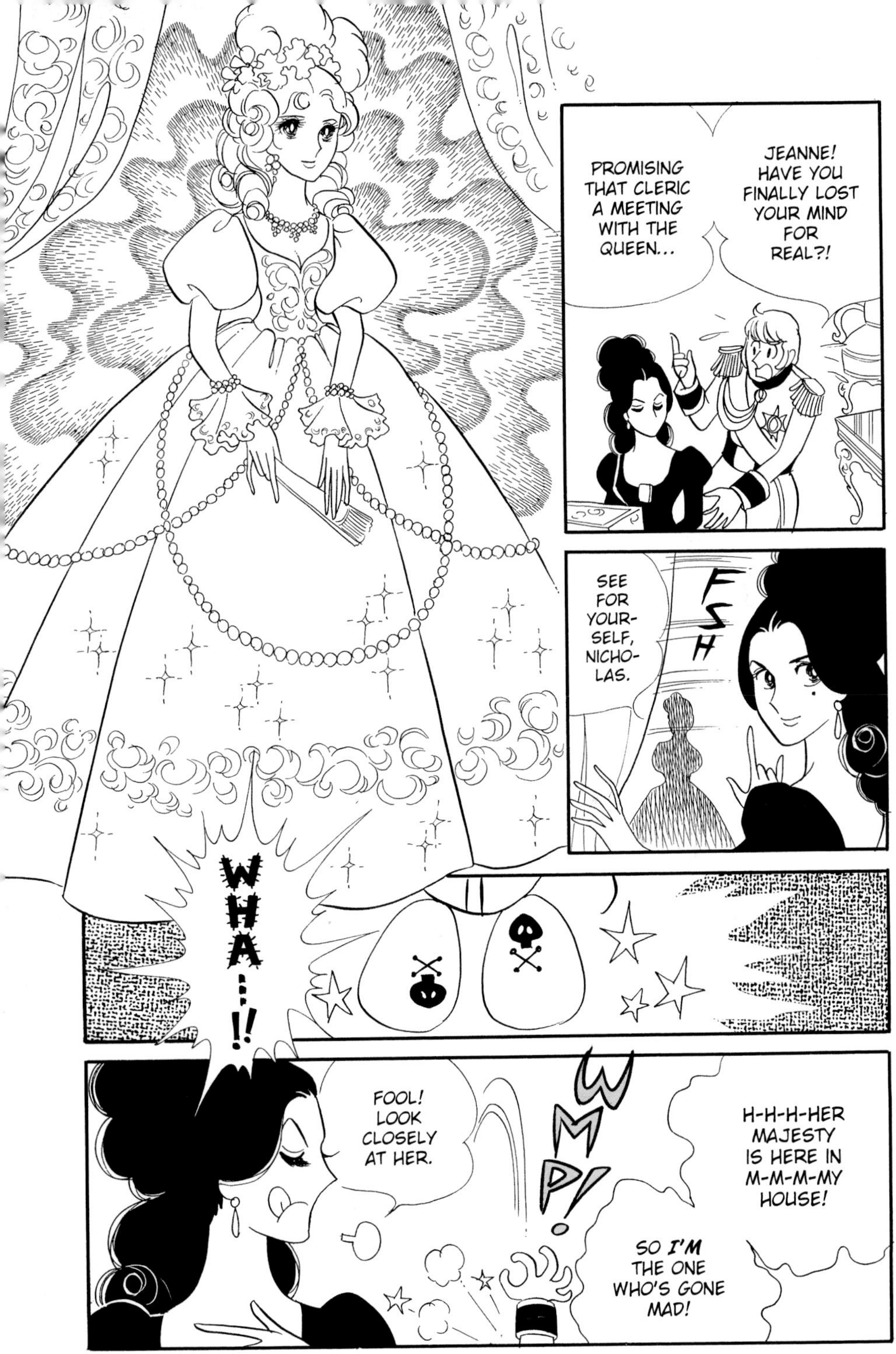
JEANNE! HAVE YOU FINALLY LOST YOUR MIND FOR REAL?!
PROMISING THAT CLERIC A MEETING WITH THE QUEEN...
FSH
SEE FOR YOURSELF, NICHOLAS.
WHA...!!
H-H-H-HER MAJESTY IS HERE IN M-M-M-MY HOUSE!
SO *I'M* THE ONE WHO'S GONE MAD!
WMP!
FOOL! LOOK CLOSELY AT HER.

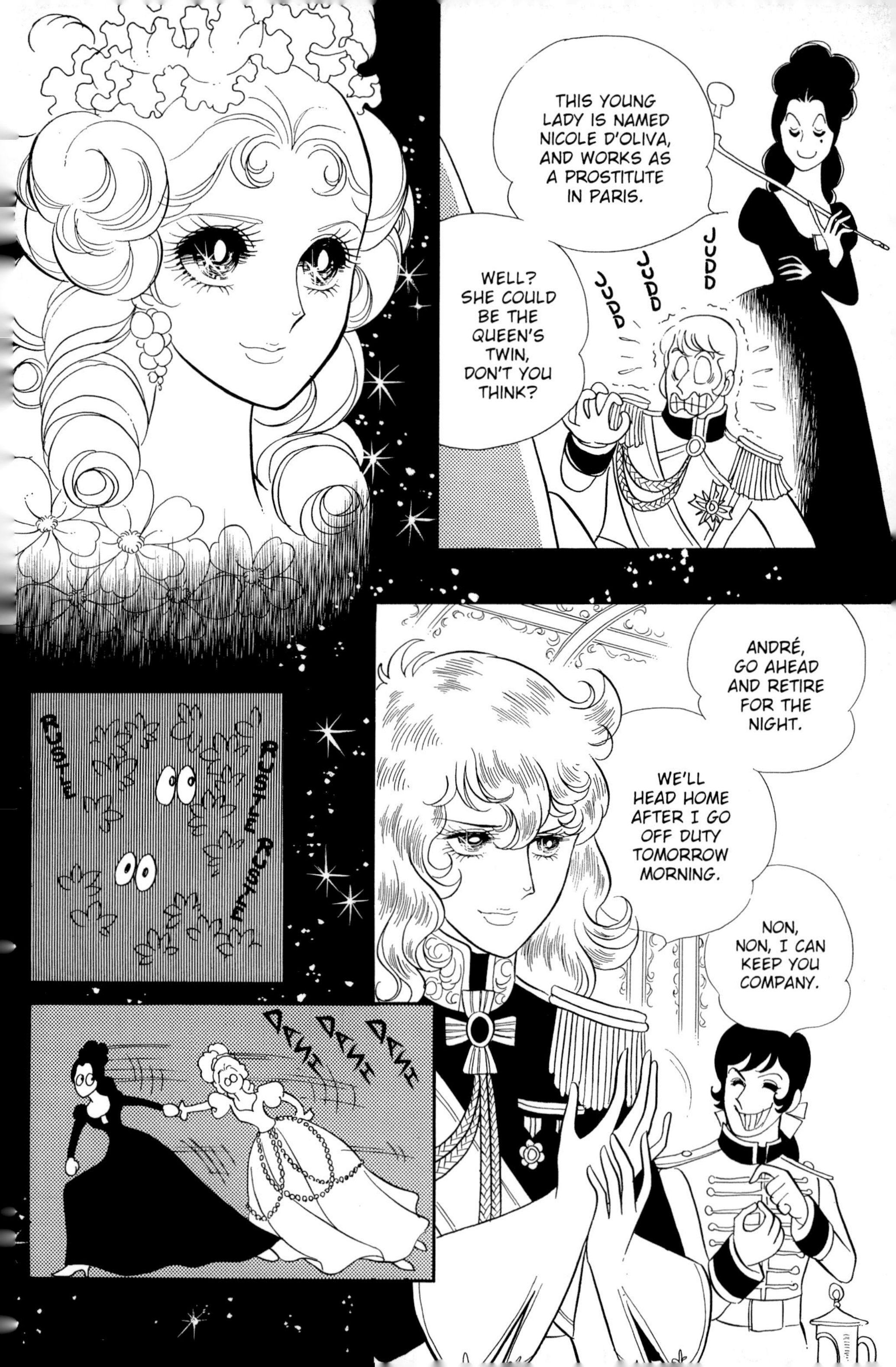
THIS YOUNG LADY IS NAMED NICOLE D'OLIVA, AND WORKS AS A PROSTITUTE IN PARIS.
WELL? SHE COULD BE THE QUEEN'S TWIN, DON'T YOU THINK?
JUDD JUDD JUDD
ANDRÉ, GO AHEAD AND RETIRE FOR THE NIGHT.
WE'LL HEAD HOME AFTER I GO OFF DUTY TOMORROW MORNING.
NON, NON, I CAN KEEP YOU COMPANY.
RUSTLE RUSTLE RUSTLE
DASH DASH DASH

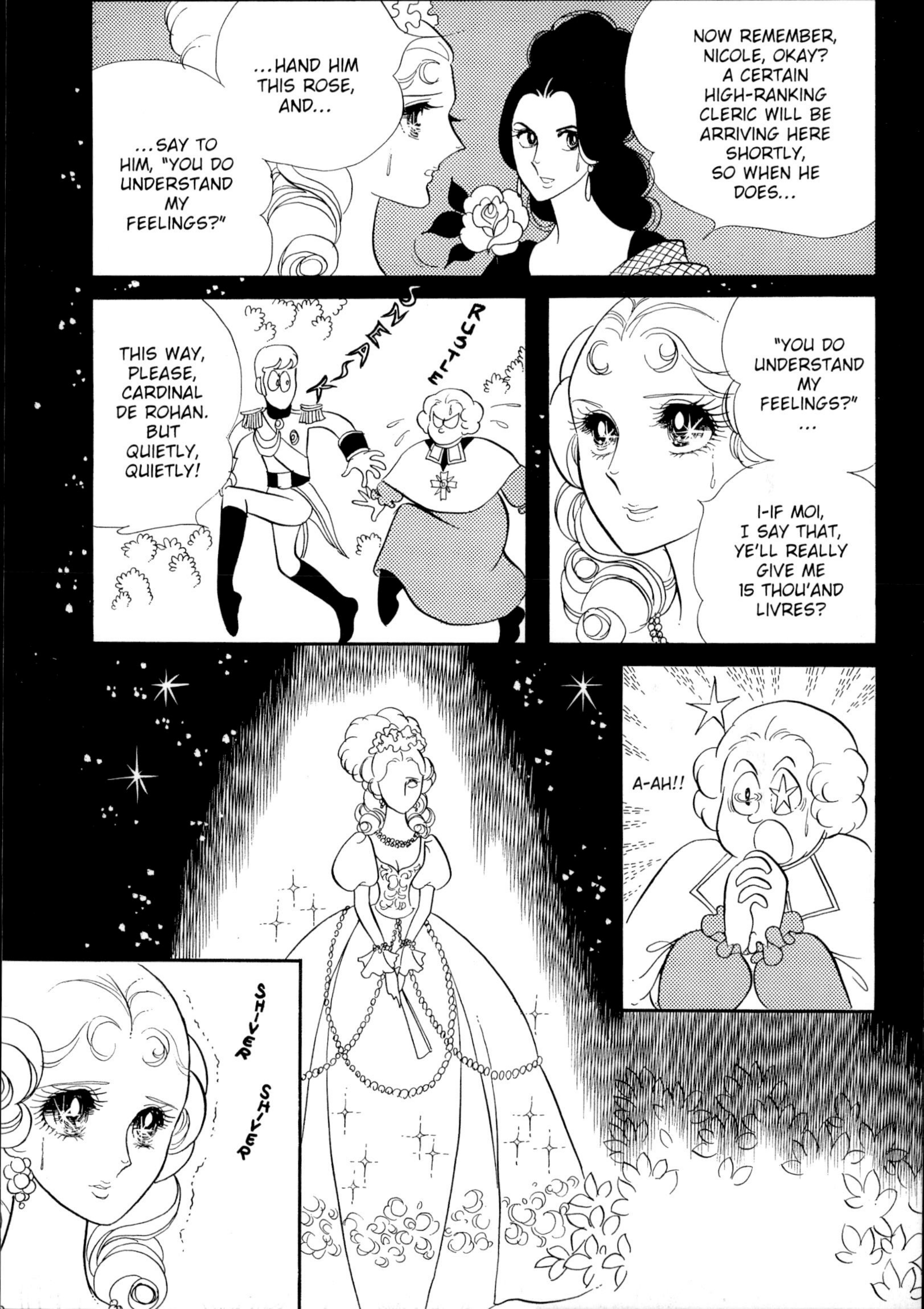
NOW REMEMBER, NICOLE, OKAY? A CERTAIN HIGH-RANKING CLERIC WILL BE ARRIVING HERE SHORTLY, SO WHEN HE DOES...
...HAND HIM THIS ROSE, AND...
...SAY TO HIM, "YOU DO UNDERSTAND MY FEELINGS?"
"YOU DO UNDERSTAND MY FEELINGS?" ...
I-IF MOI, I SAY THAT, YE'LL REALLY GIVE ME 15 THOU'AND LIVRES?
RUSTLE
SNEAK
THIS WAY, PLEASE, CARDINAL DE ROHAN. BUT QUIETLY, QUIETLY!
A-AH!!
SHIVER
SHIVER

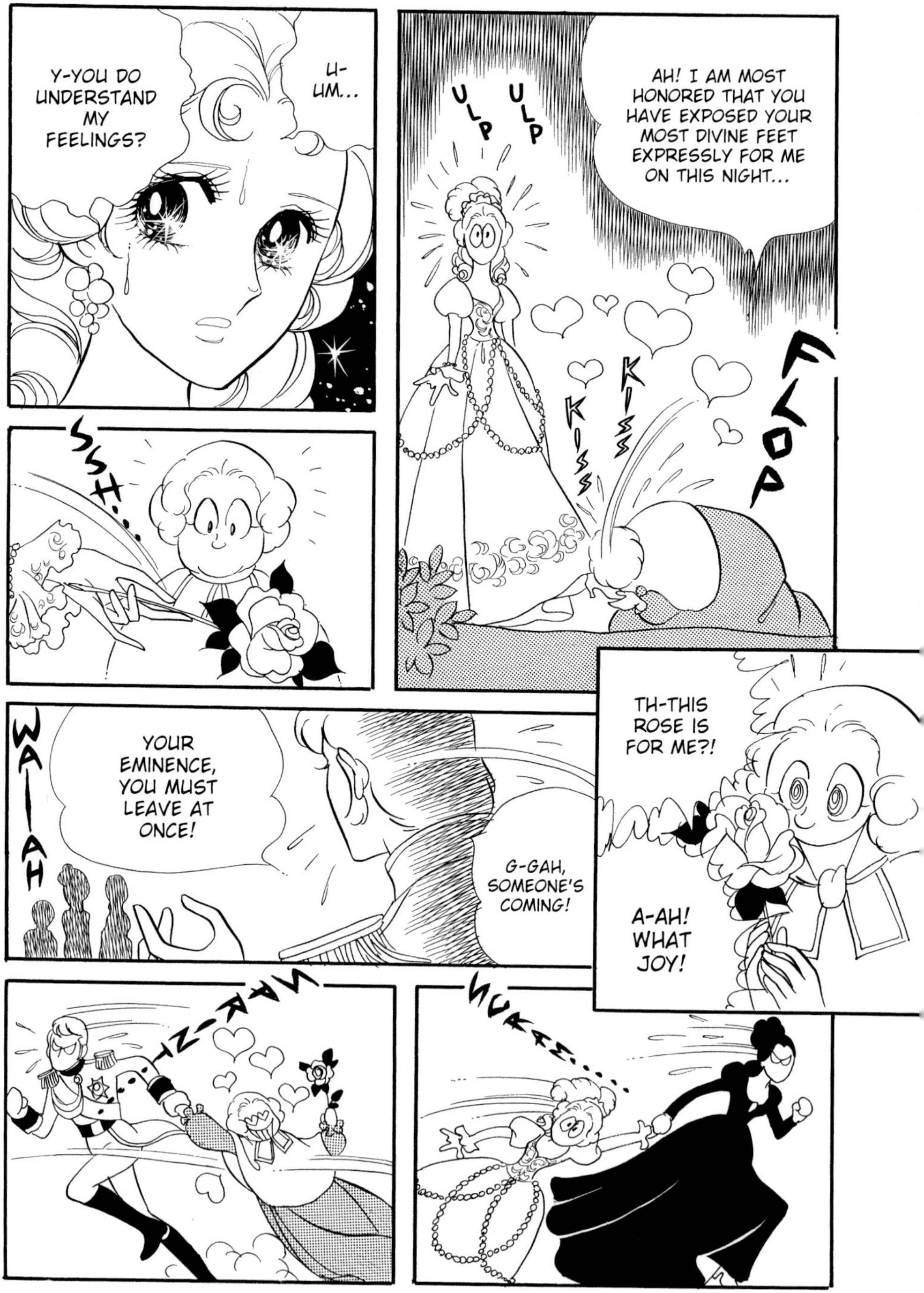
AH! I AM MOST HONORED THAT YOU HAVE EXPOSED YOUR MOST DIVINE FEET EXPRESSLY FOR ME ON THIS NIGHT...
ULP
ULP
KISS
KISS
FLOP
U-UM...
Y-YOU DO UNDERSTAND MY FEELINGS?
SSH...
TH-THIS ROSE IS FOR ME?!
A-AH! WHAT JOY!
G-GAH, SOMEONE'S COMING!
YOUR EMINENCE, YOU MUST LEAVE AT ONCE!
WA-AH

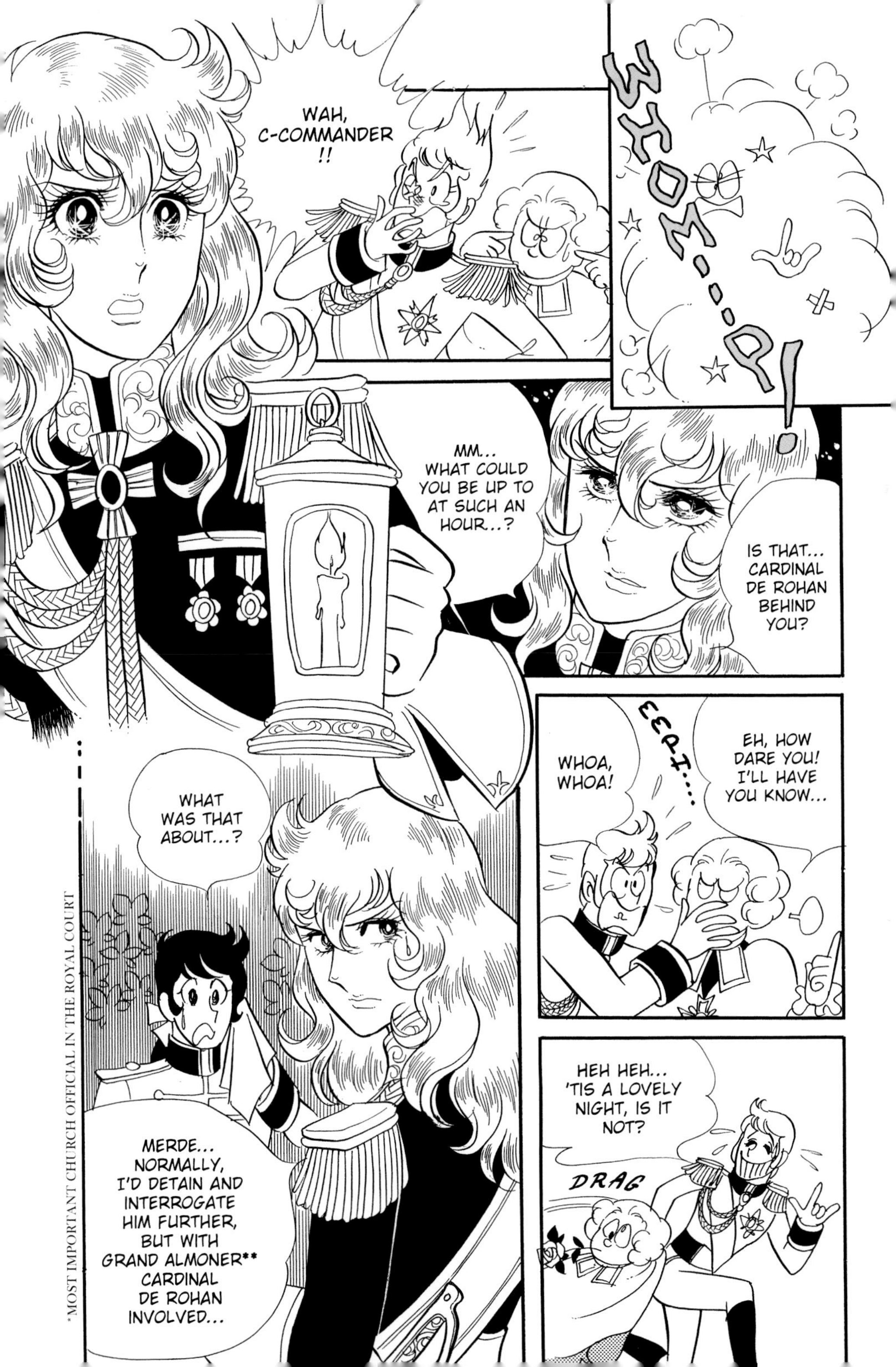
SHOOM...P!
WAH, C-COMMANDER !!
MM... WHAT COULD YOU BE UP TO AT SUCH AN HOUR...?
IS THAT... CARDINAL DE ROHAN BEHIND YOU?
EH, HOW DARE YOU! I'LL HAVE YOU KNOW...
EEP!...
WHOA, WHOA!
HEH HEH... 'TIS A LOVELY NIGHT, IS IT NOT?
DRAG
WHAT WAS THAT ABOUT...?
MERDE... NORMALLY, I'D DETAIN AND INTERROGATE HIM FURTHER, BUT WITH GRAND ALMONER** CARDINAL DE ROHAN INVOLVED...

*MOST IMPORTANT CHURCH OFFICIAL IN THE ROYAL COURT

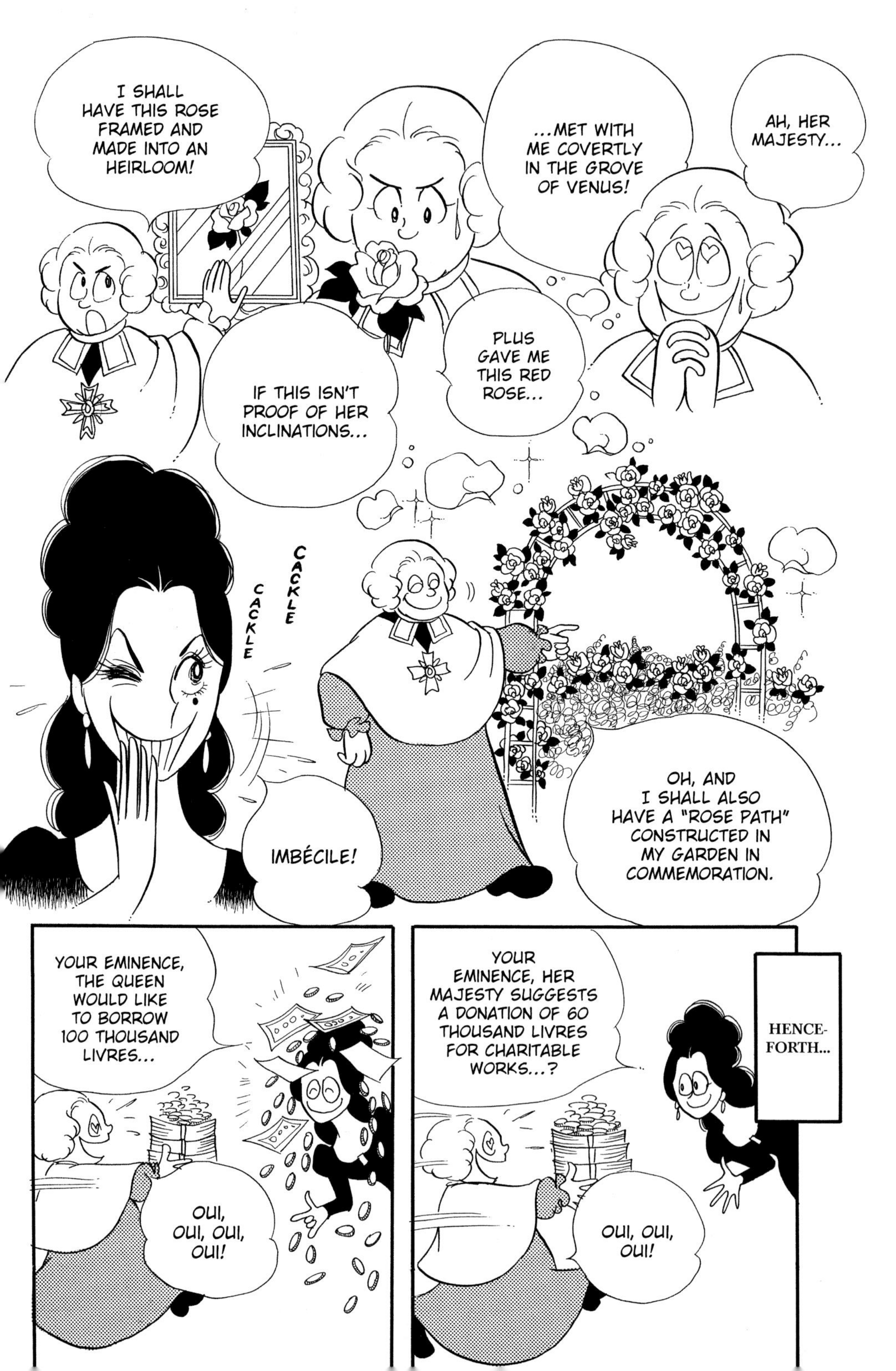
AH, HER MAJESTY...
...MET WITH ME COVERTLY IN THE GROVE OF VENUS!
PLUS GAVE ME THIS RED ROSE...
I SHALL HAVE THIS ROSE FRAMED AND MADE INTO AN HEIRLOOM!
IF THIS ISN'T PROOF OF HER INCLINATIONS...
OH, AND I SHALL ALSO HAVE A "ROSE PATH" CONSTRUCTED IN MY GARDEN IN COMMEMORATION.
CACKLE
CACKLE
IMBÉCILE!
HENCE-FORTH...
YOUR EMINENCE, HER MAJESTY SUGGESTS A DONATION OF 60 THOUSAND LIVRES FOR CHARITABLE WORKS...?
OUI, OUI, OUI!
YOUR EMINENCE, THE QUEEN WOULD LIKE TO BORROW 100 THOUSAND LIVRES...
OUI, OUI, OUI, OUI!

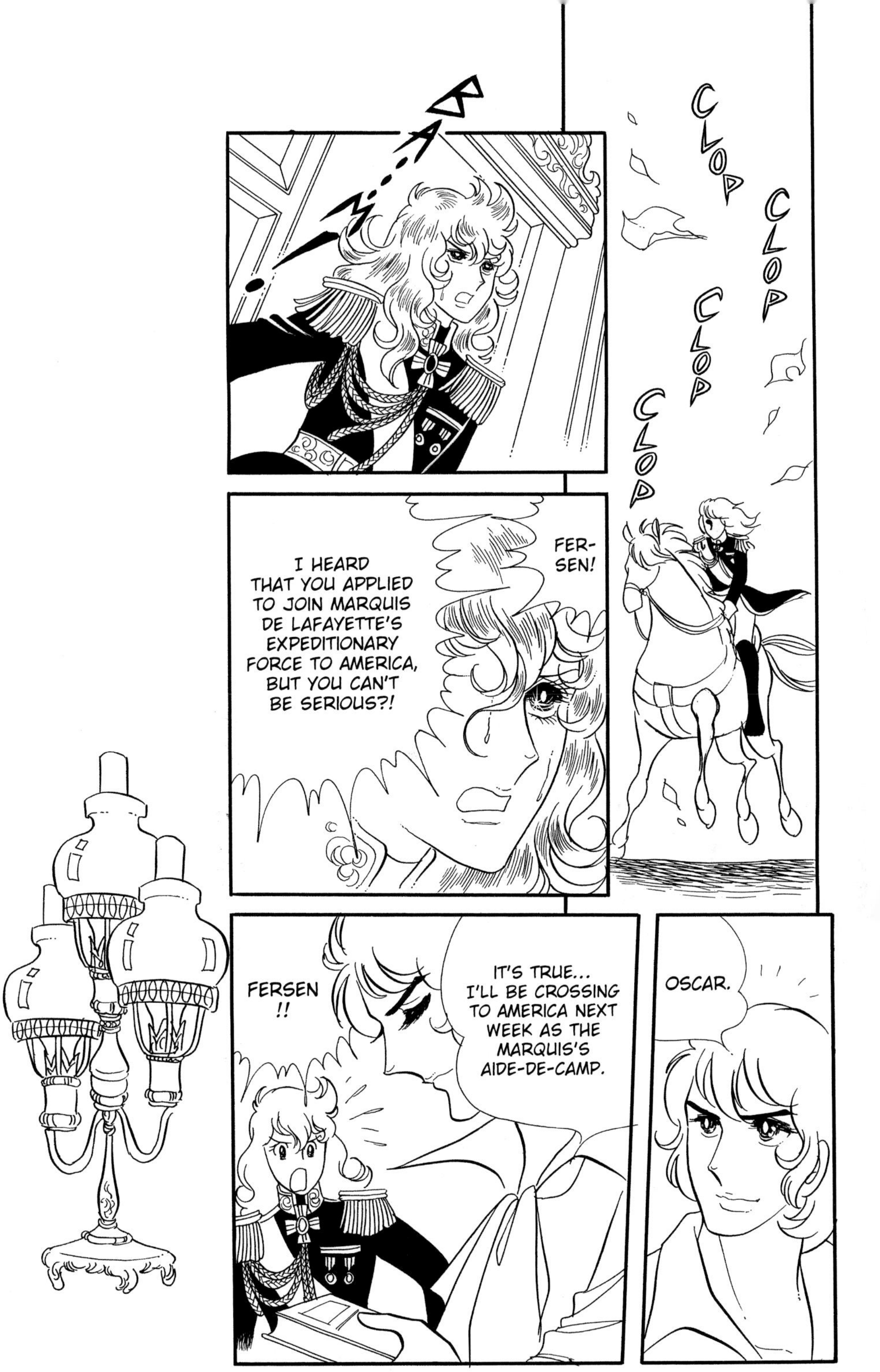
CLOP
CLOP
CLOP
CLOP
CLOP
CLOP
BA...M...!
FER-SEN!
I HEARD THAT YOU APPLIED TO JOIN MARQUIS DE LAFAYETTE'S EXPEDITIONARY FORCE TO AMERICA, BUT YOU CAN'T BE SERIOUS?!
OSCAR.
IT'S TRUE... I'LL BE CROSSING TO AMERICA NEXT WEEK AS THE MARQUIS'S AIDE-DE-CAMP.
FERSEN !!

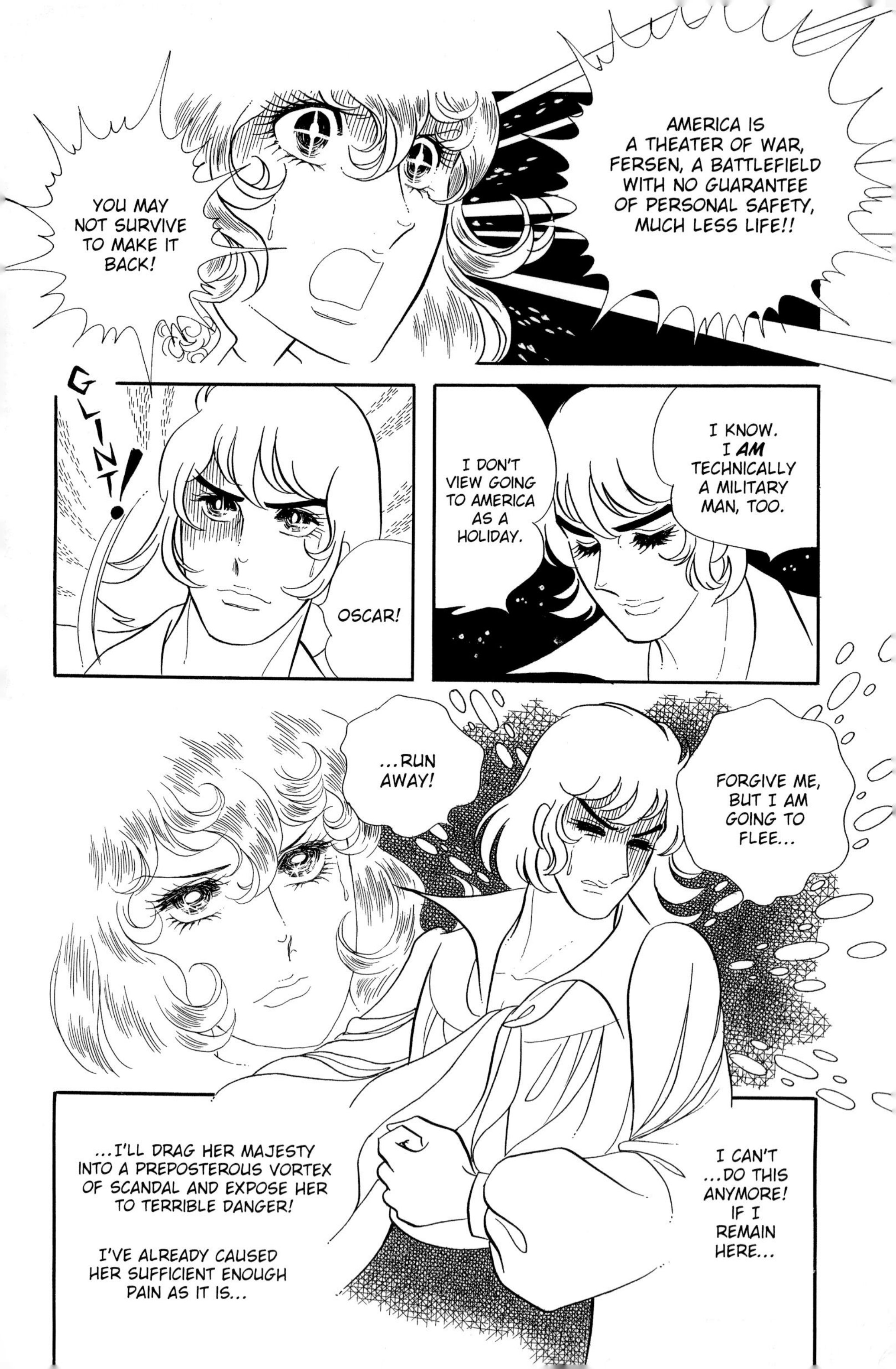
AMERICA IS A THEATER OF WAR, FERSEN, A BATTLEFIELD WITH NO GUARANTEE OF PERSONAL SAFETY, MUCH LESS LIFE!!
YOU MAY NOT SURVIVE TO MAKE IT BACK!
I KNOW. I **AM** TECHNICALLY A MILITARY MAN, TOO.
I DON'T VIEW GOING TO AMERICA AS A HOLIDAY.
GLINT!
OSCAR!
FORGIVE ME, BUT I AM GOING TO FLEE...
...RUN AWAY!
I CAN'T ...DO THIS ANYMORE! IF I REMAIN HERE...
...I'LL DRAG HER MAJESTY INTO A PREPOSTEROUS VORTEX OF SCANDAL AND EXPOSE HER TO TERRIBLE DANGER!
I'VE ALREADY CAUSED HER SUFFICIENT ENOUGH PAIN AS IT IS...

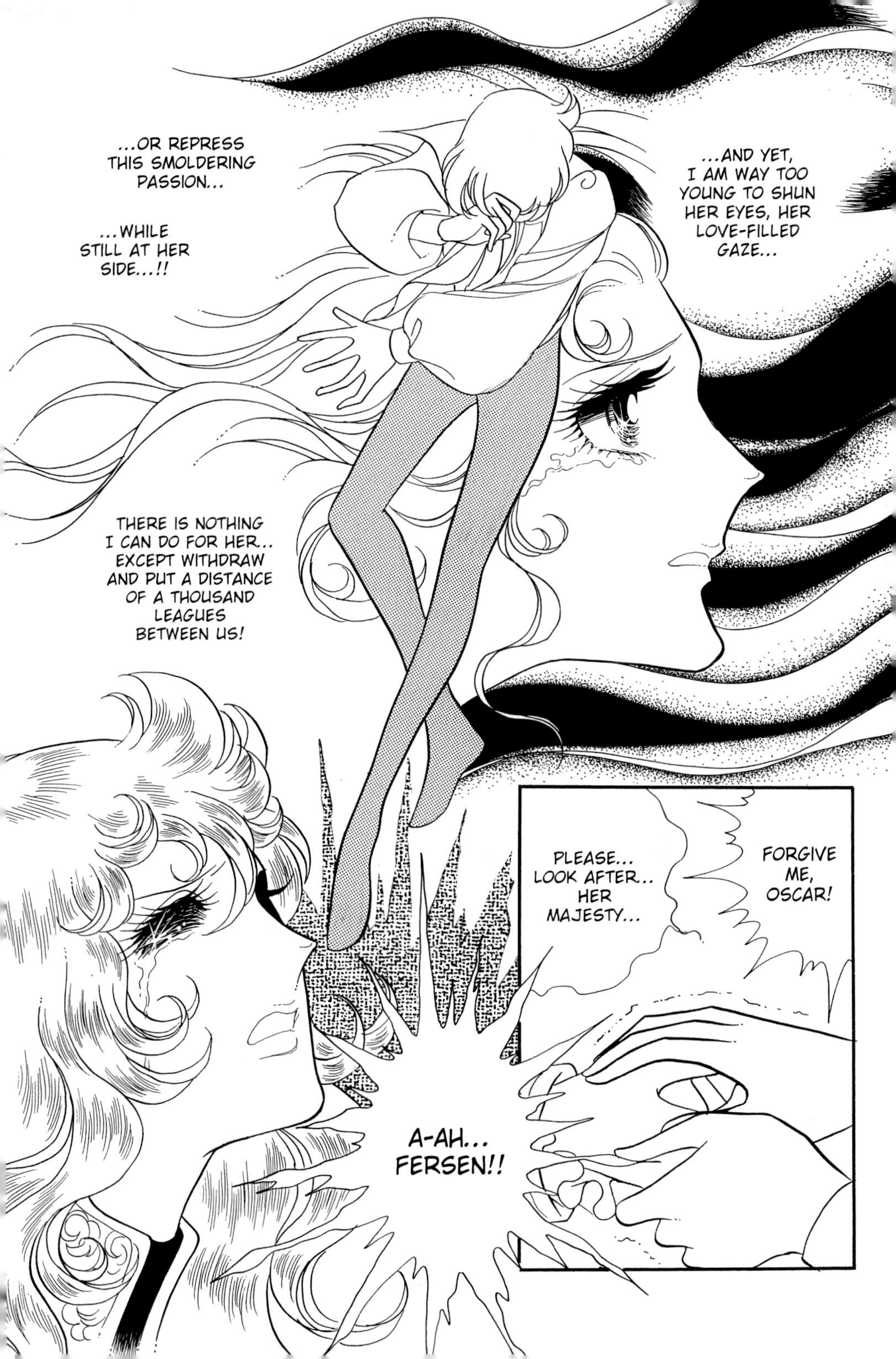
...AND YET, I AM WAY TOO YOUNG TO SHUN HER EYES, HER LOVE-FILLED GAZE...
...OR REPRESS THIS SMOLDERING PASSION...
...WHILE STILL AT HER SIDE...!!
THERE IS NOTHING I CAN DO FOR HER... EXCEPT WITHDRAW AND PUT A DISTANCE OF A THOUSAND LEAGUES BETWEEN US!
FORGIVE ME, OSCAR!
PLEASE... LOOK AFTER... HER MAJESTY...
A-AH... FERSEN!!

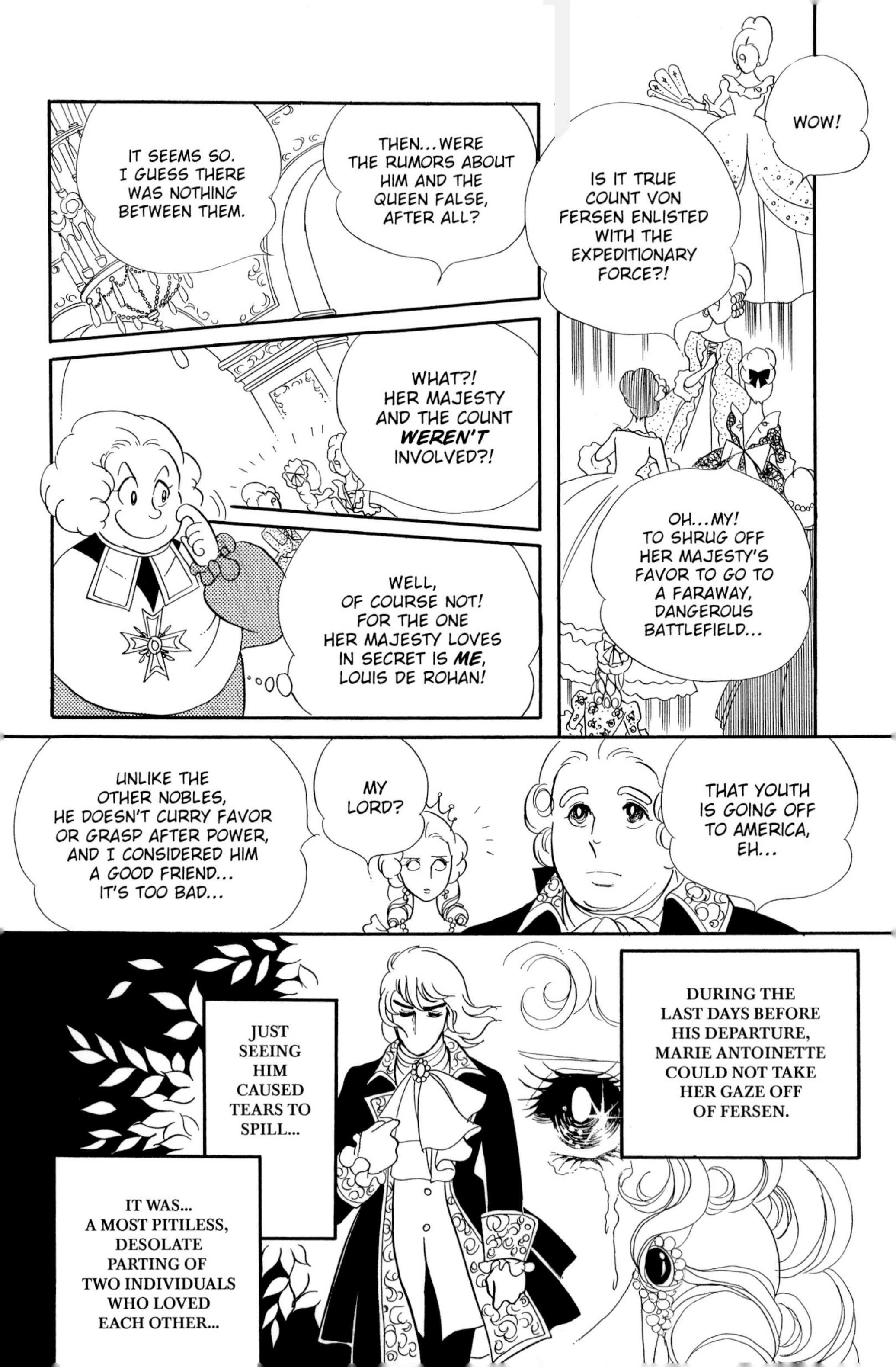
WOW!
IS IT TRUE COUNT VON FERSEN ENLISTED WITH THE EXPEDITIONARY FORCE?!
OH...MY! TO SHRUG OFF HER MAJESTY'S FAVOR TO GO TO A FARAWAY, DANGEROUS BATTLEFIELD...
THEN...WERE THE RUMORS ABOUT HIM AND THE QUEEN FALSE, AFTER ALL?
IT SEEMS SO. I GUESS THERE WAS NOTHING BETWEEN THEM.
WHAT?! HER MAJESTY AND THE COUNT *WEREN'T* INVOLVED?!
WELL, OF COURSE NOT! FOR THE ONE HER MAJESTY LOVES IN SECRET IS *ME*, LOUIS DE ROHAN!
THAT YOUTH IS GOING OFF TO AMERICA, EH...
MY LORD?
UNLIKE THE OTHER NOBLES, HE DOESN'T CURRY FAVOR OR GRASP AFTER POWER, AND I CONSIDERED HIM A GOOD FRIEND... IT'S TOO BAD...
DURING THE LAST DAYS BEFORE HIS DEPARTURE, MARIE ANTOINETTE COULD NOT TAKE HER GAZE OFF OF FERSEN.
JUST SEEING HIM CAUSED TEARS TO SPILL...
IT WAS... A MOST PITILESS, DESOLATE PARTING OF TWO INDIVIDUALS WHO LOVED EACH OTHER...

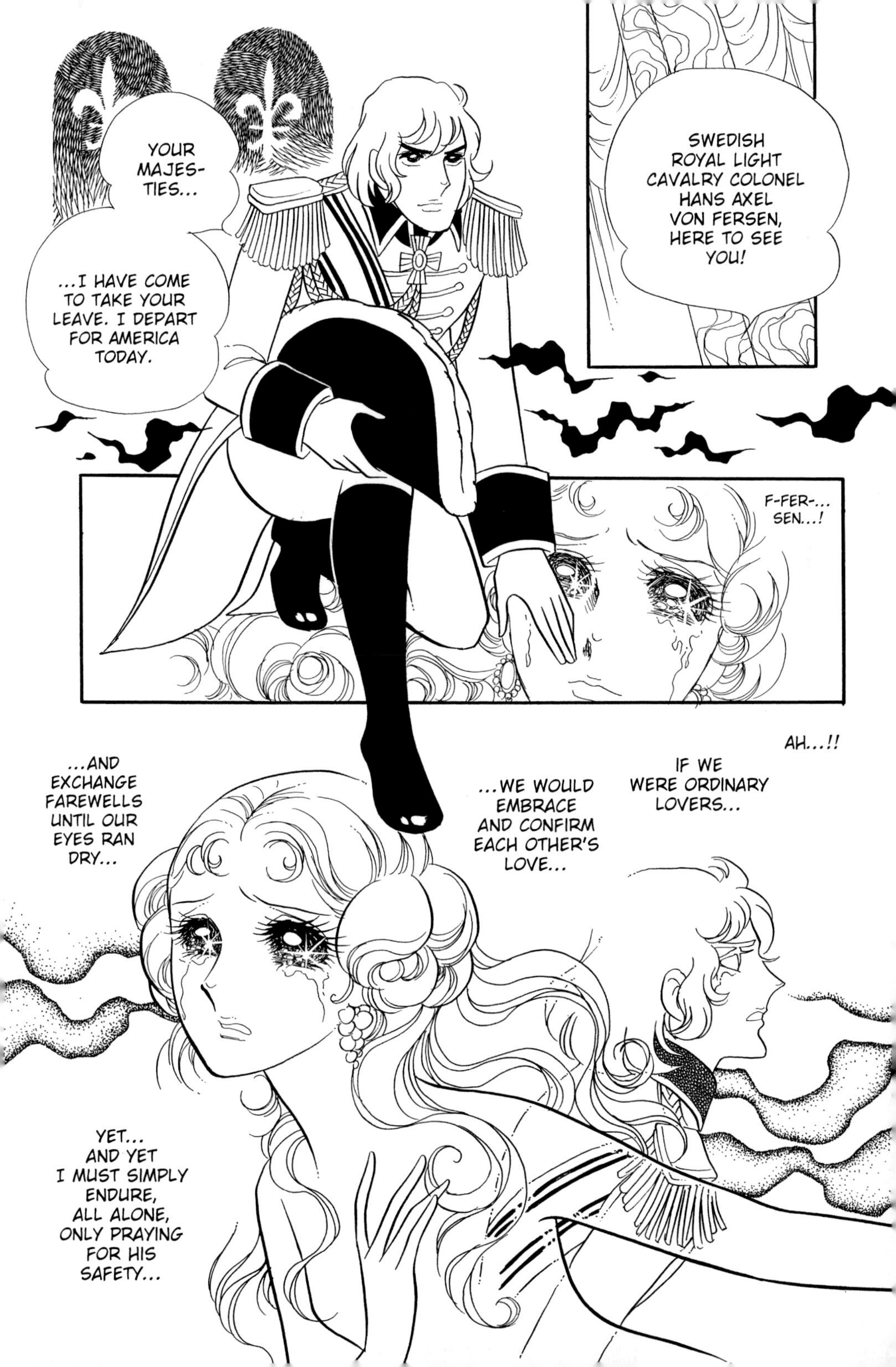
SWEDISH ROYAL LIGHT CAVALRY COLONEL HANS AXEL VON FERSEN, HERE TO SEE YOU!
YOUR MAJES-TIES...
...I HAVE COME TO TAKE YOUR LEAVE. I DEPART FOR AMERICA TODAY.
F-FER-... SEN...!
AH...!!
IF WE WERE ORDINARY LOVERS...
...WE WOULD EMBRACE AND CONFIRM EACH OTHER'S LOVE...
...AND EXCHANGE FAREWELLS UNTIL OUR EYES RAN DRY...
YET... AND YET I MUST SIMPLY ENDURE, ALL ALONE, ONLY PRAYING FOR HIS SAFETY...

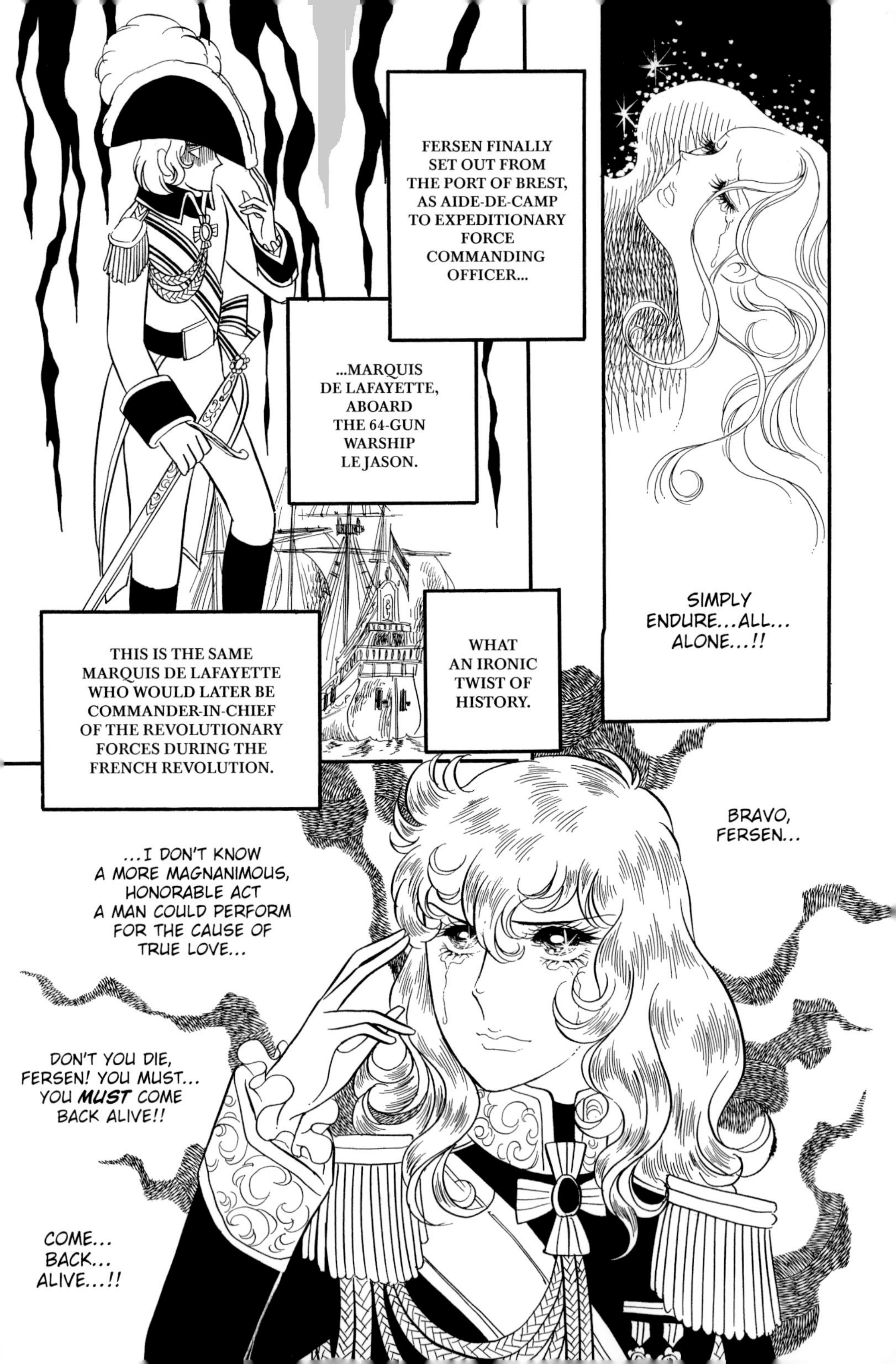
SIMPLY ENDURE...ALL... ALONE...!!
FERSEN FINALLY SET OUT FROM THE PORT OF BREST, AS AIDE-DE-CAMP TO EXPEDITIONARY FORCE COMMANDING OFFICER...
...MARQUIS DE LAFAYETTE, ABOARD THE 64-GUN WARSHIP LE JASON.
THIS IS THE SAME MARQUIS DE LAFAYETTE WHO WOULD LATER BE COMMANDER-IN-CHIEF OF THE REVOLUTIONARY FORCES DURING THE FRENCH REVOLUTION.
WHAT AN IRONIC TWIST OF HISTORY.
BRAVO, FERSEN...
...I DON'T KNOW A MORE MAGNANIMOUS, HONORABLE ACT A MAN COULD PERFORM FOR THE CAUSE OF TRUE LOVE...
DON'T YOU DIE, FERSEN! YOU MUST... YOU ***MUST*** COME BACK ALIVE!!
COME... BACK... ALIVE...!!

★OVERWHELMINGLY POPULAR! INTENSE AND IMPACTFUL!!
♥FERSEN FLESS COURT...BUT WHAT OF ANTOINETTE AND OSCAR?!

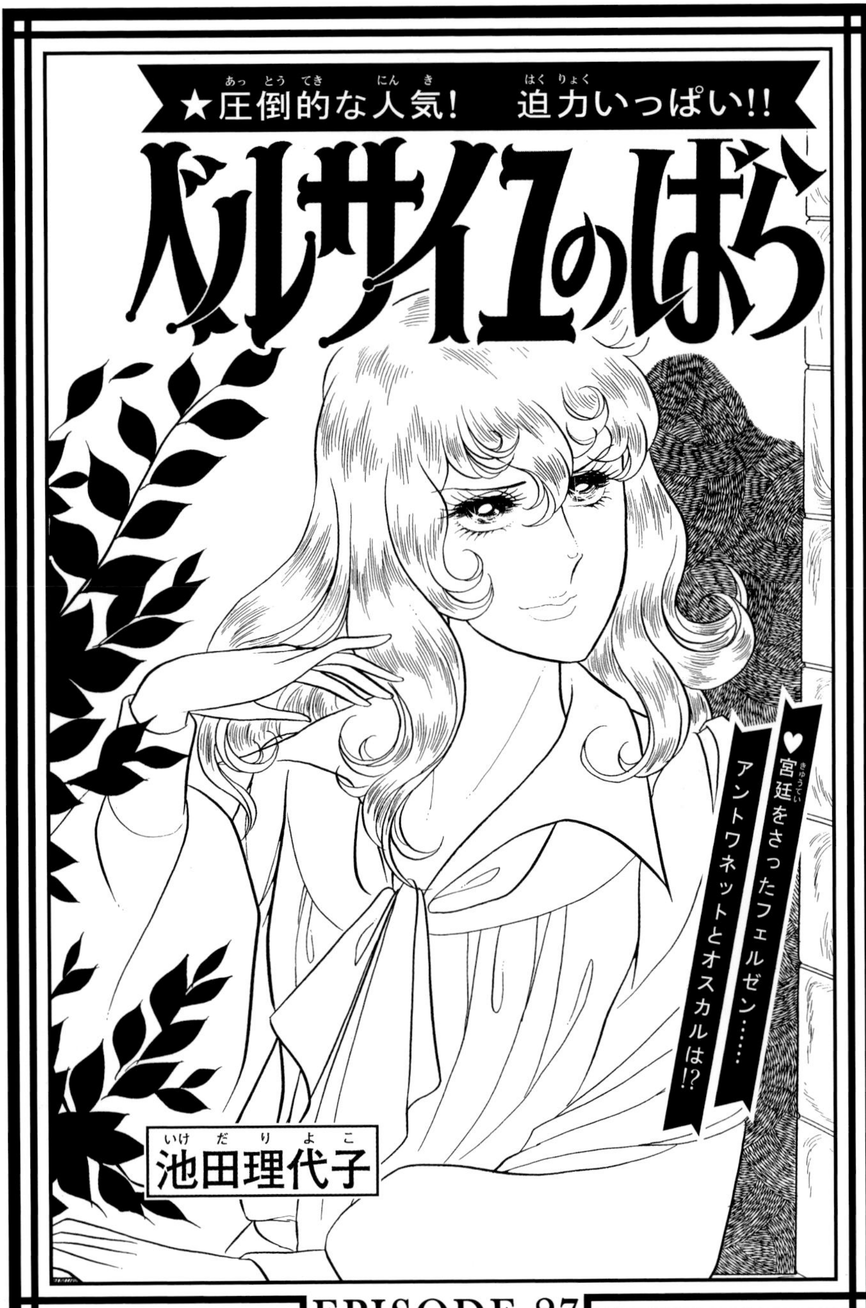
★圧倒的な人気！　迫力いっぱい!!
ベルサイユのばら
♥宮廷をさったフェルゼン……
アントワネットとオスカルは!?
池田理代子

EPISODE 27

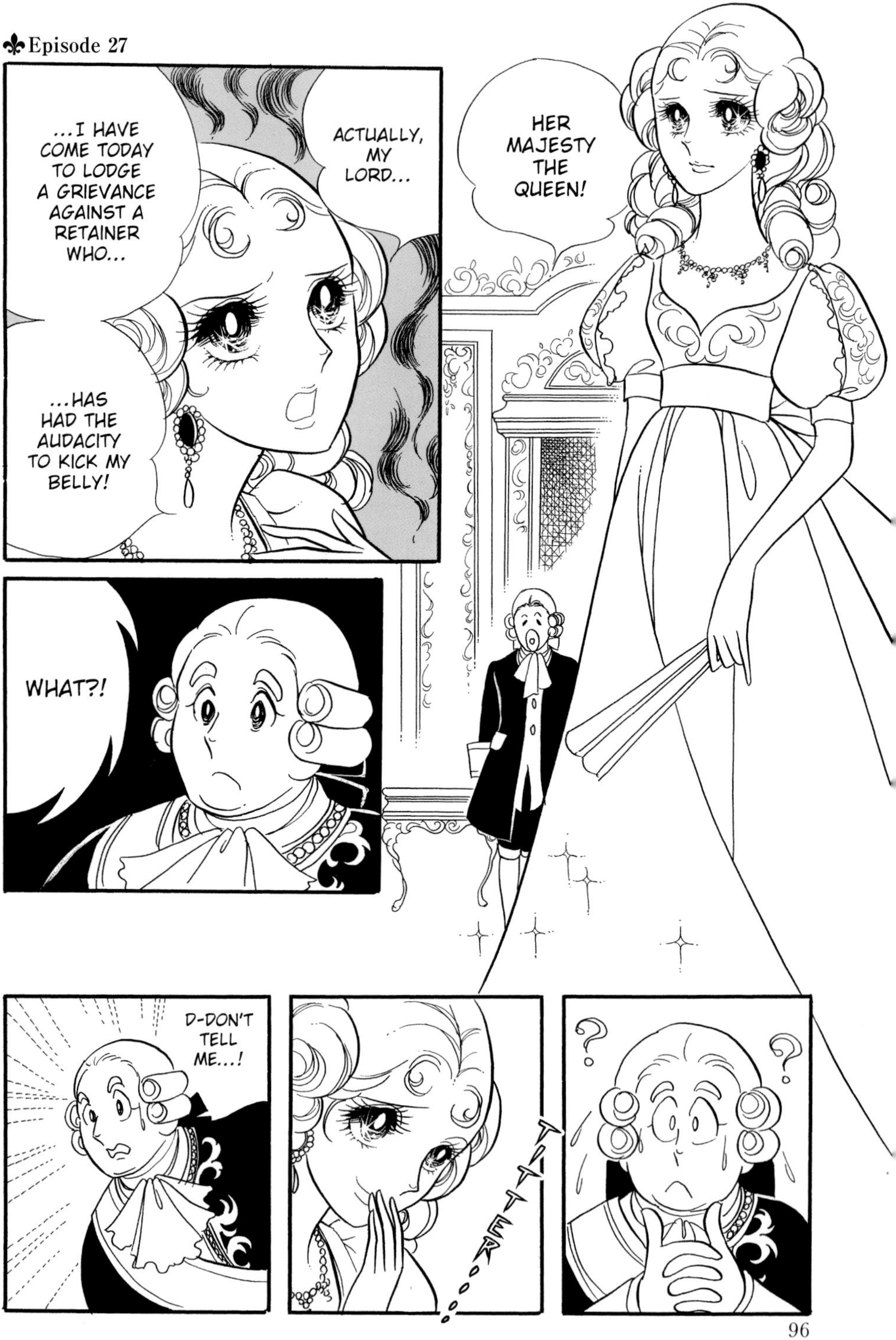
HER MAJESTY THE QUEEN!
ACTUALLY, MY LORD...
...I HAVE COME TODAY TO LODGE A GRIEVANCE AGAINST A RETAINER WHO...
...HAS HAD THE AUDACITY TO KICK MY BELLY!
WHAT?!
TITTER...
D-DON'T TELL ME...!

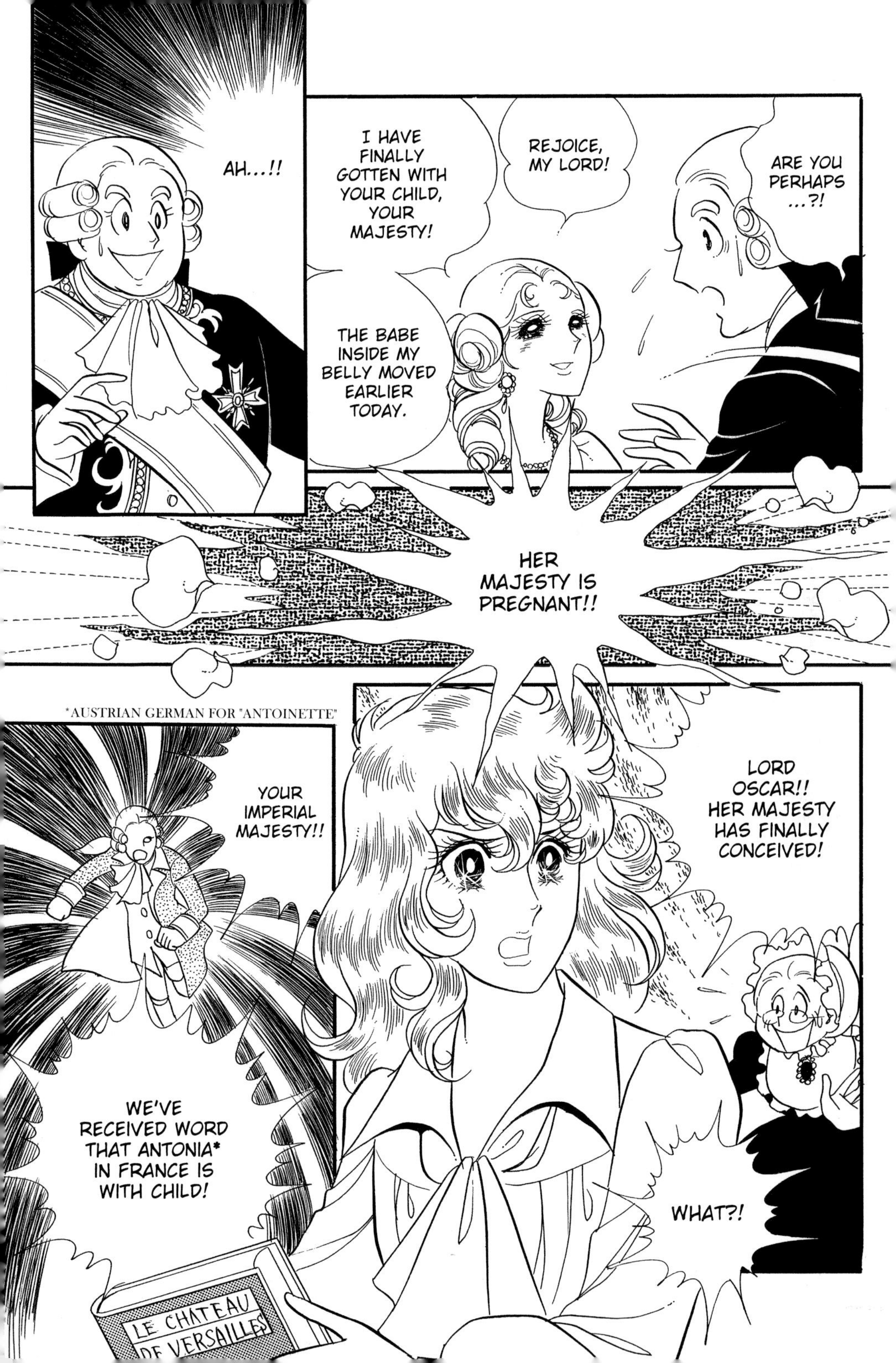
ARE YOU PERHAPS ...?!
REJOICE, MY LORD!
I HAVE FINALLY GOTTEN WITH YOUR CHILD, YOUR MAJESTY!
THE BABE INSIDE MY BELLY MOVED EARLIER TODAY.
AH...!!
HER MAJESTY IS PREGNANT!!
LORD OSCAR!! HER MAJESTY HAS FINALLY CONCEIVED!
WHAT?!
YOUR IMPERIAL MAJESTY!!
WE'VE RECEIVED WORD THAT ANTONIA* IN FRANCE IS WITH CHILD!
LE CHATEAU DE VERSAILLES

*AUSTRIAN GERMAN FOR "ANTOINETTE"

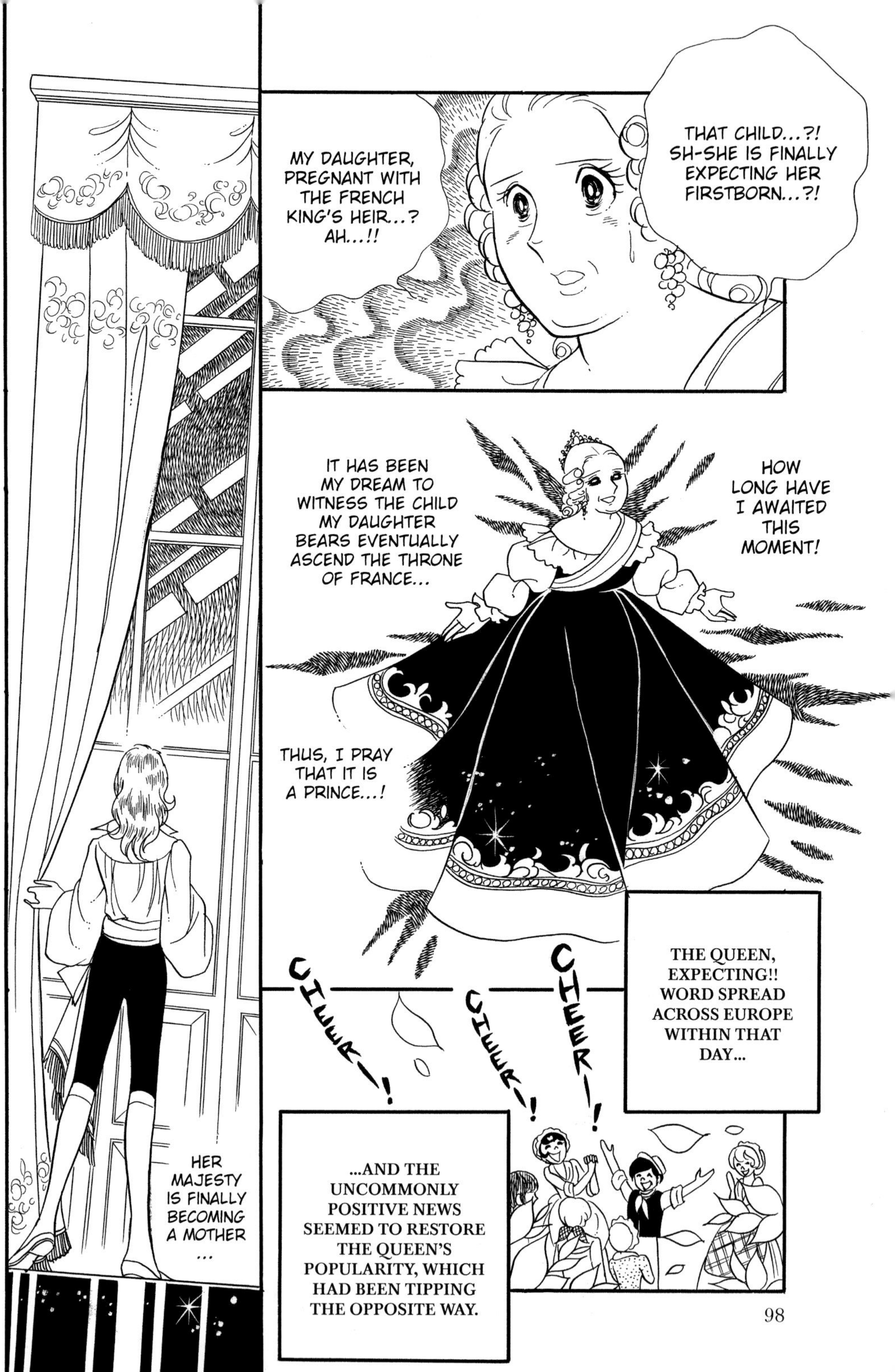
THAT CHILD...?! SH-SHE IS FINALLY EXPECTING HER FIRSTBORN...?!
MY DAUGHTER, PREGNANT WITH THE FRENCH KING'S HEIR...? AH...!!
HOW LONG HAVE I AWAITED THIS MOMENT!
IT HAS BEEN MY DREAM TO WITNESS THE CHILD MY DAUGHTER BEARS EVENTUALLY ASCEND THE THRONE OF FRANCE...
THUS, I PRAY THAT IT IS A PRINCE...!
THE QUEEN, EXPECTING!! WORD SPREAD ACROSS EUROPE WITHIN THAT DAY...
CHEER!!
CHEER!!
CHEER!!
...AND THE UNCOMMONLY POSITIVE NEWS SEEMED TO RESTORE THE QUEEN'S POPULARITY, WHICH HAD BEEN TIPPING THE OPPOSITE WAY.
HER MAJESTY IS FINALLY BECOMING A MOTHER ...

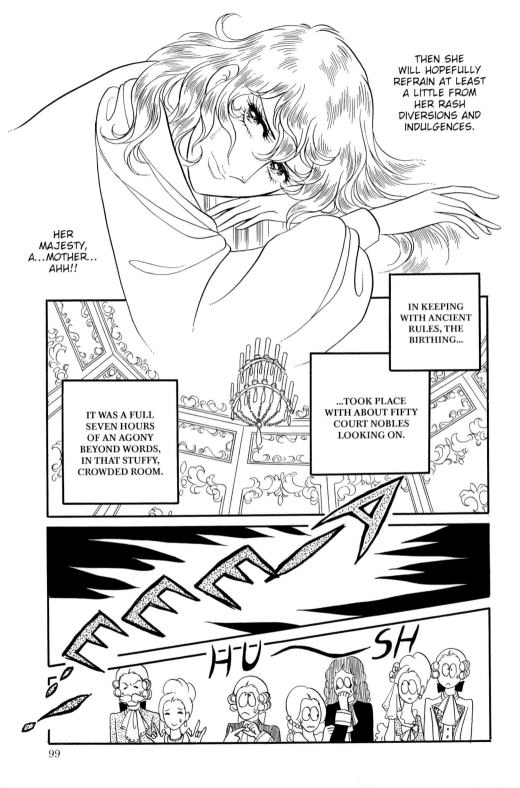

THEN SHE WILL HOPEFULLY REFRAIN AT LEAST A LITTLE FROM HER RASH DIVERSIONS AND INDULGENCES.

HER MAJESTY, A...MOTHER... AHH!!

IN KEEPING WITH ANCIENT RULES, THE BIRTHING...

...TOOK PLACE WITH ABOUT FIFTY COURT NOBLES LOOKING ON.

IT WAS A FULL SEVEN HOURS OF AN AGONY BEYOND WORDS, IN THAT STUFFY, CROWDED ROOM.

HU~SH

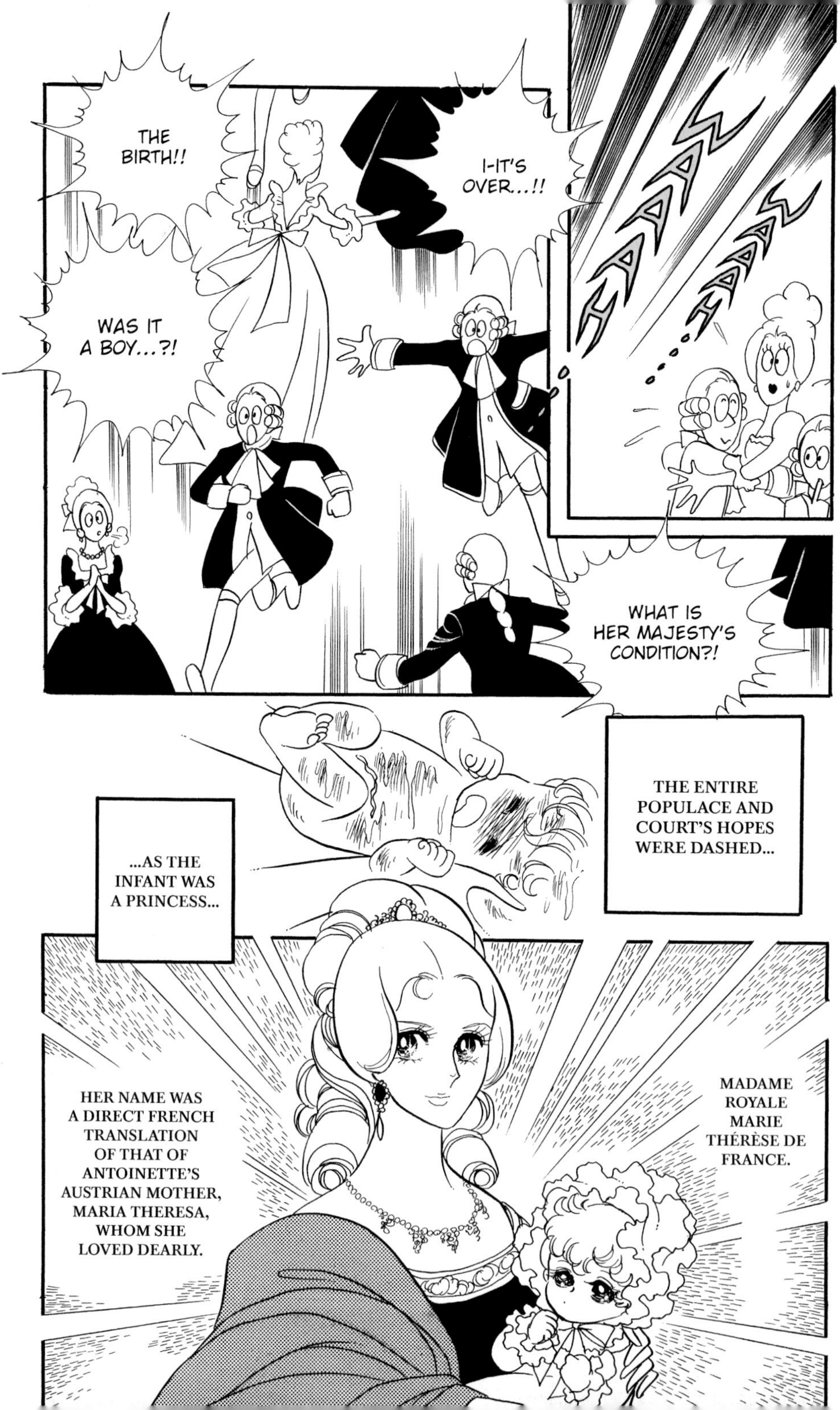
HAAAW
HAAAW
I-IT'S OVER...!!
THE BIRTH!!
WAS IT A BOY...?!
WHAT IS HER MAJESTY'S CONDITION?!
THE ENTIRE POPULACE AND COURT'S HOPES WERE DASHED...
...AS THE INFANT WAS A PRINCESS...
MADAME ROYALE MARIE THÉRÈSE DE FRANCE.
HER NAME WAS A DIRECT FRENCH TRANSLATION OF THAT OF ANTOINETTE'S AUSTRIAN MOTHER, MARIA THERESA, WHOM SHE LOVED DEARLY.

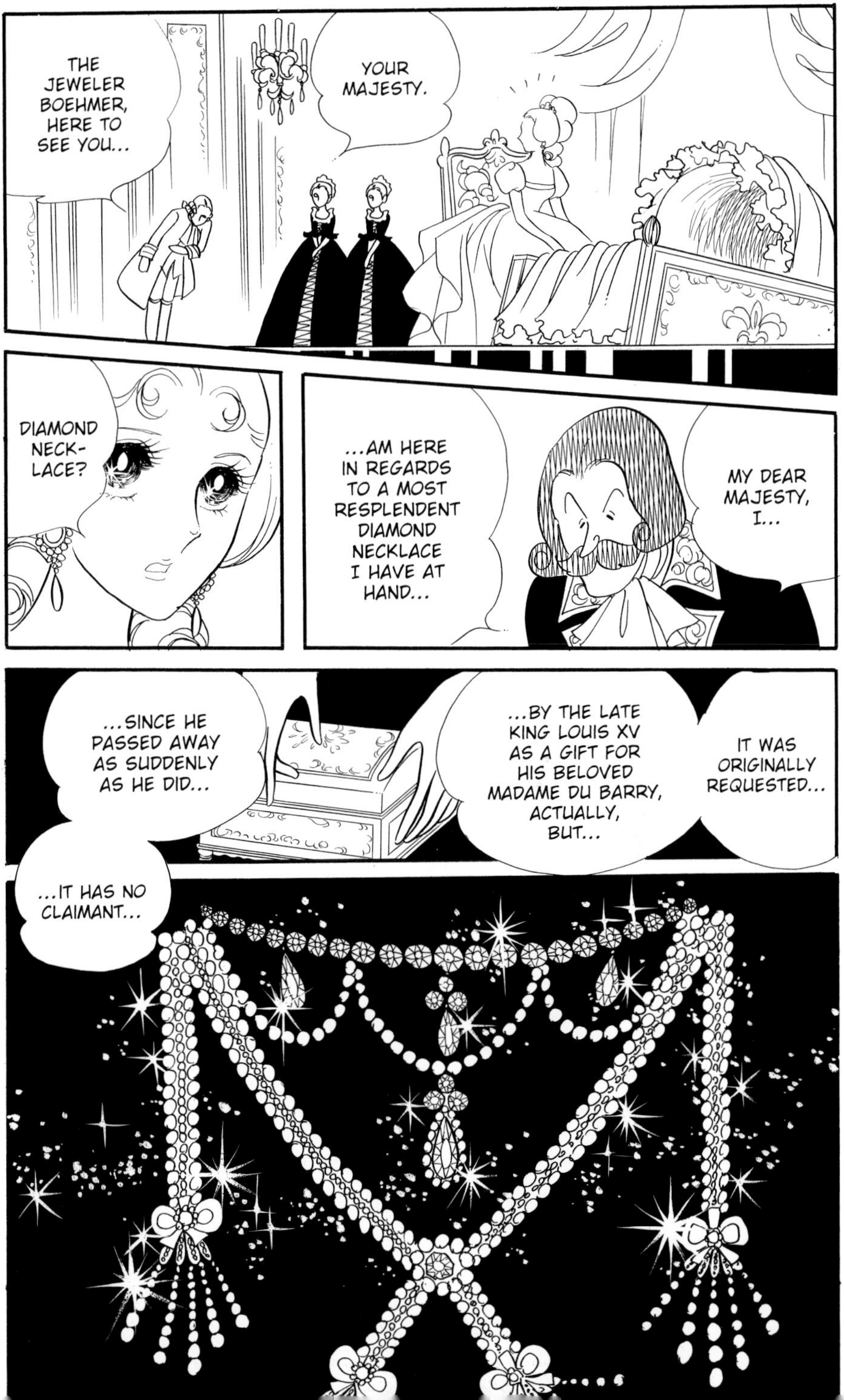
YOUR MAJESTY.
THE JEWELER BOEHMER, HERE TO SEE YOU...
MY DEAR MAJESTY, I...
...AM HERE IN REGARDS TO A MOST RESPLENDENT DIAMOND NECKLACE I HAVE AT HAND...
DIAMOND NECK-LACE?
IT WAS ORIGINALLY REQUESTED...
...BY THE LATE KING LOUIS XV AS A GIFT FOR HIS BELOVED MADAME DU BARRY, ACTUALLY, BUT...
...SINCE HE PASSED AWAY AS SUDDENLY AS HE DID...
...IT HAS NO CLAIMANT...

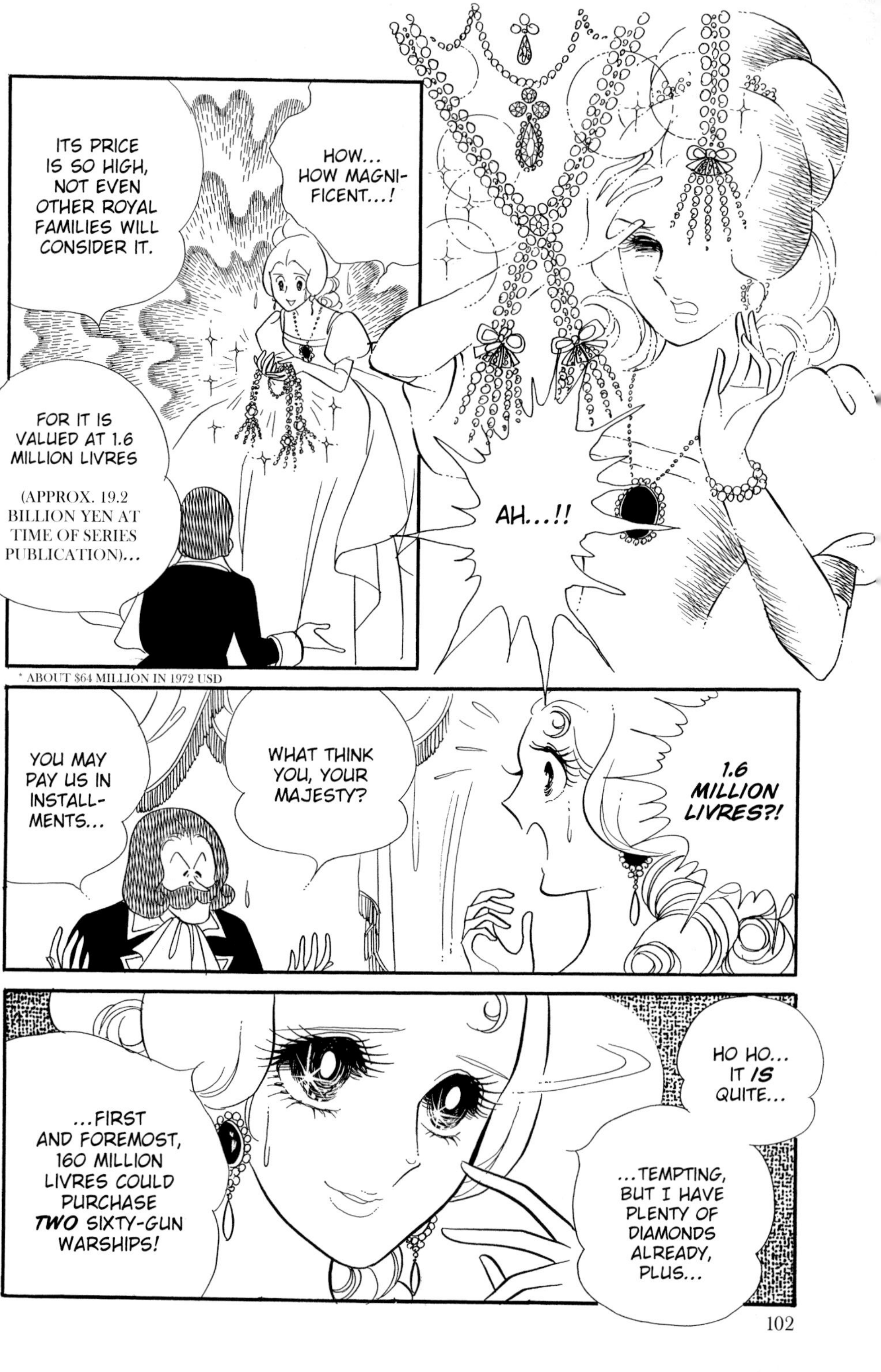
AH...!!
HOW... HOW MAGNIFICENT...!
ITS PRICE IS SO HIGH, NOT EVEN OTHER ROYAL FAMILIES WILL CONSIDER IT.
FOR IT IS VALUED AT 1.6 MILLION LIVRES (APPROX. 19.2 BILLION YEN AT TIME OF SERIES PUBLICATION)...
1.6 MILLION LIVRES?!
WHAT THINK YOU, YOUR MAJESTY?
YOU MAY PAY US IN INSTALLMENTS...
HO HO... IT *IS* QUITE...
...TEMPTING, BUT I HAVE PLENTY OF DIAMONDS ALREADY, PLUS...
...FIRST AND FOREMOST, 160 MILLION LIVRES COULD PURCHASE ***TWO*** SIXTY-GUN WARSHIPS!

* ABOUT $64 MILLION IN 1972 USD

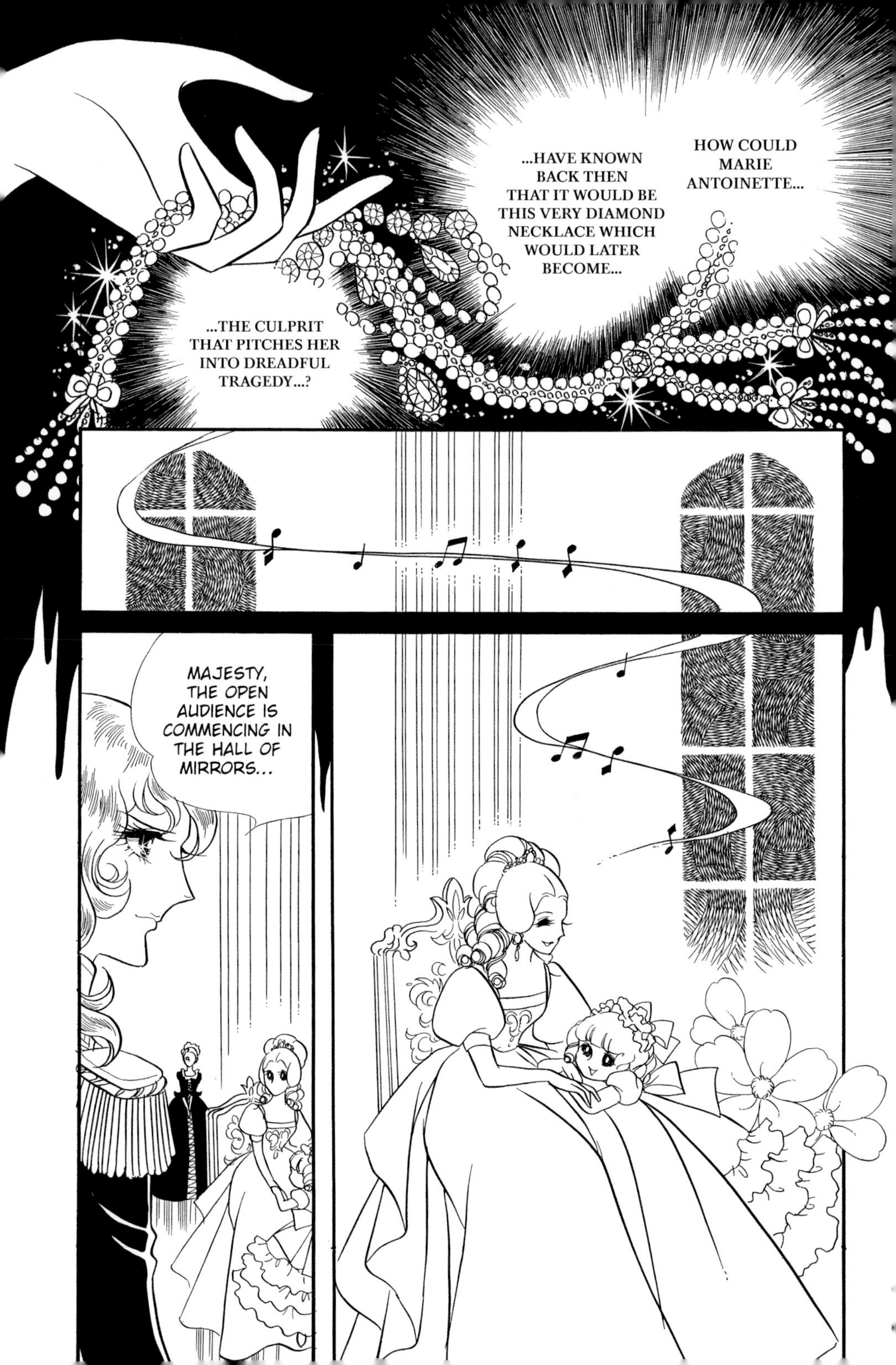
HOW COULD MARIE ANTOINETTE...
...HAVE KNOWN BACK THEN THAT IT WOULD BE THIS VERY DIAMOND NECKLACE WHICH WOULD LATER BECOME...
...THE CULPRIT THAT PITCHES HER INTO DREADFUL TRAGEDY...?
MAJESTY, THE OPEN AUDIENCE IS COMMENCING IN THE HALL OF MIRRORS...

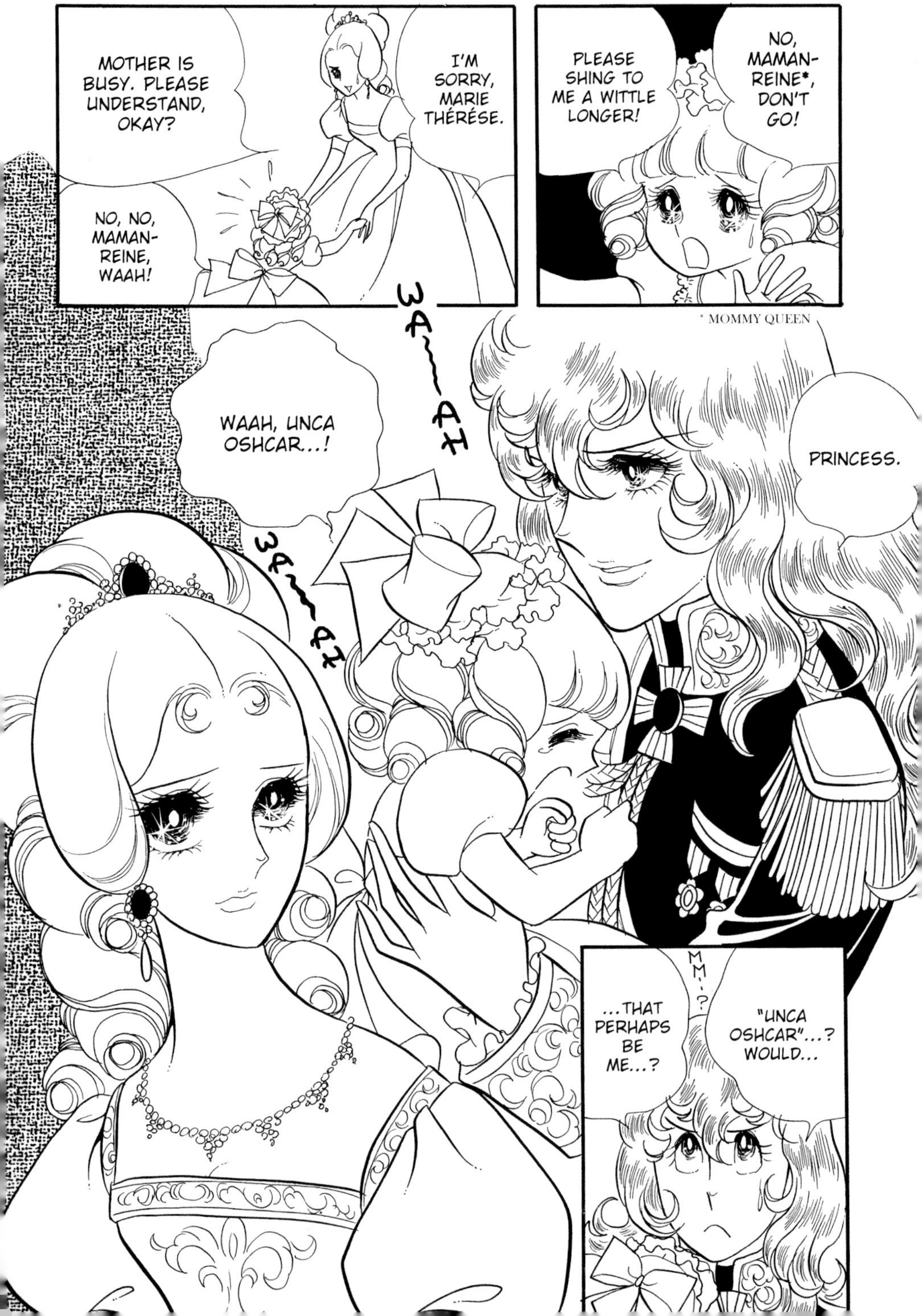
NO, MAMAN-REINE*, DON'T GO!
PLEASE SHING TO ME A WITTLE LONGER!
I'M SORRY, MARIE THÉRÉSE.
MOTHER IS BUSY. PLEASE UNDERSTAND, OKAY?
NO, NO, MAMAN-REINE, WAAH!
PRINCESS.
WA~~AH
WAAH, UNCA OSHCAR...!
WA~~AH
MM...?
"UNCA OSHCAR"...? WOULD...
...THAT PERHAPS BE ME...?

* MOMMY QUEEN

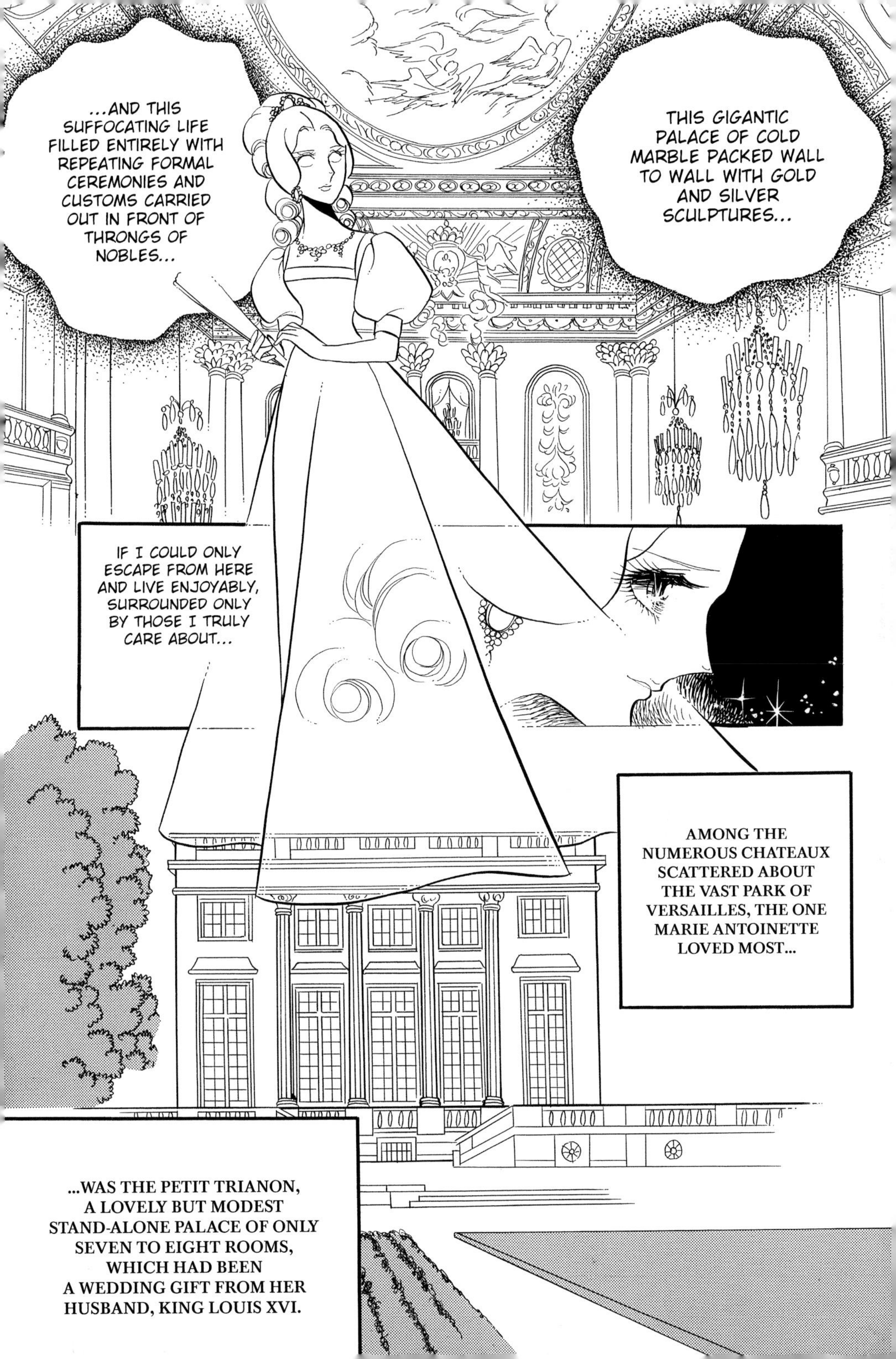
THIS GIGANTIC PALACE OF COLD MARBLE PACKED WALL TO WALL WITH GOLD AND SILVER SCULPTURES...
...AND THIS SUFFOCATING LIFE FILLED ENTIRELY WITH REPEATING FORMAL CEREMONIES AND CUSTOMS CARRIED OUT IN FRONT OF THRONGS OF NOBLES...
IF I COULD ONLY ESCAPE FROM HERE AND LIVE ENJOYABLY, SURROUNDED ONLY BY THOSE I TRULY CARE ABOUT...
AMONG THE NUMEROUS CHATEAUX SCATTERED ABOUT THE VAST PARK OF VERSAILLES, THE ONE MARIE ANTOINETTE LOVED MOST...
...WAS THE PETIT TRIANON, A LOVELY BUT MODEST STAND-ALONE PALACE OF ONLY SEVEN TO EIGHT ROOMS, WHICH HAD BEEN A WEDDING GIFT FROM HER HUSBAND, KING LOUIS XVI.

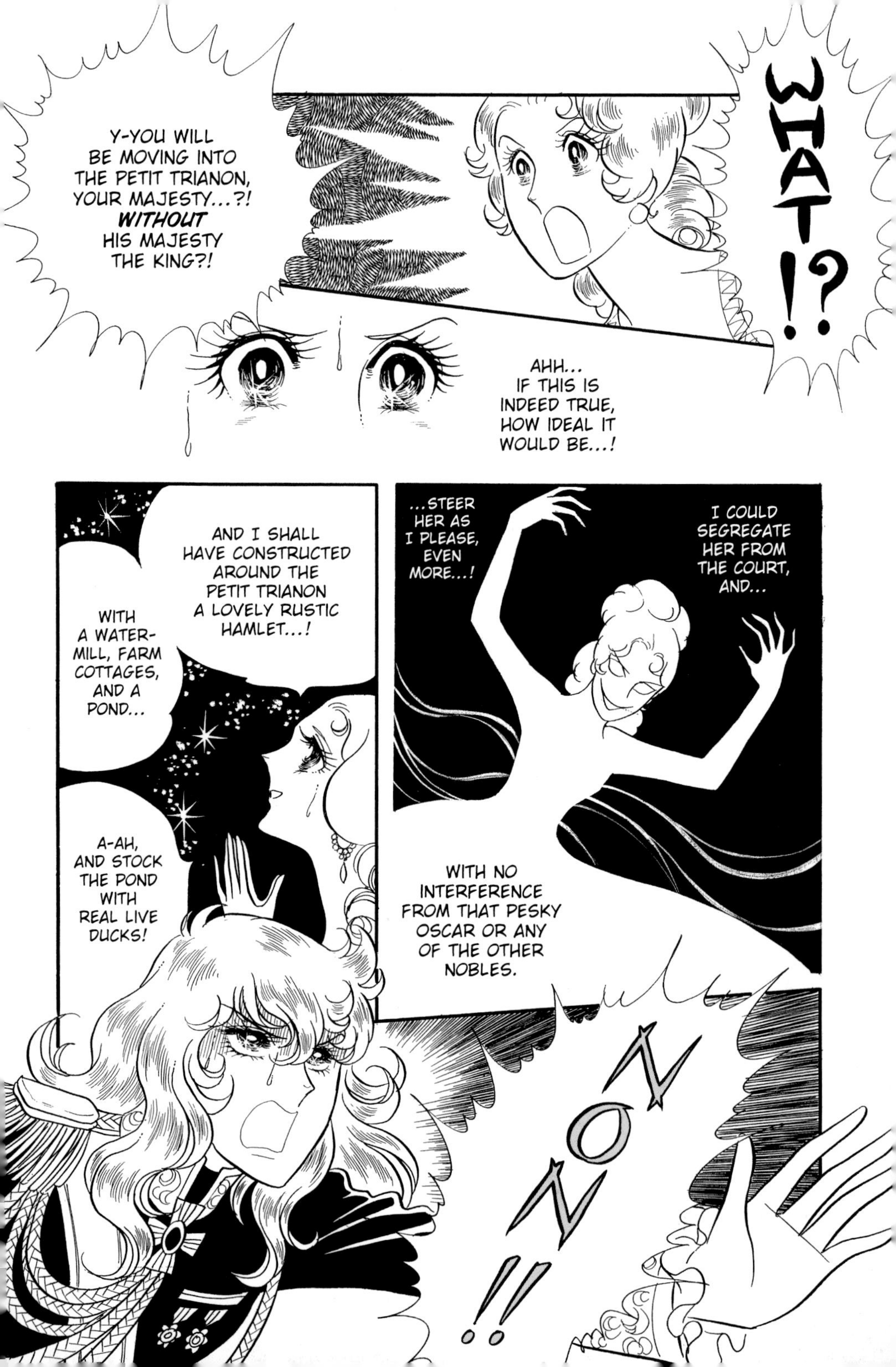
WHAT!?
Y-YOU WILL BE MOVING INTO THE PETIT TRIANON, YOUR MAJESTY...?! ***WITHOUT*** HIS MAJESTY THE KING?!
AHH... IF THIS IS INDEED TRUE, HOW IDEAL IT WOULD BE...!
I COULD SEGREGATE HER FROM THE COURT, AND...
...STEER HER AS I PLEASE, EVEN MORE...!
WITH NO INTERFERENCE FROM THAT PESKY OSCAR OR ANY OF THE OTHER NOBLES.
AND I SHALL HAVE CONSTRUCTED AROUND THE PETIT TRIANON A LOVELY RUSTIC HAMLET...!
WITH A WATER-MILL, FARM COTTAGES, AND A POND...
A-AH, AND STOCK THE POND WITH REAL LIVE DUCKS!
NON!!

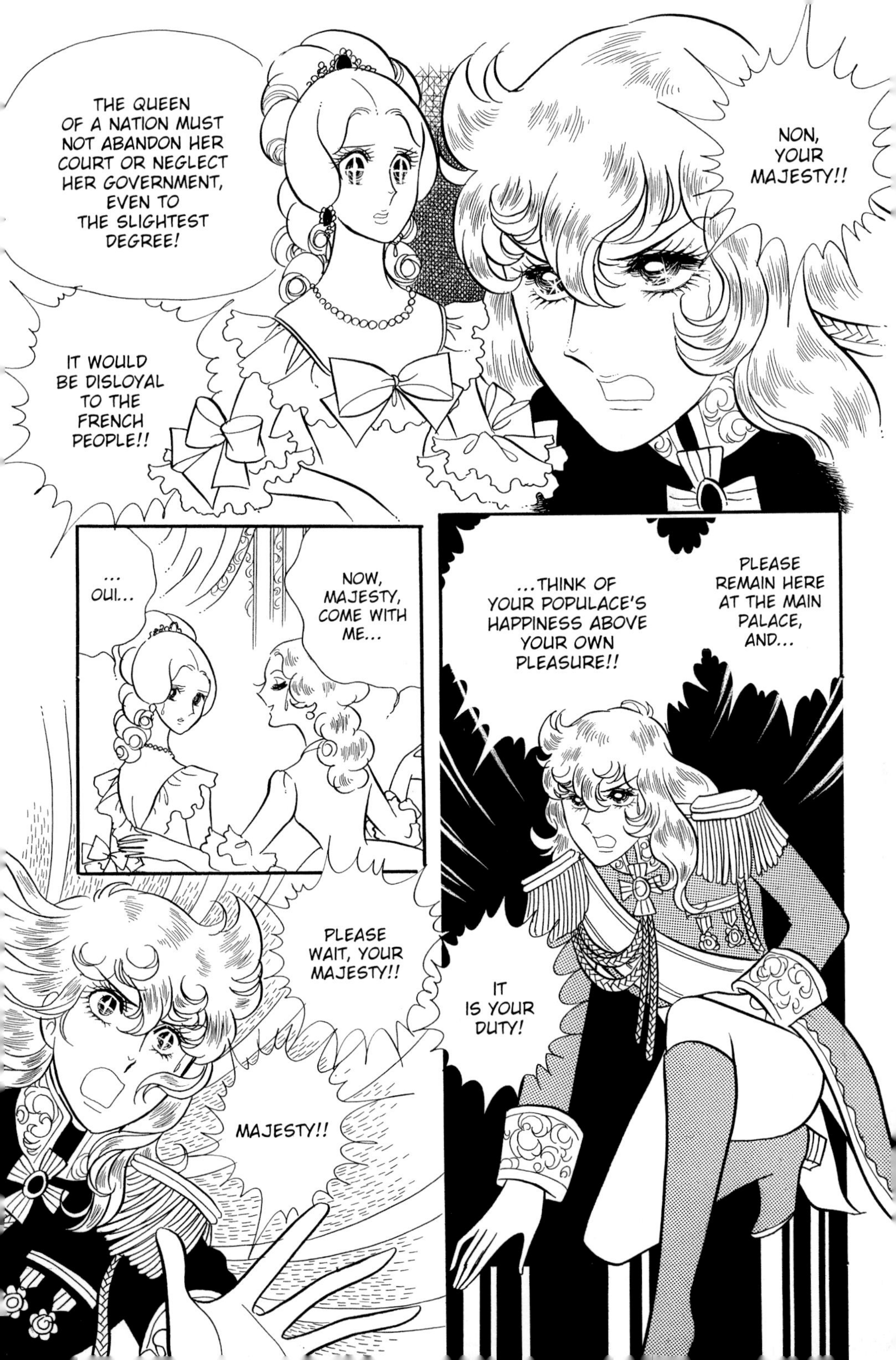
NON, YOUR MAJESTY!!
THE QUEEN OF A NATION MUST NOT ABANDON HER COURT OR NEGLECT HER GOVERNMENT, EVEN TO THE SLIGHTEST DEGREE!
IT WOULD BE DISLOYAL TO THE FRENCH PEOPLE!!
PLEASE REMAIN HERE AT THE MAIN PALACE, AND...
...THINK OF YOUR POPULACE'S HAPPINESS ABOVE YOUR OWN PLEASURE!!
IT IS YOUR DUTY!
NOW, MAJESTY, COME WITH ME...
...OUI...
PLEASE WAIT, YOUR MAJESTY!!
MAJESTY!!

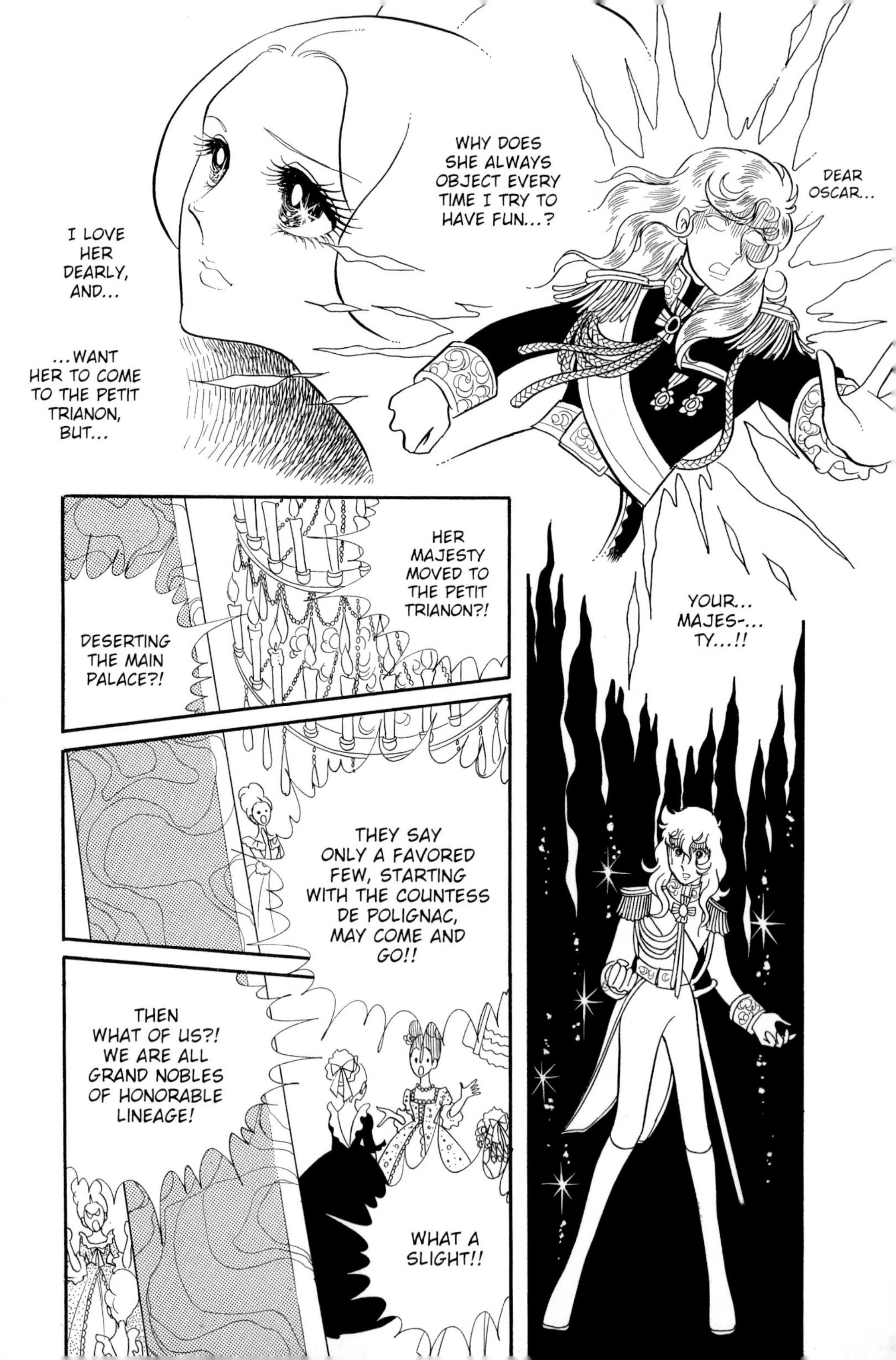
DEAR OSCAR...
WHY DOES SHE ALWAYS OBJECT EVERY TIME I TRY TO HAVE FUN...?
I LOVE HER DEARLY, AND...
...WANT HER TO COME TO THE PETIT TRIANON, BUT...
YOUR... MAJES-... TY...!!
HER MAJESTY MOVED TO THE PETIT TRIANON?!
DESERTING THE MAIN PALACE?!
THEY SAY ONLY A FAVORED FEW, STARTING WITH THE COUNTESS DE POLIGNAC, MAY COME AND GO!!
WHAT A SLIGHT!!
THEN WHAT OF US?! WE ARE ALL GRAND NOBLES OF HONORABLE LINEAGE!

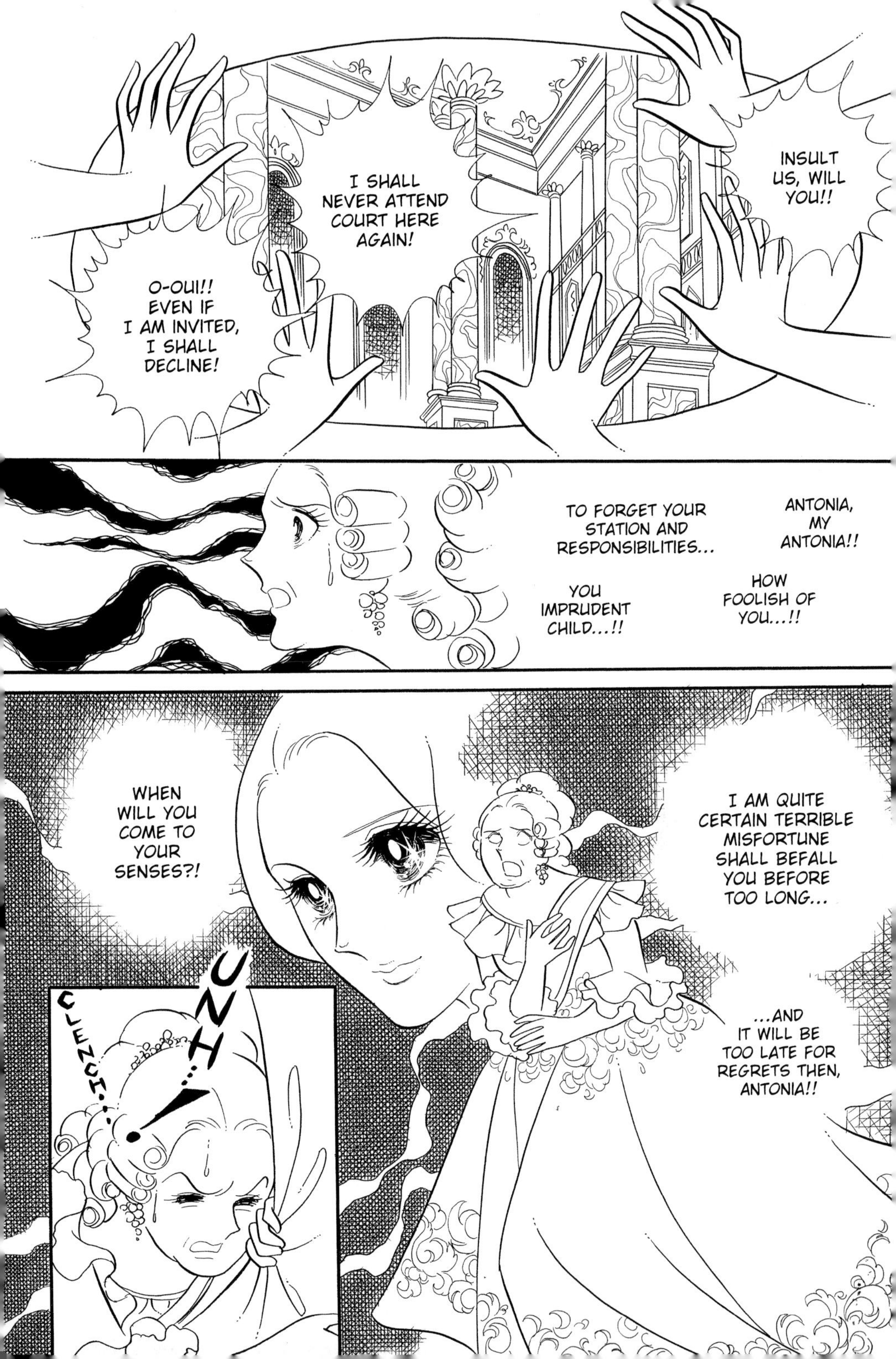
INSULT US, WILL YOU!!
I SHALL NEVER ATTEND COURT HERE AGAIN!
O-OUI!! EVEN IF I AM INVITED, I SHALL DECLINE!
ANTONIA, MY ANTONIA!!
HOW FOOLISH OF YOU...!!
TO FORGET YOUR STATION AND RESPONSIBILITIES...
YOU IMPRUDENT CHILD...!!
I AM QUITE CERTAIN TERRIBLE MISFORTUNE SHALL BEFALL YOU BEFORE TOO LONG...
...AND IT WILL BE TOO LATE FOR REGRETS THEN, ANTONIA!!
WHEN WILL YOU COME TO YOUR SENSES?!
UNH...!
CLENCH...

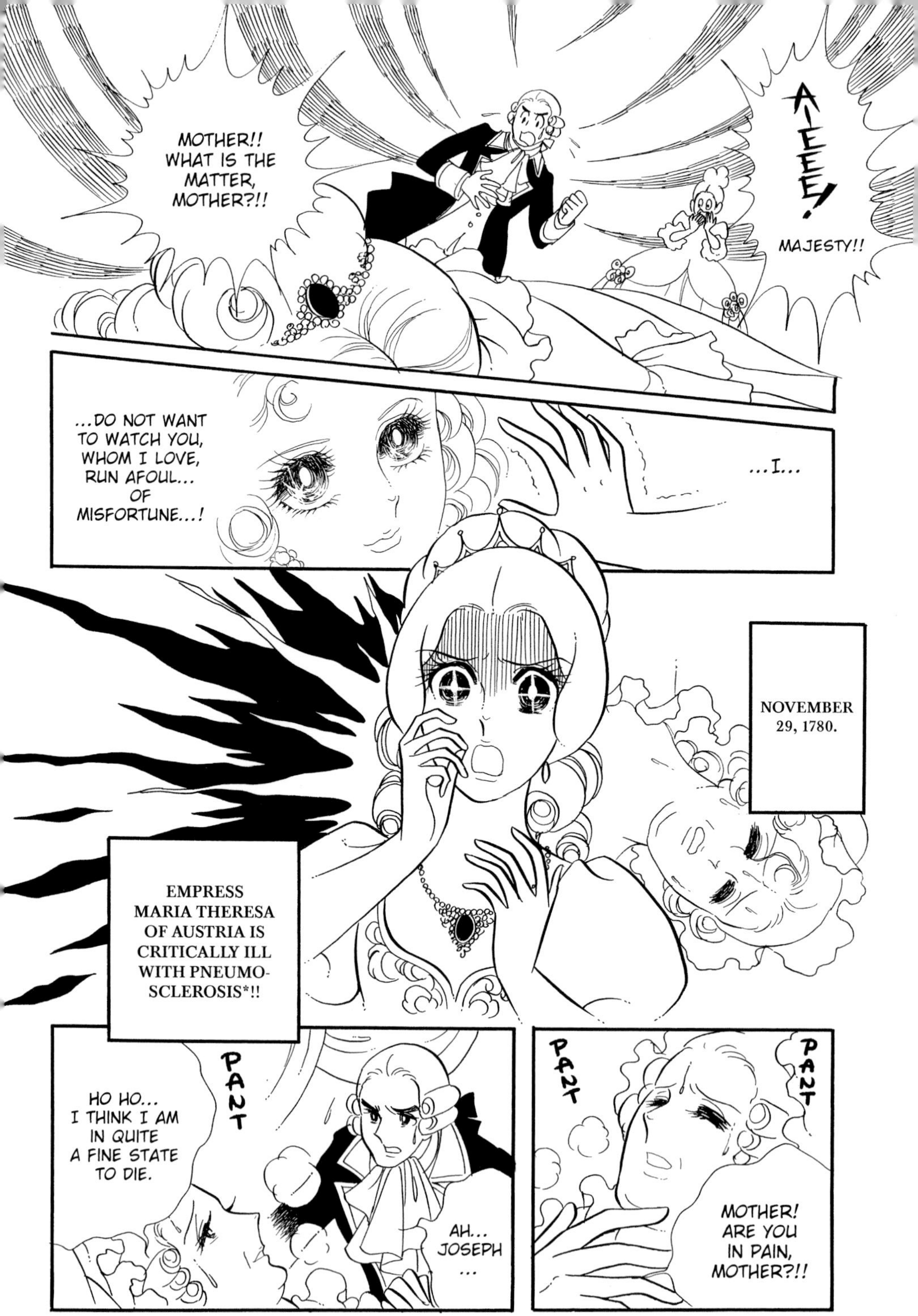

AIEEE!
MAJESTY!!
MOTHER!! WHAT IS THE MATTER, MOTHER?!!
...I...
...DO NOT WANT TO WATCH YOU, WHOM I LOVE, RUN AFOUL... OF MISFORTUNE...!
NOVEMBER 29, 1780.
EMPRESS MARIA THERESA OF AUSTRIA IS CRITICALLY ILL WITH PNEUMO-SCLEROSIS*!!
PANT
PANT
MOTHER! ARE YOU IN PAIN, MOTHER?!!
PANT
HO HO... I THINK I AM IN QUITE A FINE STATE TO DIE.
AH... JOSEPH ...

* EXCESSIVE SCARRING OF THE LUNGS

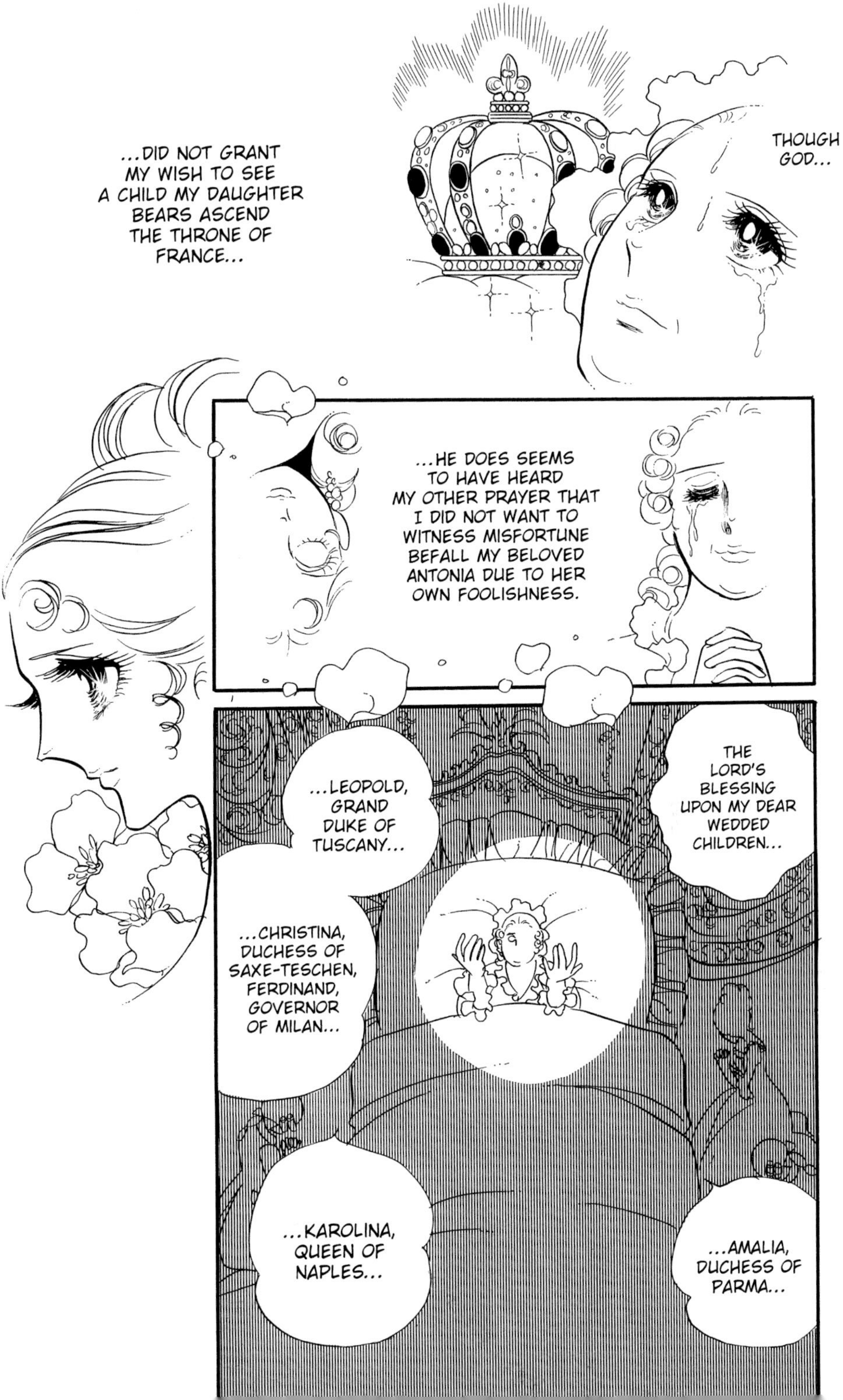
THOUGH GOD...
...DID NOT GRANT MY WISH TO SEE A CHILD MY DAUGHTER BEARS ASCEND THE THRONE OF FRANCE...
...HE DOES SEEMS TO HAVE HEARD MY OTHER PRAYER THAT I DID NOT WANT TO WITNESS MISFORTUNE BEFALL MY BELOVED ANTONIA DUE TO HER OWN FOOLISHNESS.
THE LORD'S BLESSING UPON MY DEAR WEDDED CHILDREN...
...LEOPOLD, GRAND DUKE OF TUSCANY...
...CHRISTINA, DUCHESS OF SAXE-TESCHEN, FERDINAND, GOVERNOR OF MILAN...
...AMALIA, DUCHESS OF PARMA...
...KAROLINA, QUEEN OF NAPLES...

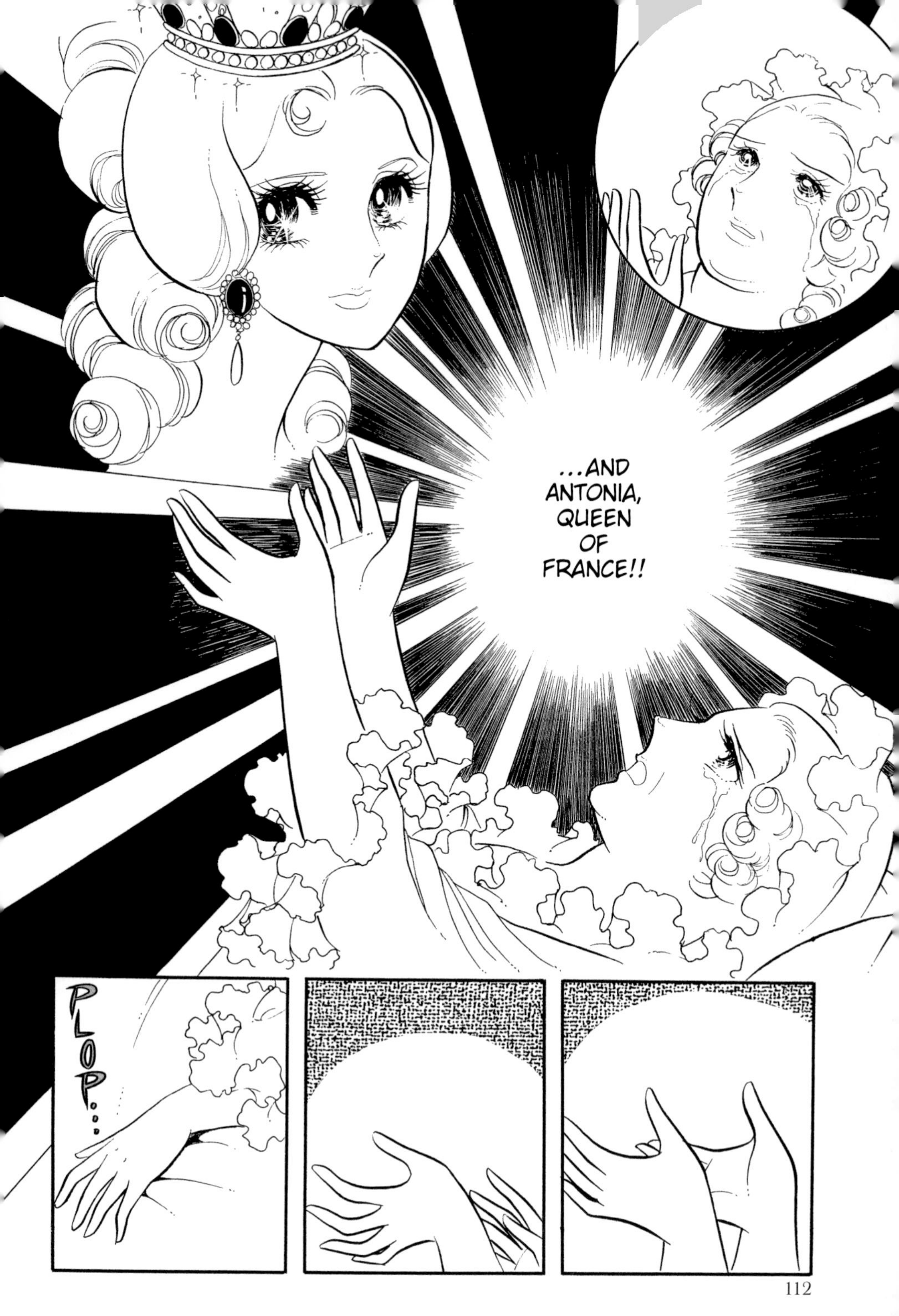
...AND ANTONIA, QUEEN OF FRANCE!!
PLOP...

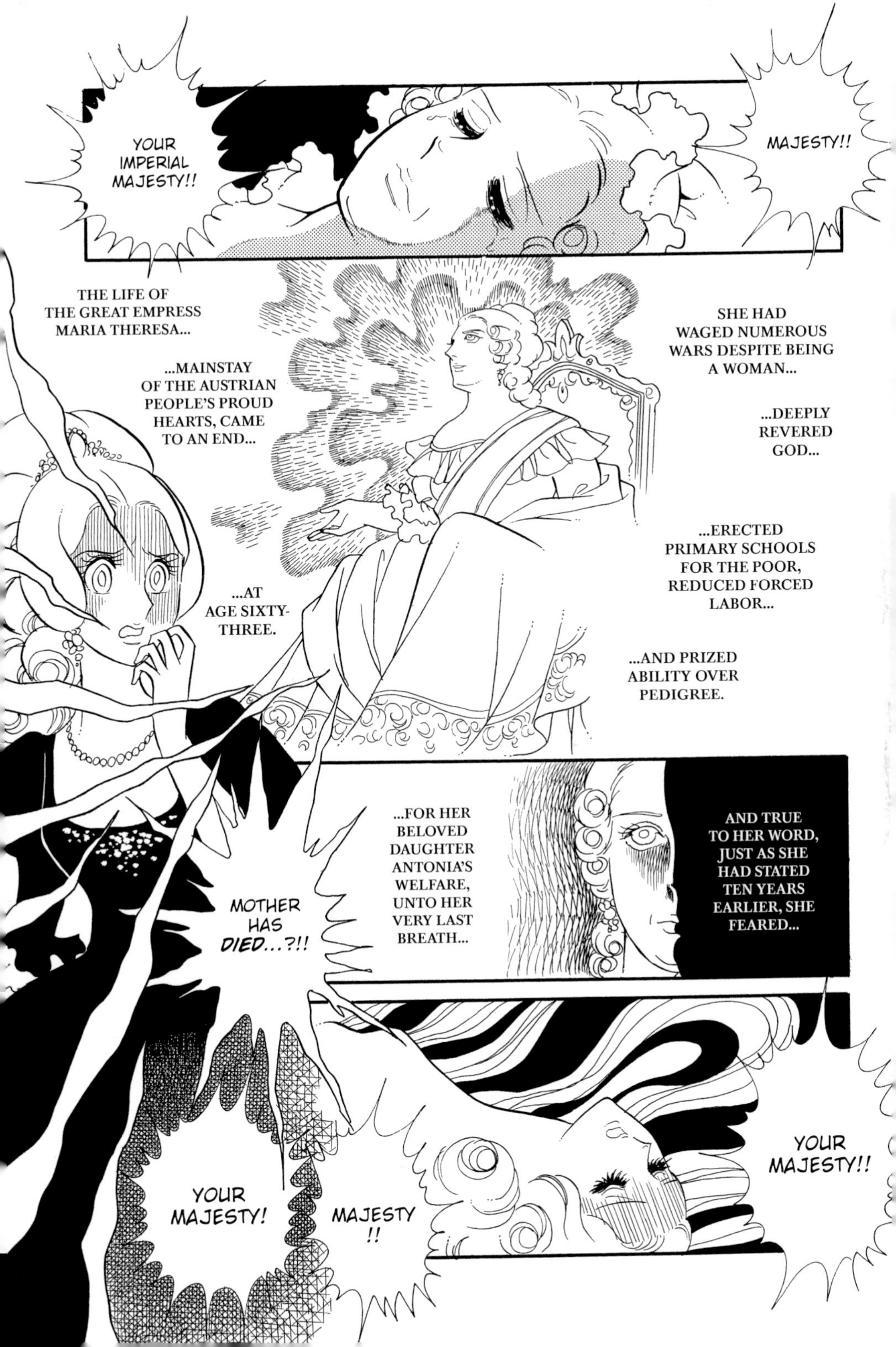

MAJESTY!!
YOUR IMPERIAL MAJESTY!!
SHE HAD WAGED NUMEROUS WARS DESPITE BEING A WOMAN...
...DEEPLY REVERED GOD...
...ERECTED PRIMARY SCHOOLS FOR THE POOR, REDUCED FORCED LABOR...
...AND PRIZED ABILITY OVER PEDIGREE.
THE LIFE OF THE GREAT EMPRESS MARIA THERESA...
...MAINSTAY OF THE AUSTRIAN PEOPLE'S PROUD HEARTS, CAME TO AN END...
...AT AGE SIXTY-THREE.
AND TRUE TO HER WORD, JUST AS SHE HAD STATED TEN YEARS EARLIER, SHE FEARED...
...FOR HER BELOVED DAUGHTER ANTONIA'S WELFARE, UNTO HER VERY LAST BREATH...
MOTHER HAS *DIED*...?!!
YOUR MAJESTY!!
MAJESTY !!
YOUR MAJESTY!

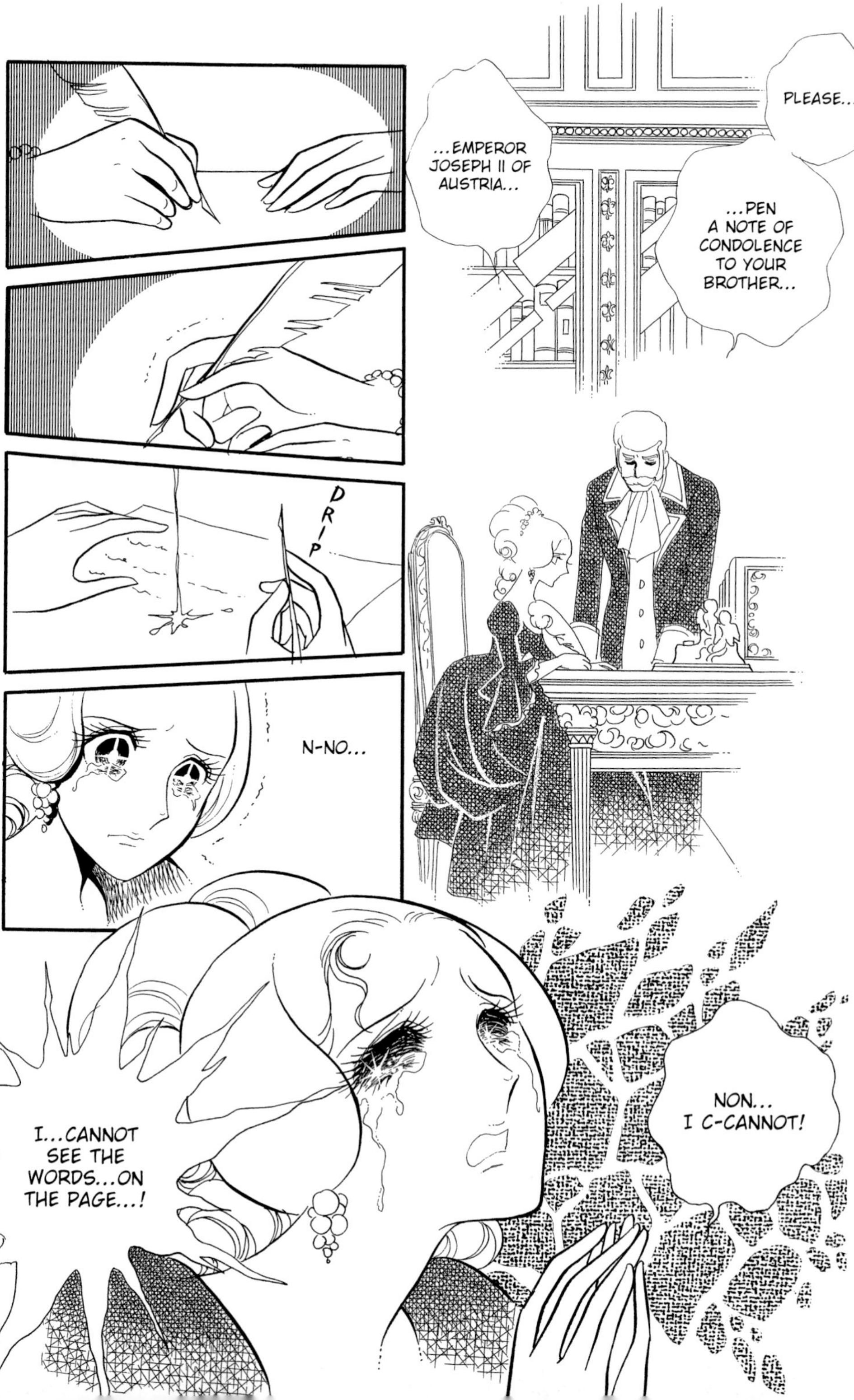
PLEASE...
...EMPEROR JOSEPH II OF AUSTRIA...
...PEN A NOTE OF CONDOLENCE TO YOUR BROTHER...
DRIP
N-NO...
NON... I C-CANNOT!
I...CANNOT SEE THE WORDS...ON THE PAGE...!

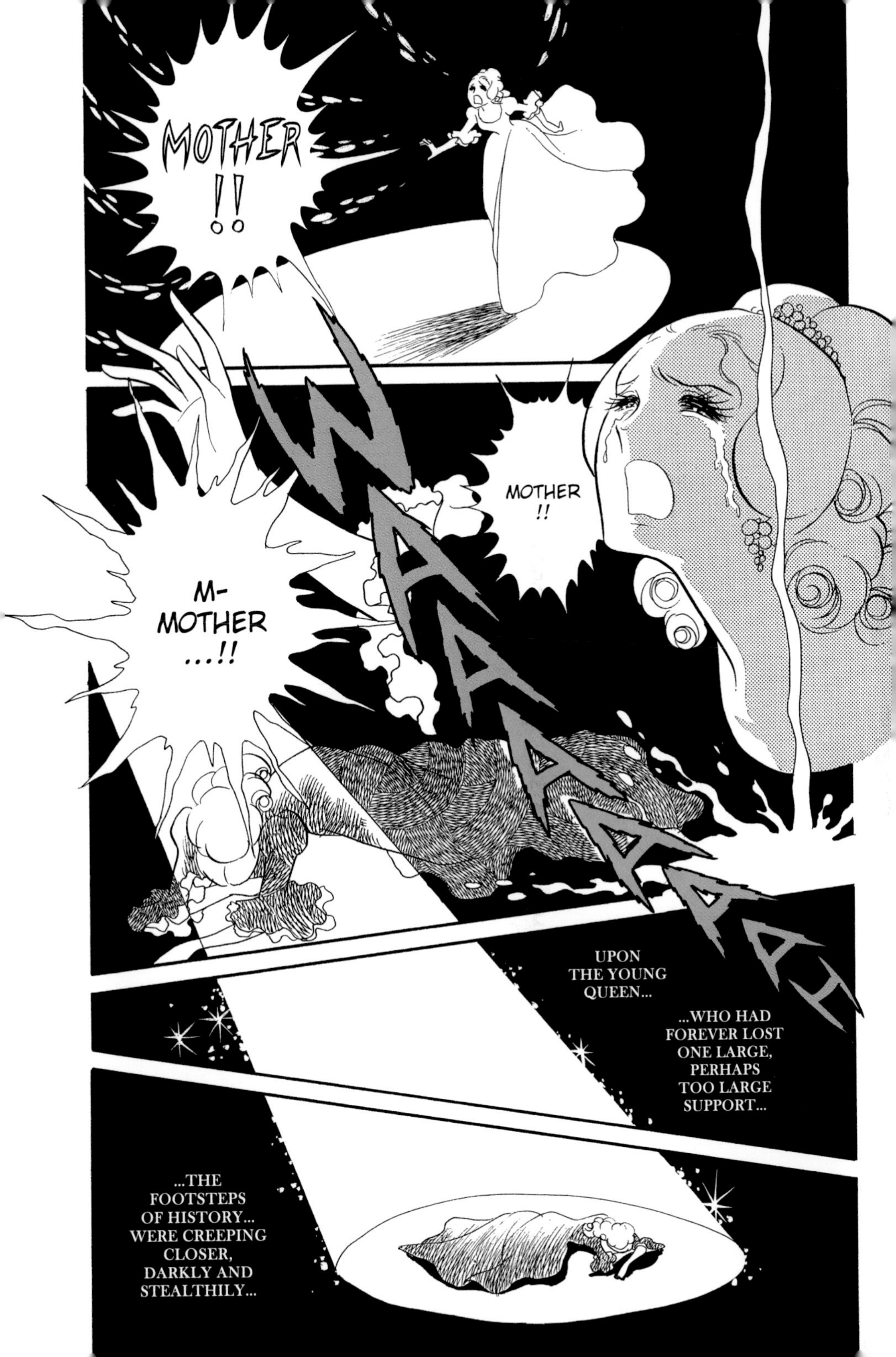
MOTHER !!
MOTHER !!
M-MOTHER ...!!
WAAAAAAH
UPON THE YOUNG QUEEN...
...WHO HAD FOREVER LOST ONE LARGE, PERHAPS TOO LARGE SUPPORT...
...THE FOOTSTEPS OF HISTORY... WERE CREEPING CLOSER, DARKLY AND STEALTHILY...

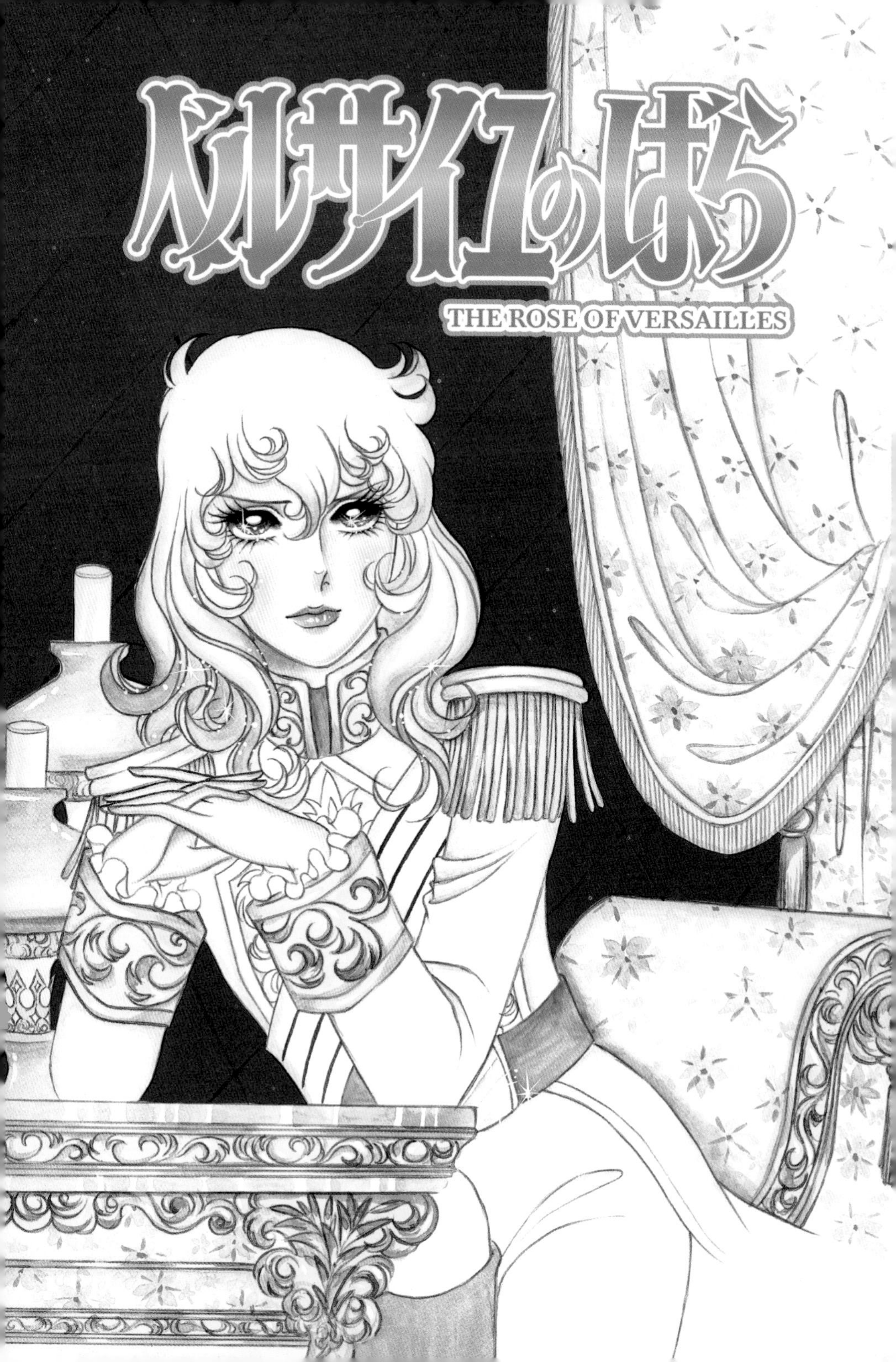
ベルサイユのばら
THE ROSE OF VERSAILLES

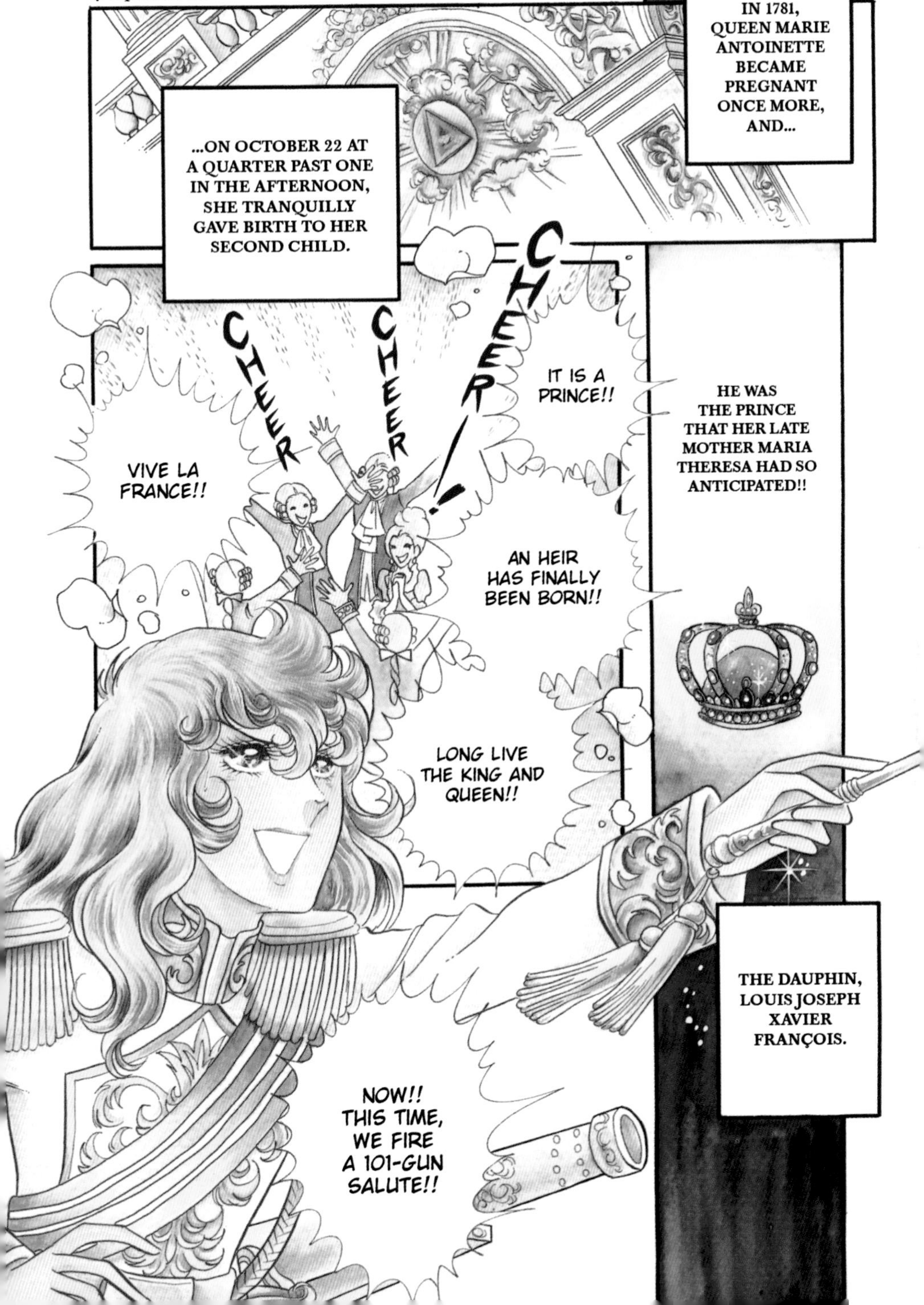
IN 1781, QUEEN MARIE ANTOINETTE BECAME PREGNANT ONCE MORE, AND...
...ON OCTOBER 22 AT A QUARTER PAST ONE IN THE AFTERNOON, SHE TRANQUILLY GAVE BIRTH TO HER SECOND CHILD.
HE WAS THE PRINCE THAT HER LATE MOTHER MARIA THERESA HAD SO ANTICIPATED!!
THE DAUPHIN, LOUIS JOSEPH XAVIER FRANÇOIS.
CHEER CHEER CHEER!!
IT IS A PRINCE!!
VIVE LA FRANCE!!
AN HEIR HAS FINALLY BEEN BORN!!
LONG LIVE THE KING AND QUEEN!!
NOW!! THIS TIME, WE FIRE A 101-GUN SALUTE!!

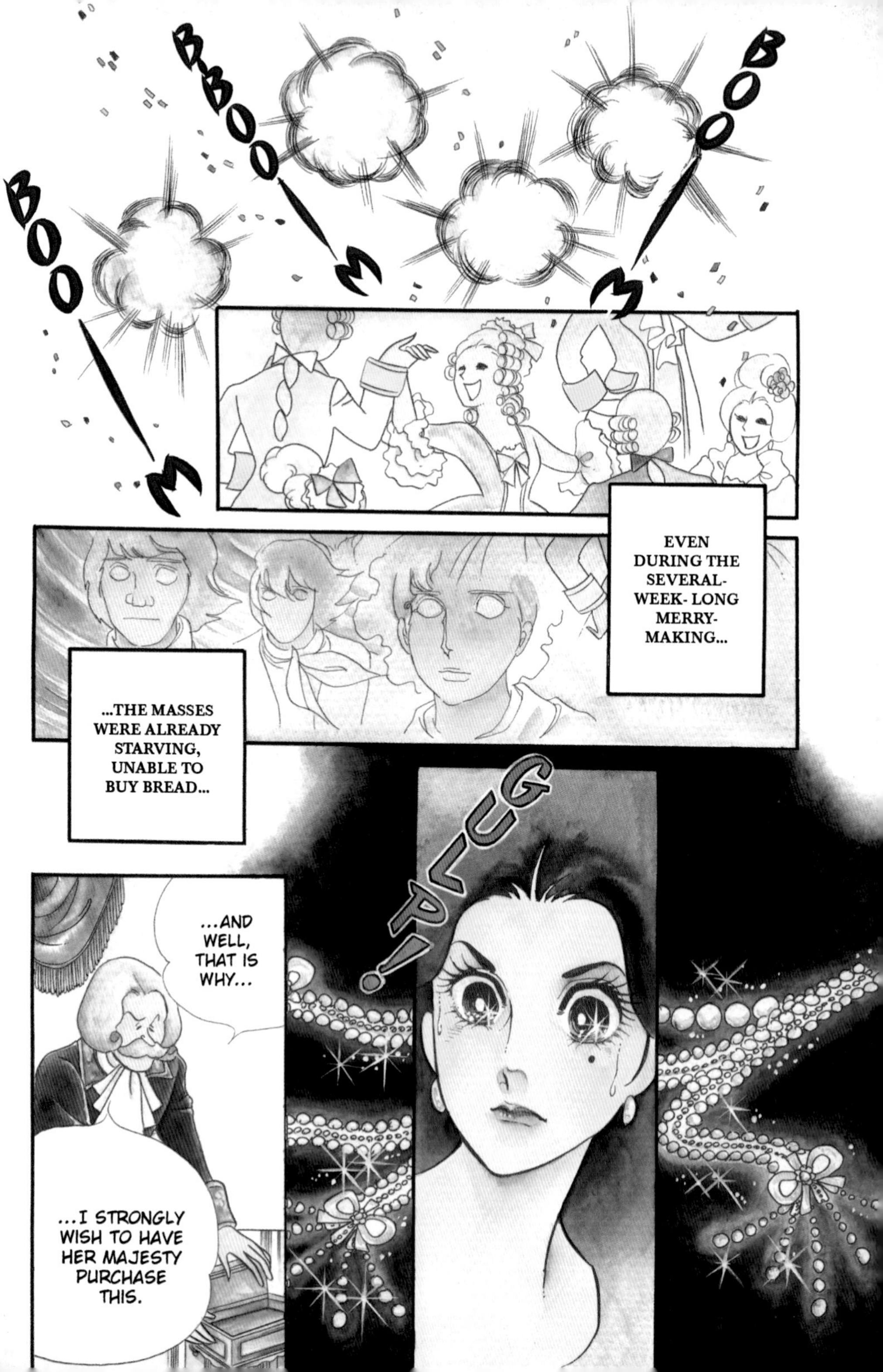
BOOM
BBOOM
BOOM
EVEN DURING THE SEVERAL-WEEK- LONG MERRY-MAKING...
...THE MASSES WERE ALREADY STARVING, UNABLE TO BUY BREAD...
GULP!
...AND WELL, THAT IS WHY...
...I STRONGLY WISH TO HAVE HER MAJESTY PURCHASE THIS.

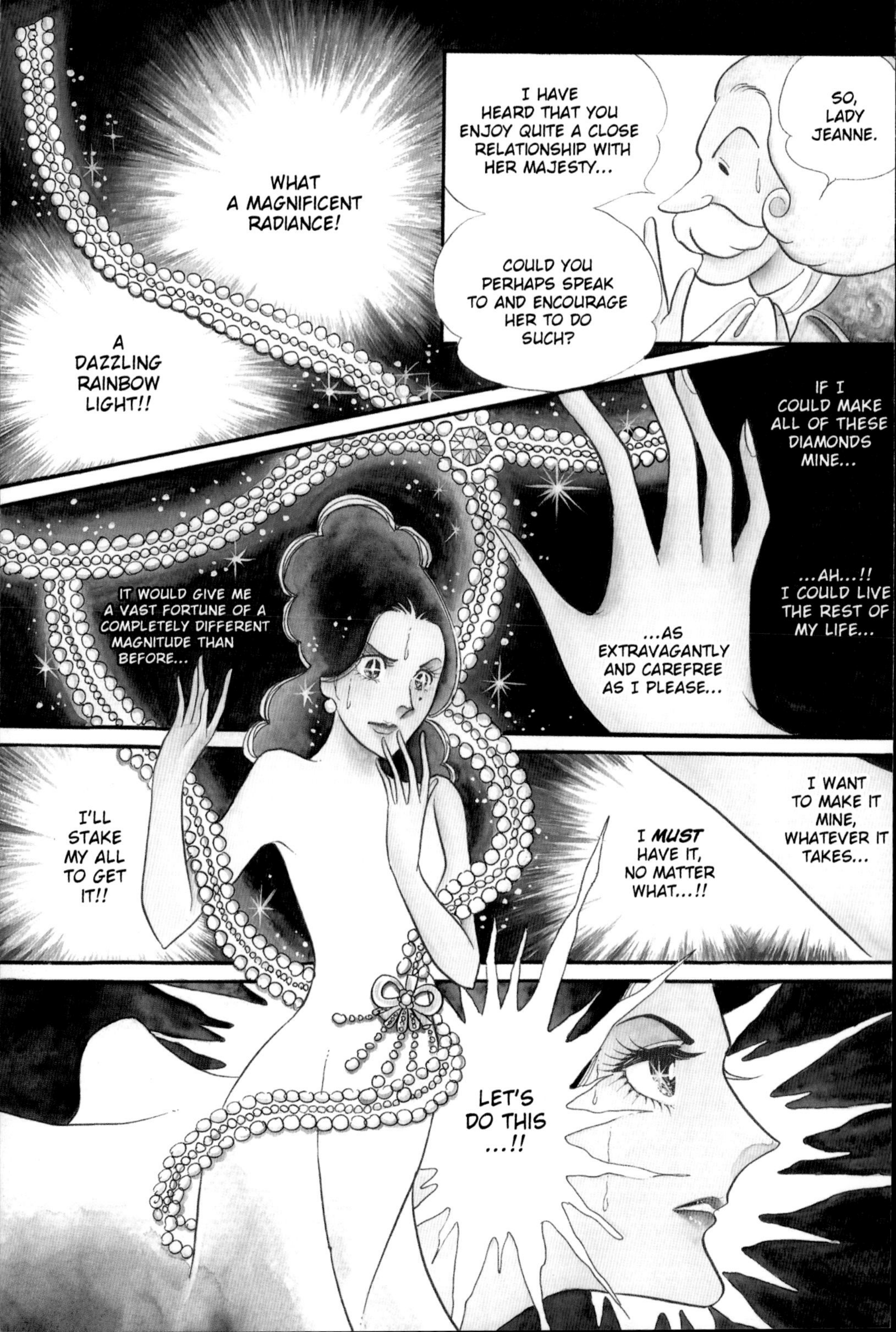
SO, LADY JEANNE.
I HAVE HEARD THAT YOU ENJOY QUITE A CLOSE RELATIONSHIP WITH HER MAJESTY...
COULD YOU PERHAPS SPEAK TO AND ENCOURAGE HER TO DO SUCH?
WHAT A MAGNIFICENT RADIANCE!
A DAZZLING RAINBOW LIGHT!!
IF I COULD MAKE ALL OF THESE DIAMONDS MINE...
IT WOULD GIVE ME A VAST FORTUNE OF A COMPLETELY DIFFERENT MAGNITUDE THAN BEFORE...
...AH...!! I COULD LIVE THE REST OF MY LIFE...
...AS EXTRAVAGANTLY AND CAREFREE AS I PLEASE...
I WANT TO MAKE IT MINE, WHATEVER IT TAKES...
I *MUST* HAVE IT, NO MATTER WHAT...!!
I'LL STAKE MY ALL TO GET IT!!
LET'S DO THIS ...!!

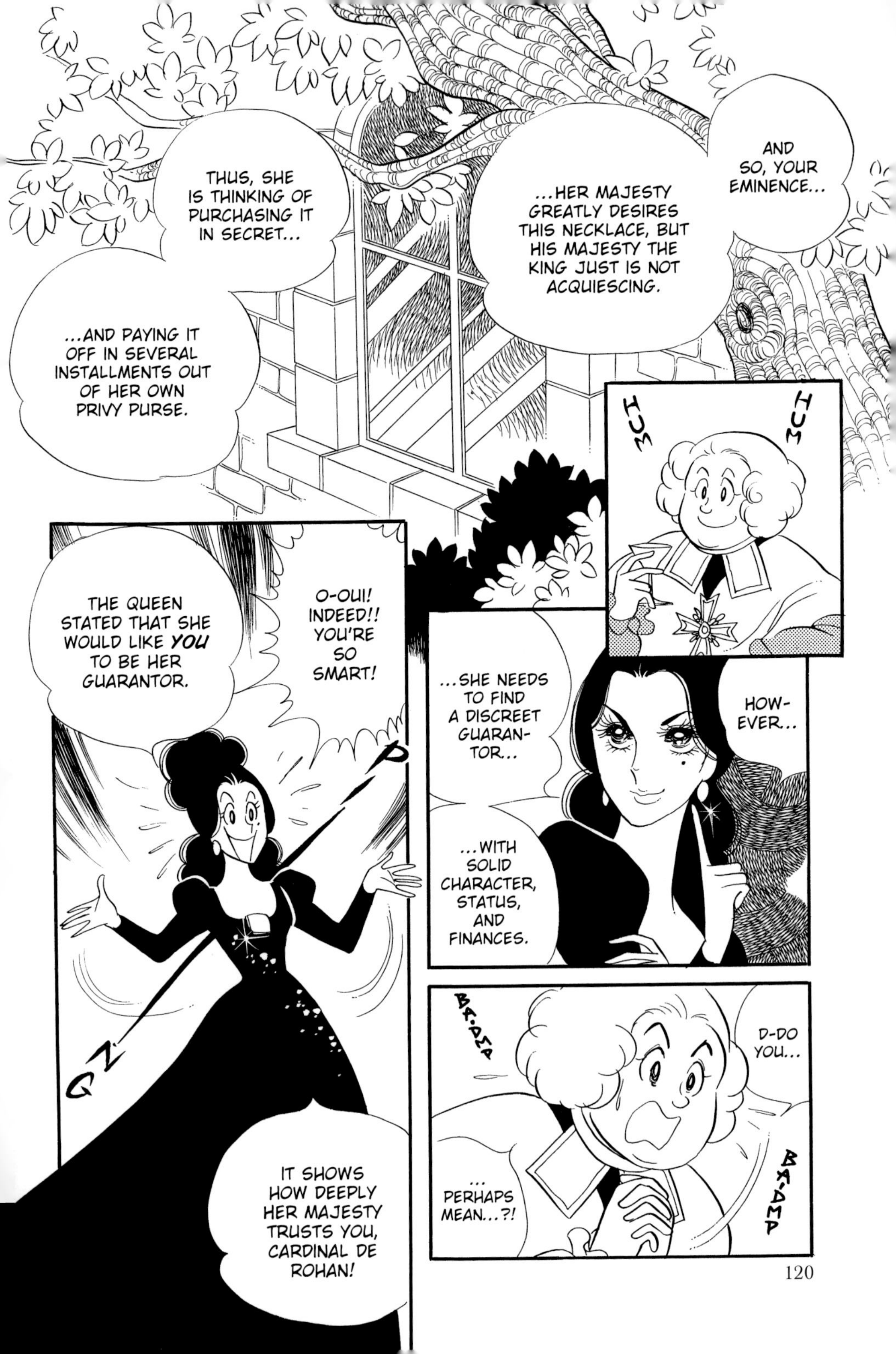
AND SO, YOUR EMINENCE...
...HER MAJESTY GREATLY DESIRES THIS NECKLACE, BUT HIS MAJESTY THE KING JUST IS NOT ACQUIESCING.
THUS, SHE IS THINKING OF PURCHASING IT IN SECRET...
...AND PAYING IT OFF IN SEVERAL INSTALLMENTS OUT OF HER OWN PRIVY PURSE.
HUM
HUM
HOW-EVER...
...SHE NEEDS TO FIND A DISCREET GUARAN-TOR...
...WITH SOLID CHARACTER, STATUS, AND FINANCES.
BA-DMP
D-DO YOU...
...PERHAPS MEAN...?!
BA-DAMP
O-OUI! INDEED!! YOU'RE SO SMART!
THE QUEEN STATED THAT SHE WOULD LIKE *YOU* TO BE HER GUARANTOR.
IT SHOWS HOW DEEPLY HER MAJESTY TRUSTS YOU, CARDINAL DE ROHAN!

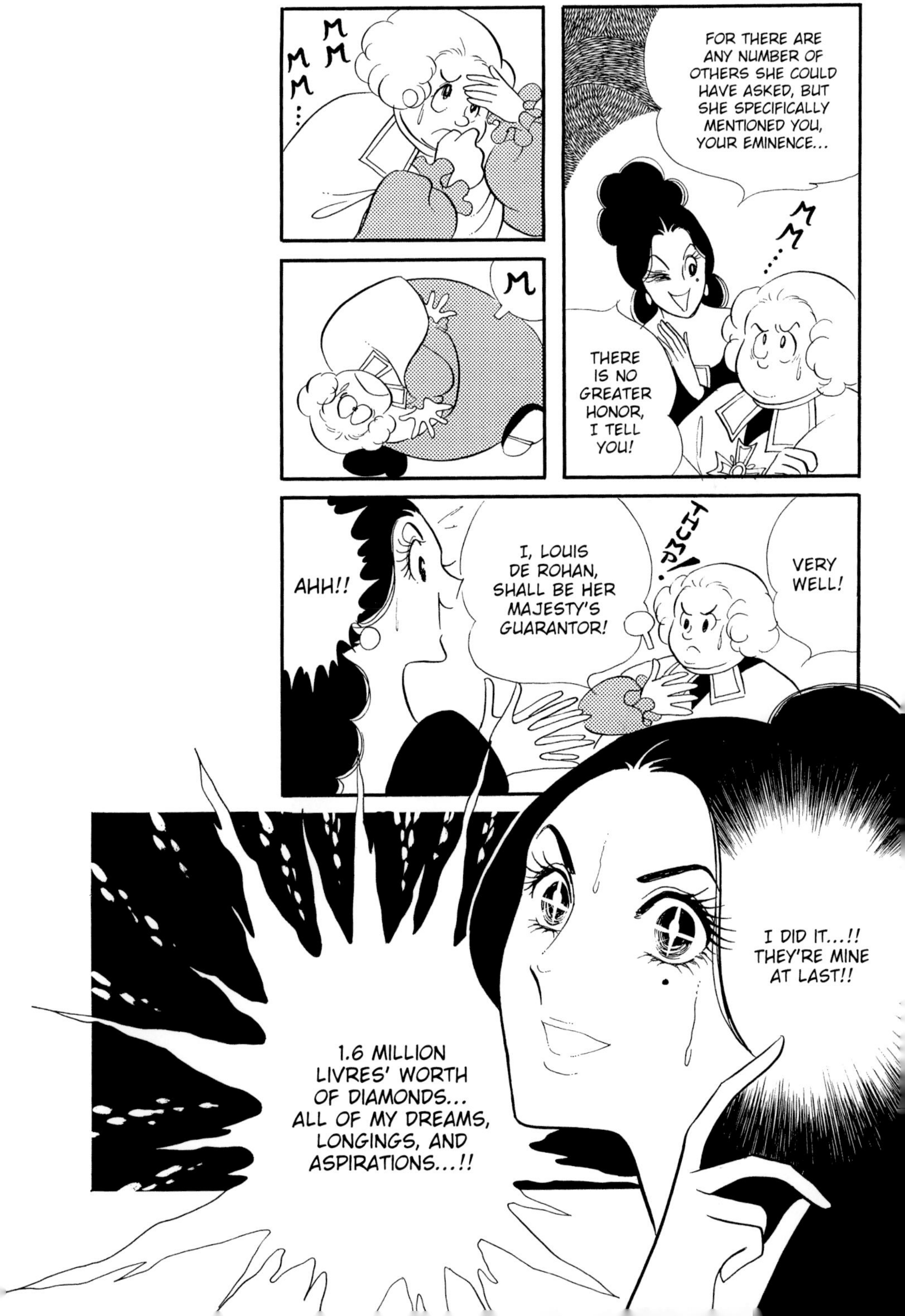
FOR THERE ARE ANY NUMBER OF OTHERS SHE COULD HAVE ASKED, BUT SHE SPECIFICALLY MENTIONED YOU, YOUR EMINENCE...
MM...
THERE IS NO GREATER HONOR, I TELL YOU!
MMMM...
M
VERY WELL!
THUMP!
I, LOUIS DE ROHAN, SHALL BE HER MAJESTY'S GUARANTOR!
AHH!!
I DID IT...!! THEY'RE MINE AT LAST!!
1.6 MILLION LIVRES' WORTH OF DIAMONDS... ALL OF MY DREAMS, LONGINGS, AND ASPIRATIONS...!!

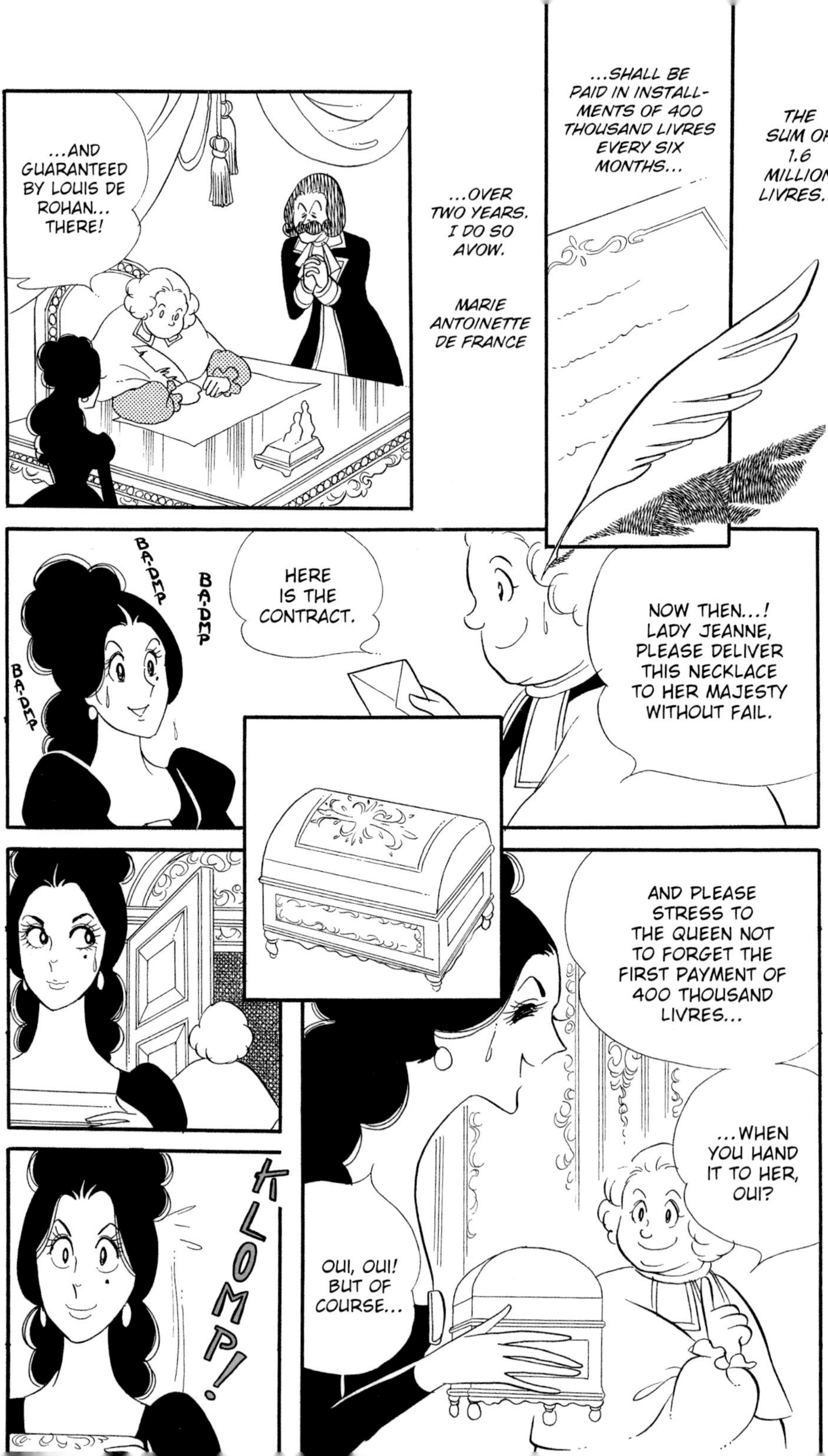

THE SUM OF 1.6 MILLION LIVRES...
...SHALL BE PAID IN INSTALLMENTS OF 400 THOUSAND LIVRES EVERY SIX MONTHS...
...OVER TWO YEARS. I DO SO AVOW.
MARIE ANTOINETTE DE FRANCE
...AND GUARANTEED BY LOUIS DE ROHAN... THERE!
NOW THEN...! LADY JEANNE, PLEASE DELIVER THIS NECKLACE TO HER MAJESTY WITHOUT FAIL.
HERE IS THE CONTRACT.
BA-DMP
BA-DMP
BA-DMP
AND PLEASE STRESS TO THE QUEEN NOT TO FORGET THE FIRST PAYMENT OF 400 THOUSAND LIVRES...
...WHEN YOU HAND IT TO HER, OUI?
OUI, OUI! BUT OF COURSE...
KLOMP!

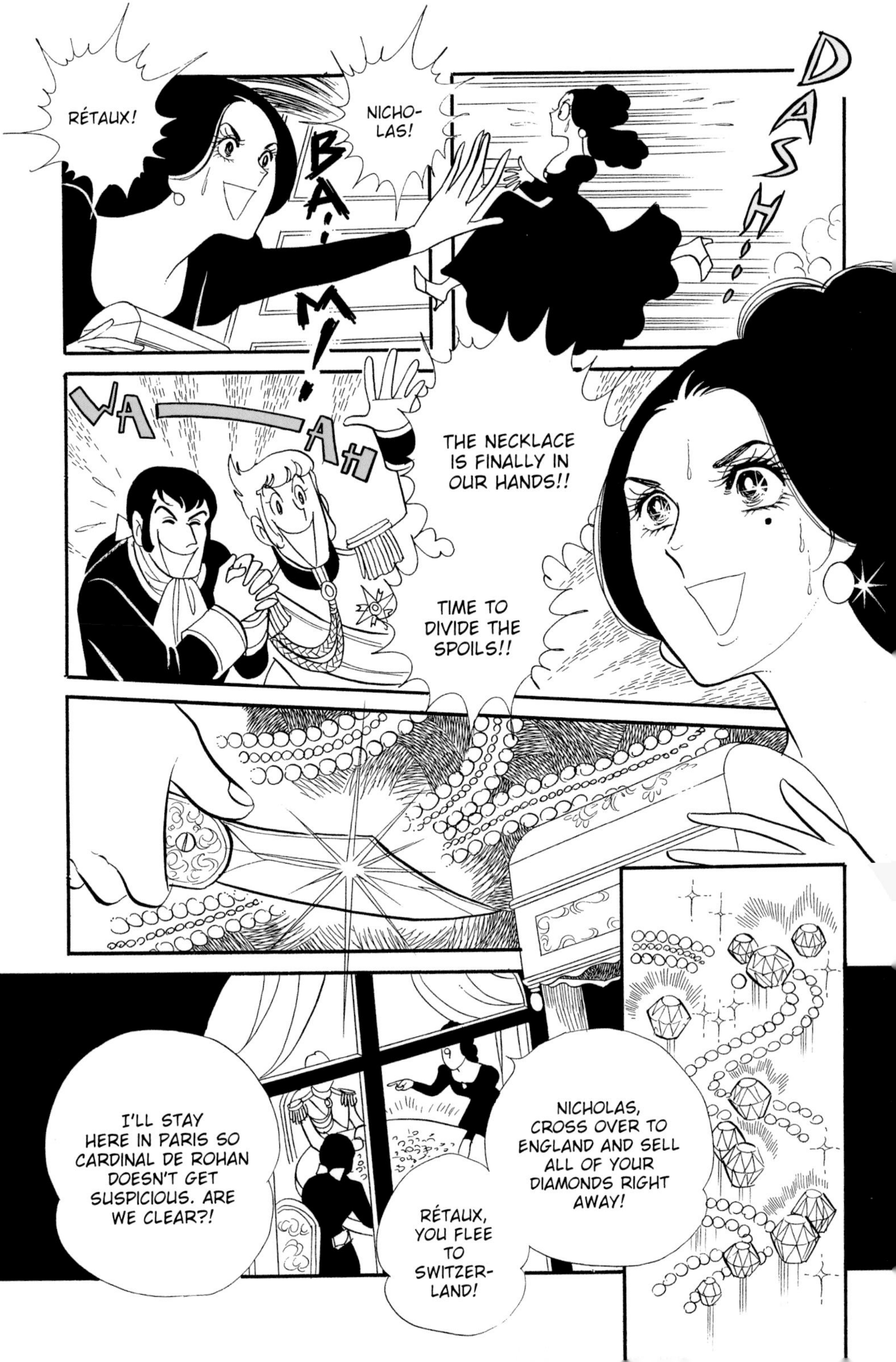
DASH!!!
NICHO-LAS!
RÉTAUX!
BAM!!
THE NECKLACE IS FINALLY IN OUR HANDS!!
TIME TO DIVIDE THE SPOILS!!
WA—AH
NICHOLAS, CROSS OVER TO ENGLAND AND SELL ALL OF YOUR DIAMONDS RIGHT AWAY!
RÉTAUX, YOU FLEE TO SWITZER-LAND!
I'LL STAY HERE IN PARIS SO CARDINAL DE ROHAN DOESN'T GET SUSPICIOUS. ARE WE CLEAR?!

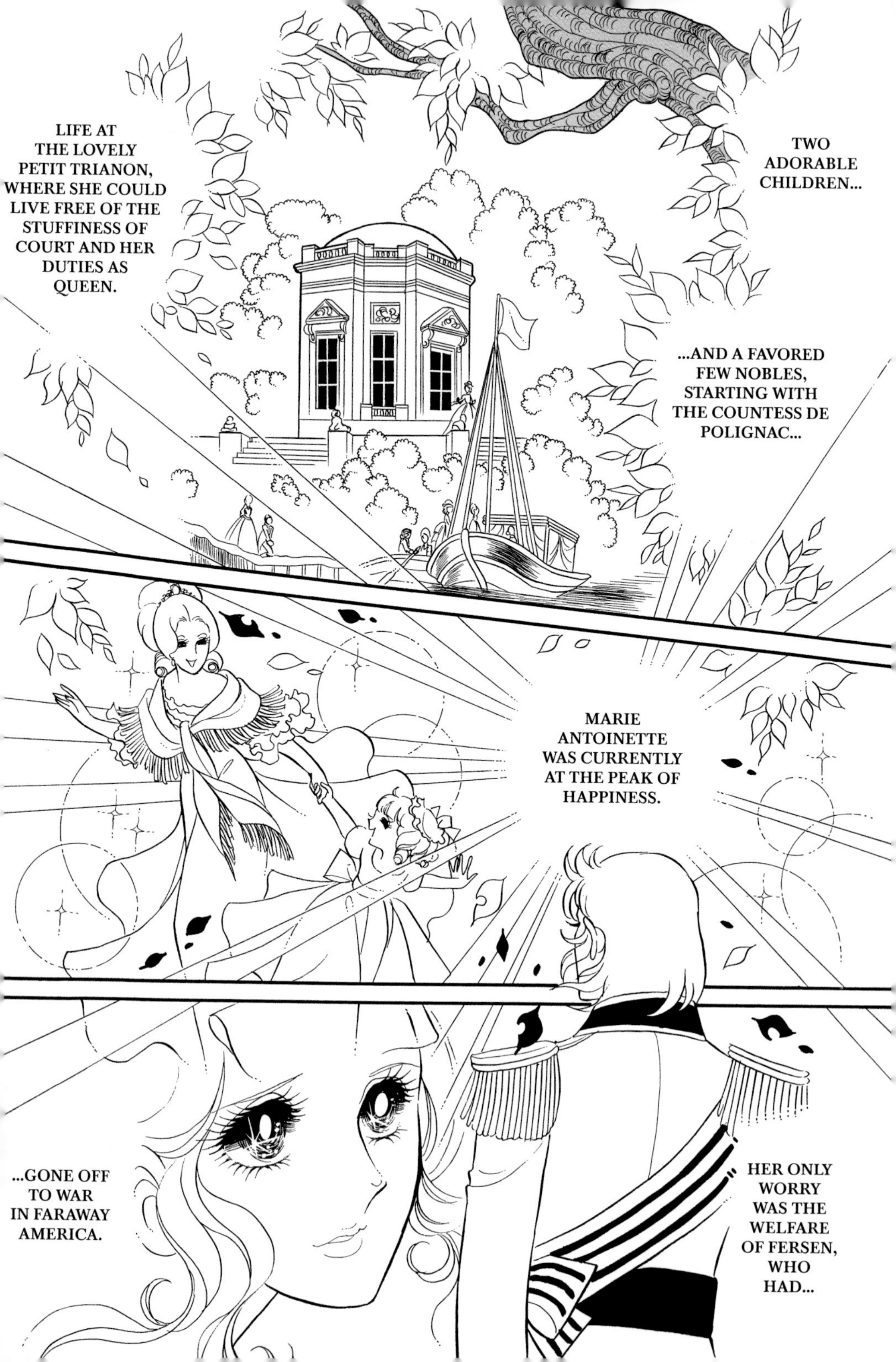
TWO ADORABLE CHILDREN...
...AND A FAVORED FEW NOBLES, STARTING WITH THE COUNTESS DE POLIGNAC...
LIFE AT THE LOVELY PETIT TRIANON, WHERE SHE COULD LIVE FREE OF THE STUFFINESS OF COURT AND HER DUTIES AS QUEEN.
MARIE ANTOINETTE WAS CURRENTLY AT THE PEAK OF HAPPINESS.
HER ONLY WORRY WAS THE WELFARE OF FERSEN, WHO HAD...
...GONE OFF TO WAR IN FARAWAY AMERICA.

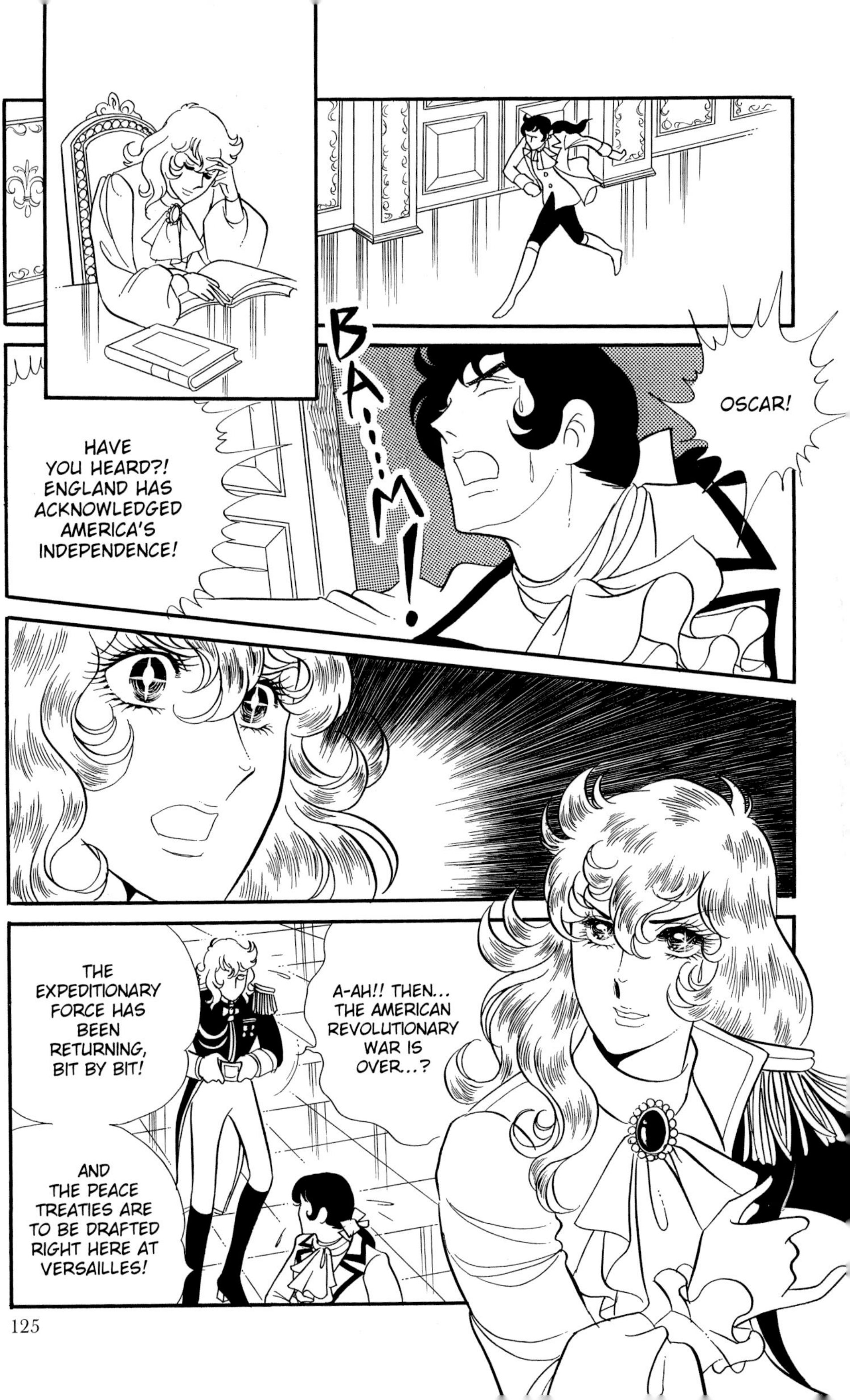
OSCAR!
BAM!
HAVE YOU HEARD?! ENGLAND HAS ACKNOWLEDGED AMERICA'S INDEPENDENCE!
A-AH!! THEN... THE AMERICAN REVOLUTIONARY WAR IS OVER...?
THE EXPEDITIONARY FORCE HAS BEEN RETURNING, BIT BY BIT!
AND THE PEACE TREATIES ARE TO BE DRAFTED RIGHT HERE AT VERSAILLES!

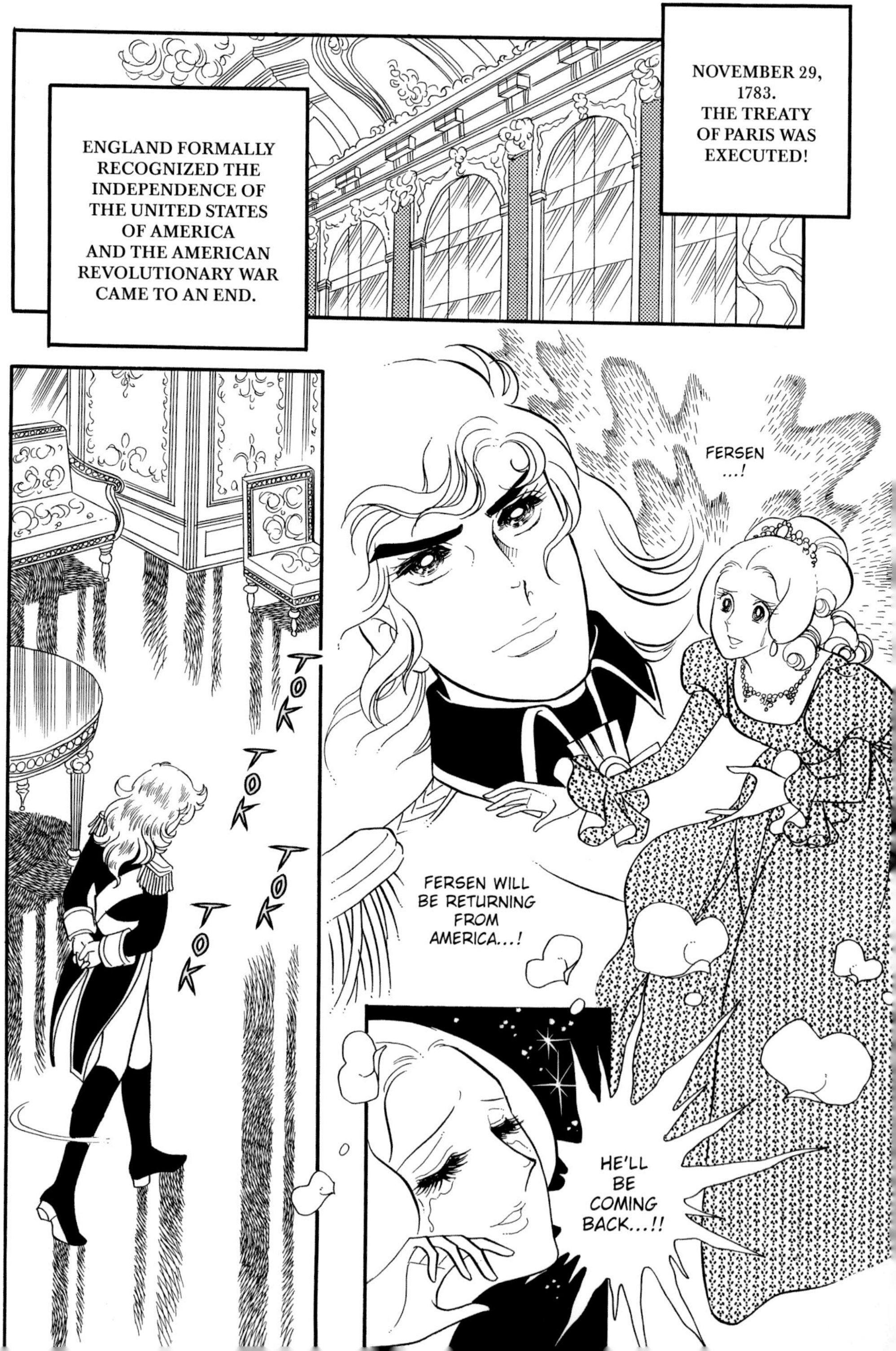

NOVEMBER 29, 1783. THE TREATY OF PARIS WAS EXECUTED!
ENGLAND FORMALLY RECOGNIZED THE INDEPENDENCE OF THE UNITED STATES OF AMERICA AND THE AMERICAN REVOLUTIONARY WAR CAME TO AN END.
FERSEN ...!
FERSEN WILL BE RETURNING FROM AMERICA...!
HE'LL BE COMING BACK...!!
TOK
TOK
TOK
TOK

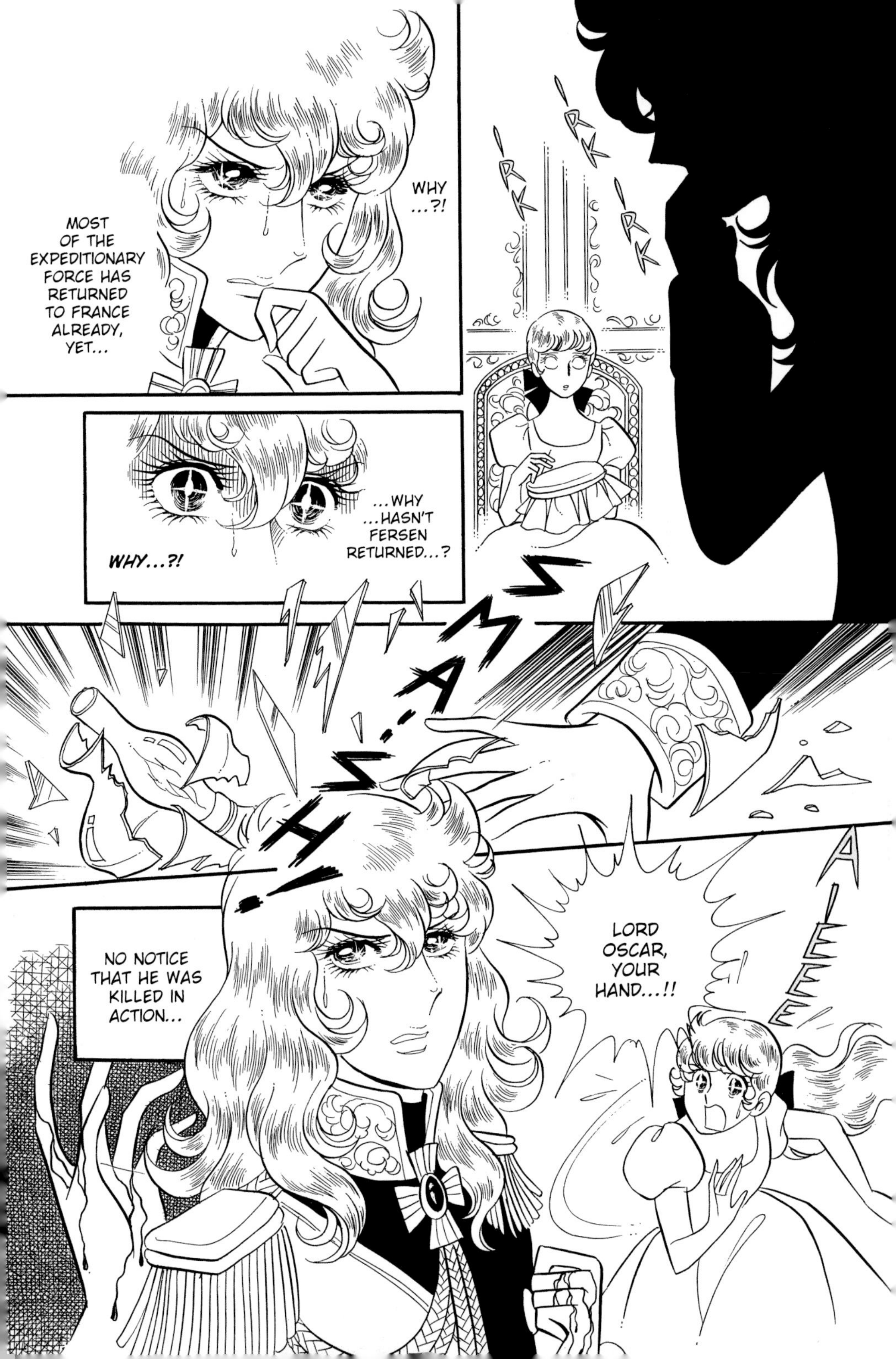

IRK
IRK
IRK
WHY ...?!
MOST OF THE EXPEDITIONARY FORCE HAS RETURNED TO FRANCE ALREADY, YET...
...WHY ...HASN'T FERSEN RETURNED...?
WHY...?!
SMASH!
AIEEEE
LORD OSCAR, YOUR HAND...!!
NO NOTICE THAT HE WAS KILLED IN ACTION...

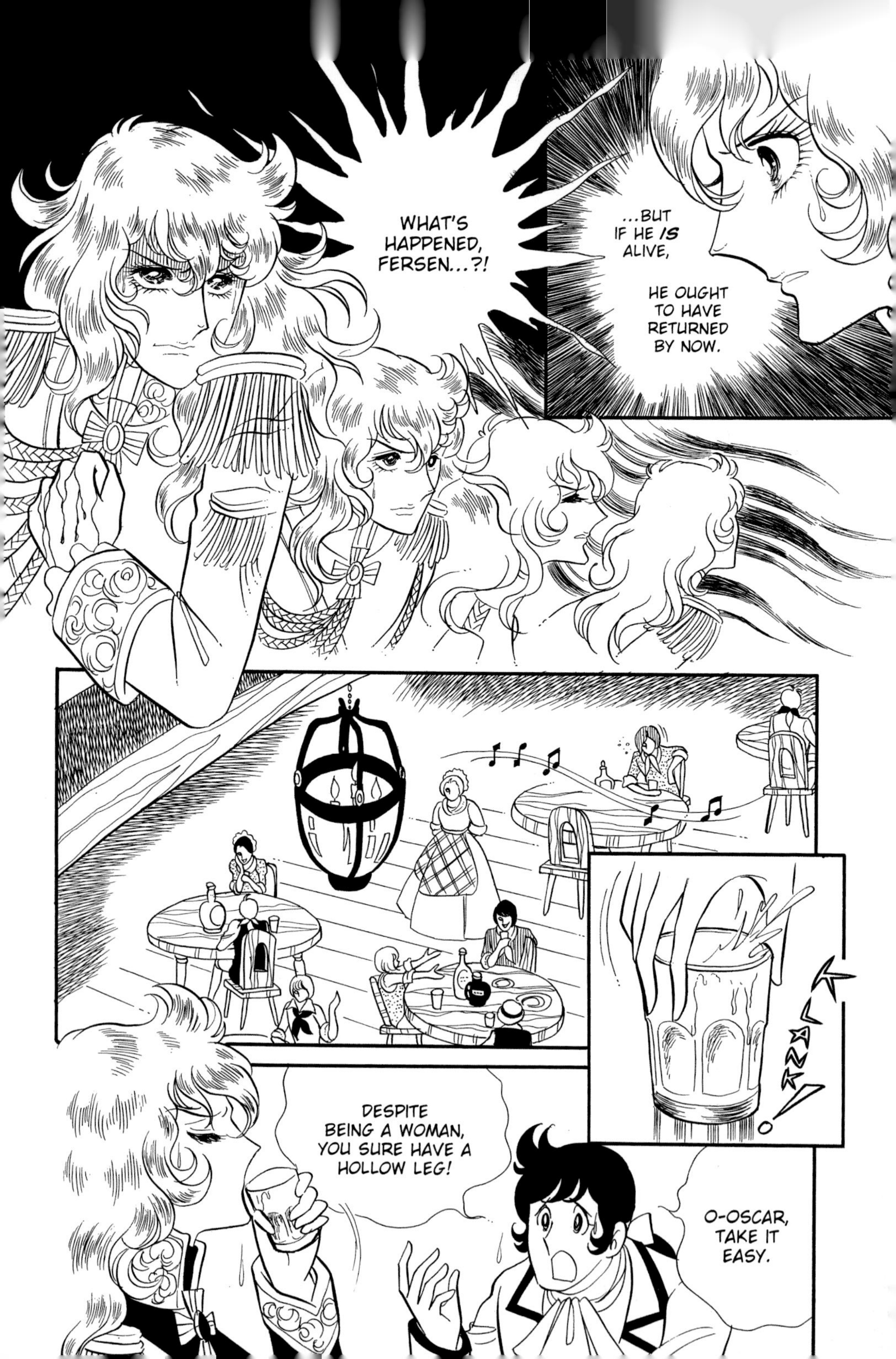
...BUT IF HE IS ALIVE,
HE OUGHT TO HAVE RETURNED BY NOW.
WHAT'S HAPPENED, FERSEN...?!
KLANK!
DESPITE BEING A WOMAN, YOU SURE HAVE A HOLLOW LEG!
O-OSCAR, TAKE IT EASY.

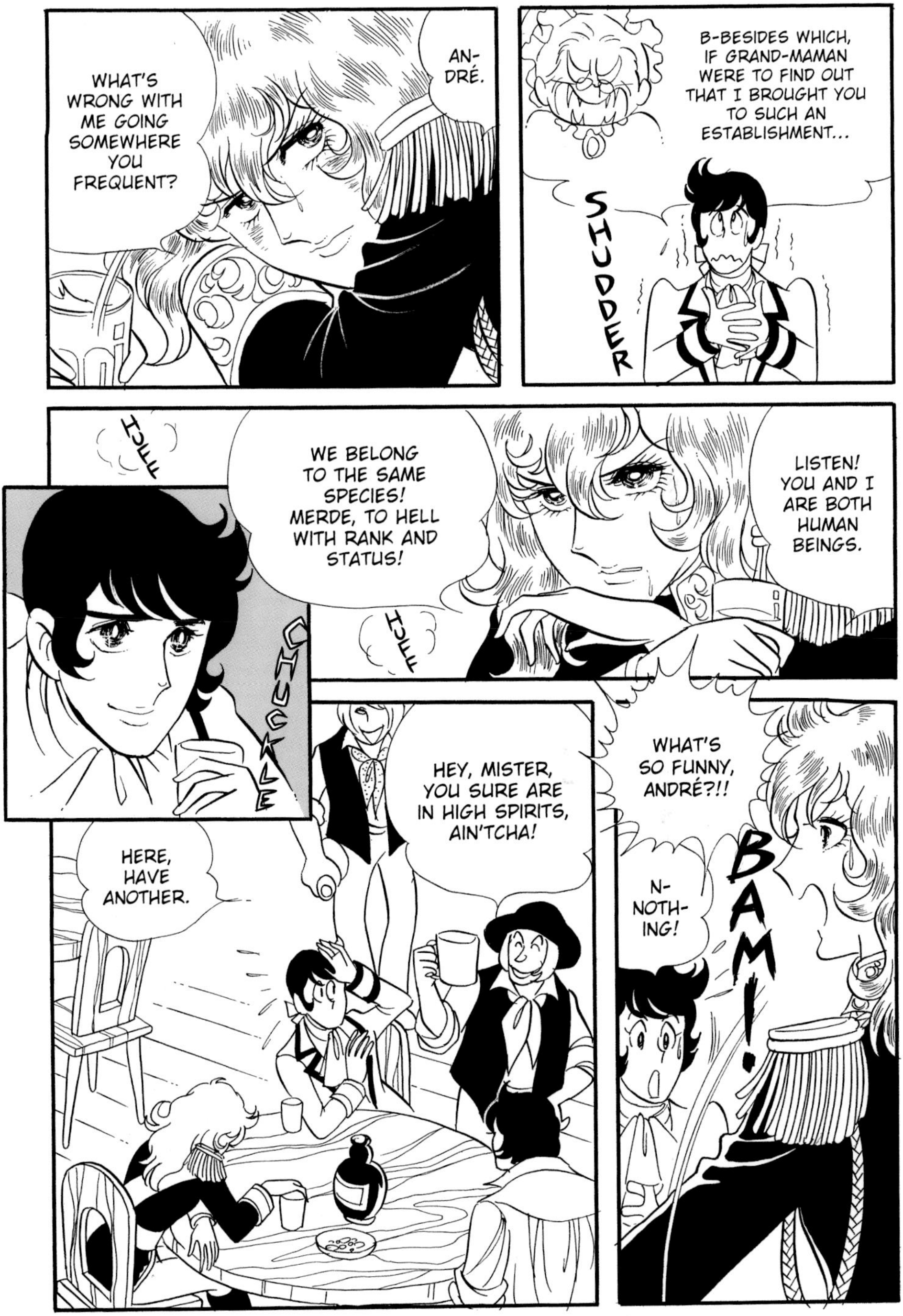
B-BESIDES WHICH, IF GRAND-MAMAN WERE TO FIND OUT THAT I BROUGHT YOU TO SUCH AN ESTABLISHMENT...
SHUDDER
AN-DRÉ.
WHAT'S WRONG WITH ME GOING SOMEWHERE YOU FREQUENT?
LISTEN! YOU AND I ARE BOTH HUMAN BEINGS.
HUFF
WE BELONG TO THE SAME SPECIES! MERDE, TO HELL WITH RANK AND STATUS!
HUFF
CHUCKLE
WHAT'S SO FUNNY, ANDRÉ?!!
BAM!
N-NOTHING!
HEY, MISTER, YOU SURE ARE IN HIGH SPIRITS, AIN'TCHA!
HERE, HAVE ANOTHER.

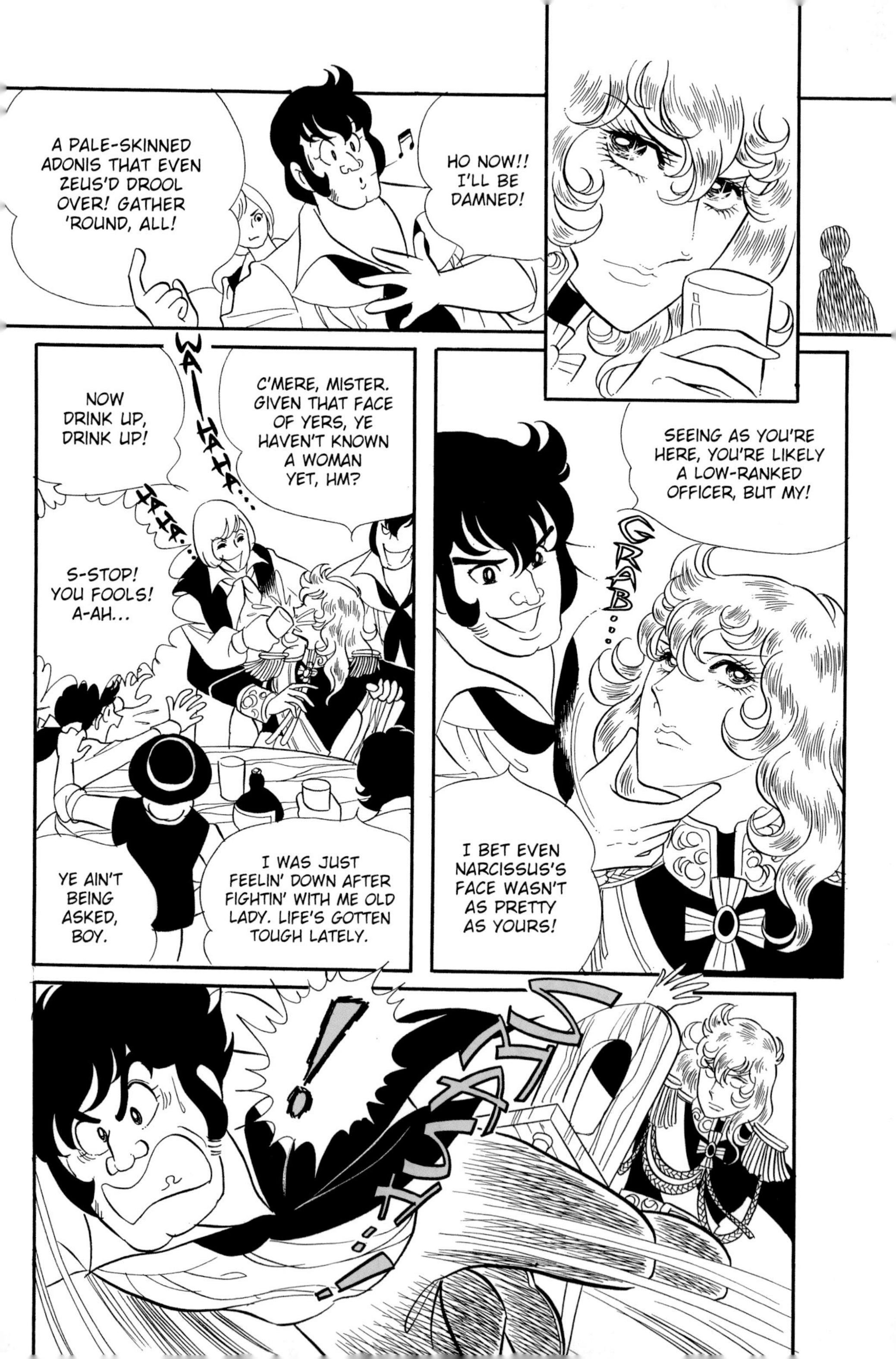
HO NOW!! I'LL BE DAMNED!
A PALE-SKINNED ADONIS THAT EVEN ZEUS'D DROOL OVER! GATHER 'ROUND, ALL!
SEEING AS YOU'RE HERE, YOU'RE LIKELY A LOW-RANKED OFFICER, BUT MY!
GRAB...
I BET EVEN NARCISSUS'S FACE WASN'T AS PRETTY AS YOURS!
C'MERE, MISTER. GIVEN THAT FACE OF YERS, YE HAVEN'T KNOWN A WOMAN YET, HM?
WAHAHAHA...
NOW DRINK UP, DRINK UP!
HAHA...
S-STOP! YOU FOOLS! A-AH...
I WAS JUST FEELIN' DOWN AFTER FIGHTIN' WITH ME OLD LADY. LIFE'S GOTTEN TOUGH LATELY.
YE AIN'T BEING ASKED, BOY.
!

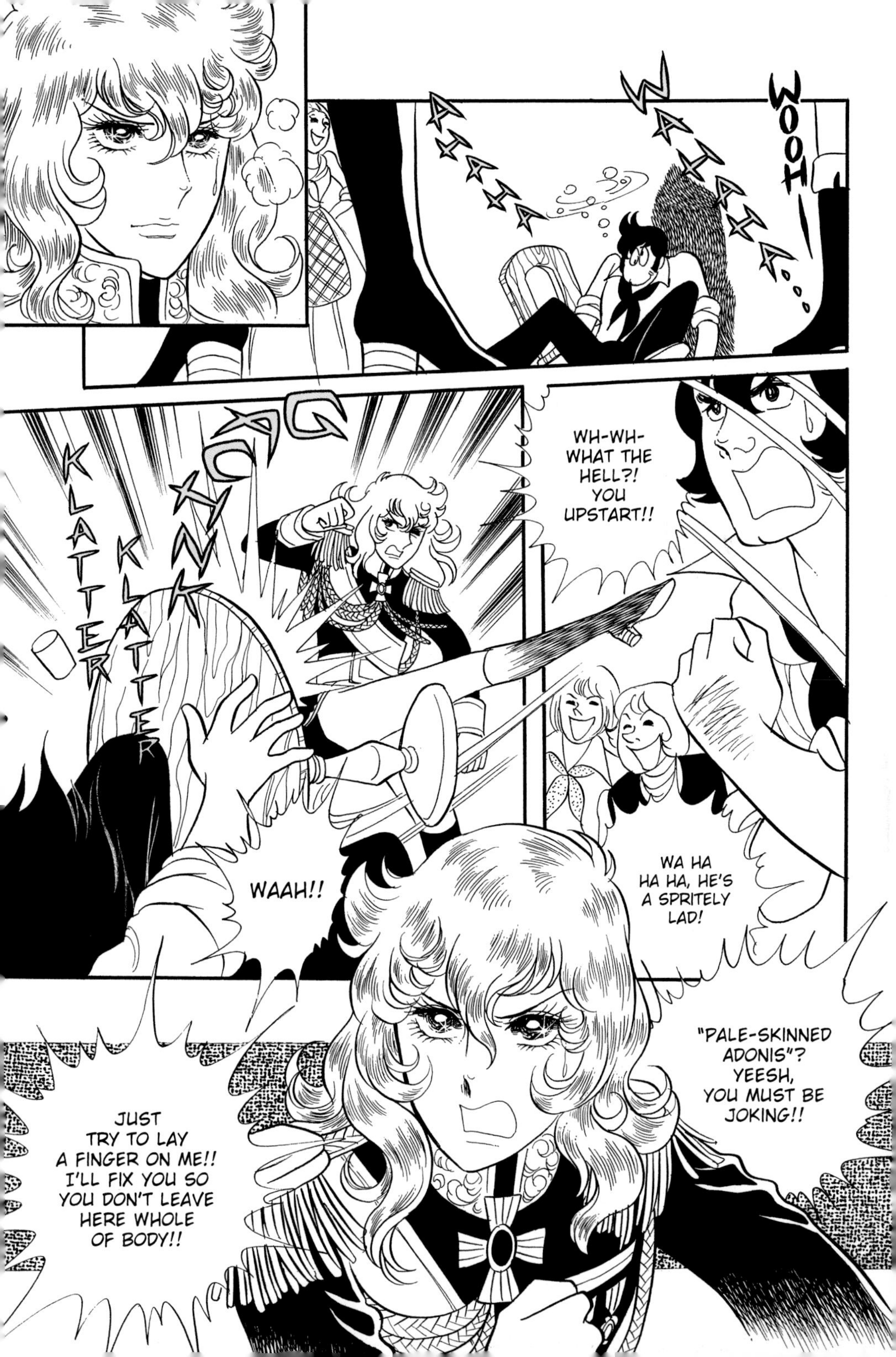
WOOOH!
WAHAHAHA...
AHAHAHA
WH-WH-WHAT THE HELL?! YOU UPSTART!!
WA HA HA HA, HE'S A SPRITELY LAD!
GAK
CLANK
KLATTER
KLATTER
WAAH!!
"PALE-SKINNED ADONIS"? YEESH, YOU MUST BE JOKING!!
JUST TRY TO LAY A FINGER ON ME!! I'LL FIX YOU SO YOU DON'T LEAVE HERE WHOLE OF BODY!!

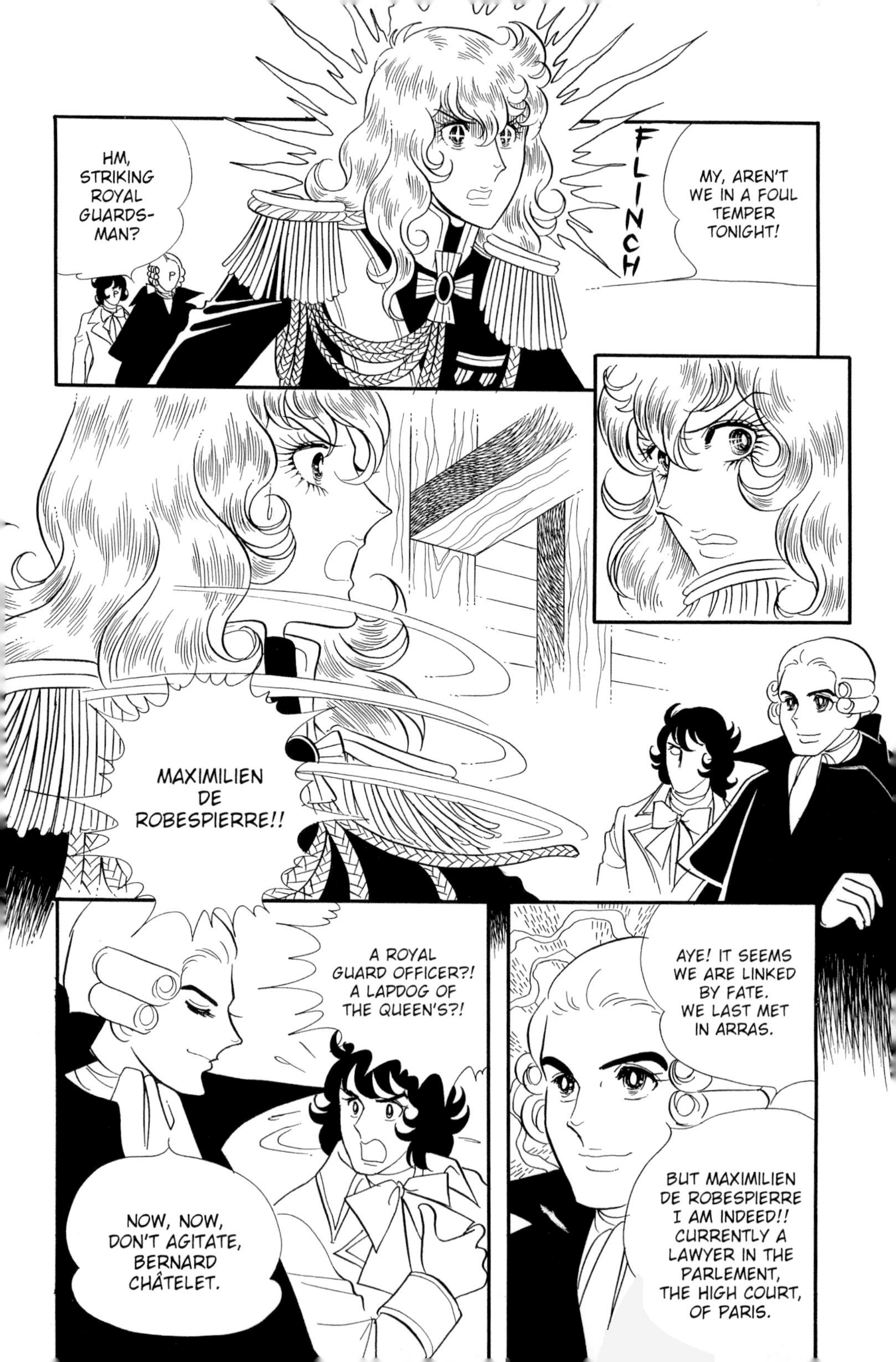
MY, AREN'T WE IN A FOUL TEMPER TONIGHT!
FLINCH
HM, STRIKING ROYAL GUARDSMAN?
MAXIMILIEN DE ROBESPIERRE!!
AYE! IT SEEMS WE ARE LINKED BY FATE. WE LAST MET IN ARRAS.
BUT MAXIMILIEN DE ROBESPIERRE I AM INDEED!! CURRENTLY A LAWYER IN THE PARLEMENT, THE HIGH COURT, OF PARIS.
A ROYAL GUARD OFFICER?! A LAPDOG OF THE QUEEN'S?!
NOW, NOW, DON'T AGITATE, BERNARD CHÂTELET.

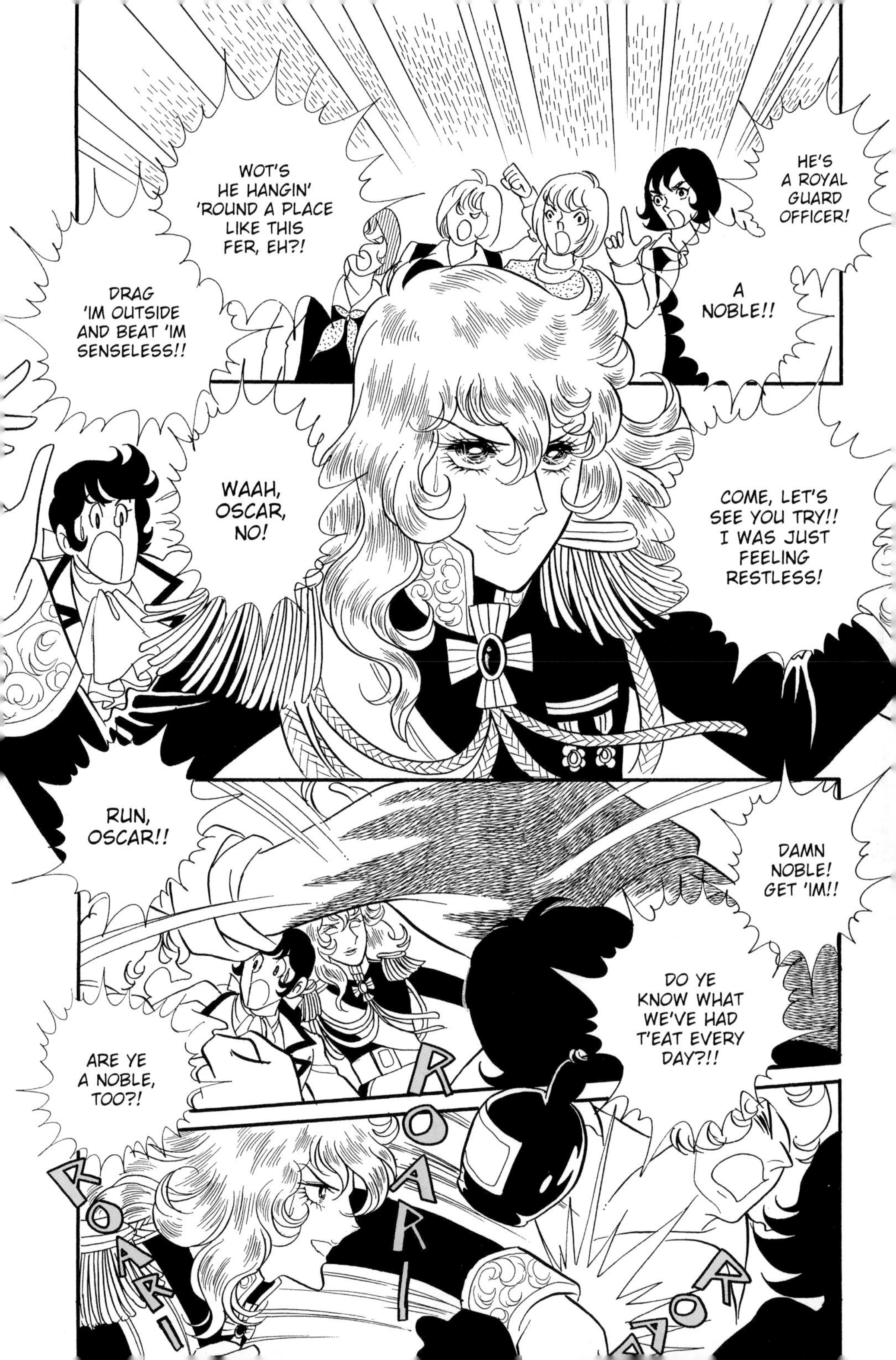

HE'S A ROYAL GUARD OFFICER!
A NOBLE!!
WOT'S HE HANGIN' 'ROUND A PLACE LIKE THIS FER, EH?!
DRAG 'IM OUTSIDE AND BEAT 'IM SENSELESS!!
COME, LET'S SEE YOU TRY!! I WAS JUST FEELING RESTLESS!
WAAH, OSCAR, NO!
DAMN NOBLE! GET 'IM!!
RUN, OSCAR!!
DO YE KNOW WHAT WE'VE HAD T'EAT EVERY DAY?!!
ARE YE A NOBLE, TOO?!
ROAR
ROAR
ROAR

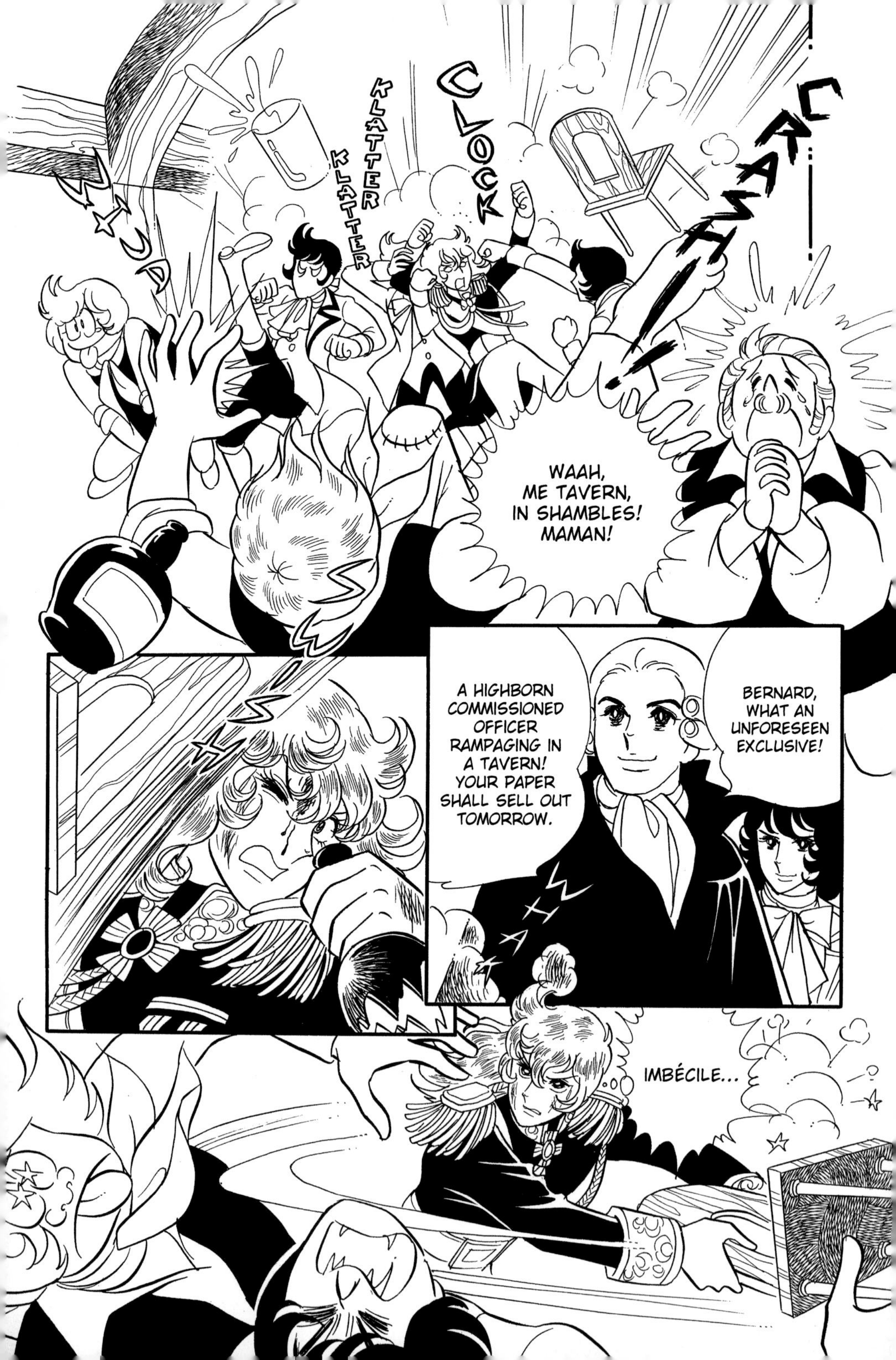
CRASH!
CLOCK
KLATTER
KLATTER
WAAH, ME TAVERN, IN SHAMBLES! MAMAN!
BERNARD, WHAT AN UNFORESEEN EXCLUSIVE!
A HIGHBORN COMMISSIONED OFFICER RAMPAGING IN A TAVERN! YOUR PAPER SHALL SELL OUT TOMORROW.
IMBÉCILE...

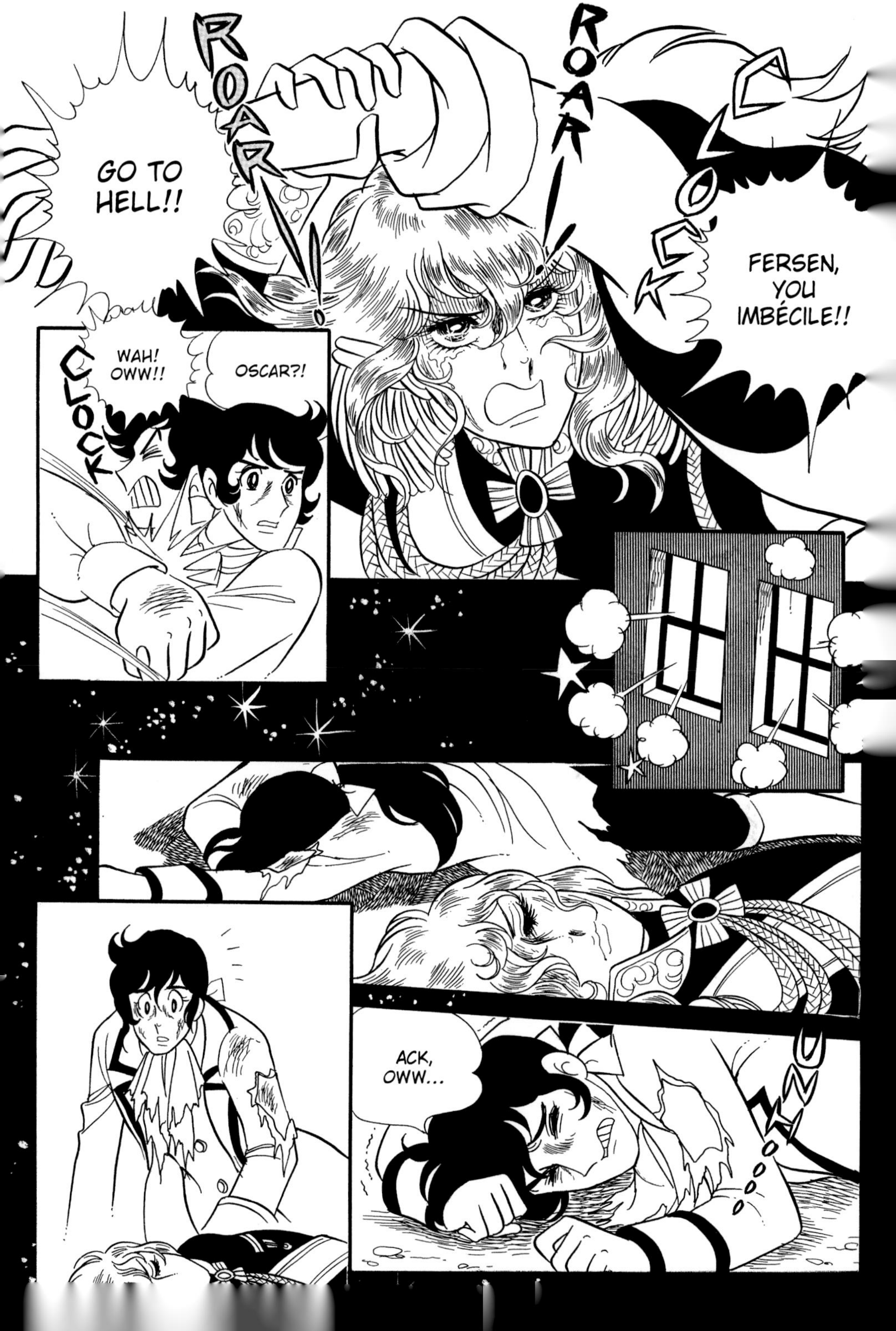
ROAR!!
CLOCK
FERSEN, YOU IMBÉCILE!!
ROAR!!
GO TO HELL!!
OSCAR?!
WAH! OWW!!
CLOCK
ACK, OWW...

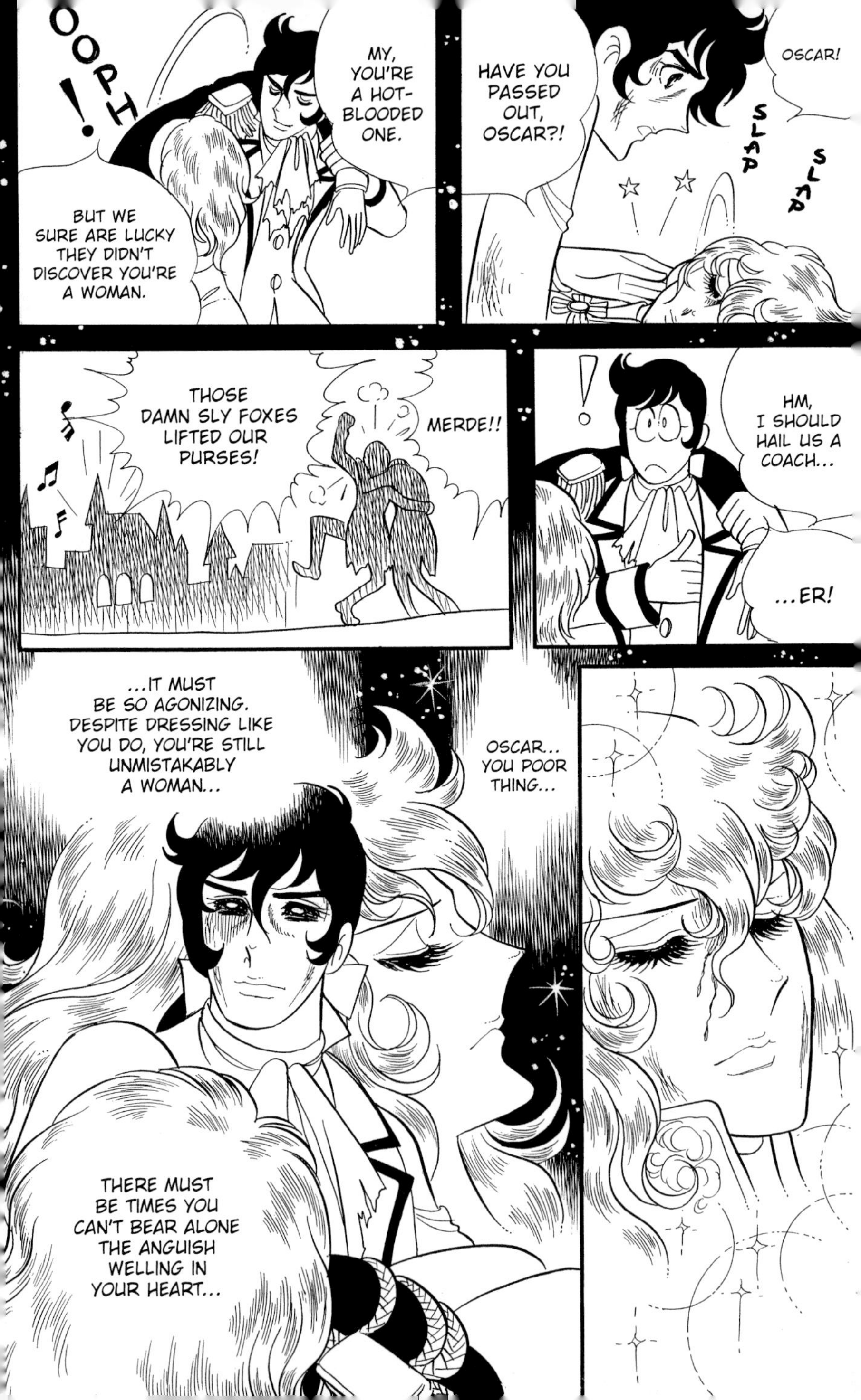
OSCAR!
SLAP
SLAP
HAVE YOU PASSED OUT, OSCAR?!
MY, YOU'RE A HOT-BLOODED ONE.
OOPH!
BUT WE SURE ARE LUCKY THEY DIDN'T DISCOVER YOU'RE A WOMAN.
HM, I SHOULD HAIL US A COACH...
...ER!
MERDE!!
THOSE DAMN SLY FOXES LIFTED OUR PURSES!
OSCAR... YOU POOR THING...
...IT MUST BE SO AGONIZING. DESPITE DRESSING LIKE YOU DO, YOU'RE STILL UNMISTAKABLY A WOMAN...
THERE MUST BE TIMES YOU CAN'T BEAR ALONE THE ANGUISH WELLING IN YOUR HEART...

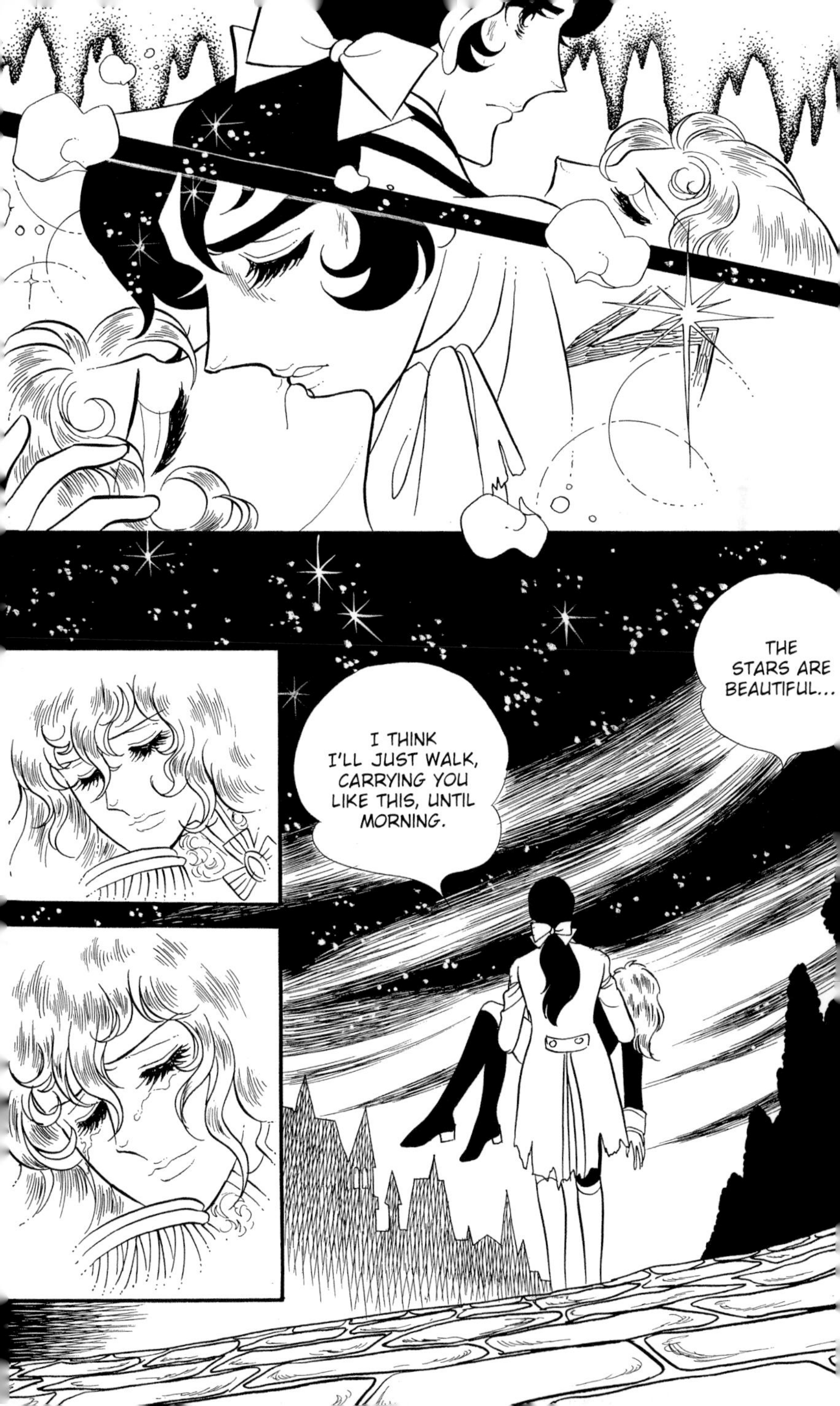
THE STARS ARE BEAUTIFUL...
I THINK I'LL JUST WALK, CARRYING YOU LIKE THIS, UNTIL MORNING.

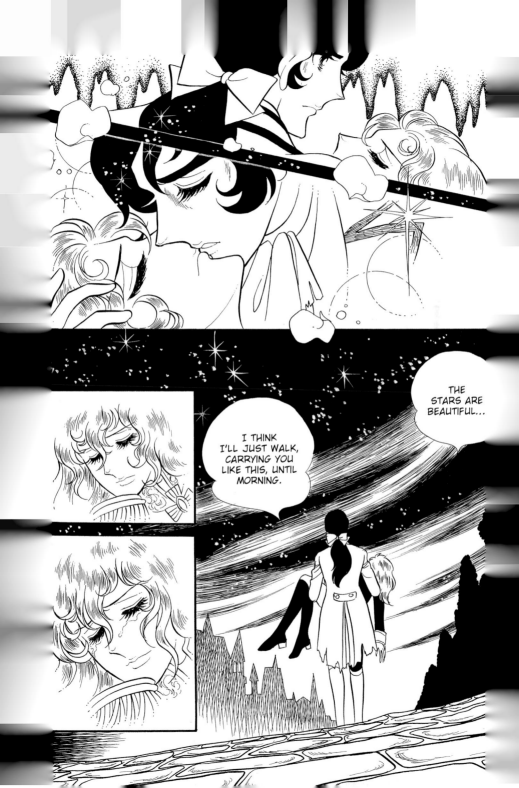

1972 WEEKLY MARGARET MAGAZINE
ISSUE 47 COVER INSERT ART

♡ HUGELY POPULAR!! CRITICALLY ACCLAIMED!!
♥ WHAT OF OSCAR, WHO IS WAITING FOR FERSEN'S RETURN...?!

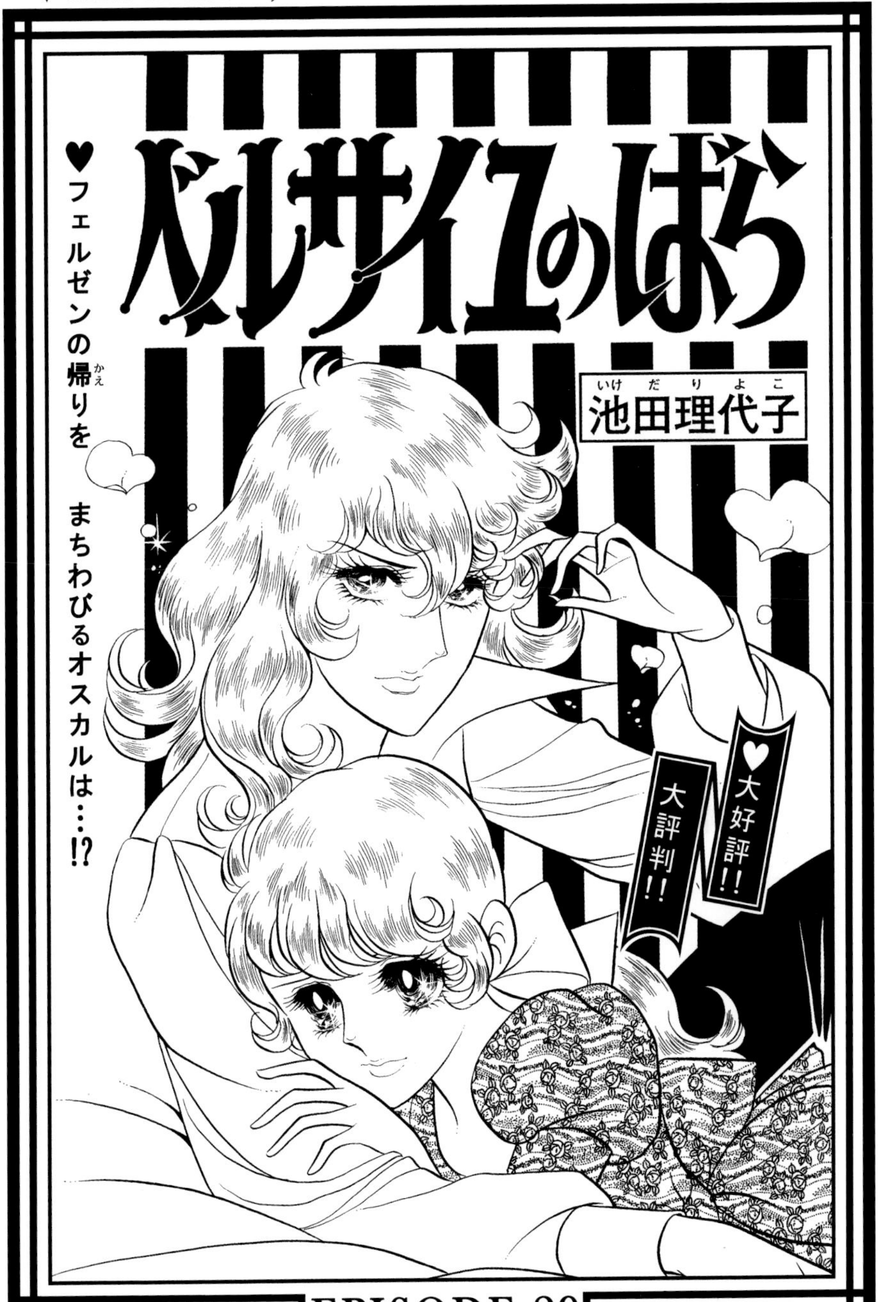
ベルサイユのばら
♥フェルゼンの帰りをまちわびるオスカルは…!?
いけだりよこ
池田理代子
♥大好評!!
大評判!!

EPISODE 29

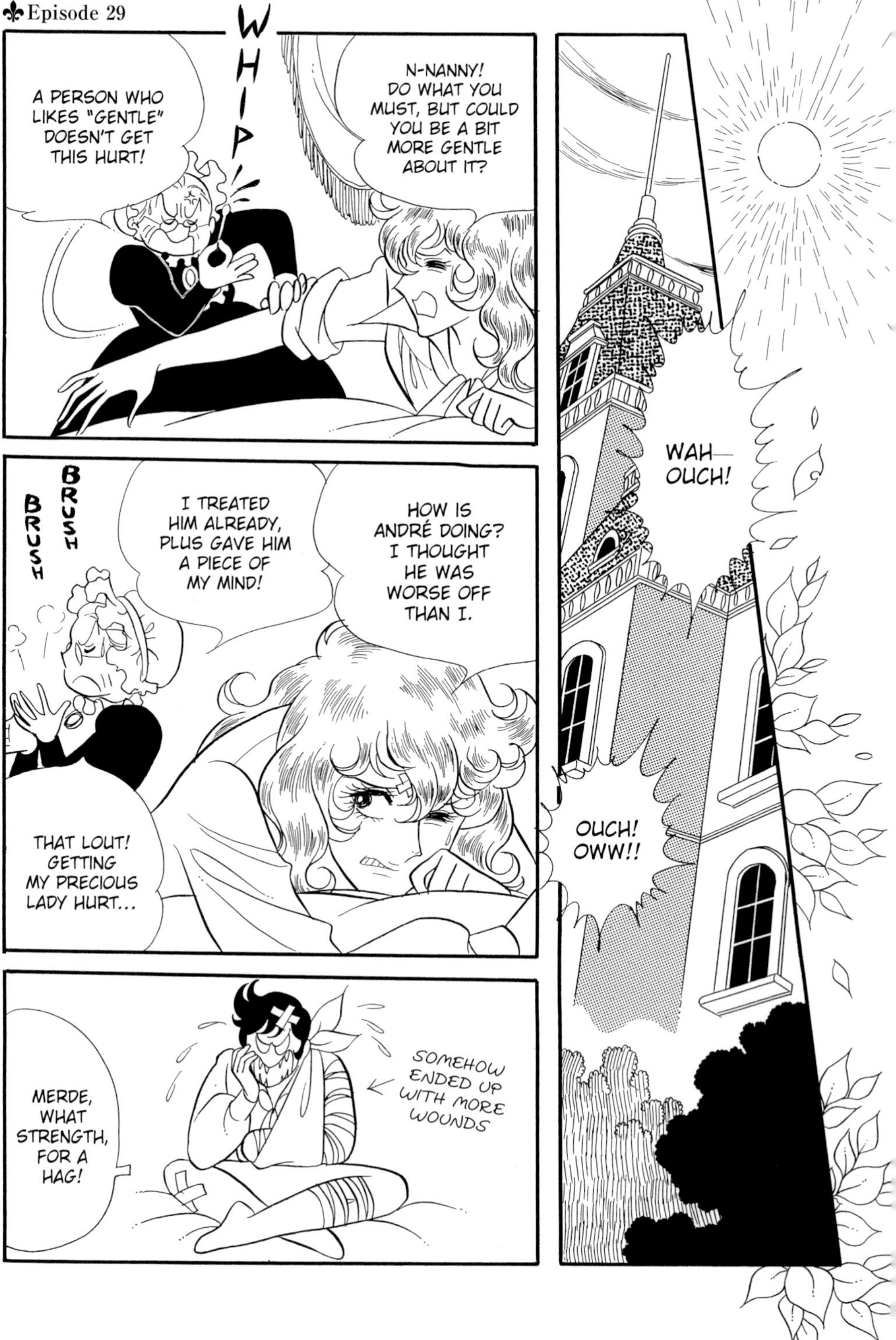
WAH— OUCH!
OUCH! OWW!!
N-NANNY! DO WHAT YOU MUST, BUT COULD YOU BE A BIT MORE GENTLE ABOUT IT?
WHIP!
A PERSON WHO LIKES "GENTLE" DOESN'T GET THIS HURT!
HOW IS ANDRÉ DOING? I THOUGHT HE WAS WORSE OFF THAN I.
I TREATED HIM ALREADY, PLUS GAVE HIM A PIECE OF MY MIND!
BRUSH
BRUSH
THAT LOUT! GETTING MY PRECIOUS LADY HURT...
SOMEHOW ENDED UP WITH MORE WOUNDS
MERDE, WHAT STRENGTH, FOR A HAG!

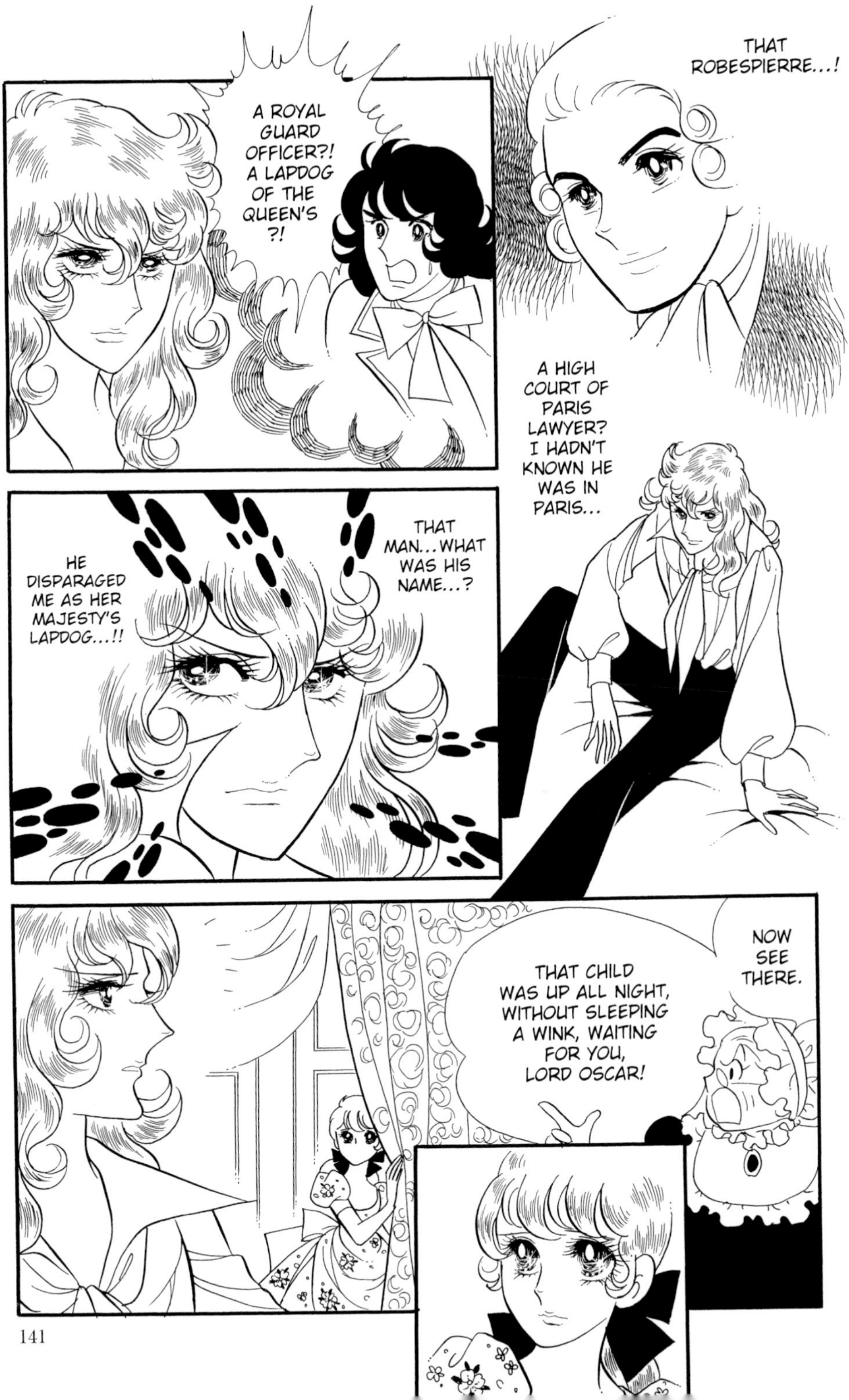
THAT ROBESPIERRE...!
A HIGH COURT OF PARIS LAWYER? I HADN'T KNOWN HE WAS IN PARIS...
A ROYAL GUARD OFFICER?! A LAPDOG OF THE QUEEN'S ?!
THAT MAN...WHAT WAS HIS NAME...?
HE DISPARAGED ME AS HER MAJESTY'S LAPDOG...!!
NOW SEE THERE.
THAT CHILD WAS UP ALL NIGHT, WITHOUT SLEEPING A WINK, WAITING FOR YOU, LORD OSCAR!

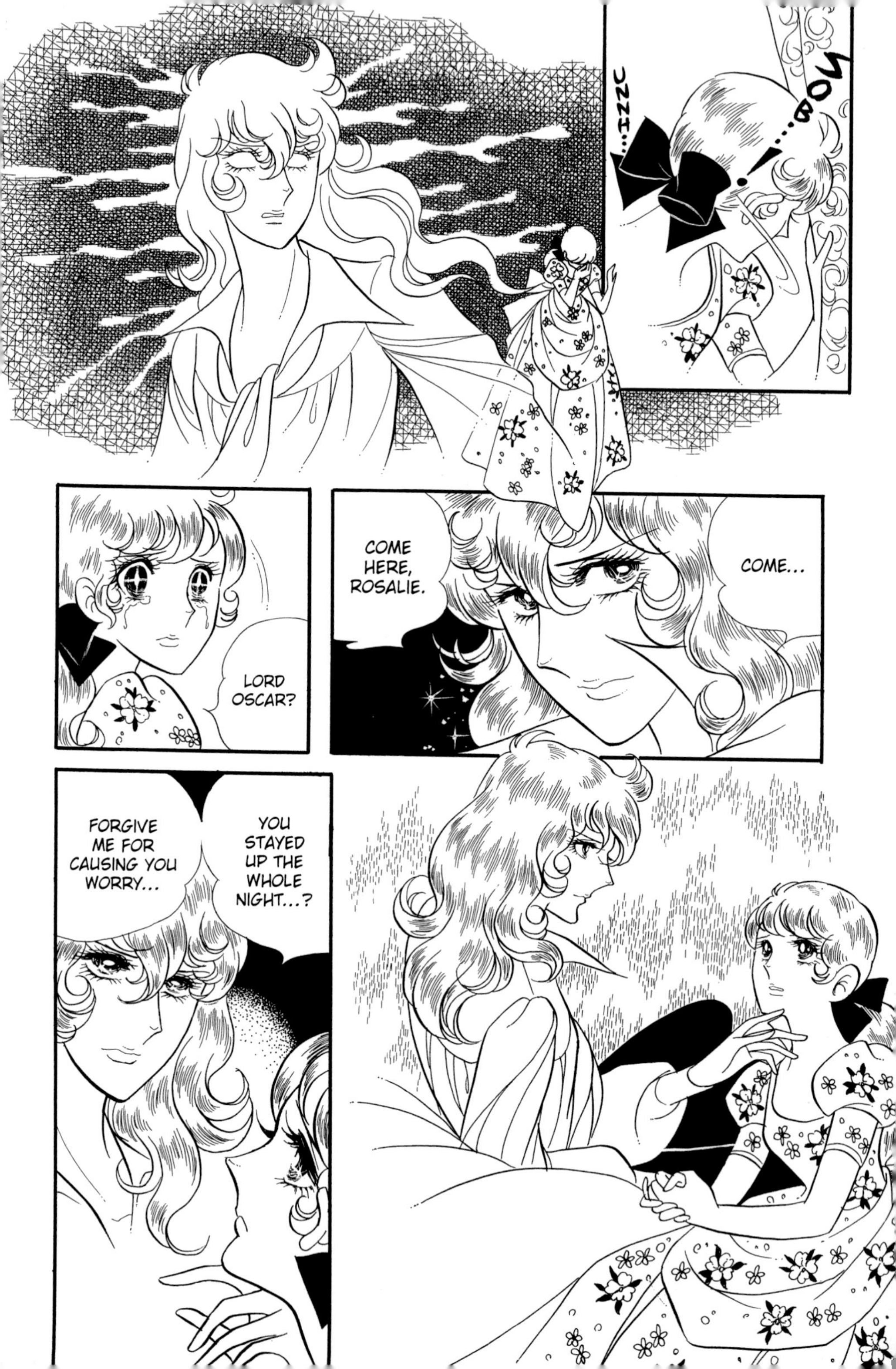
SOB...!
UNNH...
COME...
COME HERE, ROSALIE.
LORD OSCAR?
YOU STAYED UP THE WHOLE NIGHT...?
FORGIVE ME FOR CAUSING YOU WORRY...

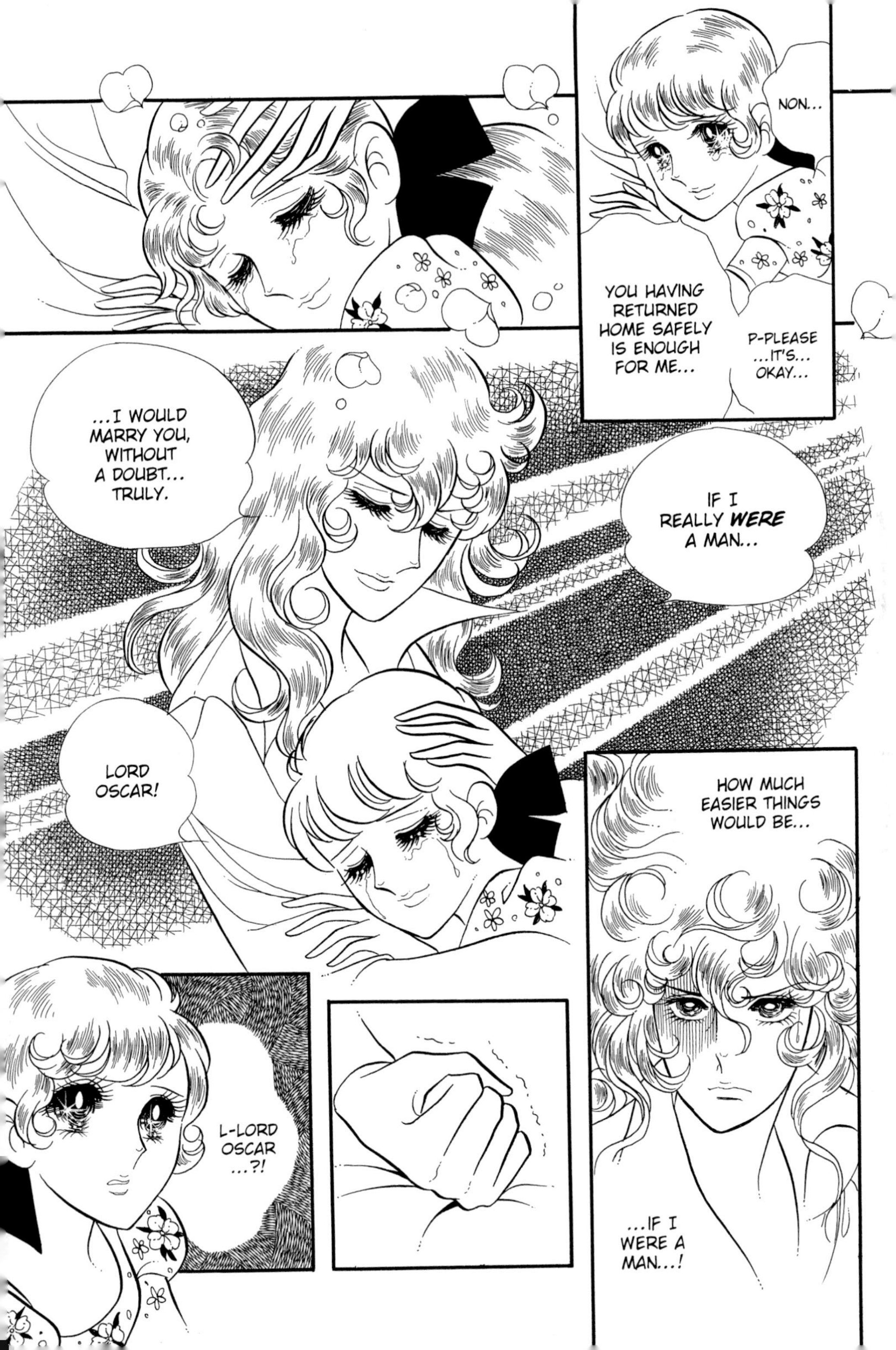
NON...
P-PLEASE ...IT'S... OKAY...
YOU HAVING RETURNED HOME SAFELY IS ENOUGH FOR ME...
IF I REALLY *WERE* A MAN...
...I WOULD MARRY YOU, WITHOUT A DOUBT... TRULY.
LORD OSCAR!
HOW MUCH EASIER THINGS WOULD BE...
...IF I WERE A MAN...!
L-LORD OSCAR ...?!

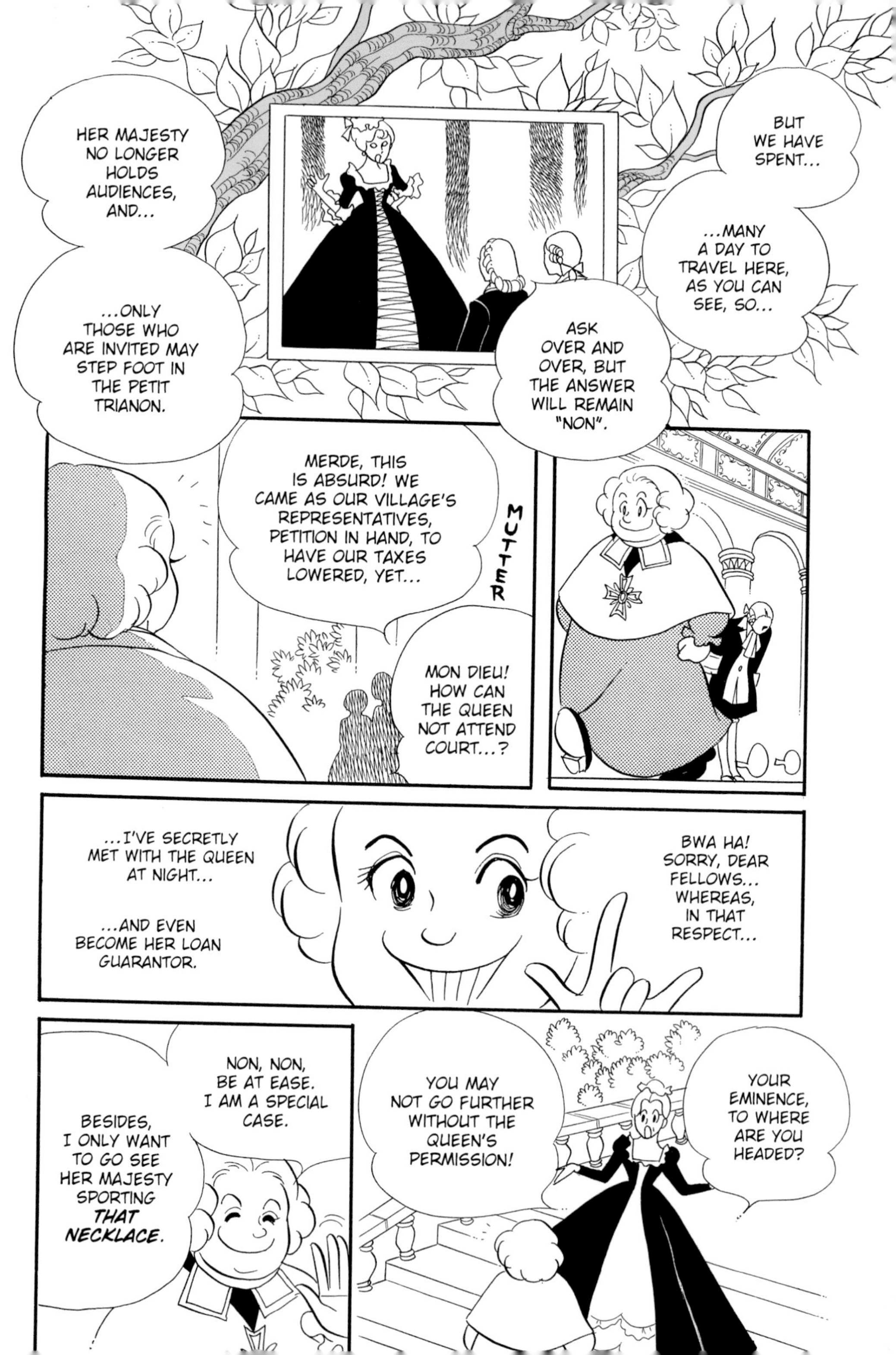

BUT WE HAVE SPENT...
...MANY A DAY TO TRAVEL HERE, AS YOU CAN SEE, SO...
HER MAJESTY NO LONGER HOLDS AUDIENCES, AND...
...ONLY THOSE WHO ARE INVITED MAY STEP FOOT IN THE PETIT TRIANON.
ASK OVER AND OVER, BUT THE ANSWER WILL REMAIN "NON".
MERDE, THIS IS ABSURD! WE CAME AS OUR VILLAGE'S REPRESENTATIVES, PETITION IN HAND, TO HAVE OUR TAXES LOWERED, YET...
MUTTER
MON DIEU! HOW CAN THE QUEEN NOT ATTEND COURT...?
BWA HA! SORRY, DEAR FELLOWS... WHEREAS, IN THAT RESPECT...
...I'VE SECRETLY MET WITH THE QUEEN AT NIGHT...
...AND EVEN BECOME HER LOAN GUARANTOR.
YOUR EMINENCE, TO WHERE ARE YOU HEADED?
YOU MAY NOT GO FURTHER WITHOUT THE QUEEN'S PERMISSION!
NON, NON, BE AT EASE. I AM A SPECIAL CASE.
BESIDES, I ONLY WANT TO GO SEE HER MAJESTY SPORTING ***THAT NECKLACE***.

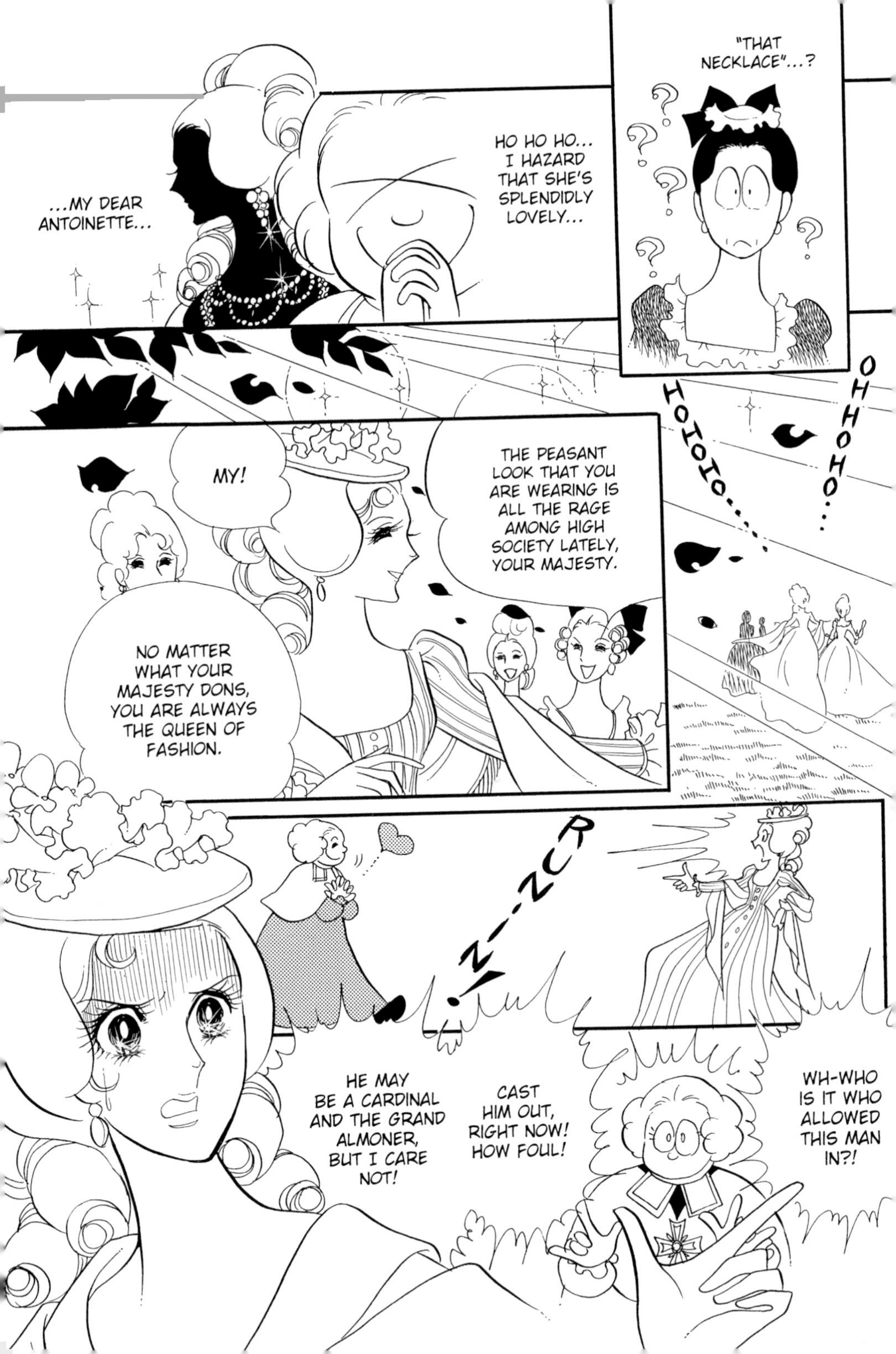
"THAT NECKLACE"...?
HO HO HO... I HAZARD THAT SHE'S SPLENDIDLY LOVELY...
...MY DEAR ANTOINETTE...
OHOHOHO...
HOHOHOHO....
THE PEASANT LOOK THAT YOU ARE WEARING IS ALL THE RAGE AMONG HIGH SOCIETY LATELY, YOUR MAJESTY.
MY!
NO MATTER WHAT YOUR MAJESTY DONS, YOU ARE ALWAYS THE QUEEN OF FASHION.
N--ZCR
WH-WHO IS IT WHO ALLOWED THIS MAN IN?!
CAST HIM OUT, RIGHT NOW! HOW FOUL!
HE MAY BE A CARDINAL AND THE GRAND ALMONER, BUT I CARE NOT!

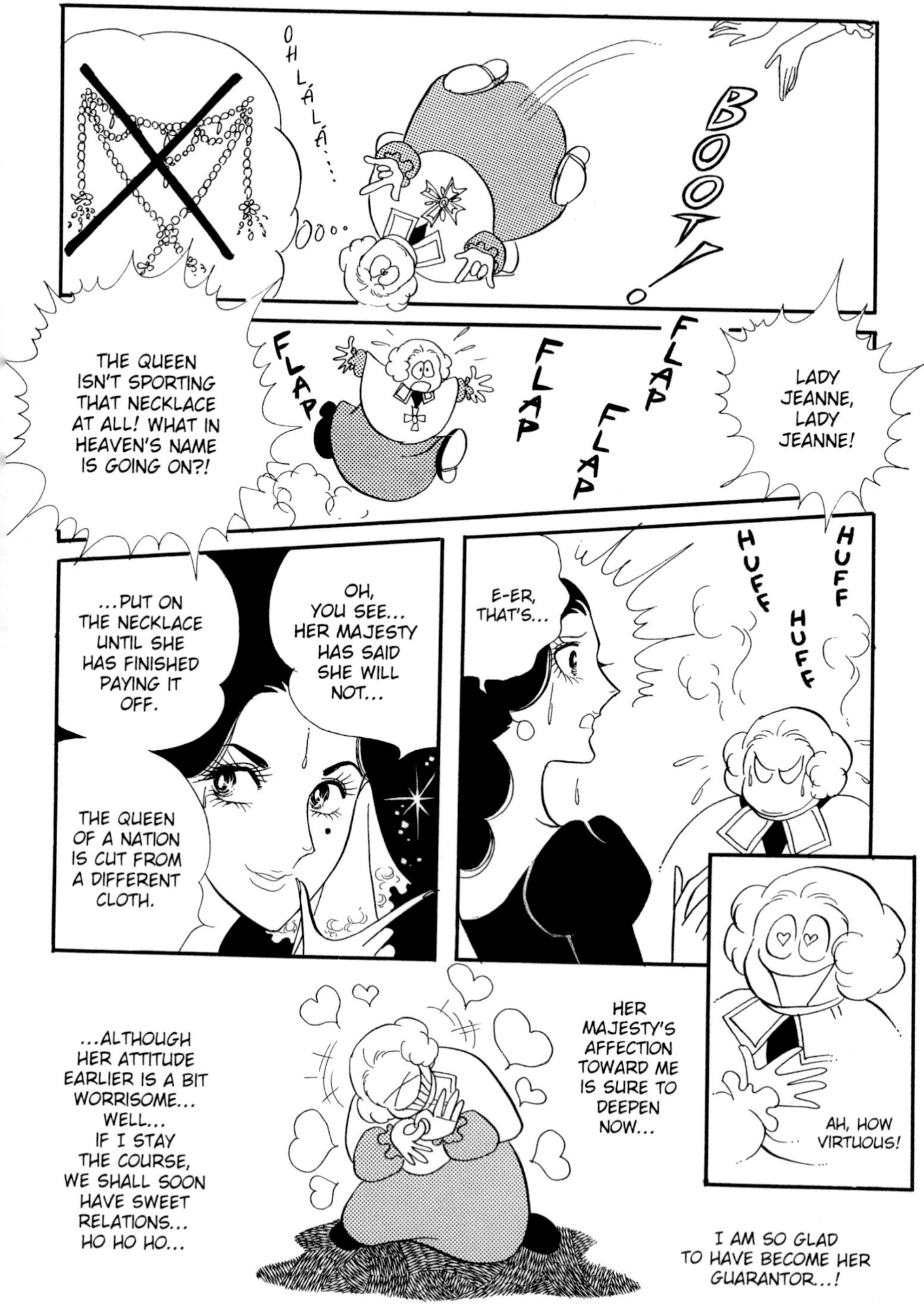
BOOT!
OH LÁ LÁ...
Ooo...
LADY JEANNE, LADY JEANNE!
FLAP
FLAP
FLAP
FLAP
THE QUEEN ISN'T SPORTING THAT NECKLACE AT ALL! WHAT IN HEAVEN'S NAME IS GOING ON?!
HUFF
HUFF
HUFF
E-ER, THAT'S...
OH, YOU SEE... HER MAJESTY HAS SAID SHE WILL NOT...
...PUT ON THE NECKLACE UNTIL SHE HAS FINISHED PAYING IT OFF.
THE QUEEN OF A NATION IS CUT FROM A DIFFERENT CLOTH.
AH, HOW VIRTUOUS!
I AM SO GLAD TO HAVE BECOME HER GUARANTOR...!
HER MAJESTY'S AFFECTION TOWARD ME IS SURE TO DEEPEN NOW...
...ALTHOUGH HER ATTITUDE EARLIER IS A BIT WORRISOME... WELL... IF I STAY THE COURSE, WE SHALL SOON HAVE SWEET RELATIONS... HO HO HO...

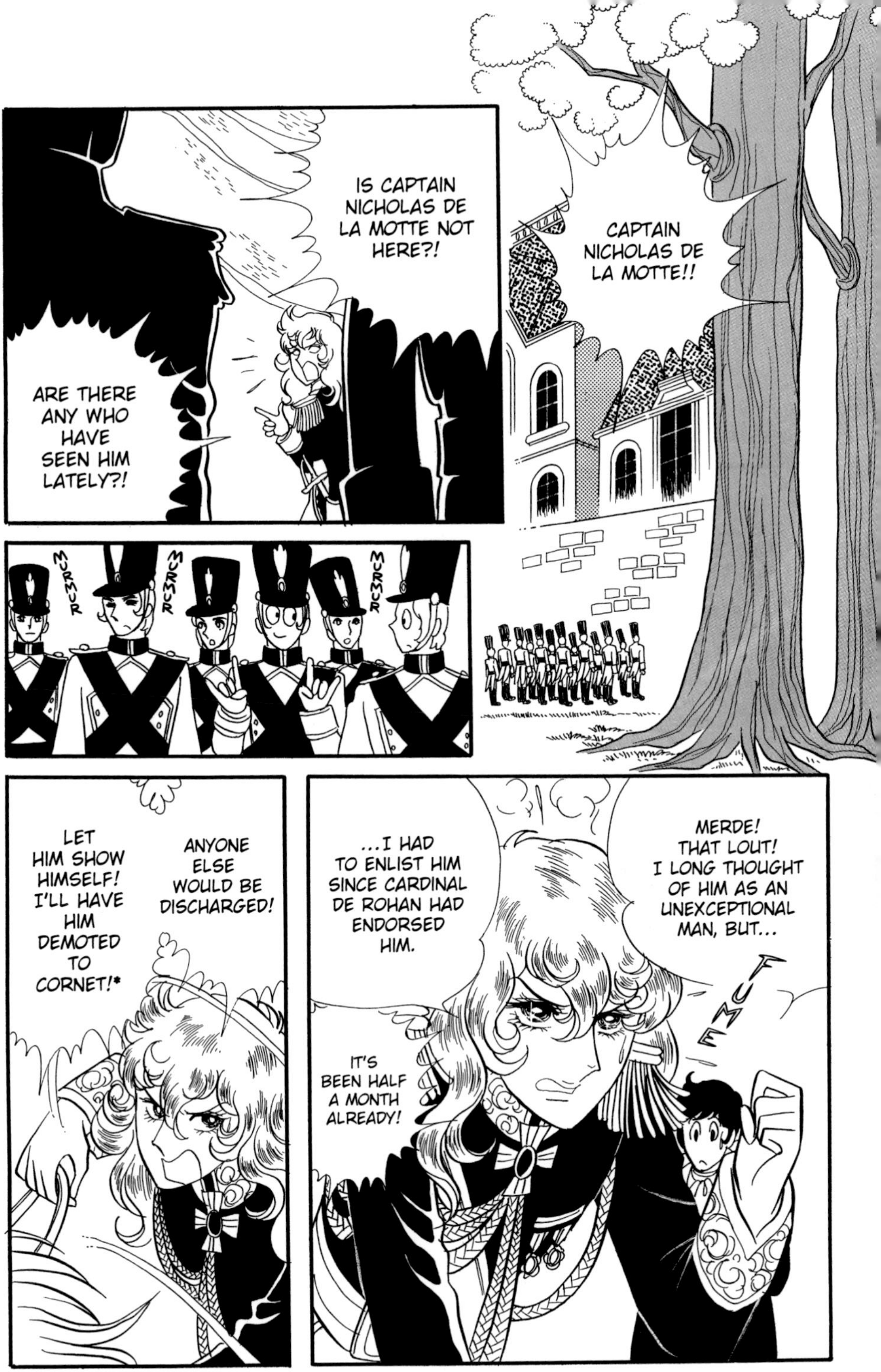
CAPTAIN NICHOLAS DE LA MOTTE!!
IS CAPTAIN NICHOLAS DE LA MOTTE NOT HERE?!
ARE THERE ANY WHO HAVE SEEN HIM LATELY?!
MURMUR
MURMUR
MURMUR
MERDE! THAT LOUT! I LONG THOUGHT OF HIM AS AN UNEXCEPTIONAL MAN, BUT...
...I HAD TO ENLIST HIM SINCE CARDINAL DE ROHAN HAD ENDORSED HIM.
FUME
IT'S BEEN HALF A MONTH ALREADY!
ANYONE ELSE WOULD BE DISCHARGED!
LET HIM SHOW HIMSELF! I'LL HAVE HIM DEMOTED TO CORNET!*

* CAVALRY EQUIVALENT OF SECOND-LIEUTENANT

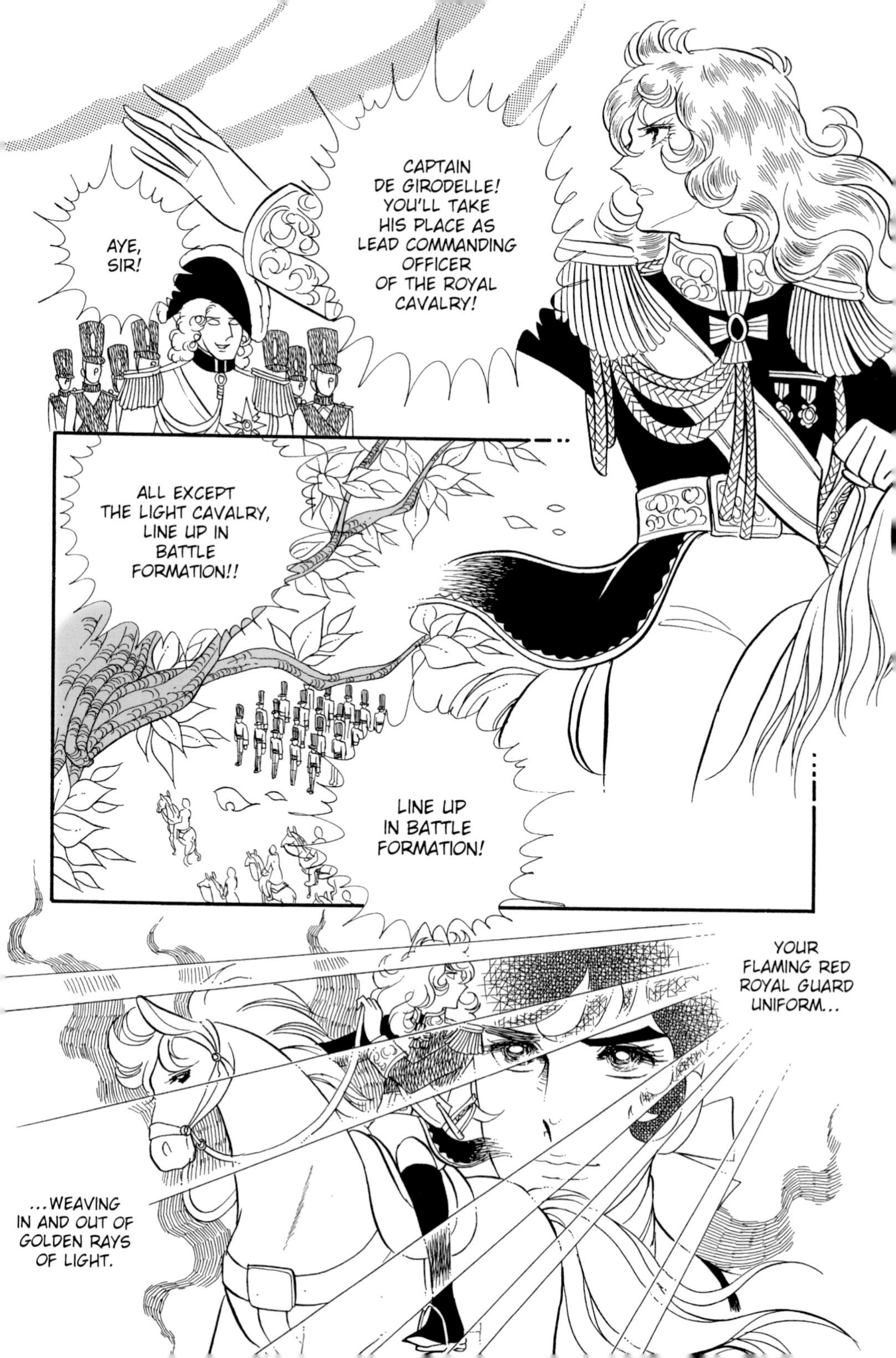
CAPTAIN DE GIRODELLE! YOU'LL TAKE HIS PLACE AS LEAD COMMANDING OFFICER OF THE ROYAL CAVALRY!
AYE, SIR!
ALL EXCEPT THE LIGHT CAVALRY, LINE UP IN BATTLE FORMATION!!
LINE UP IN BATTLE FORMATION!
YOUR FLAMING RED ROYAL GUARD UNIFORM...
...WEAVING IN AND OUT OF GOLDEN RAYS OF LIGHT.

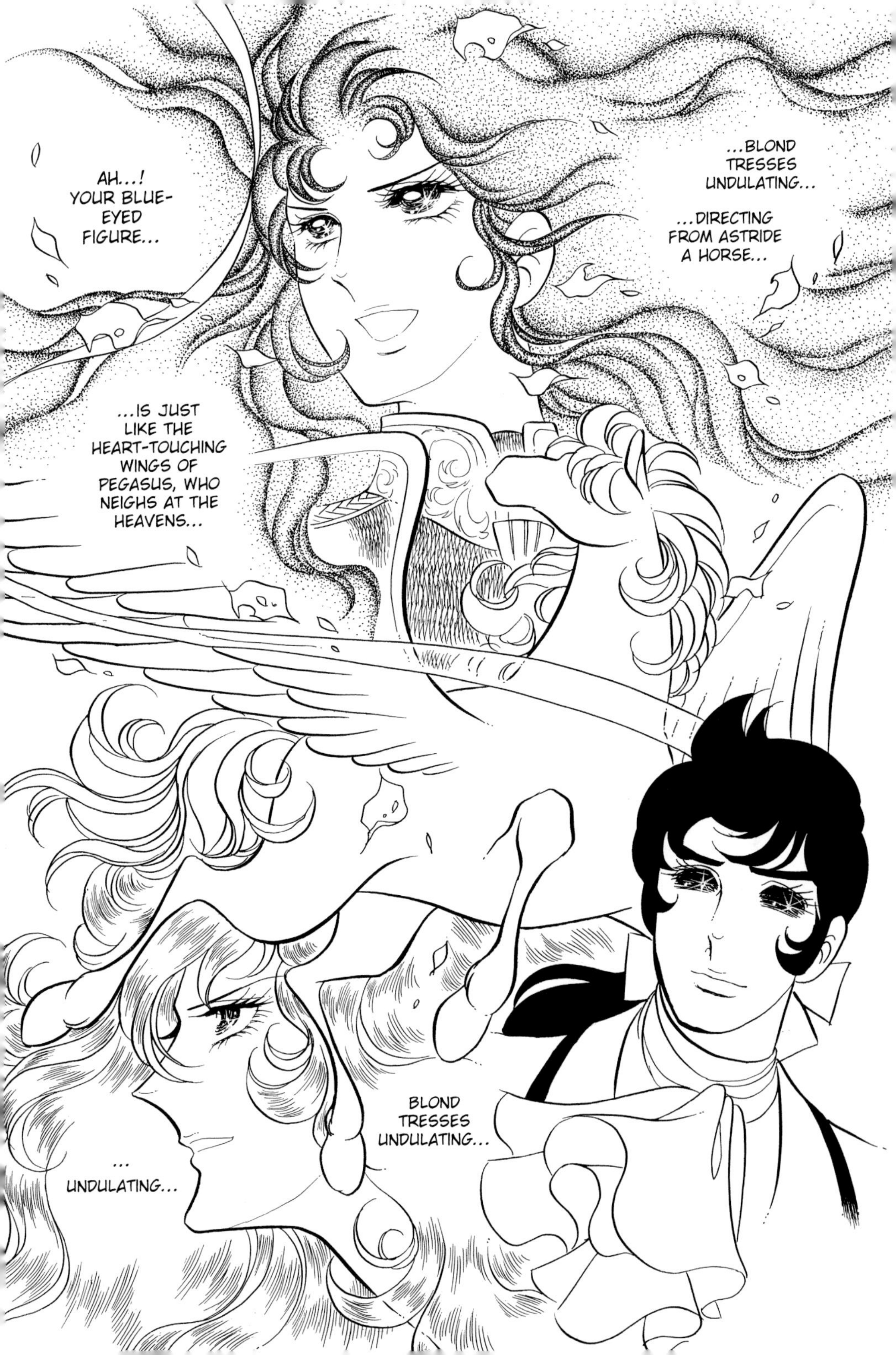
...BLOND TRESSES UNDULATING...
...DIRECTING FROM ASTRIDE A HORSE...
AH...! YOUR BLUE-EYED FIGURE...
...IS JUST LIKE THE HEART-TOUCHING WINGS OF PEGASUS, WHO NEIGHS AT THE HEAVENS...
BLOND TRESSES UNDULATING...
... UNDULATING...

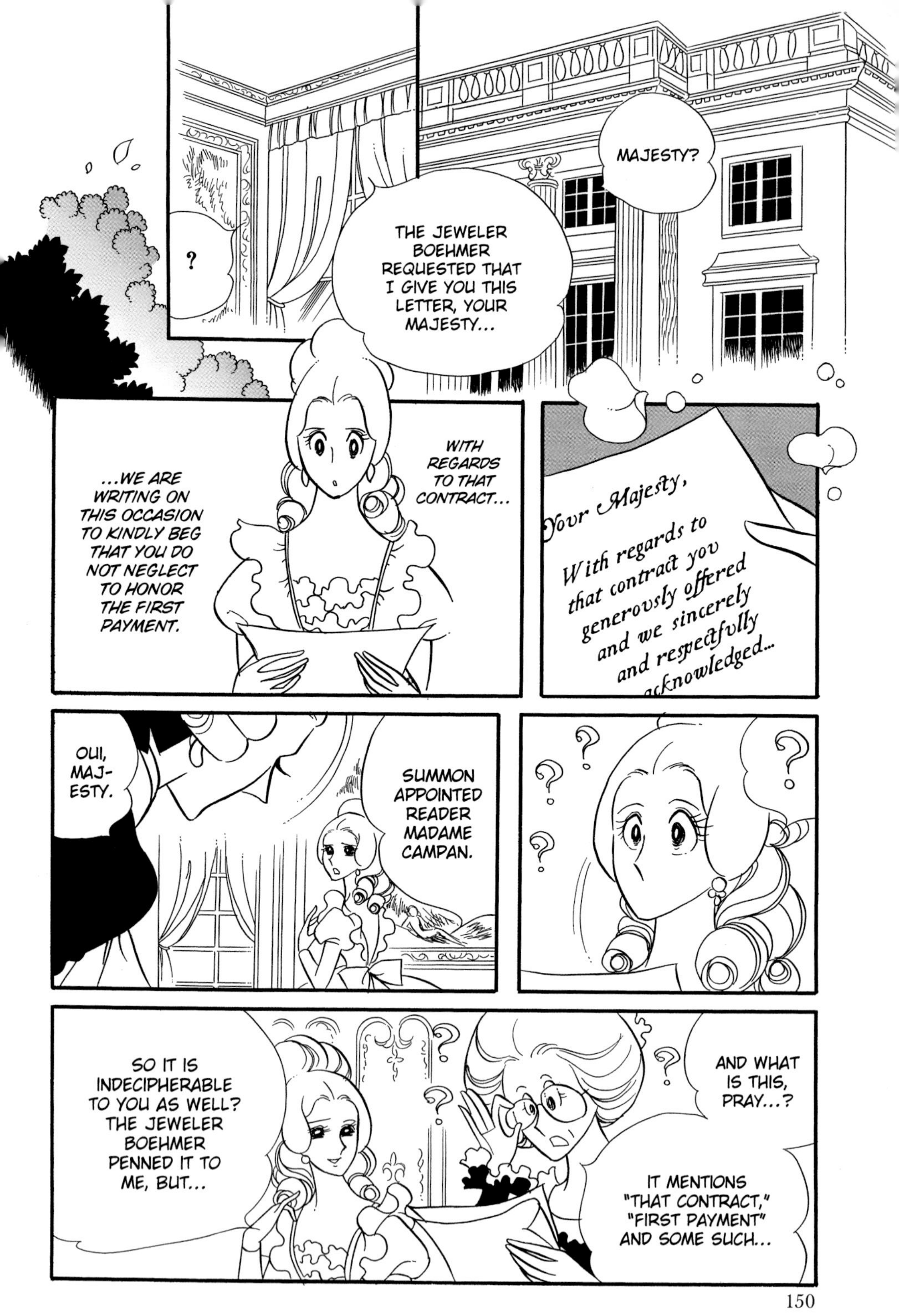
MAJESTY?
THE JEWELER BOEHMER REQUESTED THAT I GIVE YOU THIS LETTER, YOUR MAJESTY...
?
Your Majesty,
With regards to that contract you generously offered and we sincerely and respectfully acknowledged...
WITH REGARDS TO THAT CONTRACT...
...WE ARE WRITING ON THIS OCCASION TO KINDLY BEG THAT YOU DO NOT NEGLECT TO HONOR THE FIRST PAYMENT.
SUMMON APPOINTED READER MADAME CAMPAN.
OUI, MAJ-ESTY.
AND WHAT IS THIS, PRAY...?
IT MENTIONS "THAT CONTRACT," "FIRST PAYMENT" AND SOME SUCH...
SO IT IS INDECIPHERABLE TO YOU AS WELL? THE JEWELER BOEHMER PENNED IT TO ME, BUT...

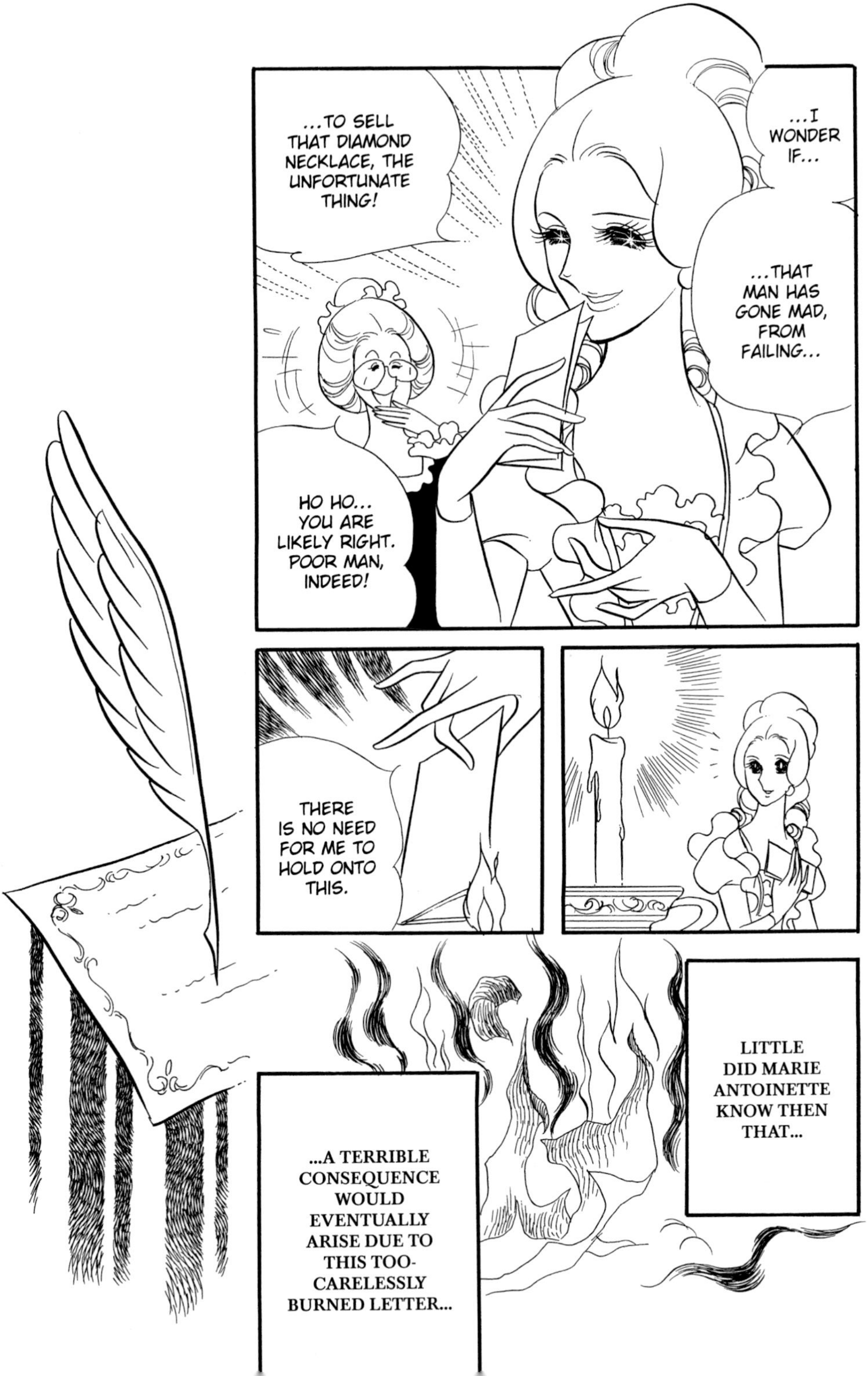
...I WONDER IF...
...THAT MAN HAS GONE MAD, FROM FAILING...
...TO SELL THAT DIAMOND NECKLACE, THE UNFORTUNATE THING!
HO HO... YOU ARE LIKELY RIGHT. POOR MAN, INDEED!
THERE IS NO NEED FOR ME TO HOLD ONTO THIS.
LITTLE DID MARIE ANTOINETTE KNOW THEN THAT...
...A TERRIBLE CONSEQUENCE WOULD EVENTUALLY ARISE DUE TO THIS TOO-CARELESSLY BURNED LETTER...

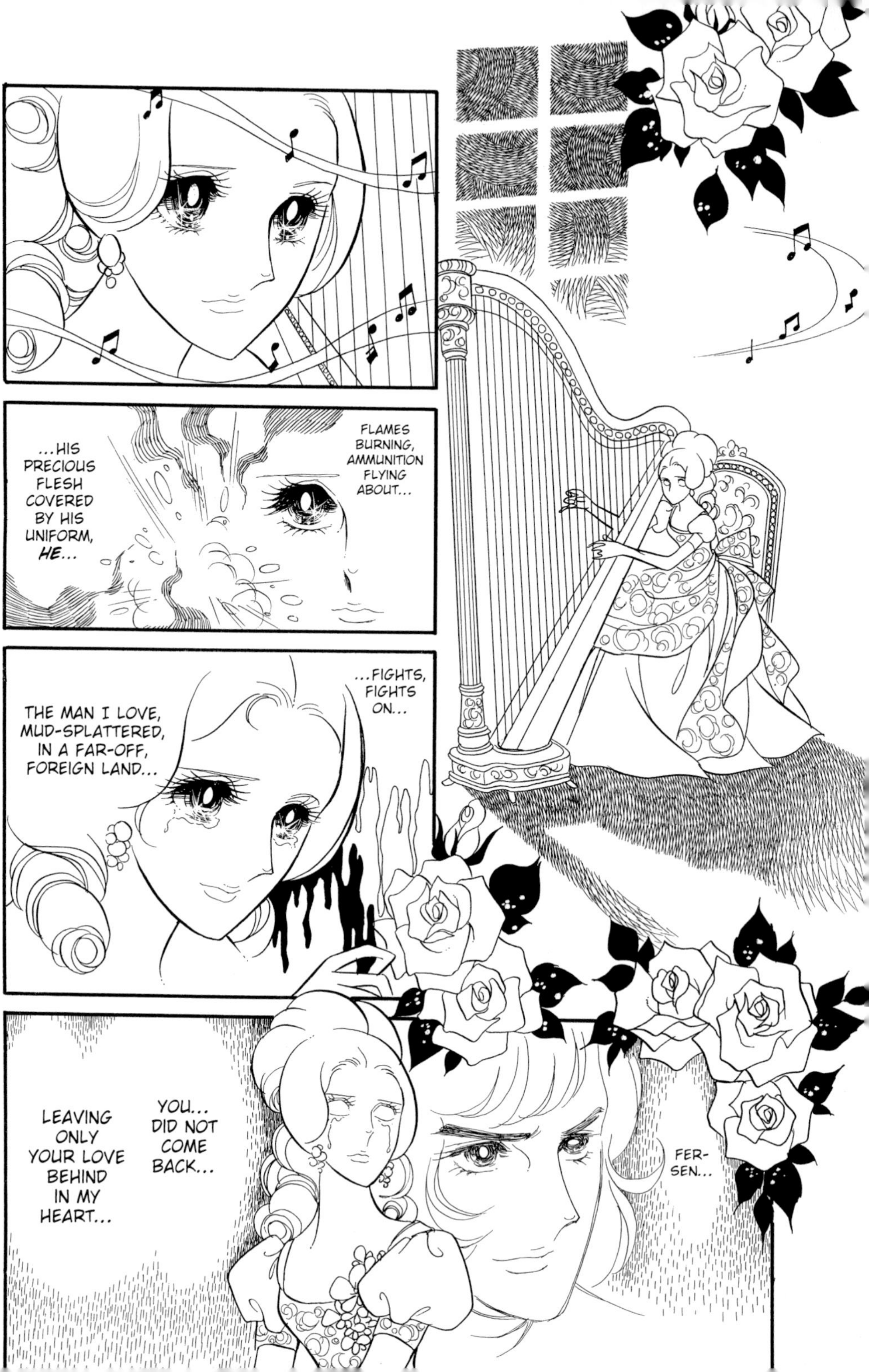
FLAMES BURNING, AMMUNITION FLYING ABOUT...
...HIS PRECIOUS FLESH COVERED BY HIS UNIFORM, *HE*...
...FIGHTS, FIGHTS ON...
THE MAN I LOVE, MUD-SPLATTERED, IN A FAR-OFF, FOREIGN LAND...
FER-SEN...
YOU... DID NOT COME BACK...
LEAVING ONLY YOUR LOVE BEHIND IN MY HEART...

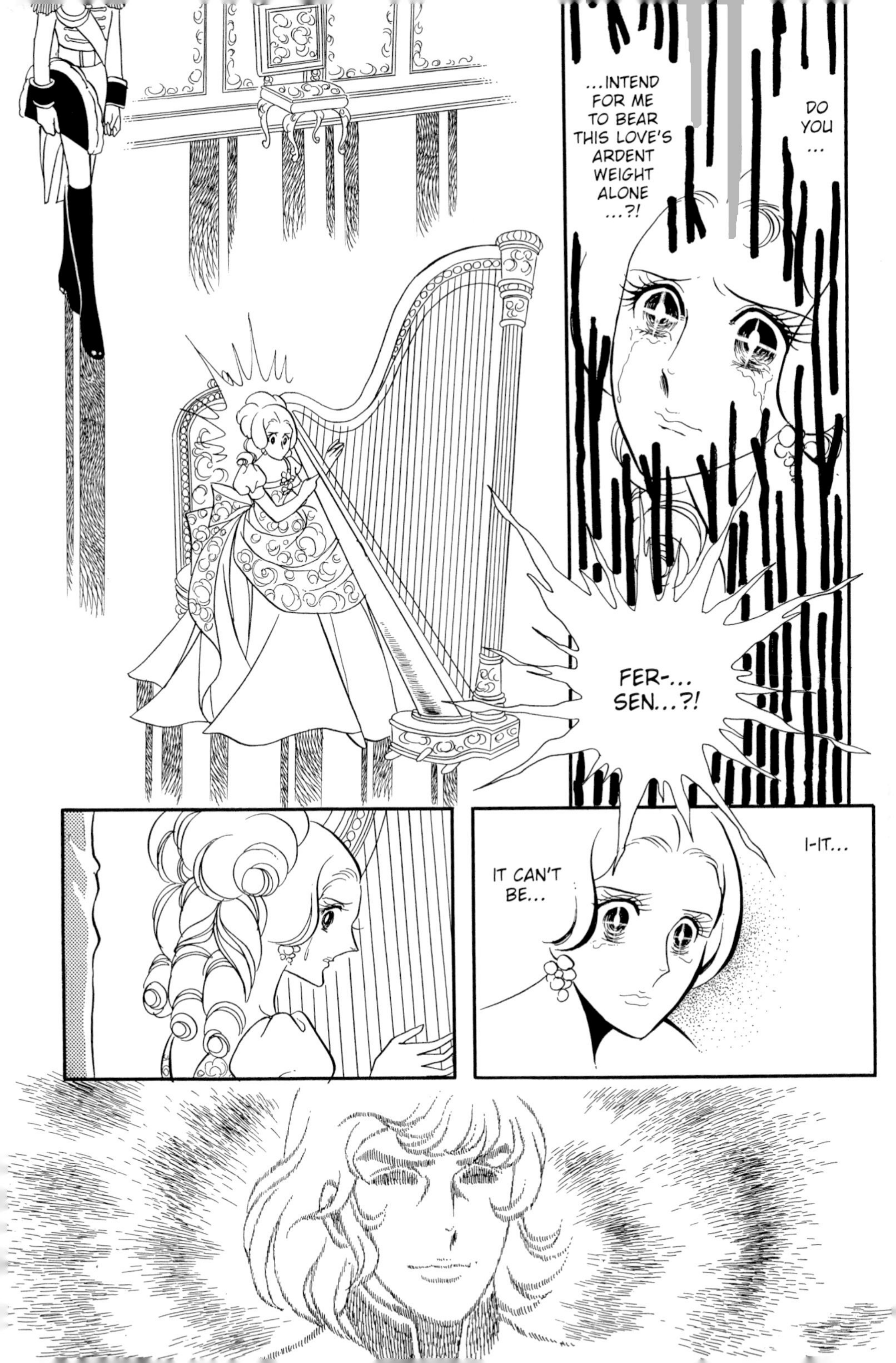
DO YOU...
...INTEND FOR ME TO BEAR THIS LOVE'S ARDENT WEIGHT ALONE...?!
FER-... SEN...?!
I-IT...
IT CAN'T BE...

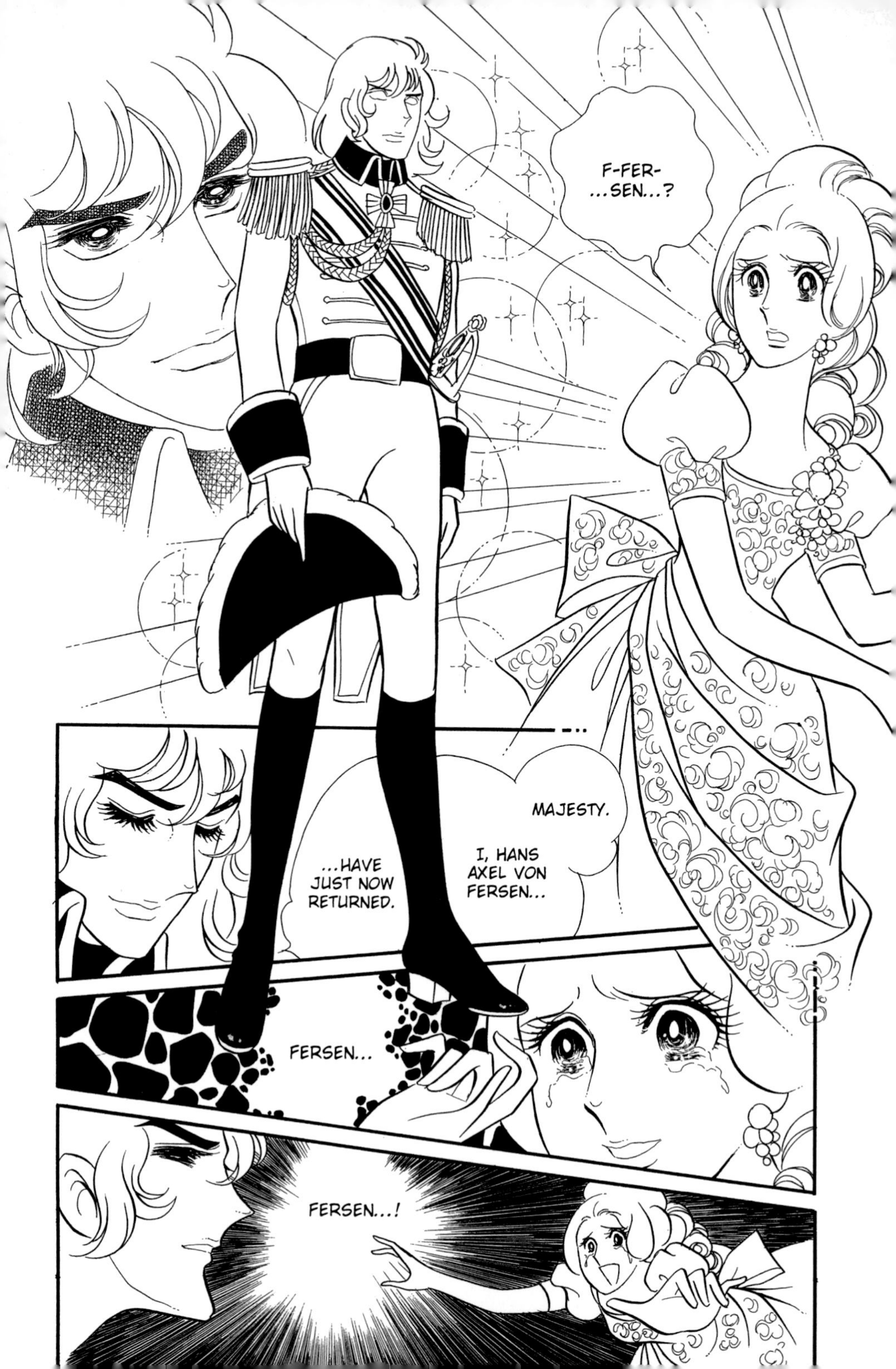
F-FER-
...SEN...?
MAJESTY.
I, HANS AXEL VON FERSEN...
...HAVE JUST NOW RETURNED.
FERSEN...
FERSEN...!

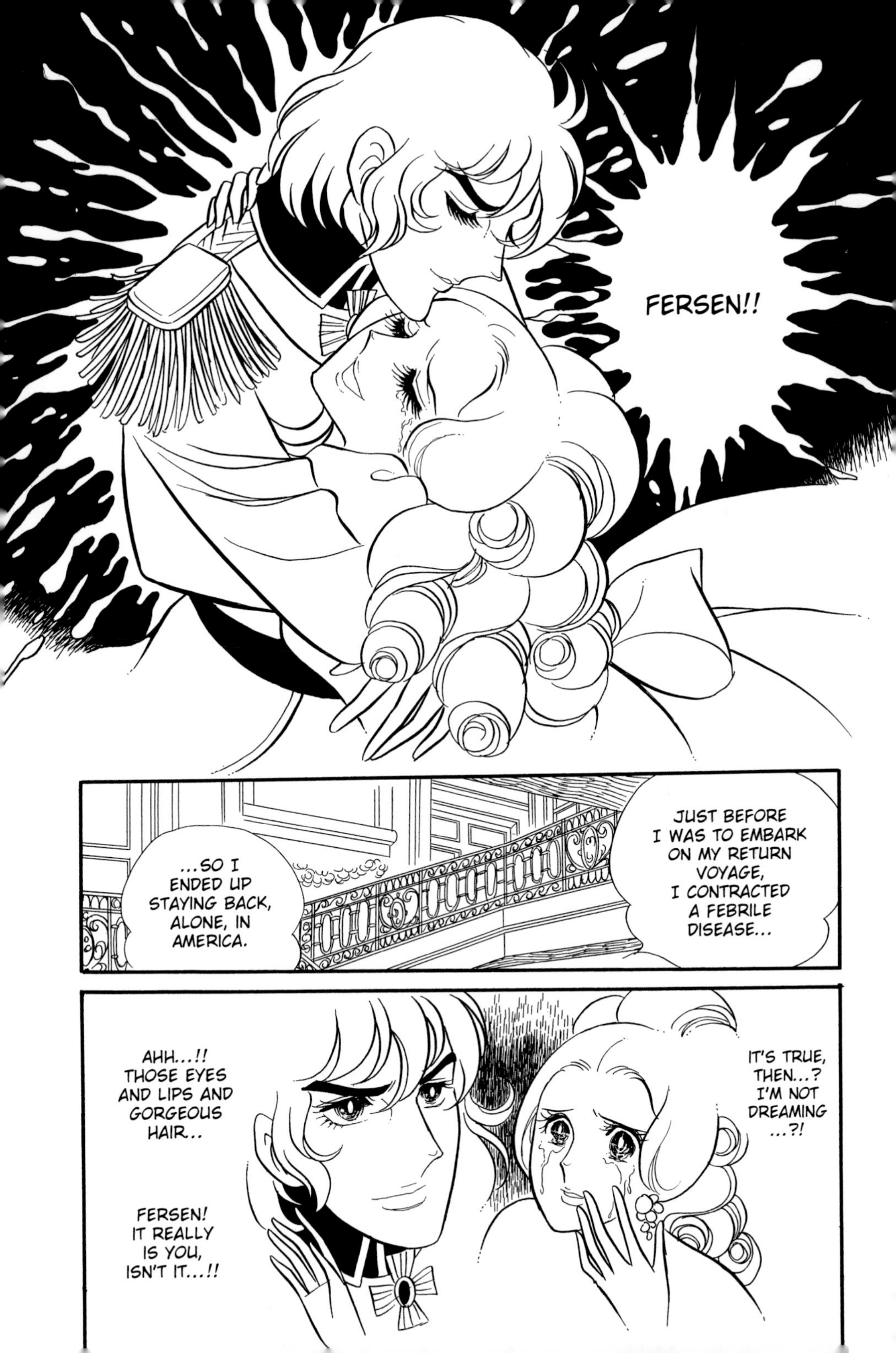
FERSEN!!
JUST BEFORE I WAS TO EMBARK ON MY RETURN VOYAGE, I CONTRACTED A FEBRILE DISEASE...
...SO I ENDED UP STAYING BACK, ALONE, IN AMERICA.
IT'S TRUE, THEN...? I'M NOT DREAMING ...?!
AHH...!! THOSE EYES AND LIPS AND GORGEOUS HAIR...
FERSEN! IT REALLY IS YOU, ISN'T IT...!!

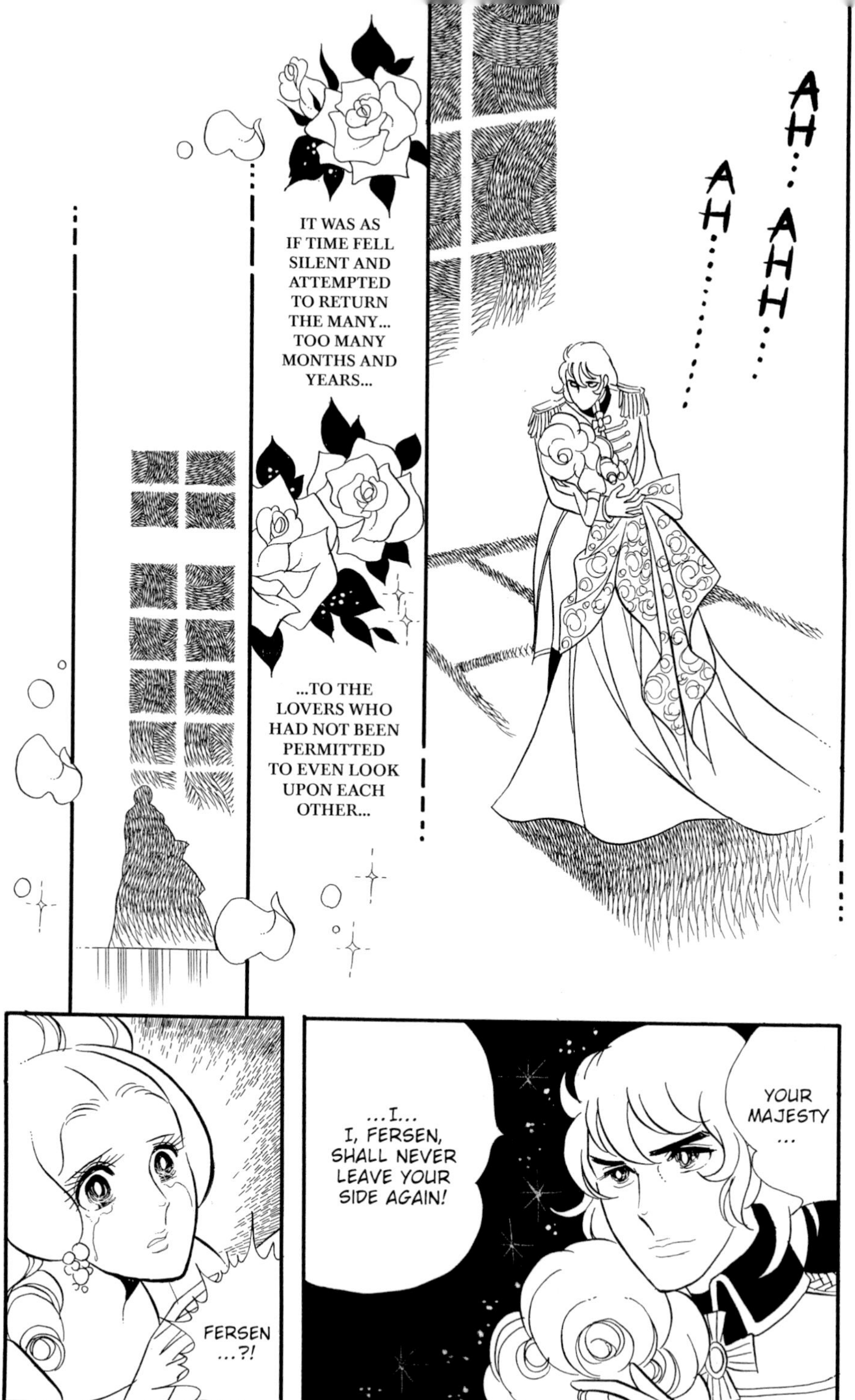
AH... AHH...
AH......
IT WAS AS IF TIME FELL SILENT AND ATTEMPTED TO RETURN THE MANY... TOO MANY MONTHS AND YEARS...
...TO THE LOVERS WHO HAD NOT BEEN PERMITTED TO EVEN LOOK UPON EACH OTHER...
YOUR MAJESTY ...
...I... I, FERSEN, SHALL NEVER LEAVE YOUR SIDE AGAIN!
FERSEN ...?!

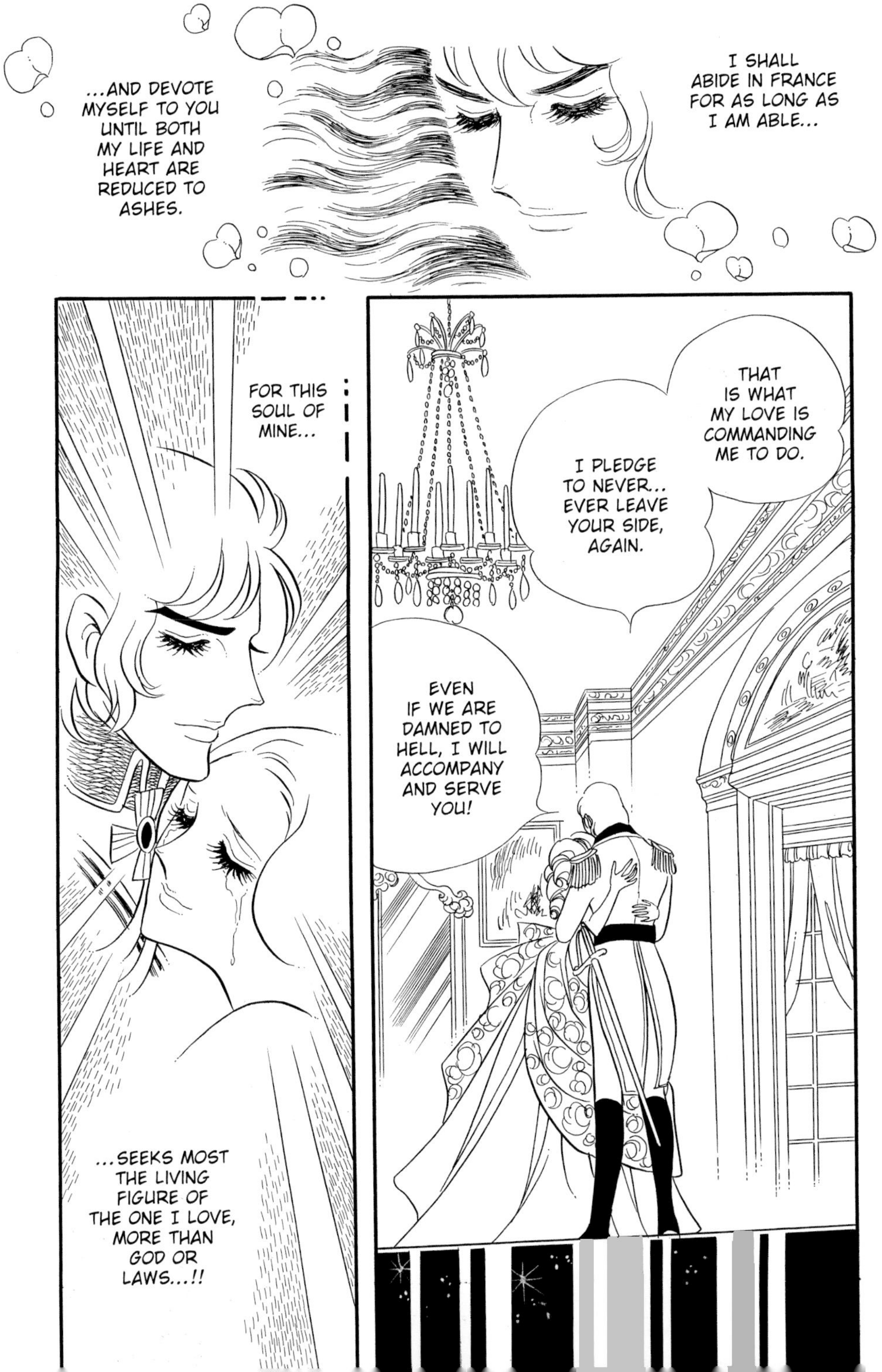
I SHALL ABIDE IN FRANCE FOR AS LONG AS I AM ABLE...
...AND DEVOTE MYSELF TO YOU UNTIL BOTH MY LIFE AND HEART ARE REDUCED TO ASHES.
THAT IS WHAT MY LOVE IS COMMANDING ME TO DO.
I PLEDGE TO NEVER... EVER LEAVE YOUR SIDE, AGAIN.
EVEN IF WE ARE DAMNED TO HELL, I WILL ACCOMPANY AND SERVE YOU!
FOR THIS SOUL OF MINE...
...SEEKS MOST THE LIVING FIGURE OF THE ONE I LOVE, MORE THAN GOD OR LAWS...!!

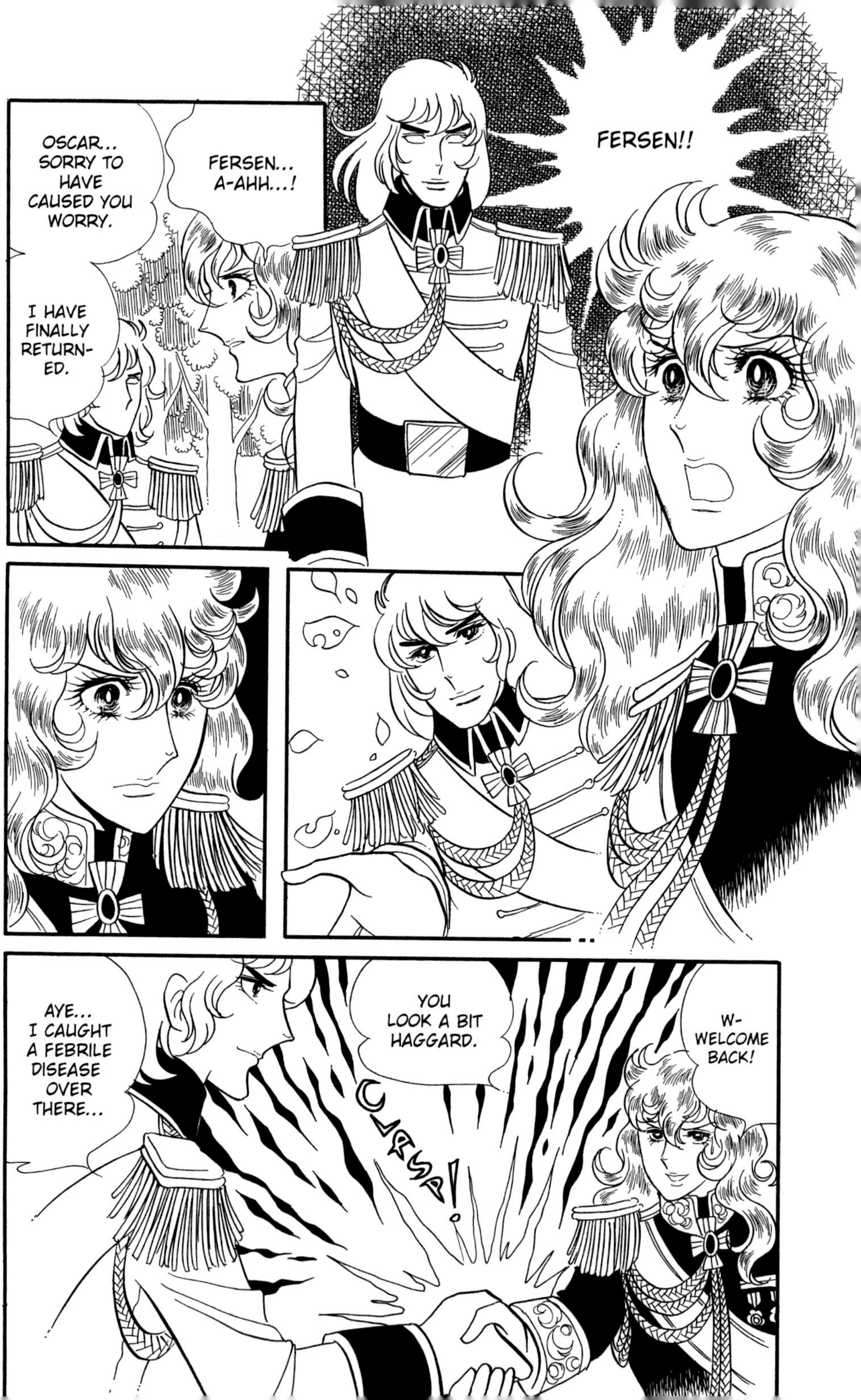
FERSEN!!
FERSEN... A-AHH...!
OSCAR... SORRY TO HAVE CAUSED YOU WORRY.
I HAVE FINALLY RETURN-ED.
W-WELCOME BACK!
YOU LOOK A BIT HAGGARD.
CLASP!
AYE... I CAUGHT A FEBRILE DISEASE OVER THERE...

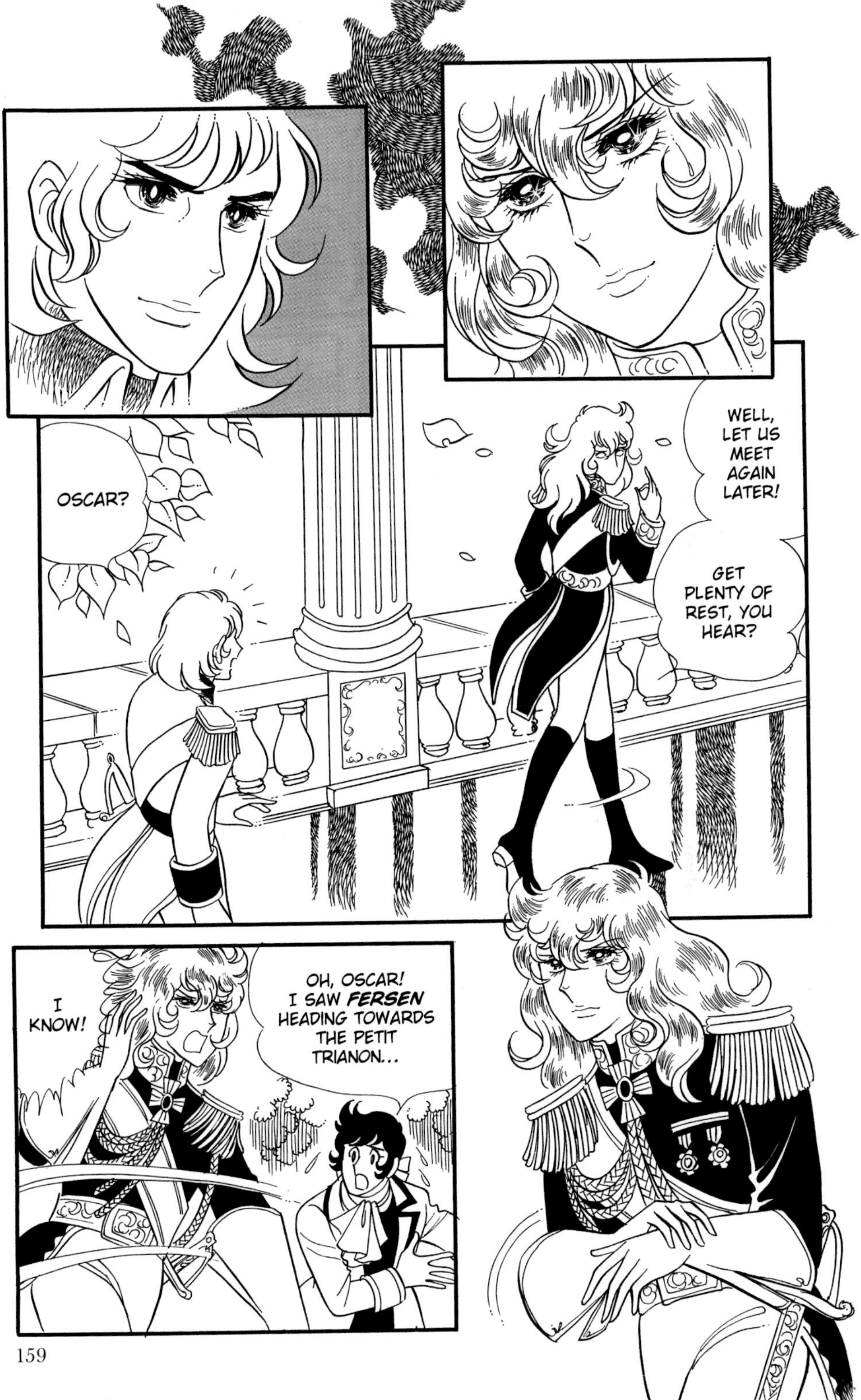
WELL, LET US MEET AGAIN LATER!
GET PLENTY OF REST, YOU HEAR?
OSCAR?
OH, OSCAR! I SAW **FERSEN** HEADING TOWARDS THE PETIT TRIANON...
I KNOW!

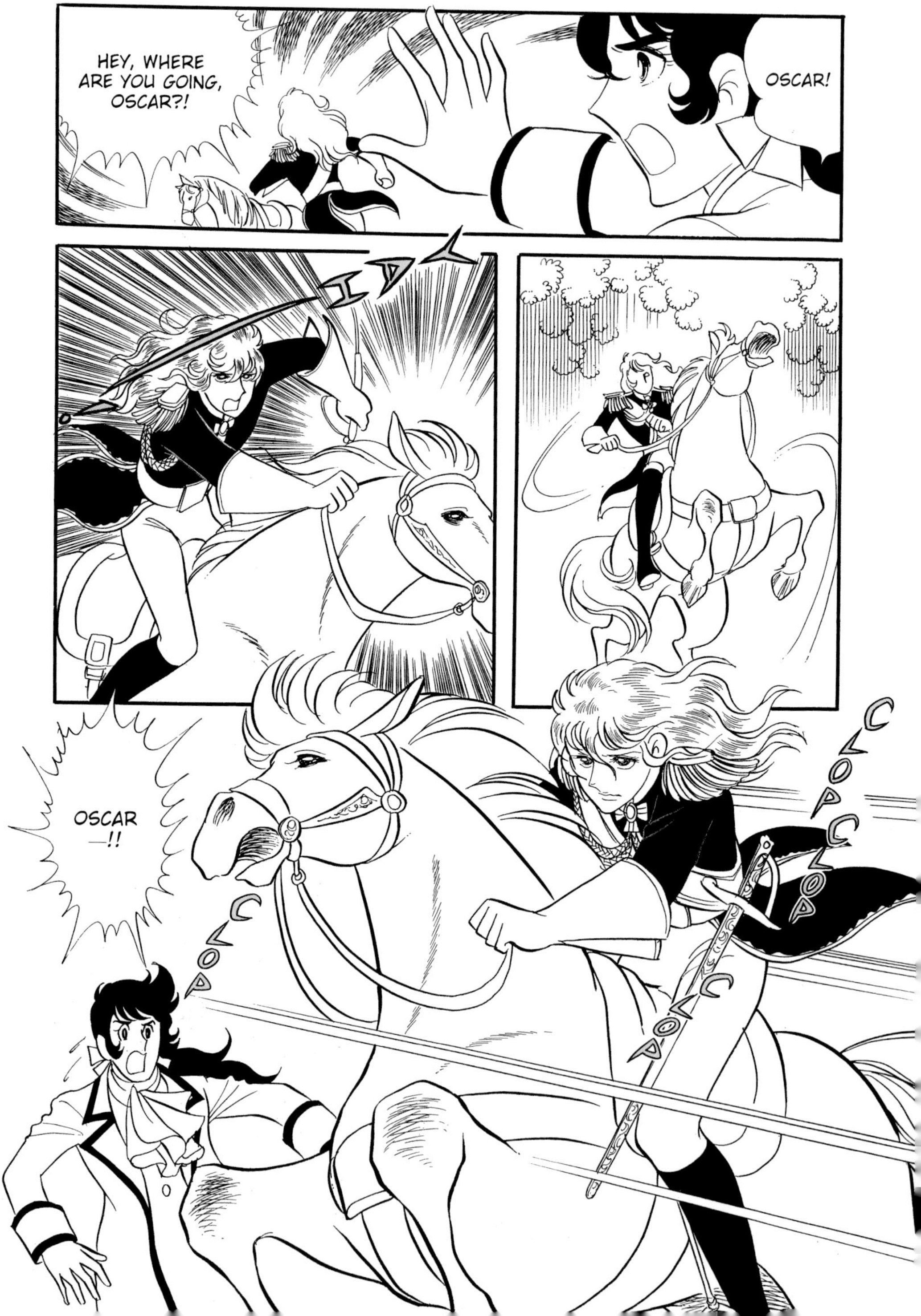
OSCAR!
HEY, WHERE ARE YOU GOING, OSCAR?!
CLOP CLOP CLOP
CLOP
OSCAR —!!
CLOP

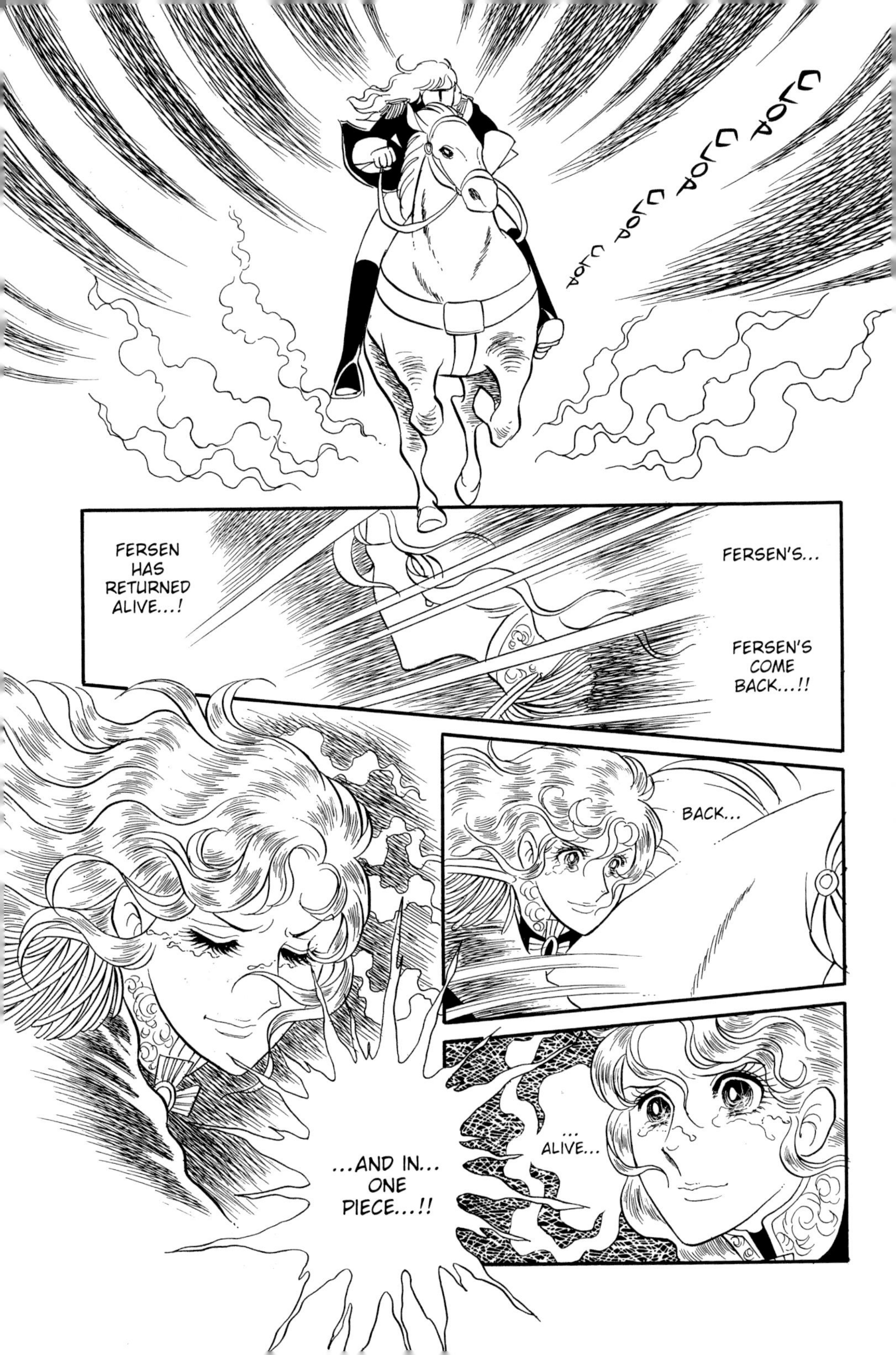
CLOP CLOP CLOP CLOP CLOP
FERSEN'S...
FERSEN'S COME BACK...!!
FERSEN HAS RETURNED ALIVE...!
BACK...
... ALIVE...
...AND IN... ONE PIECE...!!

THE ROSE OF VERSAILLES

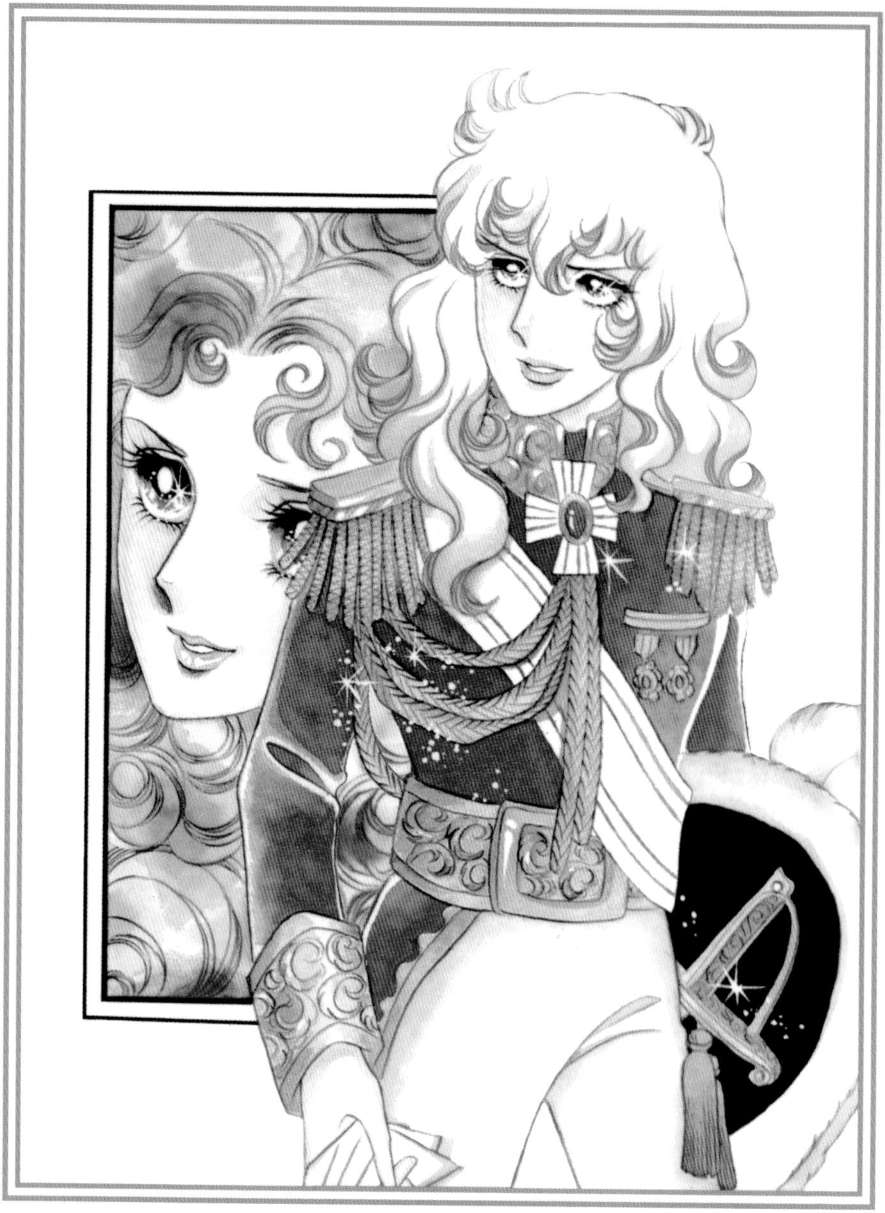

1973 MARGARET COMICS TRADE PAPERBACK
VOLUME 3 COVER

THE HUGELY POPULAR SERIES!!
♥ FERSEN RETURNS FROM THE WAR, BUT WHAT OF ANTOINETTE AND OSCAR...?!

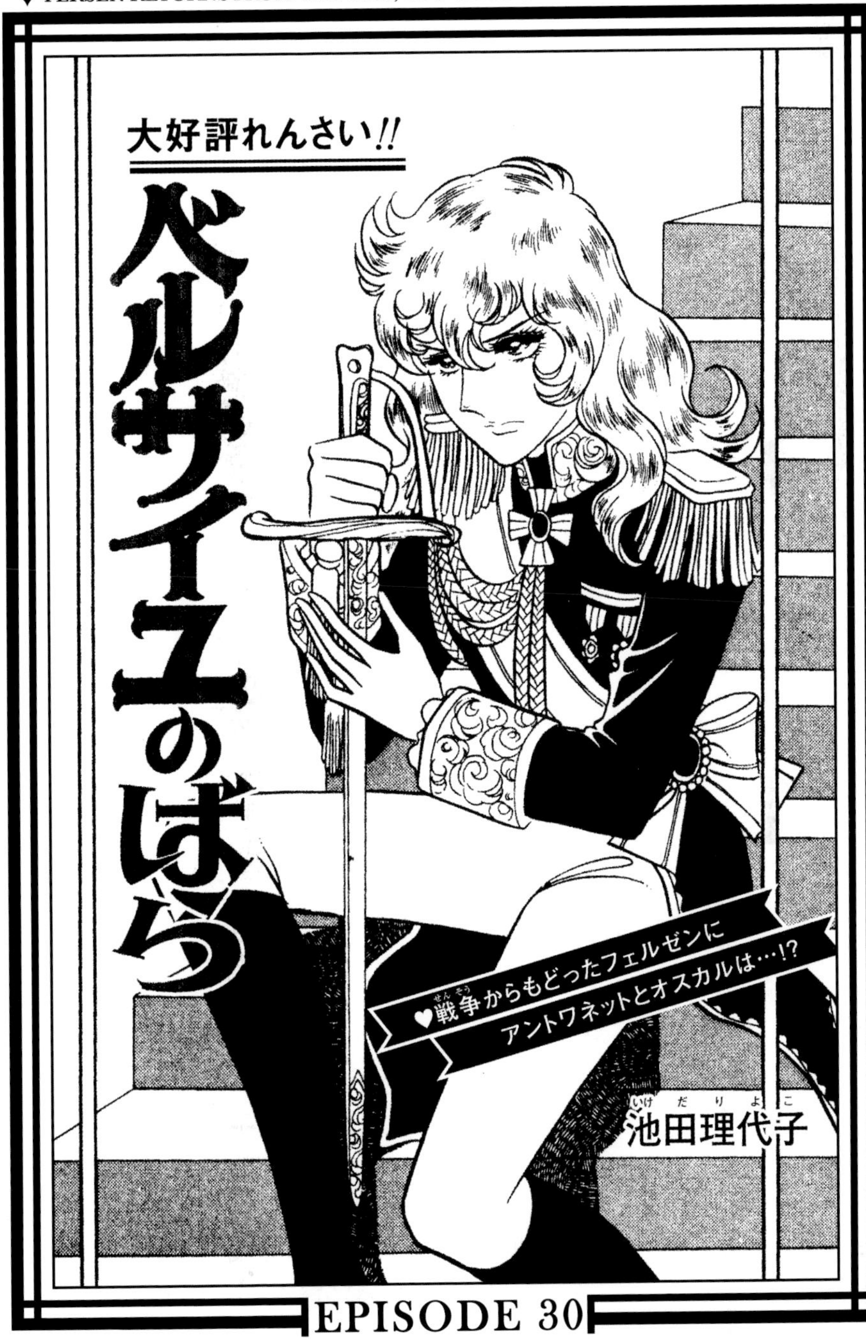
大好評れんさい!!
ベルサイユのばら
♥戦争からもどったフェルゼンに
アントワネットとオスカルは…!?
池田理代子

EPISODE 30

Episode 30

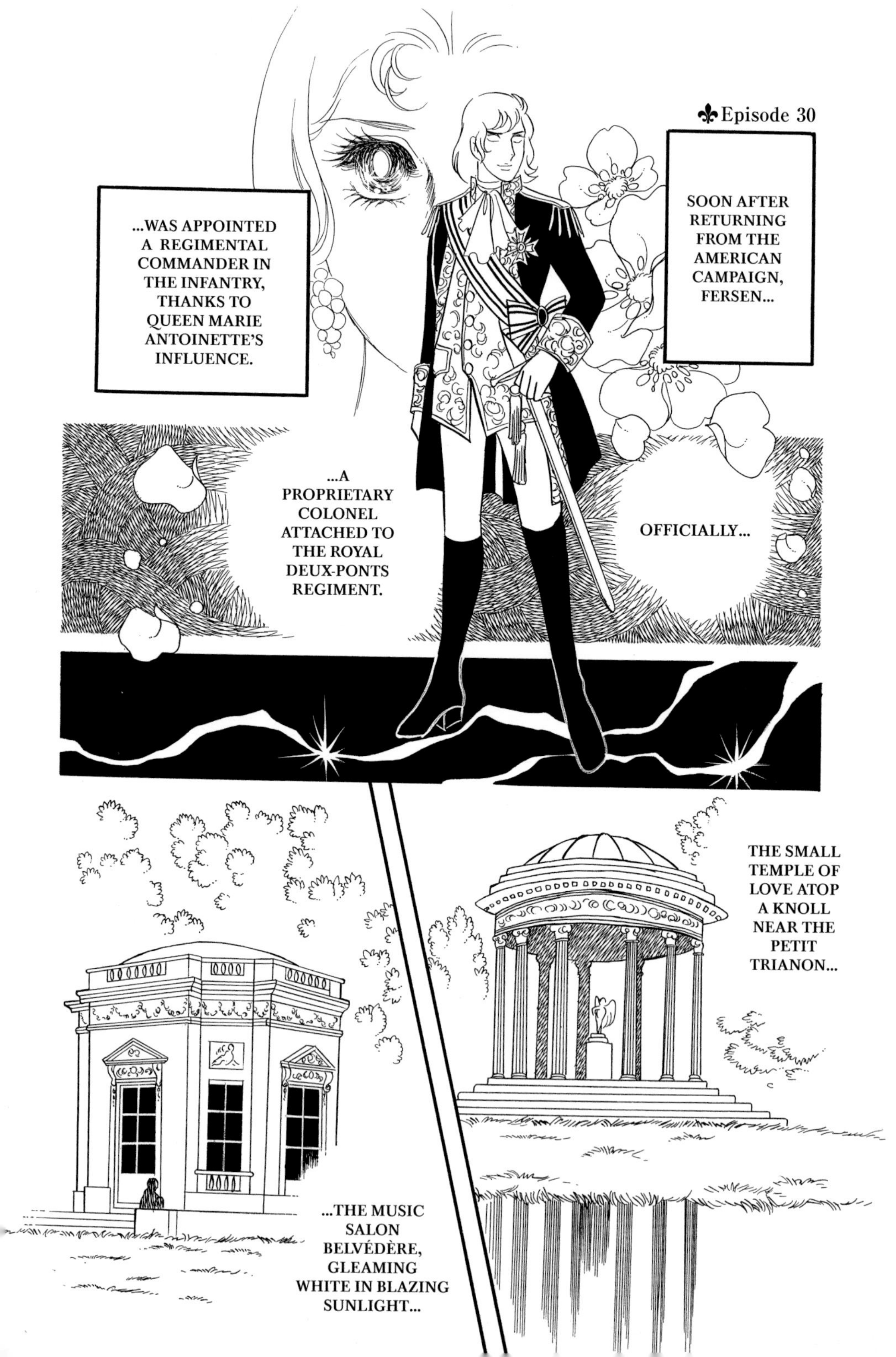

SOON AFTER RETURNING FROM THE AMERICAN CAMPAIGN, FERSEN...
...WAS APPOINTED A REGIMENTAL COMMANDER IN THE INFANTRY, THANKS TO QUEEN MARIE ANTOINETTE'S INFLUENCE.
OFFICIALLY...
...A PROPRIETARY COLONEL ATTACHED TO THE ROYAL DEUX-PONTS REGIMENT.
THE SMALL TEMPLE OF LOVE ATOP A KNOLL NEAR THE PETIT TRIANON...
...THE MUSIC SALON BELVÉDÈRE, GLEAMING WHITE IN BLAZING SUNLIGHT...

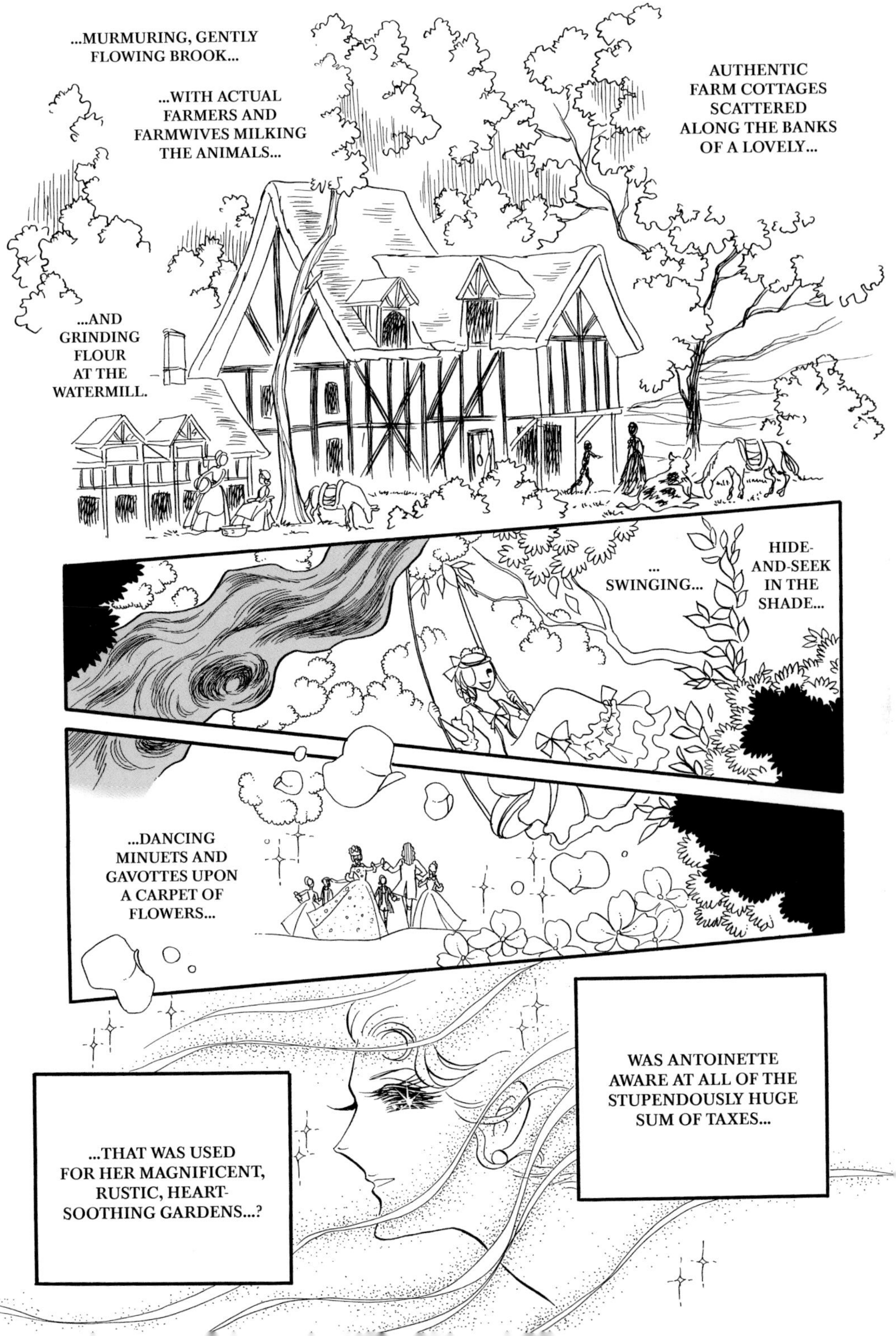
AUTHENTIC FARM COTTAGES SCATTERED ALONG THE BANKS OF A LOVELY...
...MURMURING, GENTLY FLOWING BROOK...
...WITH ACTUAL FARMERS AND FARMWIVES MILKING THE ANIMALS...
...AND GRINDING FLOUR AT THE WATERMILL.
HIDE-AND-SEEK IN THE SHADE...
...SWINGING...
...DANCING MINUETS AND GAVOTTES UPON A CARPET OF FLOWERS...
WAS ANTOINETTE AWARE AT ALL OF THE STUPENDOUSLY HUGE SUM OF TAXES...
...THAT WAS USED FOR HER MAGNIFICENT, RUSTIC, HEART-SOOTHING GARDENS...?

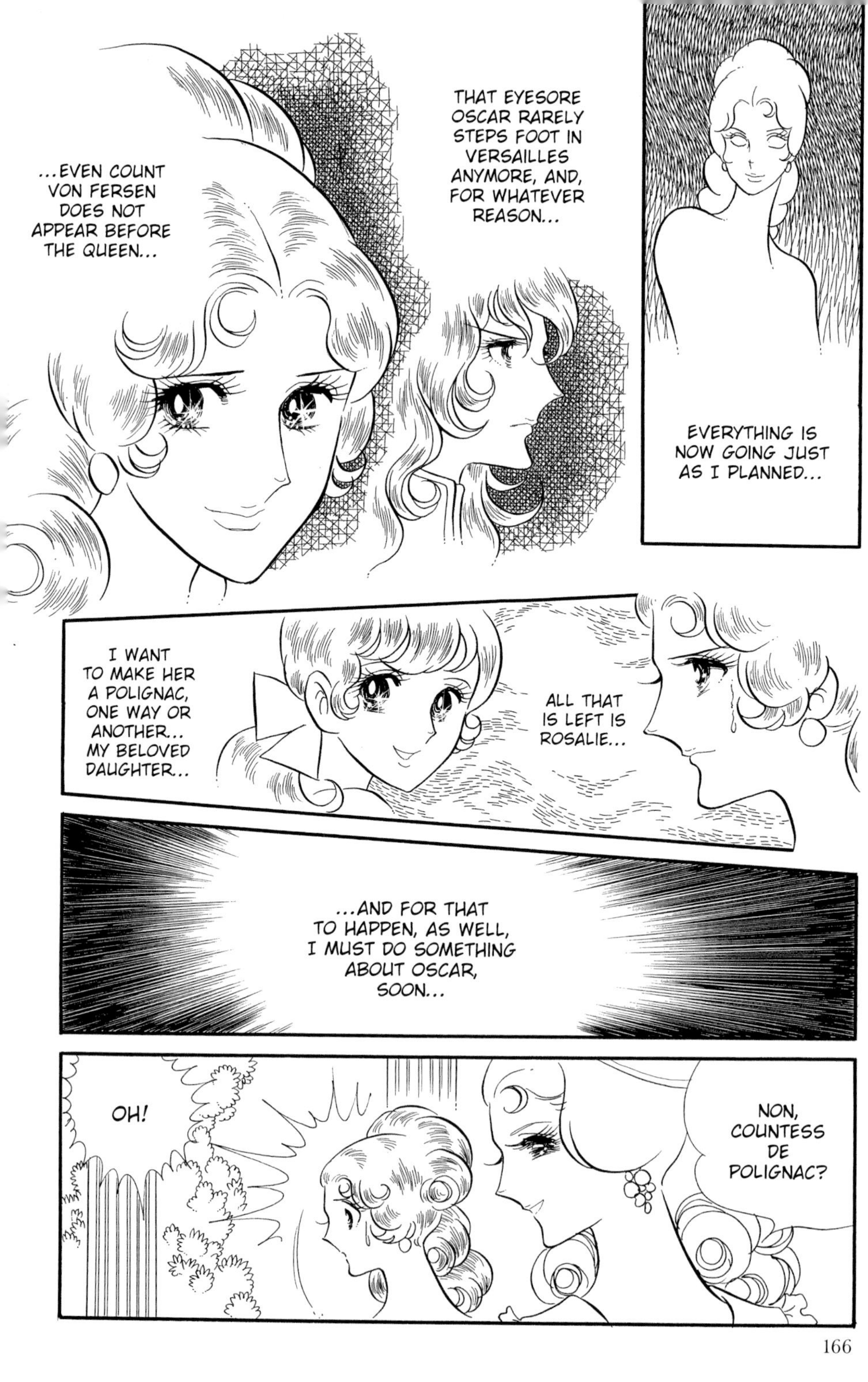
EVERYTHING IS NOW GOING JUST AS I PLANNED...
THAT EYESORE OSCAR RARELY STEPS FOOT IN VERSAILLES ANYMORE, AND, FOR WHATEVER REASON...
...EVEN COUNT VON FERSEN DOES NOT APPEAR BEFORE THE QUEEN...
ALL THAT IS LEFT IS ROSALIE...
I WANT TO MAKE HER A POLIGNAC, ONE WAY OR ANOTHER... MY BELOVED DAUGHTER...
...AND FOR THAT TO HAPPEN, AS WELL, I MUST DO SOMETHING ABOUT OSCAR, SOON...
NON, COUNTESS DE POLIGNAC?
OH!

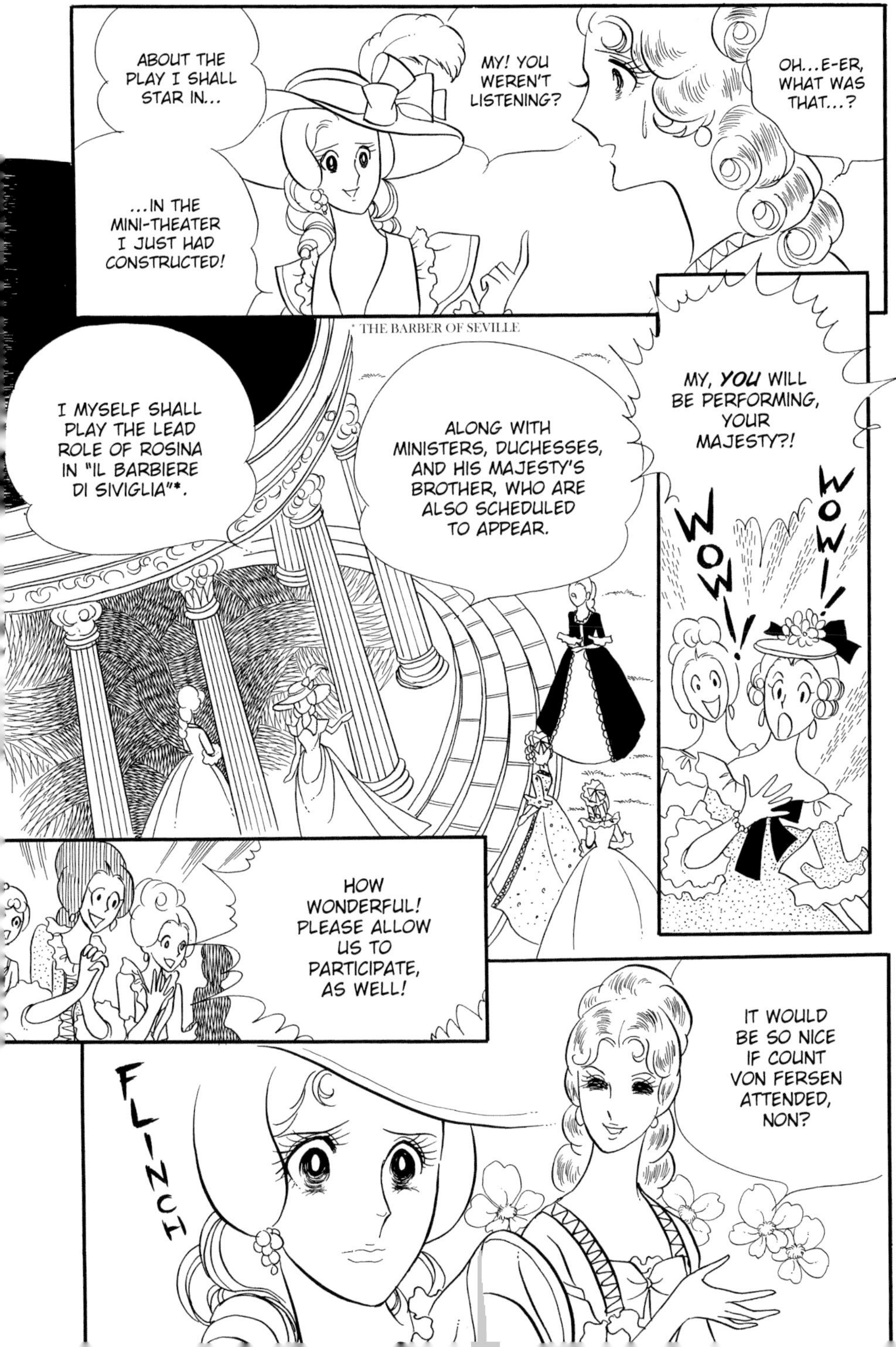
OH...E-ER, WHAT WAS THAT...?
MY! YOU WEREN'T LISTENING?
ABOUT THE PLAY I SHALL STAR IN...
...IN THE MINI-THEATER I JUST HAD CONSTRUCTED!
* THE BARBER OF SEVILLE
I MYSELF SHALL PLAY THE LEAD ROLE OF ROSINA IN "IL BARBIERE DI SIVIGLIA"*.
ALONG WITH MINISTERS, DUCHESSES, AND HIS MAJESTY'S BROTHER, WHO ARE ALSO SCHEDULED TO APPEAR.
MY, *YOU* WILL BE PERFORMING, YOUR MAJESTY?!
WOW!
WOW!
HOW WONDERFUL! PLEASE ALLOW US TO PARTICIPATE, AS WELL!
IT WOULD BE SO NICE IF COUNT VON FERSEN ATTENDED, NON?
FLINCH

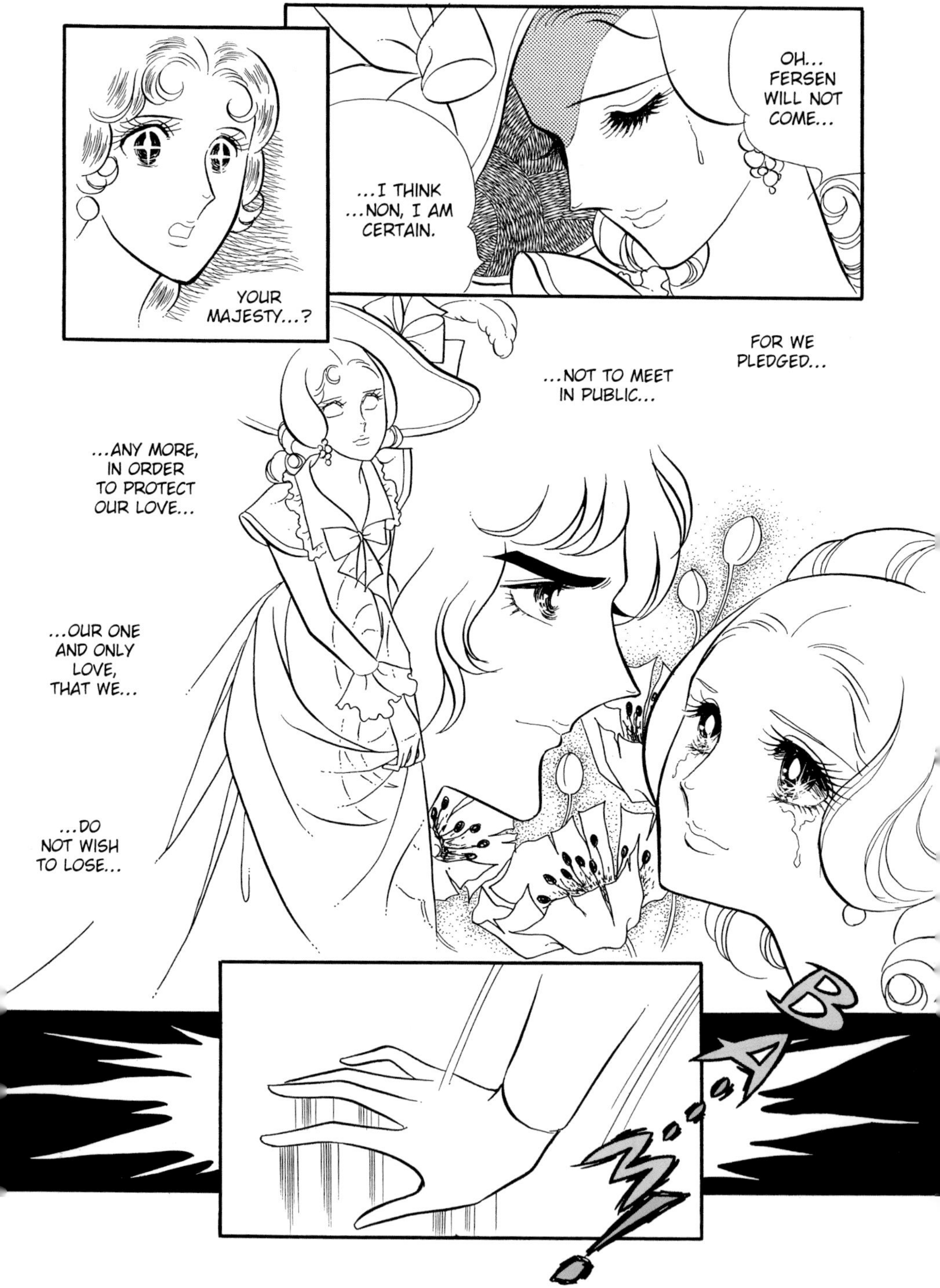
OH... FERSEN WILL NOT COME...
...I THINK ...NON, I AM CERTAIN.
YOUR MAJESTY...?
FOR WE PLEDGED...
...NOT TO MEET IN PUBLIC...
...ANY MORE, IN ORDER TO PROTECT OUR LOVE...
...OUR ONE AND ONLY LOVE, THAT WE...
...DO NOT WISH TO LOSE...
BA...M!

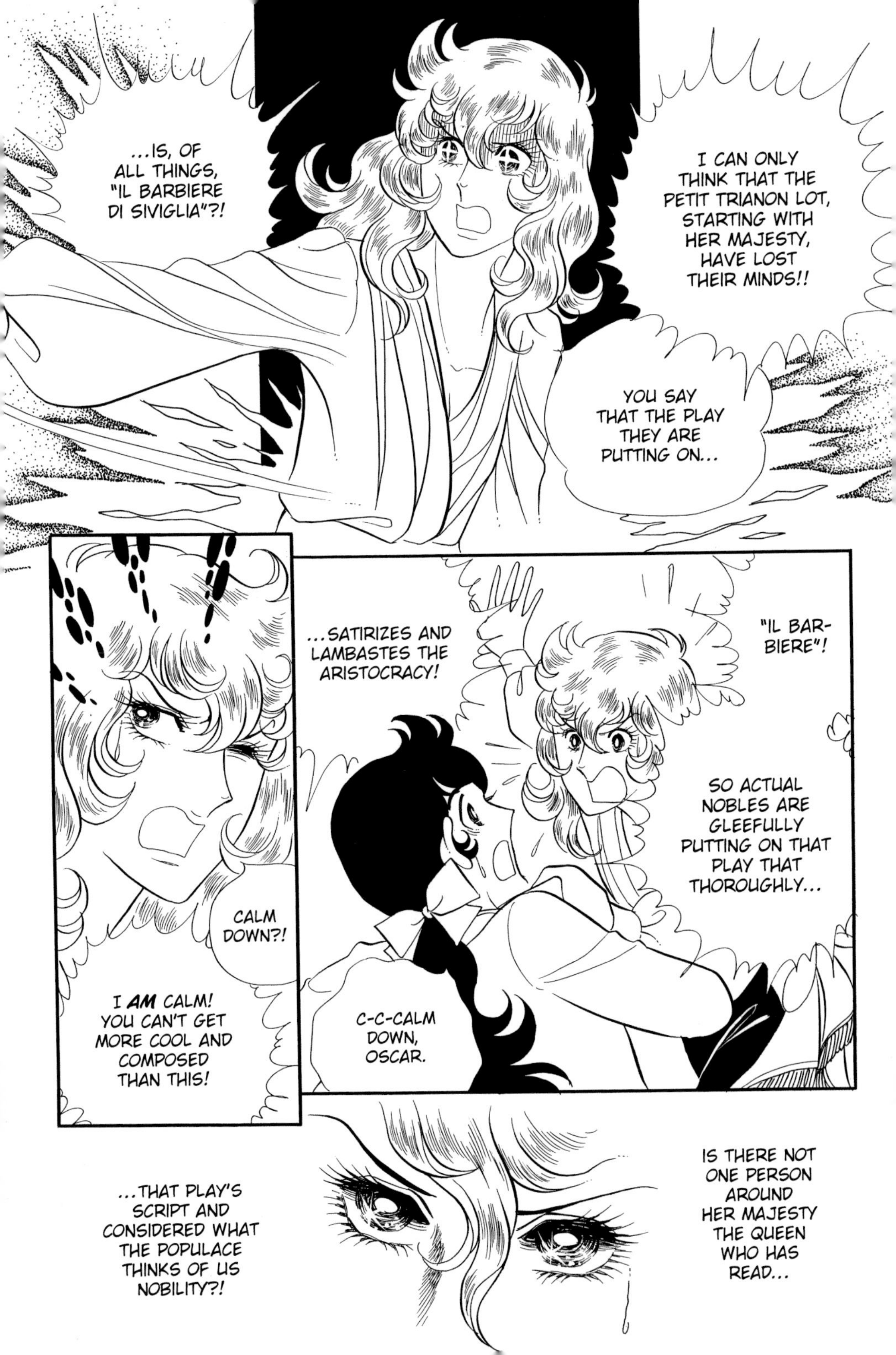
I CAN ONLY THINK THAT THE PETIT TRIANON LOT, STARTING WITH HER MAJESTY, HAVE LOST THEIR MINDS!!
YOU SAY THAT THE PLAY THEY ARE PUTTING ON...
...IS, OF ALL THINGS, "IL BARBIERE DI SIVIGLIA"?!
"IL BAR-BIERE"!
SO ACTUAL NOBLES ARE GLEEFULLY PUTTING ON THAT PLAY THAT THOROUGHLY...
...SATIRIZES AND LAMBASTES THE ARISTOCRACY!
C-C-CALM DOWN, OSCAR.
CALM DOWN?!
I *AM* CALM! YOU CAN'T GET MORE COOL AND COMPOSED THAN THIS!
IS THERE NOT ONE PERSON AROUND HER MAJESTY THE QUEEN WHO HAS READ...
...THAT PLAY'S SCRIPT AND CONSIDERED WHAT THE POPULACE THINKS OF US NOBILITY?!

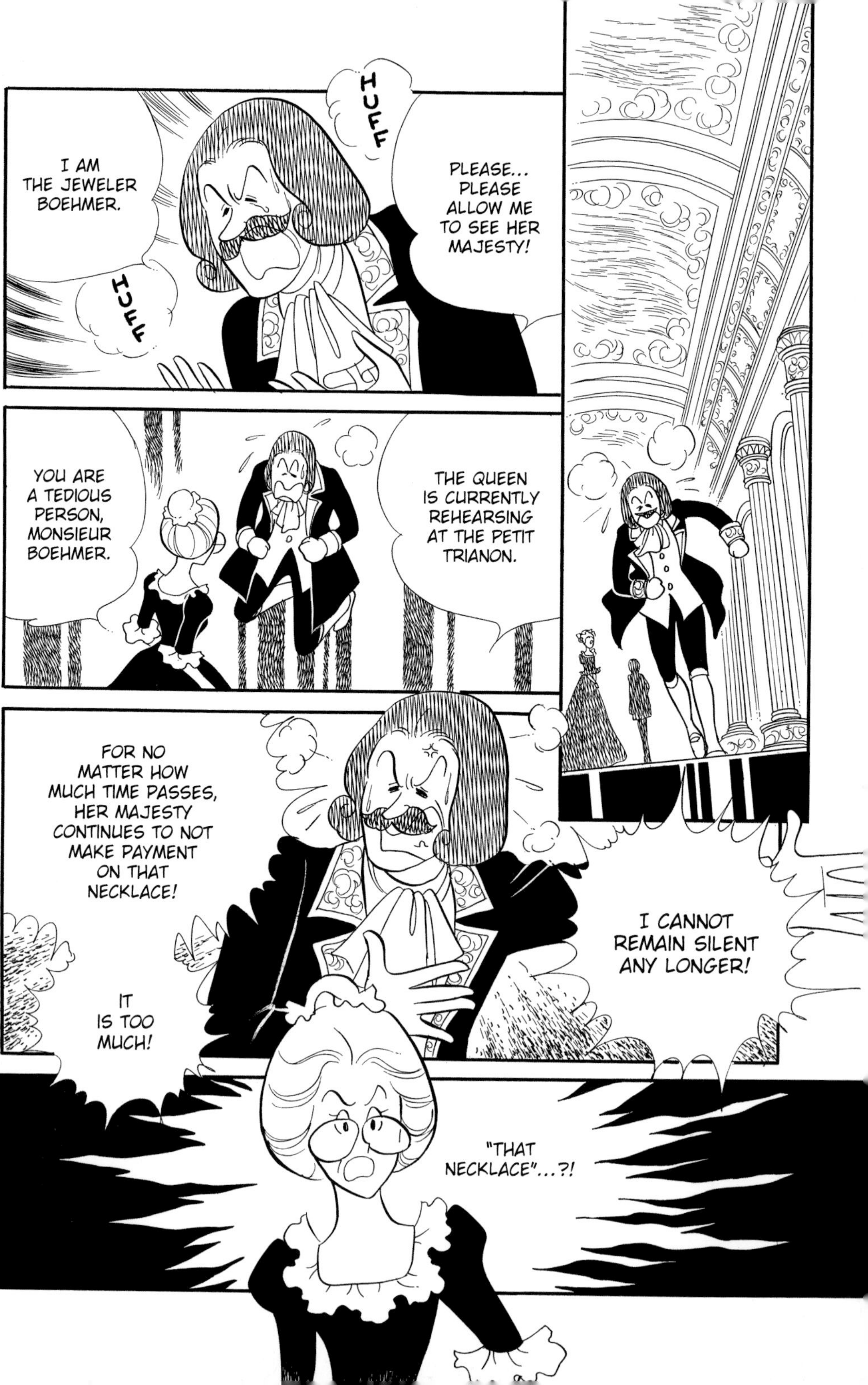
HUFF
PLEASE... PLEASE ALLOW ME TO SEE HER MAJESTY!
I AM THE JEWELER BOEHMER.
HUFF
THE QUEEN IS CURRENTLY REHEARSING AT THE PETIT TRIANON.
YOU ARE A TEDIOUS PERSON, MONSIEUR BOEHMER.
I CANNOT REMAIN SILENT ANY LONGER!
FOR NO MATTER HOW MUCH TIME PASSES, HER MAJESTY CONTINUES TO NOT MAKE PAYMENT ON THAT NECKLACE!
IT IS TOO MUCH!
"THAT NECKLACE"...?!

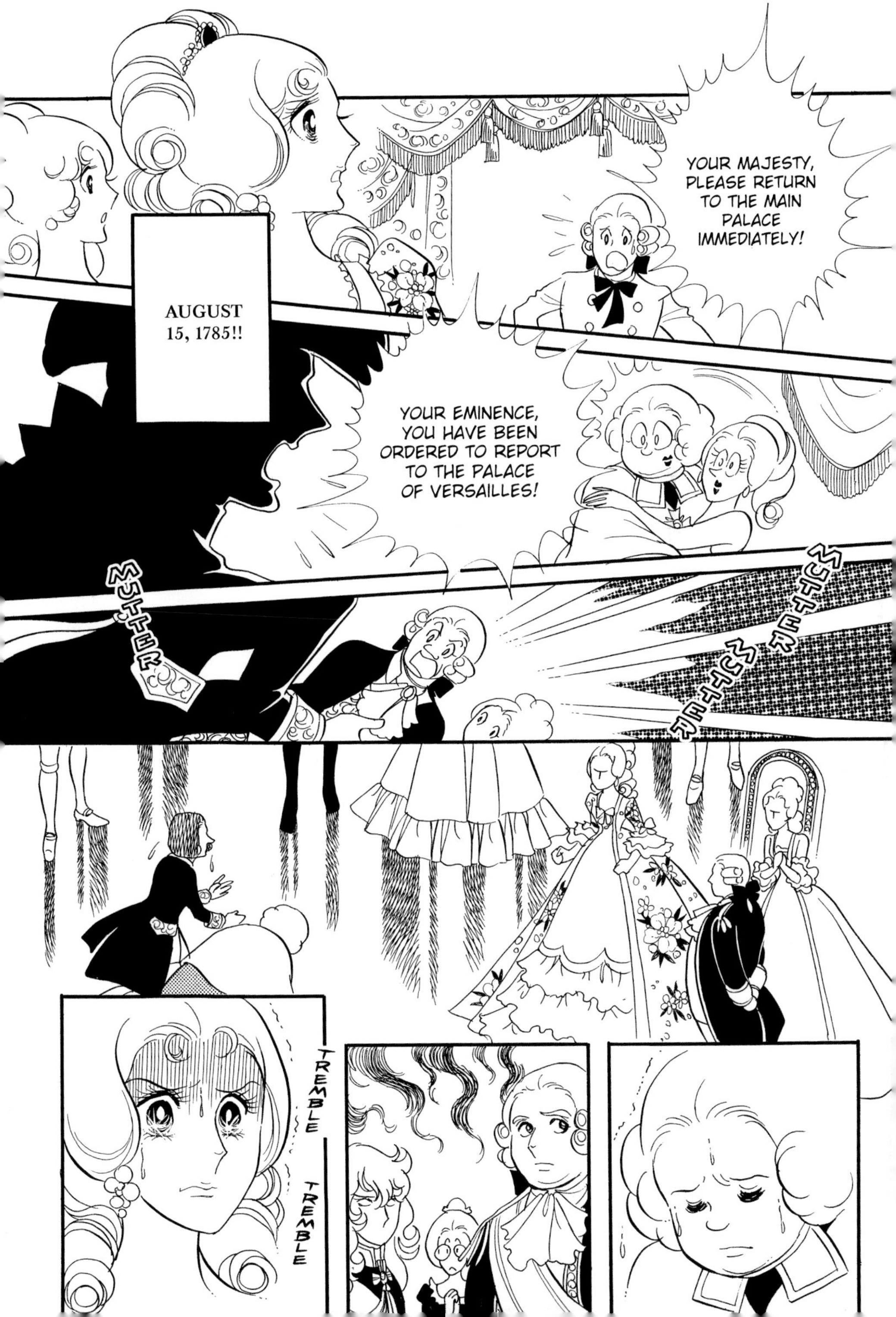
YOUR MAJESTY, PLEASE RETURN TO THE MAIN PALACE IMMEDIATELY!
AUGUST 15, 1785!!
YOUR EMINENCE, YOU HAVE BEEN ORDERED TO REPORT TO THE PALACE OF VERSAILLES!
MUTTER MUTTER
MUTTER
TREMBLE TREMBLE

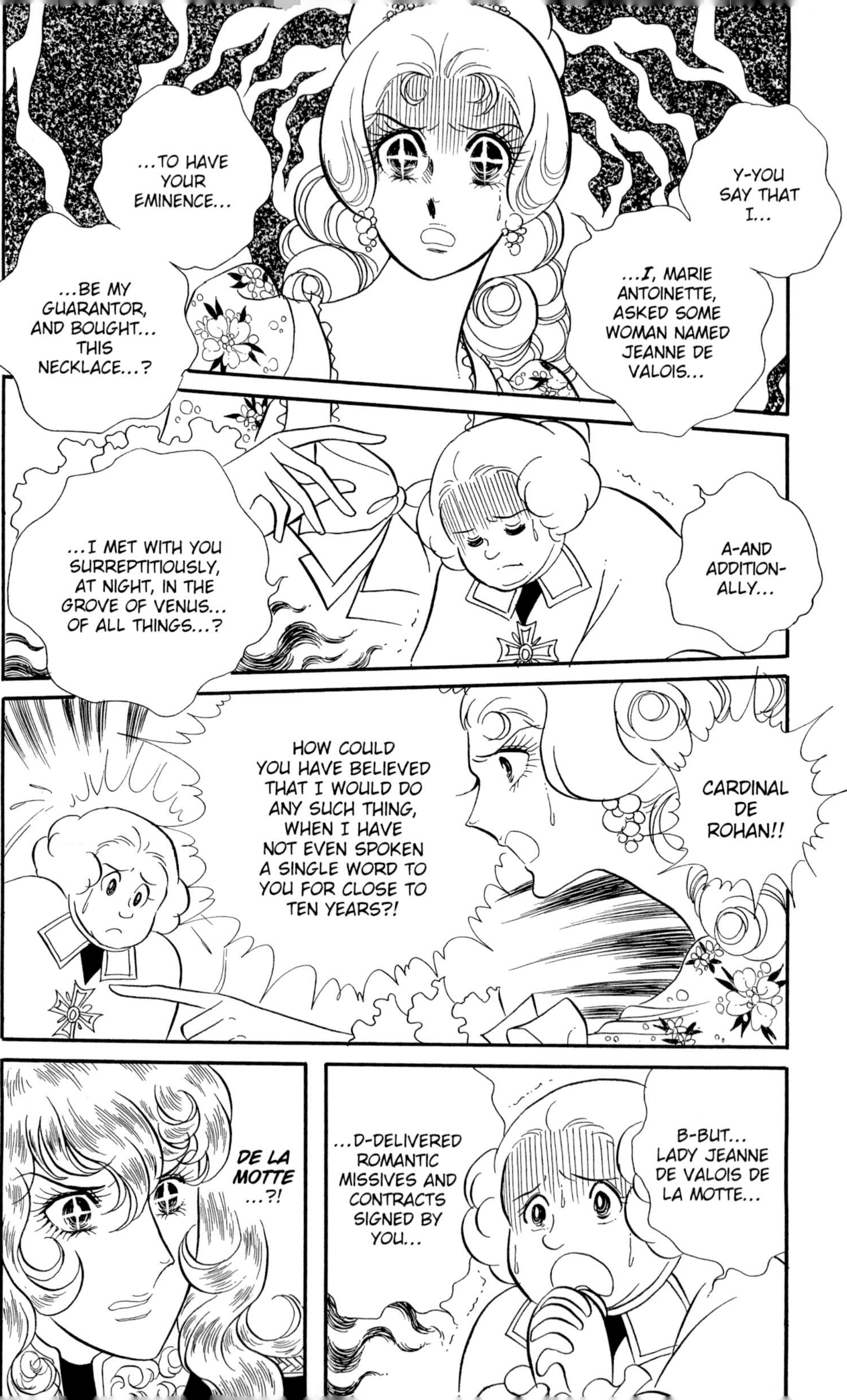
Y-YOU SAY THAT I...
...*I*, MARIE ANTOINETTE, ASKED SOME WOMAN NAMED JEANNE DE VALOIS...
...TO HAVE YOUR EMINENCE...
...BE MY GUARANTOR, AND BOUGHT... THIS NECKLACE...?
A-AND ADDITION-ALLY...
...I MET WITH YOU SURREPTITIOUSLY, AT NIGHT, IN THE GROVE OF VENUS... OF ALL THINGS...?
CARDINAL DE ROHAN!!
HOW COULD YOU HAVE BELIEVED THAT I WOULD DO ANY SUCH THING, WHEN I HAVE NOT EVEN SPOKEN A SINGLE WORD TO YOU FOR CLOSE TO TEN YEARS?!
B-BUT... LADY JEANNE DE VALOIS DE LA MOTTE...
...D-DELIVERED ROMANTIC MISSIVES AND CONTRACTS SIGNED BY YOU...
DE LA MOTTE...?!

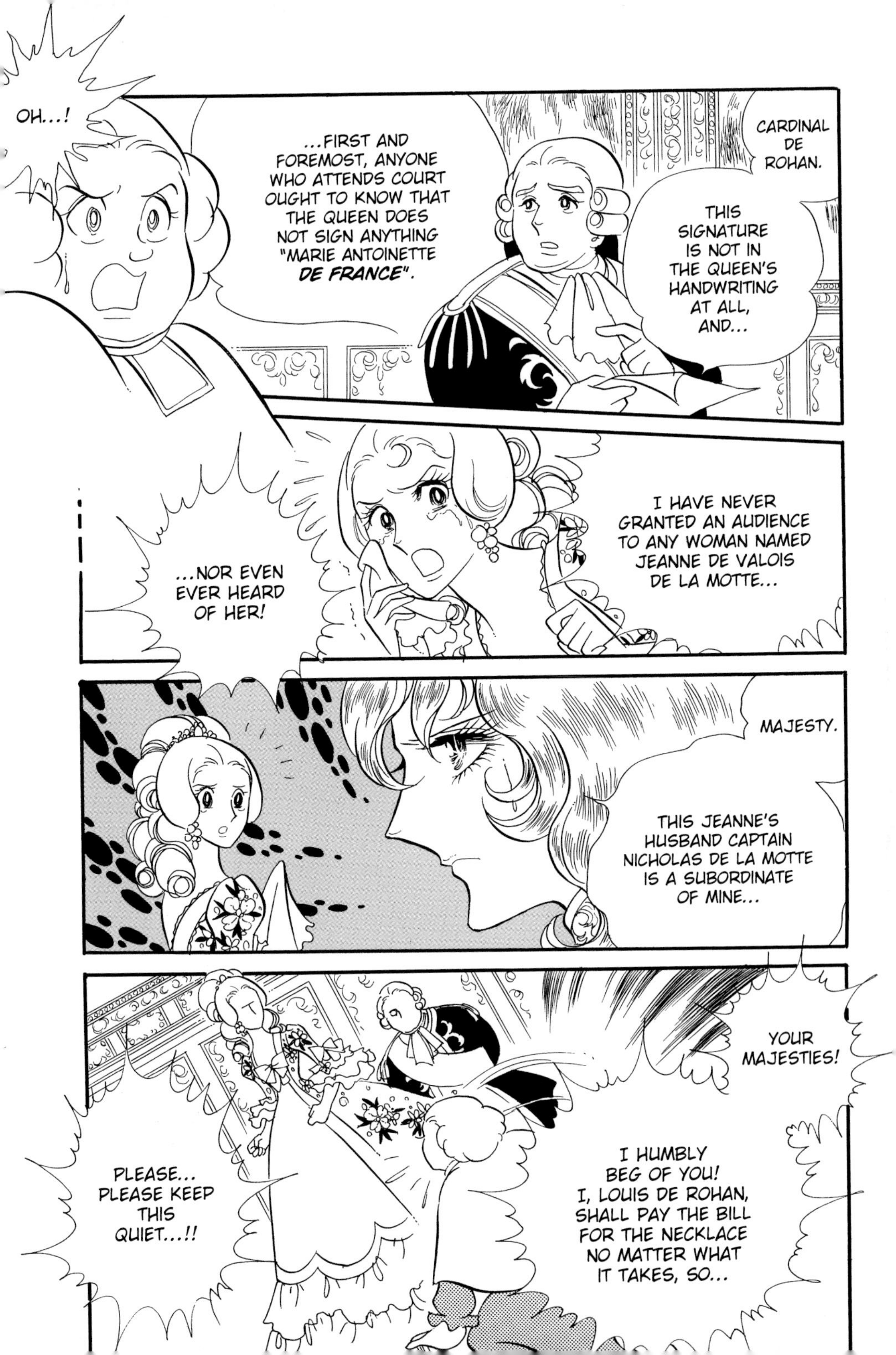
CARDINAL DE ROHAN.
THIS SIGNATURE IS NOT IN THE QUEEN'S HANDWRITING AT ALL, AND...
...FIRST AND FOREMOST, ANYONE WHO ATTENDS COURT OUGHT TO KNOW THAT THE QUEEN DOES NOT SIGN ANYTHING "MARIE ANTOINETTE ***DE FRANCE***".
OH...!
I HAVE NEVER GRANTED AN AUDIENCE TO ANY WOMAN NAMED JEANNE DE VALOIS DE LA MOTTE...
...NOR EVEN EVER HEARD OF HER!
MAJESTY.
THIS JEANNE'S HUSBAND CAPTAIN NICHOLAS DE LA MOTTE IS A SUBORDINATE OF MINE...
YOUR MAJESTIES!
I HUMBLY BEG OF YOU! I, LOUIS DE ROHAN, SHALL PAY THE BILL FOR THE NECKLACE NO MATTER WHAT IT TAKES, SO...
PLEASE... PLEASE KEEP THIS QUIET...!!

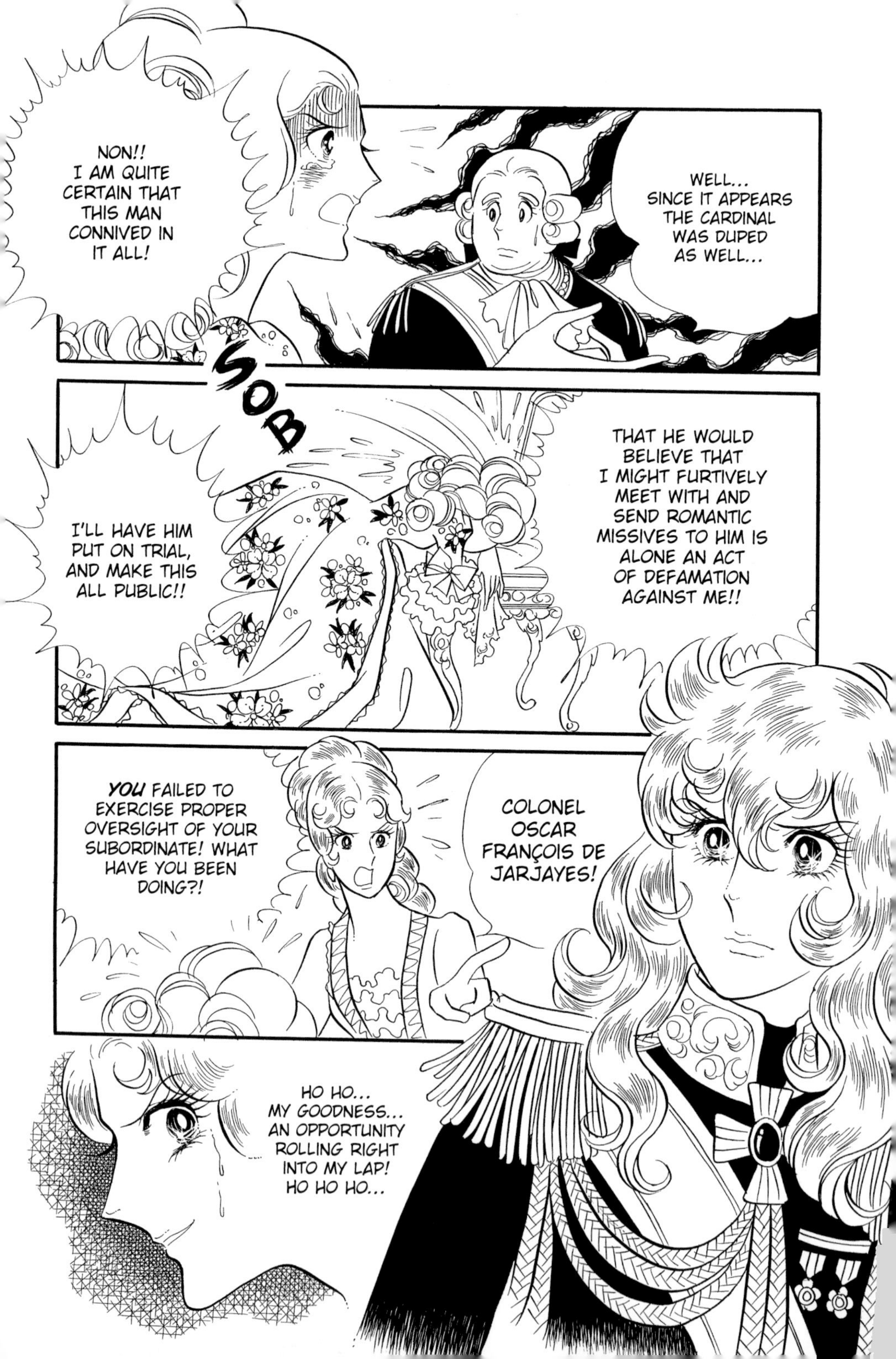
WELL... SINCE IT APPEARS THE CARDINAL WAS DUPED AS WELL...
NON!! I AM QUITE CERTAIN THAT THIS MAN CONNIVED IN IT ALL!
SOB
THAT HE WOULD BELIEVE THAT I MIGHT FURTIVELY MEET WITH AND SEND ROMANTIC MISSIVES TO HIM IS ALONE AN ACT OF DEFAMATION AGAINST ME!!
I'LL HAVE HIM PUT ON TRIAL, AND MAKE THIS ALL PUBLIC!!
COLONEL OSCAR FRANÇOIS DE JARJAYES!
YOU FAILED TO EXERCISE PROPER OVERSIGHT OF YOUR SUBORDINATE! WHAT HAVE YOU BEEN DOING?!
HO HO... MY GOODNESS... AN OPPORTUNITY ROLLING RIGHT INTO MY LAP! HO HO HO...

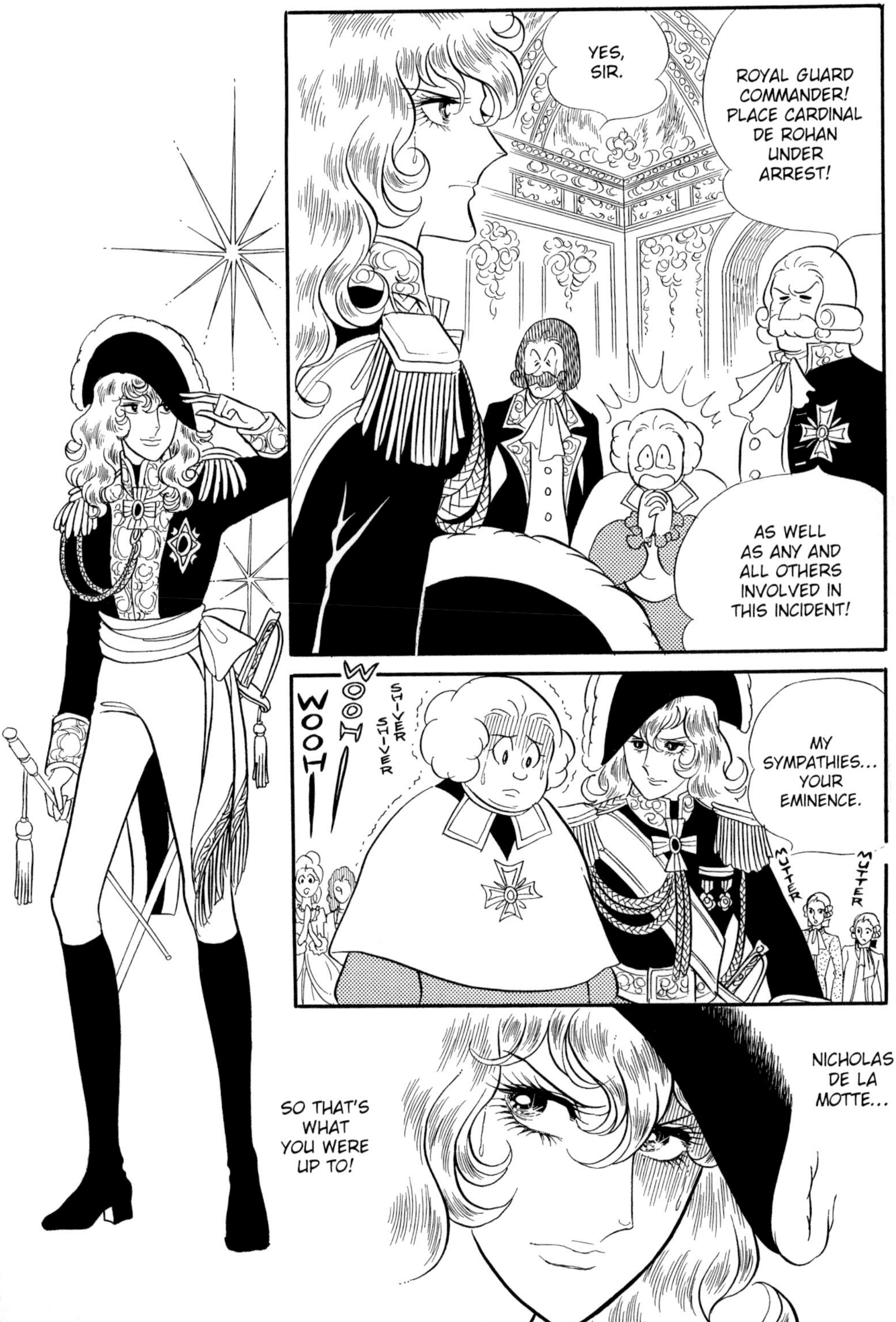
ROYAL GUARD COMMANDER! PLACE CARDINAL DE ROHAN UNDER ARREST!
AS WELL AS ANY AND ALL OTHERS INVOLVED IN THIS INCIDENT!
YES, SIR.
MY SYMPATHIES... YOUR EMINENCE.
MUTTER
MUTTER
SHIVER SHIVER
WOOH!
WOOH!
NICHOLAS DE LA MOTTE...
SO THAT'S WHAT YOU WERE UP TO!

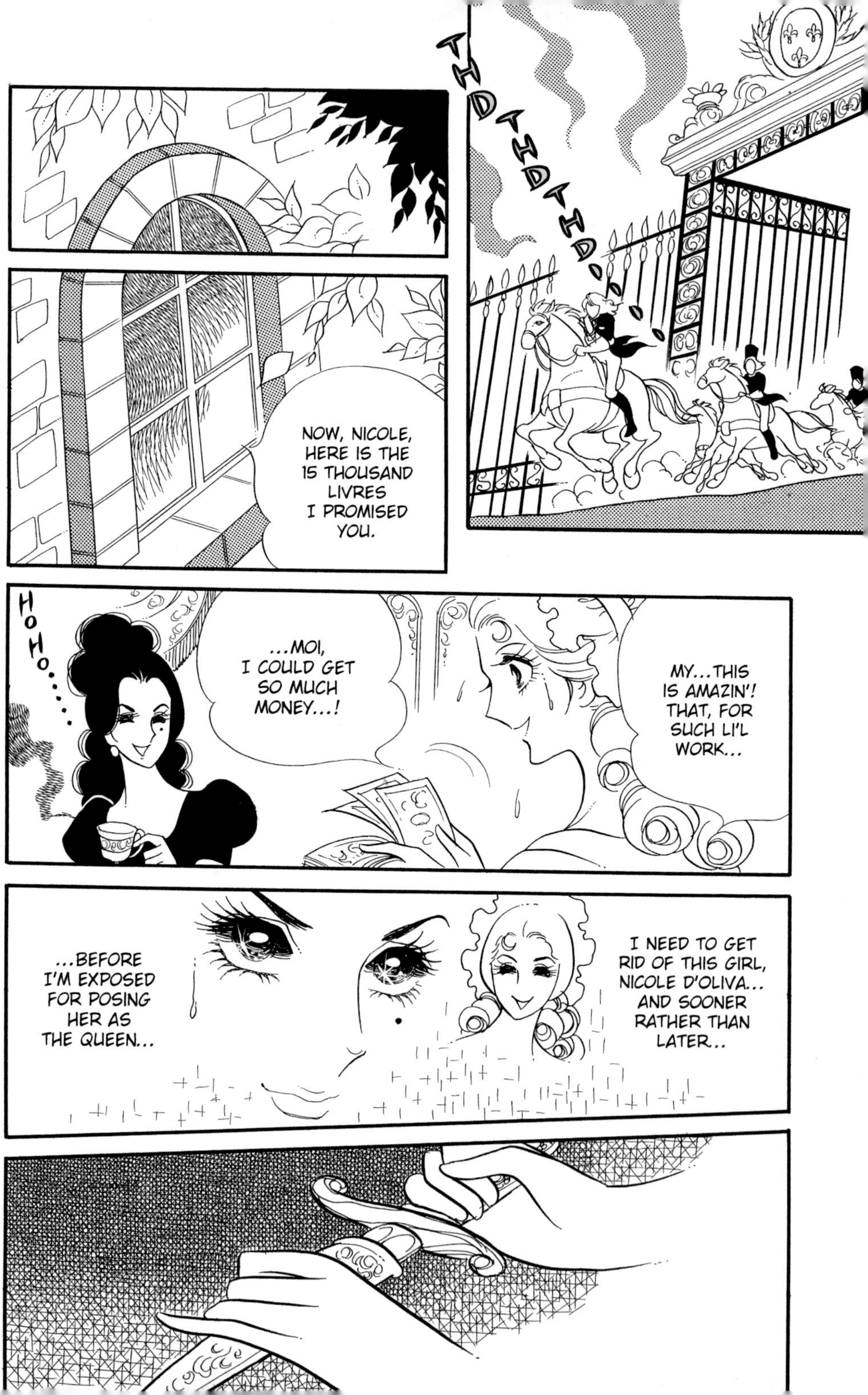
THDTHDTHDTHD...
NOW, NICOLE, HERE IS THE 15 THOUSAND LIVRES I PROMISED YOU.
MY...THIS IS AMAZIN'! THAT, FOR SUCH LI'L WORK...
...MOI, I COULD GET SO MUCH MONEY...!
HoHo.....
I NEED TO GET RID OF THIS GIRL, NICOLE D'OLIVA... AND SOONER RATHER THAN LATER...
...BEFORE I'M EXPOSED FOR POSING HER AS THE QUEEN...

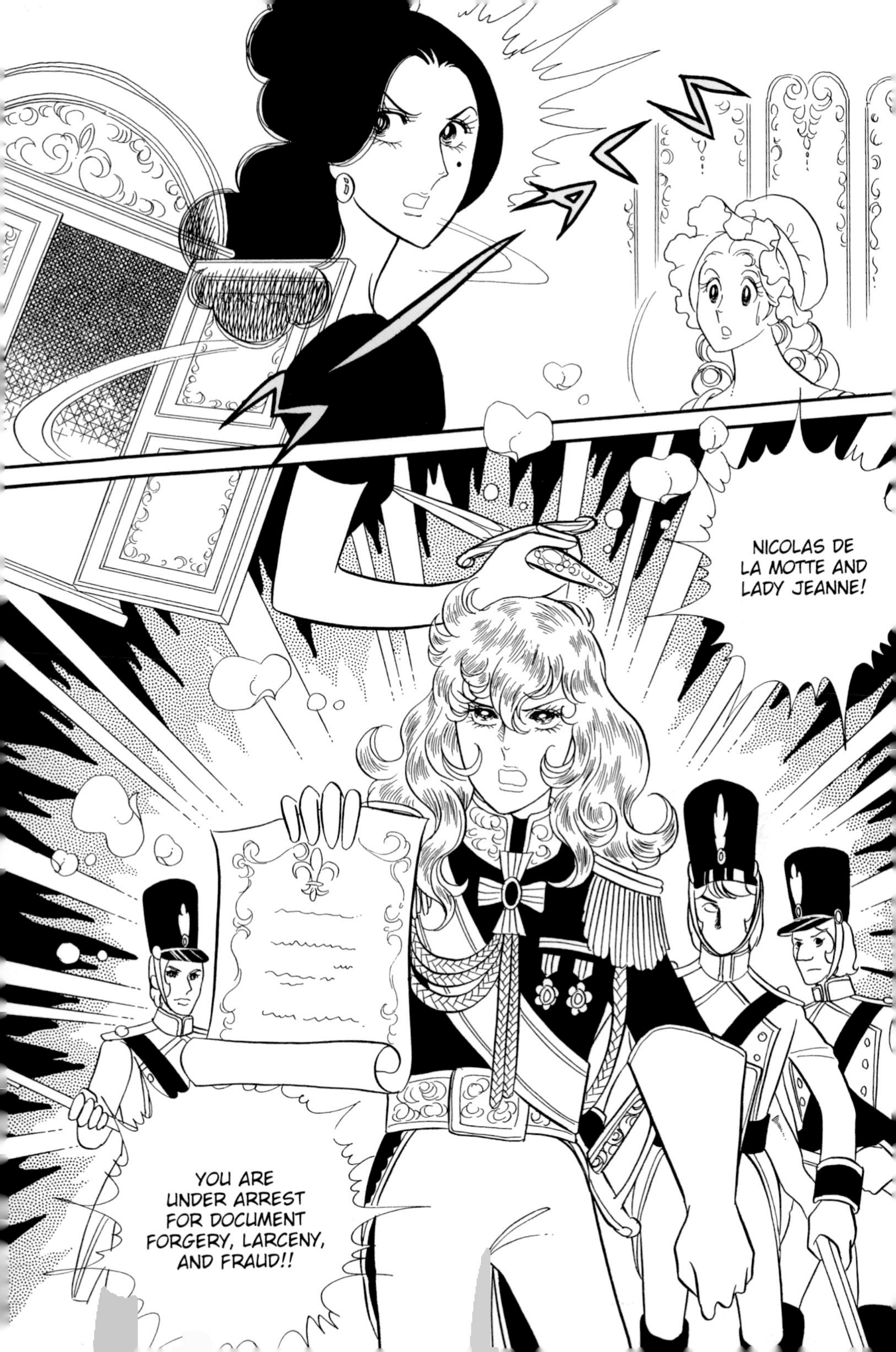
NICOLAS DE LA MOTTE AND LADY JEANNE!
YOU ARE UNDER ARREST FOR DOCUMENT FORGERY, LARCENY, AND FRAUD!!

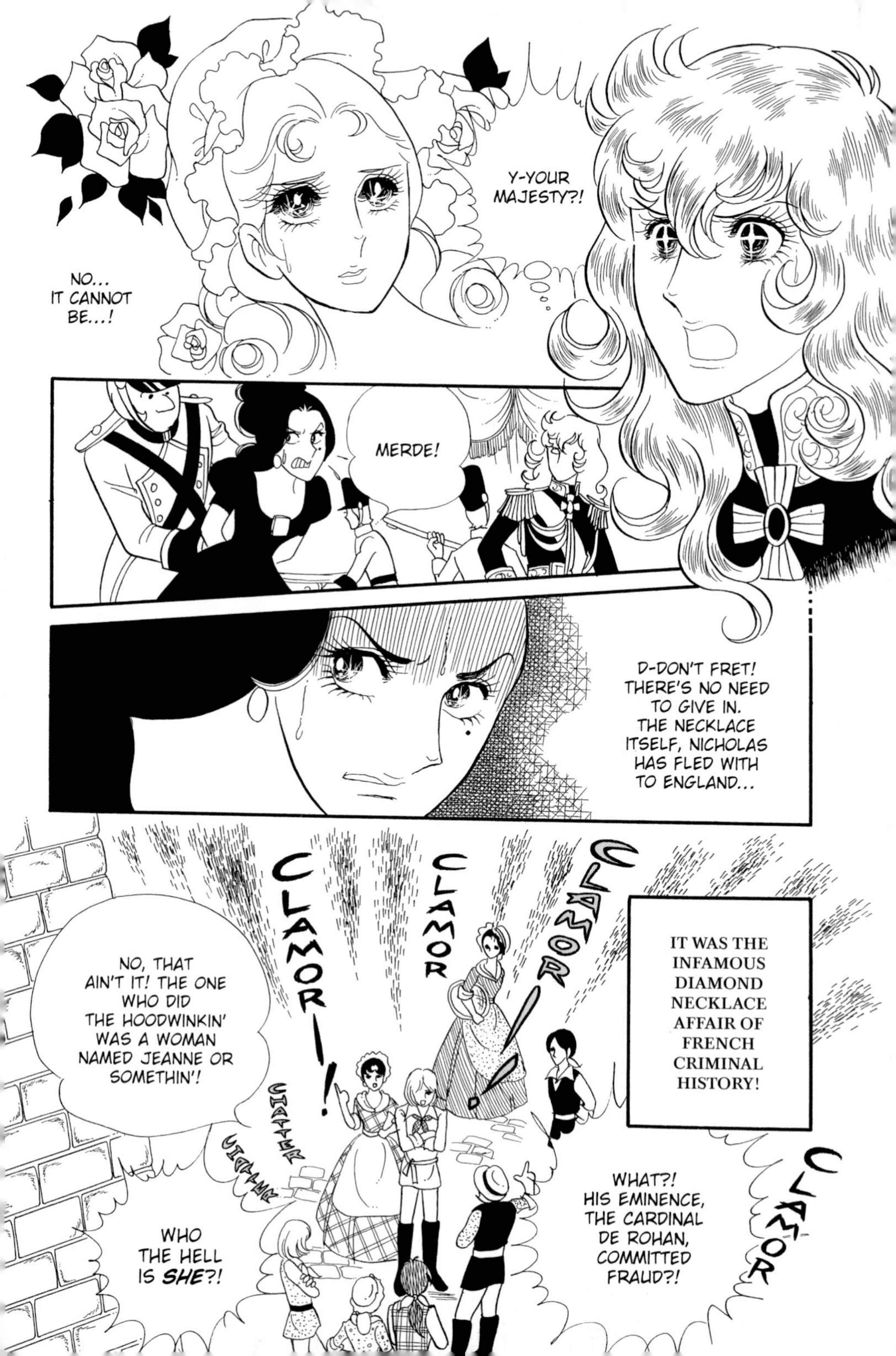

Y-YOUR MAJESTY?!
NO... IT CANNOT BE...!
MERDE!
D-DON'T FRET! THERE'S NO NEED TO GIVE IN. THE NECKLACE ITSELF, NICHOLAS HAS FLED WITH TO ENGLAND...
IT WAS THE INFAMOUS DIAMOND NECKLACE AFFAIR OF FRENCH CRIMINAL HISTORY!
CLAMOR
CLAMOR
CLAMOR!!
WHAT?! HIS EMINENCE, THE CARDINAL DE ROHAN, COMMITTED FRAUD?!
CLAMOR
NO, THAT AIN'T IT! THE ONE WHO DID THE HOODWINKIN' WAS A WOMAN NAMED JEANNE OR SOMETHIN'!
CHATTER
CHATTER
WHO THE HELL IS *SHE*?!

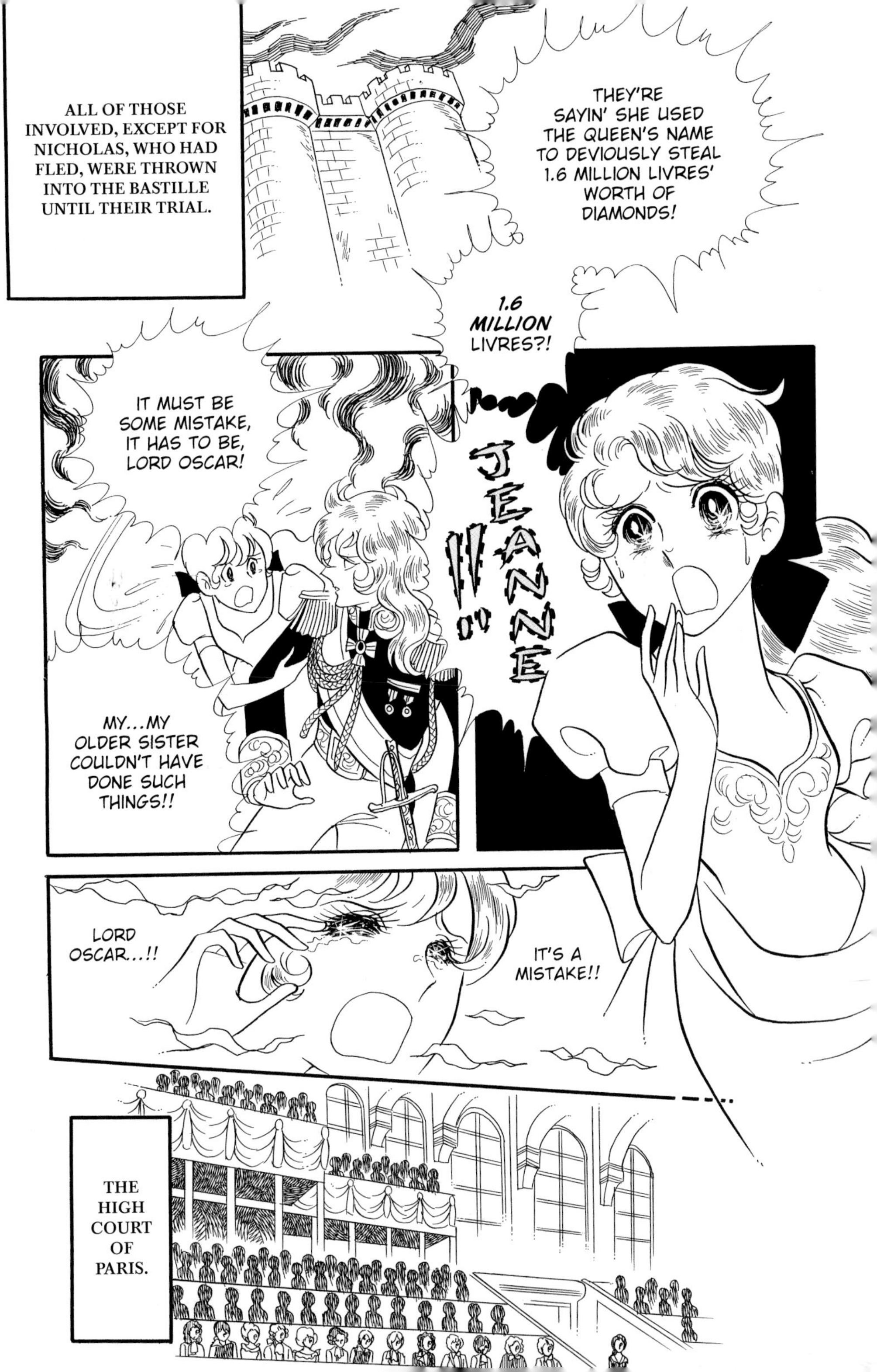

THEY'RE SAYIN' SHE USED THE QUEEN'S NAME TO DEVIOUSLY STEAL 1.6 MILLION LIVRES' WORTH OF DIAMONDS!
ALL OF THOSE INVOLVED, EXCEPT FOR NICHOLAS, WHO HAD FLED, WERE THROWN INTO THE BASTILLE UNTIL THEIR TRIAL.
1.6 MILLION LIVRES?!
JEANNE!!
IT MUST BE SOME MISTAKE, IT HAS TO BE, LORD OSCAR!
MY...MY OLDER SISTER COULDN'T HAVE DONE SUCH THINGS!!
IT'S A MISTAKE!!
LORD OSCAR...!!
THE HIGH COURT OF PARIS.

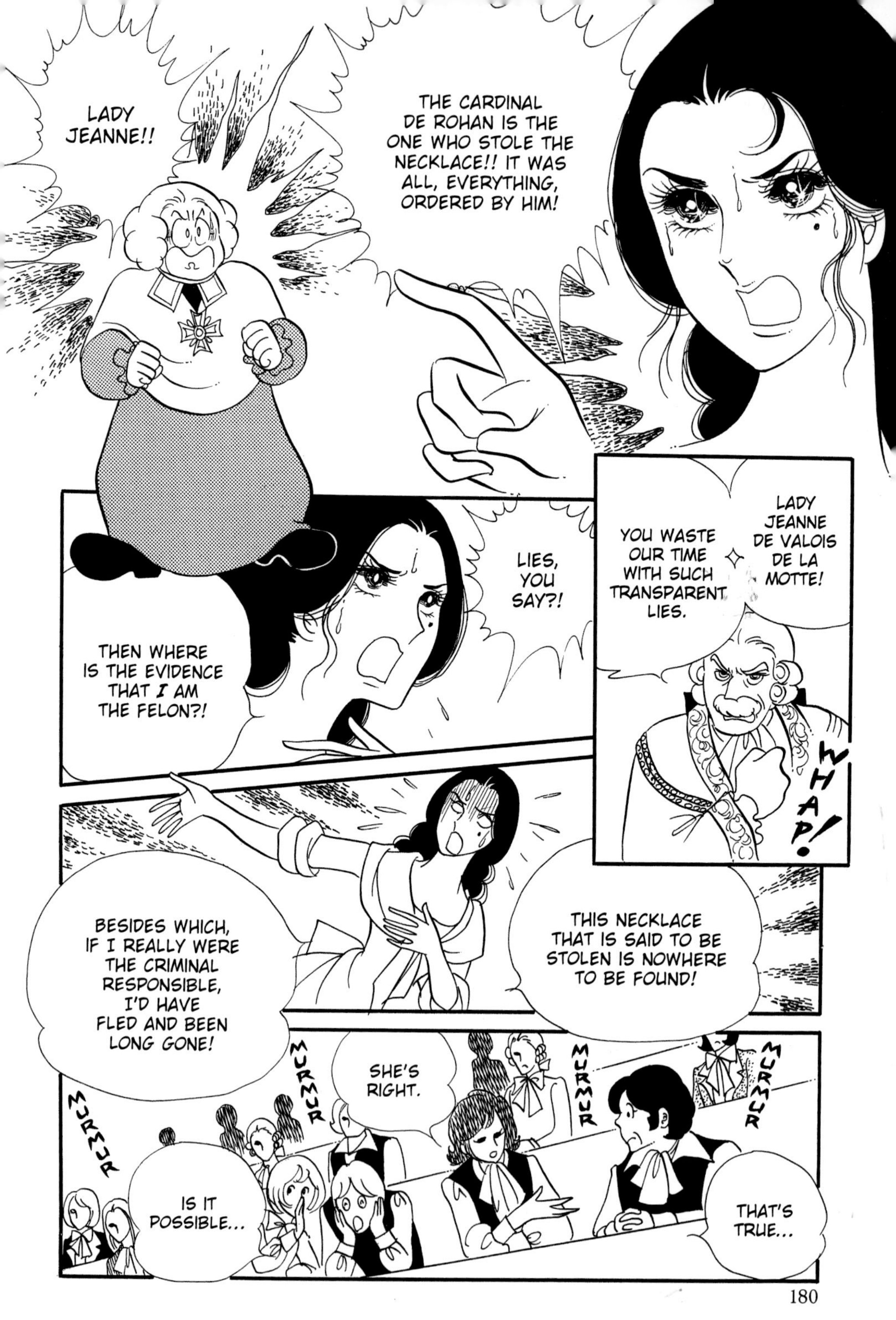
THE CARDINAL DE ROHAN IS THE ONE WHO STOLE THE NECKLACE!! IT WAS ALL, EVERYTHING, ORDERED BY HIM!
LADY JEANNE!!
LADY JEANNE DE VALOIS DE LA MOTTE!
YOU WASTE OUR TIME WITH SUCH TRANSPARENT LIES.
WHAP!
LIES, YOU SAY?!
THEN WHERE IS THE EVIDENCE THAT *I* AM THE FELON?!
THIS NECKLACE THAT IS SAID TO BE STOLEN IS NOWHERE TO BE FOUND!
BESIDES WHICH, IF I REALLY WERE THE CRIMINAL RESPONSIBLE, I'D HAVE FLED AND BEEN LONG GONE!
MURMUR
THAT'S TRUE...
MURMUR
SHE'S RIGHT.
MURMUR
IS IT POSSIBLE...
MURMUR

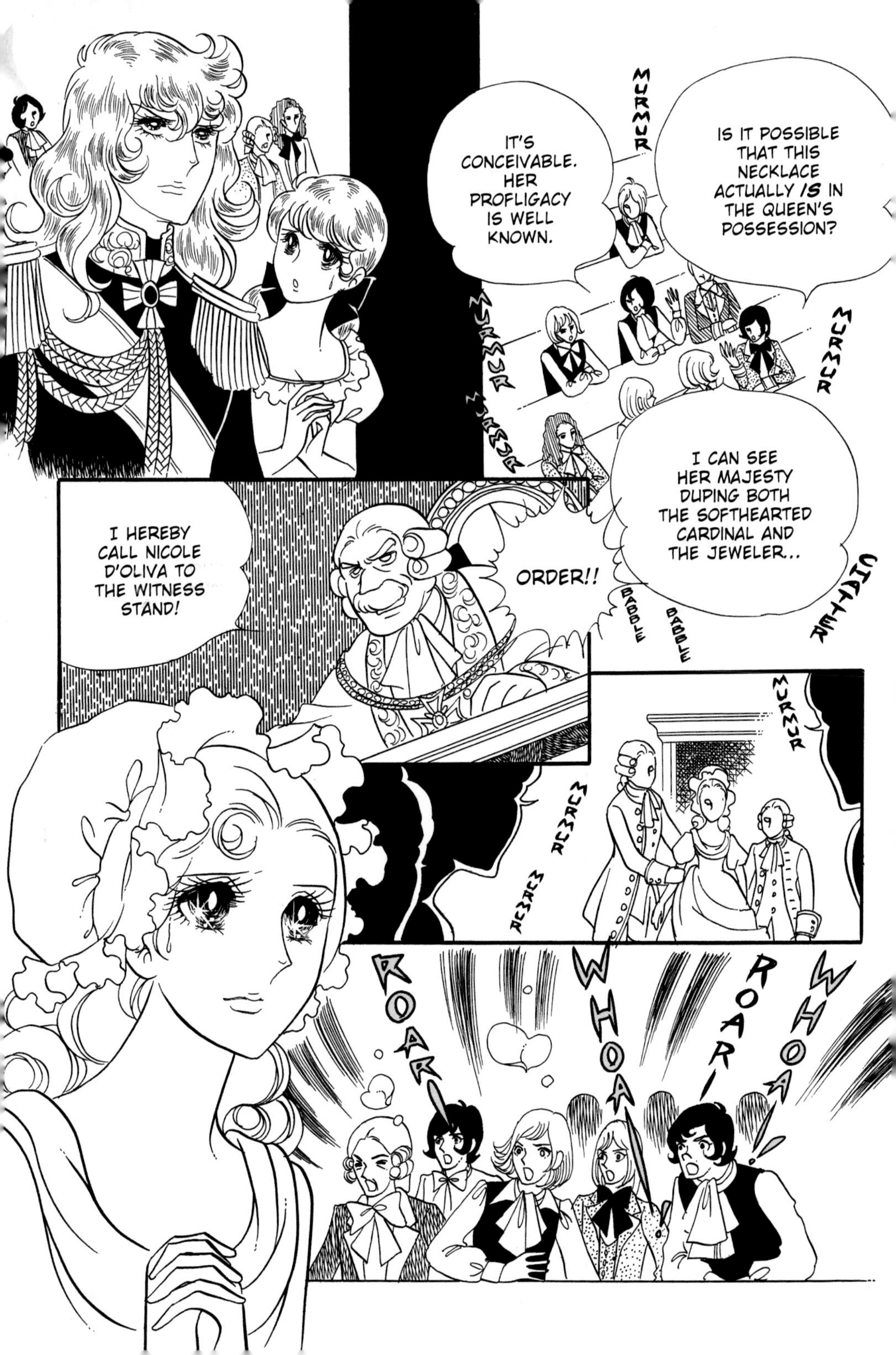
MURMUR
IS IT POSSIBLE THAT THIS NECKLACE ACTUALLY *IS* IN THE QUEEN'S POSSESSION?
IT'S CONCEIVABLE. HER PROFLIGACY IS WELL KNOWN.
MURMUR
MURMUR
MURMUR
I CAN SEE HER MAJESTY DUPING BOTH THE SOFTHEARTED CARDINAL AND THE JEWELER..
TITTER
BABBLE
BABBLE
ORDER!!
I HEREBY CALL NICOLE D'OLIVA TO THE WITNESS STAND!
MURMUR
MURMUR
MURMUR
WHOA!
ROAR!
WHOA!
ROAR!

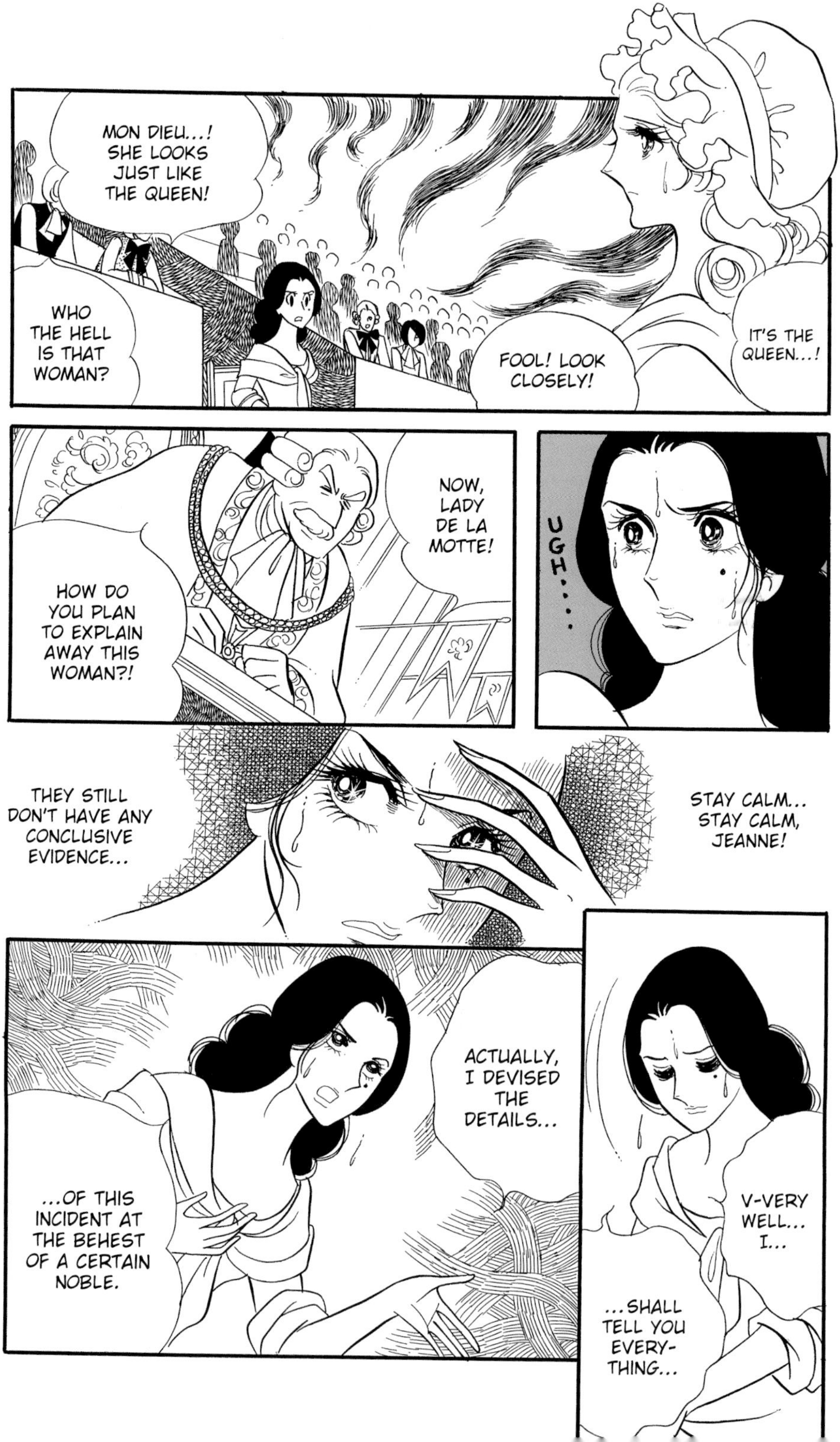
IT'S THE QUEEN...!
FOOL! LOOK CLOSELY!
MON DIEU...! SHE LOOKS JUST LIKE THE QUEEN!
WHO THE HELL IS THAT WOMAN?
UGH...
NOW, LADY DE LA MOTTE!
HOW DO YOU PLAN TO EXPLAIN AWAY THIS WOMAN?!
STAY CALM... STAY CALM, JEANNE!
THEY STILL DON'T HAVE ANY CONCLUSIVE EVIDENCE...
V-VERY WELL... I...
...SHALL TELL YOU EVERY-THING...
ACTUALLY, I DEVISED THE DETAILS...
...OF THIS INCIDENT AT THE BEHEST OF A CERTAIN NOBLE.

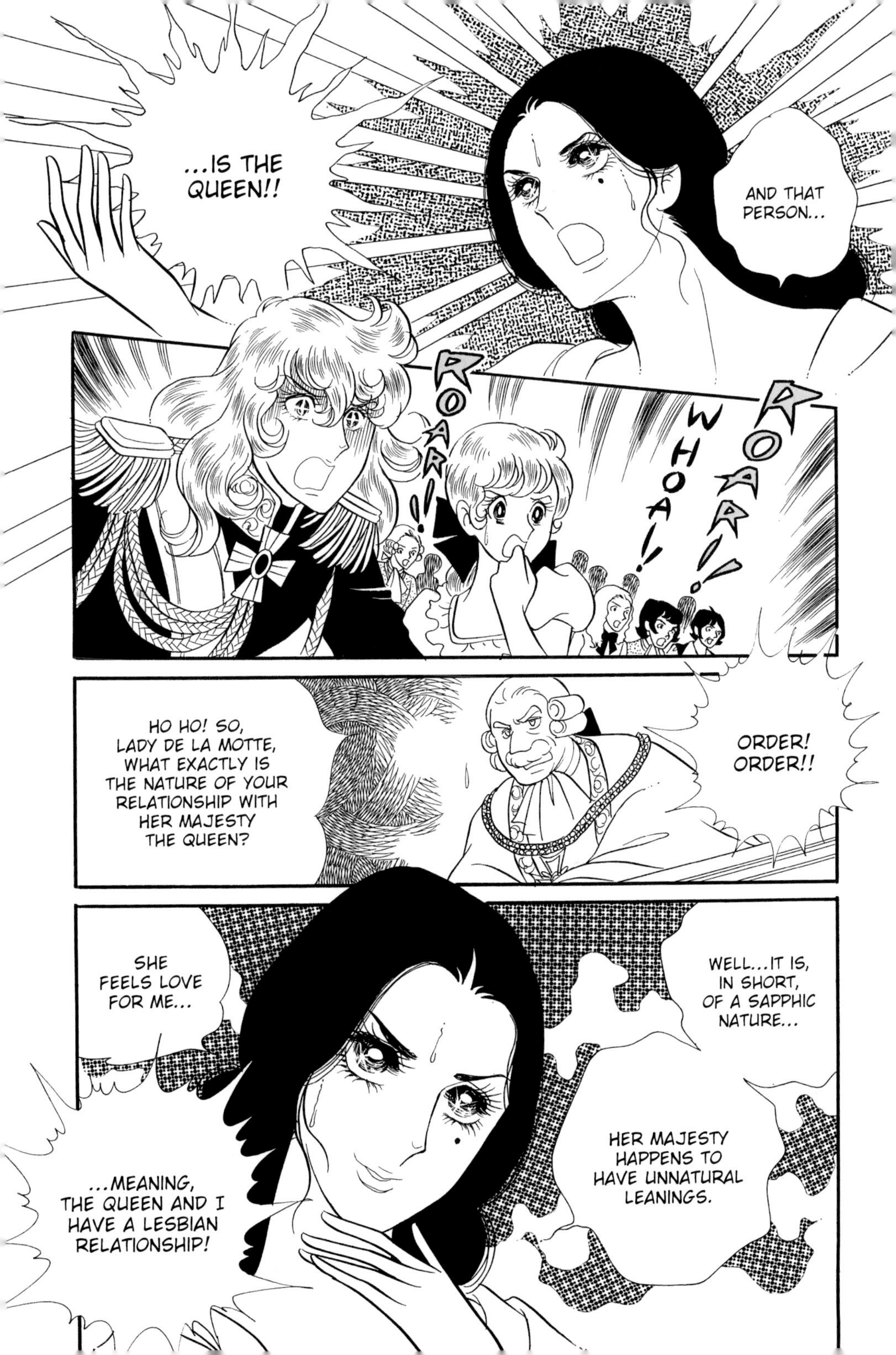
AND THAT PERSON...
...IS THE QUEEN!!
ROAR!!
WHOA!!
ROAR!!
ORDER! ORDER!!
HO HO! SO, LADY DE LA MOTTE, WHAT EXACTLY IS THE NATURE OF YOUR RELATIONSHIP WITH HER MAJESTY THE QUEEN?
WELL...IT IS, IN SHORT, OF A SAPPHIC NATURE...
SHE FEELS LOVE FOR ME...
HER MAJESTY HAPPENS TO HAVE UNNATURAL LEANINGS.
...MEANING, THE QUEEN AND I HAVE A LESBIAN RELATIONSHIP!

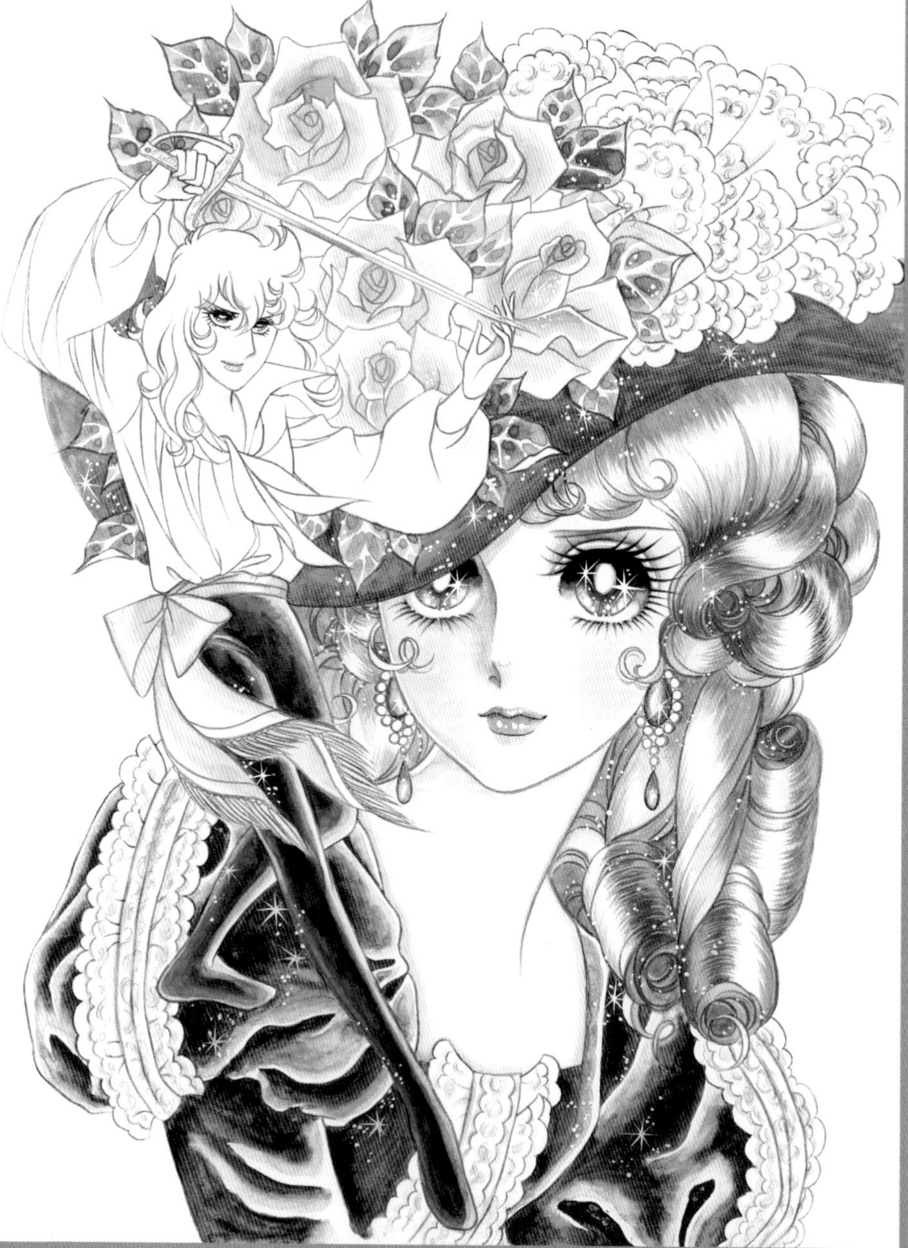

1972 WEEKLY MARGARET MAGAZINE ISSUE 50 COVER ART

★ますます快調！　大好評、大評判!!

♥おいつめられたジャンヌは、法廷で、じぶんと王妃・アントワネットはレズだったと!?

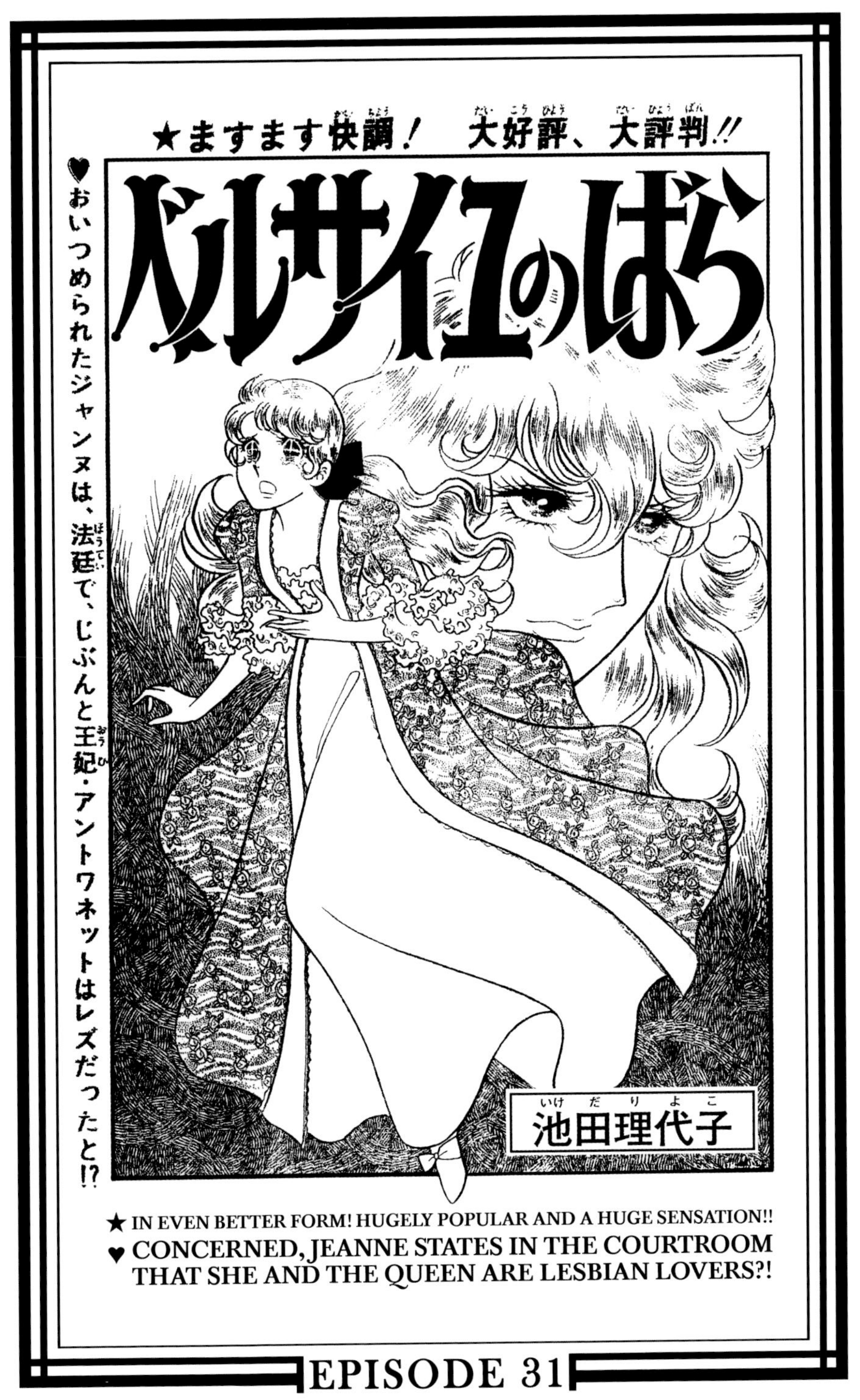
ベルサイユのばら
池田理代子

★ IN EVEN BETTER FORM! HUGELY POPULAR AND A HUGE SENSATION!!

♥ CONCERNED, JEANNE STATES IN THE COURTROOM THAT SHE AND THE QUEEN ARE LESBIAN LOVERS?!

EPISODE 31

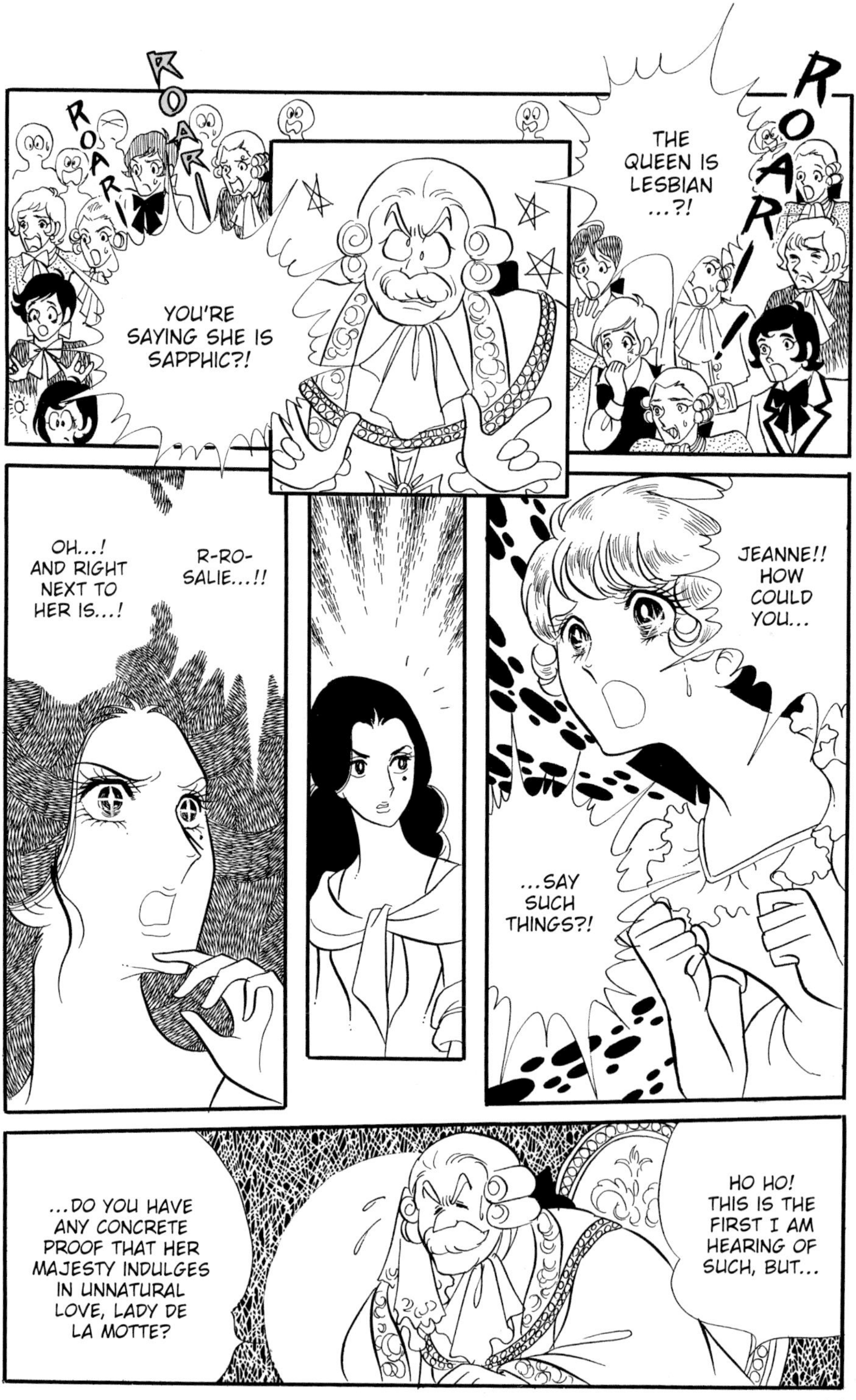
R-O-A-R-!!
THE QUEEN IS LESBIAN ...?!
YOU'RE SAYING SHE IS SAPPHIC?!
ROAR!
ROAR!
JEANNE!! HOW COULD YOU...
...SAY SUCH THINGS?!
R-RO-SALIE...!!
OH...! AND RIGHT NEXT TO HER IS...!
HO HO! THIS IS THE FIRST I AM HEARING OF SUCH, BUT...
...DO YOU HAVE ANY CONCRETE PROOF THAT HER MAJESTY INDULGES IN UNNATURAL LOVE, LADY DE LA MOTTE?

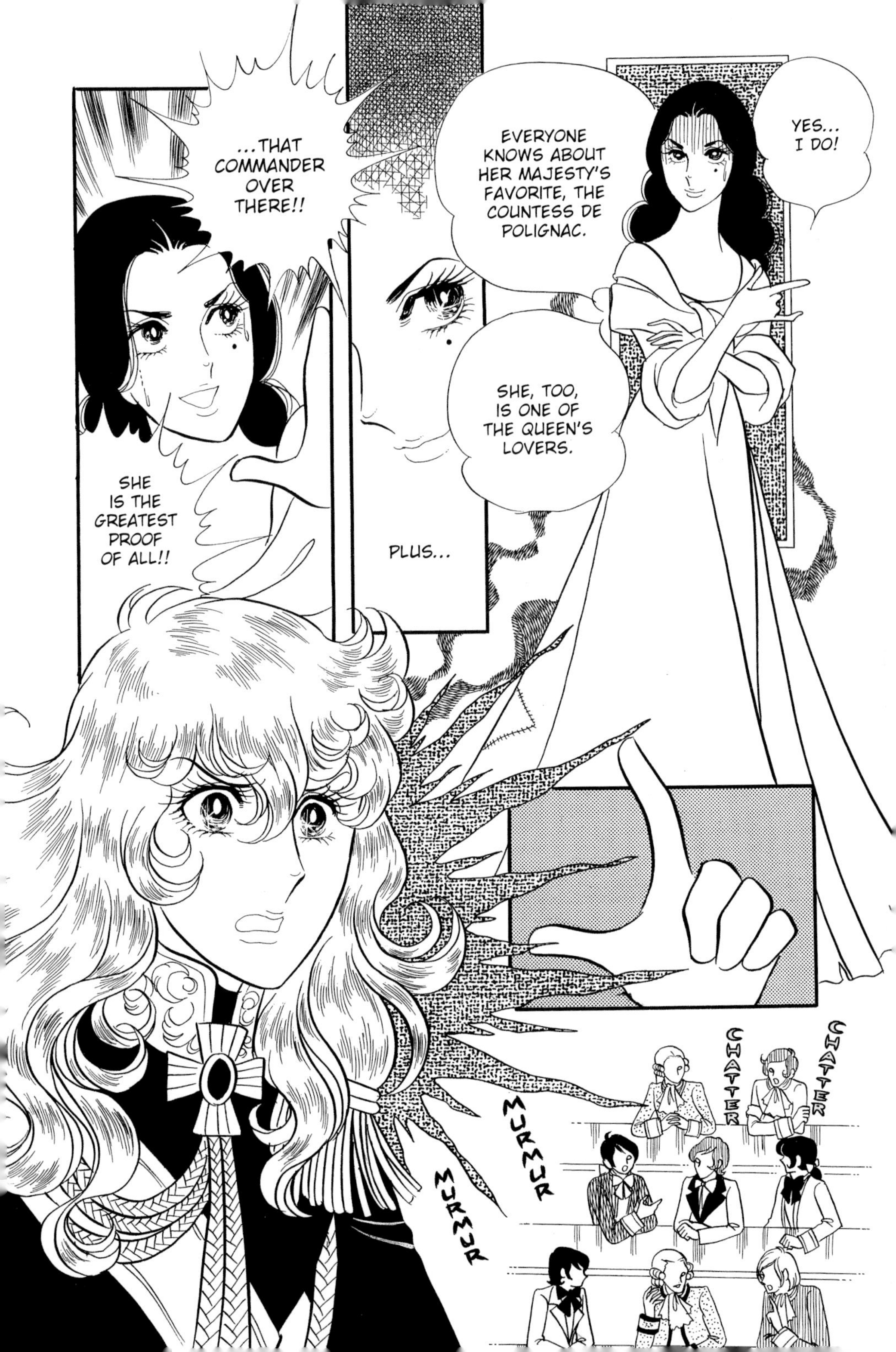
YES... I DO!
EVERYONE KNOWS ABOUT HER MAJESTY'S FAVORITE, THE COUNTESS DE POLIGNAC.
SHE, TOO, IS ONE OF THE QUEEN'S LOVERS.
PLUS...
...THAT COMMANDER OVER THERE!!
SHE IS THE GREATEST PROOF OF ALL!!
CHATTER
CHATTER
MURMUR
MURMUR

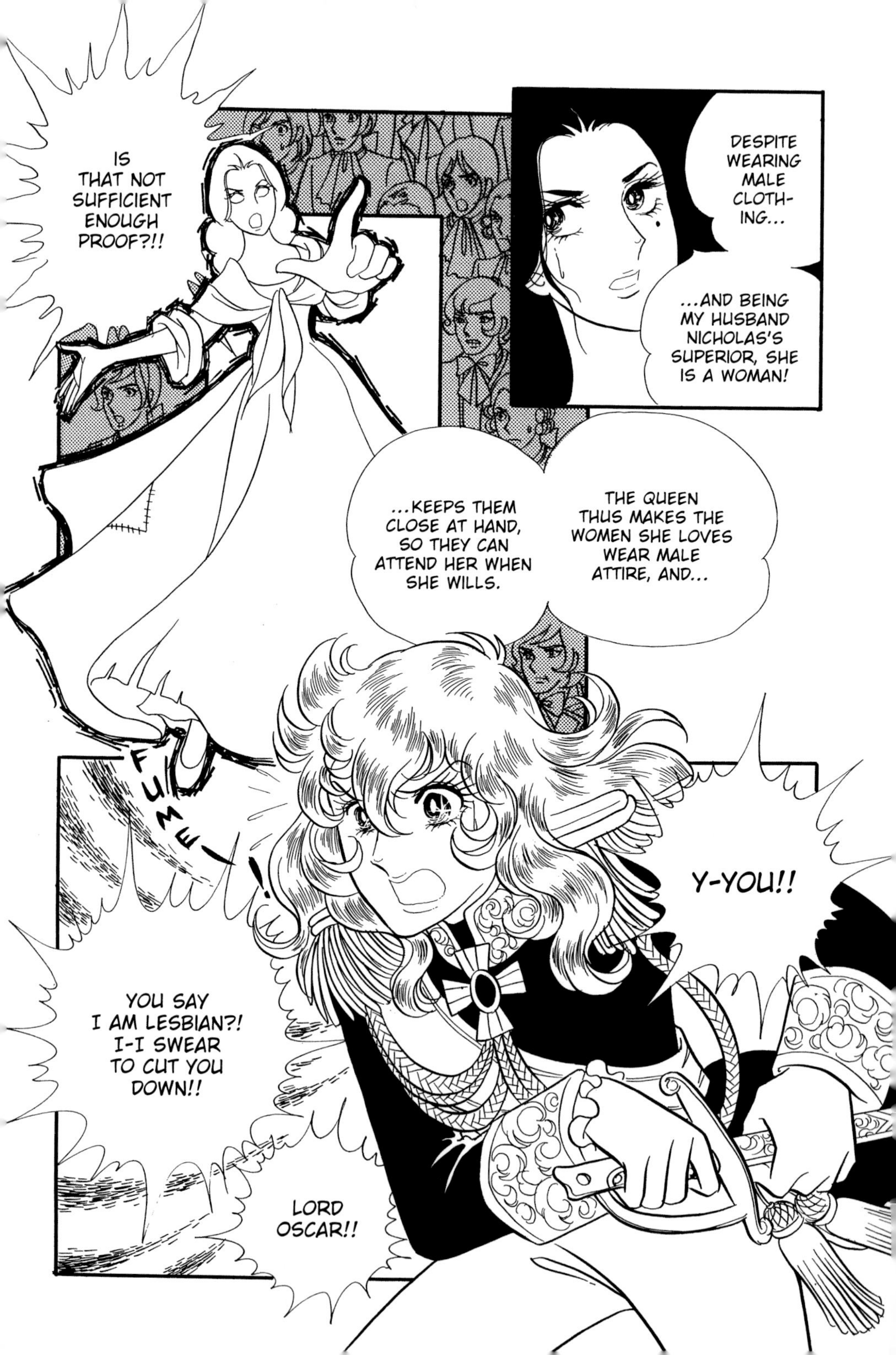
DESPITE WEARING MALE CLOTHING...
...AND BEING MY HUSBAND NICHOLAS'S SUPERIOR, SHE IS A WOMAN!
IS THAT NOT SUFFICIENT ENOUGH PROOF?!!
THE QUEEN THUS MAKES THE WOMEN SHE LOVES WEAR MALE ATTIRE, AND...
...KEEPS THEM CLOSE AT HAND, SO THEY CAN ATTEND HER WHEN SHE WILLS.
Y-YOU!!
FUME—!
YOU SAY I AM LESBIAN?! I-I SWEAR TO CUT YOU DOWN!!
LORD OSCAR!!

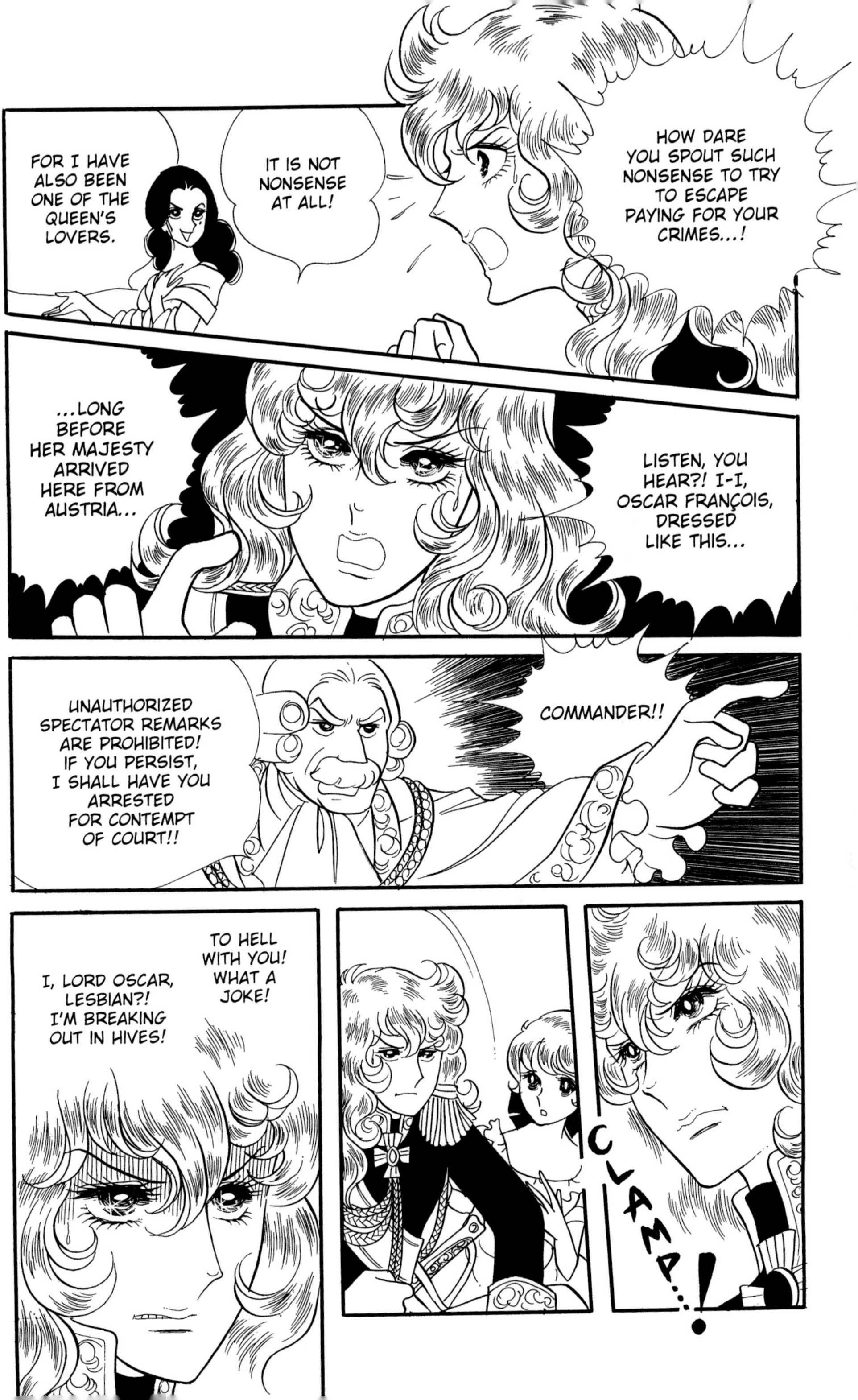

HOW DARE YOU SPOUT SUCH NONSENSE TO TRY TO ESCAPE PAYING FOR YOUR CRIMES...!
IT IS NOT NONSENSE AT ALL!
FOR I HAVE ALSO BEEN ONE OF THE QUEEN'S LOVERS.
LISTEN, YOU HEAR?! I-I, OSCAR FRANÇOIS, DRESSED LIKE THIS...
...LONG BEFORE HER MAJESTY ARRIVED HERE FROM AUSTRIA...
COMMANDER!!
UNAUTHORIZED SPECTATOR REMARKS ARE PROHIBITED! IF YOU PERSIST, I SHALL HAVE YOU ARRESTED FOR CONTEMPT OF COURT!!
CLAMP...!
TO HELL WITH YOU! WHAT A JOKE!
I, LORD OSCAR, LESBIAN?! I'M BREAKING OUT IN HIVES!

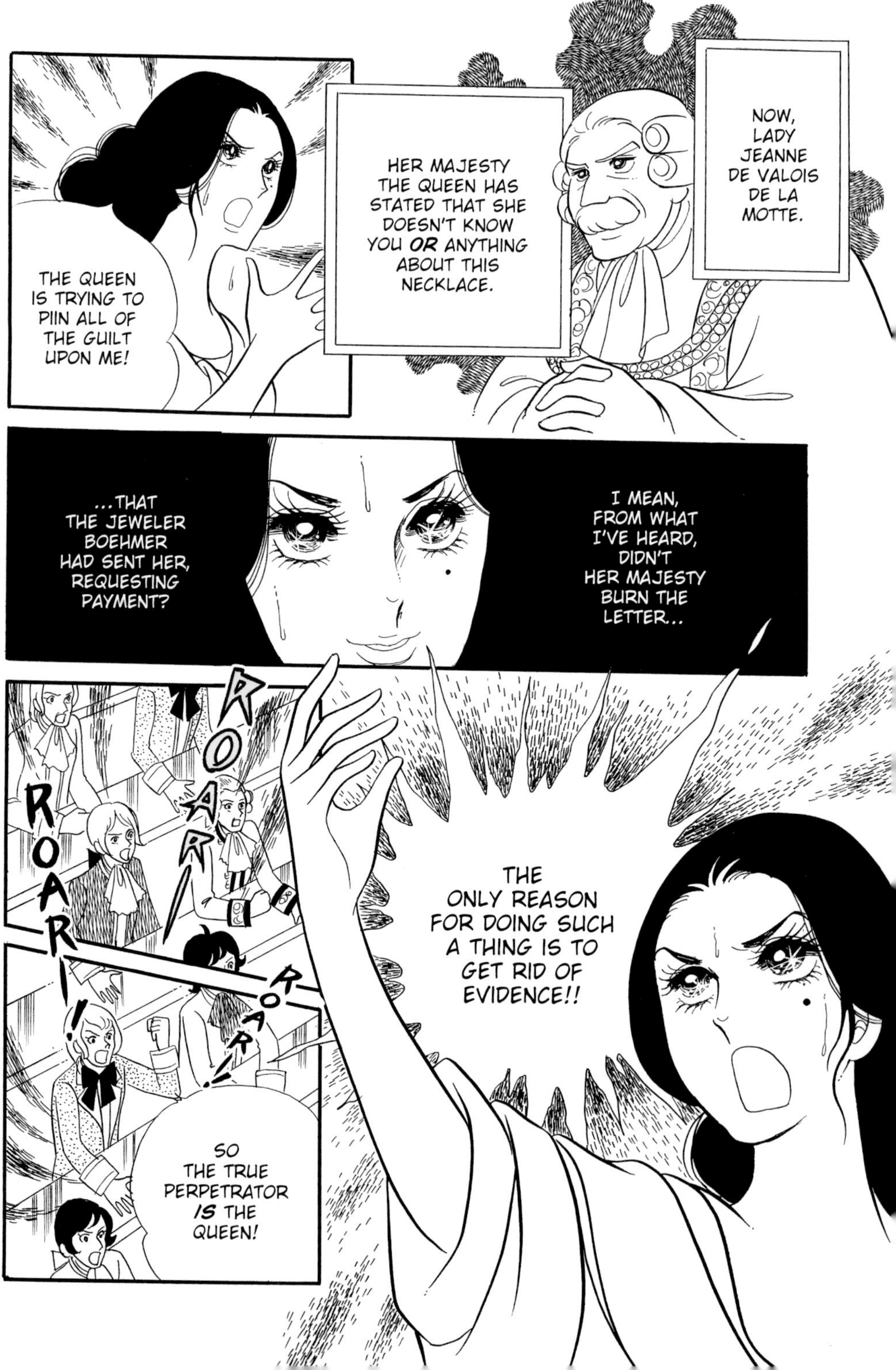
NOW, LADY JEANNE DE VALOIS DE LA MOTTE.
HER MAJESTY THE QUEEN HAS STATED THAT SHE DOESN'T KNOW YOU *OR* ANYTHING ABOUT THIS NECKLACE.
THE QUEEN IS TRYING TO PIIN ALL OF THE GUILT UPON ME!
I MEAN, FROM WHAT I'VE HEARD, DIDN'T HER MAJESTY BURN THE LETTER...
...THAT THE JEWELER BOEHMER HAD SENT HER, REQUESTING PAYMENT?
THE ONLY REASON FOR DOING SUCH A THING IS TO GET RID OF EVIDENCE!!
ROAR!
ROAR!
ROAR!!
ROAR!!
SO THE TRUE PERPETRATOR *IS* THE QUEEN!

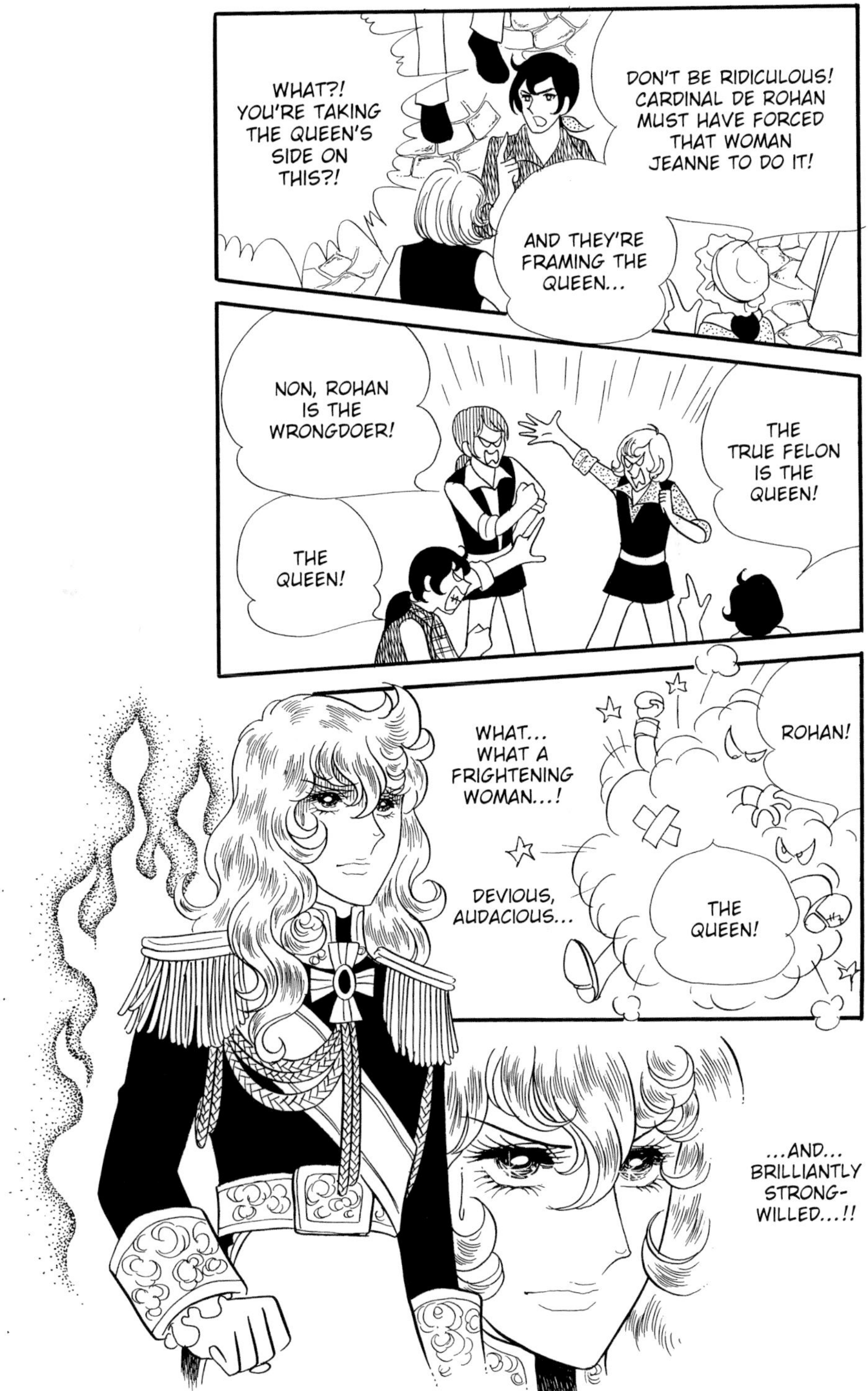
DON'T BE RIDICULOUS! CARDINAL DE ROHAN MUST HAVE FORCED THAT WOMAN JEANNE TO DO IT!
AND THEY'RE FRAMING THE QUEEN...
WHAT?! YOU'RE TAKING THE QUEEN'S SIDE ON THIS?!
THE TRUE FELON IS THE QUEEN!
NON, ROHAN IS THE WRONGDOER!
THE QUEEN!
ROHAN!
THE QUEEN!
WHAT... WHAT A FRIGHTENING WOMAN...!
DEVIOUS, AUDACIOUS...
...AND... BRILLIANTLY STRONG-WILLED...!!

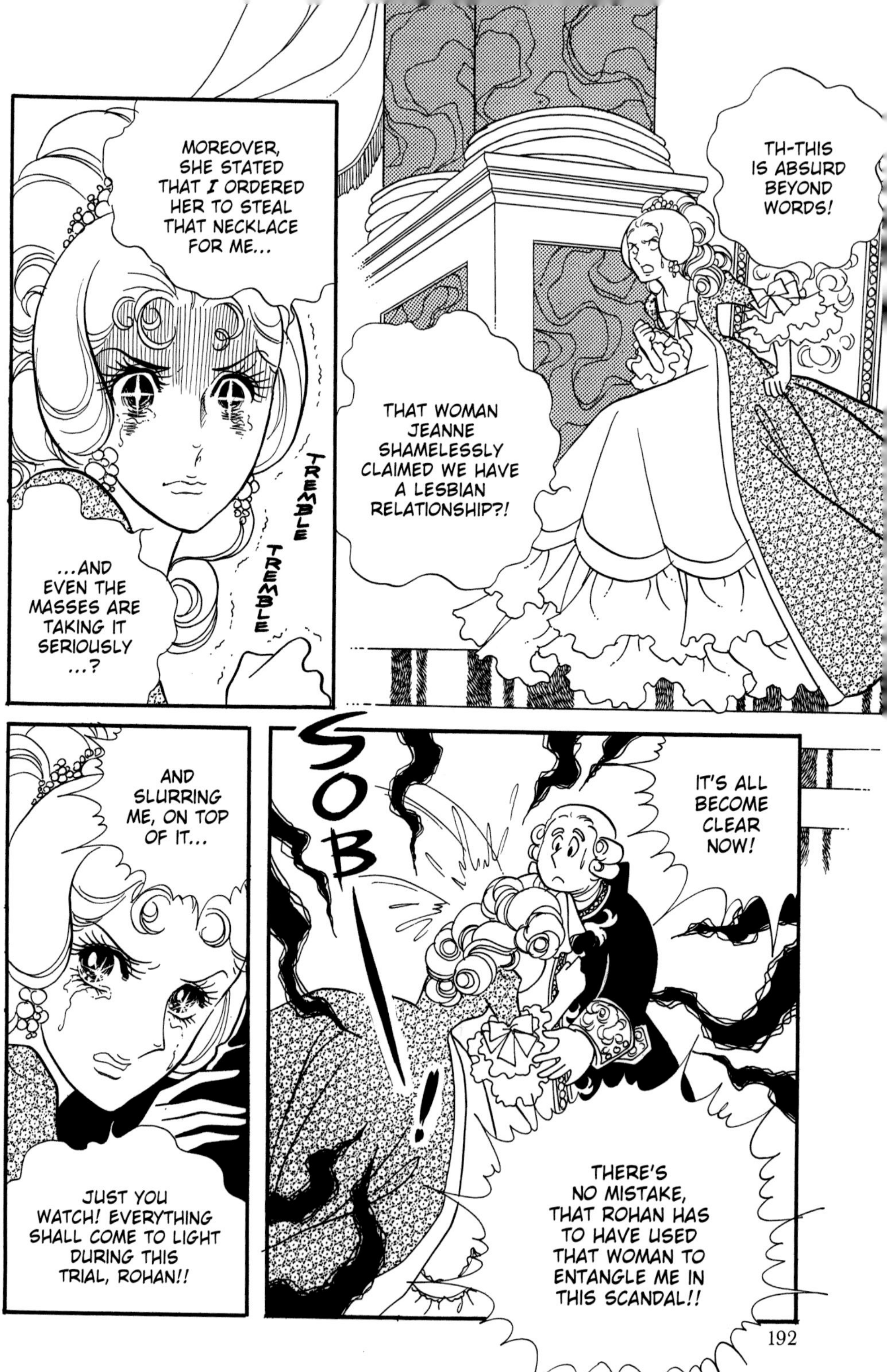
TH-THIS IS ABSURD BEYOND WORDS!
THAT WOMAN JEANNE SHAMELESSLY CLAIMED WE HAVE A LESBIAN RELATIONSHIP?!
MOREOVER, SHE STATED THAT *I* ORDERED HER TO STEAL THAT NECKLACE FOR ME...
TREMBLE
TREMBLE
...AND EVEN THE MASSES ARE TAKING IT SERIOUSLY ...?
SOB
IT'S ALL BECOME CLEAR NOW!
!
THERE'S NO MISTAKE, THAT ROHAN HAS TO HAVE USED THAT WOMAN TO ENTANGLE ME IN THIS SCANDAL!!
AND SLURRING ME, ON TOP OF IT...
JUST YOU WATCH! EVERYTHING SHALL COME TO LIGHT DURING THIS TRIAL, ROHAN!!

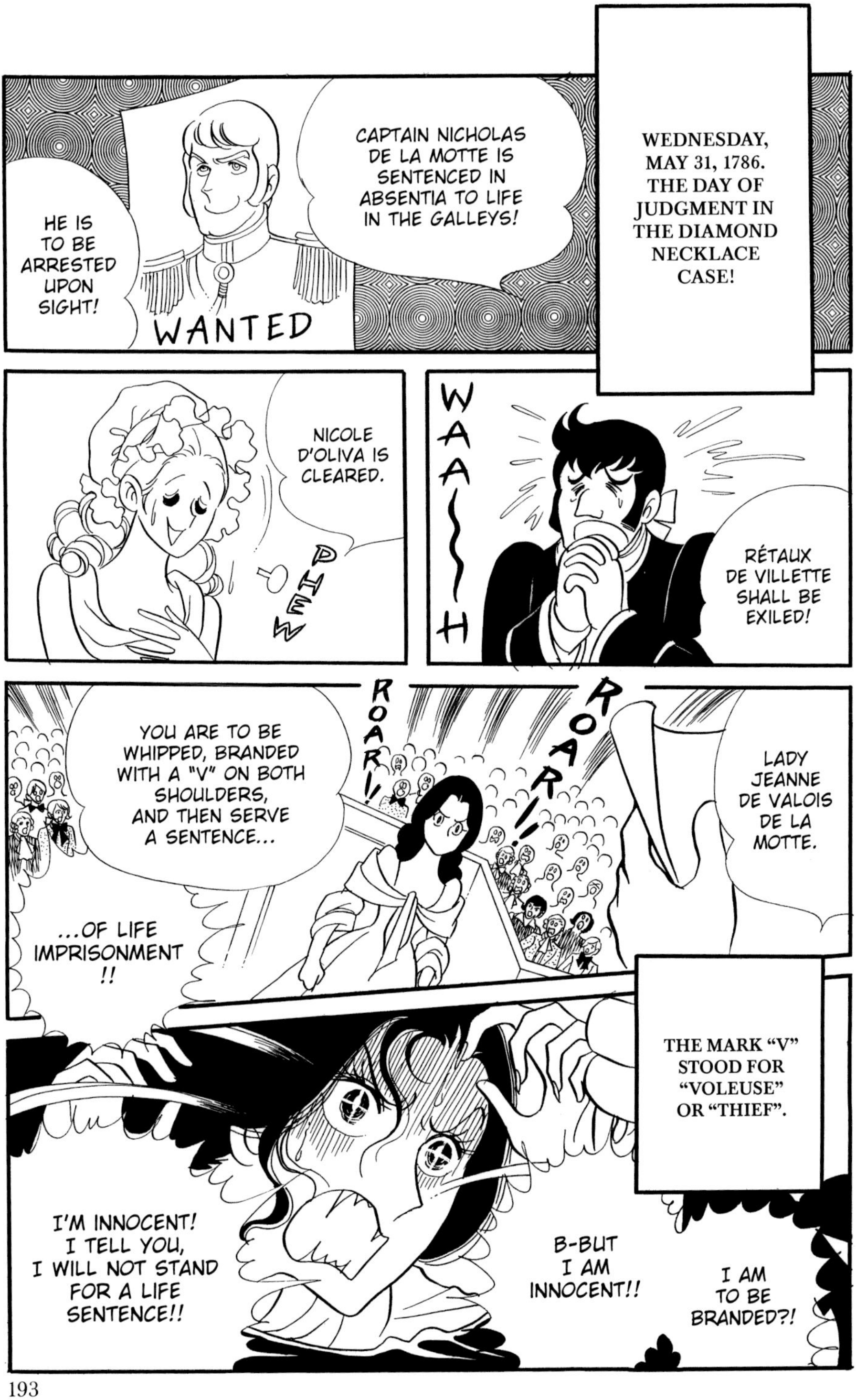
WEDNESDAY, MAY 31, 1786. THE DAY OF JUDGMENT IN THE DIAMOND NECKLACE CASE!
CAPTAIN NICHOLAS DE LA MOTTE IS SENTENCED IN ABSENTIA TO LIFE IN THE GALLEYS!
HE IS TO BE ARRESTED UPON SIGHT!
WANTED
RÉTAUX DE VILLETTE SHALL BE EXILED!
WAA~~H
NICOLE D'OLIVA IS CLEARED.
PHEW
LADY JEANNE DE VALOIS DE LA MOTTE.
ROAR!!
ROAR!!
YOU ARE TO BE WHIPPED, BRANDED WITH A "V" ON BOTH SHOULDERS, AND THEN SERVE A SENTENCE...
...OF LIFE IMPRISONMENT!!
THE MARK "V" STOOD FOR "VOLEUSE" OR "THIEF".
I AM TO BE BRANDED?!
B-BUT I AM INNOCENT!!
I'M INNOCENT! I TELL YOU, I WILL NOT STAND FOR A LIFE SENTENCE!!

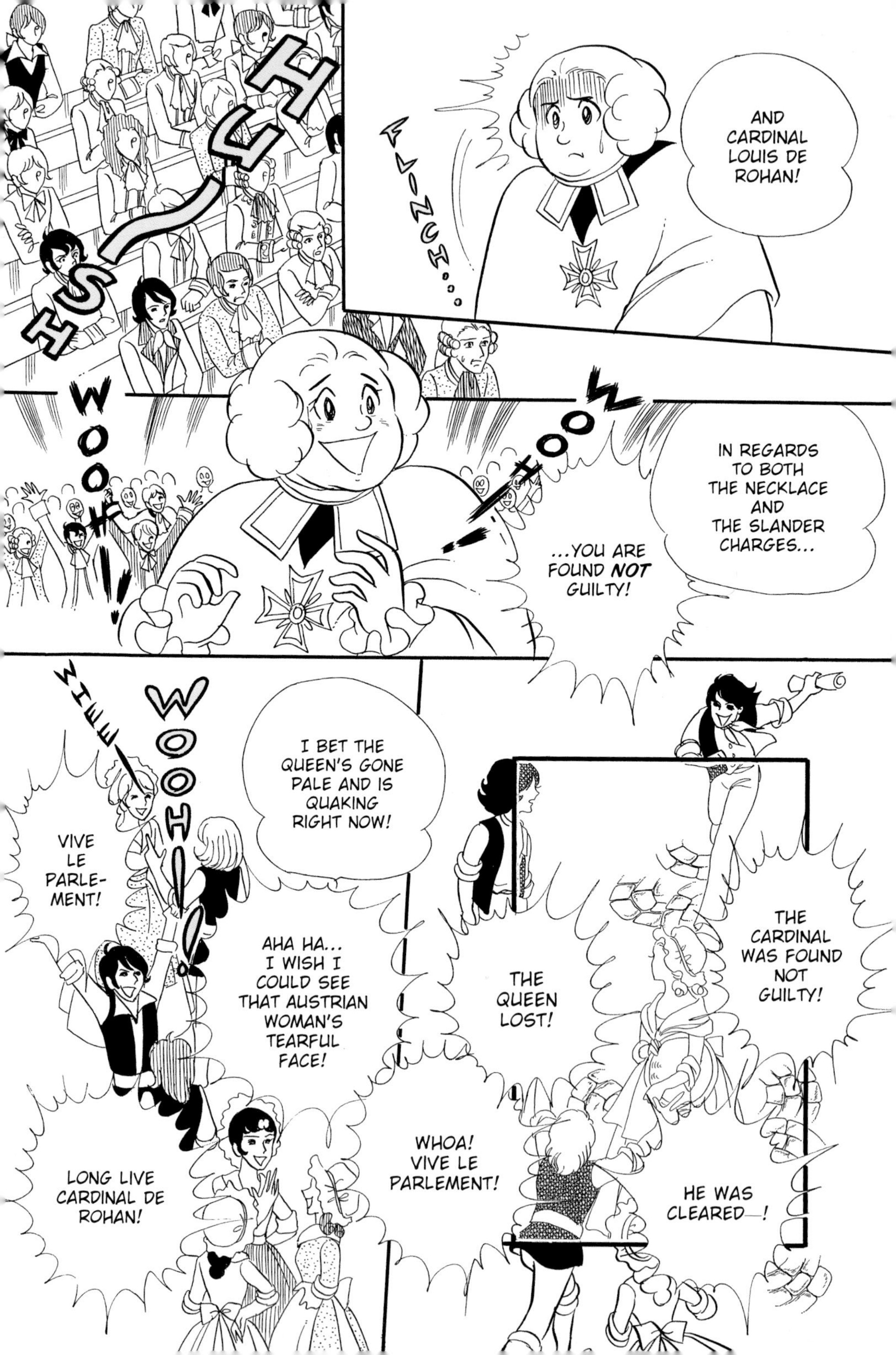

AND CARDINAL LOUIS DE ROHAN!
FLINCH...
HUSH—
IN REGARDS TO BOTH THE NECKLACE AND THE SLANDER CHARGES...
...YOU ARE FOUND **NOT** GUILTY!
WHOOW
WOOH!!
THE CARDINAL WAS FOUND NOT GUILTY!
THE QUEEN LOST!
HE WAS CLEARED—!
WHOA! VIVE LE PARLEMENT!
WOOOH!!
WHEE
I BET THE QUEEN'S GONE PALE AND IS QUAKING RIGHT NOW!
VIVE LE PARLE-MENT!
AHA HA... I WISH I COULD SEE THAT AUSTRIAN WOMAN'S TEARFUL FACE!
LONG LIVE CARDINAL DE ROHAN!

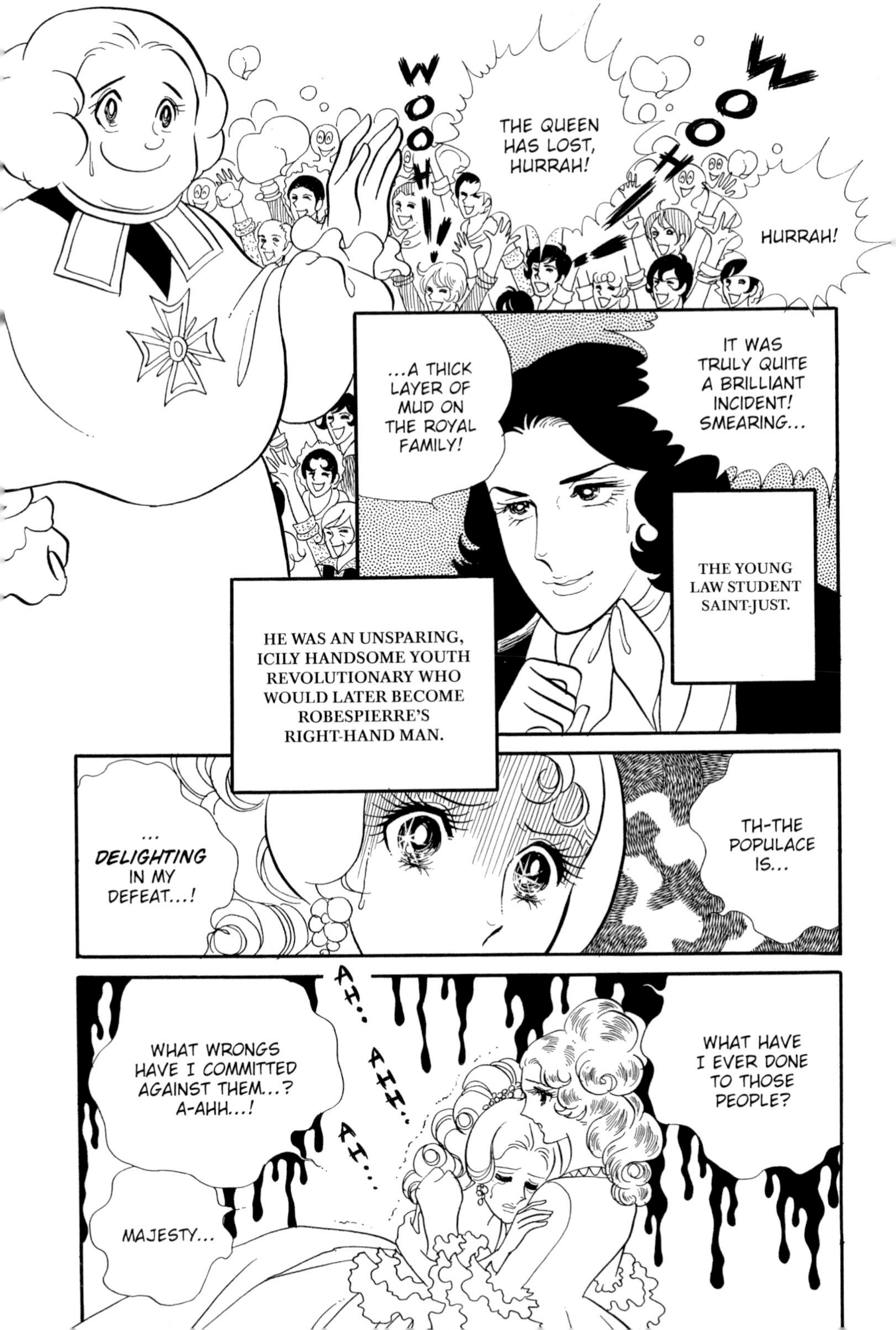
WOOH!!
HURRAH!
THE QUEEN HAS LOST, HURRAH!
WOOH!!!
IT WAS TRULY QUITE A BRILLIANT INCIDENT! SMEARING...
...A THICK LAYER OF MUD ON THE ROYAL FAMILY!
THE YOUNG LAW STUDENT SAINT-JUST.
HE WAS AN UNSPARING, ICILY HANDSOME YOUTH REVOLUTIONARY WHO WOULD LATER BECOME ROBESPIERRE'S RIGHT-HAND MAN.
TH-THE POPULACE IS...
...*DELIGHTING* IN MY DEFEAT...!
WHAT HAVE I EVER DONE TO THOSE PEOPLE?
AH... AHH... AH...
WHAT WRONGS HAVE I COMMITTED AGAINST THEM...? A-AHH...!
MAJESTY...

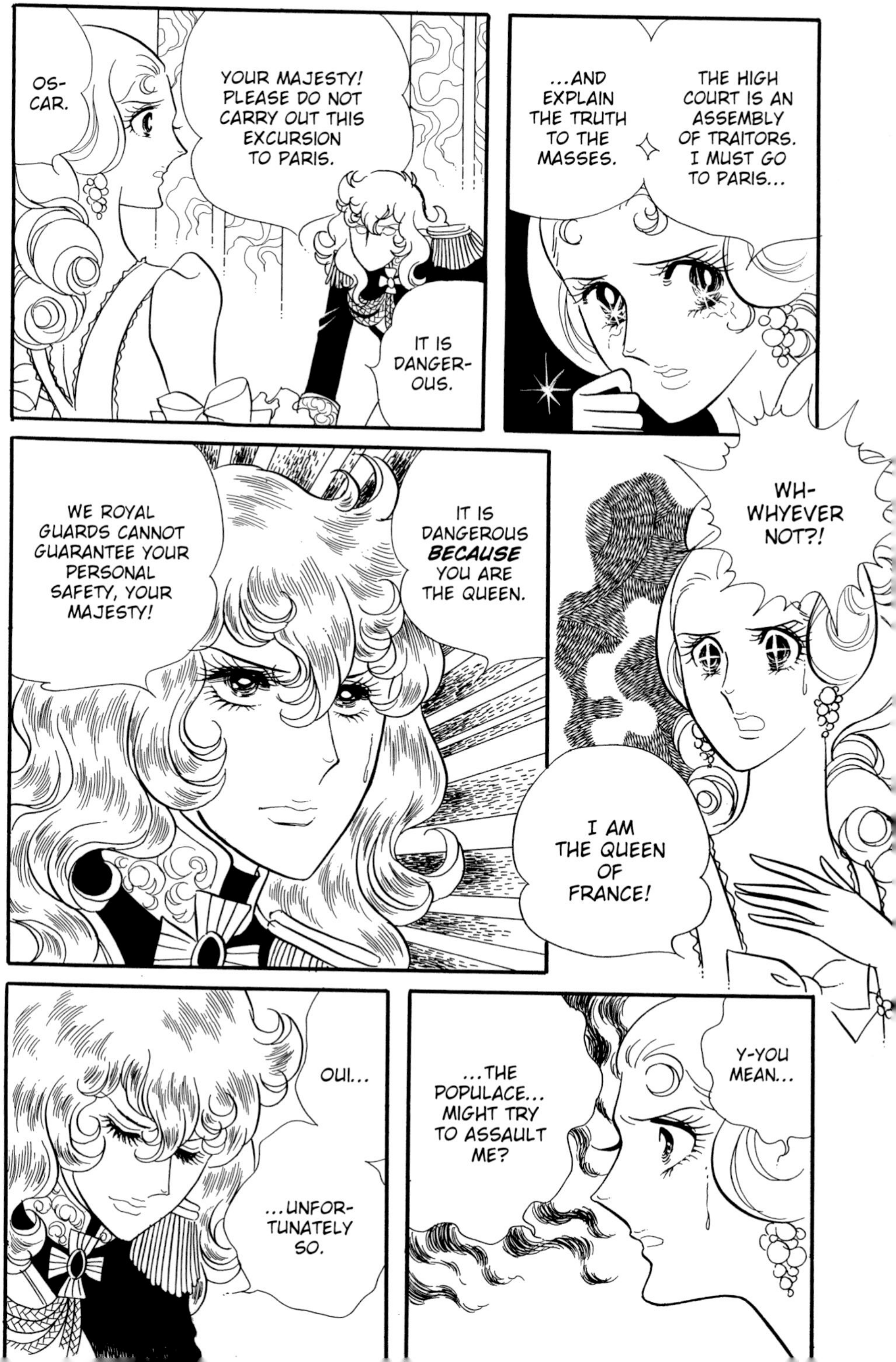
THE HIGH COURT IS AN ASSEMBLY OF TRAITORS. I MUST GO TO PARIS...
...AND EXPLAIN THE TRUTH TO THE MASSES.
OS-CAR.
YOUR MAJESTY! PLEASE DO NOT CARRY OUT THIS EXCURSION TO PARIS.
IT IS DANGER-OUS.
WH-WHYEVER NOT?!
I AM THE QUEEN OF FRANCE!
IT IS DANGEROUS ***BECAUSE*** YOU ARE THE QUEEN.
WE ROYAL GUARDS CANNOT GUARANTEE YOUR PERSONAL SAFETY, YOUR MAJESTY!
Y-YOU MEAN...
...THE POPULACE... MIGHT TRY TO ASSAULT ME?
OUI...
...UNFOR-TUNATELY SO.

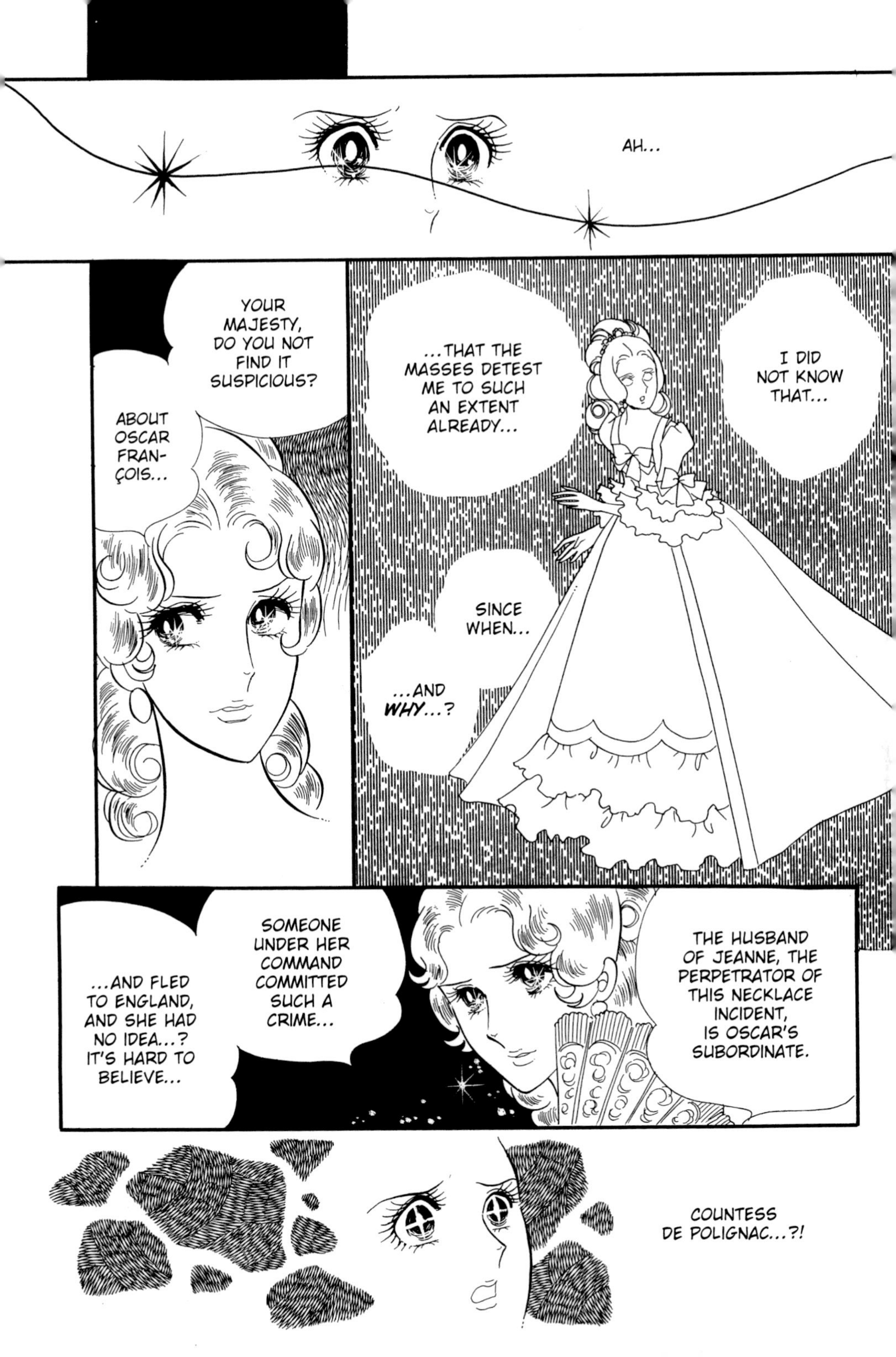
AH...
I DID NOT KNOW THAT...
...THAT THE MASSES DETEST ME TO SUCH AN EXTENT ALREADY...
SINCE WHEN...
...AND *WHY*...?
YOUR MAJESTY, DO YOU NOT FIND IT SUSPICIOUS?
ABOUT OSCAR FRAN-ÇOIS...
THE HUSBAND OF JEANNE, THE PERPETRATOR OF THIS NECKLACE INCIDENT, IS OSCAR'S SUBORDINATE.
SOMEONE UNDER HER COMMAND COMMITTED SUCH A CRIME...
...AND FLED TO ENGLAND, AND SHE HAD NO IDEA...? IT'S HARD TO BELIEVE...
COUNTESS DE POLIGNAC...?!

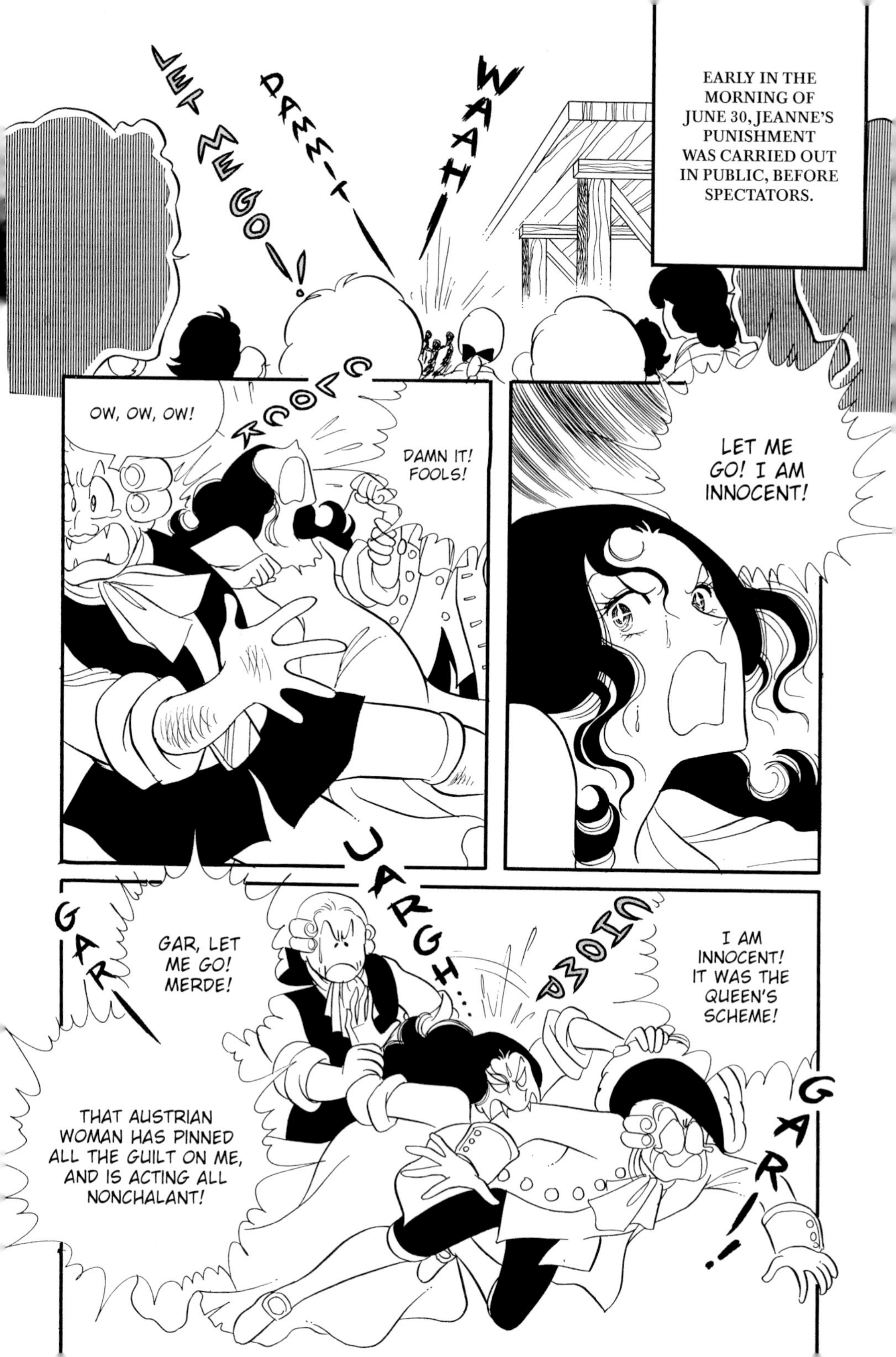
EARLY IN THE MORNING OF JUNE 30, JEANNE'S PUNISHMENT WAS CARRIED OUT IN PUBLIC, BEFORE SPECTATORS.
WAAAH!
DAMMIT!
LET ME GO!!
LET ME GO! I AM INNOCENT!
DAMN IT! FOOLS!
OW, OW, OW!
GAR!!
I AM INNOCENT! IT WAS THE QUEEN'S SCHEME!
JARGH...
GAR, LET ME GO! MERDE!
GAR!
THAT AUSTRIAN WOMAN HAS PINNED ALL THE GUILT ON ME, AND IS ACTING ALL NONCHALANT!

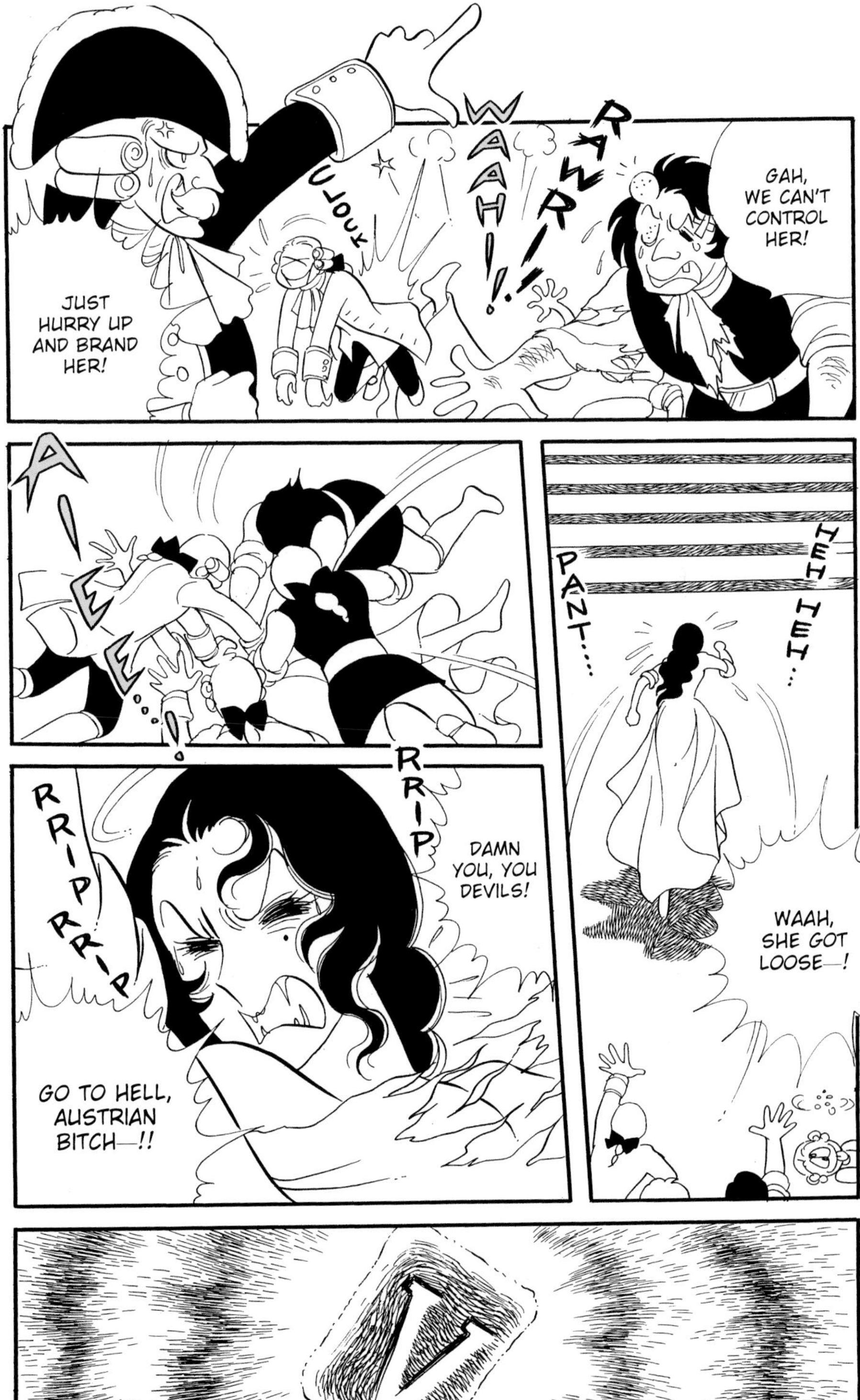
RAWR!!
GAH, WE CAN'T CONTROL HER!
WAAH!!
CLOUK
JUST HURRY UP AND BRAND HER!
HEH HEH...
PANT....
WAAH, SHE GOT LOOSE—!
AIEE!
RRIP
DAMN YOU, YOU DEVILS!
RRIPRRIP
GO TO HELL, AUSTRIAN BITCH—!!

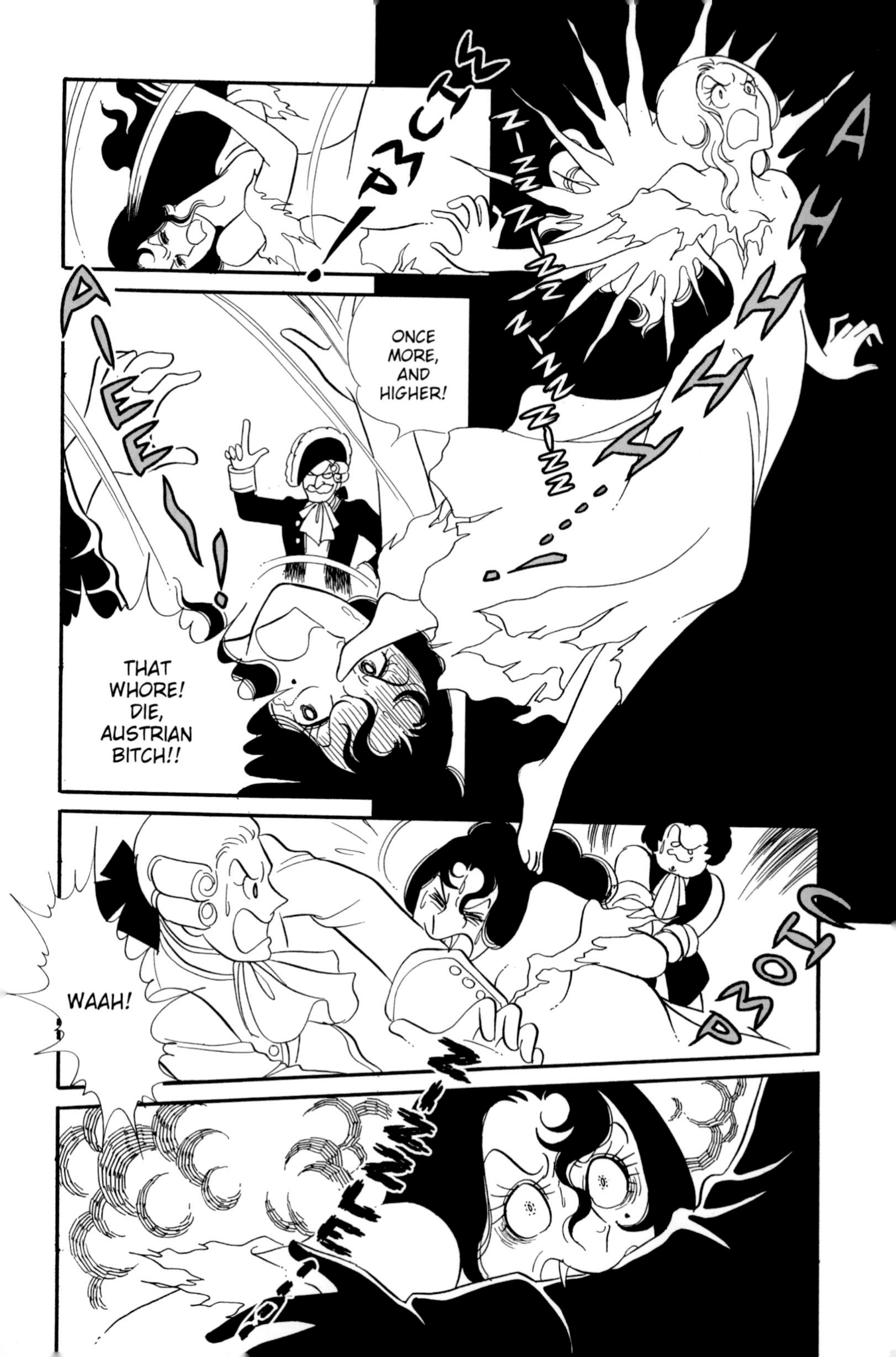
AHHHH...!
ONCE MORE, AND HIGHER!
AIEEE-!
THAT WHORE! DIE, AUSTRIAN BITCH!!
WAAH!

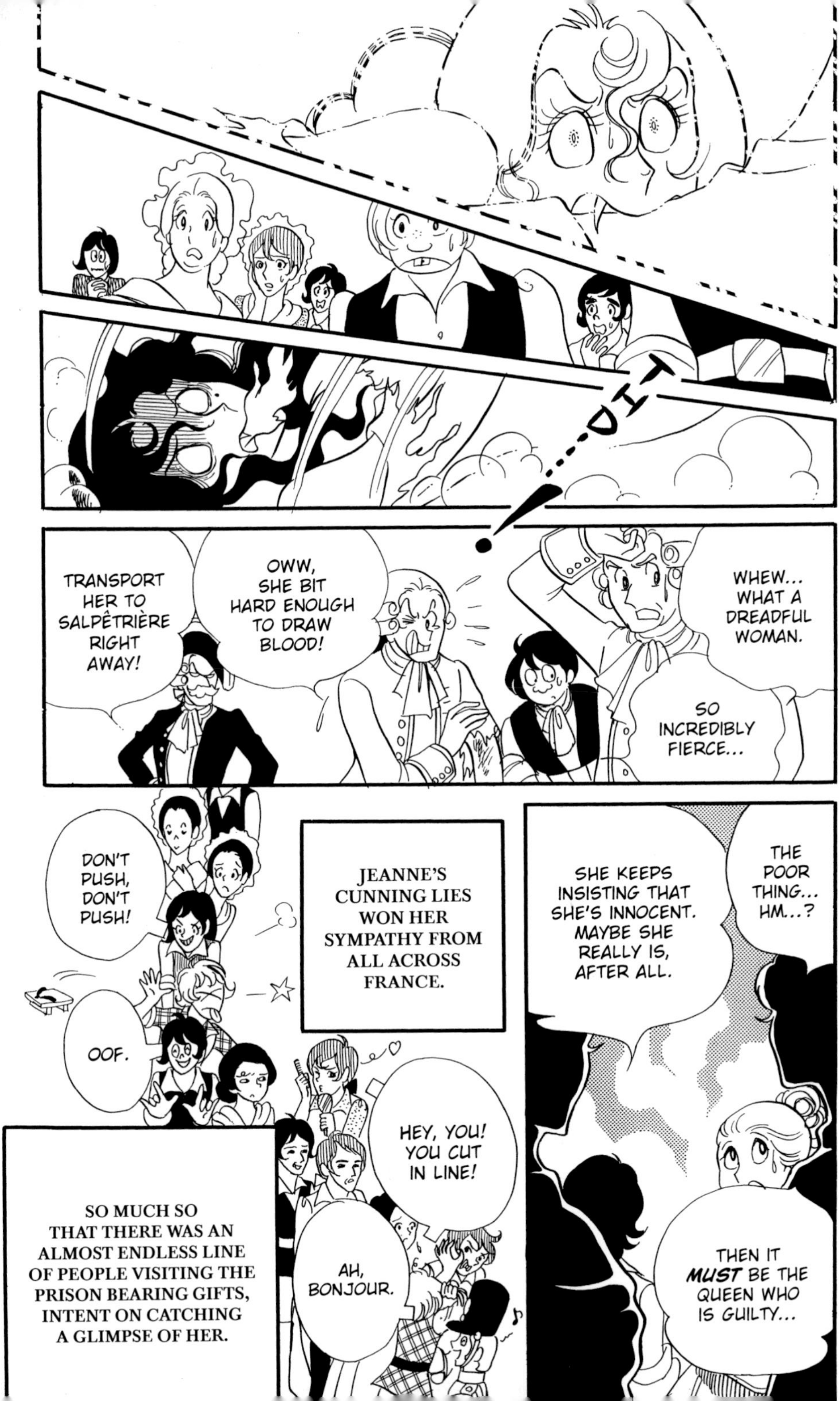
TID...!
WHEW... WHAT A DREADFUL WOMAN.
SO INCREDIBLY FIERCE...
OWW, SHE BIT HARD ENOUGH TO DRAW BLOOD!
TRANSPORT HER TO SALPÊTRIÈRE RIGHT AWAY!
THE POOR THING... HM...?
SHE KEEPS INSISTING THAT SHE'S INNOCENT. MAYBE SHE REALLY IS, AFTER ALL.
THEN IT MUST BE THE QUEEN WHO IS GUILTY...
JEANNE'S CUNNING LIES WON HER SYMPATHY FROM ALL ACROSS FRANCE.
DON'T PUSH, DON'T PUSH!
OOF.
HEY, YOU! YOU CUT IN LINE!
AH, BONJOUR.
SO MUCH SO THAT THERE WAS AN ALMOST ENDLESS LINE OF PEOPLE VISITING THE PRISON BEARING GIFTS, INTENT ON CATCHING A GLIMPSE OF HER.

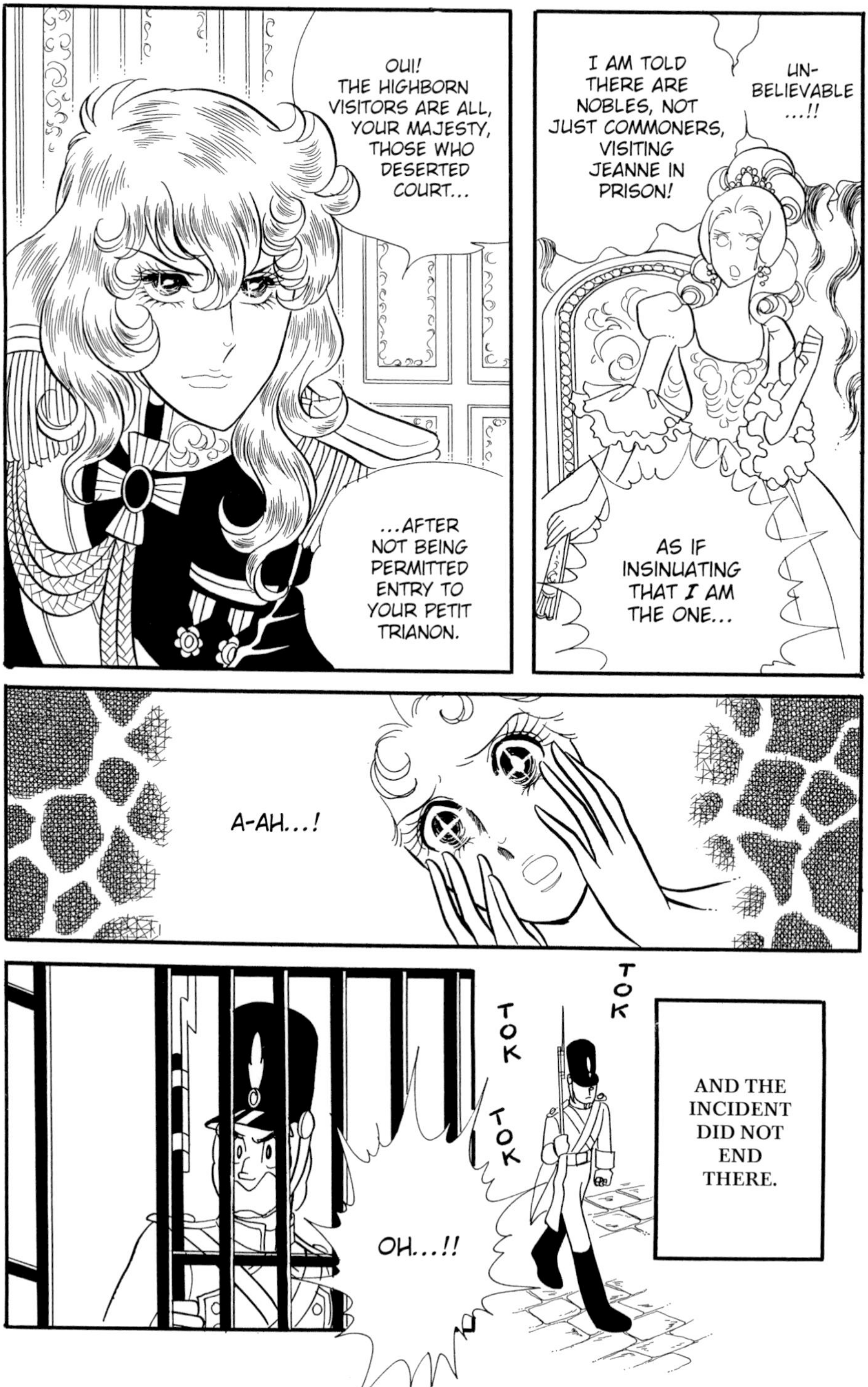
UN-BELIEVABLE ...!!
I AM TOLD THERE ARE NOBLES, NOT JUST COMMONERS, VISITING JEANNE IN PRISON!
AS IF INSINUATING THAT *I* AM THE ONE...
OUI! THE HIGHBORN VISITORS ARE ALL, YOUR MAJESTY, THOSE WHO DESERTED COURT...
...AFTER NOT BEING PERMITTED ENTRY TO YOUR PETIT TRIANON.
A-AH...!
AND THE INCIDENT DID NOT END THERE.
TOK
TOK
TOK
OH...!!

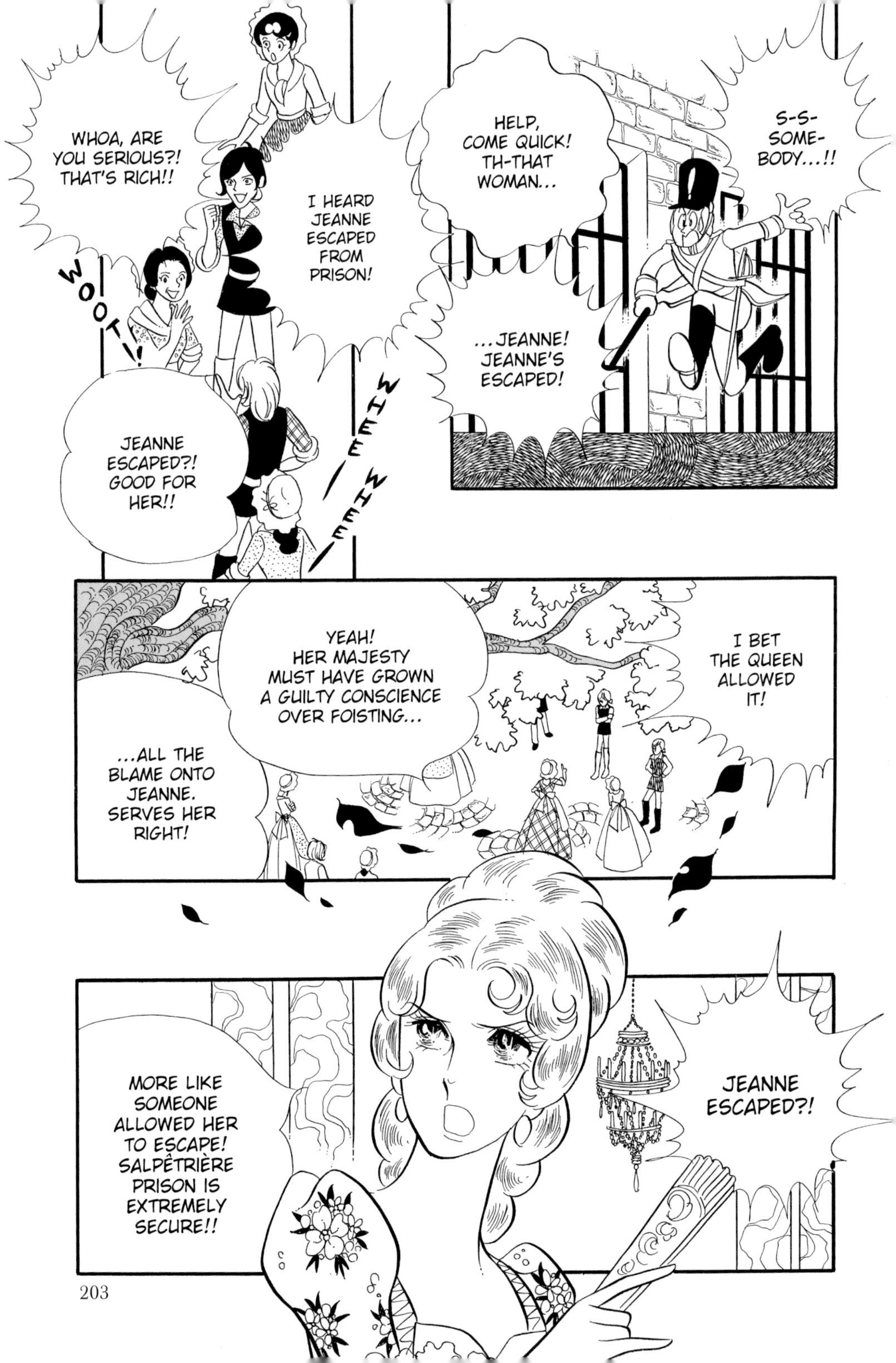
S-S-SOME-BODY...!!
HELP, COME QUICK! TH-THAT WOMAN...
...JEANNE! JEANNE'S ESCAPED!
I HEARD JEANNE ESCAPED FROM PRISON!
WHOA, ARE YOU SERIOUS?! THAT'S RICH!!
WOOT!!
JEANNE ESCAPED?! GOOD FOR HER!!
WHEE WHEE
I BET THE QUEEN ALLOWED IT!
YEAH! HER MAJESTY MUST HAVE GROWN A GUILTY CONSCIENCE OVER FOISTING...
...ALL THE BLAME ONTO JEANNE. SERVES HER RIGHT!
JEANNE ESCAPED?!
MORE LIKE SOMEONE ALLOWED HER TO ESCAPE! SALPÊTRIÈRE PRISON IS EXTREMELY SECURE!!

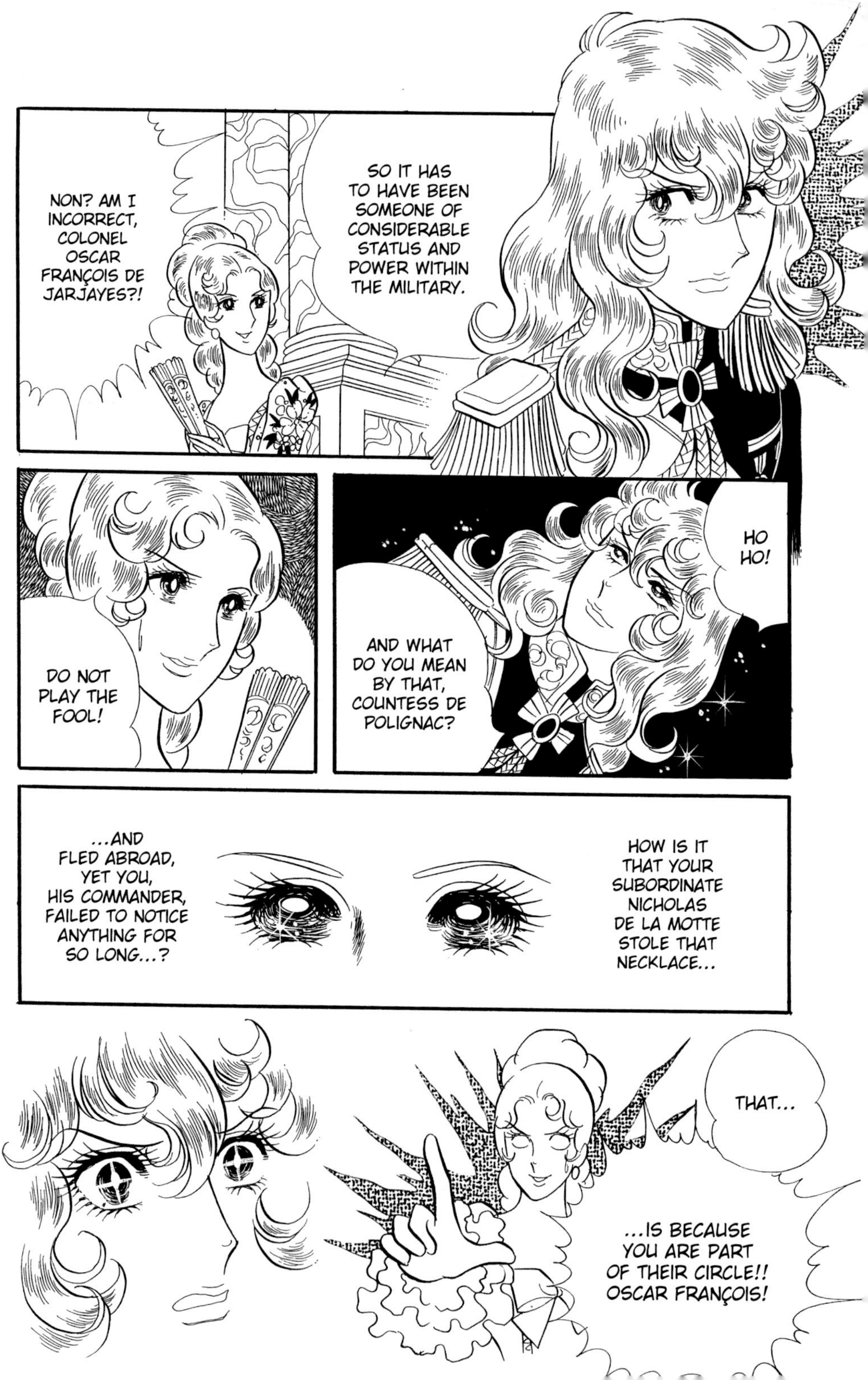
SO IT HAS TO HAVE BEEN SOMEONE OF CONSIDERABLE STATUS AND POWER WITHIN THE MILITARY.
NON? AM I INCORRECT, COLONEL OSCAR FRANÇOIS DE JARJAYES?!
HO HO!
AND WHAT DO YOU MEAN BY THAT, COUNTESS DE POLIGNAC?
DO NOT PLAY THE FOOL!
HOW IS IT THAT YOUR SUBORDINATE NICHOLAS DE LA MOTTE STOLE THAT NECKLACE...
...AND FLED ABROAD, YET YOU, HIS COMMANDER, FAILED TO NOTICE ANYTHING FOR SO LONG...?
THAT...
...IS BECAUSE YOU ARE PART OF THEIR CIRCLE!! OSCAR FRANÇOIS!

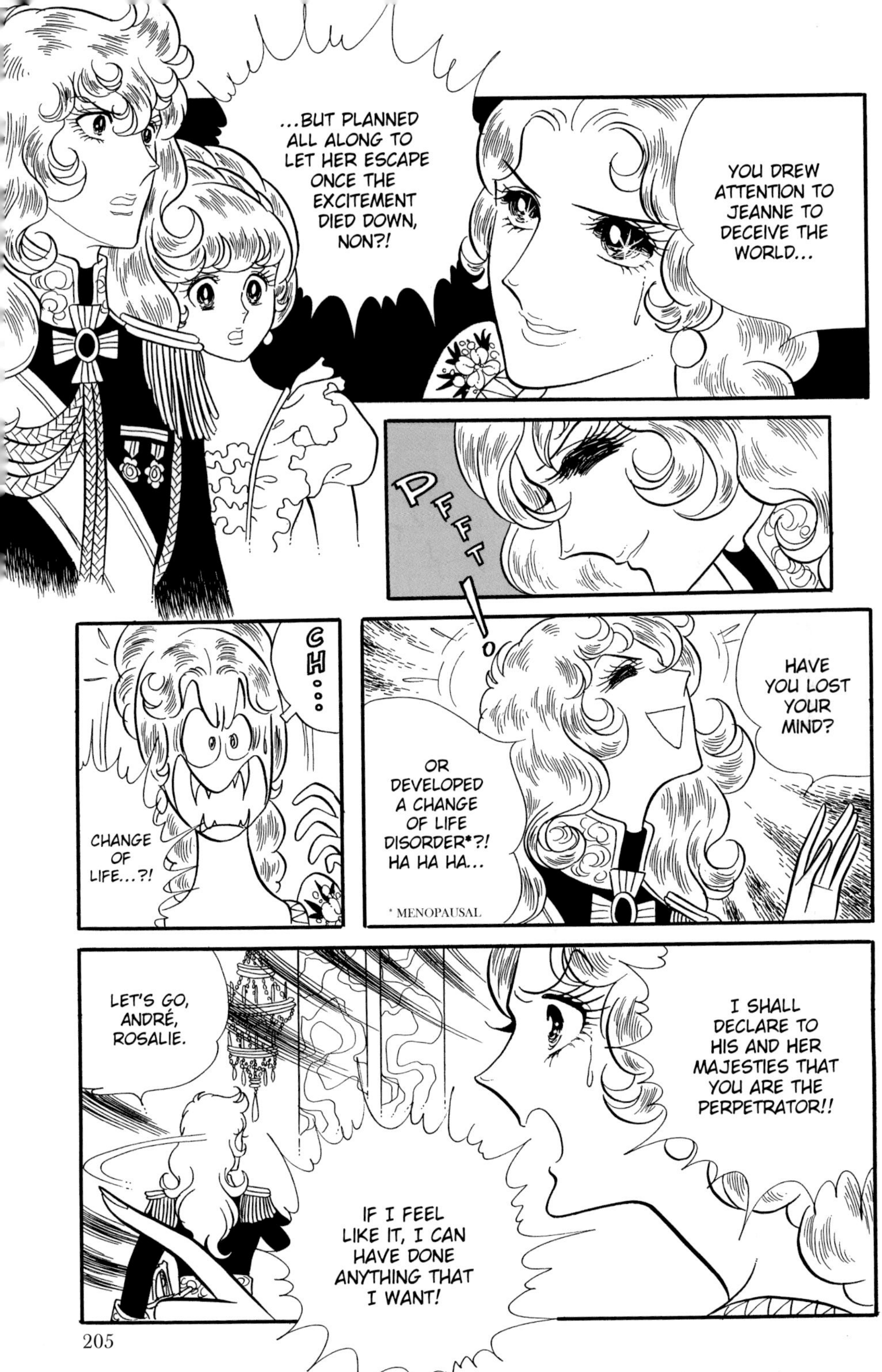

YOU DREW ATTENTION TO JEANNE TO DECEIVE THE WORLD...
...BUT PLANNED ALL ALONG TO LET HER ESCAPE ONCE THE EXCITEMENT DIED DOWN, NON?!
PFFT!
HAVE YOU LOST YOUR MIND?
OR DEVELOPED A CHANGE OF LIFE DISORDER*?! HA HA HA...
* MENOPAUSAL
CH...
CHANGE OF LIFE...?!
I SHALL DECLARE TO HIS AND HER MAJESTIES THAT YOU ARE THE PERPETRATOR!!
LET'S GO, ANDRÉ, ROSALIE.
IF I FEEL LIKE IT, I CAN HAVE DONE ANYTHING THAT I WANT!

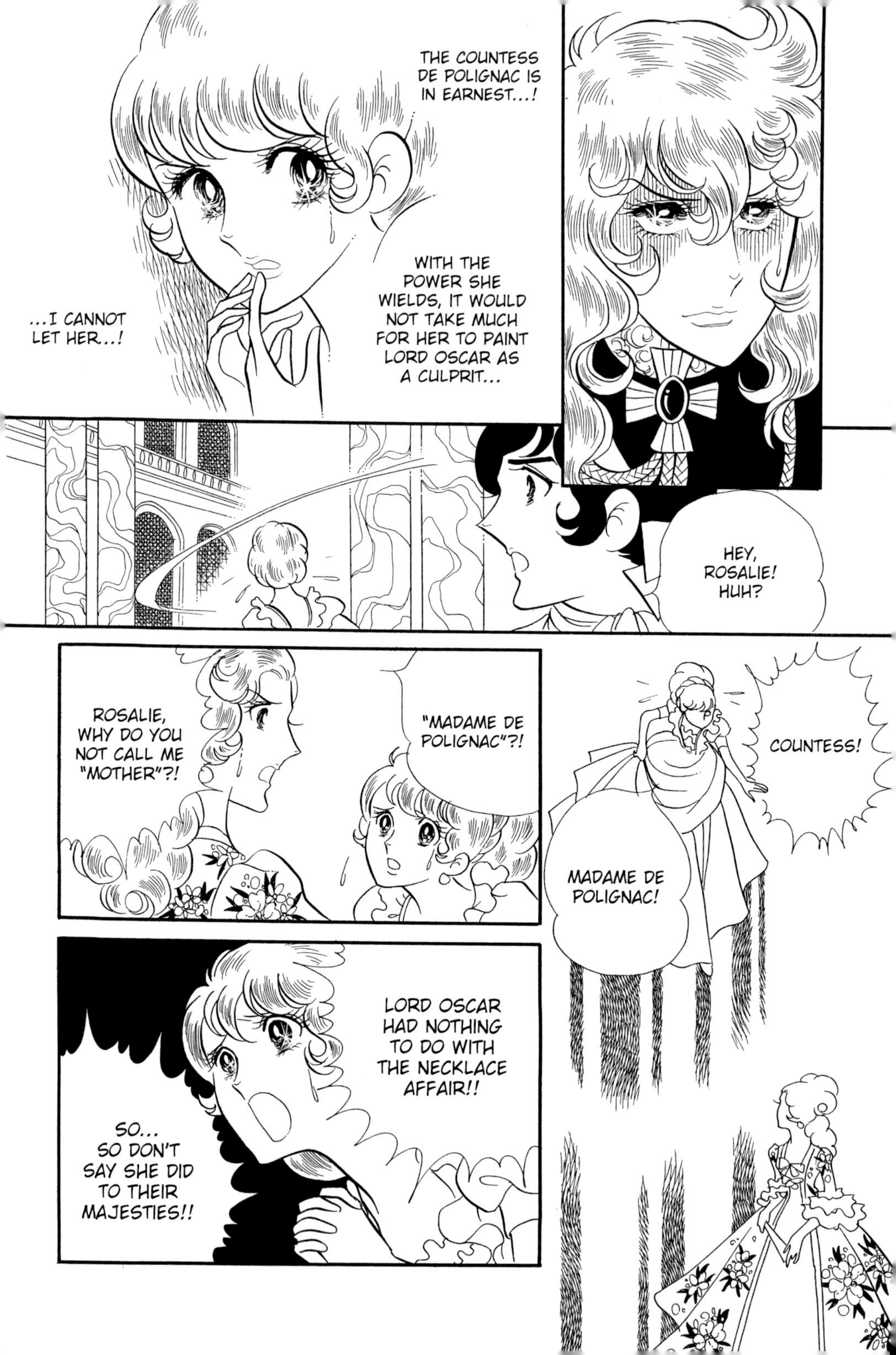
THE COUNTESS DE POLIGNAC IS IN EARNEST...!
WITH THE POWER SHE WIELDS, IT WOULD NOT TAKE MUCH FOR HER TO PAINT LORD OSCAR AS A CULPRIT...
...I CANNOT LET HER...!
HEY, ROSALIE! HUH?
COUNTESS!
MADAME DE POLIGNAC!
"MADAME DE POLIGNAC"?!
ROSALIE, WHY DO YOU NOT CALL ME "MOTHER"?!
LORD OSCAR HAD NOTHING TO DO WITH THE NECKLACE AFFAIR!!
SO... SO DON'T SAY SHE DID TO THEIR MAJESTIES!!

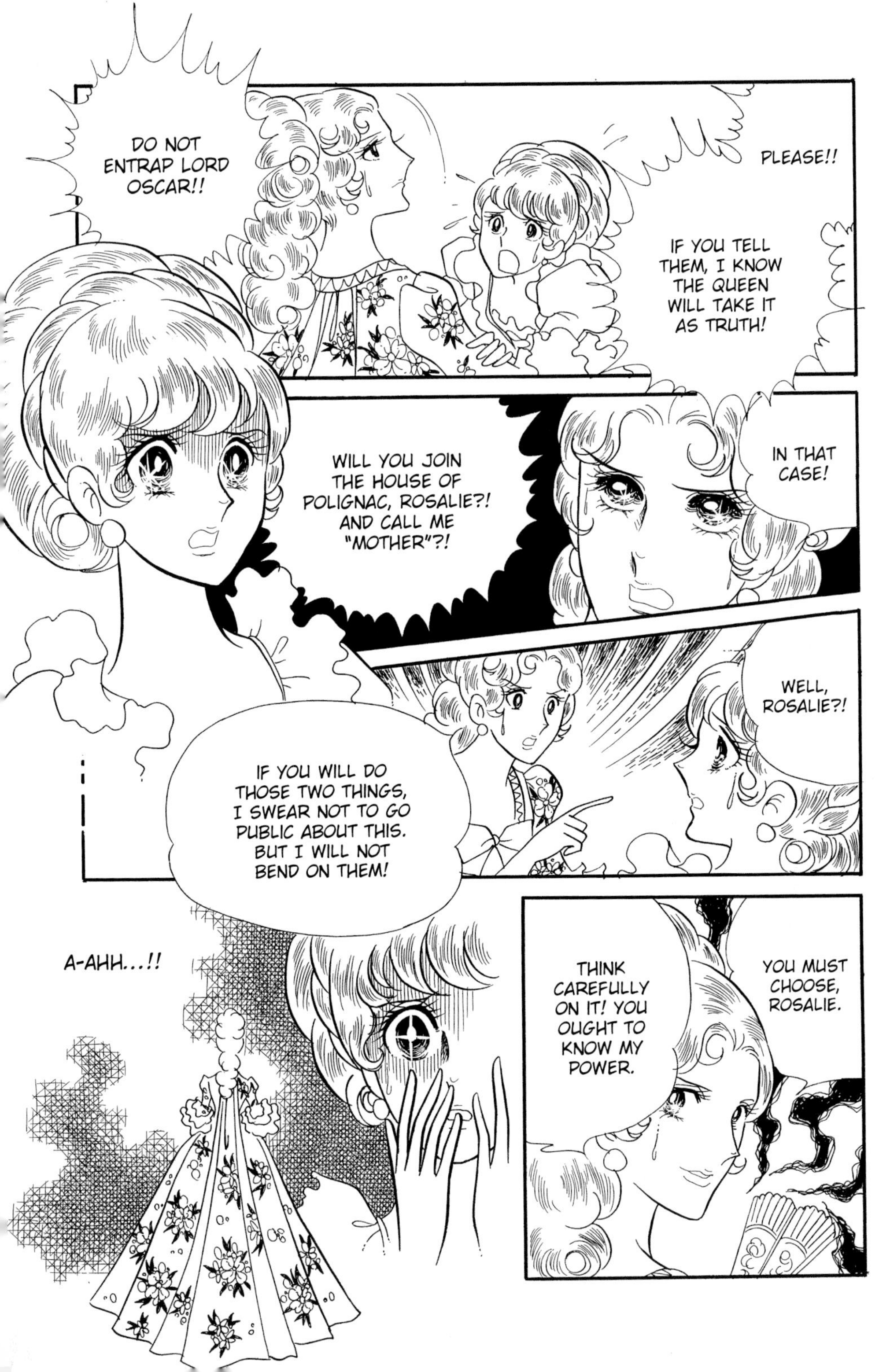
PLEASE!!
IF YOU TELL THEM, I KNOW THE QUEEN WILL TAKE IT AS TRUTH!
DO NOT ENTRAP LORD OSCAR!!
IN THAT CASE!
WILL YOU JOIN THE HOUSE OF POLIGNAC, ROSALIE?! AND CALL ME "MOTHER"?!
WELL, ROSALIE?!
IF YOU WILL DO THOSE TWO THINGS, I SWEAR NOT TO GO PUBLIC ABOUT THIS. BUT I WILL NOT BEND ON THEM!
YOU MUST CHOOSE, ROSALIE.
THINK CAREFULLY ON IT! YOU OUGHT TO KNOW MY POWER.
A-AHH...!!

THE ROSE OF VERSAILLES

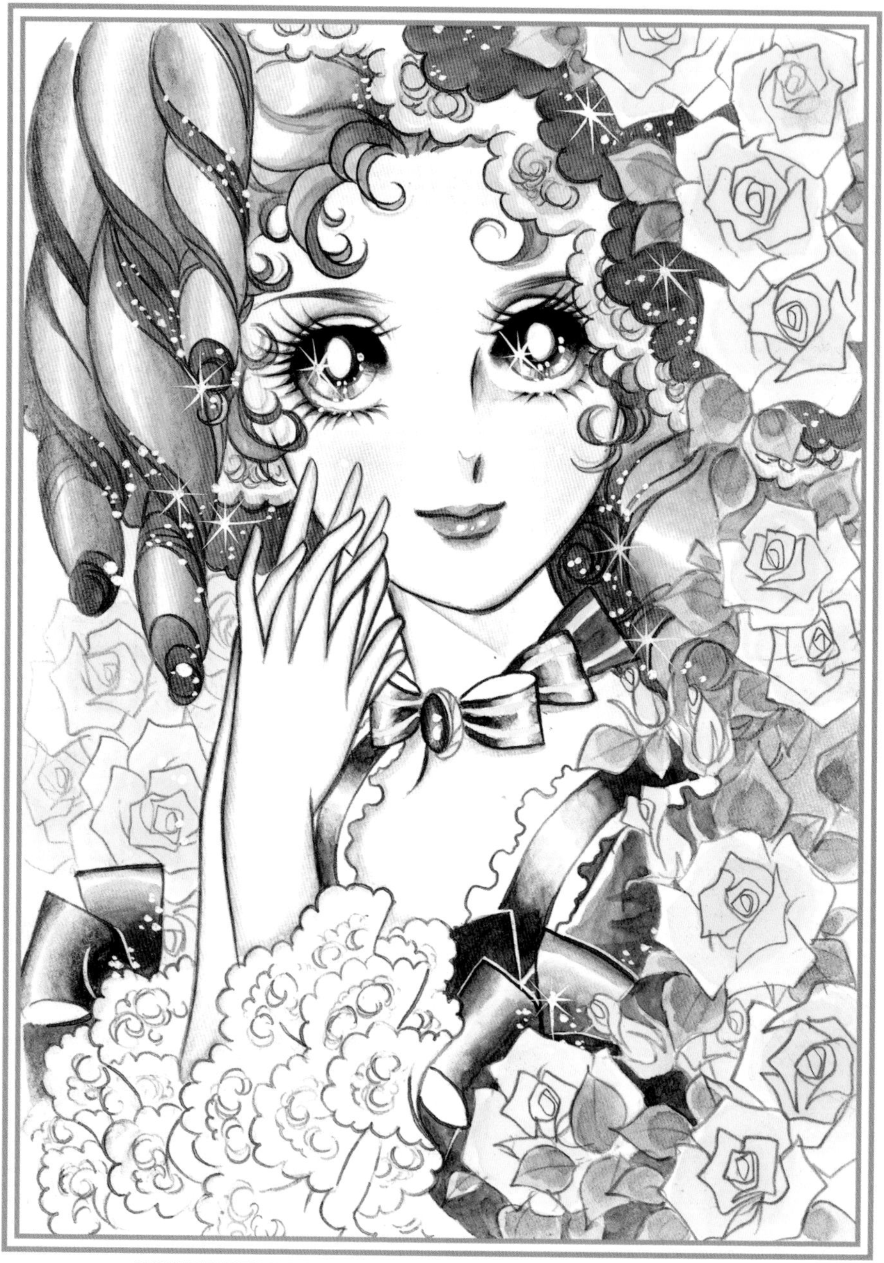

1972 WEEKLY MARGARET MAGAZINE ISSUE 52 NEW YEAR'S GREETING CARD ART

♥ WHAT WILL COUNTESS DE POLIGNAC DO UPON LEARNING OF JEANNE'S JAILBREAK?!

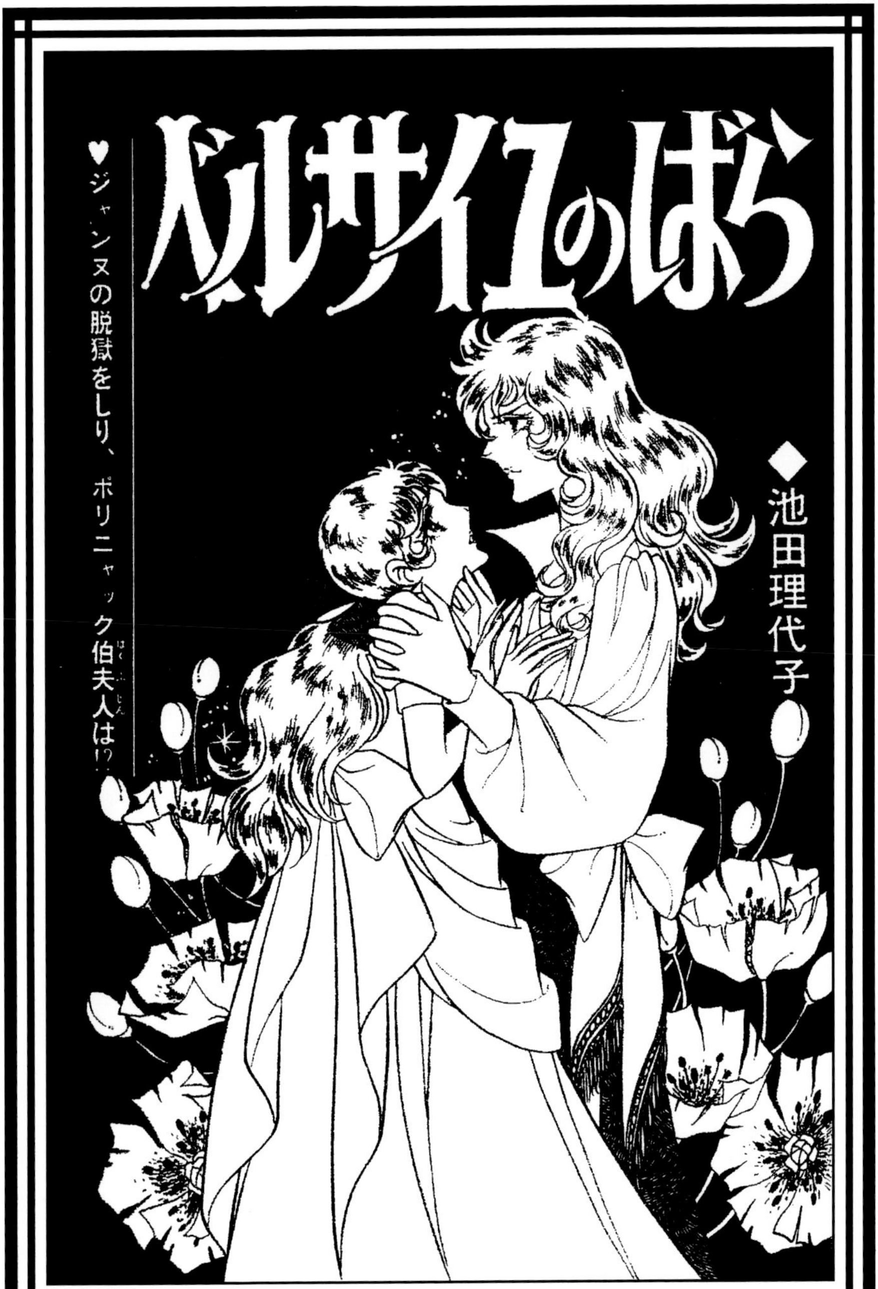
ベルサイユのばら
♥ジャンヌの脱獄をしり、ポリニャック伯夫人は!?
◆池田理代子

EPISODE 32

⚜Episode 32

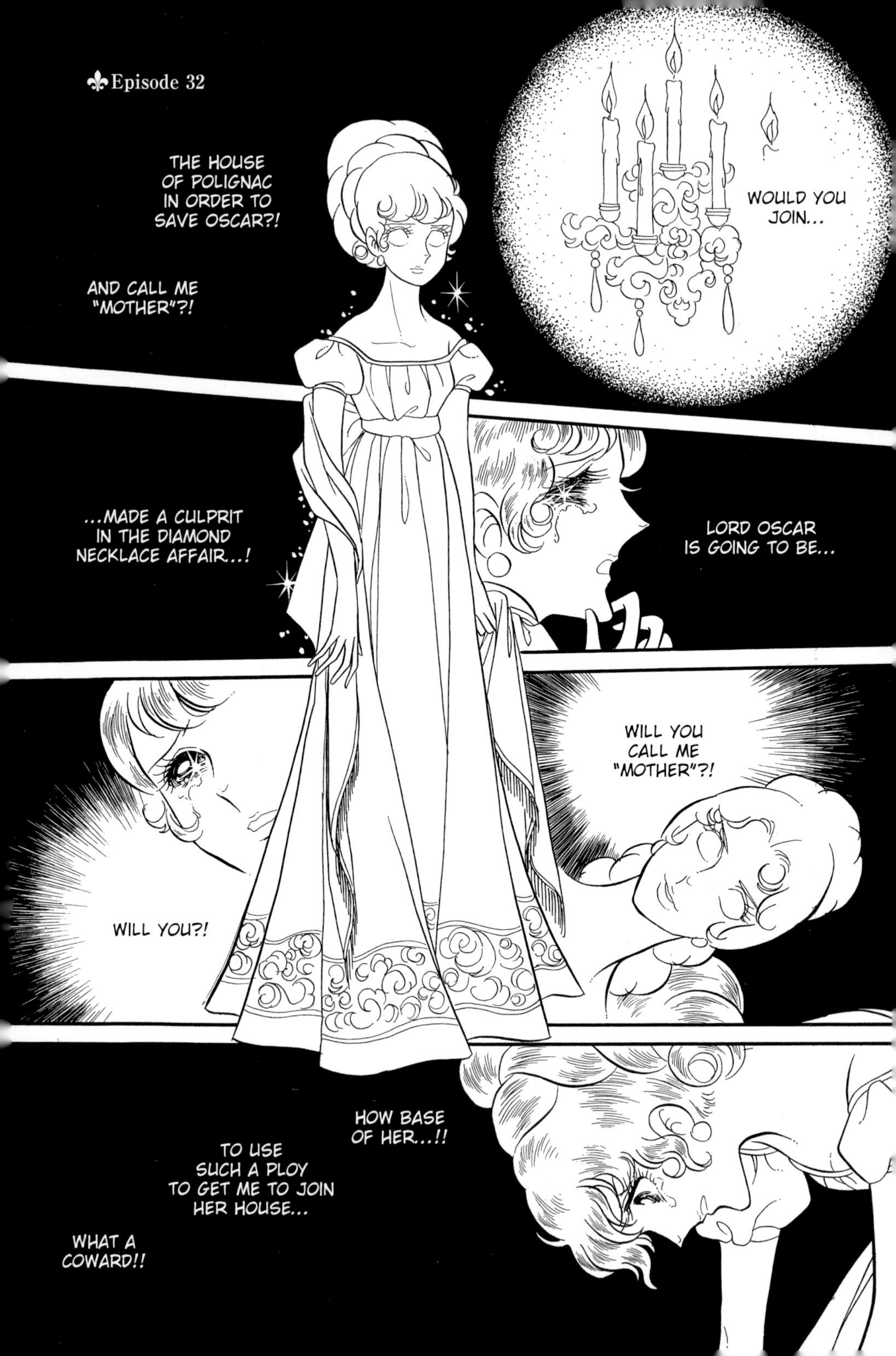
WOULD YOU JOIN...
THE HOUSE OF POLIGNAC IN ORDER TO SAVE OSCAR?!
AND CALL ME "MOTHER"?!
LORD OSCAR IS GOING TO BE...
...MADE A CULPRIT IN THE DIAMOND NECKLACE AFFAIR...!
WILL YOU CALL ME "MOTHER"?!
WILL YOU?!
HOW BASE OF HER...!!
TO USE SUCH A PLOY TO GET ME TO JOIN HER HOUSE...
WHAT A COWARD!!

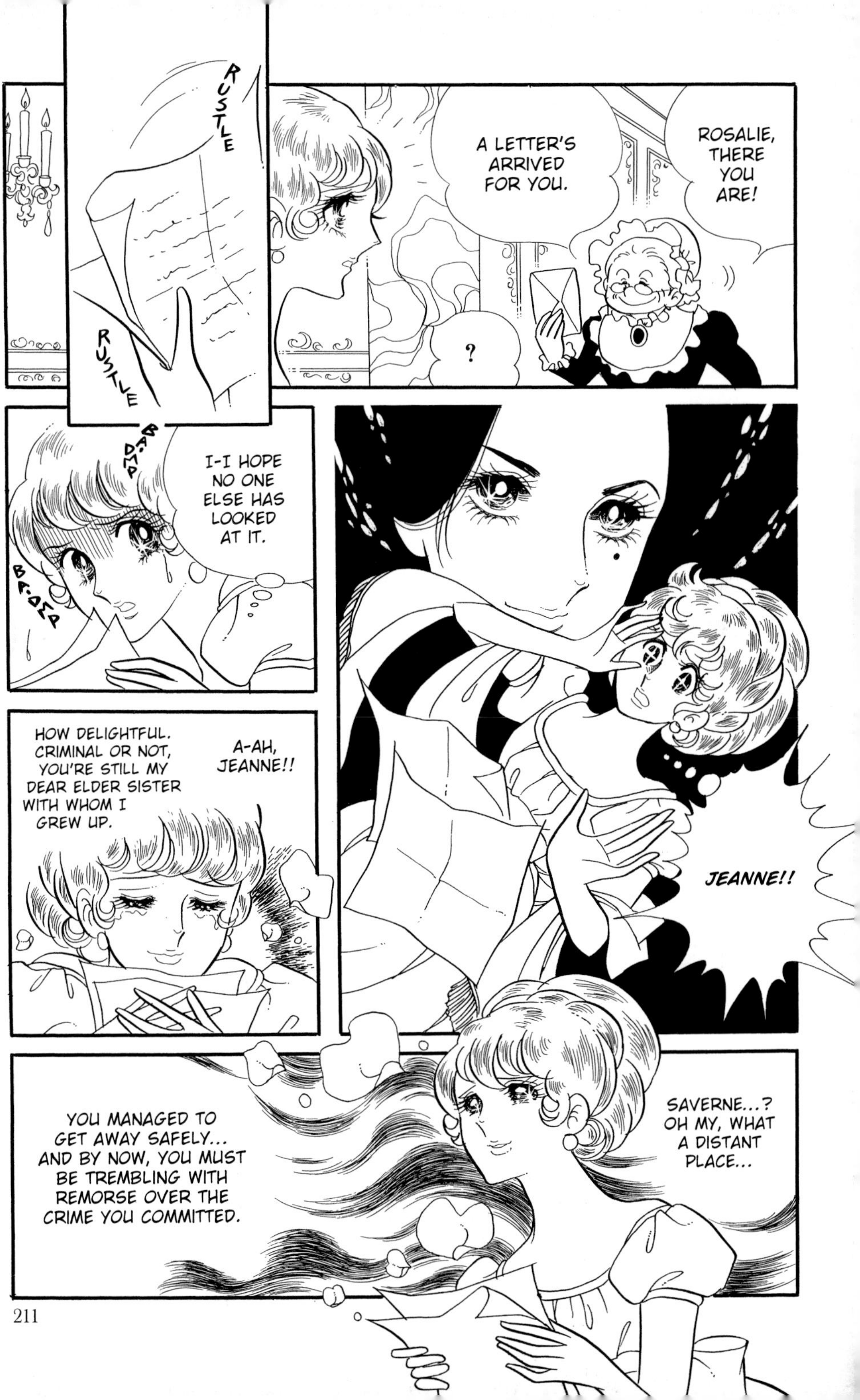
ROSALIE, THERE YOU ARE!
A LETTER'S ARRIVED FOR YOU.
?
RUSTLE
RUSTLE
JEANNE!!
BA-DMP
BA-DMP
I-I HOPE NO ONE ELSE HAS LOOKED AT IT.
A-AH, JEANNE!!
HOW DELIGHTFUL. CRIMINAL OR NOT, YOU'RE STILL MY DEAR ELDER SISTER WITH WHOM I GREW UP.
SAVERNE...? OH MY, WHAT A DISTANT PLACE...
YOU MANAGED TO GET AWAY SAFELY... AND BY NOW, YOU MUST BE TREMBLING WITH REMORSE OVER THE CRIME YOU COMMITTED.

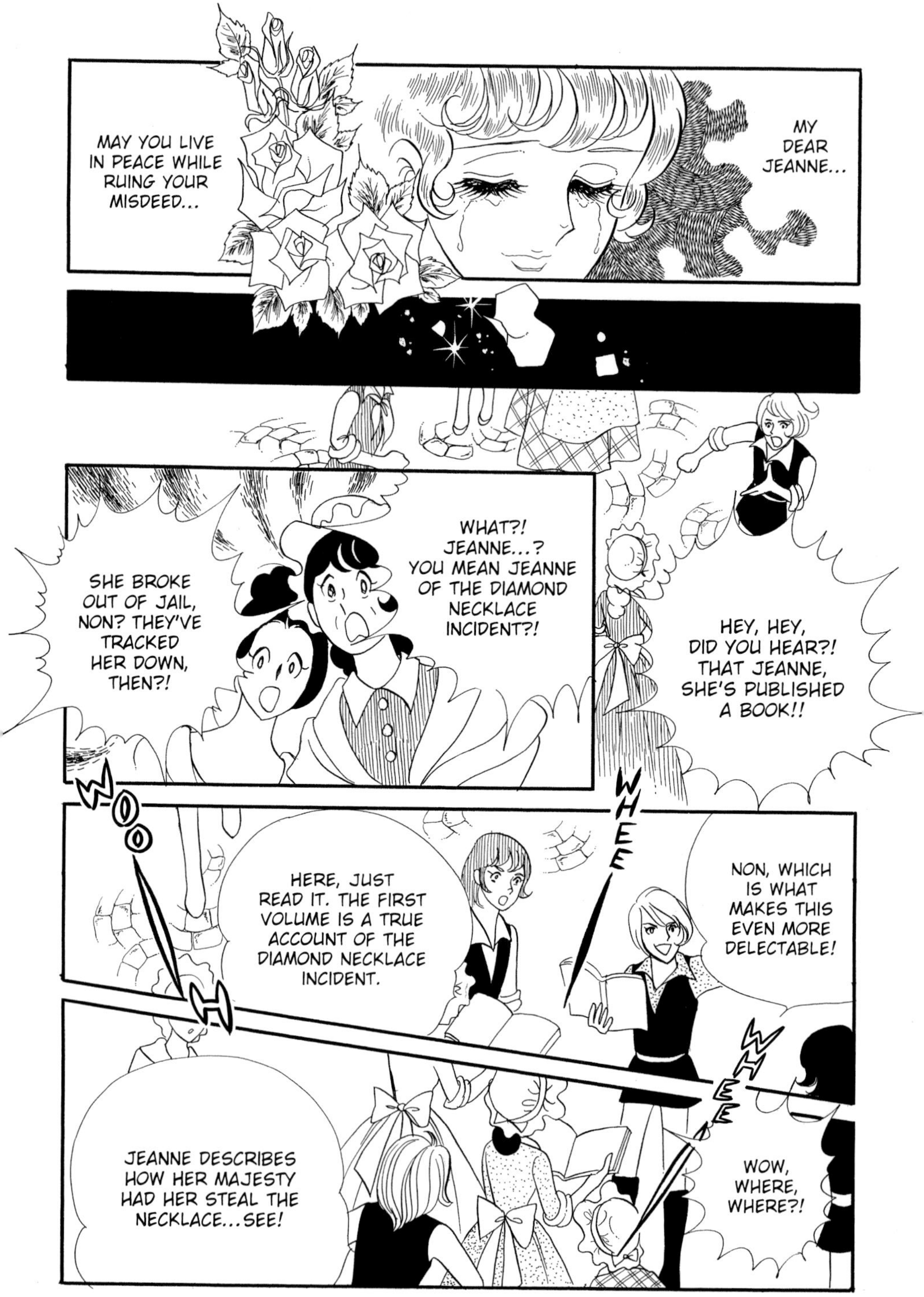
MY DEAR JEANNE...
MAY YOU LIVE IN PEACE WHILE RUING YOUR MISDEED...
HEY, HEY, DID YOU HEAR?! THAT JEANNE, SHE'S PUBLISHED A BOOK!!
WHAT?! JEANNE...? YOU MEAN JEANNE OF THE DIAMOND NECKLACE INCIDENT?!
SHE BROKE OUT OF JAIL, NON? THEY'VE TRACKED HER DOWN, THEN?!
WHEE
WOOOH
NON, WHICH IS WHAT MAKES THIS EVEN MORE DELECTABLE!
HERE, JUST READ IT. THE FIRST VOLUME IS A TRUE ACCOUNT OF THE DIAMOND NECKLACE INCIDENT.
WHEE
WOW, WHERE, WHERE?!
JEANNE DESCRIBES HOW HER MAJESTY HAD HER STEAL THE NECKLACE...SEE!

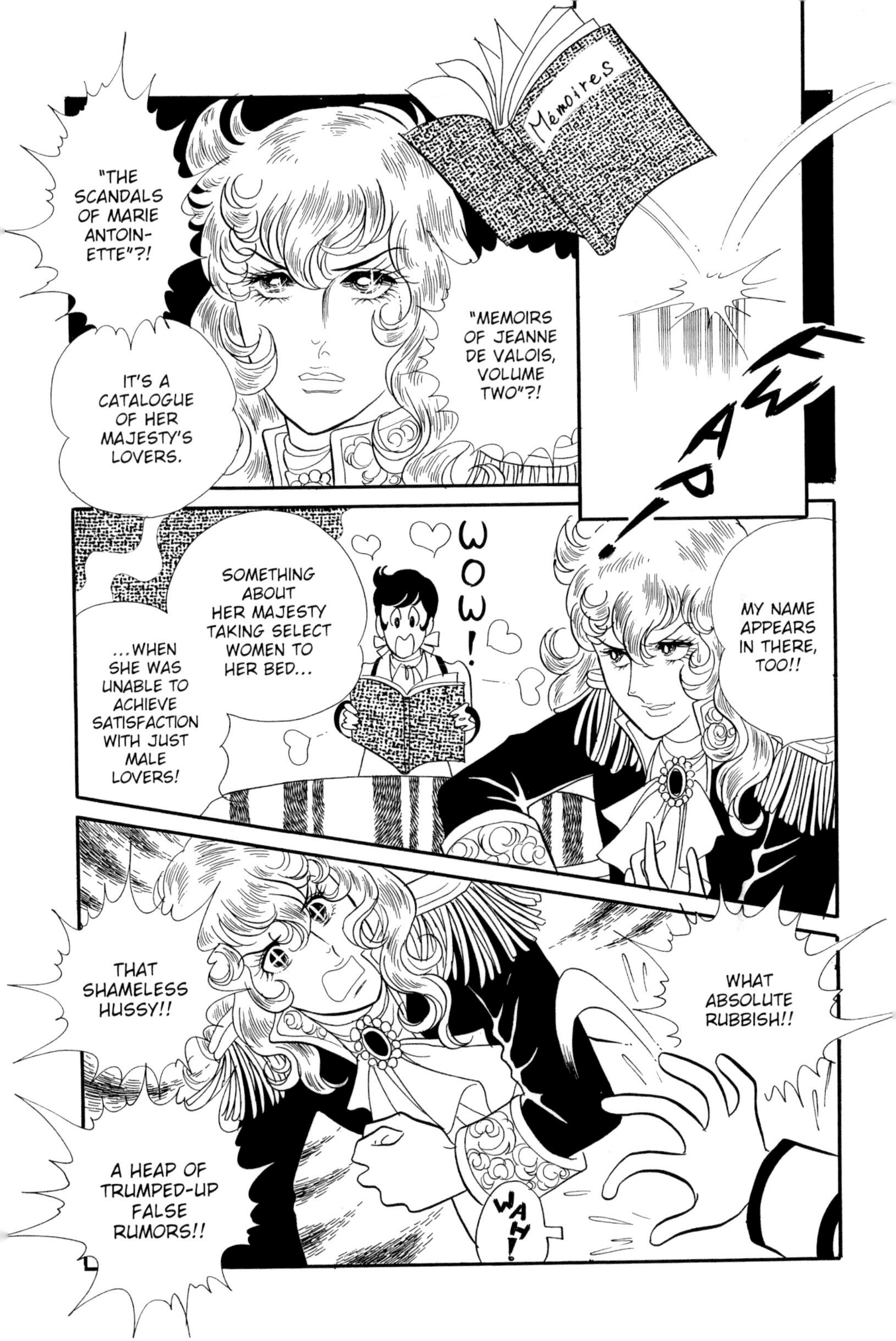
Mémoires
FWAP!
"MEMOIRS OF JEANNE DE VALOIS, VOLUME TWO"?!
"THE SCANDALS OF MARIE ANTOINETTE"?!
IT'S A CATALOGUE OF HER MAJESTY'S LOVERS.
MY NAME APPEARS IN THERE, TOO!!
WOW!
SOMETHING ABOUT HER MAJESTY TAKING SELECT WOMEN TO HER BED...
...WHEN SHE WAS UNABLE TO ACHIEVE SATISFACTION WITH JUST MALE LOVERS!
WHAT ABSOLUTE RUBBISH!!
THAT SHAMELESS HUSSY!!
A HEAP OF TRUMPED-UP FALSE RUMORS!!
WAH!

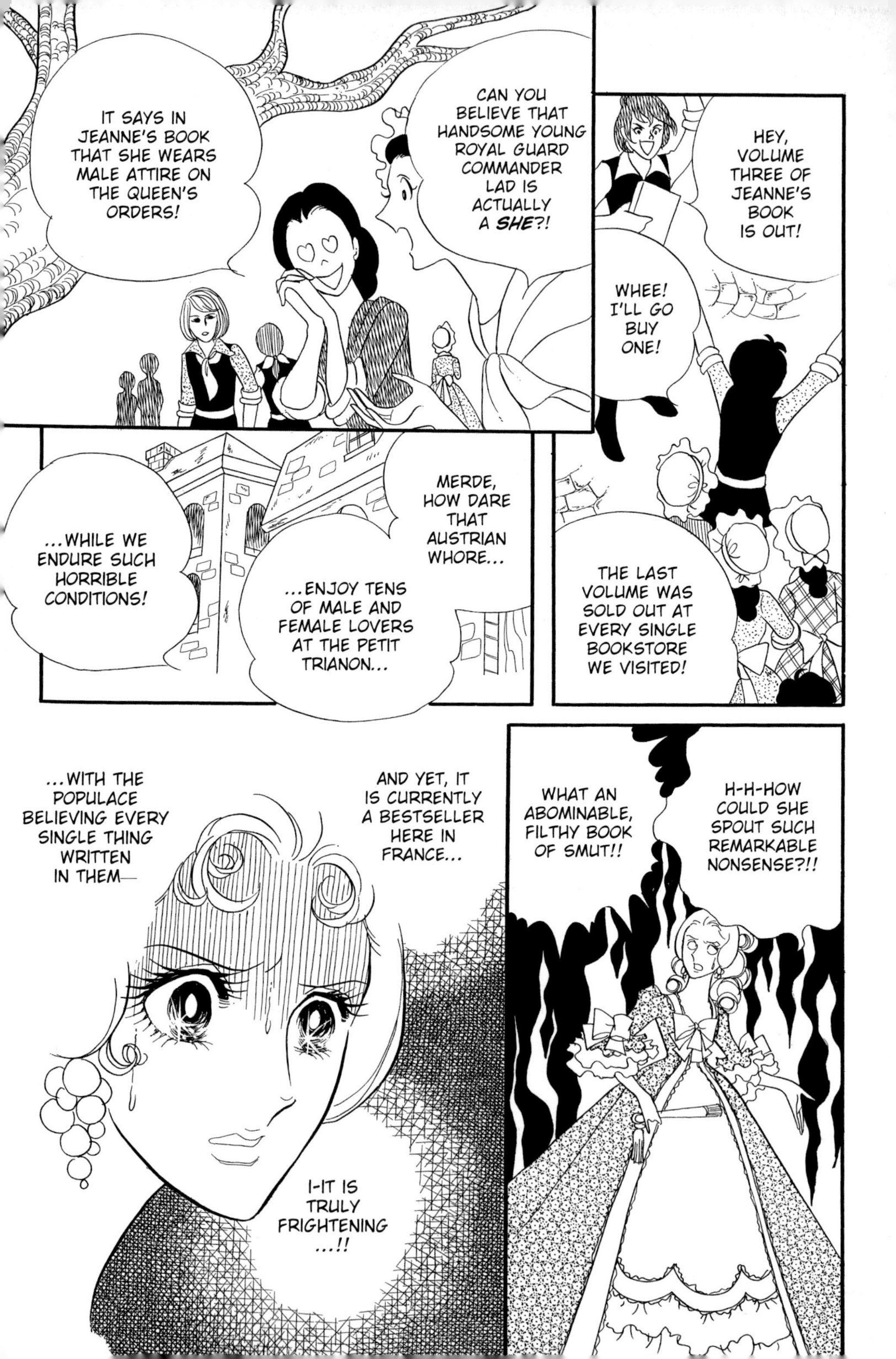
HEY, VOLUME THREE OF JEANNE'S BOOK IS OUT!
WHEE! I'LL GO BUY ONE!
THE LAST VOLUME WAS SOLD OUT AT EVERY SINGLE BOOKSTORE WE VISITED!
CAN YOU BELIEVE THAT HANDSOME YOUNG ROYAL GUARD COMMANDER LAD IS ACTUALLY A *SHE*?!
IT SAYS IN JEANNE'S BOOK THAT SHE WEARS MALE ATTIRE ON THE QUEEN'S ORDERS!
MERDE, HOW DARE THAT AUSTRIAN WHORE...
...ENJOY TENS OF MALE AND FEMALE LOVERS AT THE PETIT TRIANON...
...WHILE WE ENDURE SUCH HORRIBLE CONDITIONS!
H-H-HOW COULD SHE SPOUT SUCH REMARKABLE NONSENSE?!!
WHAT AN ABOMINABLE, FILTHY BOOK OF SMUT!!
AND YET, IT IS CURRENTLY A BESTSELLER HERE IN FRANCE...
...WITH THE POPULACE BELIEVING EVERY SINGLE THING WRITTEN IN THEM—
I-IT IS TRULY FRIGHTENING ...!!

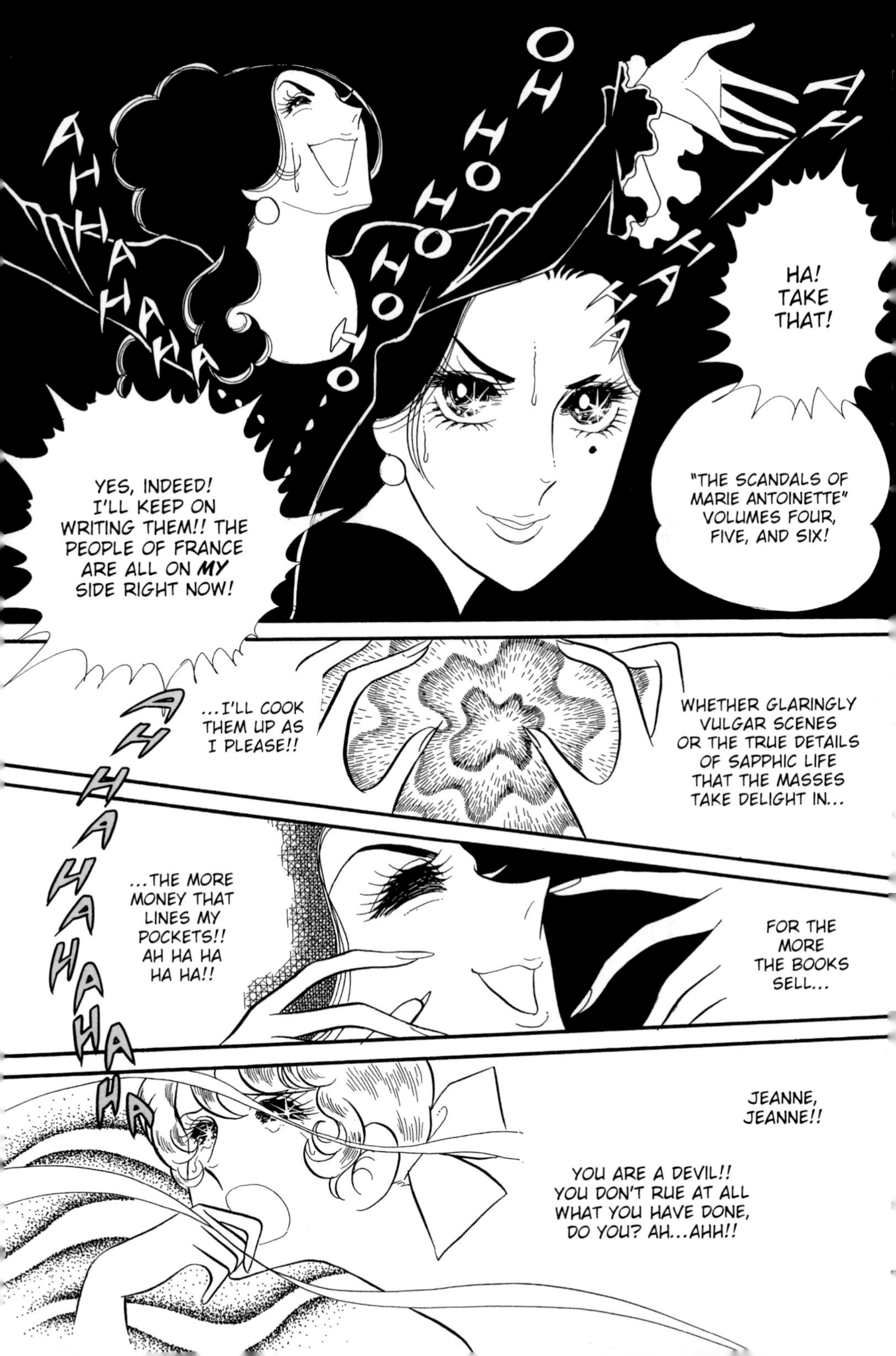
HA! TAKE THAT!
"THE SCANDALS OF MARIE ANTOINETTE" VOLUMES FOUR, FIVE, AND SIX!
OH HO HO HO HO HO HO
AH HA HA HA HA...
YES, INDEED! I'LL KEEP ON WRITING THEM!! THE PEOPLE OF FRANCE ARE ALL ON *MY* SIDE RIGHT NOW!
WHETHER GLARINGLY VULGAR SCENES OR THE TRUE DETAILS OF SAPPHIC LIFE THAT THE MASSES TAKE DELIGHT IN...
...I'LL COOK THEM UP AS I PLEASE!!
FOR THE MORE THE BOOKS SELL...
...THE MORE MONEY THAT LINES MY POCKETS!! AH HA HA HA HA!!
AH HA HA HA HA HA HA HA HA HA
JEANNE, JEANNE!!
YOU ARE A DEVIL!! YOU DON'T RUE AT ALL WHAT YOU HAVE DONE, DO YOU? AH...AHH!!

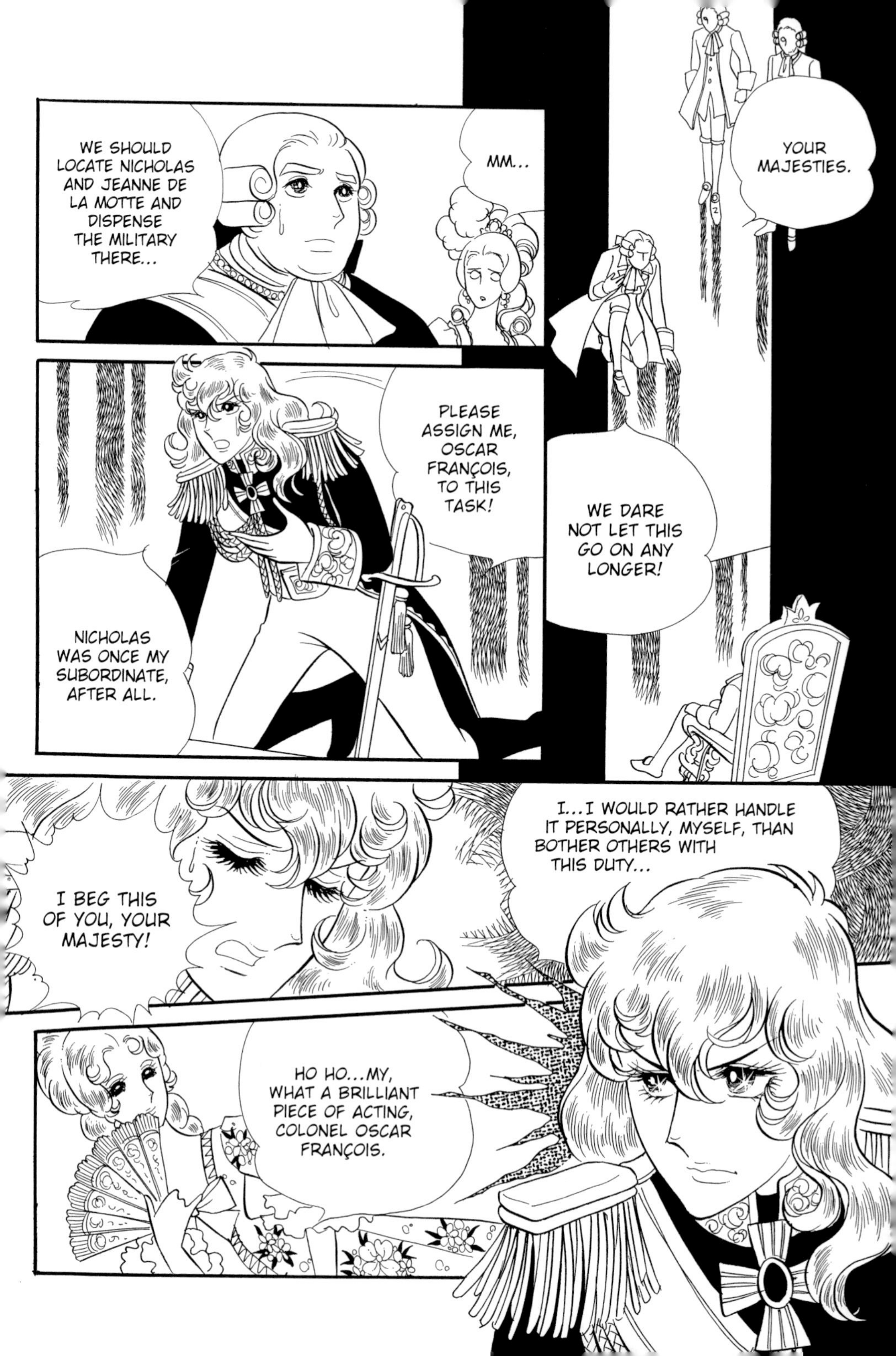
YOUR MAJESTIES.
WE DARE NOT LET THIS GO ON ANY LONGER!
MM...
WE SHOULD LOCATE NICHOLAS AND JEANNE DE LA MOTTE AND DISPENSE THE MILITARY THERE...
PLEASE ASSIGN ME, OSCAR FRANÇOIS, TO THIS TASK!
NICHOLAS WAS ONCE MY SUBORDINATE, AFTER ALL.
I...I WOULD RATHER HANDLE IT PERSONALLY, MYSELF, THAN BOTHER OTHERS WITH THIS DUTY...
I BEG THIS OF YOU, YOUR MAJESTY!
HO HO...MY, WHAT A BRILLIANT PIECE OF ACTING, COLONEL OSCAR FRANÇOIS.

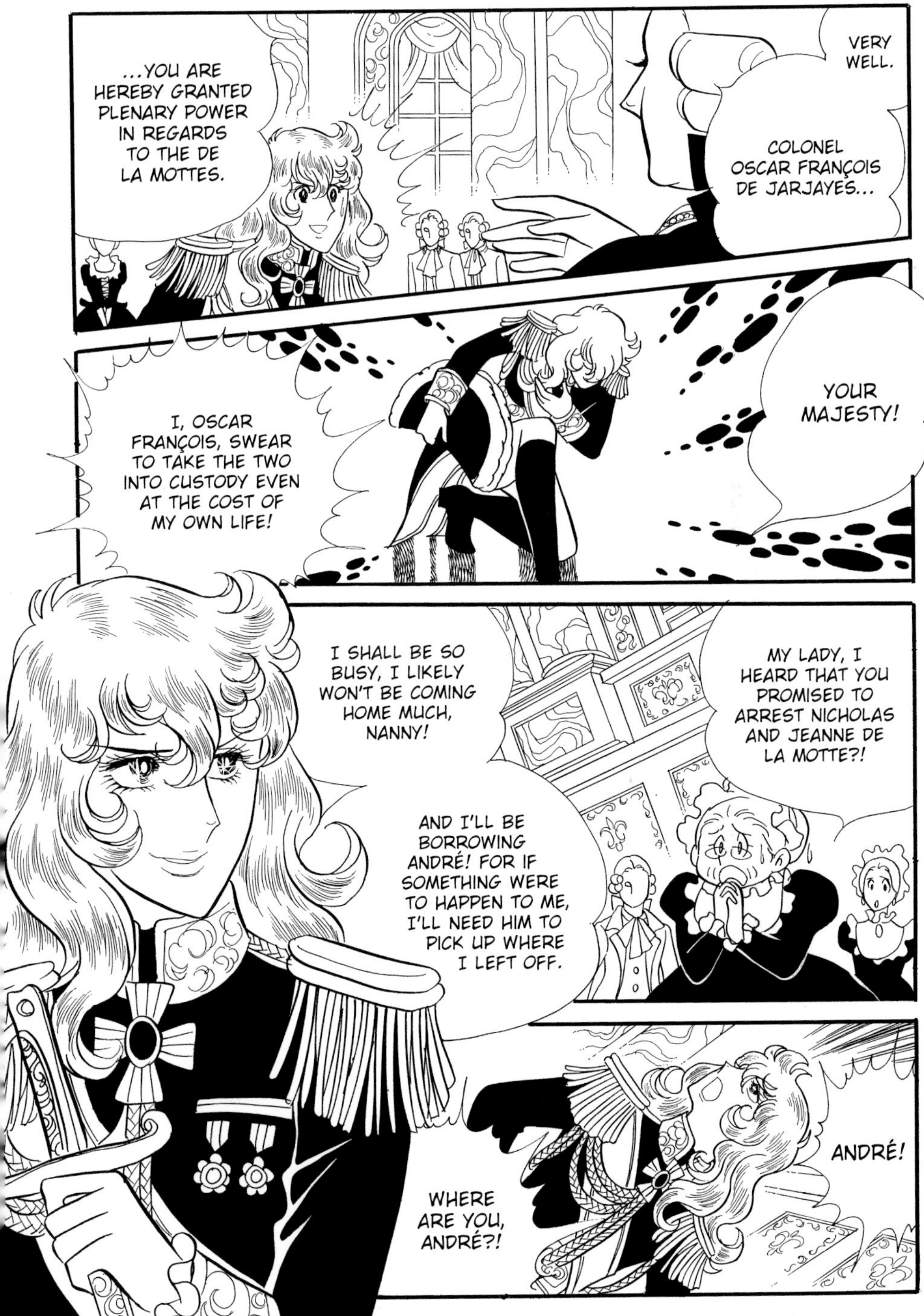
VERY WELL.
COLONEL OSCAR FRANÇOIS DE JARJAYES...
...YOU ARE HEREBY GRANTED PLENARY POWER IN REGARDS TO THE DE LA MOTTES.
YOUR MAJESTY!
I, OSCAR FRANÇOIS, SWEAR TO TAKE THE TWO INTO CUSTODY EVEN AT THE COST OF MY OWN LIFE!
MY LADY, I HEARD THAT YOU PROMISED TO ARREST NICHOLAS AND JEANNE DE LA MOTTE?!
I SHALL BE SO BUSY, I LIKELY WON'T BE COMING HOME MUCH, NANNY!
AND I'LL BE BORROWING ANDRÉ! FOR IF SOMETHING WERE TO HAPPEN TO ME, I'LL NEED HIM TO PICK UP WHERE I LEFT OFF.
ANDRÉ!
WHERE ARE YOU, ANDRÉ?!

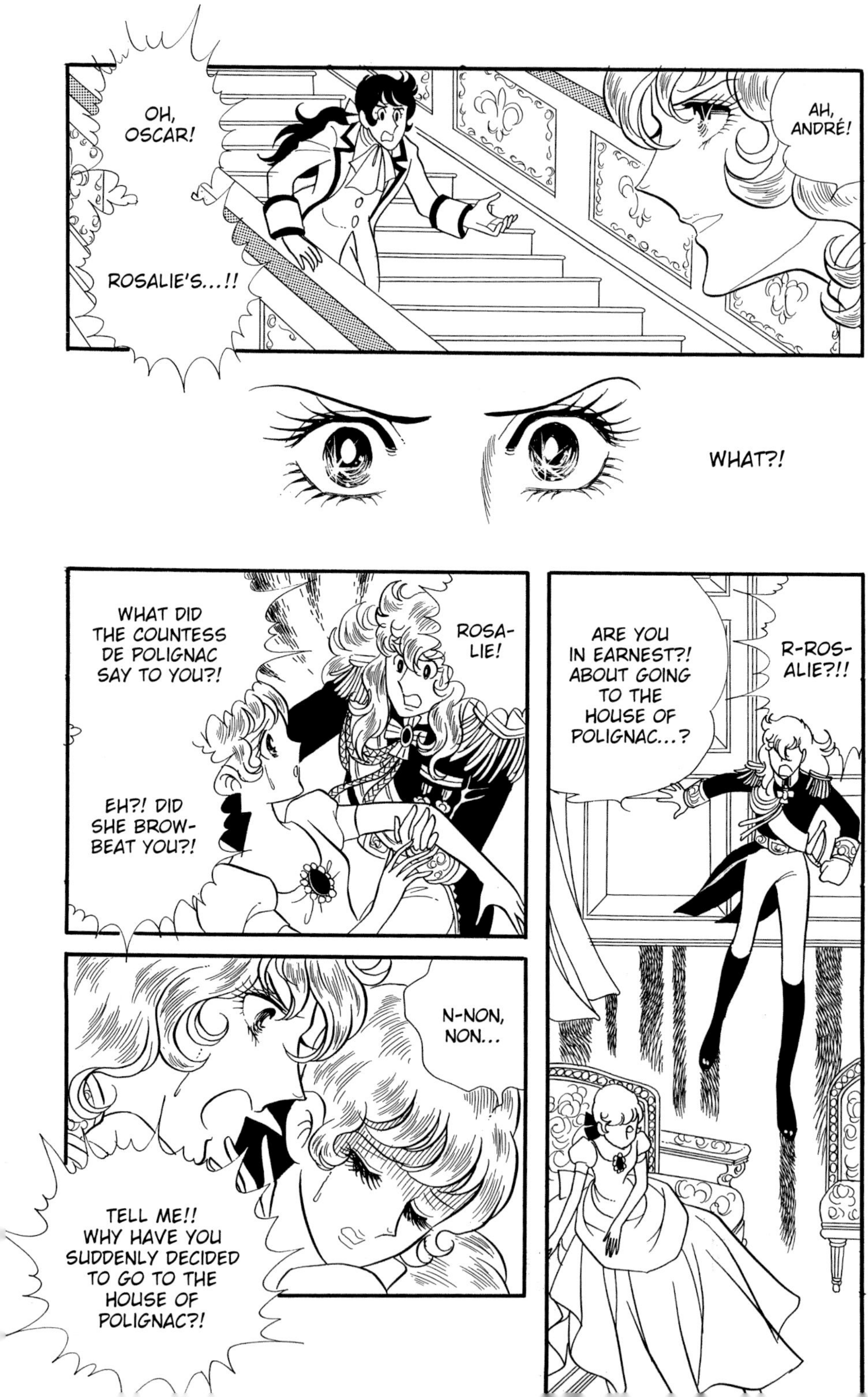
AH, ANDRÉ!
OH, OSCAR!
ROSALIE'S...!!
WHAT?!
R-ROSALIE?!!
ARE YOU IN EARNEST?! ABOUT GOING TO THE HOUSE OF POLIGNAC...?
ROSALIE!
WHAT DID THE COUNTESS DE POLIGNAC SAY TO YOU?!
EH?! DID SHE BROWBEAT YOU?!
N-NON, NON...
TELL ME!! WHY HAVE YOU SUDDENLY DECIDED TO GO TO THE HOUSE OF POLIGNAC?!

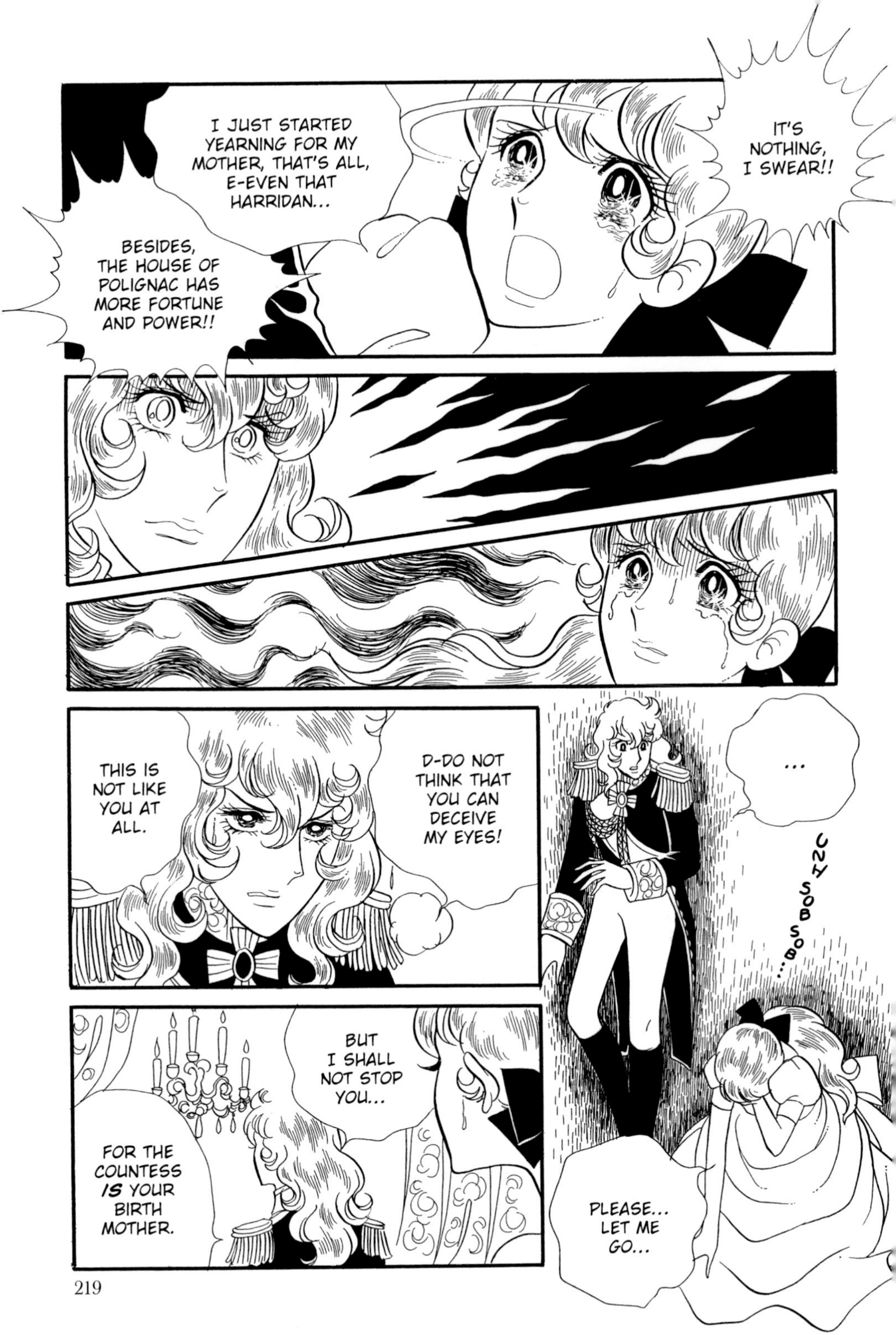
IT'S NOTHING, I SWEAR!!
I JUST STARTED YEARNING FOR MY MOTHER, THAT'S ALL, E-EVEN THAT HARRIDAN...
BESIDES, THE HOUSE OF POLIGNAC HAS MORE FORTUNE AND POWER!!
...
UNY SOB SOB...
PLEASE... LET ME GO...
D-DO NOT THINK THAT YOU CAN DECEIVE MY EYES!
THIS IS NOT LIKE YOU AT ALL.
BUT I SHALL NOT STOP YOU...
FOR THE COUNTESS *IS* YOUR BIRTH MOTHER.

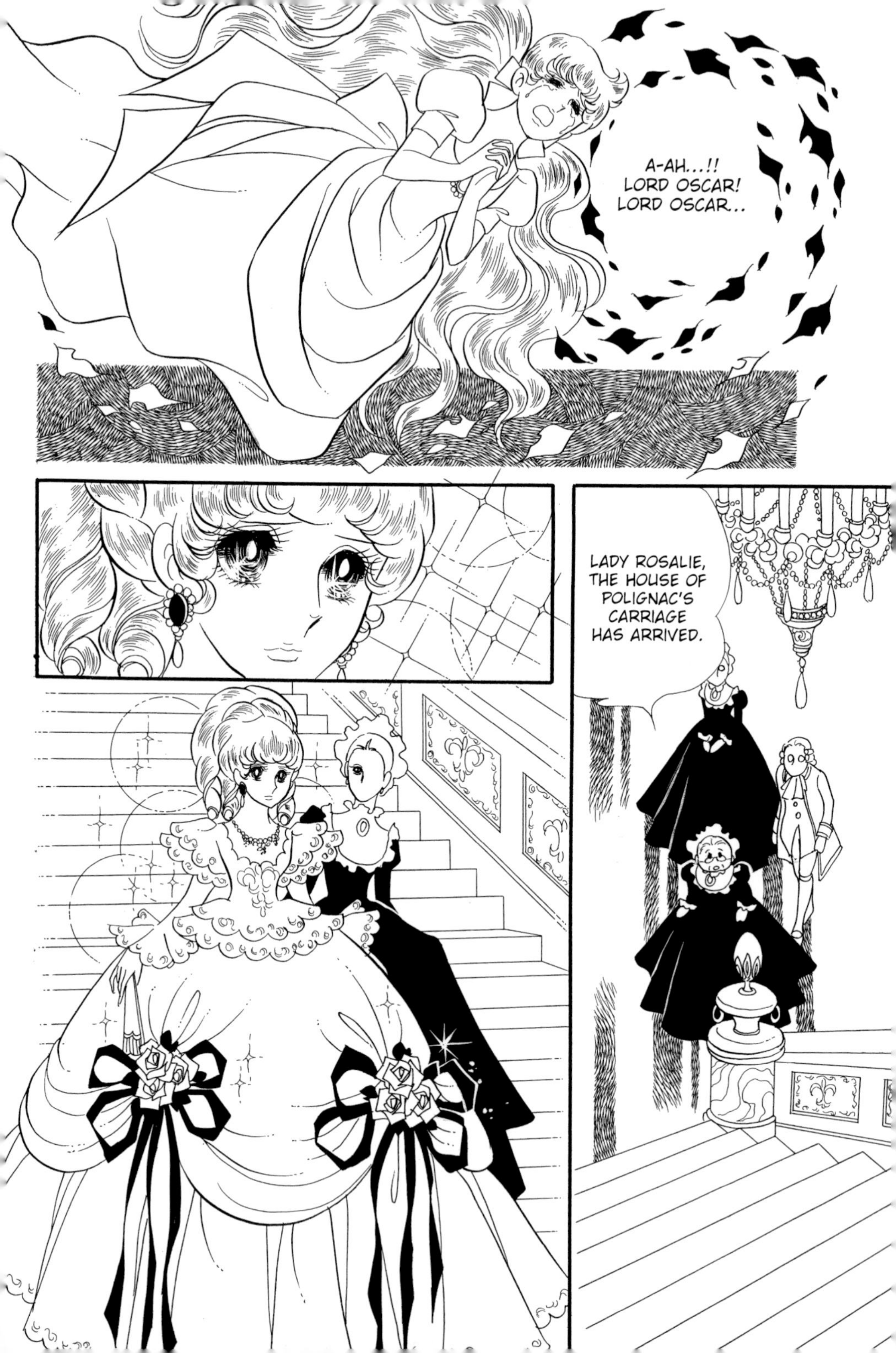
A-AH...!!
LORD OSCAR!
LORD OSCAR...
LADY ROSALIE, THE HOUSE OF POLIGNAC'S CARRIAGE HAS ARRIVED.

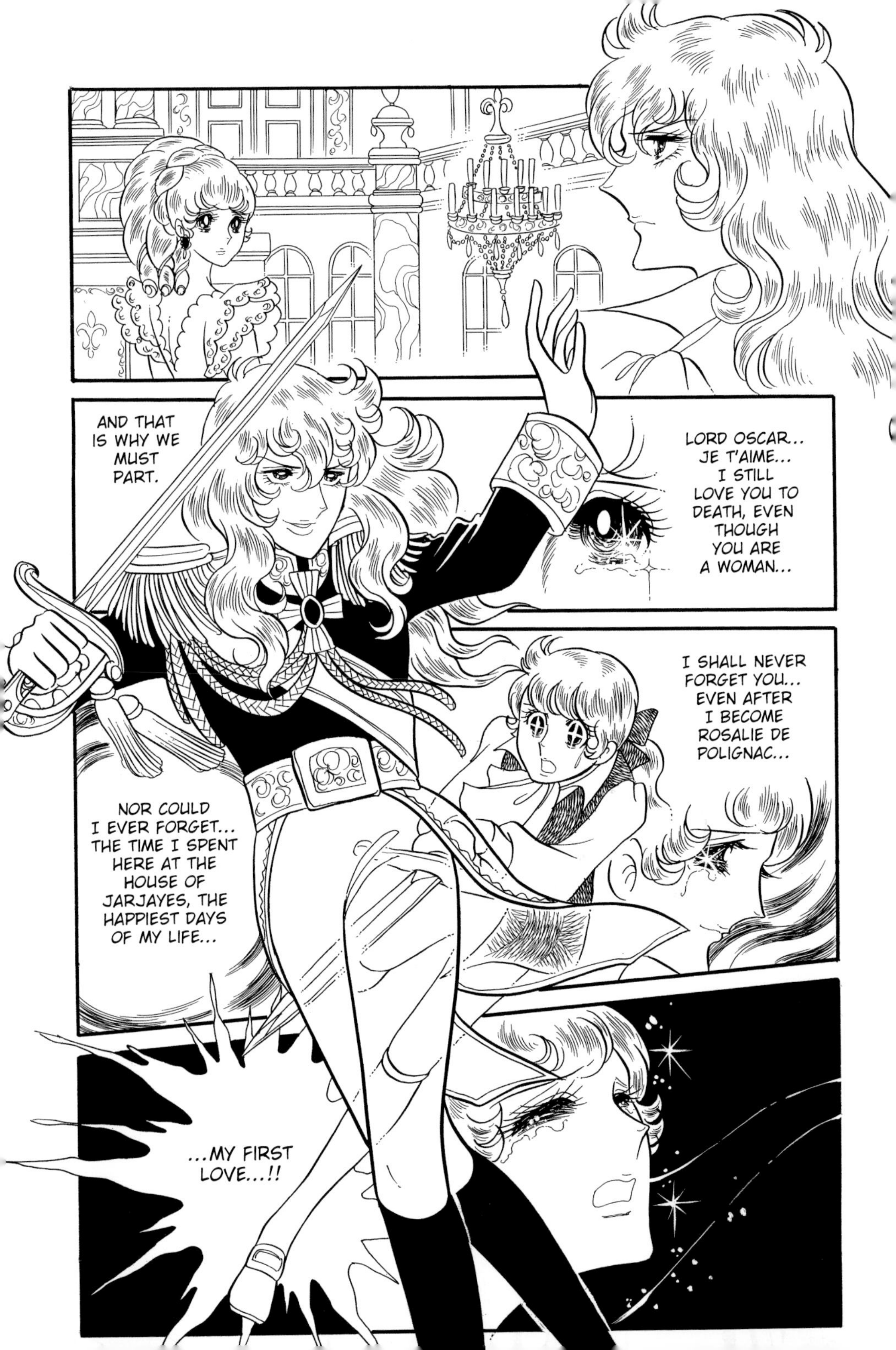
LORD OSCAR... JE T'AIME... I STILL LOVE YOU TO DEATH, EVEN THOUGH YOU ARE A WOMAN...
AND THAT IS WHY WE MUST PART.
I SHALL NEVER FORGET YOU... EVEN AFTER I BECOME ROSALIE DE POLIGNAC...
NOR COULD I EVER FORGET... THE TIME I SPENT HERE AT THE HOUSE OF JARJAYES, THE HAPPIEST DAYS OF MY LIFE...
...MY FIRST LOVE...!!

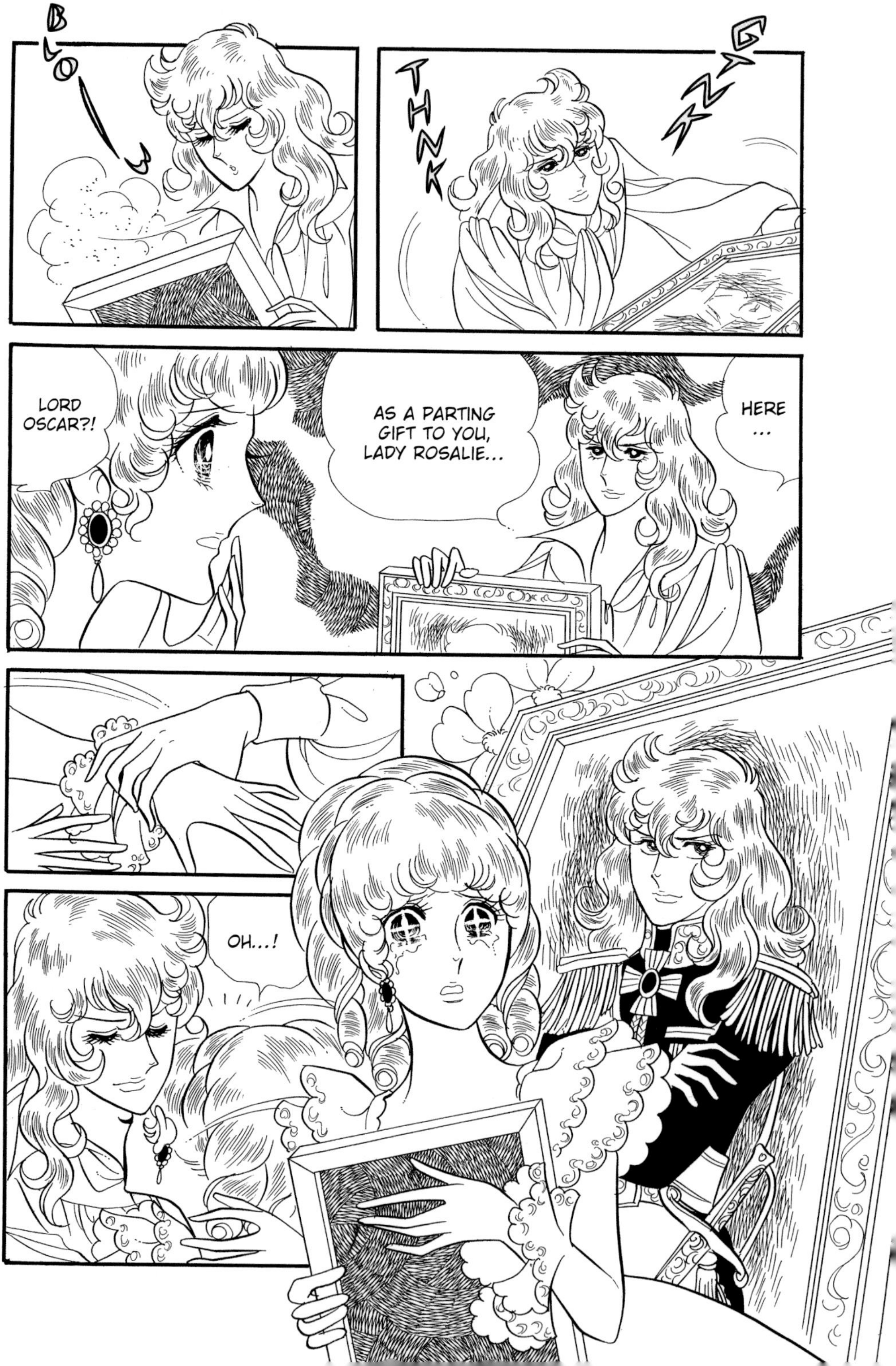
THNK
ZZZG
BLOW
HERE ...
AS A PARTING GIFT TO YOU, LADY ROSALIE...
LORD OSCAR?!
OH...!

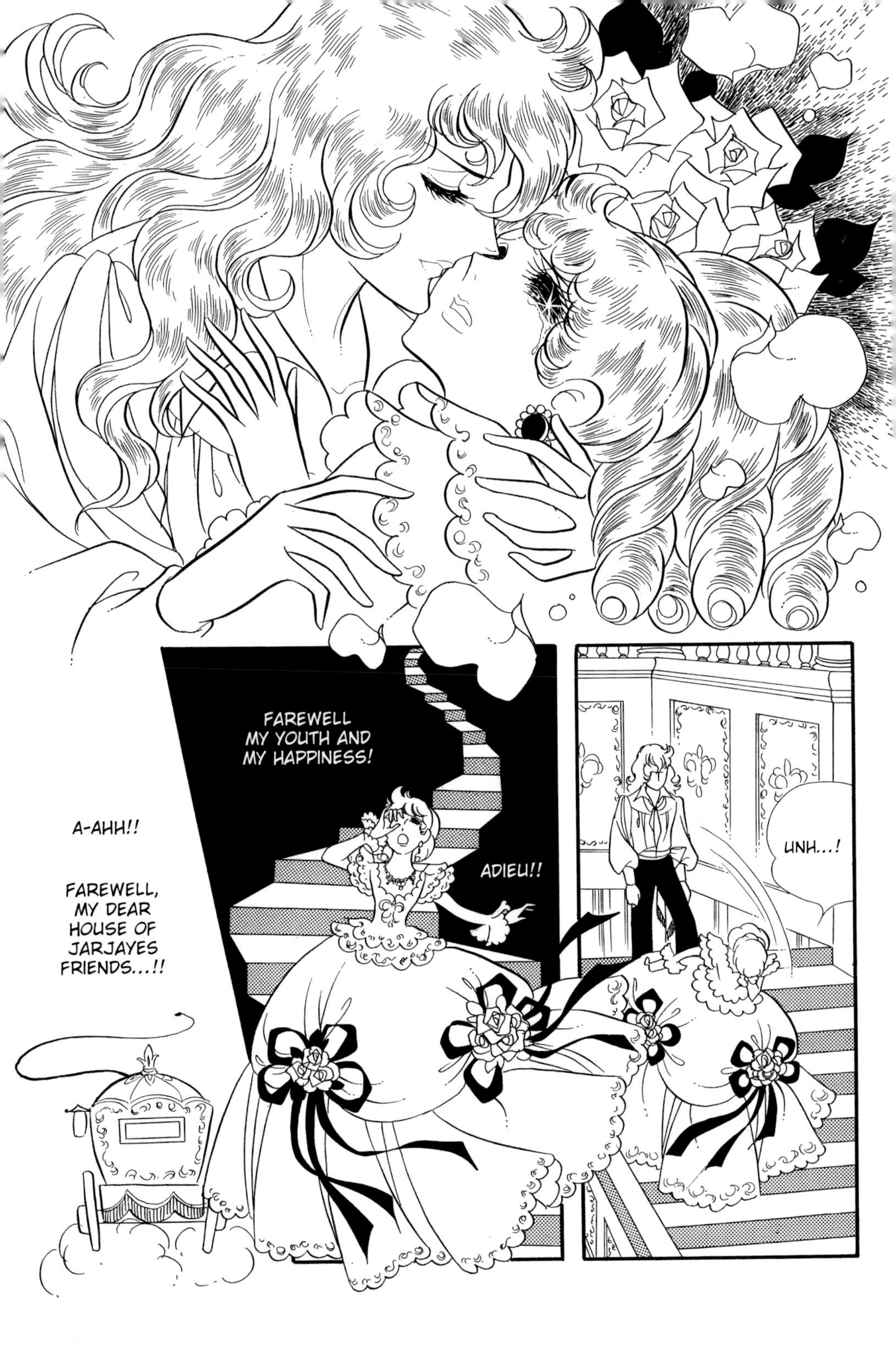
UNH...!
FAREWELL MY YOUTH AND MY HAPPINESS!
ADIEU!!
A-AHH!!
FAREWELL, MY DEAR HOUSE OF JARJAYES FRIENDS...!!

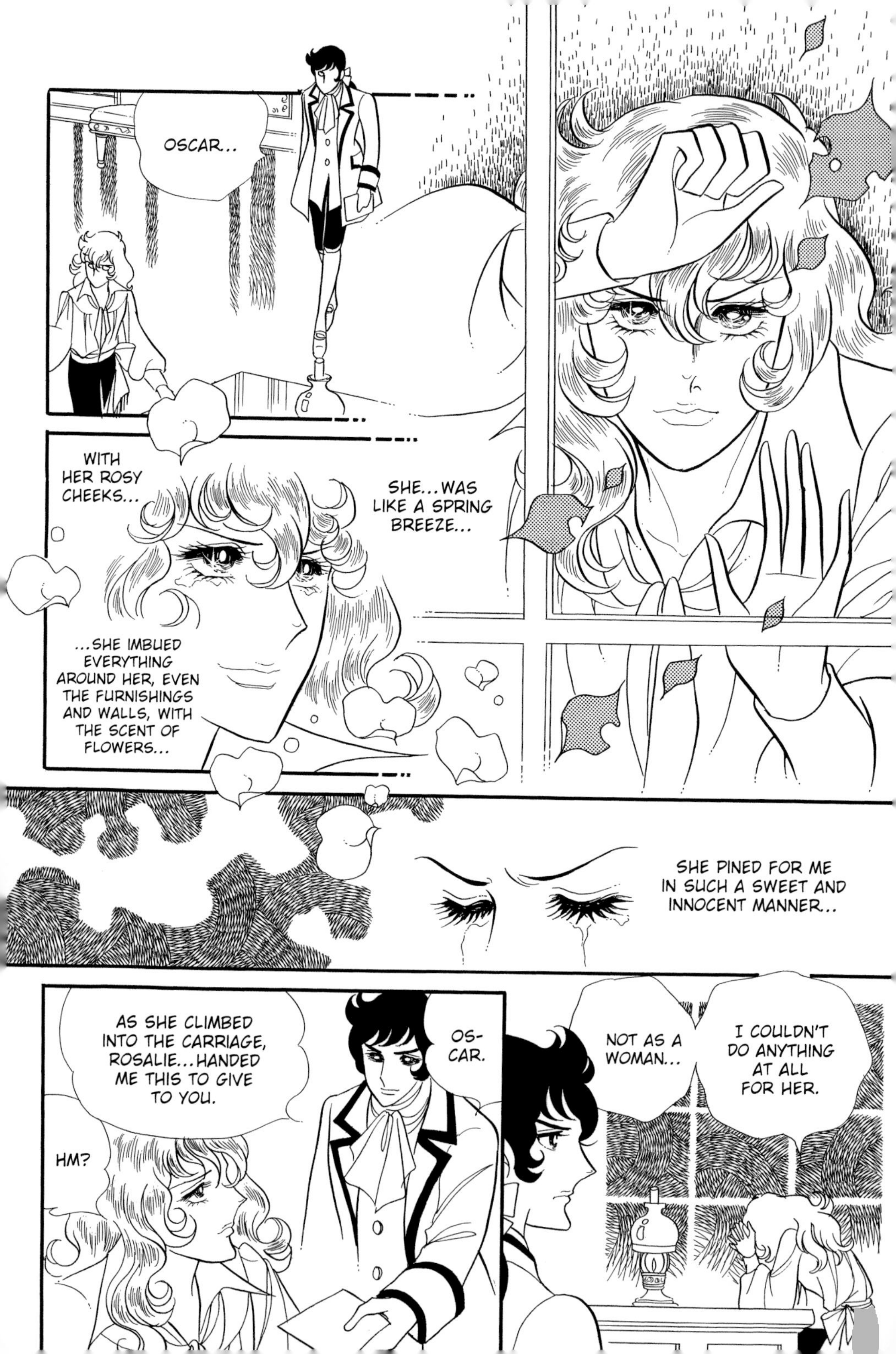
OSCAR...
SHE...WAS LIKE A SPRING BREEZE...
WITH HER ROSY CHEEKS...
...SHE IMBUED EVERYTHING AROUND HER, EVEN THE FURNISHINGS AND WALLS, WITH THE SCENT OF FLOWERS...
SHE PINED FOR ME IN SUCH A SWEET AND INNOCENT MANNER...
I COULDN'T DO ANYTHING AT ALL FOR HER.
NOT AS A WOMAN...
OS-CAR.
AS SHE CLIMBED INTO THE CARRIAGE, ROSALIE...HANDED ME THIS TO GIVE TO YOU.
HM?

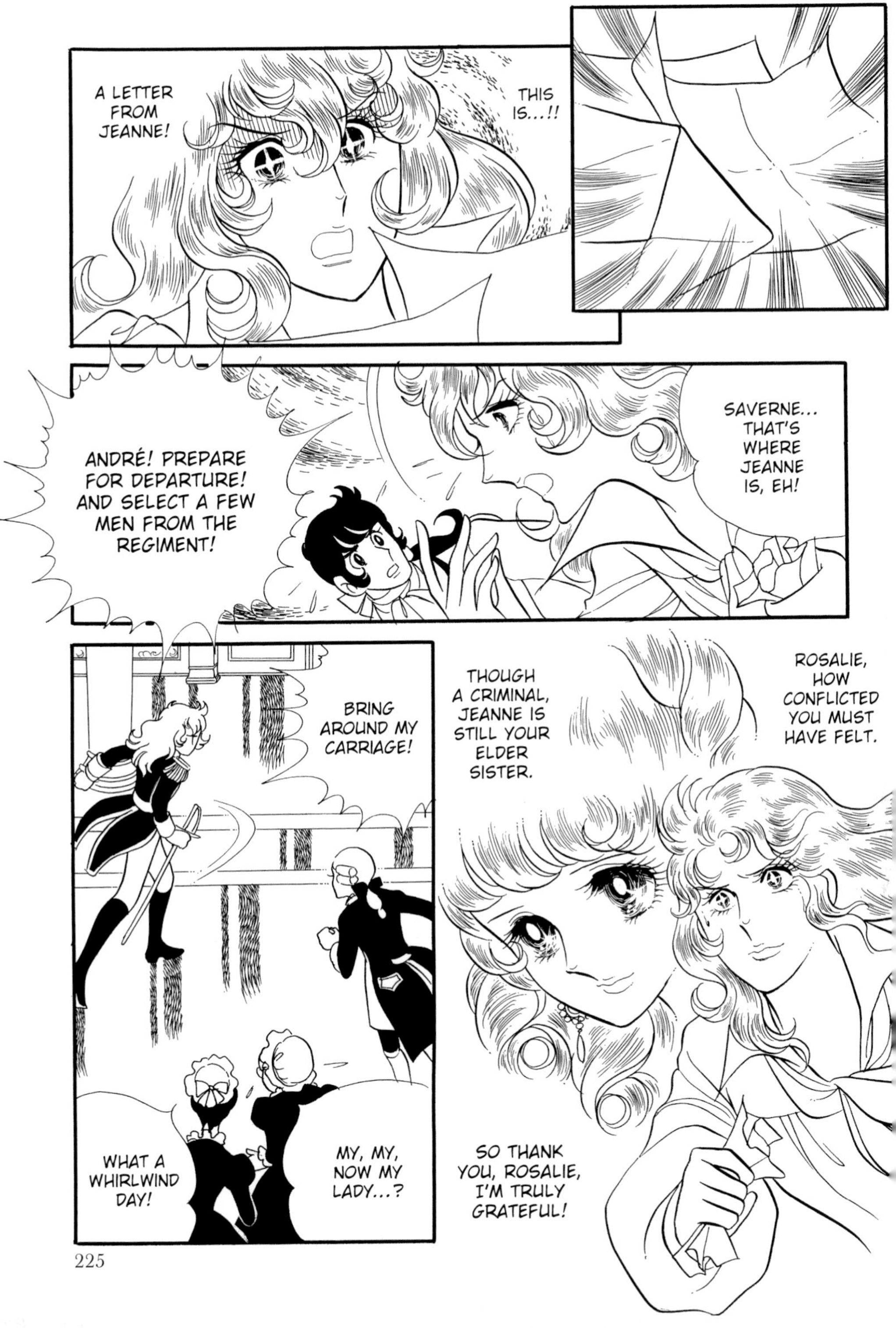
THIS IS...!!
A LETTER FROM JEANNE!
SAVERNE... THAT'S WHERE JEANNE IS, EH!
ANDRÉ! PREPARE FOR DEPARTURE! AND SELECT A FEW MEN FROM THE REGIMENT!
ROSALIE, HOW CONFLICTED YOU MUST HAVE FELT.
THOUGH A CRIMINAL, JEANNE IS STILL YOUR ELDER SISTER.
SO THANK YOU, ROSALIE, I'M TRULY GRATEFUL!
BRING AROUND MY CARRIAGE!
MY, MY, NOW MY LADY...?
WHAT A WHIRLWIND DAY!

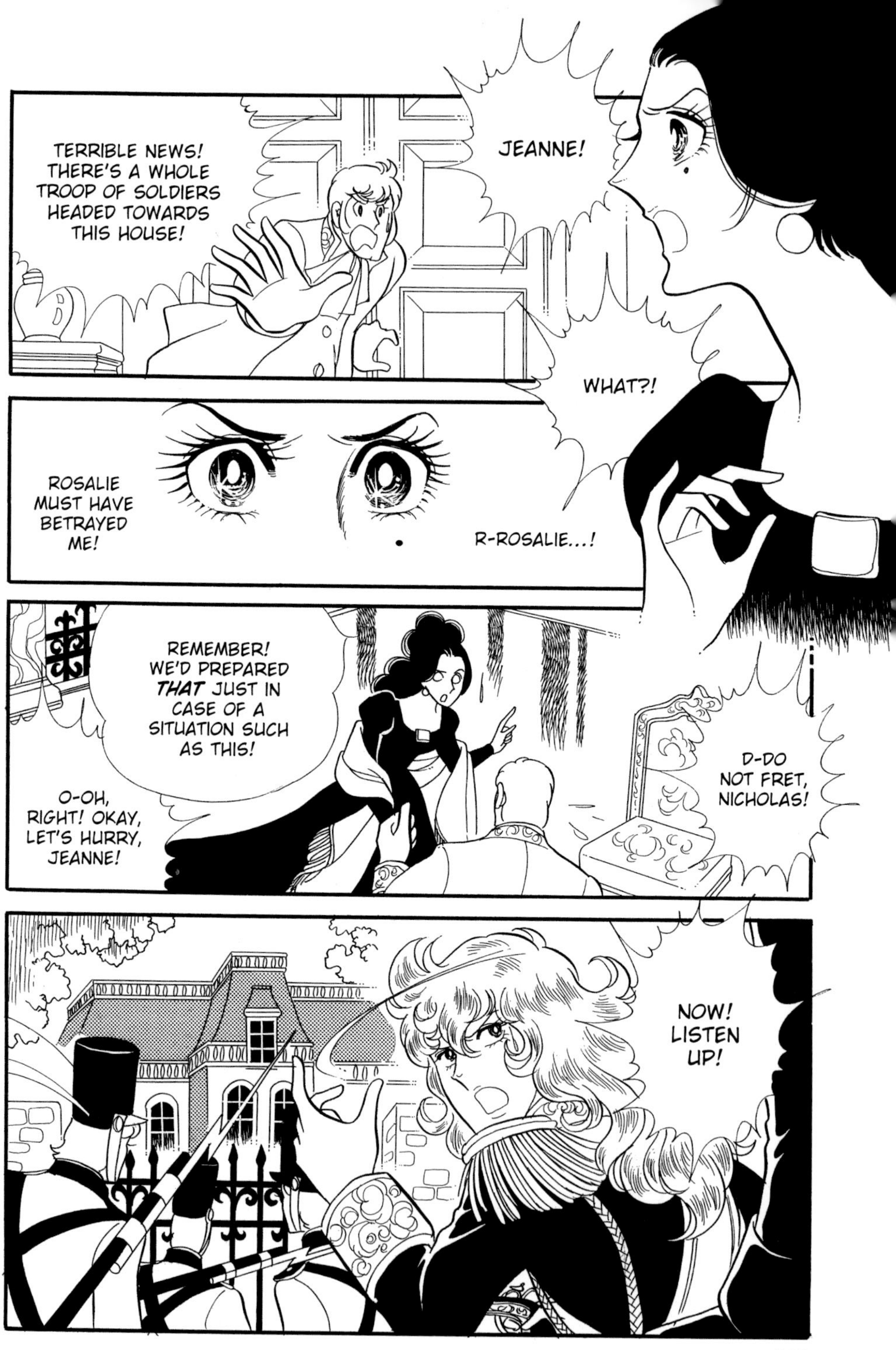
JEANNE!
TERRIBLE NEWS! THERE'S A WHOLE TROOP OF SOLDIERS HEADED TOWARDS THIS HOUSE!
WHAT?!
R-ROSALIE...!
ROSALIE MUST HAVE BETRAYED ME!
D-DO NOT FRET, NICHOLAS!
REMEMBER! WE'D PREPARED *THAT* JUST IN CASE OF A SITUATION SUCH AS THIS!
O-OH, RIGHT! OKAY, LET'S HURRY, JEANNE!
NOW! LISTEN UP!

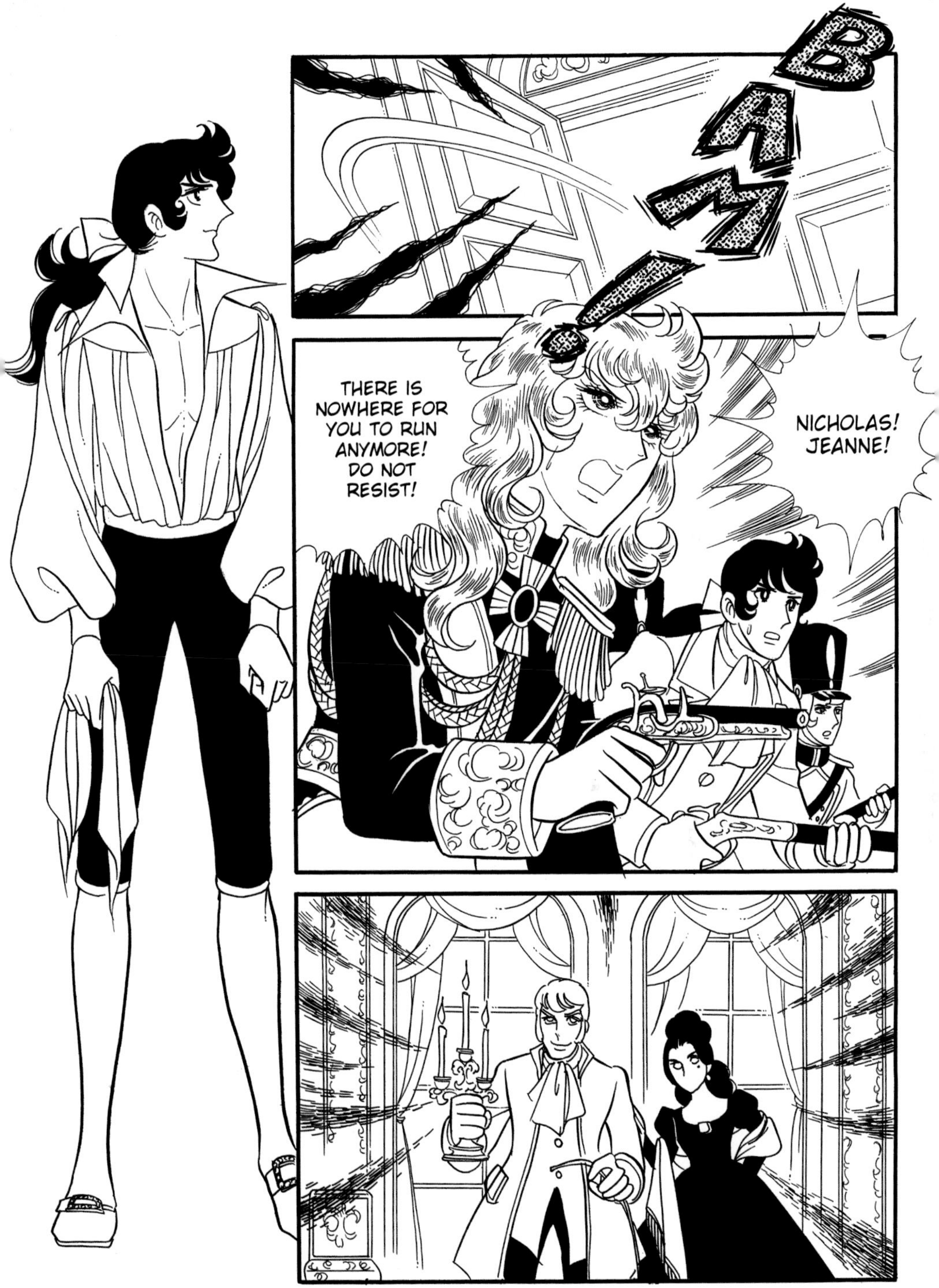
BAM!
NICHOLAS! JEANNE!
THERE IS NOWHERE FOR YOU TO RUN ANYMORE! DO NOT RESIST!

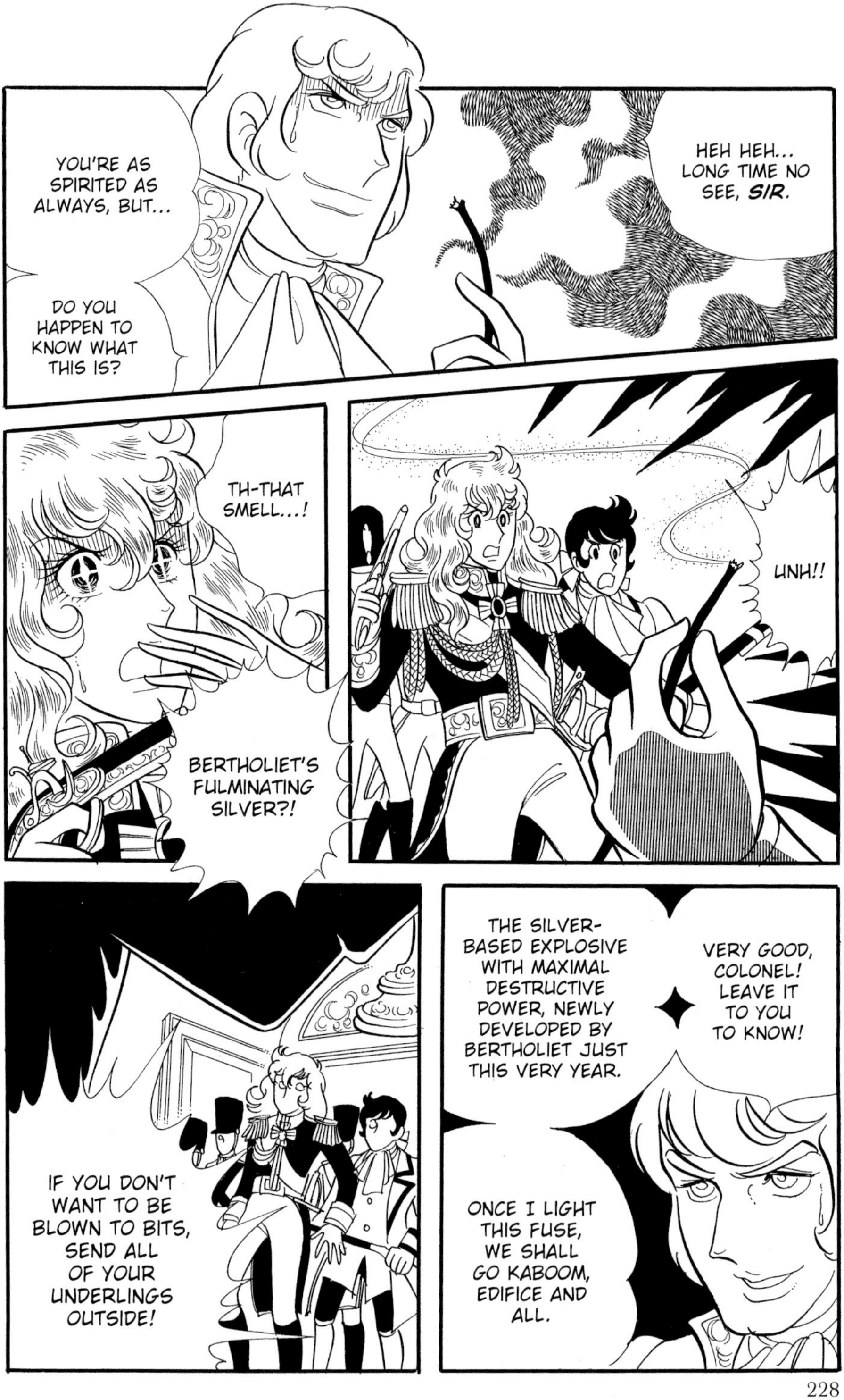
HEH HEH... LONG TIME NO SEE, *SIR*.
YOU'RE AS SPIRITED AS ALWAYS, BUT...
DO YOU HAPPEN TO KNOW WHAT THIS IS?
UNH!!
TH-THAT SMELL...!
BERTHOLIET'S FULMINATING SILVER?!
VERY GOOD, COLONEL! LEAVE IT TO YOU TO KNOW!
THE SILVER-BASED EXPLOSIVE WITH MAXIMAL DESTRUCTIVE POWER, NEWLY DEVELOPED BY BERTHOLIET JUST THIS VERY YEAR.
ONCE I LIGHT THIS FUSE, WE SHALL GO KABOOM, EDIFICE AND ALL.
IF YOU DON'T WANT TO BE BLOWN TO BITS, SEND ALL OF YOUR UNDERLINGS OUTSIDE!

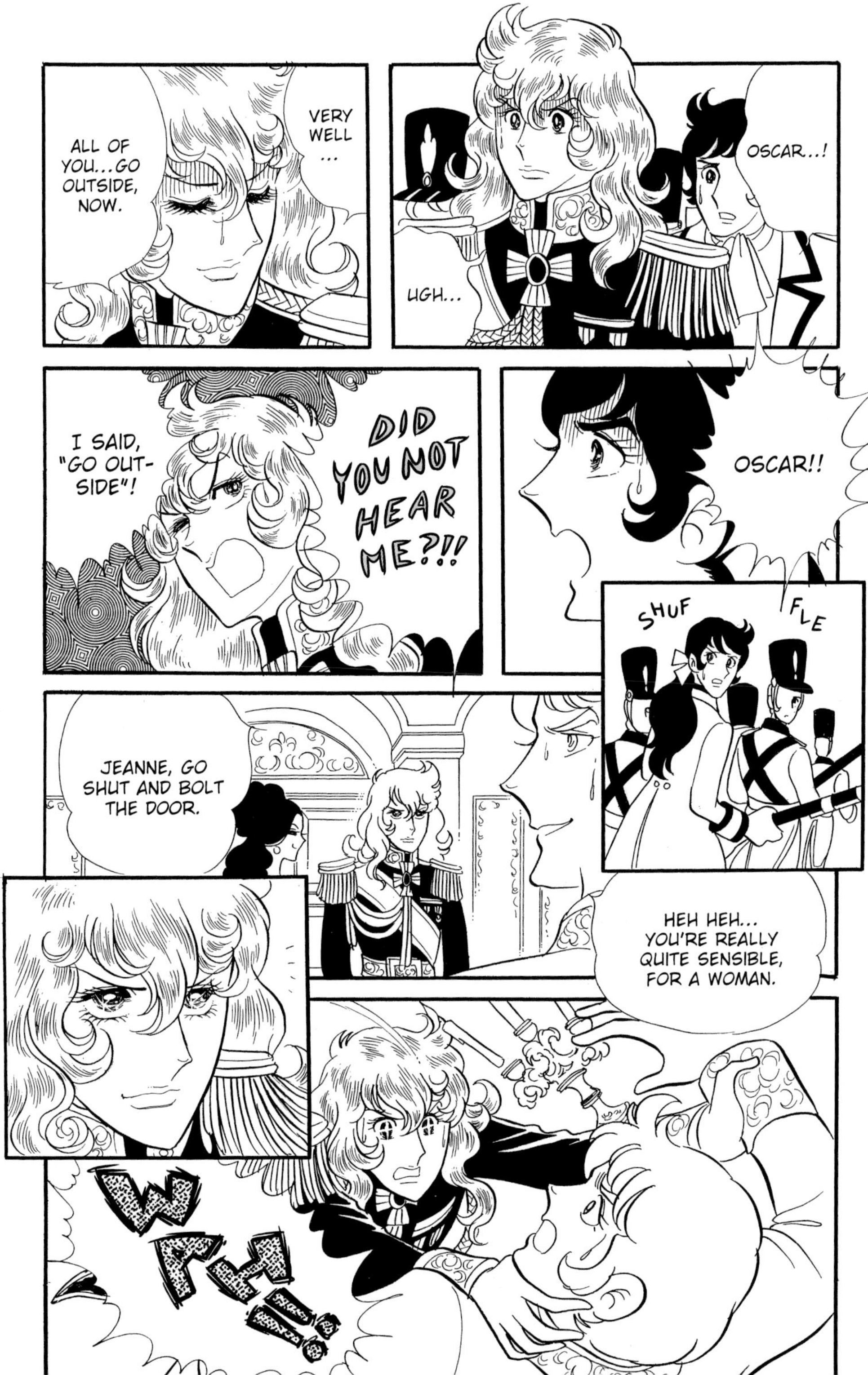
OSCAR...!
UGH...
VERY WELL ...
ALL OF YOU...GO OUTSIDE, NOW.
OSCAR!!
SHUF FLE
DID YOU NOT HEAR ME?!!
I SAID, "GO OUT-SIDE"!
HEH HEH... YOU'RE REALLY QUITE SENSIBLE, FOR A WOMAN.
JEANNE, GO SHUT AND BOLT THE DOOR.
WAH!!

the ROSE of VERSAILLES

ベルサイユのばら

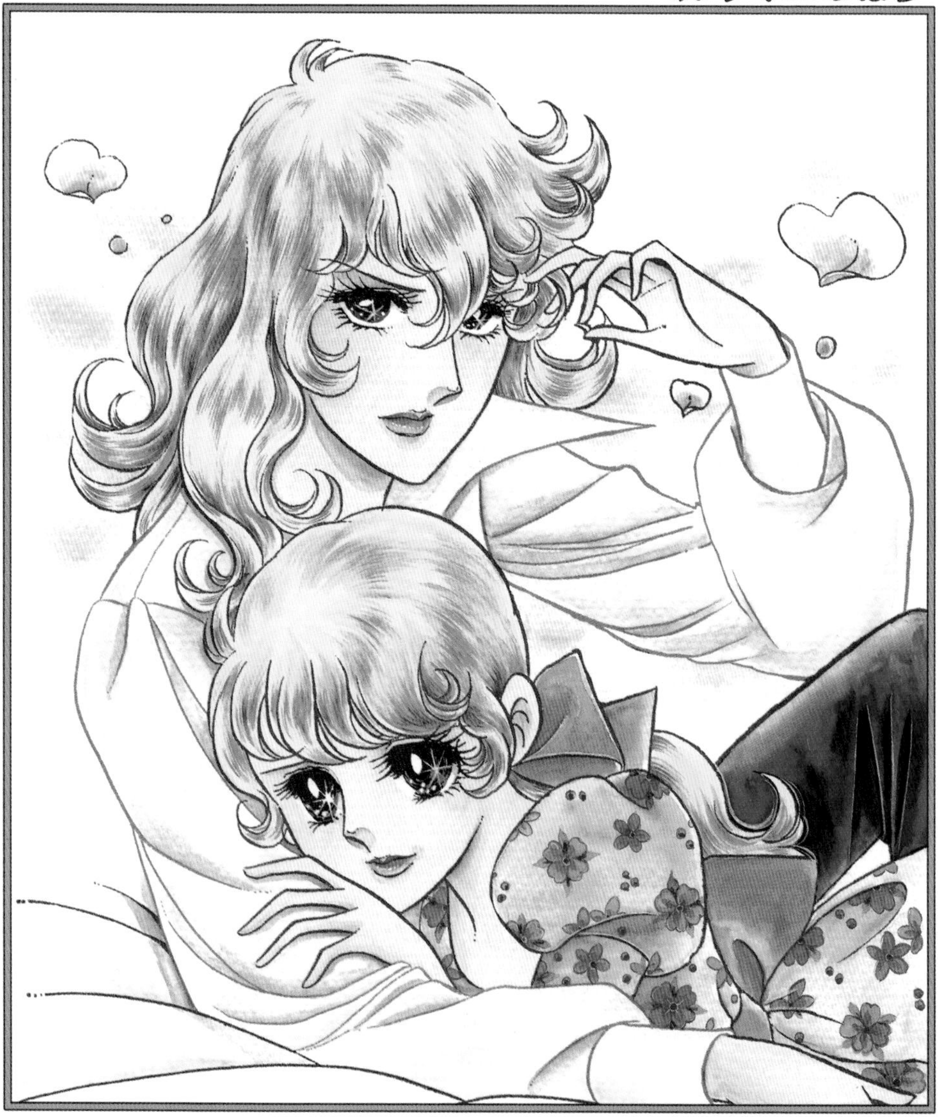

1972 WEEKLY MARGARET MAGAZINE ISSUE 49 COVER PAGE
(SPECIAL COLORIZED VERSION)

★うずまく興奮、ますますもりあがる大ロマン!!
ベルサイユのばら
♥オスカルがあぶない!! ジャンヌとニコラスにおいつめられ オスカルは…!?
池田理代子

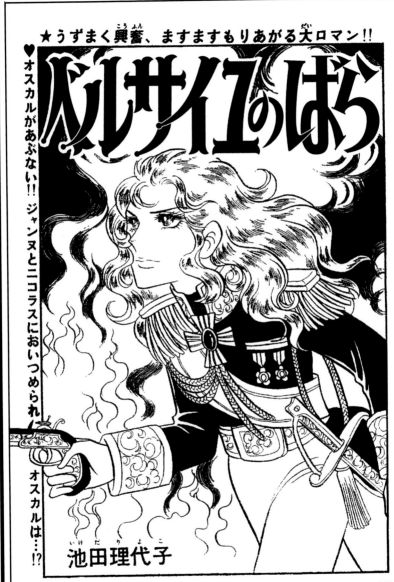

★ THE SWIRLING EXCITEMENT, THE INCREASINGLY THRILLING GRAND ROMANCE!!

♥ OSCAR IN DANGER!! DRIVEN BY JEANNE AND NICHOLAS AGAINST THE WALL, WHAT WILL OSCAR DO...?!

EPISODE 33

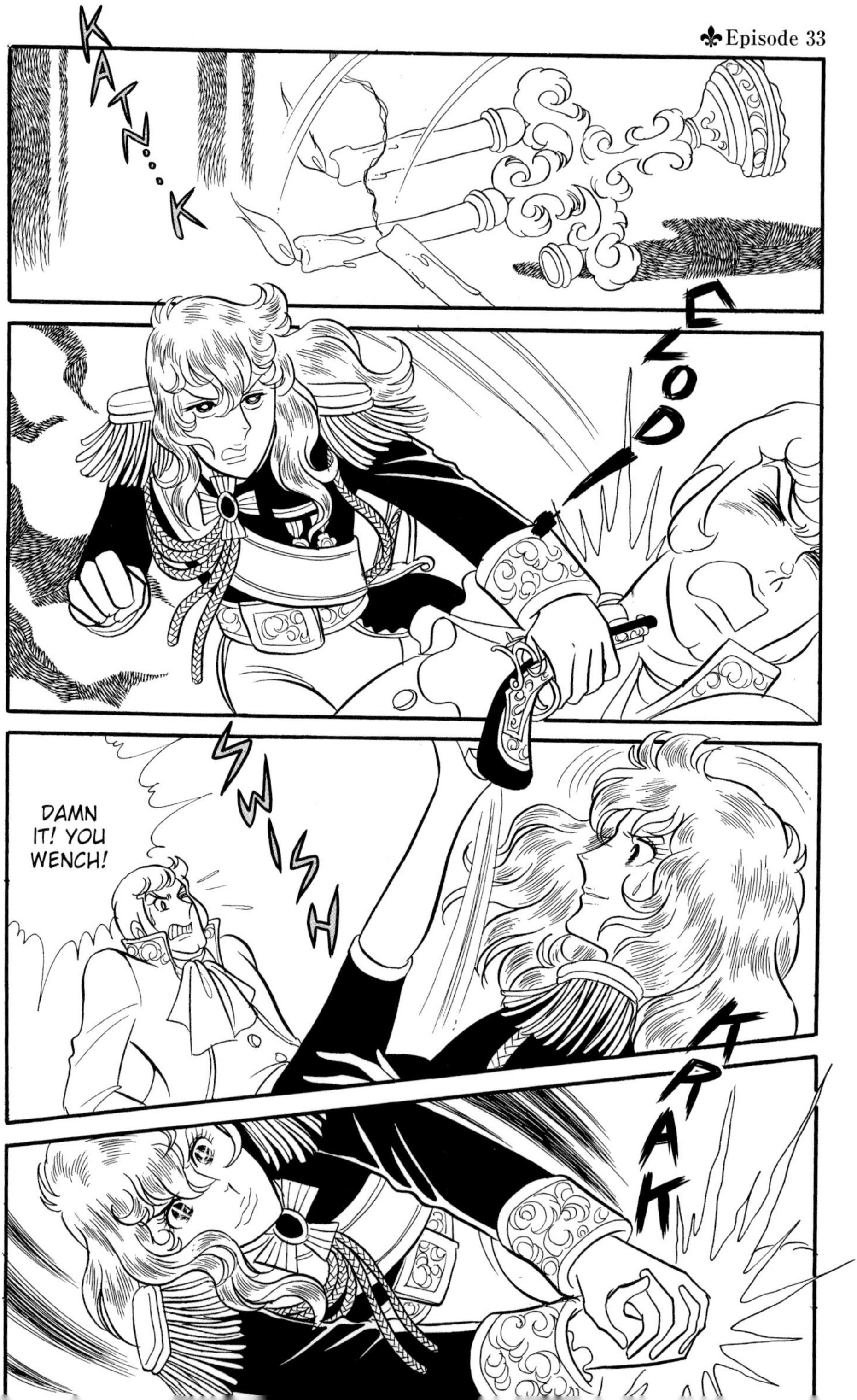
KATN...K
CLOD!
SWISH
DAMN IT! YOU WENCH!
KRAK

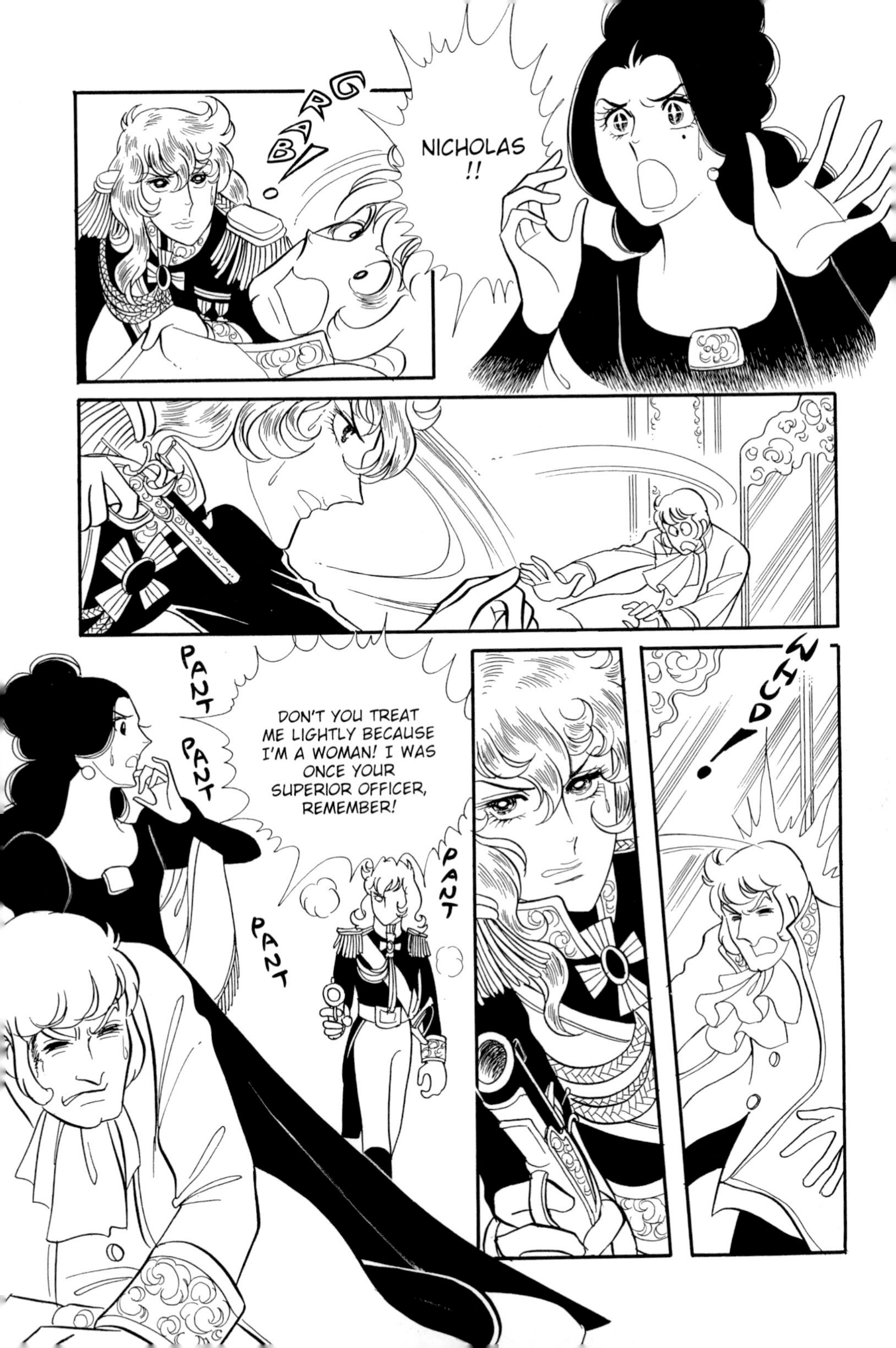
NICHOLAS !!
BARG!
WHUD!
PANT PANT
DON'T YOU TREAT ME LIGHTLY BECAUSE I'M A WOMAN! I WAS ONCE YOUR SUPERIOR OFFICER, REMEMBER!
PANT PANT
PANT
PANT

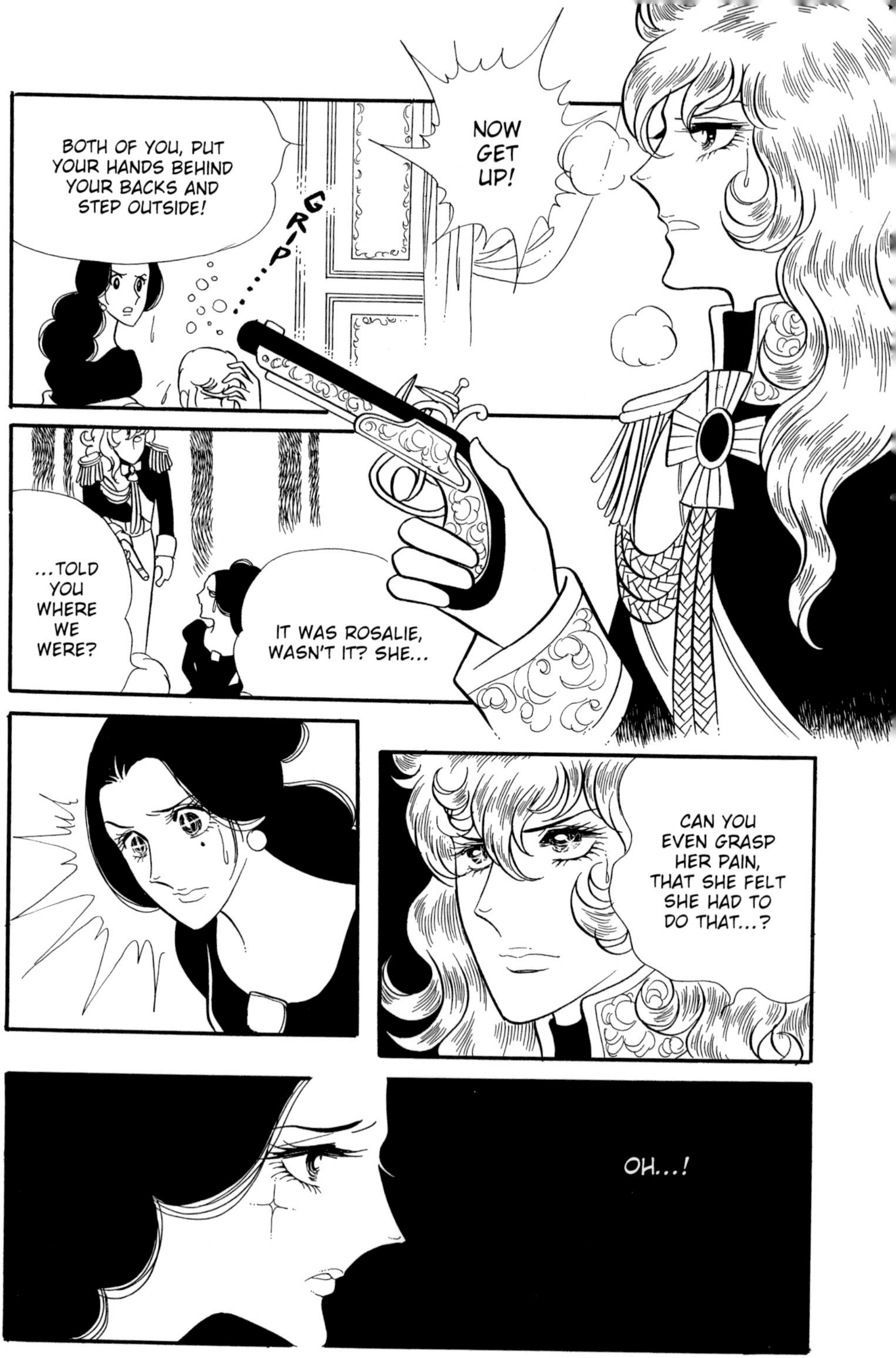

NOW GET UP!
BOTH OF YOU, PUT YOUR HANDS BEHIND YOUR BACKS AND STEP OUTSIDE!
GRIP...
IT WAS ROSALIE, WASN'T IT? SHE...
...TOLD YOU WHERE WE WERE?
CAN YOU EVEN GRASP HER PAIN, THAT SHE FELT SHE HAD TO DO THAT...?
OH...!

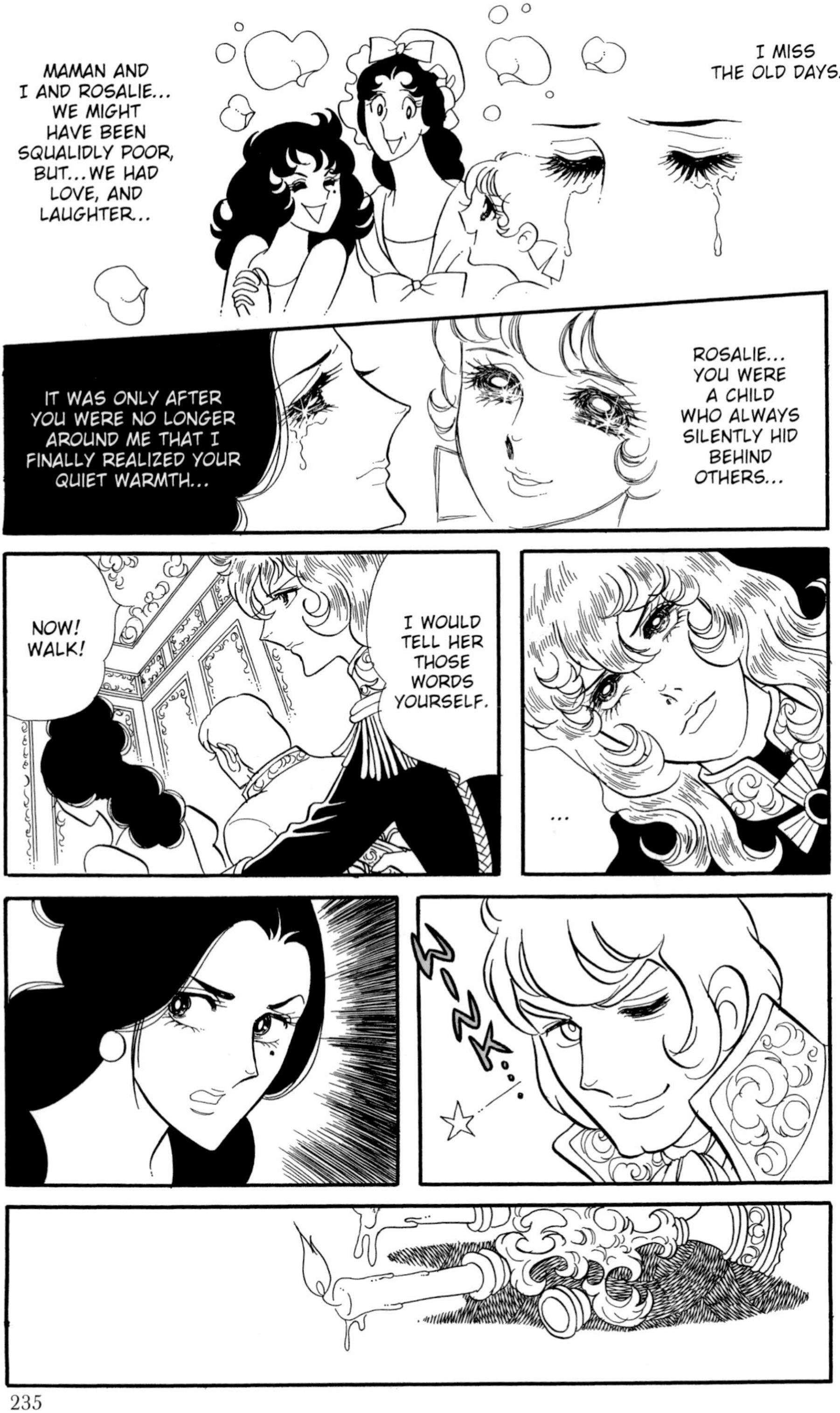
I MISS THE OLD DAYS...
MAMAN AND I AND ROSALIE... WE MIGHT HAVE BEEN SQUALIDLY POOR, BUT...WE HAD LOVE, AND LAUGHTER...
ROSALIE... YOU WERE A CHILD WHO ALWAYS SILENTLY HID BEHIND OTHERS...
IT WAS ONLY AFTER YOU WERE NO LONGER AROUND ME THAT I FINALLY REALIZED YOUR QUIET WARMTH...
...
I WOULD TELL HER THOSE WORDS YOURSELF.
NOW! WALK!
WINK

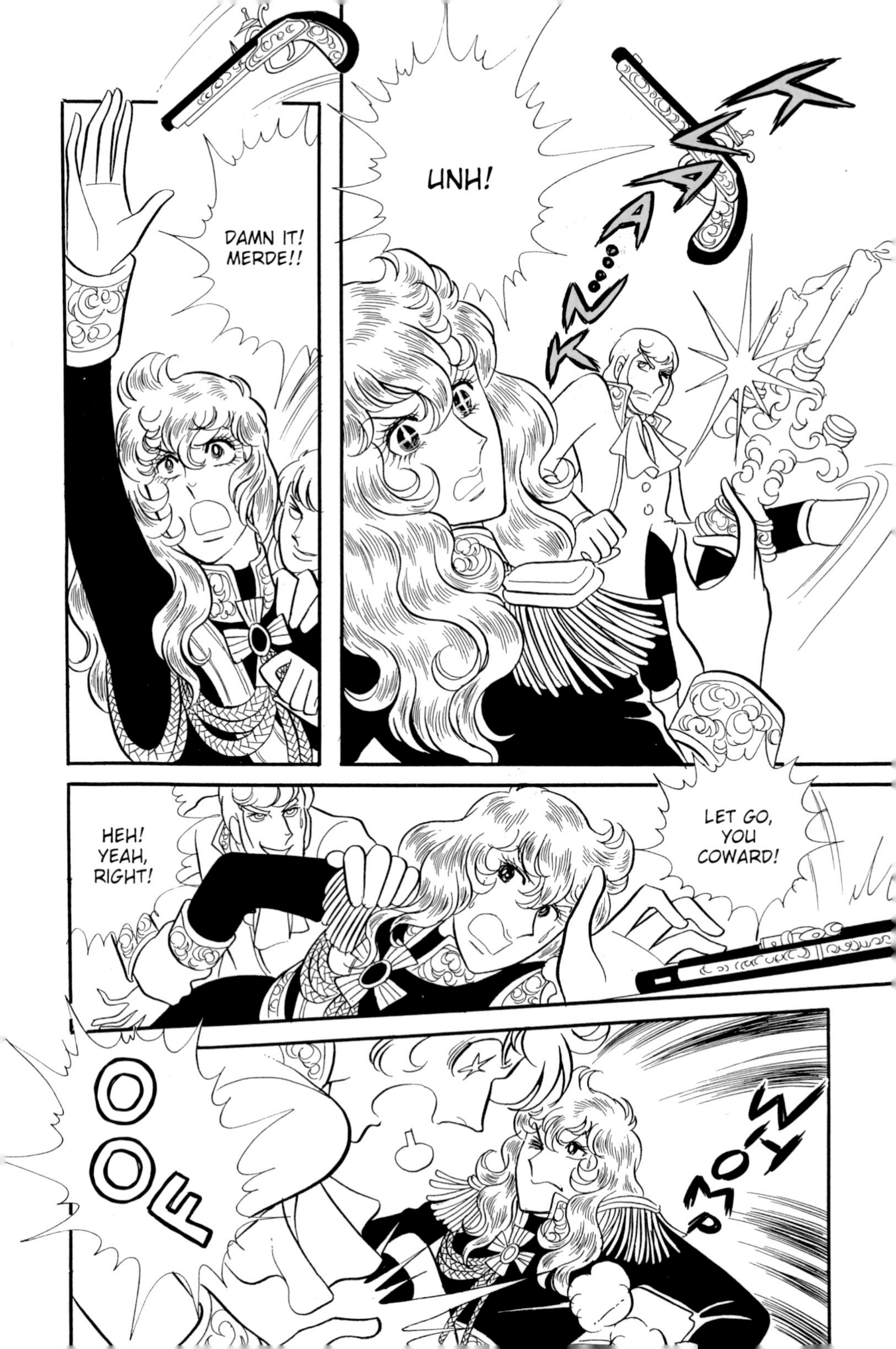
UNH!
DAMN IT! MERDE!!
LET GO, YOU COWARD!
HEH! YEAH, RIGHT!
OOF

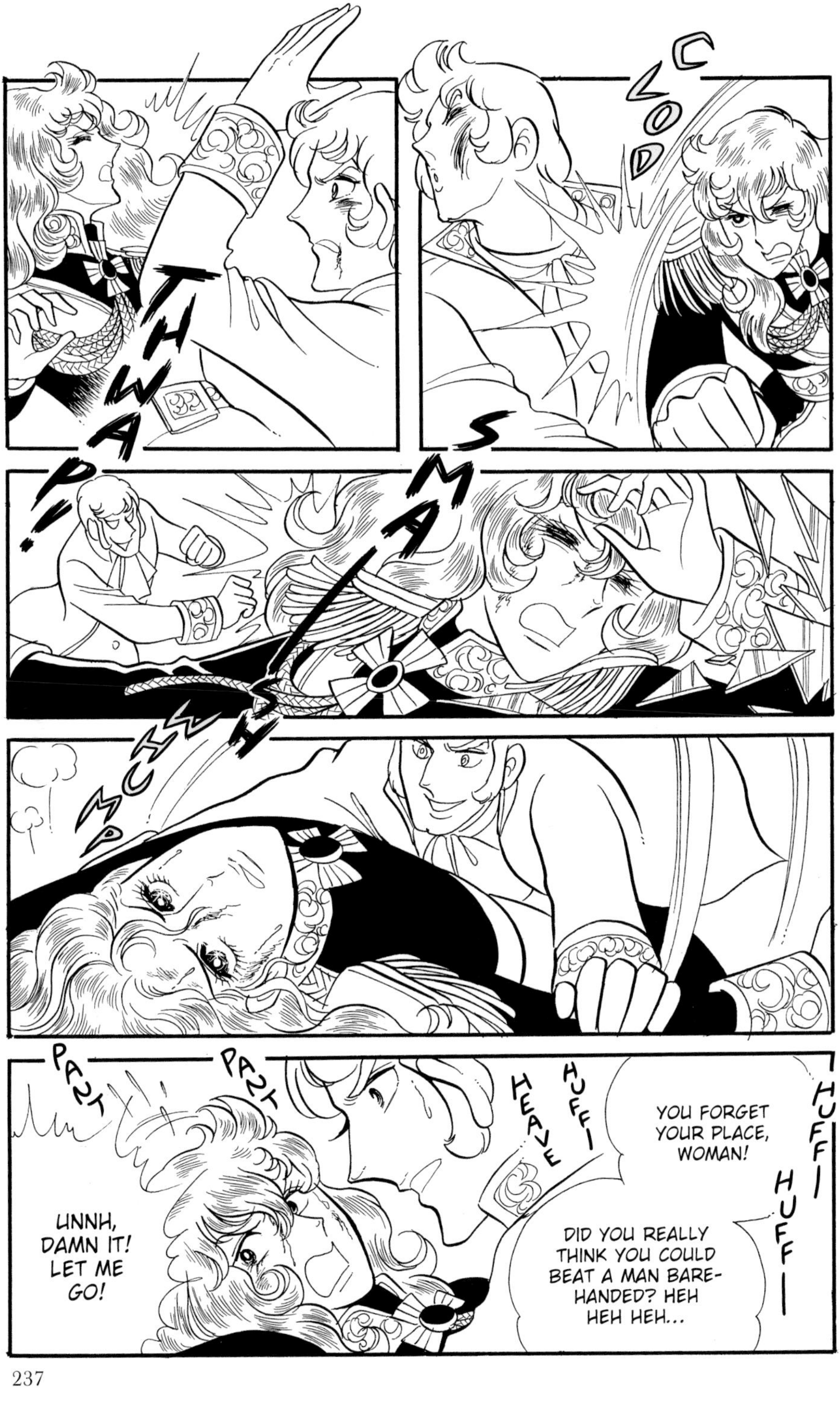
CLODD
THWAP!!
SMASH
WHUMP
HUFF!
HUFF!
YOU FORGET YOUR PLACE, WOMAN!
DID YOU REALLY THINK YOU COULD BEAT A MAN BARE-HANDED? HEH HEH HEH...
HUFF!
HEAVE
PANT
PANT
UNNH, DAMN IT! LET ME GO!

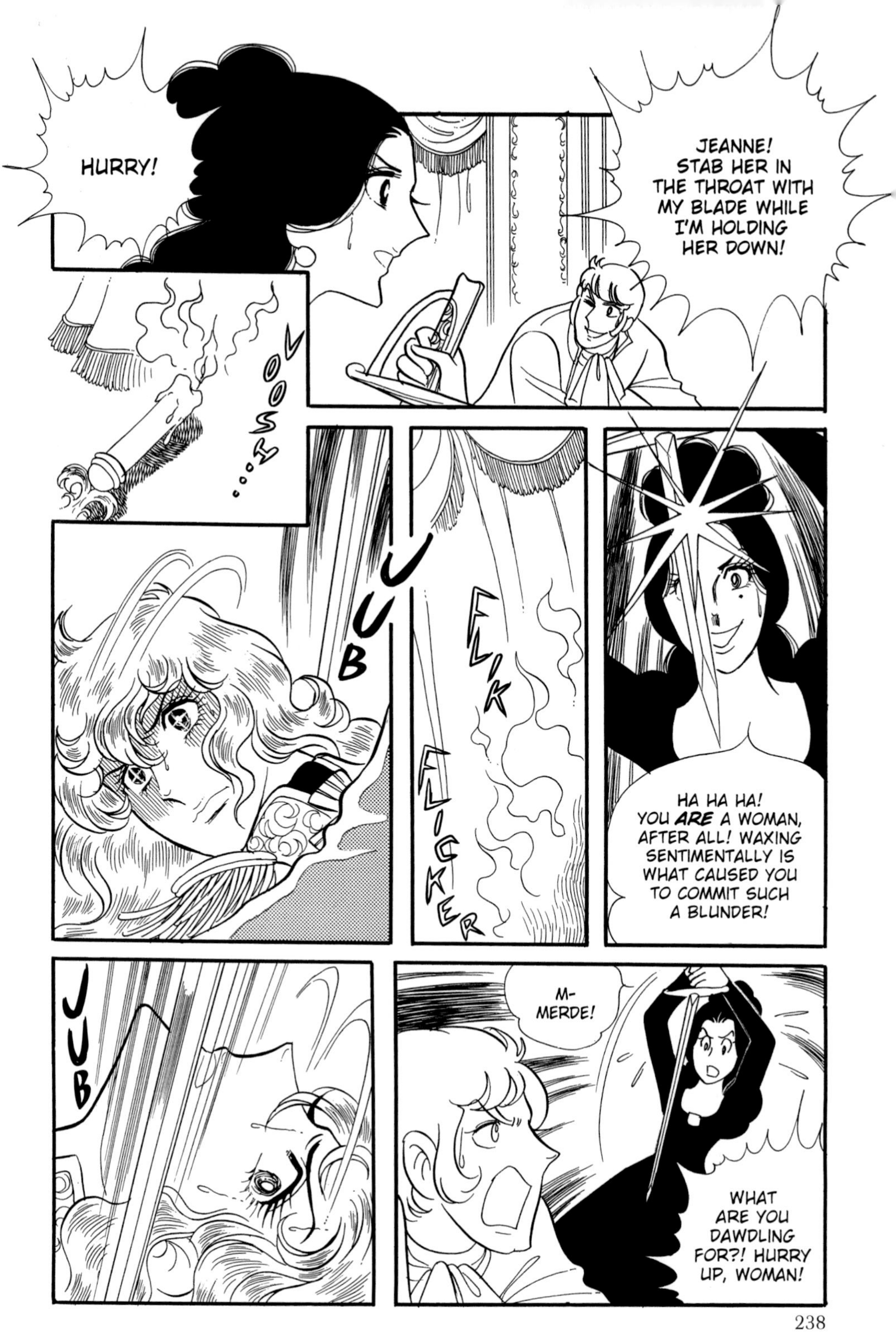
JEANNE! STAB HER IN THE THROAT WITH MY BLADE WHILE I'M HOLDING HER DOWN!
HURRY!
WOOSH...
HA HA HA! YOU *ARE* A WOMAN, AFTER ALL! WAXING SENTIMENTALLY IS WHAT CAUSED YOU TO COMMIT SUCH A BLUNDER!
FLIK
FLICKER
JUB
M-MERDE!
WHAT ARE YOU DAWDLING FOR?! HURRY UP, WOMAN!
JUB

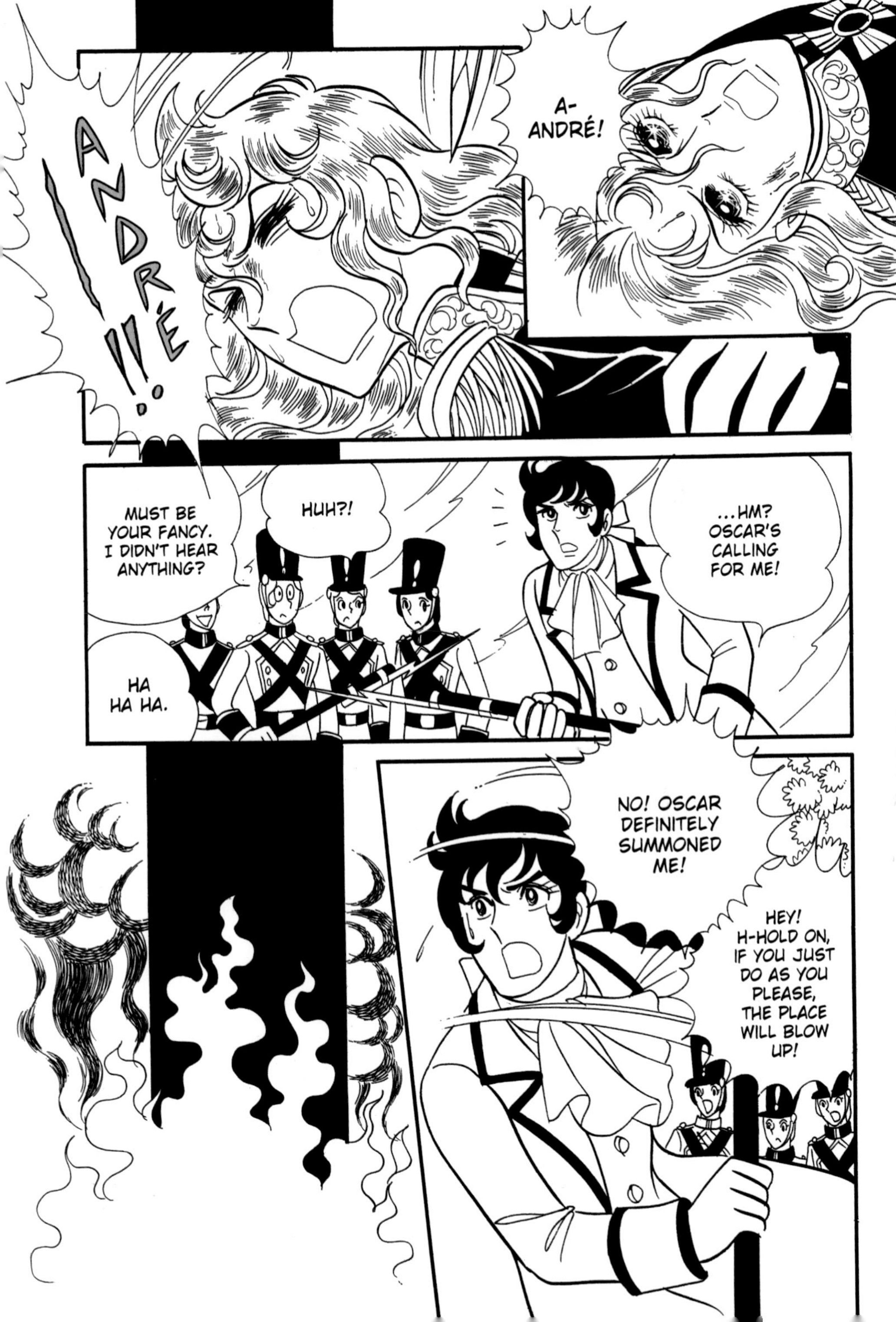
A- ANDRÉ!
ANDRÉ!!
...HM? OSCAR'S CALLING FOR ME!
HUH?!
MUST BE YOUR FANCY. I DIDN'T HEAR ANYTHING?
HA HA HA.
NO! OSCAR DEFINITELY SUMMONED ME!
HEY! H-HOLD ON, IF YOU JUST DO AS YOU PLEASE, THE PLACE WILL BLOW UP!

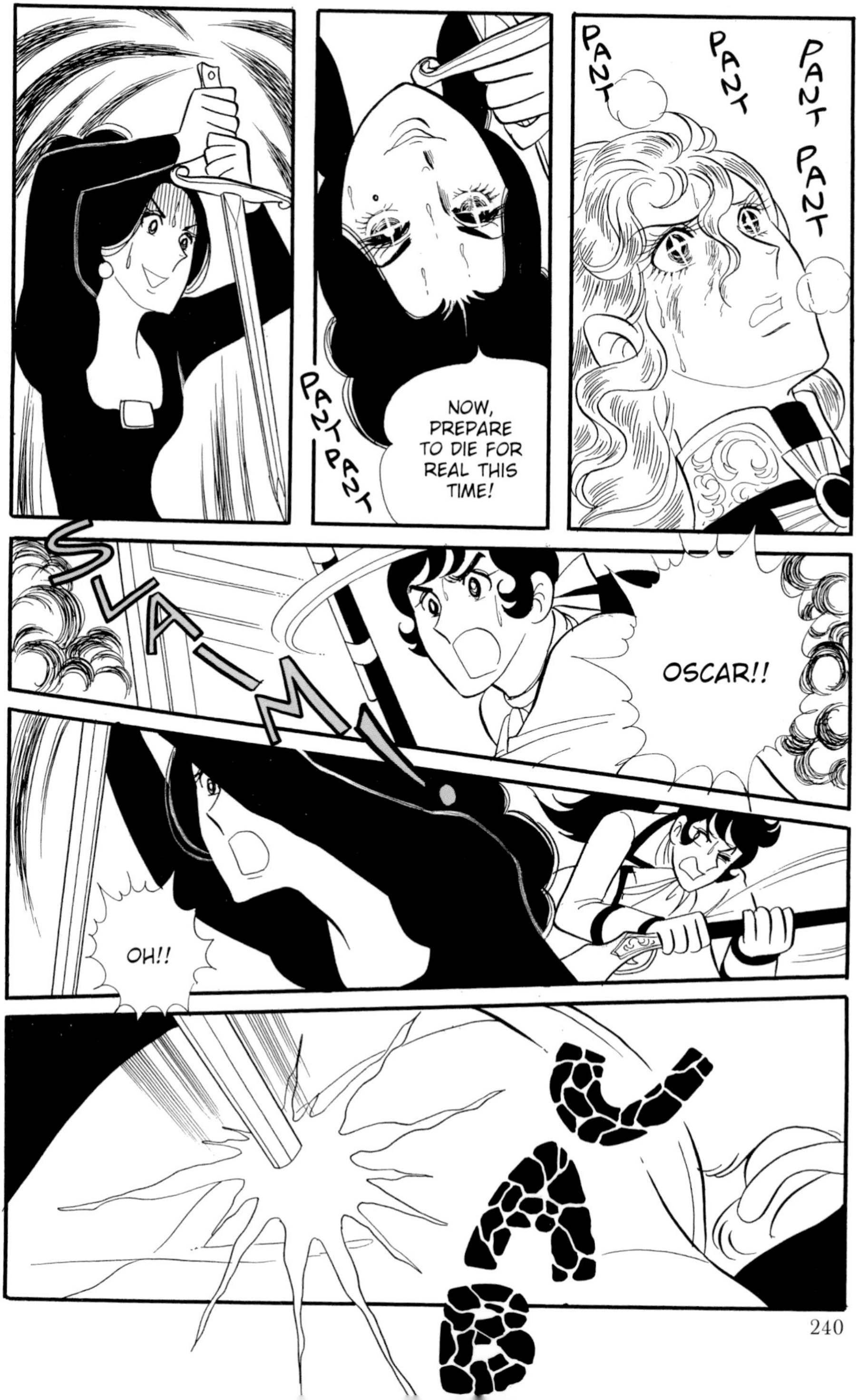
PANT PANT PANT PANT
PANT PANT
NOW, PREPARE TO DIE FOR REAL THIS TIME!
OSCAR!!
SLA-M!
OH!!

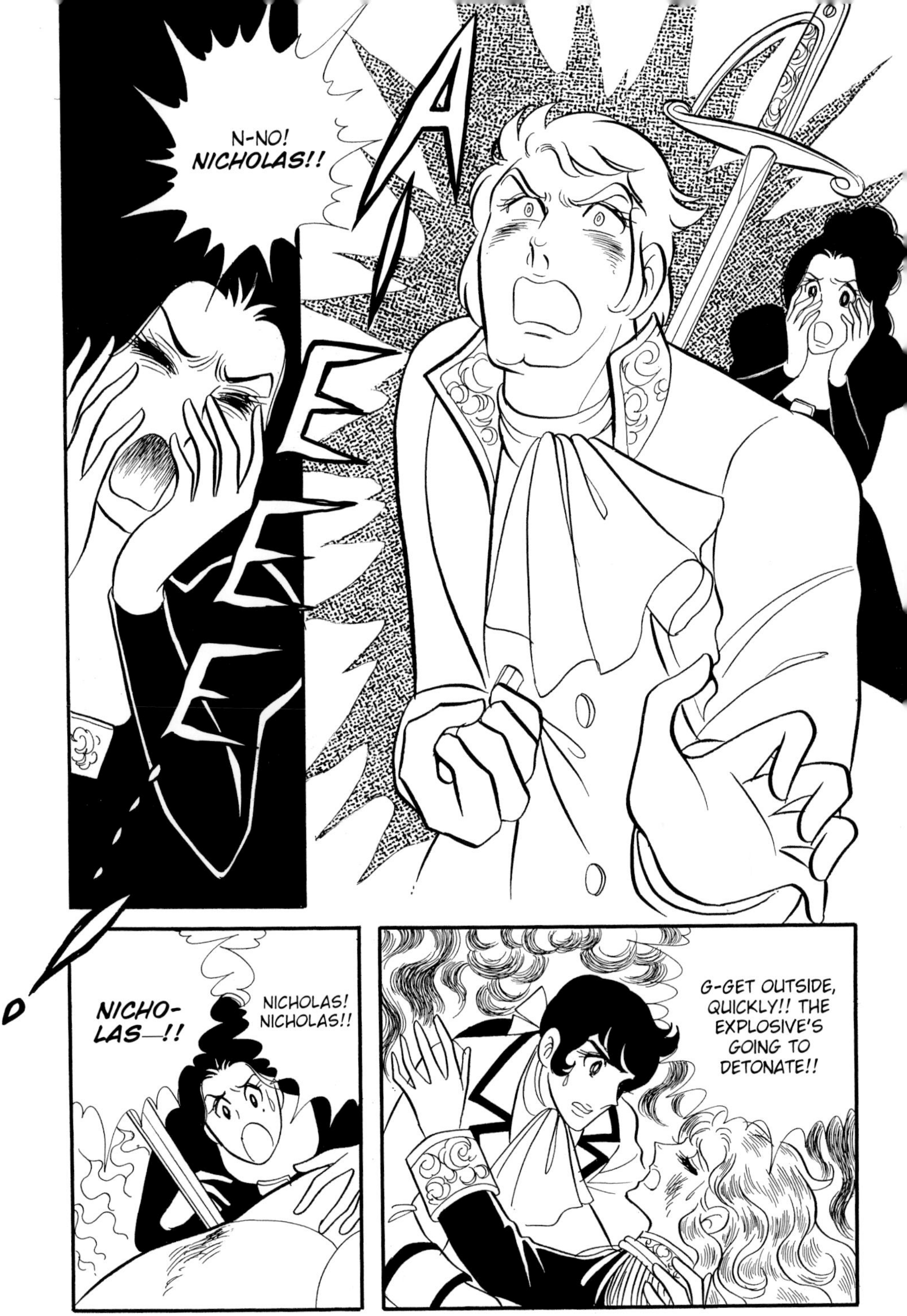
N-NO! NICHOLAS!!
G-GET OUTSIDE, QUICKLY!! THE EXPLOSIVE'S GOING TO DETONATE!!
NICHOLAS! NICHOLAS!!
NICHO-LAS—!!

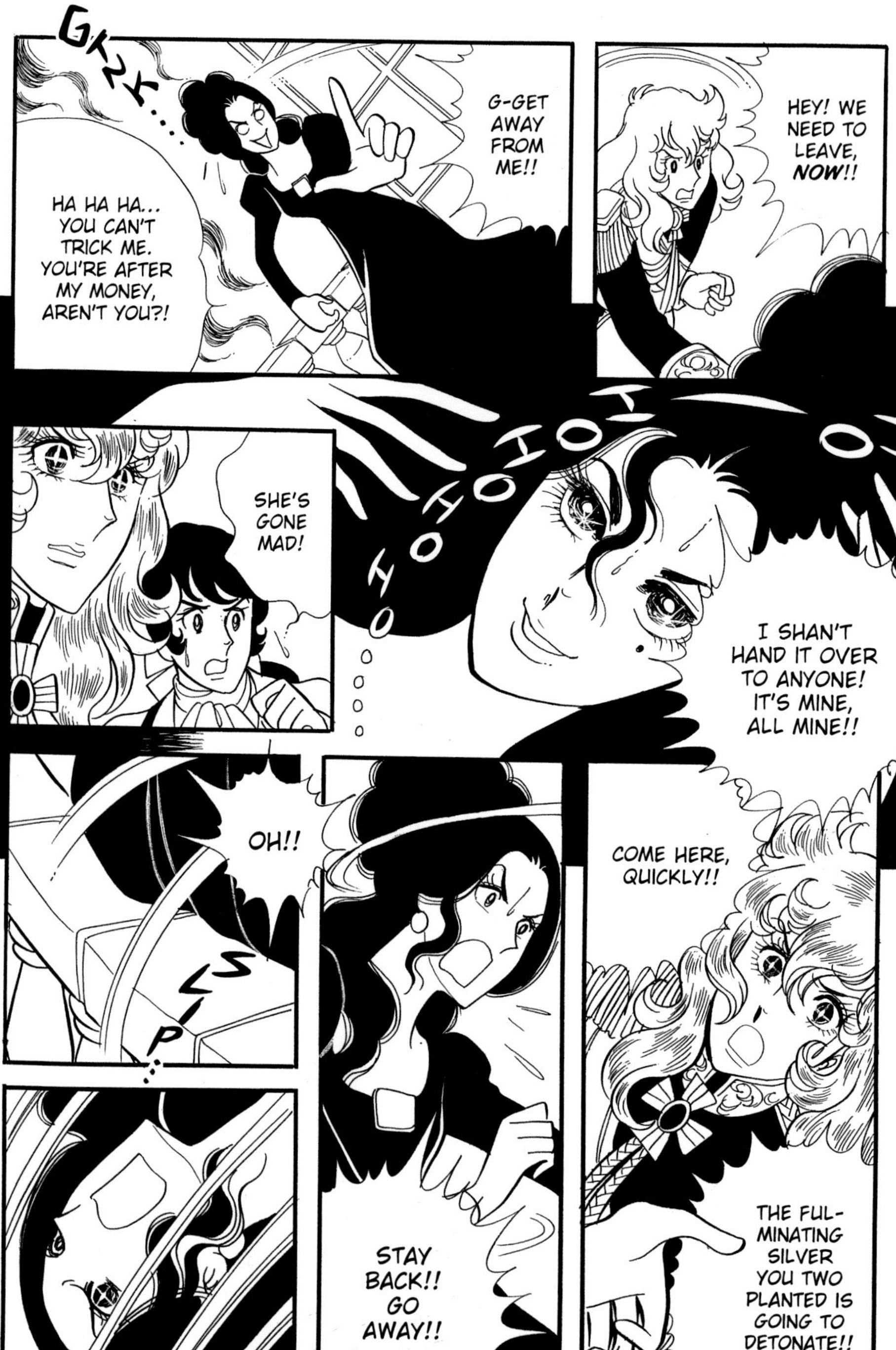
HEY! WE NEED TO LEAVE, **NOW**!!
G-GET AWAY FROM ME!!
GKZK...
HA HA HA... YOU CAN'T TRICK ME. YOU'RE AFTER MY MONEY, AREN'T YOU?!
HO HO HO HO HO HO HO...
I SHAN'T HAND IT OVER TO ANYONE! IT'S MINE, ALL MINE!!
SHE'S GONE MAD!
COME HERE, QUICKLY!!
THE FUL-MINATING SILVER YOU TWO PLANTED IS GOING TO DETONATE!!
STAY BACK!! GO AWAY!!
OH!!
SLIP...

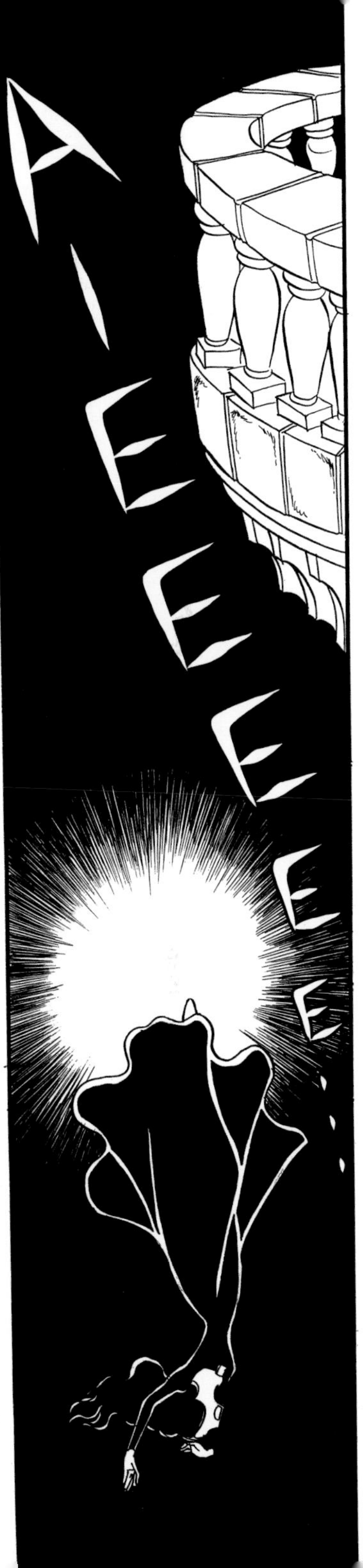
AIEEEEEE...

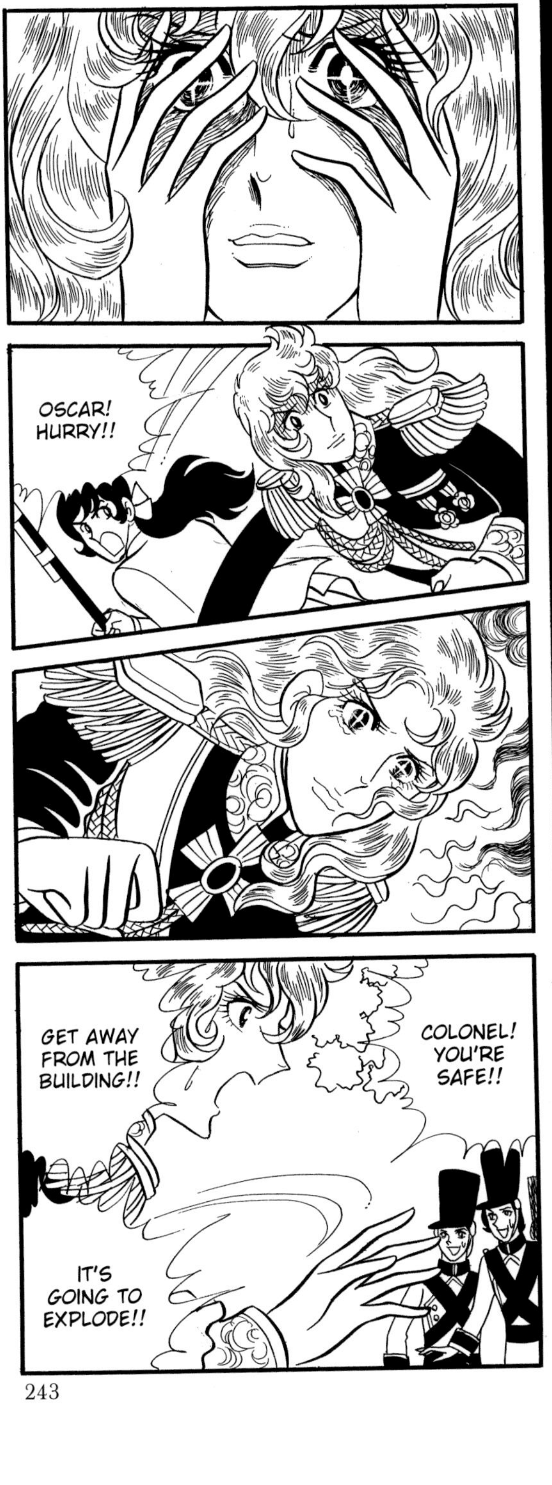
OSCAR! HURRY!!
COLONEL! YOU'RE SAFE!!
GET AWAY FROM THE BUILDING!!
IT'S GOING TO EXPLODE!!

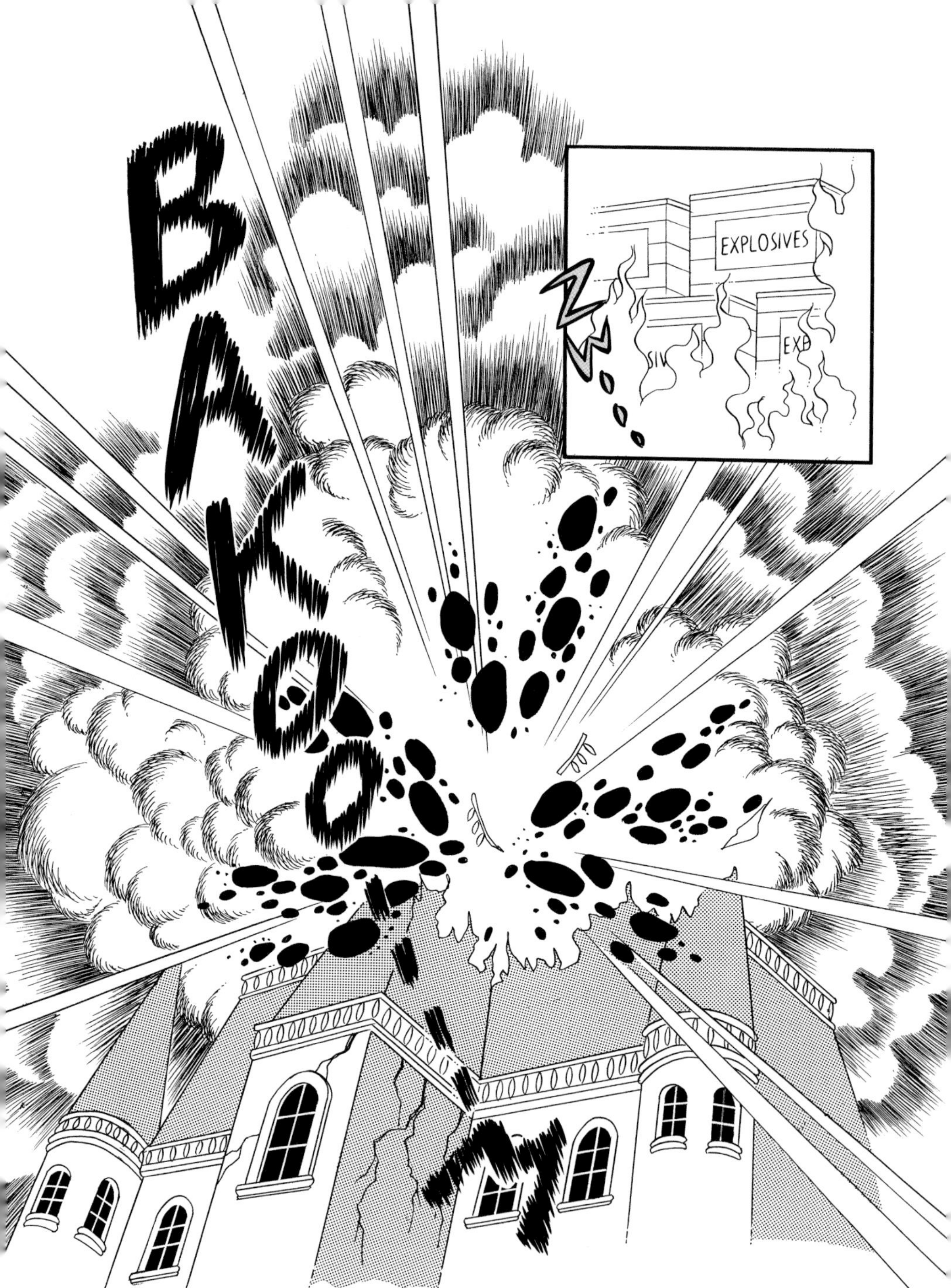
ZWOO..
EXPLOSIVES
EXP
BAKOO!!

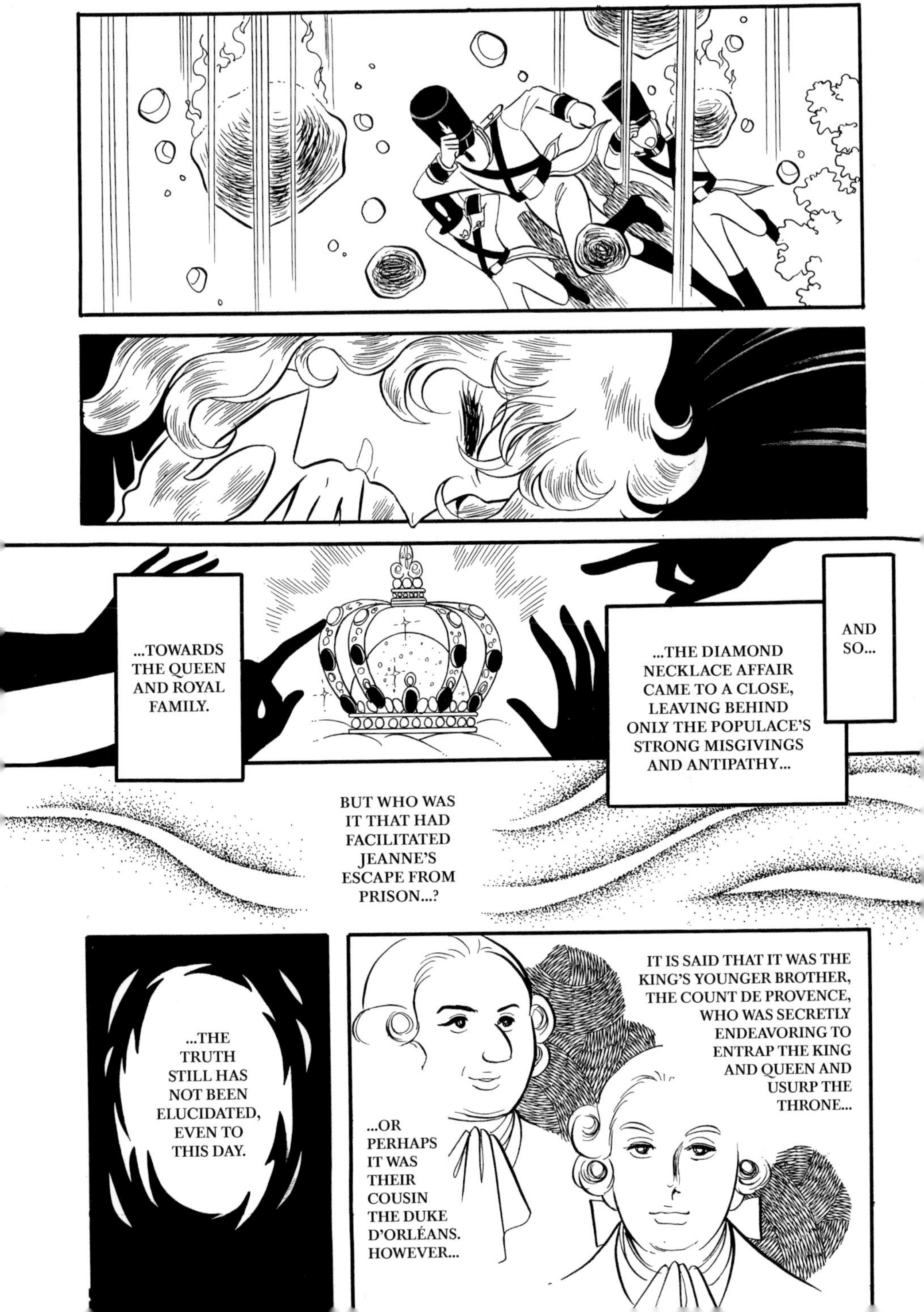
AND SO...
...THE DIAMOND NECKLACE AFFAIR CAME TO A CLOSE, LEAVING BEHIND ONLY THE POPULACE'S STRONG MISGIVINGS AND ANTIPATHY...
...TOWARDS THE QUEEN AND ROYAL FAMILY.
BUT WHO WAS IT THAT HAD FACILITATED JEANNE'S ESCAPE FROM PRISON...?
IT IS SAID THAT IT WAS THE KING'S YOUNGER BROTHER, THE COUNT DE PROVENCE, WHO WAS SECRETLY ENDEAVORING TO ENTRAP THE KING AND QUEEN AND USURP THE THRONE...
...OR PERHAPS IT WAS THEIR COUSIN THE DUKE D'ORLÉANS. HOWEVER...
...THE TRUTH STILL HAS NOT BEEN ELUCIDATED, EVEN TO THIS DAY.

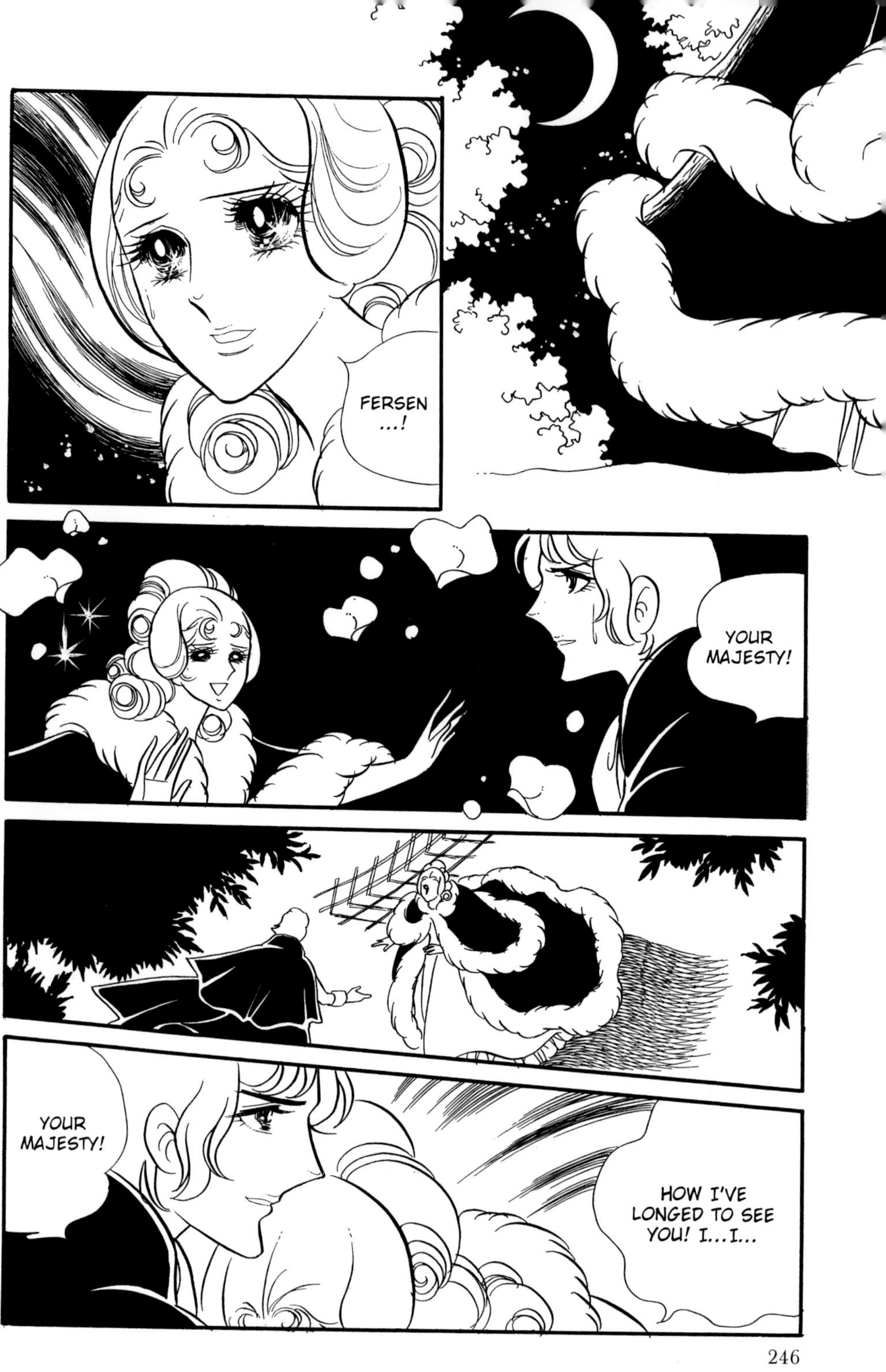
FERSEN
...!
YOUR MAJESTY!
HOW I'VE LONGED TO SEE YOU! I...I...
YOUR MAJESTY!

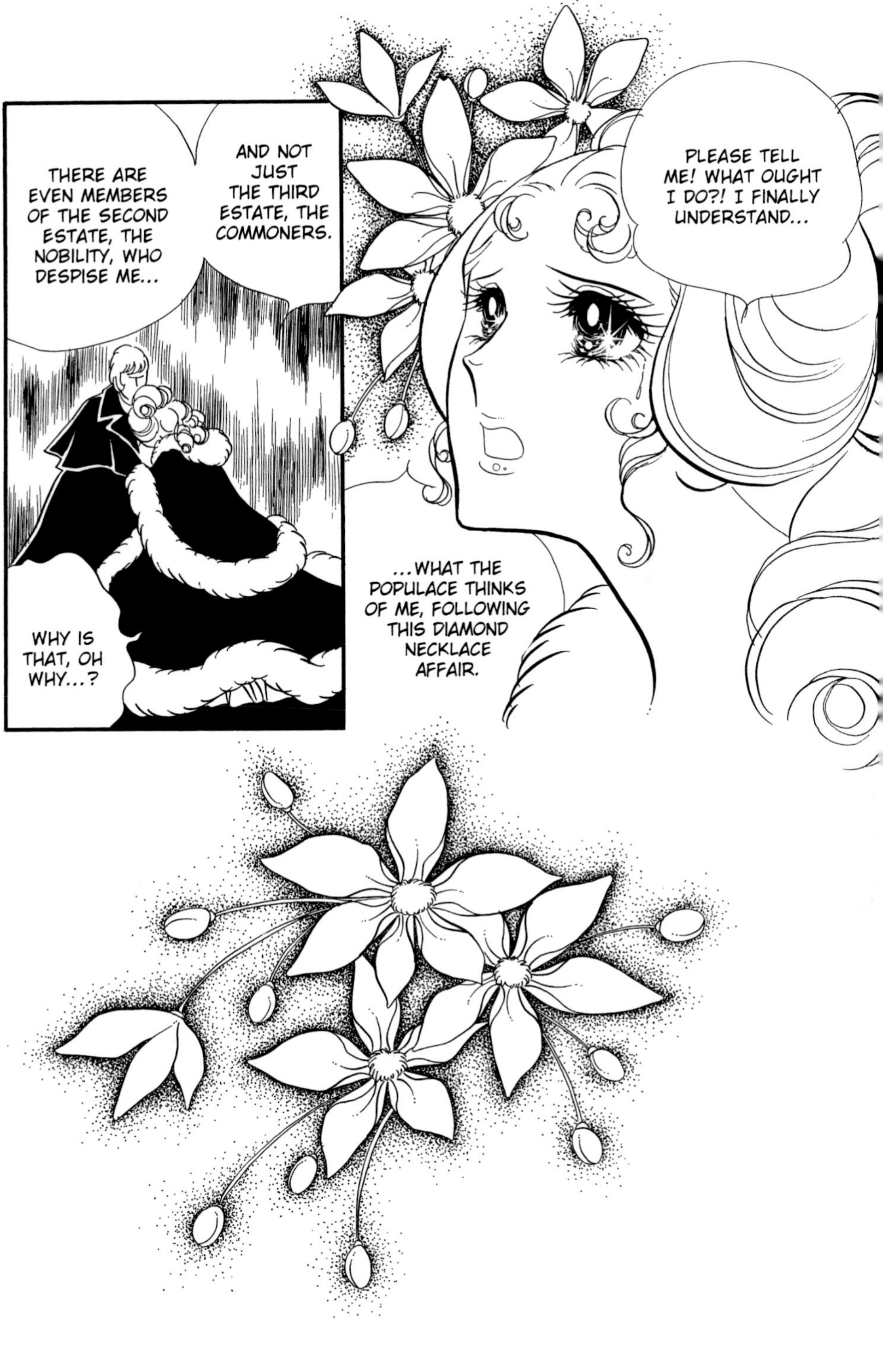
PLEASE TELL ME! WHAT OUGHT I DO?! I FINALLY UNDERSTAND...
...WHAT THE POPULACE THINKS OF ME, FOLLOWING THIS DIAMOND NECKLACE AFFAIR.
AND NOT JUST THE THIRD ESTATE, THE COMMONERS.
THERE ARE EVEN MEMBERS OF THE SECOND ESTATE, THE NOBILITY, WHO DESPISE ME...
WHY IS THAT, OH WHY...?

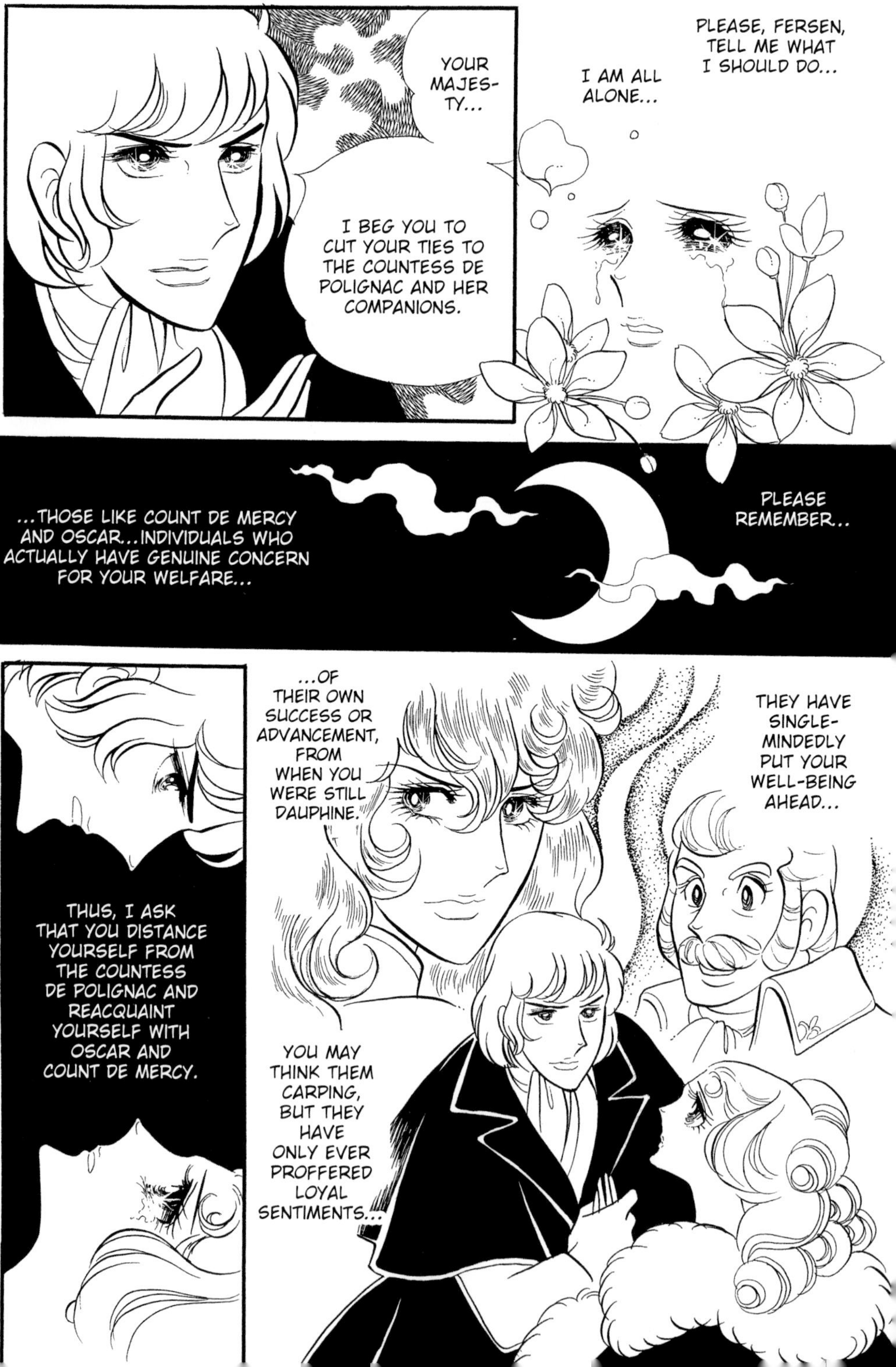
PLEASE, FERSEN, TELL ME WHAT I SHOULD DO...
I AM ALL ALONE...
YOUR MAJES-TY...
I BEG YOU TO CUT YOUR TIES TO THE COUNTESS DE POLIGNAC AND HER COMPANIONS.
PLEASE REMEMBER...
...THOSE LIKE COUNT DE MERCY AND OSCAR...INDIVIDUALS WHO ACTUALLY HAVE GENUINE CONCERN FOR YOUR WELFARE...
THEY HAVE SINGLE-MINDEDLY PUT YOUR WELL-BEING AHEAD...
...OF THEIR OWN SUCCESS OR ADVANCEMENT, FROM WHEN YOU WERE STILL DAUPHINE.
YOU MAY THINK THEM CARPING, BUT THEY HAVE ONLY EVER PROFFERED LOYAL SENTIMENTS...
THUS, I ASK THAT YOU DISTANCE YOURSELF FROM THE COUNTESS DE POLIGNAC AND REACQUAINT YOURSELF WITH OSCAR AND COUNT DE MERCY.

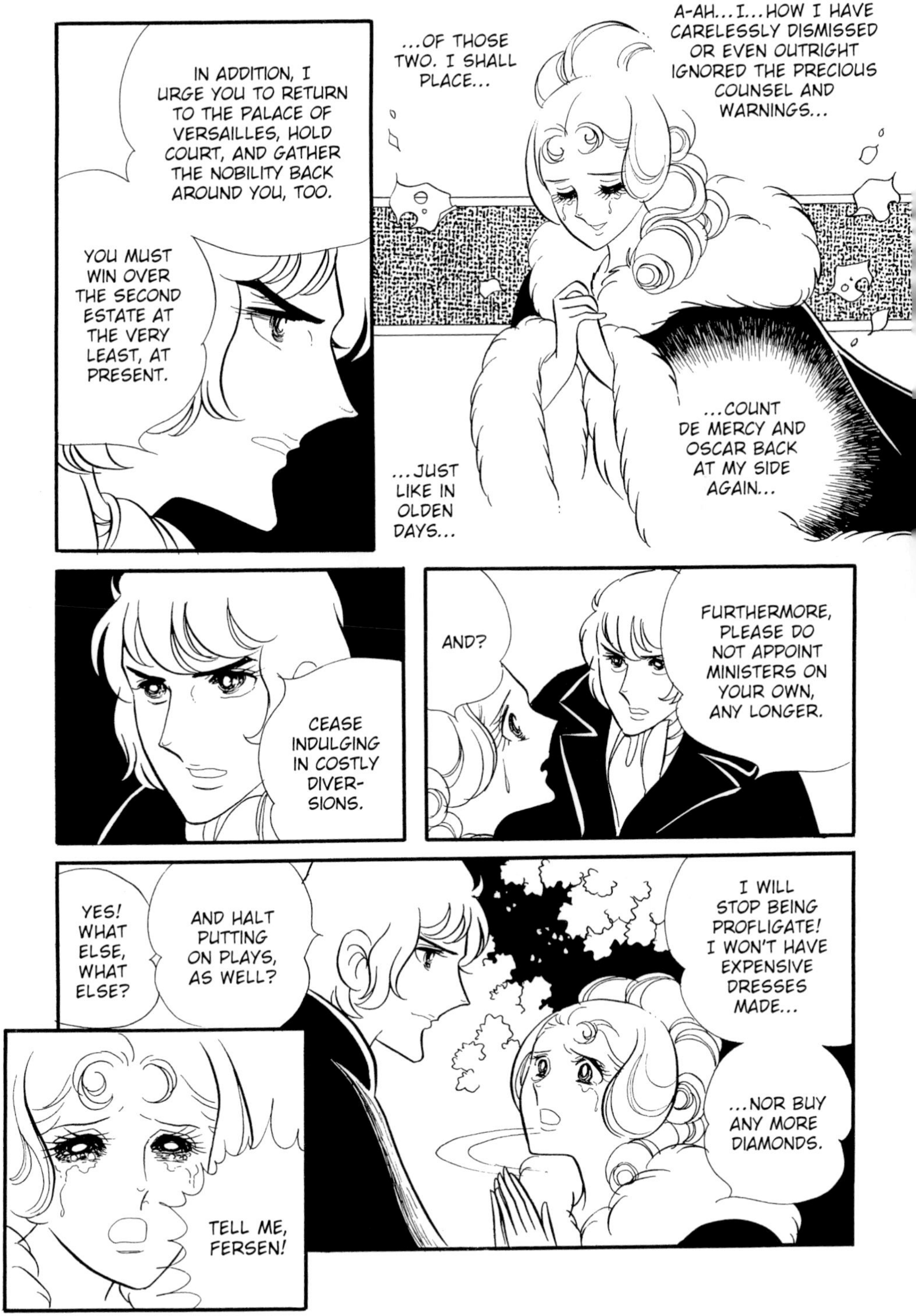
A-AH...I...HOW I HAVE CARELESSLY DISMISSED OR EVEN OUTRIGHT IGNORED THE PRECIOUS COUNSEL AND WARNINGS...
...OF THOSE TWO. I SHALL PLACE...
...COUNT DE MERCY AND OSCAR BACK AT MY SIDE AGAIN...
...JUST LIKE IN OLDEN DAYS...
IN ADDITION, I URGE YOU TO RETURN TO THE PALACE OF VERSAILLES, HOLD COURT, AND GATHER THE NOBILITY BACK AROUND YOU, TOO.
YOU MUST WIN OVER THE SECOND ESTATE AT THE VERY LEAST, AT PRESENT.
FURTHERMORE, PLEASE DO NOT APPOINT MINISTERS ON YOUR OWN, ANY LONGER.
AND?
CEASE INDULGING IN COSTLY DIVERSIONS.
I WILL STOP BEING PROFLIGATE! I WON'T HAVE EXPENSIVE DRESSES MADE...
...NOR BUY ANY MORE DIAMONDS.
AND HALT PUTTING ON PLAYS, AS WELL?
YES! WHAT ELSE, WHAT ELSE?
TELL ME, FERSEN!

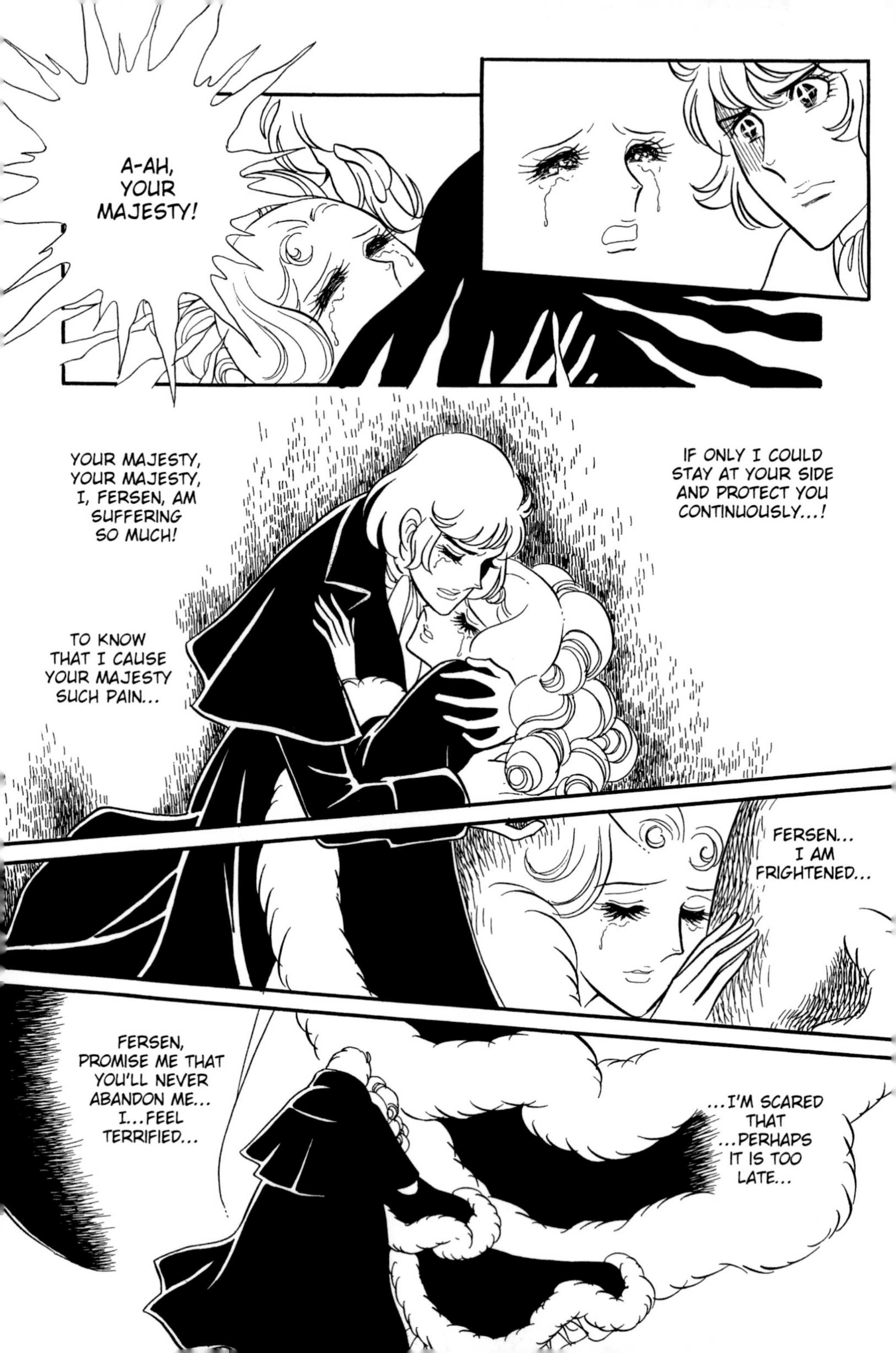
A-AH, YOUR MAJESTY!
IF ONLY I COULD STAY AT YOUR SIDE AND PROTECT YOU CONTINUOUSLY...!
YOUR MAJESTY, YOUR MAJESTY, I, FERSEN, AM SUFFERING SO MUCH!
TO KNOW THAT I CAUSE YOUR MAJESTY SUCH PAIN...
FERSEN... I AM FRIGHTENED...
...I'M SCARED THAT ...PERHAPS IT IS TOO LATE...
FERSEN, PROMISE ME THAT YOU'LL NEVER ABANDON ME... I...FEEL TERRIFIED...

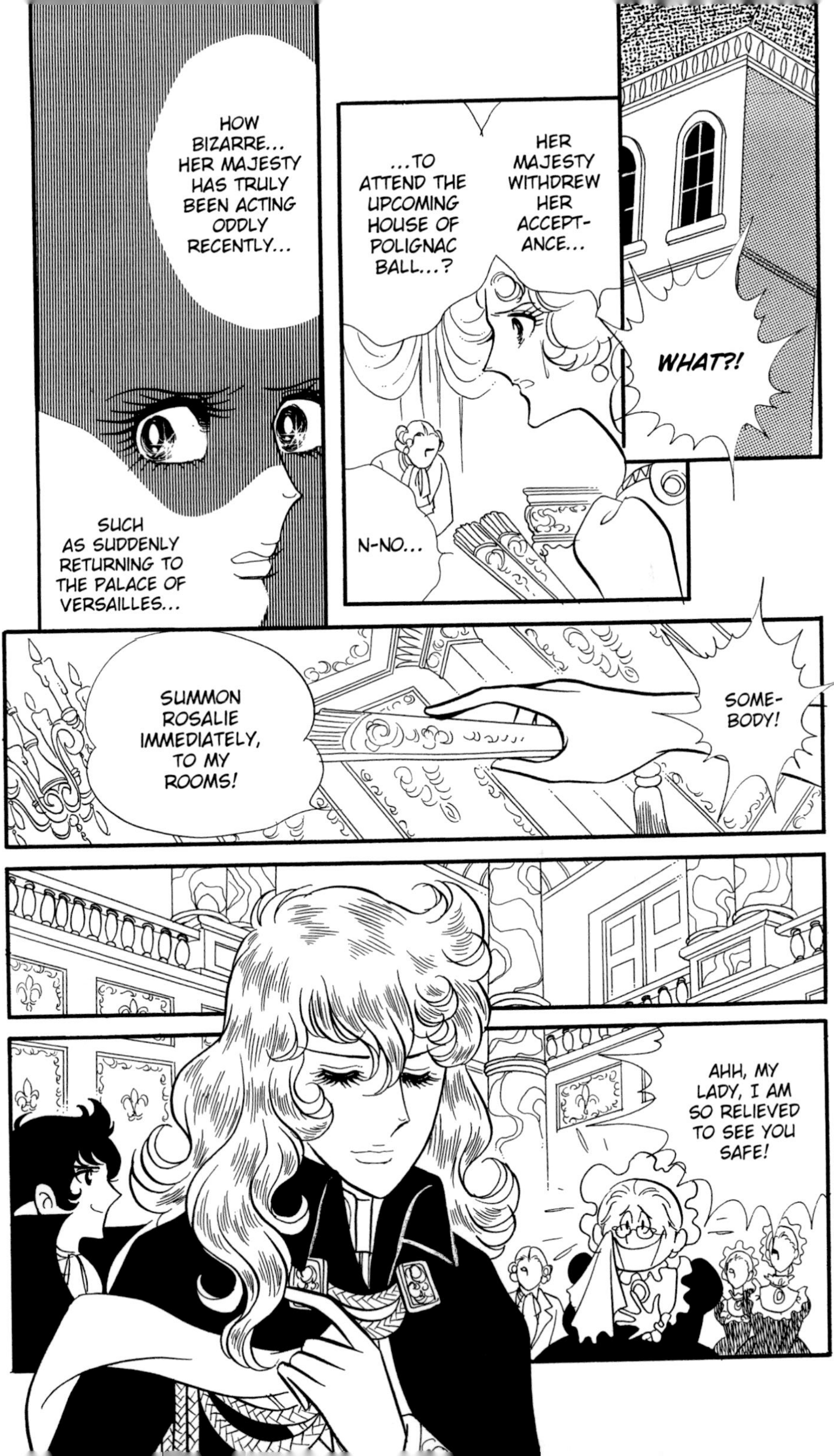

WHAT?!
HER MAJESTY WITHDREW HER ACCEPT-ANCE...
...TO ATTEND THE UPCOMING HOUSE OF POLIGNAC BALL...?
N-NO...
HOW BIZARRE... HER MAJESTY HAS TRULY BEEN ACTING ODDLY RECENTLY...
SUCH AS SUDDENLY RETURNING TO THE PALACE OF VERSAILLES...
SOME-BODY!
SUMMON ROSALIE IMMEDIATELY, TO MY ROOMS!
AHH, MY LADY, I AM SO RELIEVED TO SEE YOU SAFE!

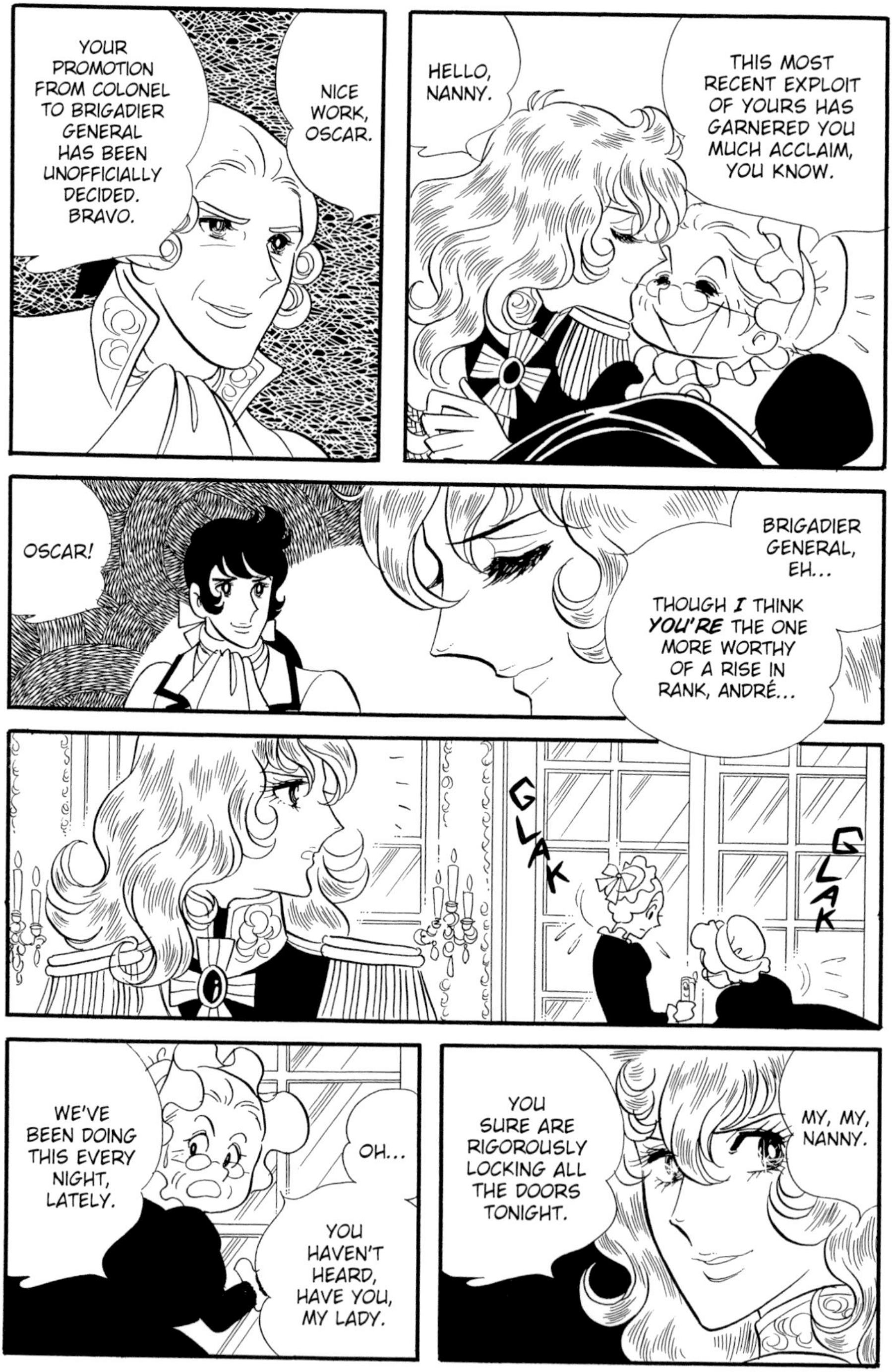
THIS MOST RECENT EXPLOIT OF YOURS HAS GARNERED YOU MUCH ACCLAIM, YOU KNOW.
HELLO, NANNY.
NICE WORK, OSCAR.
YOUR PROMOTION FROM COLONEL TO BRIGADIER GENERAL HAS BEEN UNOFFICIALLY DECIDED. BRAVO.
BRIGADIER GENERAL, EH...
THOUGH *I* THINK ***YOU'RE*** THE ONE MORE WORTHY OF A RISE IN RANK, ANDRÉ...
OSCAR!
GLAK
GLAK
MY, MY, NANNY.
YOU SURE ARE RIGOROUSLY LOCKING ALL THE DOORS TONIGHT.
OH...
YOU HAVEN'T HEARD, HAVE YOU, MY LADY.
WE'VE BEEN DOING THIS EVERY NIGHT, LATELY.

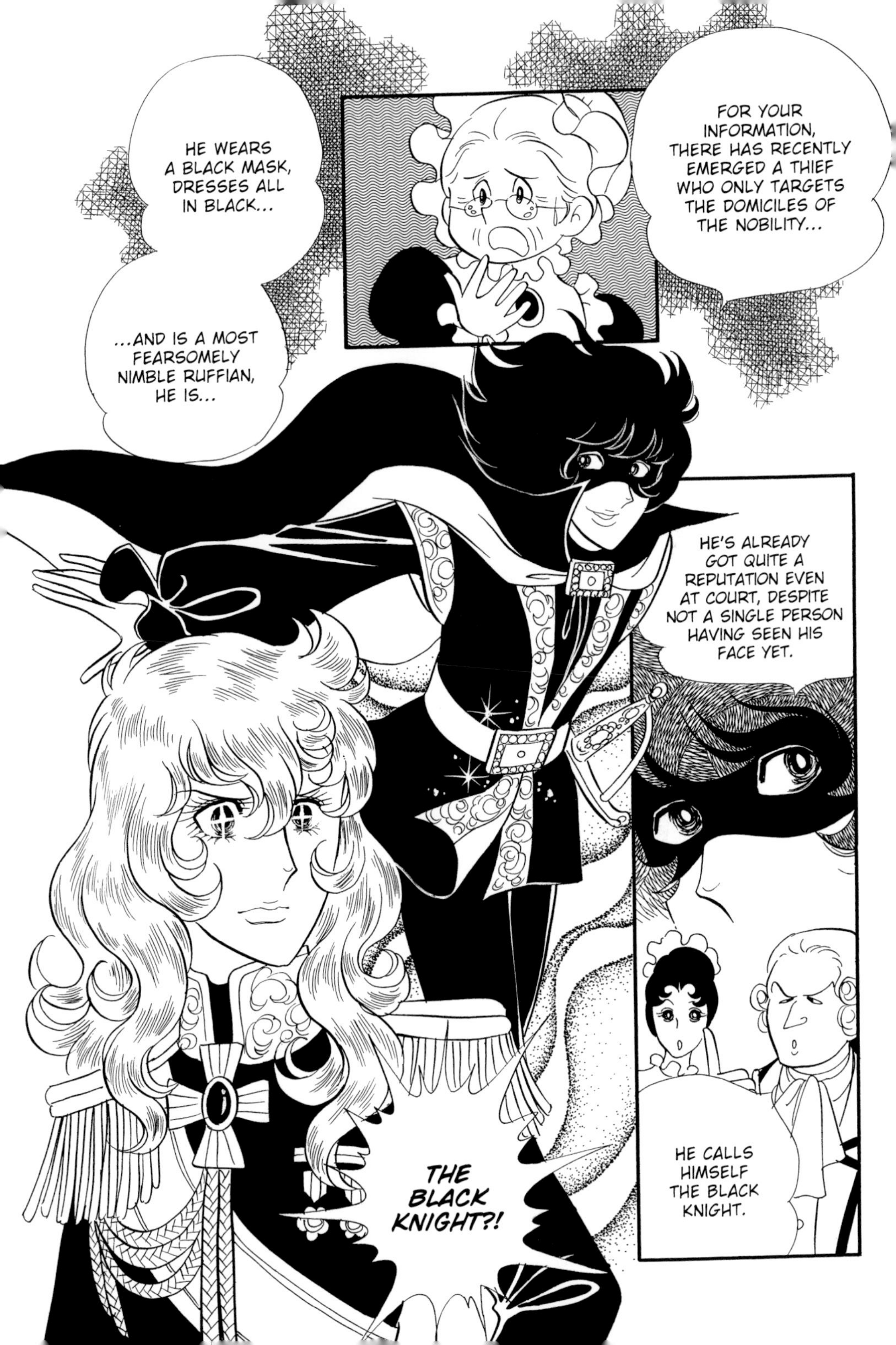
FOR YOUR INFORMATION, THERE HAS RECENTLY EMERGED A THIEF WHO ONLY TARGETS THE DOMICILES OF THE NOBILITY...
HE WEARS A BLACK MASK, DRESSES ALL IN BLACK...
...AND IS A MOST FEARSOMELY NIMBLE RUFFIAN, HE IS...
HE'S ALREADY GOT QUITE A REPUTATION EVEN AT COURT, DESPITE NOT A SINGLE PERSON HAVING SEEN HIS FACE YET.
HE CALLS HIMSELF THE BLACK KNIGHT.
THE BLACK KNIGHT?!

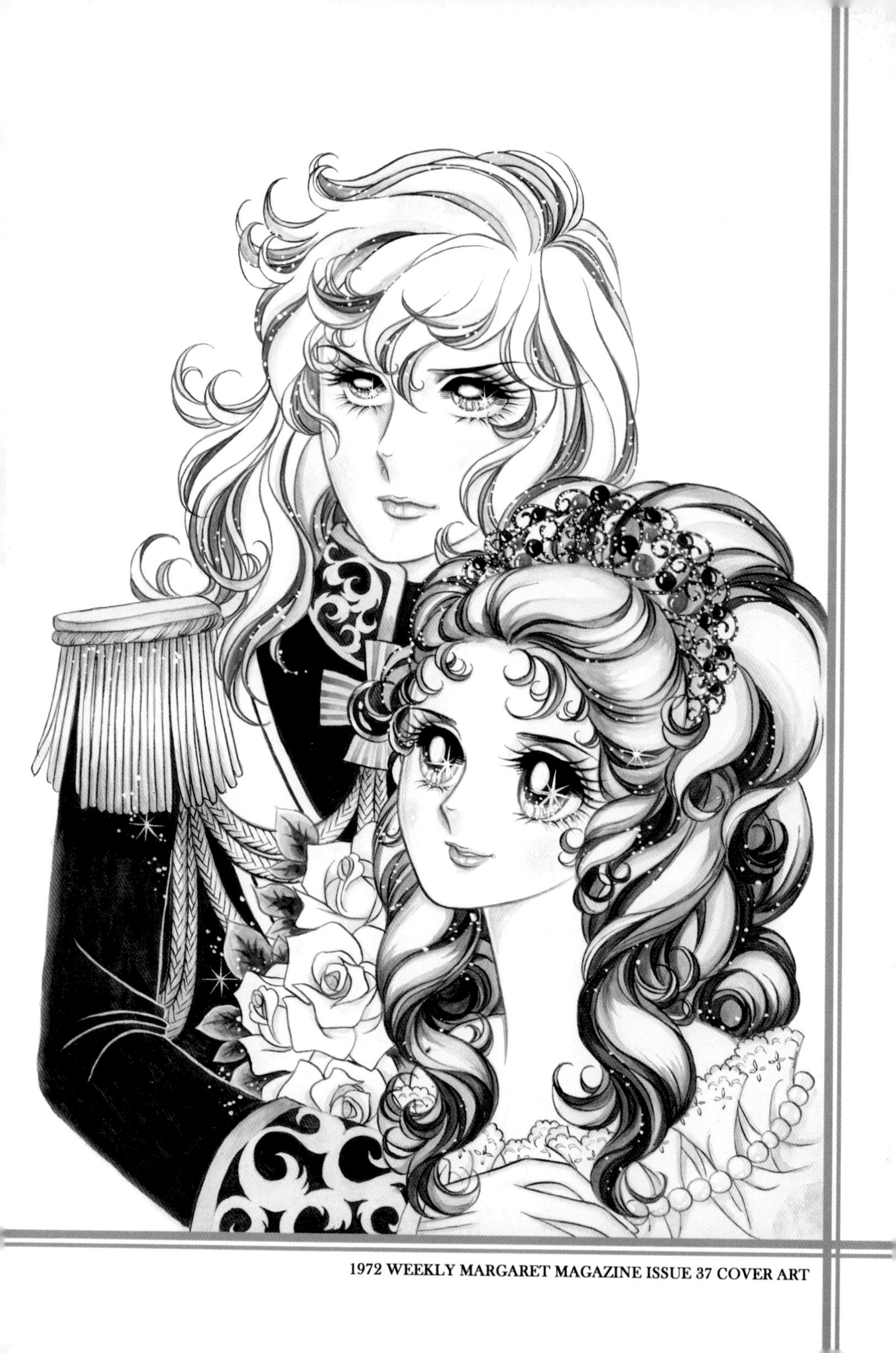

1972 WEEKLY MARGARET MAGAZINE ISSUE 37 COVER ART

ベルサイユのばら

THE ROSE OF VERSAILLES

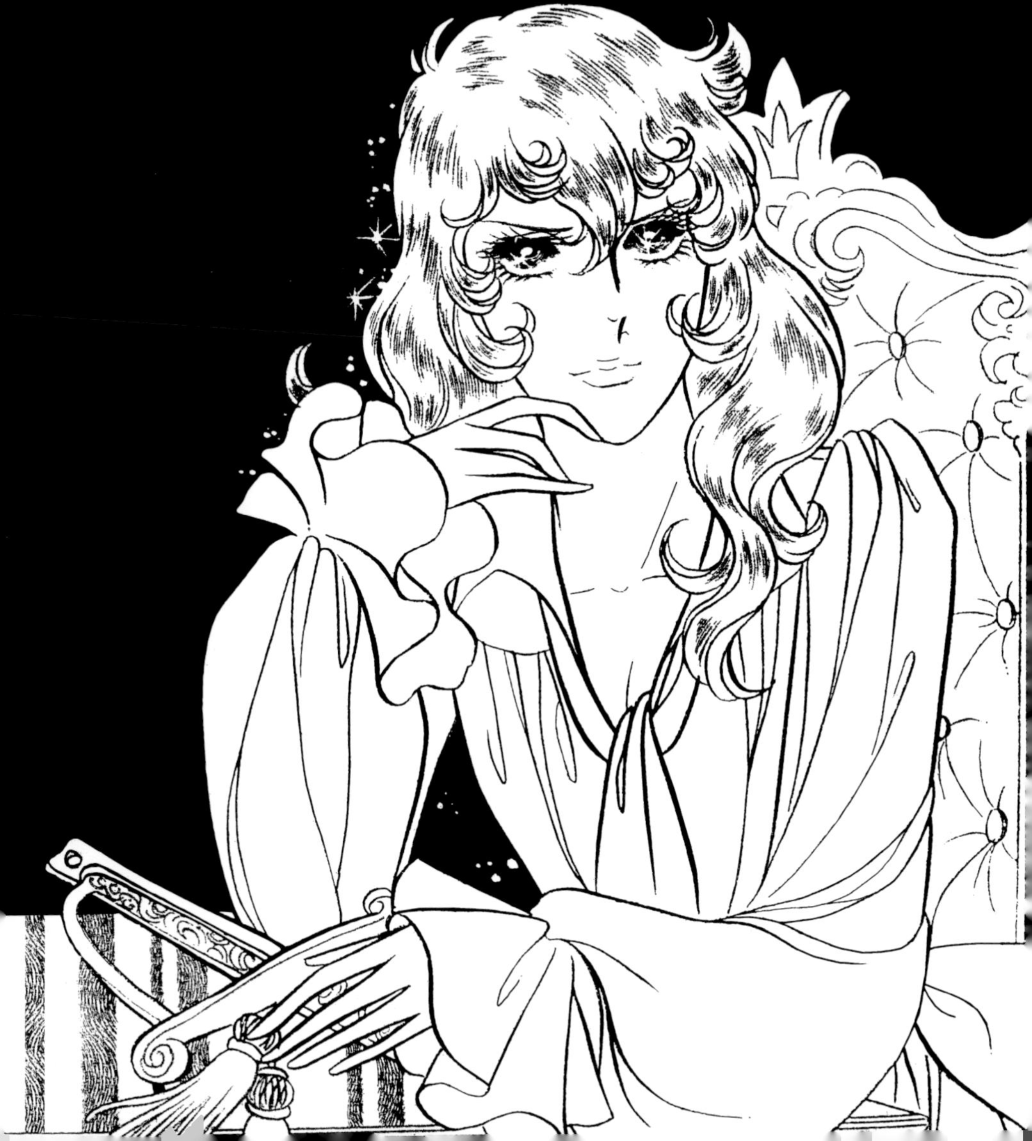

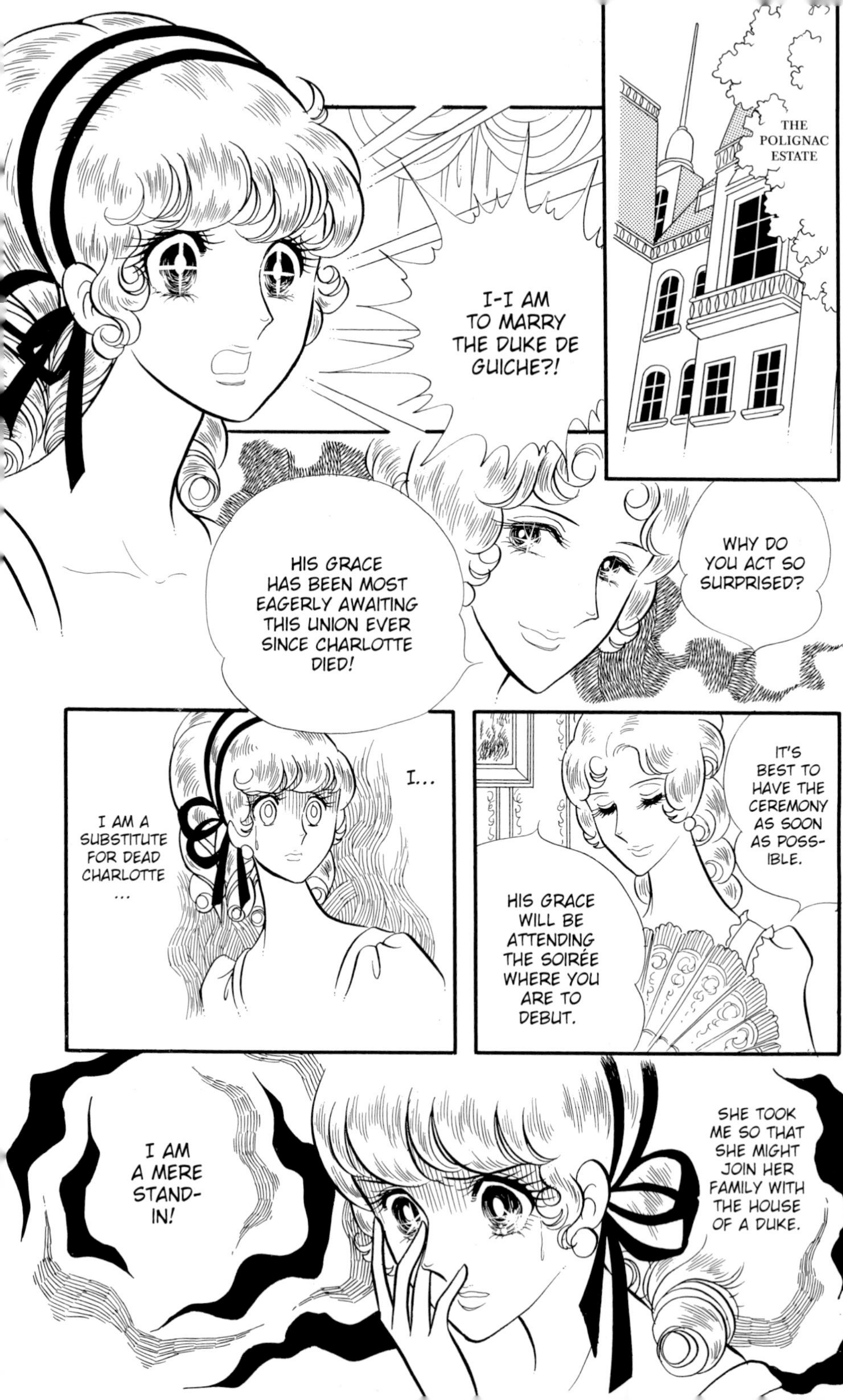
THE POLIGNAC ESTATE
I-I AM TO MARRY THE DUKE DE GUICHE?!
WHY DO YOU ACT SO SURPRISED?
HIS GRACE HAS BEEN MOST EAGERLY AWAITING THIS UNION EVER SINCE CHARLOTTE DIED!
IT'S BEST TO HAVE THE CEREMONY AS SOON AS POSS-IBLE.
HIS GRACE WILL BE ATTENDING THE SOIRÉE WHERE YOU ARE TO DEBUT.
I...
I AM A SUBSTITUTE FOR DEAD CHARLOTTE ...
SHE TOOK ME SO THAT SHE MIGHT JOIN HER FAMILY WITH THE HOUSE OF A DUKE.
I AM A MERE STAND-IN!

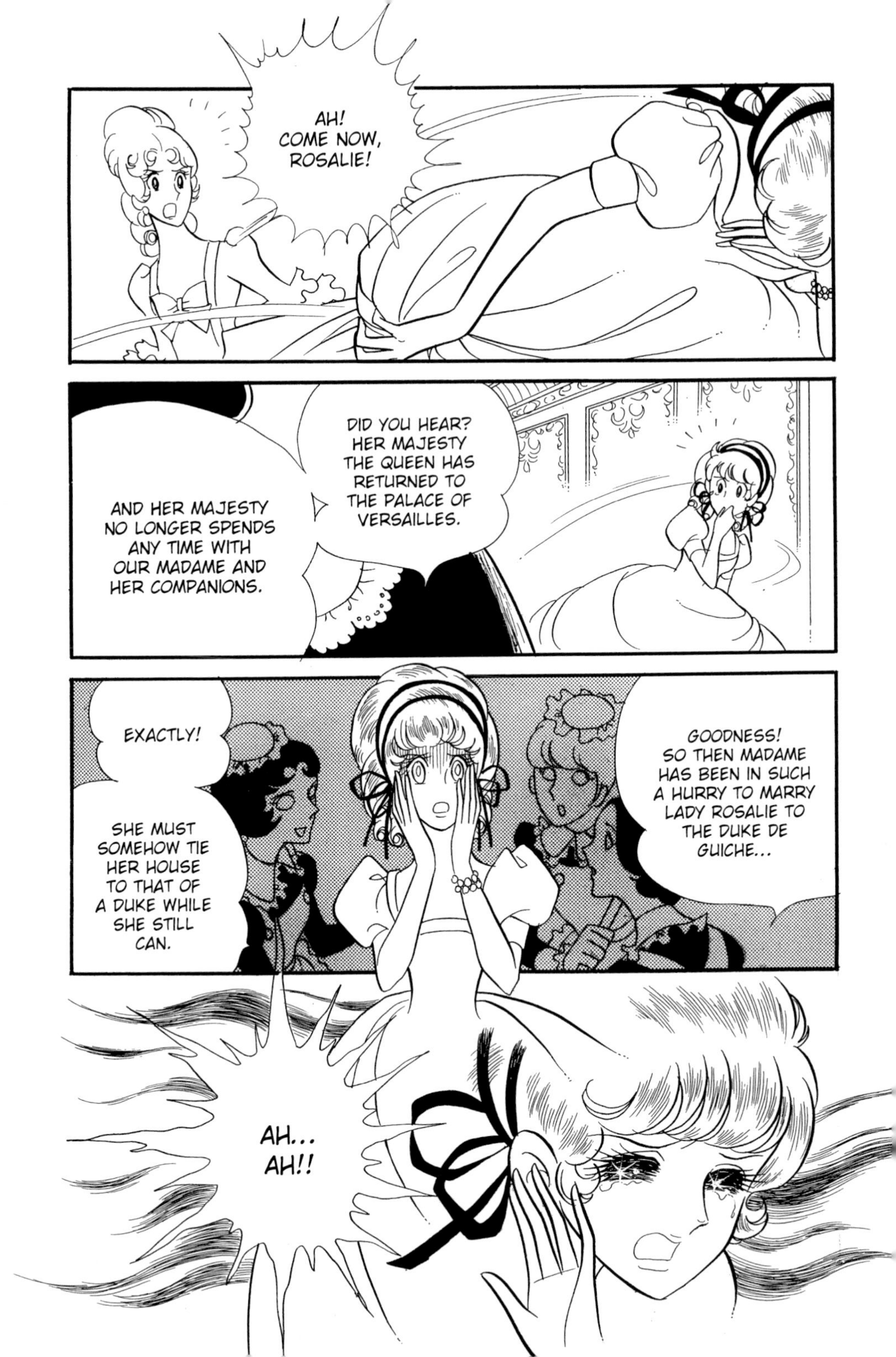
AH! COME NOW, ROSALIE!
DID YOU HEAR? HER MAJESTY THE QUEEN HAS RETURNED TO THE PALACE OF VERSAILLES.
AND HER MAJESTY NO LONGER SPENDS ANY TIME WITH OUR MADAME AND HER COMPANIONS.
GOODNESS! SO THEN MADAME HAS BEEN IN SUCH A HURRY TO MARRY LADY ROSALIE TO THE DUKE DE GUICHE...
EXACTLY!
SHE MUST SOMEHOW TIE HER HOUSE TO THAT OF A DUKE WHILE SHE STILL CAN.
AH... AH!!

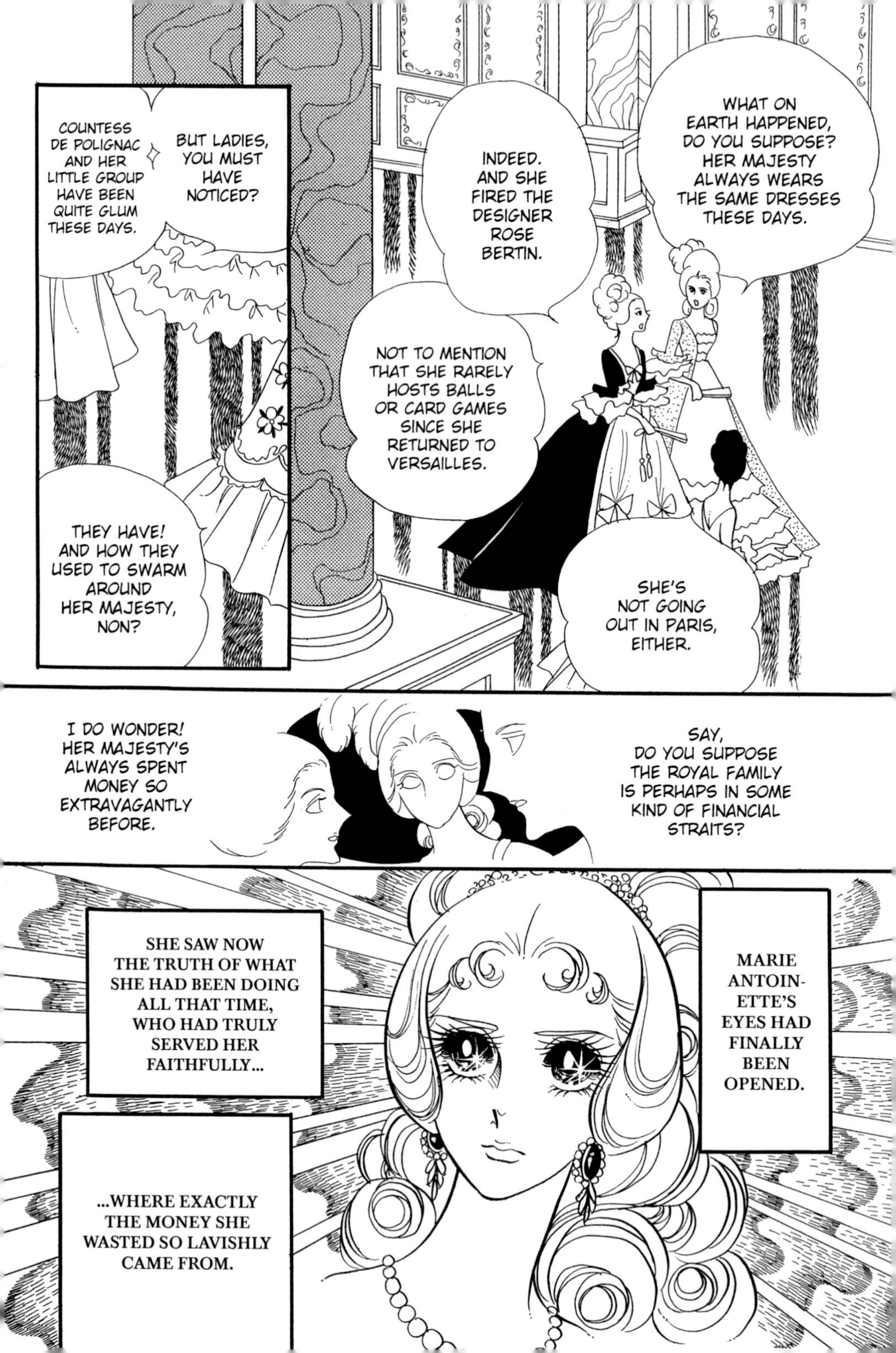
WHAT ON EARTH HAPPENED, DO YOU SUPPOSE? HER MAJESTY ALWAYS WEARS THE SAME DRESSES THESE DAYS.
INDEED. AND SHE FIRED THE DESIGNER ROSE BERTIN.
NOT TO MENTION THAT SHE RARELY HOSTS BALLS OR CARD GAMES SINCE SHE RETURNED TO VERSAILLES.
SHE'S NOT GOING OUT IN PARIS, EITHER.
BUT LADIES, YOU MUST HAVE NOTICED?
COUNTESS DE POLIGNAC AND HER LITTLE GROUP HAVE BEEN QUITE GLUM THESE DAYS.
THEY HAVE! AND HOW THEY USED TO SWARM AROUND HER MAJESTY, NON?
SAY, DO YOU SUPPOSE THE ROYAL FAMILY IS PERHAPS IN SOME KIND OF FINANCIAL STRAITS?
I DO WONDER! HER MAJESTY'S ALWAYS SPENT MONEY SO EXTRAVAGANTLY BEFORE.
MARIE ANTOIN-ETTE'S EYES HAD FINALLY BEEN OPENED.
SHE SAW NOW THE TRUTH OF WHAT SHE HAD BEEN DOING ALL THAT TIME, WHO HAD TRULY SERVED HER FAITHFULLY...
...WHERE EXACTLY THE MONEY SHE WASTED SO LAVISHLY CAME FROM.

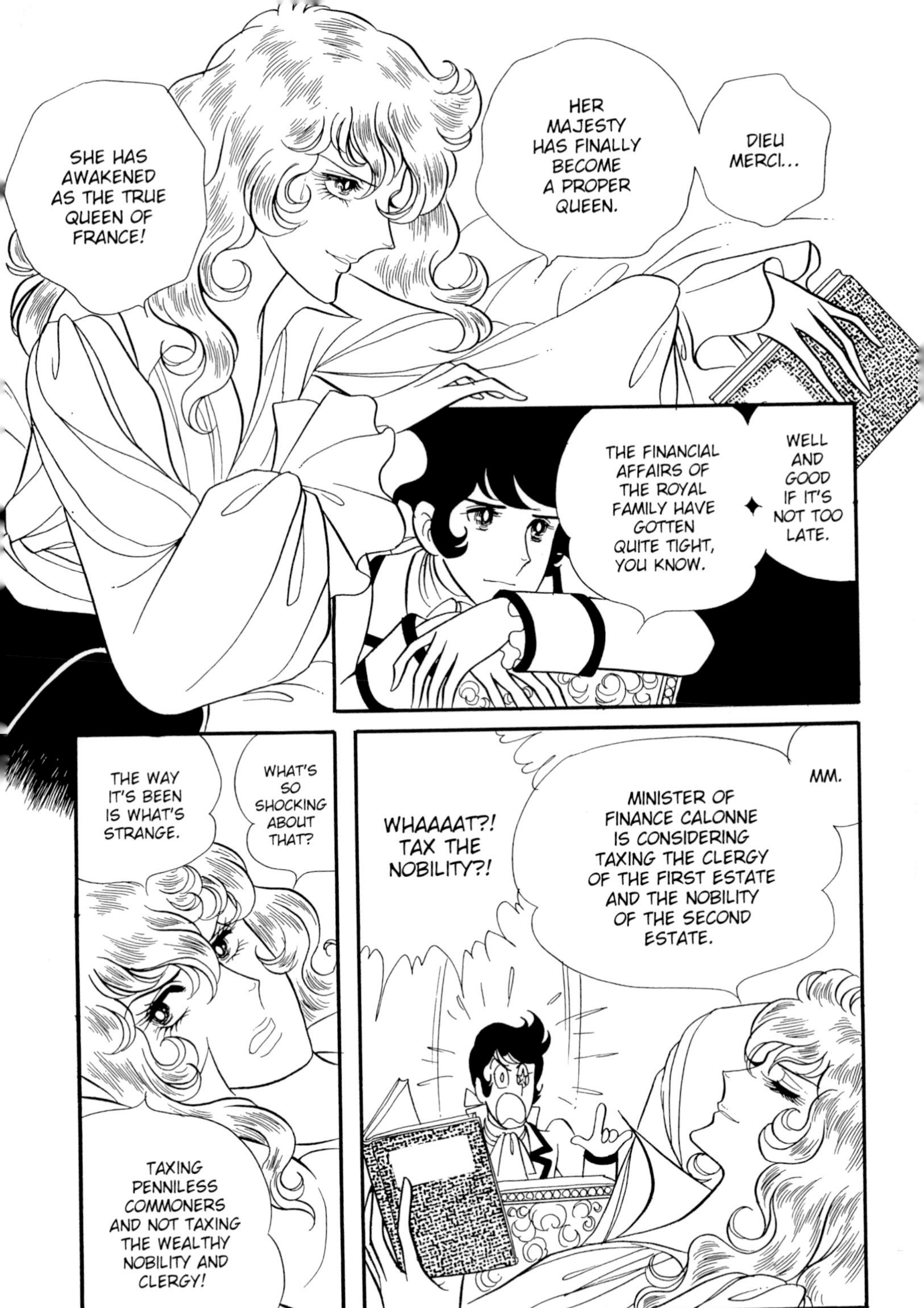
DIEU MERCI...
HER MAJESTY HAS FINALLY BECOME A PROPER QUEEN.
SHE HAS AWAKENED AS THE TRUE QUEEN OF FRANCE!
WELL AND GOOD IF IT'S NOT TOO LATE.
THE FINANCIAL AFFAIRS OF THE ROYAL FAMILY HAVE GOTTEN QUITE TIGHT, YOU KNOW.
MM.
MINISTER OF FINANCE CALONNE IS CONSIDERING TAXING THE CLERGY OF THE FIRST ESTATE AND THE NOBILITY OF THE SECOND ESTATE.
WHAAAAT?! TAX THE NOBILITY?!
WHAT'S SO SHOCKING ABOUT THAT?
THE WAY IT'S BEEN IS WHAT'S STRANGE.
TAXING PENNILESS COMMONERS AND NOT TAXING THE WEALTHY NOBILITY AND CLERGY!

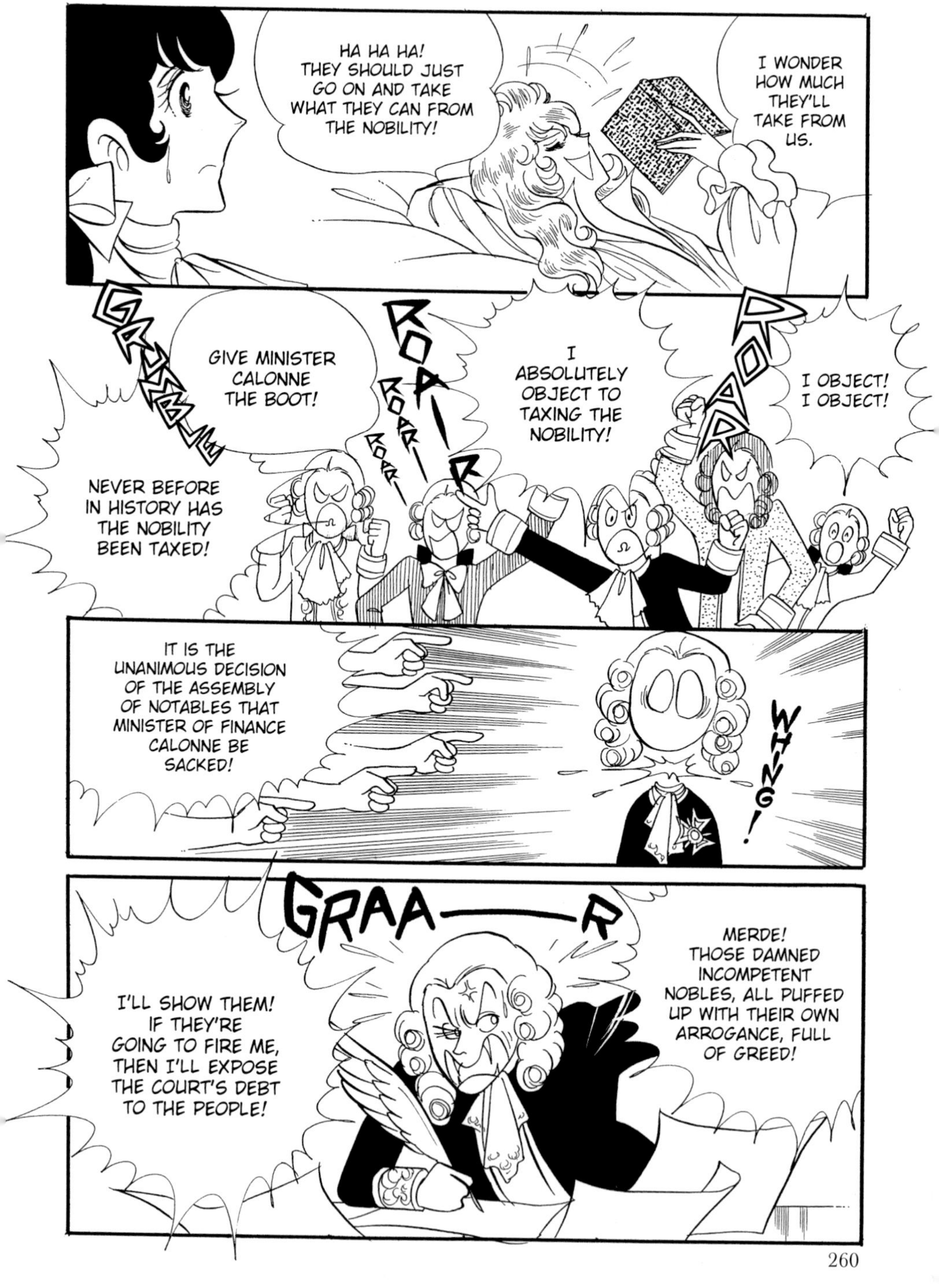
I WONDER HOW MUCH THEY'LL TAKE FROM US.
HA HA HA! THEY SHOULD JUST GO ON AND TAKE WHAT THEY CAN FROM THE NOBILITY!
I OBJECT! I OBJECT!
I ABSOLUTELY OBJECT TO TAXING THE NOBILITY!
GIVE MINISTER CALONNE THE BOOT!
GRUMBLE
NEVER BEFORE IN HISTORY HAS THE NOBILITY BEEN TAXED!
WHING!
IT IS THE UNANIMOUS DECISION OF THE ASSEMBLY OF NOTABLES THAT MINISTER OF FINANCE CALONNE BE SACKED!
MERDE! THOSE DAMNED INCOMPETENT NOBLES, ALL PUFFED UP WITH THEIR OWN ARROGANCE, FULL OF GREED!
GRAA—R
I'LL SHOW THEM! IF THEY'RE GOING TO FIRE ME, THEN I'LL EXPOSE THE COURT'S DEBT TO THE PEOPLE!

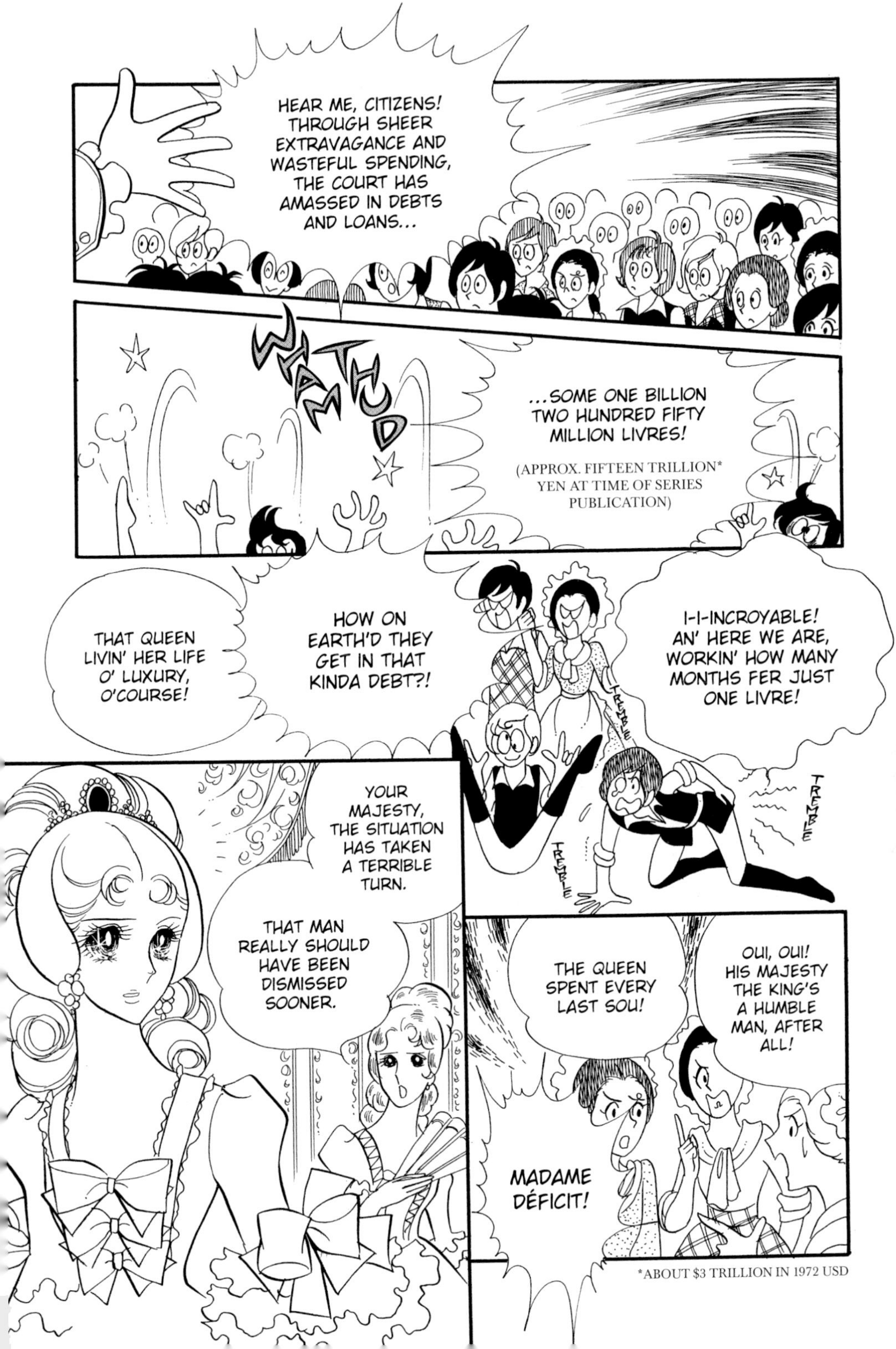
HEAR ME, CITIZENS! THROUGH SHEER EXTRAVAGANCE AND WASTEFUL SPENDING, THE COURT HAS AMASSED IN DEBTS AND LOANS...
...SOME ONE BILLION TWO HUNDRED FIFTY MILLION LIVRES!
(APPROX. FIFTEEN TRILLION* YEN AT TIME OF SERIES PUBLICATION)
WHAM
THUD
I-I-INCROYABLE! AN' HERE WE ARE, WORKIN' HOW MANY MONTHS FER JUST ONE LIVRE!
HOW ON EARTH'D THEY GET IN THAT KINDA DEBT?!
THAT QUEEN LIVIN' HER LIFE O' LUXURY, O'COURSE!
TREMBLE
TREMBLE
TREMBLE
OUI, OUI! HIS MAJESTY THE KING'S A HUMBLE MAN, AFTER ALL!
THE QUEEN SPENT EVERY LAST SOU!
MADAME DÉFICIT!
YOUR MAJESTY, THE SITUATION HAS TAKEN A TERRIBLE TURN.
THAT MAN REALLY SHOULD HAVE BEEN DISMISSED SOONER.

*ABOUT $3 TRILLION IN 1972 USD

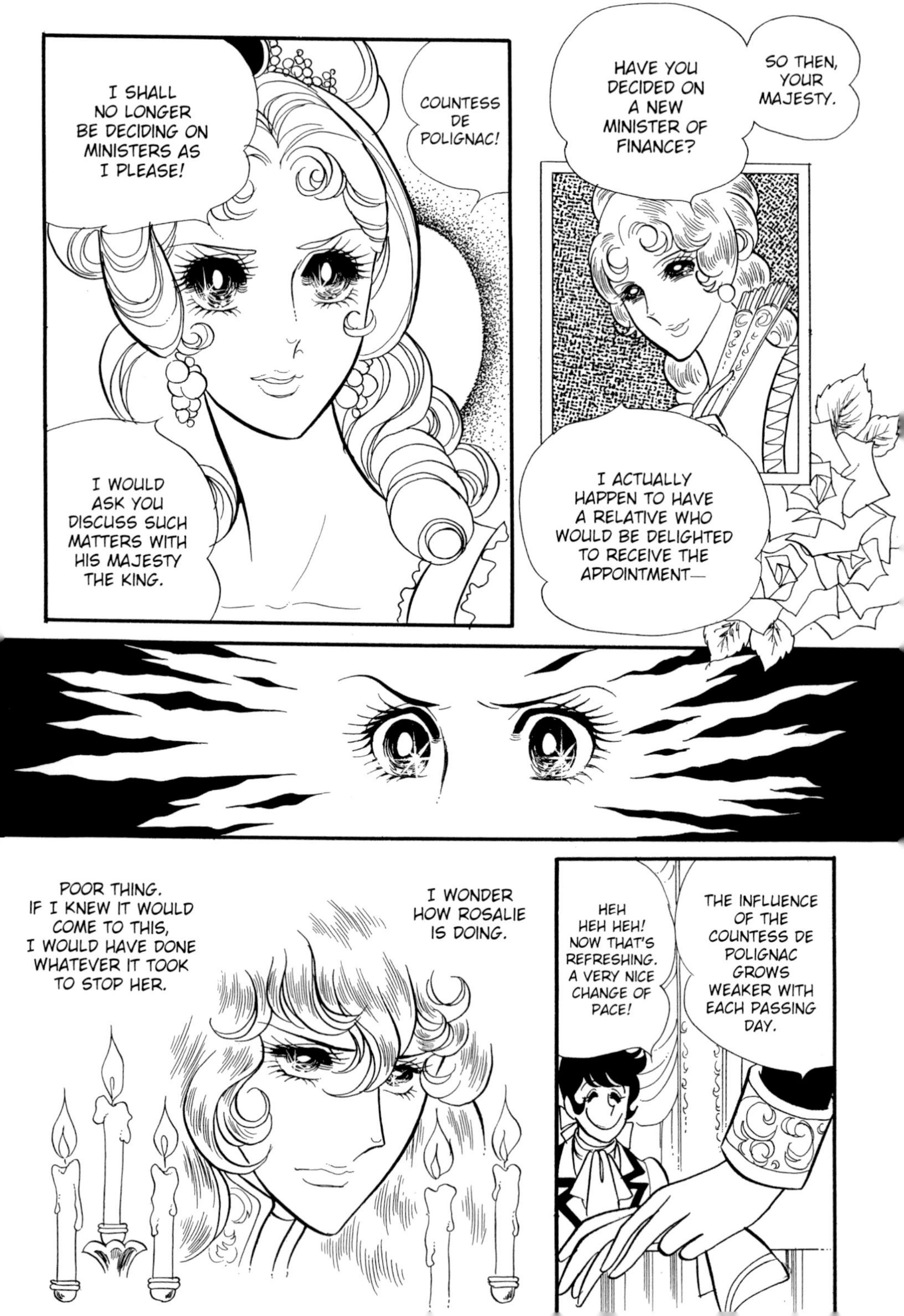
SO THEN, YOUR MAJESTY.
HAVE YOU DECIDED ON A NEW MINISTER OF FINANCE?
I ACTUALLY HAPPEN TO HAVE A RELATIVE WHO WOULD BE DELIGHTED TO RECEIVE THE APPOINTMENT—
COUNTESS DE POLIGNAC!
I SHALL NO LONGER BE DECIDING ON MINISTERS AS I PLEASE!
I WOULD ASK YOU DISCUSS SUCH MATTERS WITH HIS MAJESTY THE KING.
THE INFLUENCE OF THE COUNTESS DE POLIGNAC GROWS WEAKER WITH EACH PASSING DAY.
HEH HEH HEH! NOW THAT'S REFRESHING. A VERY NICE CHANGE OF PACE!
I WONDER HOW ROSALIE IS DOING.
POOR THING. IF I KNEW IT WOULD COME TO THIS, I WOULD HAVE DONE WHATEVER IT TOOK TO STOP HER.

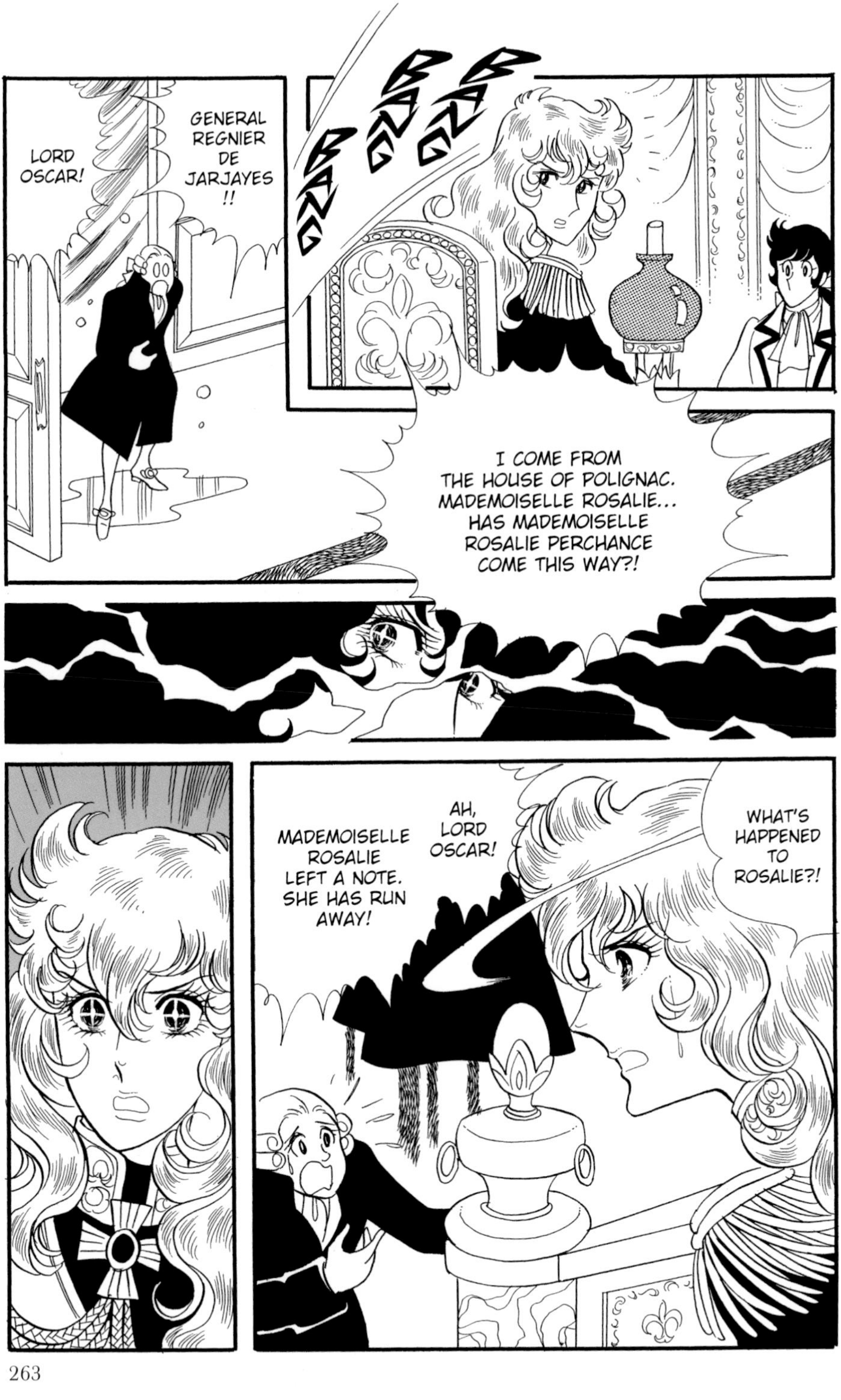
BANG
BANG
BANG
GENERAL REGNIER DE JARJAYES!!
LORD OSCAR!
I COME FROM THE HOUSE OF POLIGNAC. MADEMOISELLE ROSALIE... HAS MADEMOISELLE ROSALIE PERCHANCE COME THIS WAY?!
WHAT'S HAPPENED TO ROSALIE?!
AH, LORD OSCAR!
MADEMOISELLE ROSALIE LEFT A NOTE. SHE HAS RUN AWAY!

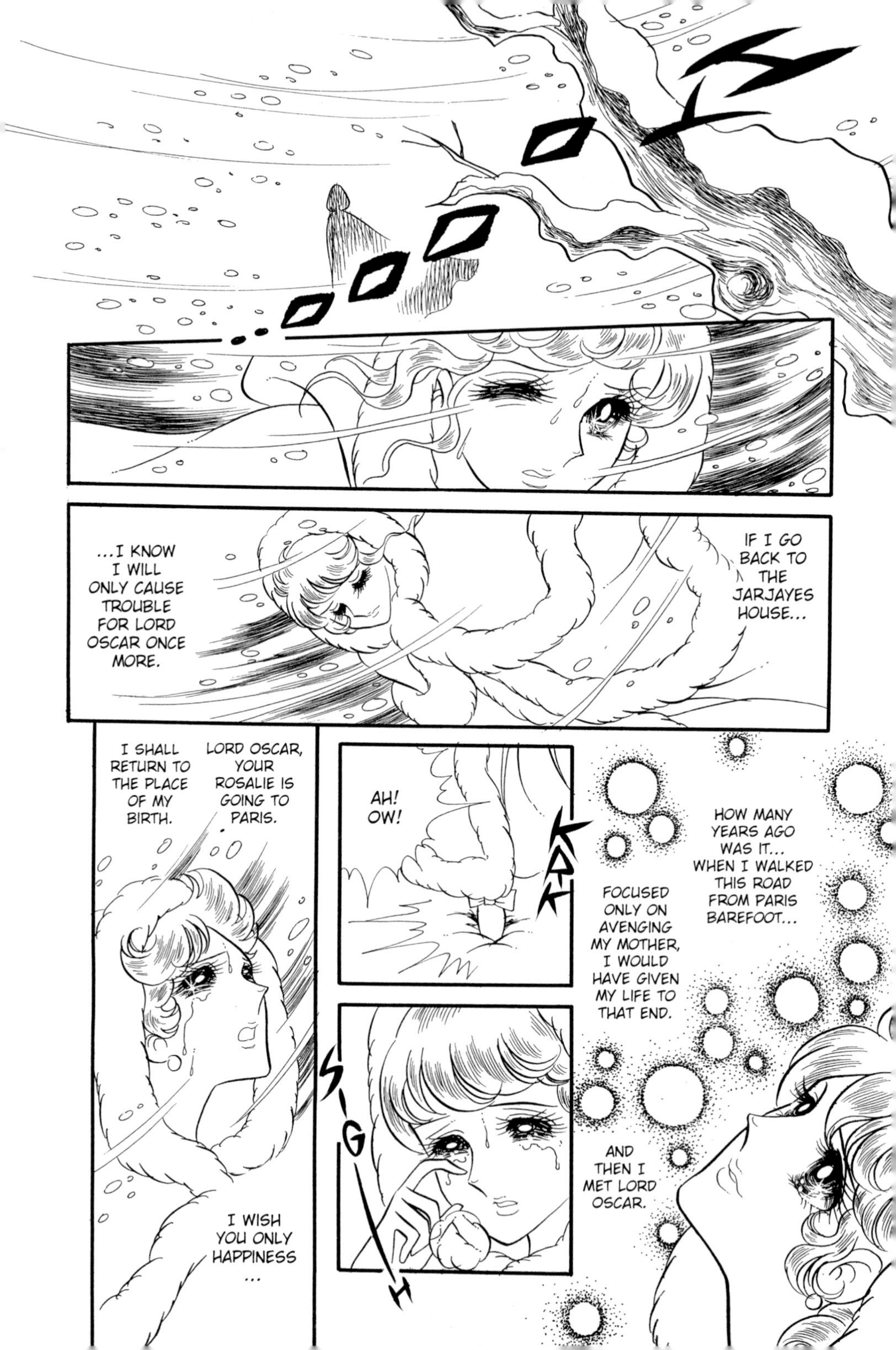
IF I GO BACK TO THE JARJAYES HOUSE...
...I KNOW I WILL ONLY CAUSE TROUBLE FOR LORD OSCAR ONCE MORE.
HOW MANY YEARS AGO WAS IT... WHEN I WALKED THIS ROAD FROM PARIS BAREFOOT...
FOCUSED ONLY ON AVENGING MY MOTHER, I WOULD HAVE GIVEN MY LIFE TO THAT END.
AND THEN I MET LORD OSCAR.
KAK
AH! OW!
SIGH
LORD OSCAR, YOUR ROSALIE IS GOING TO PARIS.
I SHALL RETURN TO THE PLACE OF MY BIRTH.
I WISH YOU ONLY HAPPINESS ...

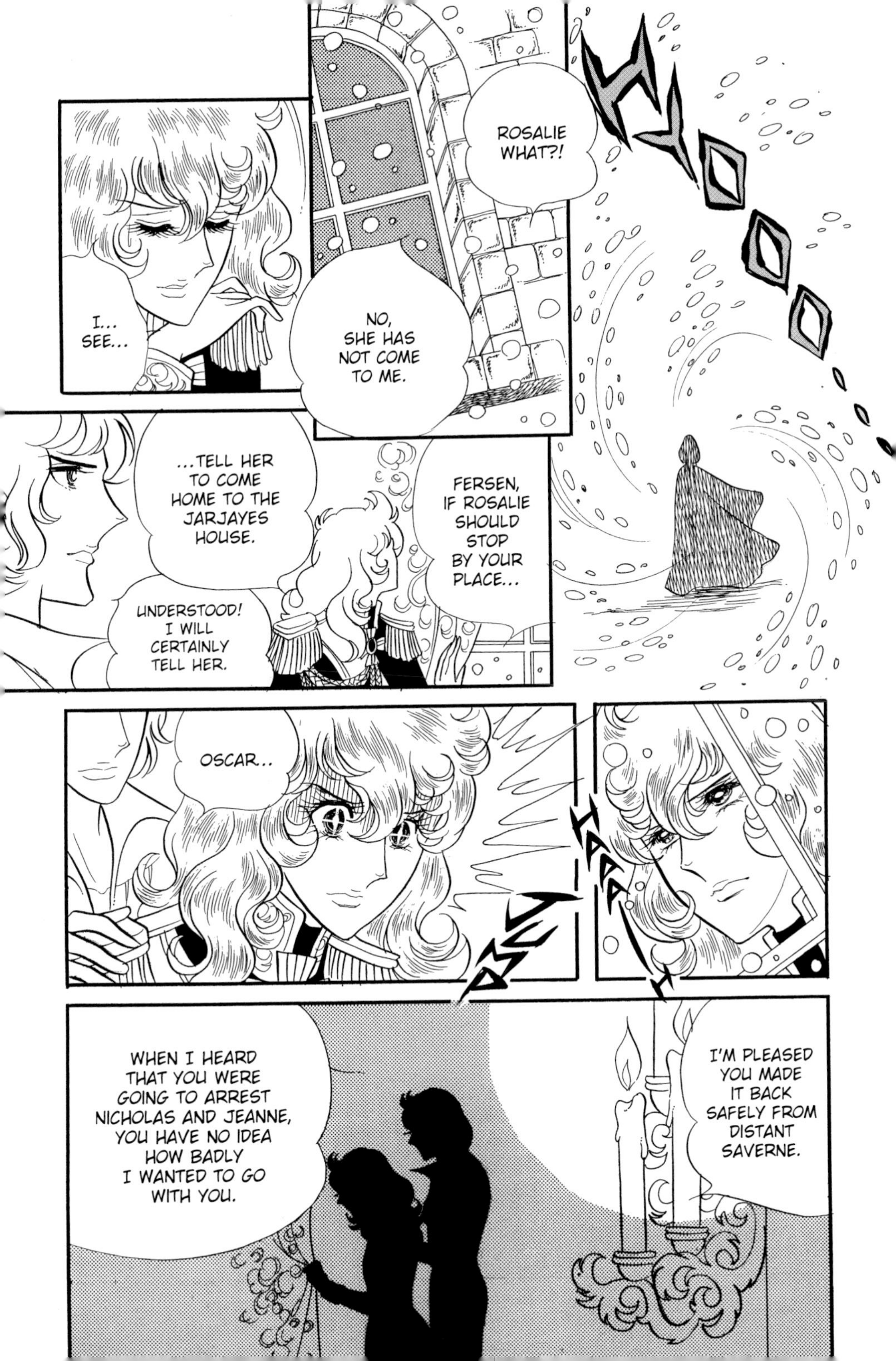
HYOOOO...
ROSALIE WHAT?!
NO, SHE HAS NOT COME TO ME.
I... SEE...
FERSEN, IF ROSALIE SHOULD STOP BY YOUR PLACE...
...TELL HER TO COME HOME TO THE JARJAYES HOUSE.
UNDERSTOOD! I WILL CERTAINLY TELL HER.
OSCAR...
I'M PLEASED YOU MADE IT BACK SAFELY FROM DISTANT SAVERNE.
WHEN I HEARD THAT YOU WERE GOING TO ARREST NICHOLAS AND JEANNE, YOU HAVE NO IDEA HOW BADLY I WANTED TO GO WITH YOU.

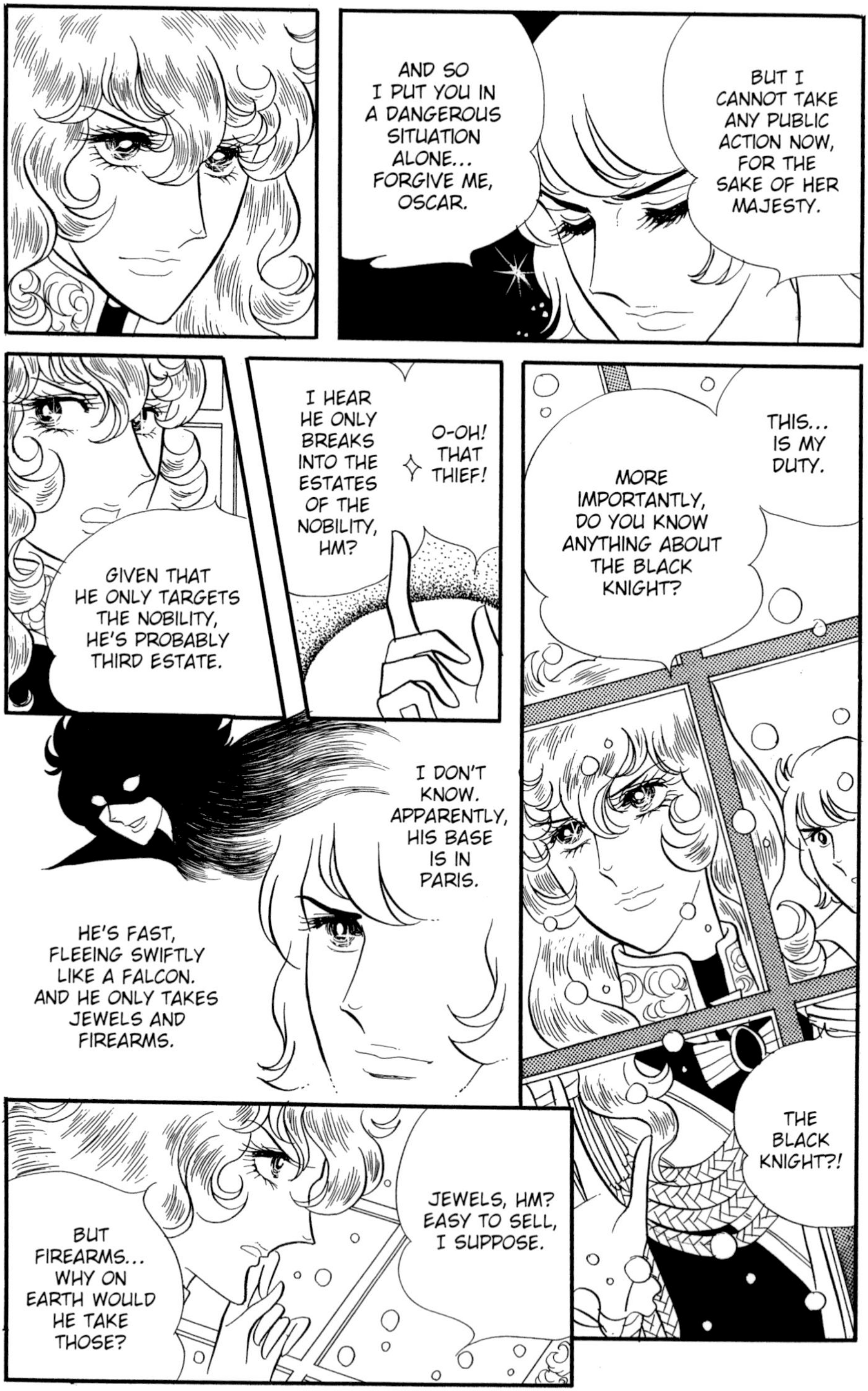

BUT I CANNOT TAKE ANY PUBLIC ACTION NOW, FOR THE SAKE OF HER MAJESTY.
AND SO I PUT YOU IN A DANGEROUS SITUATION ALONE... FORGIVE ME, OSCAR.
THIS... IS MY DUTY.
MORE IMPORTANTLY, DO YOU KNOW ANYTHING ABOUT THE BLACK KNIGHT?
THE BLACK KNIGHT?!
O-OH! THAT THIEF!
I HEAR HE ONLY BREAKS INTO THE ESTATES OF THE NOBILITY, HM?
GIVEN THAT HE ONLY TARGETS THE NOBILITY, HE'S PROBABLY THIRD ESTATE.
I DON'T KNOW. APPARENTLY, HIS BASE IS IN PARIS.
HE'S FAST, FLEEING SWIFTLY LIKE A FALCON. AND HE ONLY TAKES JEWELS AND FIREARMS.
JEWELS, HM? EASY TO SELL, I SUPPOSE.
BUT FIREARMS... WHY ON EARTH WOULD HE TAKE THOSE?

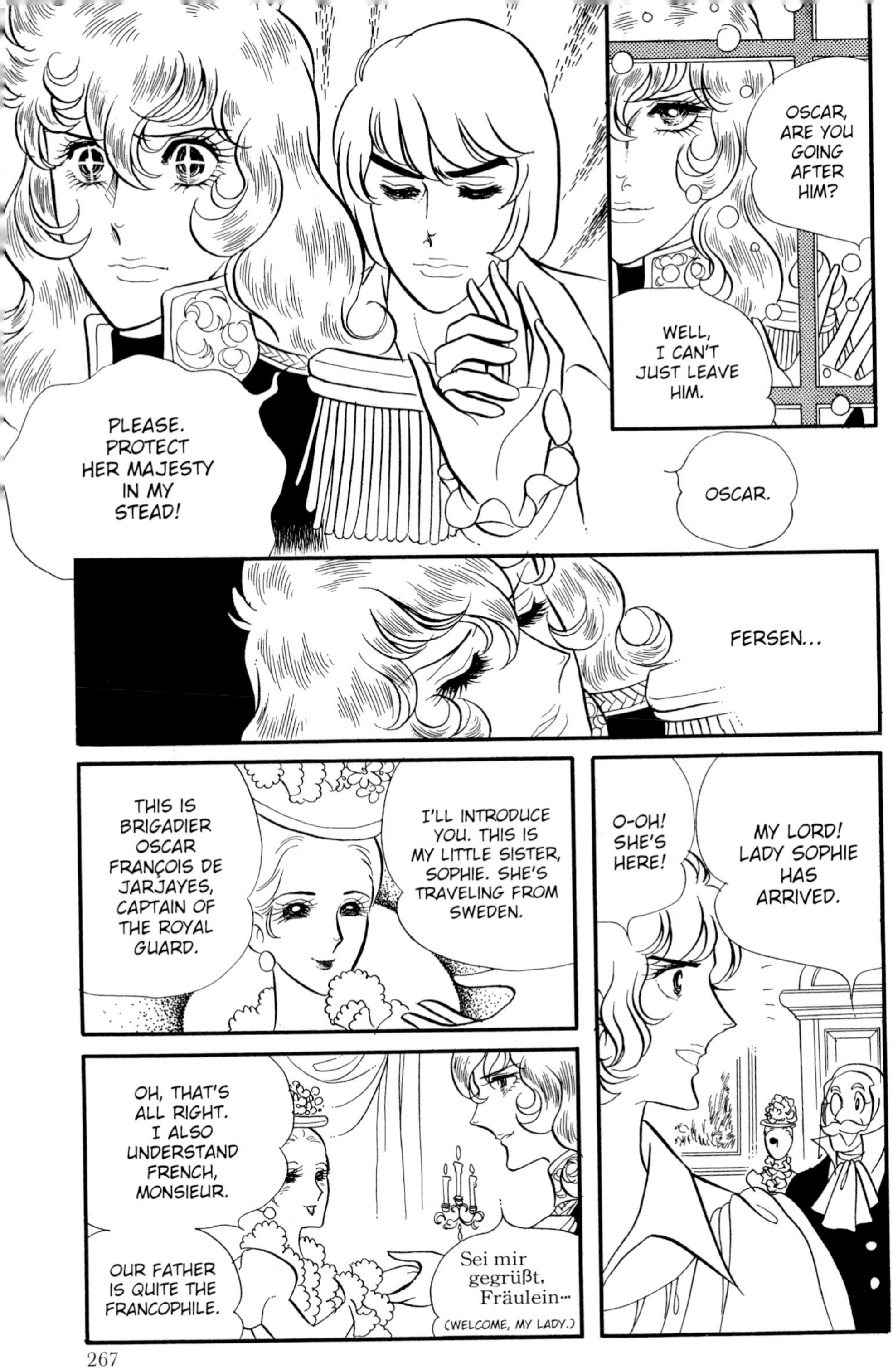
OSCAR, ARE YOU GOING AFTER HIM?
WELL, I CAN'T JUST LEAVE HIM.
OSCAR.
PLEASE. PROTECT HER MAJESTY IN MY STEAD!
FERSEN...
MY LORD! LADY SOPHIE HAS ARRIVED.
O-OH! SHE'S HERE!
I'LL INTRODUCE YOU. THIS IS MY LITTLE SISTER, SOPHIE. SHE'S TRAVELING FROM SWEDEN.
THIS IS BRIGADIER OSCAR FRANÇOIS DE JARJAYES, CAPTAIN OF THE ROYAL GUARD.
Sei mir gegrüßt, Fräulein…
(WELCOME, MY LADY.)
OH, THAT'S ALL RIGHT. I ALSO UNDERSTAND FRENCH, MONSIEUR.
OUR FATHER IS QUITE THE FRANCOPHILE.

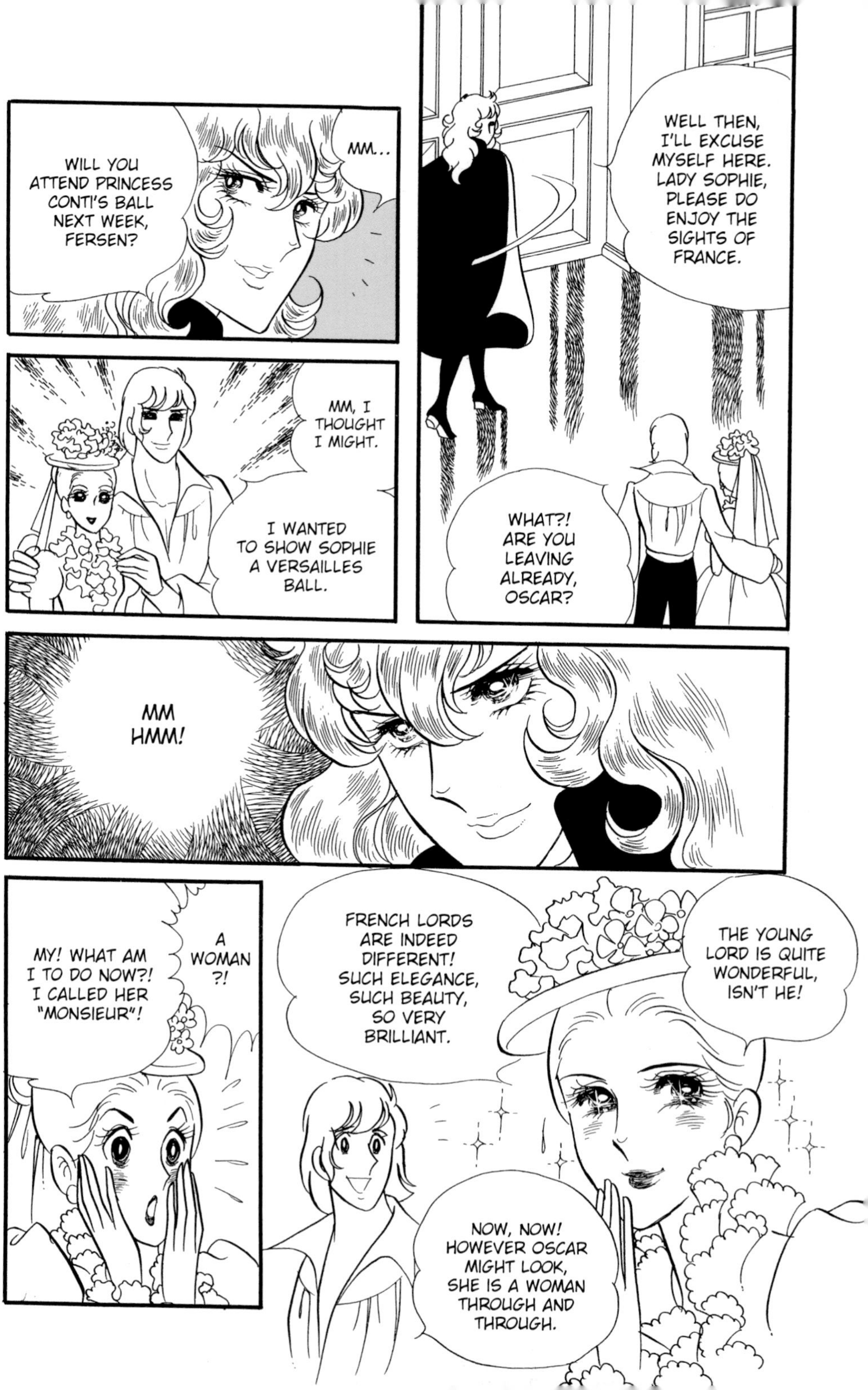
WELL THEN, I'LL EXCUSE MYSELF HERE. LADY SOPHIE, PLEASE DO ENJOY THE SIGHTS OF FRANCE.
WHAT?! ARE YOU LEAVING ALREADY, OSCAR?
MM...
WILL YOU ATTEND PRINCESS CONTI'S BALL NEXT WEEK, FERSEN?
MM, I THOUGHT I MIGHT.
I WANTED TO SHOW SOPHIE A VERSAILLES BALL.
MM HMM!
THE YOUNG LORD IS QUITE WONDERFUL, ISN'T HE!
FRENCH LORDS ARE INDEED DIFFERENT! SUCH ELEGANCE, SUCH BEAUTY, SO VERY BRILLIANT.
NOW, NOW! HOWEVER OSCAR MIGHT LOOK, SHE IS A WOMAN THROUGH AND THROUGH.
A WOMAN ?!
MY! WHAT AM I TO DO NOW?! I CALLED HER "MONSIEUR"!

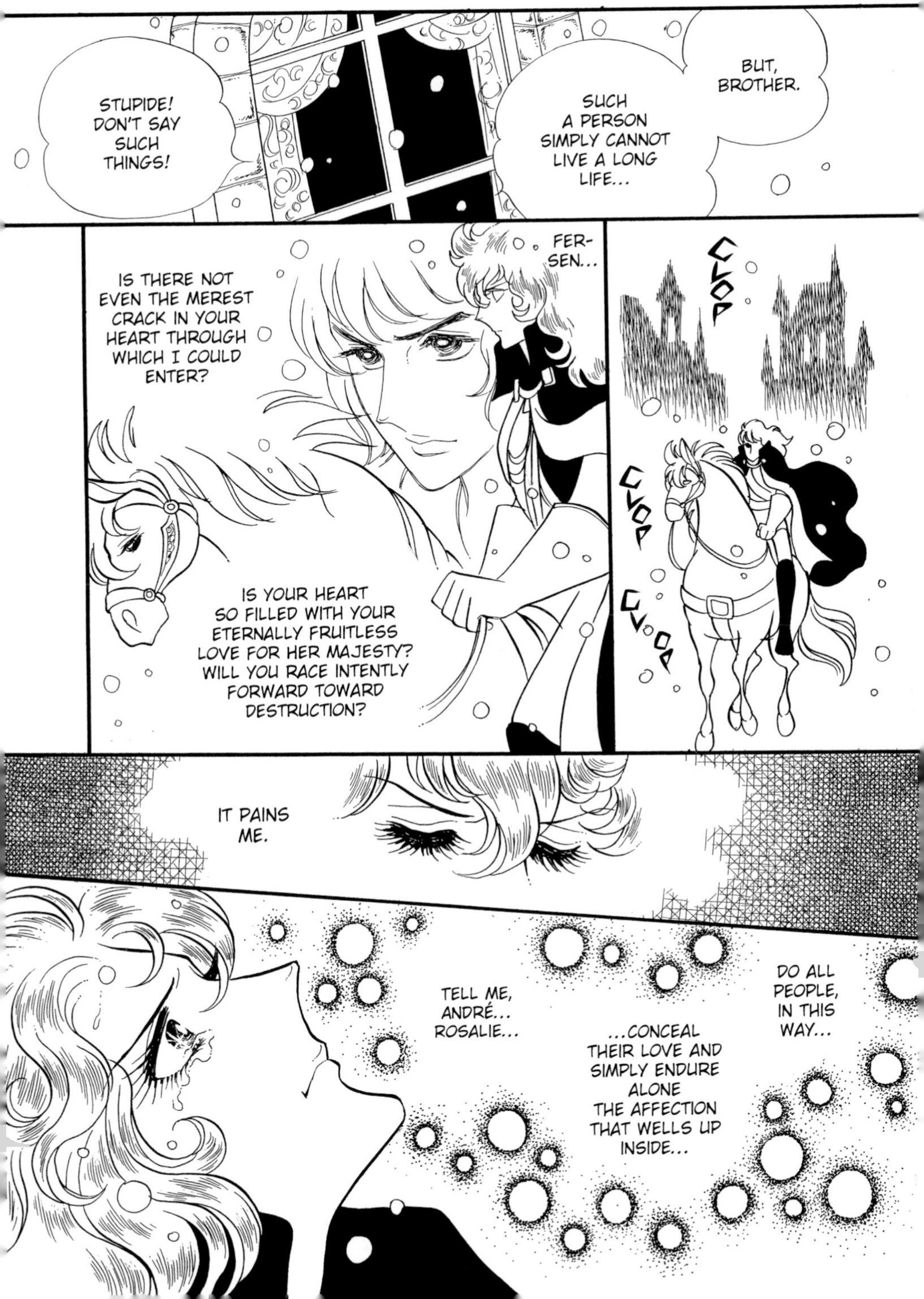
BUT, BROTHER.
SUCH A PERSON SIMPLY CANNOT LIVE A LONG LIFE...
STUPIDE! DON'T SAY SUCH THINGS!
CLOP
CLOP
CLOP
FER-SEN...
IS THERE NOT EVEN THE MEREST CRACK IN YOUR HEART THROUGH WHICH I COULD ENTER?
IS YOUR HEART SO FILLED WITH YOUR ETERNALLY FRUITLESS LOVE FOR HER MAJESTY? WILL YOU RACE INTENTLY FORWARD TOWARD DESTRUCTION?
IT PAINS ME.
DO ALL PEOPLE, IN THIS WAY...
...CONCEAL THEIR LOVE AND SIMPLY ENDURE ALONE THE AFFECTION THAT WELLS UP INSIDE...
TELL ME, ANDRÉ... ROSALIE...

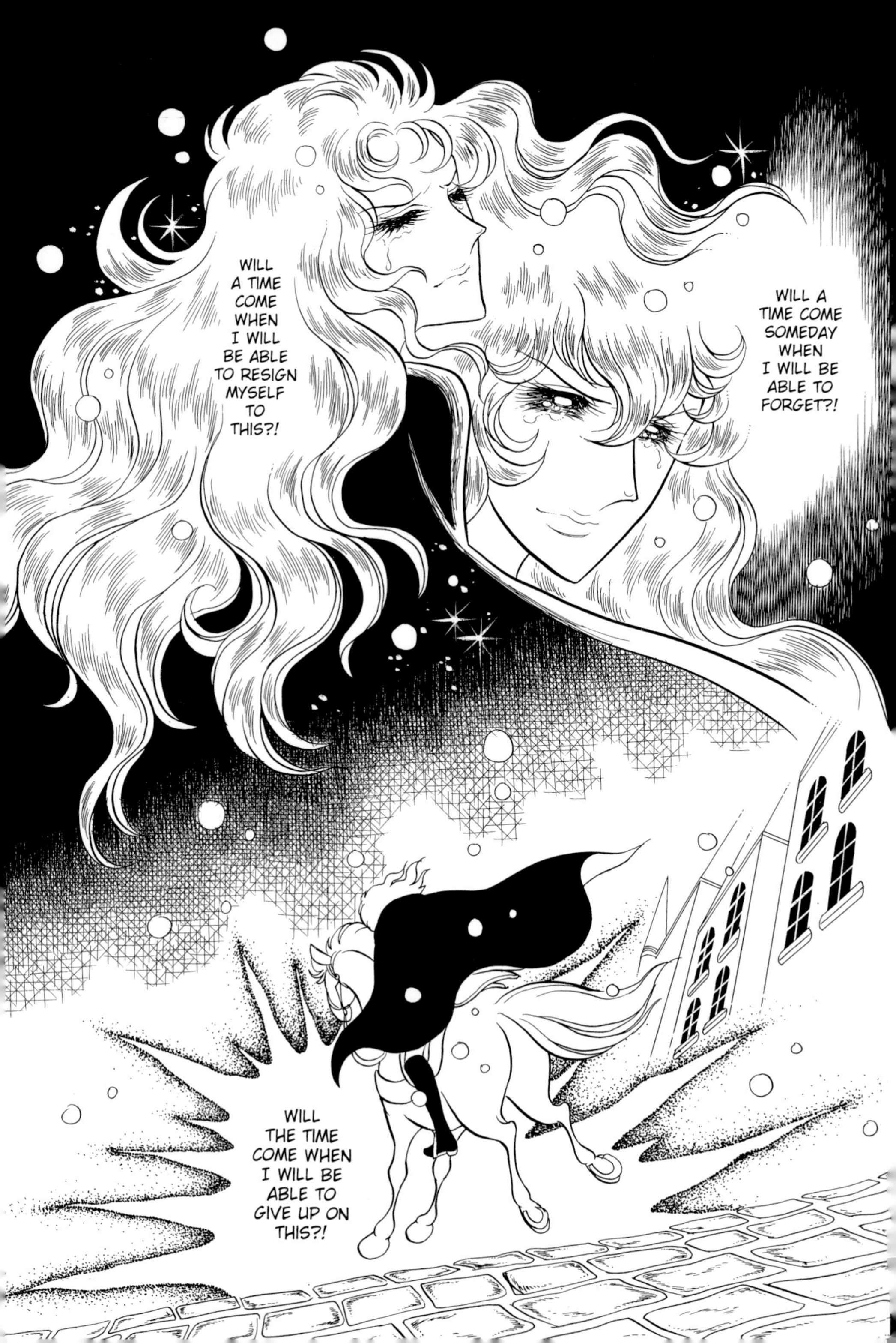
WILL A TIME COME SOMEDAY WHEN I WILL BE ABLE TO FORGET?!
WILL A TIME COME WHEN I WILL BE ABLE TO RESIGN MYSELF TO THIS?!
WILL THE TIME COME WHEN I WILL BE ABLE TO GIVE UP ON THIS?!

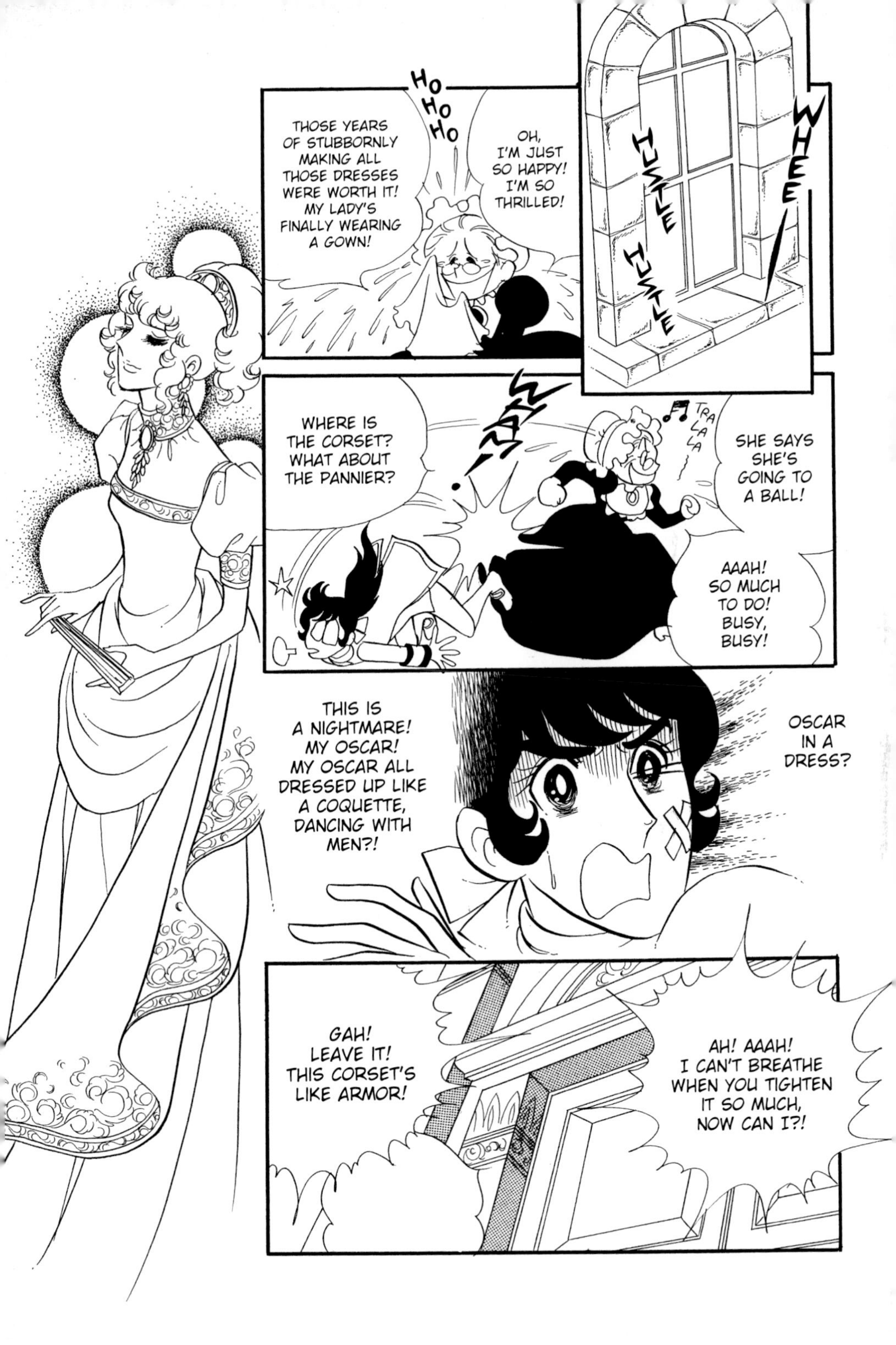
WHEE!
HUSTLE
HUSTLE
OH, I'M JUST SO HAPPY! I'M SO THRILLED!
HO HO HO
THOSE YEARS OF STUBBORNLY MAKING ALL THOSE DRESSES WERE WORTH IT! MY LADY'S FINALLY WEARING A GOWN!
TRA LA LA
SHE SAYS SHE'S GOING TO A BALL!
WHAM!
WHERE IS THE CORSET? WHAT ABOUT THE PANNIER?
AAAH! SO MUCH TO DO! BUSY, BUSY!
OSCAR IN A DRESS?
THIS IS A NIGHTMARE! MY OSCAR! MY OSCAR ALL DRESSED UP LIKE A COQUETTE, DANCING WITH MEN?!
AH! AAAH! I CAN'T BREATHE WHEN YOU TIGHTEN IT SO MUCH, NOW CAN I?!
GAH! LEAVE IT! THIS CORSET'S LIKE ARMOR!

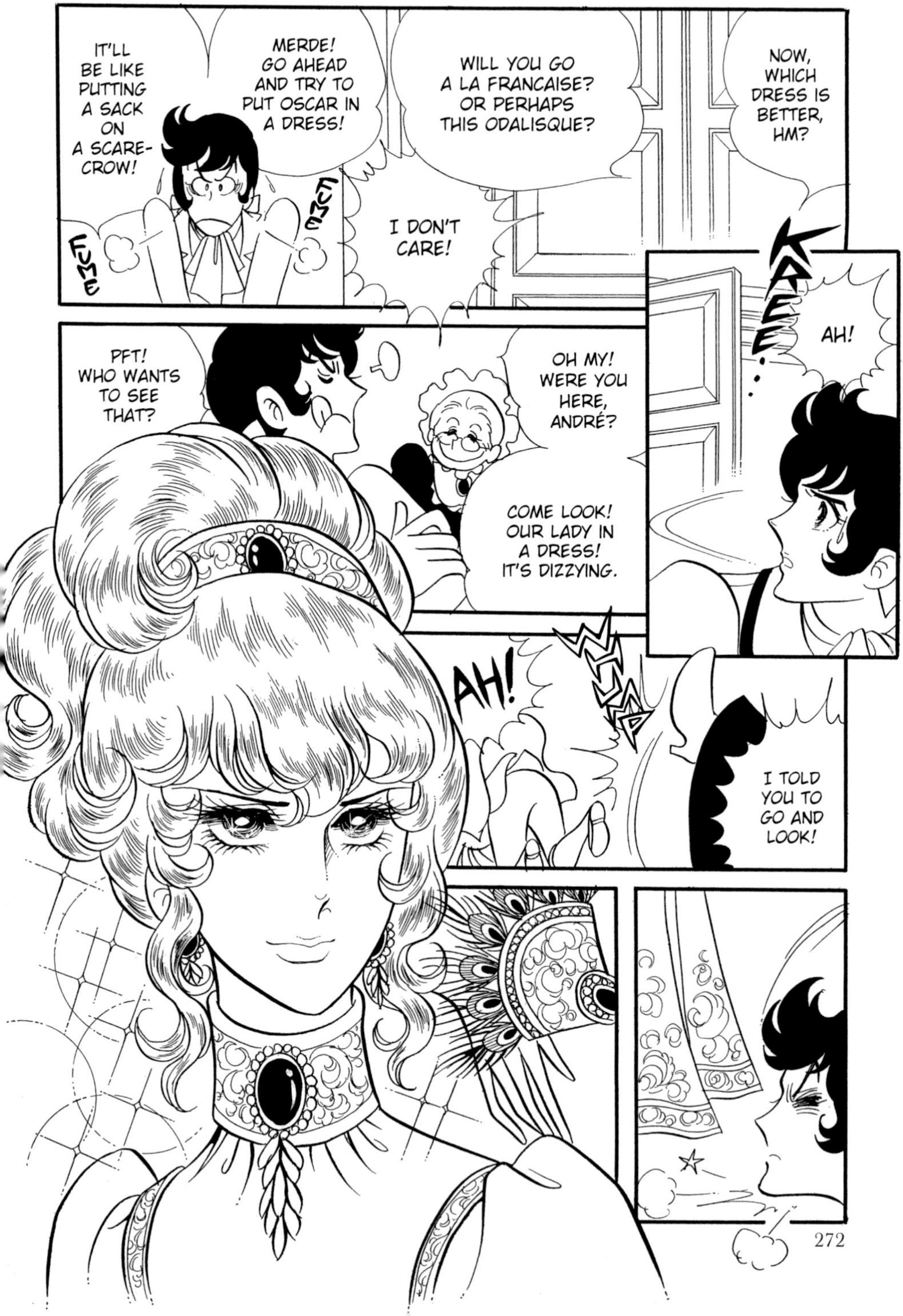
NOW, WHICH DRESS IS BETTER, HM?
WILL YOU GO A LA FRANCAISE? OR PERHAPS THIS ODALISQUE?
I DON'T CARE!
MERDE! GO AHEAD AND TRY TO PUT OSCAR IN A DRESS!
IT'LL BE LIKE PUTTING A SACK ON A SCARE-CROW!
FUME
FUME
KREE...
AH!
OH MY! WERE YOU HERE, ANDRÉ?
COME LOOK! OUR LADY IN A DRESS! IT'S DIZZYING.
PFT! WHO WANTS TO SEE THAT?
I TOLD YOU TO GO AND LOOK!
THUMP
AH!

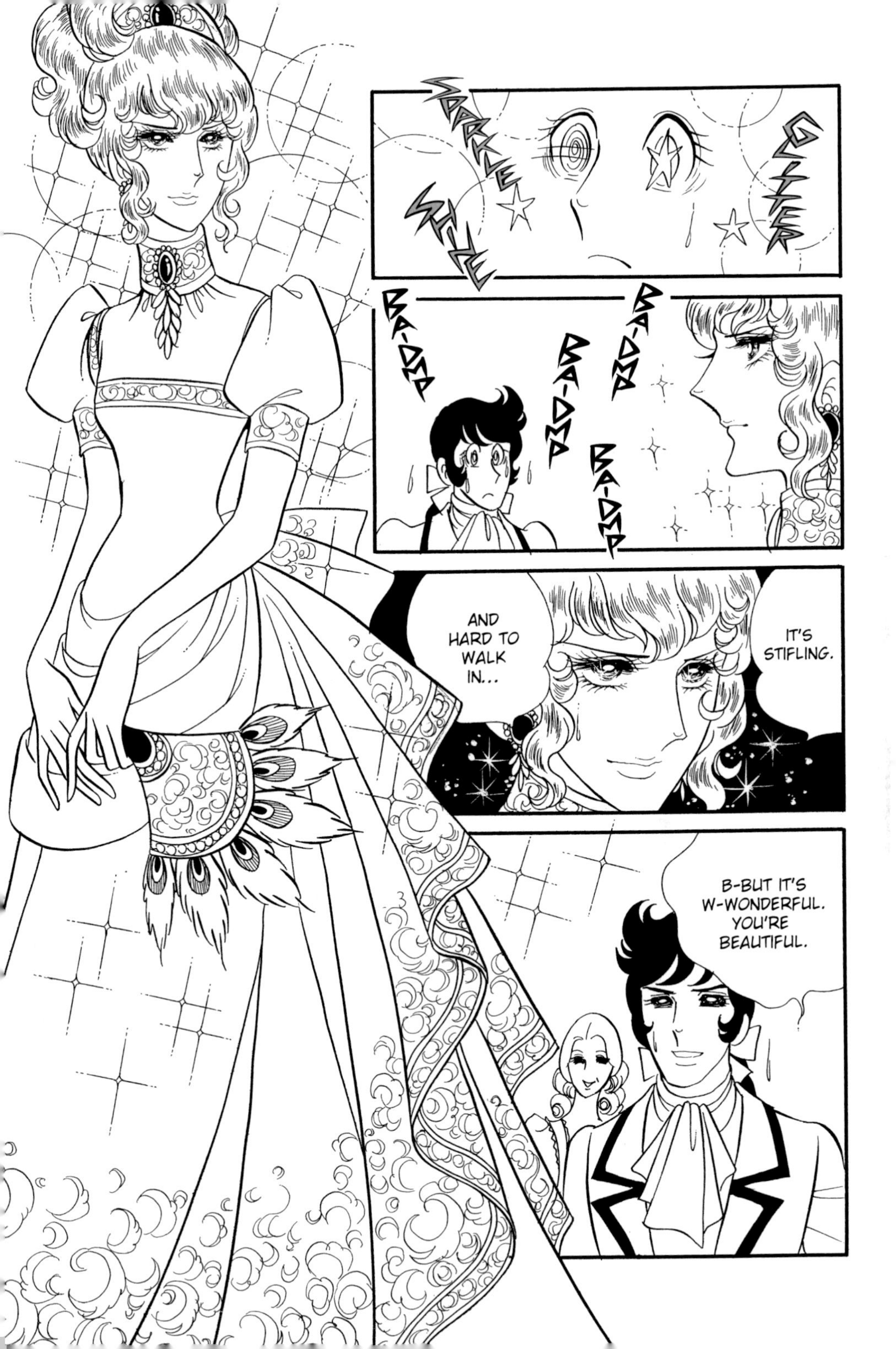
GLITTER
SPARKLE
SHINE
BA-DMP
BA-DMP
BA-DMP
BA-DMP
IT'S STIFLING.
AND HARD TO WALK IN...
B-BUT IT'S W-WONDERFUL. YOU'RE BEAUTIFUL.

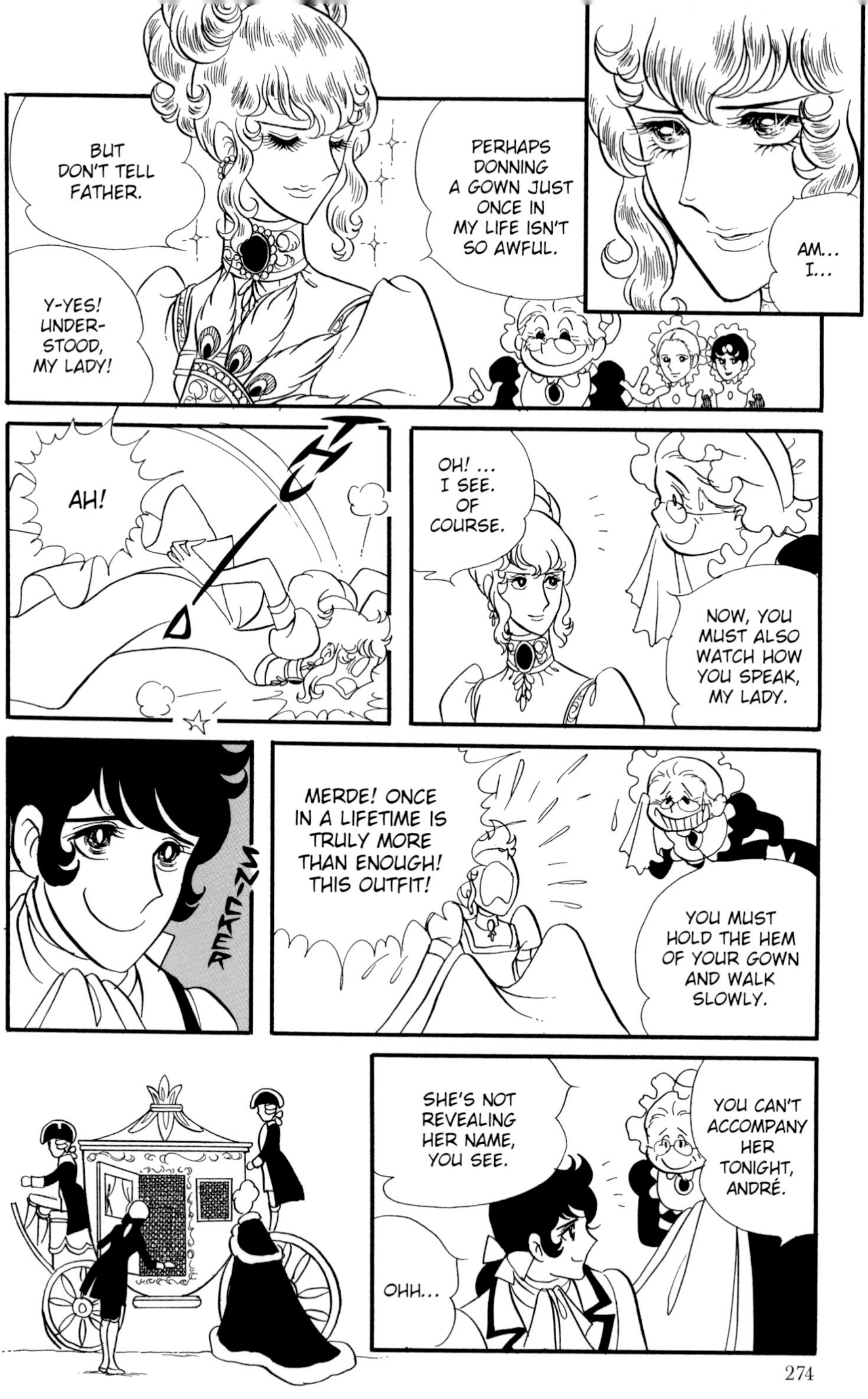
AM... I...
PERHAPS DONNING A GOWN JUST ONCE IN MY LIFE ISN'T SO AWFUL.
BUT DON'T TELL FATHER.
Y-YES! UNDERSTOOD, MY LADY!
OH! ... I SEE. OF COURSE.
NOW, YOU MUST ALSO WATCH HOW YOU SPEAK, MY LADY.
THUD
AH!
MERDE! ONCE IN A LIFETIME IS TRULY MORE THAN ENOUGH! THIS OUTFIT!
YOU MUST HOLD THE HEM OF YOUR GOWN AND WALK SLOWLY.
SNICKER
YOU CAN'T ACCOMPANY HER TONIGHT, ANDRÉ.
SHE'S NOT REVEALING HER NAME, YOU SEE.
OHH...

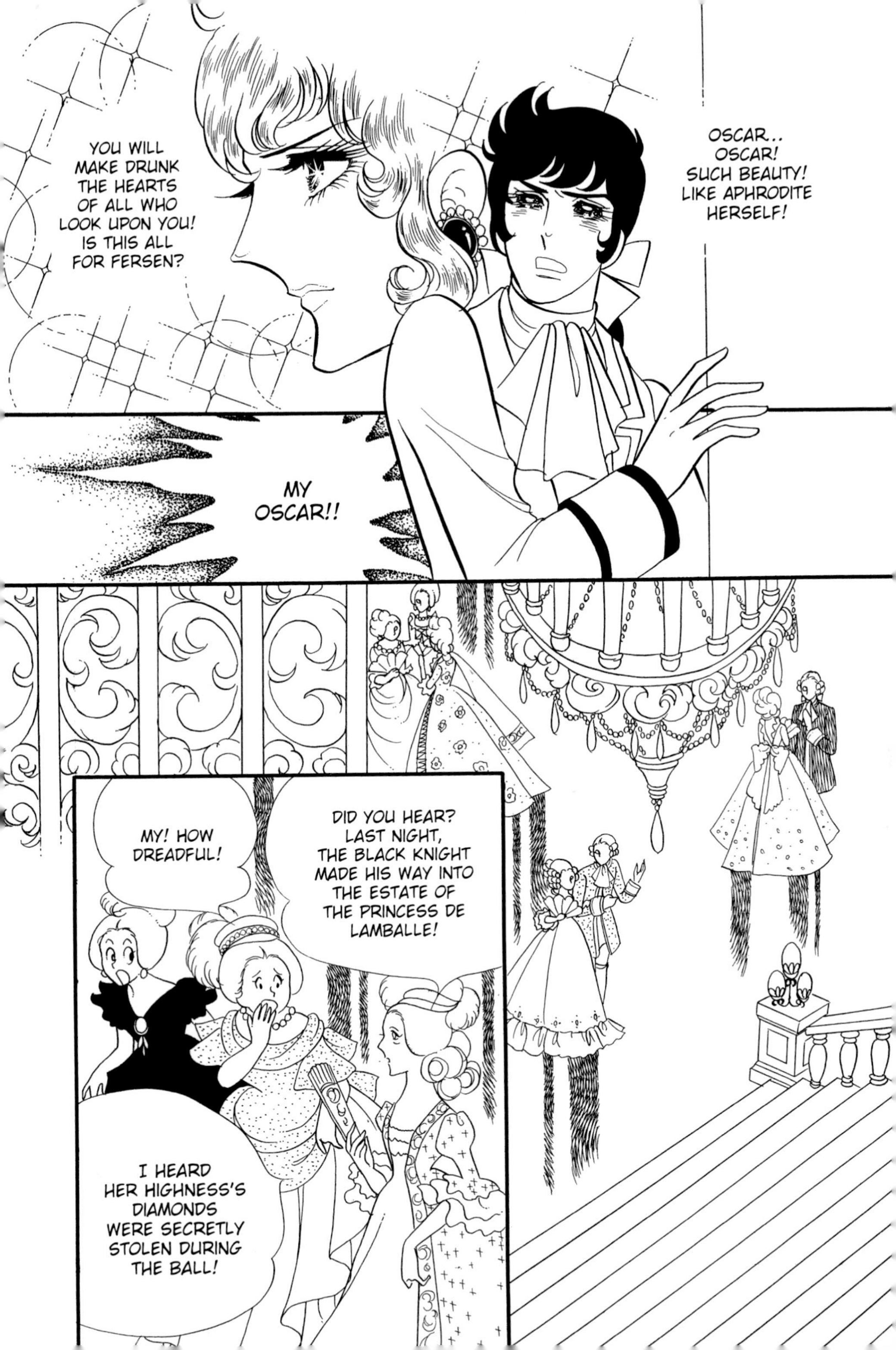
OSCAR.. OSCAR! SUCH BEAUTY! LIKE APHRODITE HERSELF!
YOU WILL MAKE DRUNK THE HEARTS OF ALL WHO LOOK UPON YOU! IS THIS ALL FOR FERSEN?
MY OSCAR!!
DID YOU HEAR? LAST NIGHT, THE BLACK KNIGHT MADE HIS WAY INTO THE ESTATE OF THE PRINCESS DE LAMBALLE!
MY! HOW DREADFUL!
I HEARD HER HIGHNESS'S DIAMONDS WERE SECRETLY STOLEN DURING THE BALL!

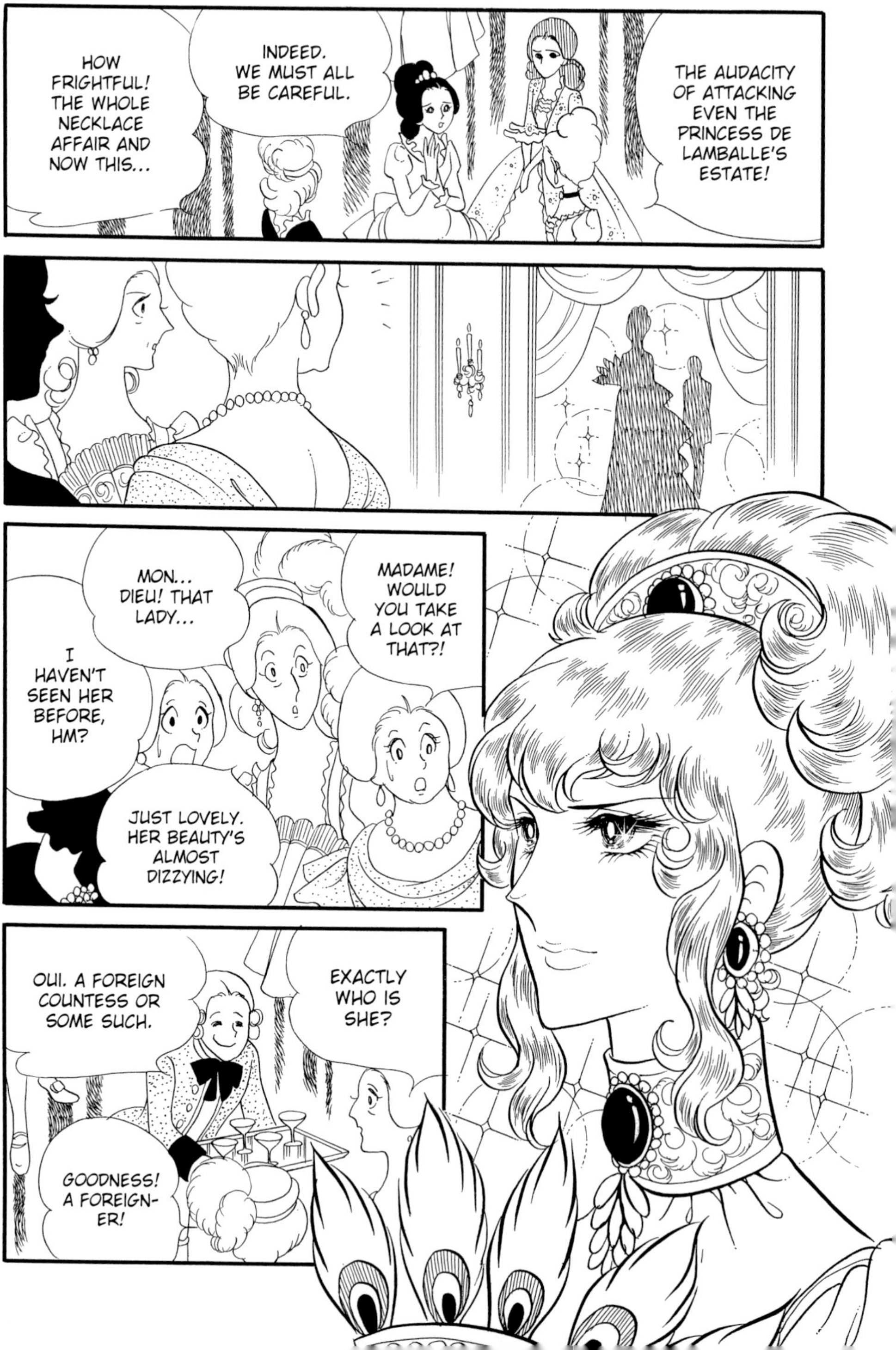
THE AUDACITY OF ATTACKING EVEN THE PRINCESS DE LAMBALLE'S ESTATE!
INDEED. WE MUST ALL BE CAREFUL.
HOW FRIGHTFUL! THE WHOLE NECKLACE AFFAIR AND NOW THIS...
MADAME! WOULD YOU TAKE A LOOK AT THAT?!
MON... DIEU! THAT LADY...
I HAVEN'T SEEN HER BEFORE, HM?
JUST LOVELY. HER BEAUTY'S ALMOST DIZZYING!
EXACTLY WHO IS SHE?
OUI. A FOREIGN COUNTESS OR SOME SUCH.
GOODNESS! A FOREIGN-ER!

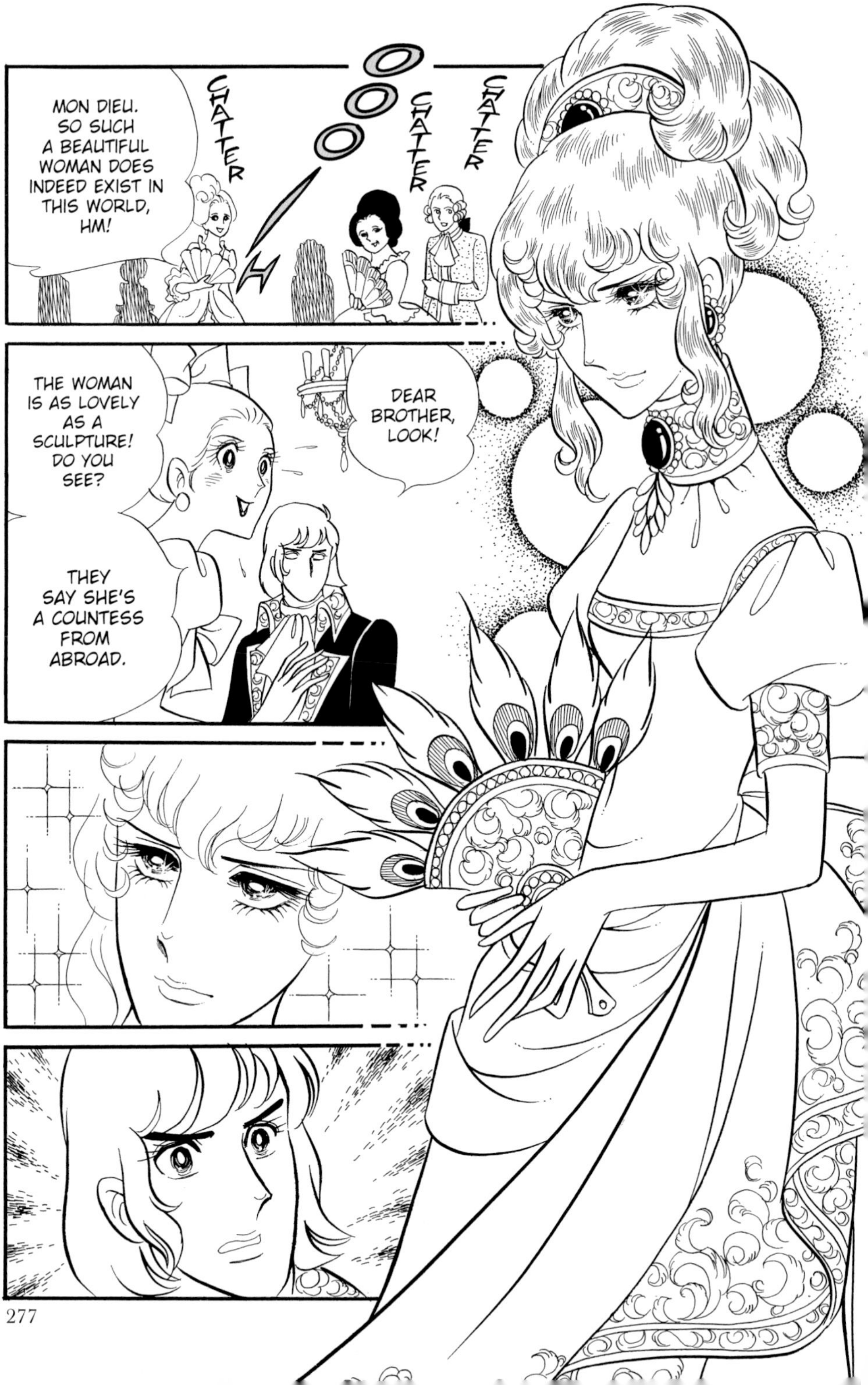
CHATTER
OOOH
CHATTER
CHATTER
MON DIEU. SO SUCH A BEAUTIFUL WOMAN DOES INDEED EXIST IN THIS WORLD, HM!
DEAR BROTHER, LOOK!
THE WOMAN IS AS LOVELY AS A SCULPTURE! DO YOU SEE?
THEY SAY SHE'S A COUNTESS FROM ABROAD.

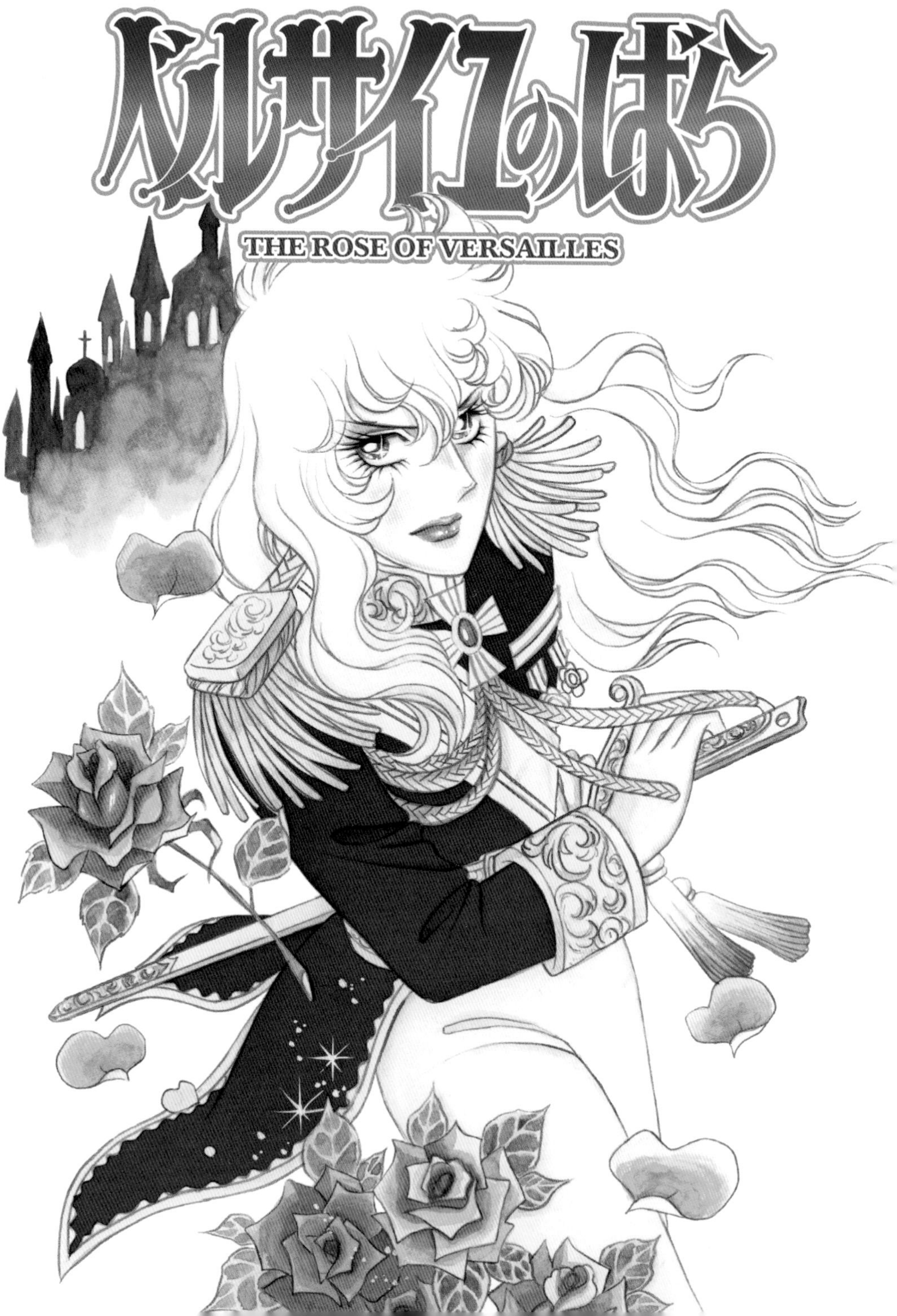
ベルサイユのばら
THE ROSE OF VERSAILLES

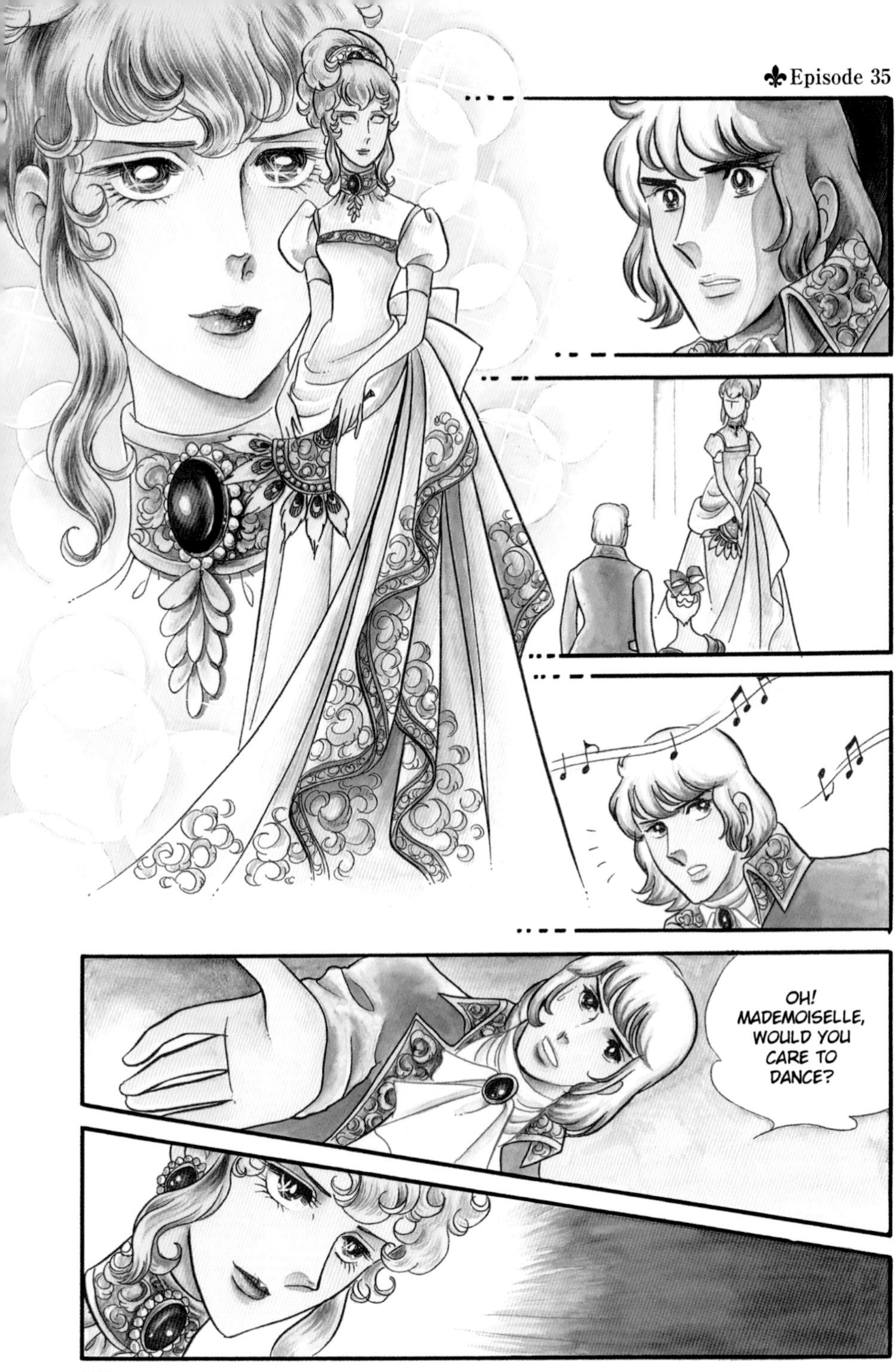
OH! MADEMOISELLE, WOULD YOU CARE TO DANCE?

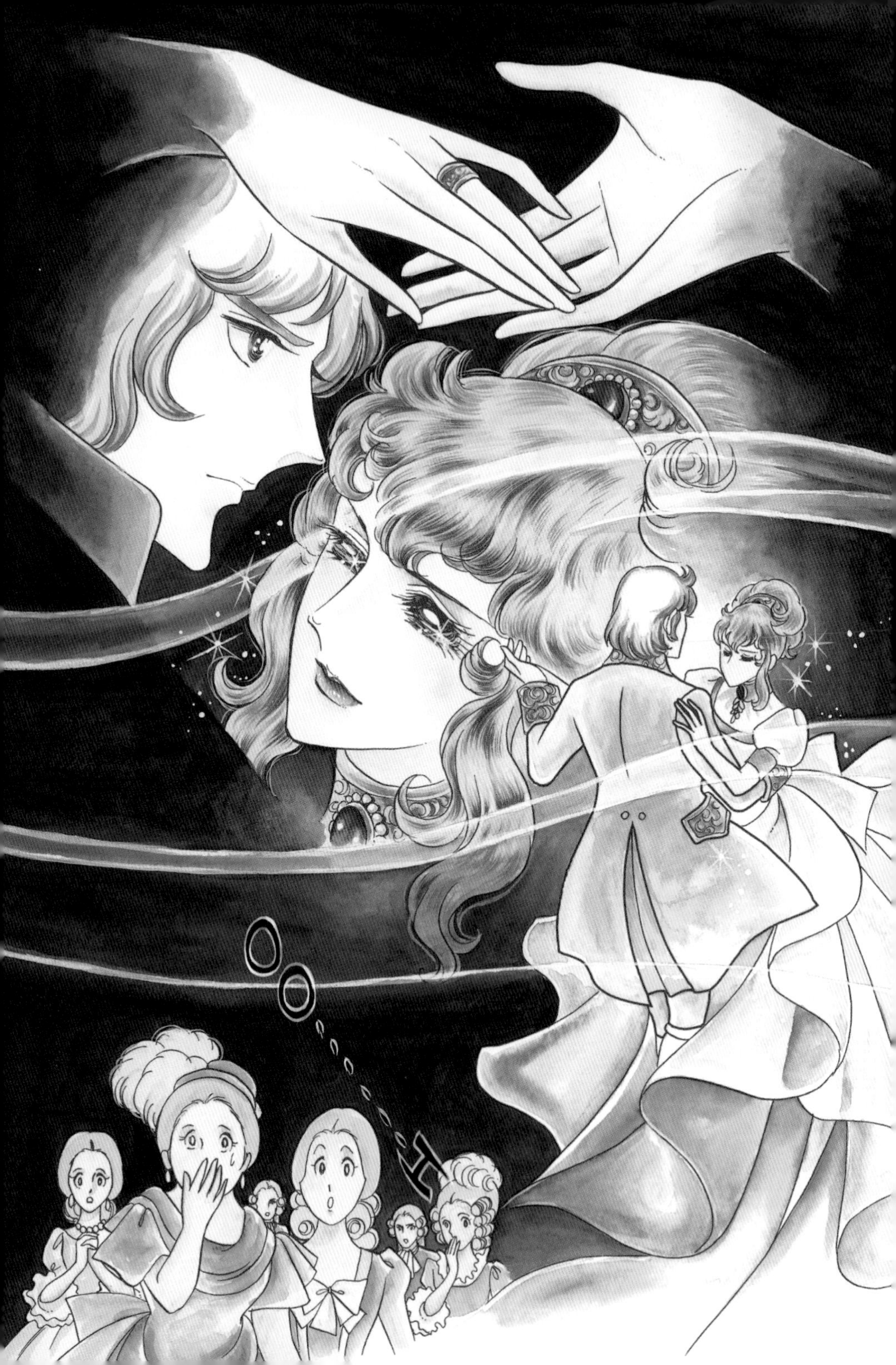
OOoooooooH

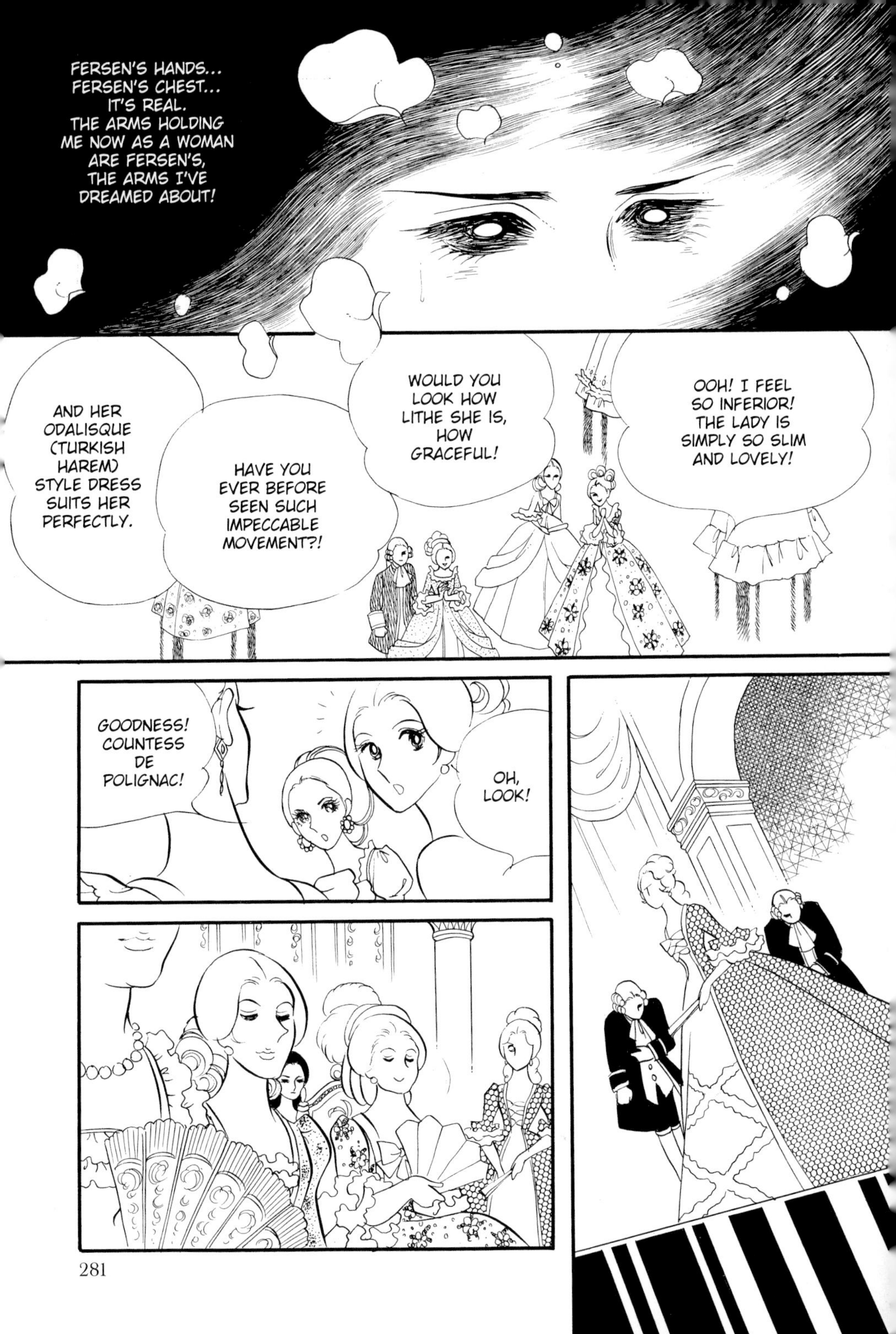
FERSEN'S HANDS... FERSEN'S CHEST... IT'S REAL. THE ARMS HOLDING ME NOW AS A WOMAN ARE FERSEN'S, THE ARMS I'VE DREAMED ABOUT!
OOH! I FEEL SO INFERIOR! THE LADY IS SIMPLY SO SLIM AND LOVELY!
WOULD YOU LOOK HOW LITHE SHE IS, HOW GRACEFUL!
HAVE YOU EVER BEFORE SEEN SUCH IMPECCABLE MOVEMENT?!
AND HER ODALISQUE (TURKISH HAREM) STYLE DRESS SUITS HER PERFECTLY.
OH, LOOK!
GOODNESS! COUNTESS DE POLIGNAC!

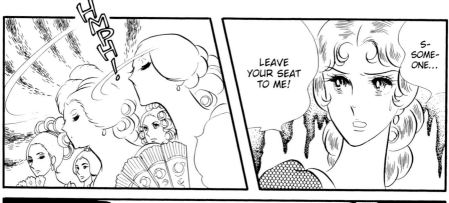

S-SOME-ONE...

LEAVE YOUR SEAT TO ME!

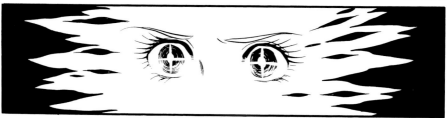

FROM WHICH LAND DO YOU HAIL?

MY LADY.

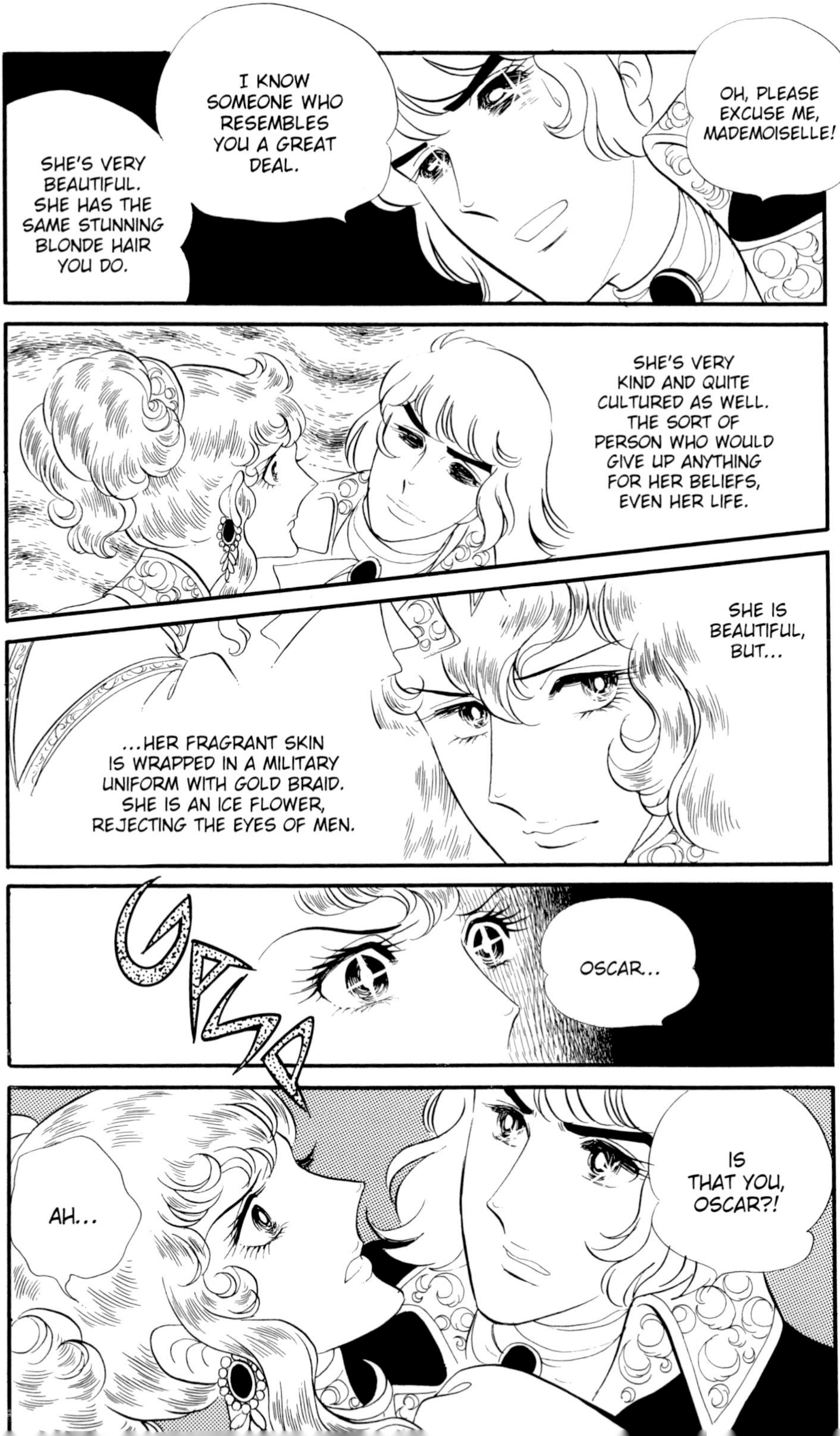
OH, PLEASE EXCUSE ME, MADEMOISELLE!
I KNOW SOMEONE WHO RESEMBLES YOU A GREAT DEAL.
SHE'S VERY BEAUTIFUL. SHE HAS THE SAME STUNNING BLONDE HAIR YOU DO.
SHE'S VERY KIND AND QUITE CULTURED AS WELL. THE SORT OF PERSON WHO WOULD GIVE UP ANYTHING FOR HER BELIEFS, EVEN HER LIFE.
SHE IS BEAUTIFUL, BUT...
...HER FRAGRANT SKIN IS WRAPPED IN A MILITARY UNIFORM WITH GOLD BRAID. SHE IS AN ICE FLOWER, REJECTING THE EYES OF MEN.
OSCAR...
IS THAT YOU, OSCAR?!
AH...

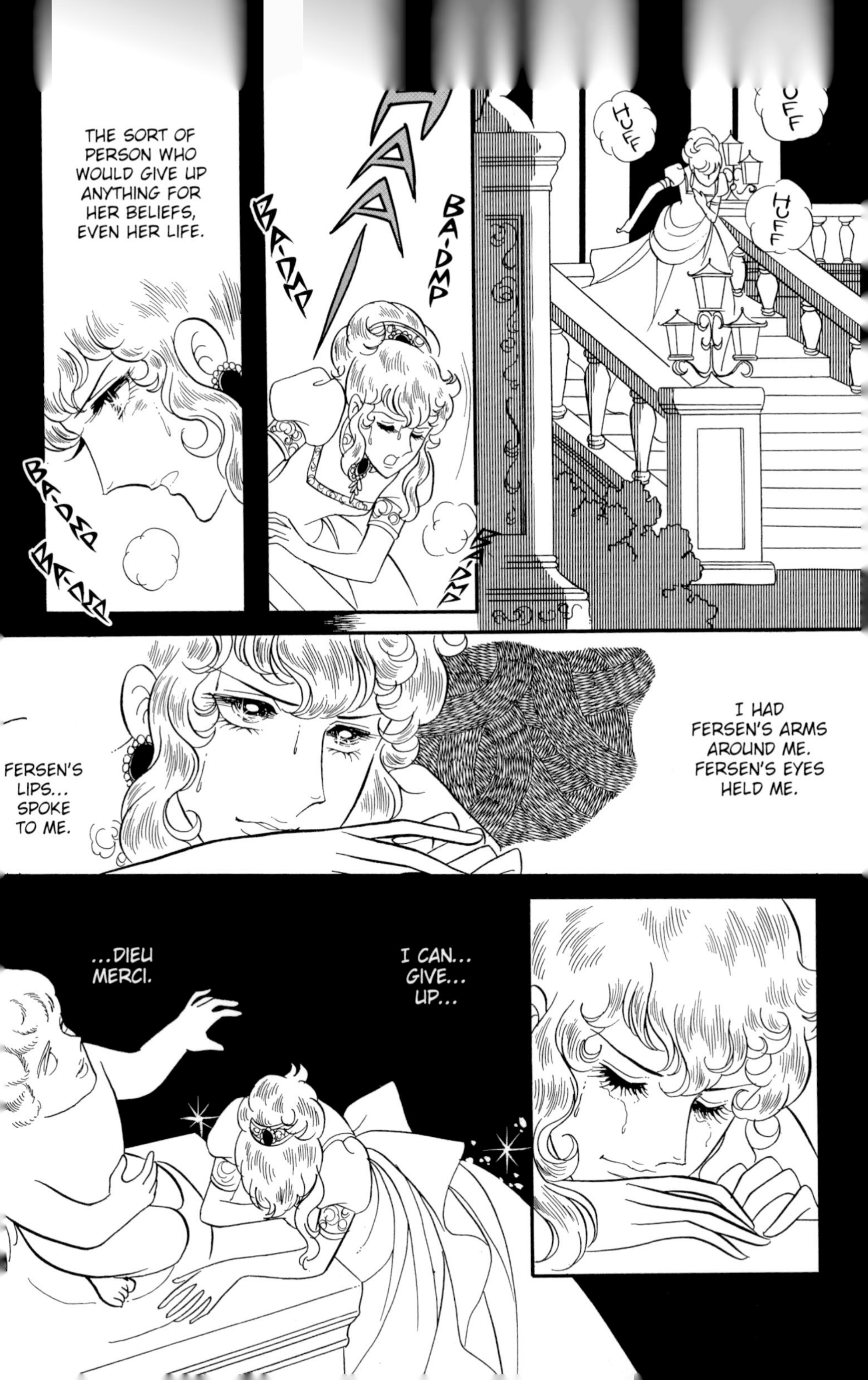
HUFF
HUFF
HUFF
HAA
BA-DMP
BA-DMP
THE SORT OF PERSON WHO WOULD GIVE UP ANYTHING FOR HER BELIEFS, EVEN HER LIFE.
BA-DMP
BA-DMP
I HAD FERSEN'S ARMS AROUND ME. FERSEN'S EYES HELD ME.
FERSEN'S LIPS... SPOKE TO ME.
I CAN... GIVE... UP...
...DIEU MERCI.

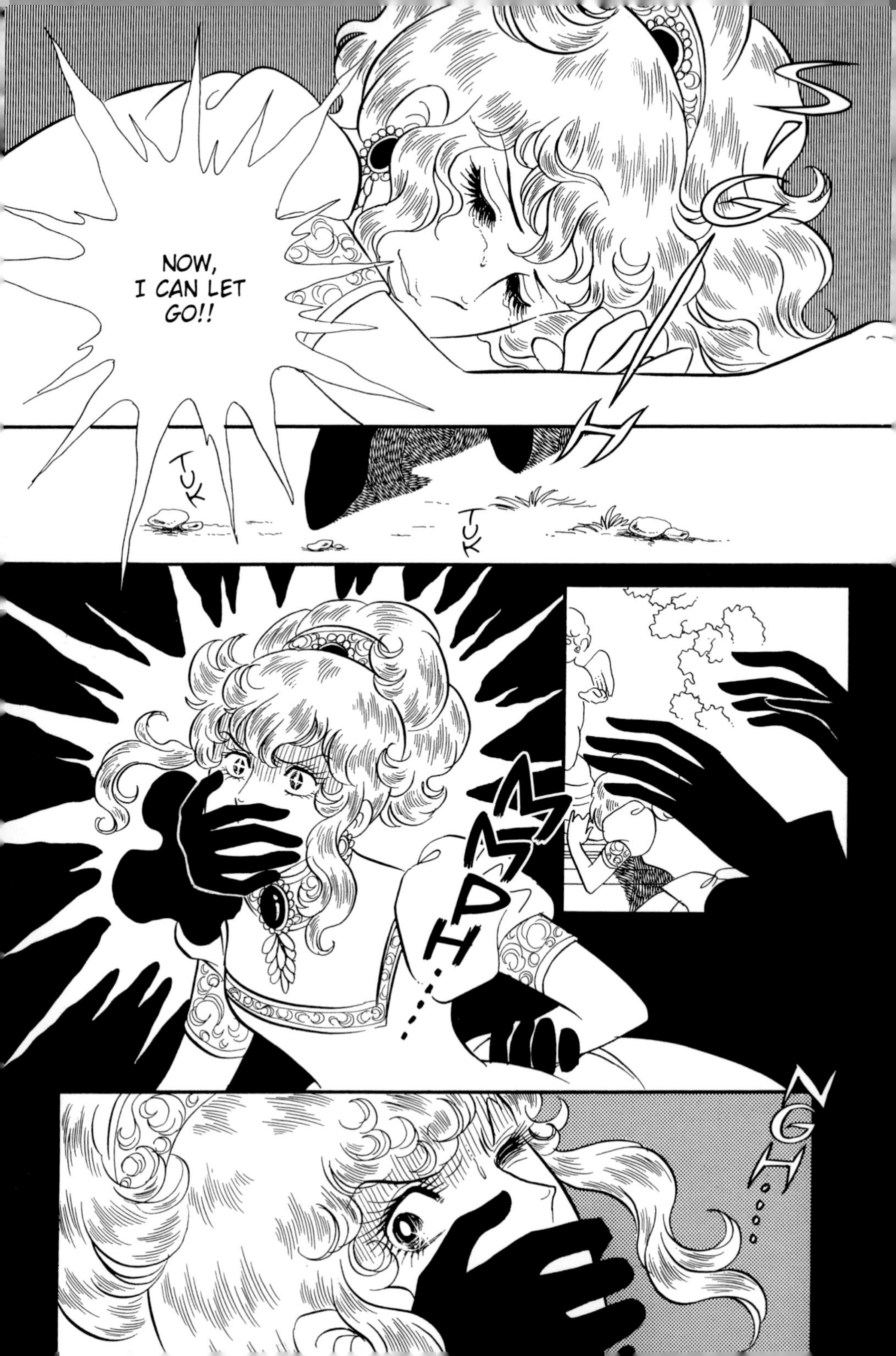
SIGH
NOW, I CAN LET GO!!
TUK
TUK
MMPH....
NGH....

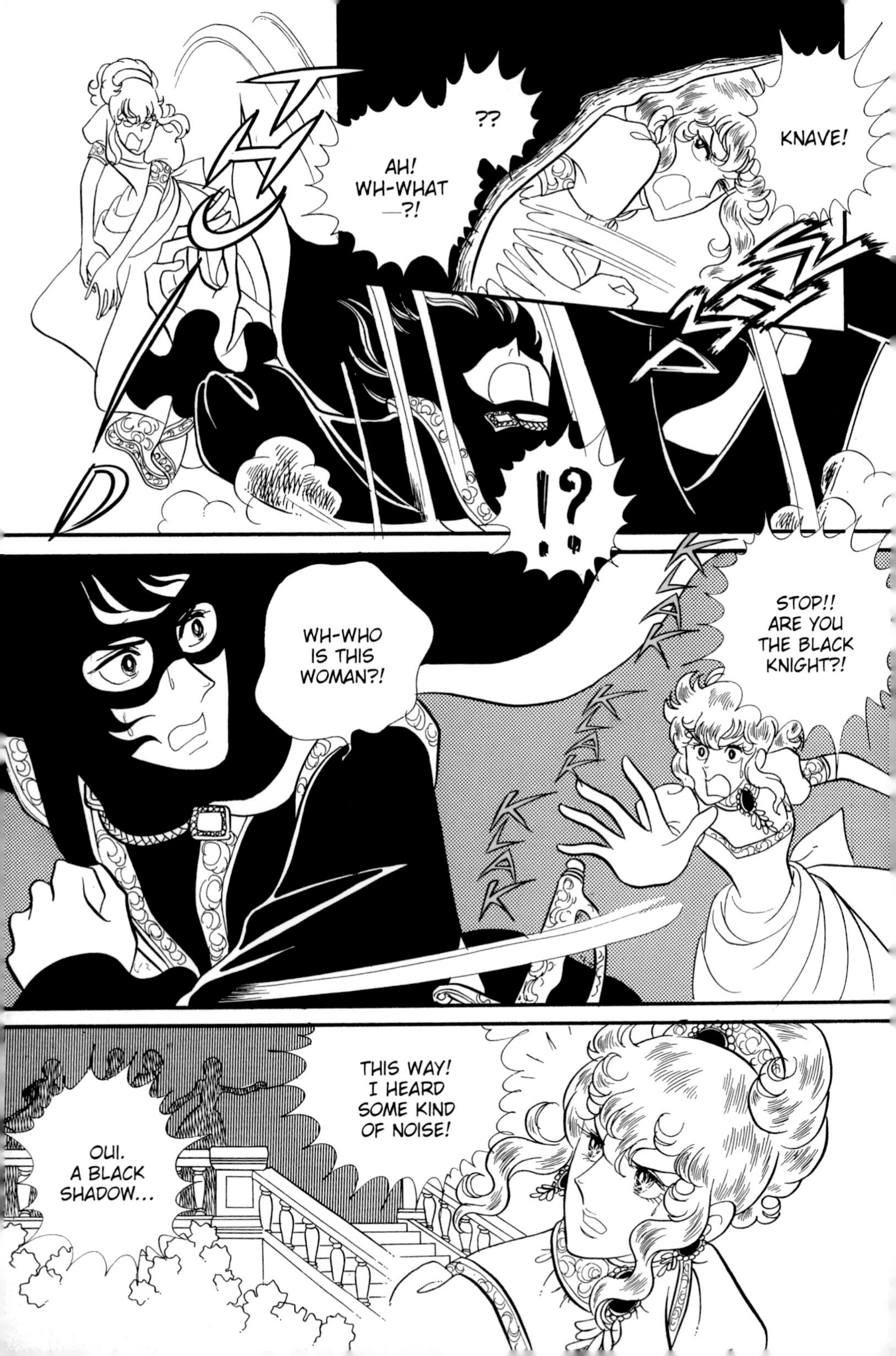
KNAVE!
??
AH! WH-WHAT —?!
!?
STOP!! ARE YOU THE BLACK KNIGHT?!
WH-WHO IS THIS WOMAN?!
THIS WAY! I HEARD SOME KIND OF NOISE!
OUI. A BLACK SHADOW...

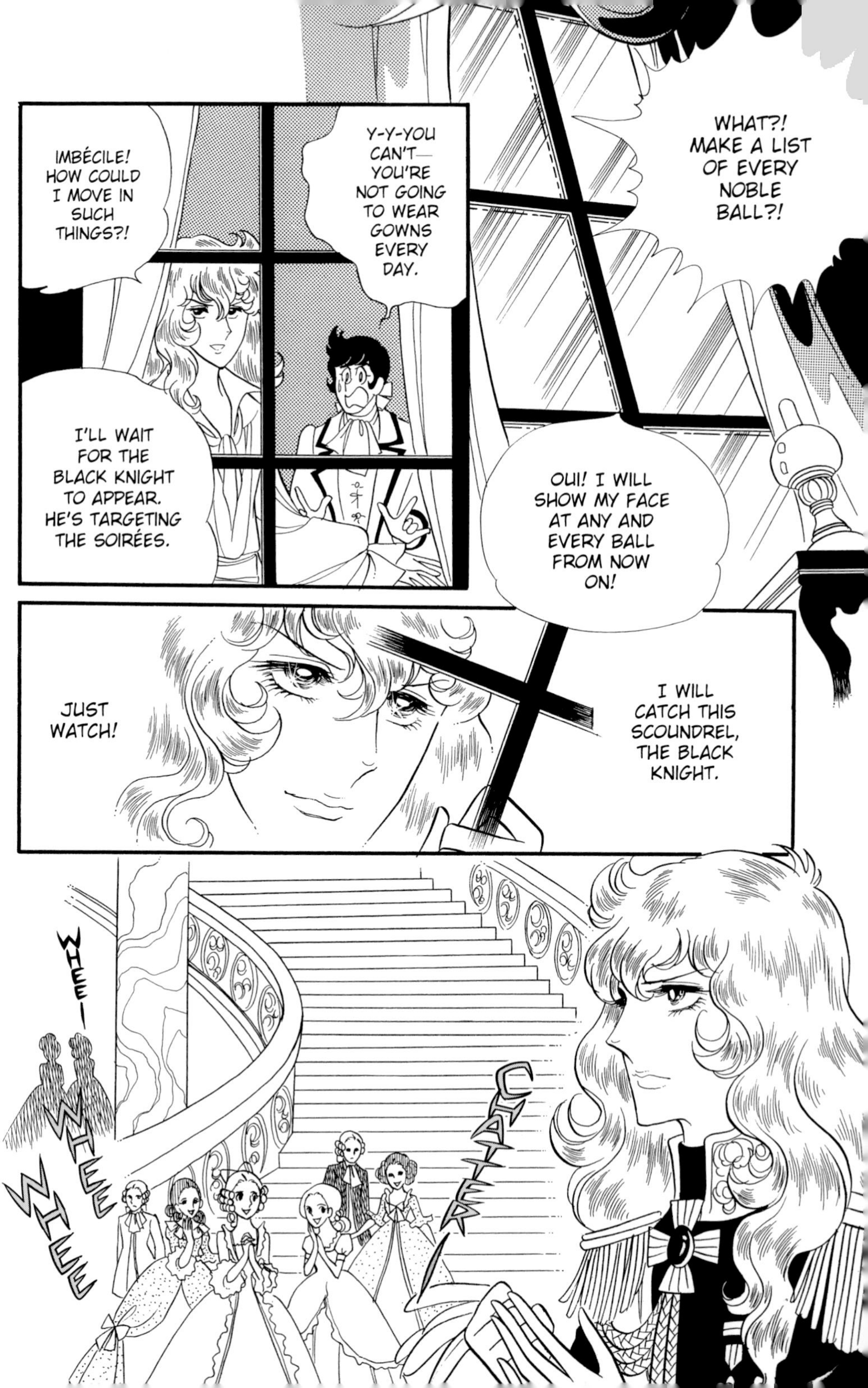
WHAT?! MAKE A LIST OF EVERY NOBLE BALL?!
OUI! I WILL SHOW MY FACE AT ANY AND EVERY BALL FROM NOW ON!
Y-Y-YOU CAN'T— YOU'RE NOT GOING TO WEAR GOWNS EVERY DAY.
IMBÉCILE! HOW COULD I MOVE IN SUCH THINGS?!
I'LL WAIT FOR THE BLACK KNIGHT TO APPEAR. HE'S TARGETING THE SOIRÉES.
I WILL CATCH THIS SCOUNDREL, THE BLACK KNIGHT.
JUST WATCH!
CHATTER
WHEE
WHEE
WHEE

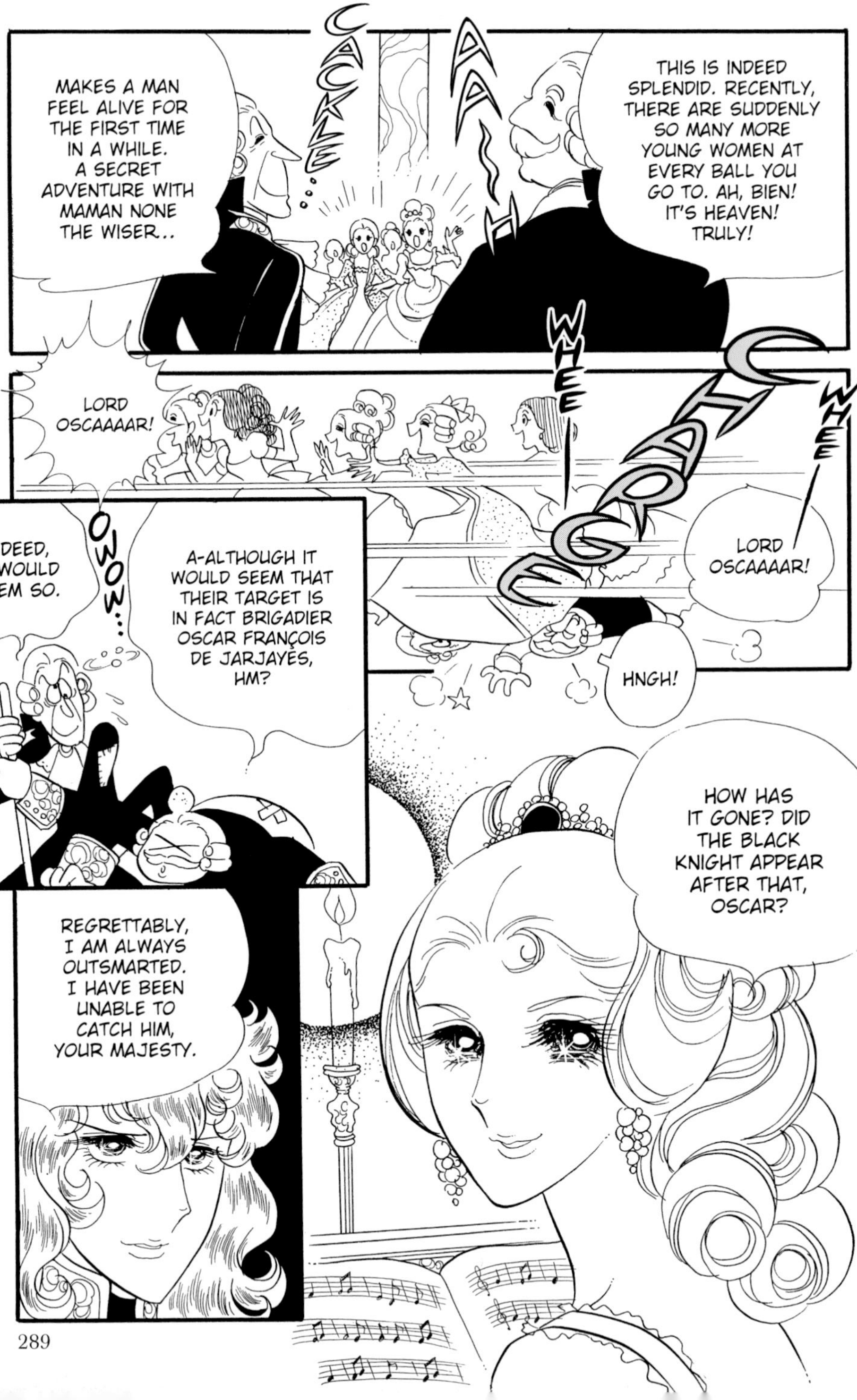
THIS IS INDEED SPLENDID. RECENTLY, THERE ARE SUDDENLY SO MANY MORE YOUNG WOMEN AT EVERY BALL YOU GO TO. AH, BIEN! IT'S HEAVEN! TRULY!
AAAH
CACKLE...
MAKES A MAN FEEL ALIVE FOR THE FIRST TIME IN A WHILE. A SECRET ADVENTURE WITH MAMAN NONE THE WISER...
WHEE!
CHARGE
WHEE!
LORD OSCAAAAR!
LORD OSCAAAAR!
HNGH!
A-ALTHOUGH IT WOULD SEEM THAT THEIR TARGET IS IN FACT BRIGADIER OSCAR FRANÇOIS DE JARJAYES, HM?
INDEED, IT WOULD SEEM SO.
OWOW...
HOW HAS IT GONE? DID THE BLACK KNIGHT APPEAR AFTER THAT, OSCAR?
REGRETTABLY, I AM ALWAYS OUTSMARTED. I HAVE BEEN UNABLE TO CATCH HIM, YOUR MAJESTY.

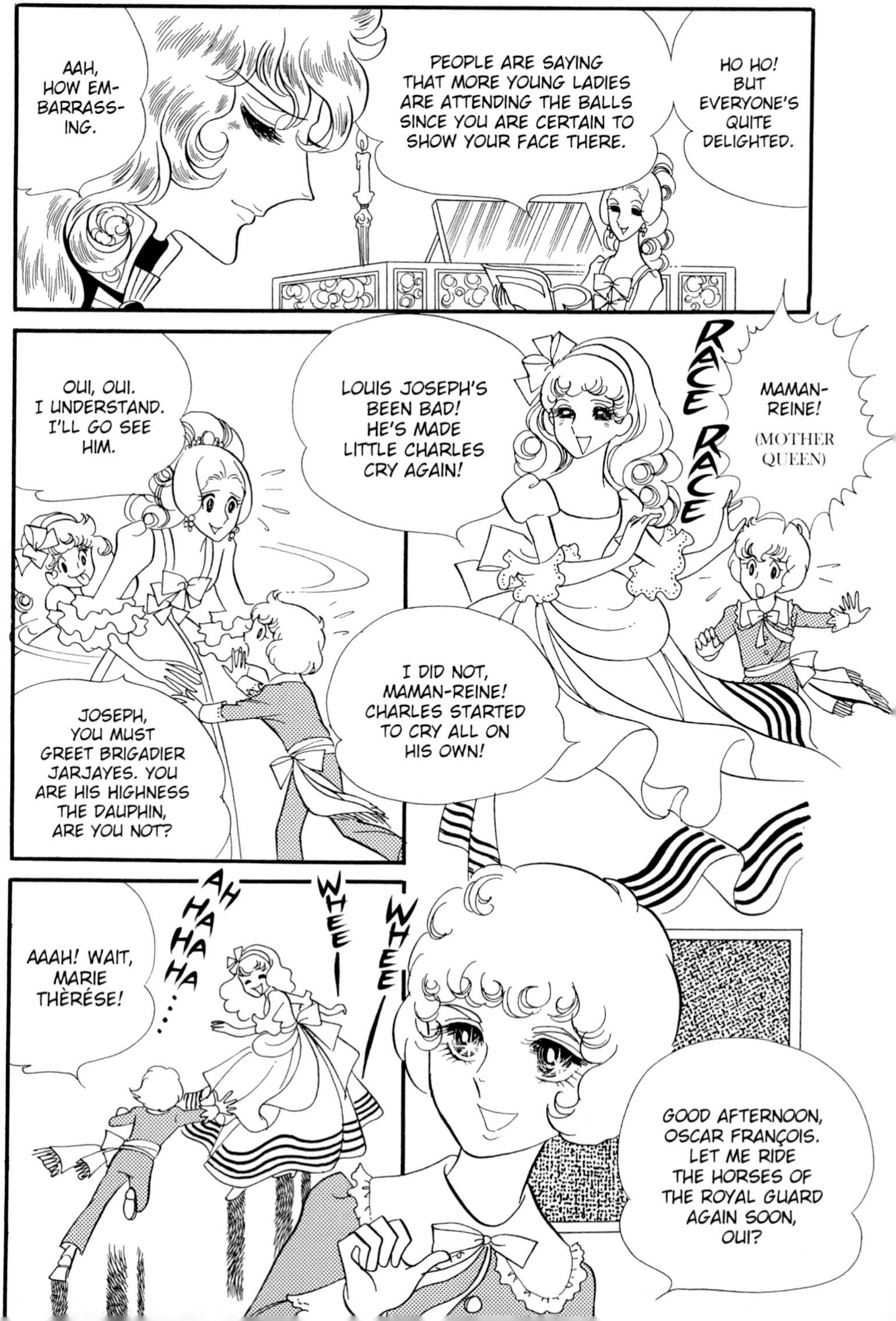
HO HO! BUT EVERYONE'S QUITE DELIGHTED.
PEOPLE ARE SAYING THAT MORE YOUNG LADIES ARE ATTENDING THE BALLS SINCE YOU ARE CERTAIN TO SHOW YOUR FACE THERE.
AAH, HOW EM-BARRASS-ING.
RACE RACE
MAMAN-REINE! (MOTHER QUEEN)
LOUIS JOSEPH'S BEEN BAD! HE'S MADE LITTLE CHARLES CRY AGAIN!
I DID NOT, MAMAN-REINE! CHARLES STARTED TO CRY ALL ON HIS OWN!
GOOD AFTERNOON, OSCAR FRANÇOIS. LET ME RIDE THE HORSES OF THE ROYAL GUARD AGAIN SOON, OUI?
OUI, OUI. I UNDERSTAND. I'LL GO SEE HIM.
JOSEPH, YOU MUST GREET BRIGADIER JARJAYES. YOU ARE HIS HIGHNESS THE DAUPHIN, ARE YOU NOT?
WHEE WHEE
AH HA HA HA HA...
AAAH! WAIT, MARIE THÈRÉSE!

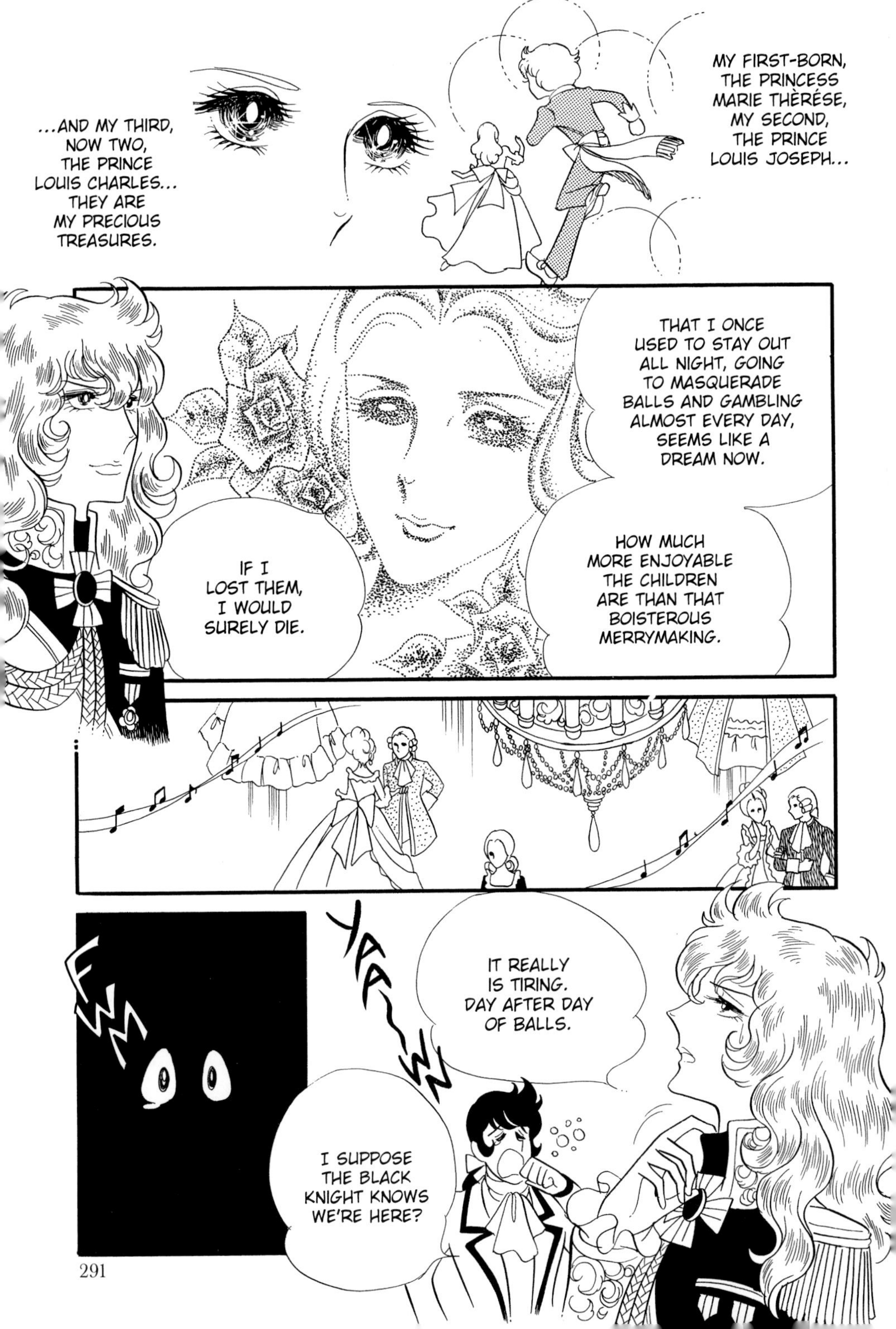
MY FIRST-BORN, THE PRINCESS MARIE THÈRÉSE, MY SECOND, THE PRINCE LOUIS JOSEPH...
...AND MY THIRD, NOW TWO, THE PRINCE LOUIS CHARLES... THEY ARE MY PRECIOUS TREASURES.
THAT I ONCE USED TO STAY OUT ALL NIGHT, GOING TO MASQUERADE BALLS AND GAMBLING ALMOST EVERY DAY, SEEMS LIKE A DREAM NOW.
HOW MUCH MORE ENJOYABLE THE CHILDREN ARE THAN THAT BOISTEROUS MERRYMAKING.
IF I LOST THEM, I WOULD SURELY DIE.
YAA~WN
IT REALLY IS TIRING. DAY AFTER DAY OF BALLS.
I SUPPOSE THE BLACK KNIGHT KNOWS WE'RE HERE?
FWM

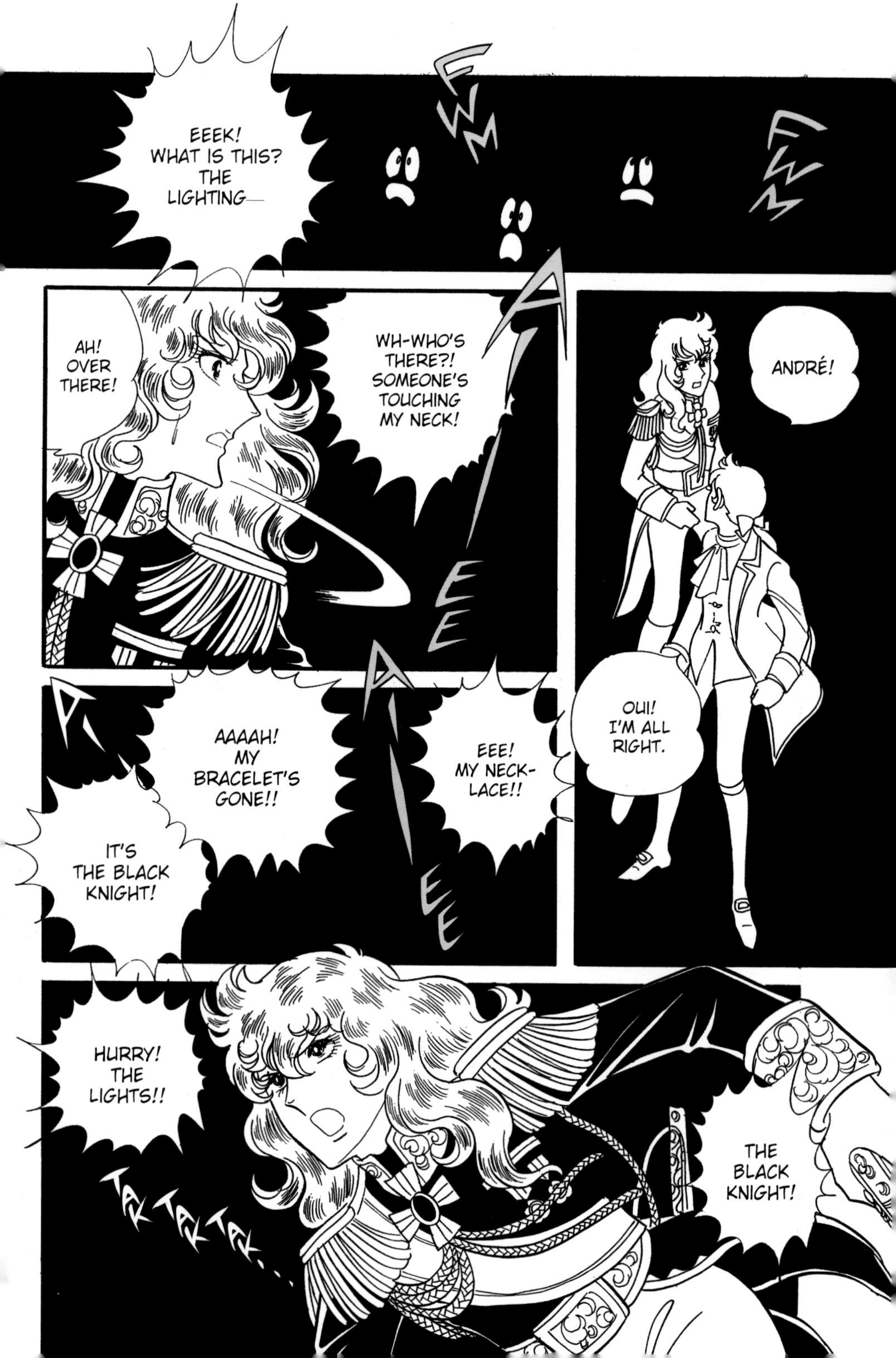
FWM
FWM
EEEK! WHAT IS THIS? THE LIGHTING—
ANDRÉ!
OUI! I'M ALL RIGHT.
WH-WHO'S THERE?! SOMEONE'S TOUCHING MY NECK!
AH! OVER THERE!
EEE! MY NECK-LACE!!
AAAAH! MY BRACELET'S GONE!!
IT'S THE BLACK KNIGHT!
THE BLACK KNIGHT!
HURRY! THE LIGHTS!!
TAK TAK TAK...

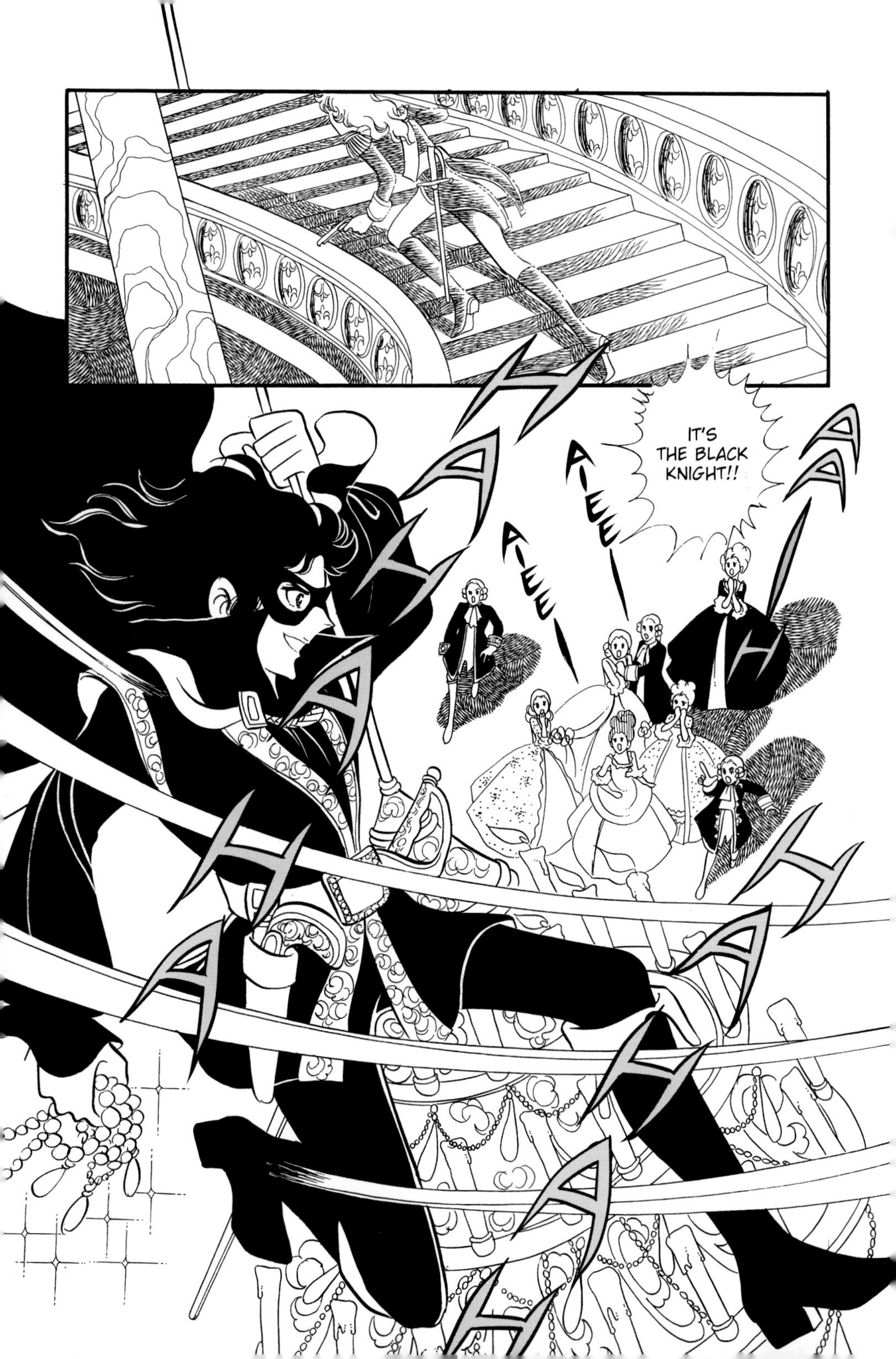
IT'S THE BLACK KNIGHT!!
AIEE!
AIEE!
HAHAHA

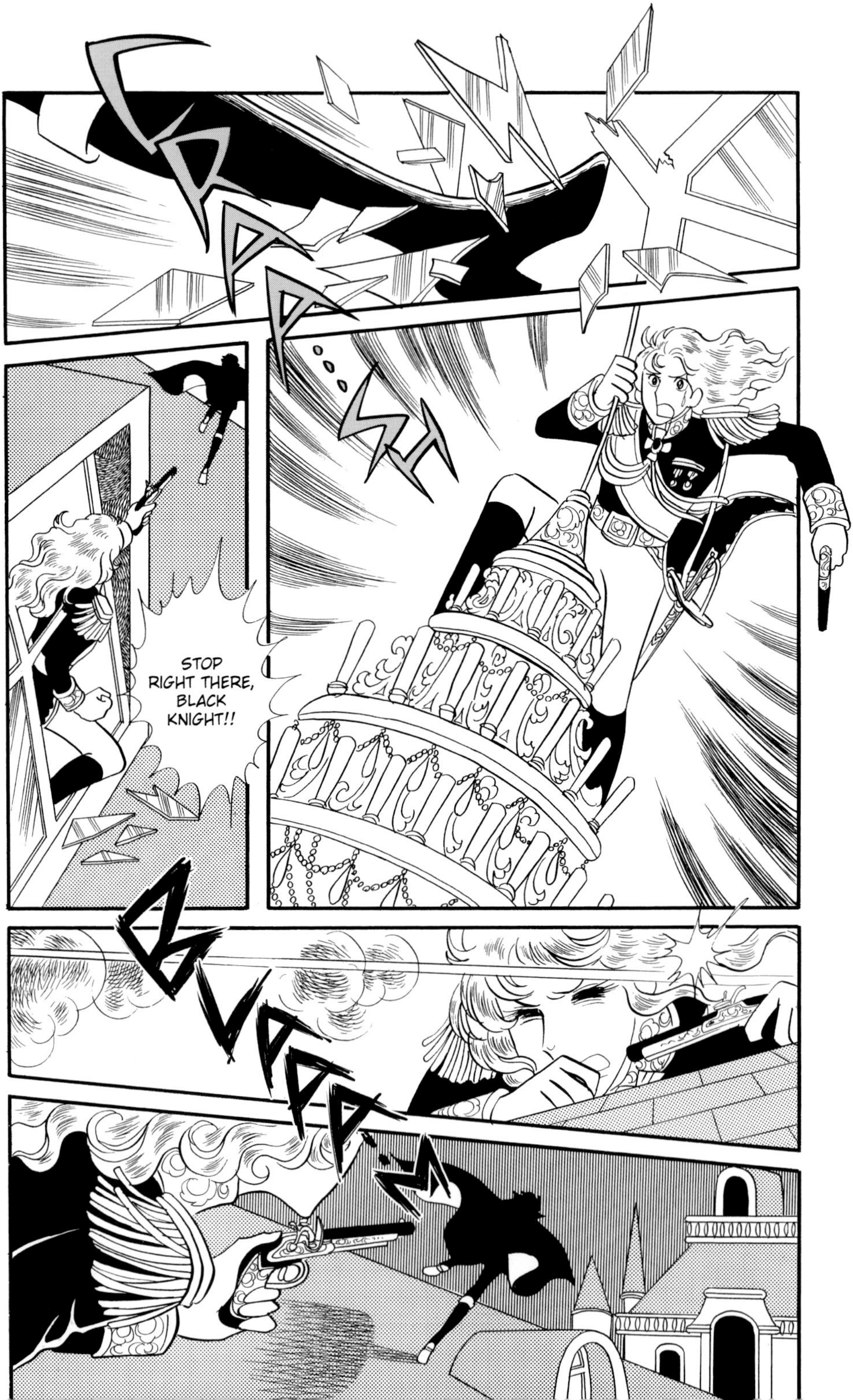
CRAASH...
STOP RIGHT THERE, BLACK KNIGHT!!
BLAAAM

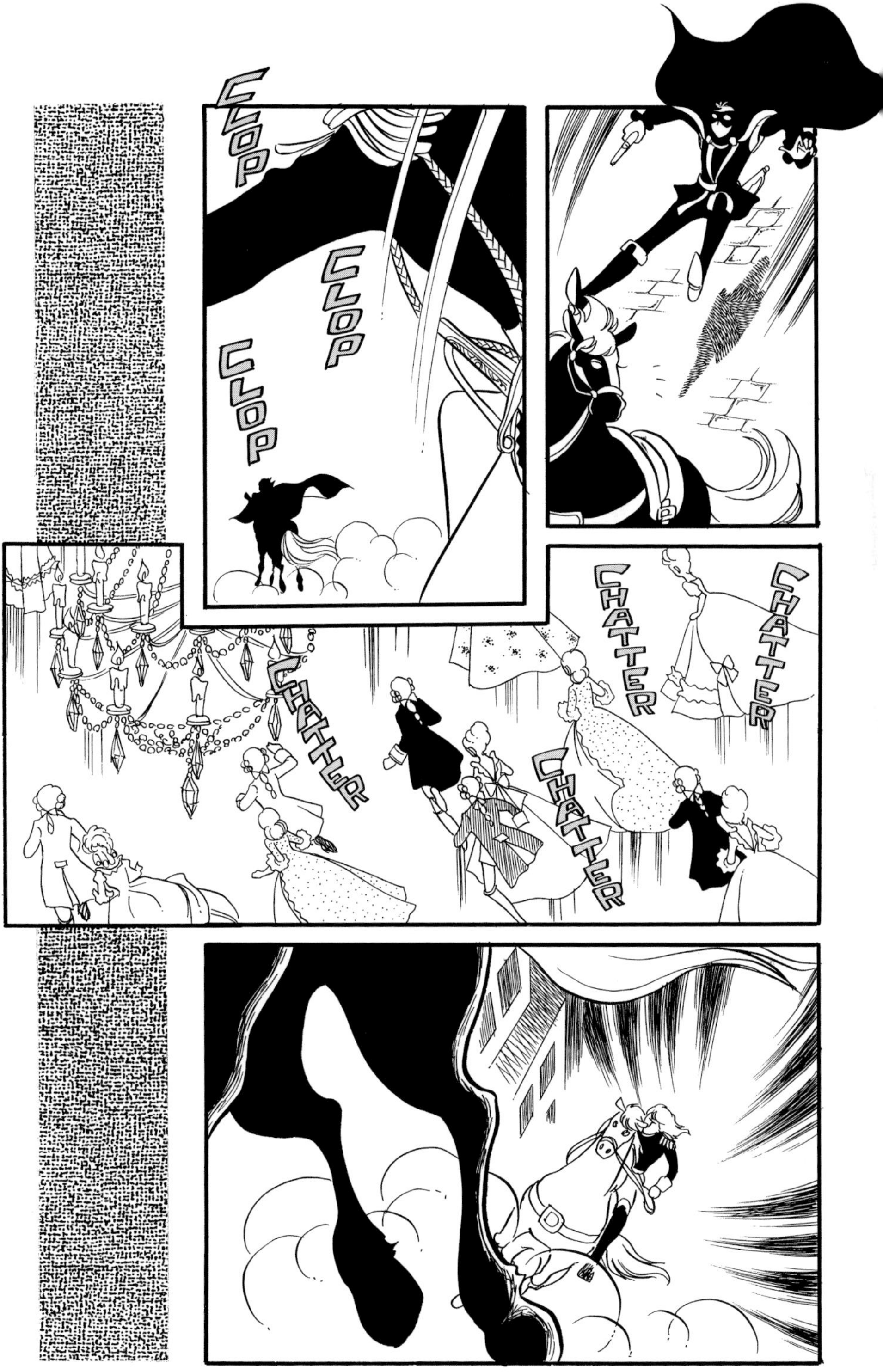
CLOP
CLOP
CLOP
CHATTER
CHATTER
CHATTER
CHATTER

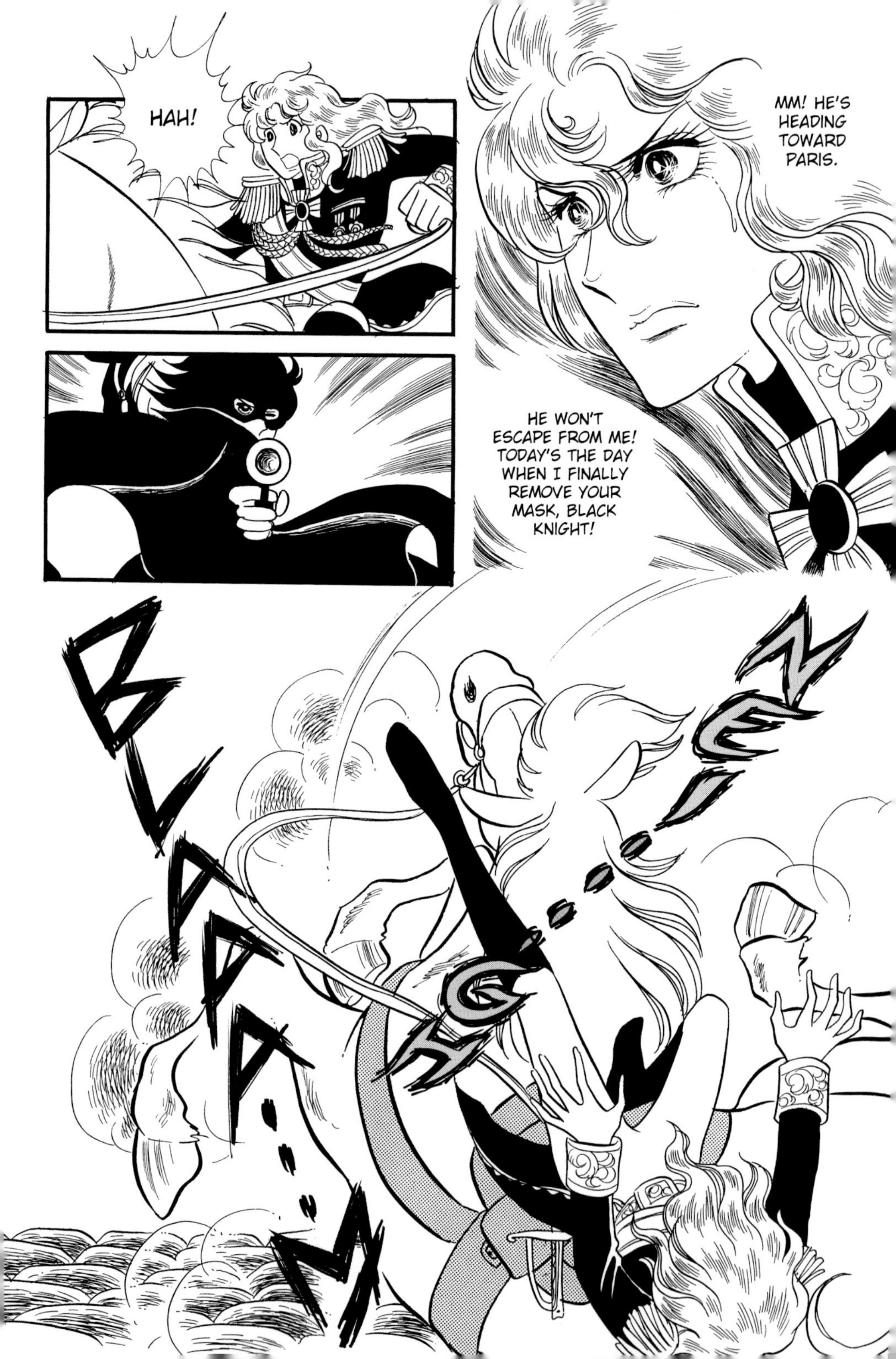
MM! HE'S HEADING TOWARD PARIS.
HE WON'T ESCAPE FROM ME! TODAY'S THE DAY WHEN I FINALLY REMOVE YOUR MASK, BLACK KNIGHT!
HAH!
BLAAAM

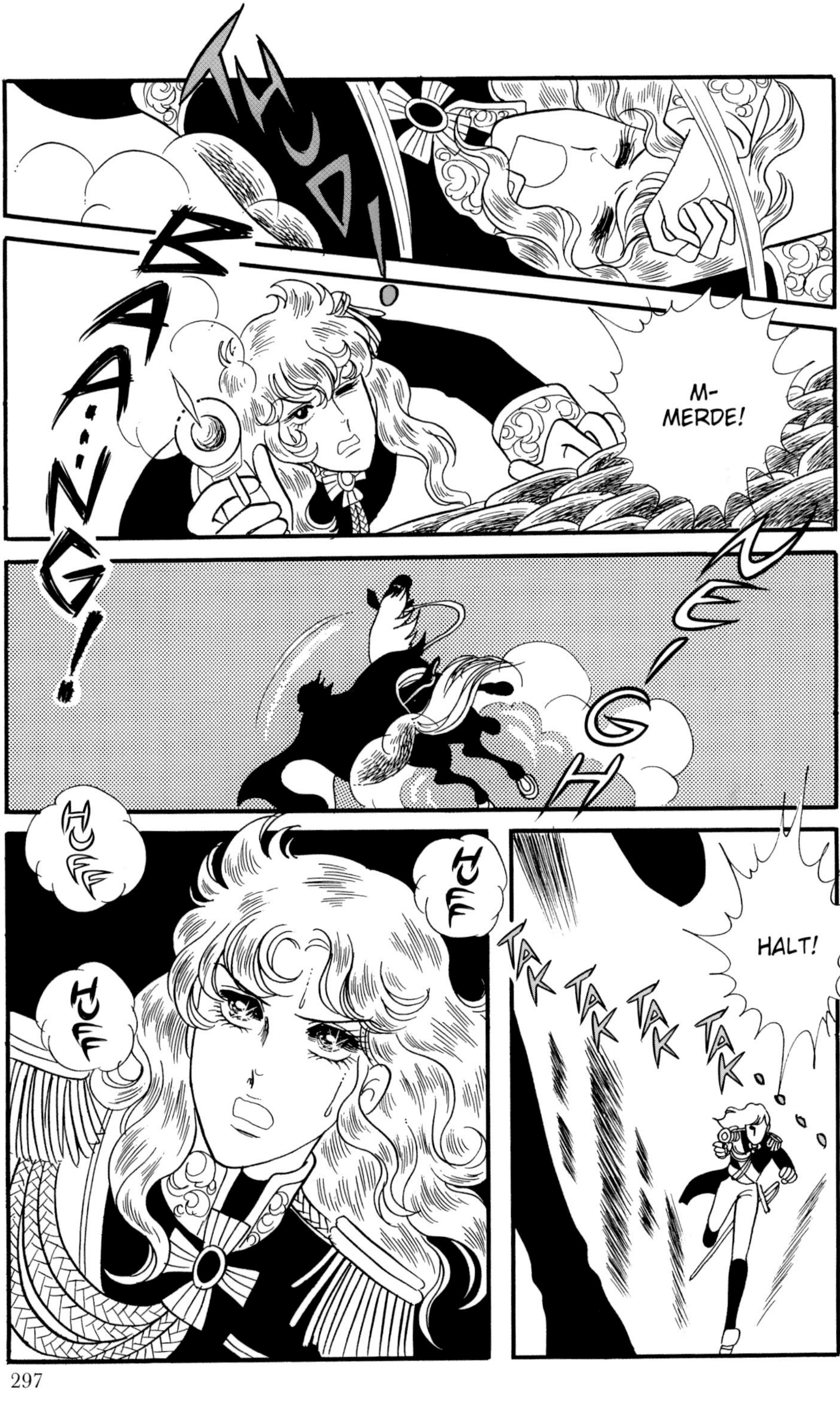
THUD!
BAA...NG!
M-MERDE!
NEIGH
HALT!
TAK TAK TAK TAK
HUFF
HUFF
HUFF

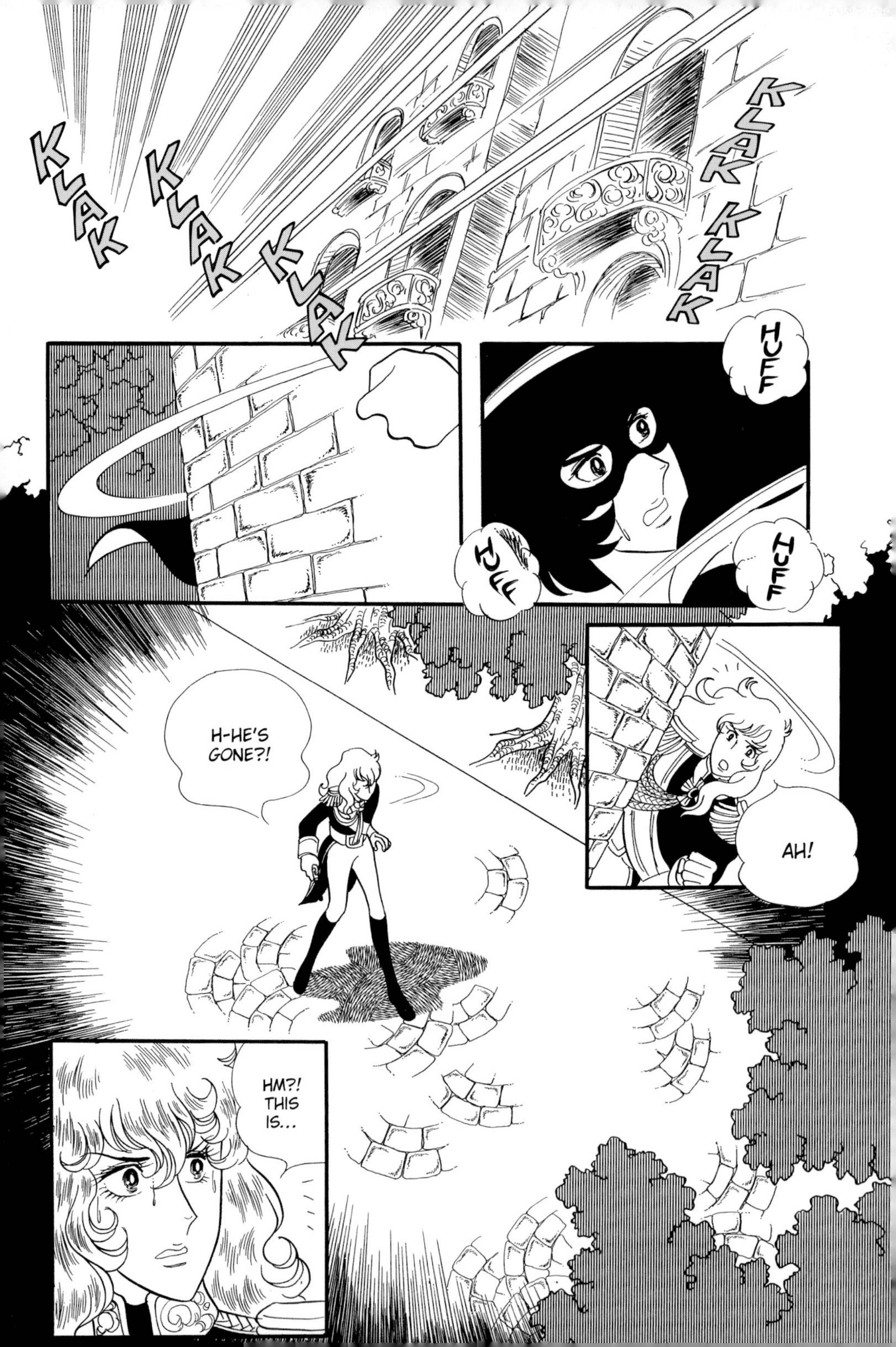
KLAK KLAK KLAK
KVAK KVAK KVAK
HUFF
HUFF
HUFF
AH!
H-HE'S GONE?!
HM?! THIS IS...

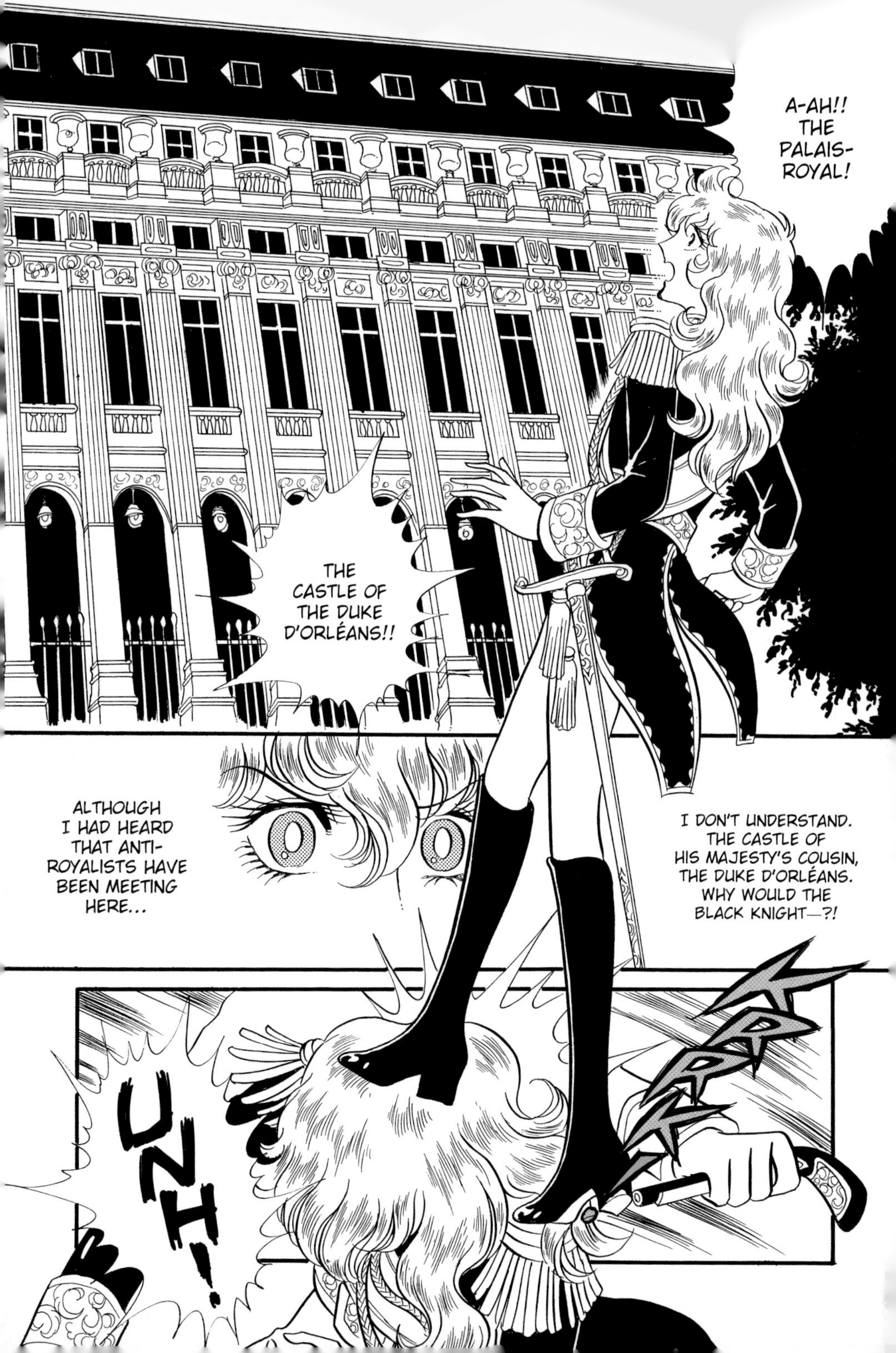
A-AH!! THE PALAIS-ROYAL!
THE CASTLE OF THE DUKE D'ORLÉANS!!
I DON'T UNDERSTAND. THE CASTLE OF HIS MAJESTY'S COUSIN, THE DUKE D'ORLÉANS. WHY WOULD THE BLACK KNIGHT—?!
ALTHOUGH I HAD HEARD THAT ANTI-ROYALISTS HAVE BEEN MEETING HERE...
UNH!!

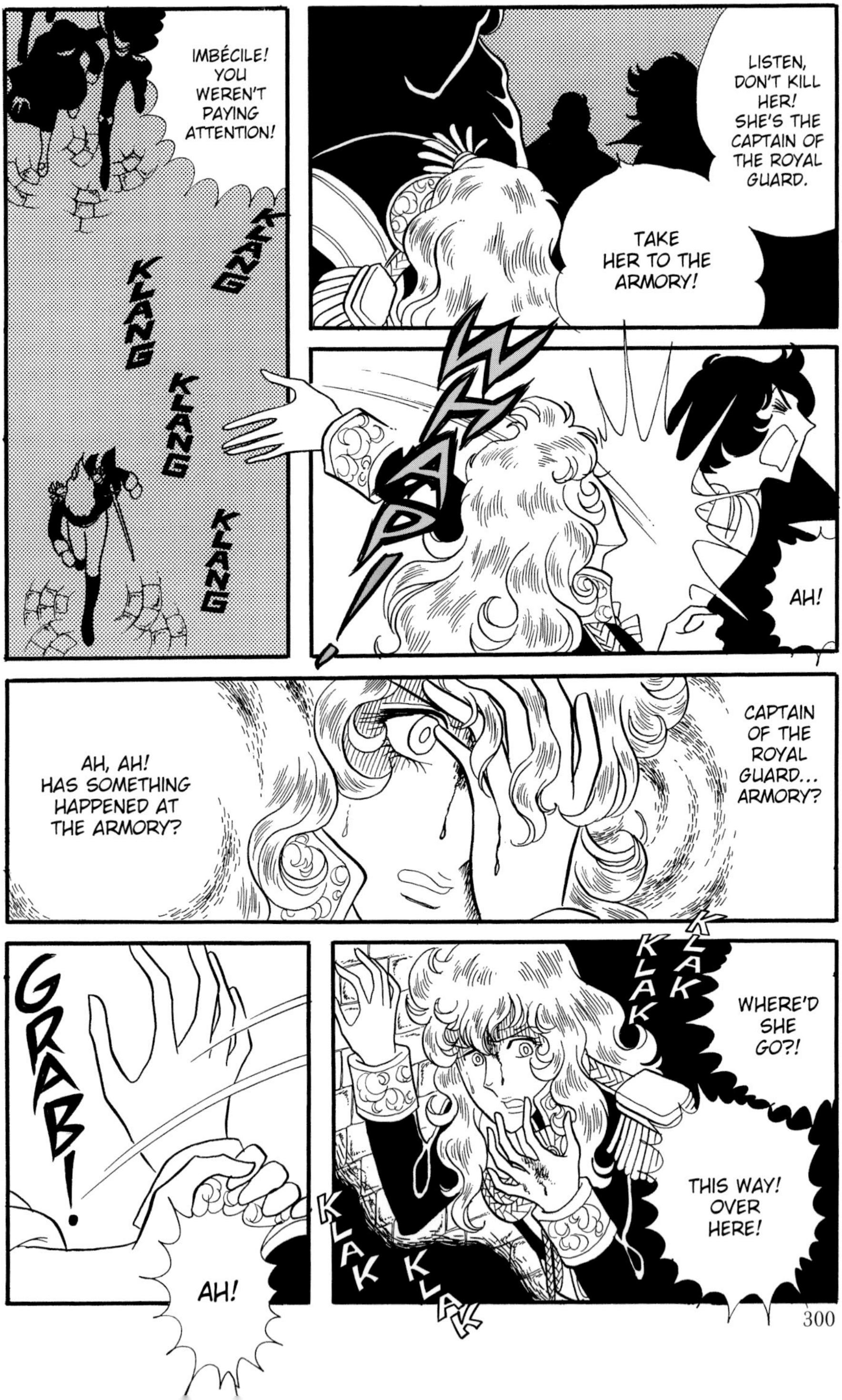

LISTEN, DON'T KILL HER! SHE'S THE CAPTAIN OF THE ROYAL GUARD.
TAKE HER TO THE ARMORY!
WHAP
AH!
IMBÉCILE! YOU WEREN'T PAYING ATTENTION!
KLANG
KLANG
KLANG
KLANG
CAPTAIN OF THE ROYAL GUARD... ARMORY?
AH, AH! HAS SOMETHING HAPPENED AT THE ARMORY?
KLAK
KLAK
WHERE'D SHE GO?!
THIS WAY! OVER HERE!
KLAK
KLAK
GRAB!
AH!

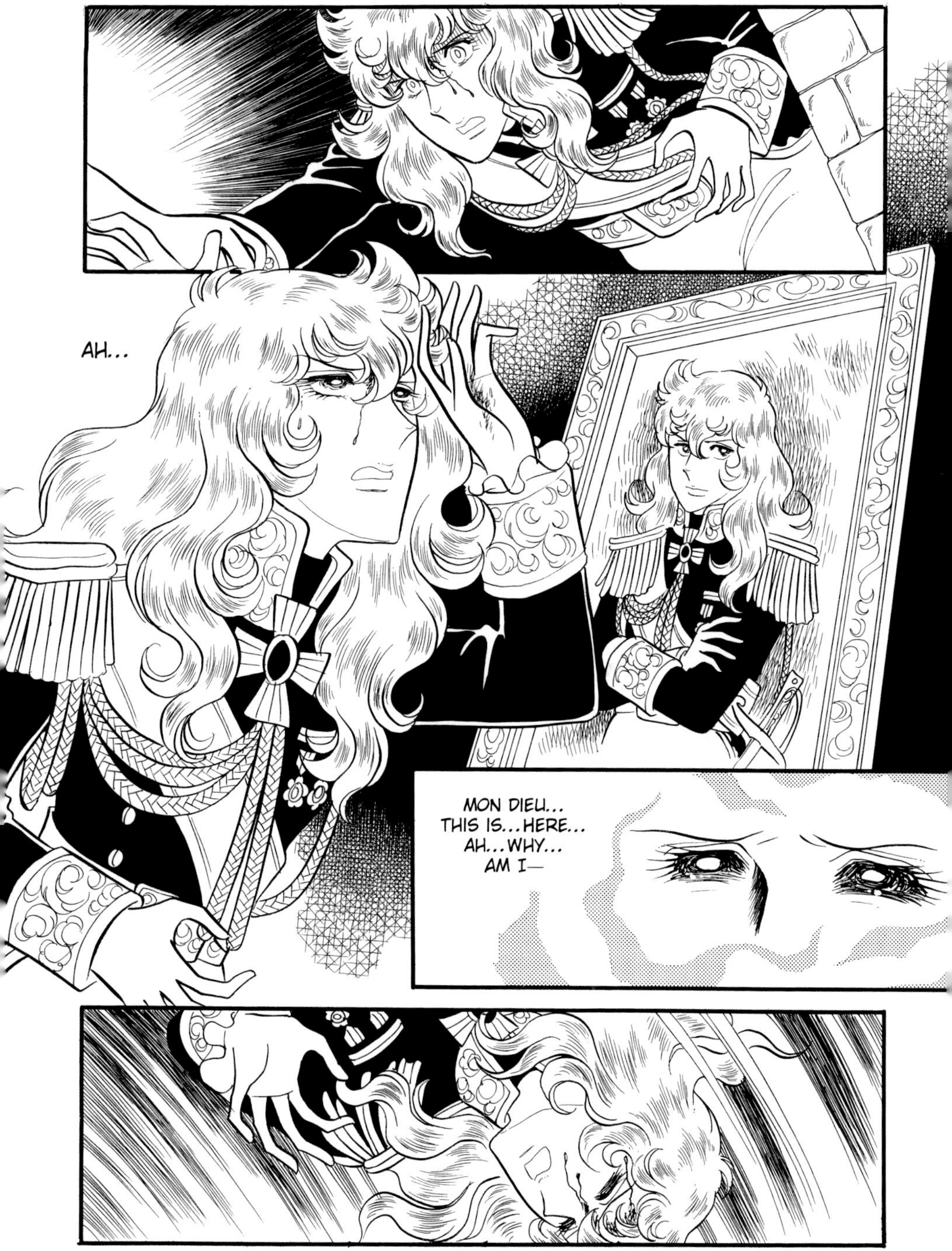
AH...
MON DIEU... THIS IS...HERE... AH...WHY... AM I—

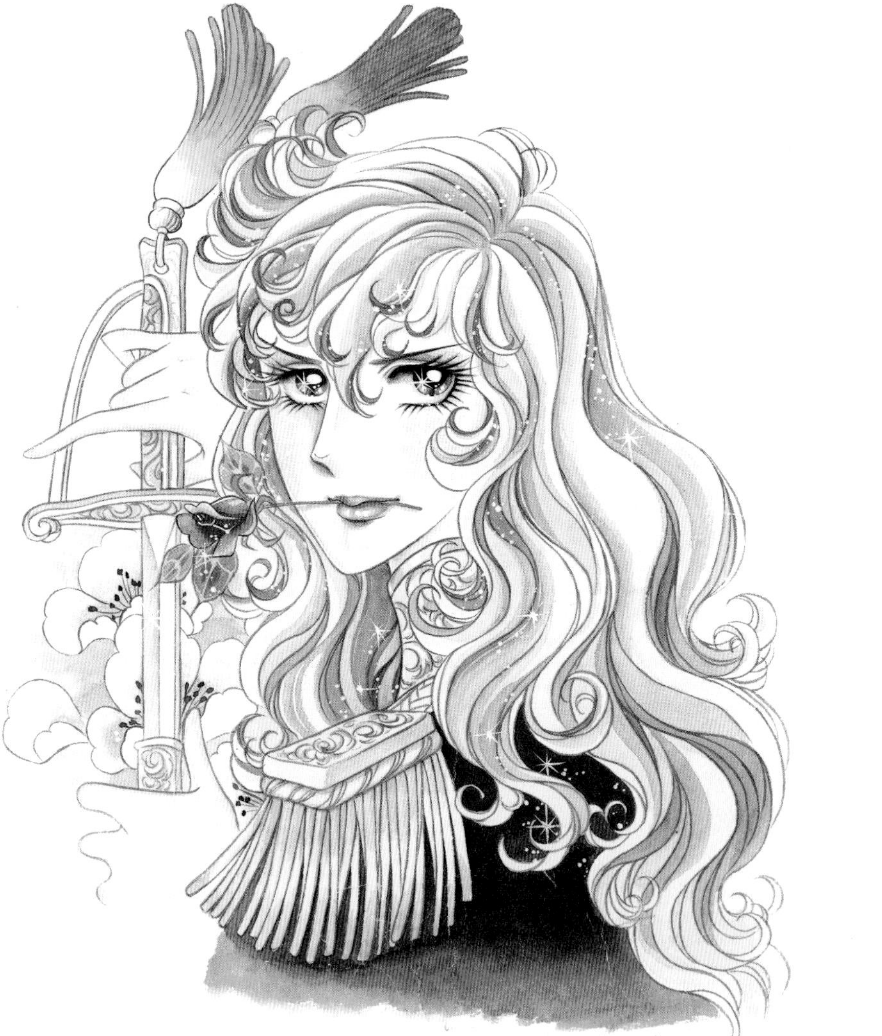

1973 WEEKLY MARGARET MAGAZINE
ISSUE 6 COVER ART

✤OVERWHELMINGLY POPULAR!!
CRITICALLY ACCLAIMED TOUR DE FORCE
◆INJURED CHASING THE BLACK KNIGHT, WHAT WILL HAPPEN TO OSCAR?!

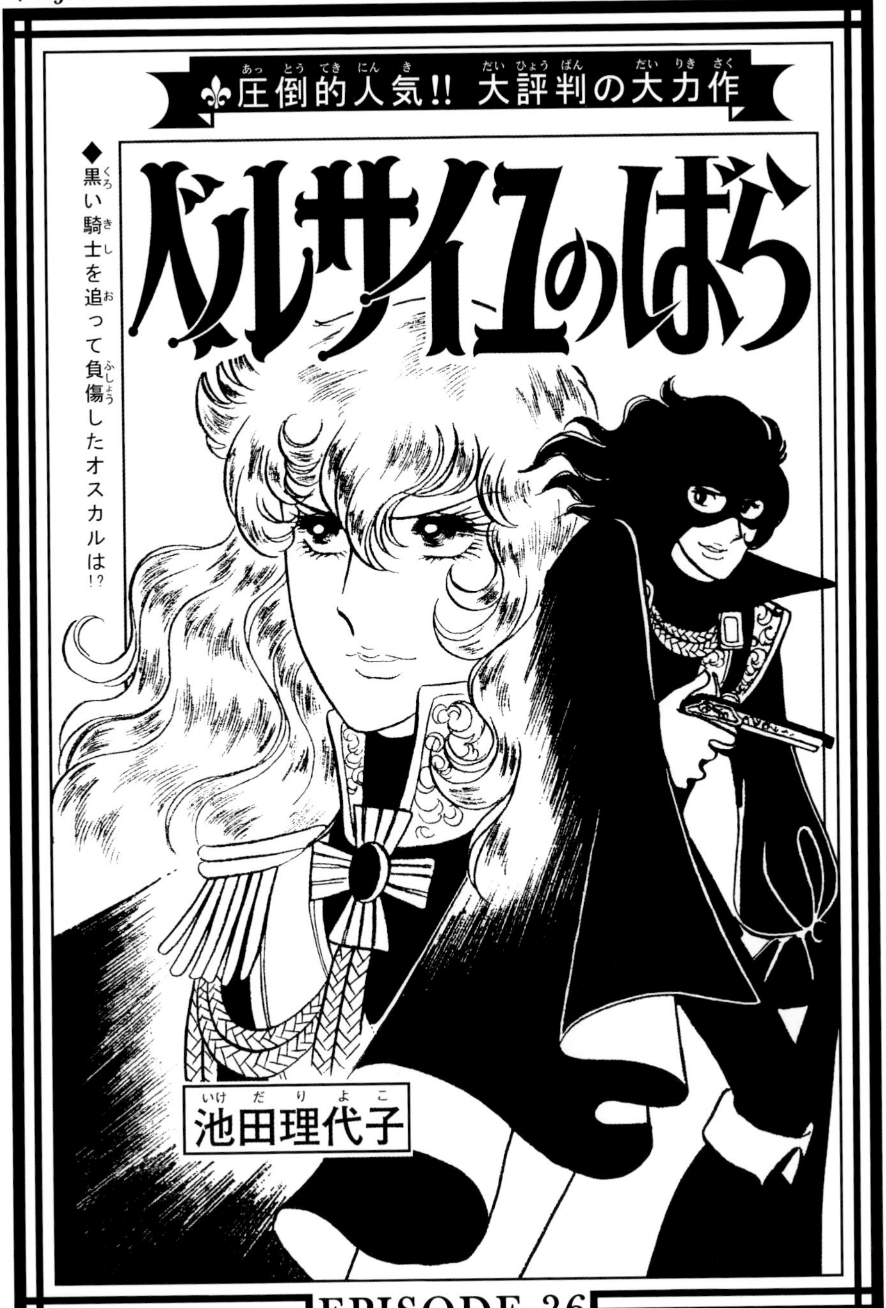
✤圧倒的人気!! 大評判の大力作
ベルサイユのばら
◆黒い騎士を追って負傷したオスカルは!?
池田理代子
EPISODE 36

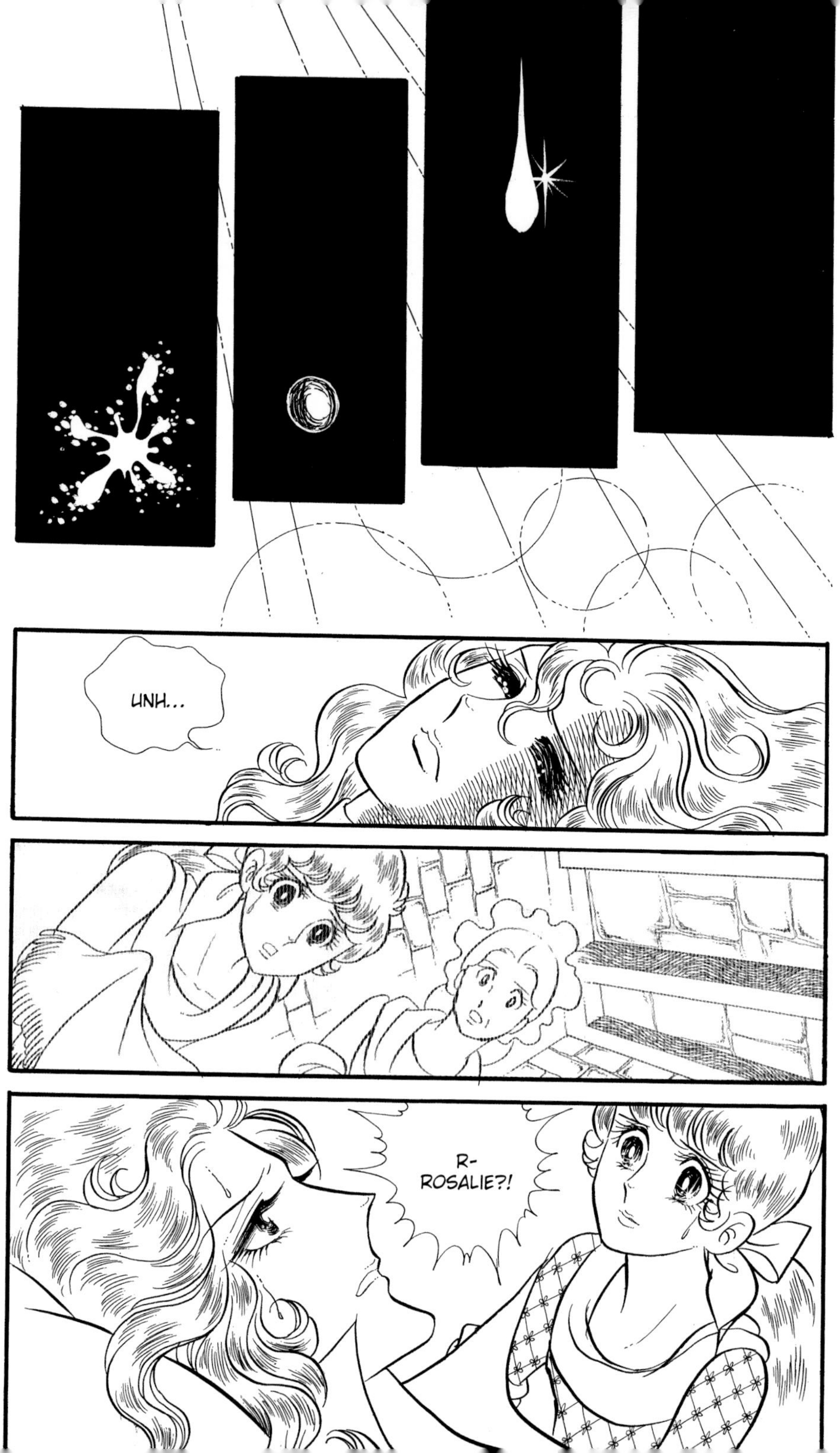
UNH...
R-ROSALIE?!

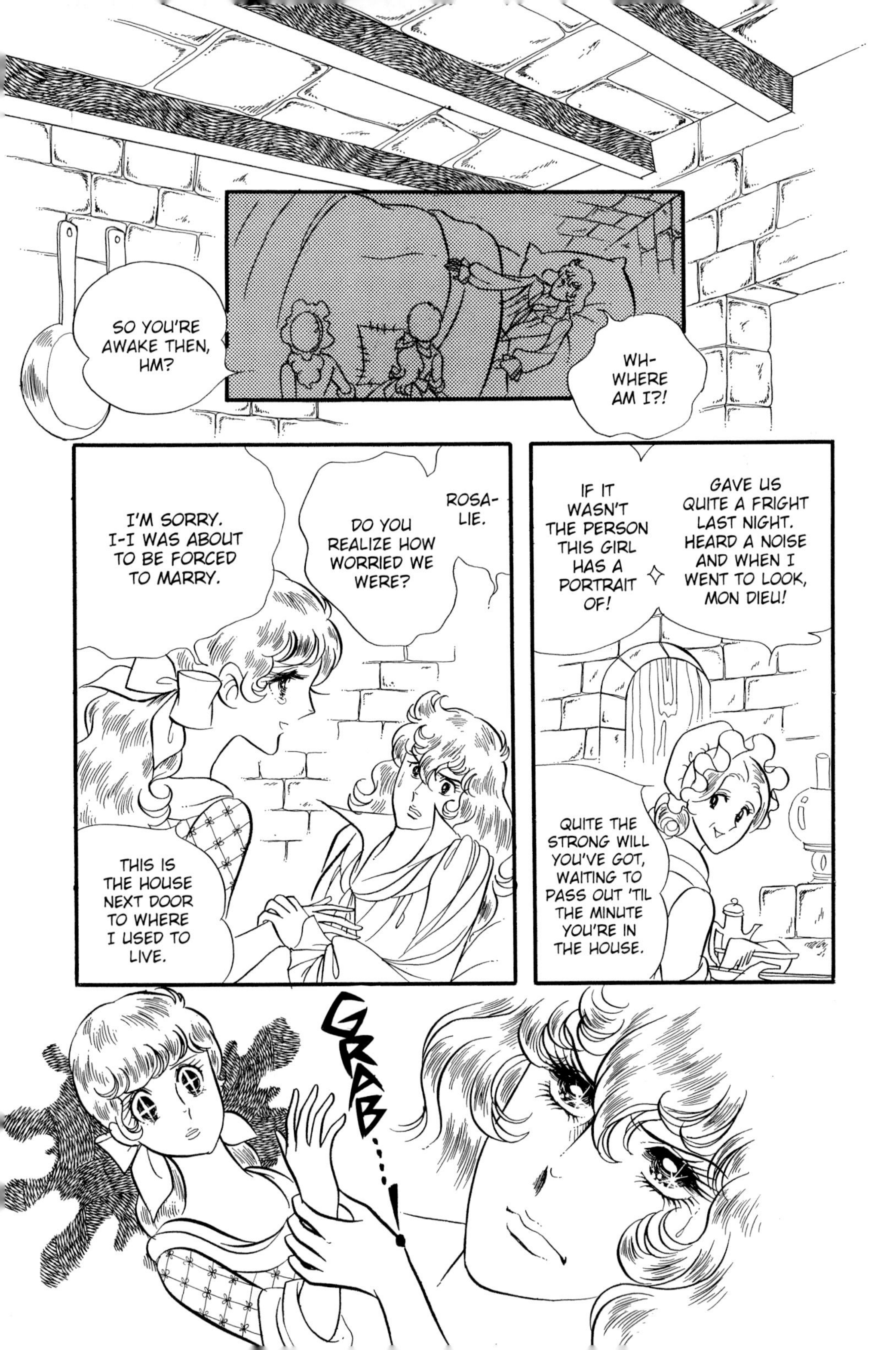
WH- WHERE AM I?!
SO YOU'RE AWAKE THEN, HM?
GAVE US QUITE A FRIGHT LAST NIGHT. HEARD A NOISE AND WHEN I WENT TO LOOK, MON DIEU!
IF IT WASN'T THE PERSON THIS GIRL HAS A PORTRAIT OF!
QUITE THE STRONG WILL YOU'VE GOT, WAITING TO PASS OUT 'TIL THE MINUTE YOU'RE IN THE HOUSE.
ROSA- LIE.
DO YOU REALIZE HOW WORRIED WE WERE?
I'M SORRY. I-I WAS ABOUT TO BE FORCED TO MARRY.
THIS IS THE HOUSE NEXT DOOR TO WHERE I USED TO LIVE.
GRAB...!

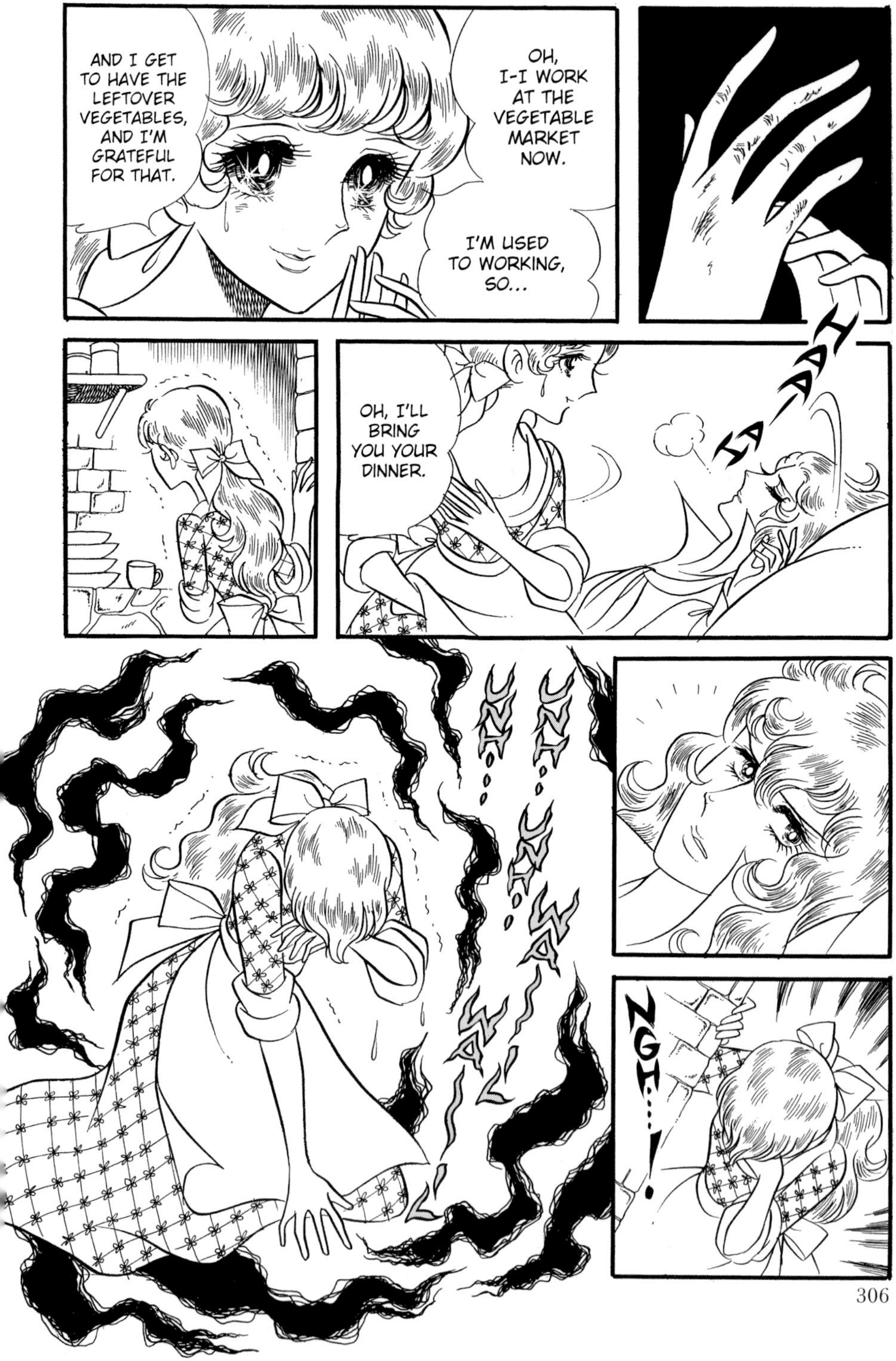
OH, I-I WORK AT THE VEGETABLE MARKET NOW.
I'M USED TO WORKING, SO...
AND I GET TO HAVE THE LEFTOVER VEGETABLES, AND I'M GRATEFUL FOR THAT.
HAA-HA
OH, I'LL BRING YOU YOUR DINNER.
NGH...!
UNH... UNH... WA—
UNH... WA—

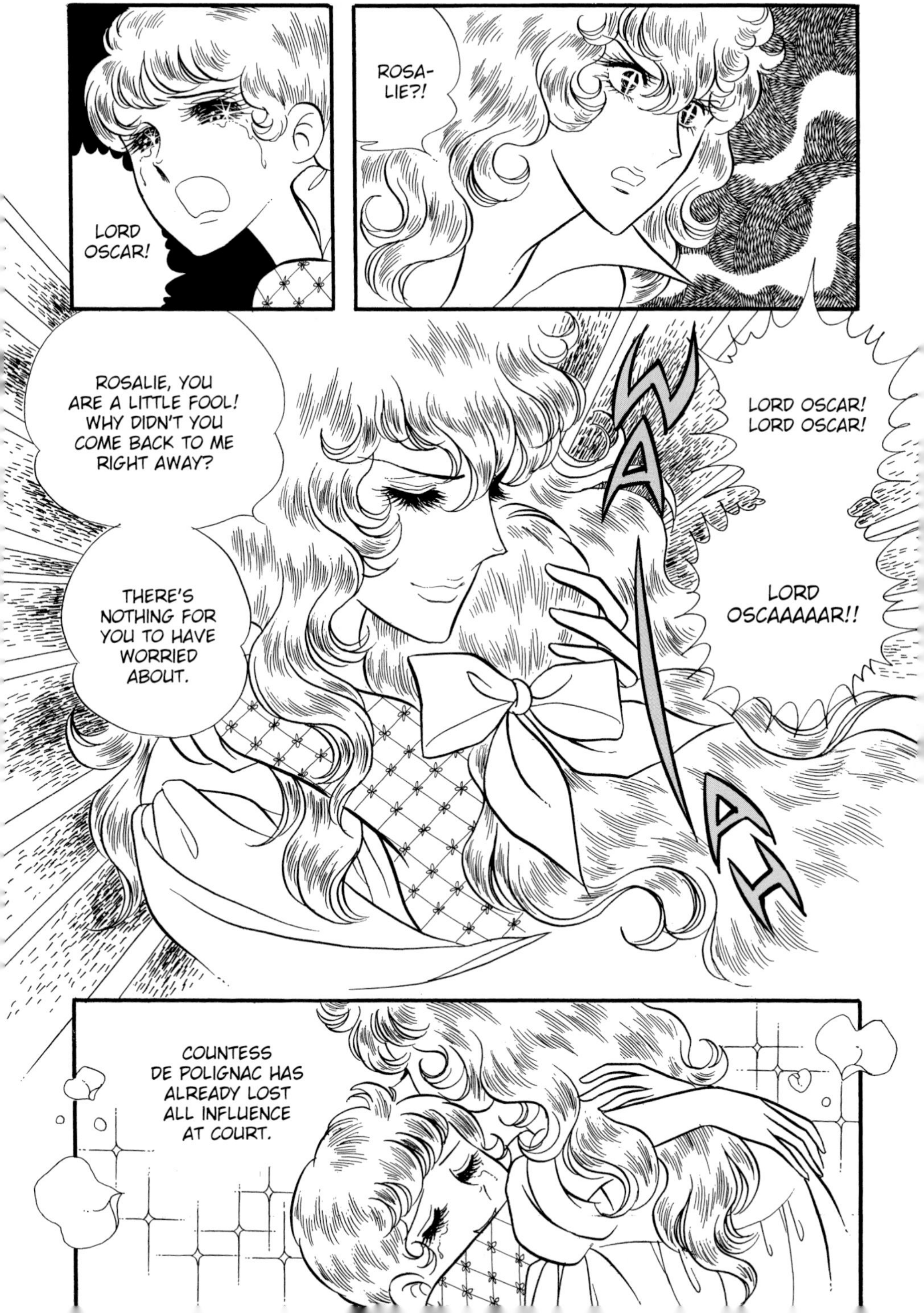

ROSA-LIE?!
LORD OSCAR!
LORD OSCAR! LORD OSCAR!
LORD OSCAAAAAR!!
WAAH
ROSALIE, YOU ARE A LITTLE FOOL! WHY DIDN'T YOU COME BACK TO ME RIGHT AWAY?
THERE'S NOTHING FOR YOU TO HAVE WORRIED ABOUT.
COUNTESS DE POLIGNAC HAS ALREADY LOST ALL INFLUENCE AT COURT.

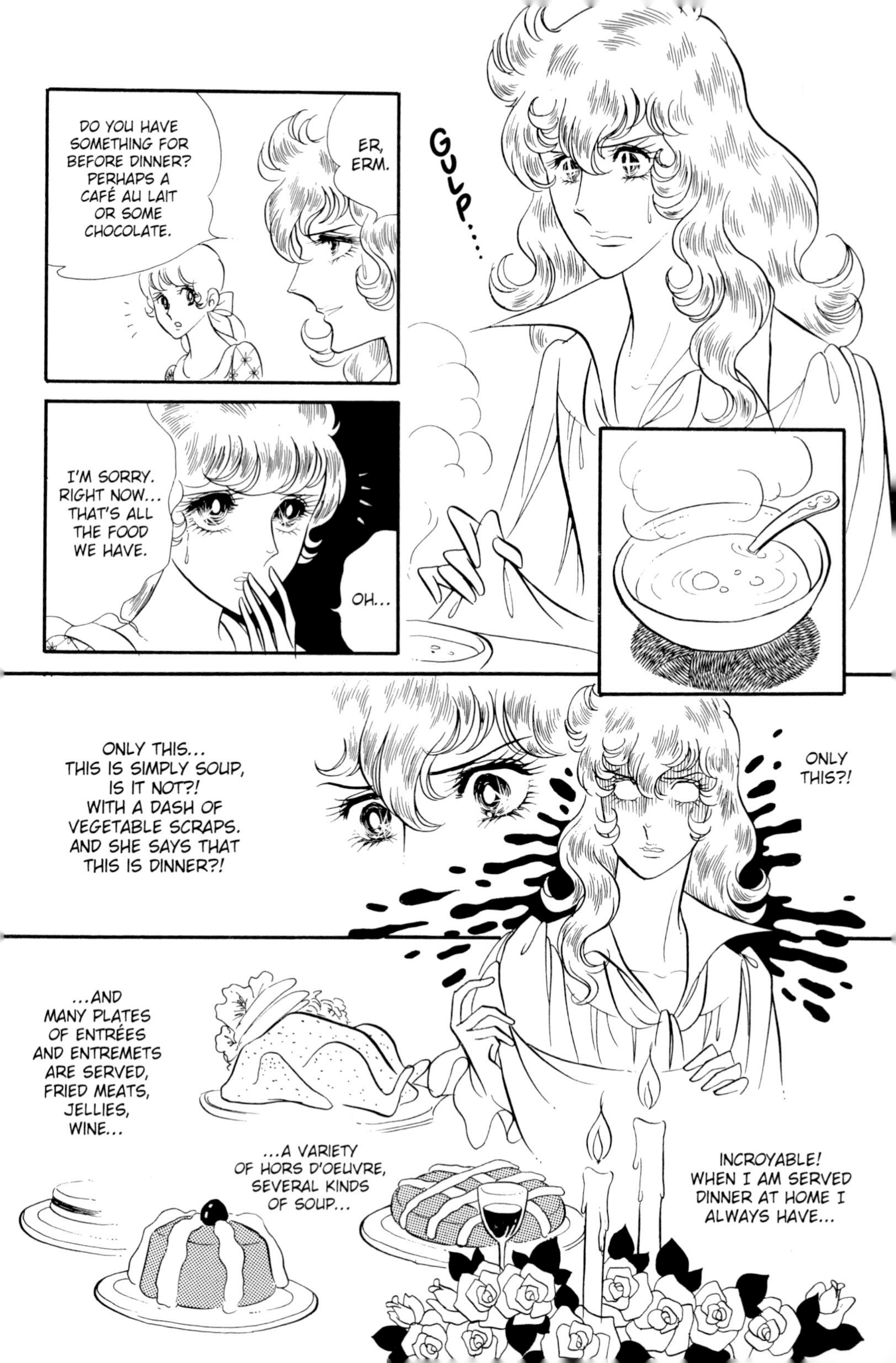
GULP...
ER, ERM.
DO YOU HAVE SOMETHING FOR BEFORE DINNER? PERHAPS A CAFÉ AU LAIT OR SOME CHOCOLATE.
I'M SORRY. RIGHT NOW... THAT'S ALL THE FOOD WE HAVE.
OH...
ONLY THIS?!
ONLY THIS... THIS IS SIMPLY SOUP, IS IT NOT?! WITH A DASH OF VEGETABLE SCRAPS. AND SHE SAYS THAT THIS IS DINNER?!
INCROYABLE! WHEN I AM SERVED DINNER AT HOME I ALWAYS HAVE...
...A VARIETY OF HORS D'OEUVRE, SEVERAL KINDS OF SOUP...
...AND MANY PLATES OF ENTRÉES AND ENTREMETS ARE SERVED, FRIED MEATS, JELLIES, WINE...

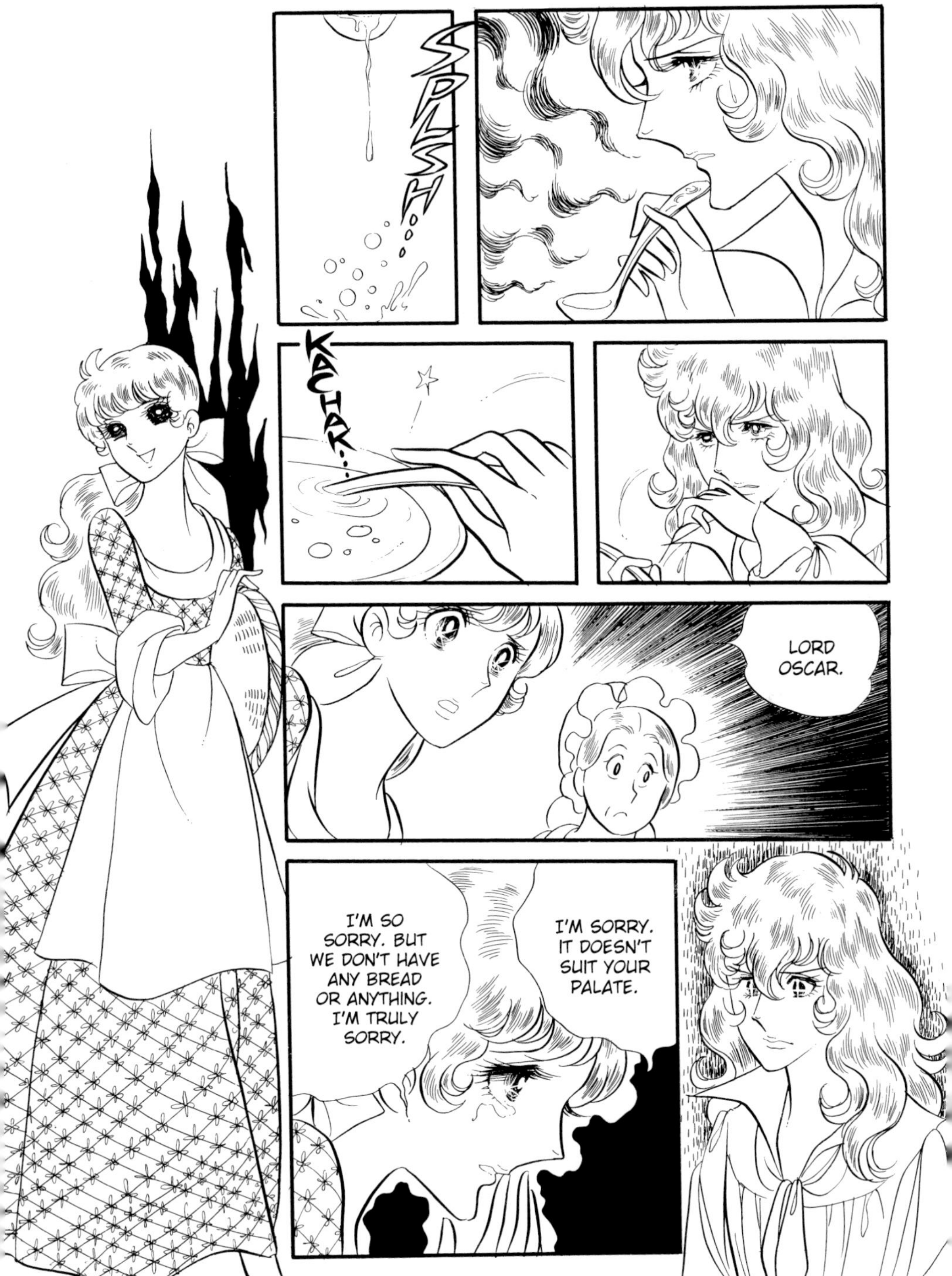
SPLSH...
KACHAK...
LORD OSCAR.
I'M SORRY. IT DOESN'T SUIT YOUR PALATE.
I'M SO SORRY. BUT WE DON'T HAVE ANY BREAD OR ANYTHING. I'M TRULY SORRY.

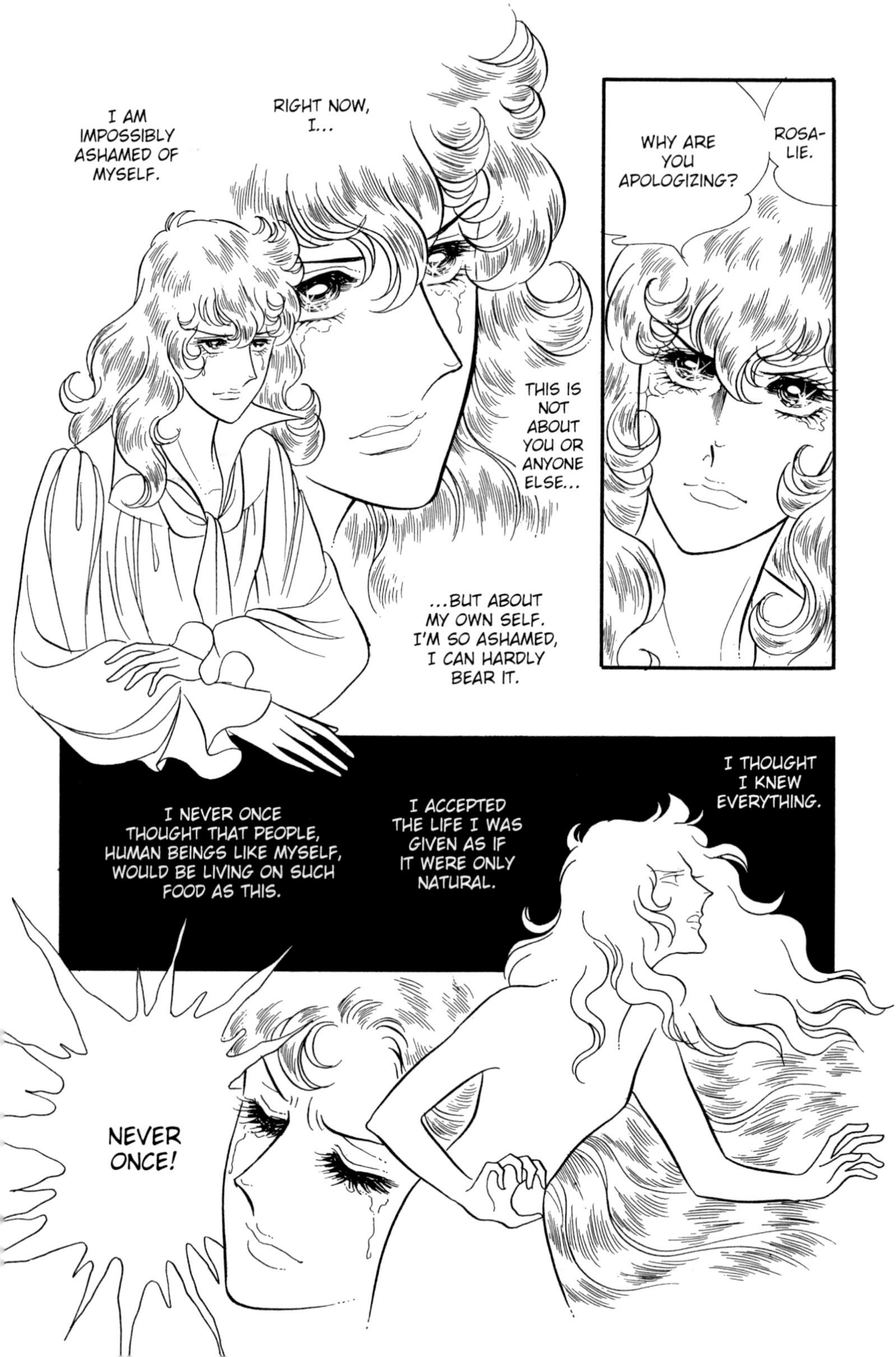
ROSA-LIE.
WHY ARE YOU APOLOGIZING?
RIGHT NOW, I...
I AM IMPOSSIBLY ASHAMED OF MYSELF.
THIS IS NOT ABOUT YOU OR ANYONE ELSE...
...BUT ABOUT MY OWN SELF. I'M SO ASHAMED, I CAN HARDLY BEAR IT.
I THOUGHT I KNEW EVERYTHING.
I ACCEPTED THE LIFE I WAS GIVEN AS IF IT WERE ONLY NATURAL.
I NEVER ONCE THOUGHT THAT PEOPLE, HUMAN BEINGS LIKE MYSELF, WOULD BE LIVING ON SUCH FOOD AS THIS.
NEVER ONCE!

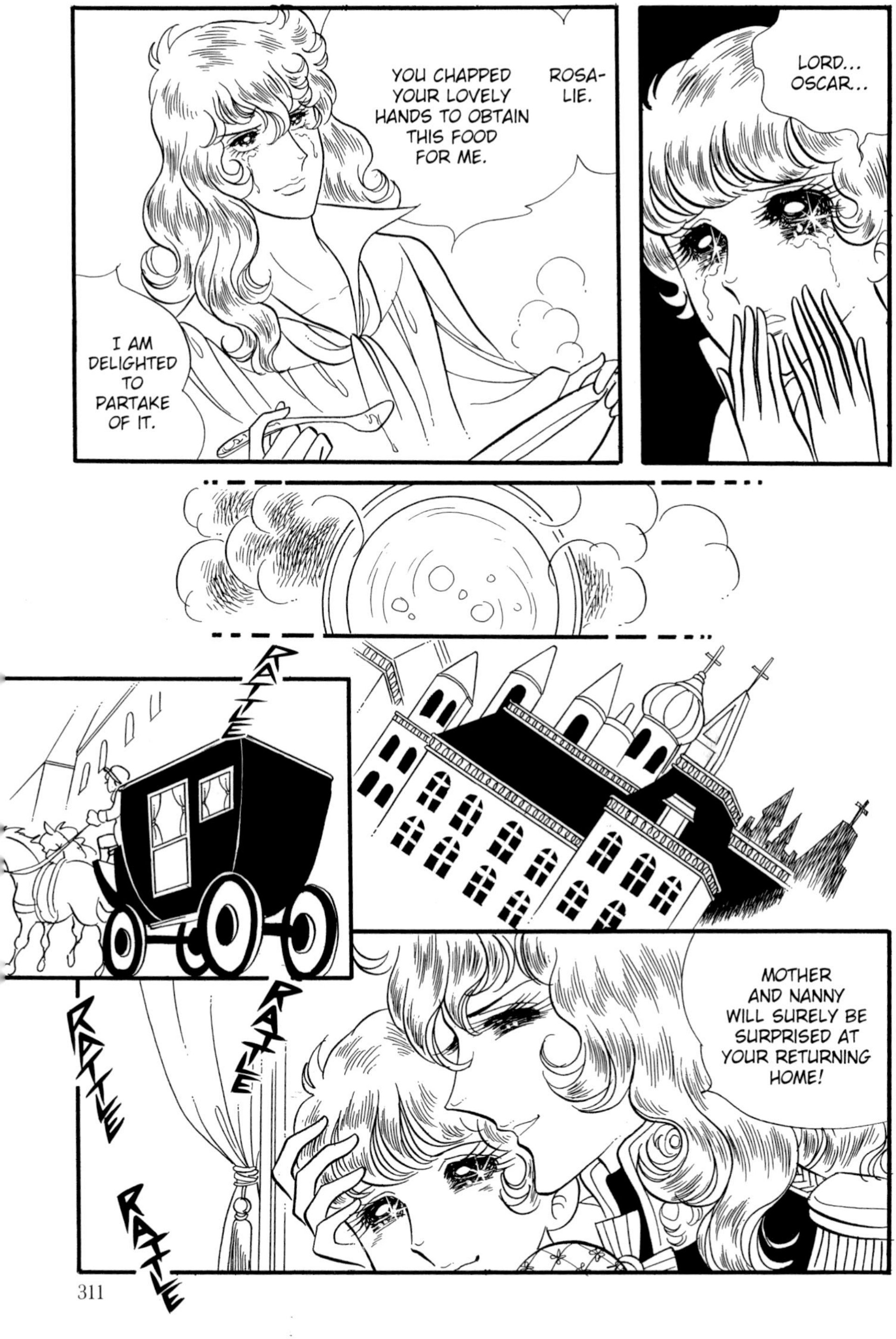
LORD... OSCAR...
ROSA- LIE.
YOU CHAPPED YOUR LOVELY HANDS TO OBTAIN THIS FOOD FOR ME.
I AM DELIGHTED TO PARTAKE OF IT.
RATTLE
MOTHER AND NANNY WILL SURELY BE SURPRISED AT YOUR RETURNING HOME!
RATTLE
RATTLE
RATTLE

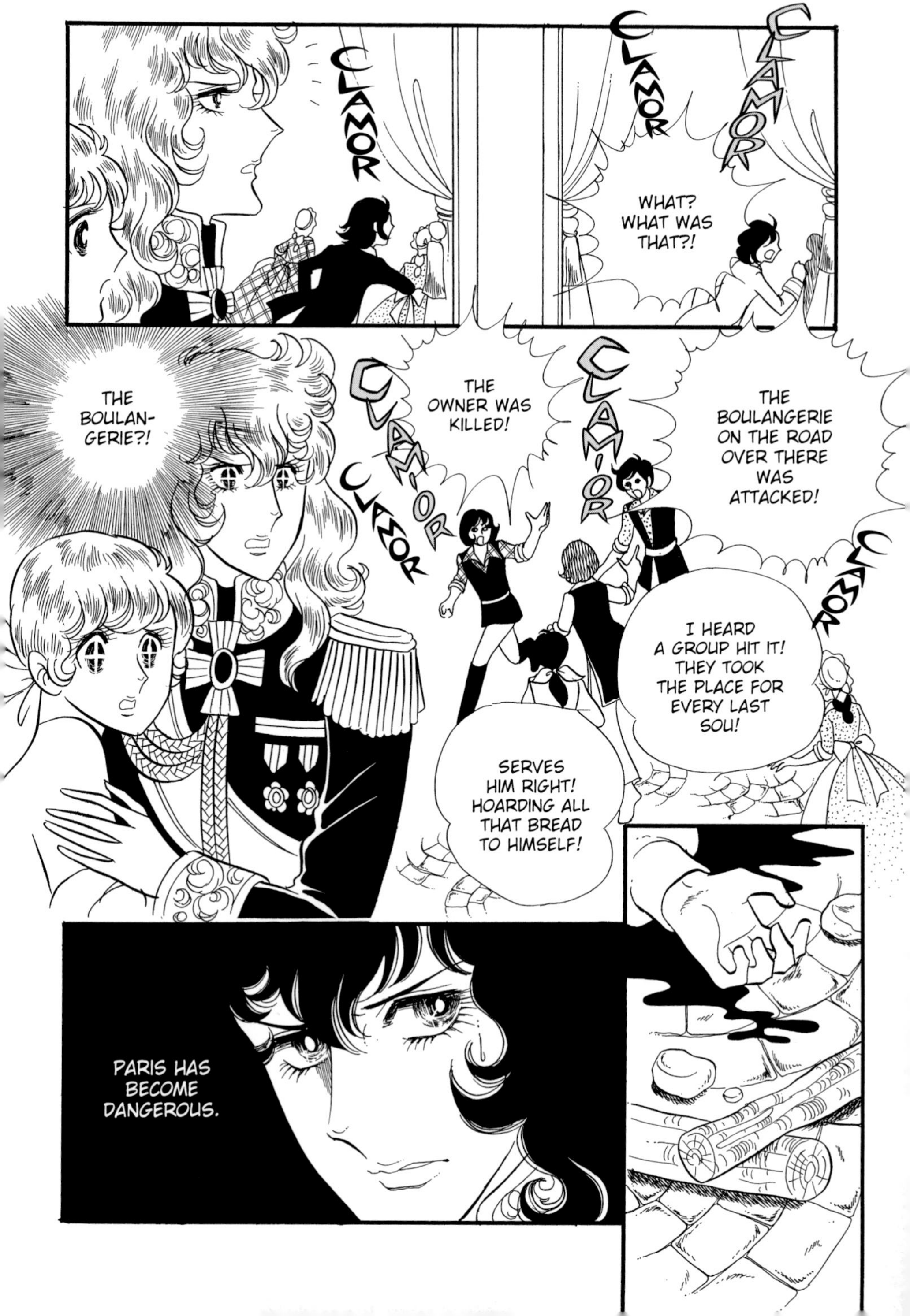
CLAMOR
CLAMOR
WHAT? WHAT WAS THAT?!
CLAMOR
CLAMOR
THE BOULANGERIE ON THE ROAD OVER THERE WAS ATTACKED!
CLAMOR
I HEARD A GROUP HIT IT! THEY TOOK THE PLACE FOR EVERY LAST SOU!
THE OWNER WAS KILLED!
SERVES HIM RIGHT! HOARDING ALL THAT BREAD TO HIMSELF!
CLAMOR
CLAMOR
THE BOULAN-GERIE?!
PARIS HAS BECOME DANGEROUS.

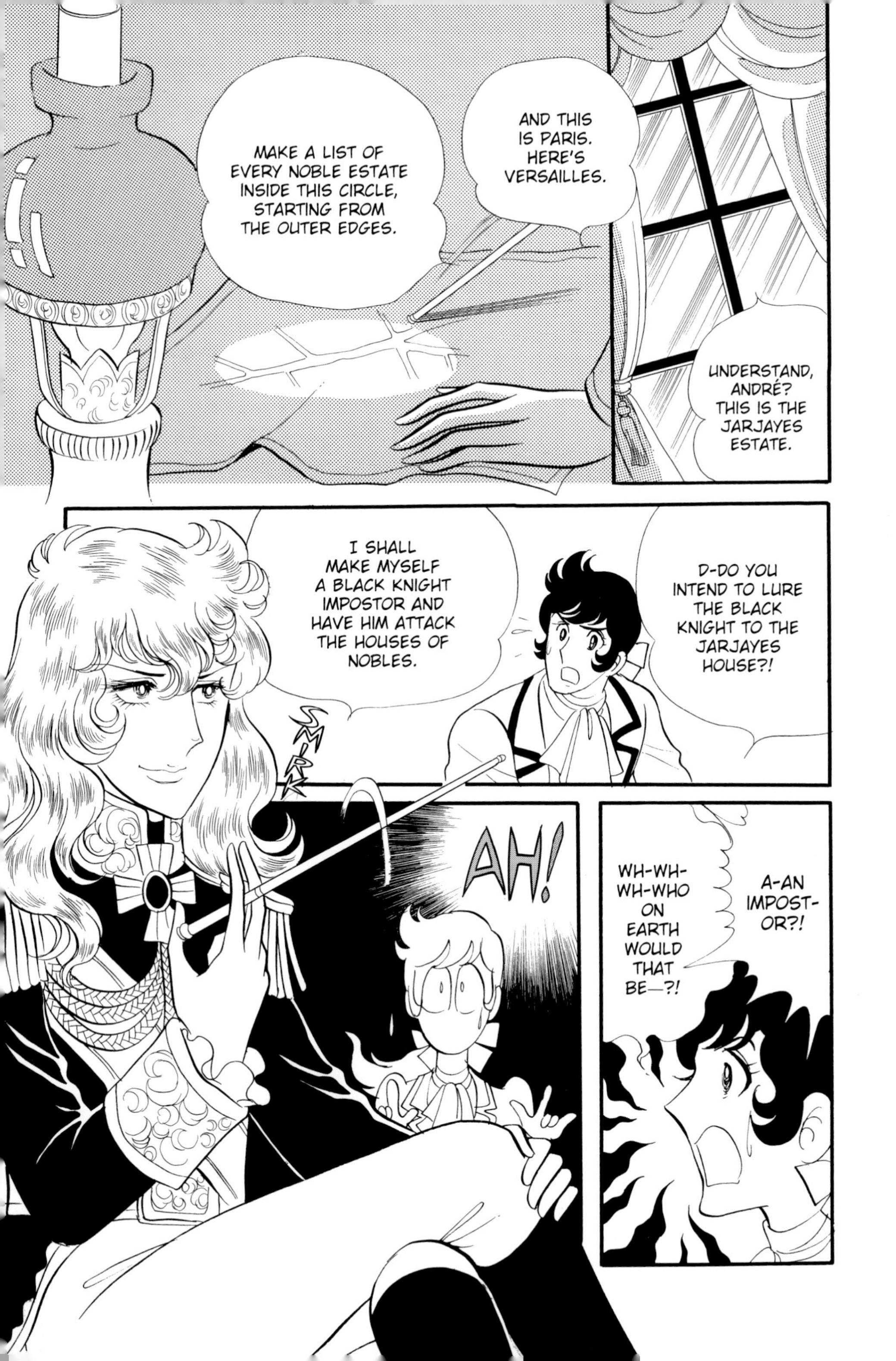
UNDERSTAND, ANDRÉ? THIS IS THE JARJAYES ESTATE.
AND THIS IS PARIS. HERE'S VERSAILLES.
MAKE A LIST OF EVERY NOBLE ESTATE INSIDE THIS CIRCLE, STARTING FROM THE OUTER EDGES.
D-DO YOU INTEND TO LURE THE BLACK KNIGHT TO THE JARJAYES HOUSE?!
I SHALL MAKE MYSELF A BLACK KNIGHT IMPOSTOR AND HAVE HIM ATTACK THE HOUSES OF NOBLES.
SMIRK
A-AN IMPOST-OR?!
WH-WH-WH-WHO ON EARTH WOULD THAT BE—?!
AH!

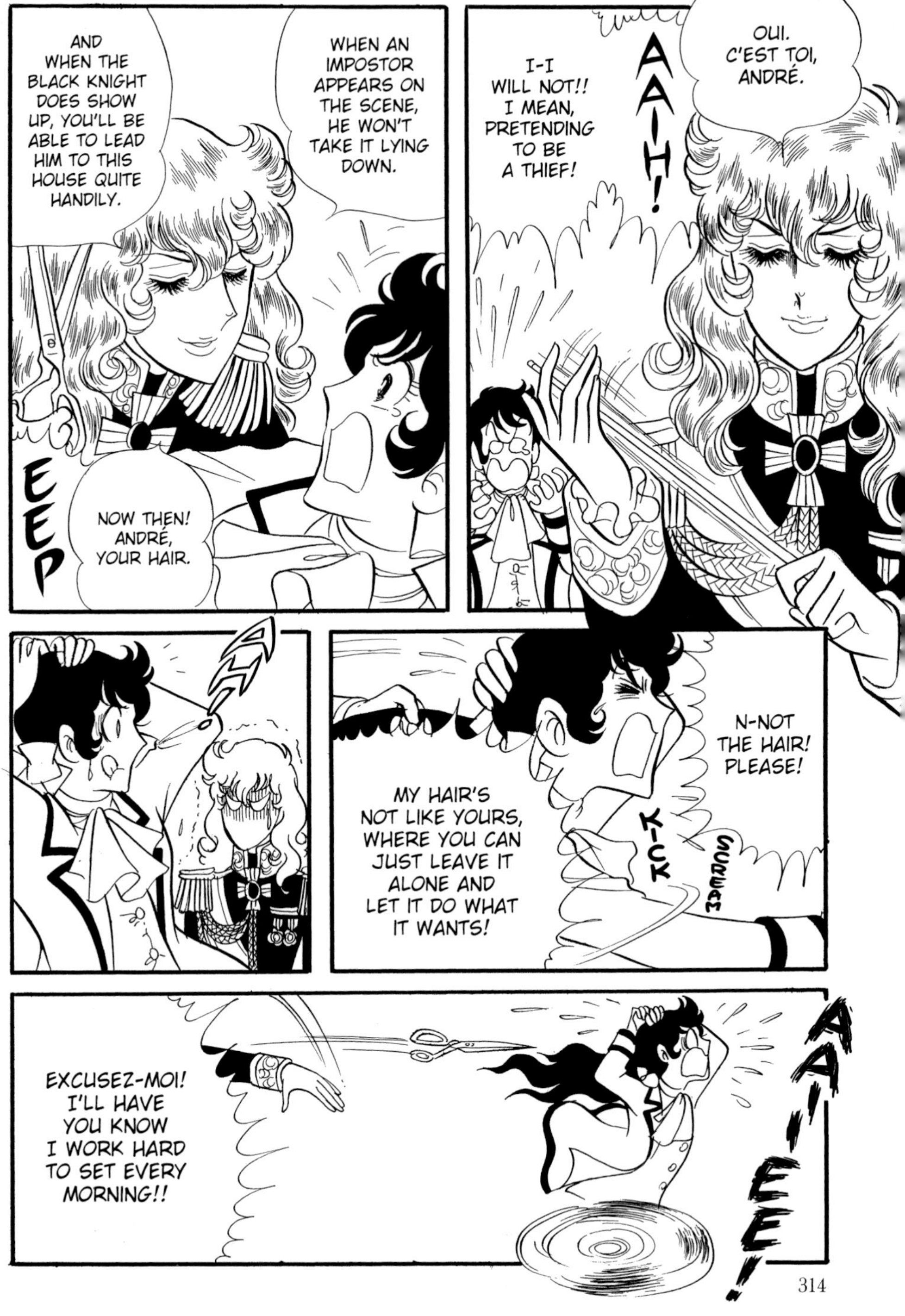
OUI. C'EST TOI, ANDRÉ.
AAIH!
I-I WILL NOT!! I MEAN, PRETENDING TO BE A THIEF!
WHEN AN IMPOSTOR APPEARS ON THE SCENE, HE WON'T TAKE IT LYING DOWN.
AND WHEN THE BLACK KNIGHT DOES SHOW UP, YOU'LL BE ABLE TO LEAD HIM TO THIS HOUSE QUITE HANDILY.
NOW THEN! ANDRÉ, YOUR HAIR.
EEP
N-NOT THE HAIR! PLEASE!
SCREAM
KICK
MY HAIR'S NOT LIKE YOURS, WHERE YOU CAN JUST LEAVE IT ALONE AND LET IT DO WHAT IT WANTS!
AAIEEE!
EXCUSEZ-MOI! I'LL HAVE YOU KNOW I WORK HARD TO SET EVERY MORNING!!

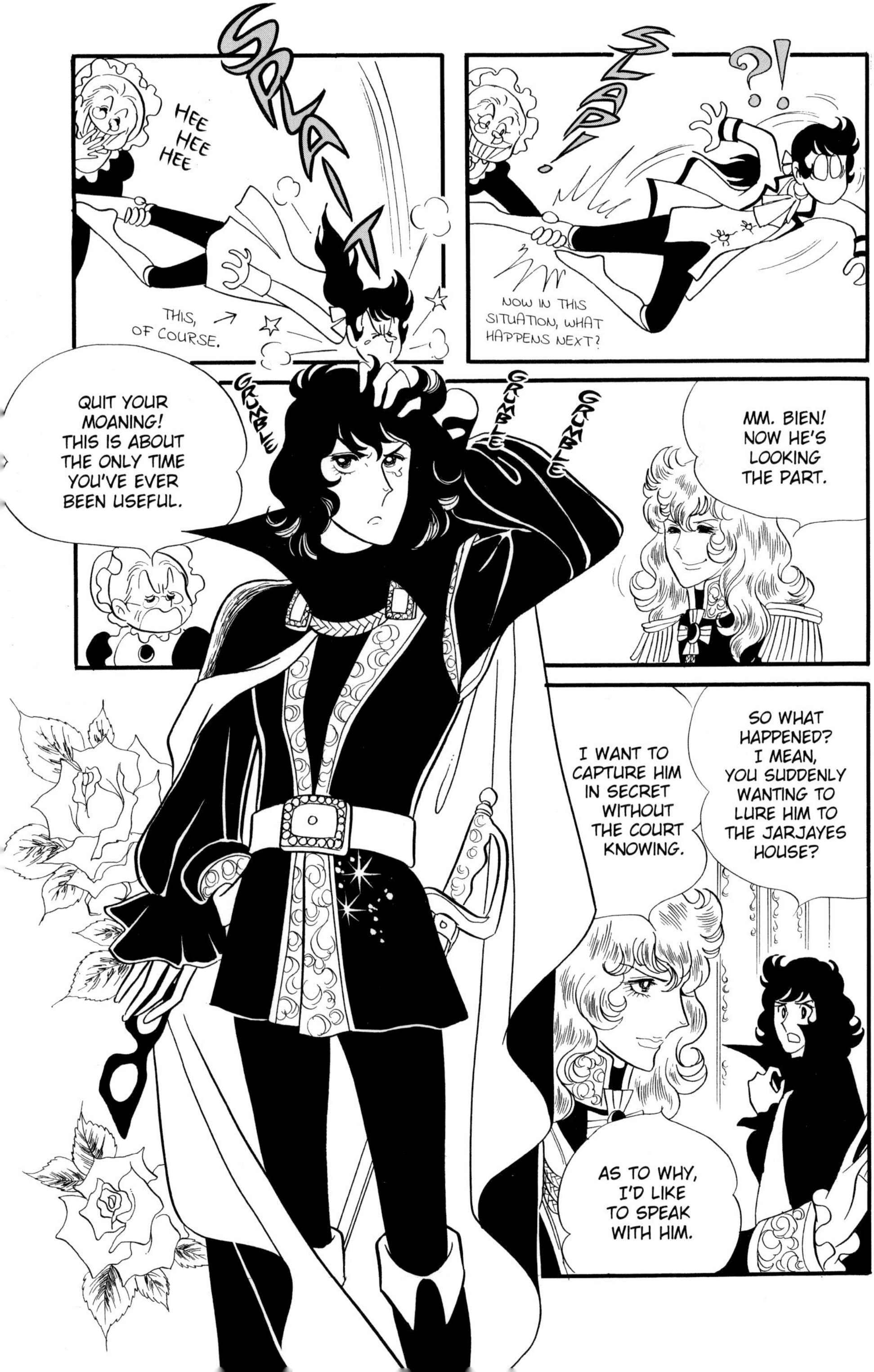
SLAP!
?!
NOW IN THIS SITUATION, WHAT HAPPENS NEXT?
HEE HEE HEE
SPLA-T
THIS, OF COURSE.
MM. BIEN! NOW HE'S LOOKING THE PART.
QUIT YOUR MOANING! THIS IS ABOUT THE ONLY TIME YOU'VE EVER BEEN USEFUL.
GRUMBLE GRUMBLE GRUMBLE
SO WHAT HAPPENED? I MEAN, YOU SUDDENLY WANTING TO LURE HIM TO THE JARJAYES HOUSE?
I WANT TO CAPTURE HIM IN SECRET WITHOUT THE COURT KNOWING.
AS TO WHY, I'D LIKE TO SPEAK WITH HIM.

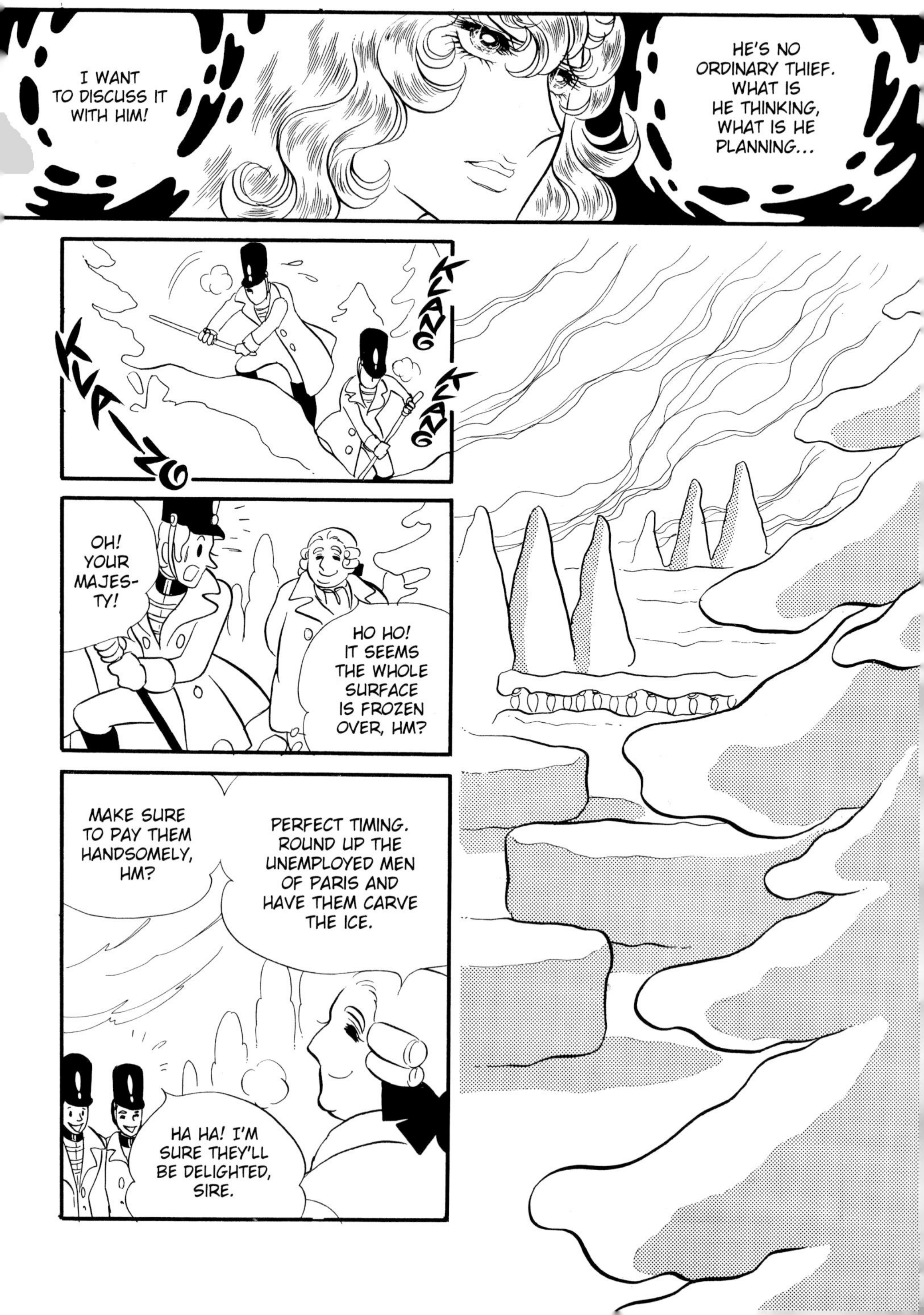
HE'S NO ORDINARY THIEF. WHAT IS HE THINKING, WHAT IS HE PLANNING...
I WANT TO DISCUSS IT WITH HIM!
KLANG KLANG
KVA-ZG
OH! YOUR MAJES-TY!
HO HO! IT SEEMS THE WHOLE SURFACE IS FROZEN OVER, HM?
PERFECT TIMING. ROUND UP THE UNEMPLOYED MEN OF PARIS AND HAVE THEM CARVE THE ICE.
MAKE SURE TO PAY THEM HANDSOMELY, HM?
HA HA! I'M SURE THEY'LL BE DELIGHTED, SIRE.

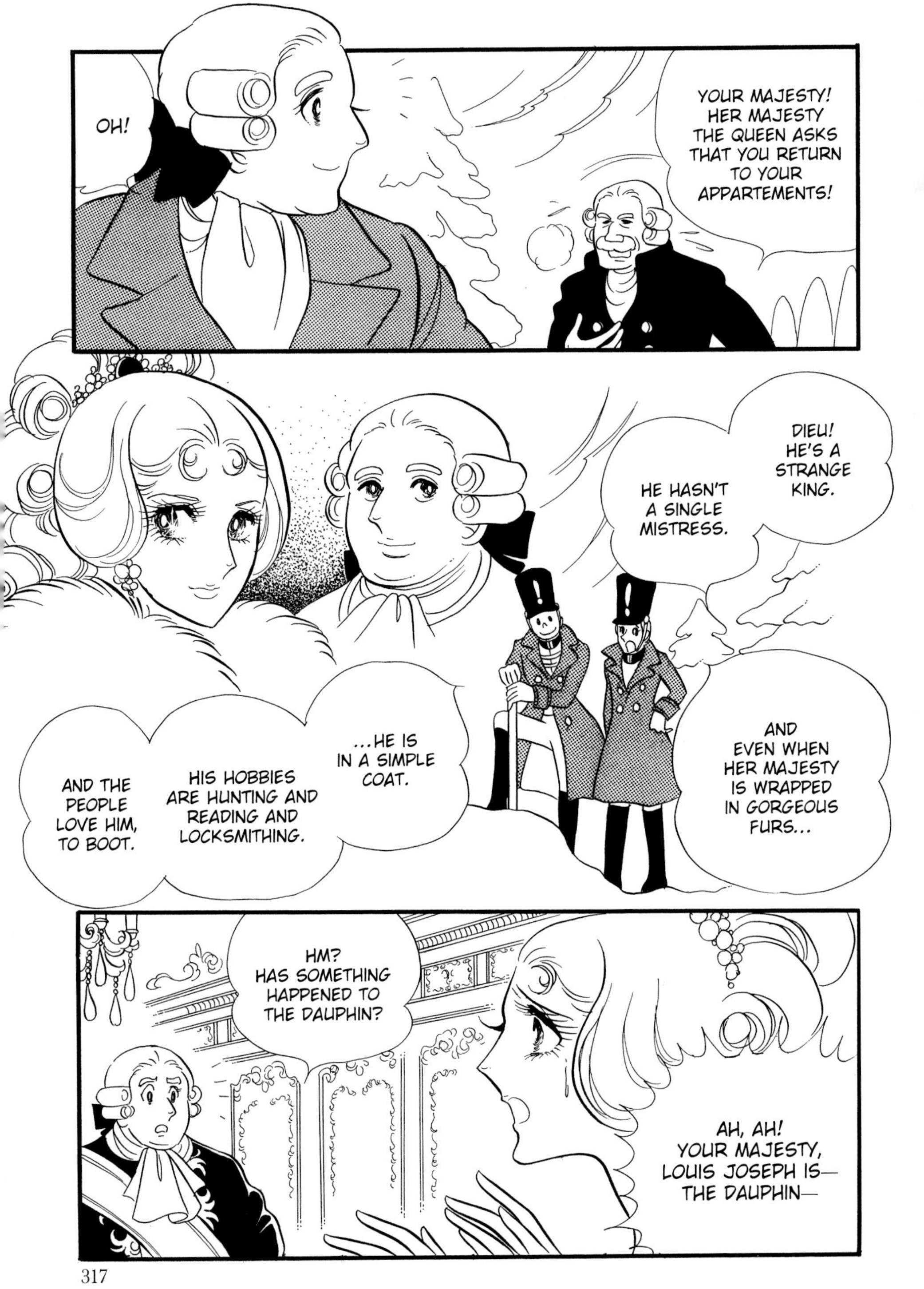
YOUR MAJESTY! HER MAJESTY THE QUEEN ASKS THAT YOU RETURN TO YOUR APPARTEMENTS!
OH!
DIEU! HE'S A STRANGE KING.
HE HASN'T A SINGLE MISTRESS.
AND EVEN WHEN HER MAJESTY IS WRAPPED IN GORGEOUS FURS...
...HE IS IN A SIMPLE COAT.
HIS HOBBIES ARE HUNTING AND READING AND LOCKSMITHING.
AND THE PEOPLE LOVE HIM, TO BOOT.
HM? HAS SOMETHING HAPPENED TO THE DAUPHIN?
AH, AH! YOUR MAJESTY, LOUIS JOSEPH IS— THE DAUPHIN—

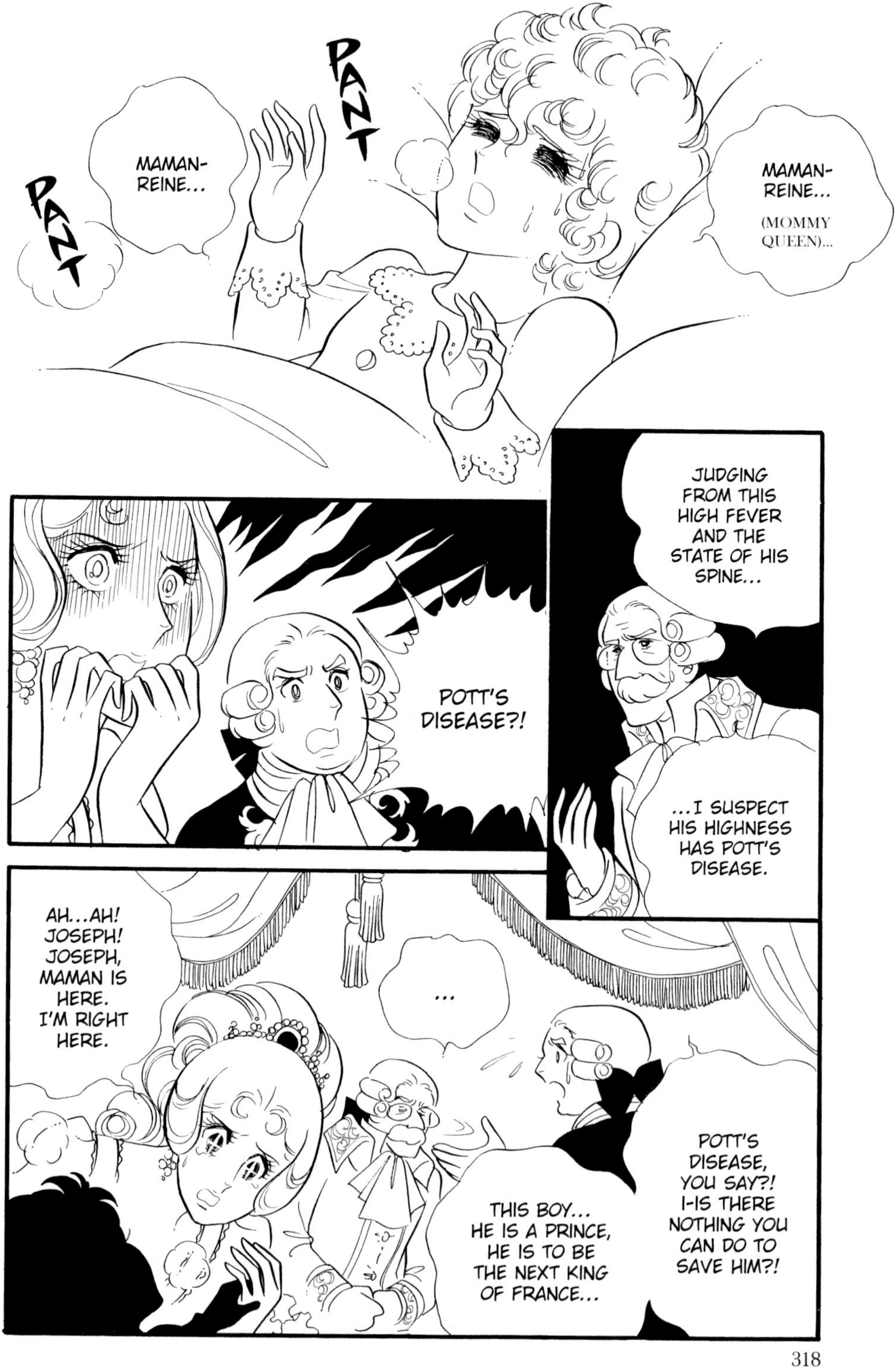

MAMAN-REINE... (MOMMY QUEEN)...
PANT
MAMAN-REINE...
PANT
JUDGING FROM THIS HIGH FEVER AND THE STATE OF HIS SPINE...
...I SUSPECT HIS HIGHNESS HAS POTT'S DISEASE.
POTT'S DISEASE?!
POTT'S DISEASE, YOU SAY?! I-IS THERE NOTHING YOU CAN DO TO SAVE HIM?!
THIS BOY... HE IS A PRINCE, HE IS TO BE THE NEXT KING OF FRANCE...
...
AH...AH! JOSEPH! JOSEPH, MAMAN IS HERE. I'M RIGHT HERE.

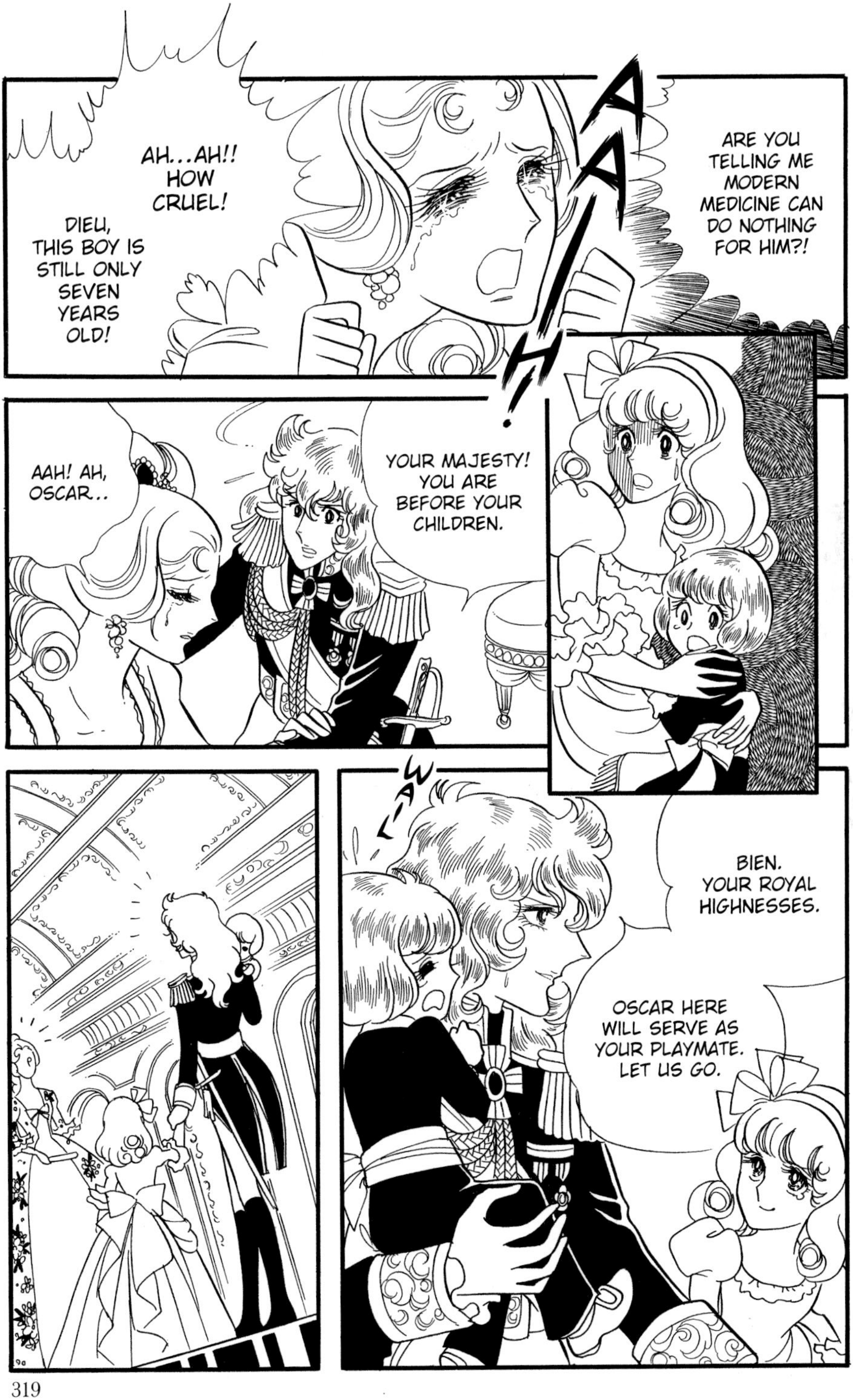
ARE YOU TELLING ME MODERN MEDICINE CAN DO NOTHING FOR HIM?!
AAAH!
AH...AH!! HOW CRUEL!
DIEU, THIS BOY IS STILL ONLY SEVEN YEARS OLD!
YOUR MAJESTY! YOU ARE BEFORE YOUR CHILDREN.
AAH! AH, OSCAR..
WA-I
BIEN. YOUR ROYAL HIGHNESSES.
OSCAR HERE WILL SERVE AS YOUR PLAYMATE. LET US GO.

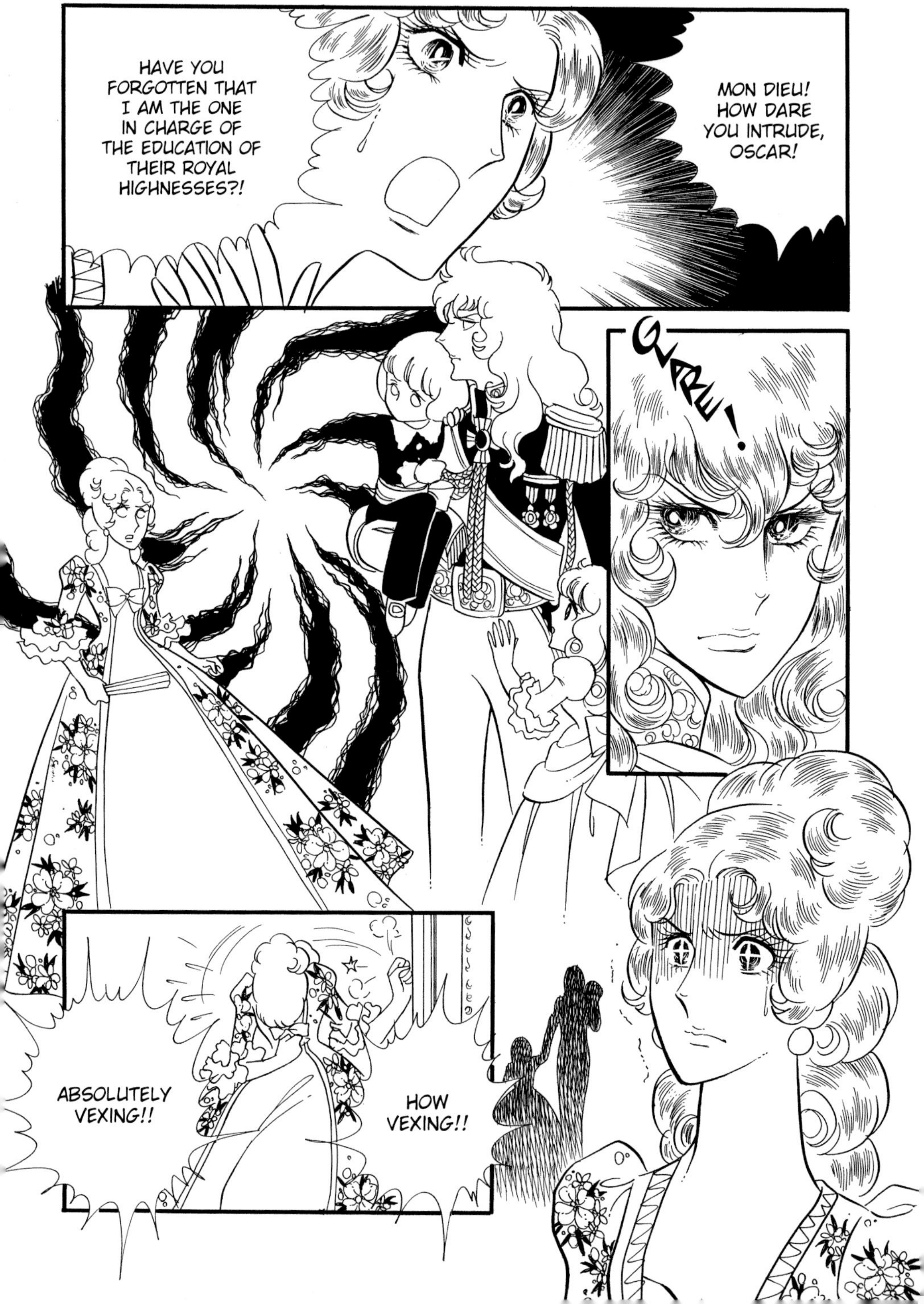
MON DIEU! HOW DARE YOU INTRUDE, OSCAR!
HAVE YOU FORGOTTEN THAT I AM THE ONE IN CHARGE OF THE EDUCATION OF THEIR ROYAL HIGHNESSES?!
GLARE!
HOW VEXING!!
ABSOLUTELY VEXING!!

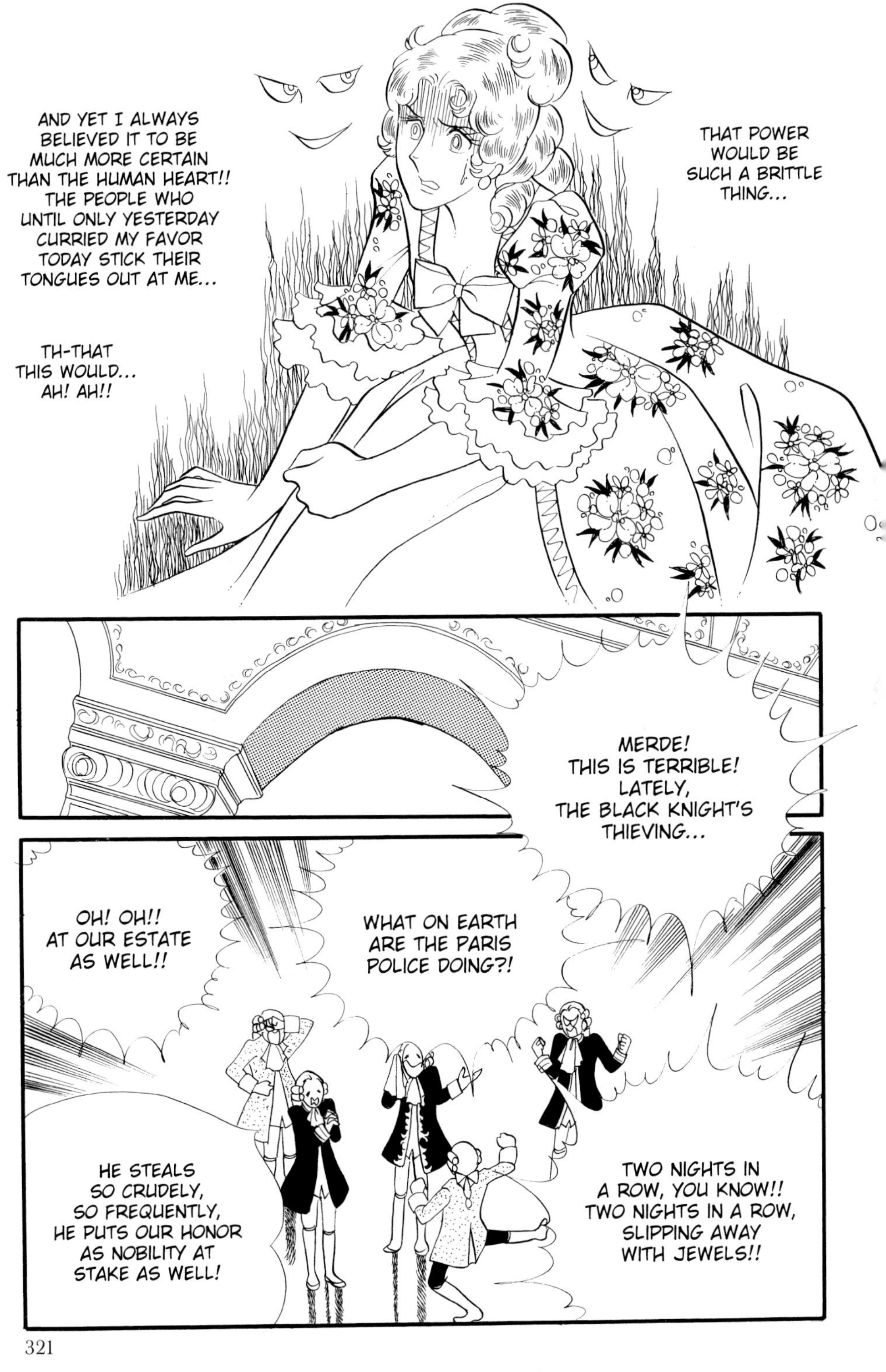
THAT POWER WOULD BE SUCH A BRITTLE THING...
AND YET I ALWAYS BELIEVED IT TO BE MUCH MORE CERTAIN THAN THE HUMAN HEART!! THE PEOPLE WHO UNTIL ONLY YESTERDAY CURRIED MY FAVOR TODAY STICK THEIR TONGUES OUT AT ME...
TH-THAT THIS WOULD... AH! AH!!
MERDE! THIS IS TERRIBLE! LATELY, THE BLACK KNIGHT'S THIEVING...
WHAT ON EARTH ARE THE PARIS POLICE DOING?!
OH! OH!! AT OUR ESTATE AS WELL!!
TWO NIGHTS IN A ROW, YOU KNOW!! TWO NIGHTS IN A ROW, SLIPPING AWAY WITH JEWELS!!
HE STEALS SO CRUDELY, SO FREQUENTLY, HE PUTS OUR HONOR AS NOBILITY AT STAKE AS WELL!

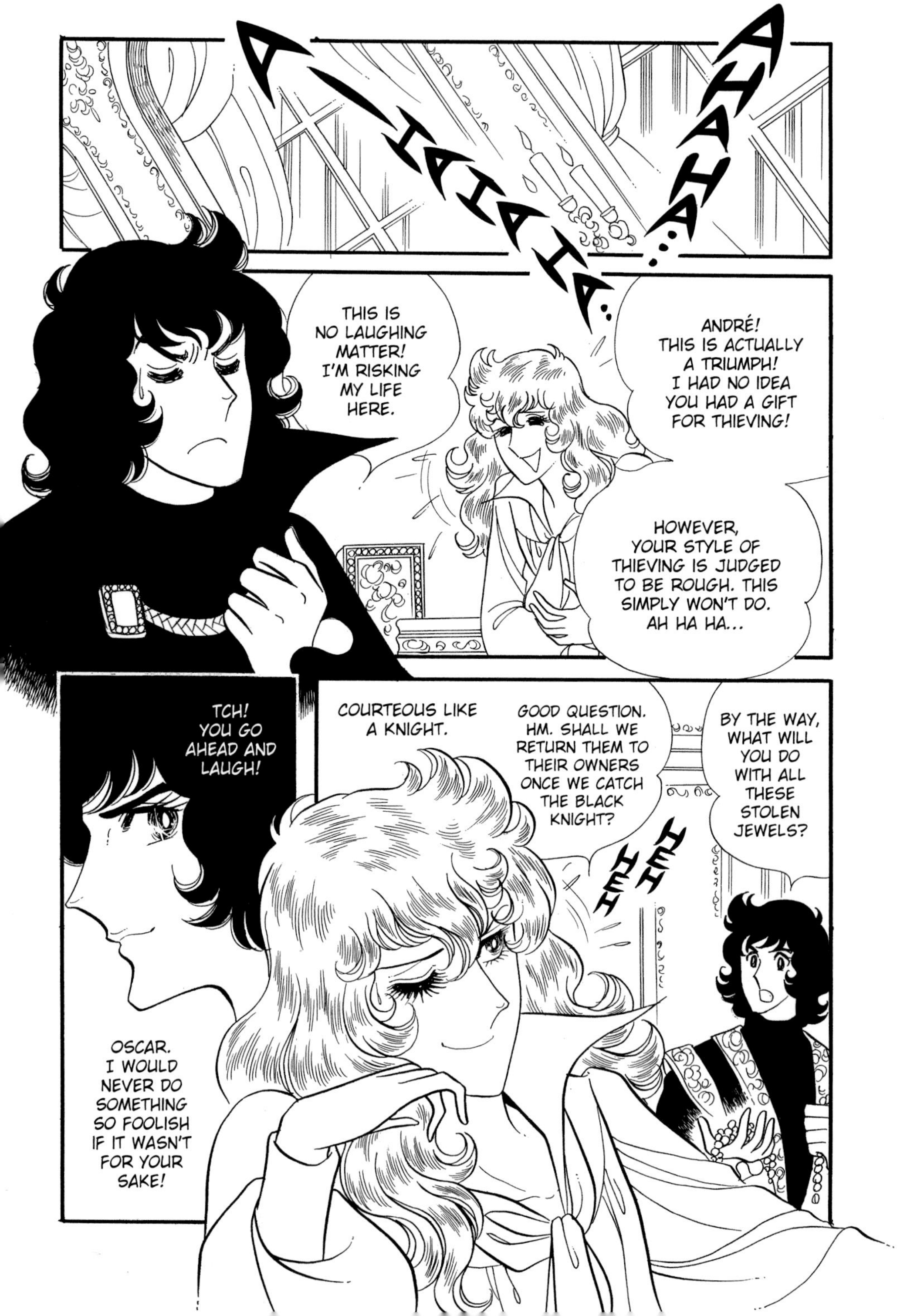

AHAHA...
A—HAHAHAHA..
ANDRÉ! THIS IS ACTUALLY A TRIUMPH! I HAD NO IDEA YOU HAD A GIFT FOR THIEVING!
HOWEVER, YOUR STYLE OF THIEVING IS JUDGED TO BE ROUGH. THIS SIMPLY WON'T DO. AH HA HA...
THIS IS NO LAUGHING MATTER! I'M RISKING MY LIFE HERE.
BY THE WAY, WHAT WILL YOU DO WITH ALL THESE STOLEN JEWELS?
HEH HEH
GOOD QUESTION. HM. SHALL WE RETURN THEM TO THEIR OWNERS ONCE WE CATCH THE BLACK KNIGHT?
COURTEOUS LIKE A KNIGHT.
TCH! YOU GO AHEAD AND LAUGH!
OSCAR. I WOULD NEVER DO SOMETHING SO FOOLISH IF IT WASN'T FOR YOUR SAKE!

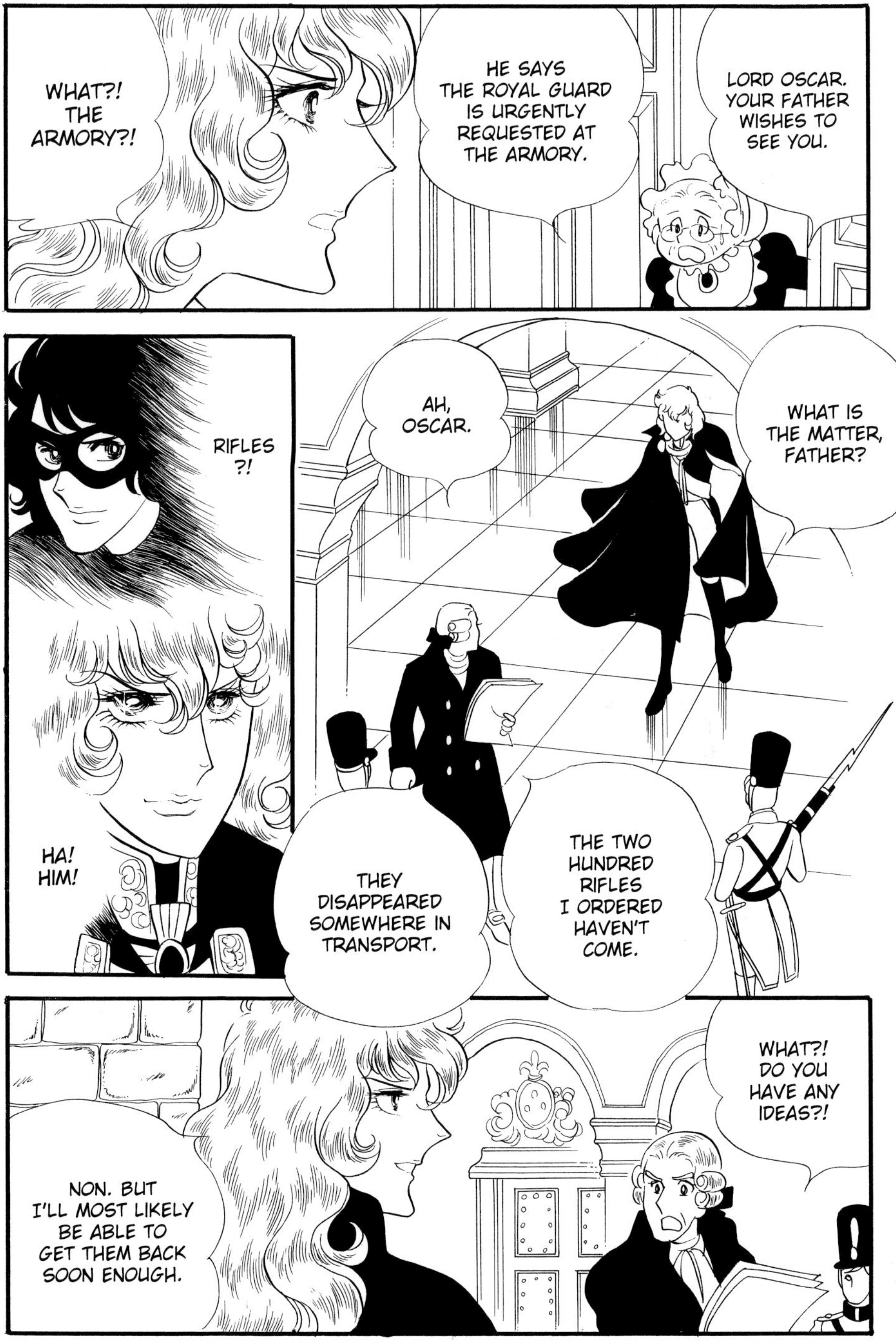
LORD OSCAR. YOUR FATHER WISHES TO SEE YOU.
HE SAYS THE ROYAL GUARD IS URGENTLY REQUESTED AT THE ARMORY.
WHAT?! THE ARMORY?!
WHAT IS THE MATTER, FATHER?
AH, OSCAR.
THE TWO HUNDRED RIFLES I ORDERED HAVEN'T COME.
THEY DISAPPEARED SOMEWHERE IN TRANSPORT.
RIFLES?!
HA! HIM!
WHAT?! DO YOU HAVE ANY IDEAS?!
NON. BUT I'LL MOST LIKELY BE ABLE TO GET THEM BACK SOON ENOUGH.

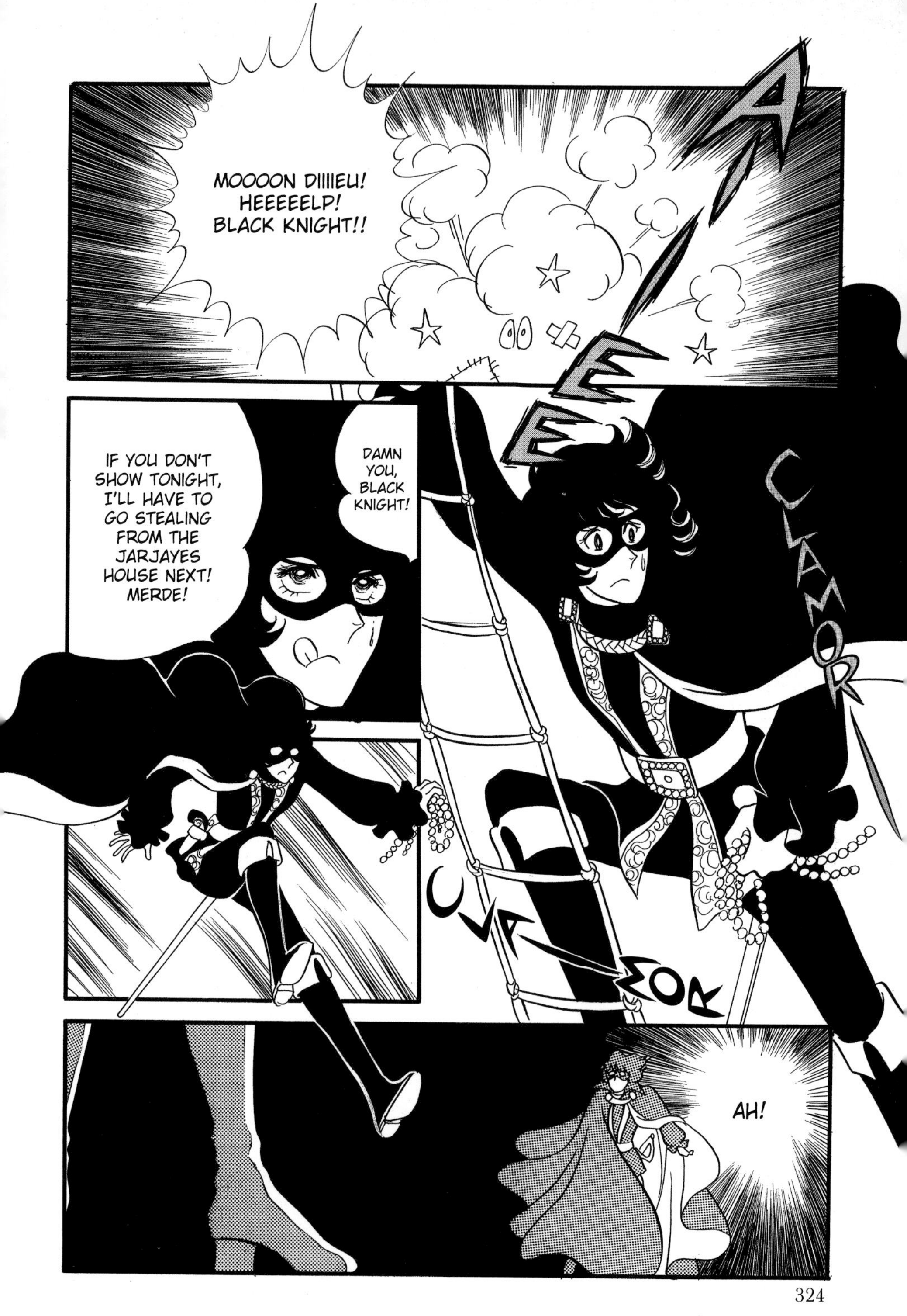
AIEEE
MOOOON DIIIIEU! HEEEEELP! BLACK KNIGHT!!
DAMN YOU, BLACK KNIGHT!
CLAMOR
CLAMOR
IF YOU DON'T SHOW TONIGHT, I'LL HAVE TO GO STEALING FROM THE JARJAYES HOUSE NEXT! MERDE!
AH!

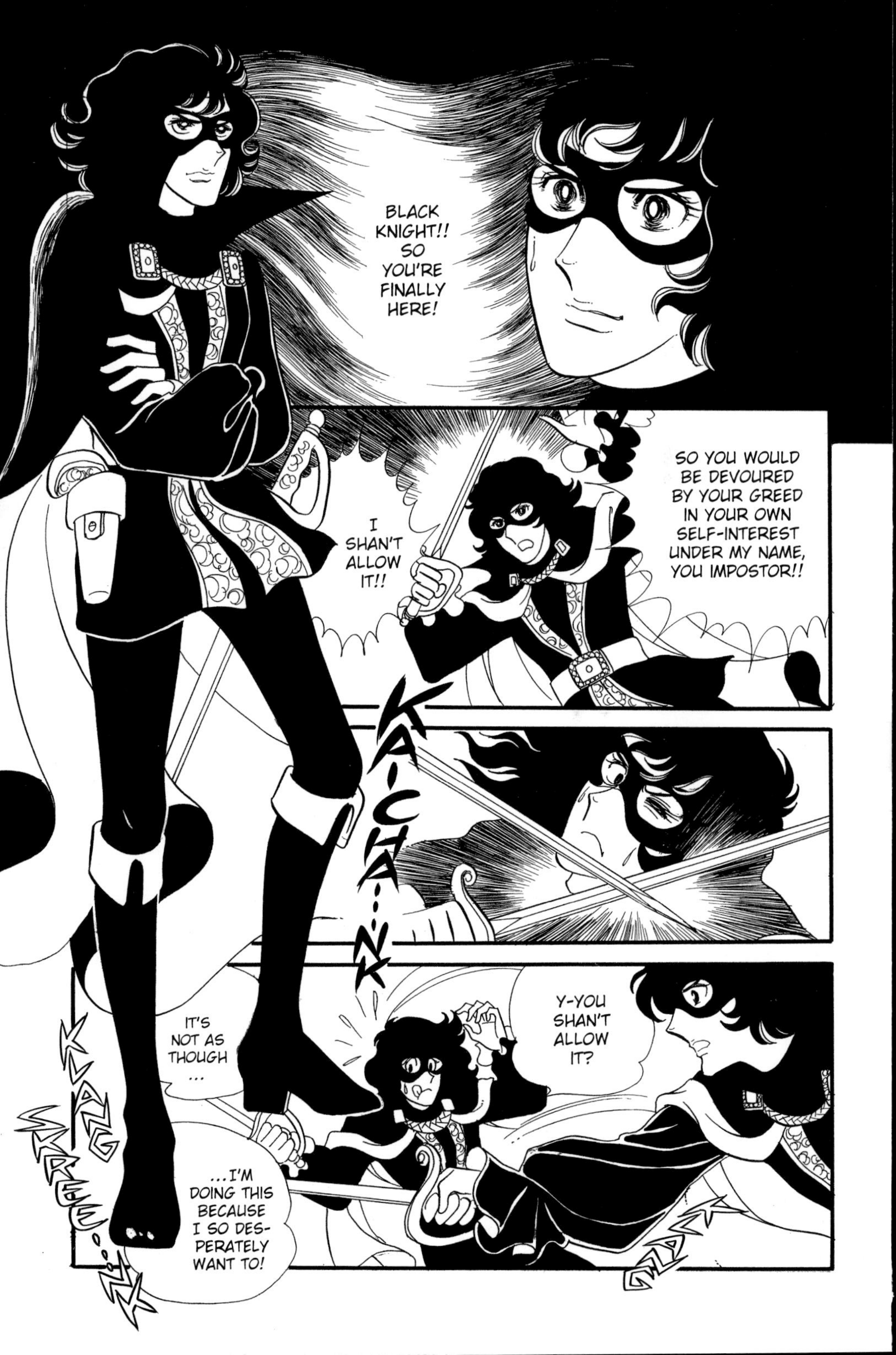
BLACK KNIGHT!! SO YOU'RE FINALLY HERE!
SO YOU WOULD BE DEVOURED BY YOUR GREED IN YOUR OWN SELF-INTEREST UNDER MY NAME, YOU IMPOSTOR!!
I SHAN'T ALLOW IT!!
KA-CHA...NK
Y-YOU SHAN'T ALLOW IT?
IT'S NOT AS THOUGH ...
...I'M DOING THIS BECAUSE I SO DES-PERATELY WANT TO!
KWANG
SKREEE...NK

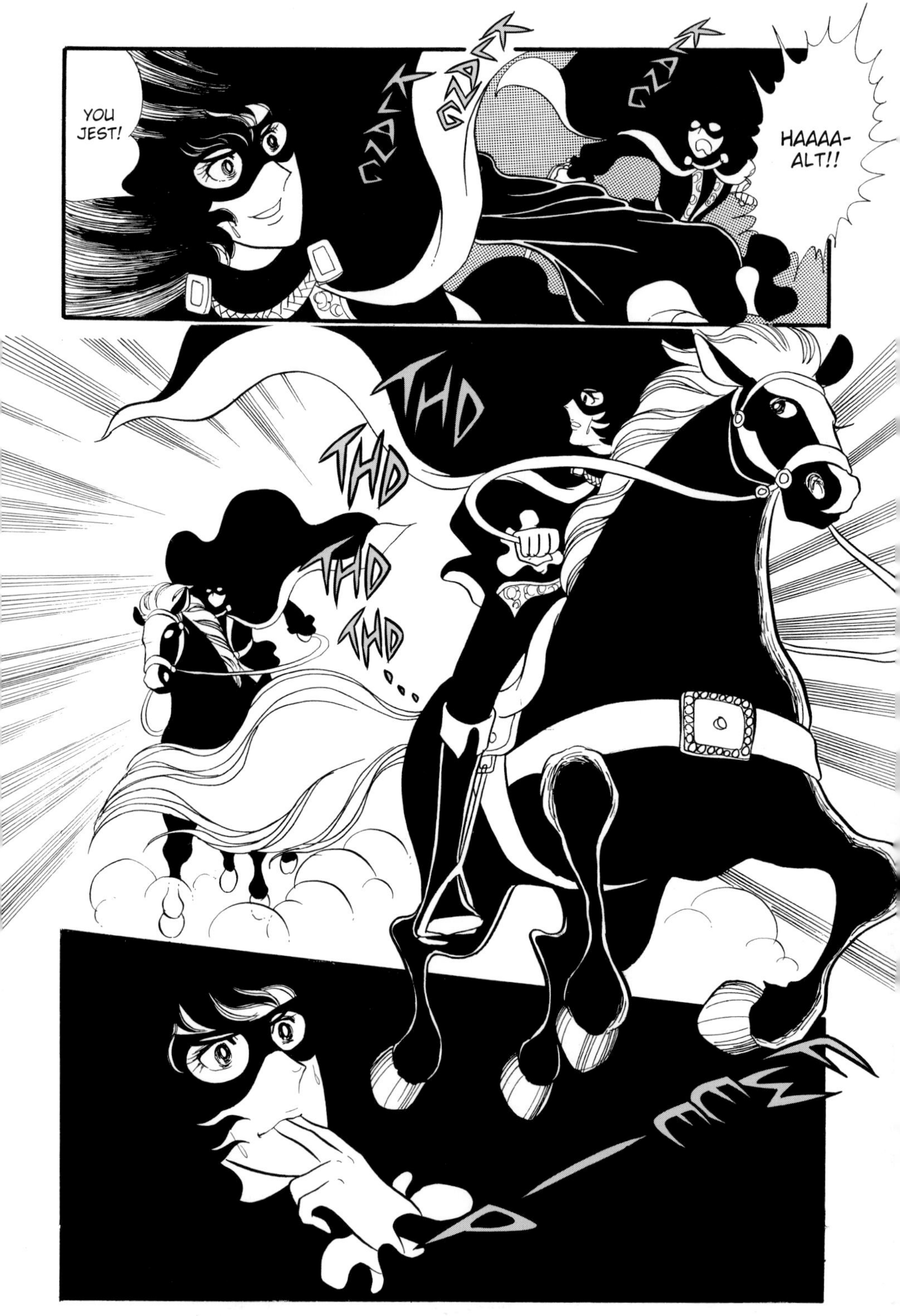
HAAAAA-
ALT!!
GZACK
GZACK
GZACK
YOU
JEST!
THD
THD
THD
THD...

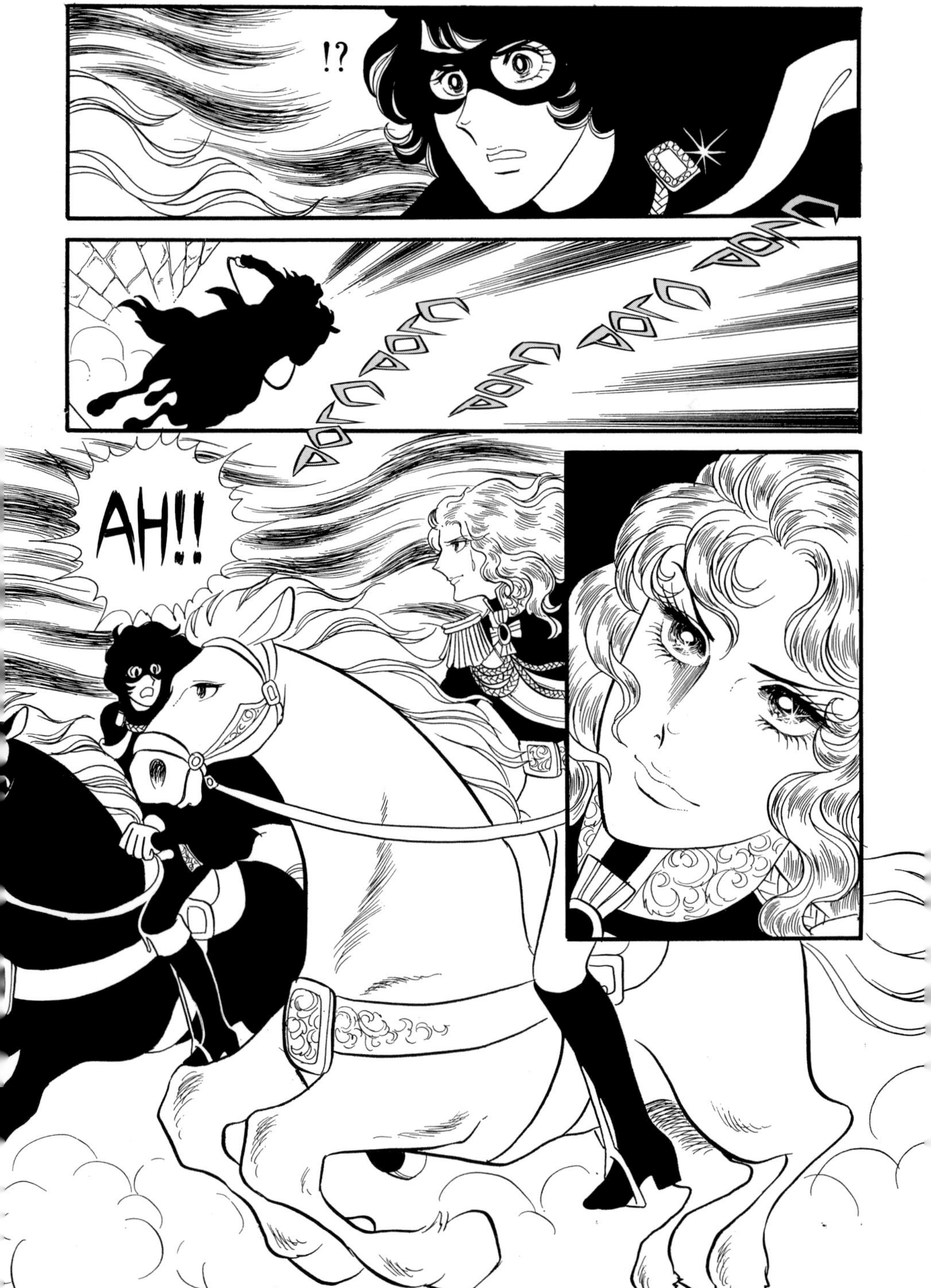
!?
AH!!

SPECIAL TREASURED GALLERY

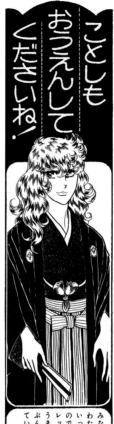

ことしも
おうえんして
くださいね！
みなさん、お正月はいかがでしたか？
わたくしは、和服でくつろいだオスカルと
いっしょに、のんびりすごそうと思っていた
のですが、4日から大阪でひらかれたマーガ
レットまんが展に出席したりして、あっとい
うまにすぎた感じ。ことしこそは、もっとじ
ぶんの時間をつくって、すきなことをと思っ
ているのですが、どうなることやら……！
池田理代子

PLEASE JOIN US AGAIN THIS YEAR!

HOW WAS YOUR NEW YEAR HOLIDAY, EVERYONE? I WAS PLANNING TO TAKE IT EASY WITH OSCAR LOUNGING IN JAPANESE STYLE CLOTHES, BUT I ENDED UP ATTENDING AN EXHIBIT PUT ON BY MARGARET IN OSAKA STARTING ON THE 4TH. IT SEEMED LIKE THE HOLIDAY WAS OVER BEFORE I KNEW IT. THIS YEAR, FOR SURE, I'D LIKE TO MAKE SOME TIME FOR MYSELF AND DO THE THINGS I LIKE, BUT I DON'T KNOW HOW THAT WILL GO!

RIYOKO IKEDA

1973 WEEKLY MARGARET MAGAZINE ISSUE 06 NEW YEAR'S GREETING INSET

⚜EXPLODING IN POPULARITY!!
A GRAND MASTERPIECE SWIRLING WITH EXCITEMENT AND EMOTION!!

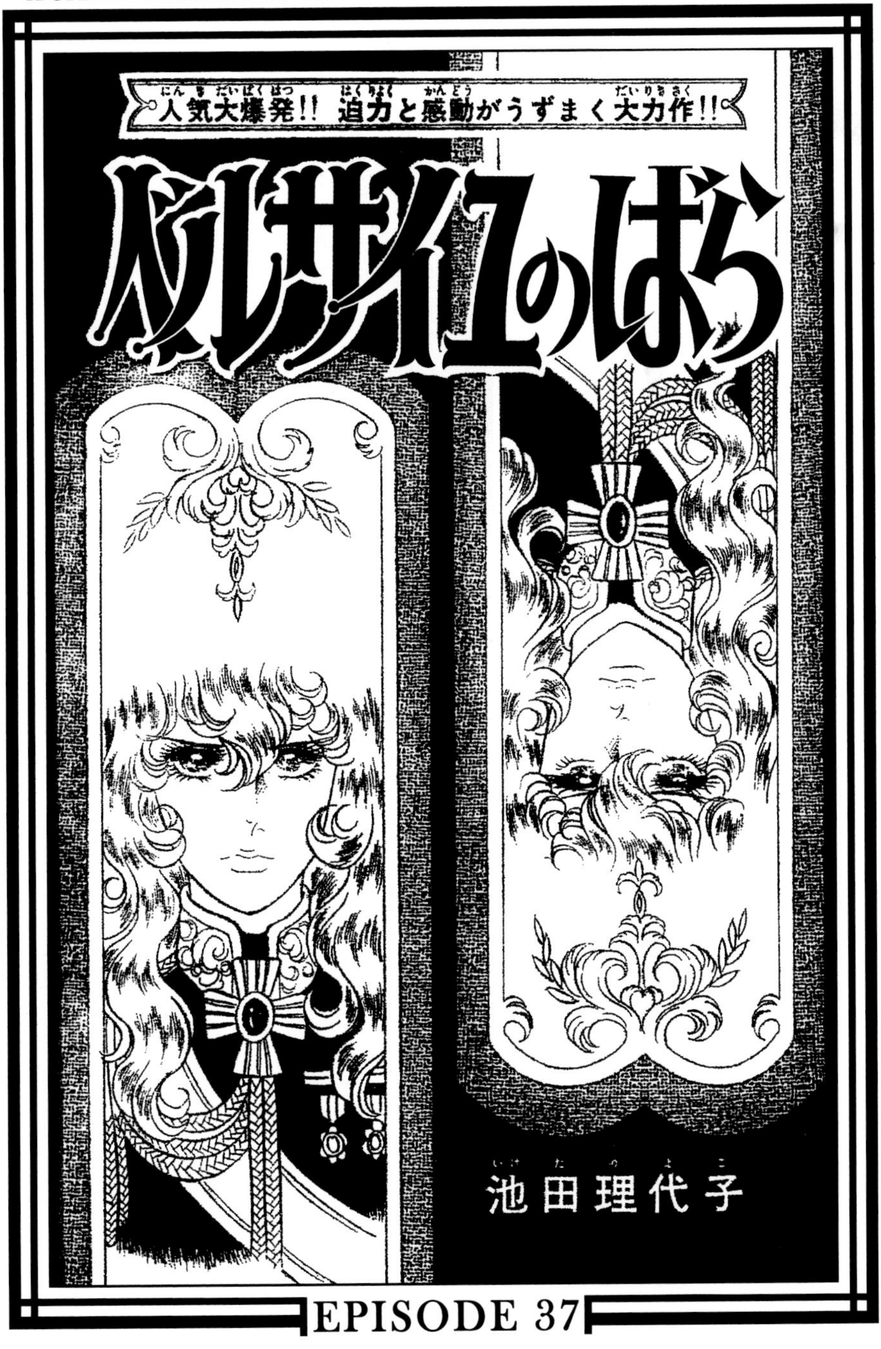
人気大爆発!! 迫力と感動がうずまく大力作!!
ベルサイユのばら
池田理代子
EPISODE 37

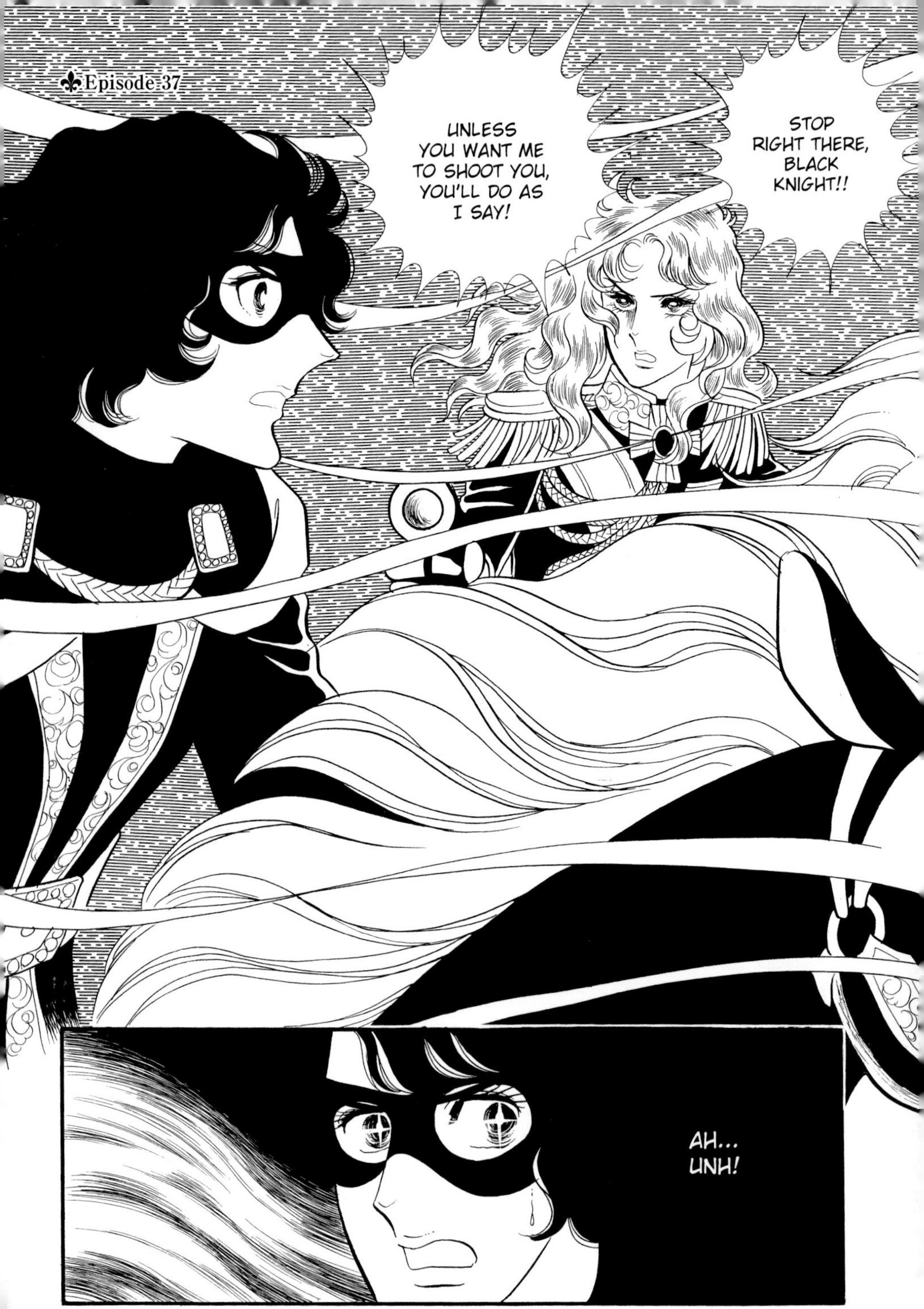
STOP RIGHT THERE, BLACK KNIGHT!!
UNLESS YOU WANT ME TO SHOOT YOU, YOU'LL DO AS I SAY!
AH... UNH!

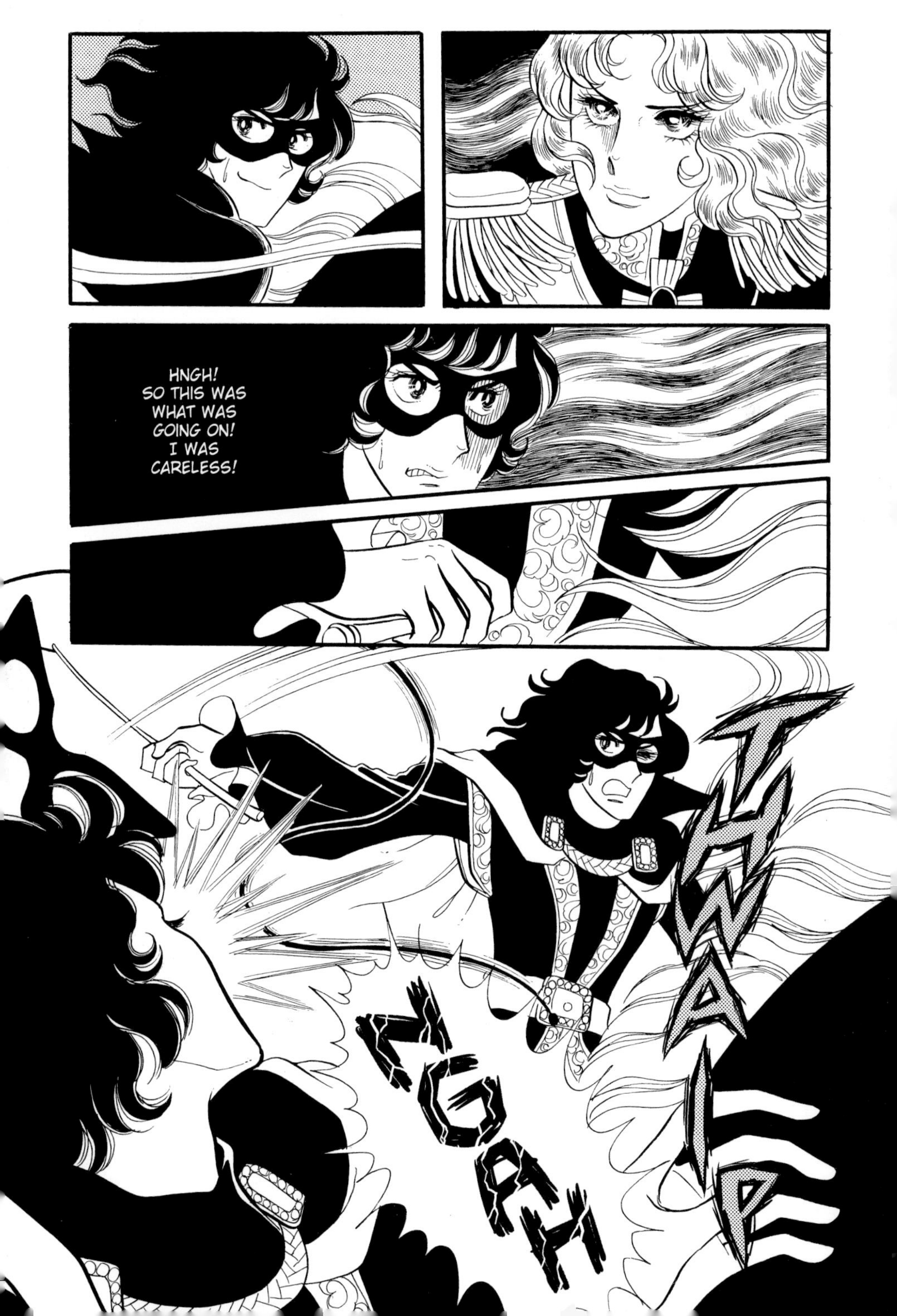
HNGH! SO THIS WAS WHAT WAS GOING ON! I WAS CARELESS!
THWAP
NGAH

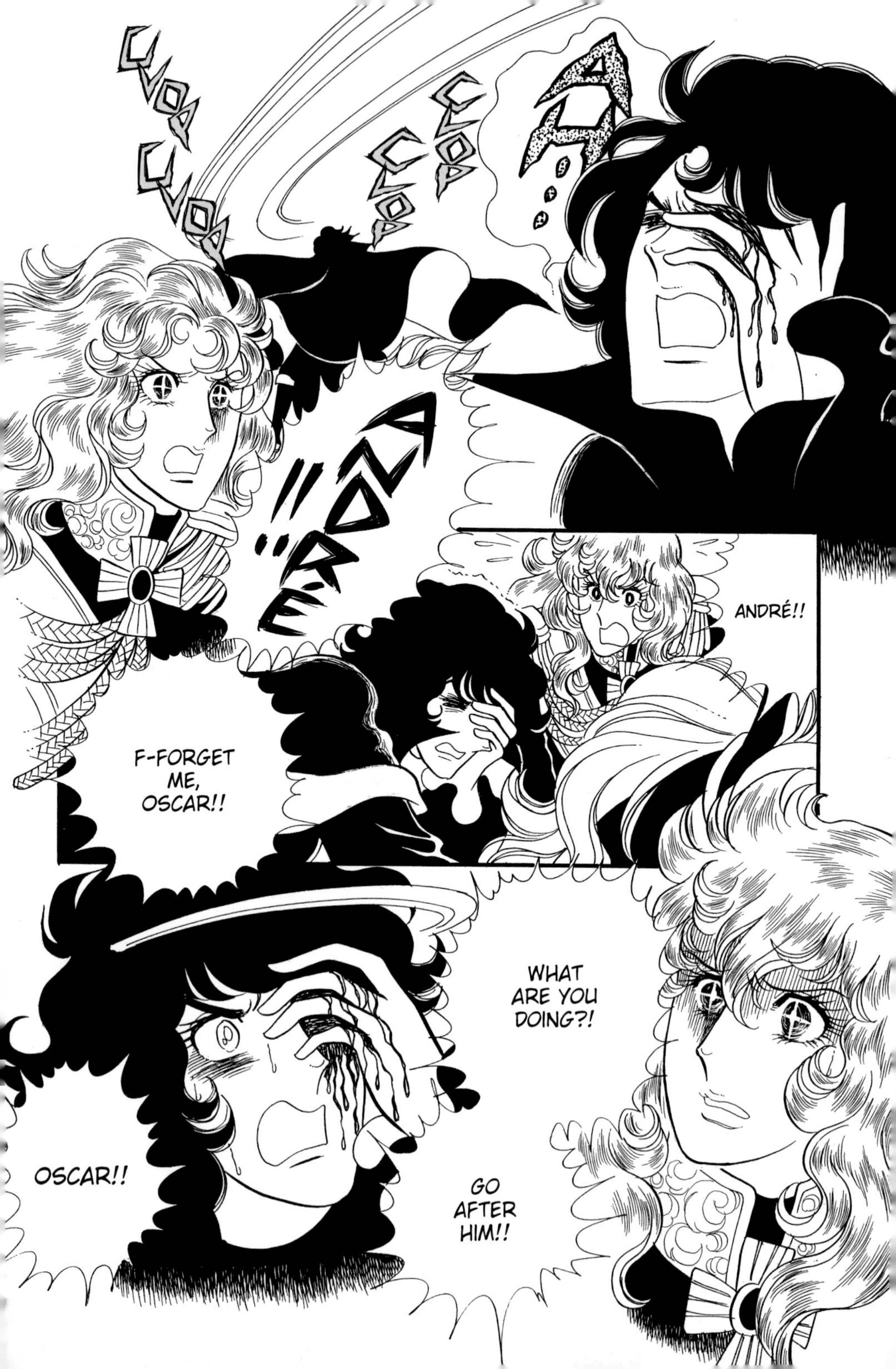
AA
CLOP CLOP
CLOP CLOP
ANDRÉ!!
ANDRÉ!!
F-FORGET ME, OSCAR!!
WHAT ARE YOU DOING?!
GO AFTER HIM!!
OSCAR!!

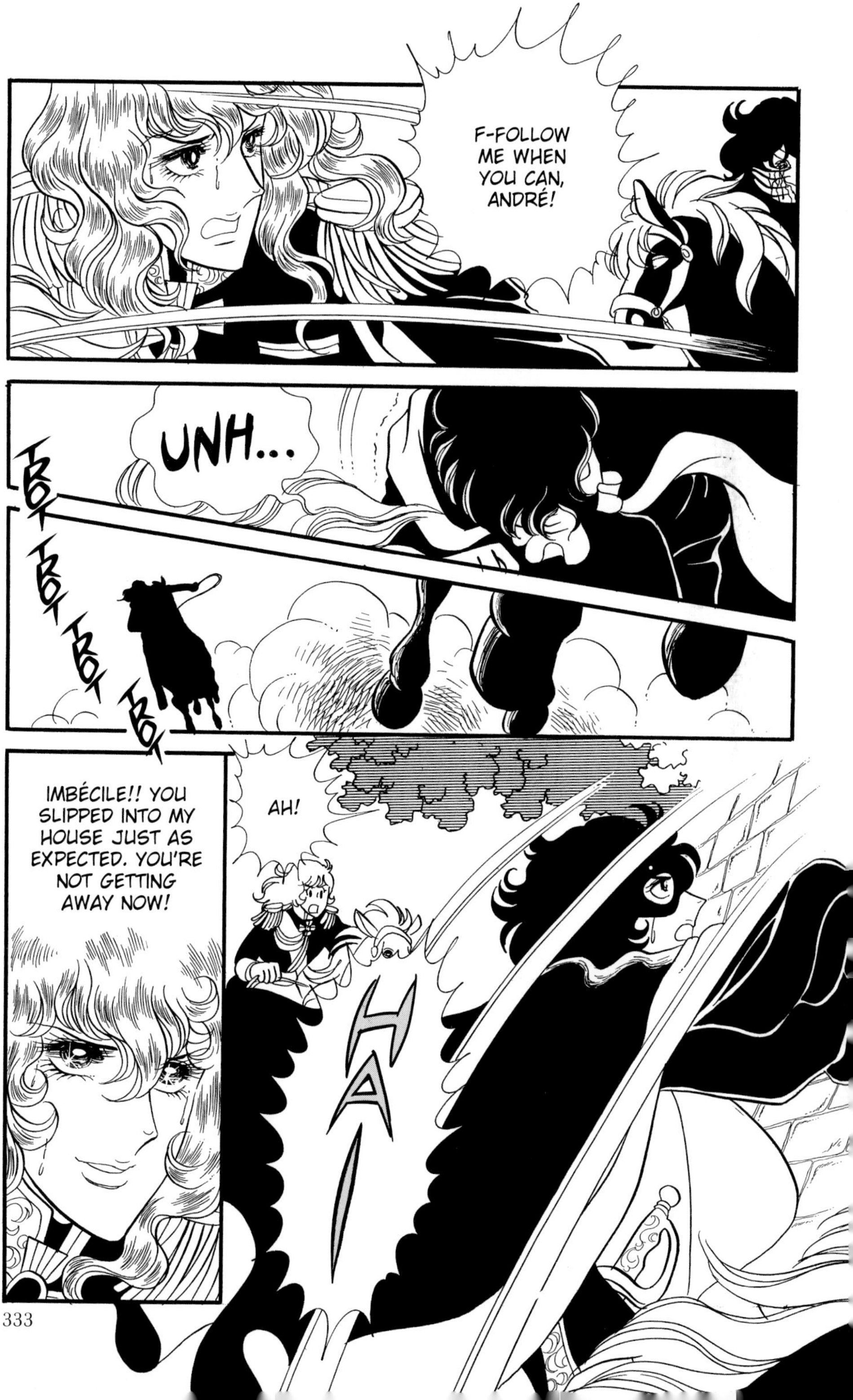
F-FOLLOW ME WHEN YOU CAN, ANDRÉ!
UNH...
TROT TROT TROT TROT
AH!
HAI
IMBÉCILE!! YOU SLIPPED INTO MY HOUSE JUST AS EXPECTED. YOU'RE NOT GETTING AWAY NOW!

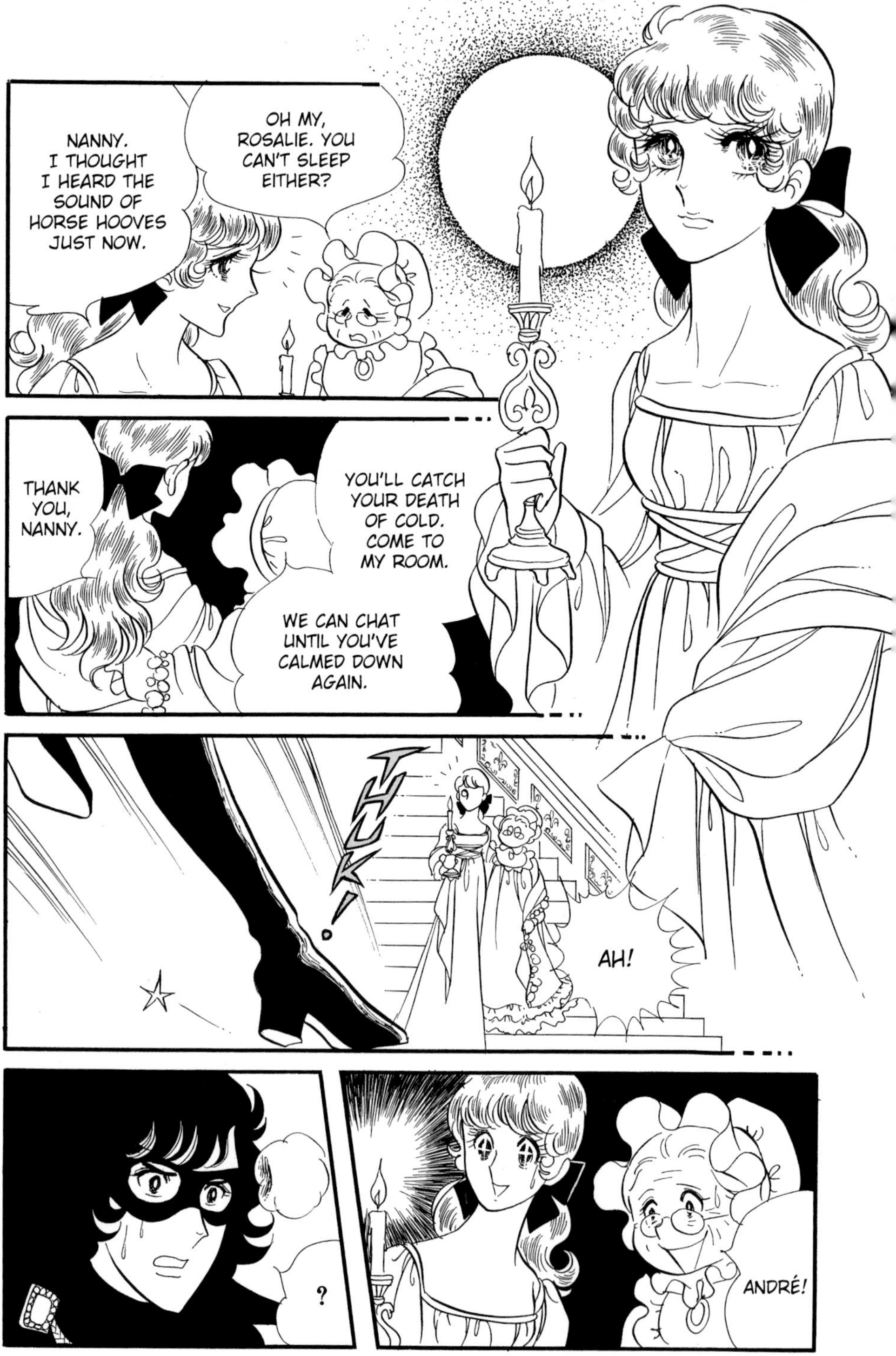
OH MY, ROSALIE. YOU CAN'T SLEEP EITHER?
NANNY. I THOUGHT I HEARD THE SOUND OF HORSE HOOVES JUST NOW.
YOU'LL CATCH YOUR DEATH OF COLD. COME TO MY ROOM.
WE CAN CHAT UNTIL YOU'VE CALMED DOWN AGAIN.
THANK YOU, NANNY.
THUNK!
AH!
ANDRÉ!
?

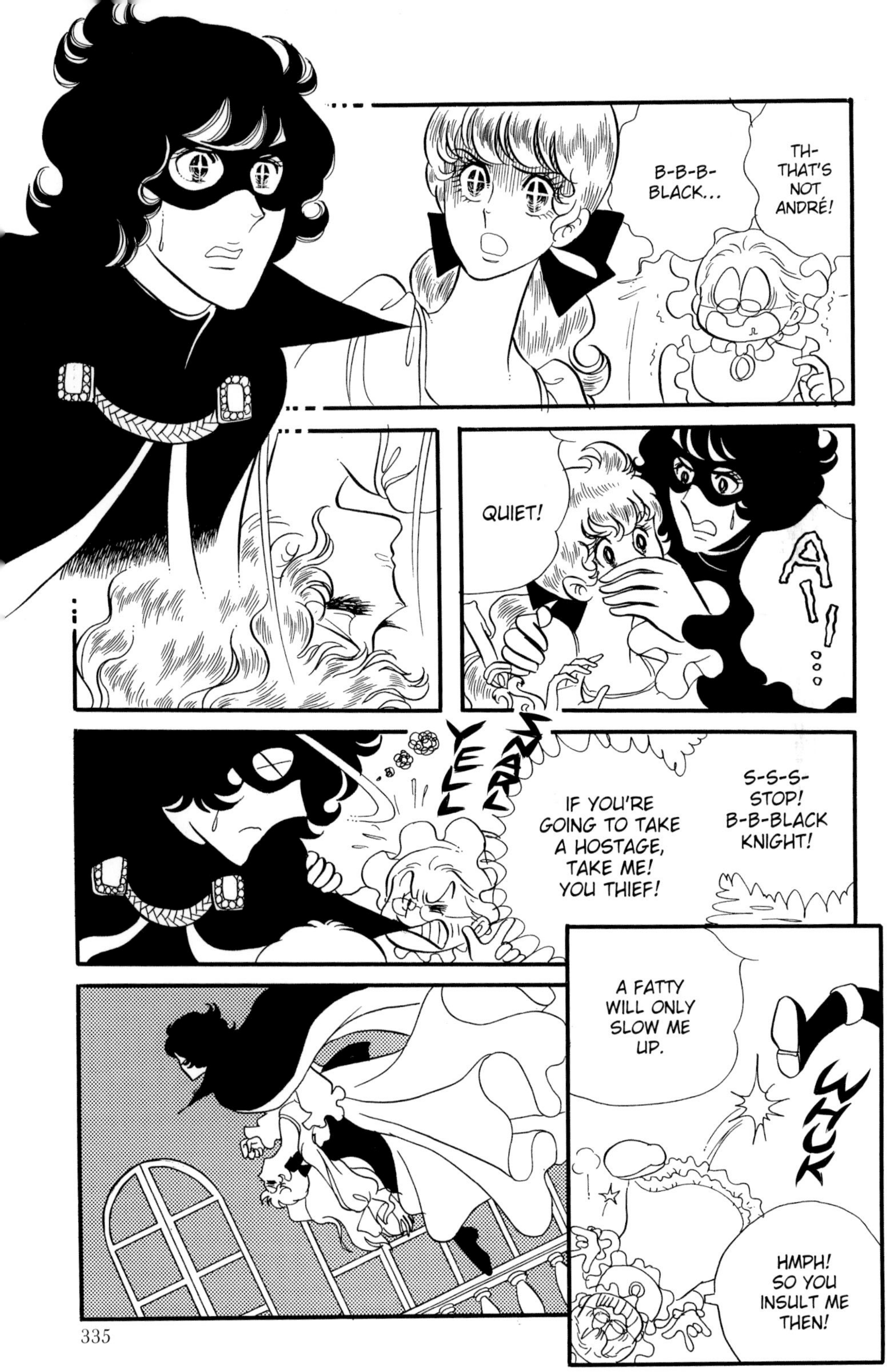
TH-THAT'S NOT ANDRÉ!
B-B-B-BLACK...
QUIET!
A!!...
S-S-S-STOP! B-B-BLACK KNIGHT!
IF YOU'RE GOING TO TAKE A HOSTAGE, TAKE ME! YOU THIEF!
YELL
A FATTY WILL ONLY SLOW ME UP.
WHUK
HMPH! SO YOU INSULT ME THEN!

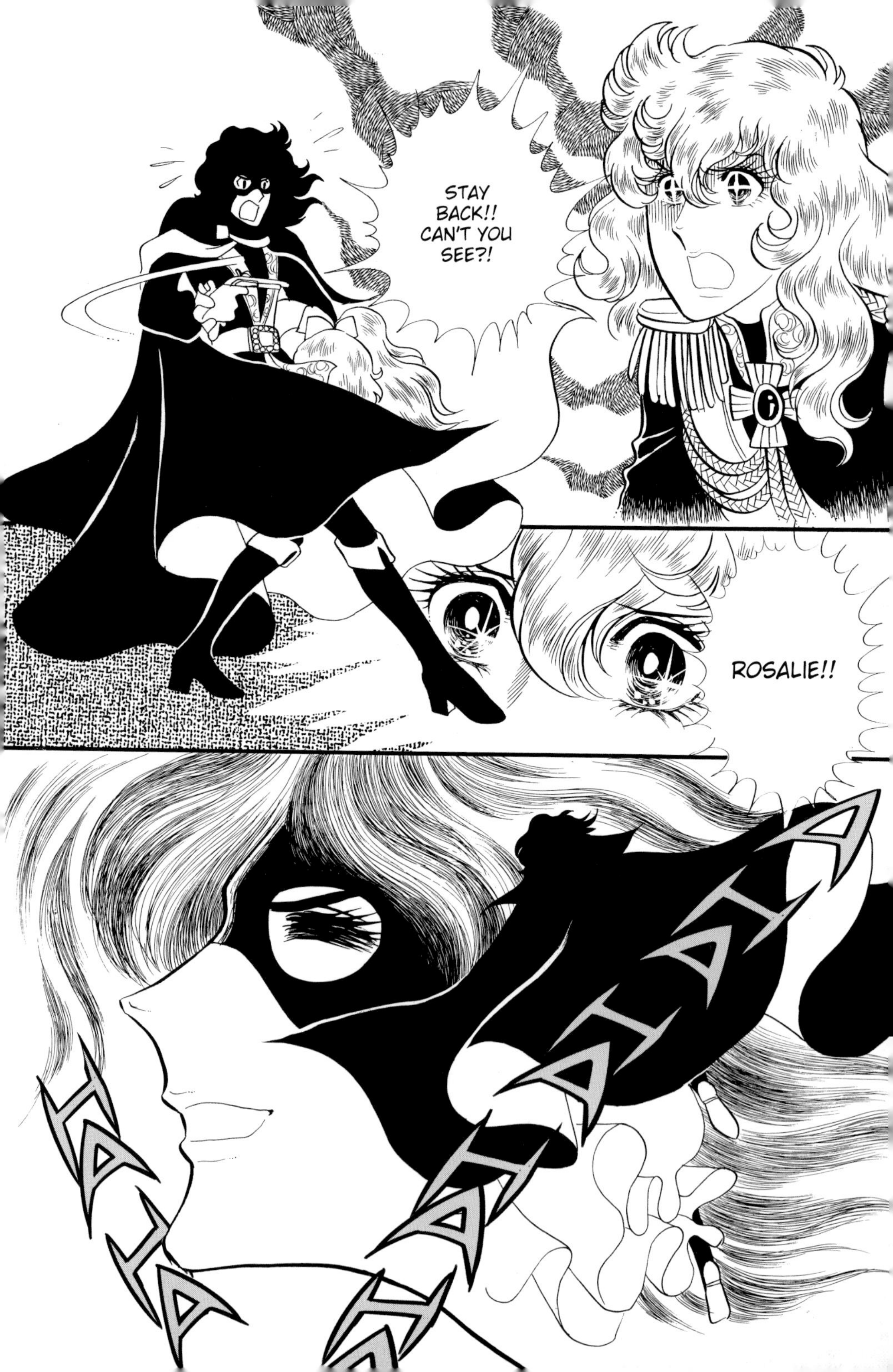
STAY BACK!! CAN'T YOU SEE?!
ROSALIE!!
HAHAHAHAHAHA
HAHAHA

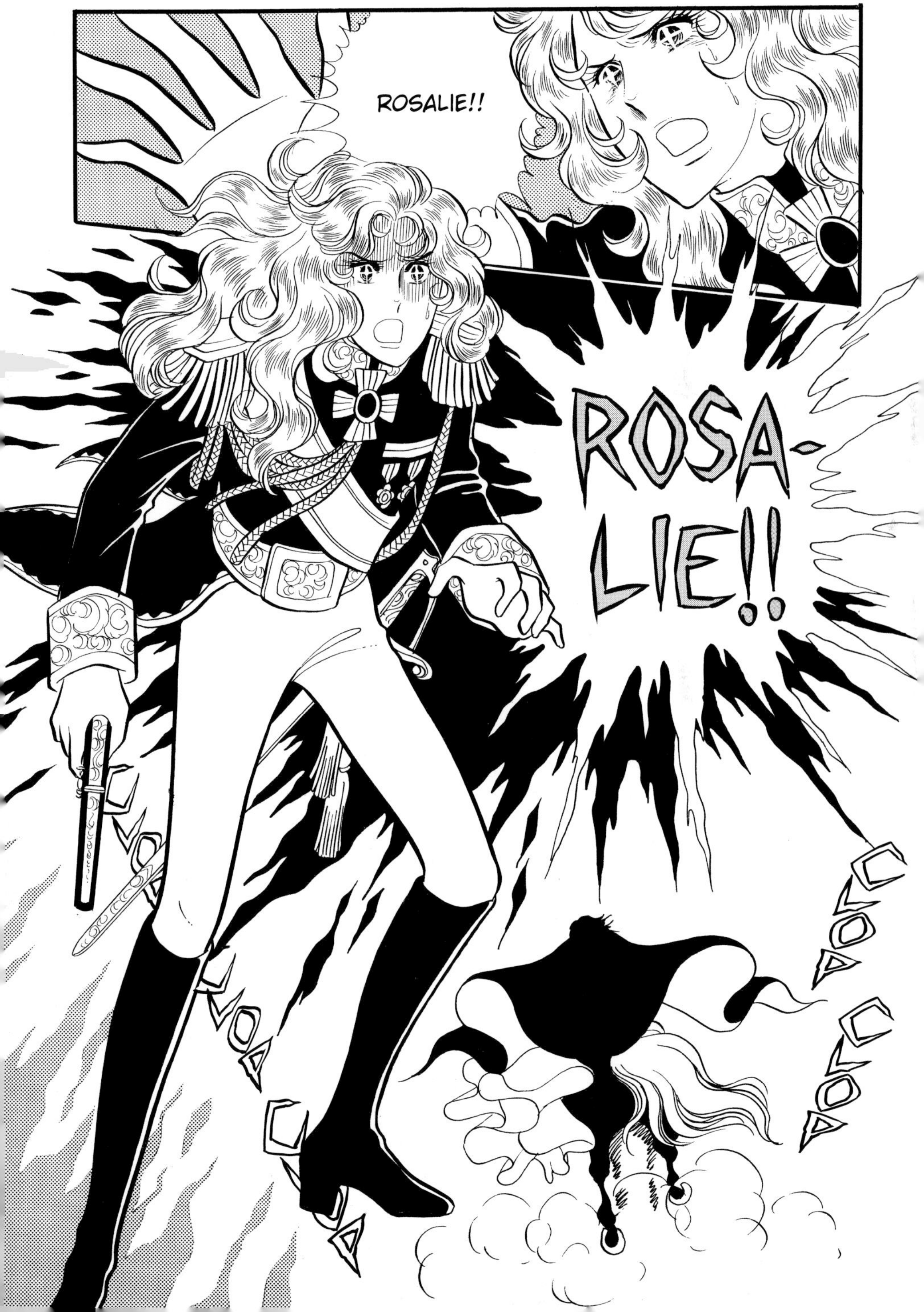
ROSALIE!!
ROSA-
LIE!!

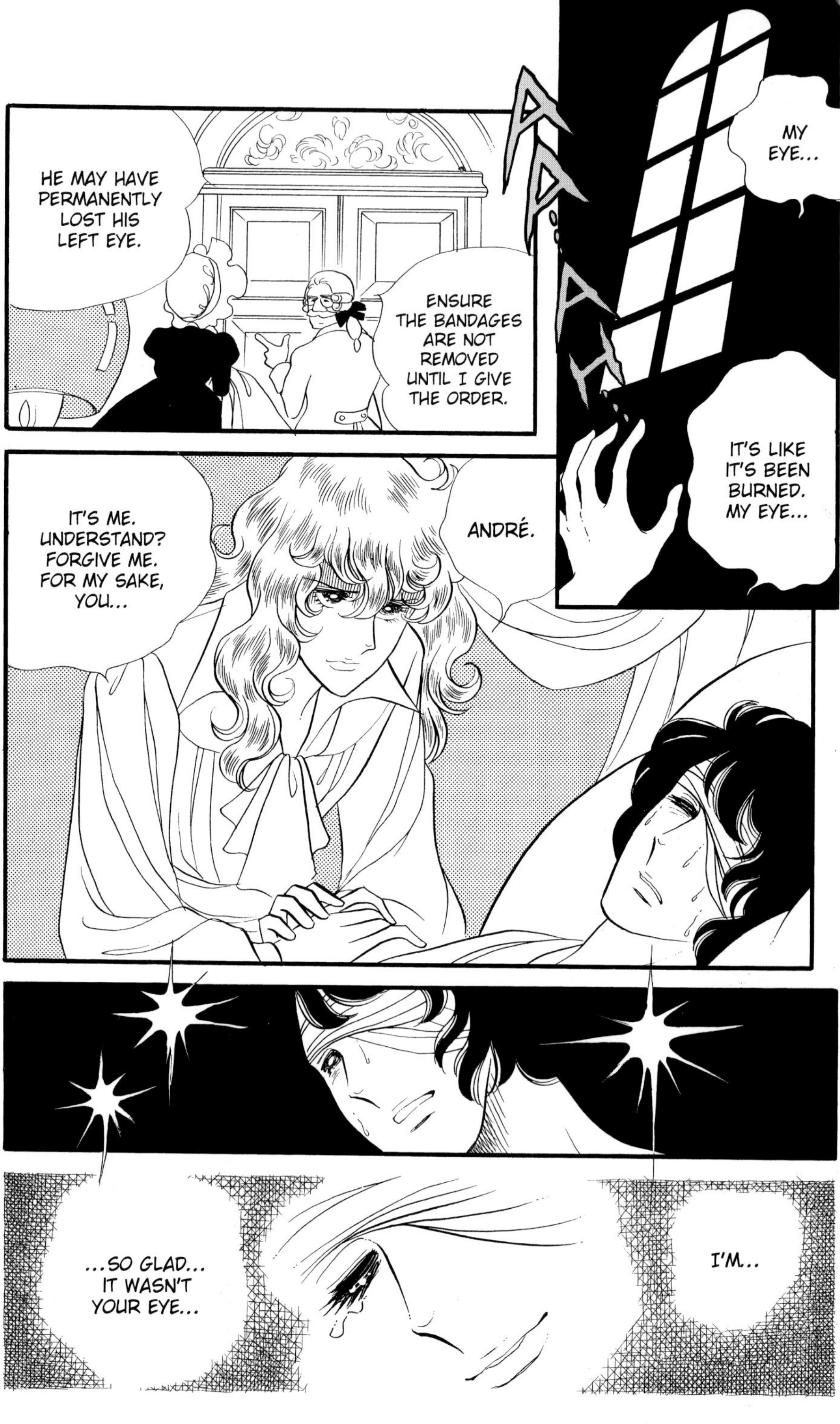
AAAH
MY EYE...
IT'S LIKE IT'S BEEN BURNED. MY EYE...
HE MAY HAVE PERMANENTLY LOST HIS LEFT EYE.
ENSURE THE BANDAGES ARE NOT REMOVED UNTIL I GIVE THE ORDER.
ANDRÉ.
IT'S ME. UNDERSTAND? FORGIVE ME. FOR MY SAKE, YOU...
I'M...
...SO GLAD... IT WASN'T YOUR EYE...

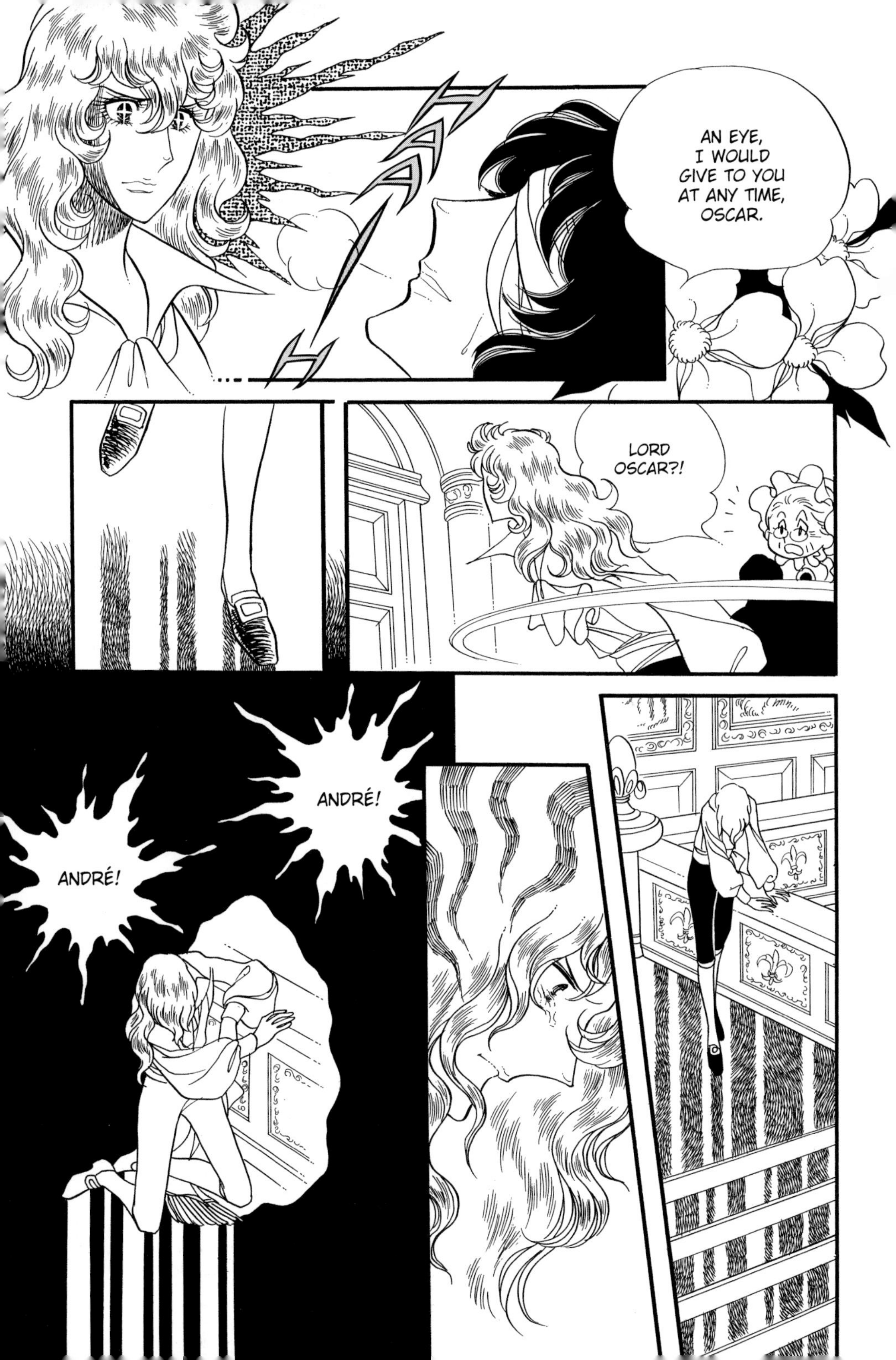
AN EYE, I WOULD GIVE TO YOU AT ANY TIME, OSCAR.
HAAH
LORD OSCAR?!
ANDRÉ!
ANDRÉ!

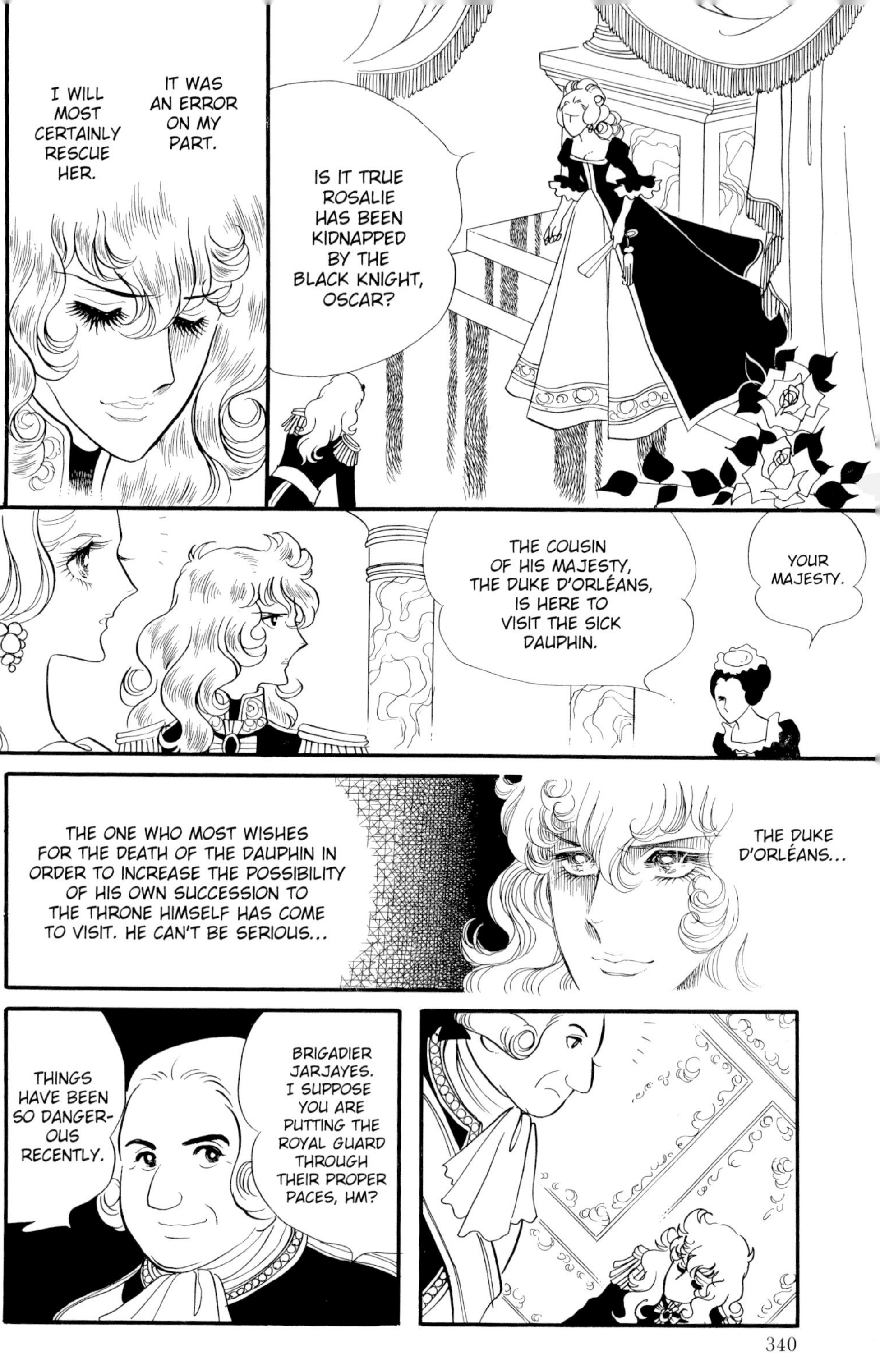
IS IT TRUE ROSALIE HAS BEEN KIDNAPPED BY THE BLACK KNIGHT, OSCAR?
IT WAS AN ERROR ON MY PART.
I WILL MOST CERTAINLY RESCUE HER.
YOUR MAJESTY.
THE COUSIN OF HIS MAJESTY, THE DUKE D'ORLÉANS, IS HERE TO VISIT THE SICK DAUPHIN.
THE DUKE D'ORLÉANS...
THE ONE WHO MOST WISHES FOR THE DEATH OF THE DAUPHIN IN ORDER TO INCREASE THE POSSIBILITY OF HIS OWN SUCCESSION TO THE THRONE HIMSELF HAS COME TO VISIT. HE CAN'T BE SERIOUS...
BRIGADIER JARJAYES. I SUPPOSE YOU ARE PUTTING THE ROYAL GUARD THROUGH THEIR PROPER PACES, HM?
THINGS HAVE BEEN SO DANGER-OUS RECENTLY.

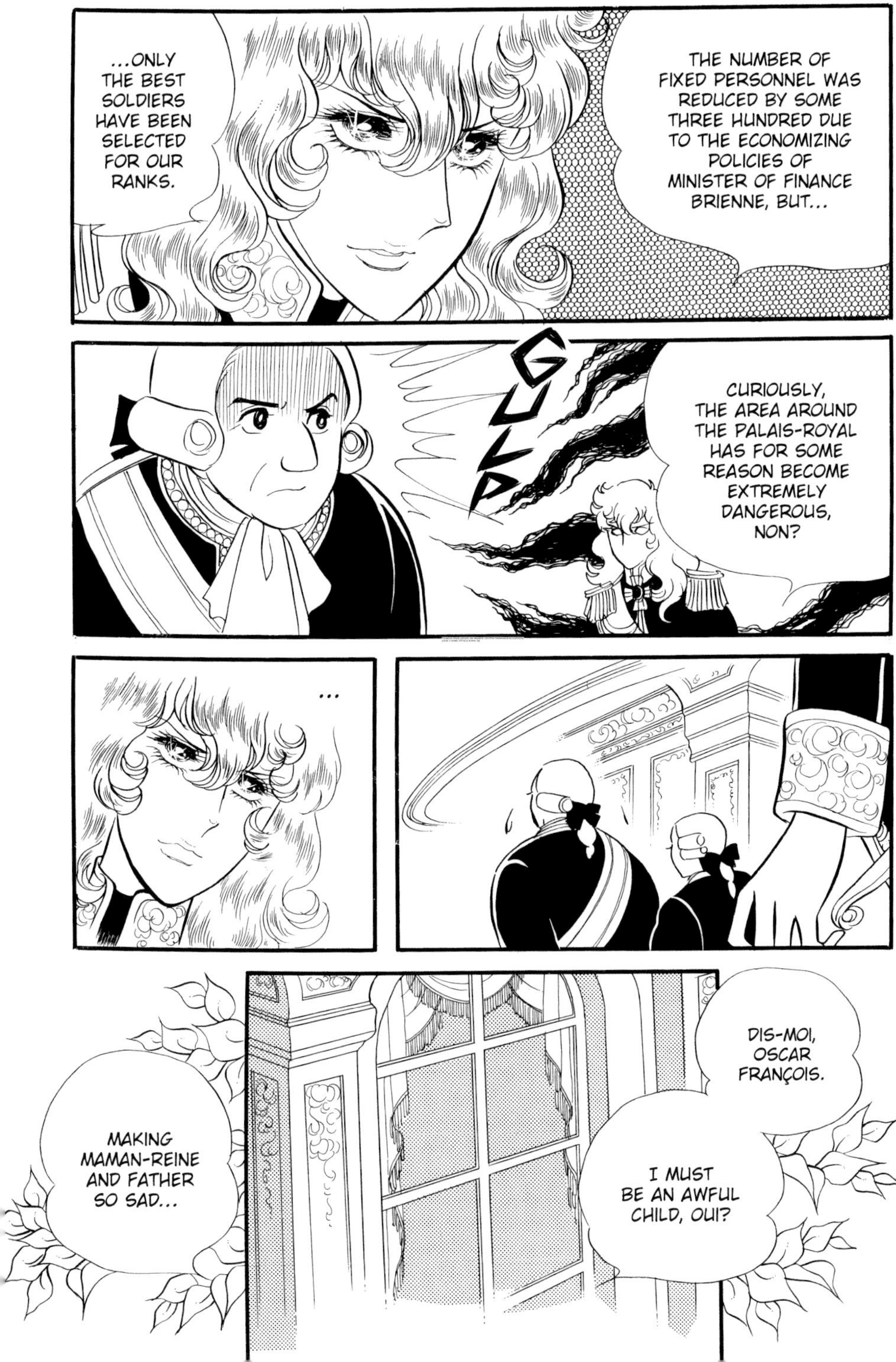
THE NUMBER OF FIXED PERSONNEL WAS REDUCED BY SOME THREE HUNDRED DUE TO THE ECONOMIZING POLICIES OF MINISTER OF FINANCE BRIENNE, BUT...
...ONLY THE BEST SOLDIERS HAVE BEEN SELECTED FOR OUR RANKS.
CURIOUSLY, THE AREA AROUND THE PALAIS-ROYAL HAS FOR SOME REASON BECOME EXTREMELY DANGEROUS, NON?
GULP
...
DIS-MOI, OSCAR FRANÇOIS.
I MUST BE AN AWFUL CHILD, OUI?
MAKING MAMAN-REINE AND FATHER SO SAD...

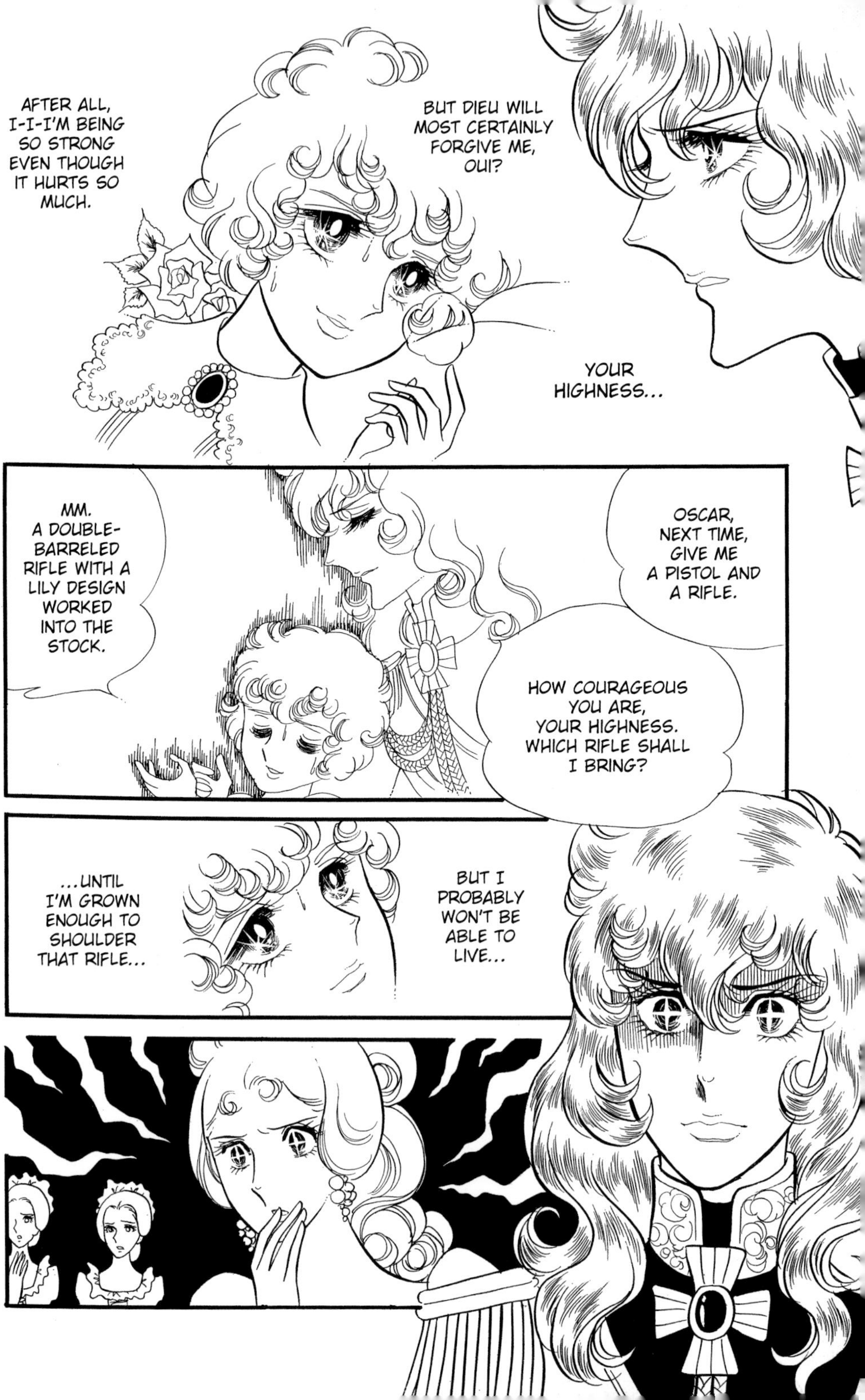
BUT DIEU WILL MOST CERTAINLY FORGIVE ME, OUI?
AFTER ALL, I-I-I'M BEING SO STRONG EVEN THOUGH IT HURTS SO MUCH.
YOUR HIGHNESS...
OSCAR, NEXT TIME, GIVE ME A PISTOL AND A RIFLE.
HOW COURAGEOUS YOU ARE, YOUR HIGHNESS. WHICH RIFLE SHALL I BRING?
MM. A DOUBLE-BARRELED RIFLE WITH A LILY DESIGN WORKED INTO THE STOCK.
BUT I PROBABLY WON'T BE ABLE TO LIVE...
...UNTIL I'M GROWN ENOUGH TO SHOULDER THAT RIFLE...

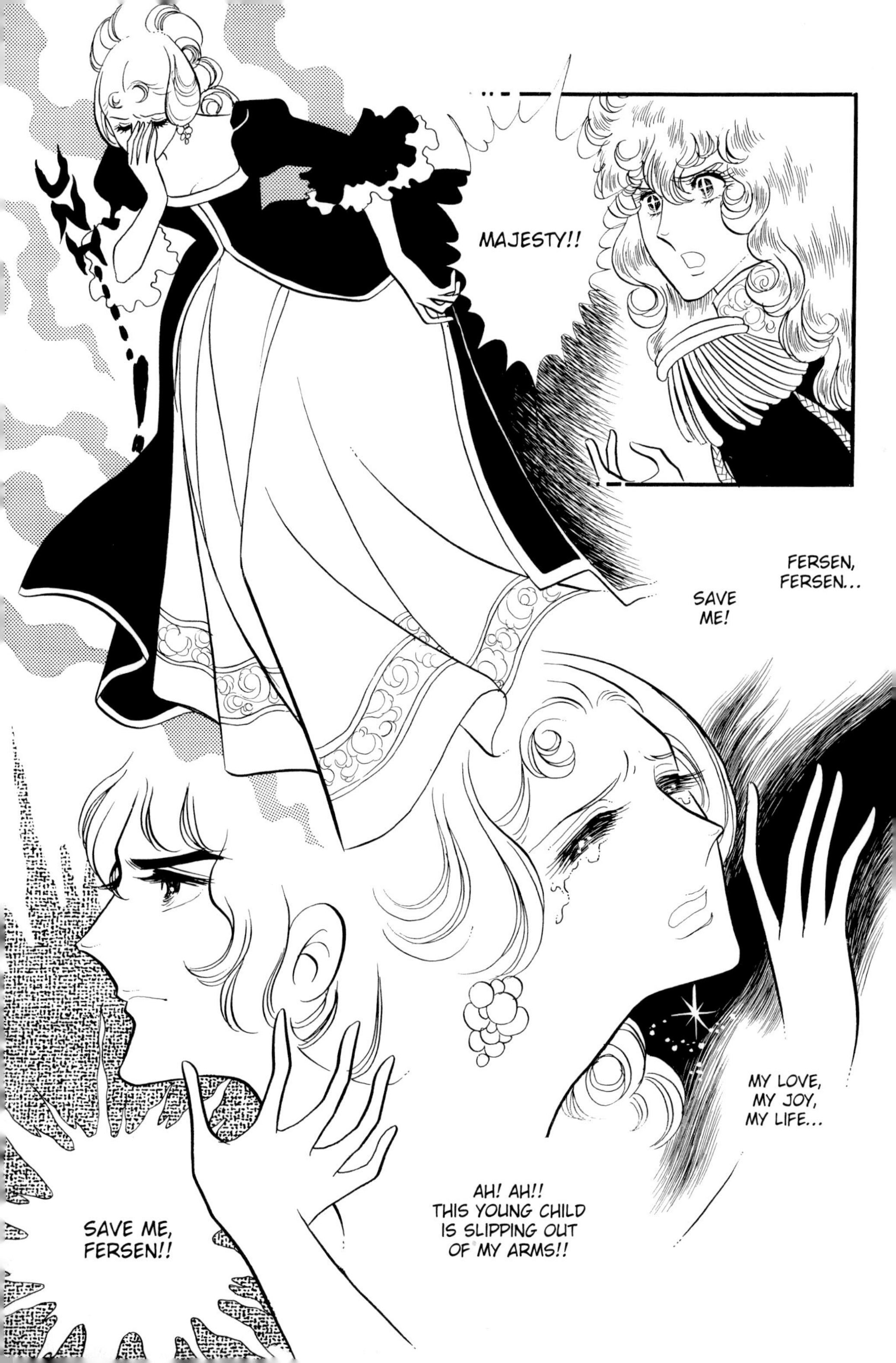
MAJESTY!!
FERSEN, FERSEN...
SAVE ME!
MY LOVE, MY JOY, MY LIFE...
AH! AH!! THIS YOUNG CHILD IS SLIPPING OUT OF MY ARMS!!
SAVE ME, FERSEN!!

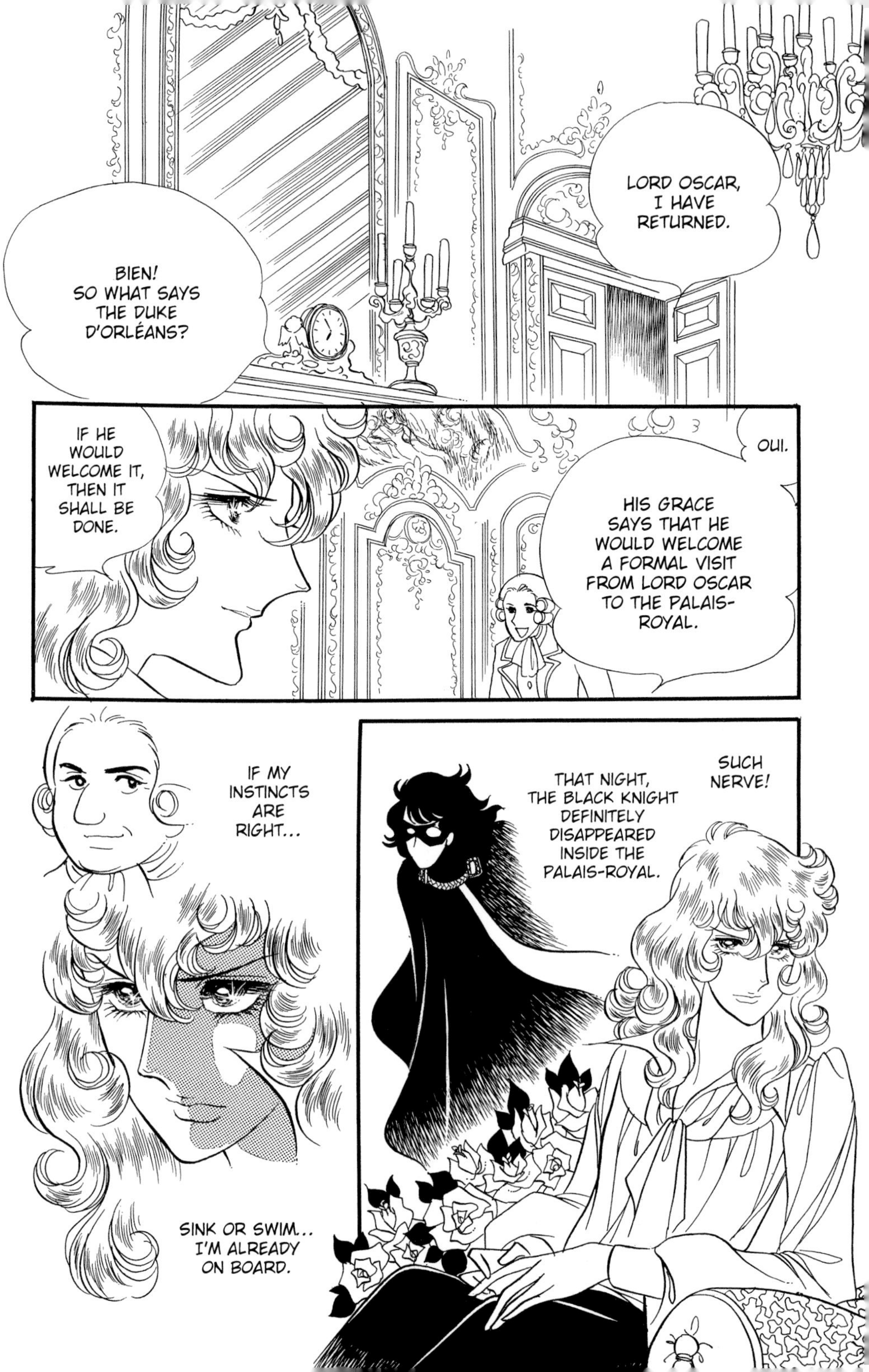
LORD OSCAR, I HAVE RETURNED.
BIEN! SO WHAT SAYS THE DUKE D'ORLÉANS?
OUI.
HIS GRACE SAYS THAT HE WOULD WELCOME A FORMAL VISIT FROM LORD OSCAR TO THE PALAIS-ROYAL.
IF HE WOULD WELCOME IT, THEN IT SHALL BE DONE.
SUCH NERVE!
THAT NIGHT, THE BLACK KNIGHT DEFINITELY DISAPPEARED INSIDE THE PALAIS-ROYAL.
IF MY INSTINCTS ARE RIGHT...
SINK OR SWIM... I'M ALREADY ON BOARD.

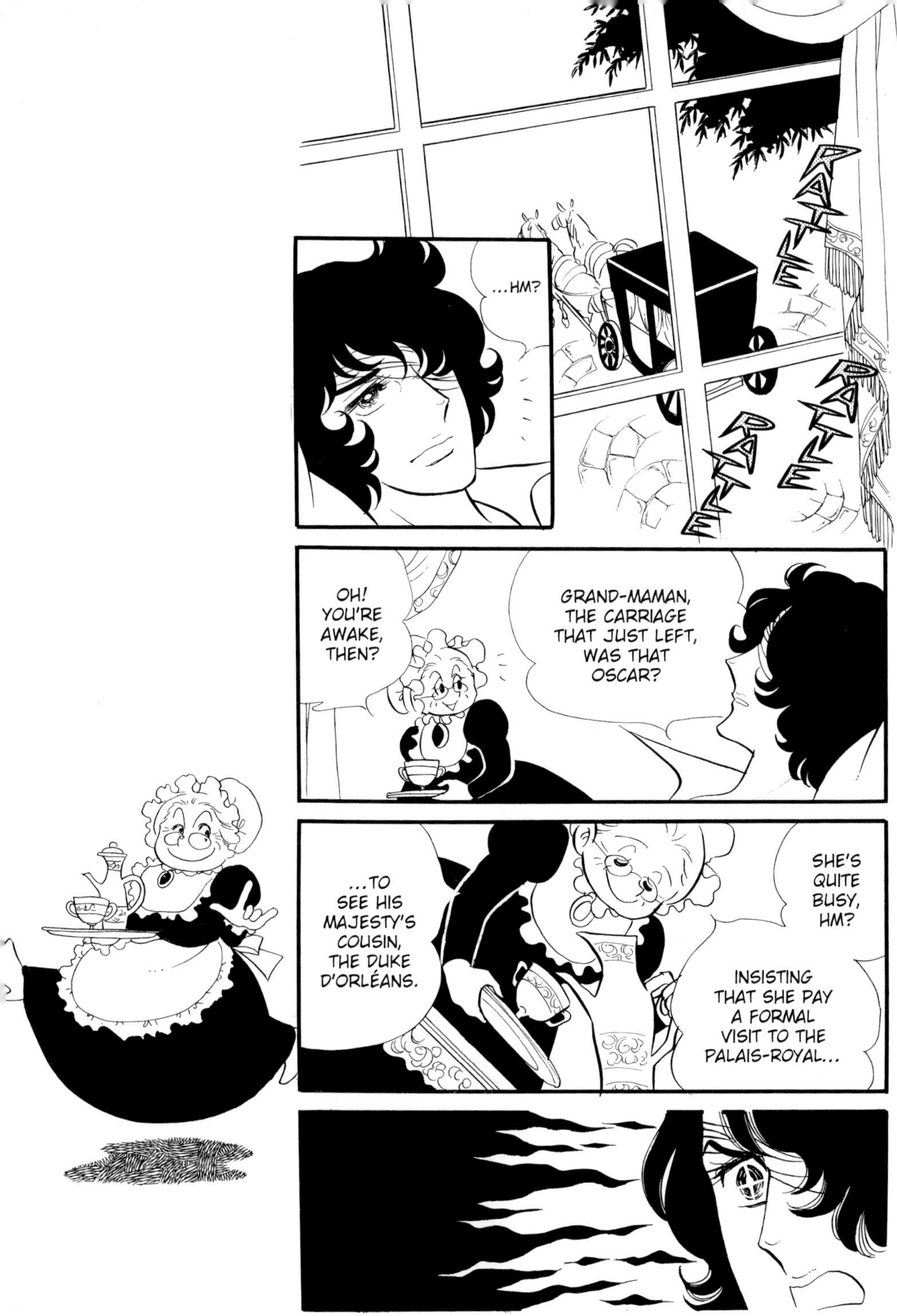
RATTLE
RATTLE
RATTLE
...HM?
GRAND-MAMAN, THE CARRIAGE THAT JUST LEFT, WAS THAT OSCAR?
OH! YOU'RE AWAKE, THEN?
SHE'S QUITE BUSY, HM?
INSISTING THAT SHE PAY A FORMAL VISIT TO THE PALAIS-ROYAL...
...TO SEE HIS MAJESTY'S COUSIN, THE DUKE D'ORLÉANS.

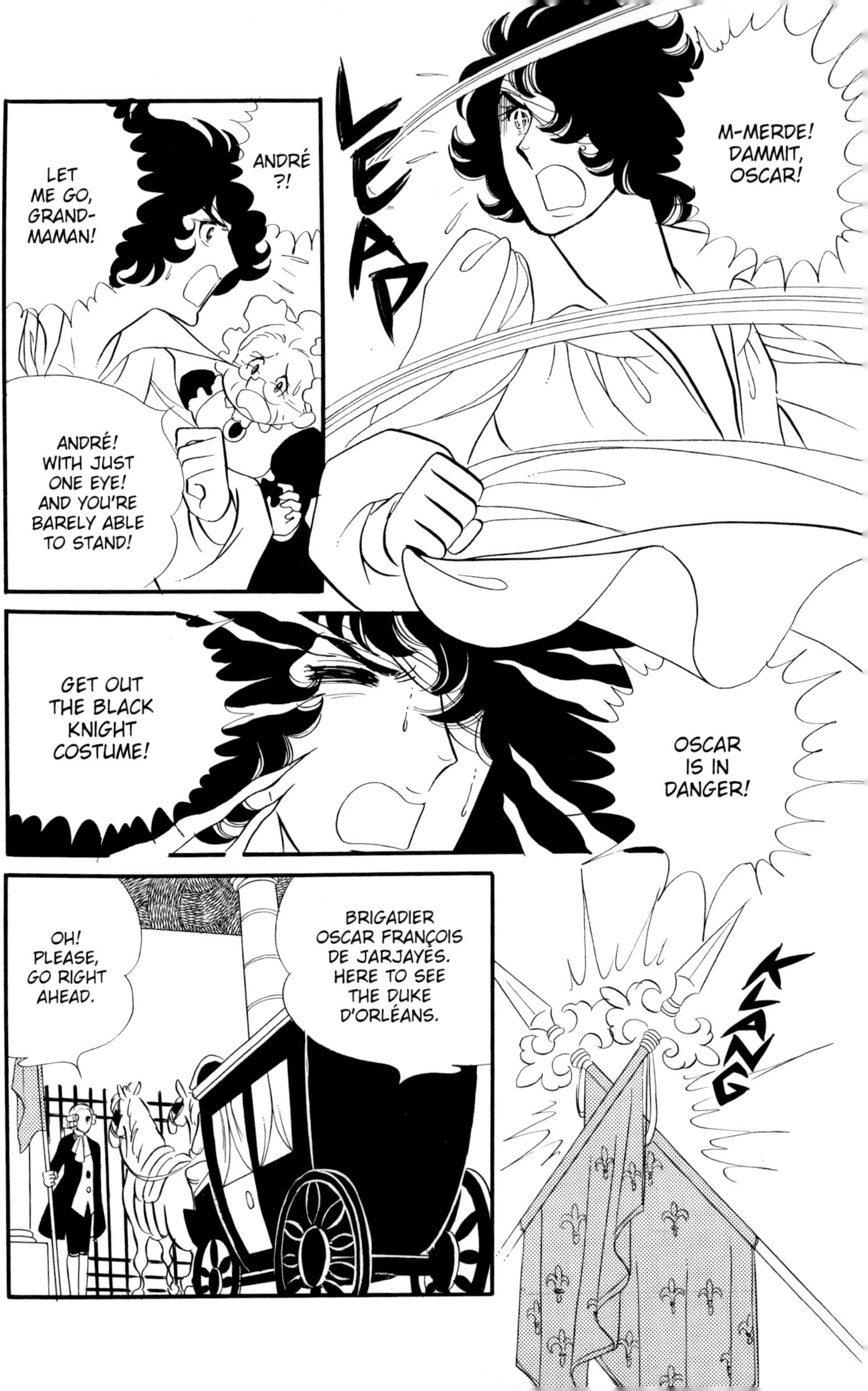
LEAP
M-MERDE! DAMMIT, OSCAR!
OSCAR IS IN DANGER!
ANDRÉ ?!
LET ME GO, GRAND-MAMAN!
ANDRÉ! WITH JUST ONE EYE! AND YOU'RE BARELY ABLE TO STAND!
GET OUT THE BLACK KNIGHT COSTUME!
KLANG
BRIGADIER OSCAR FRANÇOIS DE JARJAYÉS. HERE TO SEE THE DUKE D'ORLÉANS.
OH! PLEASE, GO RIGHT AHEAD.

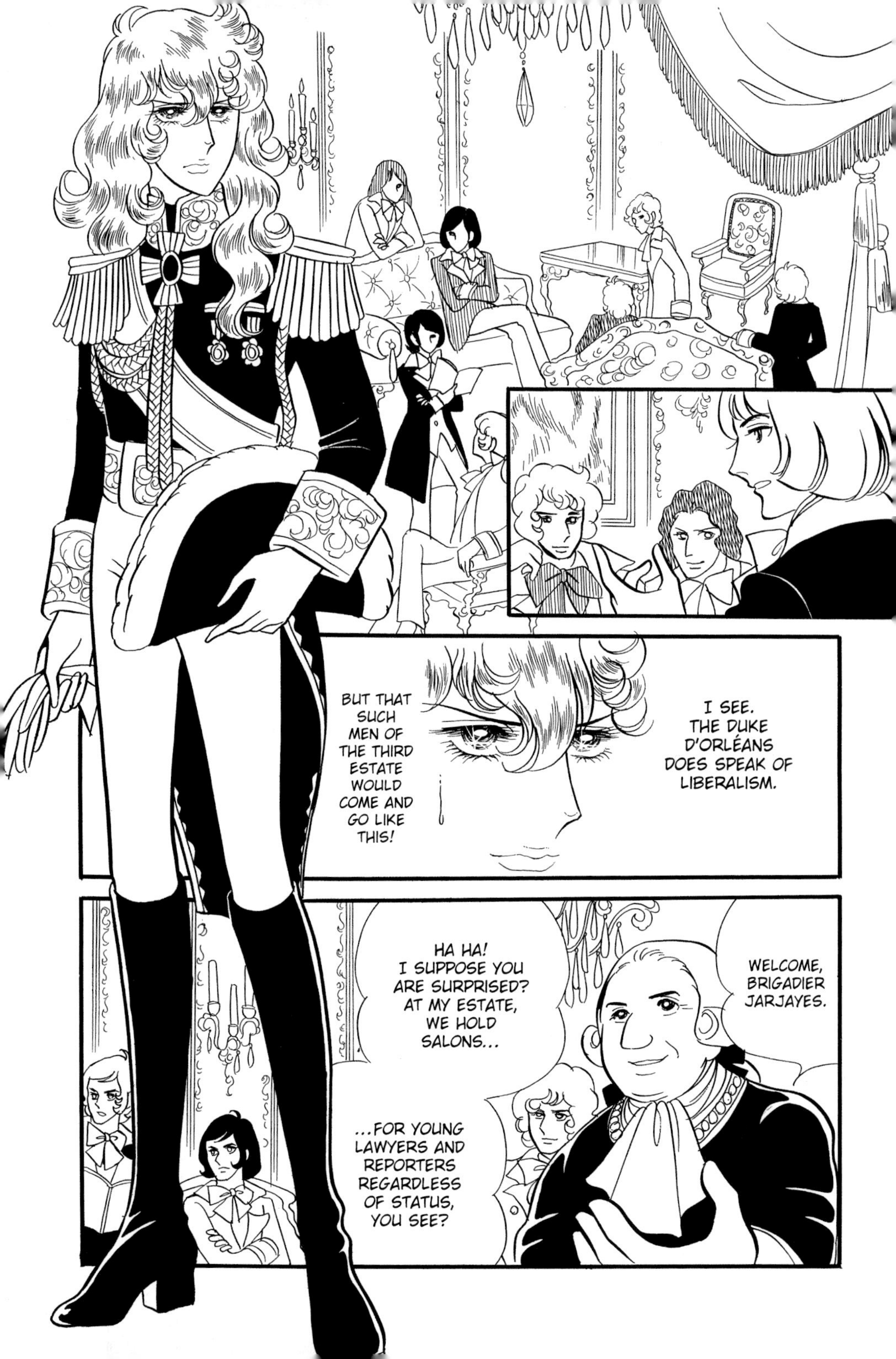
I SEE. THE DUKE D'ORLÉANS DOES SPEAK OF LIBERALISM.
BUT THAT SUCH MEN OF THE THIRD ESTATE WOULD COME AND GO LIKE THIS!
WELCOME, BRIGADIER JARJAYES.
HA HA! I SUPPOSE YOU ARE SURPRISED? AT MY ESTATE, WE HOLD SALONS...
...FOR YOUNG LAWYERS AND REPORTERS REGARDLESS OF STATUS, YOU SEE?

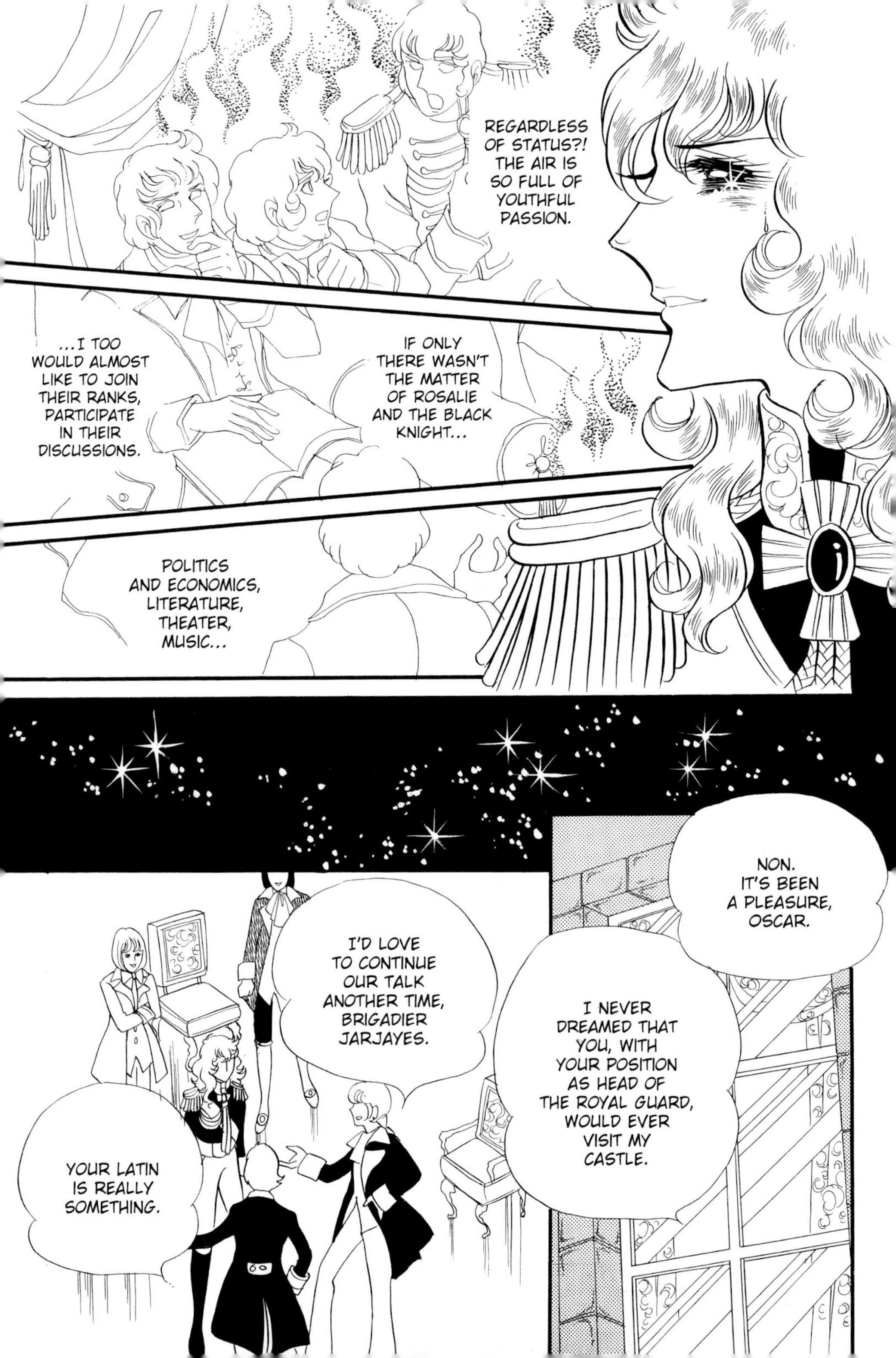
REGARDLESS OF STATUS?! THE AIR IS SO FULL OF YOUTHFUL PASSION.
IF ONLY THERE WASN'T THE MATTER OF ROSALIE AND THE BLACK KNIGHT...
...I TOO WOULD ALMOST LIKE TO JOIN THEIR RANKS, PARTICIPATE IN THEIR DISCUSSIONS.
POLITICS AND ECONOMICS, LITERATURE, THEATER, MUSIC...
NON. IT'S BEEN A PLEASURE, OSCAR.
I NEVER DREAMED THAT YOU, WITH YOUR POSITION AS HEAD OF THE ROYAL GUARD, WOULD EVER VISIT MY CASTLE.
I'D LOVE TO CONTINUE OUR TALK ANOTHER TIME, BRIGADIER JARJAYES.
YOUR LATIN IS REALLY SOMETHING.

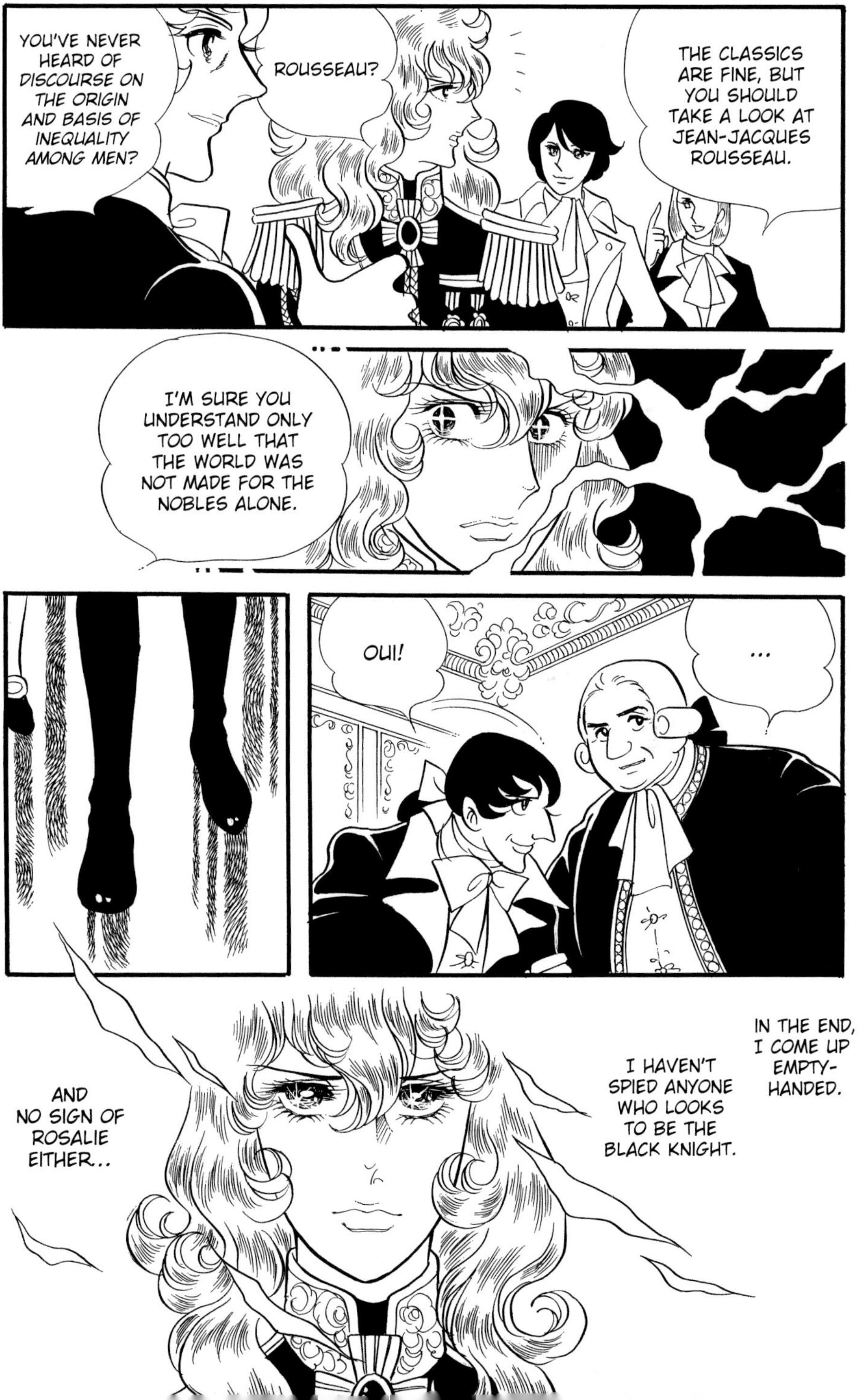
THE CLASSICS ARE FINE, BUT YOU SHOULD TAKE A LOOK AT JEAN-JACQUES ROUSSEAU.
ROUSSEAU?
YOU'VE NEVER HEARD OF DISCOURSE ON THE ORIGIN AND BASIS OF INEQUALITY AMONG MEN?
I'M SURE YOU UNDERSTAND ONLY TOO WELL THAT THE WORLD WAS NOT MADE FOR THE NOBLES ALONE.
...
OUI!
IN THE END, I COME UP EMPTY-HANDED.
I HAVEN'T SPIED ANYONE WHO LOOKS TO BE THE BLACK KNIGHT.
AND NO SIGN OF ROSALIE EITHER...

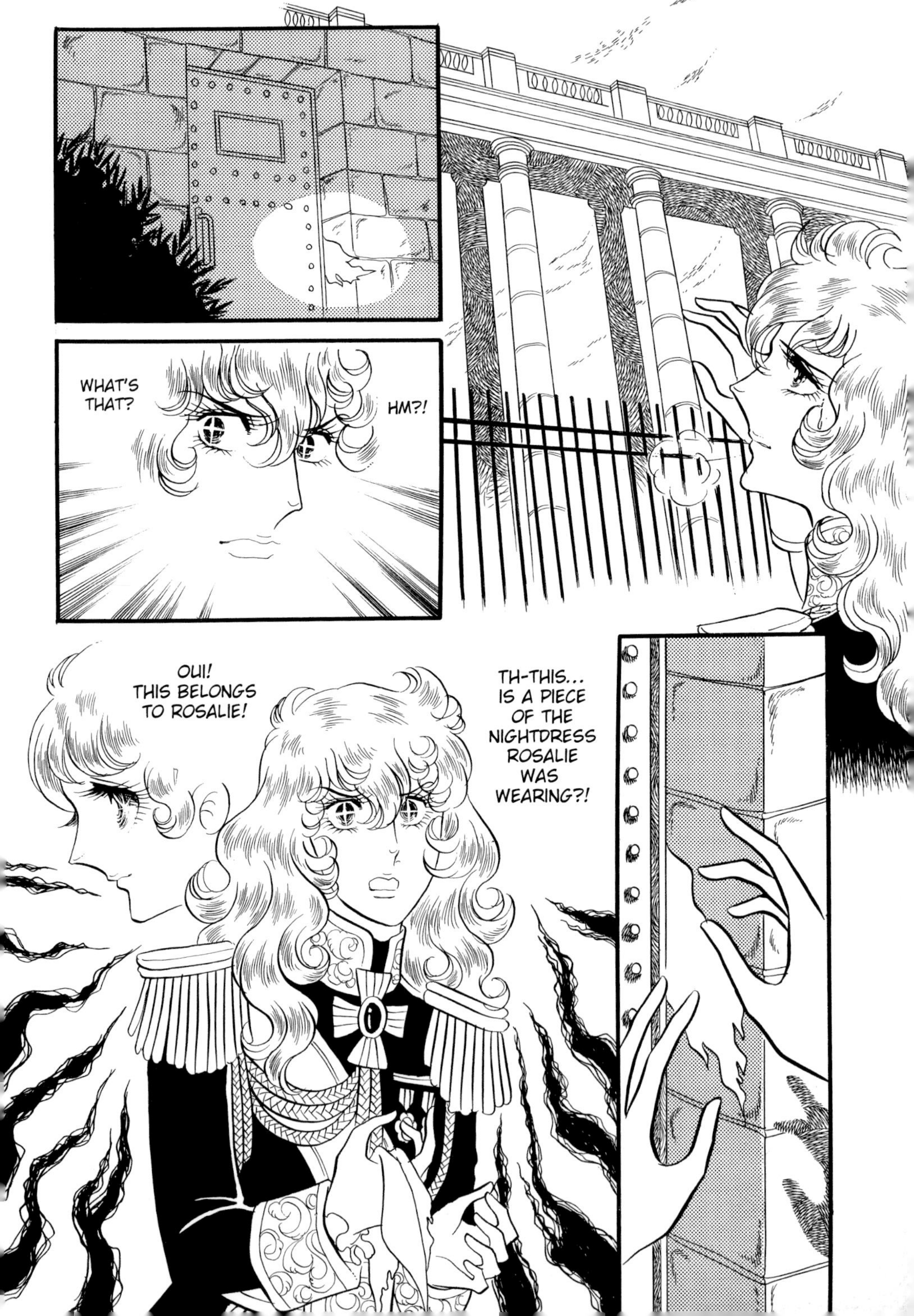
HM?!
WHAT'S THAT?
TH-THIS... IS A PIECE OF THE NIGHTDRESS ROSALIE WAS WEARING?!
OUI! THIS BELONGS TO ROSALIE!

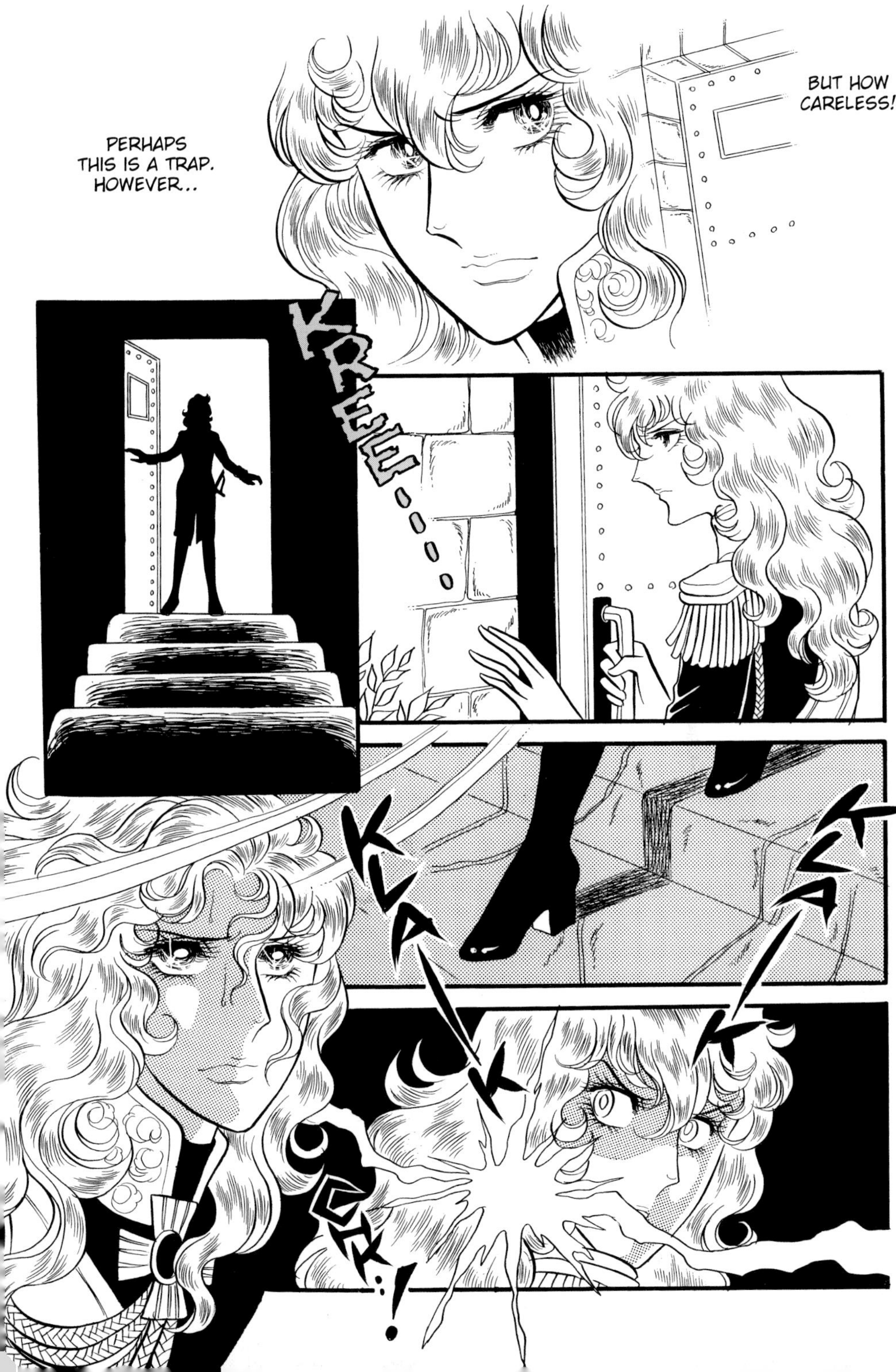
BUT HOW CARELESS!
PERHAPS THIS IS A TRAP. HOWEVER...
KREEE....
KLAK
KLAK
CHK..!

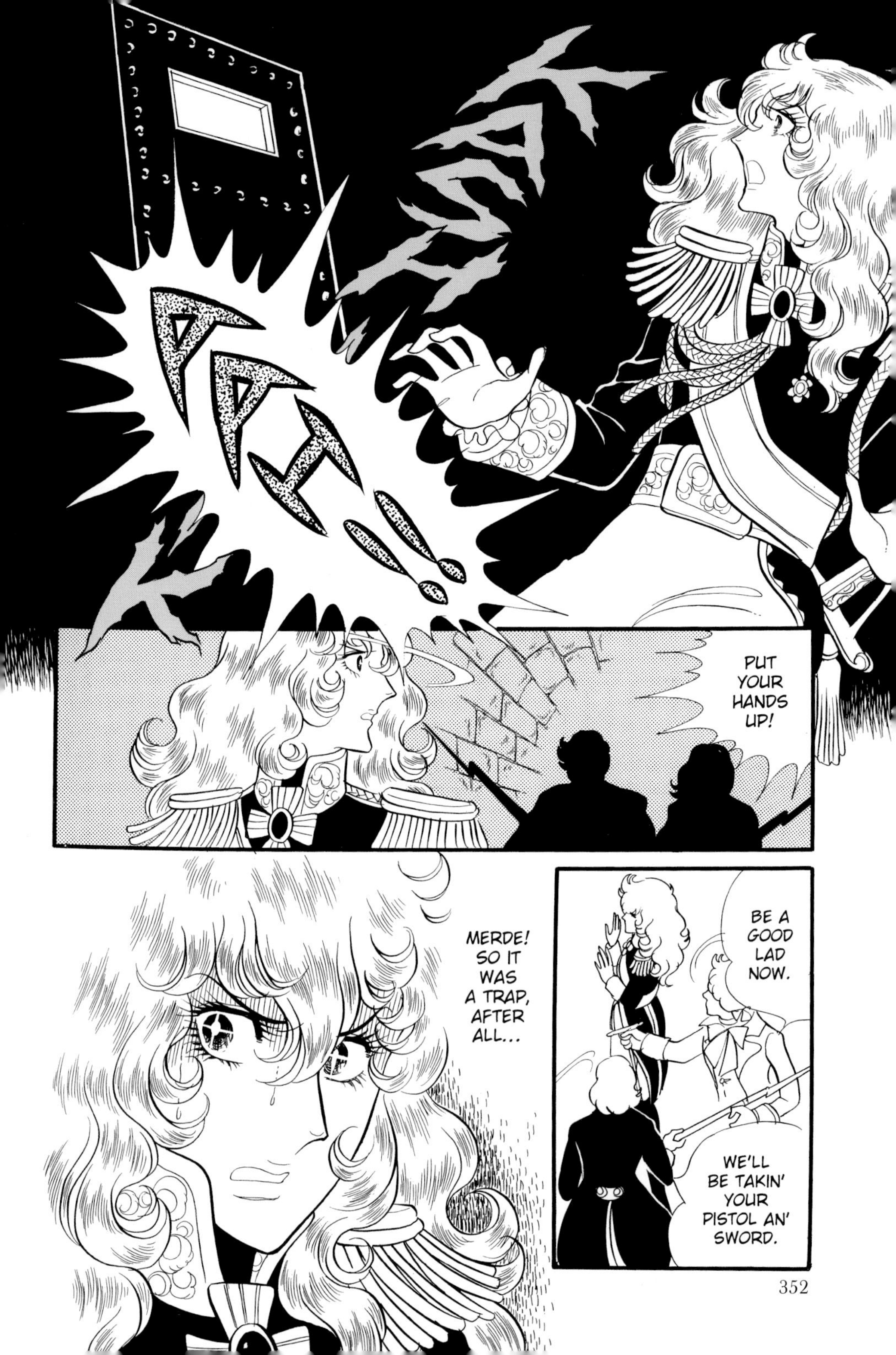
PUT YOUR HANDS UP!
BE A GOOD LAD NOW.
WE'LL BE TAKIN' YOUR PISTOL AN' SWORD.
MERDE! SO IT WAS A TRAP, AFTER ALL...

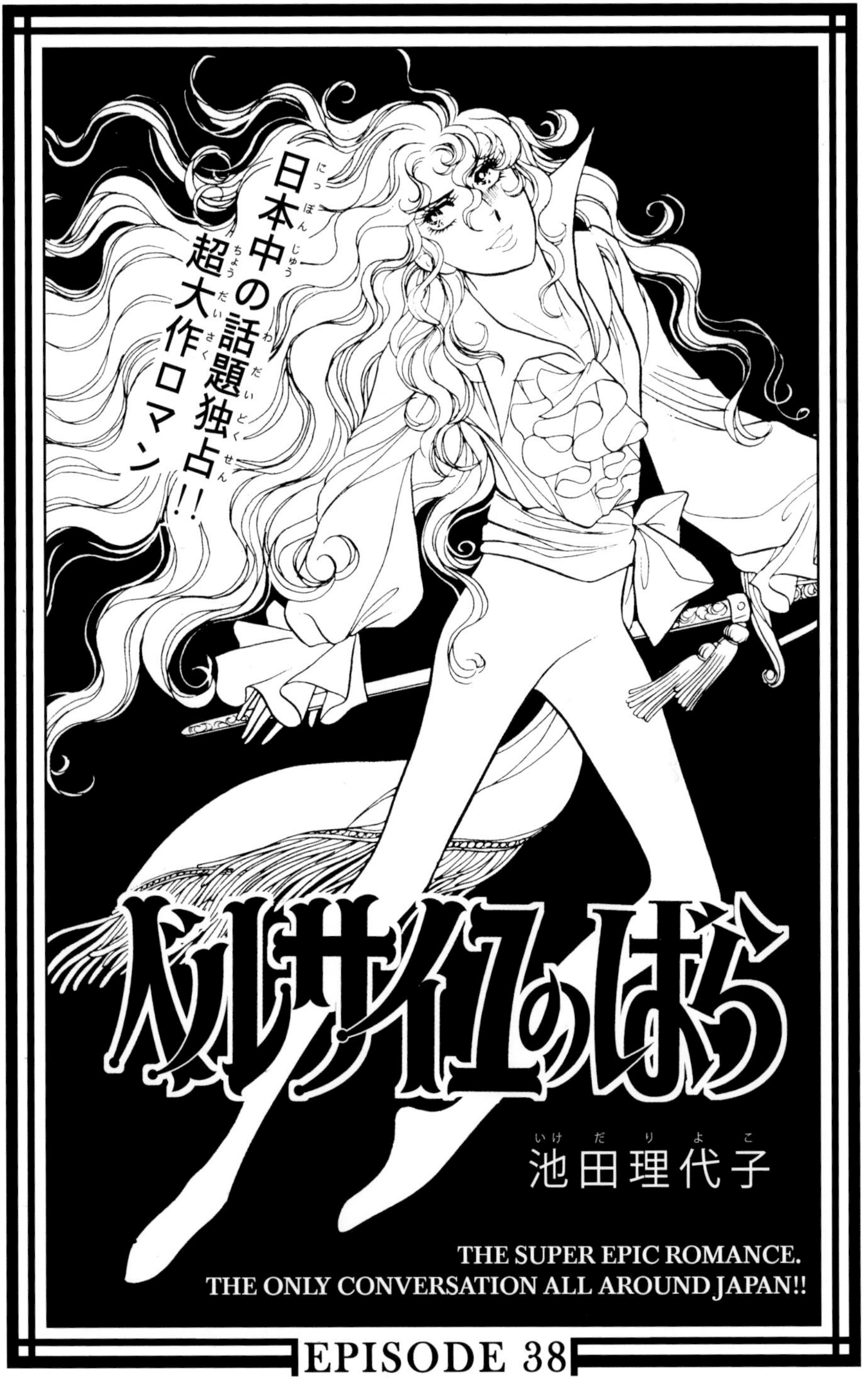
日本中の話題独占!!
超大作ロマン
ベルサイユのばら
池田理代子
THE SUPER EPIC ROMANCE.
THE ONLY CONVERSATION ALL AROUND JAPAN!!
EPISODE 38

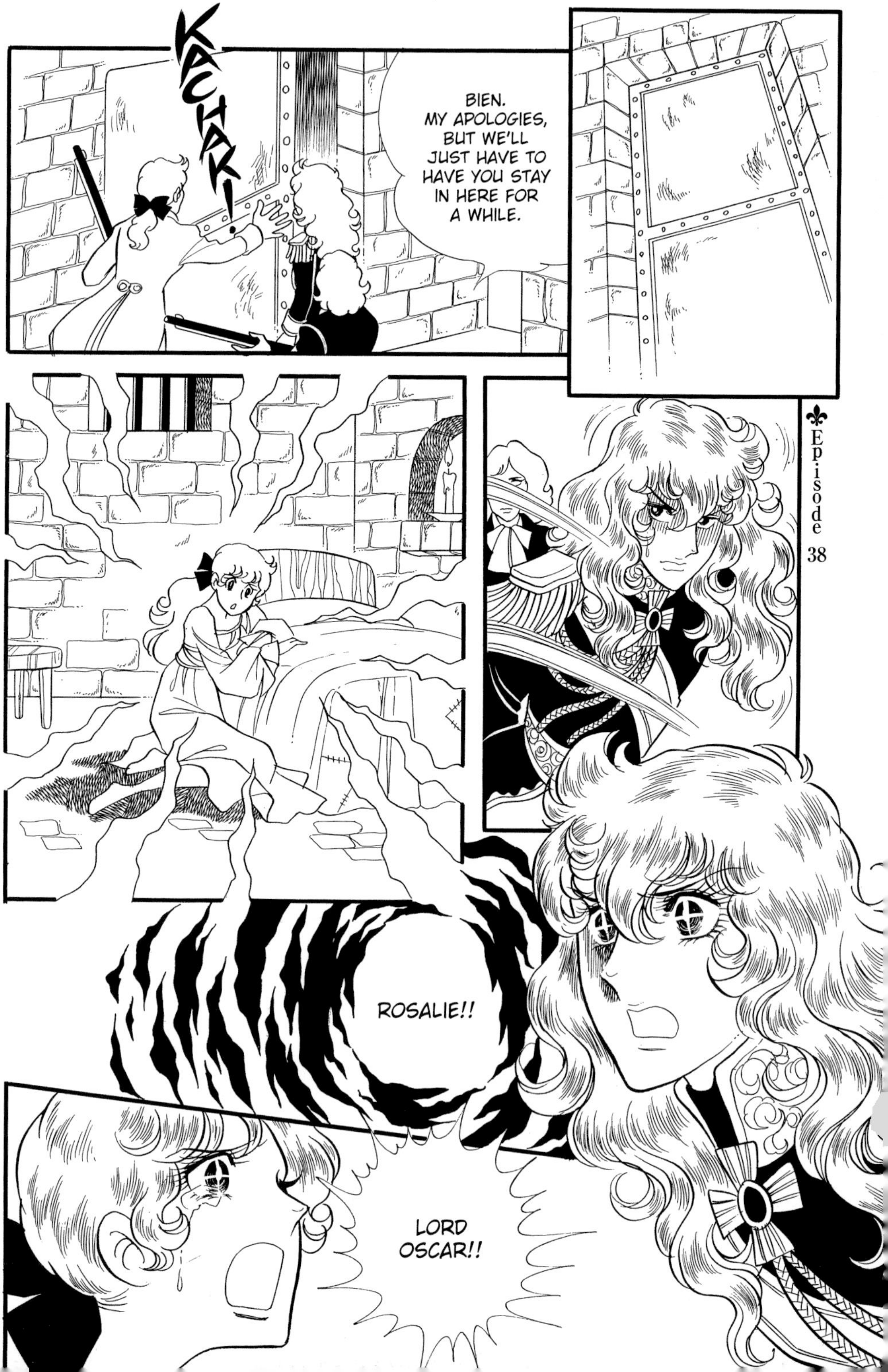
BIEN. MY APOLOGIES, BUT WE'LL JUST HAVE TO HAVE YOU STAY IN HERE FOR A WHILE.
KACHAK!
ROSALIE!!
LORD OSCAR!!

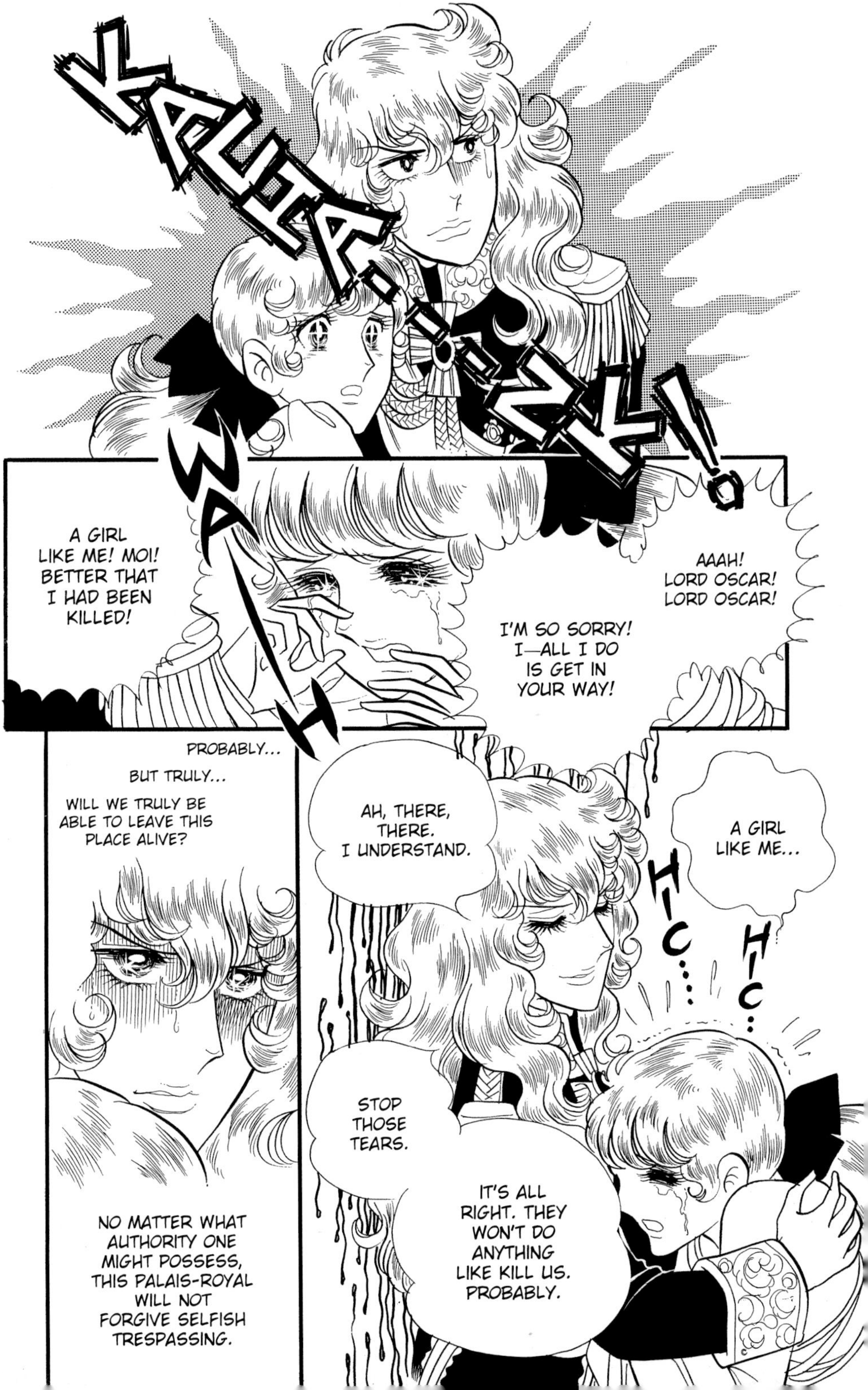
AAAH! LORD OSCAR! LORD OSCAR!
I'M SO SORRY! I—ALL I DO IS GET IN YOUR WAY!
A GIRL LIKE ME! MOI! BETTER THAT I HAD BEEN KILLED!
WAAH
A GIRL LIKE ME...
HIC... HIC...
AH, THERE, THERE. I UNDERSTAND.
STOP THOSE TEARS.
IT'S ALL RIGHT. THEY WON'T DO ANYTHING LIKE KILL US. PROBABLY.
PROBABLY...
BUT TRULY...
WILL WE TRULY BE ABLE TO LEAVE THIS PLACE ALIVE?
NO MATTER WHAT AUTHORITY ONE MIGHT POSSESS, THIS PALAIS-ROYAL WILL NOT FORGIVE SELFISH TRESPASSING.

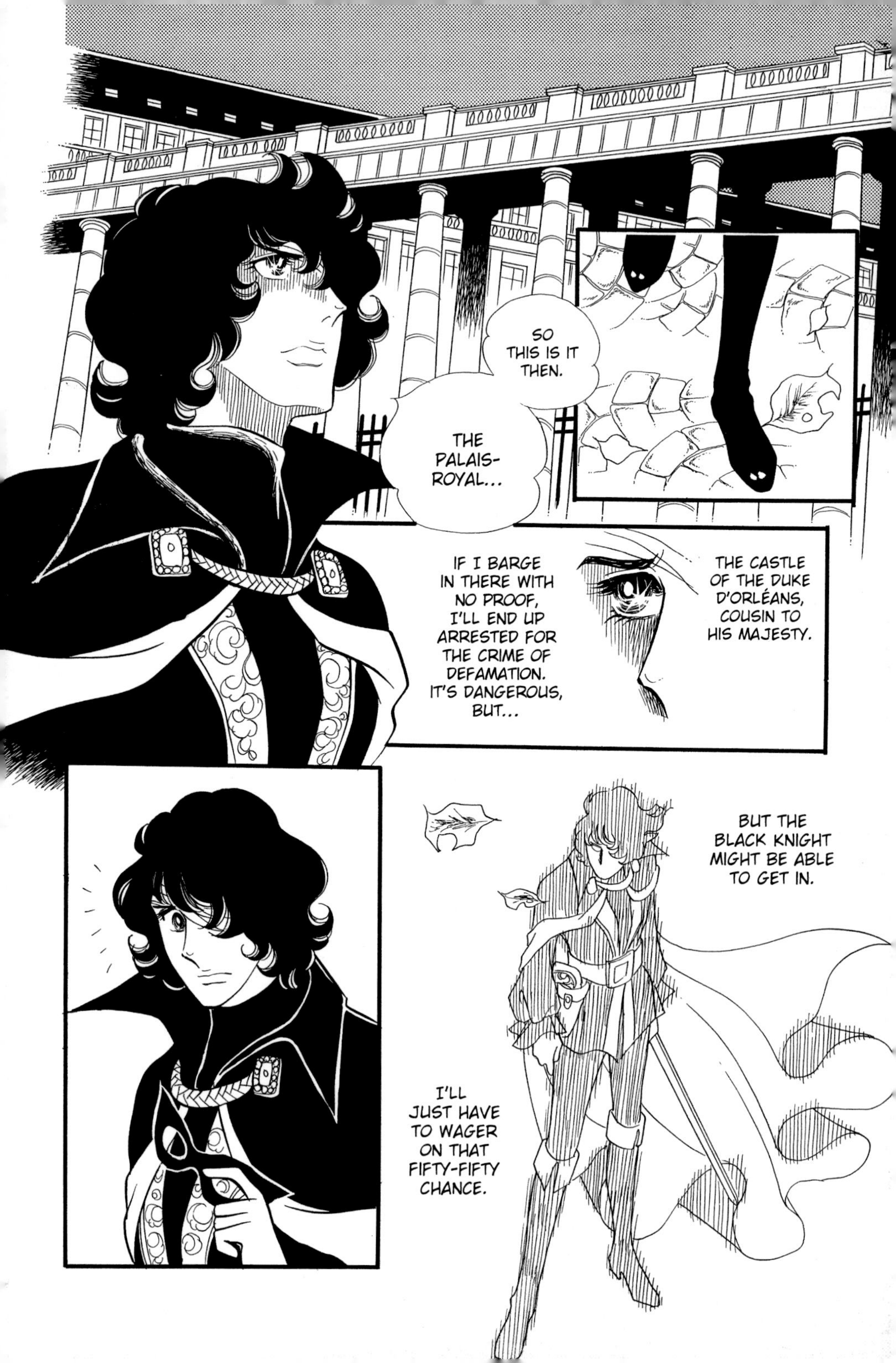
SO THIS IS IT THEN.
THE PALAIS-ROYAL…
THE CASTLE OF THE DUKE D'ORLÉANS, COUSIN TO HIS MAJESTY.
IF I BARGE IN THERE WITH NO PROOF, I'LL END UP ARRESTED FOR THE CRIME OF DEFAMATION. IT'S DANGEROUS, BUT…
BUT THE BLACK KNIGHT MIGHT BE ABLE TO GET IN.
I'LL JUST HAVE TO WAGER ON THAT FIFTY-FIFTY CHANCE.

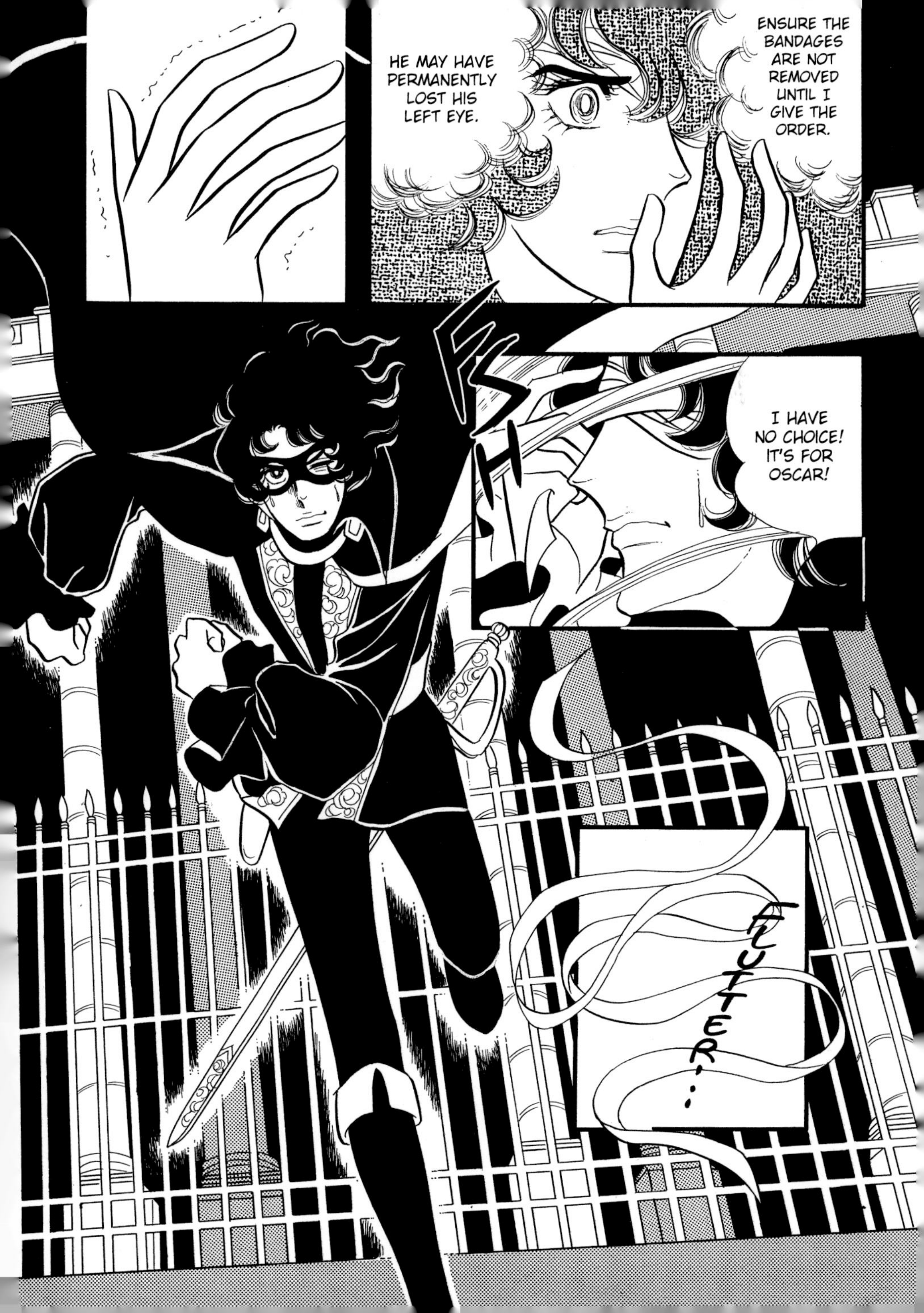
ENSURE THE BANDAGES ARE NOT REMOVED UNTIL I GIVE THE ORDER.
HE MAY HAVE PERMANENTLY LOST HIS LEFT EYE.
I HAVE NO CHOICE! IT'S FOR OSCAR!
FSH
FLUTTER...

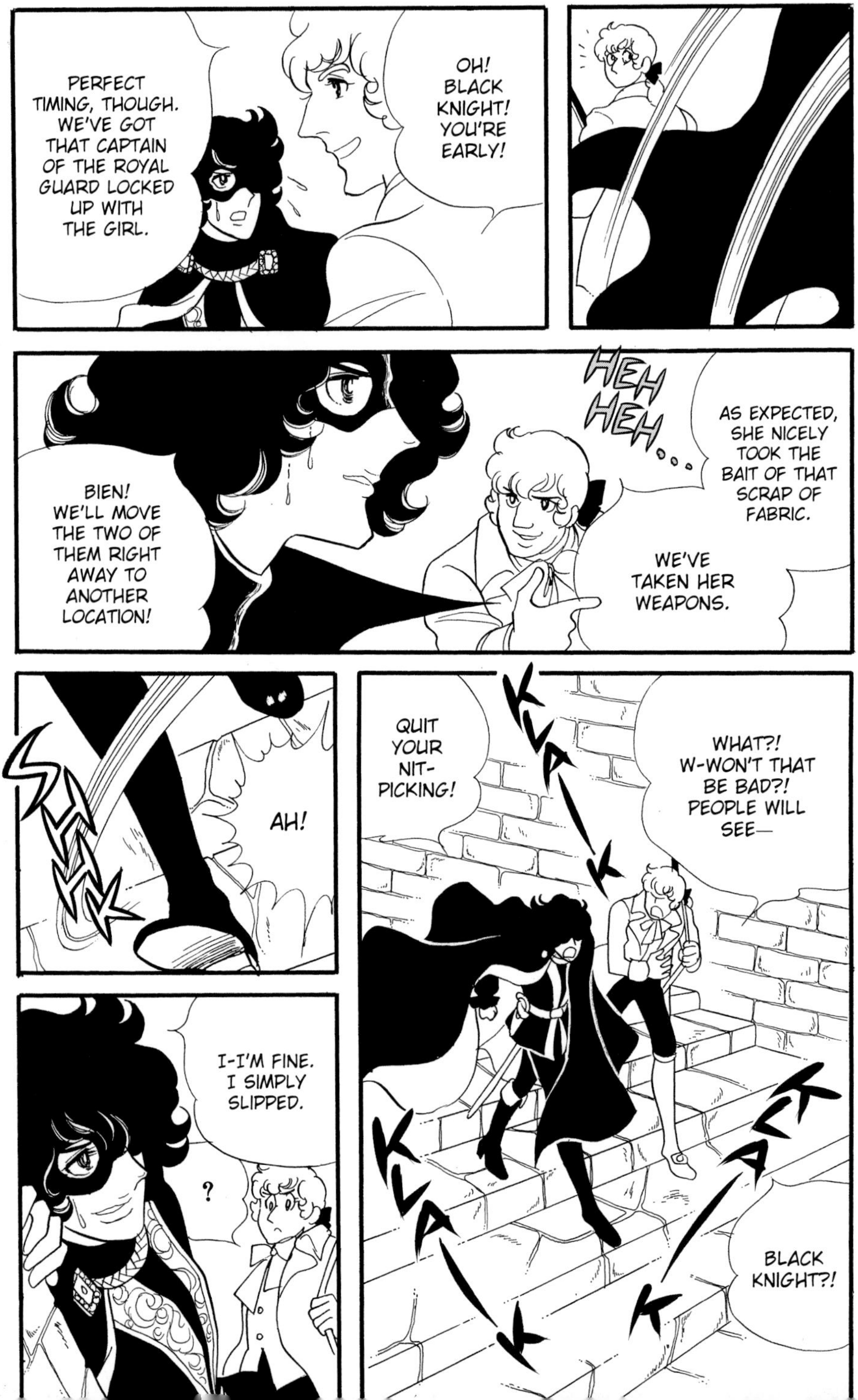
OH! BLACK KNIGHT! YOU'RE EARLY!
PERFECT TIMING, THOUGH. WE'VE GOT THAT CAPTAIN OF THE ROYAL GUARD LOCKED UP WITH THE GIRL.
HEH HEH...
AS EXPECTED, SHE NICELY TOOK THE BAIT OF THAT SCRAP OF FABRIC.
WE'VE TAKEN HER WEAPONS.
BIEN! WE'LL MOVE THE TWO OF THEM RIGHT AWAY TO ANOTHER LOCATION!
WHAT?! W-WON'T THAT BE BAD?! PEOPLE WILL SEE—
KLAK
QUIT YOUR NIT-PICKING!
KLAK
BLACK KNIGHT?!
KLAK
SHKK
AH!
I-I'M FINE. I SIMPLY SLIPPED.
?

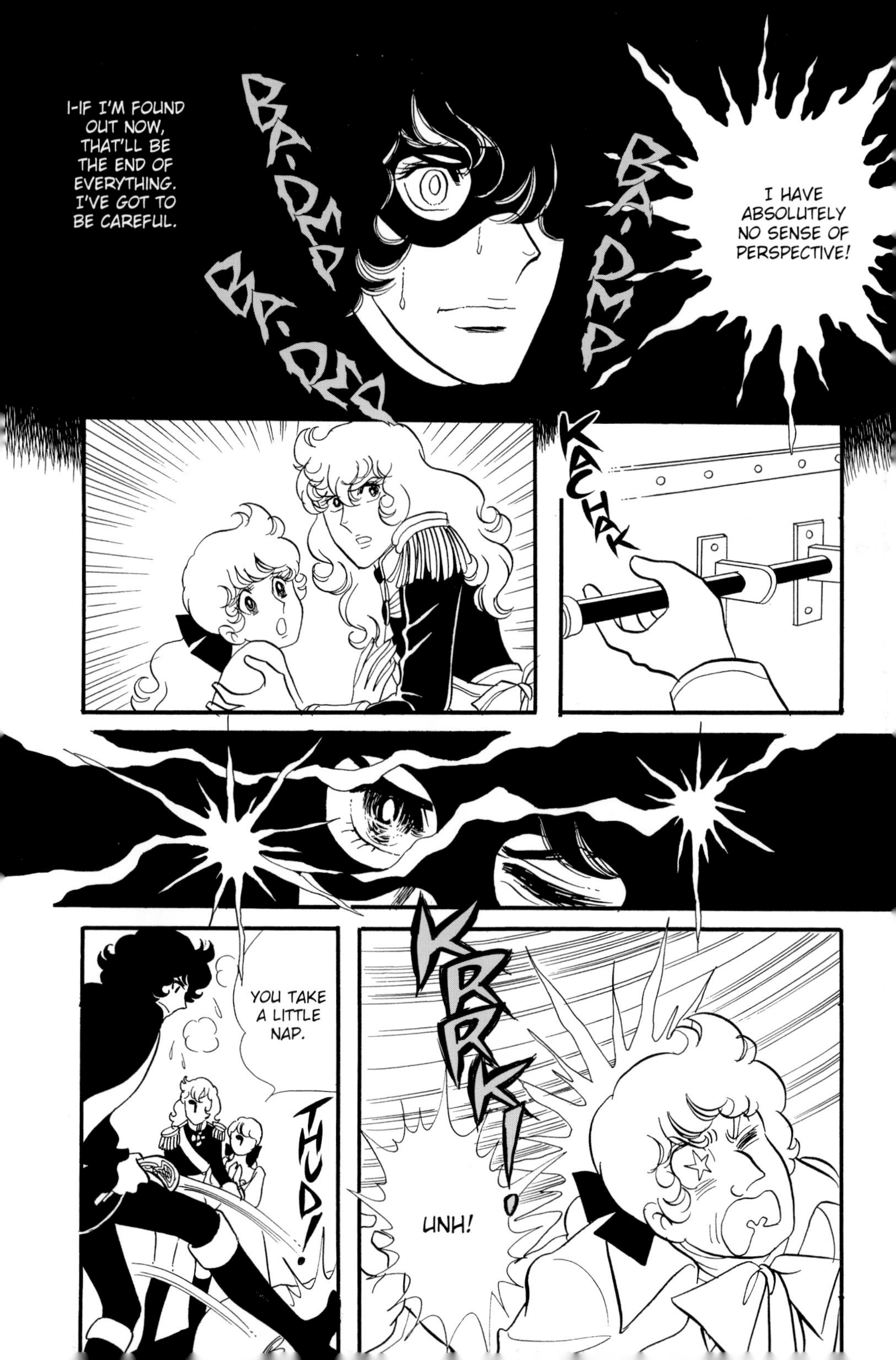
BA-DMP
I HAVE ABSOLUTELY NO SENSE OF PERSPECTIVE!
I-IF I'M FOUND OUT NOW, THAT'LL BE THE END OF EVERYTHING. I'VE GOT TO BE CAREFUL.
BA-DMP
BA-DEP
KACHAK
KRRK!
UNH!
YOU TAKE A LITTLE NAP.
THUD!

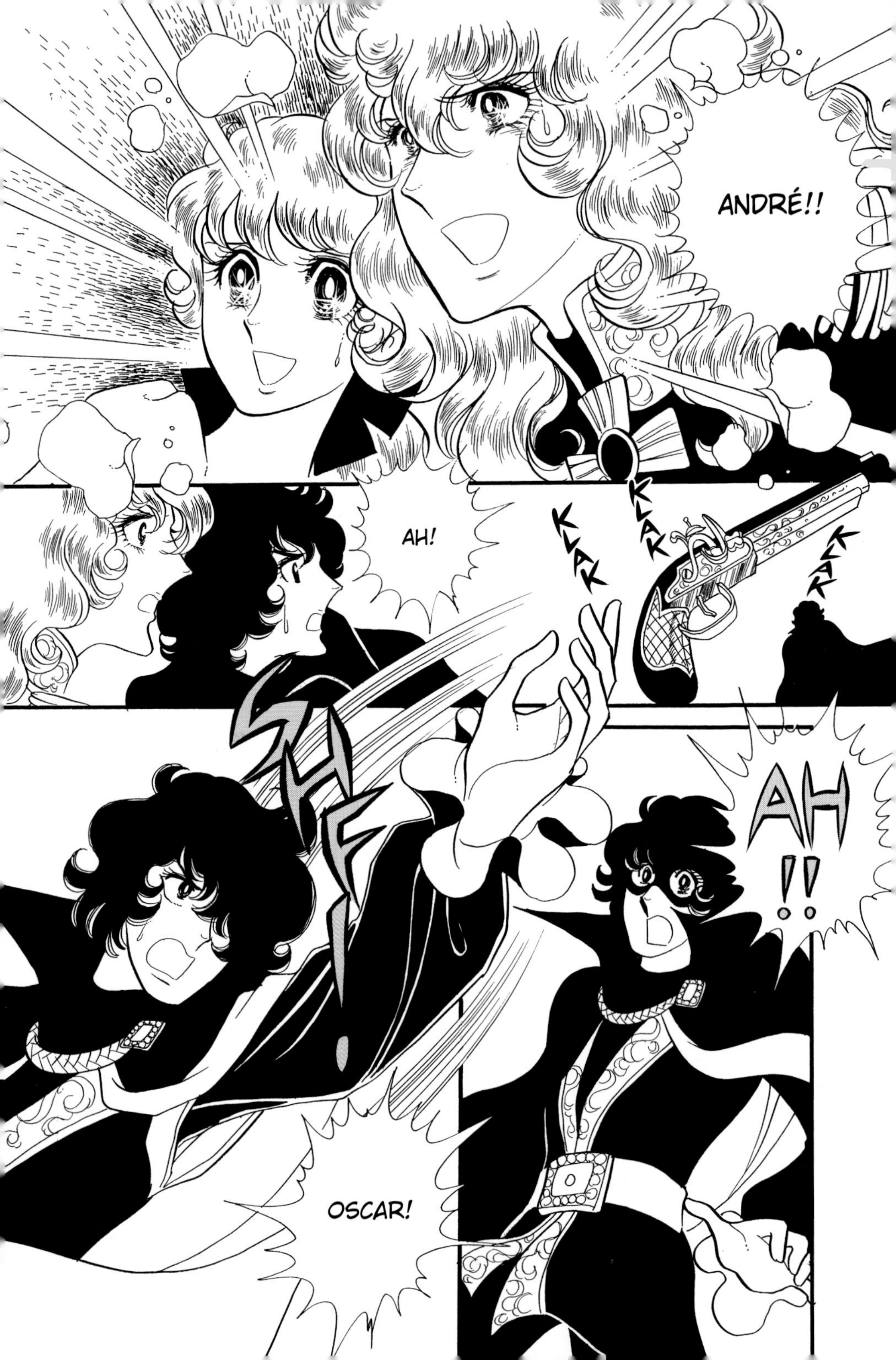
ANDRÉ!!
KLAK
KLAK
KLAK
AH!
AH!!
SHF
OSCAR!

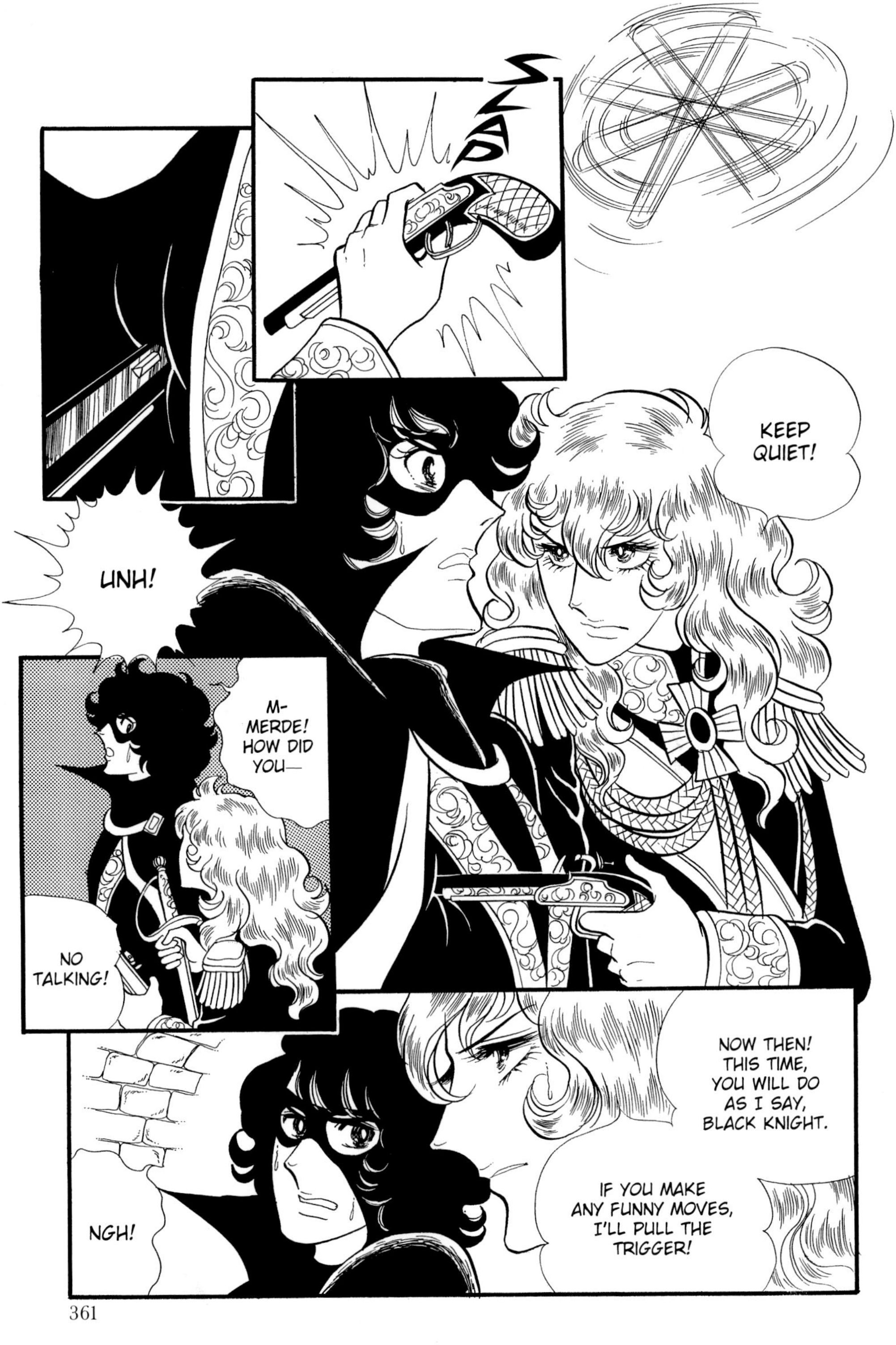
SLAP
KEEP QUIET!
UNH!
M-MERDE! HOW DID YOU—
NO TALKING!
NOW THEN! THIS TIME, YOU WILL DO AS I SAY, BLACK KNIGHT.
IF YOU MAKE ANY FUNNY MOVES, I'LL PULL THE TRIGGER!
NGH!

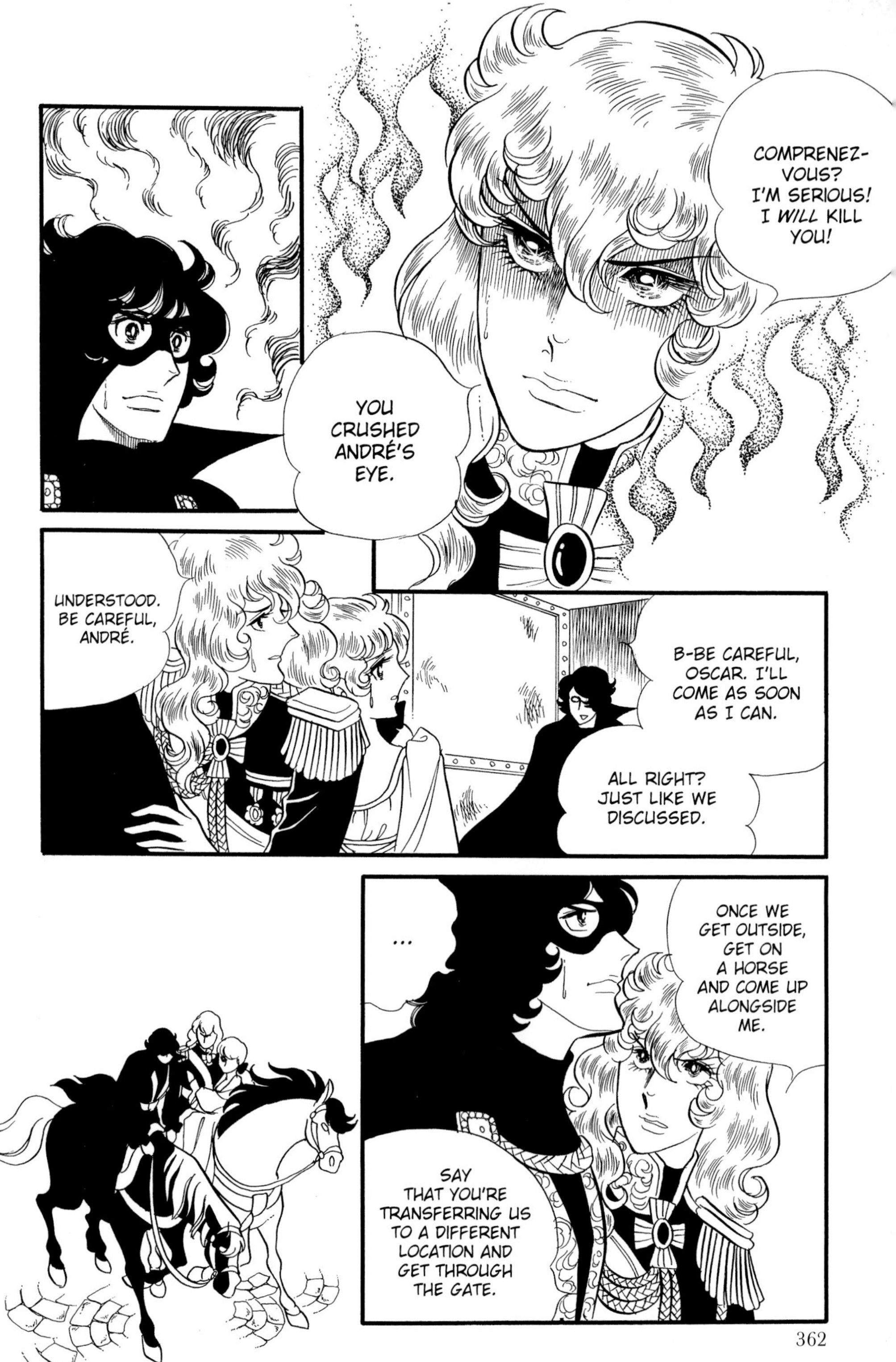
COMPRENEZ-VOUS? I'M SERIOUS! I *WILL* KILL YOU!
YOU CRUSHED ANDRÉ'S EYE.
B-BE CAREFUL, OSCAR. I'LL COME AS SOON AS I CAN.
ALL RIGHT? JUST LIKE WE DISCUSSED.
UNDERSTOOD. BE CAREFUL, ANDRÉ.
ONCE WE GET OUTSIDE, GET ON A HORSE AND COME UP ALONGSIDE ME.
...
SAY THAT YOU'RE TRANSFERRING US TO A DIFFERENT LOCATION AND GET THROUGH THE GATE.

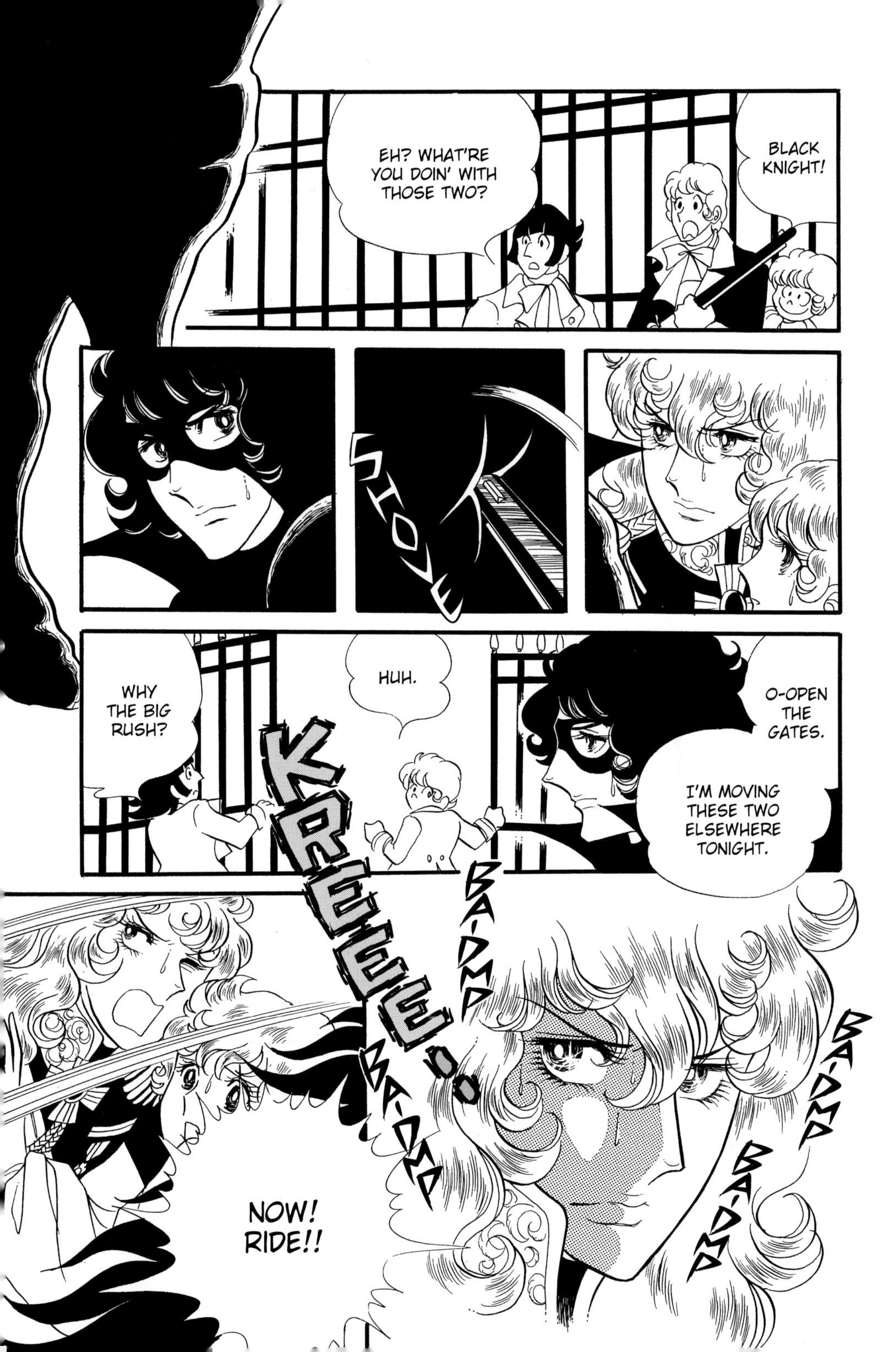
BLACK KNIGHT!
EH? WHAT'RE YOU DOIN' WITH THOSE TWO?
SHOVE
O-OPEN THE GATES.
I'M MOVING THESE TWO ELSEWHERE TONIGHT.
HUH.
WHY THE BIG RUSH?
KREEE..
BA-DMP
BA-DMP
BA-DMP
BA-DMP
BA-DMP
NOW! RIDE!!

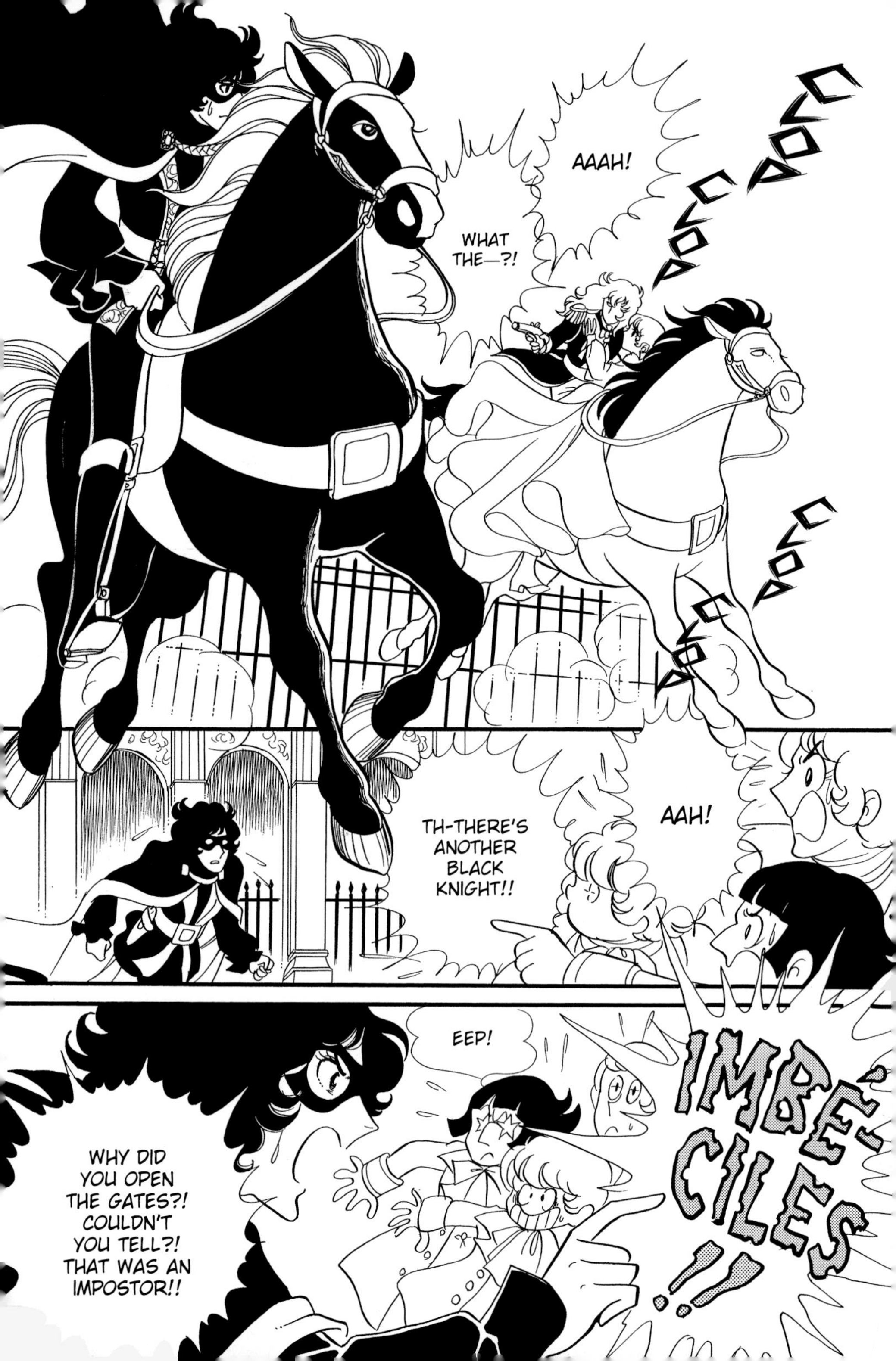
AAAH!
WHAT THE—?!
AAH!
TH-THERE'S ANOTHER BLACK KNIGHT!!
IMBÉCILES!!
EEP!
WHY DID YOU OPEN THE GATES?! COULDN'T YOU TELL?! THAT WAS AN IMPOSTOR!!

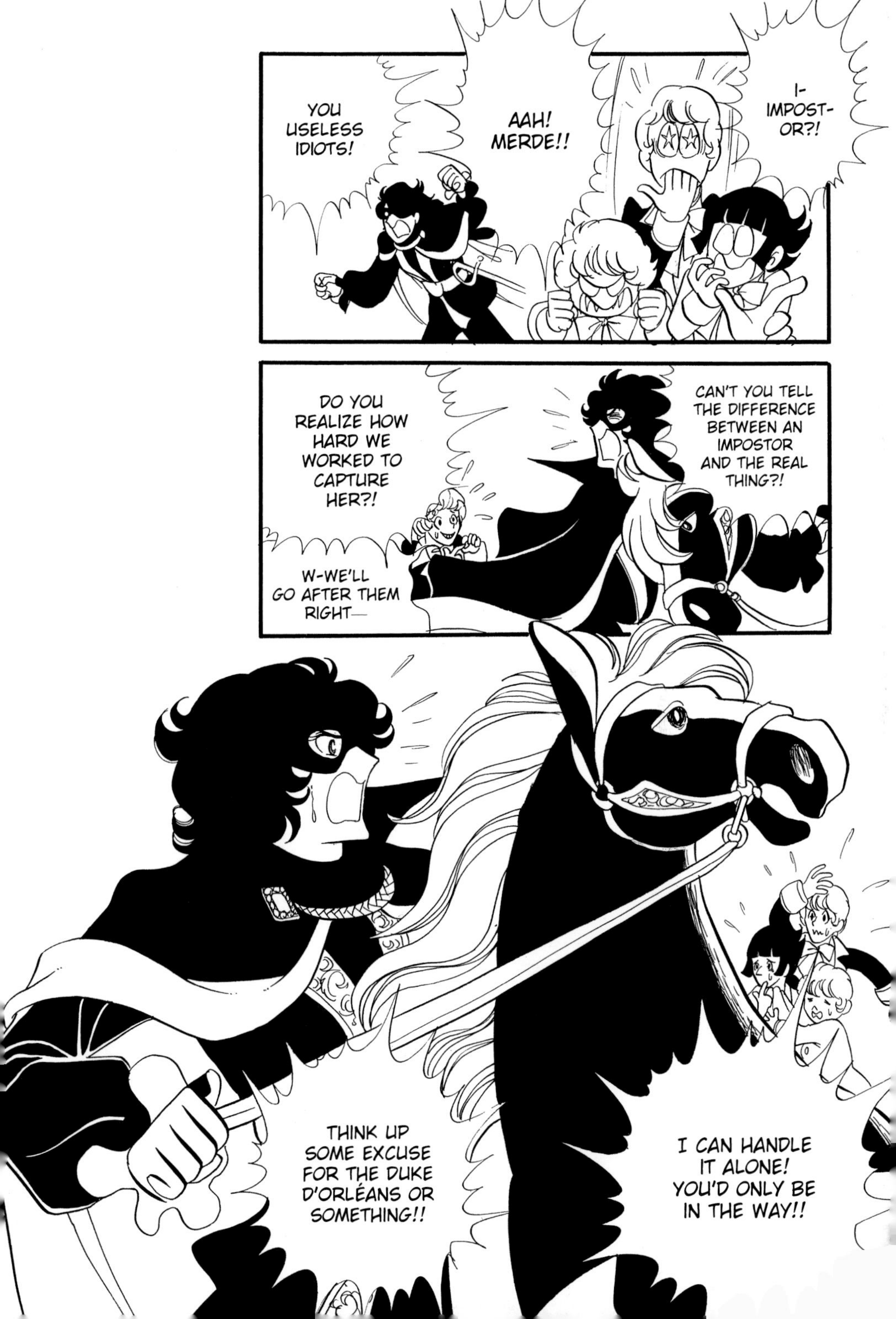
I- IMPOST- OR?!
AAH! MERDE!!
YOU USELESS IDIOTS!
CAN'T YOU TELL THE DIFFERENCE BETWEEN AN IMPOSTOR AND THE REAL THING?!
DO YOU REALIZE HOW HARD WE WORKED TO CAPTURE HER?!
W-WE'LL GO AFTER THEM RIGHT—
I CAN HANDLE IT ALONE! YOU'D ONLY BE IN THE WAY!!
THINK UP SOME EXCUSE FOR THE DUKE D'ORLÉANS OR SOMETHING!!

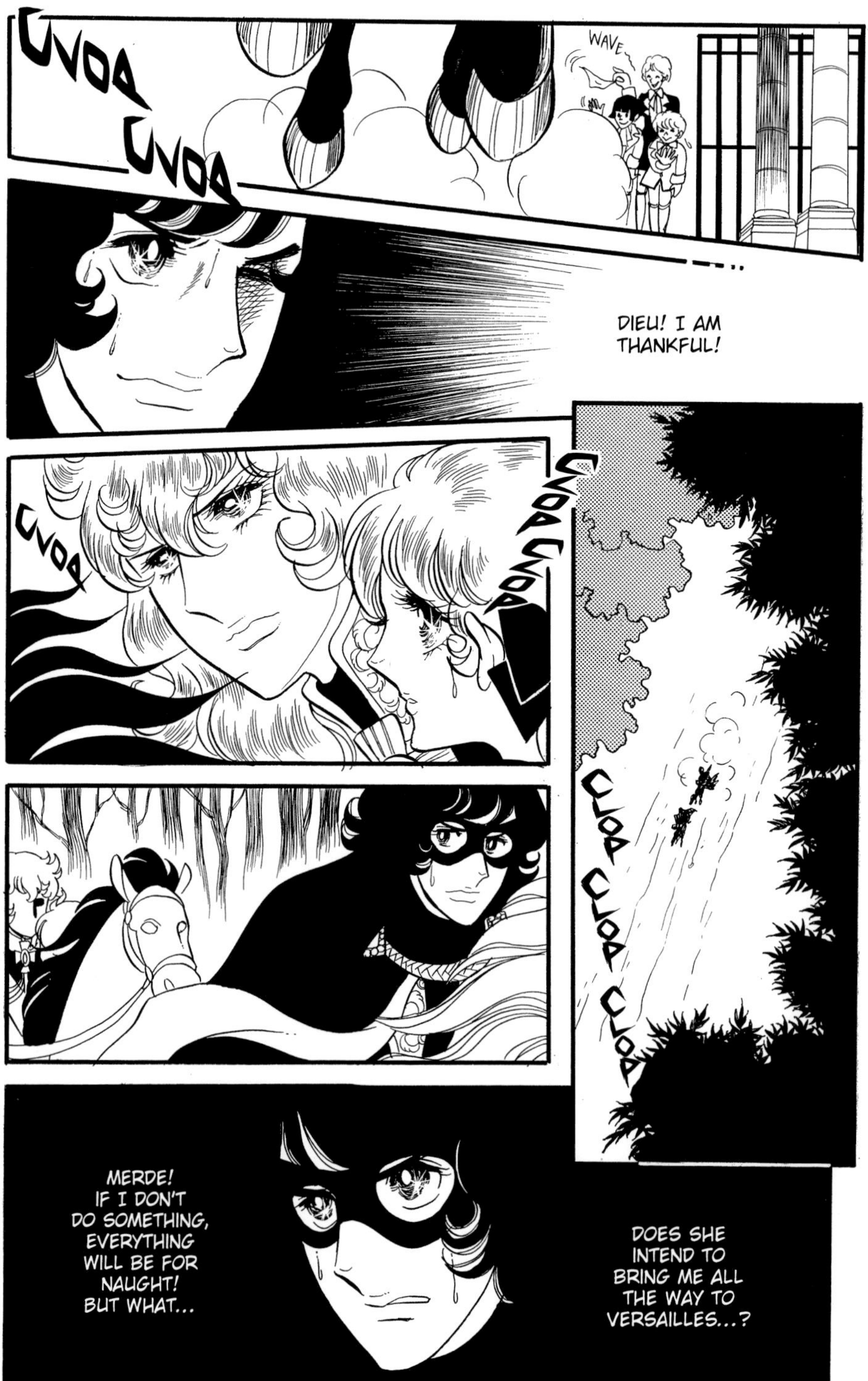
WAVE
CLOP
CLOP
CLOP
DIEU! I AM THANKFUL!
CLOP
CLOP
CLOP
CLOP
CLOP
CLOP
CLOP
DOES SHE INTEND TO BRING ME ALL THE WAY TO VERSAILLES...?
MERDE! IF I DON'T DO SOMETHING, EVERYTHING WILL BE FOR NAUGHT! BUT WHAT...

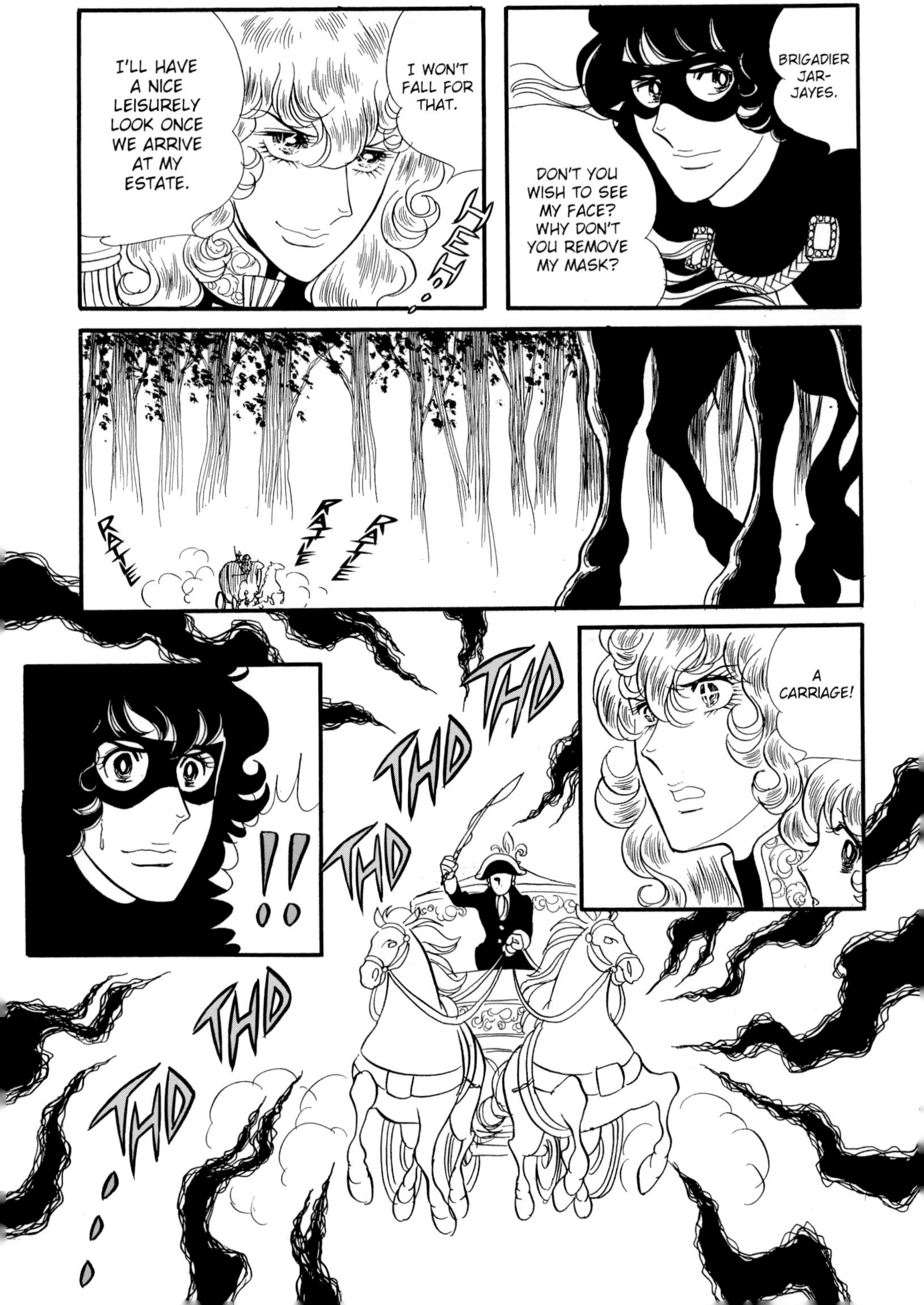
BRIGADIER JARJAYES.
DON'T YOU WISH TO SEE MY FACE? WHY DON'T YOU REMOVE MY MASK?
I WON'T FALL FOR THAT.
I'LL HAVE A NICE LEISURELY LOOK ONCE WE ARRIVE AT MY ESTATE.
HEH...
RATTLE
RATTLE
RATTLE
A CARRIAGE!
THD
THD
THD
THD
THD
!!

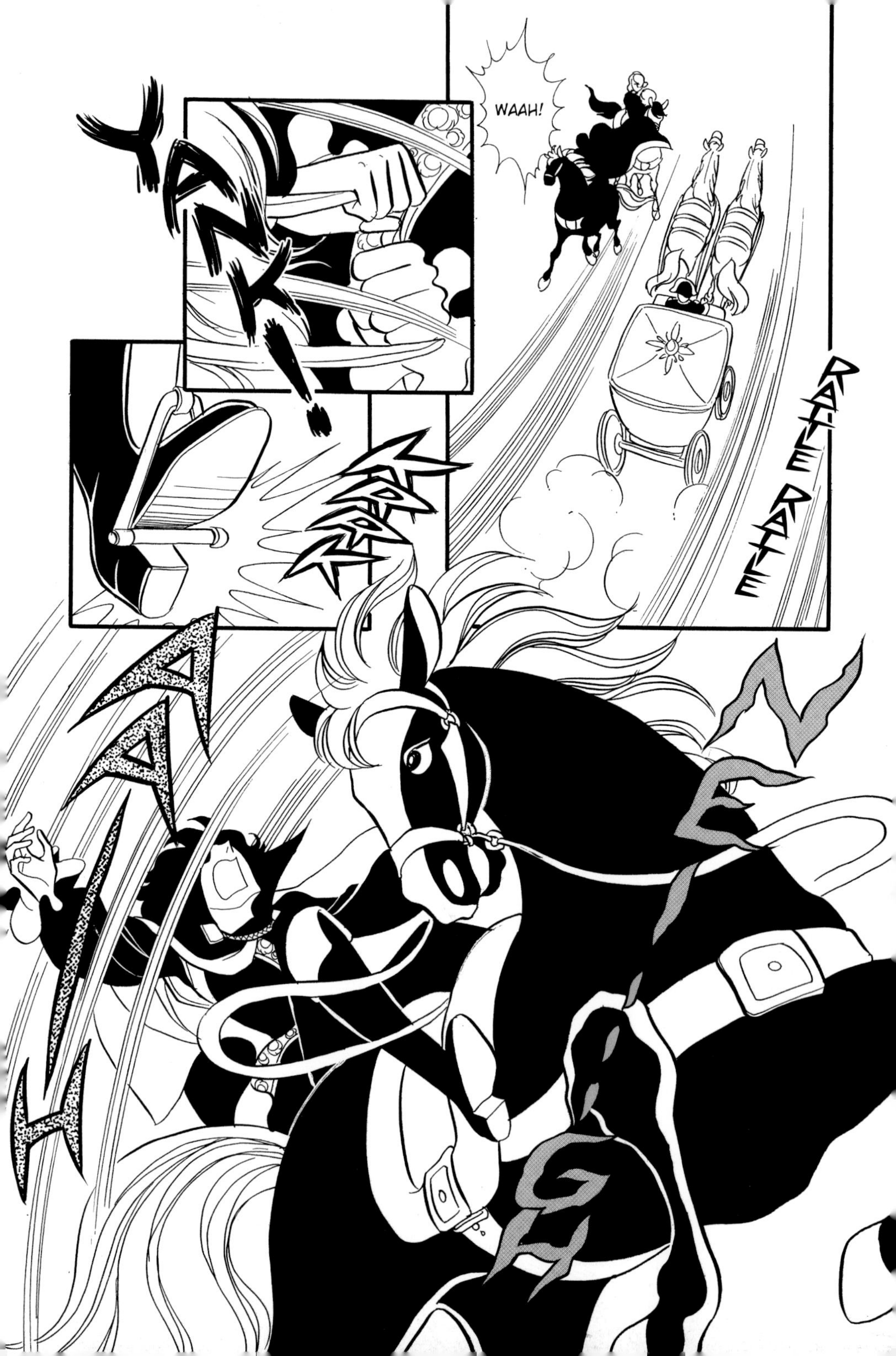
WAAH!
RATTLE RATTLE
YANK!
NEIGH
HAAA

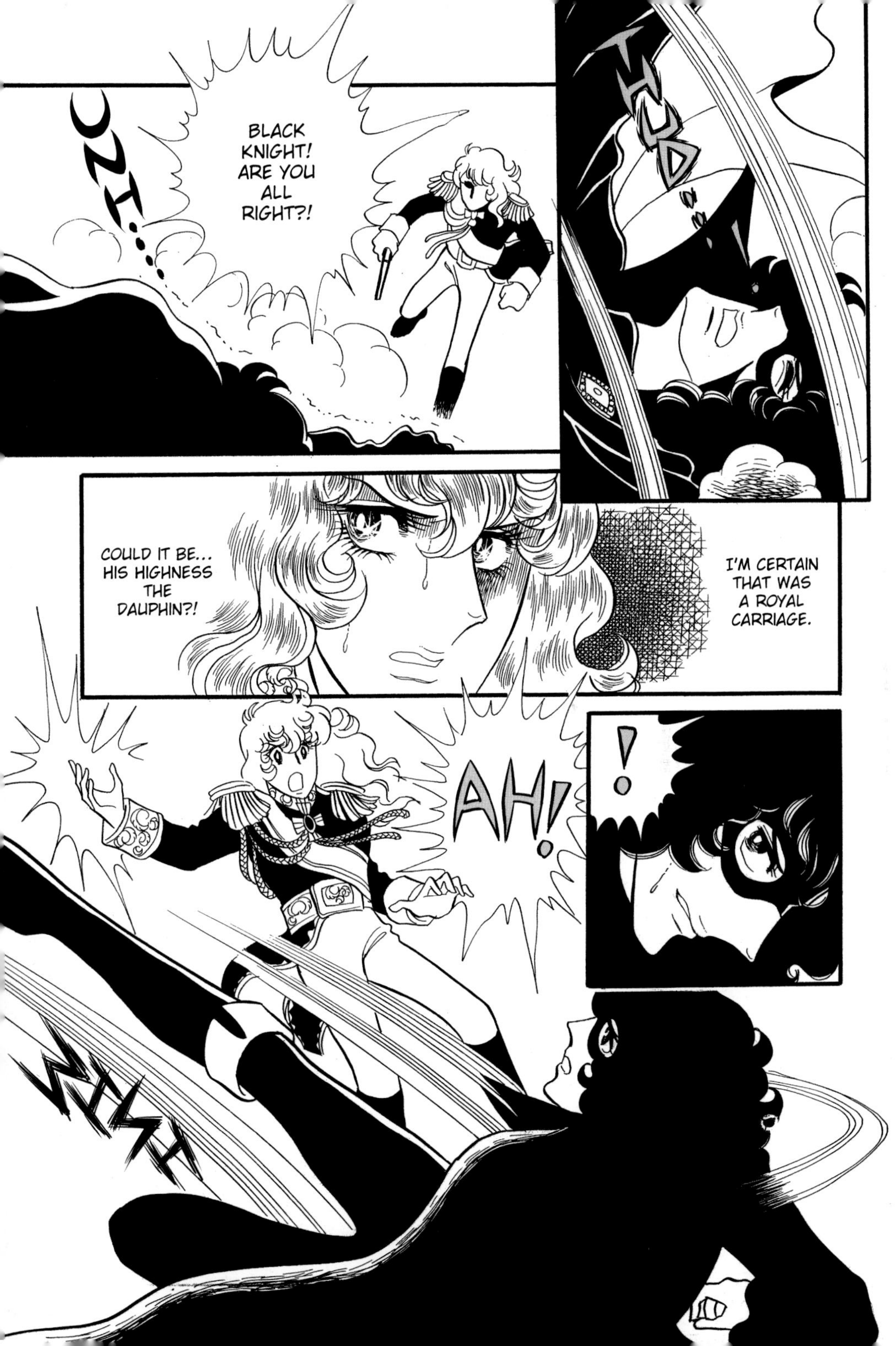
THUD
UNH...
BLACK KNIGHT! ARE YOU ALL RIGHT?!
I'M CERTAIN THAT WAS A ROYAL CARRIAGE.
COULD IT BE... HIS HIGHNESS THE DAUPHIN?!
!
AH!
WHSH

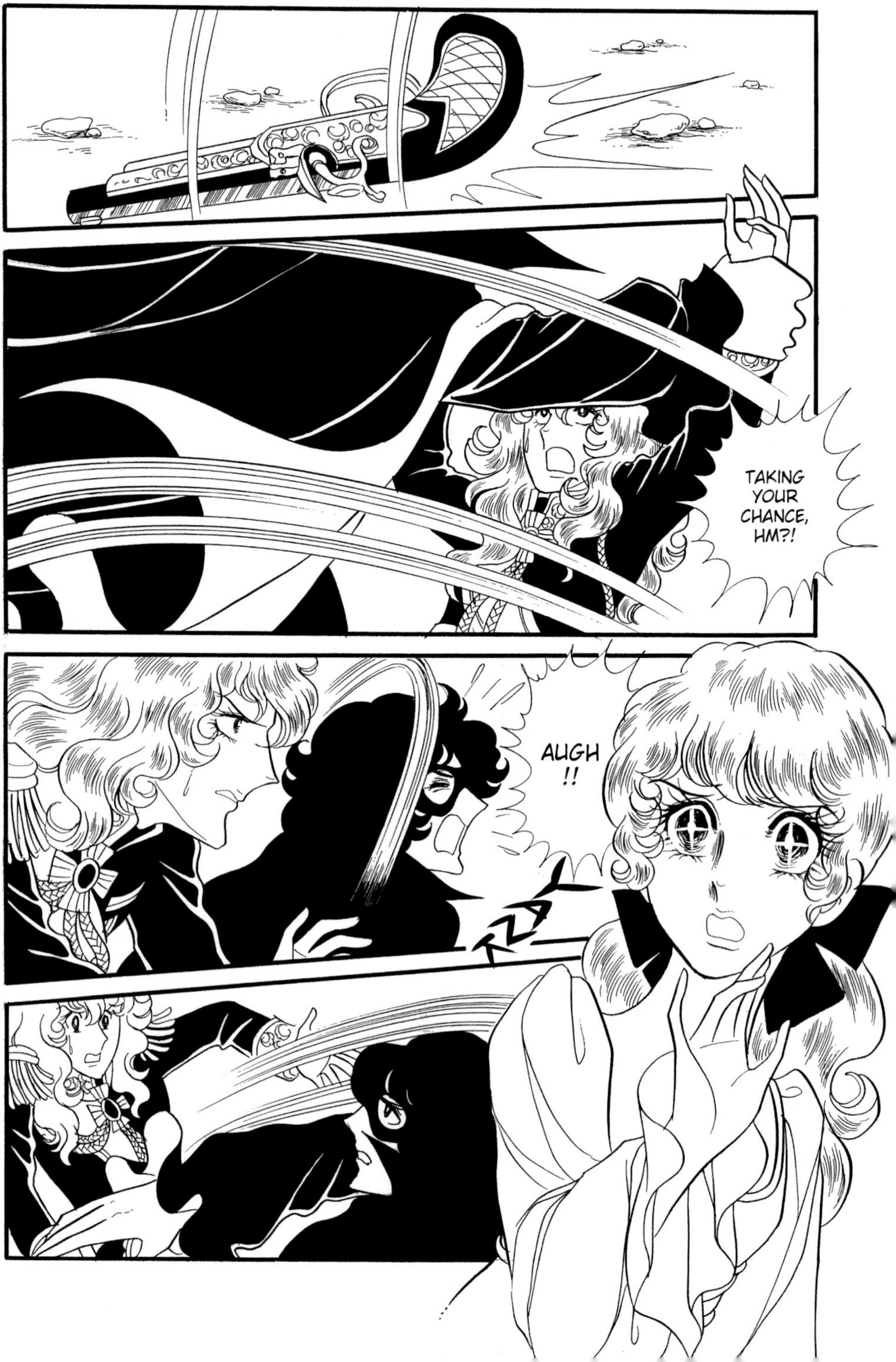
TAKING YOUR CHANCE, HM?!
AUGH !!

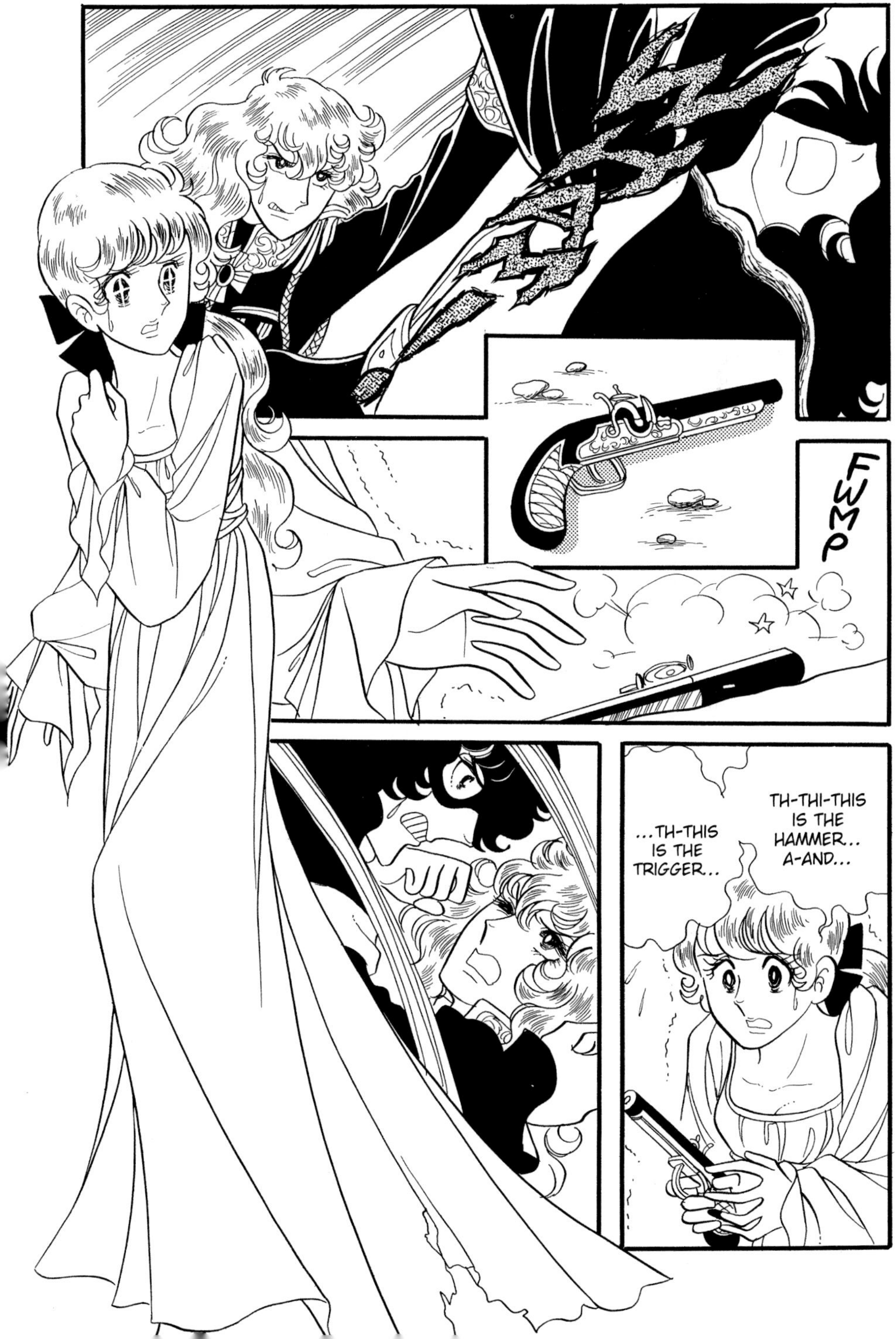
FWMP
TH-THI-THIS IS THE HAMMER... A-AND...
...TH-THIS IS THE TRIGGER...

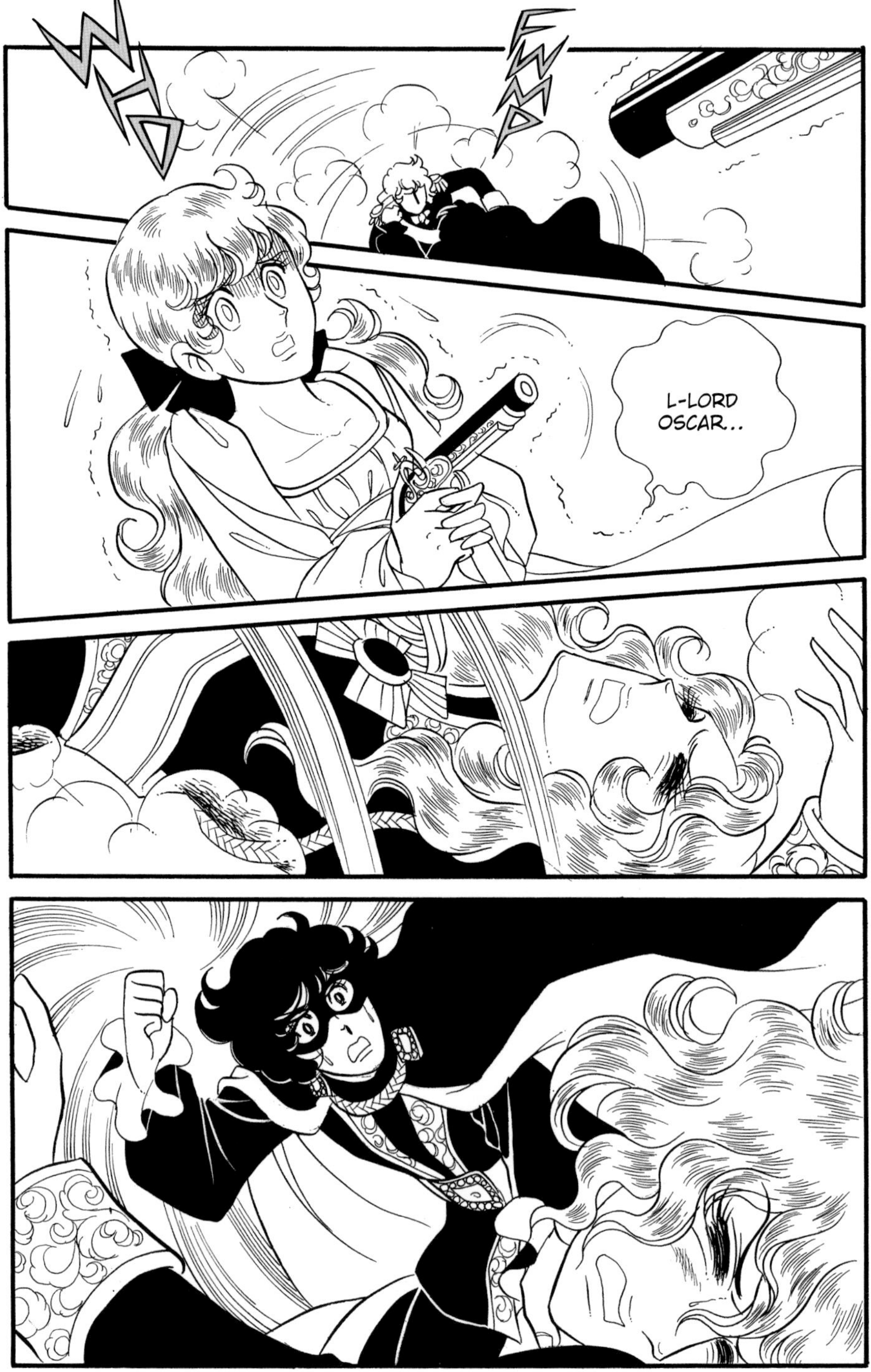
FWMP
WHO
L-LORD OSCAR...

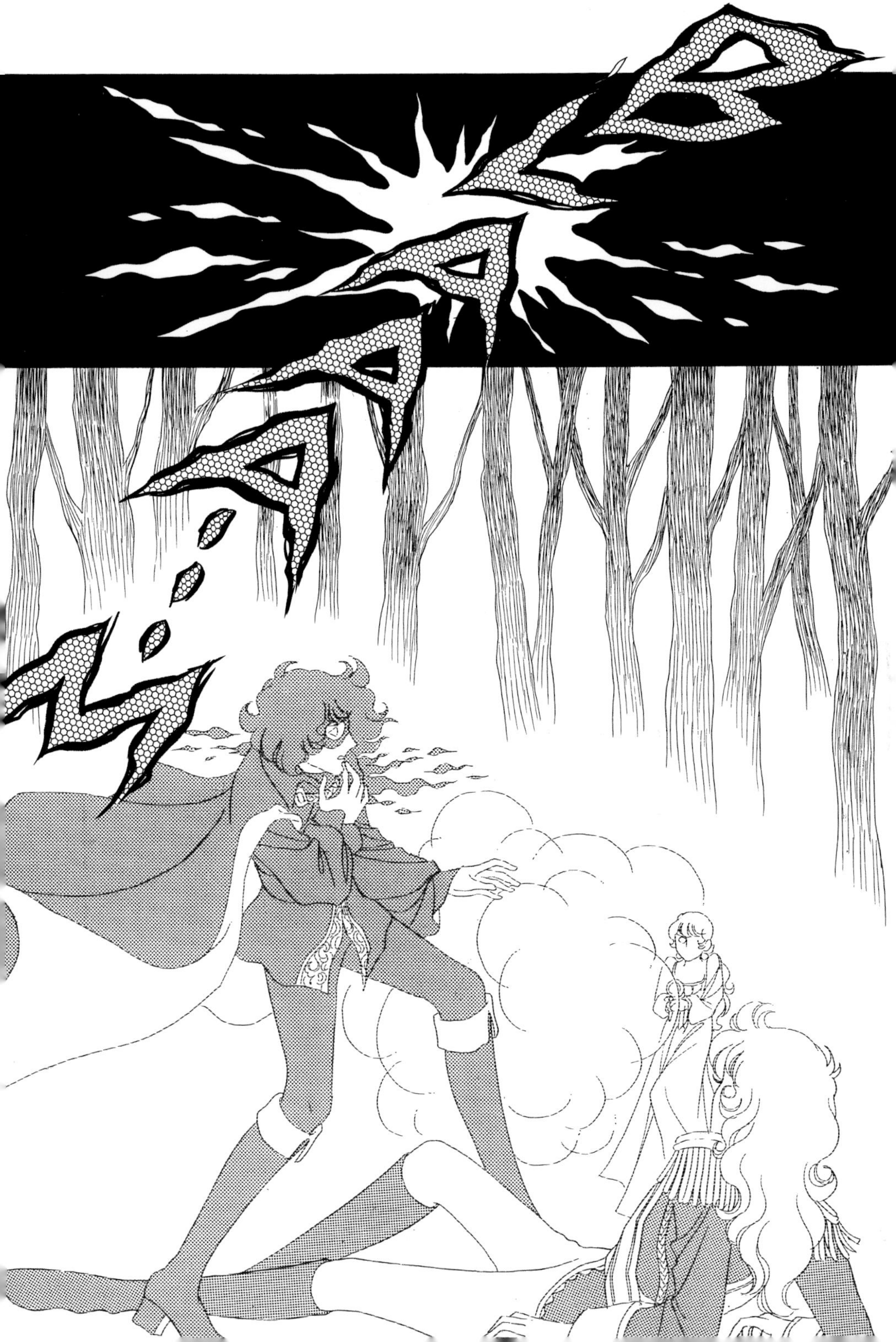

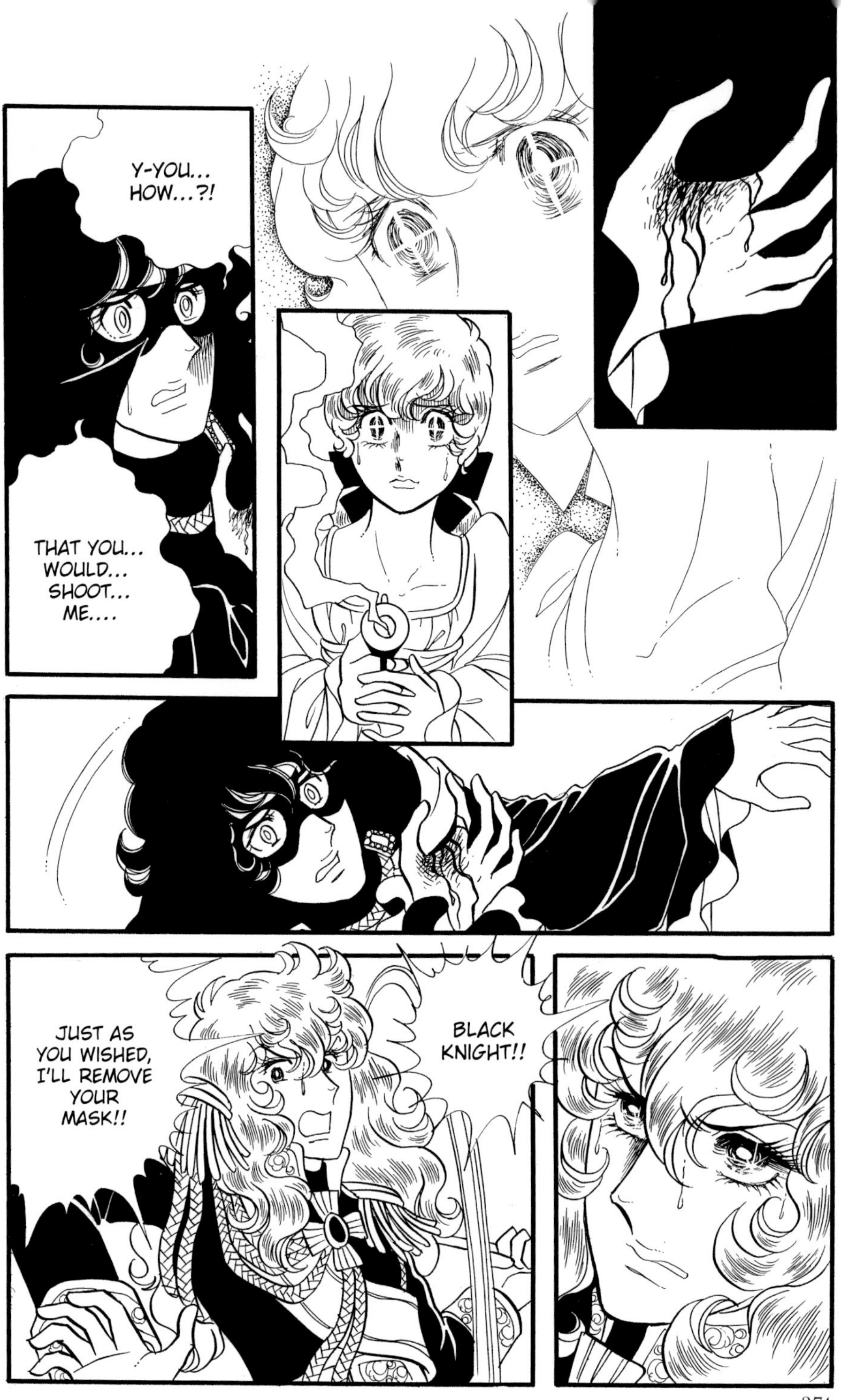
Y-YOU... HOW...?!
THAT YOU... WOULD... SHOOT... ME....
BLACK KNIGHT!!
JUST AS YOU WISHED, I'LL REMOVE YOUR MASK!!

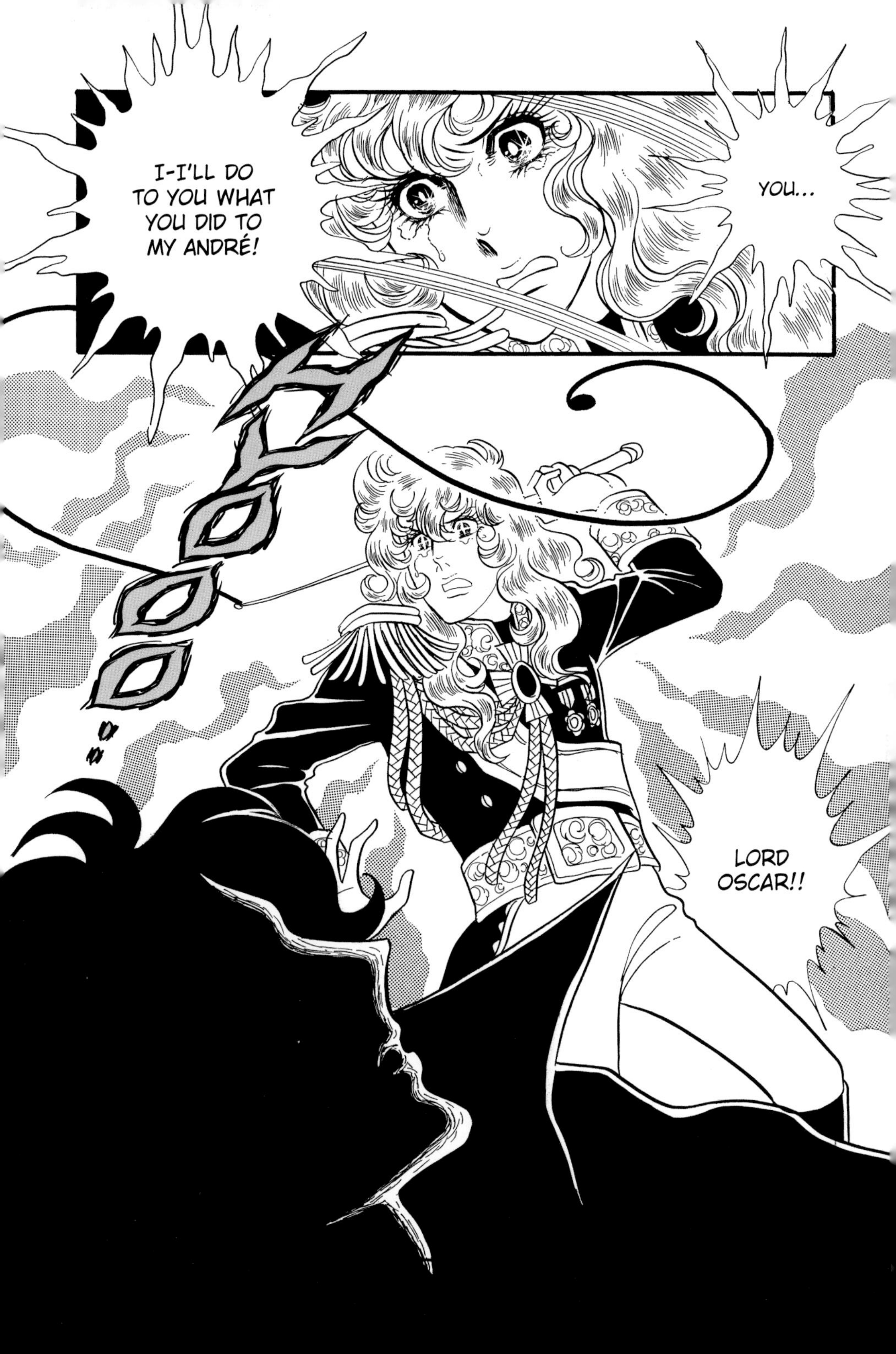
YOU...
I-I'LL DO TO YOU WHAT YOU DID TO MY ANDRÉ!
HYOOOO
LORD OSCAR!!

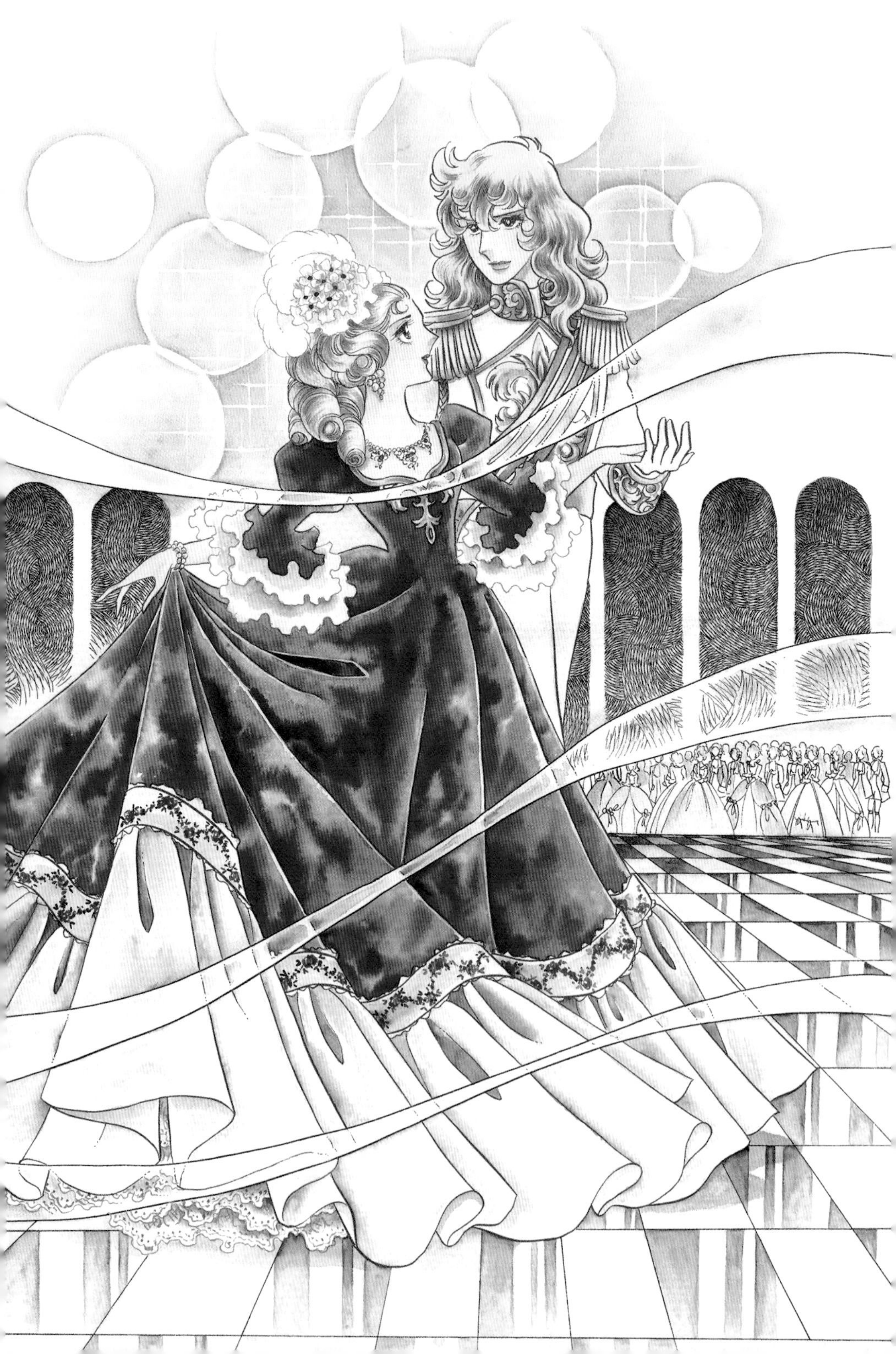

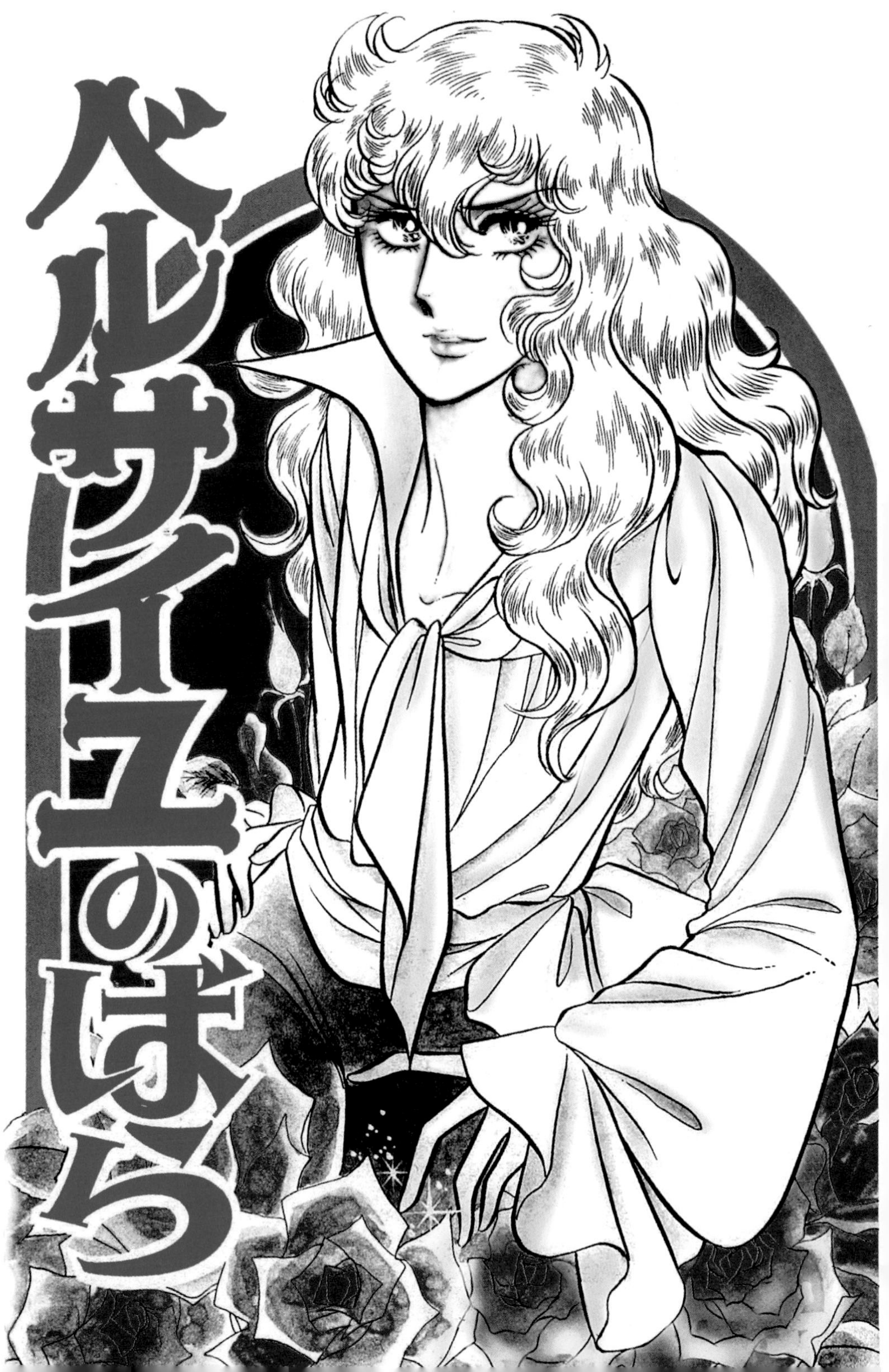
ベルサイユのばら

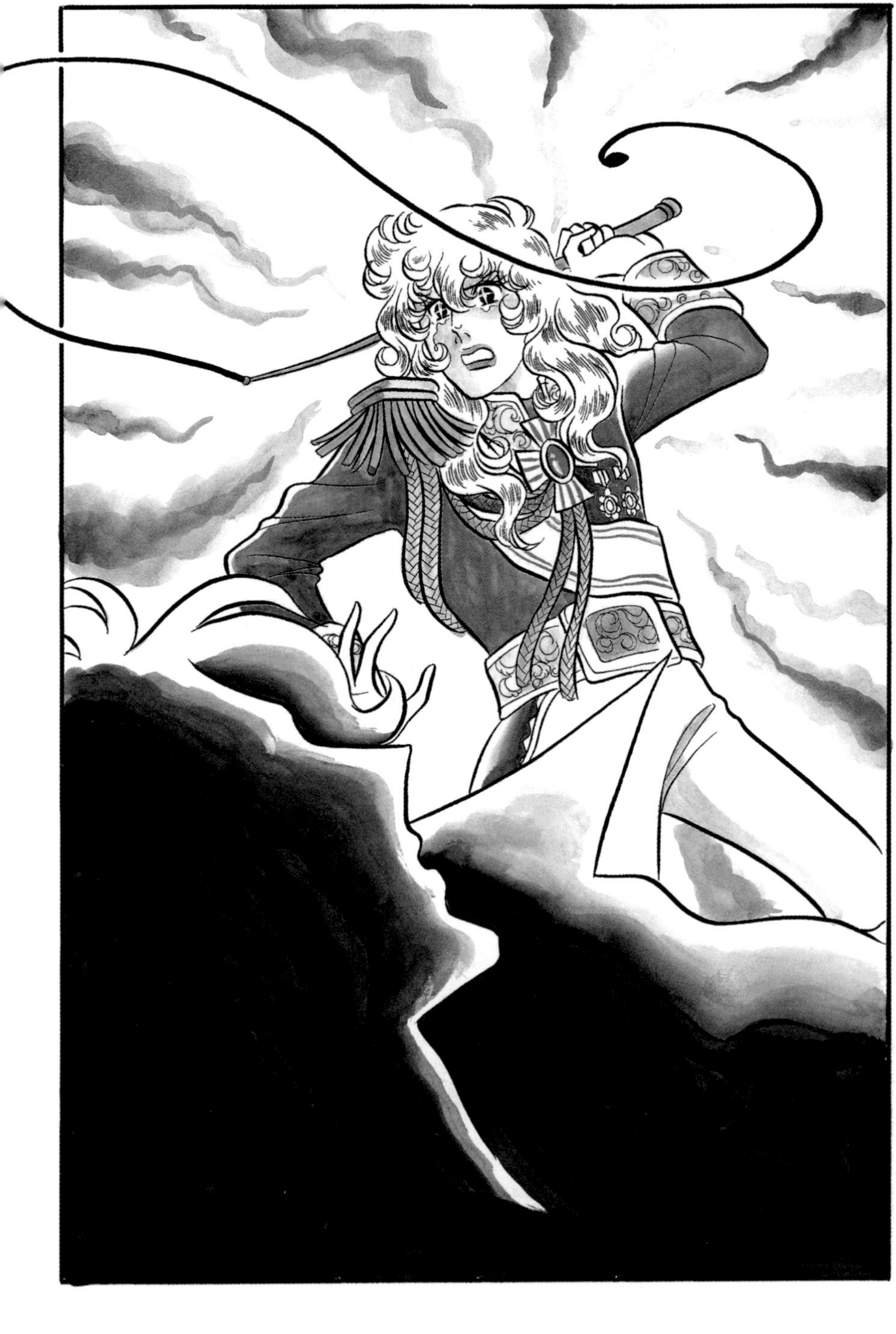

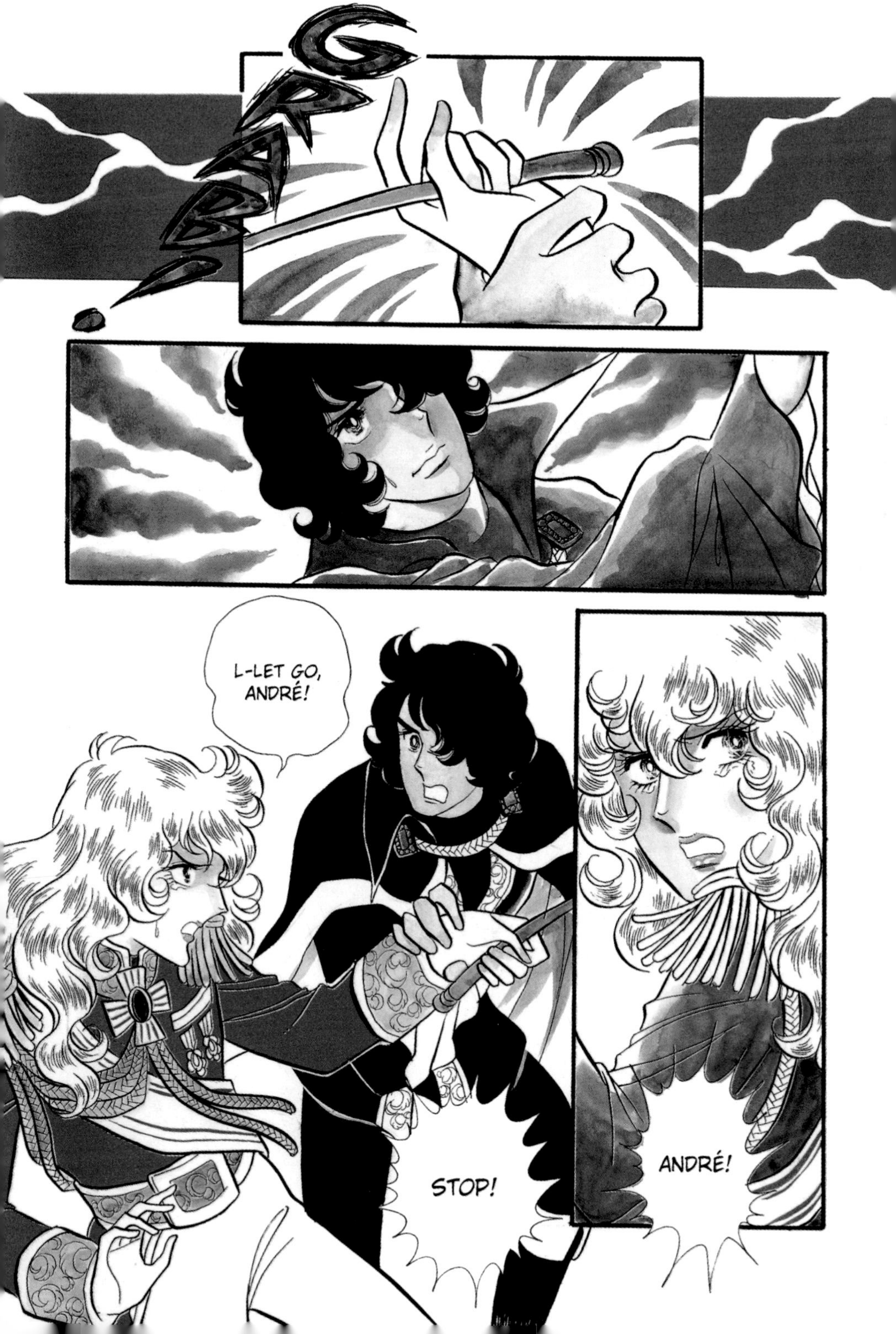
GRAB!
ANDRÉ!
L-LET GO, ANDRÉ!
STOP!

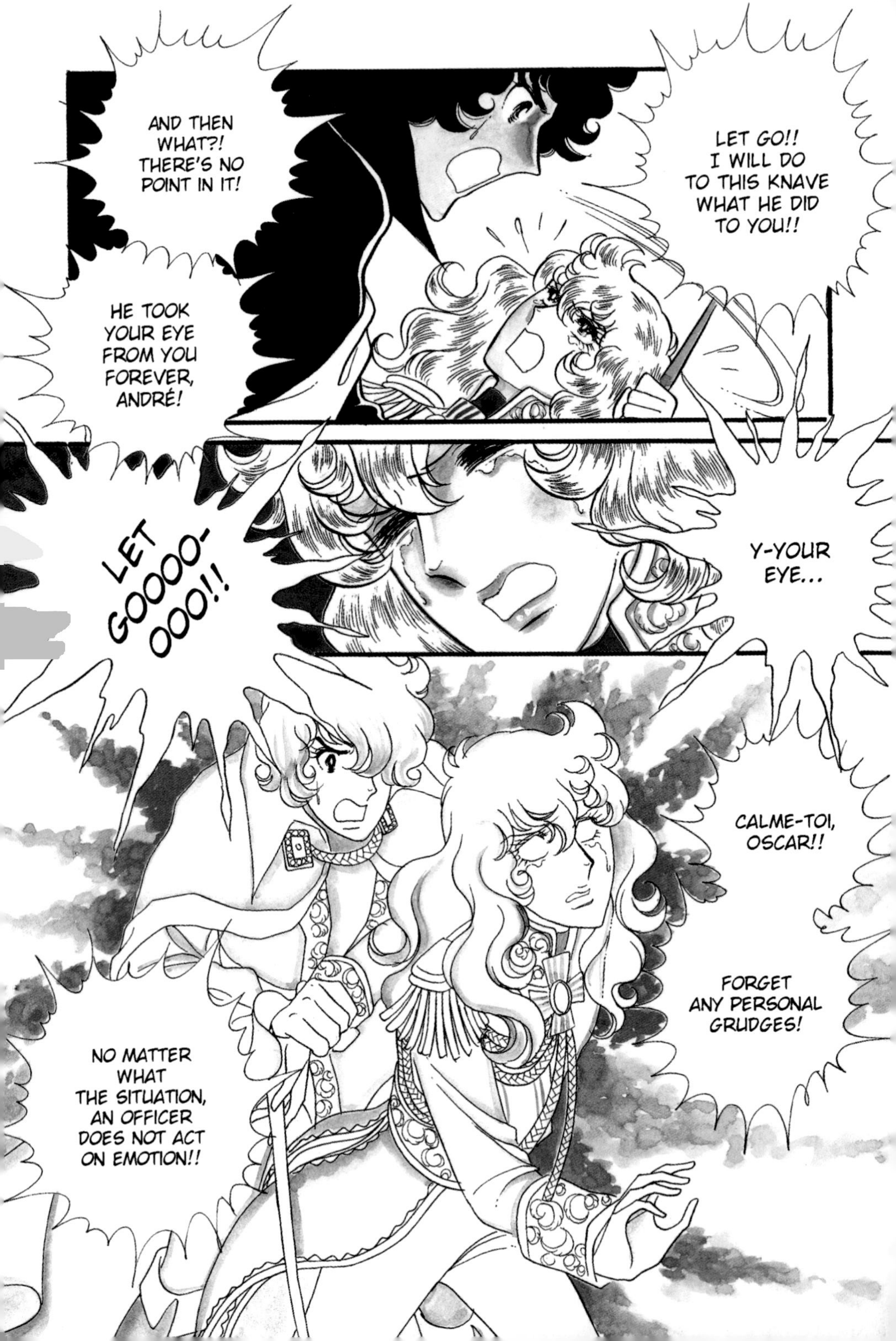

LET GO!! I WILL DO TO THIS KNAVE WHAT HE DID TO YOU!!
AND THEN WHAT?! THERE'S NO POINT IN IT!
HE TOOK YOUR EYE FROM YOU FOREVER, ANDRÉ!
Y-YOUR EYE...
LET GOOOO-OOO!!
CALME-TOI, OSCAR!!
FORGET ANY PERSONAL GRUDGES!
NO MATTER WHAT THE SITUATION, AN OFFICER DOES NOT ACT ON EMOTION!!

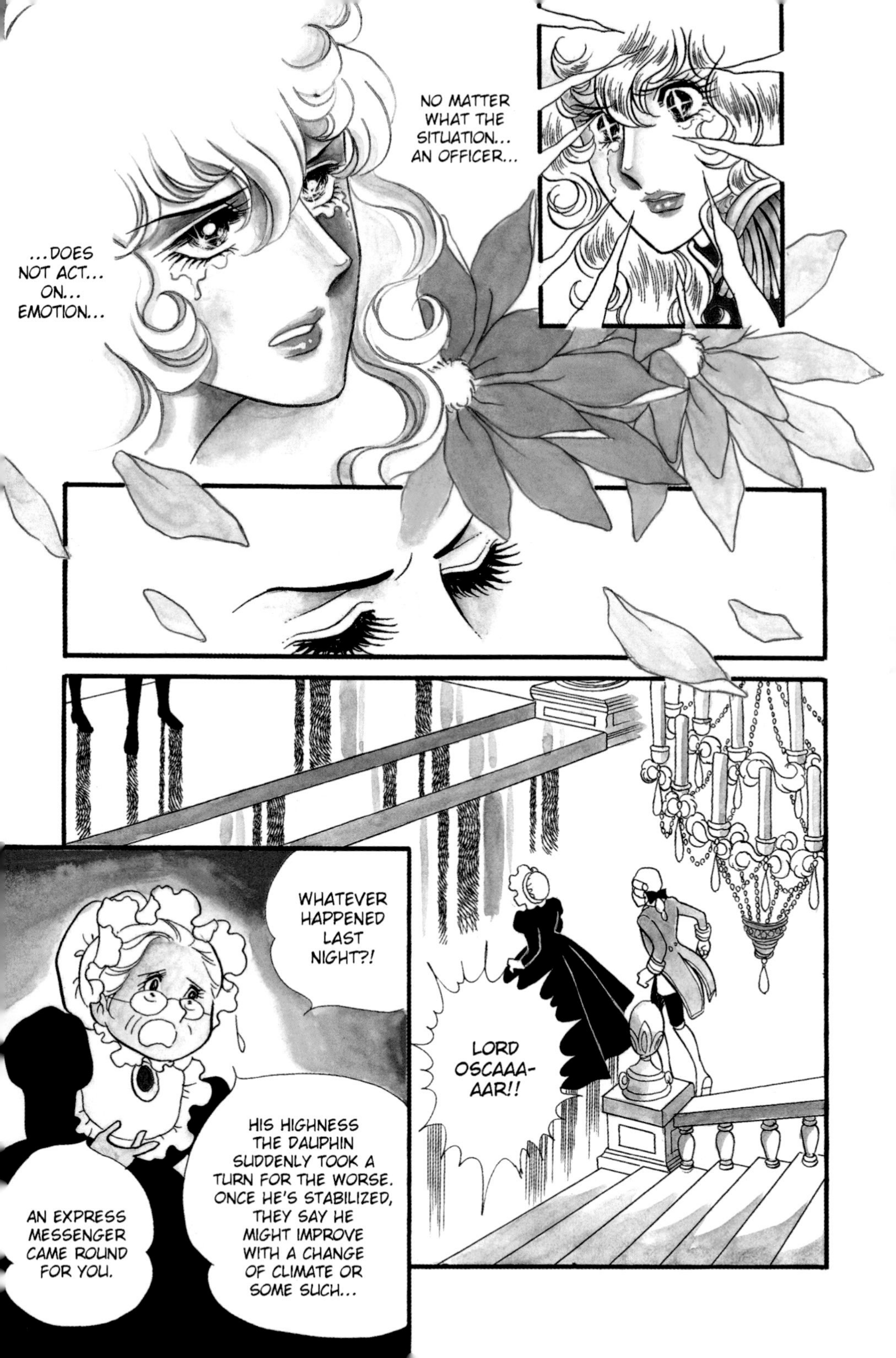
NO MATTER WHAT THE SITUATION... AN OFFICER...
...DOES NOT ACT... ON... EMOTION...
LORD OSCAAA-AAR!!
WHATEVER HAPPENED LAST NIGHT?!
HIS HIGHNESS THE DAUPHIN SUDDENLY TOOK A TURN FOR THE WORSE. ONCE HE'S STABILIZED, THEY SAY HE MIGHT IMPROVE WITH A CHANGE OF CLIMATE OR SOME SUCH...
AN EXPRESS MESSENGER CAME ROUND FOR YOU.

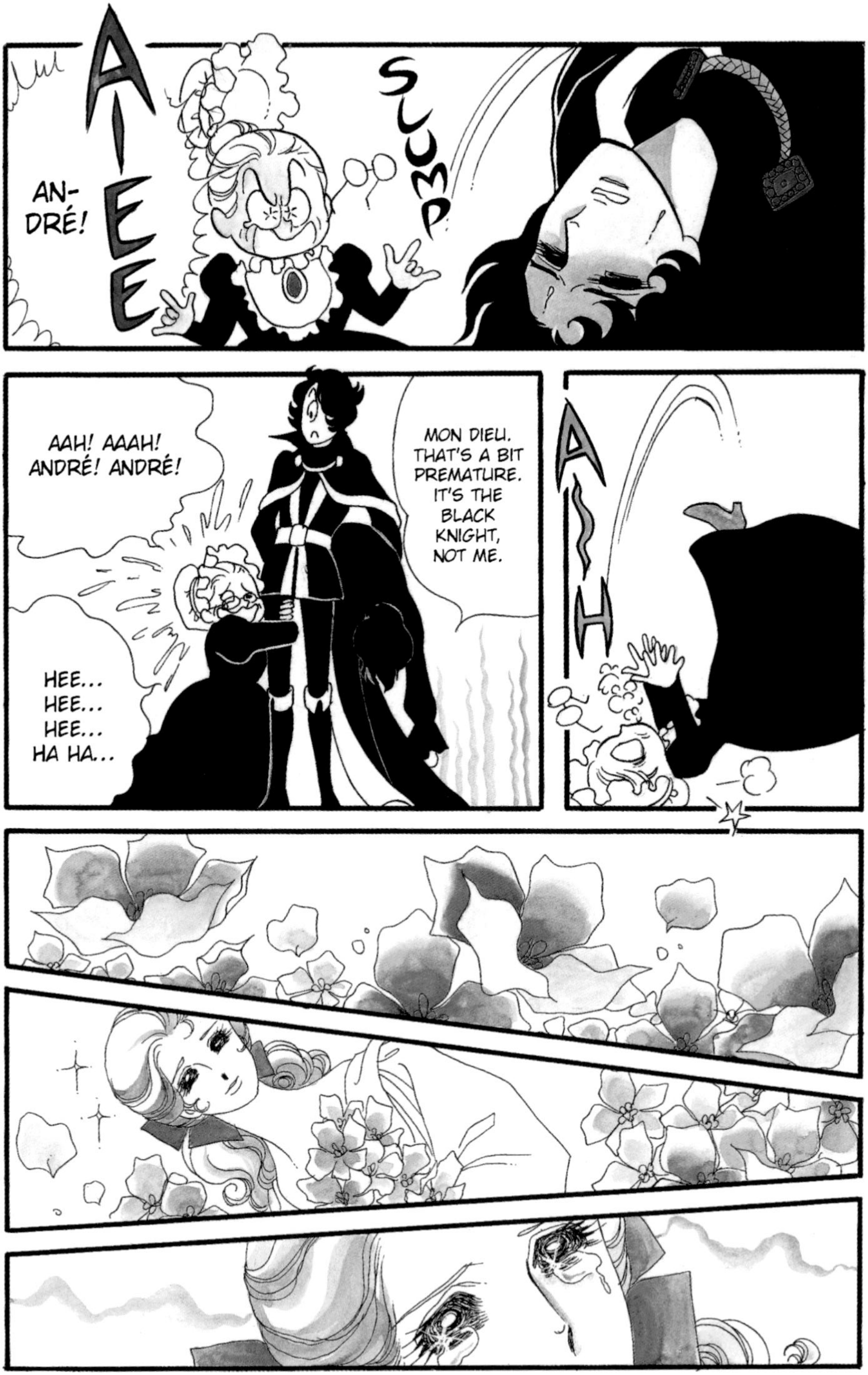
SLUMP
AIEE
AN-DRÉ!
AH
MON DIEU. THAT'S A BIT PREMATURE. IT'S THE BLACK KNIGHT, NOT ME.
AAH! AAAH! ANDRÉ! ANDRÉ!
HEE... HEE... HEE... HA HA...

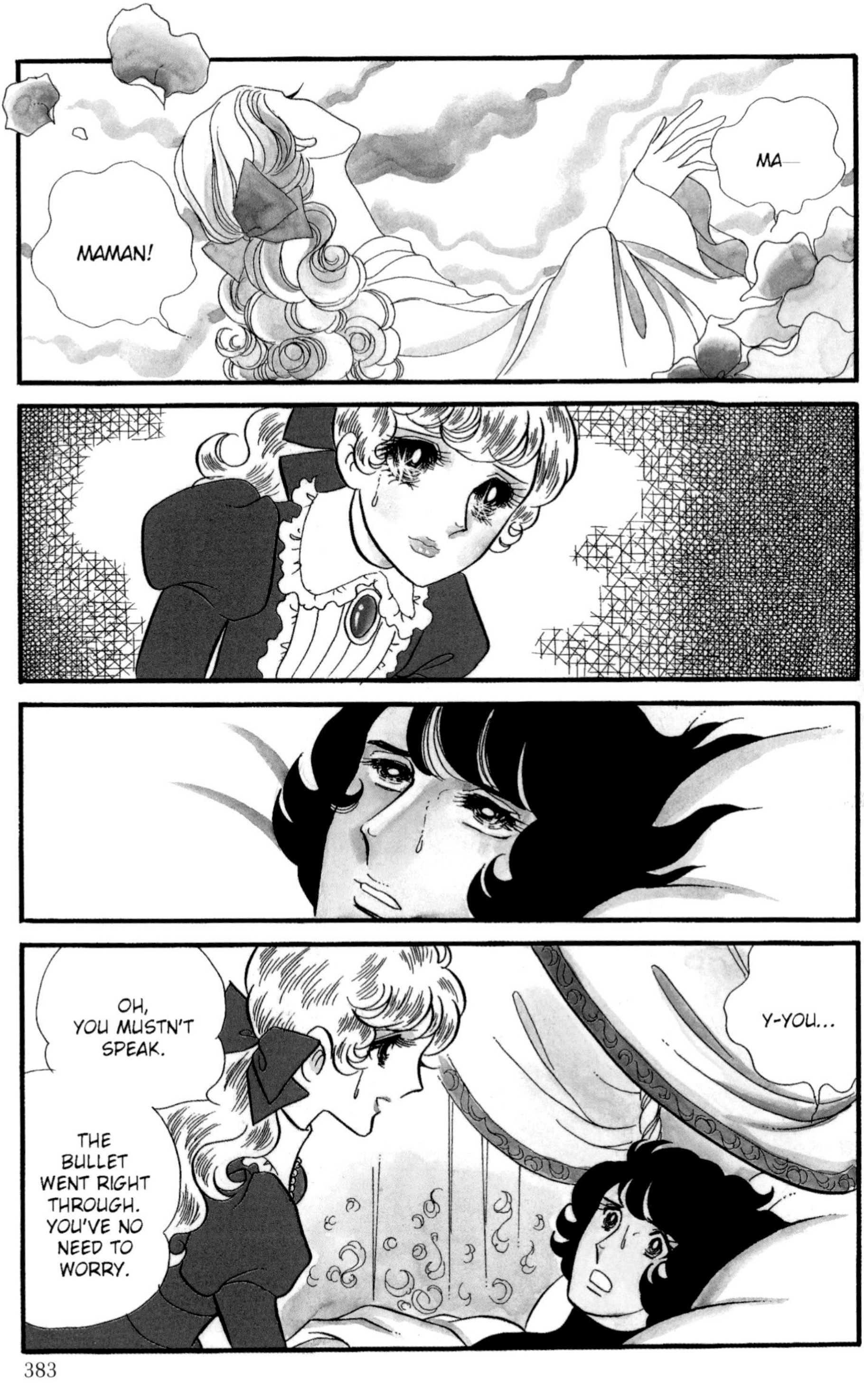
MA—
MAMAN!
Y-YOU...
OH, YOU MUSTN'T SPEAK.
THE BULLET WENT RIGHT THROUGH. YOU'VE NO NEED TO WORRY.

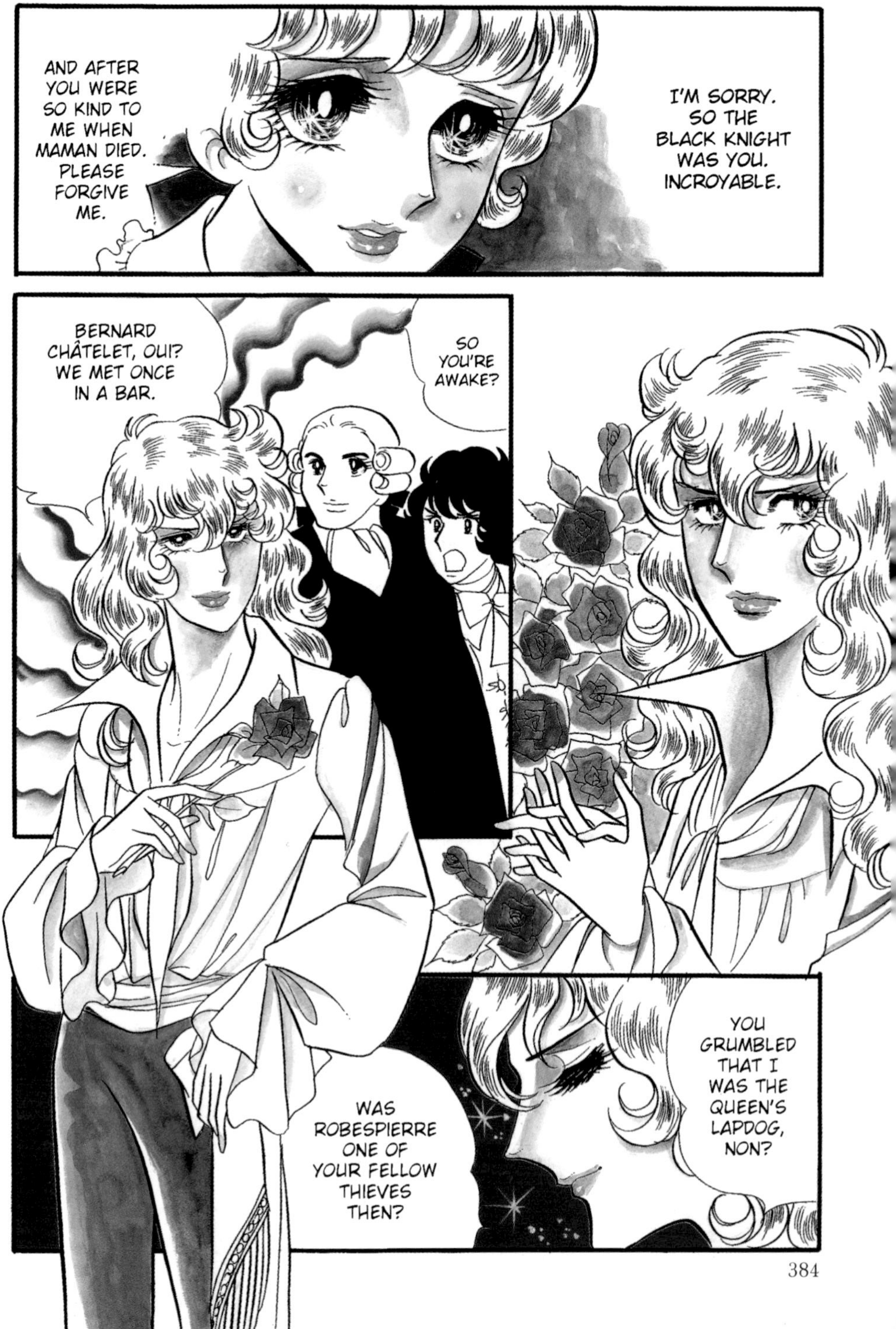
I'M SORRY. SO THE BLACK KNIGHT WAS YOU. INCROYABLE.
AND AFTER YOU WERE SO KIND TO ME WHEN MAMAN DIED. PLEASE FORGIVE ME.
SO YOU'RE AWAKE?
BERNARD CHÂTELET, OUI? WE MET ONCE IN A BAR.
YOU GRUMBLED THAT I WAS THE QUEEN'S LAPDOG, NON?
WAS ROBESPIERRE ONE OF YOUR FELLOW THIEVES THEN?

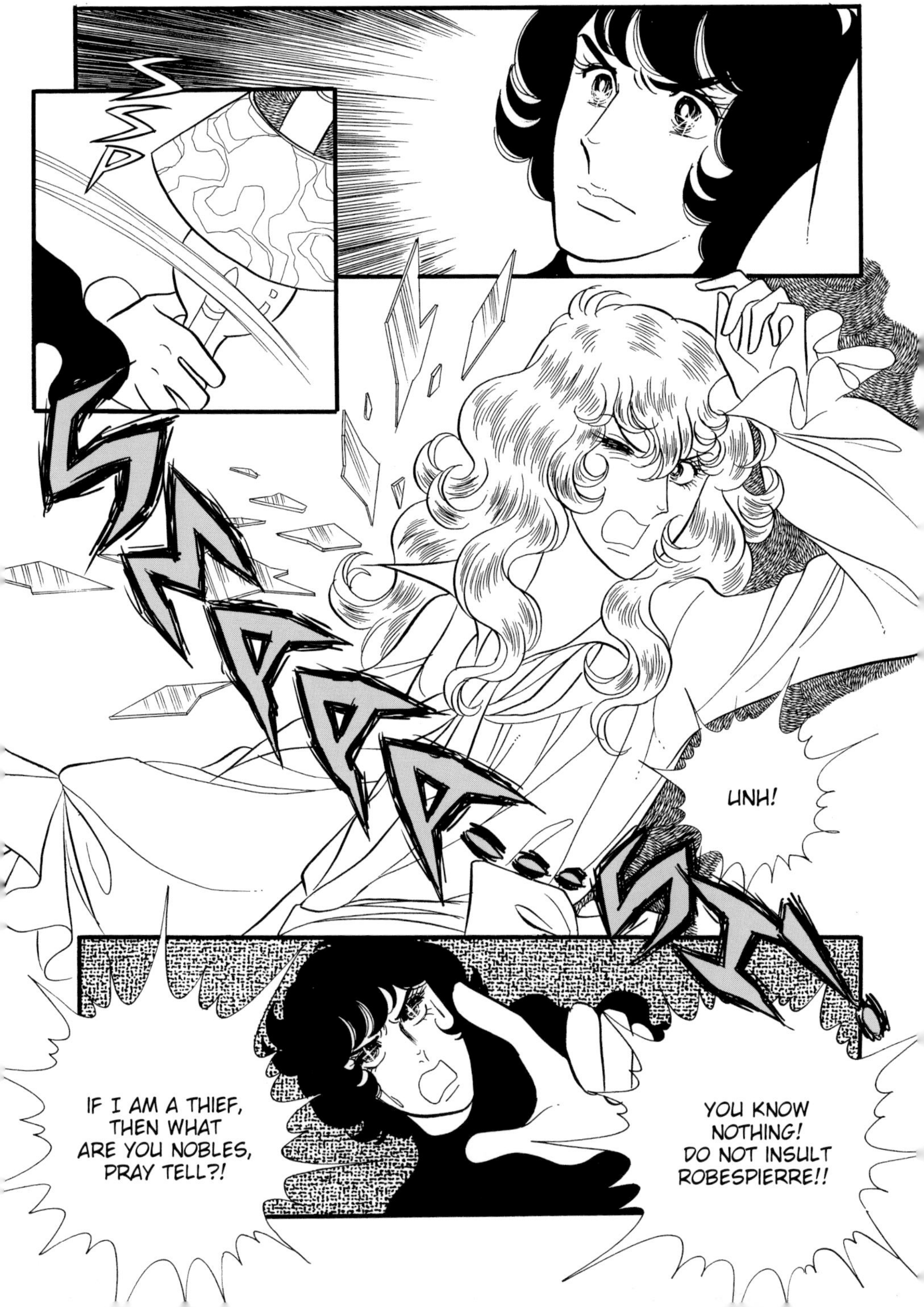
SSP
SMAAAASH!
UNH!
YOU KNOW NOTHING! DO NOT INSULT ROBESPIERRE!!
IF I AM A THIEF, THEN WHAT ARE YOU NOBLES, PRAY TELL?!

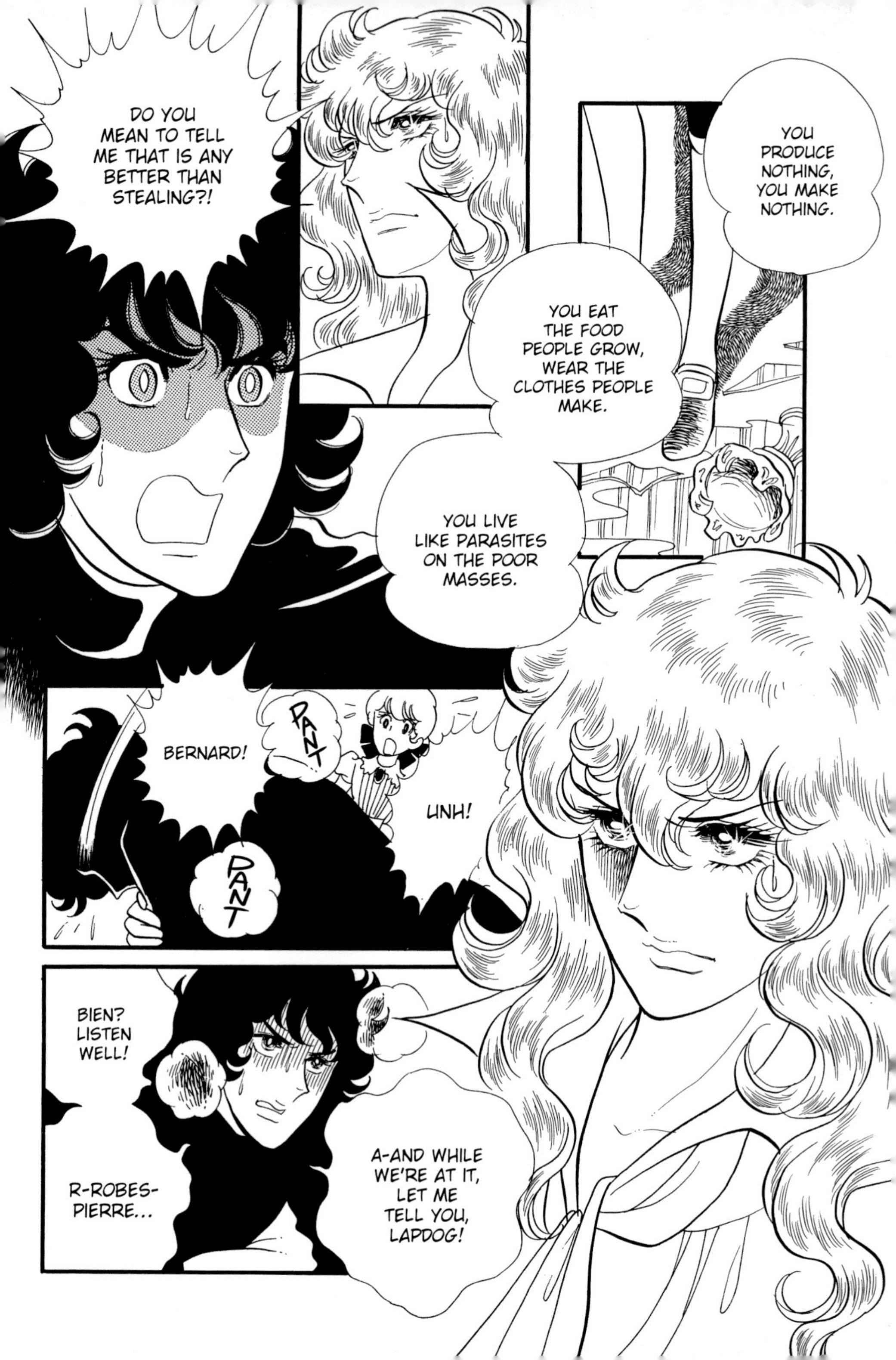
YOU PRODUCE NOTHING, YOU MAKE NOTHING.
YOU EAT THE FOOD PEOPLE GROW, WEAR THE CLOTHES PEOPLE MAKE.
YOU LIVE LIKE PARASITES ON THE POOR MASSES.
DO YOU MEAN TO TELL ME THAT IS ANY BETTER THAN STEALING?!
UNH!
PANT
BERNARD!
PANT
BIEN? LISTEN WELL!
R-ROBES-PIERRE...
A-AND WHILE WE'RE AT IT, LET ME TELL YOU, LAPDOG!

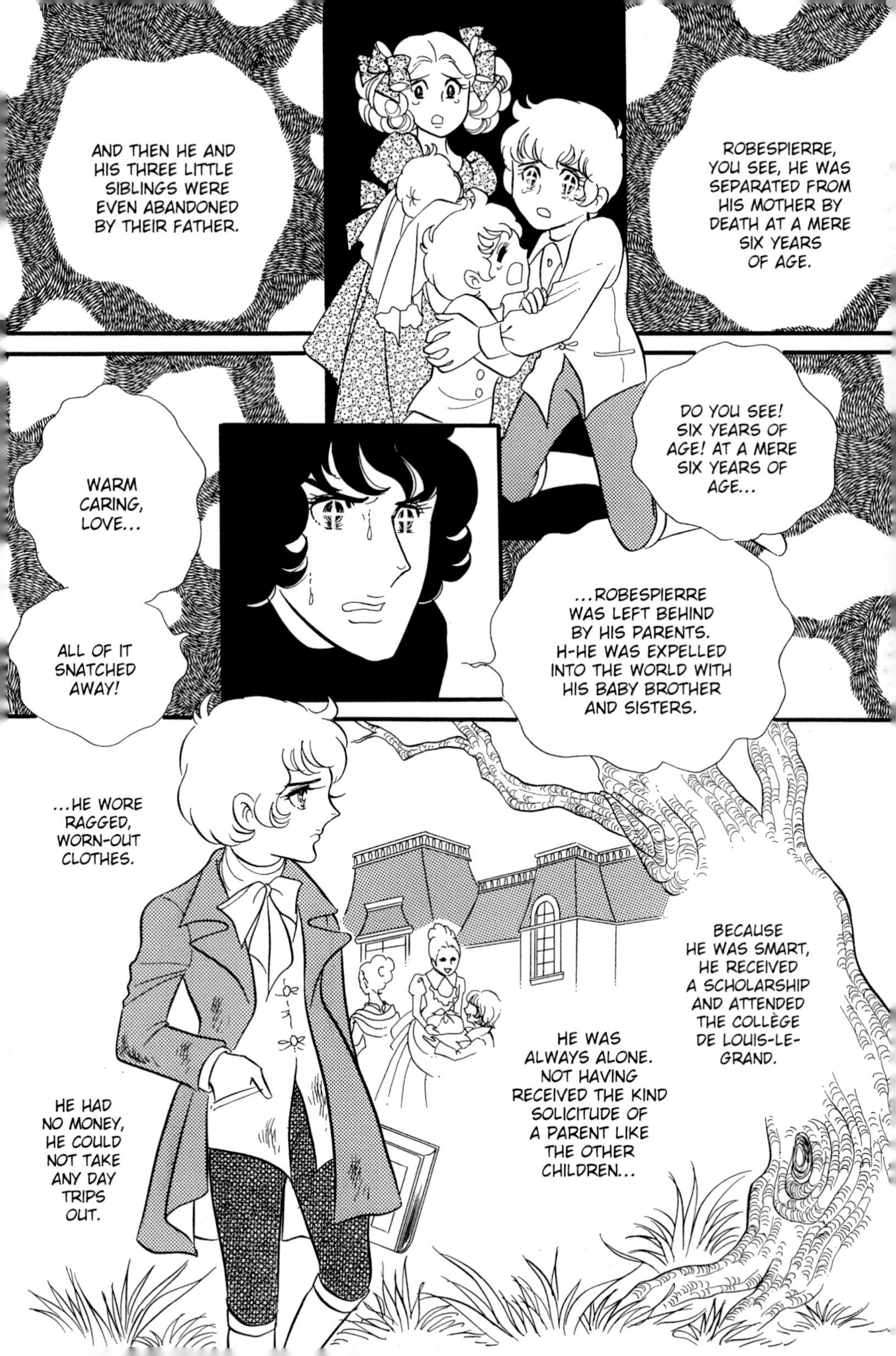
ROBESPIERRE, YOU SEE, HE WAS SEPARATED FROM HIS MOTHER BY DEATH AT A MERE SIX YEARS OF AGE.
AND THEN HE AND HIS THREE LITTLE SIBLINGS WERE EVEN ABANDONED BY THEIR FATHER.
DO YOU SEE! SIX YEARS OF AGE! AT A MERE SIX YEARS OF AGE...
...ROBESPIERRE WAS LEFT BEHIND BY HIS PARENTS. H-HE WAS EXPELLED INTO THE WORLD WITH HIS BABY BROTHER AND SISTERS.
WARM CARING, LOVE...
ALL OF IT SNATCHED AWAY!
BECAUSE HE WAS SMART, HE RECEIVED A SCHOLARSHIP AND ATTENDED THE COLLÈGE DE LOUIS-LE-GRAND.
HE WAS ALWAYS ALONE. NOT HAVING RECEIVED THE KIND SOLICITUDE OF A PARENT LIKE THE OTHER CHILDREN...
...HE WORE RAGGED, WORN-OUT CLOTHES.
HE HAD NO MONEY, HE COULD NOT TAKE ANY DAY TRIPS OUT.

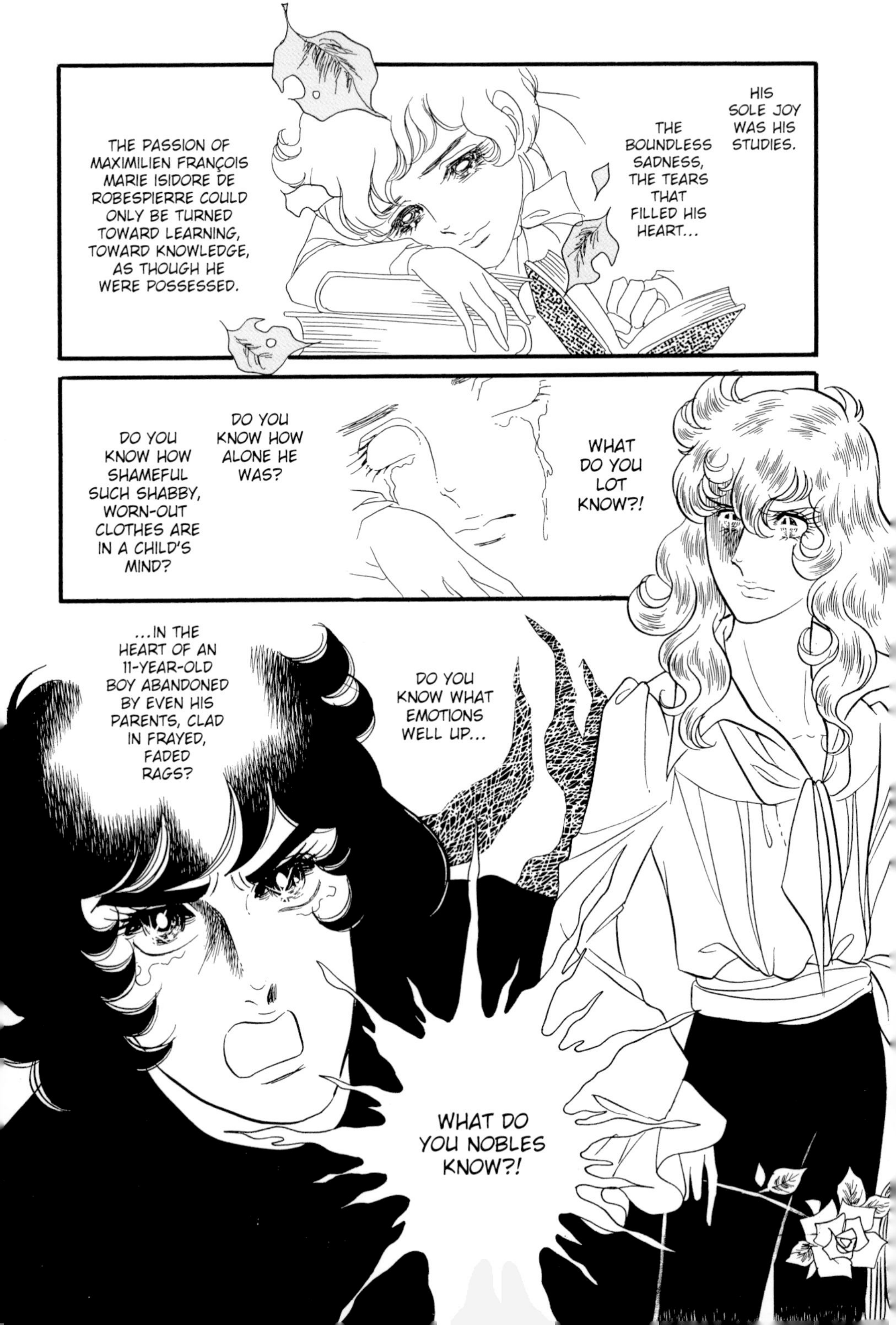
HIS SOLE JOY WAS HIS STUDIES.
THE BOUNDLESS SADNESS, THE TEARS THAT FILLED HIS HEART...
THE PASSION OF MAXIMILIEN FRANÇOIS MARIE ISIDORE DE ROBESPIERRE COULD ONLY BE TURNED TOWARD LEARNING, TOWARD KNOWLEDGE, AS THOUGH HE WERE POSSESSED.
WHAT DO YOU LOT KNOW?!
DO YOU KNOW HOW ALONE HE WAS?
DO YOU KNOW HOW SHAMEFUL SUCH SHABBY, WORN-OUT CLOTHES ARE IN A CHILD'S MIND?
DO YOU KNOW WHAT EMOTIONS WELL UP...
...IN THE HEART OF AN 11-YEAR-OLD BOY ABANDONED BY EVEN HIS PARENTS, CLAD IN FRAYED, FADED RAGS?
WHAT DO YOU NOBLES KNOW?!

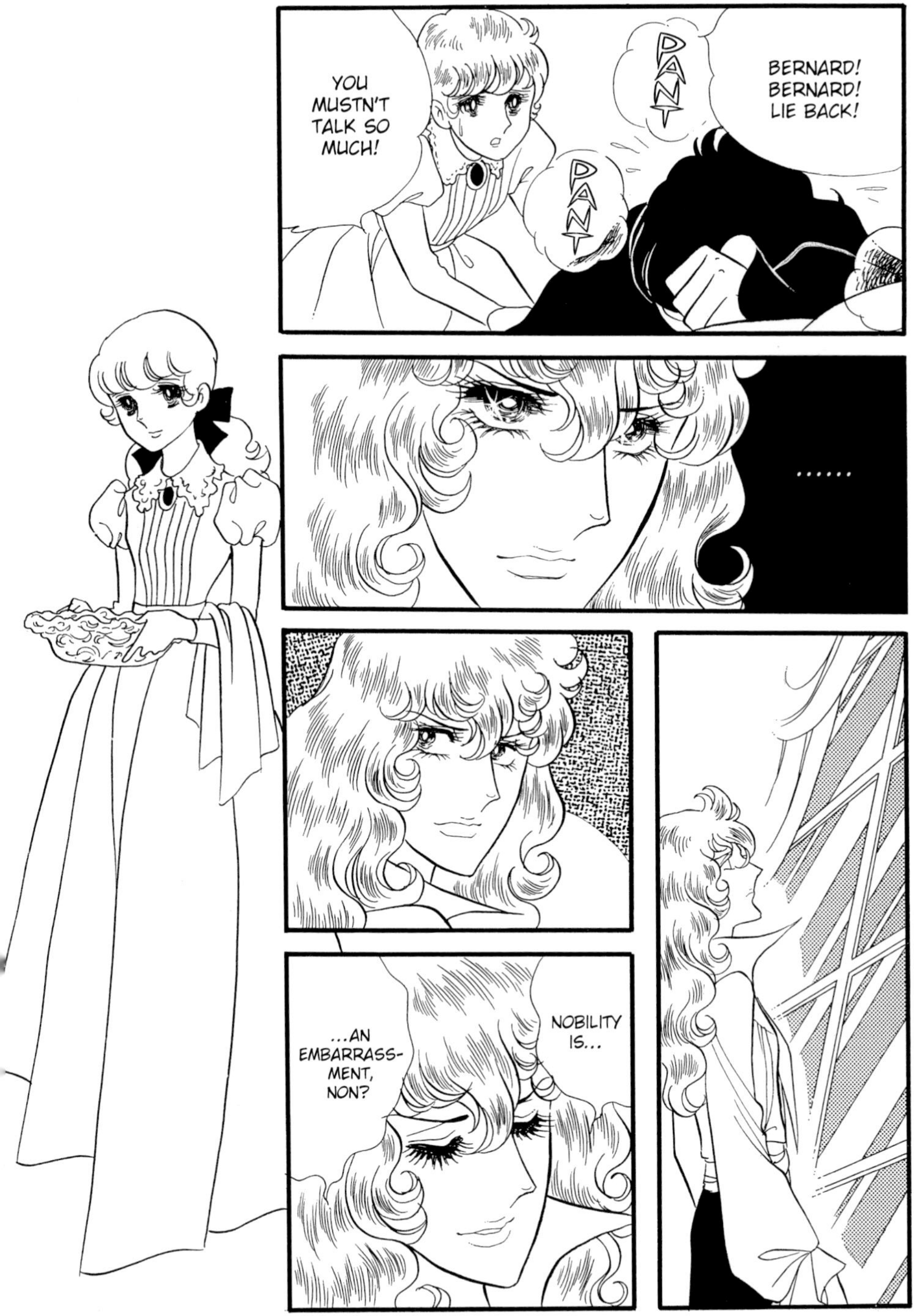
BERNARD! BERNARD! LIE BACK!
PANT
PANT
YOU MUSTN'T TALK SO MUCH!
......
NOBILITY IS...
...AN EMBARRASS-MENT, NON?

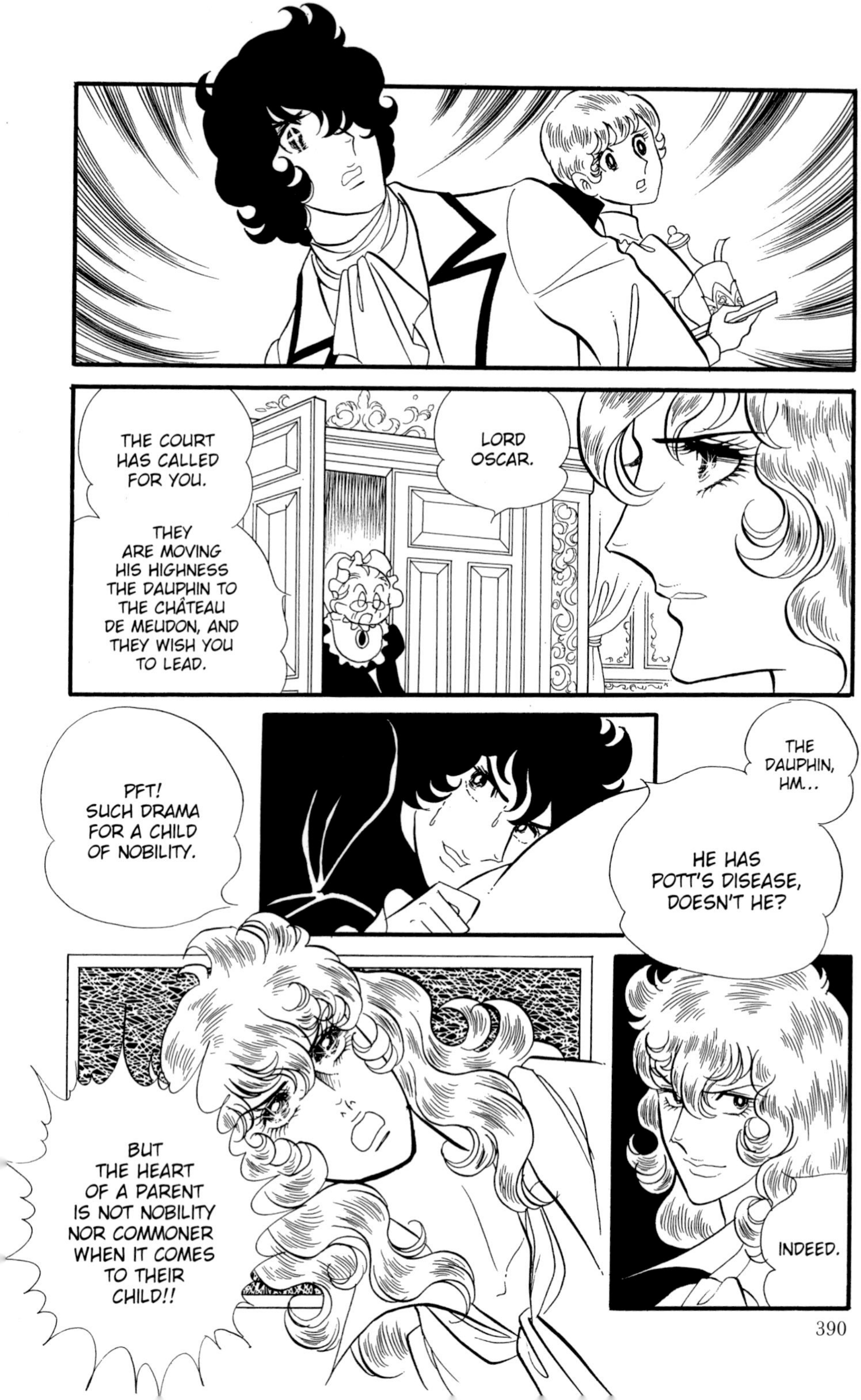

LORD OSCAR.
THE COURT HAS CALLED FOR YOU.
THEY ARE MOVING HIS HIGHNESS THE DAUPHIN TO THE CHÂTEAU DE MEUDON, AND THEY WISH YOU TO LEAD.
THE DAUPHIN, HM...
PFT! SUCH DRAMA FOR A CHILD OF NOBILITY.
HE HAS POTT'S DISEASE, DOESN'T HE?
INDEED.
BUT THE HEART OF A PARENT IS NOT NOBILITY NOR COMMONER WHEN IT COMES TO THEIR CHILD!!

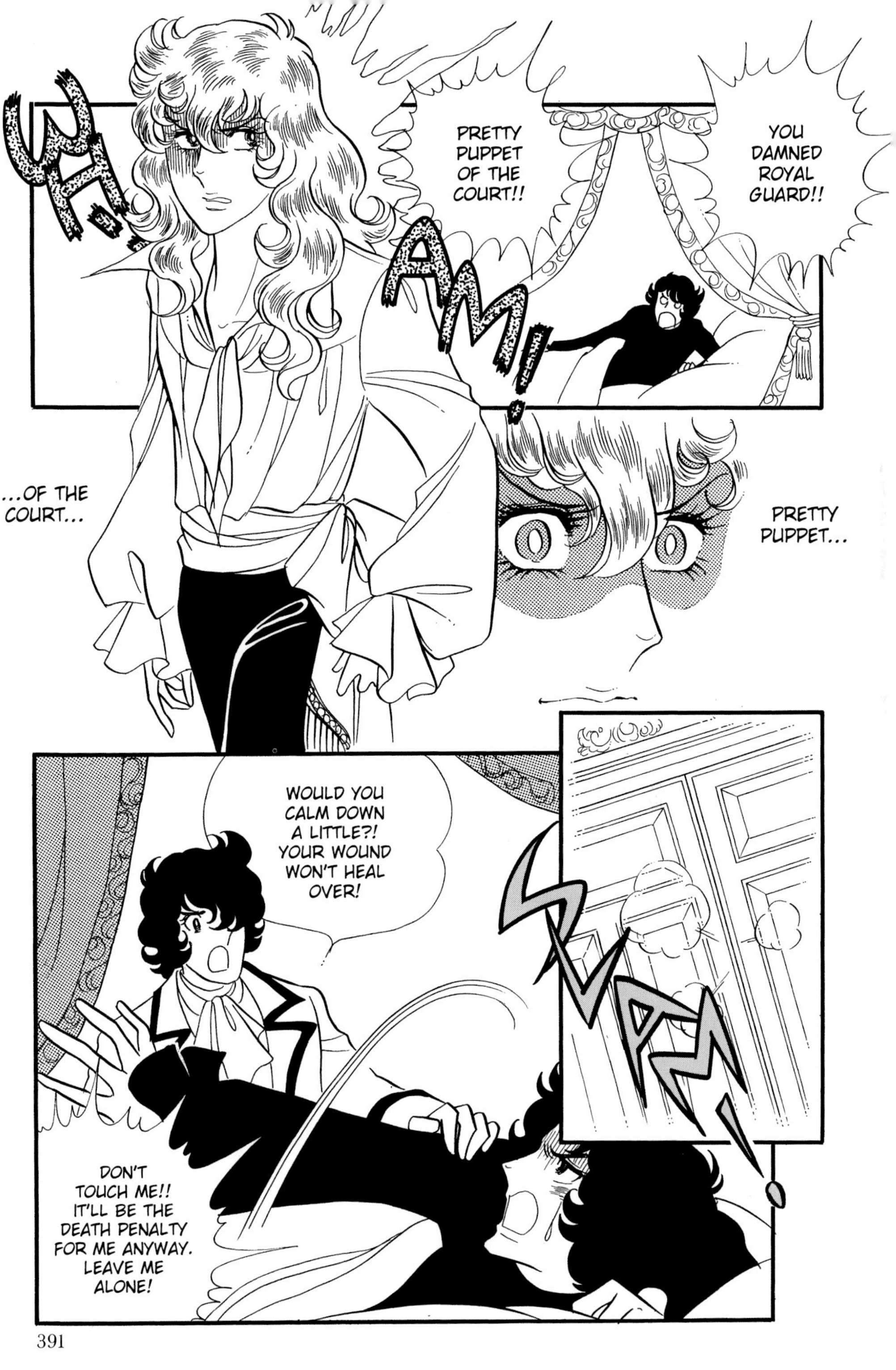
YOU DAMNED ROYAL GUARD!!
PRETTY PUPPET OF THE COURT!!
WHAM!
PRETTY PUPPET...
...OF THE COURT...
SLAM!
WOULD YOU CALM DOWN A LITTLE?! YOUR WOUND WON'T HEAL OVER!
DON'T TOUCH ME!! IT'LL BE THE DEATH PENALTY FOR ME ANYWAY. LEAVE ME ALONE!

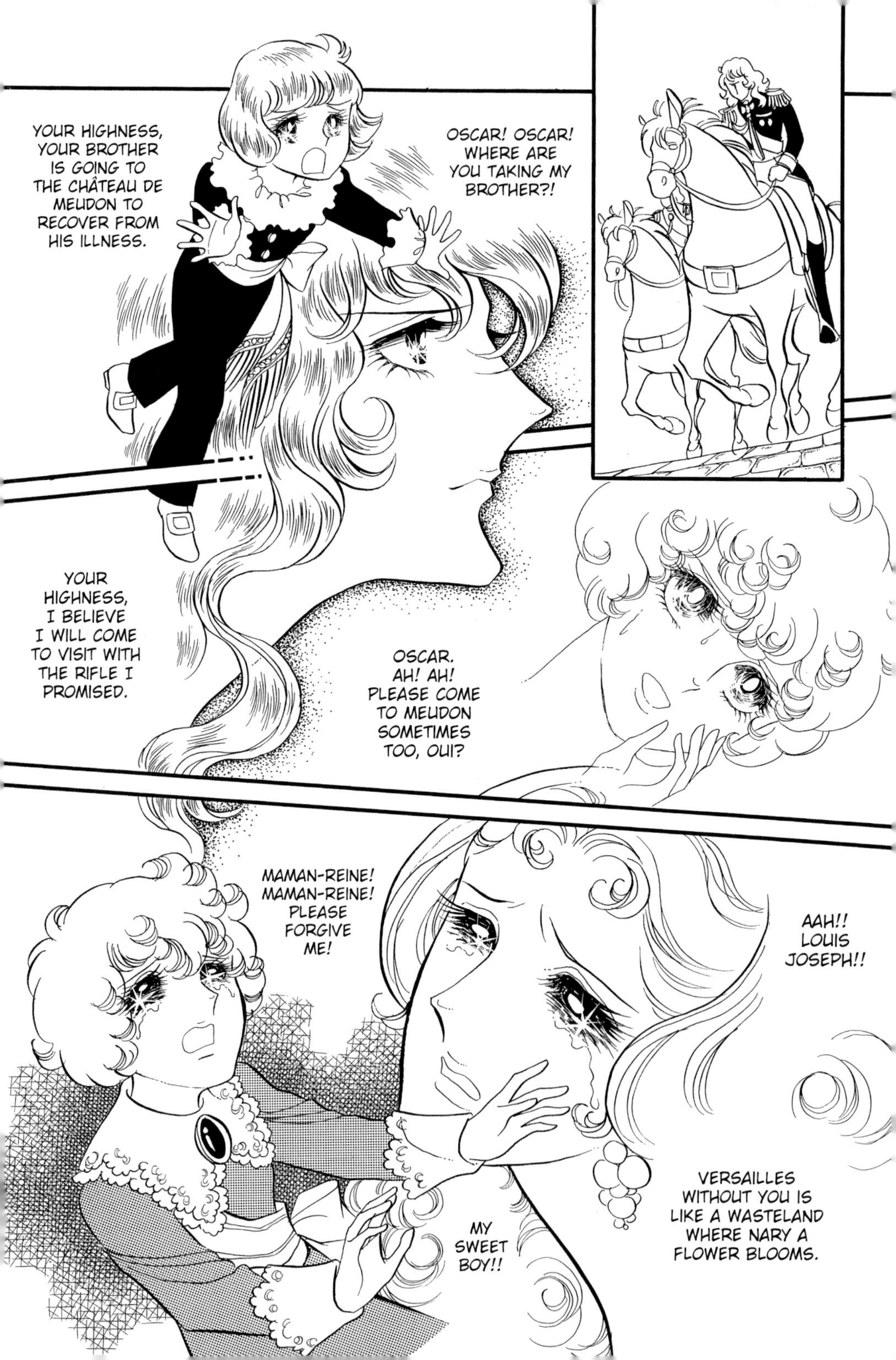
OSCAR! OSCAR! WHERE ARE YOU TAKING MY BROTHER?!
YOUR HIGHNESS, YOUR BROTHER IS GOING TO THE CHÂTEAU DE MEUDON TO RECOVER FROM HIS ILLNESS.
OSCAR. AH! AH! PLEASE COME TO MEUDON SOMETIMES TOO, OUI?
YOUR HIGHNESS, I BELIEVE I WILL COME TO VISIT WITH THE RIFLE I PROMISED.
AAH!! LOUIS JOSEPH!!
MAMAN-REINE! MAMAN-REINE! PLEASE FORGIVE ME!
VERSAILLES WITHOUT YOU IS LIKE A WASTELAND WHERE NARY A FLOWER BLOOMS.
MY SWEET BOY!!

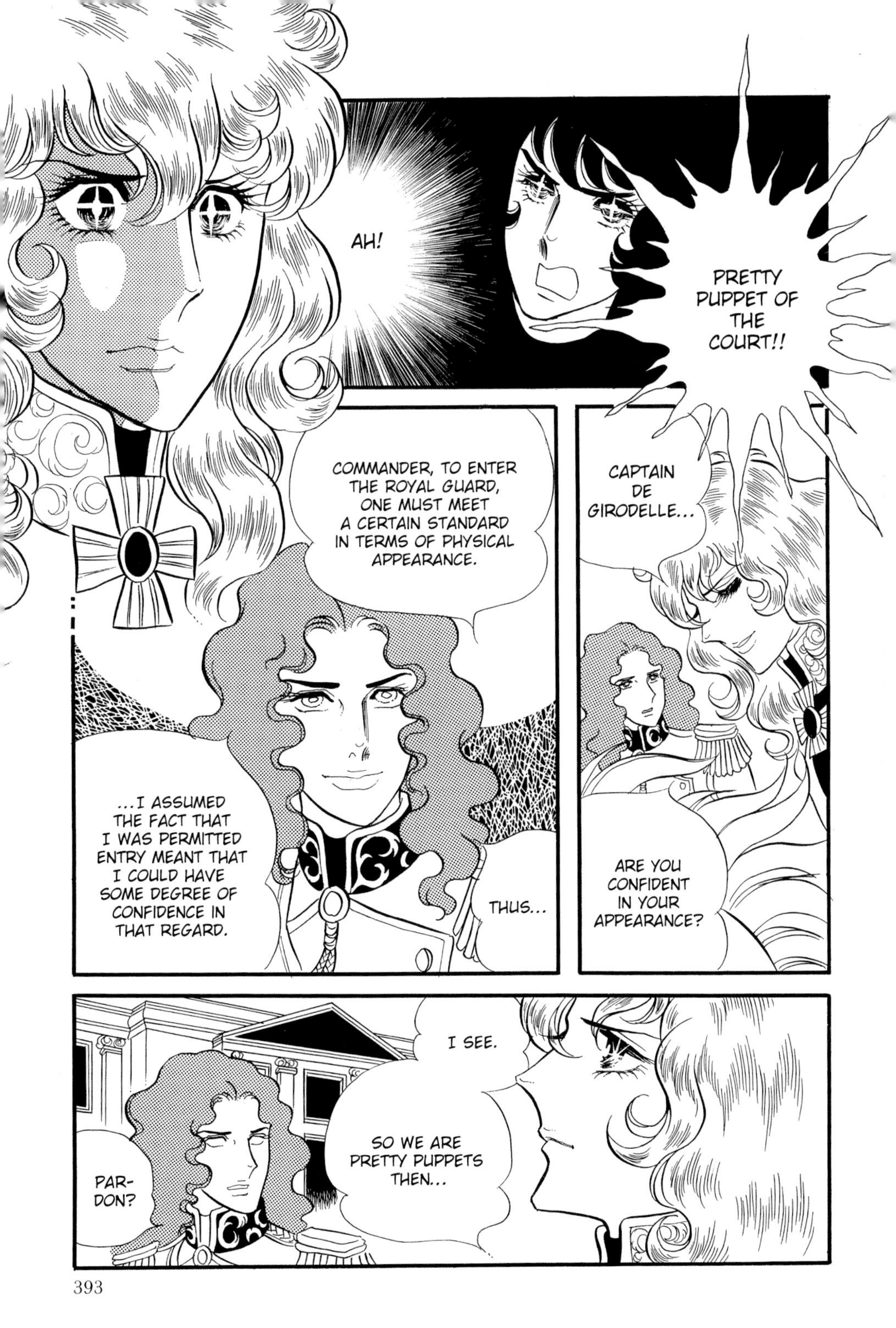

PRETTY PUPPET OF THE COURT!!
AH!
CAPTAIN DE GIRODELLE...
ARE YOU CONFIDENT IN YOUR APPEARANCE?
COMMANDER, TO ENTER THE ROYAL GUARD, ONE MUST MEET A CERTAIN STANDARD IN TERMS OF PHYSICAL APPEARANCE.
THUS...
...I ASSUMED THE FACT THAT I WAS PERMITTED ENTRY MEANT THAT I COULD HAVE SOME DEGREE OF CONFIDENCE IN THAT REGARD.
I SEE.
SO WE ARE PRETTY PUPPETS THEN...
PAR-DON?

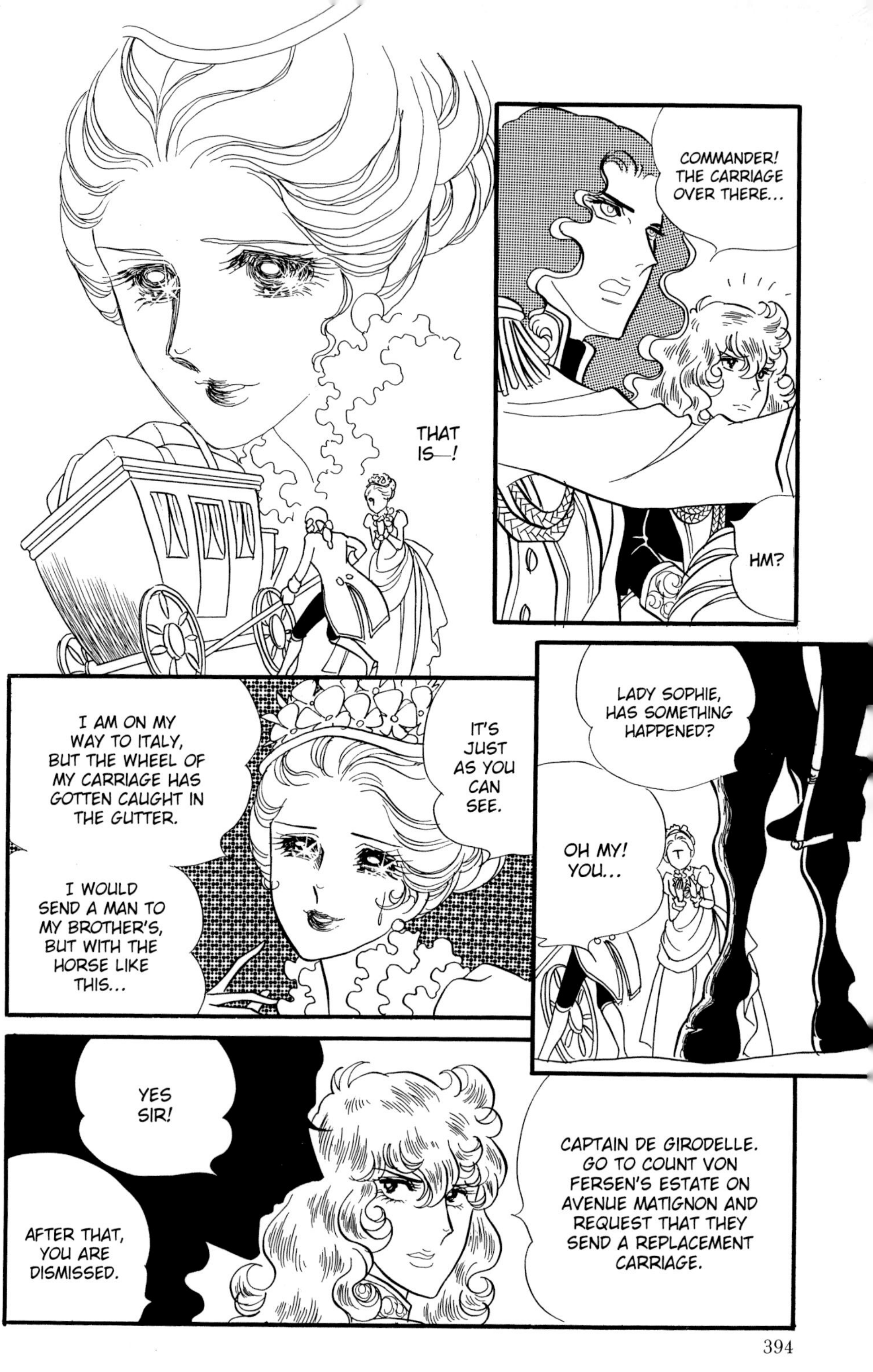
COMMANDER! THE CARRIAGE OVER THERE...
HM?
THAT IS—!
LADY SOPHIE, HAS SOMETHING HAPPENED?
OH MY! YOU...
IT'S JUST AS YOU CAN SEE.
I AM ON MY WAY TO ITALY, BUT THE WHEEL OF MY CARRIAGE HAS GOTTEN CAUGHT IN THE GUTTER.
I WOULD SEND A MAN TO MY BROTHER'S, BUT WITH THE HORSE LIKE THIS...
CAPTAIN DE GIRODELLE. GO TO COUNT VON FERSEN'S ESTATE ON AVENUE MATIGNON AND REQUEST THAT THEY SEND A REPLACEMENT CARRIAGE.
YES SIR!
AFTER THAT, YOU ARE DISMISSED.

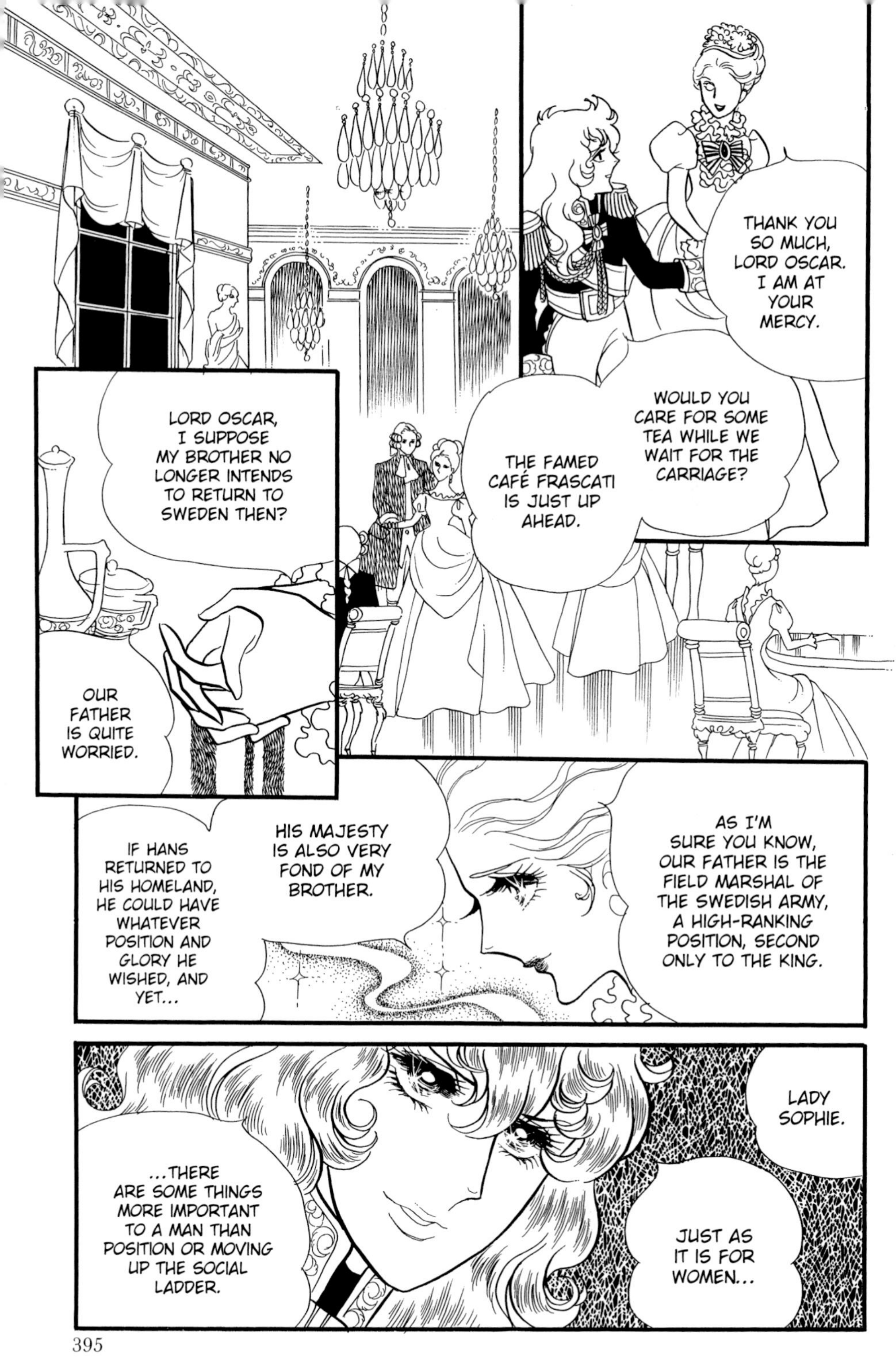
THANK YOU SO MUCH, LORD OSCAR. I AM AT YOUR MERCY.
WOULD YOU CARE FOR SOME TEA WHILE WE WAIT FOR THE CARRIAGE?
THE FAMED CAFÉ FRASCATI IS JUST UP AHEAD.
LORD OSCAR, I SUPPOSE MY BROTHER NO LONGER INTENDS TO RETURN TO SWEDEN THEN?
OUR FATHER IS QUITE WORRIED.
AS I'M SURE YOU KNOW, OUR FATHER IS THE FIELD MARSHAL OF THE SWEDISH ARMY, A HIGH-RANKING POSITION, SECOND ONLY TO THE KING.
HIS MAJESTY IS ALSO VERY FOND OF MY BROTHER.
IF HANS RETURNED TO HIS HOMELAND, HE COULD HAVE WHATEVER POSITION AND GLORY HE WISHED, AND YET...
LADY SOPHIE.
JUST AS IT IS FOR WOMEN...
...THERE ARE SOME THINGS MORE IMPORTANT TO A MAN THAN POSITION OR MOVING UP THE SOCIAL LADDER.

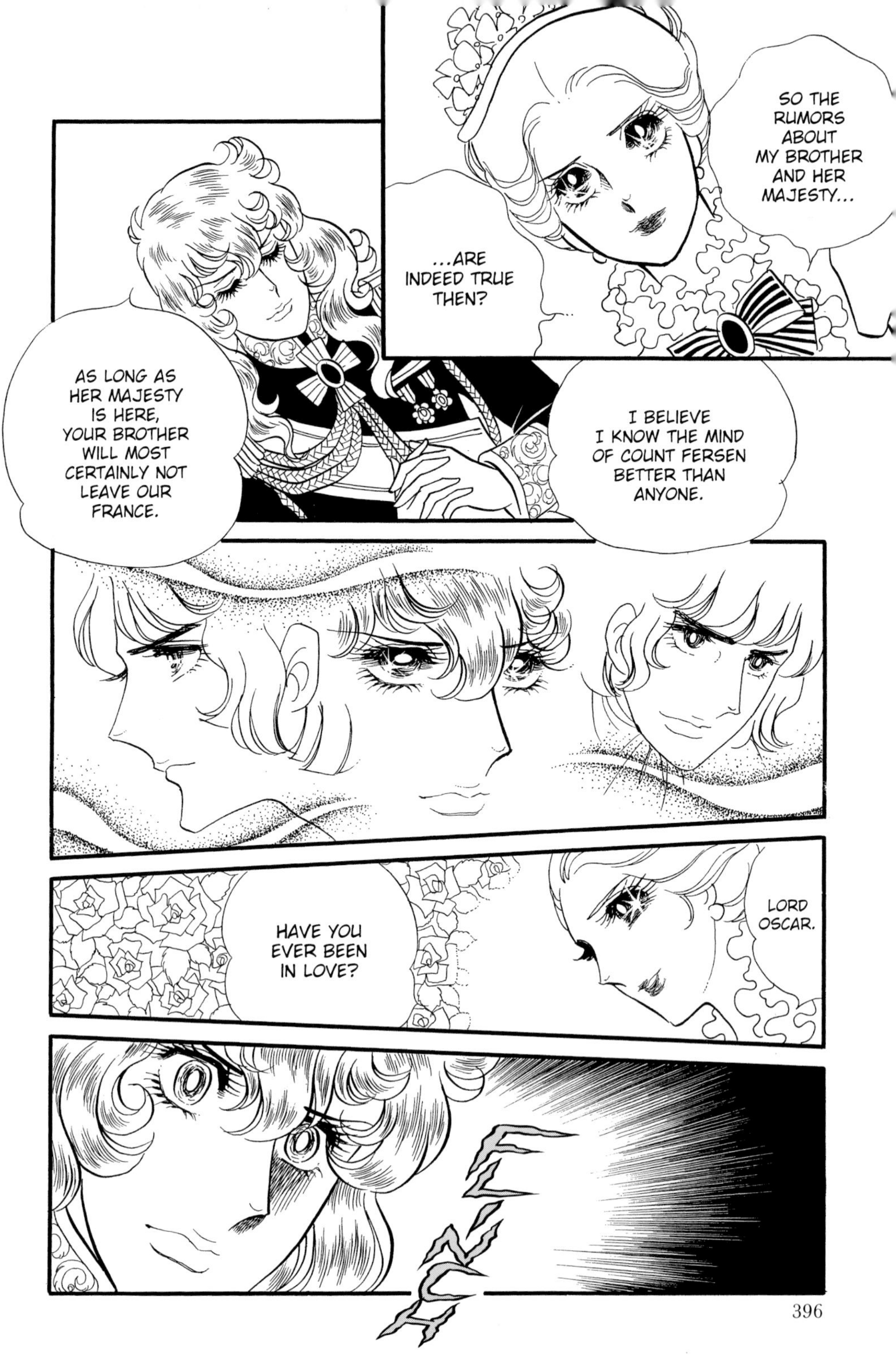
SO THE RUMORS ABOUT MY BROTHER AND HER MAJESTY...
...ARE INDEED TRUE THEN?
I BELIEVE I KNOW THE MIND OF COUNT FERSEN BETTER THAN ANYONE.
AS LONG AS HER MAJESTY IS HERE, YOUR BROTHER WILL MOST CERTAINLY NOT LEAVE OUR FRANCE.
LORD OSCAR.
HAVE YOU EVER BEEN IN LOVE?

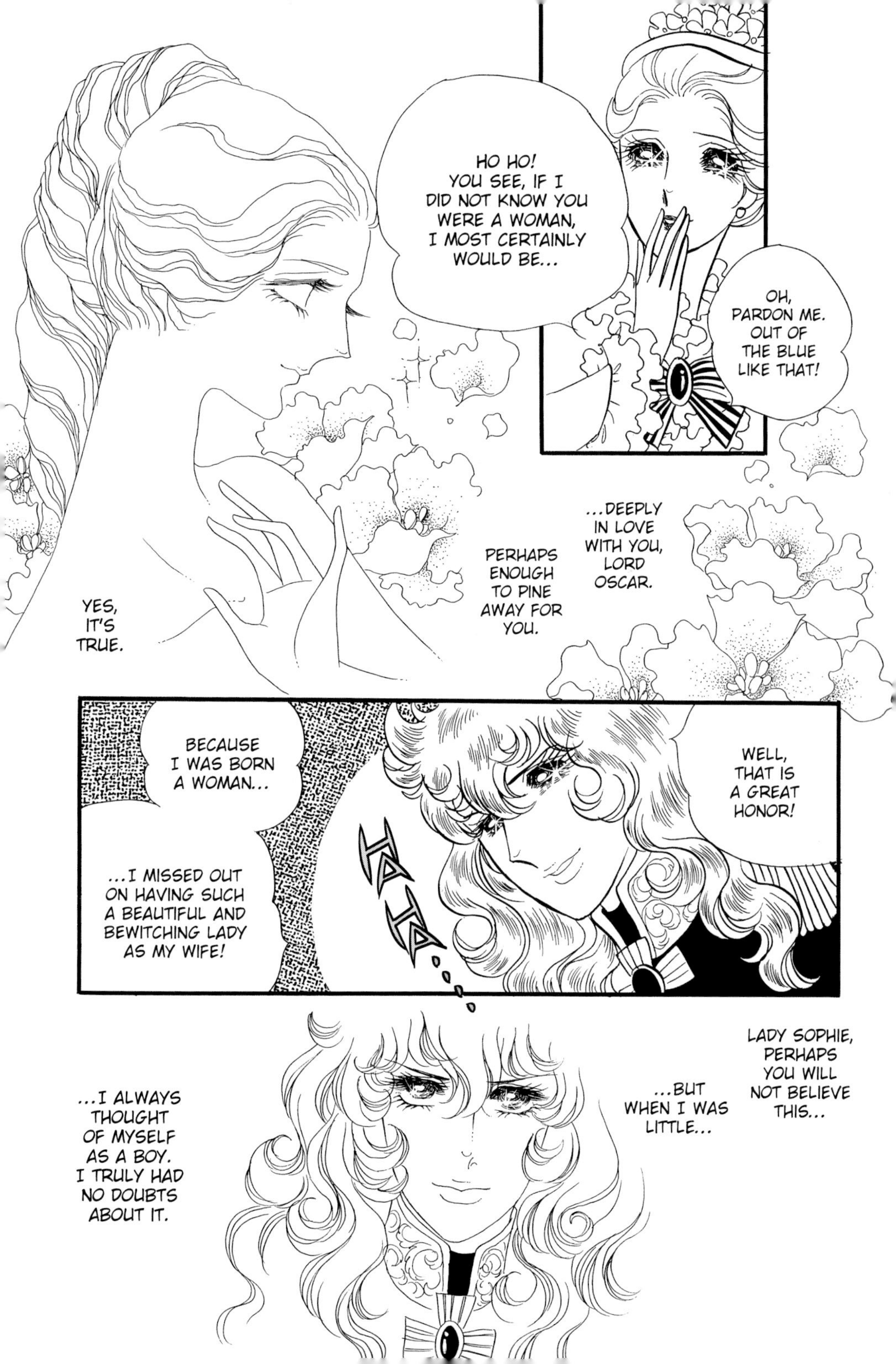
HO HO! YOU SEE, IF I DID NOT KNOW YOU WERE A WOMAN, I MOST CERTAINLY WOULD BE...
...DEEPLY IN LOVE WITH YOU, LORD OSCAR.
PERHAPS ENOUGH TO PINE AWAY FOR YOU.
OH, PARDON ME. OUT OF THE BLUE LIKE THAT!
YES, IT'S TRUE.
WELL, THAT IS A GREAT HONOR!
BECAUSE I WAS BORN A WOMAN...
...I MISSED OUT ON HAVING SUCH A BEAUTIFUL AND BEWITCHING LADY AS MY WIFE!
HA HA
LADY SOPHIE, PERHAPS YOU WILL NOT BELIEVE THIS...
...BUT WHEN I WAS LITTLE...
...I ALWAYS THOUGHT OF MYSELF AS A BOY. I TRULY HAD NO DOUBTS ABOUT IT.

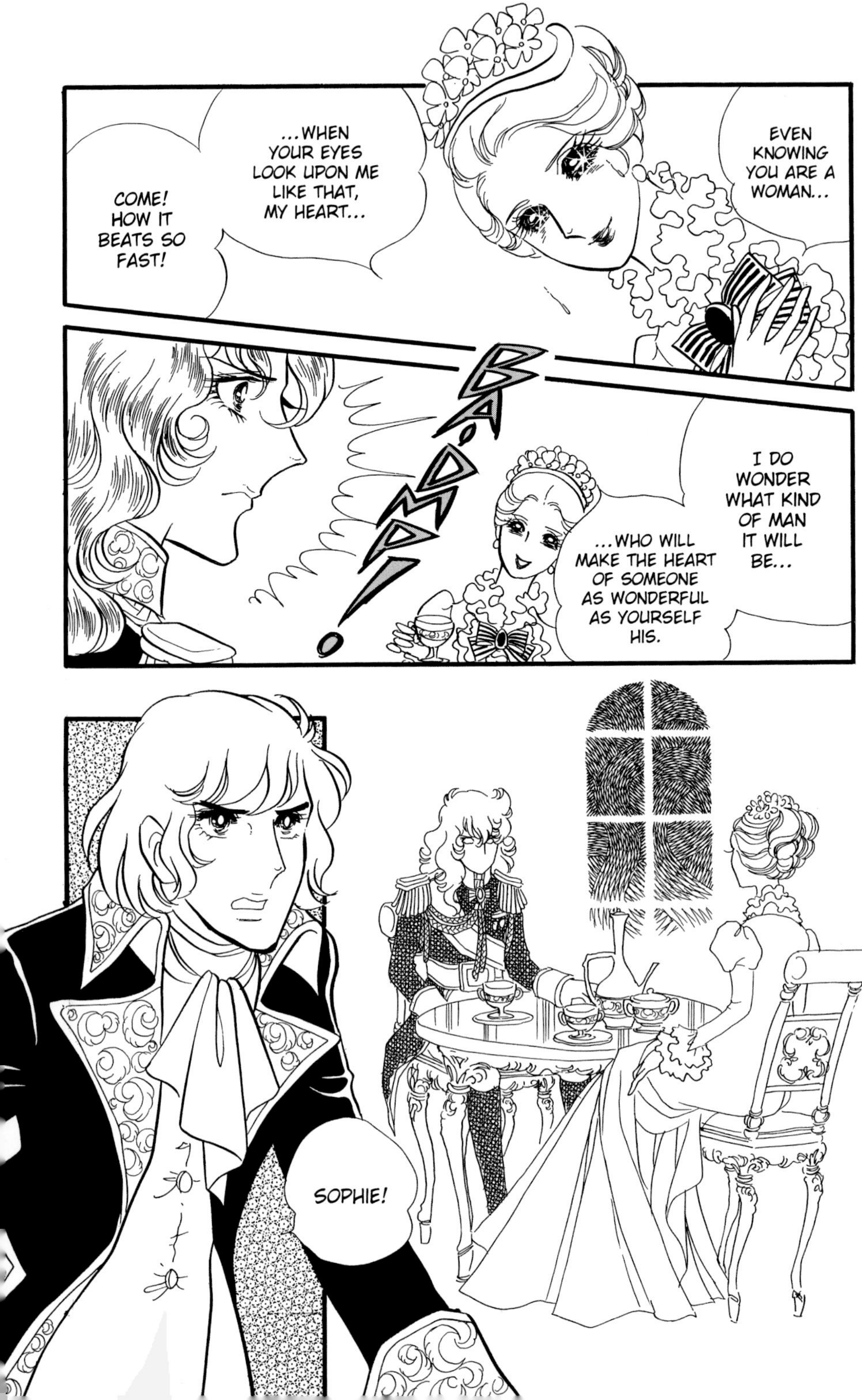
EVEN KNOWING YOU ARE A WOMAN...
...WHEN YOUR EYES LOOK UPON ME LIKE THAT, MY HEART...
COME! HOW IT BEATS SO FAST!
I DO WONDER WHAT KIND OF MAN IT WILL BE...
...WHO WILL MAKE THE HEART OF SOMEONE AS WONDERFUL AS YOURSELF HIS.
BA-DMP!
SOPHIE!

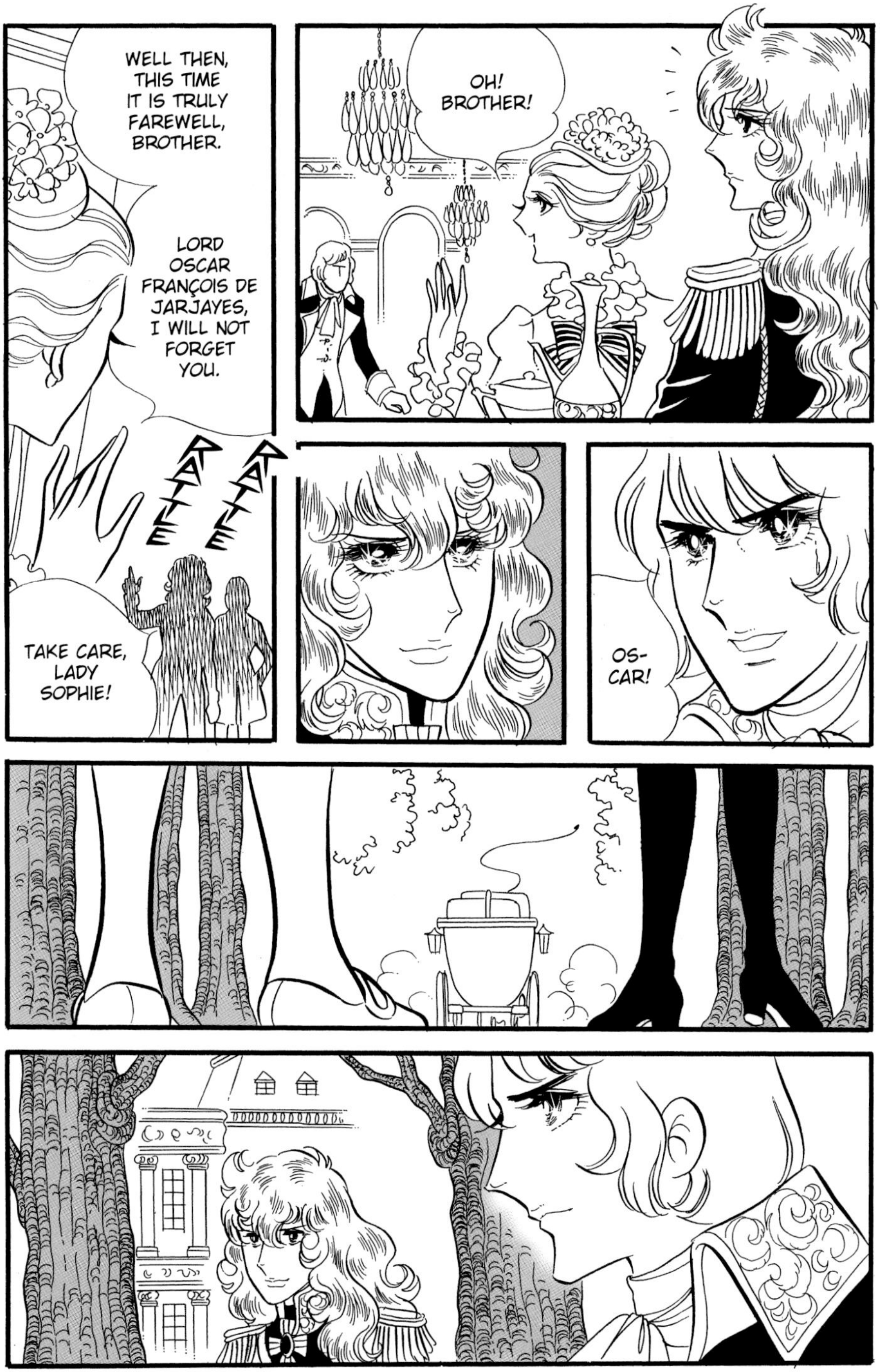

OH! BROTHER!
OS-CAR!
WELL THEN, THIS TIME IT IS TRULY FAREWELL, BROTHER.
LORD OSCAR FRANÇOIS DE JARJAYES, I WILL NOT FORGET YOU.
RATTLE RATTLE
TAKE CARE, LADY SOPHIE!

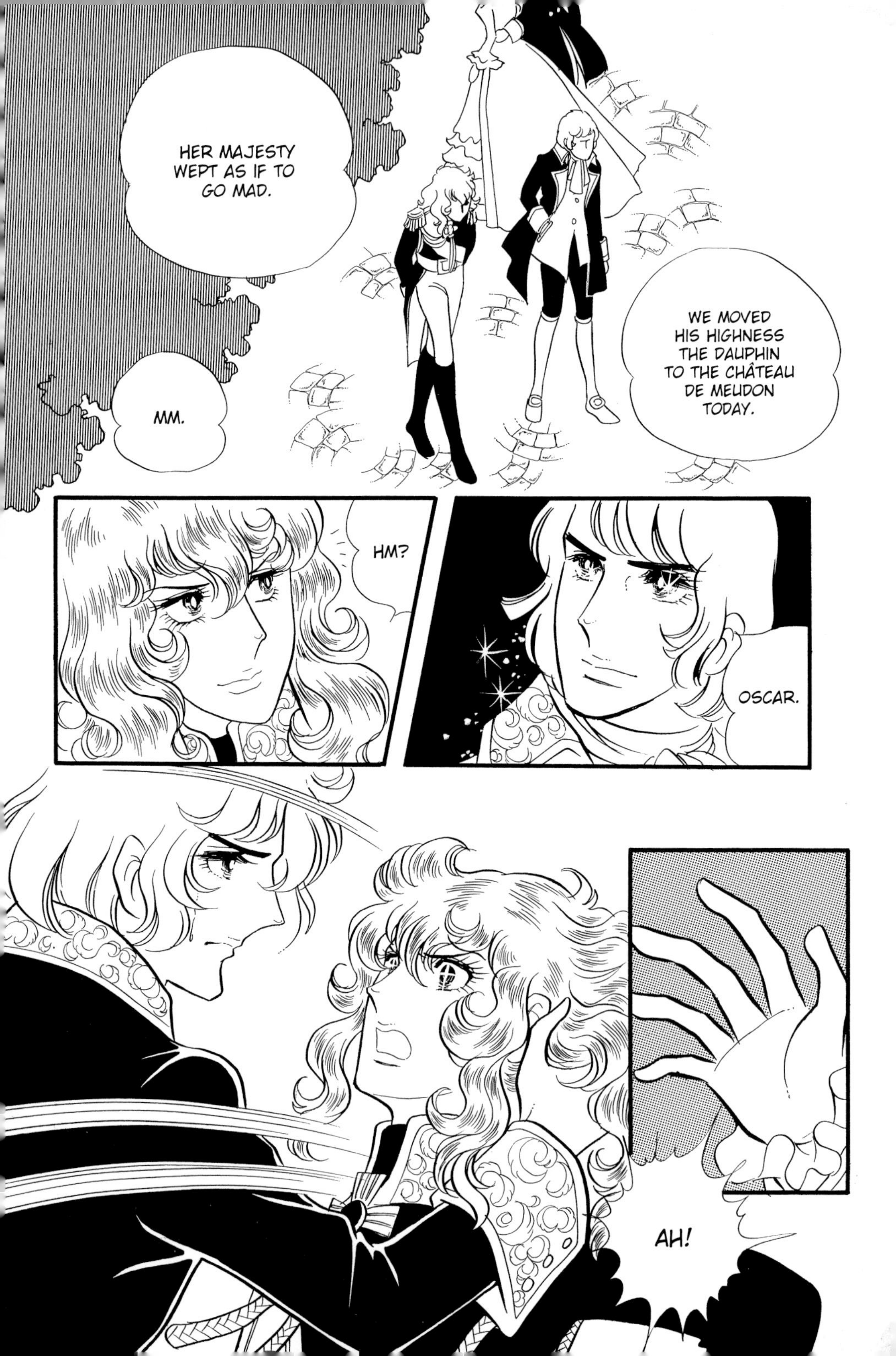
WE MOVED HIS HIGHNESS THE DAUPHIN TO THE CHÂTEAU DE MEUDON TODAY.
HER MAJESTY WEPT AS IF TO GO MAD.
MM.
OSCAR.
HM?
AH!

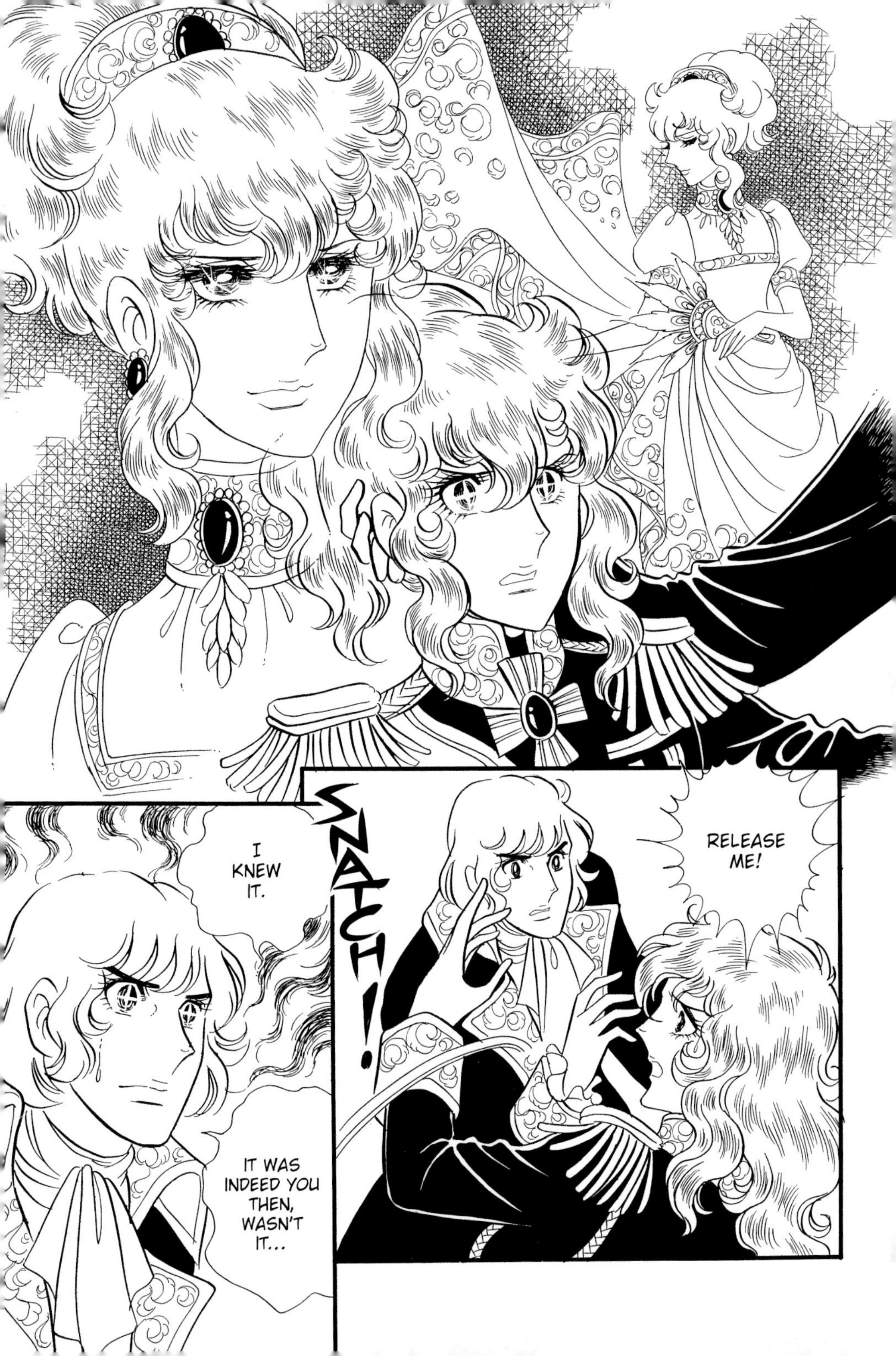
SNATCH!!
RELEASE ME!
I KNEW IT.
IT WAS INDEED YOU THEN, WASN'T IT...

the ROSE of VERSAILLES
ベルサイユのばら

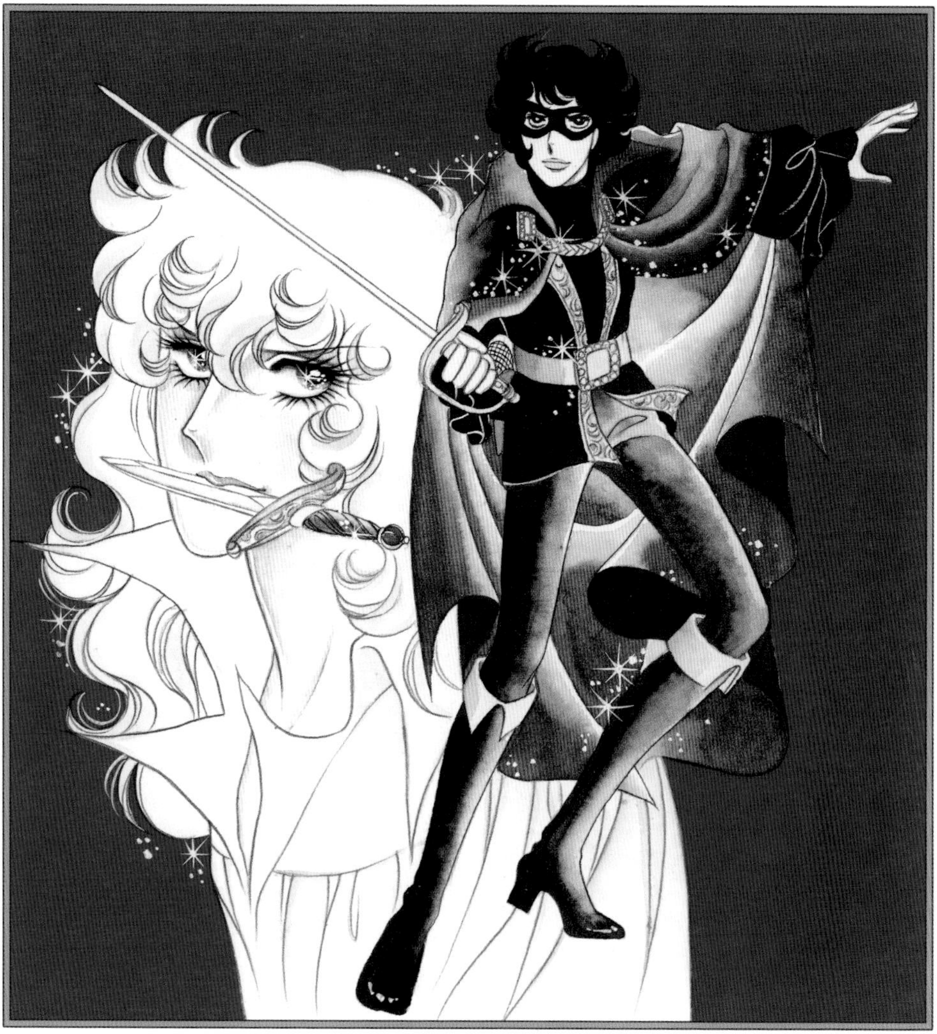

1973 MARGARET COMICS TRADE PAPERBACK
VOLUME 4 COVER

EXPLODING IN POPULARITY!! A GRAND MASTERPIECE FULL OF LOVE AND STORMY TURNS!!

♥OSCAR HAS A CHANCE MEETING WITH FERSEN! BUT FERSEN IS...?!

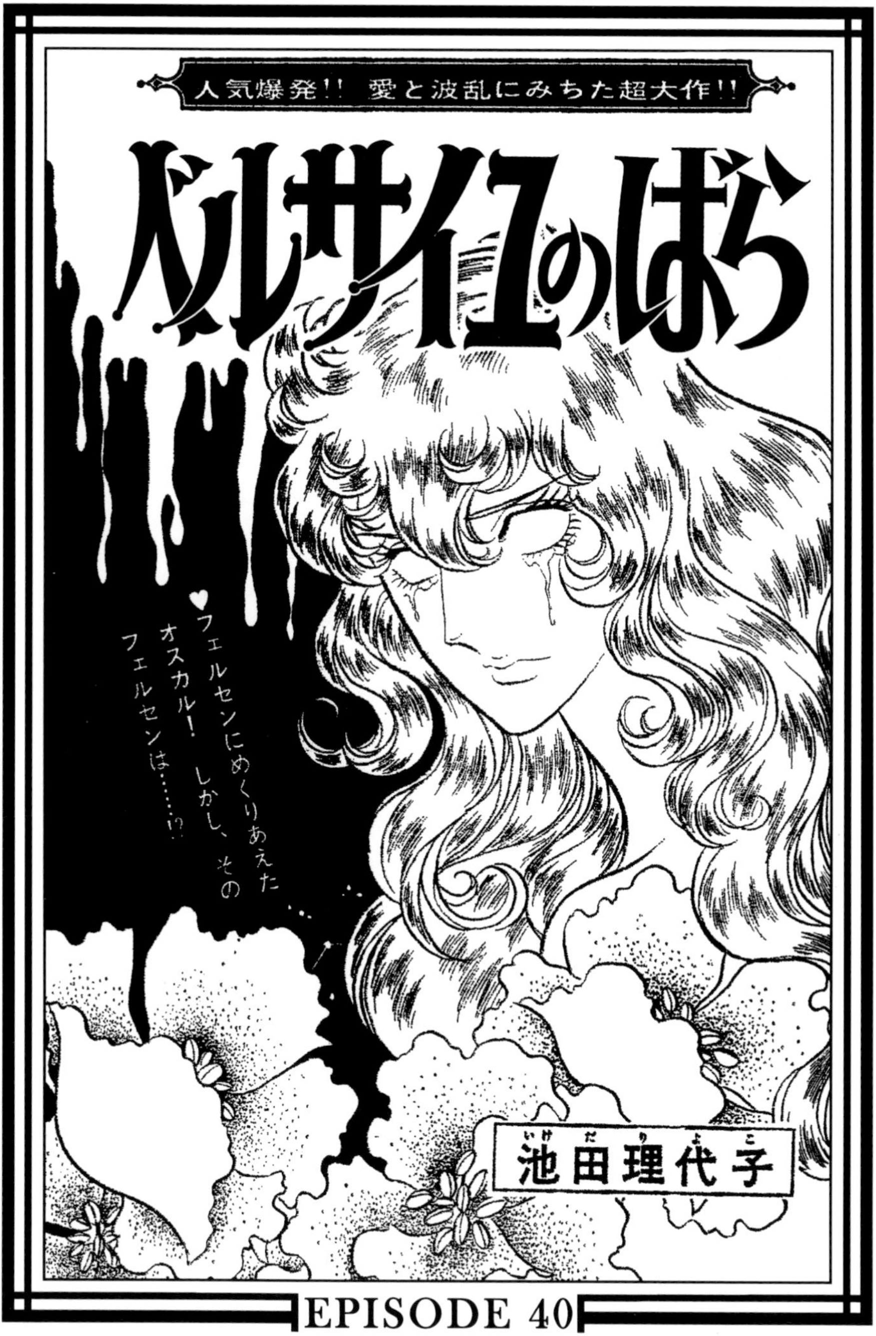
人気爆発!! 愛と波乱にみちた超大作!!
ベルサイユのばら
♥フェルセンにめぐりあえたオスカル! しかし、そのフェルセンは……!?
池田理代子

EPISODE 40

⚜Episode 40

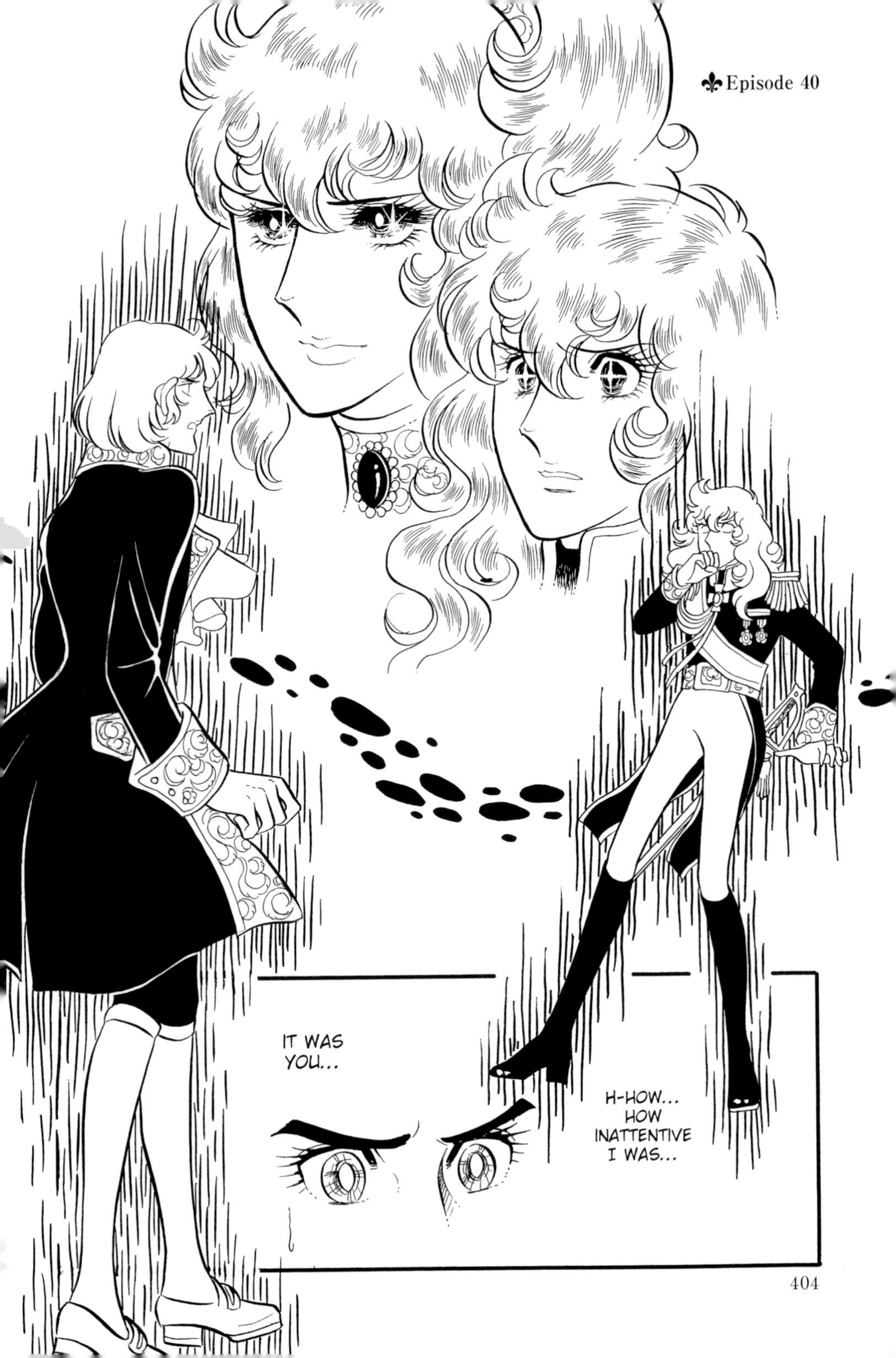
IT WAS YOU…
H-HOW… HOW INATTENTIVE I WAS…

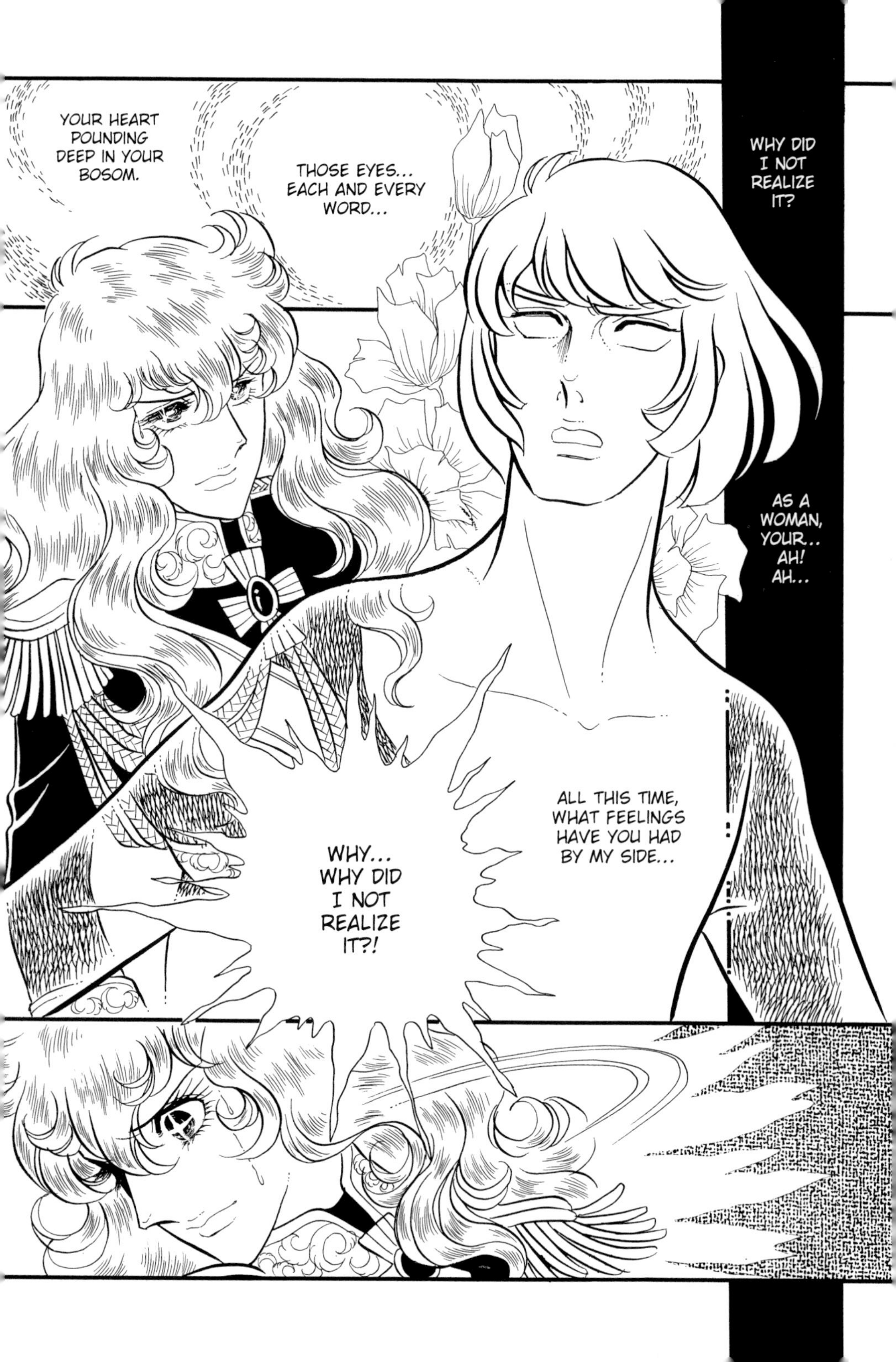
WHY DID I NOT REALIZE IT?
THOSE EYES... EACH AND EVERY WORD...
YOUR HEART POUNDING DEEP IN YOUR BOSOM.
AS A WOMAN, YOUR... AH! AH...
ALL THIS TIME, WHAT FEELINGS HAVE YOU HAD BY MY SIDE...
WHY... WHY DID I NOT REALIZE IT?!

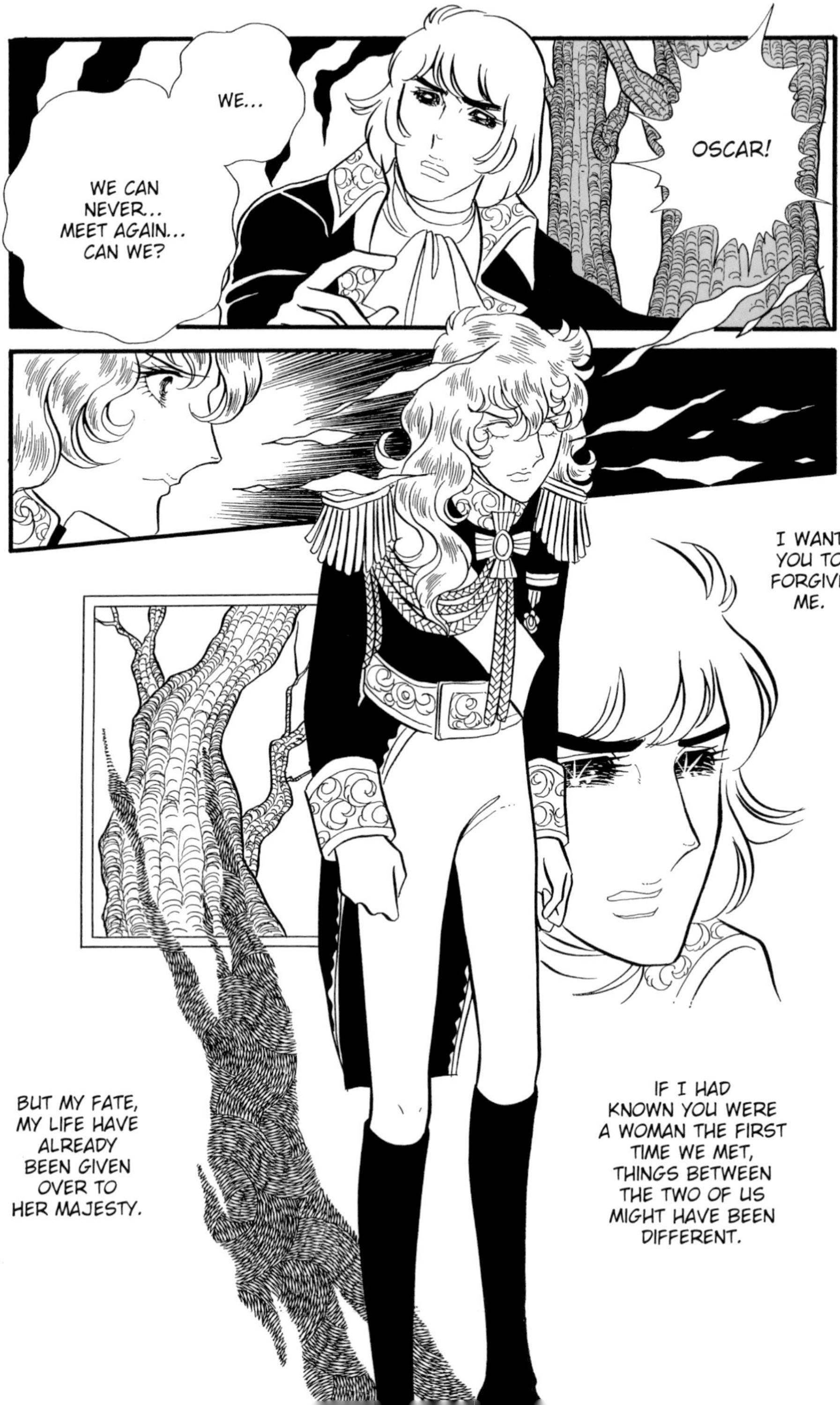
OSCAR!
WE...
WE CAN NEVER.. MEET AGAIN... CAN WE?
I WANT YOU TO FORGIVE ME.
IF I HAD KNOWN YOU WERE A WOMAN THE FIRST TIME WE MET, THINGS BETWEEN THE TWO OF US MIGHT HAVE BEEN DIFFERENT.
BUT MY FATE, MY LIFE HAVE ALREADY BEEN GIVEN OVER TO HER MAJESTY.

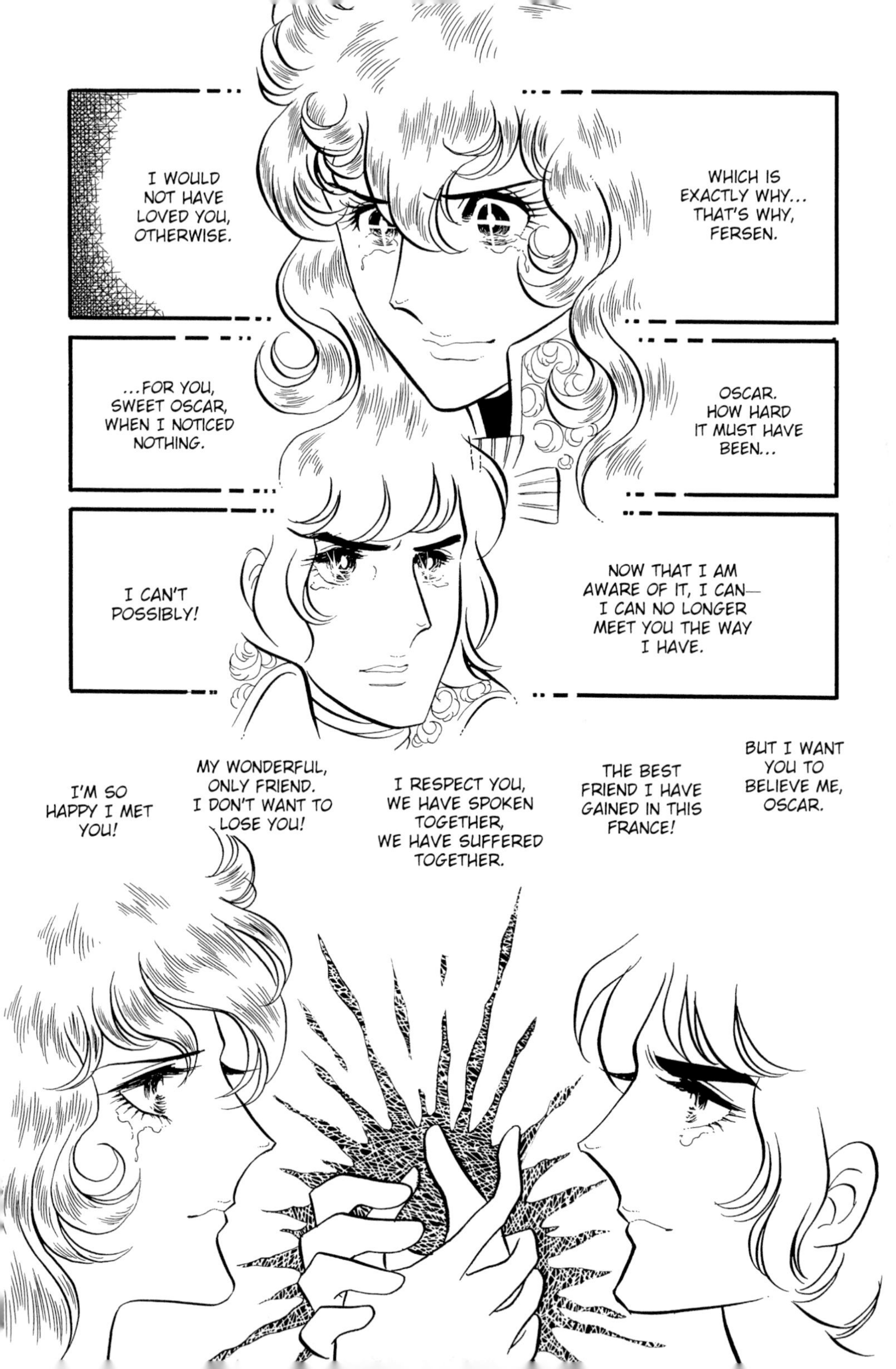
WHICH IS EXACTLY WHY... THAT'S WHY, FERSEN.
I WOULD NOT HAVE LOVED YOU, OTHERWISE.
OSCAR. HOW HARD IT MUST HAVE BEEN...
...FOR YOU, SWEET OSCAR, WHEN I NOTICED NOTHING.
NOW THAT I AM AWARE OF IT, I CAN— I CAN NO LONGER MEET YOU THE WAY I HAVE.
I CAN'T POSSIBLY!
BUT I WANT YOU TO BELIEVE ME, OSCAR.
THE BEST FRIEND I HAVE GAINED IN THIS FRANCE!
I RESPECT YOU, WE HAVE SPOKEN TOGETHER, WE HAVE SUFFERED TOGETHER.
MY WONDERFUL, ONLY FRIEND. I DON'T WANT TO LOSE YOU!
I'M SO HAPPY I MET YOU!

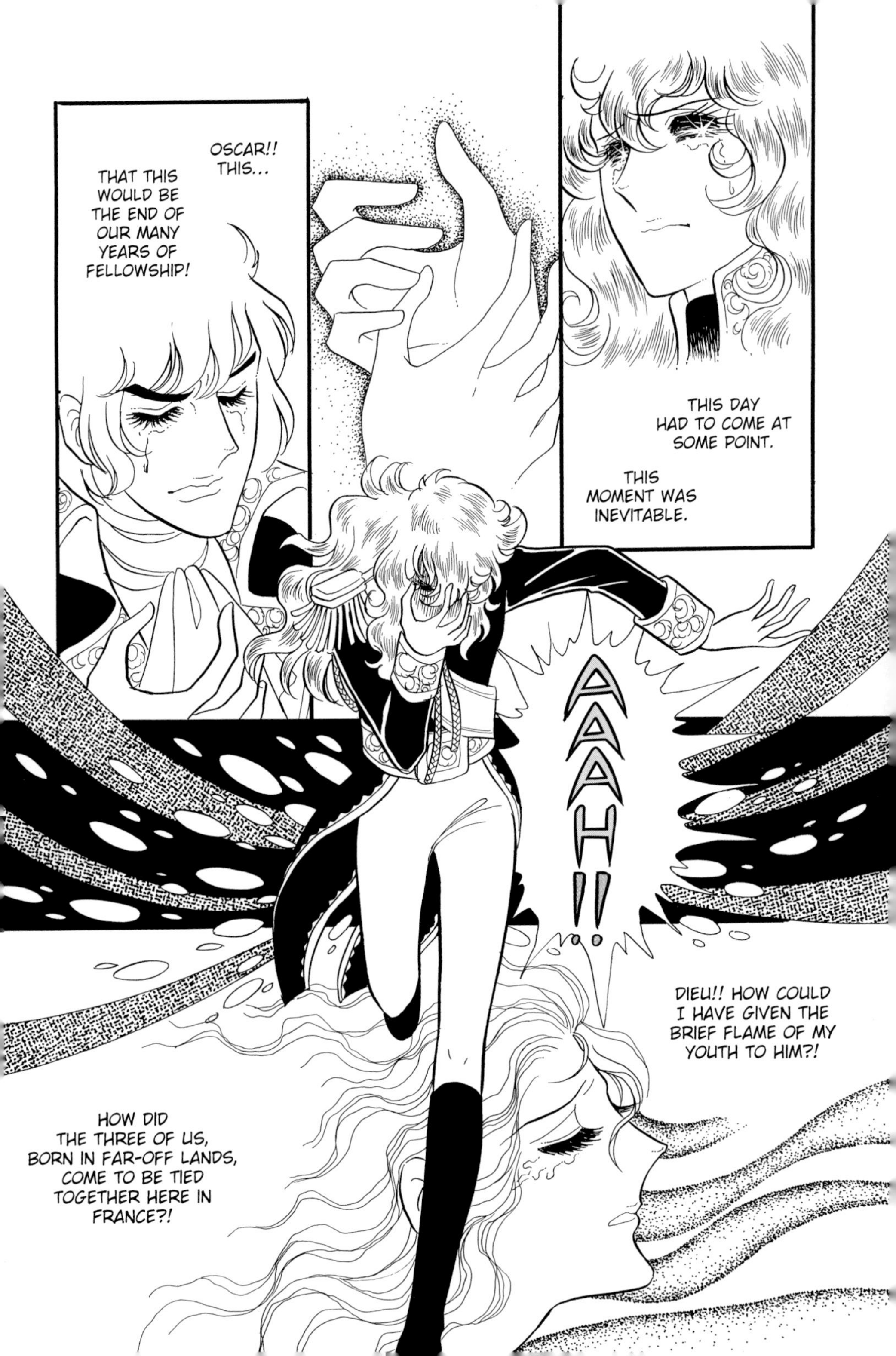
THIS DAY HAD TO COME AT SOME POINT.
THIS MOMENT WAS INEVITABLE.
OSCAR!! THIS...
THAT THIS WOULD BE THE END OF OUR MANY YEARS OF FELLOWSHIP!
AAAH!!
DIEU!! HOW COULD I HAVE GIVEN THE BRIEF FLAME OF MY YOUTH TO HIM?!
HOW DID THE THREE OF US, BORN IN FAR-OFF LANDS, COME TO BE TIED TOGETHER HERE IN FRANCE?!

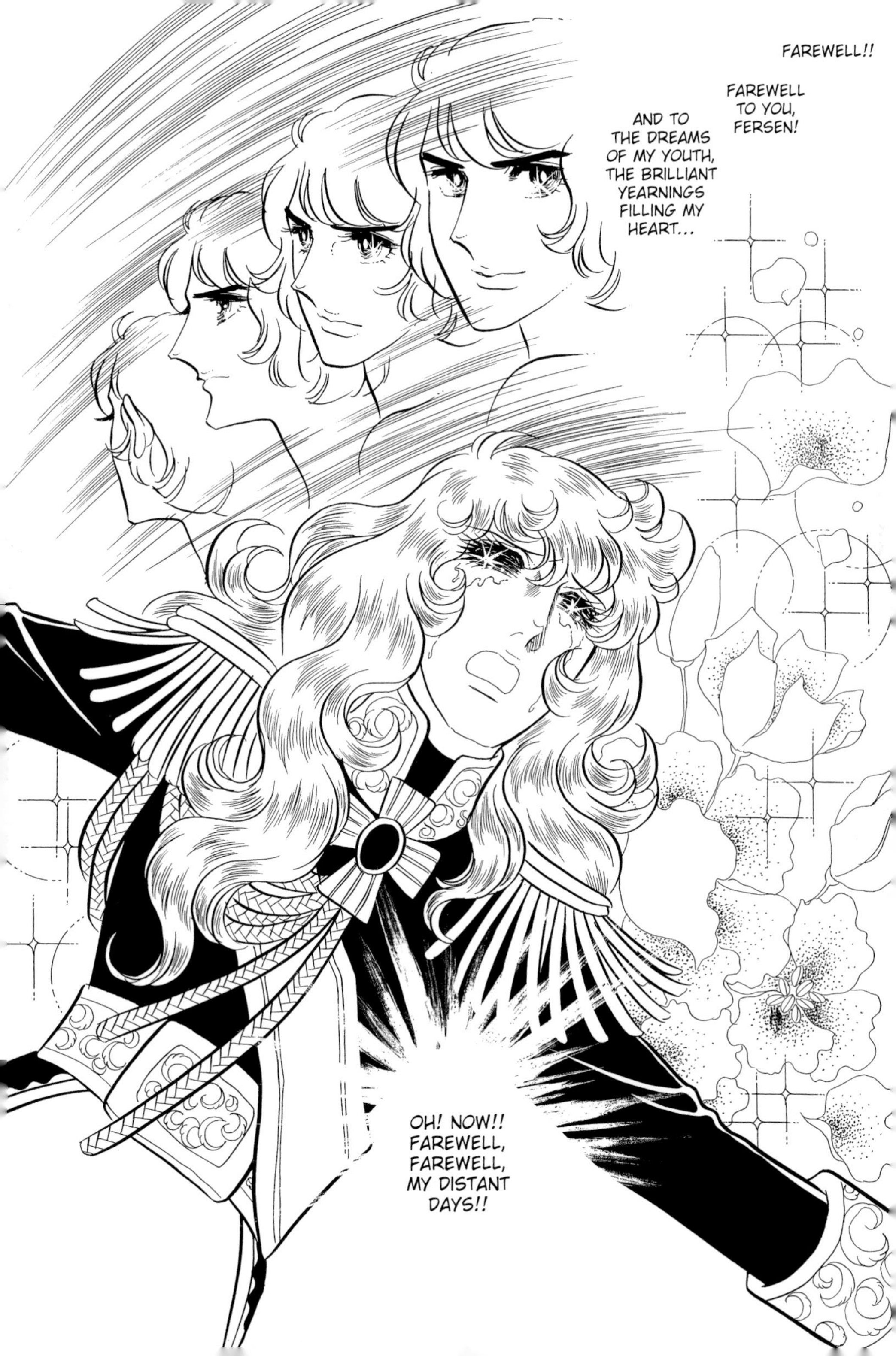
FAREWELL!!
FAREWELL TO YOU, FERSEN!
AND TO THE DREAMS OF MY YOUTH, THE BRILLIANT YEARNINGS FILLING MY HEART...
OH! NOW!! FAREWELL, FAREWELL, MY DISTANT DAYS!!

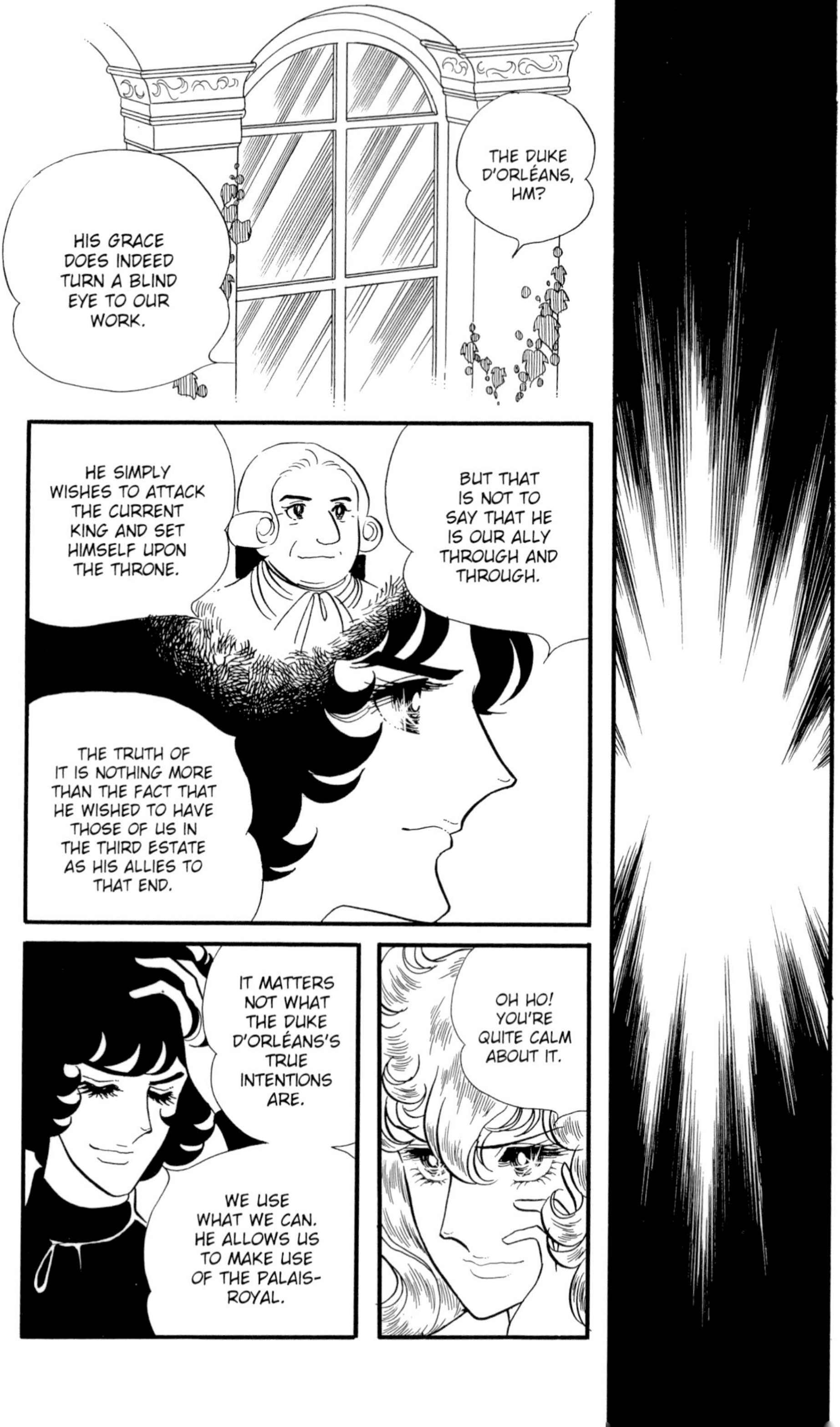
THE DUKE D'ORLÉANS, HM?
HIS GRACE DOES INDEED TURN A BLIND EYE TO OUR WORK.
BUT THAT IS NOT TO SAY THAT HE IS OUR ALLY THROUGH AND THROUGH.
HE SIMPLY WISHES TO ATTACK THE CURRENT KING AND SET HIMSELF UPON THE THRONE.
THE TRUTH OF IT IS NOTHING MORE THAN THE FACT THAT HE WISHED TO HAVE THOSE OF US IN THE THIRD ESTATE AS HIS ALLIES TO THAT END.
OH HO! YOU'RE QUITE CALM ABOUT IT.
IT MATTERS NOT WHAT THE DUKE D'ORLÉANS'S TRUE INTENTIONS ARE.
WE USE WHAT WE CAN. HE ALLOWS US TO MAKE USE OF THE PALAIS-ROYAL.

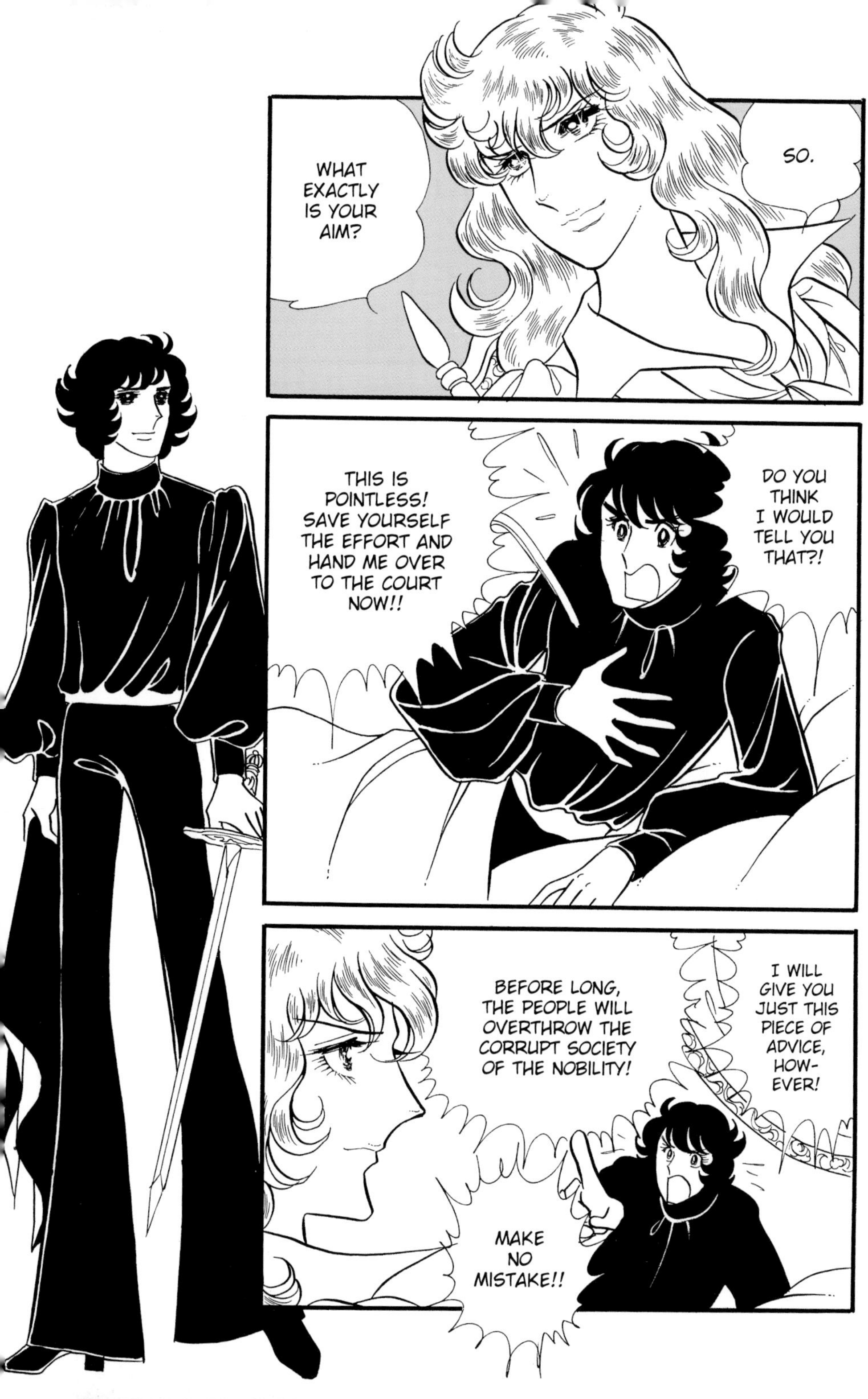
SO.
WHAT EXACTLY IS YOUR AIM?
DO YOU THINK I WOULD TELL YOU THAT?!
THIS IS POINTLESS! SAVE YOURSELF THE EFFORT AND HAND ME OVER TO THE COURT NOW!!
I WILL GIVE YOU JUST THIS PIECE OF ADVICE, HOW-EVER!
BEFORE LONG, THE PEOPLE WILL OVERTHROW THE CORRUPT SOCIETY OF THE NOBILITY!
MAKE NO MISTAKE!!

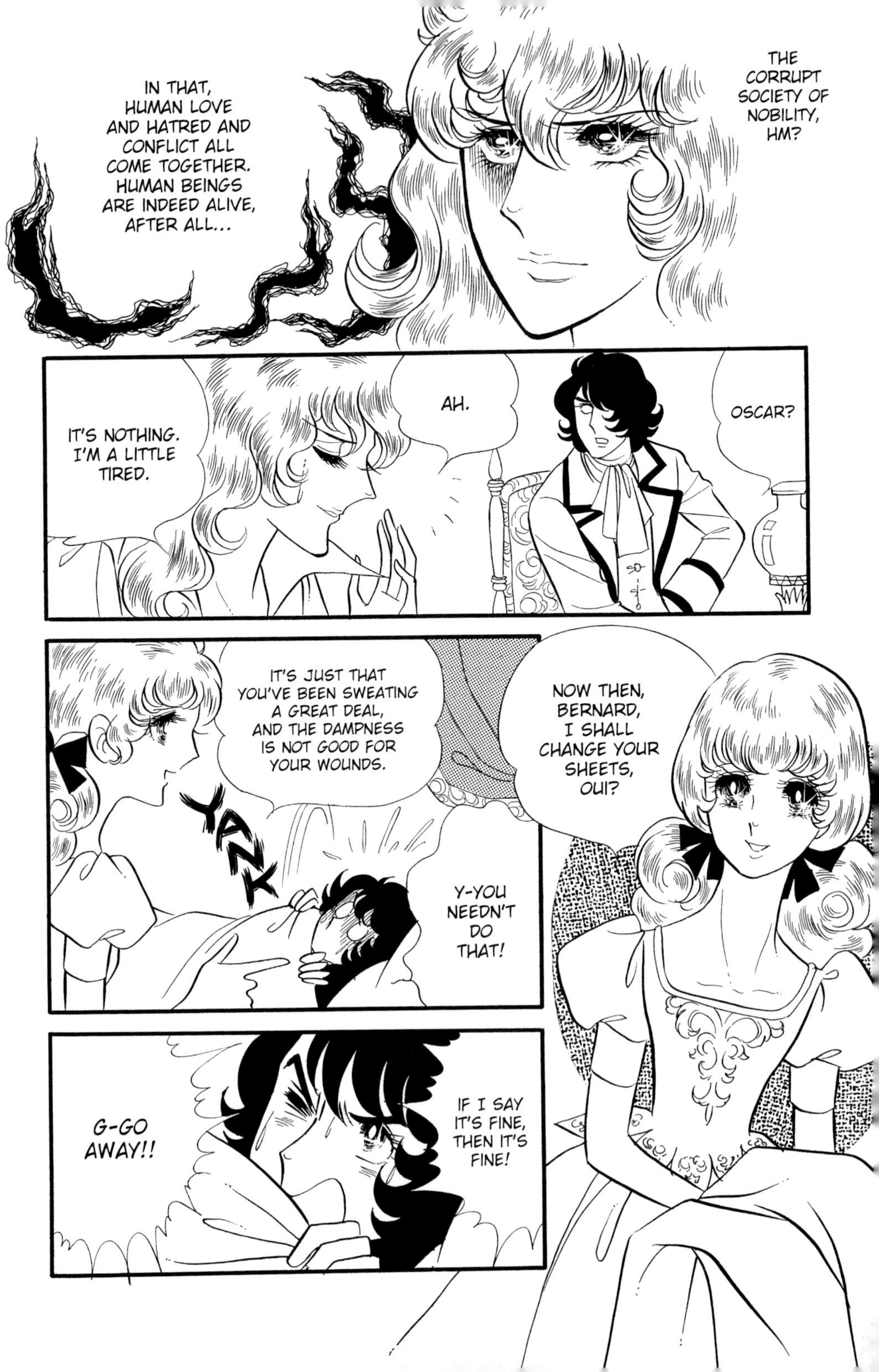
THE CORRUPT SOCIETY OF NOBILITY, HM?
IN THAT, HUMAN LOVE AND HATRED AND CONFLICT ALL COME TOGETHER. HUMAN BEINGS ARE INDEED ALIVE, AFTER ALL...
OSCAR?
AH.
IT'S NOTHING. I'M A LITTLE TIRED.
NOW THEN, BERNARD, I SHALL CHANGE YOUR SHEETS, OUI?
IT'S JUST THAT YOU'VE BEEN SWEATING A GREAT DEAL, AND THE DAMPNESS IS NOT GOOD FOR YOUR WOUNDS.
YANK
Y-YOU NEEDN'T DO THAT!
IF I SAY IT'S FINE, THEN IT'S FINE!
G-GO AWAY!!

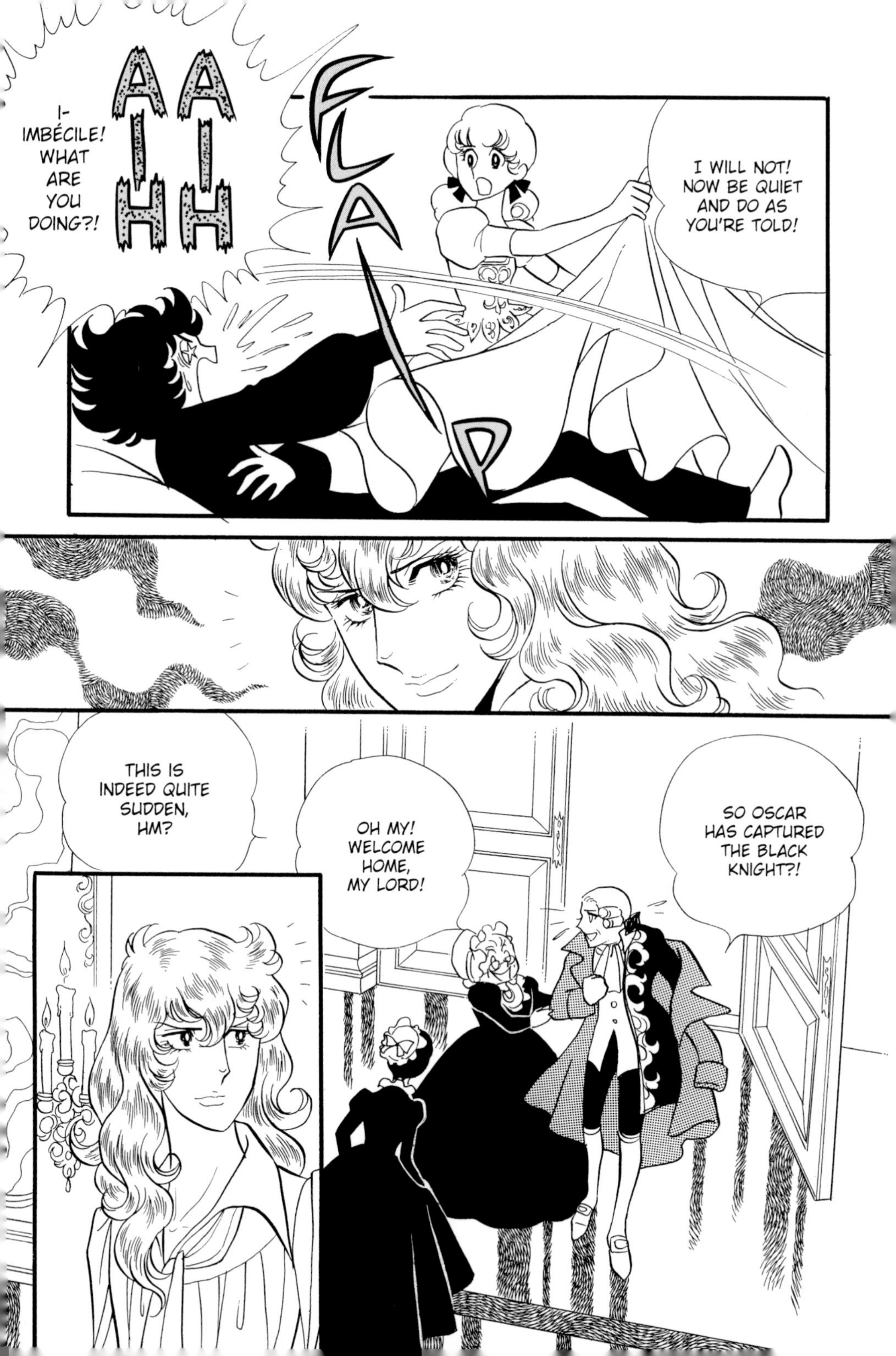
I WILL NOT! NOW BE QUIET AND DO AS YOU'RE TOLD!
FLAP
AAIIHH
I-IMBÉCILE! WHAT ARE YOU DOING?!
SO OSCAR HAS CAPTURED THE BLACK KNIGHT?!
OH MY! WELCOME HOME, MY LORD!
THIS IS INDEED QUITE SUDDEN, HM?

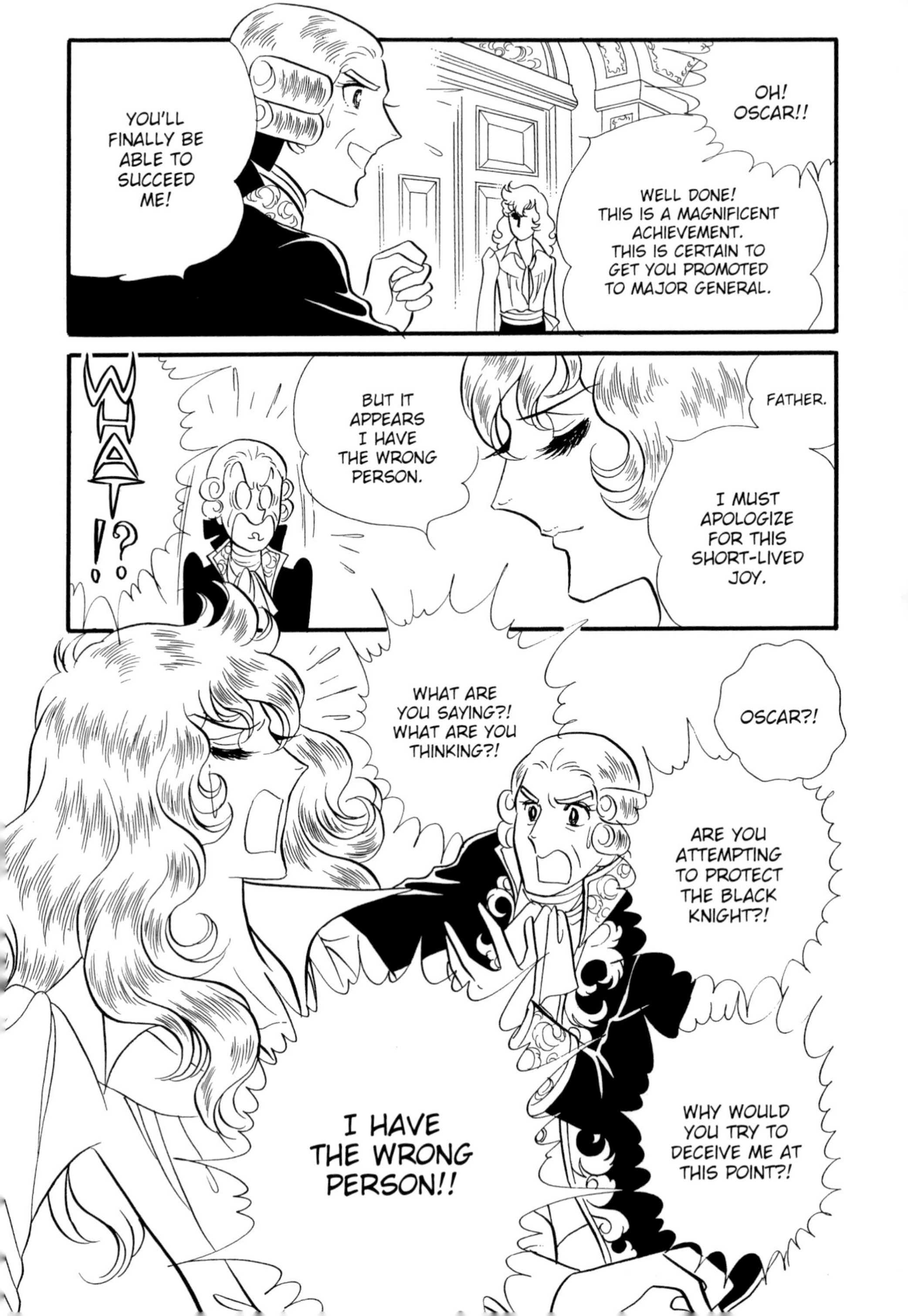
OH! OSCAR!!
WELL DONE! THIS IS A MAGNIFICENT ACHIEVEMENT. THIS IS CERTAIN TO GET YOU PROMOTED TO MAJOR GENERAL.
YOU'LL FINALLY BE ABLE TO SUCCEED ME!
FATHER.
I MUST APOLOGIZE FOR THIS SHORT-LIVED JOY.
BUT IT APPEARS I HAVE THE WRONG PERSON.
WHAT!?
OSCAR?!
WHAT ARE YOU SAYING?! WHAT ARE YOU THINKING?!
ARE YOU ATTEMPTING TO PROTECT THE BLACK KNIGHT?!
WHY WOULD YOU TRY TO DECEIVE ME AT THIS POINT?!
I HAVE THE WRONG PERSON!!

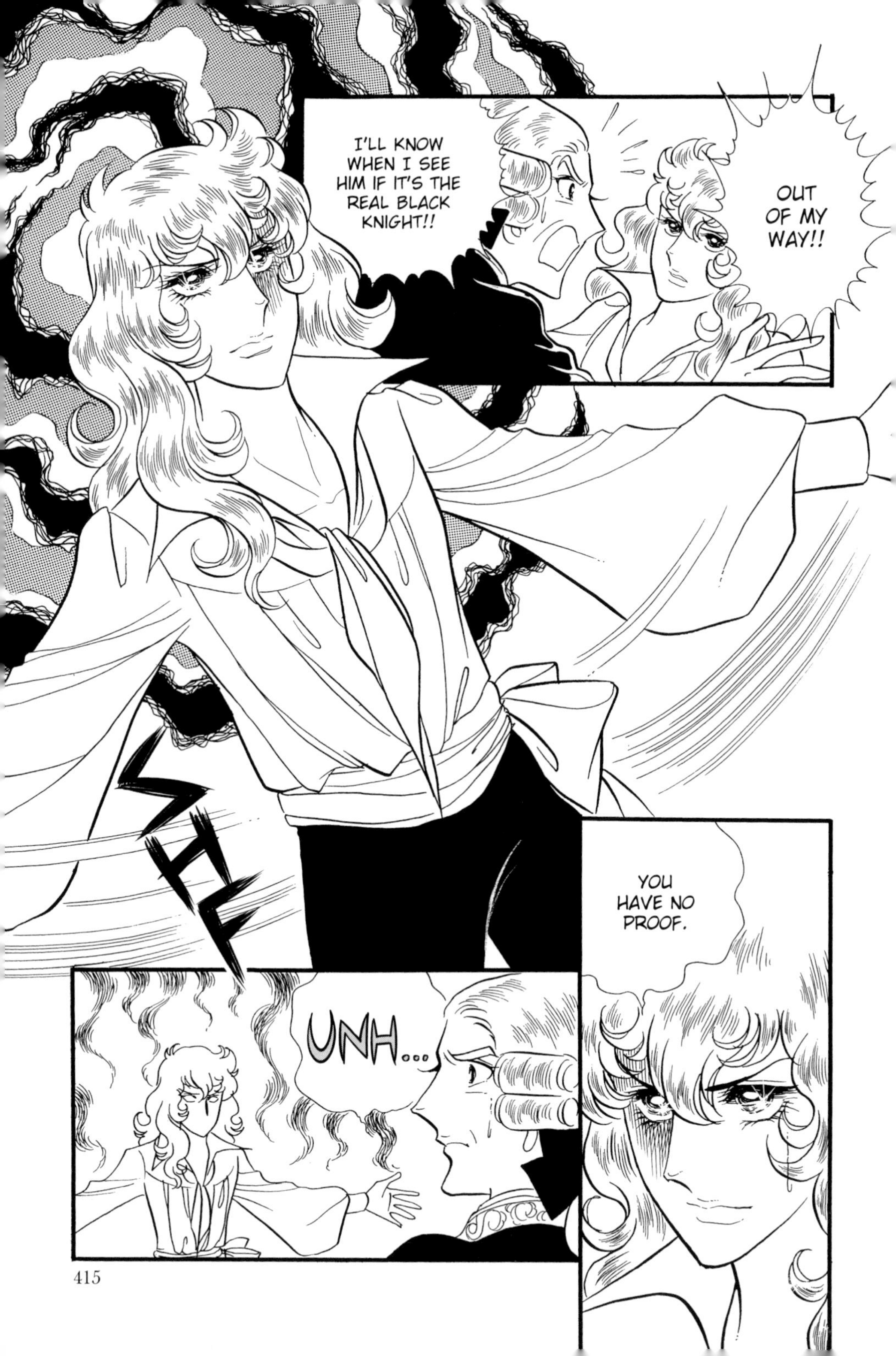
OUT OF MY WAY!!
I'LL KNOW WHEN I SEE HIM IF IT'S THE REAL BLACK KNIGHT!!
SHFF
YOU HAVE NO PROOF.
UNH...

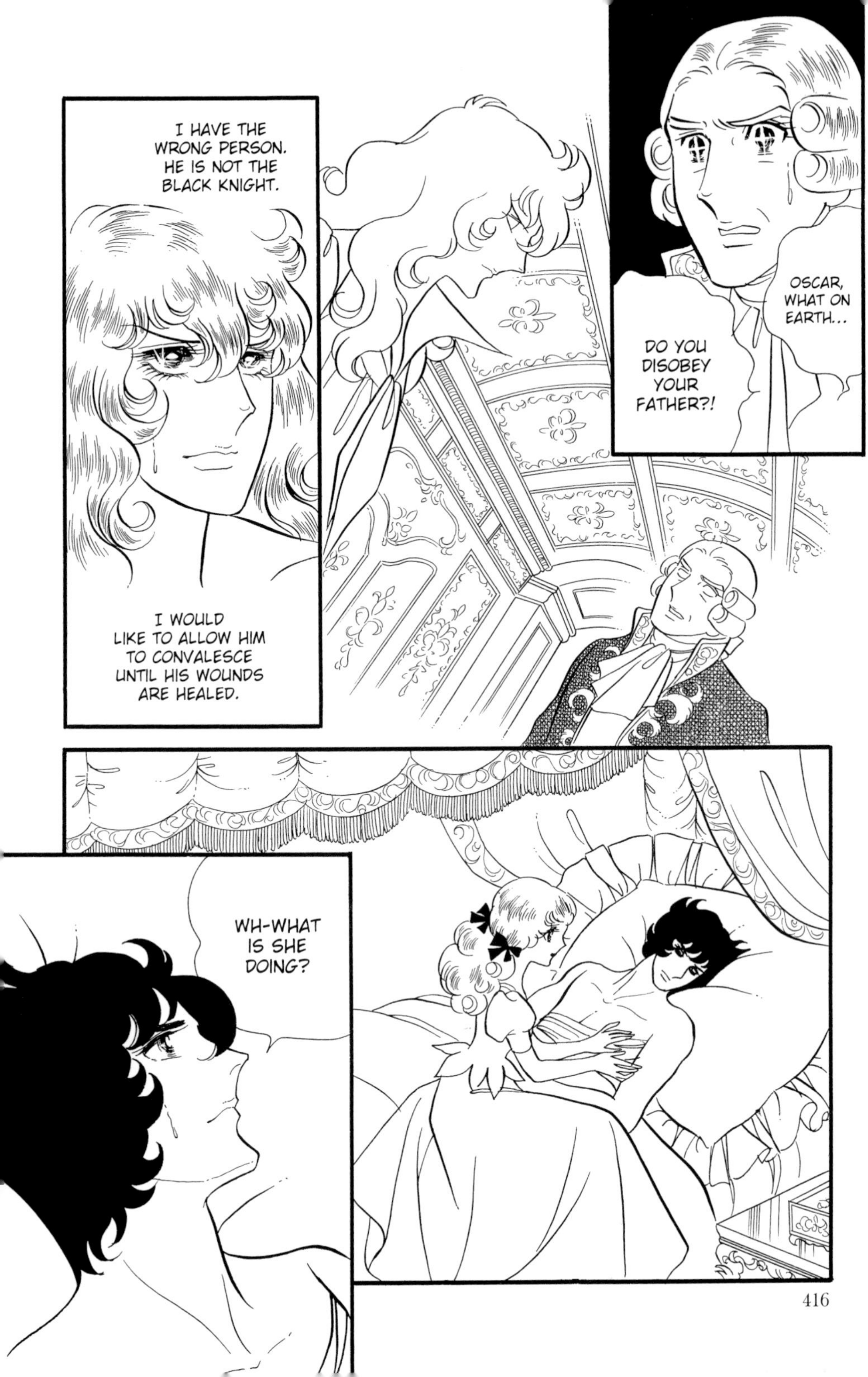
OSCAR, WHAT ON EARTH...
DO YOU DISOBEY YOUR FATHER?!
I HAVE THE WRONG PERSON. HE IS NOT THE BLACK KNIGHT.
I WOULD LIKE TO ALLOW HIM TO CONVALESCE UNTIL HIS WOUNDS ARE HEALED.
WH-WHAT IS SHE DOING?

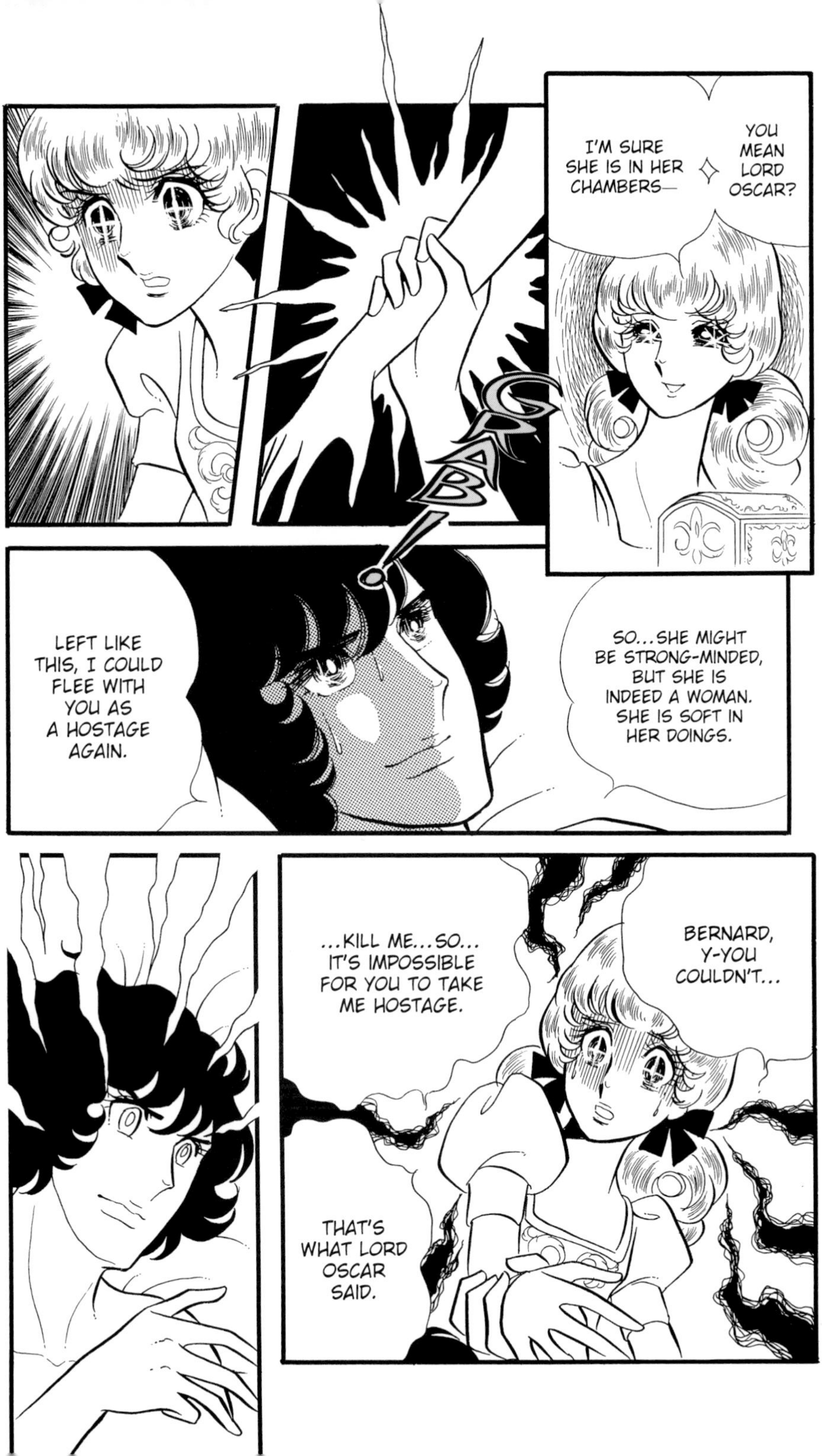
YOU MEAN LORD OSCAR?
I'M SURE SHE IS IN HER CHAMBERS—
GRAB!
SO...SHE MIGHT BE STRONG-MINDED, BUT SHE IS INDEED A WOMAN. SHE IS SOFT IN HER DOINGS.
LEFT LIKE THIS, I COULD FLEE WITH YOU AS A HOSTAGE AGAIN.
BERNARD, Y-YOU COULDN'T...
...KILL ME...SO... IT'S IMPOSSIBLE FOR YOU TO TAKE ME HOSTAGE.
THAT'S WHAT LORD OSCAR SAID.

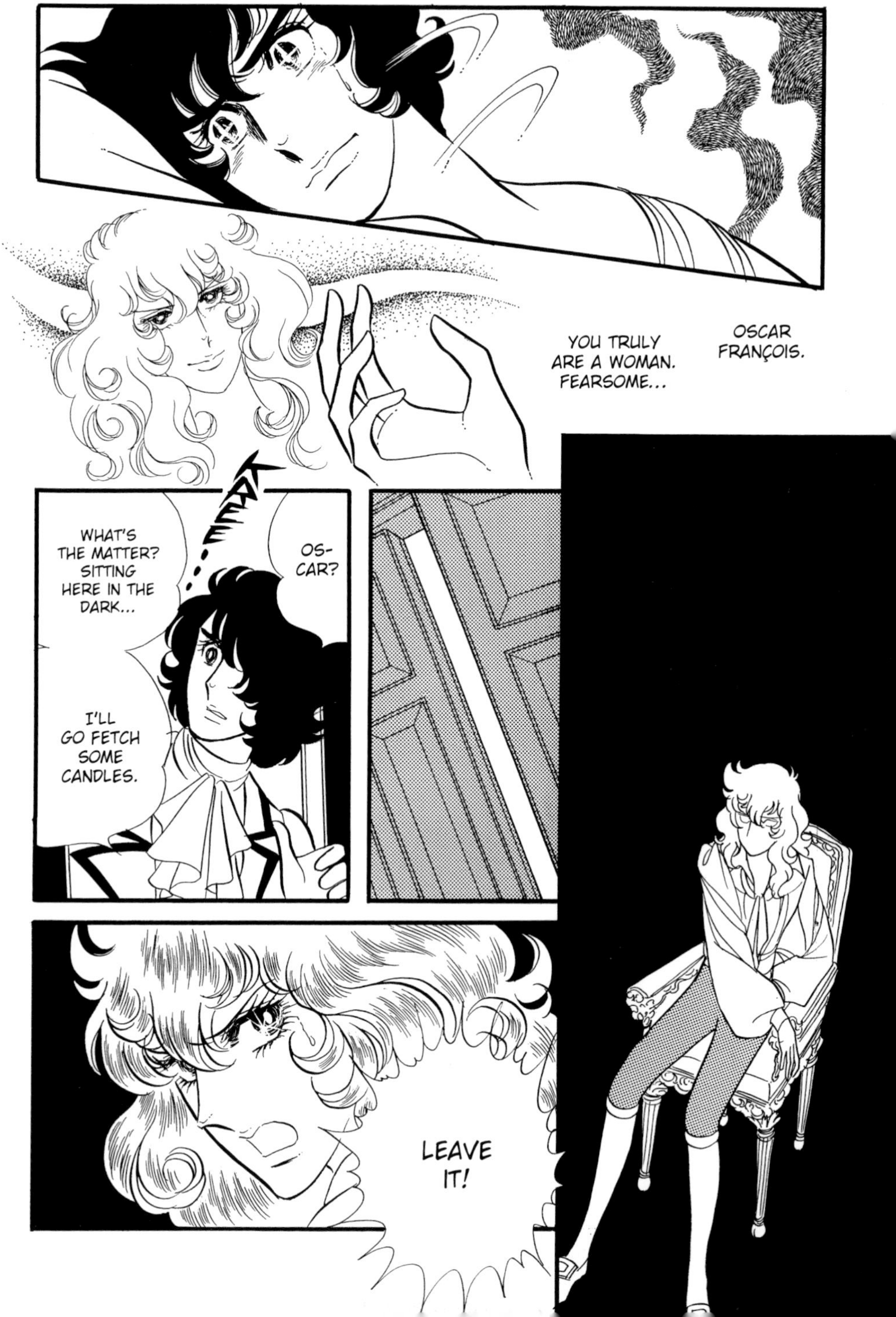

OSCAR FRANÇOIS.
YOU TRULY ARE A WOMAN. FEARSOME...
KREEE...
OS-CAR?
WHAT'S THE MATTER? SITTING HERE IN THE DARK...
I'LL GO FETCH SOME CANDLES.
LEAVE IT!

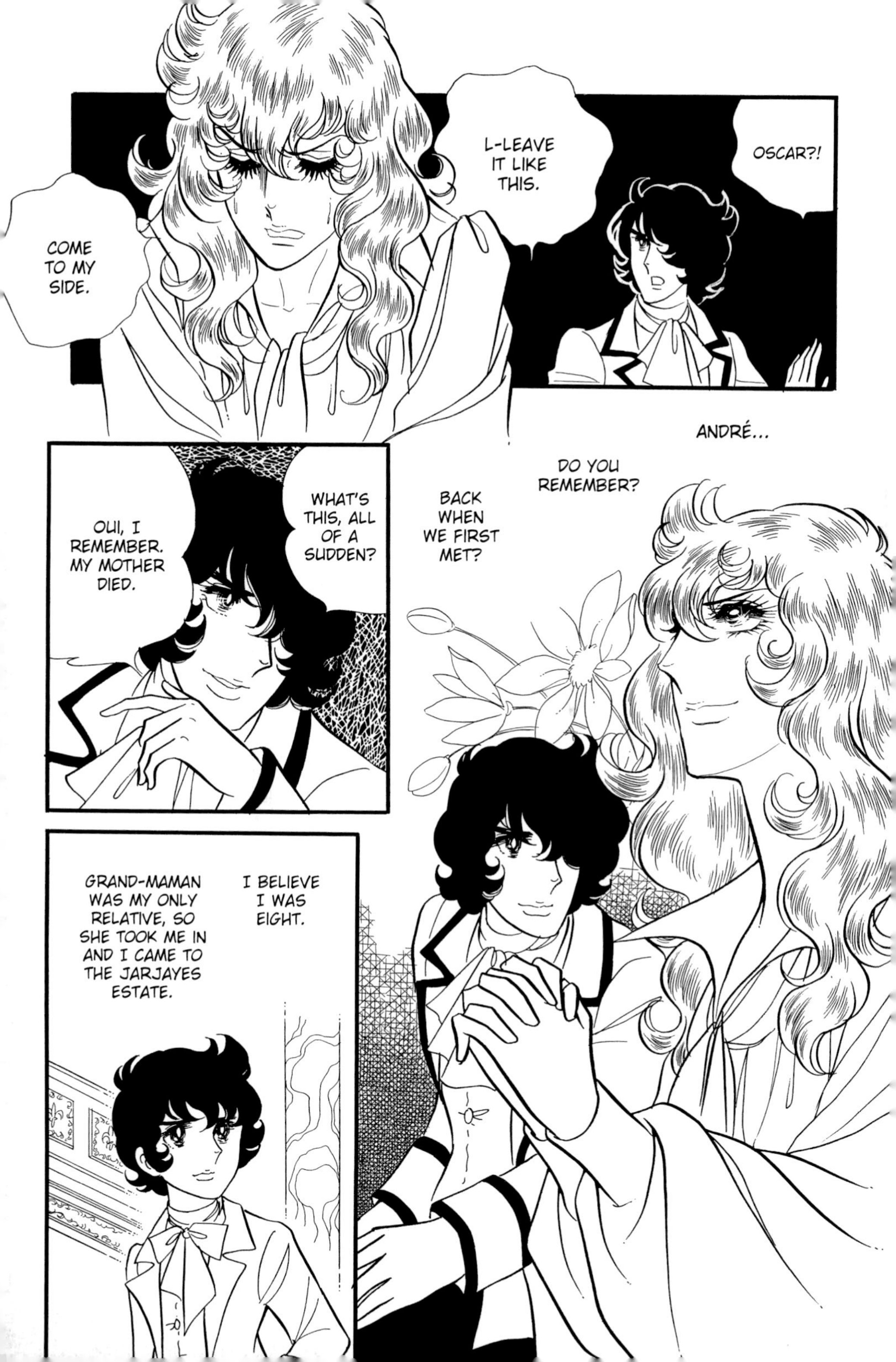

OSCAR?!
L-LEAVE IT LIKE THIS.
COME TO MY SIDE.
ANDRÉ...
DO YOU REMEMBER?
BACK WHEN WE FIRST MET?
WHAT'S THIS, ALL OF A SUDDEN?
OUI, I REMEMBER. MY MOTHER DIED.
I BELIEVE I WAS EIGHT.
GRAND-MAMAN WAS MY ONLY RELATIVE, SO SHE TOOK ME IN AND I CAME TO THE JARJAYES ESTATE.

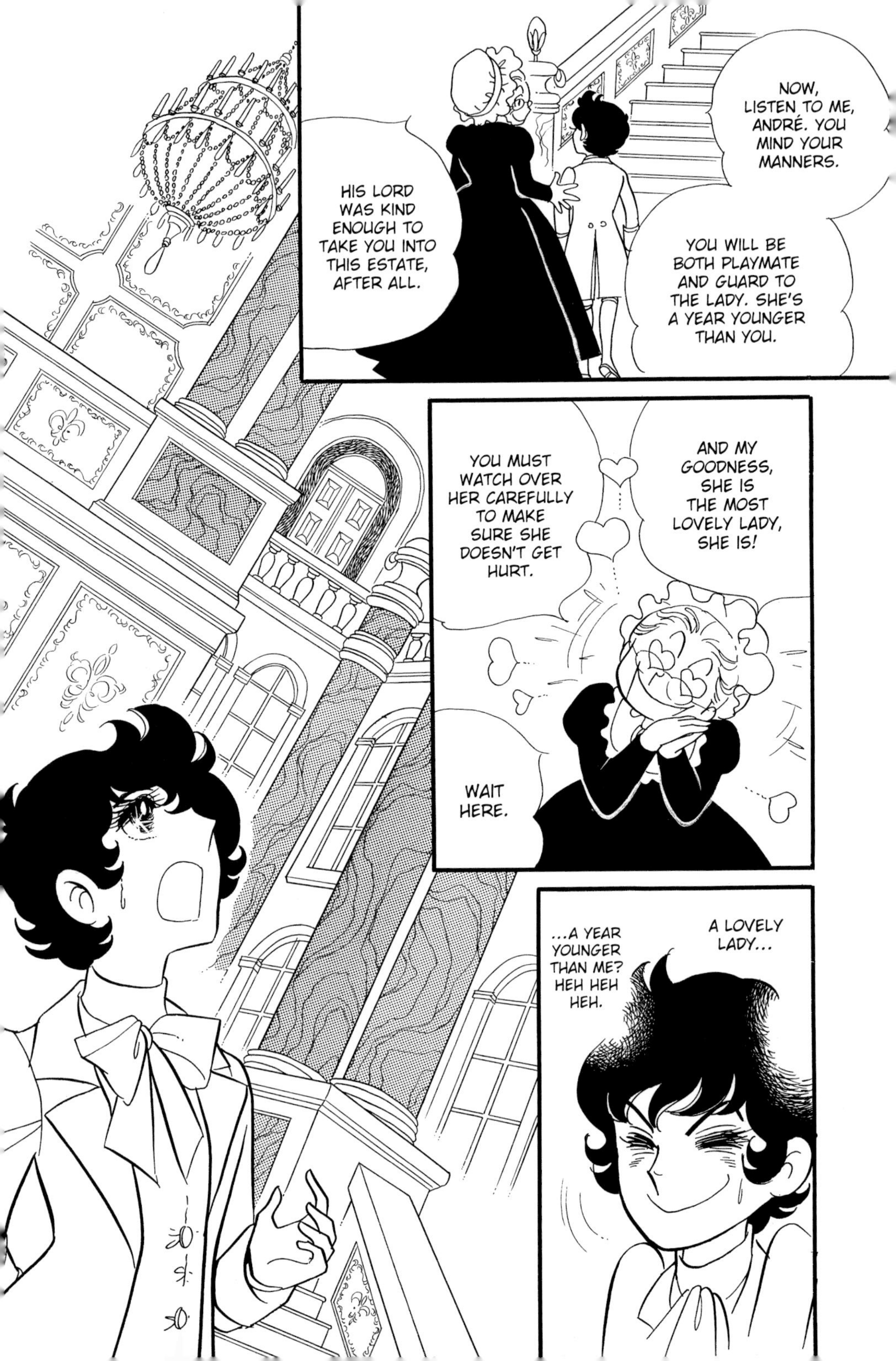
NOW, LISTEN TO ME, ANDRÉ. YOU MIND YOUR MANNERS.
HIS LORD WAS KIND ENOUGH TO TAKE YOU INTO THIS ESTATE, AFTER ALL.
YOU WILL BE BOTH PLAYMATE AND GUARD TO THE LADY. SHE'S A YEAR YOUNGER THAN YOU.
AND MY GOODNESS, SHE IS THE MOST LOVELY LADY, SHE IS!
YOU MUST WATCH OVER HER CAREFULLY TO MAKE SURE SHE DOESN'T GET HURT.
WAIT HERE.
A LOVELY LADY...
...A YEAR YOUNGER THAN ME? HEH HEH HEH.

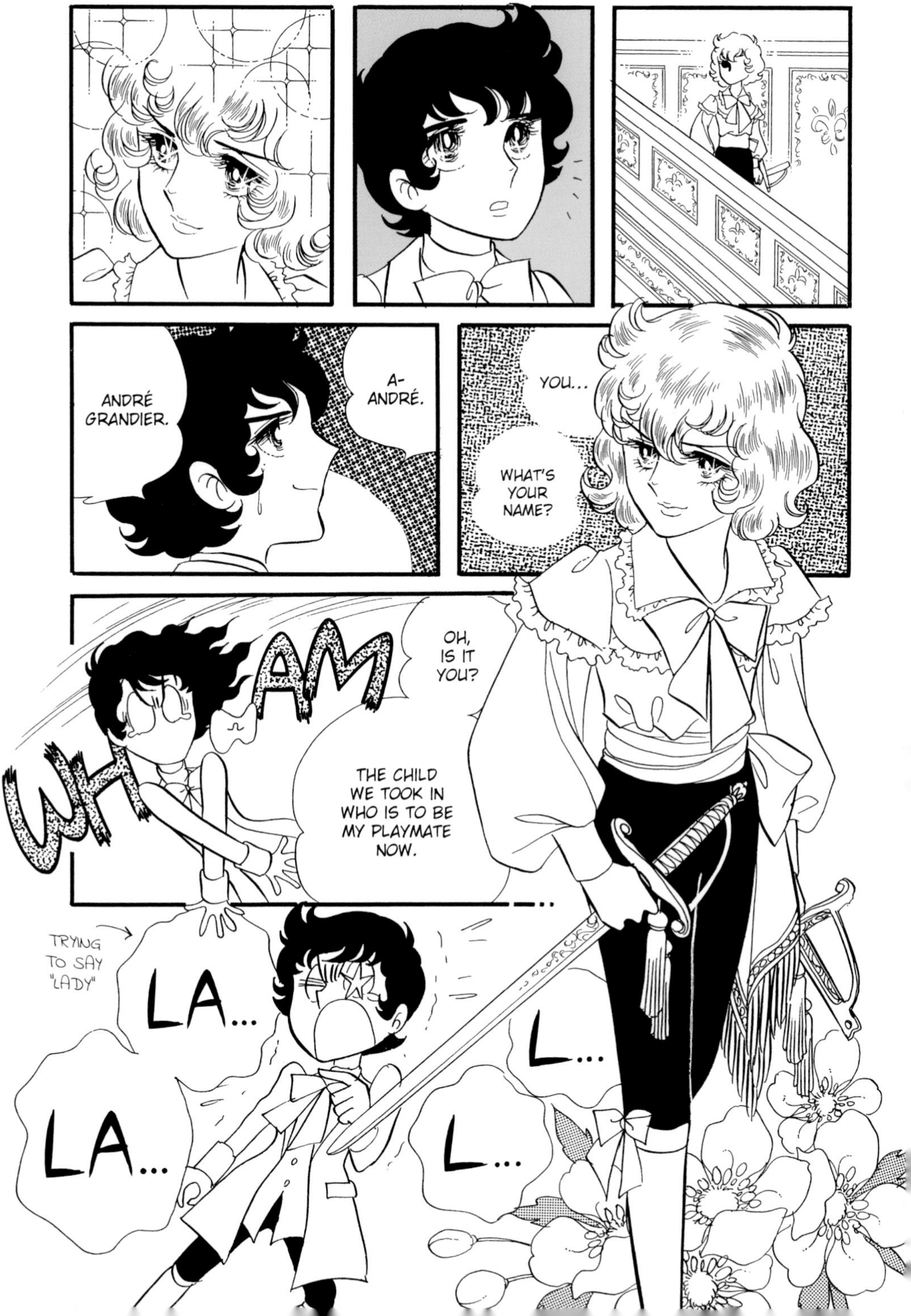
YOU...
WHAT'S YOUR NAME?
A- ANDRÉ.
ANDRÉ GRANDIER.
OH, IS IT YOU?
THE CHILD WE TOOK IN WHO IS TO BE MY PLAYMATE NOW.
WHAM
L...
L...
TRYING TO SAY "LADY"
LA...
LA...

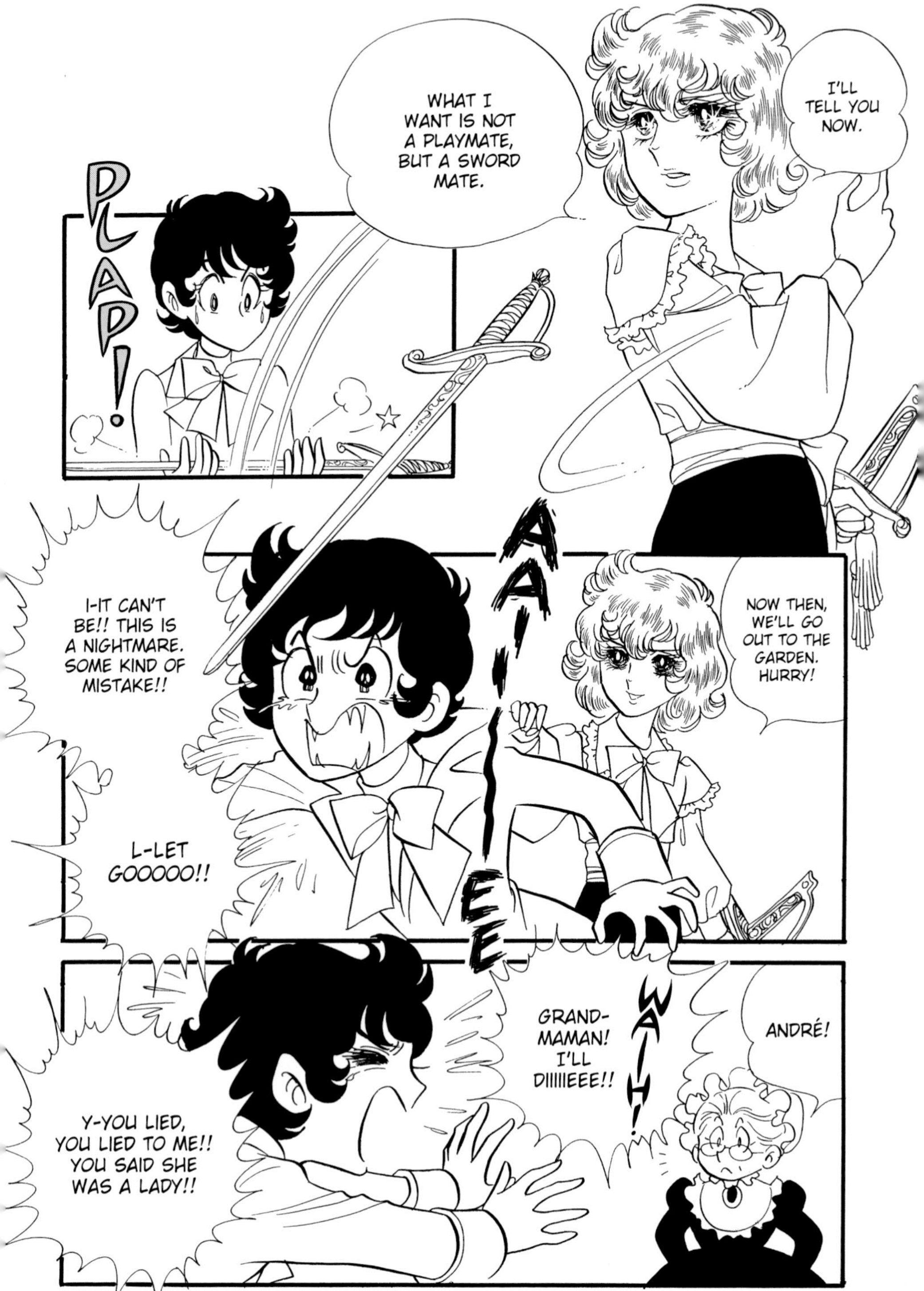
I'LL TELL YOU NOW.
WHAT I WANT IS NOT A PLAYMATE, BUT A SWORD MATE.
PLAP!
NOW THEN, WE'LL GO OUT TO THE GARDEN. HURRY!
AAIIIIEE
I-IT CAN'T BE!! THIS IS A NIGHTMARE. SOME KIND OF MISTAKE!!
L-LET GOOOOO!!
ANDRÉ!
WAH!
GRAND-MAMAN! I'LL DIIIIIEEE!!
Y-YOU LIED, YOU LIED TO ME!! YOU SAID SHE WAS A LADY!!

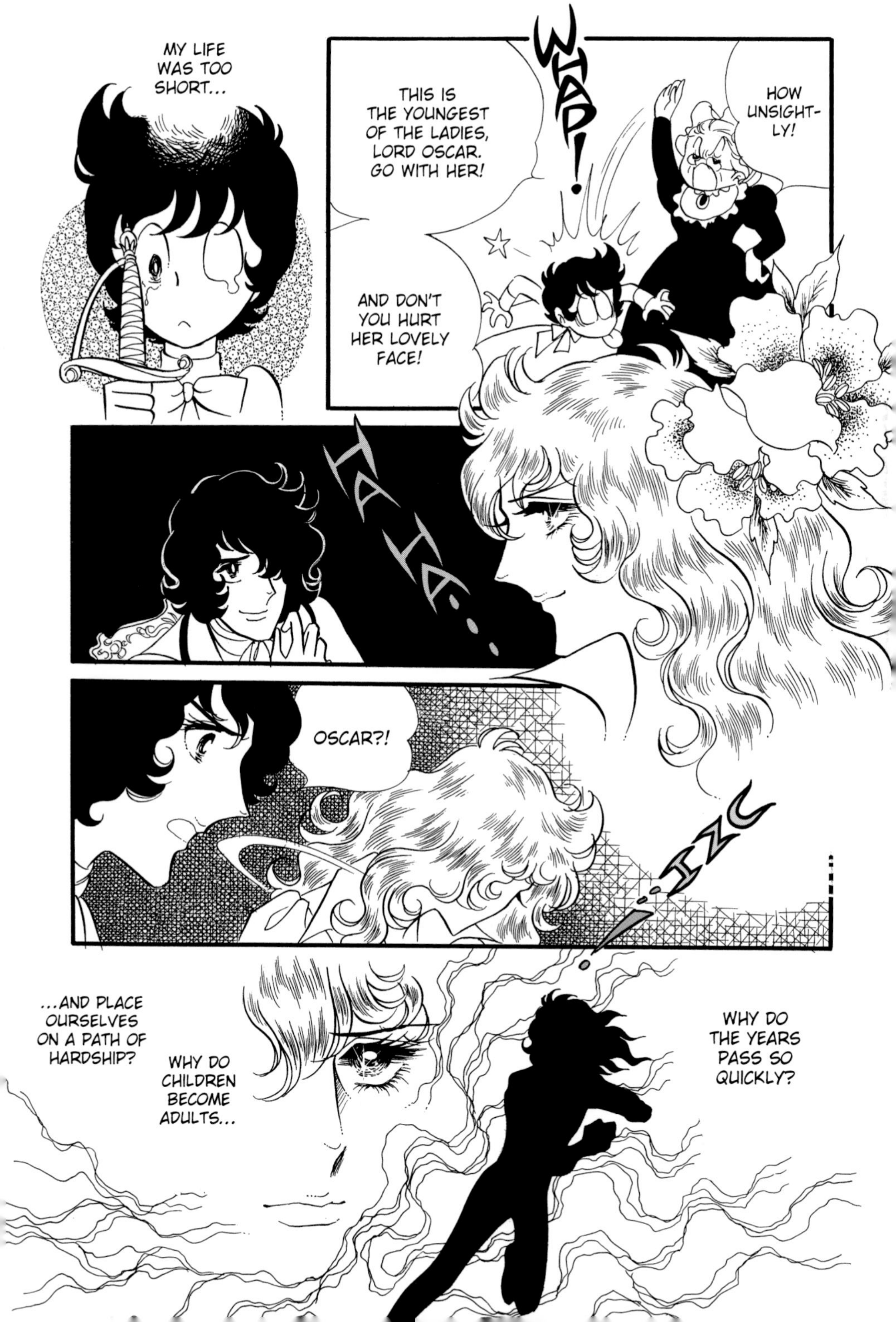
HOW UNSIGHTLY!
WHAP!
THIS IS THE YOUNGEST OF THE LADIES, LORD OSCAR. GO WITH HER!
AND DON'T YOU HURT HER LOVELY FACE!
MY LIFE WAS TOO SHORT...
HA HA HA...
OSCAR?!
WHY DO THE YEARS PASS SO QUICKLY?
WHY DO CHILDREN BECOME ADULTS...
...AND PLACE OURSELVES ON A PATH OF HARDSHIP?

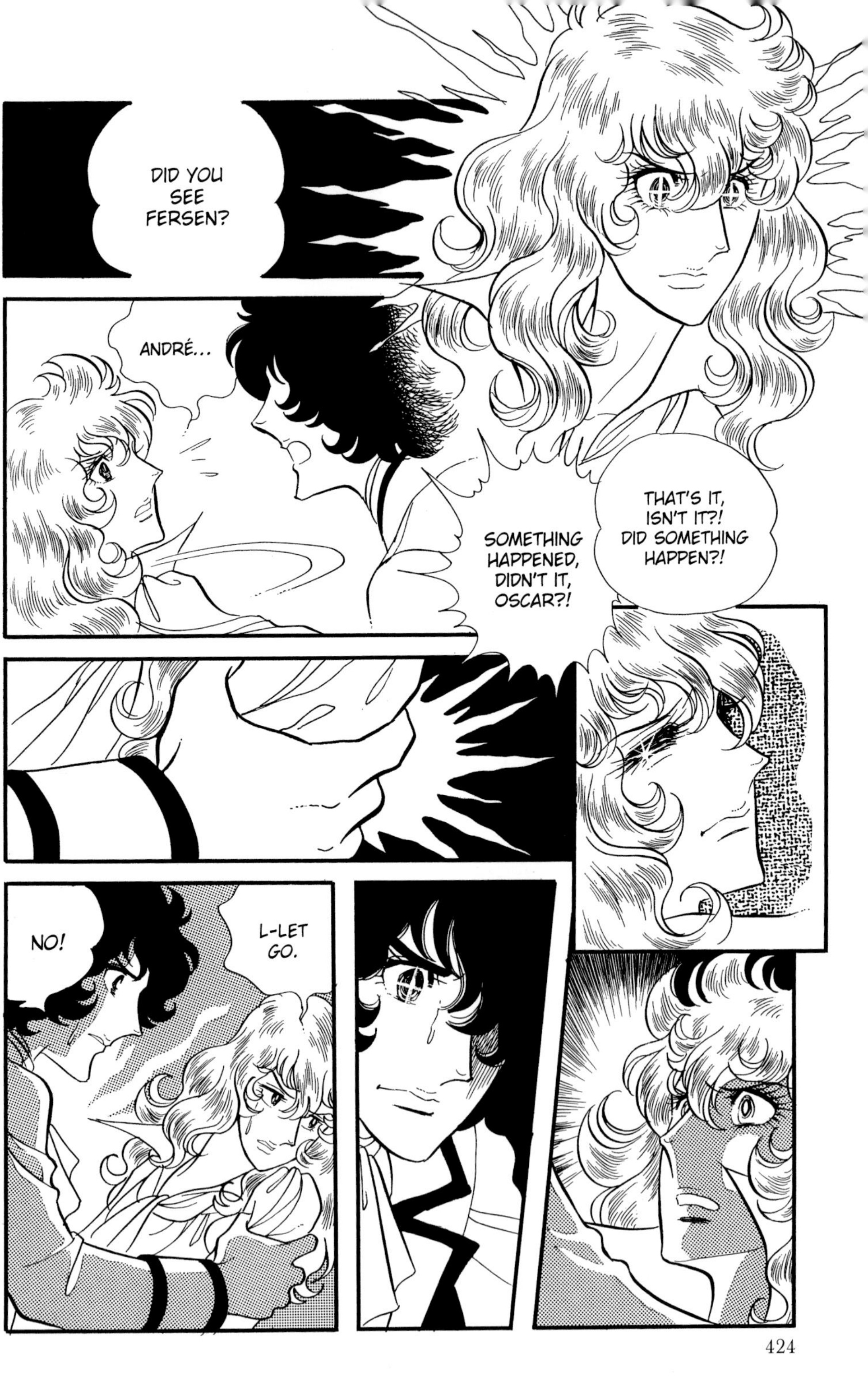
DID YOU SEE FERSEN?
THAT'S IT, ISN'T IT?! DID SOMETHING HAPPEN?!
SOMETHING HAPPENED, DIDN'T IT, OSCAR?!
ANDRÉ...
L-LET GO.
NO!

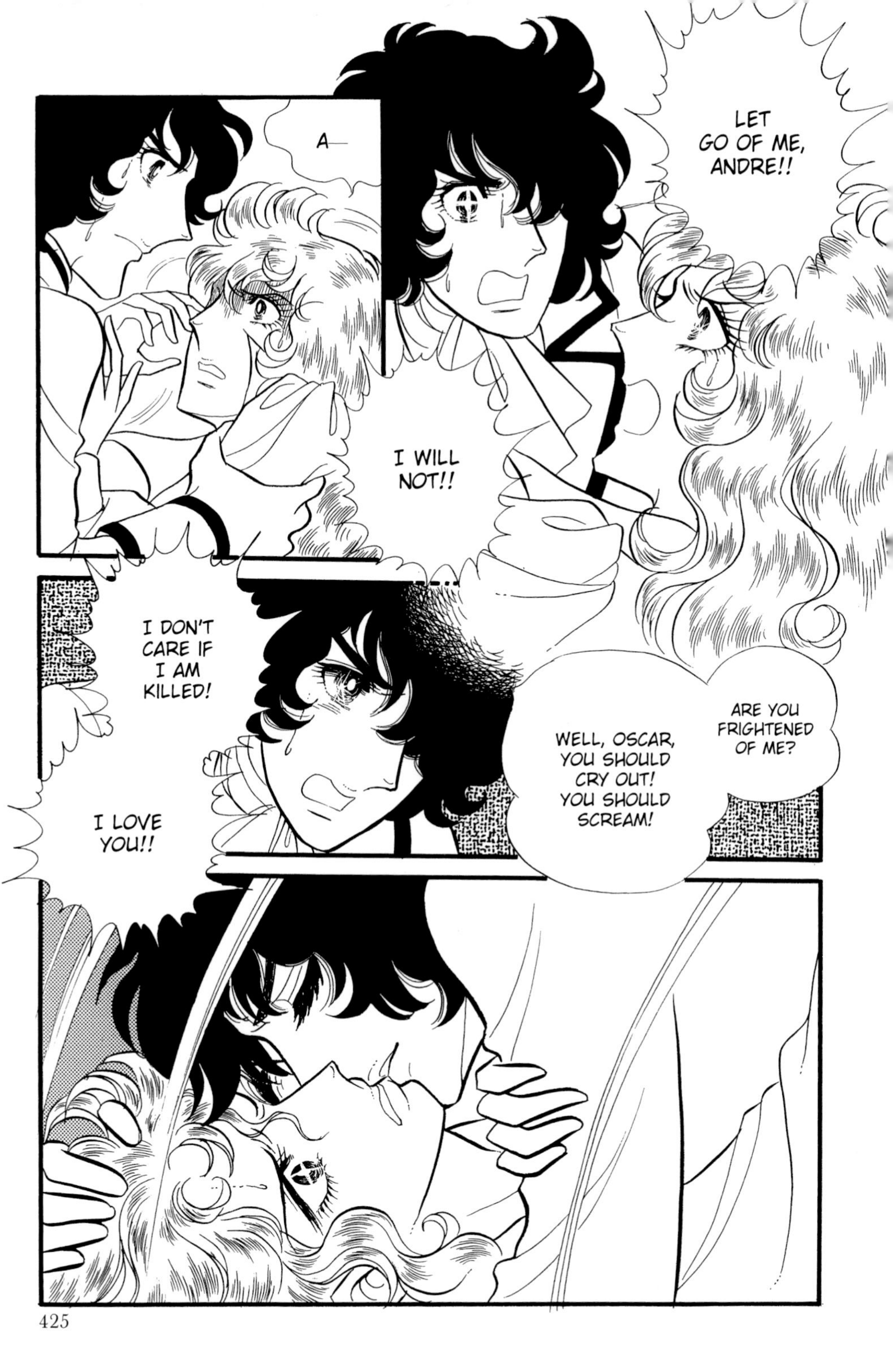
LET GO OF ME, ANDRE!!
I WILL NOT!!
A—
ARE YOU FRIGHTENED OF ME?
WELL, OSCAR, YOU SHOULD CRY OUT! YOU SHOULD SCREAM!
I DON'T CARE IF I AM KILLED!
I LOVE YOU!!

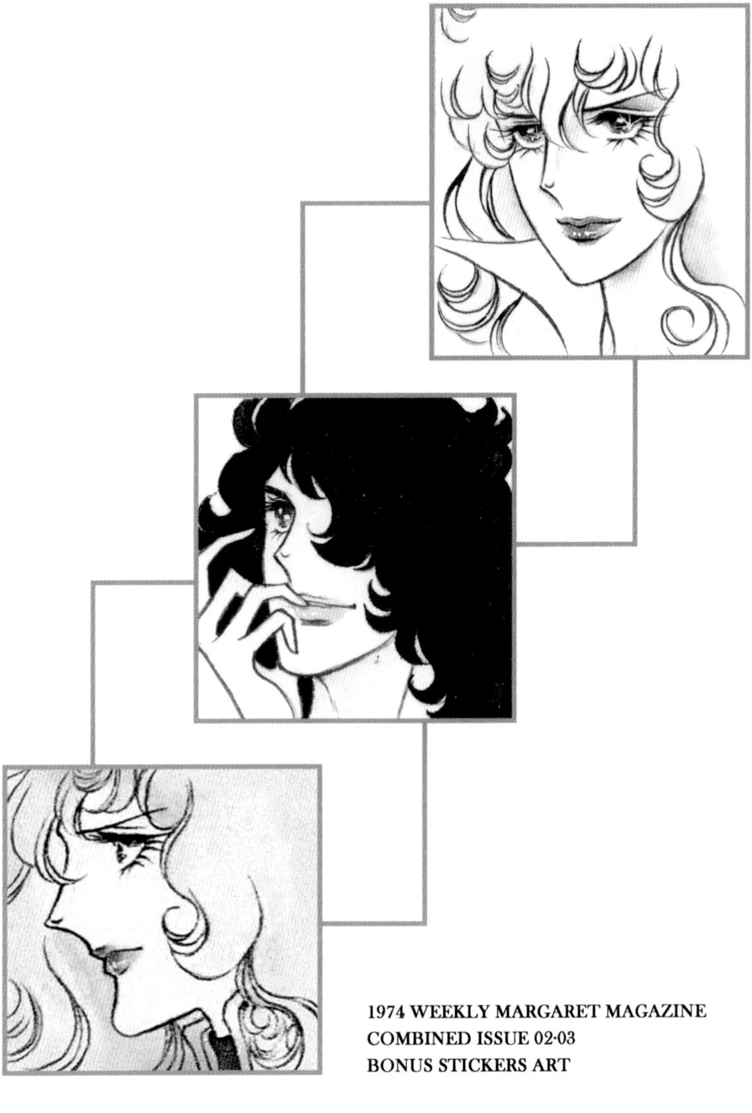

1974 WEEKLY MARGARET MAGAZINE
COMBINED ISSUE 02·03
BONUS STICKERS ART

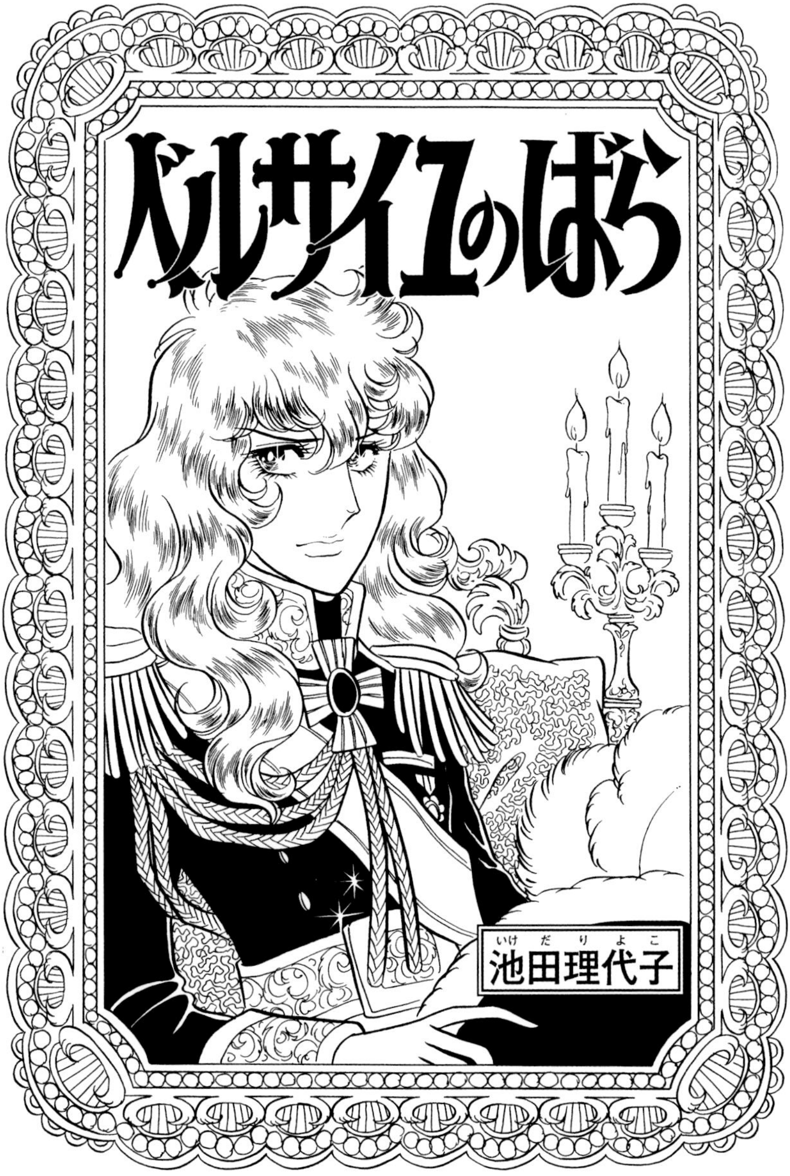
ベルサイユのばら
いけだりよこ
池田理代子

EPISODE 41

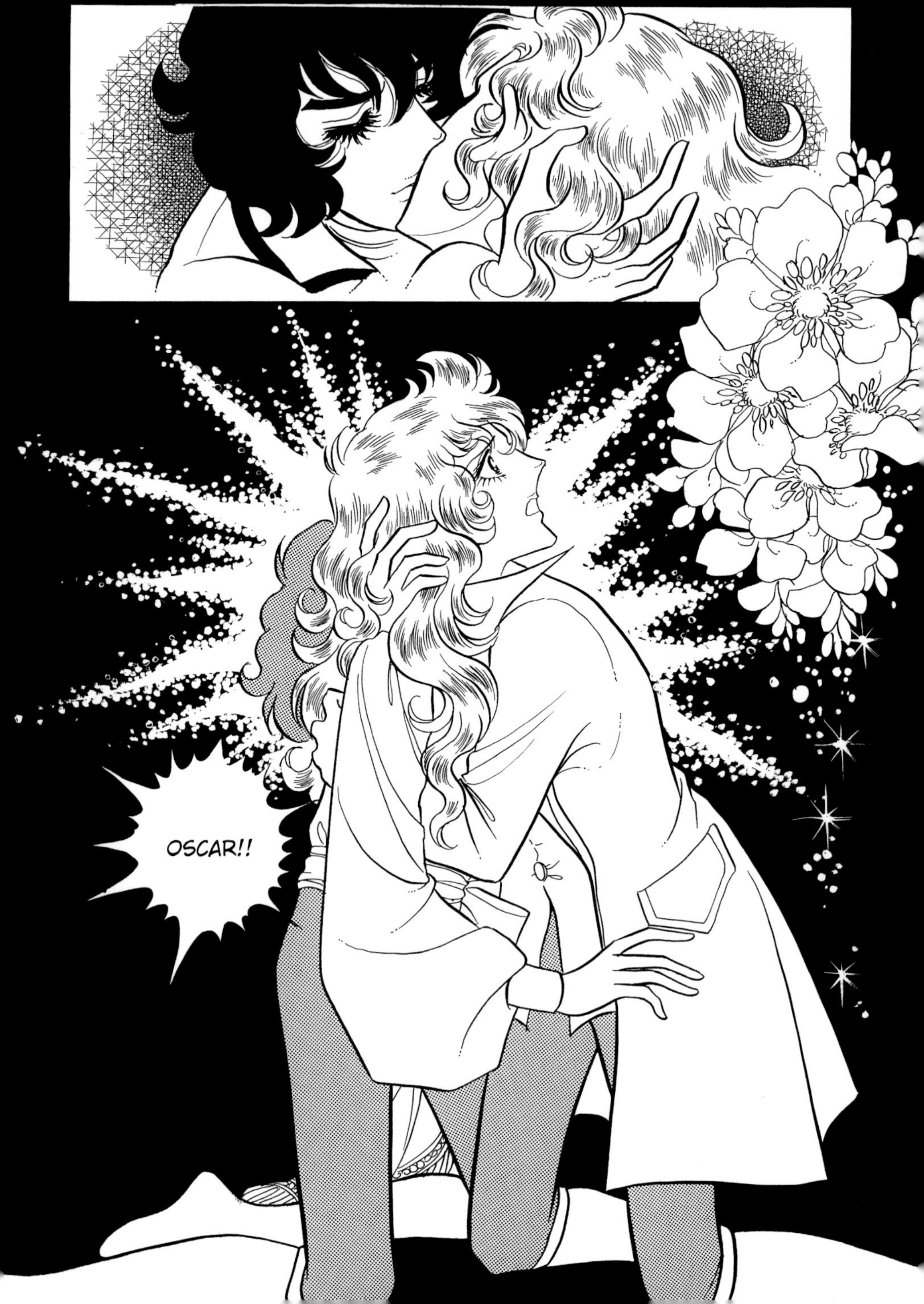
OSCAR!!

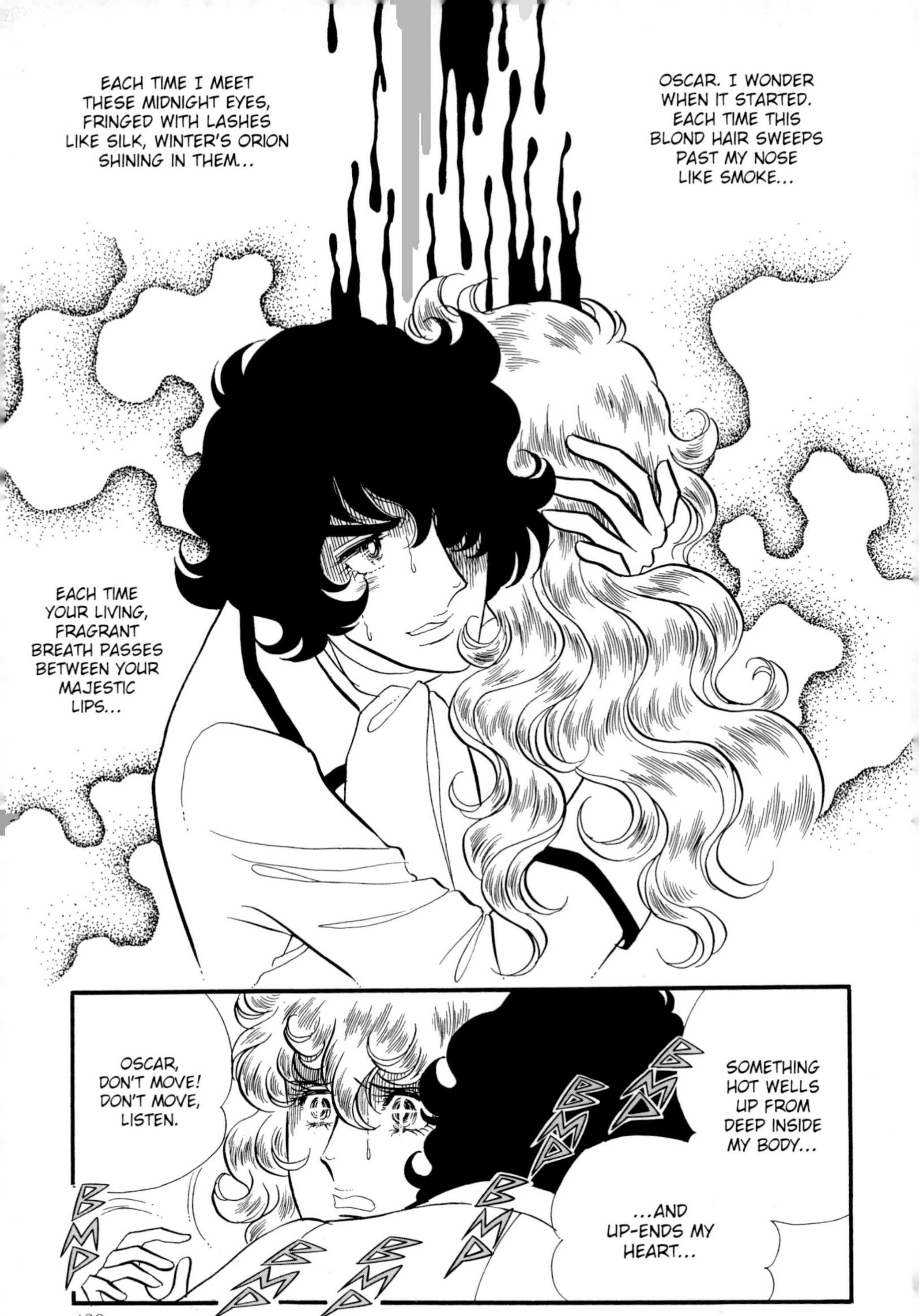
OSCAR. I WONDER WHEN IT STARTED. EACH TIME THIS BLOND HAIR SWEEPS PAST MY NOSE LIKE SMOKE...
EACH TIME I MEET THESE MIDNIGHT EYES, FRINGED WITH LASHES LIKE SILK, WINTER'S ORION SHINING IN THEM...
EACH TIME YOUR LIVING, FRAGRANT BREATH PASSES BETWEEN YOUR MAJESTIC LIPS...
BMP
BMP
BMP
SOMETHING HOT WELLS UP FROM DEEP INSIDE MY BODY...
OSCAR, DON'T MOVE! DON'T MOVE, LISTEN.
BMP
...AND UP-ENDS MY HEART...
BMP
BMP
BMP

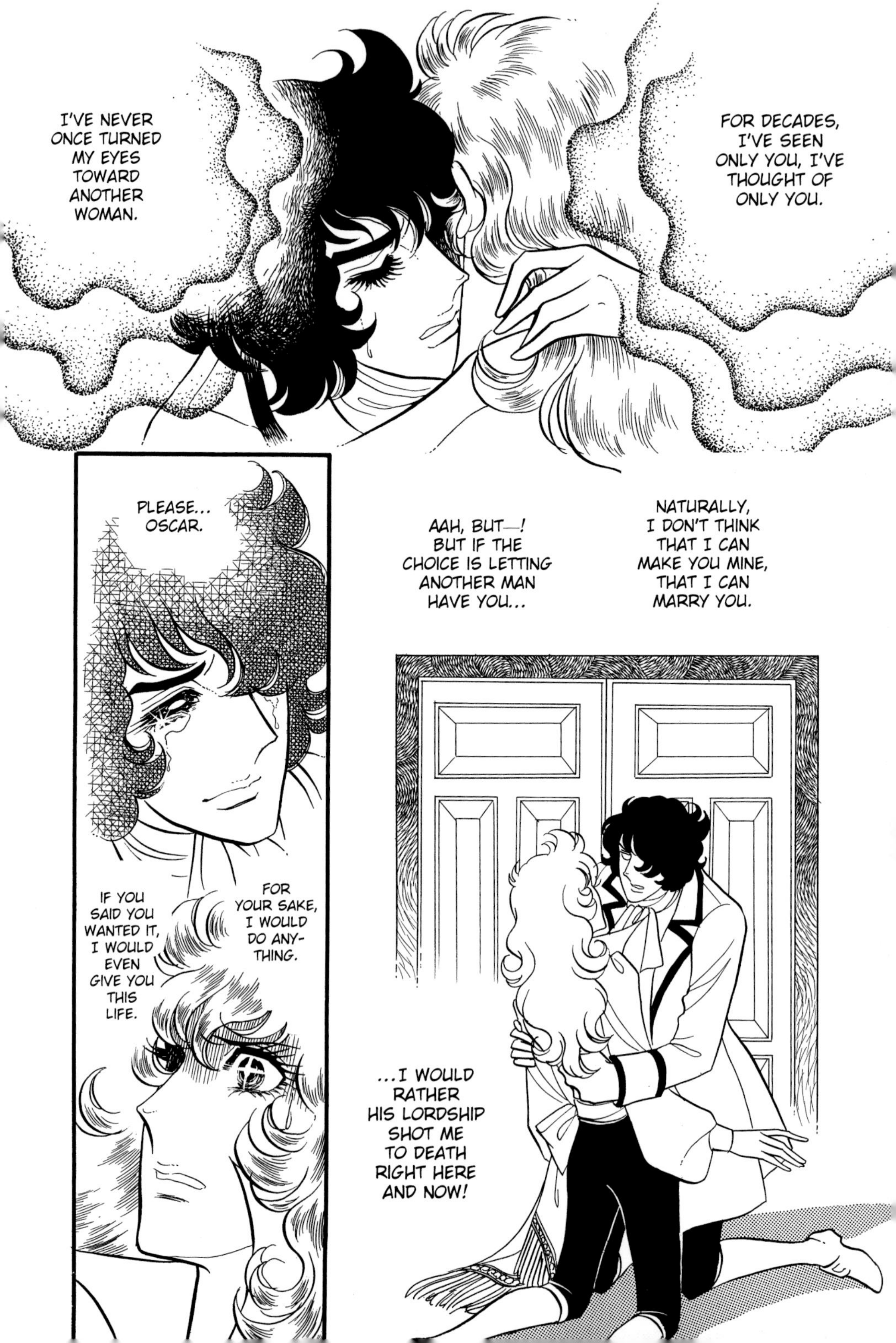
FOR DECADES, I'VE SEEN ONLY YOU, I'VE THOUGHT OF ONLY YOU.
I'VE NEVER ONCE TURNED MY EYES TOWARD ANOTHER WOMAN.
NATURALLY, I DON'T THINK THAT I CAN MAKE YOU MINE, THAT I CAN MARRY YOU.
AAH, BUT—! BUT IF THE CHOICE IS LETTING ANOTHER MAN HAVE YOU...
...I WOULD RATHER HIS LORDSHIP SHOT ME TO DEATH RIGHT HERE AND NOW!
PLEASE... OSCAR.
FOR YOUR SAKE, I WOULD DO ANY-THING.
IF YOU SAID YOU WANTED IT, I WOULD EVEN GIVE YOU THIS LIFE.

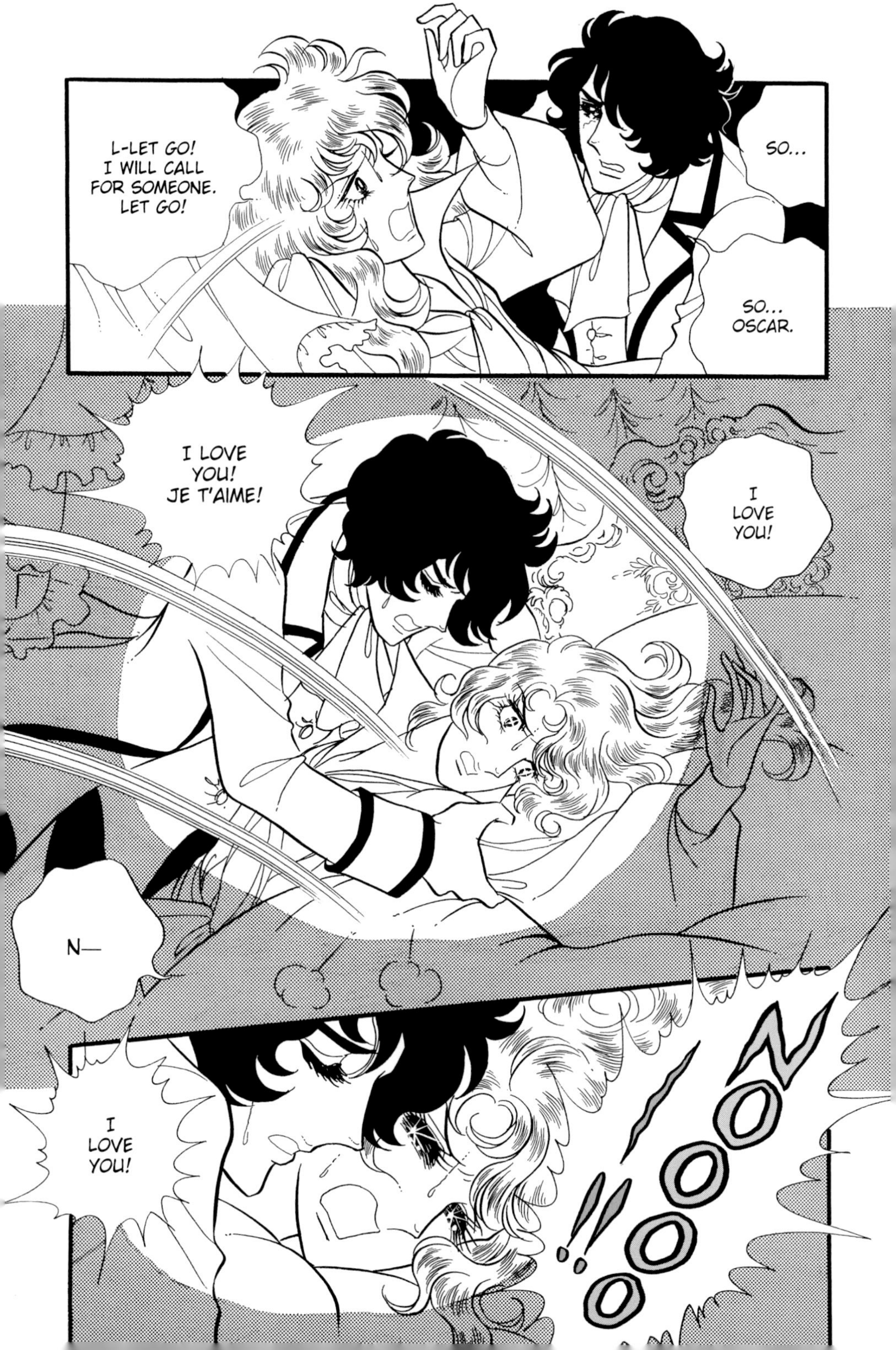
SO…
L-LET GO! I WILL CALL FOR SOMEONE. LET GO!
SO… OSCAR.
I LOVE YOU!
I LOVE YOU! JE T'AIME!
N—
NOOOOOO!!
I LOVE YOU!

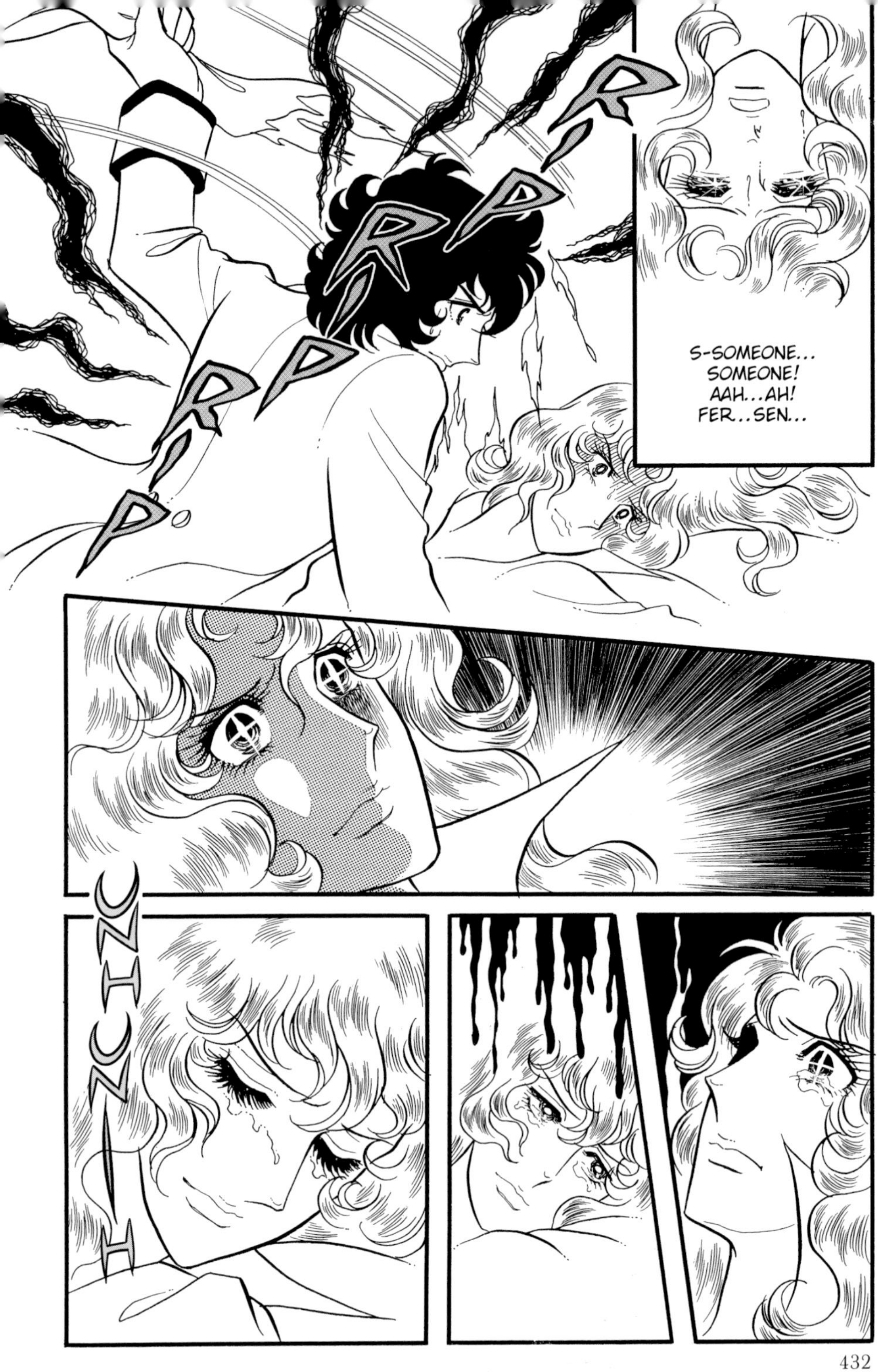
S-SOMEONE... SOMEONE! AAH...AH! FER...SEN...
RIP RIP RIP

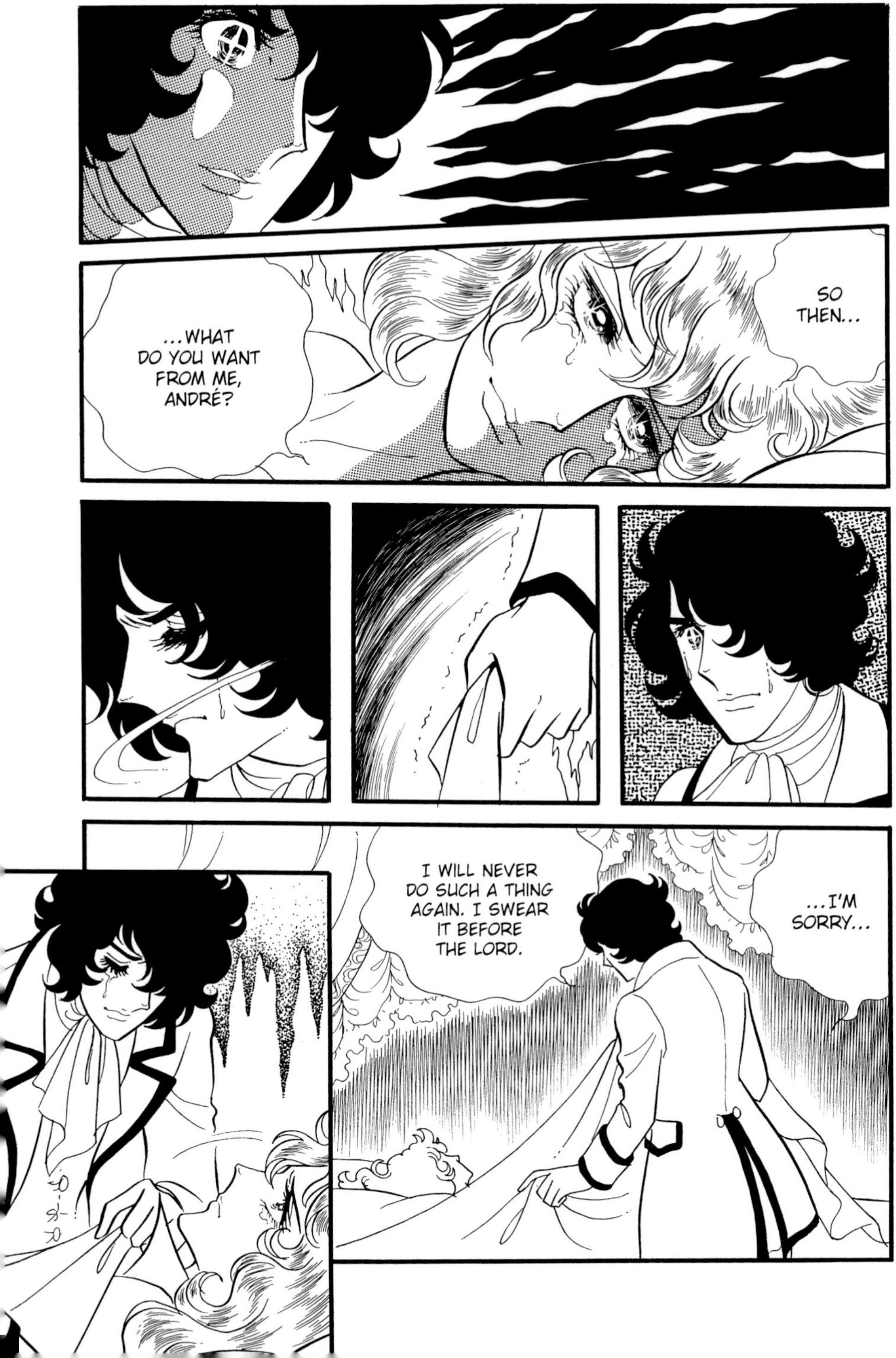
SO THEN...
...WHAT DO YOU WANT FROM ME, ANDRÉ?
...I'M SORRY...
I WILL NEVER DO SUCH A THING AGAIN. I SWEAR IT BEFORE THE LORD.

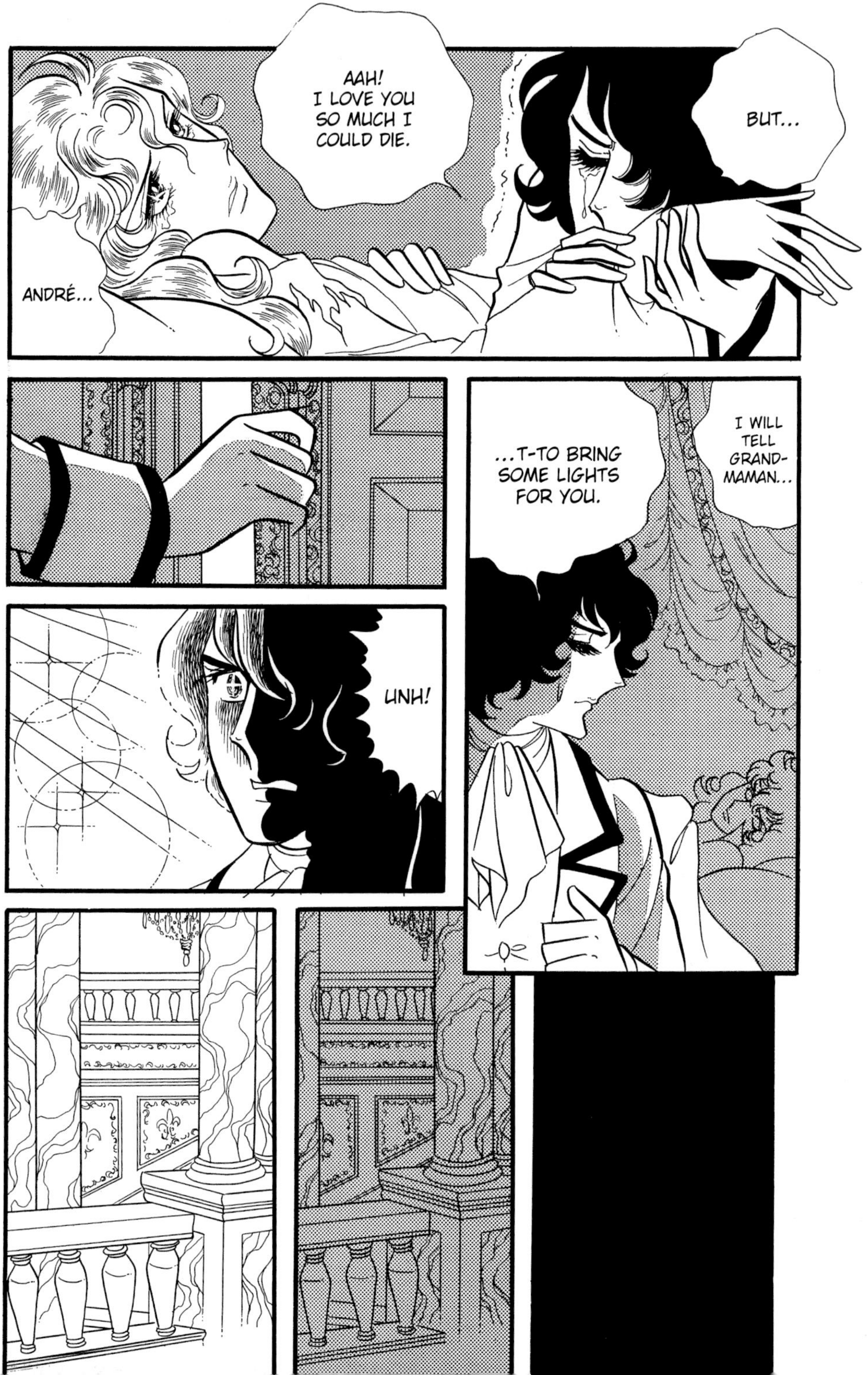
BUT...
AAH! I LOVE YOU SO MUCH I COULD DIE.
ANDRÉ...
I WILL TELL GRAND-MAMAN...
...T-TO BRING SOME LIGHTS FOR YOU.
UNH!

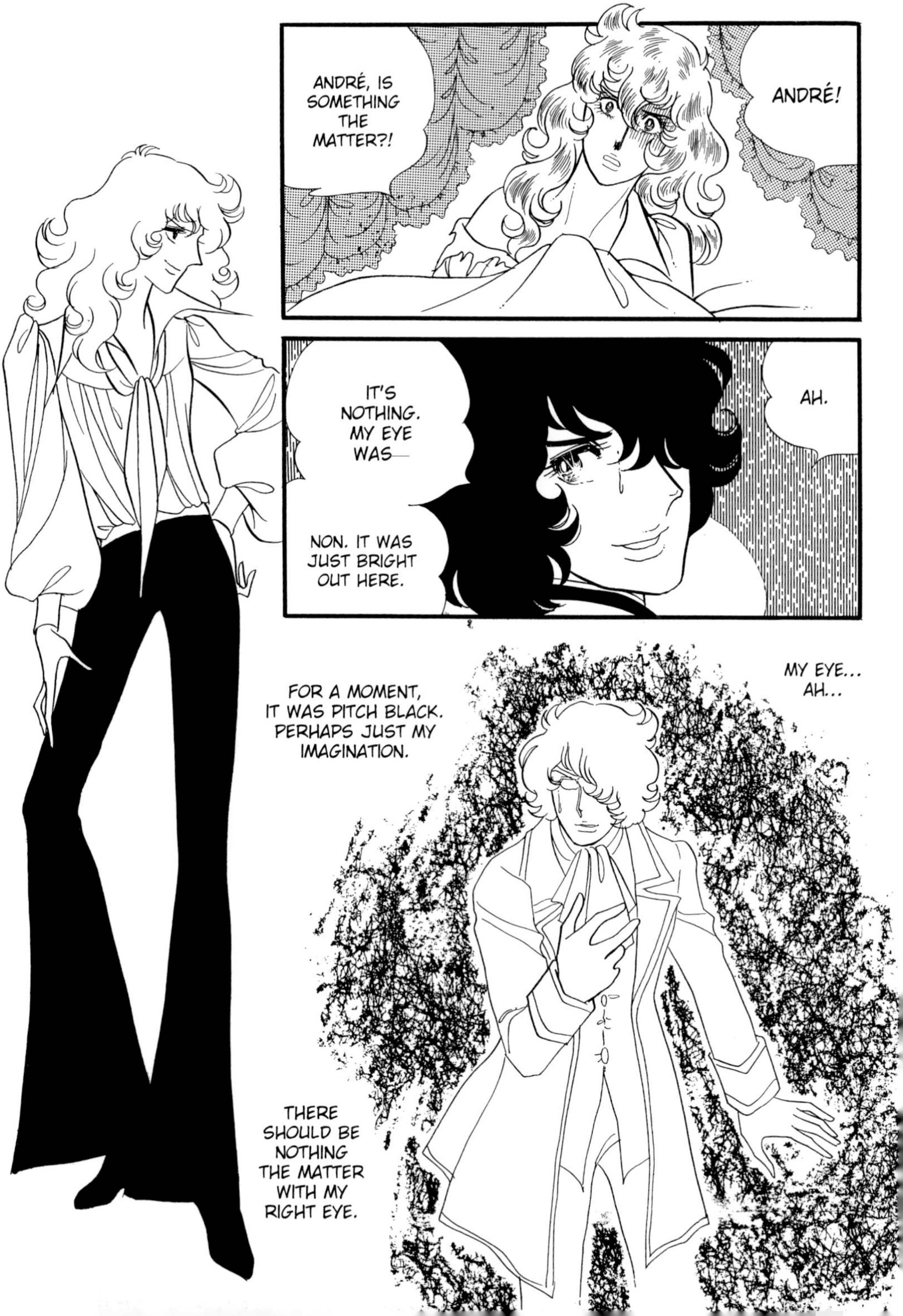
ANDRÉ!
ANDRÉ, IS SOMETHING THE MATTER?!
AH.
IT'S NOTHING. MY EYE WAS—
NON. IT WAS JUST BRIGHT OUT HERE.
MY EYE... AH...
FOR A MOMENT, IT WAS PITCH BLACK. PERHAPS JUST MY IMAGINATION.
THERE SHOULD BE NOTHING THE MATTER WITH MY RIGHT EYE.

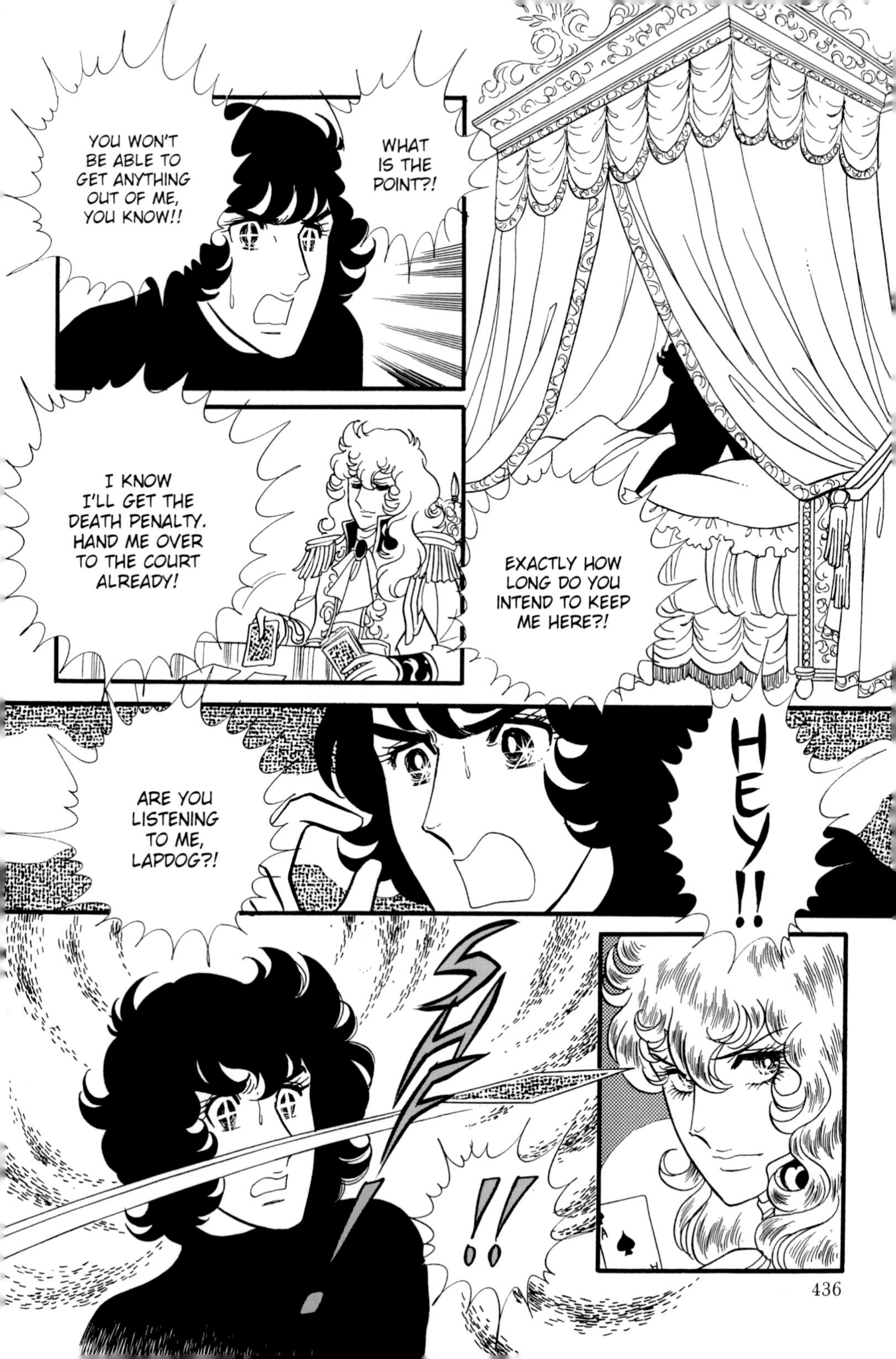
EXACTLY HOW LONG DO YOU INTEND TO KEEP ME HERE?!
WHAT IS THE POINT?!
YOU WON'T BE ABLE TO GET ANYTHING OUT OF ME, YOU KNOW!!
I KNOW I'LL GET THE DEATH PENALTY. HAND ME OVER TO THE COURT ALREADY!
HEY!!
ARE YOU LISTENING TO ME, LAPDOG?!
!!

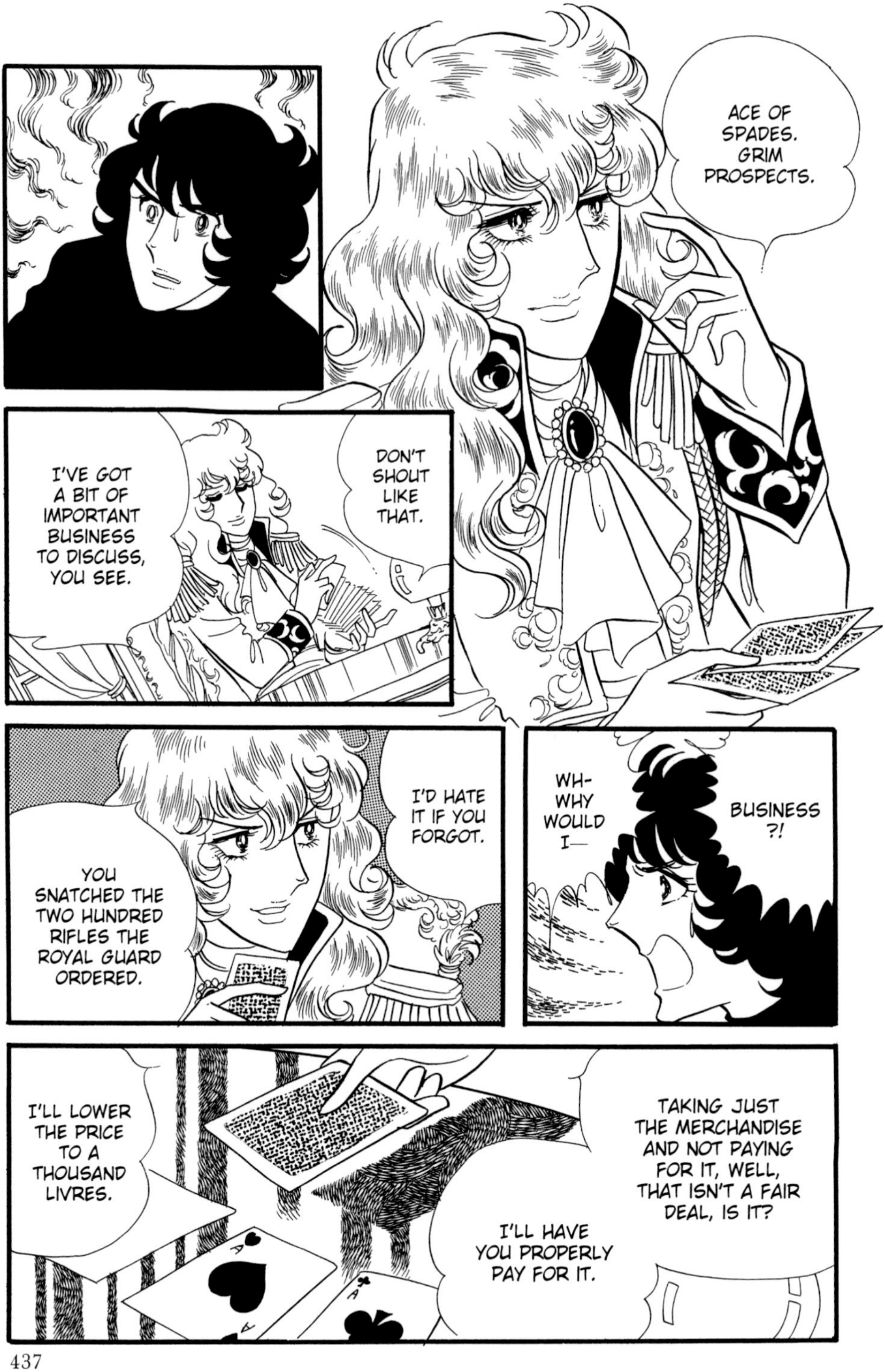
ACE OF SPADES. GRIM PROSPECTS.
DON'T SHOUT LIKE THAT.
I'VE GOT A BIT OF IMPORTANT BUSINESS TO DISCUSS, YOU SEE.
BUSINESS?!
WH- WHY WOULD I—
I'D HATE IT IF YOU FORGOT.
YOU SNATCHED THE TWO HUNDRED RIFLES THE ROYAL GUARD ORDERED.
TAKING JUST THE MERCHANDISE AND NOT PAYING FOR IT, WELL, THAT ISN'T A FAIR DEAL, IS IT?
I'LL HAVE YOU PROPERLY PAY FOR IT.
I'LL LOWER THE PRICE TO A THOUSAND LIVRES.

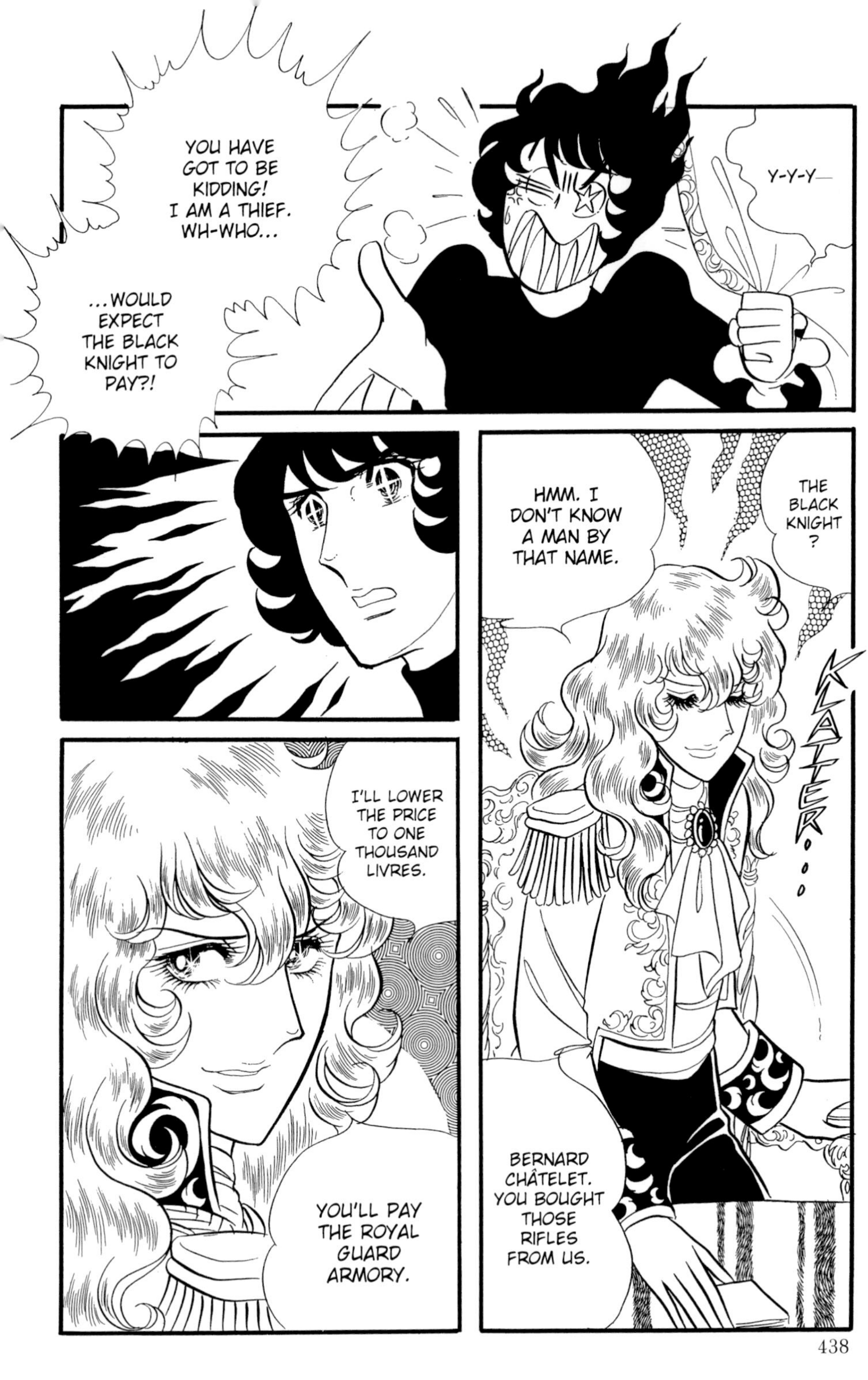
Y-Y-Y—
YOU HAVE GOT TO BE KIDDING! I AM A THIEF. WH-WHO...
...WOULD EXPECT THE BLACK KNIGHT TO PAY?!
THE BLACK KNIGHT ?
HMM. I DON'T KNOW A MAN BY THAT NAME.
KLATTER...
BERNARD CHÂTELET. YOU BOUGHT THOSE RIFLES FROM US.
I'LL LOWER THE PRICE TO ONE THOUSAND LIVRES.
YOU'LL PAY THE ROYAL GUARD ARMORY.

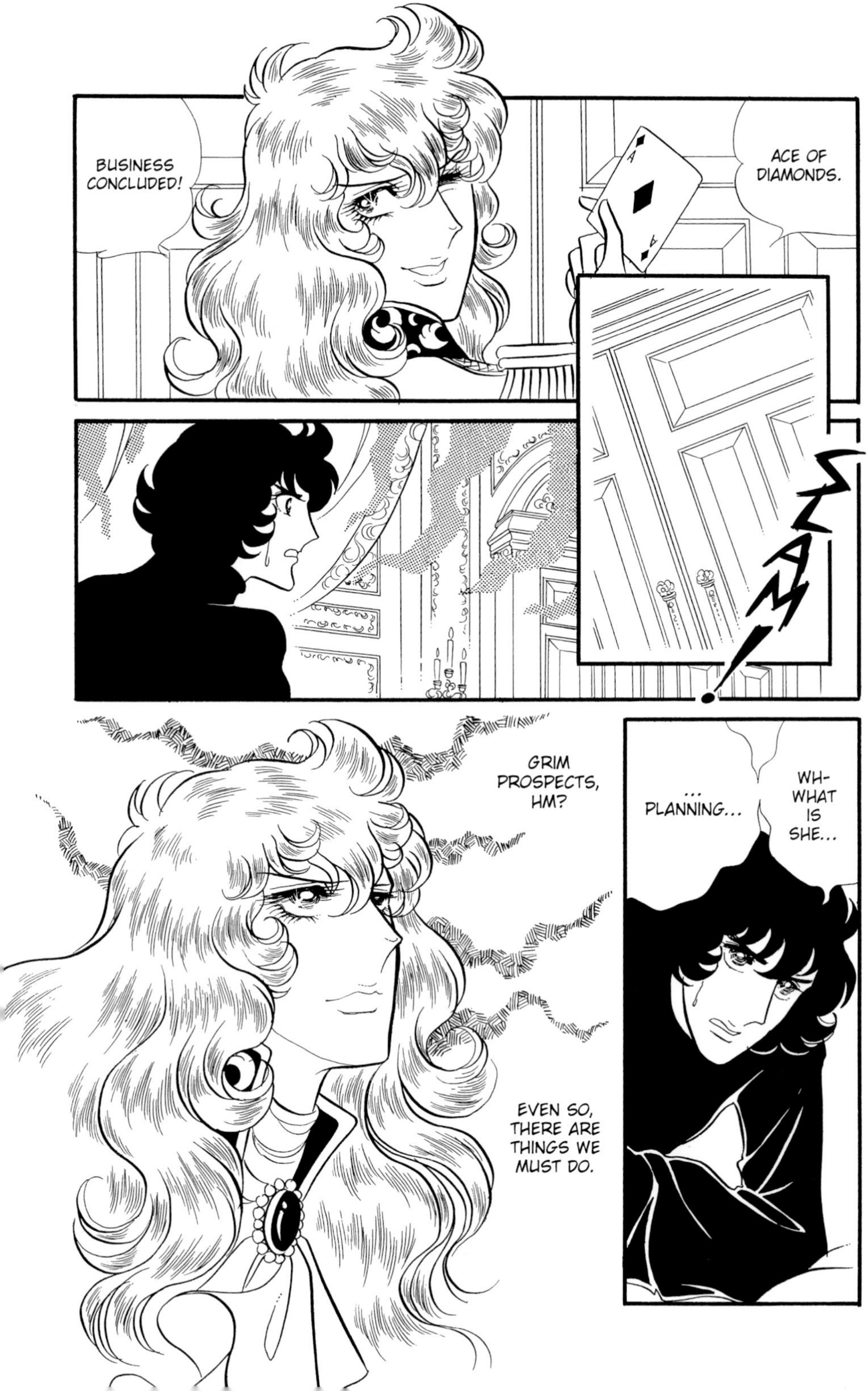
ACE OF DIAMONDS.
BUSINESS CONCLUDED!
SLAM!
WH- WHAT IS SHE...
...PLANNING...
GRIM PROSPECTS, HM?
EVEN SO, THERE ARE THINGS WE MUST DO.

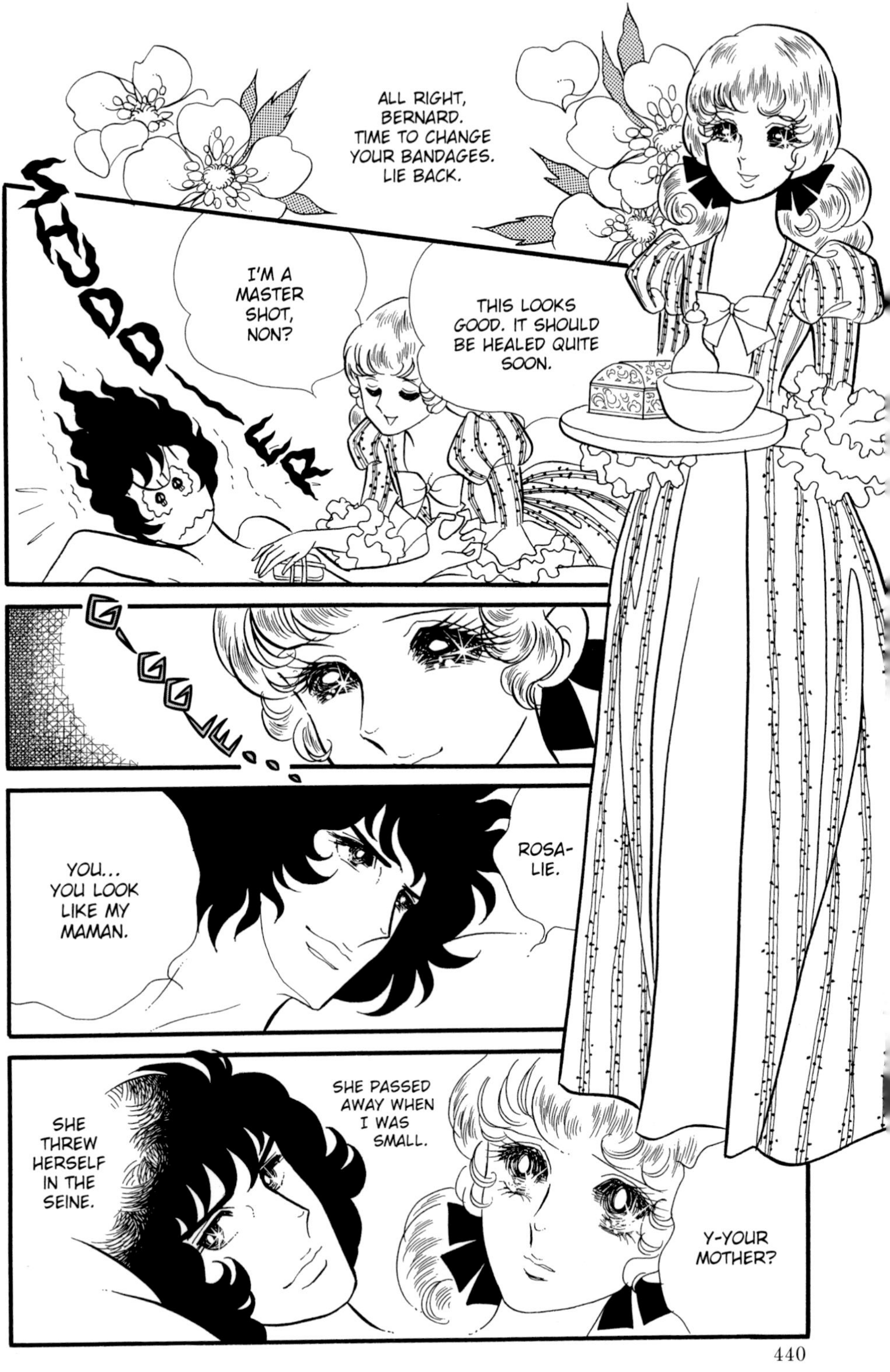
ALL RIGHT, BERNARD. TIME TO CHANGE YOUR BANDAGES. LIE BACK.
THIS LOOKS GOOD. IT SHOULD BE HEALED QUITE SOON.
I'M A MASTER SHOT, NON?
SHUDD-ER
G-GGLE...
ROSA-LIE.
YOU... YOU LOOK LIKE MY MAMAN.
Y-YOUR MOTHER?
SHE PASSED AWAY WHEN I WAS SMALL.
SHE THREW HERSELF IN THE SEINE.

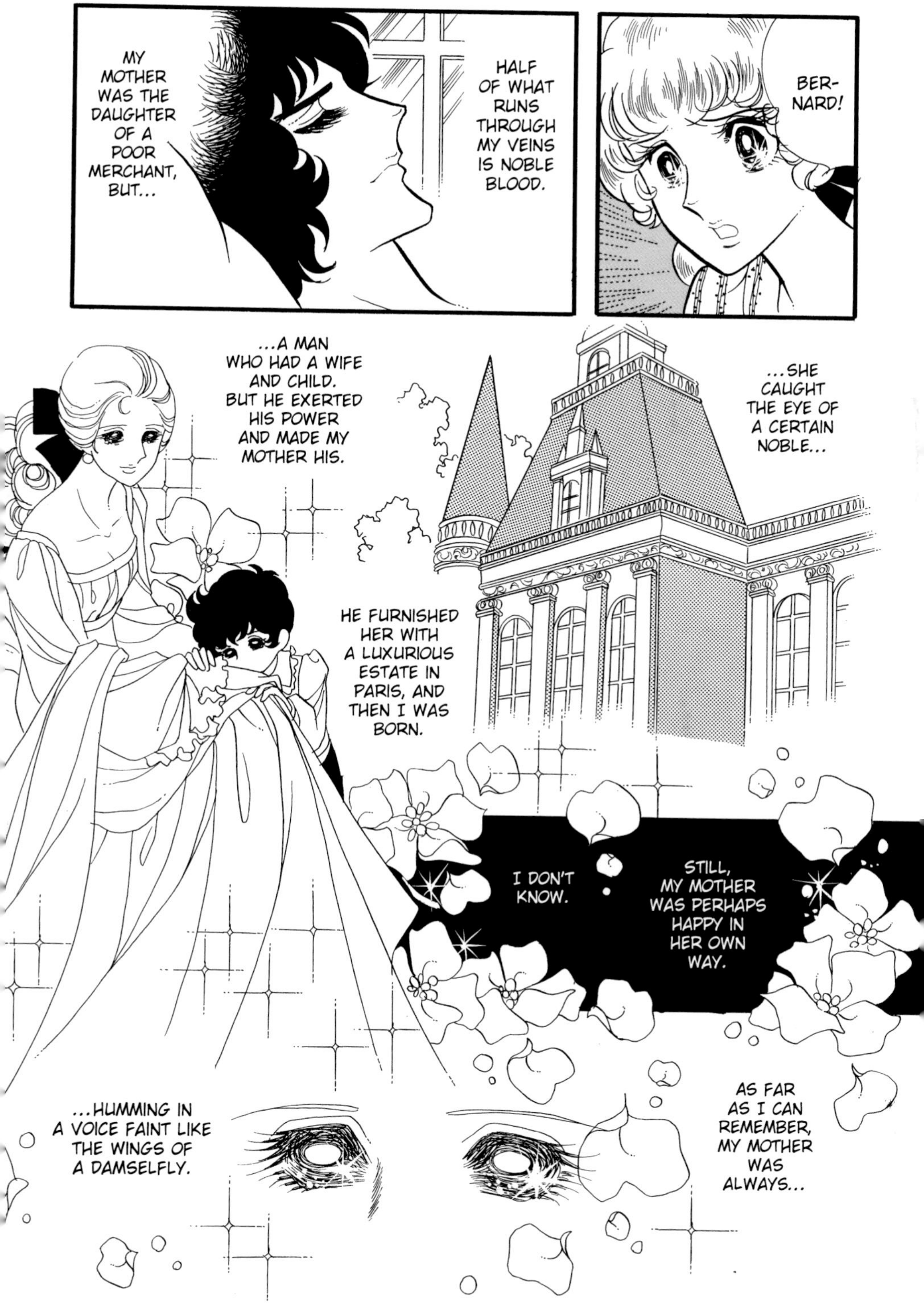
BER-NARD!
HALF OF WHAT RUNS THROUGH MY VEINS IS NOBLE BLOOD.
MY MOTHER WAS THE DAUGHTER OF A POOR MERCHANT, BUT...
...SHE CAUGHT THE EYE OF A CERTAIN NOBLE...
...A MAN WHO HAD A WIFE AND CHILD. BUT HE EXERTED HIS POWER AND MADE MY MOTHER HIS.
HE FURNISHED HER WITH A LUXURIOUS ESTATE IN PARIS, AND THEN I WAS BORN.
STILL, MY MOTHER WAS PERHAPS HAPPY IN HER OWN WAY.
I DON'T KNOW.
AS FAR AS I CAN REMEMBER, MY MOTHER WAS ALWAYS...
...HUMMING IN A VOICE FAINT LIKE THE WINGS OF A DAMSELFLY.

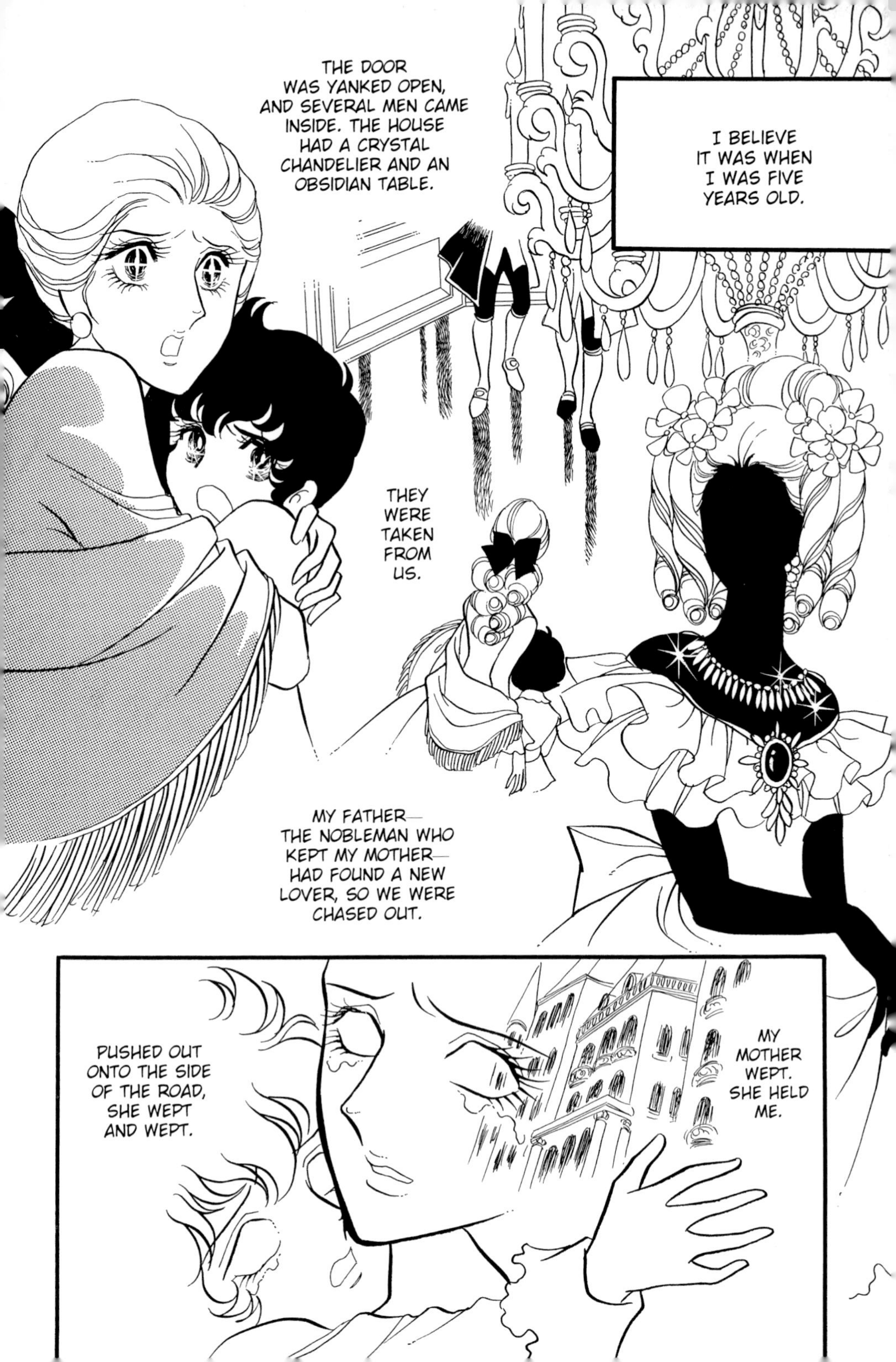
I BELIEVE IT WAS WHEN I WAS FIVE YEARS OLD.
THE DOOR WAS YANKED OPEN, AND SEVERAL MEN CAME INSIDE. THE HOUSE HAD A CRYSTAL CHANDELIER AND AN OBSIDIAN TABLE.
THEY WERE TAKEN FROM US.
MY FATHER—THE NOBLEMAN WHO KEPT MY MOTHER—HAD FOUND A NEW LOVER, SO WE WERE CHASED OUT.
MY MOTHER WEPT. SHE HELD ME.
PUSHED OUT ONTO THE SIDE OF THE ROAD, SHE WEPT AND WEPT.

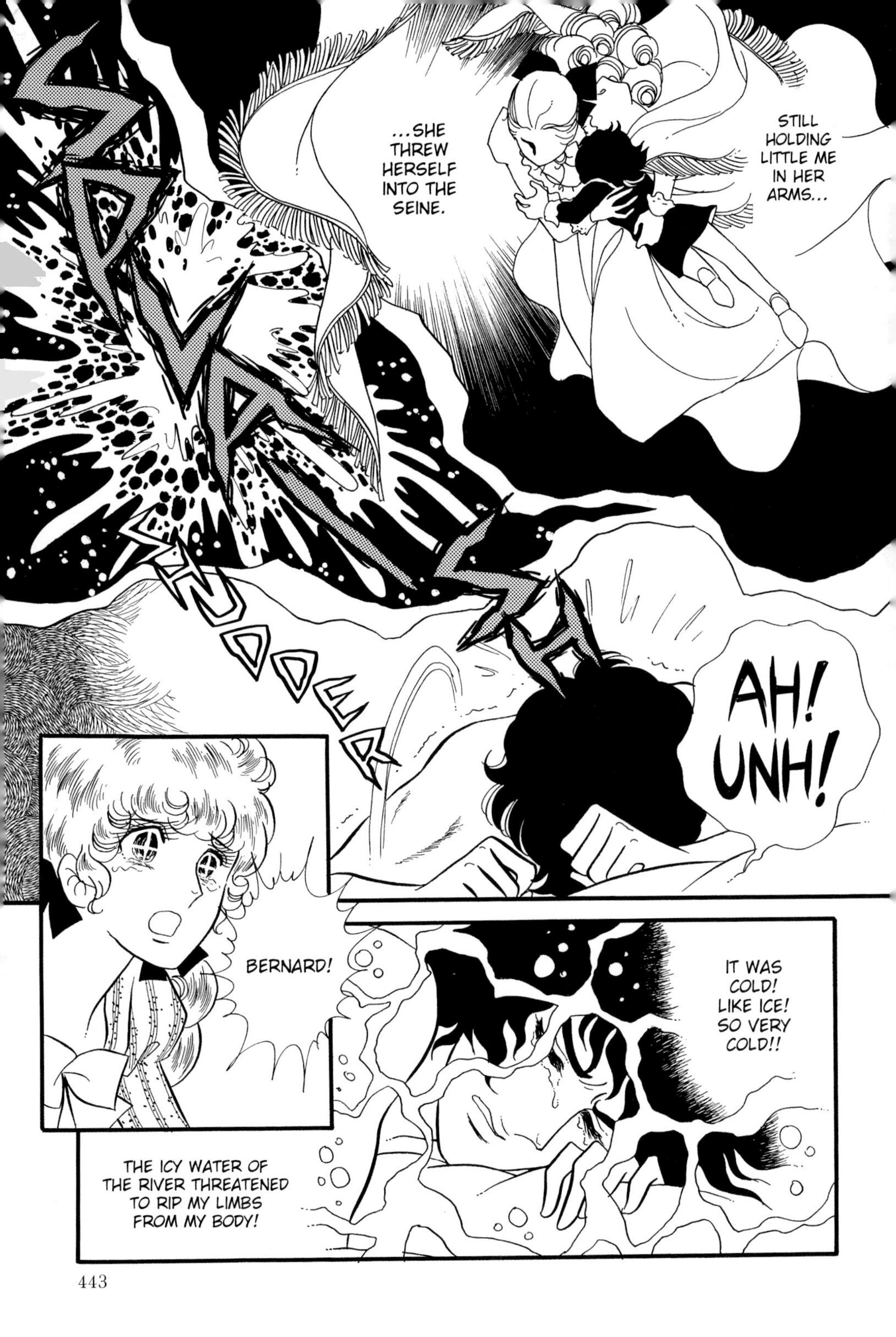
STILL HOLDING LITTLE ME IN HER ARMS...
...SHE THREW HERSELF INTO THE SEINE.
SPLASH
SHUDDER
AH! UNH!
IT WAS COLD! LIKE ICE! SO VERY COLD!!
BERNARD!
THE ICY WATER OF THE RIVER THREATENED TO RIP MY LIMBS FROM MY BODY!

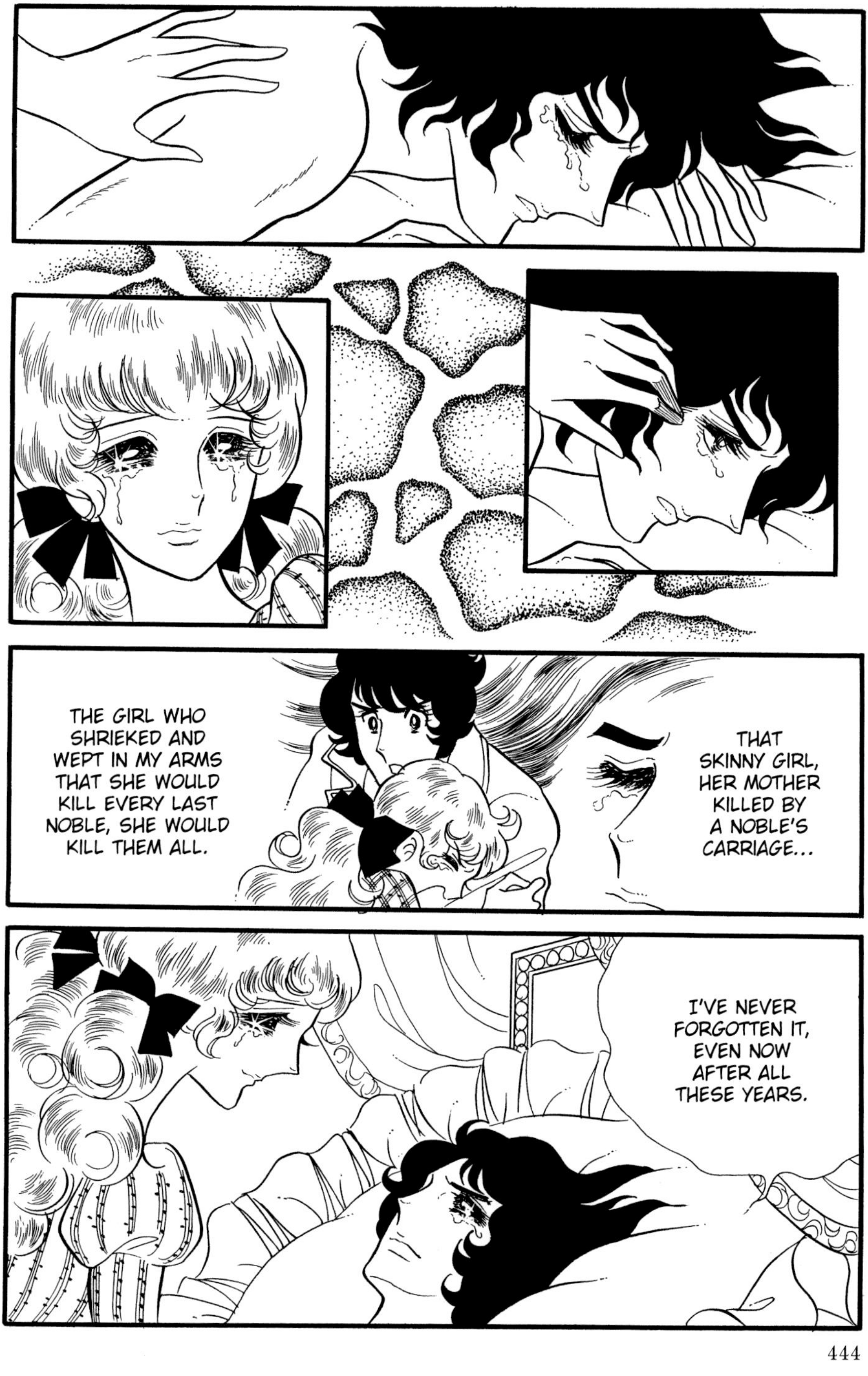
THAT SKINNY GIRL, HER MOTHER KILLED BY A NOBLE'S CARRIAGE...
THE GIRL WHO SHRIEKED AND WEPT IN MY ARMS THAT SHE WOULD KILL EVERY LAST NOBLE, SHE WOULD KILL THEM ALL.
I'VE NEVER FORGOTTEN IT, EVEN NOW AFTER ALL THESE YEARS.

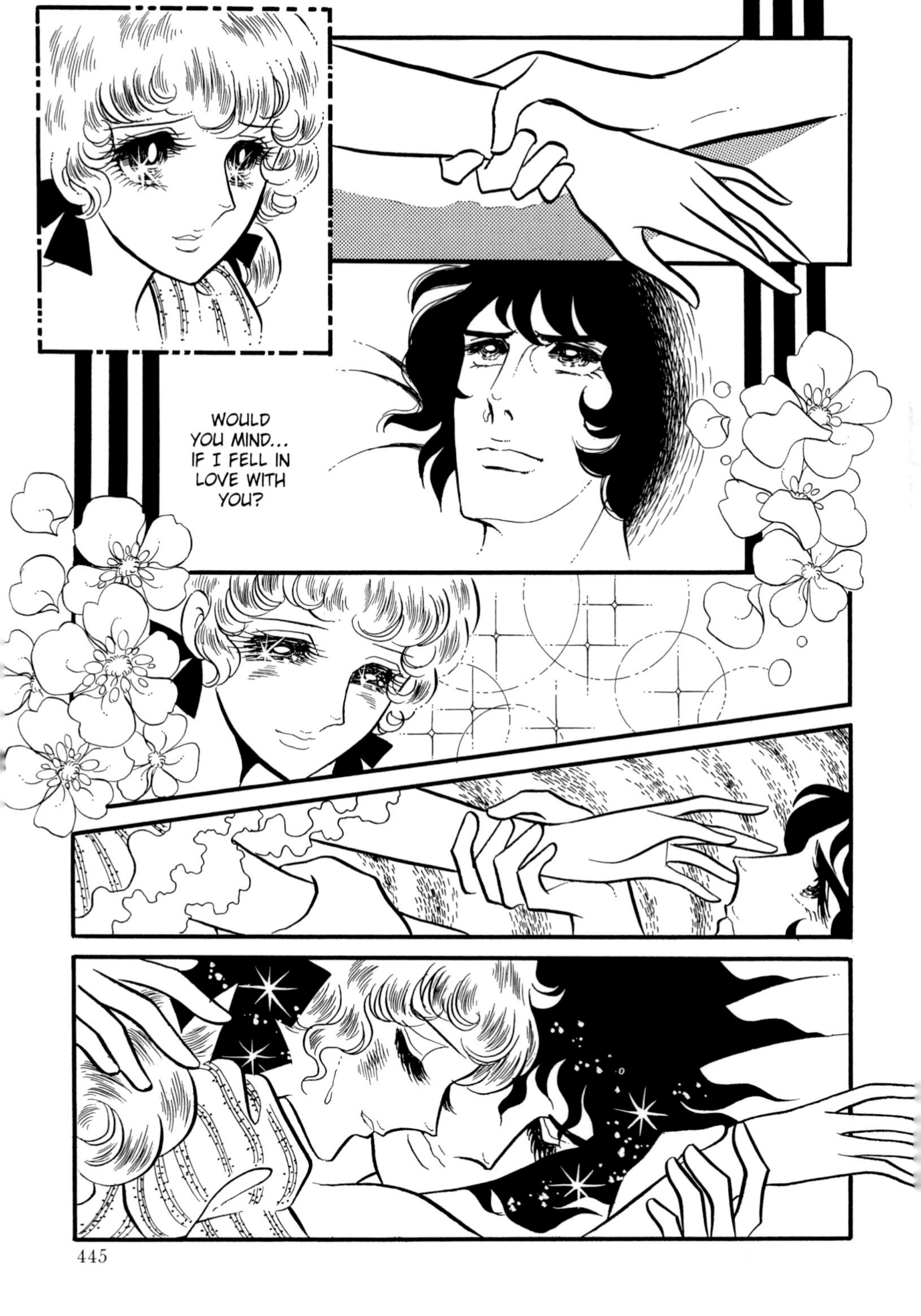
WOULD YOU MIND... IF I FELL IN LOVE WITH YOU?

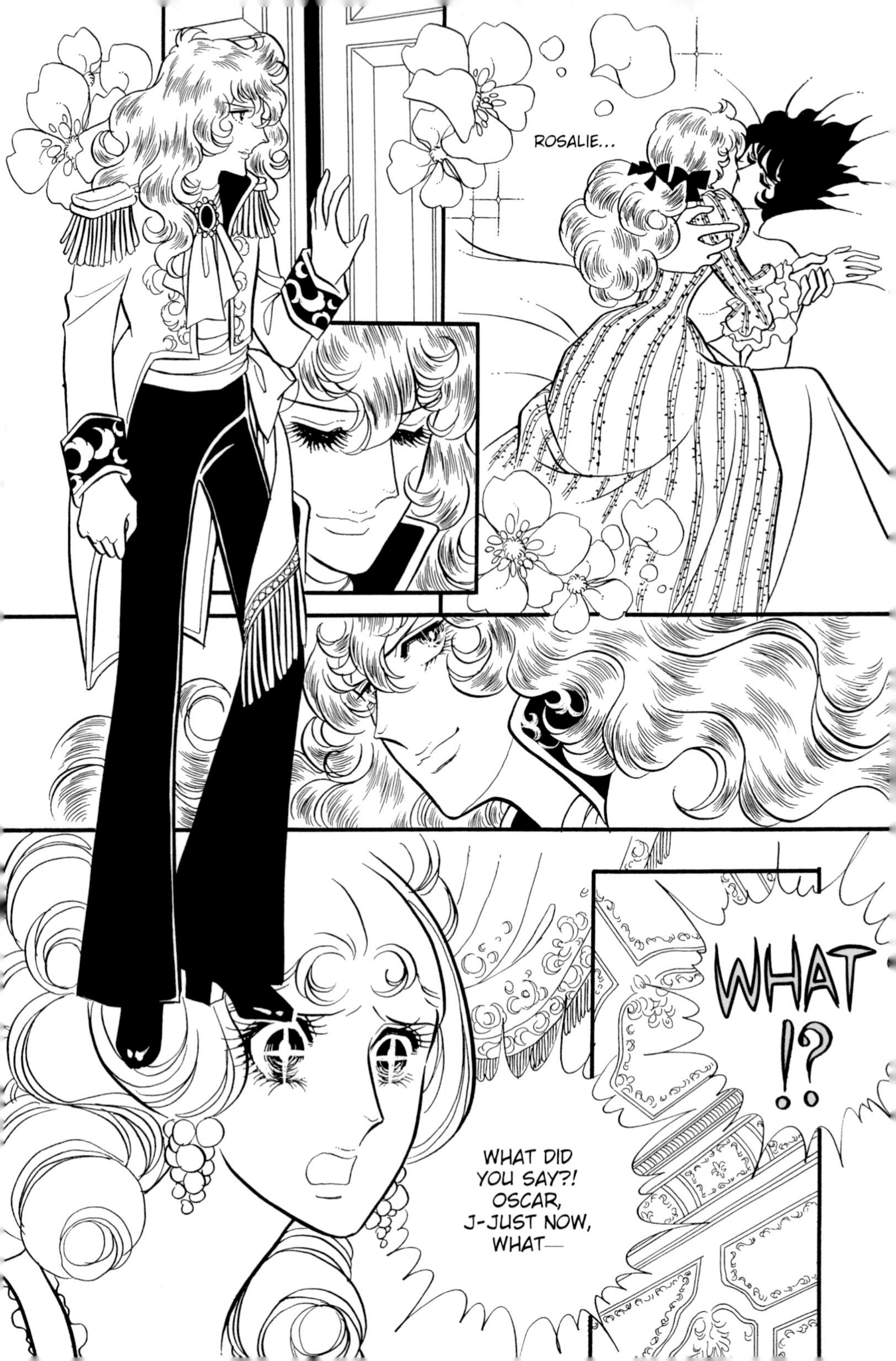
ROSALIE...
WHAT !?
WHAT DID YOU SAY?! OSCAR, J-JUST NOW, WHAT—

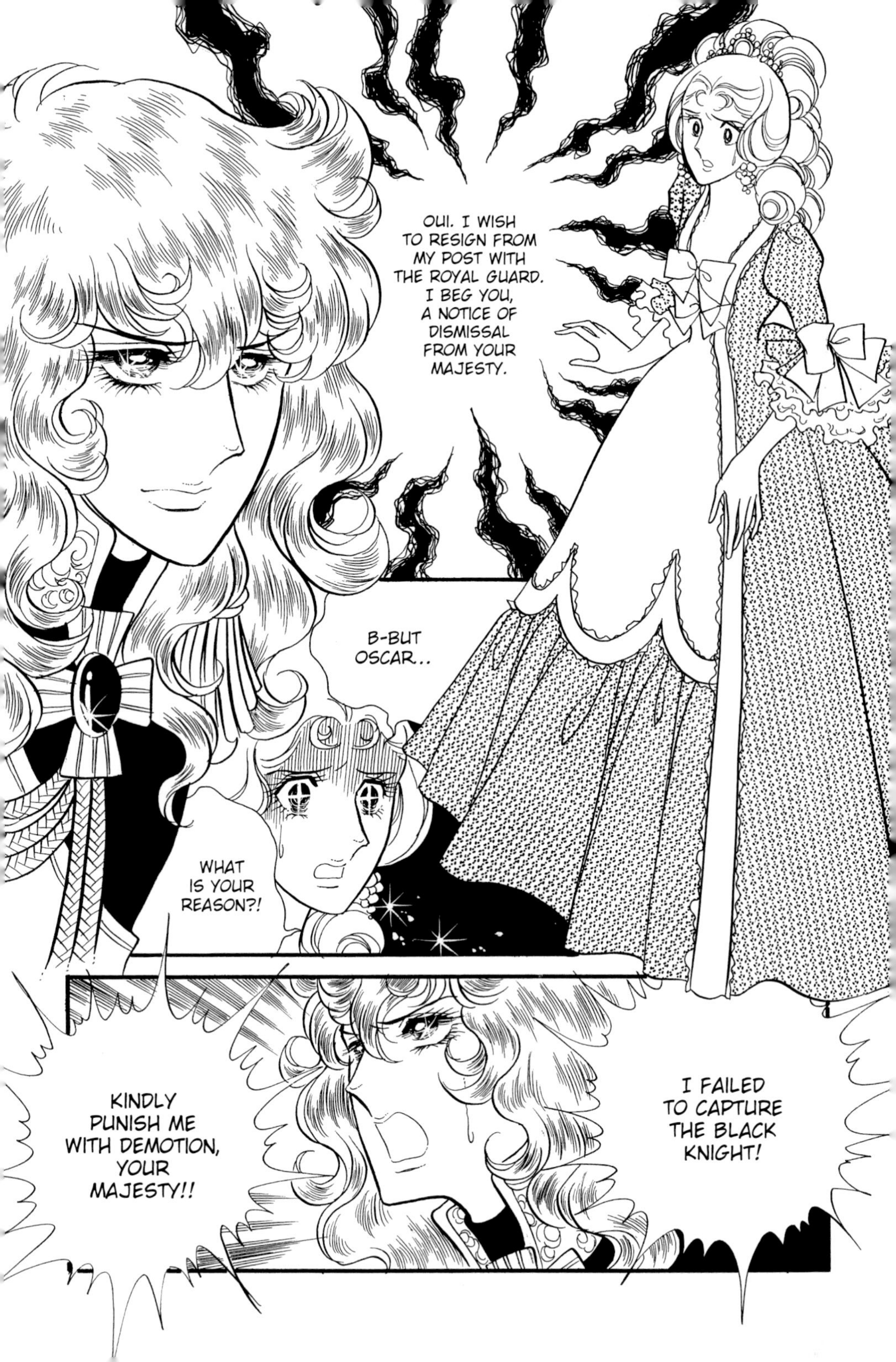

OUI. I WISH TO RESIGN FROM MY POST WITH THE ROYAL GUARD. I BEG YOU, A NOTICE OF DISMISSAL FROM YOUR MAJESTY.
B-BUT OSCAR...
WHAT IS YOUR REASON?!
I FAILED TO CAPTURE THE BLACK KNIGHT!
KINDLY PUNISH ME WITH DEMOTION, YOUR MAJESTY!!

1973 WEEKLY MARGARET MAGAZINE
ISSUE 11 INSERT ART

THE SUPER EPIC ROMANCE OF ROILING EXCITEMENT AND EMOTION
♥ OSCAR SUDDENLY ASKS ANTOINETTE TO LET HER LEAVE
THE IMPERIAL GUARD. WHAT WILL HAPPEN...?!

わきあがる興奮と感動の超大作ロマン

ベルサイユのばら

♥とつぜん、アントワネットに、近衛隊をやめさせてくれとたのむオスカル。はたして…!?

池田理代子

EPISODE 42

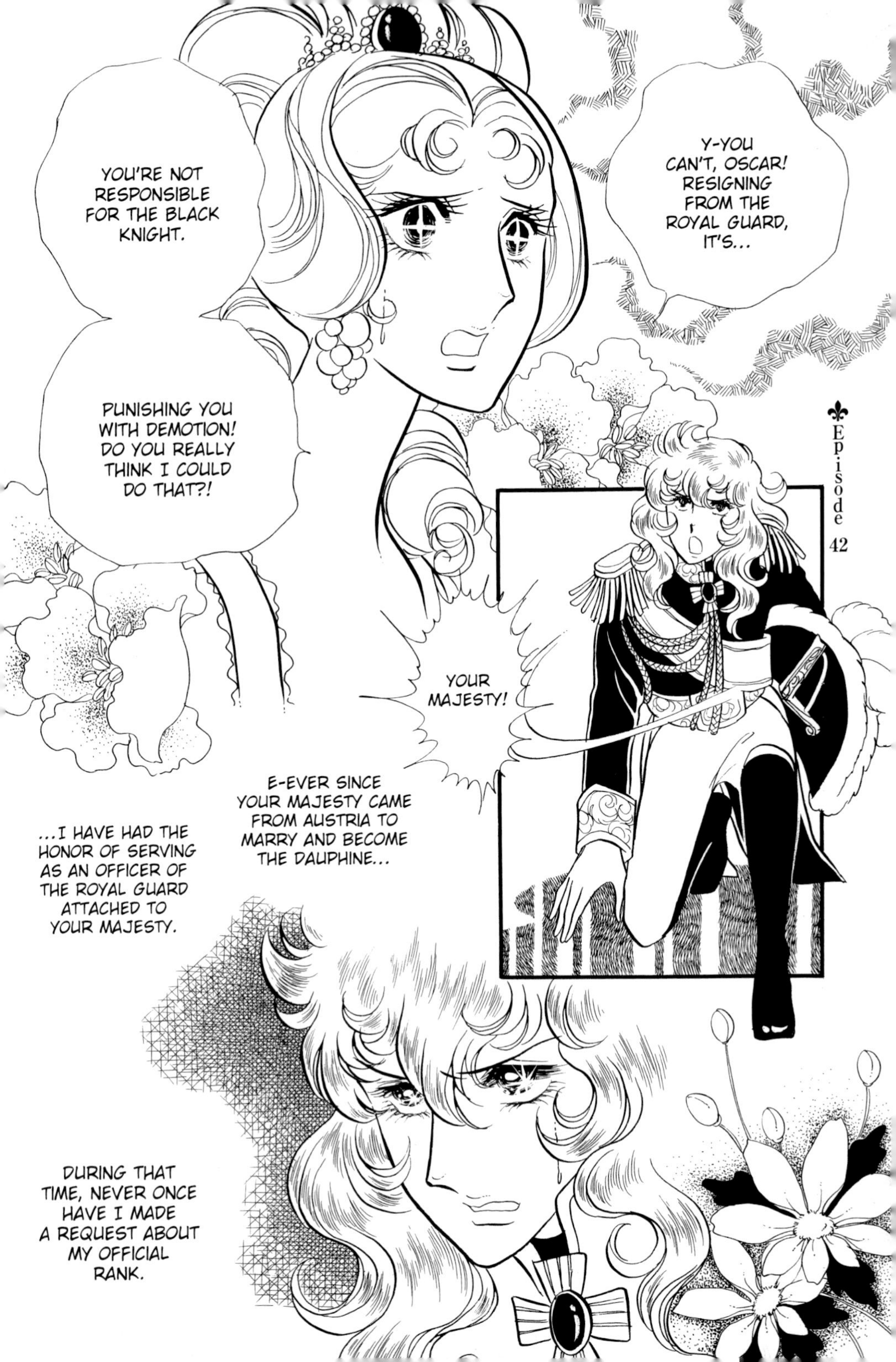
Y-YOU CAN'T, OSCAR! RESIGNING FROM THE ROYAL GUARD, IT'S...
YOU'RE NOT RESPONSIBLE FOR THE BLACK KNIGHT.
PUNISHING YOU WITH DEMOTION! DO YOU REALLY THINK I COULD DO THAT?!
Episode 42
YOUR MAJESTY!
E-EVER SINCE YOUR MAJESTY CAME FROM AUSTRIA TO MARRY AND BECOME THE DAUPHINE...
...I HAVE HAD THE HONOR OF SERVING AS AN OFFICER OF THE ROYAL GUARD ATTACHED TO YOUR MAJESTY.
DURING THAT TIME, NEVER ONCE HAVE I MADE A REQUEST ABOUT MY OFFICIAL RANK.

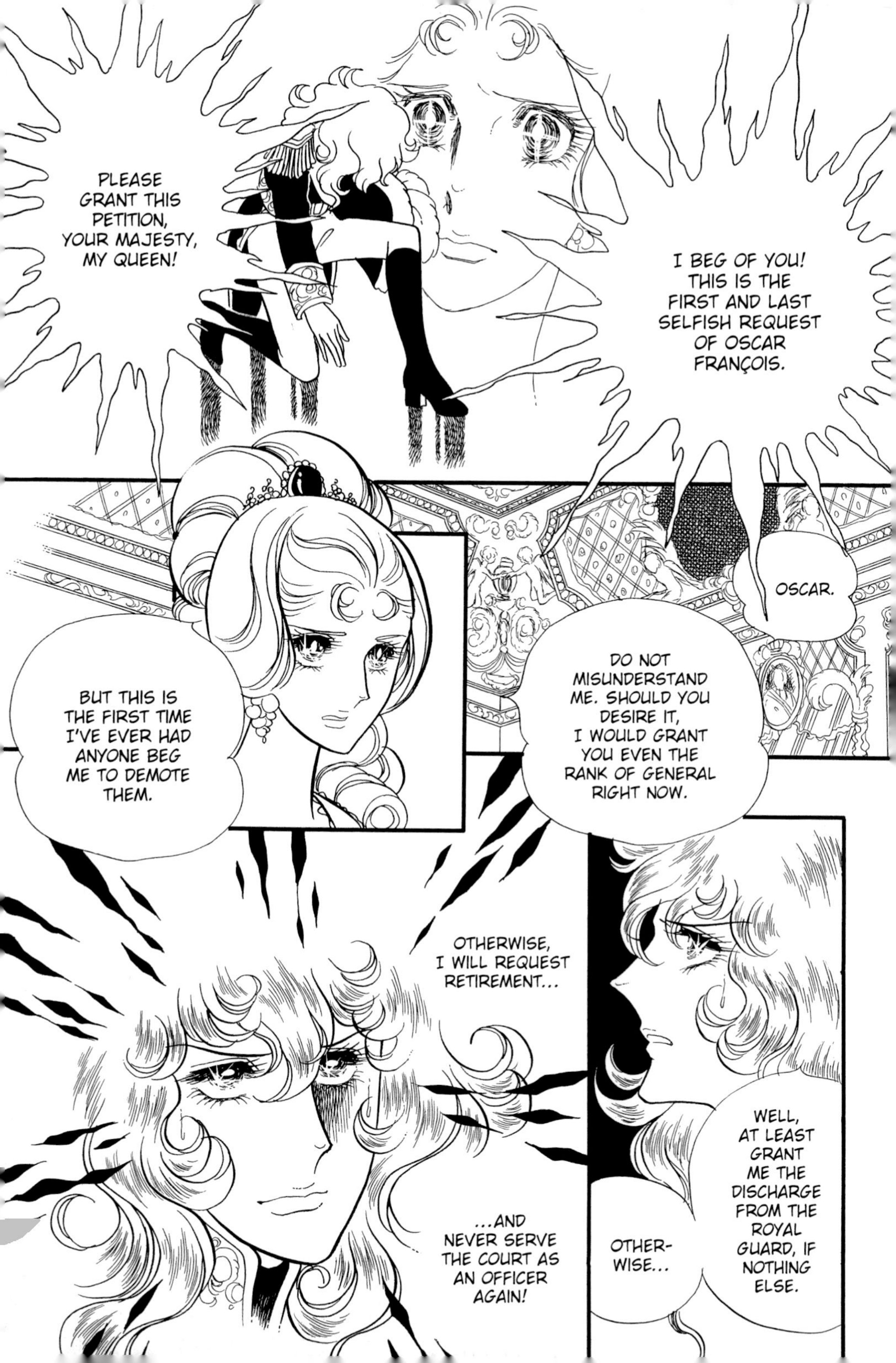
I BEG OF YOU! THIS IS THE FIRST AND LAST SELFISH REQUEST OF OSCAR FRANÇOIS.
PLEASE GRANT THIS PETITION, YOUR MAJESTY, MY QUEEN!
OSCAR.
DO NOT MISUNDERSTAND ME. SHOULD YOU DESIRE IT, I WOULD GRANT YOU EVEN THE RANK OF GENERAL RIGHT NOW.
BUT THIS IS THE FIRST TIME I'VE EVER HAD ANYONE BEG ME TO DEMOTE THEM.
WELL, AT LEAST GRANT ME THE DISCHARGE FROM THE ROYAL GUARD, IF NOTHING ELSE.
OTHER-WISE...
OTHERWISE, I WILL REQUEST RETIREMENT...
...AND NEVER SERVE THE COURT AS AN OFFICER AGAIN!

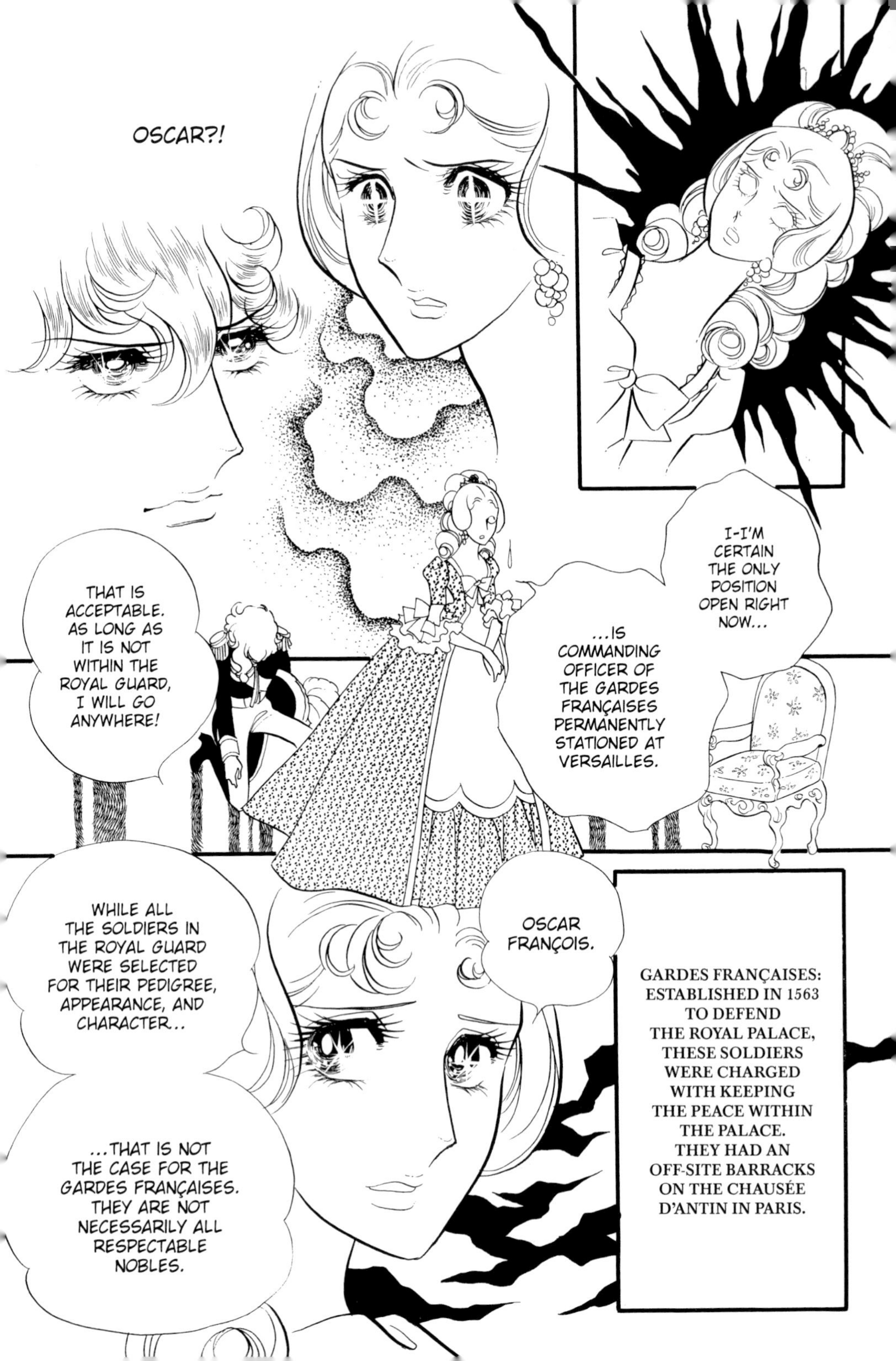

OSCAR?!
I-I'M CERTAIN THE ONLY POSITION OPEN RIGHT NOW...
...IS COMMANDING OFFICER OF THE GARDES FRANÇAISES PERMANENTLY STATIONED AT VERSAILLES.
THAT IS ACCEPTABLE. AS LONG AS IT IS NOT WITHIN THE ROYAL GUARD, I WILL GO ANYWHERE!
GARDES FRANÇAISES: ESTABLISHED IN 1563 TO DEFEND THE ROYAL PALACE, THESE SOLDIERS WERE CHARGED WITH KEEPING THE PEACE WITHIN THE PALACE. THEY HAD AN OFF-SITE BARRACKS ON THE CHAUSÉE D'ANTIN IN PARIS.
OSCAR FRANÇOIS.
WHILE ALL THE SOLDIERS IN THE ROYAL GUARD WERE SELECTED FOR THEIR PEDIGREE, APPEARANCE, AND CHARACTER...
...THAT IS NOT THE CASE FOR THE GARDES FRANÇAISES. THEY ARE NOT NECESSARILY ALL RESPECTABLE NOBLES.

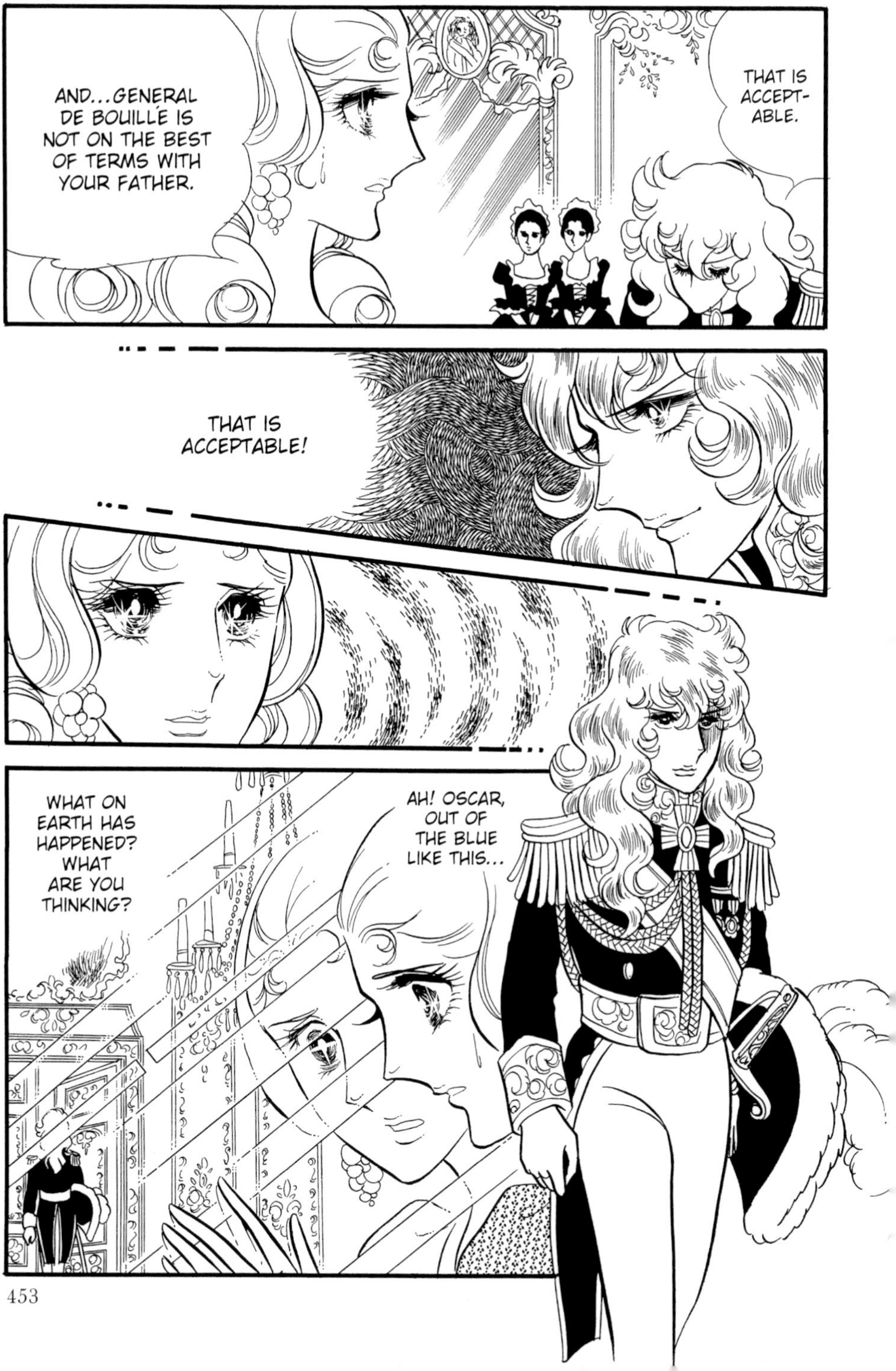
THAT IS ACCEPT-ABLE.
AND...GENERAL DE BOUILLÉ IS NOT ON THE BEST OF TERMS WITH YOUR FATHER.
THAT IS ACCEPTABLE!
AH! OSCAR, OUT OF THE BLUE LIKE THIS...
WHAT ON EARTH HAS HAPPENED? WHAT ARE YOU THINKING?

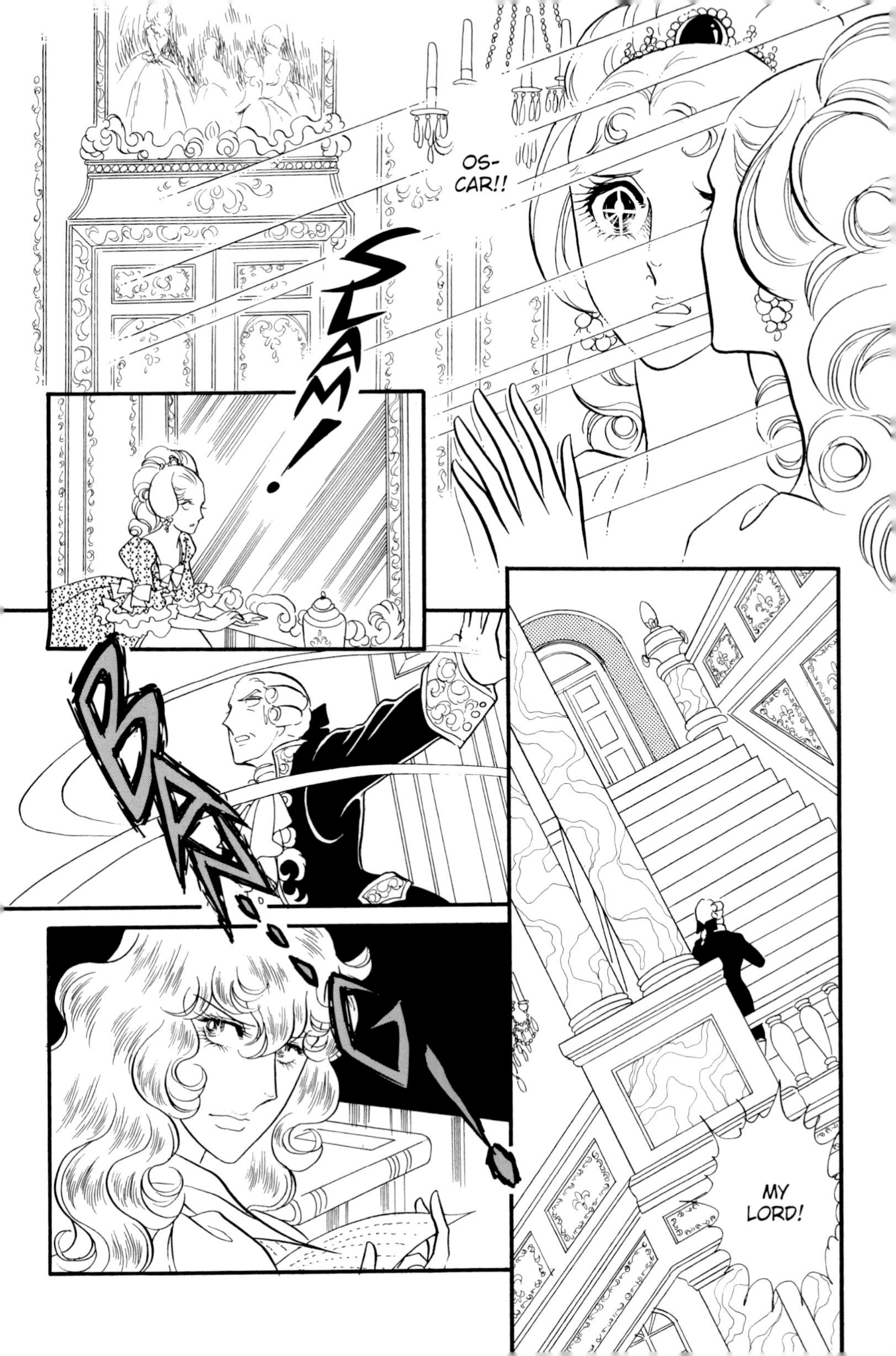

OS-CAR!!
SLAM!
MY LORD!
BAM...

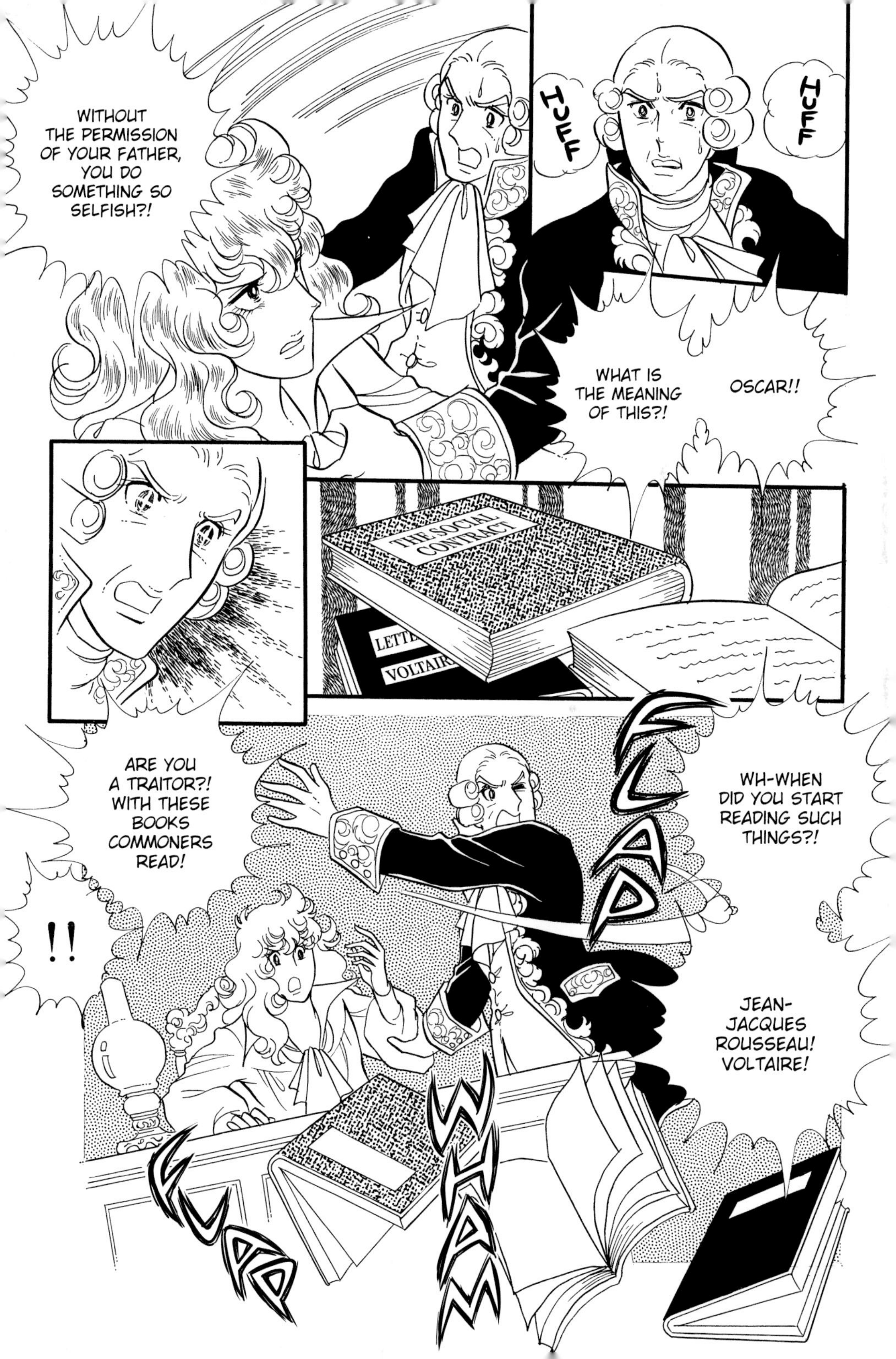
HUFF
HUFF
OSCAR!!
WHAT IS THE MEANING OF THIS?!
WITHOUT THE PERMISSION OF YOUR FATHER, YOU DO SOMETHING SO SELFISH?!
THE SOCIAL CONTRACT
FLAP
JEAN-JACQUES ROUSSEAU! VOLTAIRE!
WH-WHEN DID YOU START READING SUCH THINGS?!
ARE YOU A TRAITOR?! WITH THESE BOOKS COMMONERS READ!
!!
WHAM
FLAP

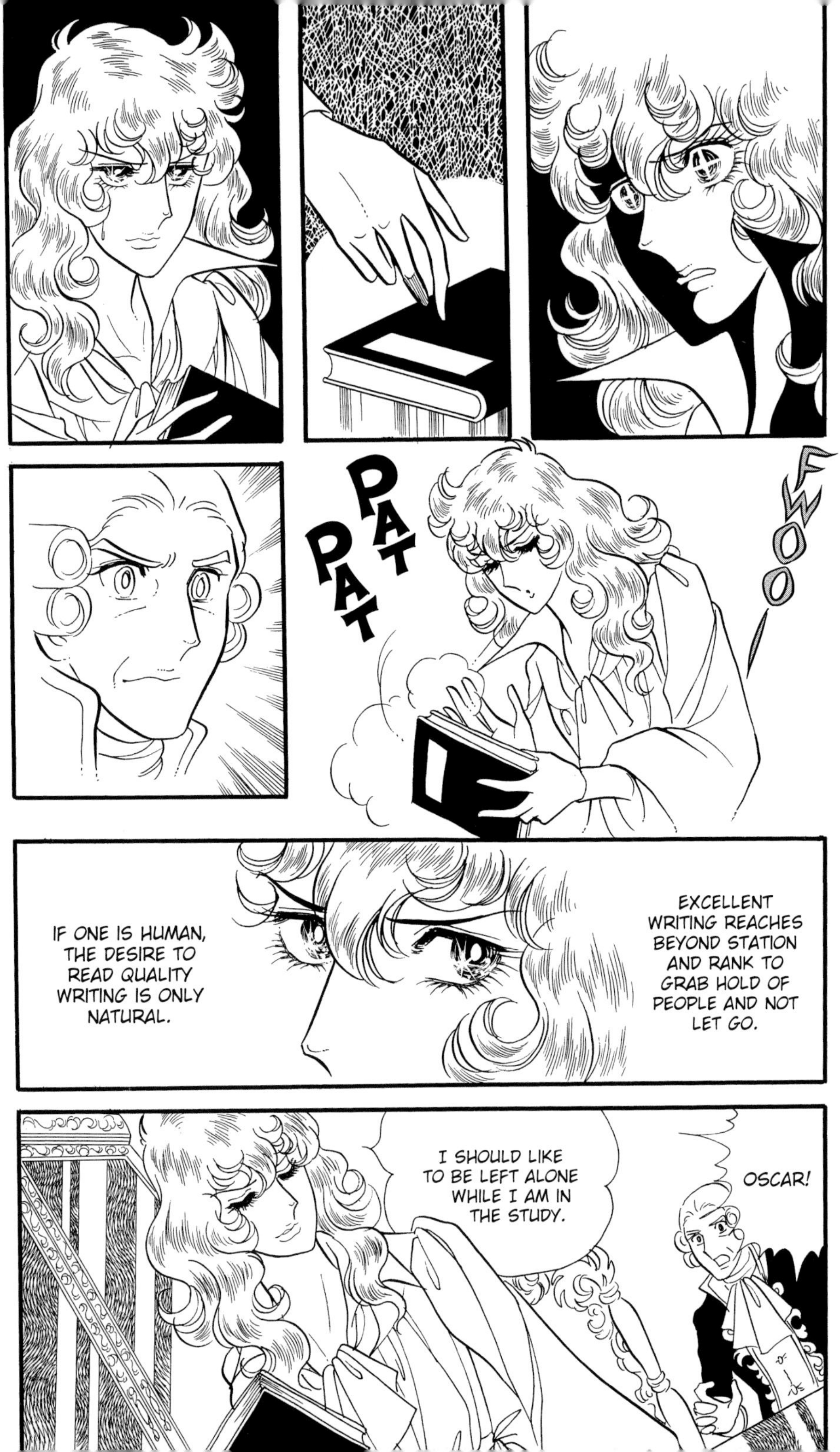
FWOO
PAT PAT PAT
EXCELLENT WRITING REACHES BEYOND STATION AND RANK TO GRAB HOLD OF PEOPLE AND NOT LET GO.
IF ONE IS HUMAN, THE DESIRE TO READ QUALITY WRITING IS ONLY NATURAL.
OSCAR!
I SHOULD LIKE TO BE LEFT ALONE WHILE I AM IN THE STUDY.

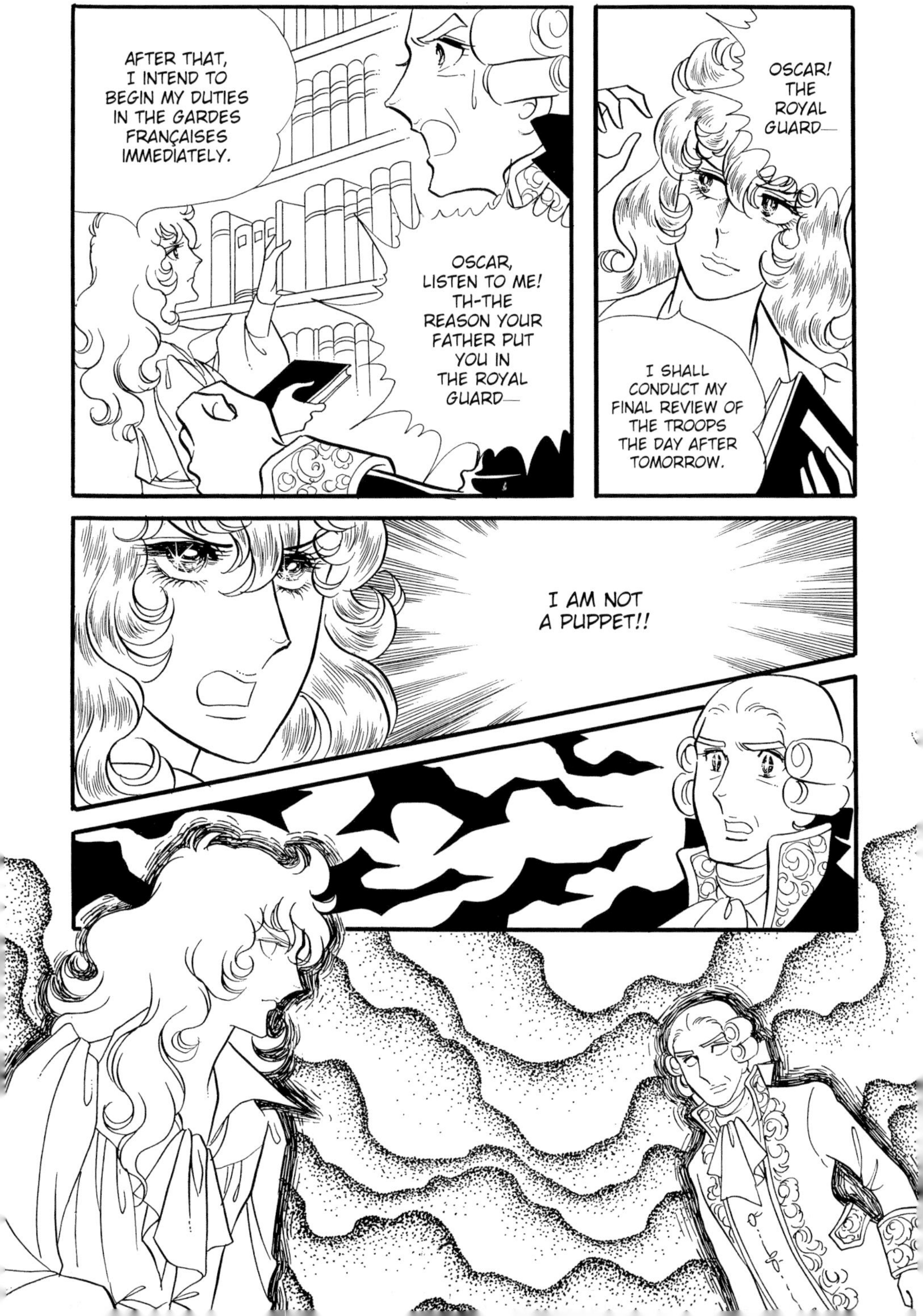

OSCAR! THE ROYAL GUARD—
I SHALL CONDUCT MY FINAL REVIEW OF THE TROOPS THE DAY AFTER TOMORROW.
AFTER THAT, I INTEND TO BEGIN MY DUTIES IN THE GARDES FRANÇAISES IMMEDIATELY.
OSCAR, LISTEN TO ME! TH-THE REASON YOUR FATHER PUT YOU IN THE ROYAL GUARD—
I AM NOT A PUPPET!!

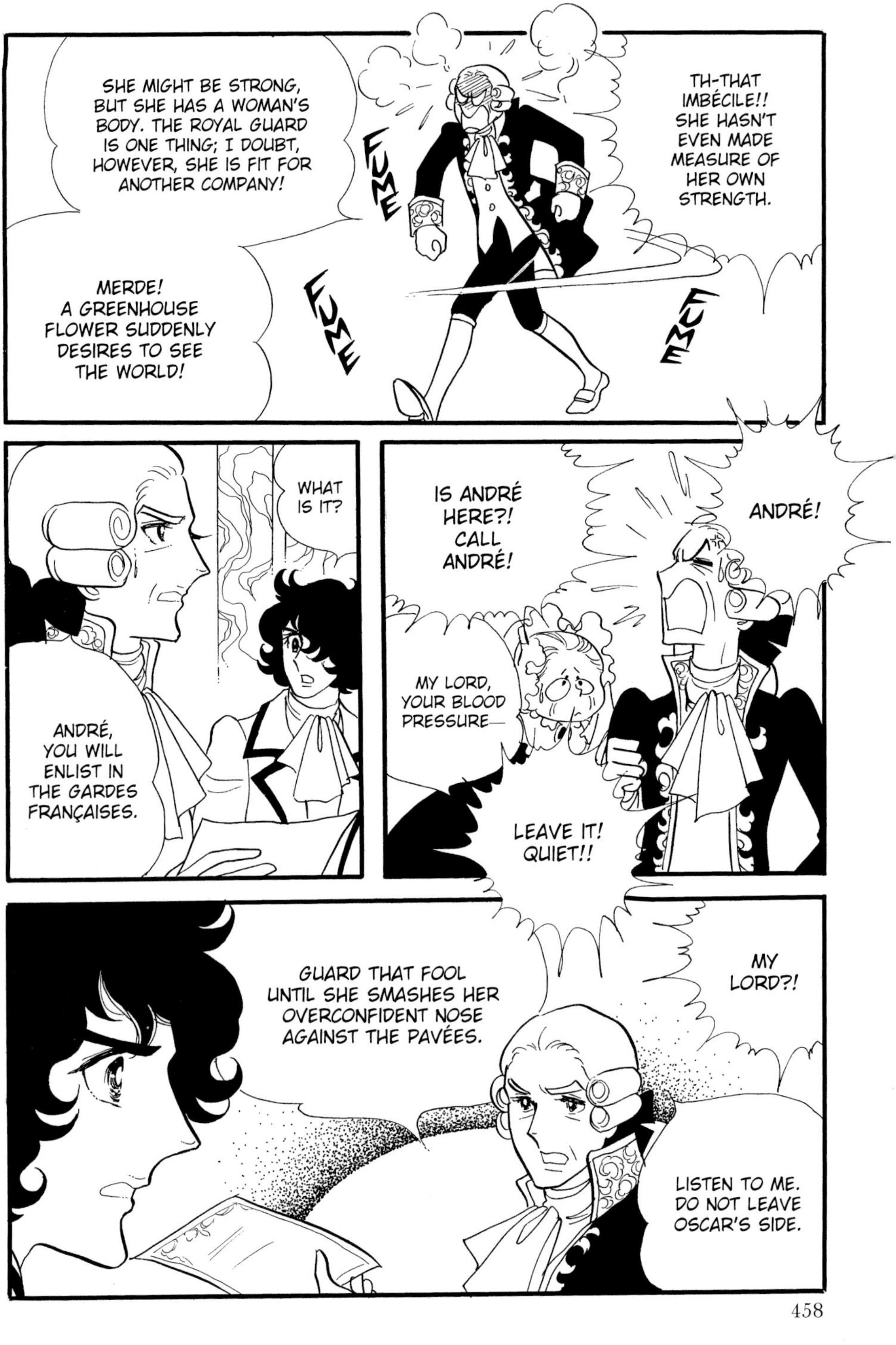
TH-THAT IMBÉCILE!! SHE HASN'T EVEN MADE MEASURE OF HER OWN STRENGTH.
FUME
FUME
SHE MIGHT BE STRONG, BUT SHE HAS A WOMAN'S BODY. THE ROYAL GUARD IS ONE THING; I DOUBT, HOWEVER, SHE IS FIT FOR ANOTHER COMPANY!
FUME
MERDE! A GREENHOUSE FLOWER SUDDENLY DESIRES TO SEE THE WORLD!
ANDRÉ!
IS ANDRÉ HERE?! CALL ANDRÉ!
MY LORD, YOUR BLOOD PRESSURE—
LEAVE IT! QUIET!!
WHAT IS IT?
ANDRÉ, YOU WILL ENLIST IN THE GARDES FRANÇAISES.
MY LORD?!
GUARD THAT FOOL UNTIL SHE SMASHES HER OVERCONFIDENT NOSE AGAINST THE PAVÉES.
LISTEN TO ME. DO NOT LEAVE OSCAR'S SIDE.

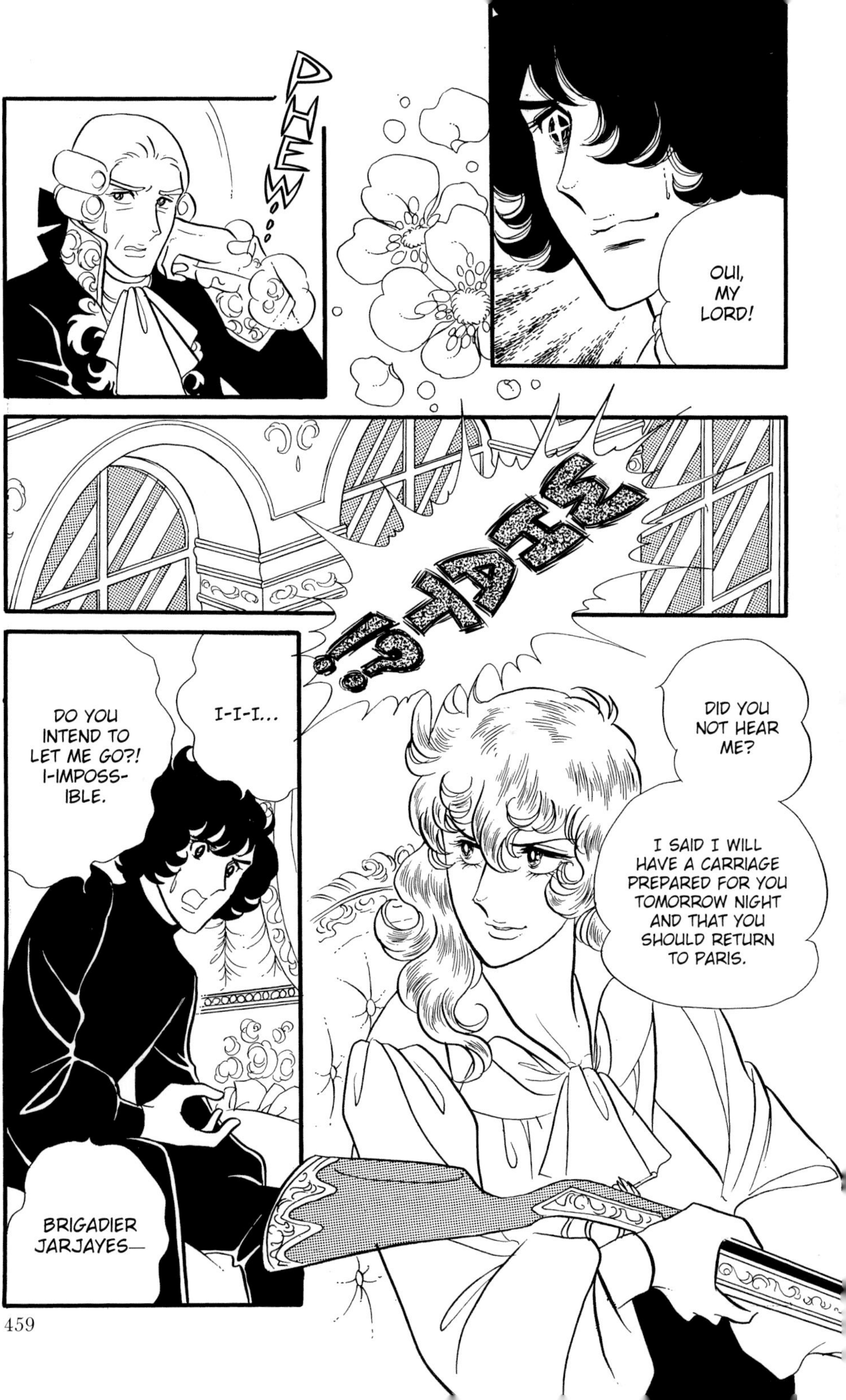
OUI, MY LORD!
PHEW...
WHAT!?
DID YOU NOT HEAR ME?
I SAID I WILL HAVE A CARRIAGE PREPARED FOR YOU TOMORROW NIGHT AND THAT YOU SHOULD RETURN TO PARIS.
I-I-I...
DO YOU INTEND TO LET ME GO?! I-IMPOSS-IBLE.
BRIGADIER JARJAYES—

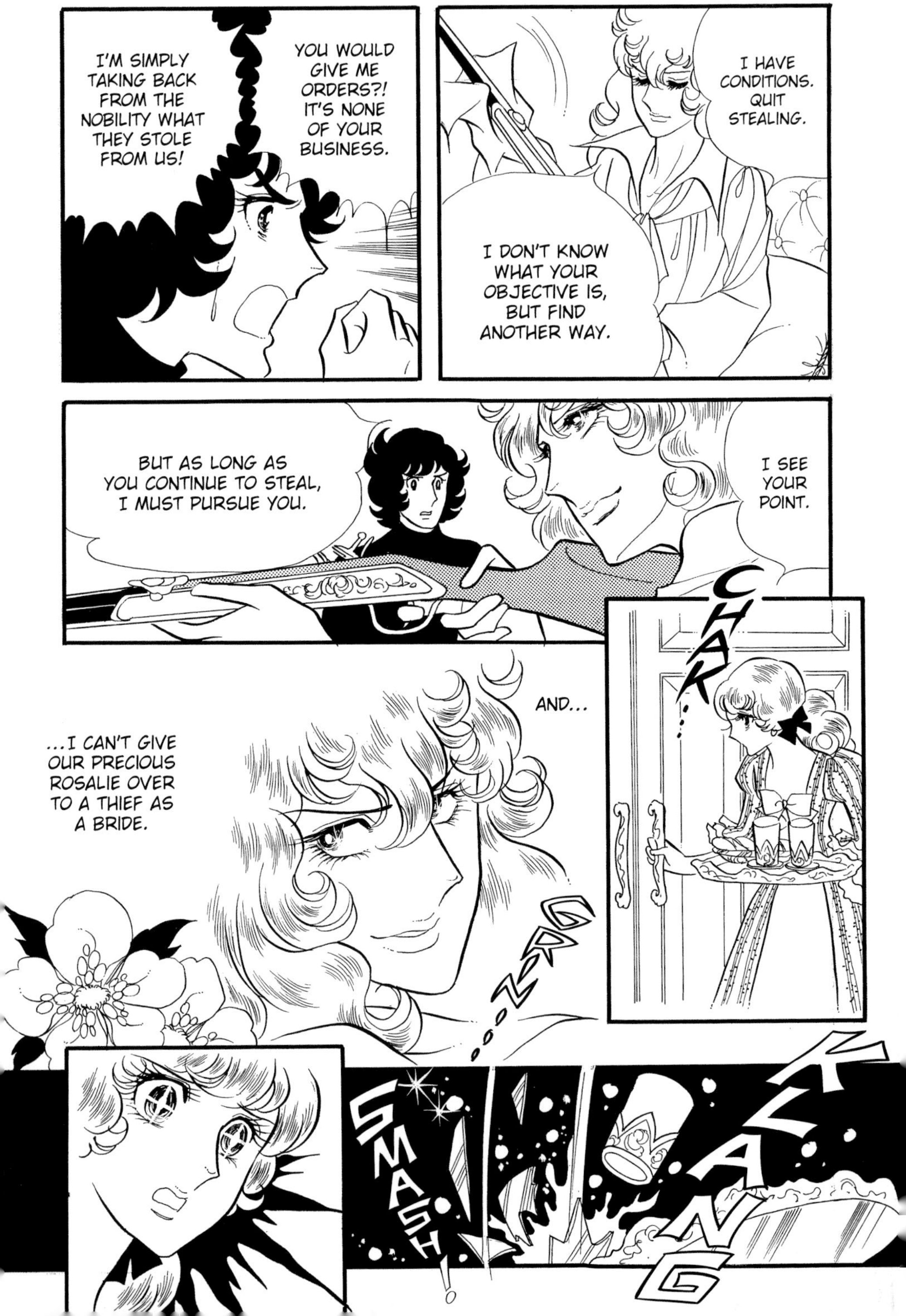
I HAVE CONDITIONS. QUIT STEALING.
I DON'T KNOW WHAT YOUR OBJECTIVE IS, BUT FIND ANOTHER WAY.
YOU WOULD GIVE ME ORDERS?! IT'S NONE OF YOUR BUSINESS.
I'M SIMPLY TAKING BACK FROM THE NOBILITY WHAT THEY STOLE FROM US!
I SEE YOUR POINT.
BUT AS LONG AS YOU CONTINUE TO STEAL, I MUST PURSUE YOU.
CHAR...
AND...
...I CAN'T GIVE OUR PRECIOUS ROSALIE OVER TO A THIEF AS A BRIDE.
KLANG
SMASH!

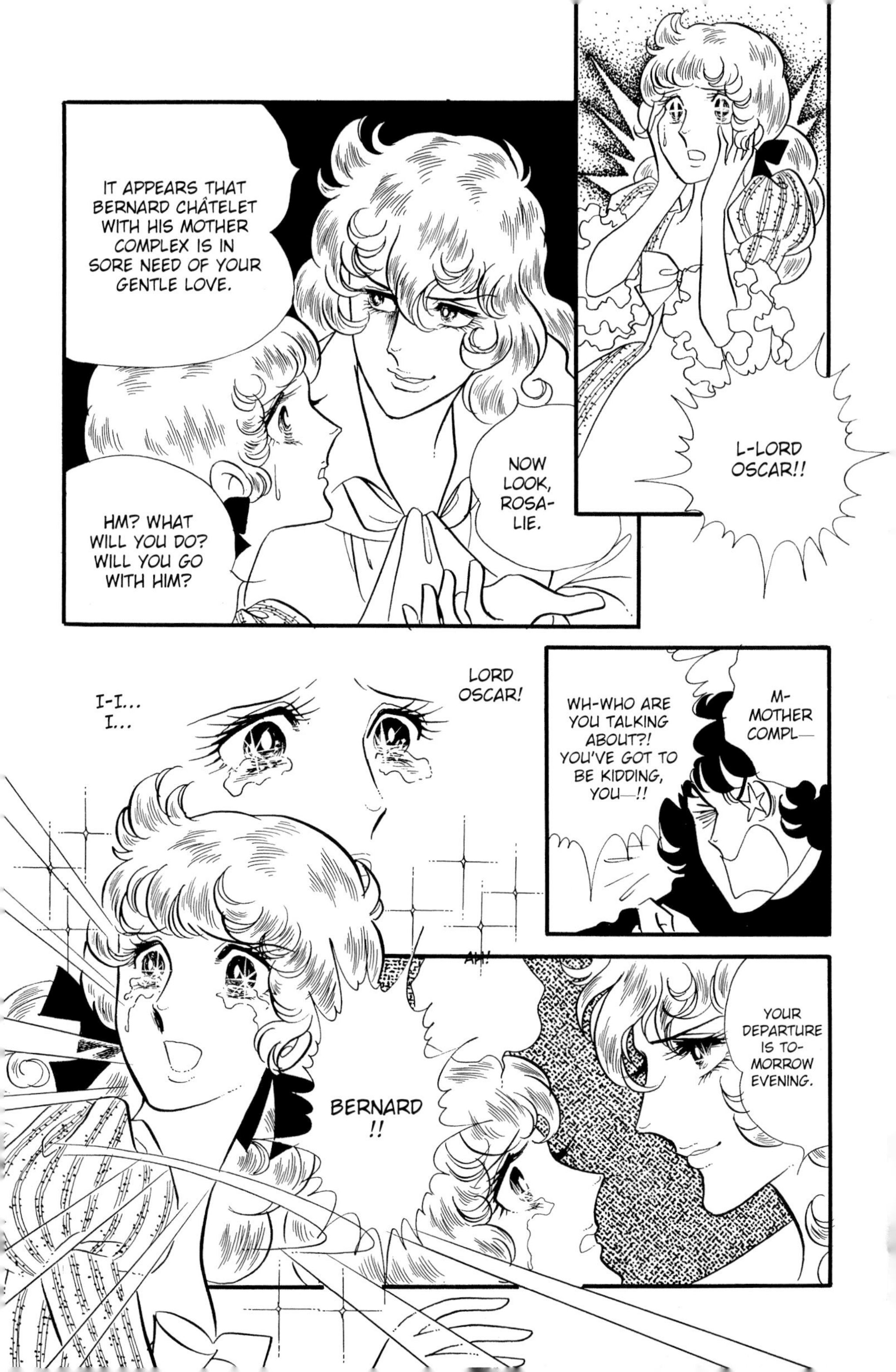

L-LORD OSCAR!!
NOW LOOK, ROSA-LIE.
IT APPEARS THAT BERNARD CHÂTELET WITH HIS MOTHER COMPLEX IS IN SORE NEED OF YOUR GENTLE LOVE.
HM? WHAT WILL YOU DO? WILL YOU GO WITH HIM?
M-MOTHER COMPL—
WH-WHO ARE YOU TALKING ABOUT?! YOU'VE GOT TO BE KIDDING, YOU—!!
LORD OSCAR!
I-I... I...
YOUR DEPARTURE IS TO-MORROW EVENING.
AH!
BERNARD !!

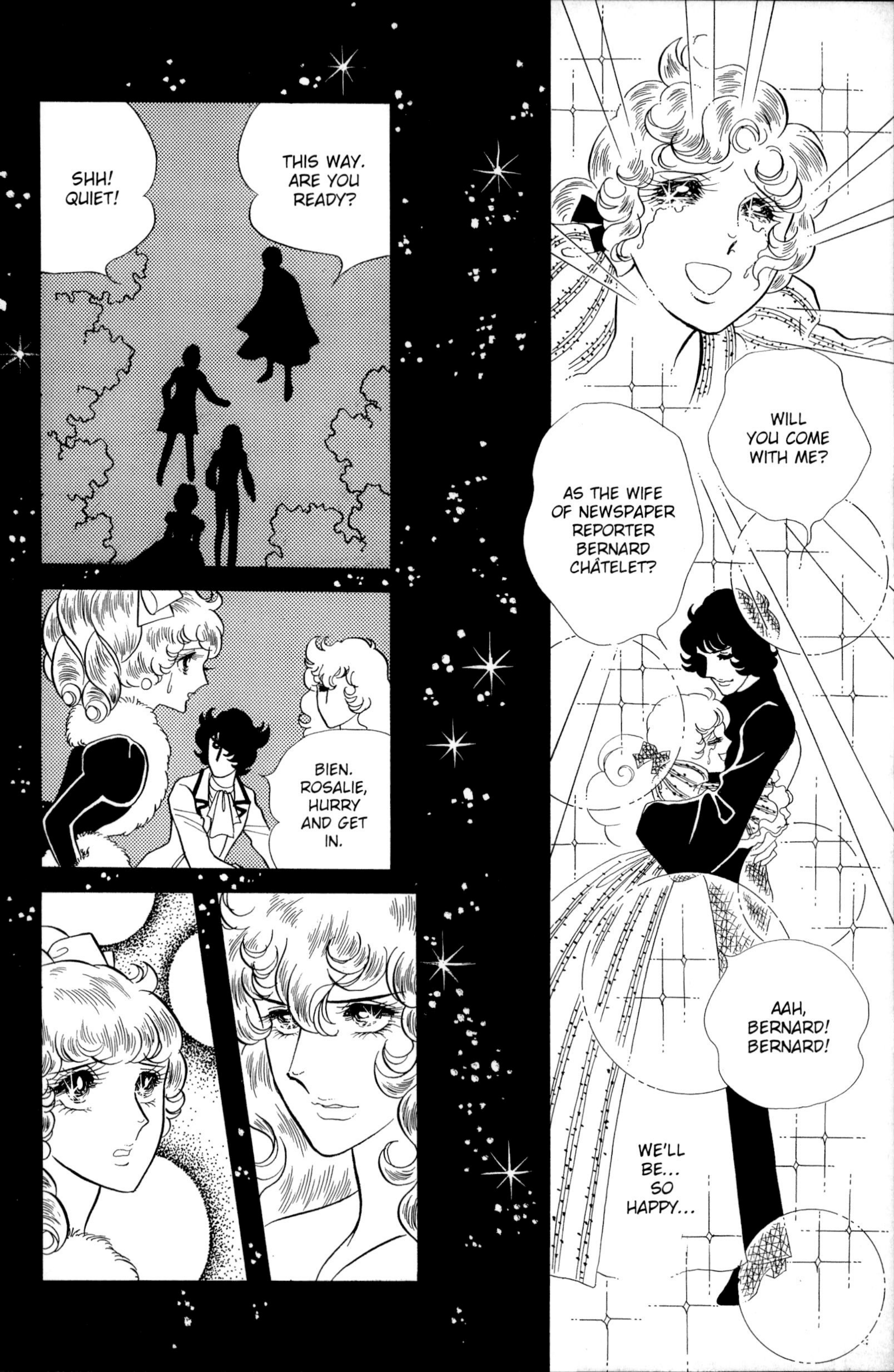
WILL YOU COME WITH ME?
AS THE WIFE OF NEWSPAPER REPORTER BERNARD CHÂTELET?
AAH, BERNARD! BERNARD!
WE'LL BE... SO HAPPY...
THIS WAY. ARE YOU READY?
SHH! QUIET!
BIEN. ROSALIE, HURRY AND GET IN.

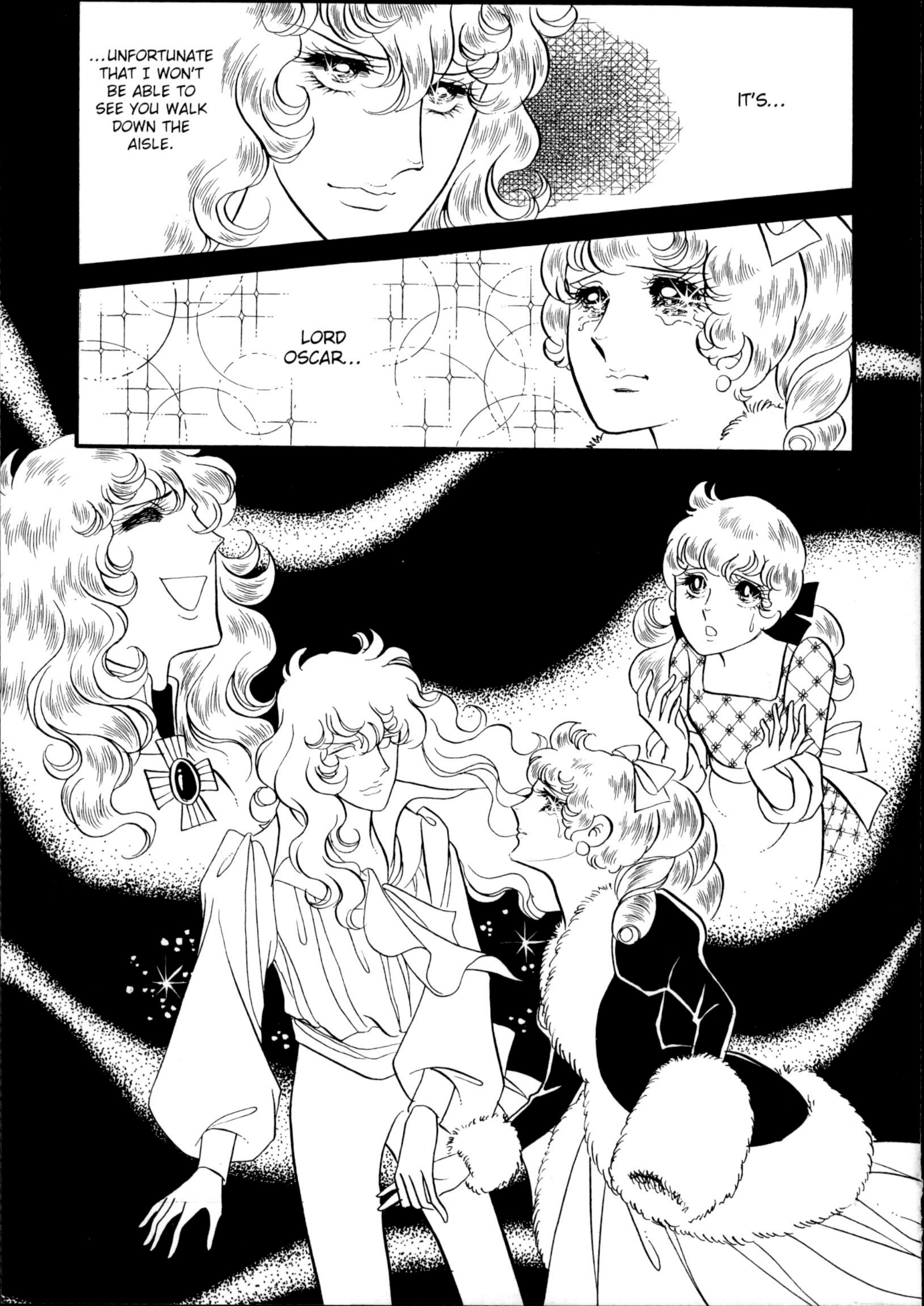
IT'S...
...UNFORTUNATE THAT I WON'T BE ABLE TO SEE YOU WALK DOWN THE AISLE.
LORD OSCAR..

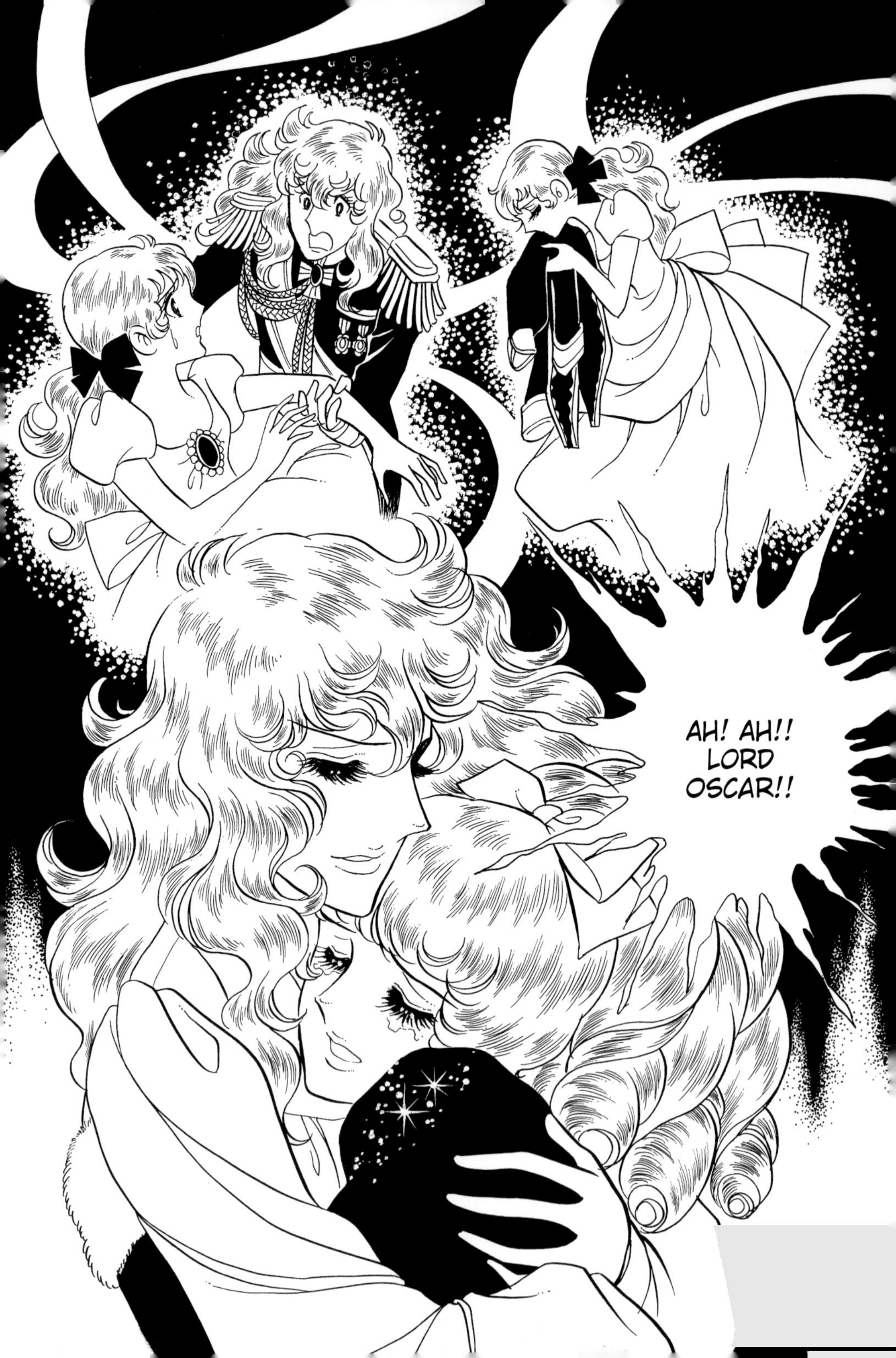
AH! AH!!
LORD
OSCAR!!

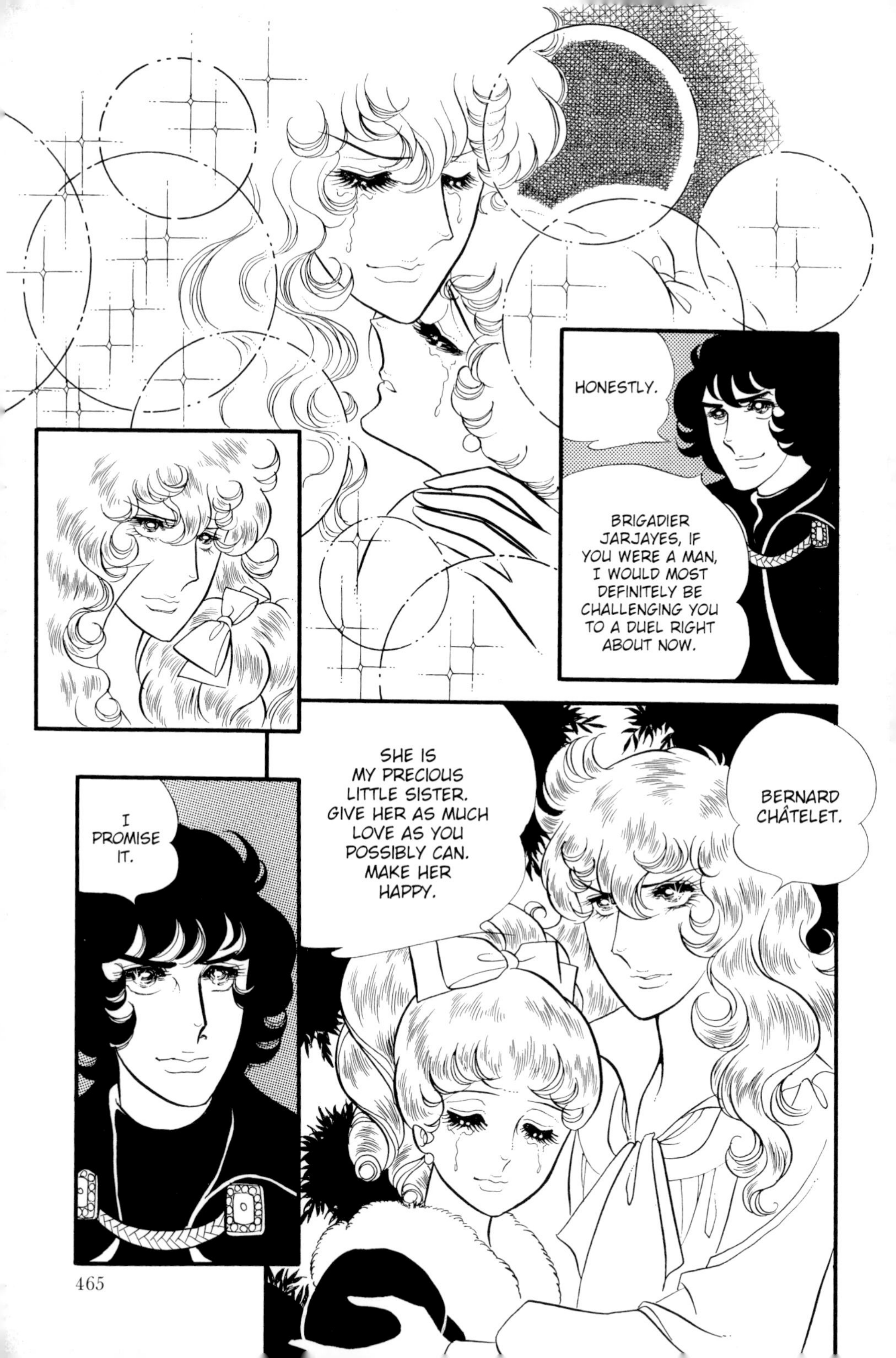
HONESTLY.
BRIGADIER JARJAYES, IF YOU WERE A MAN, I WOULD MOST DEFINITELY BE CHALLENGING YOU TO A DUEL RIGHT ABOUT NOW.
BERNARD CHÂTELET.
SHE IS MY PRECIOUS LITTLE SISTER. GIVE HER AS MUCH LOVE AS YOU POSSIBLY CAN. MAKE HER HAPPY.
I PROMISE IT.

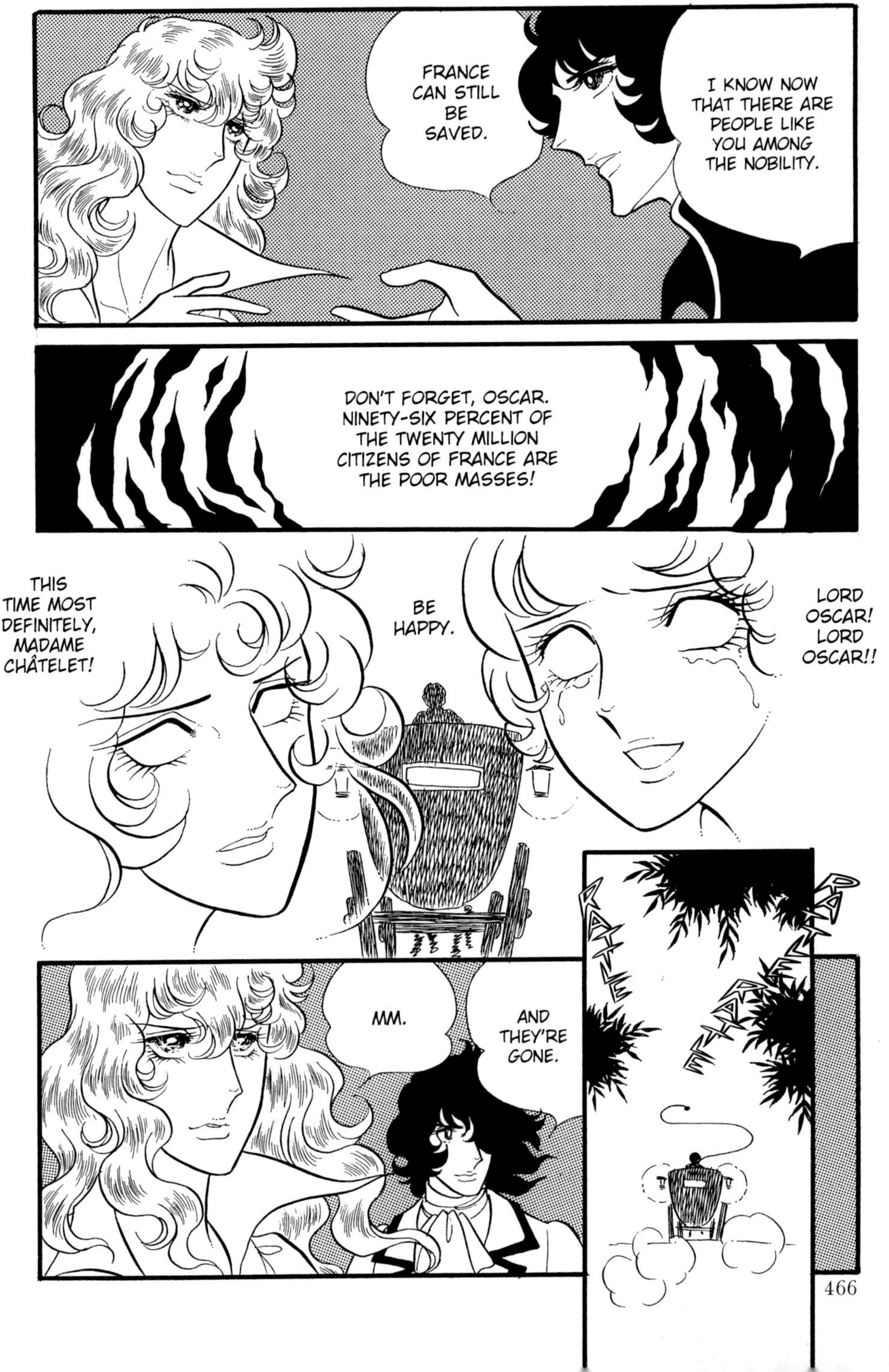
I KNOW NOW THAT THERE ARE PEOPLE LIKE YOU AMONG THE NOBILITY.
FRANCE CAN STILL BE SAVED.
DON'T FORGET, OSCAR. NINETY-SIX PERCENT OF THE TWENTY MILLION CITIZENS OF FRANCE ARE THE POOR MASSES!
LORD OSCAR! LORD OSCAR!!
BE HAPPY.
THIS TIME MOST DEFINITELY, MADAME CHÂTELET!
RATTLE RATTLE
RATTLE
AND THEY'RE GONE.
MM.

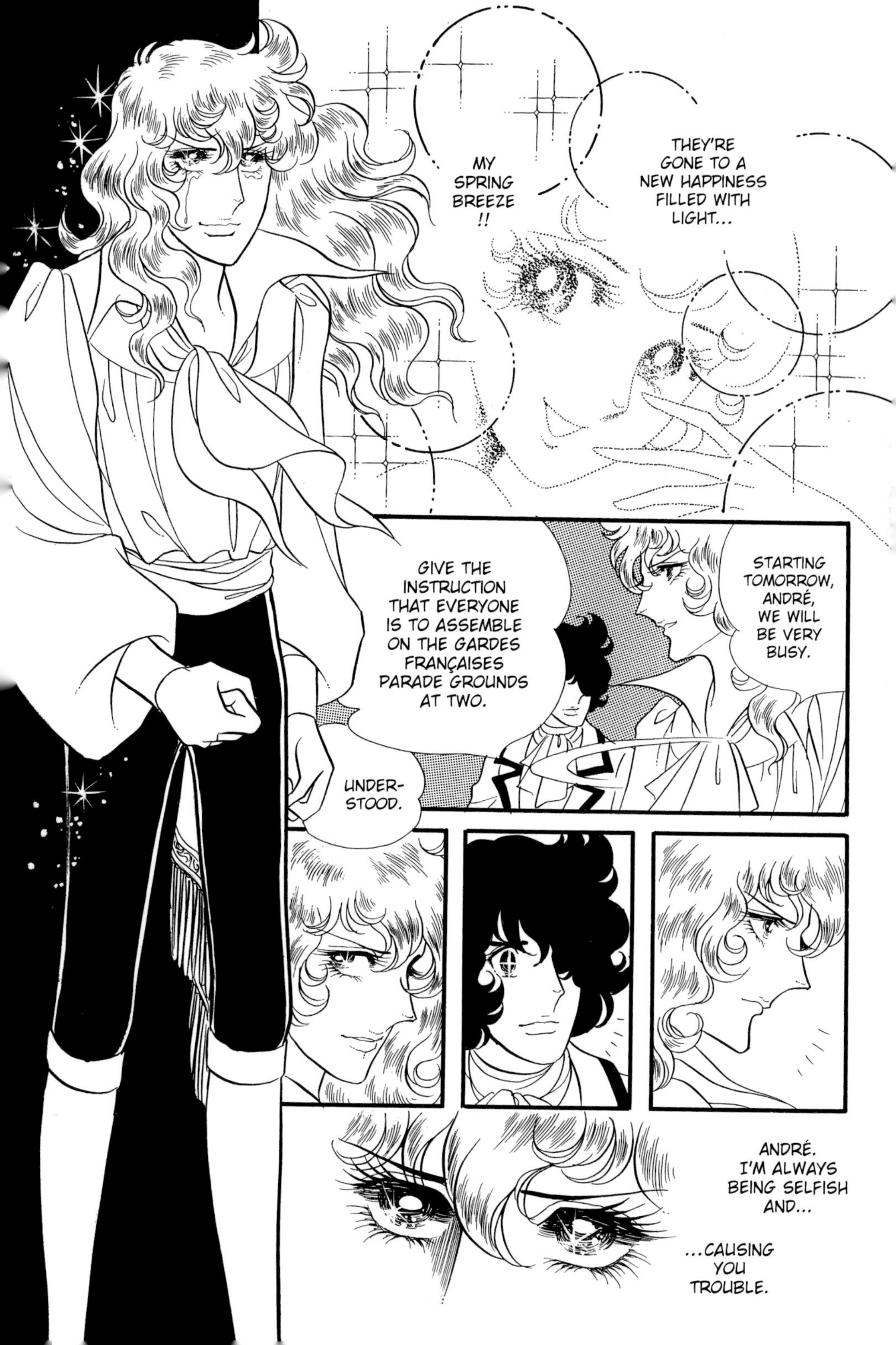
THEY'RE GONE TO A NEW HAPPINESS FILLED WITH LIGHT...
MY SPRING BREEZE !!
STARTING TOMORROW, ANDRÉ, WE WILL BE VERY BUSY.
GIVE THE INSTRUCTION THAT EVERYONE IS TO ASSEMBLE ON THE GARDES FRANÇAISES PARADE GROUNDS AT TWO.
UNDER-STOOD.
ANDRÉ. I'M ALWAYS BEING SELFISH AND...
...CAUSING YOU TROUBLE.

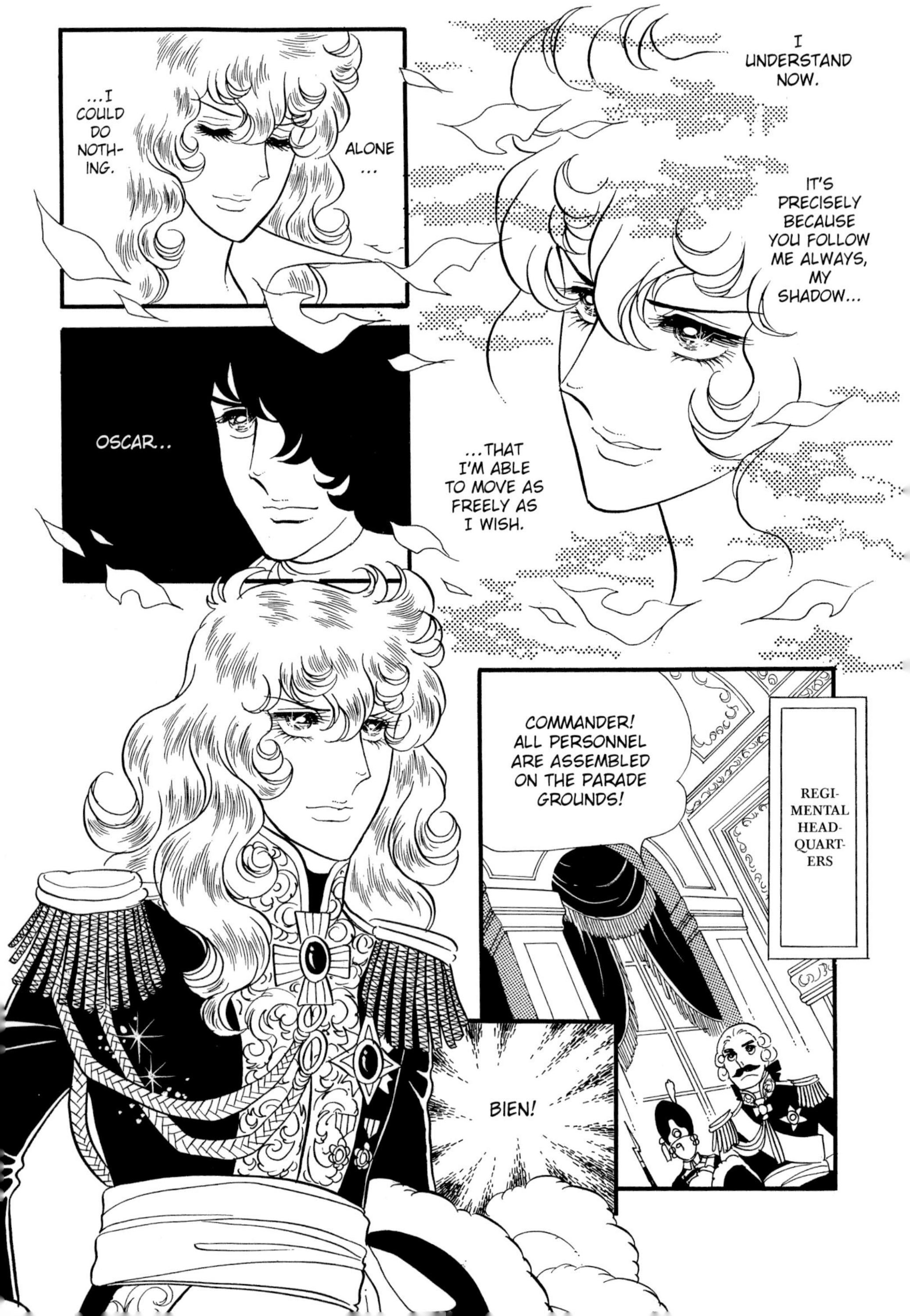
I UNDERSTAND NOW.
IT'S PRECISELY BECAUSE YOU FOLLOW ME ALWAYS, MY SHADOW...
...THAT I'M ABLE TO MOVE AS FREELY AS I WISH.
ALONE ...
...I COULD DO NOTHING.
OSCAR..
REGIMENTAL HEADQUARTERS
COMMANDER! ALL PERSONNEL ARE ASSEMBLED ON THE PARADE GROUNDS!
BIEN!

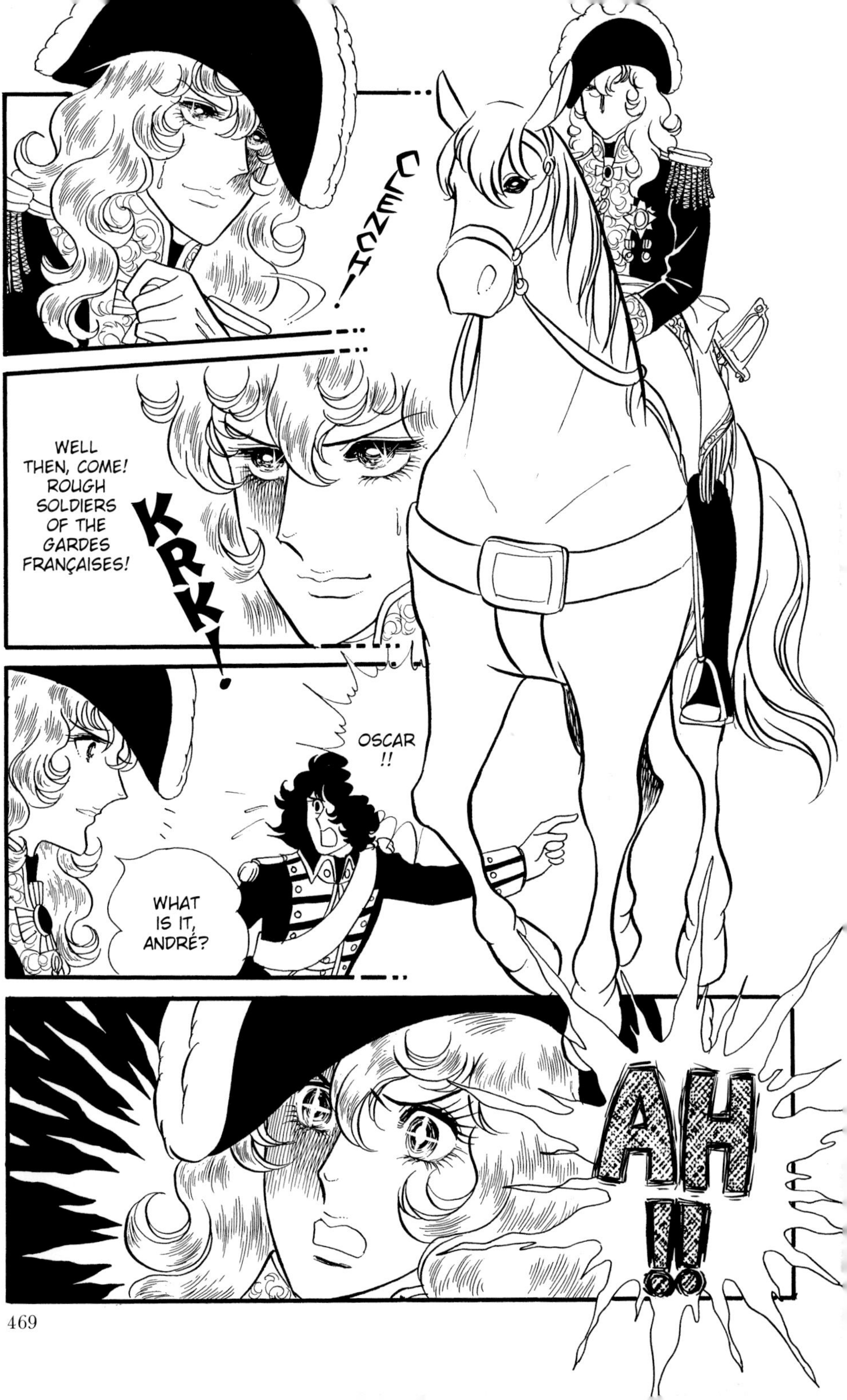
CLENCH!
WELL THEN, COME! ROUGH SOLDIERS OF THE GARDES FRANÇAISES!
KRK!
OSCAR !!
WHAT IS IT, ANDRÉ?
AH!!

THE ROSE OF VERSAILLES

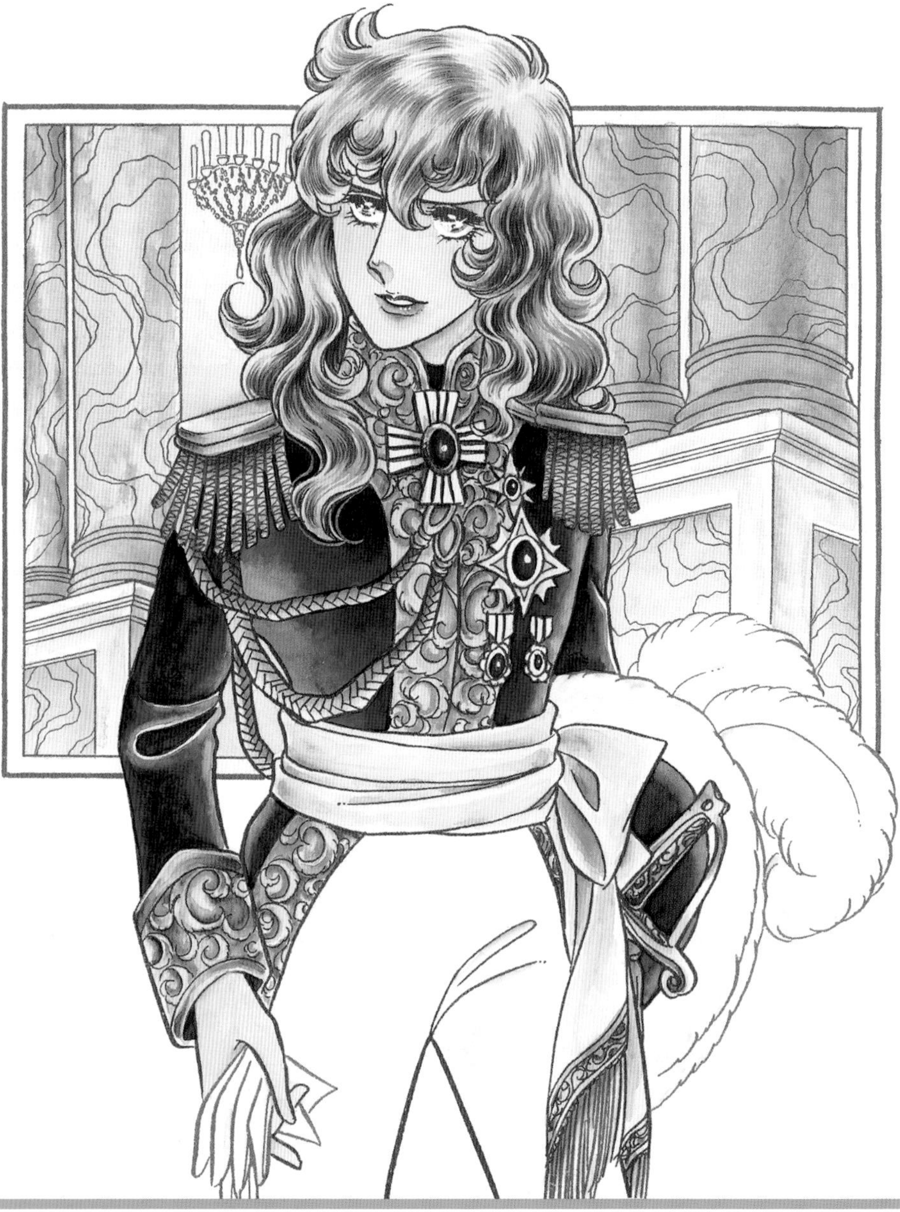

1973 WEEKLY MARGARET MAGAZINE ISSUE 12 COVER PAGE
(SPECIAL COLORIZED VERSION)

THE SUPER EPIC ROMANCE OF ROILING EXCITEMENT AND EMOTION

♥ ADVANCING ON HIS OWN, OSCAR HAS THROWN HIMSELF INTO THE GUARD FILL OF ROWDY SOLDIERS AND NOW...?!

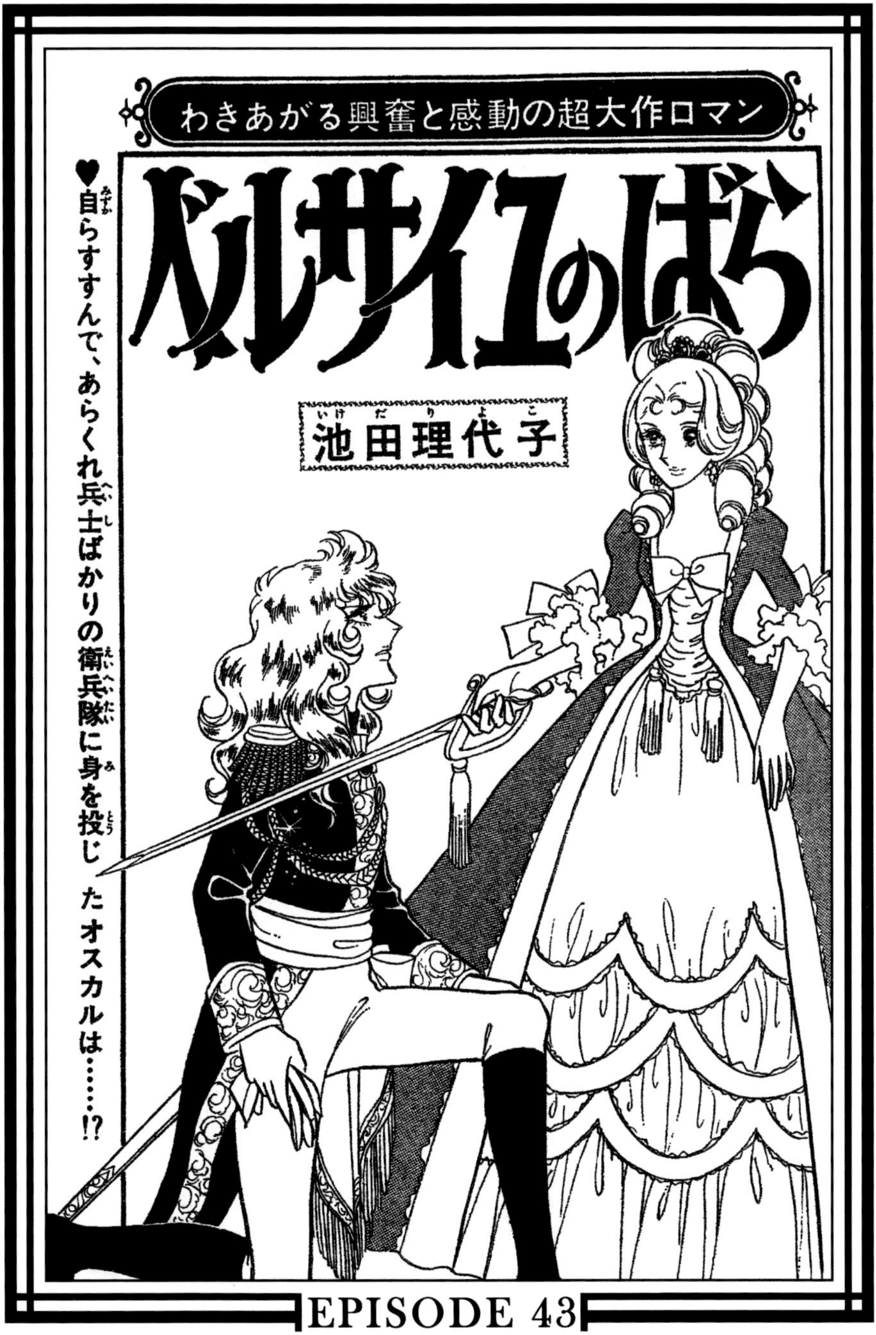
わきあがる興奮と感動の超大作ロマン
ベルサイユのばら
池田理代子
♥自らすすんで、あらくれ兵士ばかりの衛兵隊に身を投じたオスカルは……!?
EPISODE 43

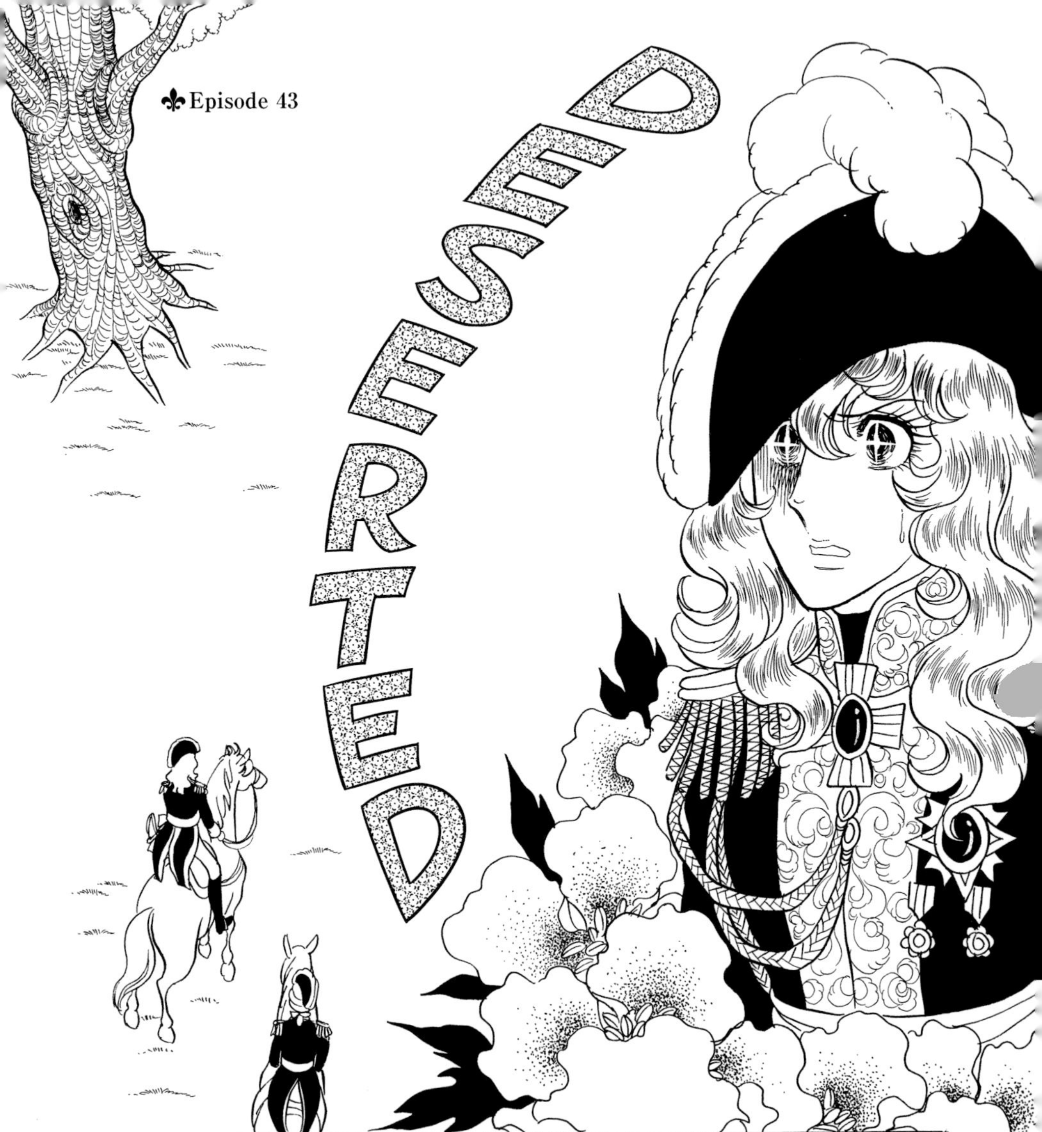
Episode 43
DESERTED

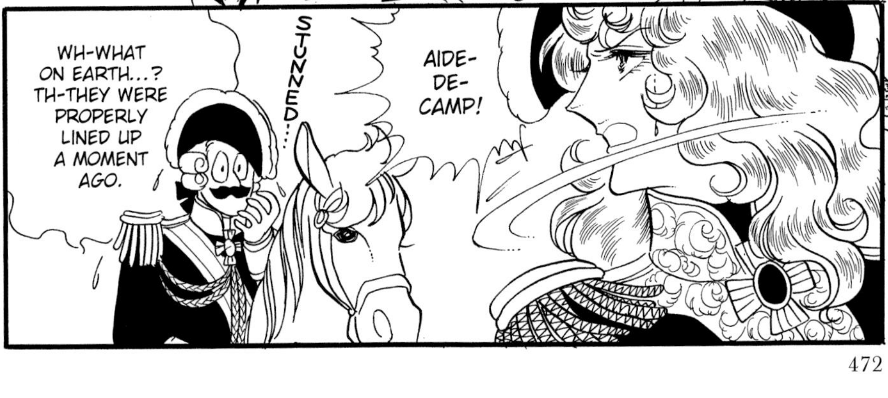
AIDE-DE-CAMP!
STUNNED...
WH-WHAT ON EARTH...? TH-THEY WERE PROPERLY LINED UP A MOMENT AGO.

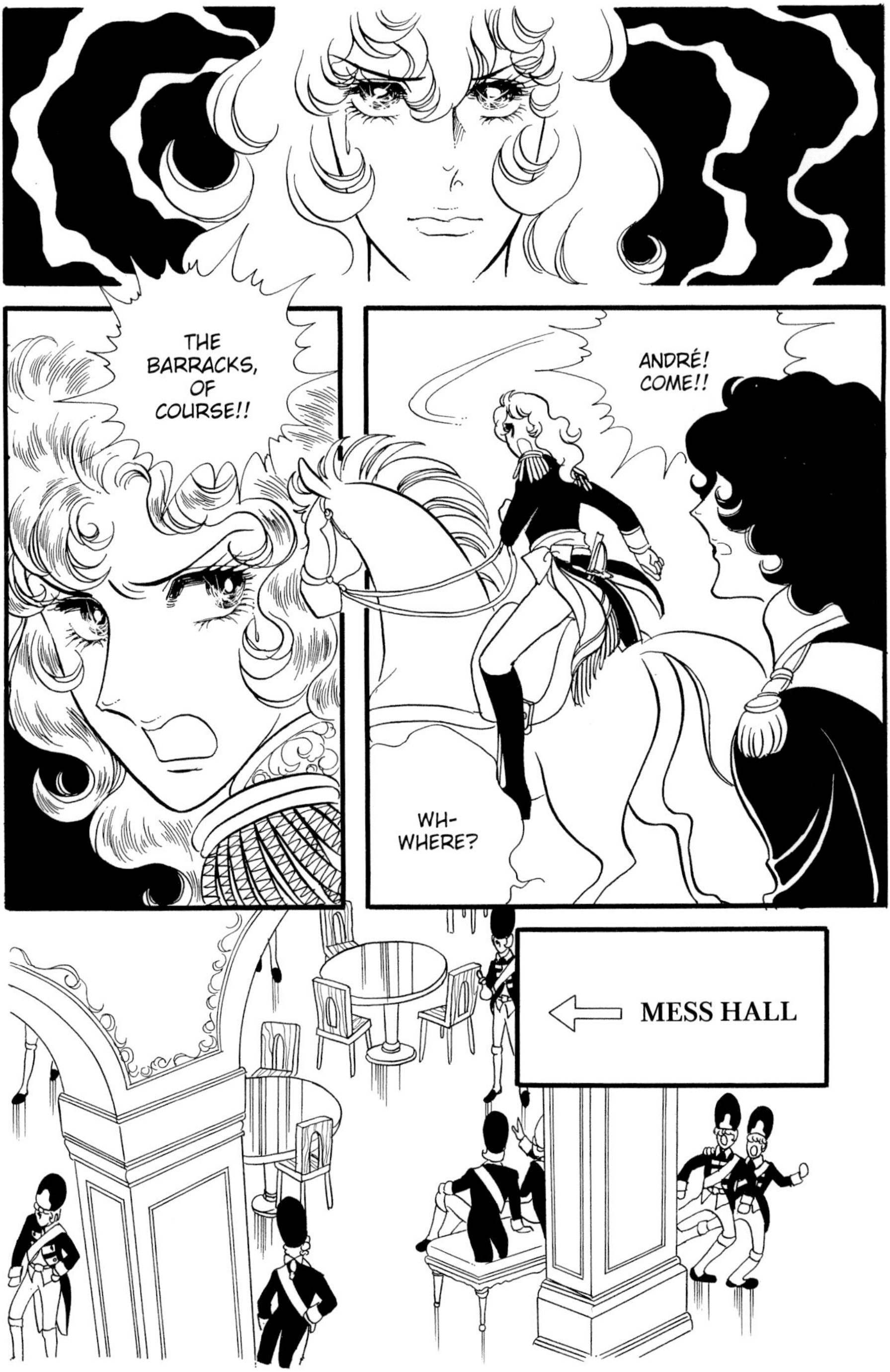
ANDRÉ! COME!!
WH- WHERE?
THE BARRACKS, OF COURSE!!
MESS HALL

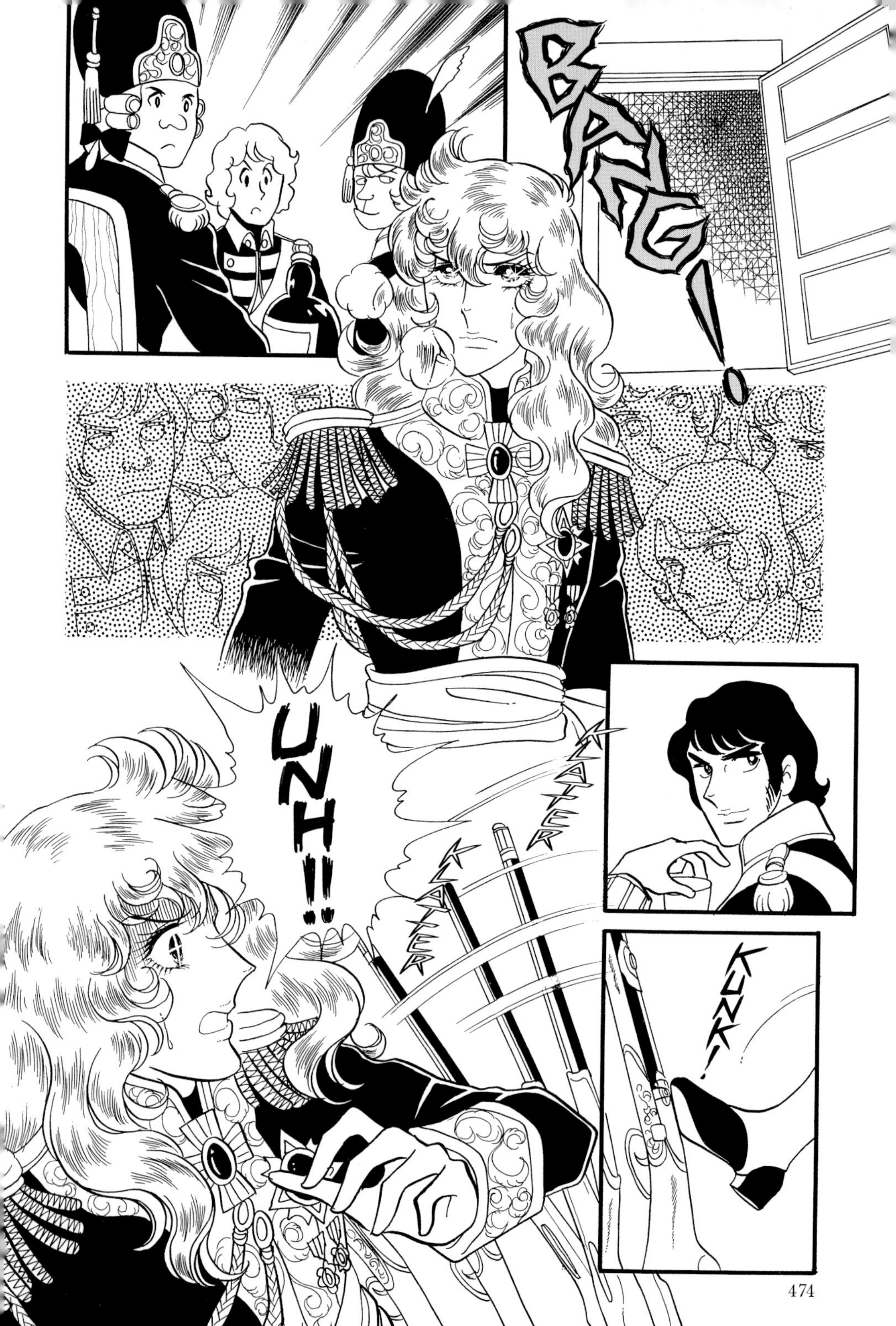
BANG!
KLATTER
KLATTER
UNH!!
KUNK!

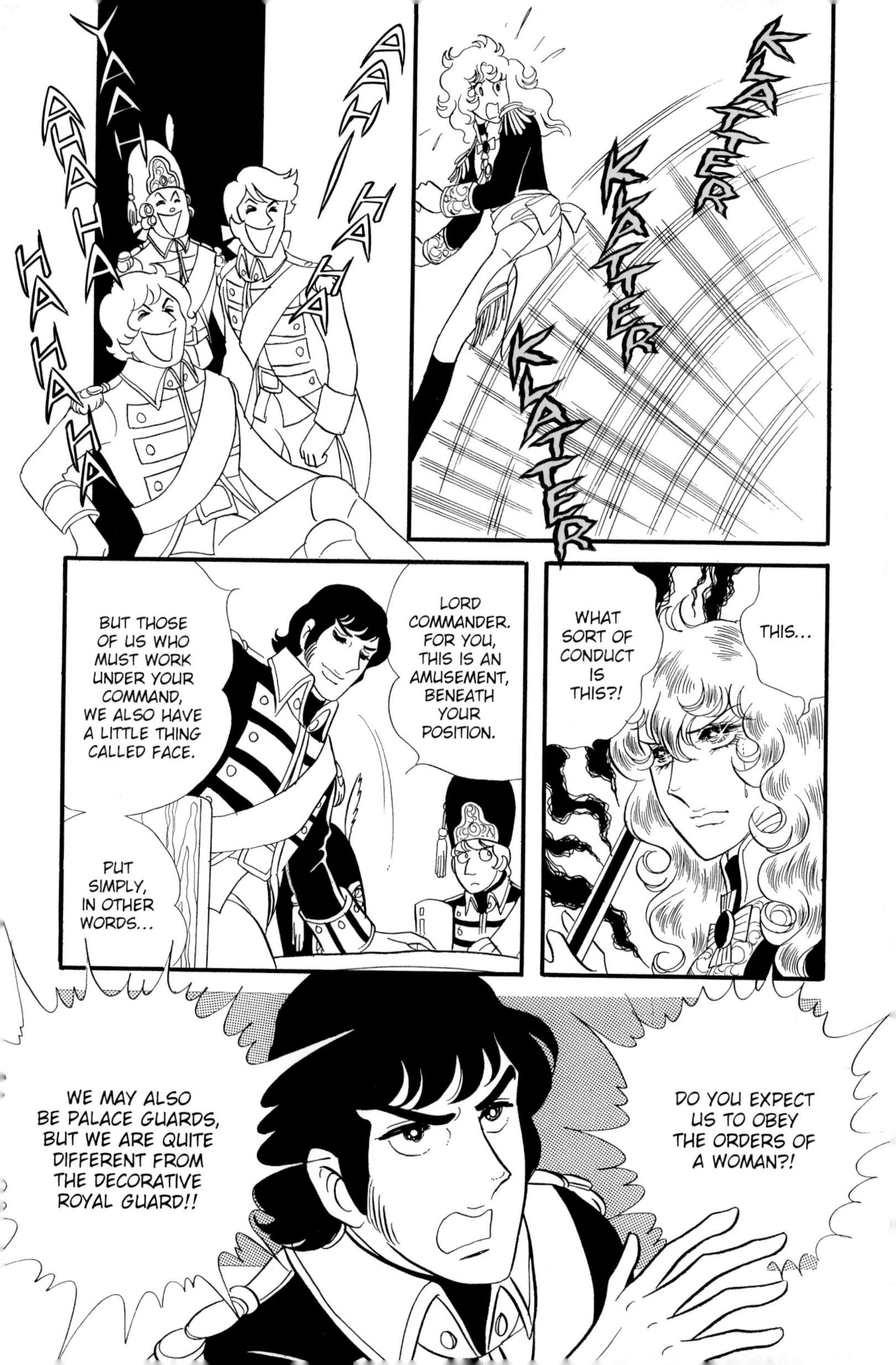
KLATTER
KLATTER
KLATTER
AAH! HAHA
YAAH
AHAHA
HAHAHA
THIS...
WHAT SORT OF CONDUCT IS THIS?!
LORD COMMANDER. FOR YOU, THIS IS AN AMUSEMENT, BENEATH YOUR POSITION.
BUT THOSE OF US WHO MUST WORK UNDER YOUR COMMAND, WE ALSO HAVE A LITTLE THING CALLED FACE.
PUT SIMPLY, IN OTHER WORDS...
DO YOU EXPECT US TO OBEY THE ORDERS OF A WOMAN?!
WE MAY ALSO BE PALACE GUARDS, BUT WE ARE QUITE DIFFERENT FROM THE DECORATIVE ROYAL GUARD!!

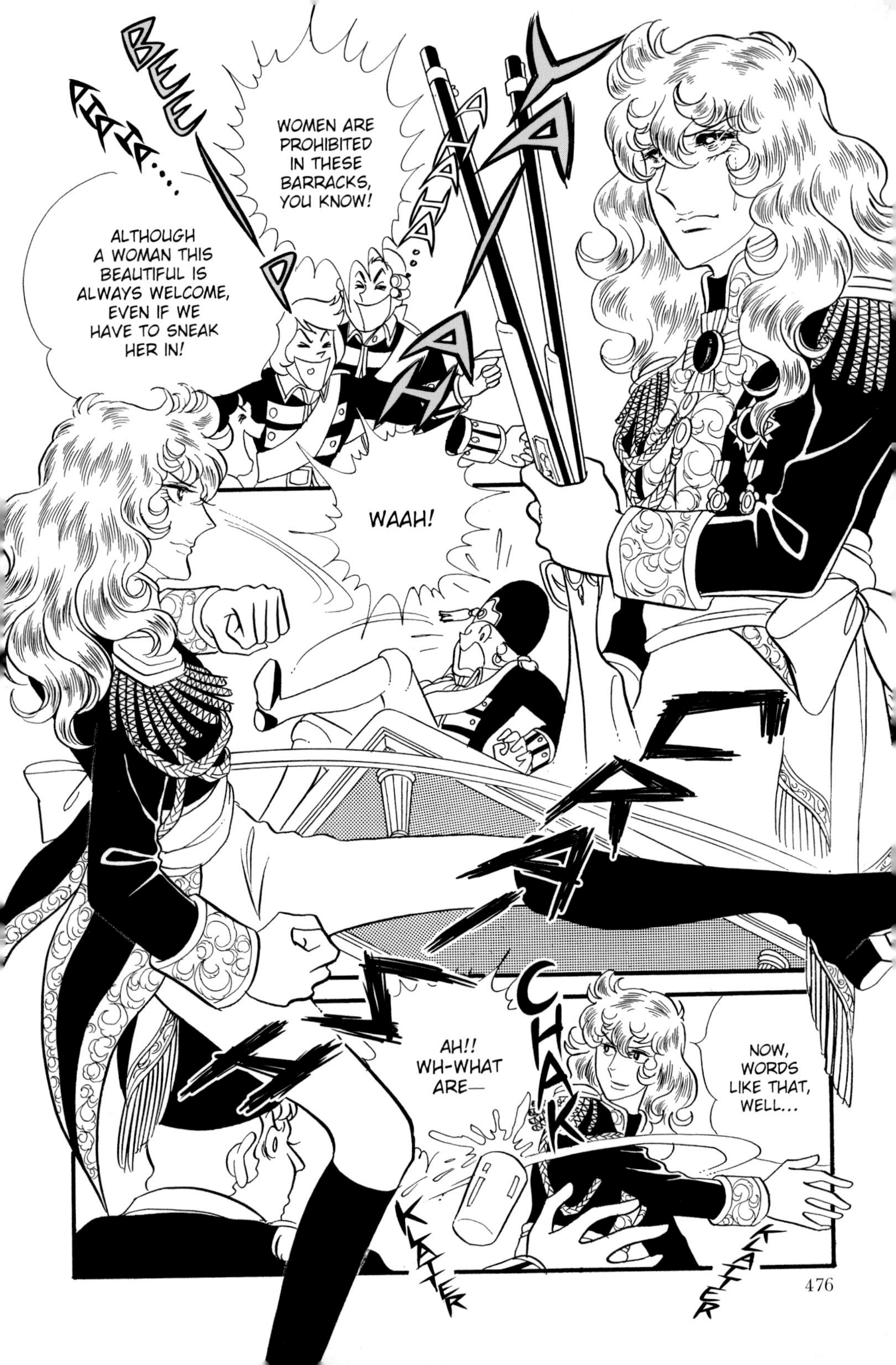
WOMEN ARE PROHIBITED IN THESE BARRACKS, YOU KNOW!
BEEE—P
HAHAHA....
ALTHOUGH A WOMAN THIS BEAUTIFUL IS ALWAYS WELCOME, EVEN IF WE HAVE TO SNEAK HER IN!
WAAH!
NOW, WORDS LIKE THAT, WELL...
CHAK
AH!! WH-WHAT ARE—
KLATTER
KLATTER

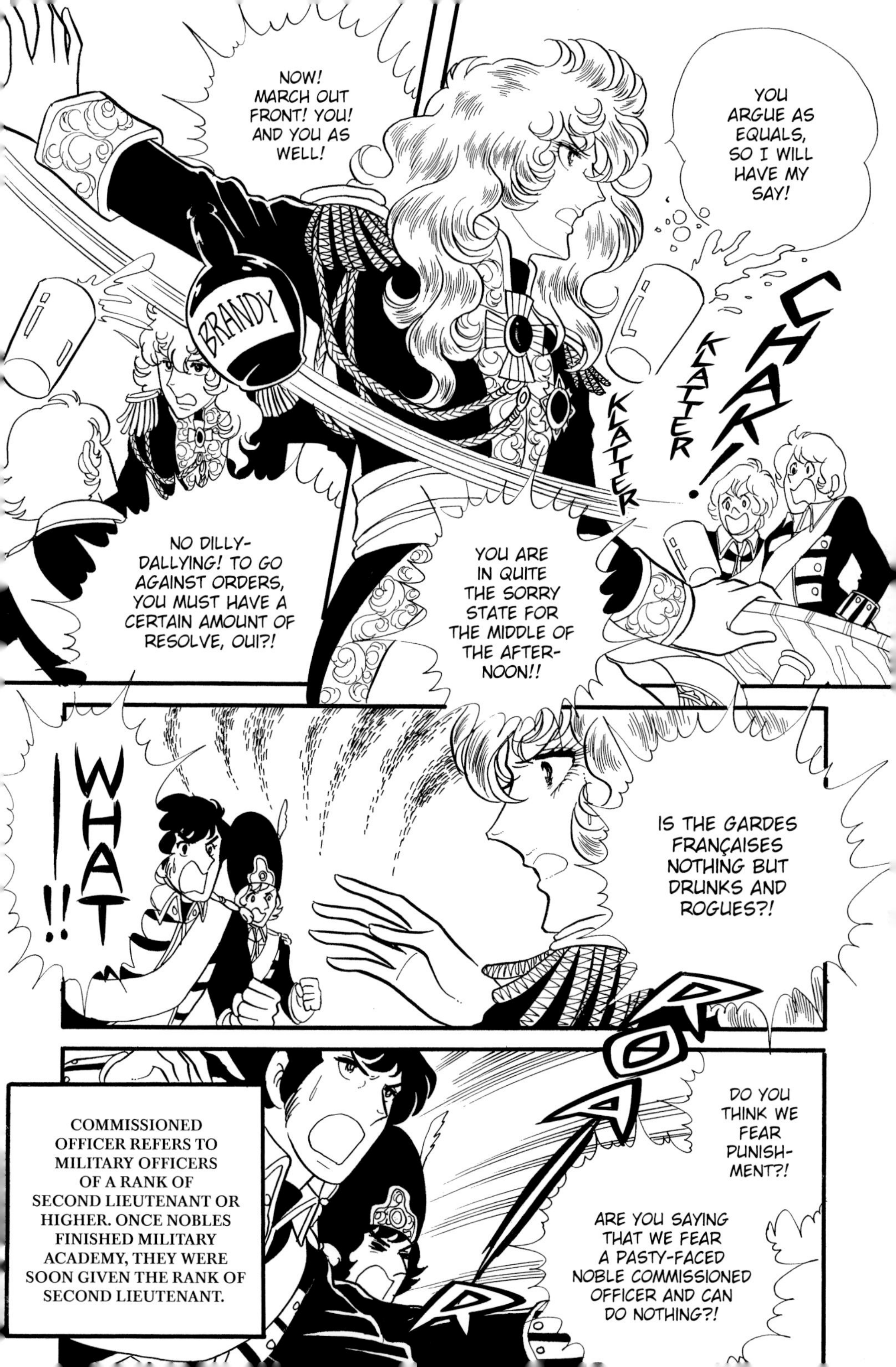
YOU ARGUE AS EQUALS, SO I WILL HAVE MY SAY!
NOW! MARCH OUT FRONT! YOU! AND YOU AS WELL!
BRANDY
CHAK!
KLATTER
KLATTER
YOU ARE IN QUITE THE SORRY STATE FOR THE MIDDLE OF THE AFTER-NOON!!
NO DILLY-DALLYING! TO GO AGAINST ORDERS, YOU MUST HAVE A CERTAIN AMOUNT OF RESOLVE, OUI?!
IS THE GARDES FRANÇAISES NOTHING BUT DRUNKS AND ROGUES?!
WHAT!!
ROAR
DO YOU THINK WE FEAR PUNISH-MENT?!
ARE YOU SAYING THAT WE FEAR A PASTY-FACED NOBLE COMMISSIONED OFFICER AND CAN DO NOTHING?!
COMMISSIONED OFFICER REFERS TO MILITARY OFFICERS OF A RANK OF SECOND LIEUTENANT OR HIGHER. ONCE NOBLES FINISHED MILITARY ACADEMY, THEY WERE SOON GIVEN THE RANK OF SECOND LIEUTENANT.

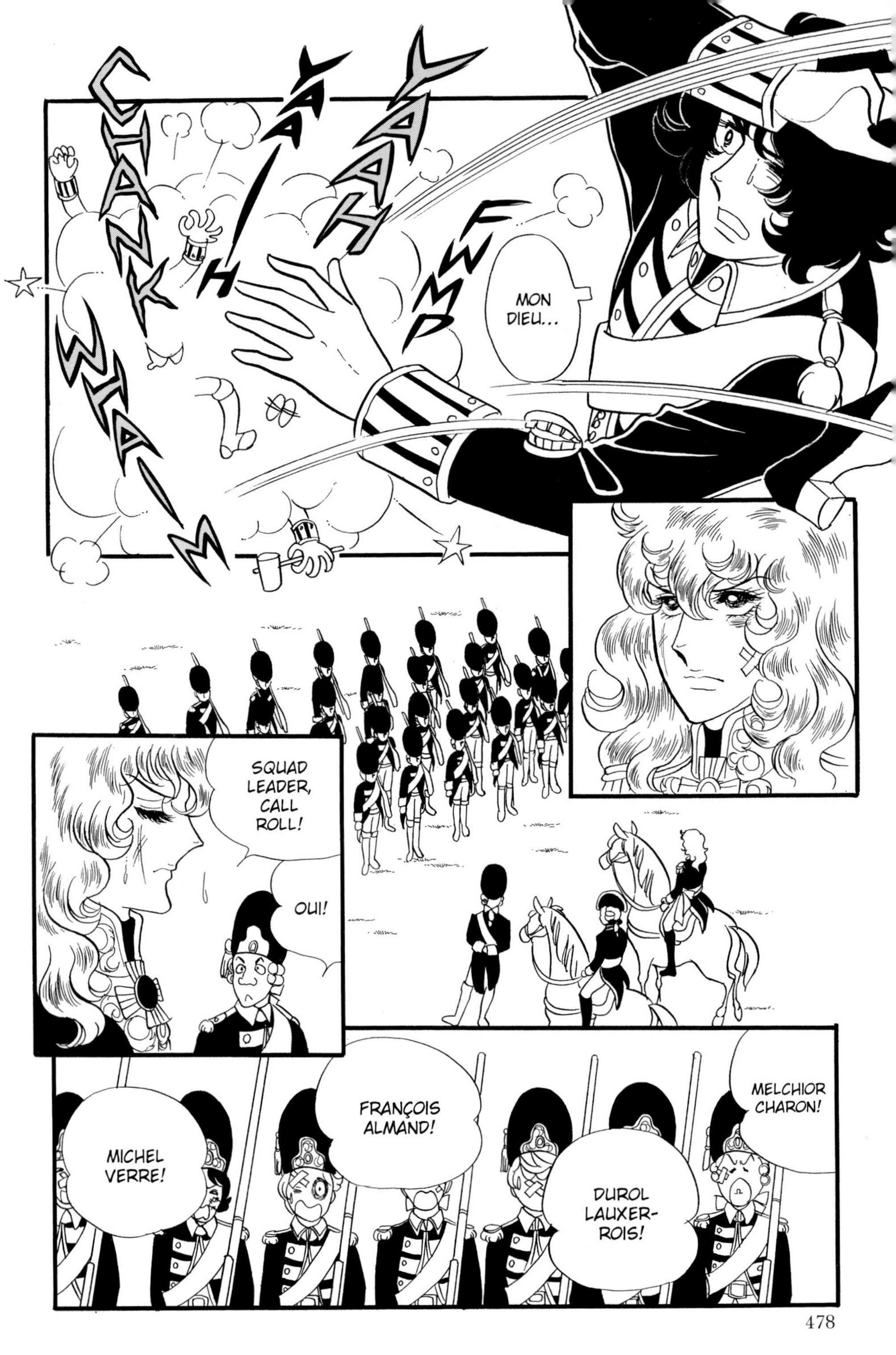
MON DIEU...
FWMP
YAAAH
YAA!H
CHANK
WHAM
SQUAD LEADER, CALL ROLL!
OUI!
MELCHIOR CHARON!
DUROL LAUXER-ROIS!
FRANÇOIS ALMAND!
MICHEL VERRE!

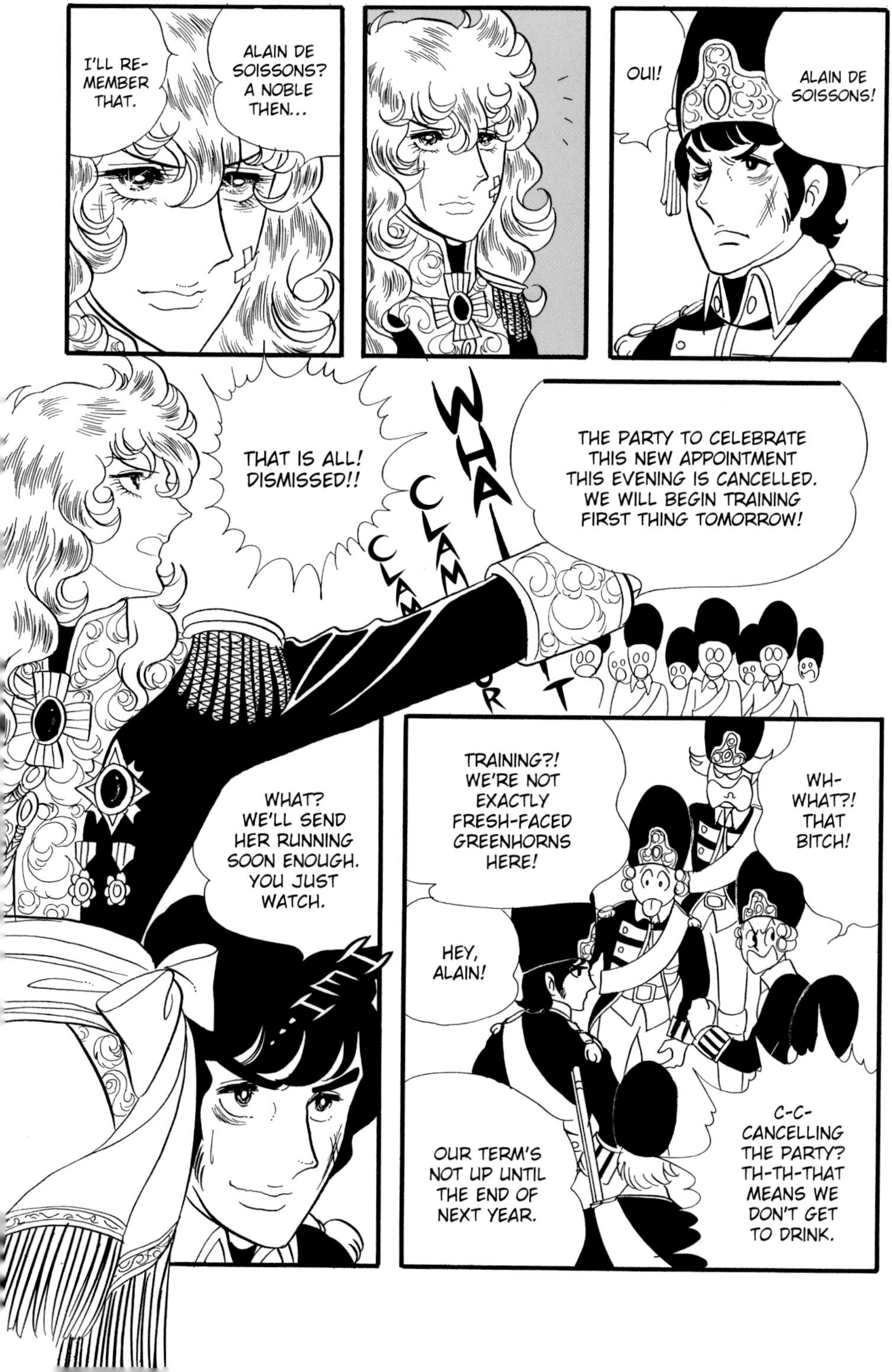
ALAIN DE SOISSONS!
OUI!
ALAIN DE SOISSONS? A NOBLE THEN...
I'LL RE-MEMBER THAT.
THE PARTY TO CELEBRATE THIS NEW APPOINTMENT THIS EVENING IS CANCELLED. WE WILL BEGIN TRAINING FIRST THING TOMORROW!
THAT IS ALL! DISMISSED!!
WHAT
CLAMOR
CLAM
WH-WHAT?! THAT BITCH!
TRAINING?! WE'RE NOT EXACTLY FRESH-FACED GREENHORNS HERE!
HEY, ALAIN!
C-C-CANCELLING THE PARTY? TH-TH-THAT MEANS WE DON'T GET TO DRINK.
OUR TERM'S NOT UP UNTIL THE END OF NEXT YEAR.
WHAT? WE'LL SEND HER RUNNING SOON ENOUGH. YOU JUST WATCH.

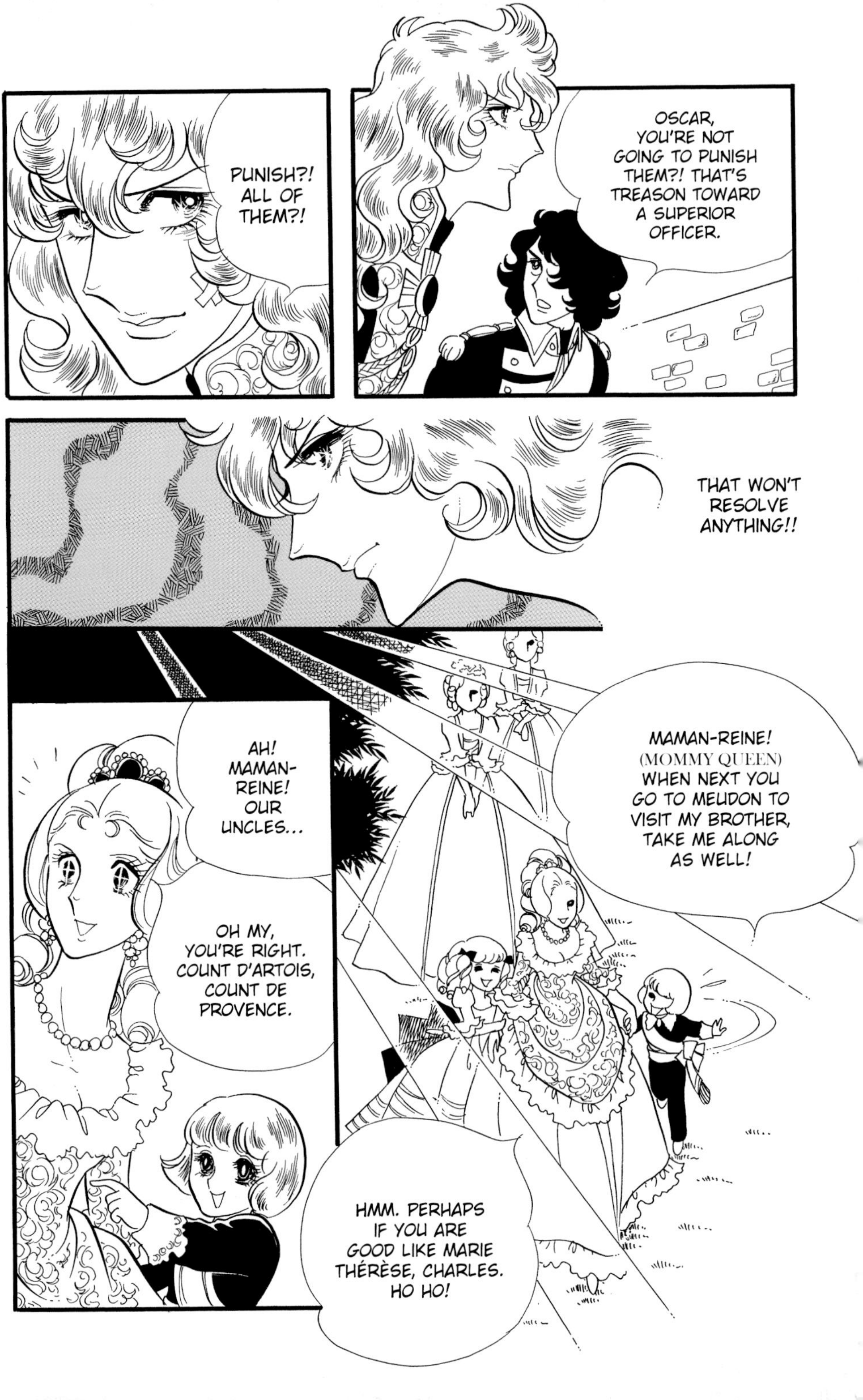

OSCAR, YOU'RE NOT GOING TO PUNISH THEM?! THAT'S TREASON TOWARD A SUPERIOR OFFICER.
PUNISH?! ALL OF THEM?!
THAT WON'T RESOLVE ANYTHING!!
MAMAN-REINE! (MOMMY QUEEN) WHEN NEXT YOU GO TO MEUDON TO VISIT MY BROTHER, TAKE ME ALONG AS WELL!
AH! MAMAN-REINE! OUR UNCLES...
OH MY, YOU'RE RIGHT. COUNT D'ARTOIS, COUNT DE PROVENCE.
HMM. PERHAPS IF YOU ARE GOOD LIKE MARIE THÉRÈSE, CHARLES. HO HO!

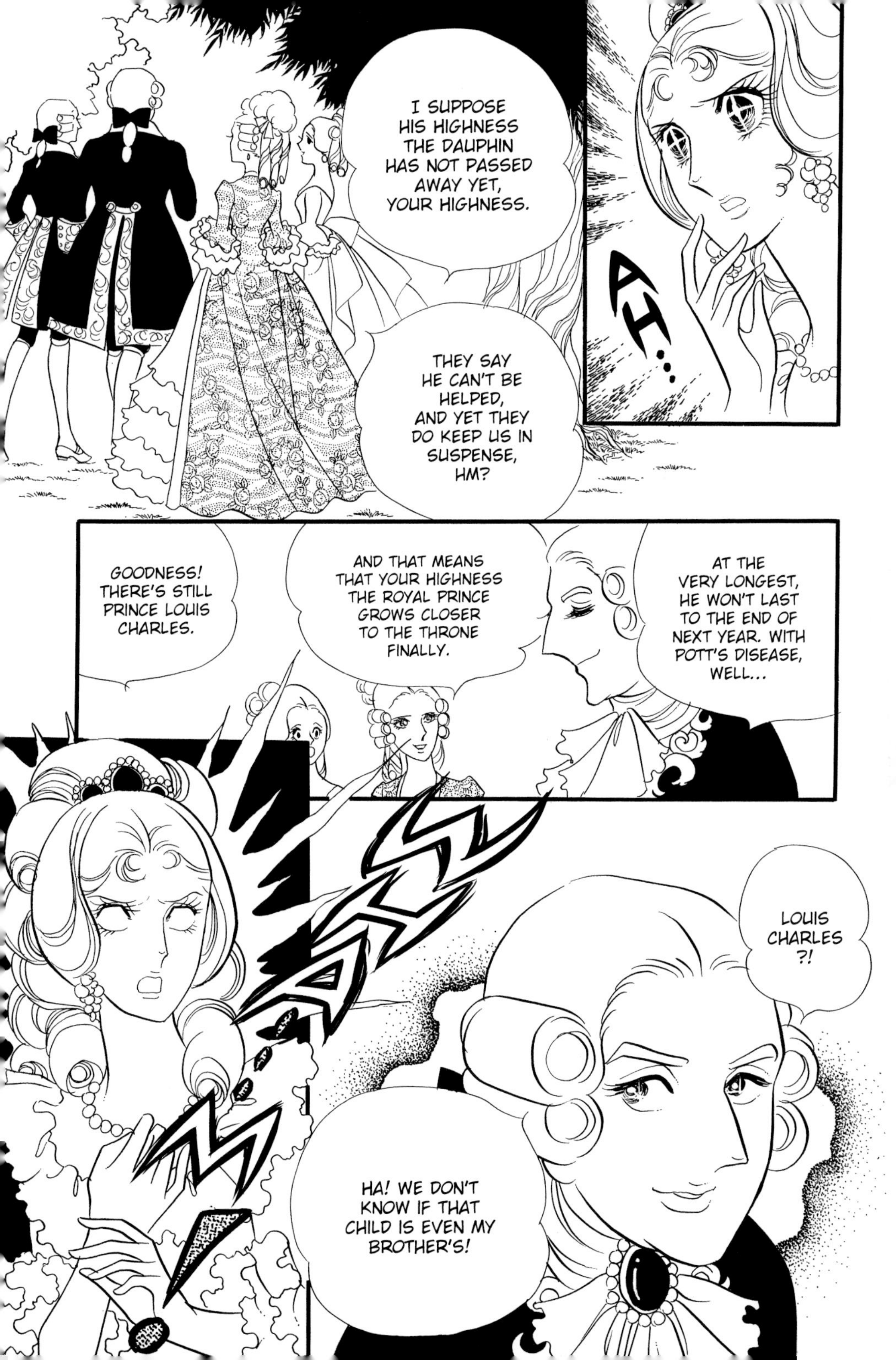
AH...
I SUPPOSE HIS HIGHNESS THE DAUPHIN HAS NOT PASSED AWAY YET, YOUR HIGHNESS.
THEY SAY HE CAN'T BE HELPED, AND YET THEY DO KEEP US IN SUSPENSE, HM?
AT THE VERY LONGEST, HE WON'T LAST TO THE END OF NEXT YEAR. WITH POTT'S DISEASE, WELL...
AND THAT MEANS THAT YOUR HIGHNESS THE ROYAL PRINCE GROWS CLOSER TO THE THRONE FINALLY.
GOODNESS! THERE'S STILL PRINCE LOUIS CHARLES.
LOUIS CHARLES ?!
HA! WE DON'T KNOW IF THAT CHILD IS EVEN MY BROTHER'S!

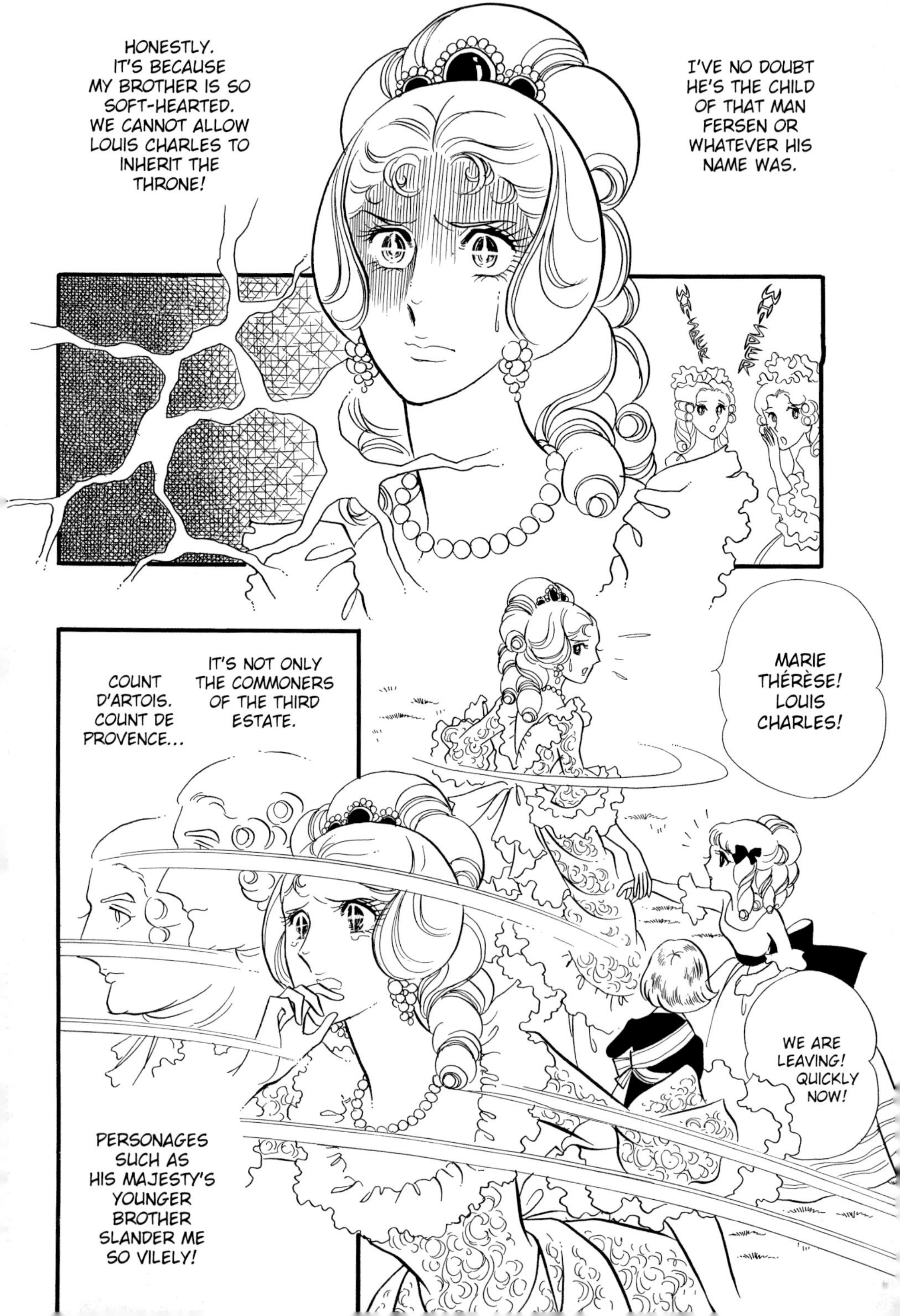
I'VE NO DOUBT HE'S THE CHILD OF THAT MAN FERSEN OR WHATEVER HIS NAME WAS.
WHISPER
WHISPER
HONESTLY. IT'S BECAUSE MY BROTHER IS SO SOFT-HEARTED. WE CANNOT ALLOW LOUIS CHARLES TO INHERIT THE THRONE!
MARIE THÉRÈSE! LOUIS CHARLES!
WE ARE LEAVING! QUICKLY NOW!
IT'S NOT ONLY THE COMMONERS OF THE THIRD ESTATE.
COUNT D'ARTOIS. COUNT DE PROVENCE...
PERSONAGES SUCH AS HIS MAJESTY'S YOUNGER BROTHER SLANDER ME SO VILELY!

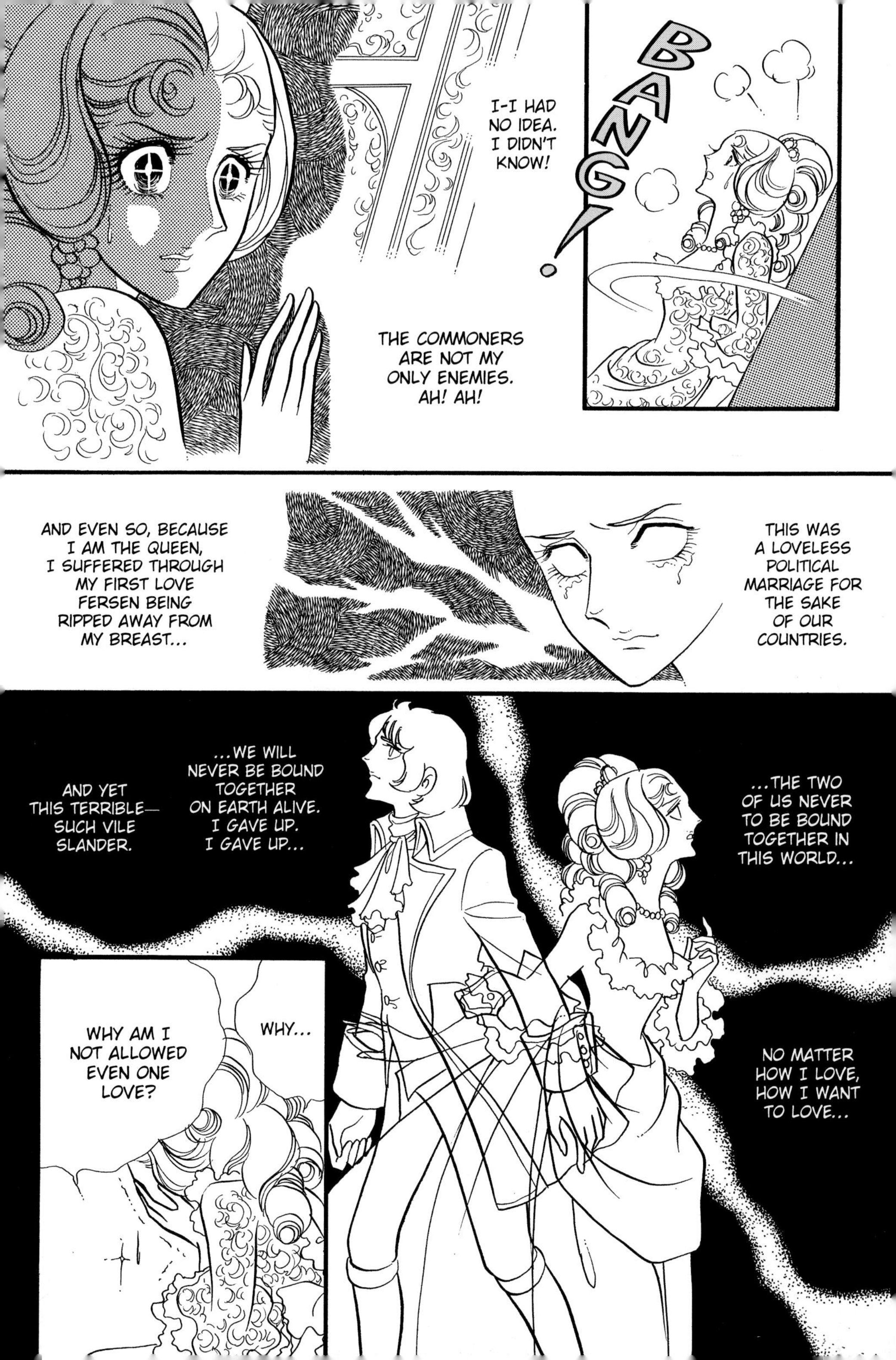
BANG!
I-I HAD NO IDEA. I DIDN'T KNOW!
THE COMMONERS ARE NOT MY ONLY ENEMIES. AH! AH!
THIS WAS A LOVELESS POLITICAL MARRIAGE FOR THE SAKE OF OUR COUNTRIES.
AND EVEN SO, BECAUSE I AM THE QUEEN, I SUFFERED THROUGH MY FIRST LOVE FERSEN BEING RIPPED AWAY FROM MY BREAST...
...THE TWO OF US NEVER TO BE BOUND TOGETHER IN THIS WORLD...
...WE WILL NEVER BE BOUND TOGETHER ON EARTH ALIVE. I GAVE UP. I GAVE UP...
AND YET THIS TERRIBLE— SUCH VILE SLANDER.
NO MATTER HOW I LOVE, HOW I WANT TO LOVE...
WHY...
WHY AM I NOT ALLOWED EVEN ONE LOVE?

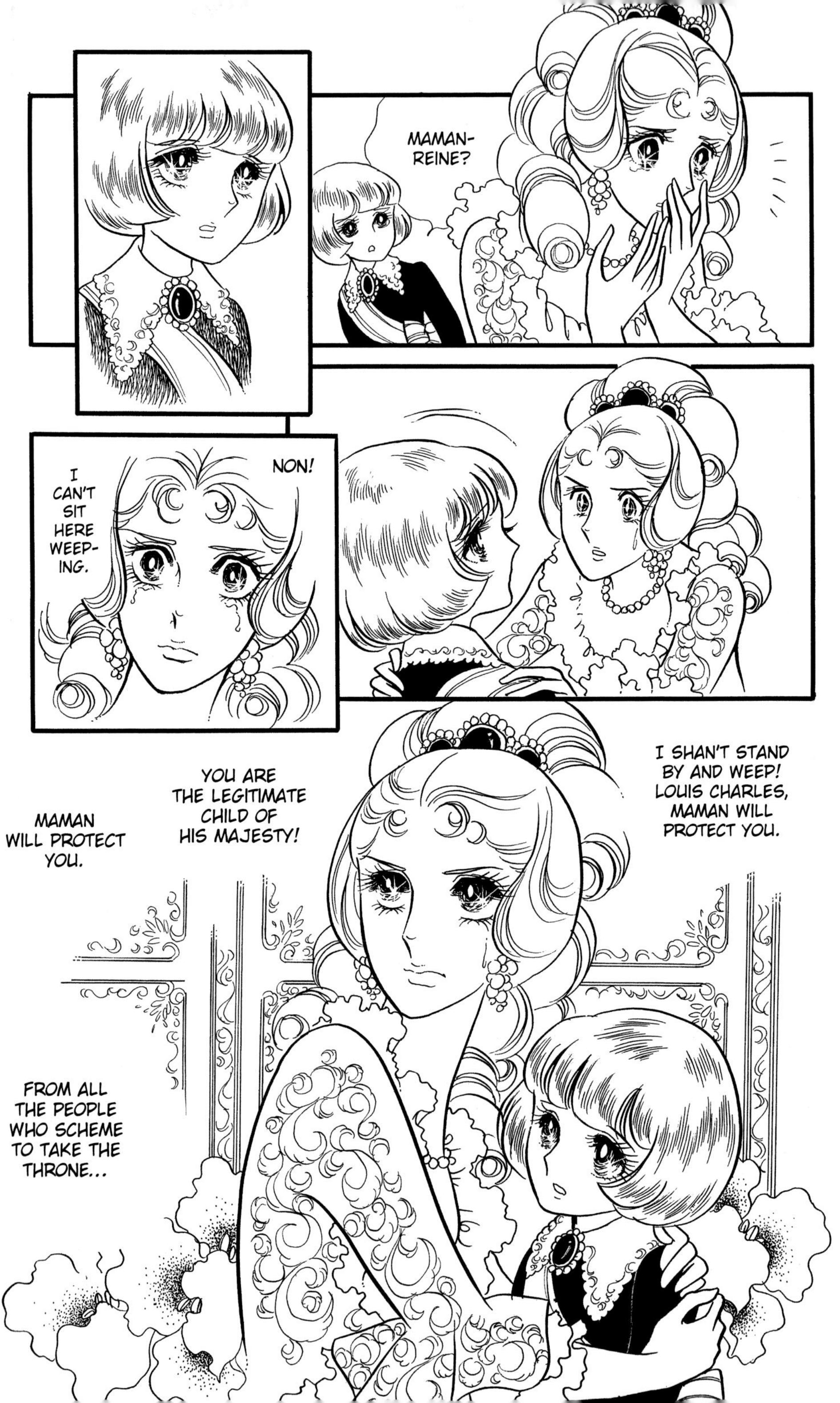
MAMAN-REINE?
NON!
I CAN'T SIT HERE WEEP-ING.
I SHAN'T STAND BY AND WEEP! LOUIS CHARLES, MAMAN WILL PROTECT YOU.
YOU ARE THE LEGITIMATE CHILD OF HIS MAJESTY!
MAMAN WILL PROTECT YOU.
FROM ALL THE PEOPLE WHO SCHEME TO TAKE THE THRONE...

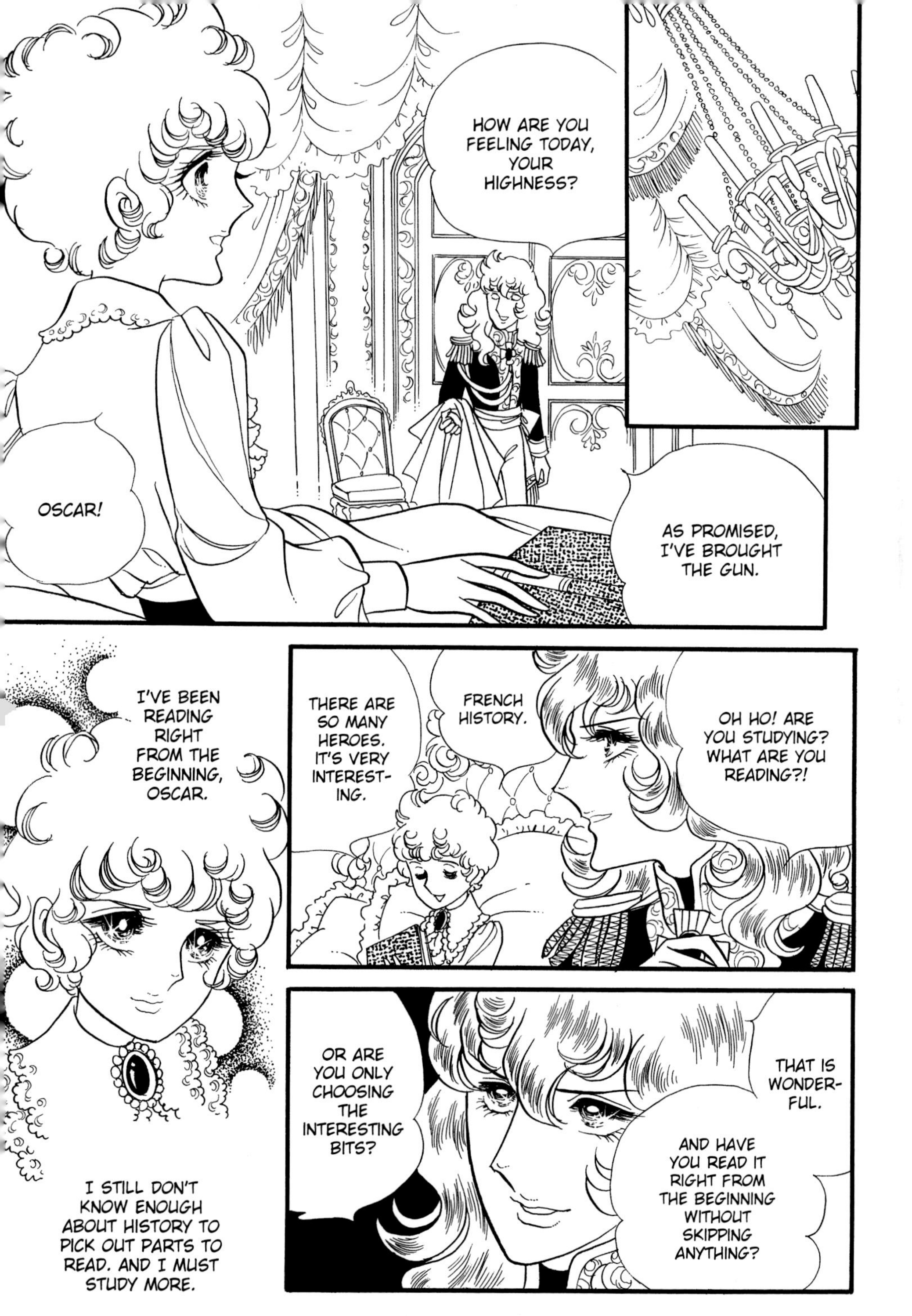
HOW ARE YOU FEELING TODAY, YOUR HIGHNESS?
OSCAR!
AS PROMISED, I'VE BROUGHT THE GUN.
OH HO! ARE YOU STUDYING? WHAT ARE YOU READING?!
FRENCH HISTORY.
THERE ARE SO MANY HEROES. IT'S VERY INTEREST-ING.
THAT IS WONDER-FUL.
AND HAVE YOU READ IT RIGHT FROM THE BEGINNING WITHOUT SKIPPING ANYTHING?
OR ARE YOU ONLY CHOOSING THE INTERESTING BITS?
I'VE BEEN READING RIGHT FROM THE BEGINNING, OSCAR.
I STILL DON'T KNOW ENOUGH ABOUT HISTORY TO PICK OUT PARTS TO READ. AND I MUST STUDY MORE.

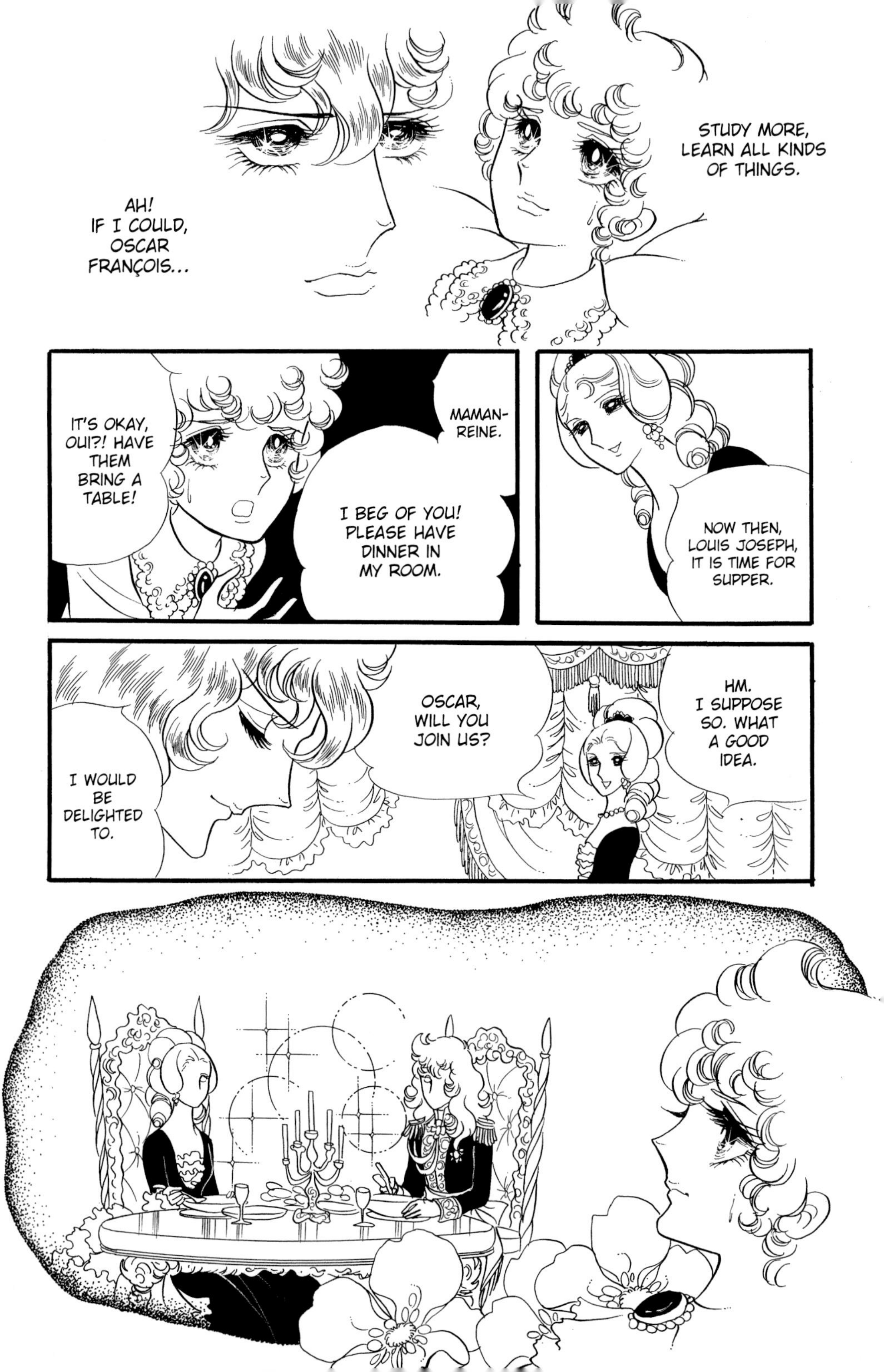
STUDY MORE, LEARN ALL KINDS OF THINGS.
AH! IF I COULD, OSCAR FRANÇOIS...
NOW THEN, LOUIS JOSEPH, IT IS TIME FOR SUPPER.
MAMAN-REINE.
I BEG OF YOU! PLEASE HAVE DINNER IN MY ROOM.
IT'S OKAY, OUI?! HAVE THEM BRING A TABLE!
HM. I SUPPOSE SO. WHAT A GOOD IDEA.
OSCAR, WILL YOU JOIN US?
I WOULD BE DELIGHTED TO.

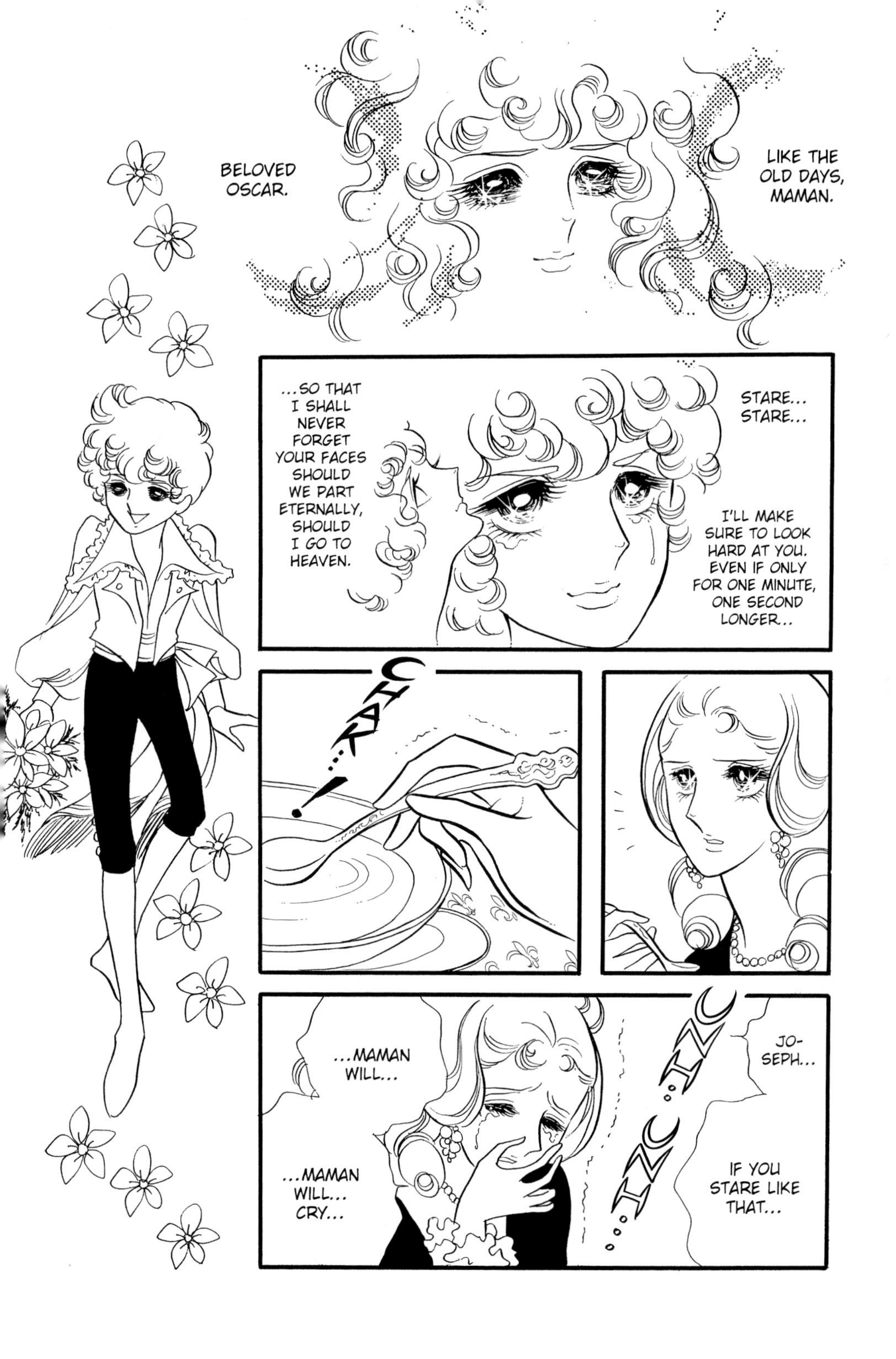

LIKE THE OLD DAYS, MAMAN.
BELOVED OSCAR.
STARE... STARE...
I'LL MAKE SURE TO LOOK HARD AT YOU. EVEN IF ONLY FOR ONE MINUTE, ONE SECOND LONGER...
...SO THAT I SHALL NEVER FORGET YOUR FACES SHOULD WE PART ETERNALLY, SHOULD I GO TO HEAVEN.
CHAR...!
JO-SEPH...
IF YOU STARE LIKE THAT...
HIC... HIC...
...MAMAN WILL...
...MAMAN WILL... CRY...

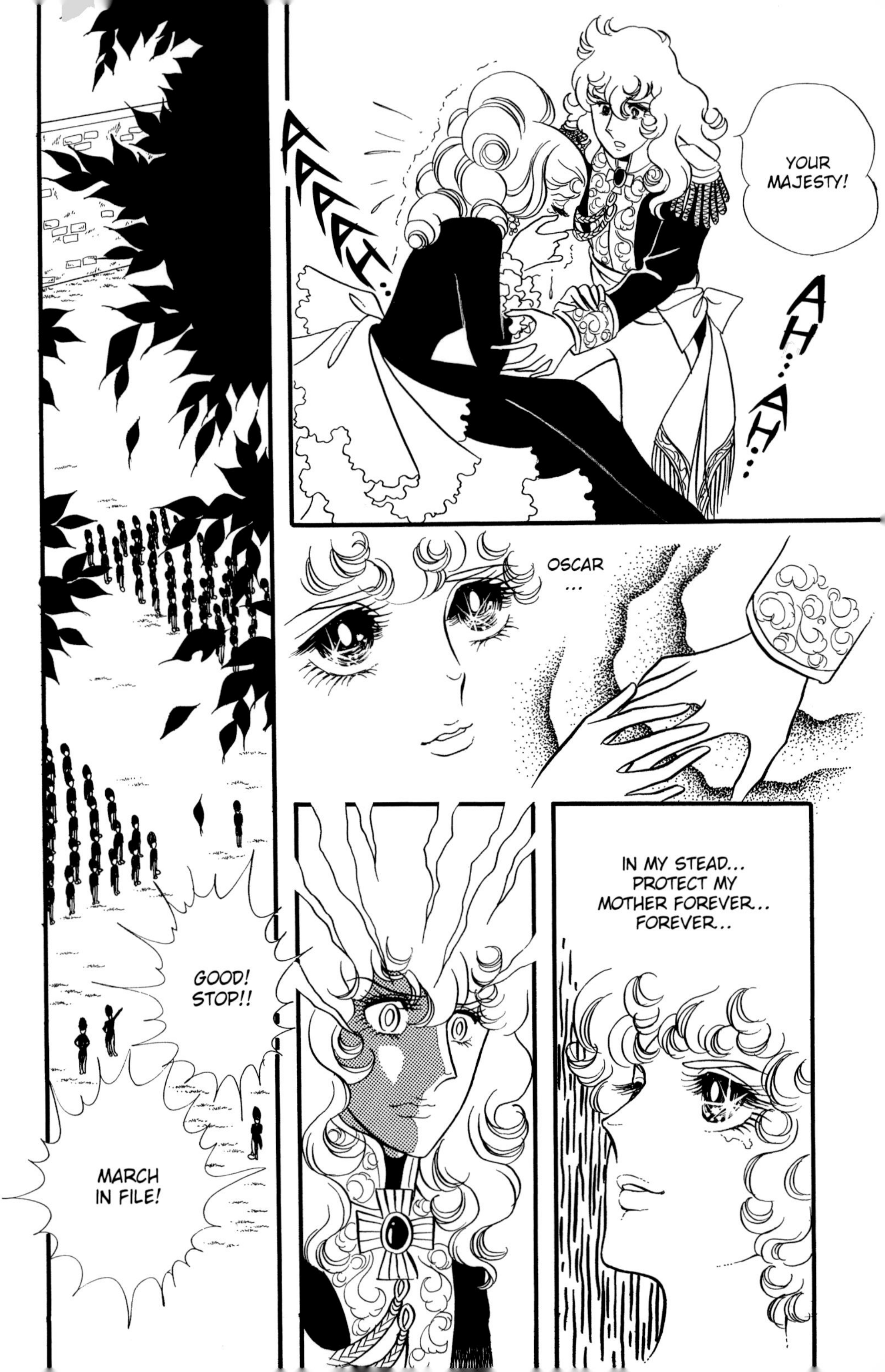
YOUR MAJESTY!
AH...AH...
AAAAH..
OSCAR ...
IN MY STEAD... PROTECT MY MOTHER FOREVER.. FOREVER..
GOOD! STOP!!
MARCH IN FILE!

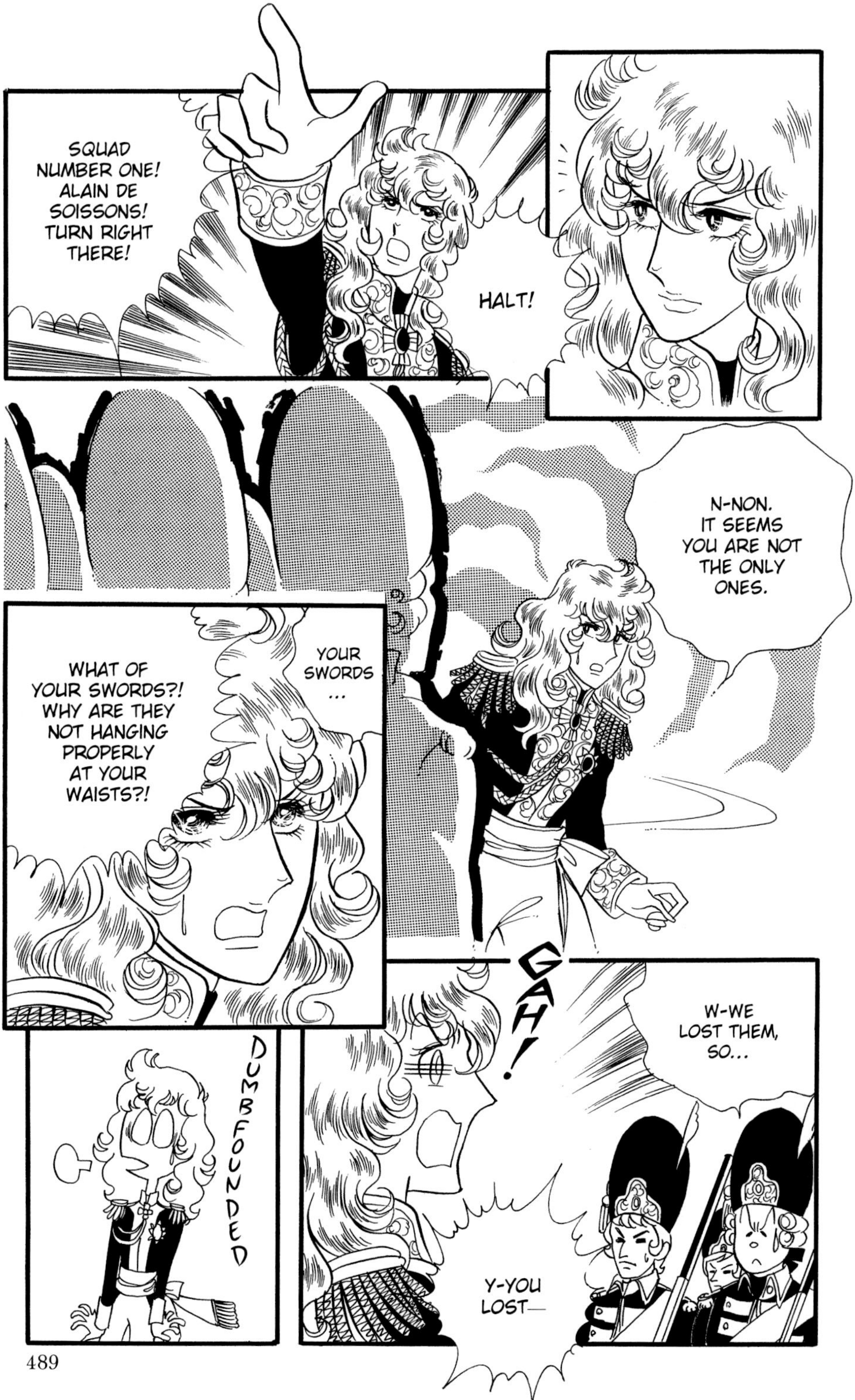
SQUAD NUMBER ONE! ALAIN DE SOISSONS! TURN RIGHT THERE!
HALT!
N-NON. IT SEEMS YOU ARE NOT THE ONLY ONES.
YOUR SWORDS ...
WHAT OF YOUR SWORDS?! WHY ARE THEY NOT HANGING PROPERLY AT YOUR WAISTS?!
GAH!
W-WE LOST THEM, SO...
Y-YOU LOST—
DUMBFOUNDED

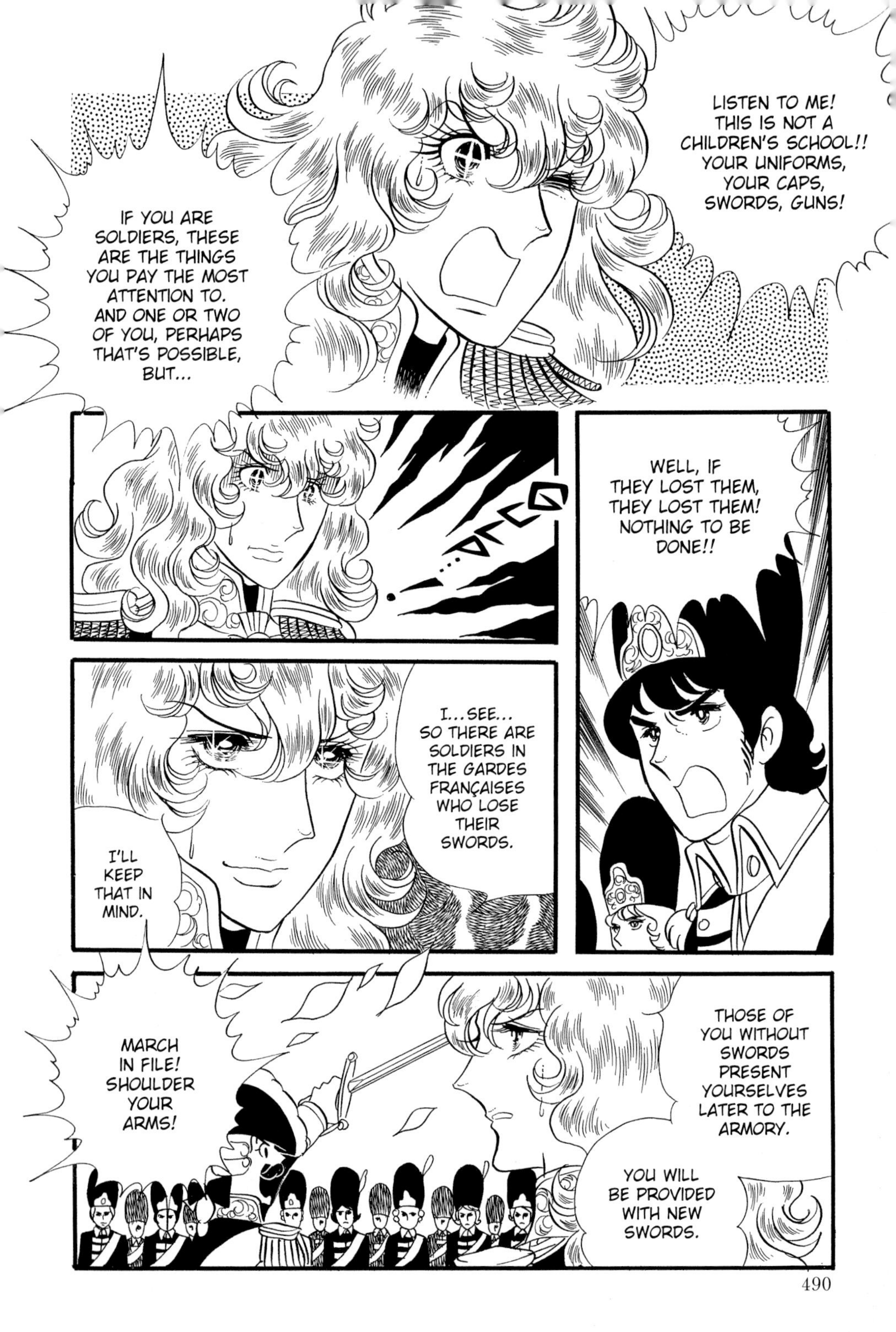
LISTEN TO ME! THIS IS NOT A CHILDREN'S SCHOOL!! YOUR UNIFORMS, YOUR CAPS, SWORDS, GUNS!
IF YOU ARE SOLDIERS, THESE ARE THE THINGS YOU PAY THE MOST ATTENTION TO. AND ONE OR TWO OF YOU, PERHAPS THAT'S POSSIBLE, BUT...
WELL, IF THEY LOST THEM, THEY LOST THEM! NOTHING TO BE DONE!!
I...SEE... SO THERE ARE SOLDIERS IN THE GARDES FRANÇAISES WHO LOSE THEIR SWORDS.
I'LL KEEP THAT IN MIND.
THOSE OF YOU WITHOUT SWORDS PRESENT YOURSELVES LATER TO THE ARMORY.
YOU WILL BE PROVIDED WITH NEW SWORDS.
MARCH IN FILE! SHOULDER YOUR ARMS!

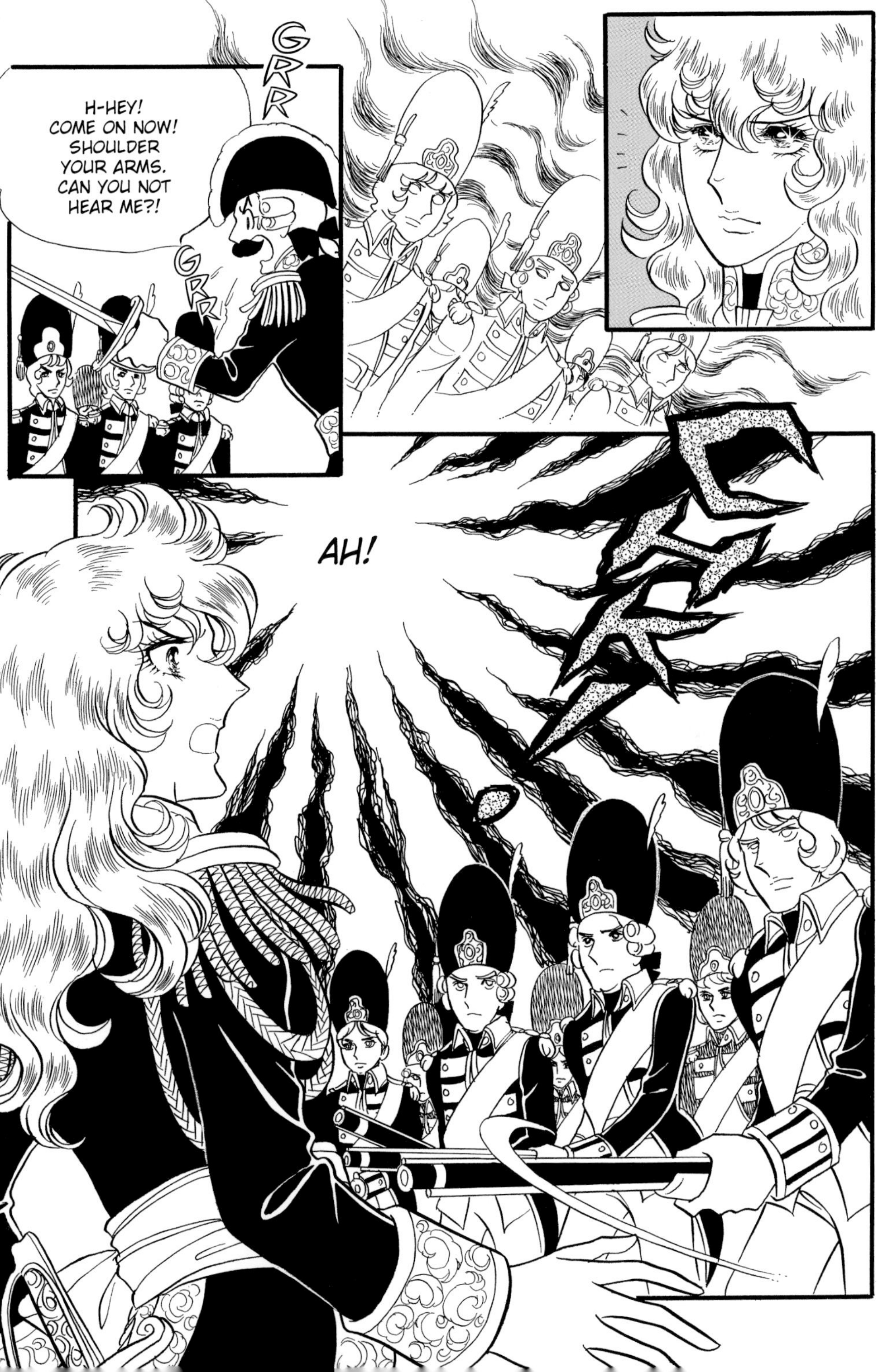
GRR
H-HEY! COME ON NOW! SHOULDER YOUR ARMS. CAN YOU NOT HEAR ME?!
GRR
AH!

1973 WEEKLY MARGARET MAGAZINE
ISSUE 29 BONUS CARD ART

THE SUPER EPIC ROMANCE OF ROILING EXCITEMENT AND EMOTION
♥ THE SOLDIERS POINT THEIR GUNS AT OSCAR AND...?!

わきあがる興奮と感動の超大作ロマン

ベルサイユのばら

♥オスカルめがけて兵士たちの銃が…!?

池田理代子

EPISODE 44

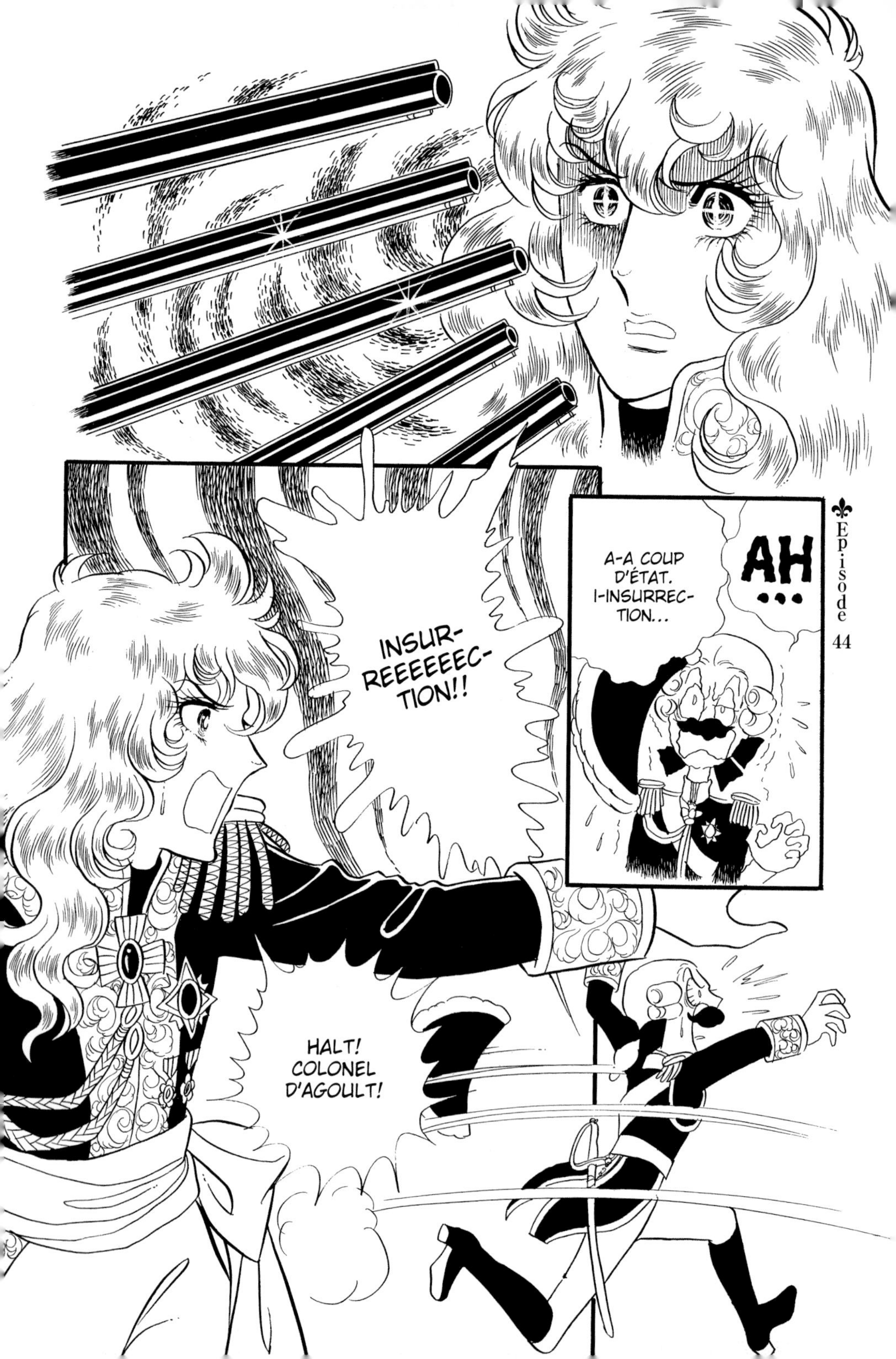
AH...
A-A COUP D'ÉTAT. I-INSURRECTION...
INSUR-REEEEEEEC-TION!!
HALT! COLONEL D'AGOULT!

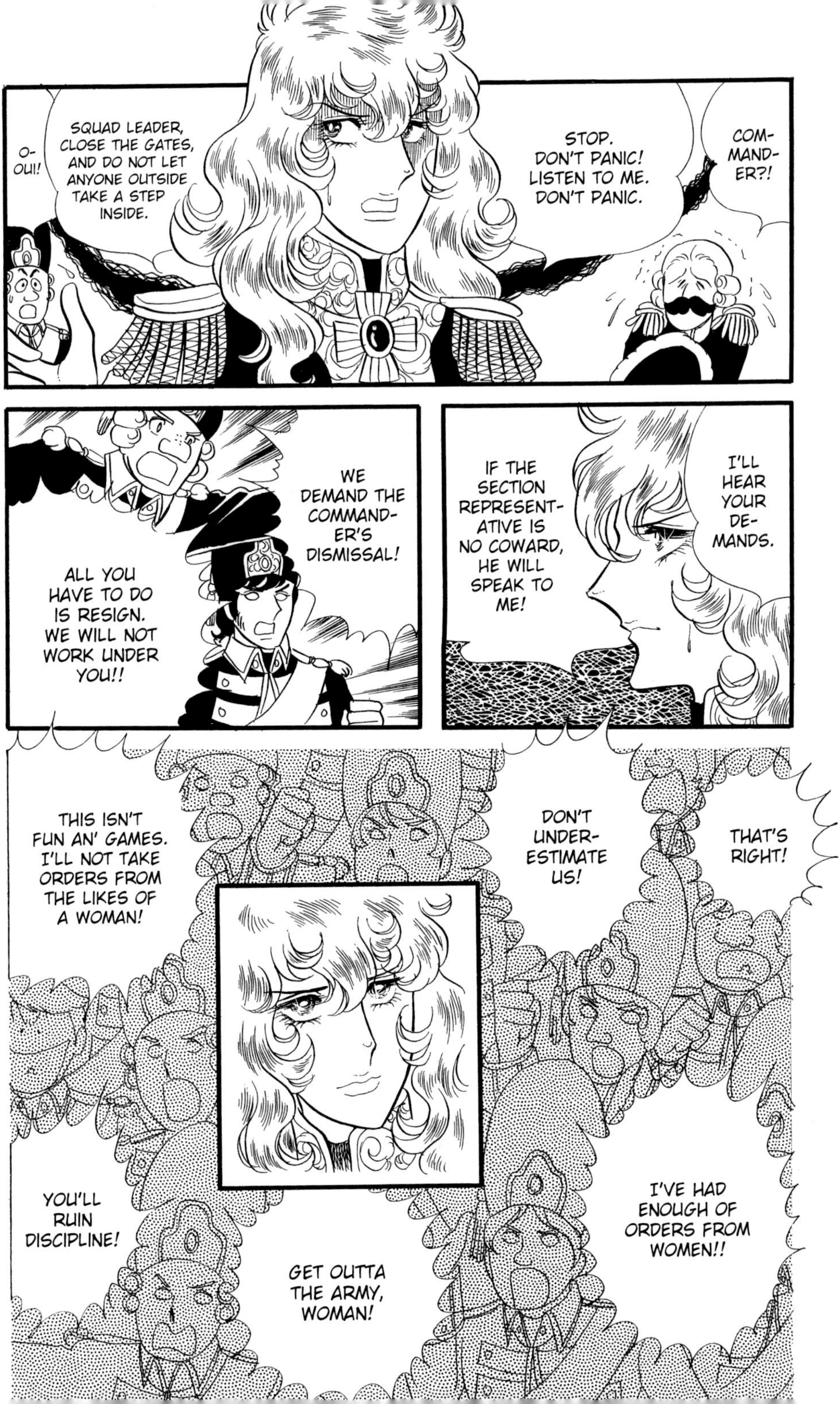
COM-MAND-ER?!
STOP. DON'T PANIC! LISTEN TO ME. DON'T PANIC.
SQUAD LEADER, CLOSE THE GATES, AND DO NOT LET ANYONE OUTSIDE TAKE A STEP INSIDE.
O-OUI!
I'LL HEAR YOUR DE-MANDS.
IF THE SECTION REPRESENT-ATIVE IS NO COWARD, HE WILL SPEAK TO ME!
WE DEMAND THE COMMAND-ER'S DISMISSAL!
ALL YOU HAVE TO DO IS RESIGN. WE WILL NOT WORK UNDER YOU!!
THAT'S RIGHT!
DON'T UNDER-ESTIMATE US!
THIS ISN'T FUN AN' GAMES. I'LL NOT TAKE ORDERS FROM THE LIKES OF A WOMAN!
I'VE HAD ENOUGH OF ORDERS FROM WOMEN!!
GET OUTTA THE ARMY, WOMAN!
YOU'LL RUIN DISCIPLINE!

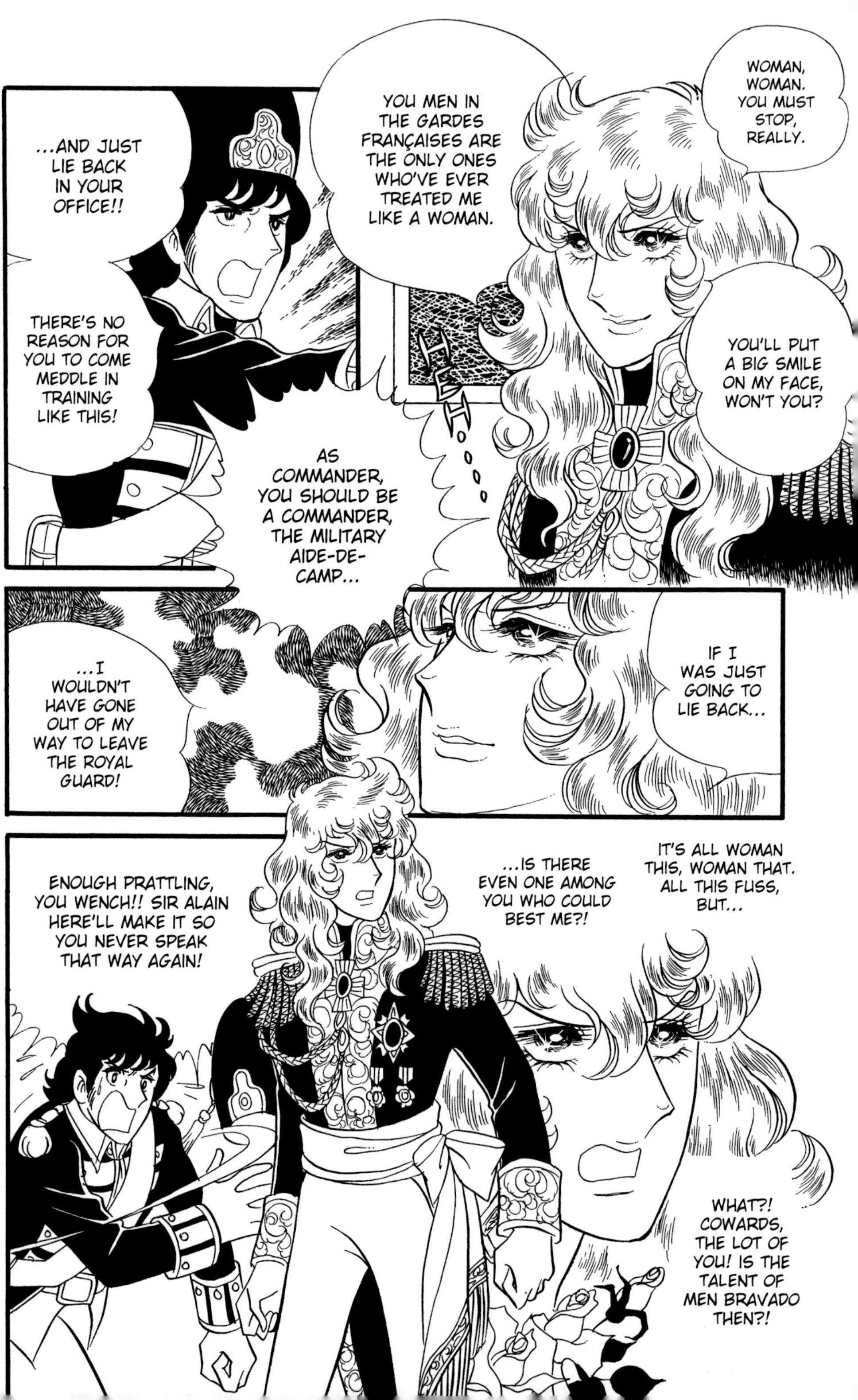
WOMAN, WOMAN. YOU MUST STOP, REALLY.
YOU MEN IN THE GARDES FRANÇAISES ARE THE ONLY ONES WHO'VE EVER TREATED ME LIKE A WOMAN.
YOU'LL PUT A BIG SMILE ON MY FACE, WON'T YOU?
HEH HOOOO
...AND JUST LIE BACK IN YOUR OFFICE!!
AS COMMANDER, YOU SHOULD BE A COMMANDER, THE MILITARY AIDE-DE-CAMP...
THERE'S NO REASON FOR YOU TO COME MEDDLE IN TRAINING LIKE THIS!
IF I WAS JUST GOING TO LIE BACK...
...I WOULDN'T HAVE GONE OUT OF MY WAY TO LEAVE THE ROYAL GUARD!
IT'S ALL WOMAN THIS, WOMAN THAT. ALL THIS FUSS, BUT...
...IS THERE EVEN ONE AMONG YOU WHO COULD BEST ME?!
ENOUGH PRATTLING, YOU WENCH!! SIR ALAIN HERE'LL MAKE IT SO YOU NEVER SPEAK THAT WAY AGAIN!
WHAT?! COWARDS, THE LOT OF YOU! IS THE TALENT OF MEN BRAVADO THEN?!

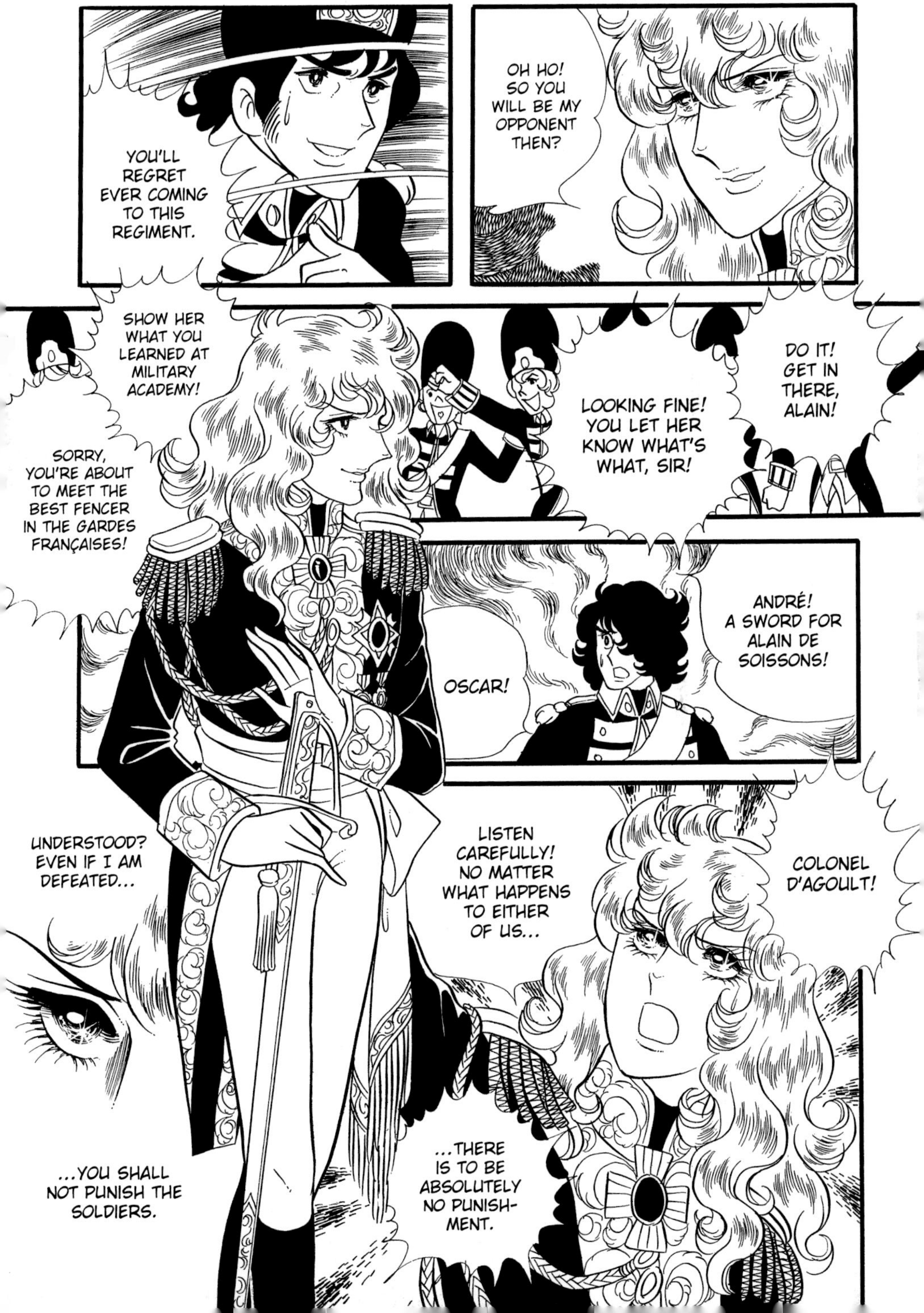

OH HO! SO YOU WILL BE MY OPPONENT THEN?
YOU'LL REGRET EVER COMING TO THIS REGIMENT.
DO IT! GET IN THERE, ALAIN!
LOOKING FINE! YOU LET HER KNOW WHAT'S WHAT, SIR!
SHOW HER WHAT YOU LEARNED AT MILITARY ACADEMY!
SORRY, YOU'RE ABOUT TO MEET THE BEST FENCER IN THE GARDES FRANÇAISES!
ANDRÉ! A SWORD FOR ALAIN DE SOISSONS!
OSCAR!
COLONEL D'AGOULT!
LISTEN CAREFULLY! NO MATTER WHAT HAPPENS TO EITHER OF US...
...THERE IS TO BE ABSOLUTELY NO PUNISH-MENT.
UNDERSTOOD? EVEN IF I AM DEFEATED...
...YOU SHALL NOT PUNISH THE SOLDIERS.

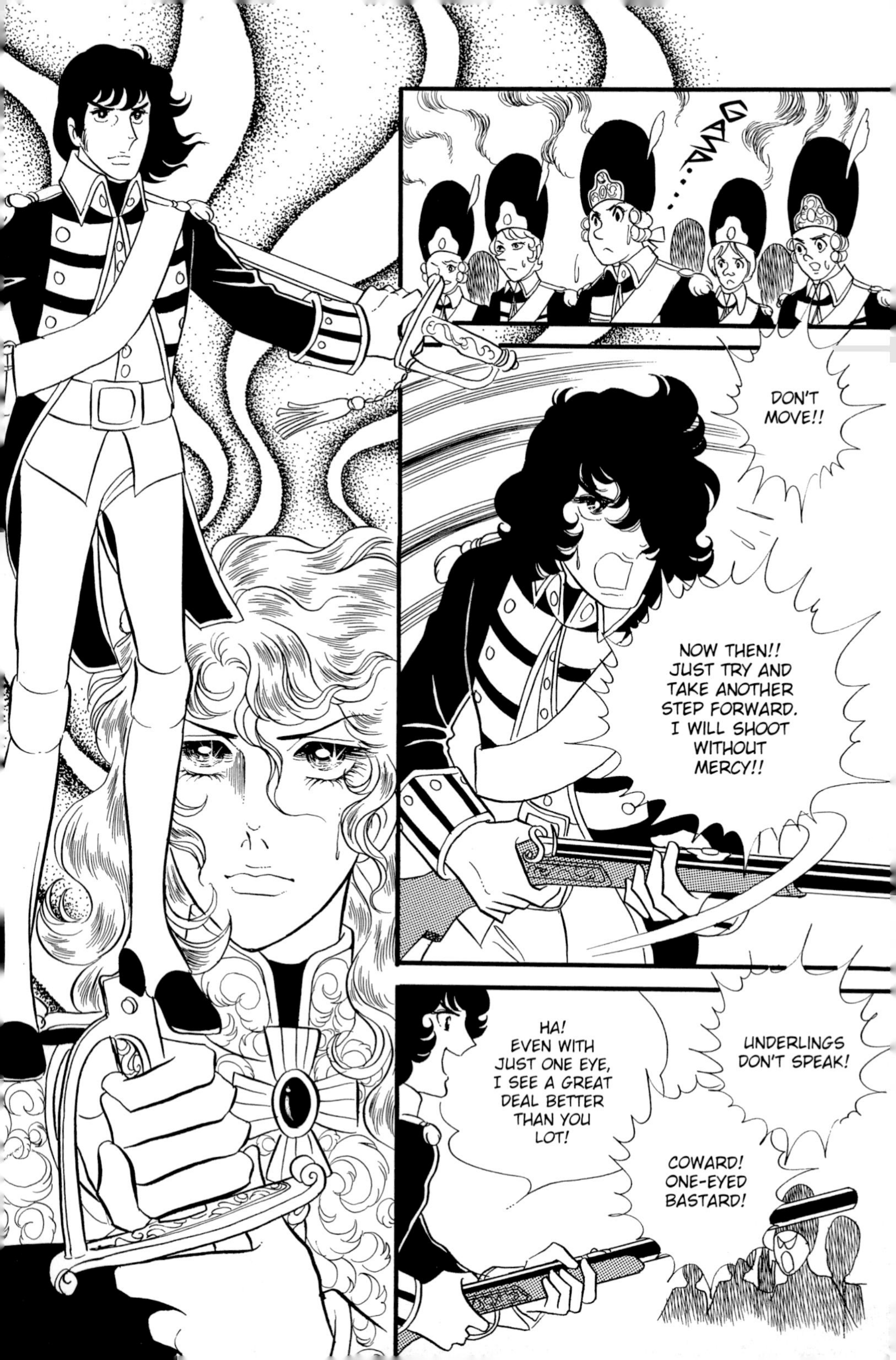
DON'T MOVE!!
NOW THEN!! JUST TRY AND TAKE ANOTHER STEP FORWARD. I WILL SHOOT WITHOUT MERCY!!
UNDERLINGS DON'T SPEAK!
COWARD! ONE-EYED BASTARD!
HA! EVEN WITH JUST ONE EYE, I SEE A GREAT DEAL BETTER THAN YOU LOT!

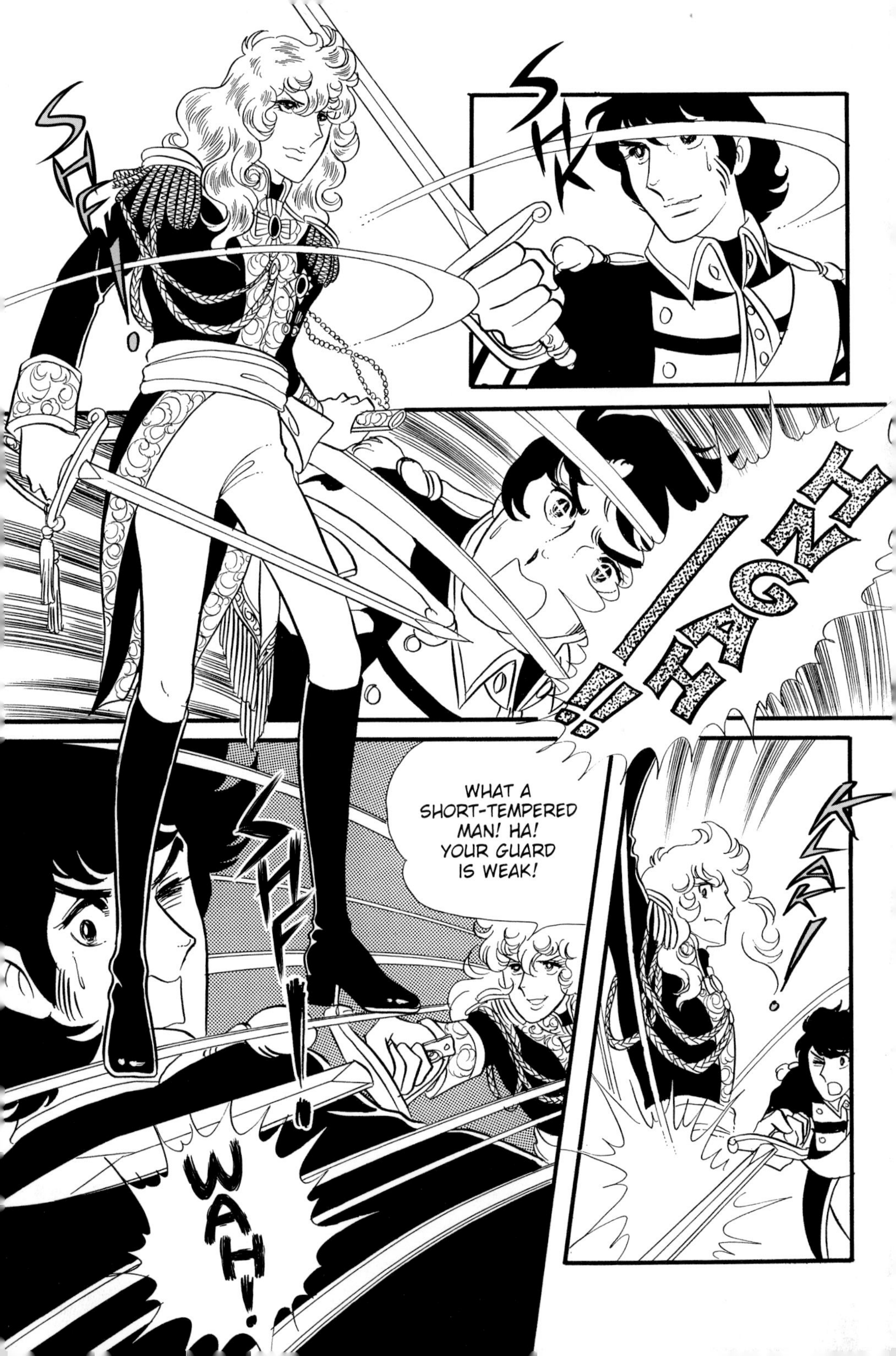
SHK
SHF
WHAT A SHORT-TEMPERED MAN! HA! YOUR GUARD IS WEAK!
SHF!
WAH!

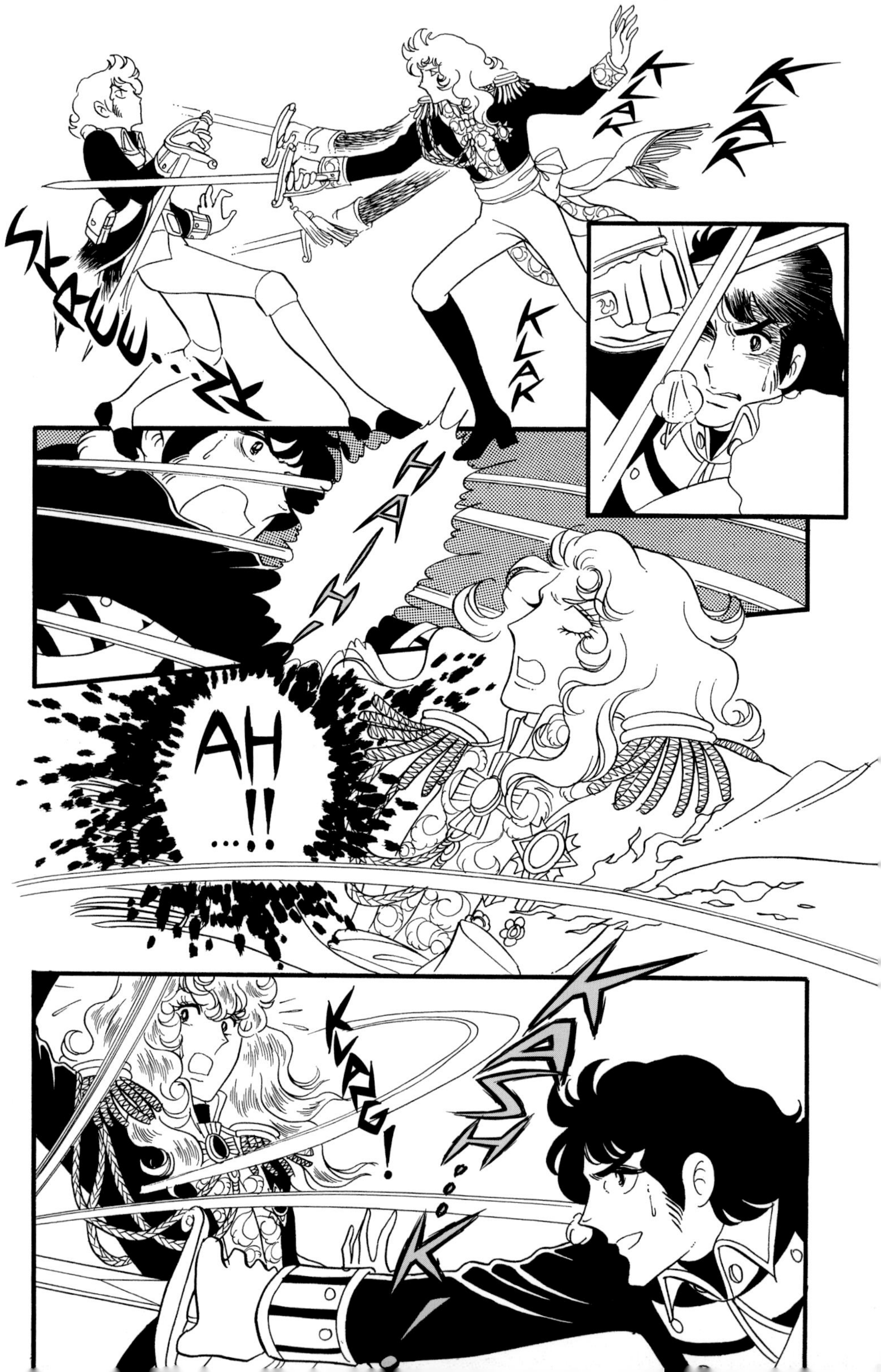
KLAK
KLAK
KLAK
SKREEE...ZZK
HA—H—
AH...!!
KASH...K
KVANG!

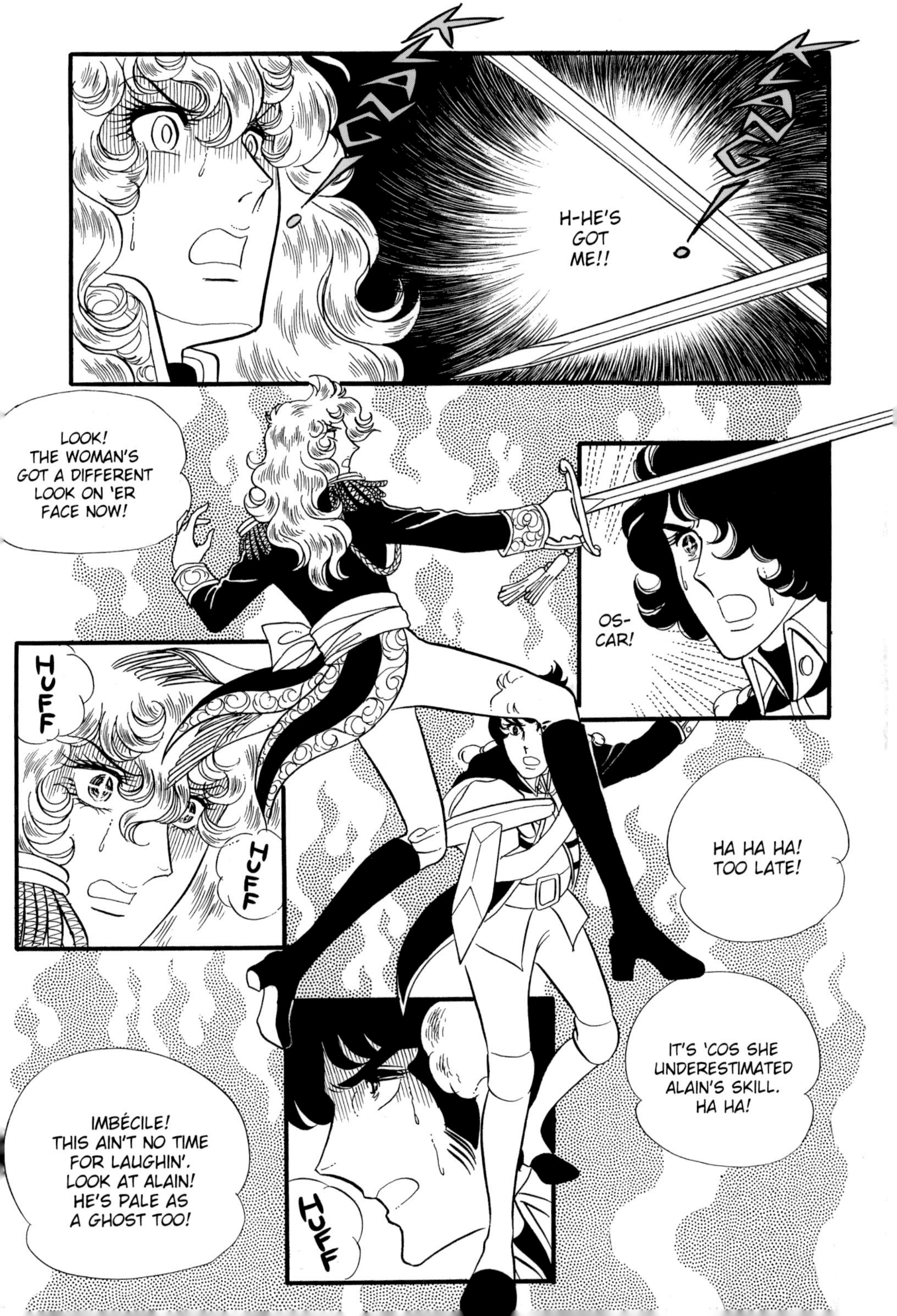
KANG!
KANG!
H-HE'S GOT ME!!
OS-CAR!
LOOK! THE WOMAN'S GOT A DIFFERENT LOOK ON 'ER FACE NOW!
HA HA HA! TOO LATE!
HUFF
HUFF
IT'S 'COS SHE UNDERESTIMATED ALAIN'S SKILL. HA HA!
HUFF
IMBÉCILE! THIS AIN'T NO TIME FOR LAUGHIN'. LOOK AT ALAIN! HE'S PALE AS A GHOST TOO!

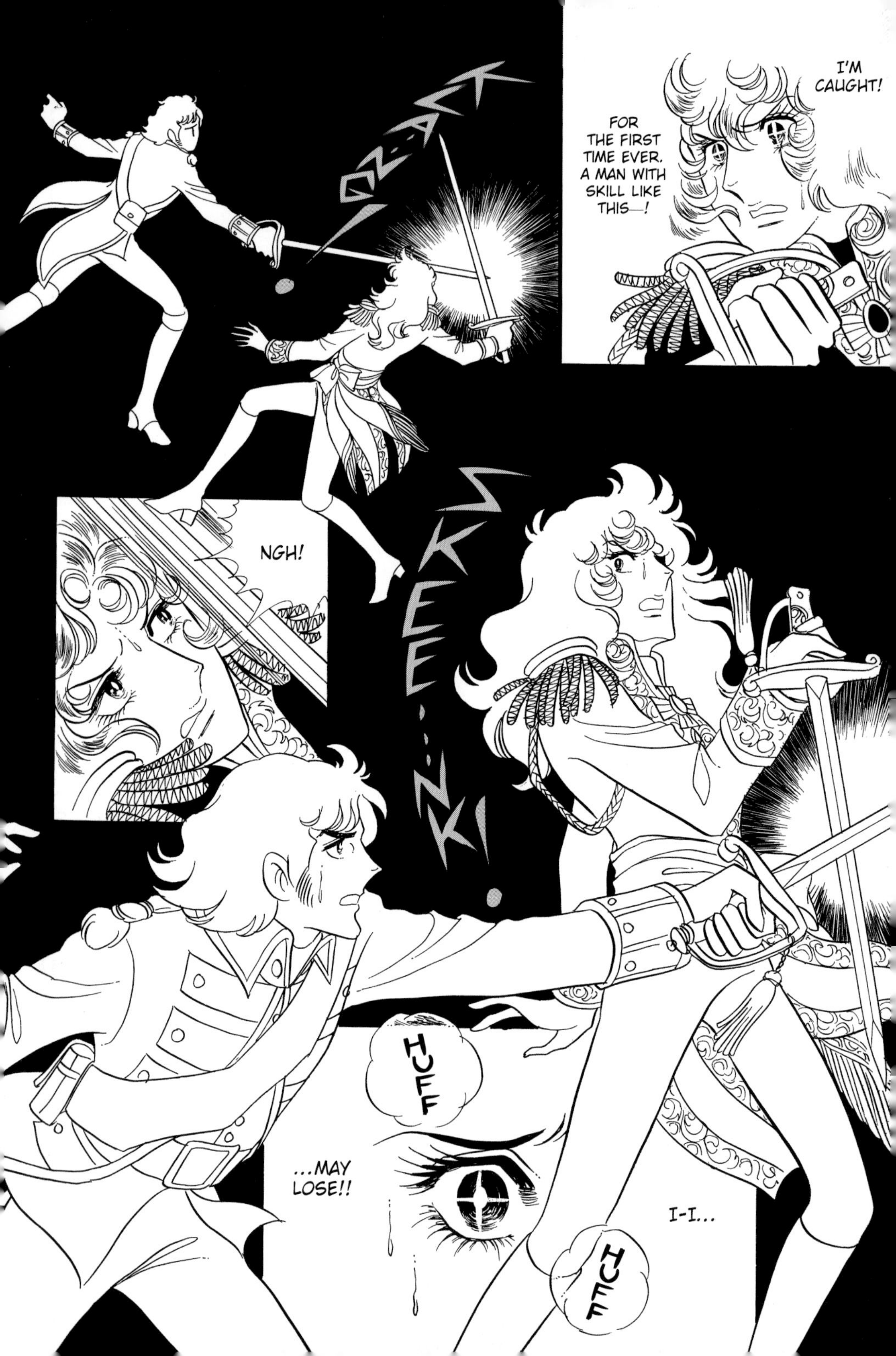
I'M CAUGHT!
FOR THE FIRST TIME EVER, A MAN WITH SKILL LIKE THIS—!
GZ-ACK
SKEE...NK!
NGH!
HUFF
I-I...
...MAY LOSE!!
HUFF

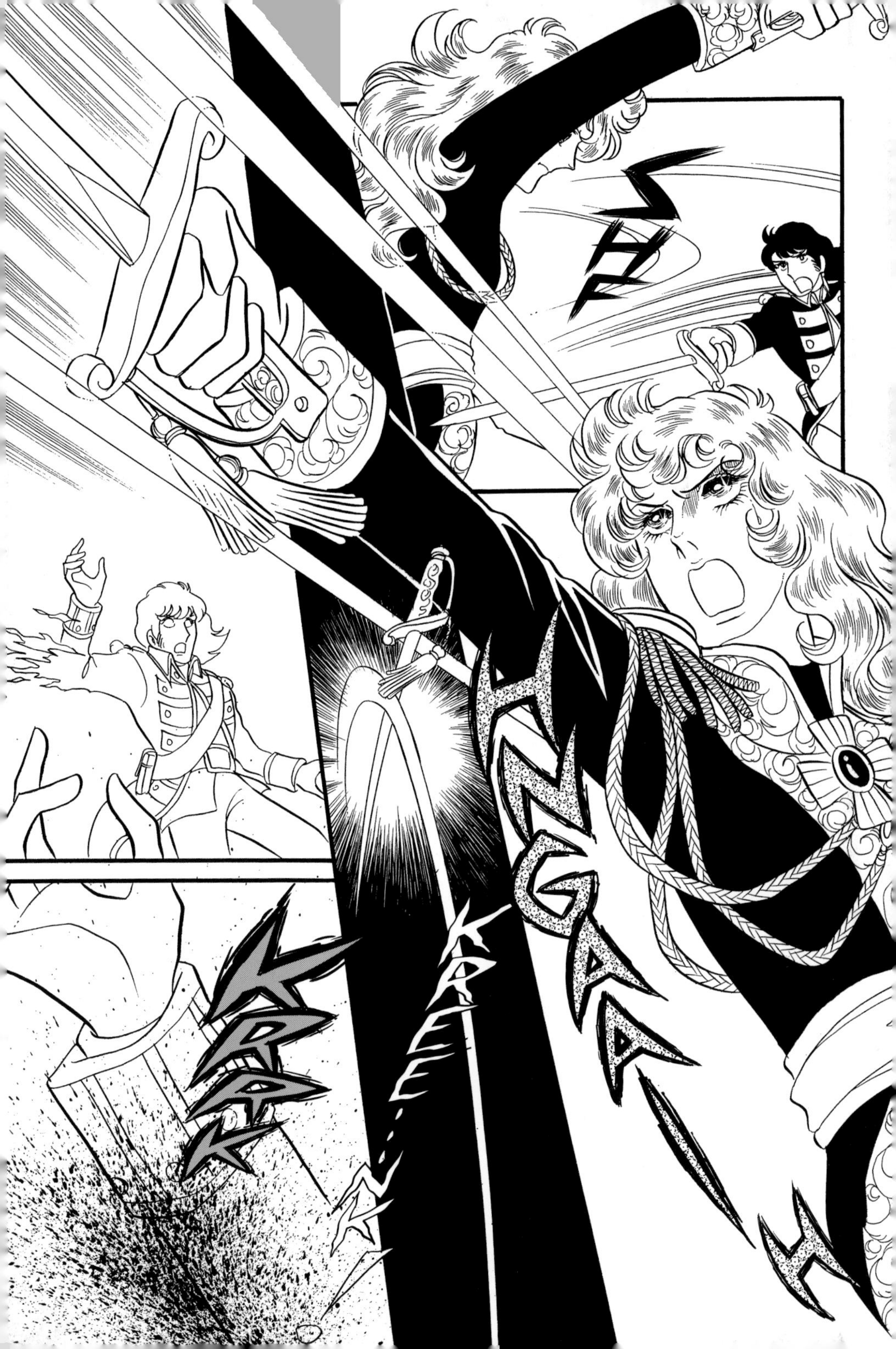
HNGAAH
KREE...K
KRRK

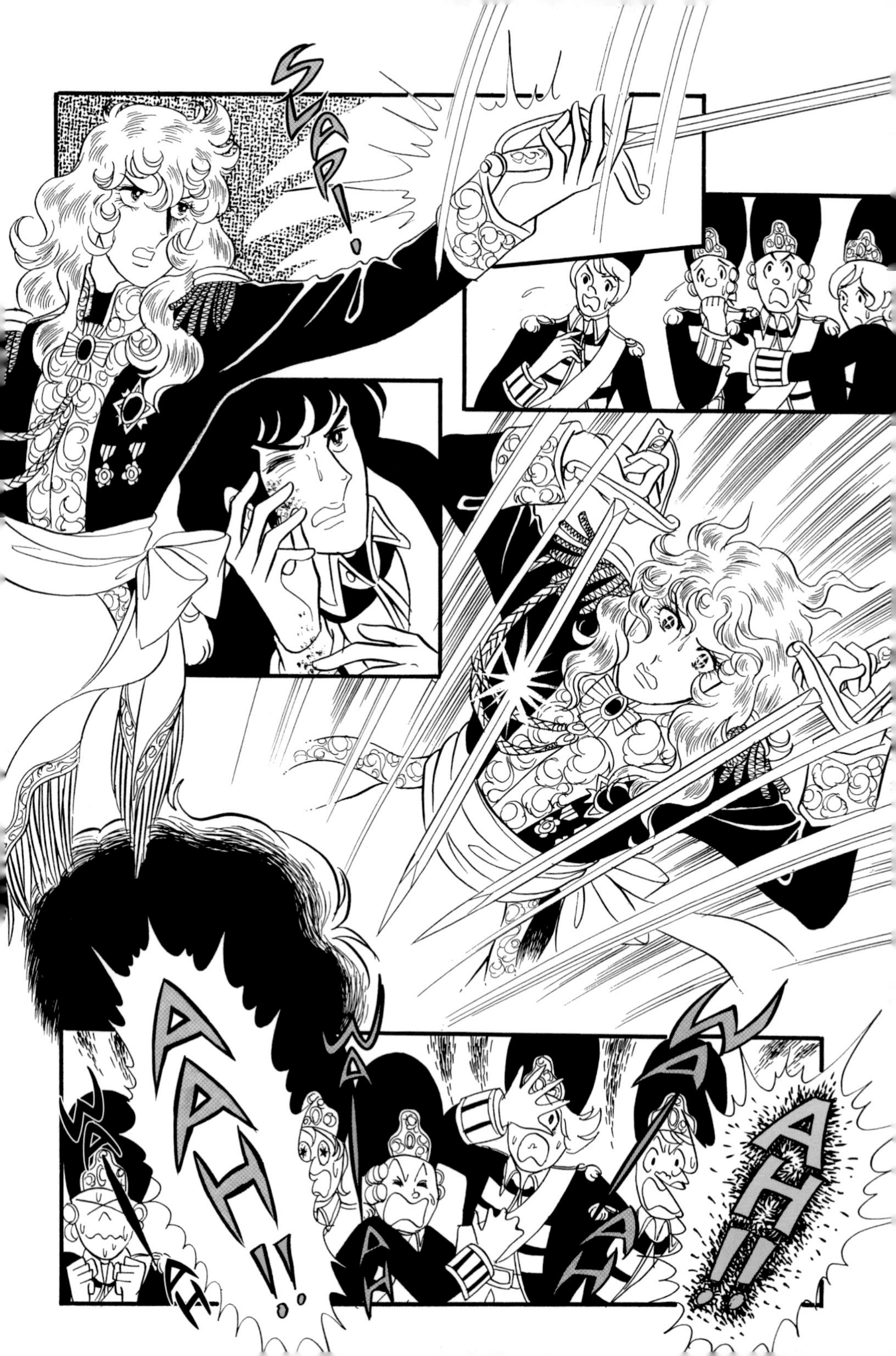
SLAP!
AH!!
AAAH!!

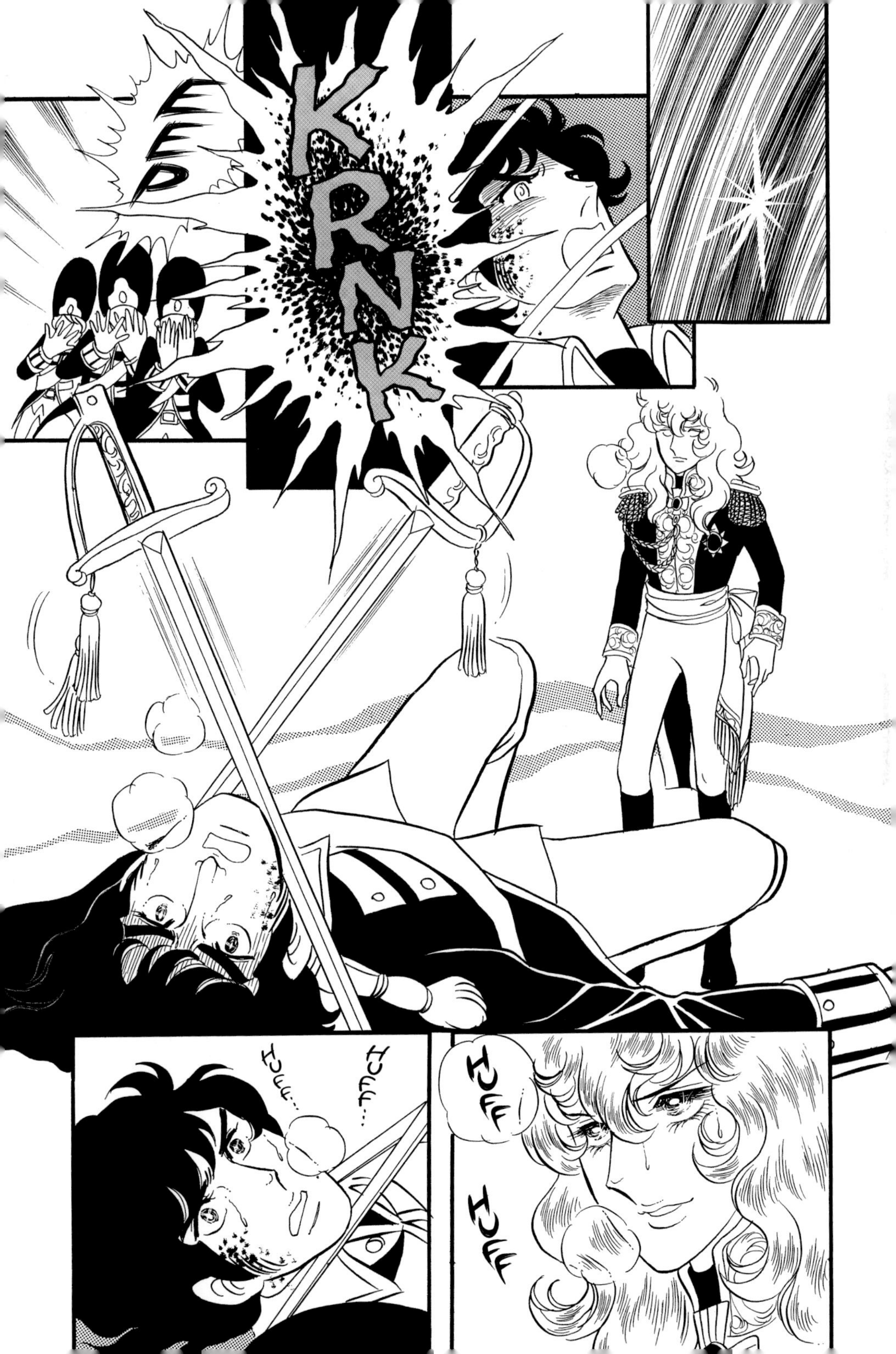
KRNK
HUFF
HUFF
HUFF...
HUFF...

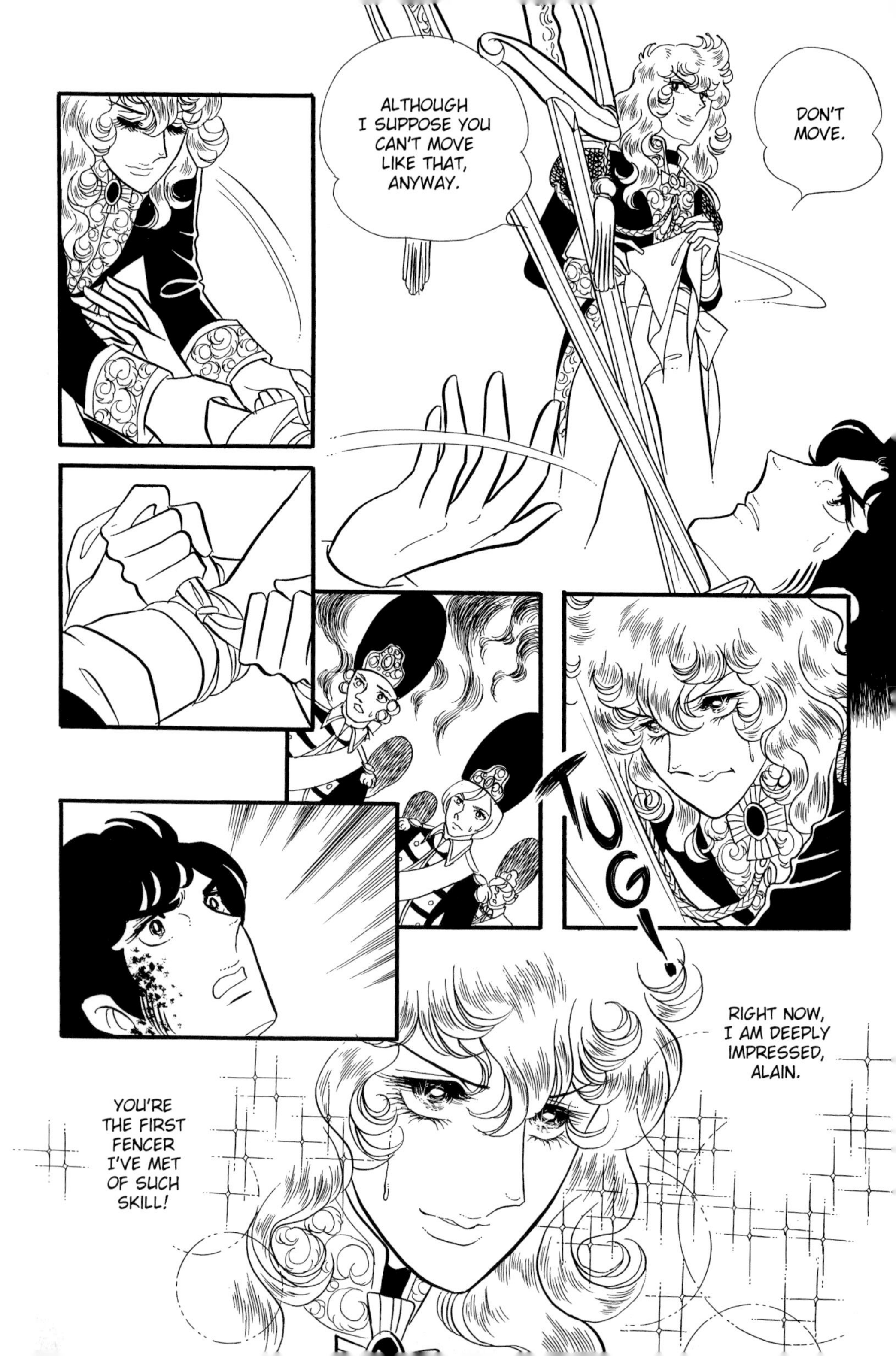
DON'T MOVE.
ALTHOUGH I SUPPOSE YOU CAN'T MOVE LIKE THAT, ANYWAY.
TUG!
RIGHT NOW, I AM DEEPLY IMPRESSED, ALAIN.
YOU'RE THE FIRST FENCER I'VE MET OF SUCH SKILL!

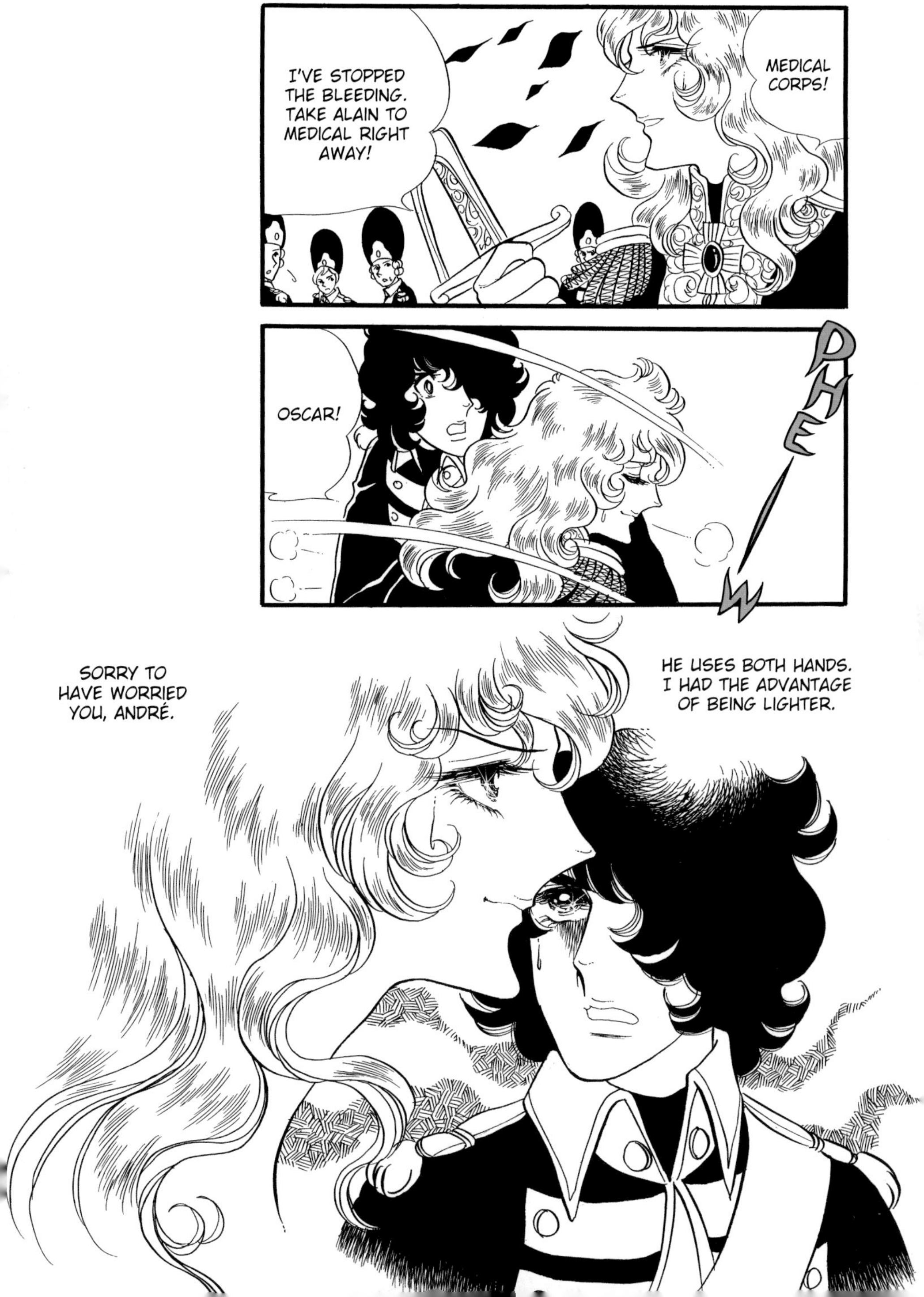
MEDICAL CORPS!
I'VE STOPPED THE BLEEDING. TAKE ALAIN TO MEDICAL RIGHT AWAY!
DHEW
OSCAR!
HE USES BOTH HANDS. I HAD THE ADVANTAGE OF BEING LIGHTER.
SORRY TO HAVE WORRIED YOU, ANDRÉ.

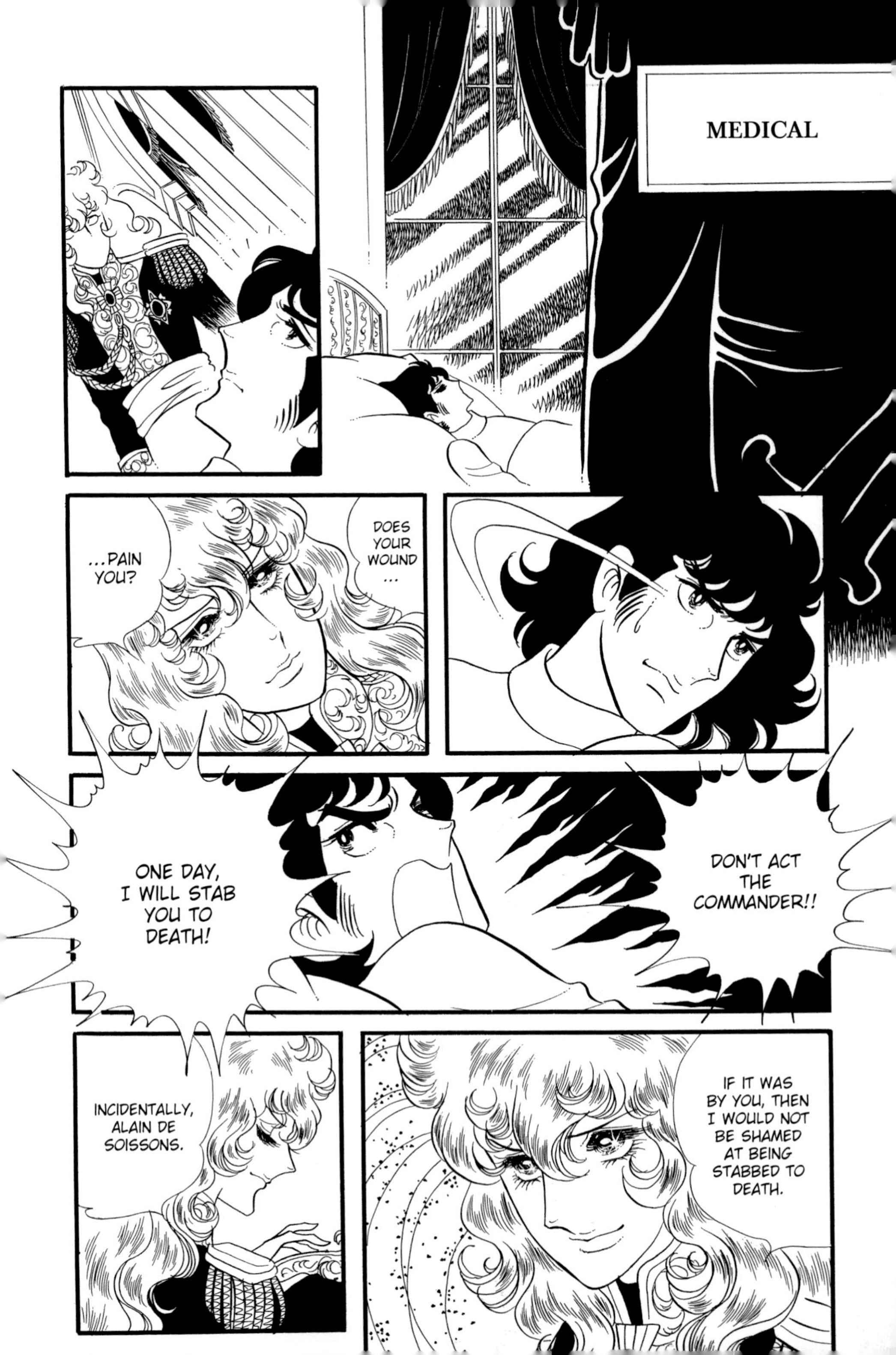
MEDICAL
DOES YOUR WOUND ...
...PAIN YOU?
DON'T ACT THE COMMANDER!!
ONE DAY, I WILL STAB YOU TO DEATH!
IF IT WAS BY YOU, THEN I WOULD NOT BE SHAMED AT BEING STABBED TO DEATH.
INCIDENTALLY, ALAIN DE SOISSONS.

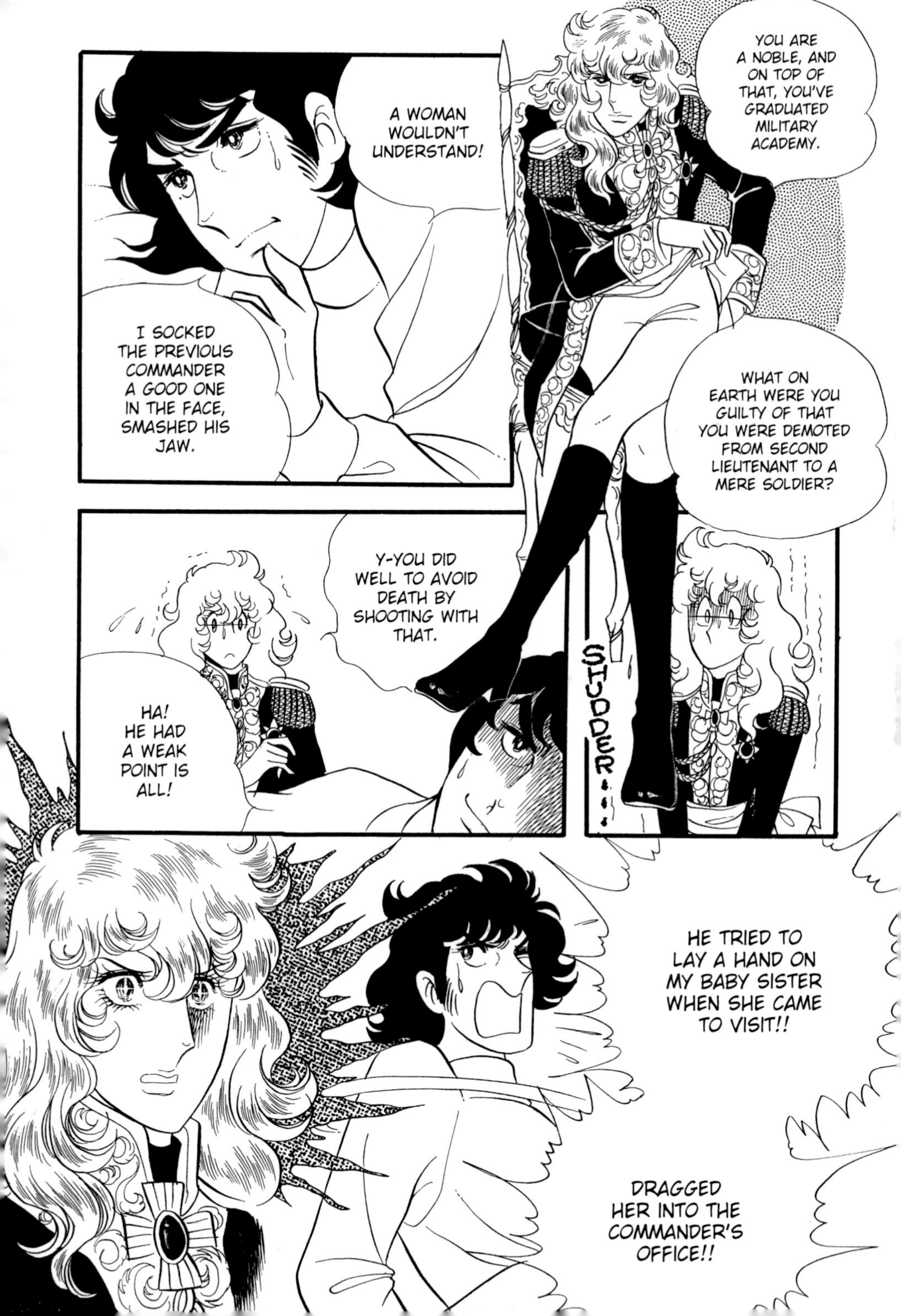
YOU ARE A NOBLE, AND ON TOP OF THAT, YOU'VE GRADUATED MILITARY ACADEMY.
WHAT ON EARTH WERE YOU GUILTY OF THAT YOU WERE DEMOTED FROM SECOND LIEUTENANT TO A MERE SOLDIER?
A WOMAN WOULDN'T UNDERSTAND!
I SOCKED THE PREVIOUS COMMANDER A GOOD ONE IN THE FACE, SMASHED HIS JAW.
SHUDDER...
Y-YOU DID WELL TO AVOID DEATH BY SHOOTING WITH THAT.
HA! HE HAD A WEAK POINT IS ALL!
HE TRIED TO LAY A HAND ON MY BABY SISTER WHEN SHE CAME TO VISIT!!
DRAGGED HER INTO THE COMMANDER'S OFFICE!!

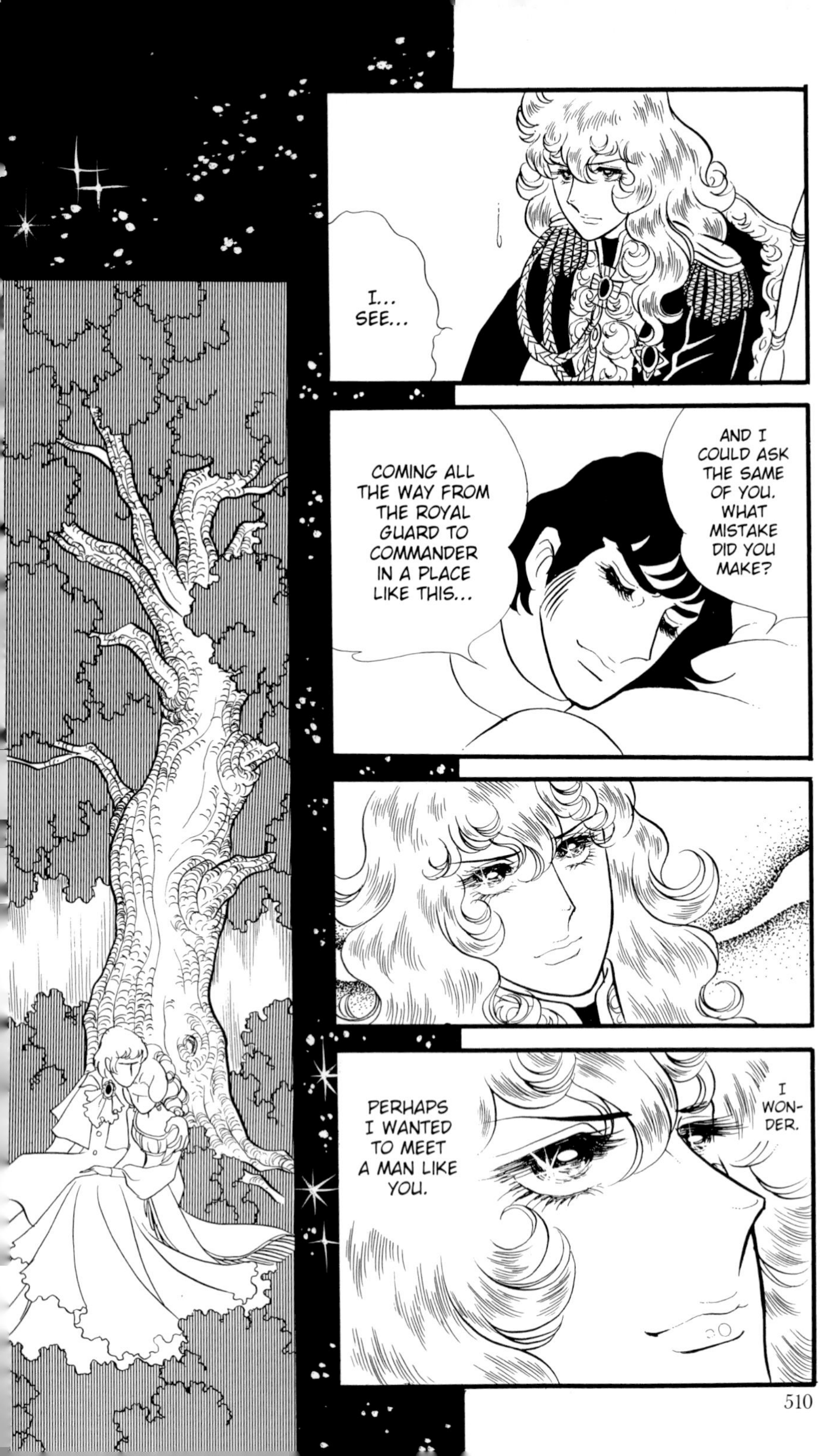
I... SEE...
COMING ALL THE WAY FROM THE ROYAL GUARD TO COMMANDER IN A PLACE LIKE THIS...
AND I COULD ASK THE SAME OF YOU. WHAT MISTAKE DID YOU MAKE?
PERHAPS I WANTED TO MEET A MAN LIKE YOU.
I WON-DER.

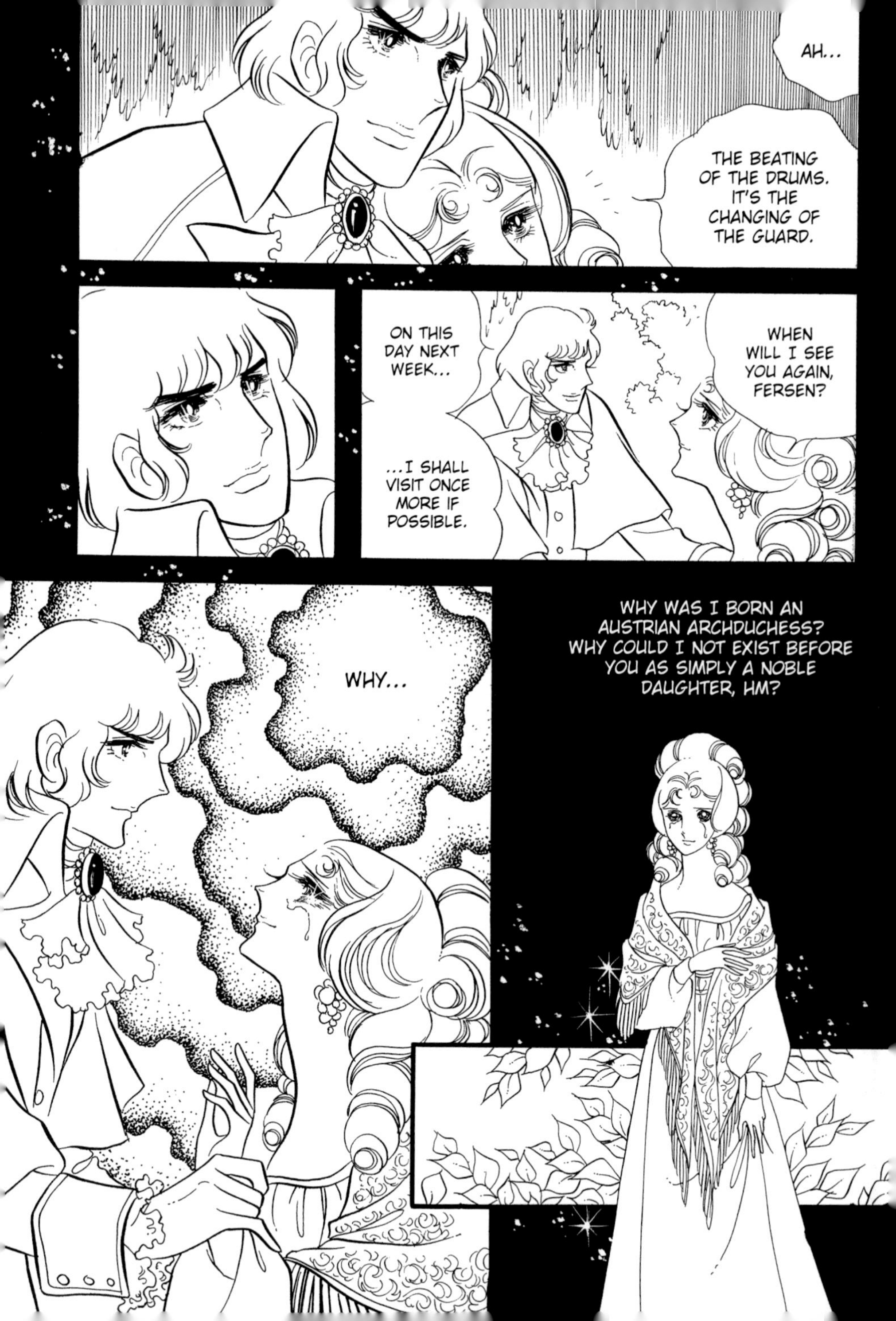
AH...
THE BEATING OF THE DRUMS. IT'S THE CHANGING OF THE GUARD.
WHEN WILL I SEE YOU AGAIN, FERSEN?
ON THIS DAY NEXT WEEK...
...I SHALL VISIT ONCE MORE IF POSSIBLE.
WHY WAS I BORN AN AUSTRIAN ARCHDUCHESS? WHY COULD I NOT EXIST BEFORE YOU AS SIMPLY A NOBLE DAUGHTER, HM?
WHY...

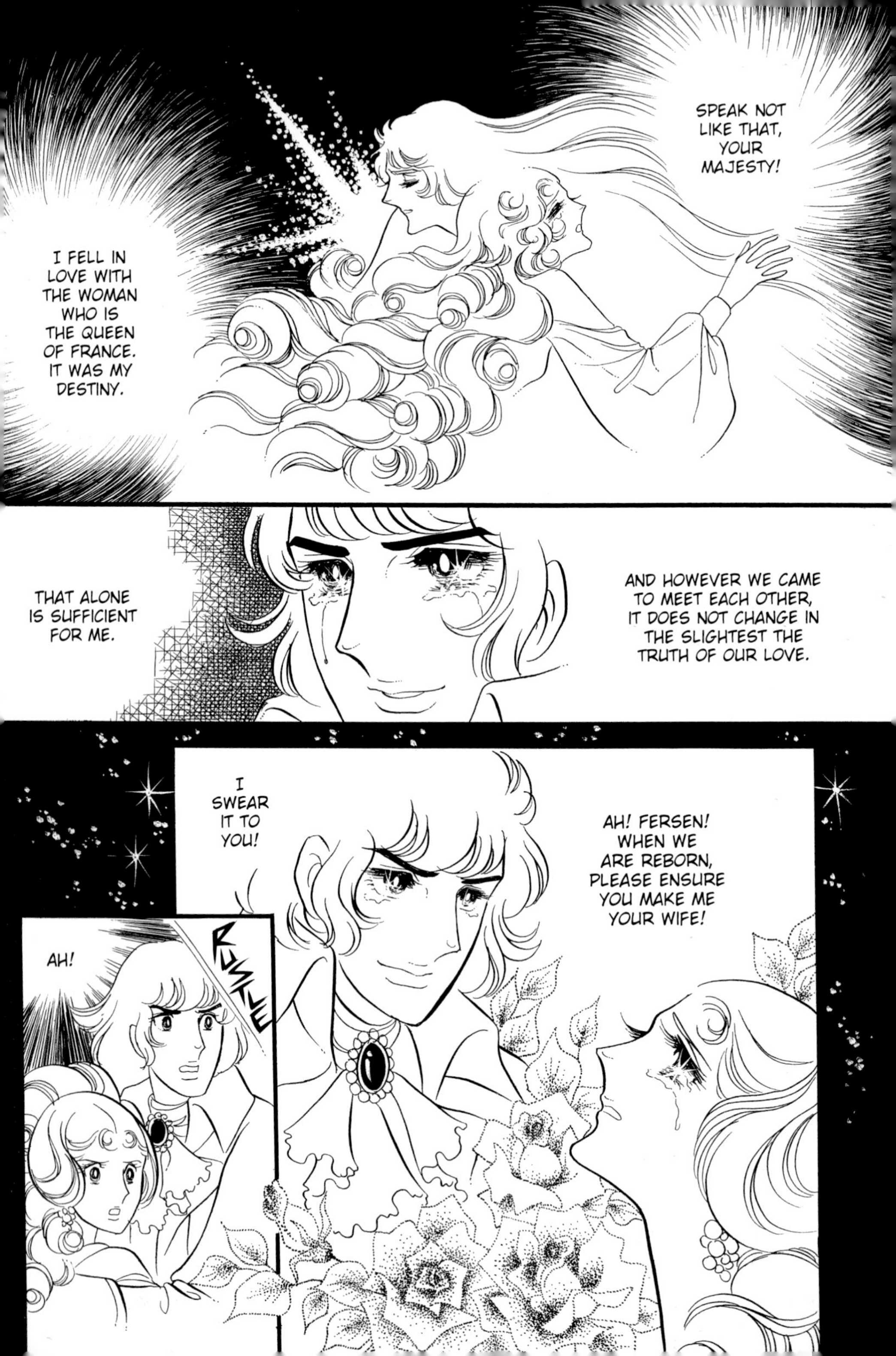
SPEAK NOT LIKE THAT, YOUR MAJESTY!
I FELL IN LOVE WITH THE WOMAN WHO IS THE QUEEN OF FRANCE. IT WAS MY DESTINY.
AND HOWEVER WE CAME TO MEET EACH OTHER, IT DOES NOT CHANGE IN THE SLIGHTEST THE TRUTH OF OUR LOVE.
THAT ALONE IS SUFFICIENT FOR ME.
AH! FERSEN! WHEN WE ARE REBORN, PLEASE ENSURE YOU MAKE ME YOUR WIFE!
I SWEAR IT TO YOU!
RUSTLE
AH!

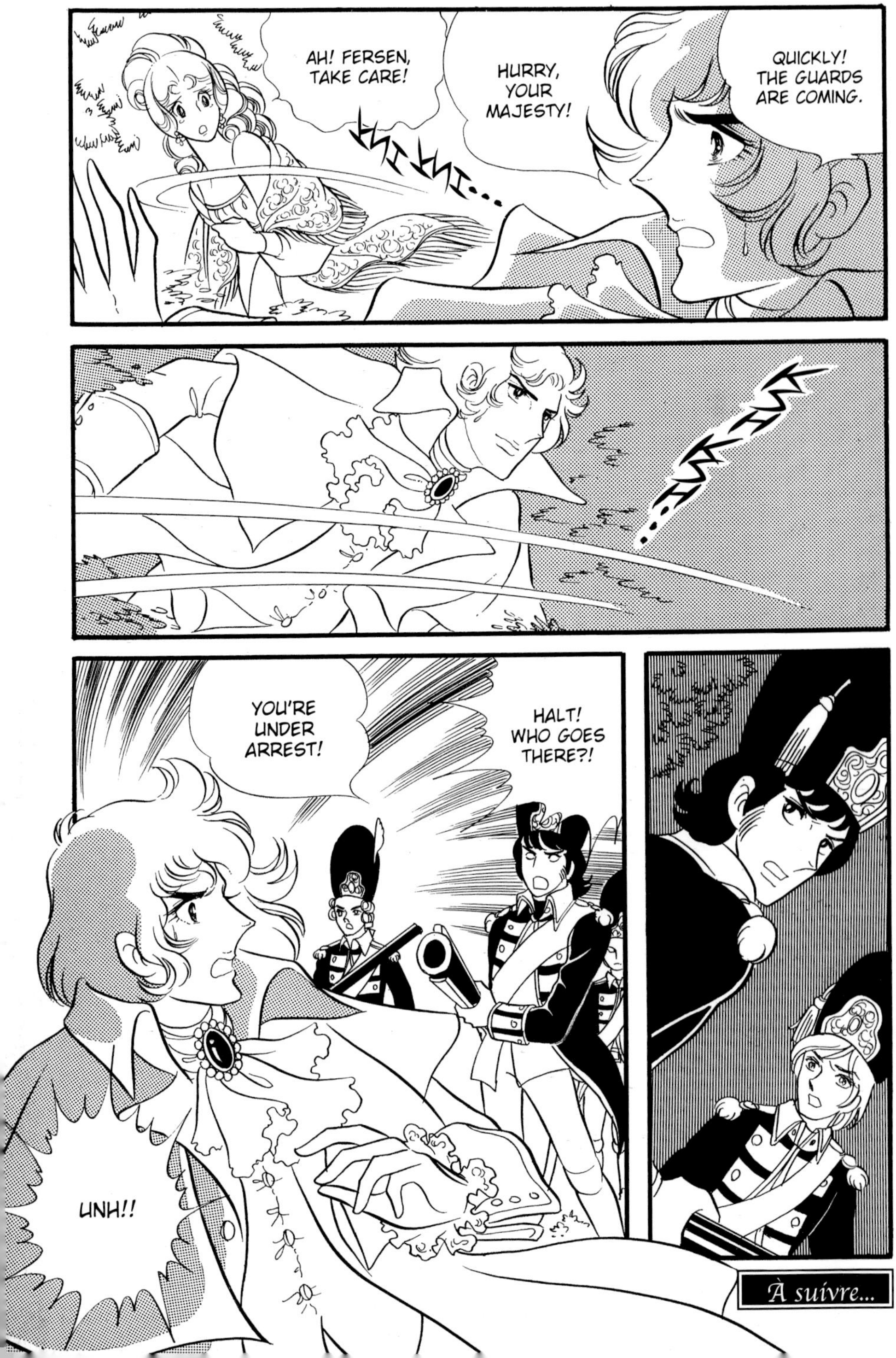
QUICKLY! THE GUARDS ARE COMING.
HURRY, YOUR MAJESTY!
AH! FERSEN, TAKE CARE!
HALT! WHO GOES THERE?!
YOU'RE UNDER ARREST!
UNH!!
À suivre...

RIYOKO IKEDA

Manga artist, author, essayist, vocalist. Born 1947 in Osaka.

Started drawing graphic novels while enrolled at Tokyo University of Education
(now University of Tsukuba), Department of Philosophy.

This work, *The Rose of Versailles*, which began serialization in *Weekly Margaret* in 1972,
became the rage across near all of society, a smash hit that was adapted for the stage by
the Takarazuka Revue and into anime and feature films, crossing media barriers
and changing the history of shojo manga.

Since then, she has continued drawing manga works based on her deep perception of history and
humankind, and written essays and critiques full of insight, to the present day.

Other representative works include *Orpheus no Mado (The Window of Orpheus)*,
which was awarded the 9th Japan Cartoonists Association Award in 1980, *Eikô no Napoleon – Eroika*
(*Eroica – The Glory of Napoleon*), and *Shôtoku Taishi (Prince Shôtoku)*.

Ms. Ikeda entered Tokyo College of Music, Voice Department, in 1995,
and graduated the same institution in 1999.

In 2006, she was active as a soprano in theatrical and musical performances.

In addition, her 4-panel color comic strip *Berubara Kids (Rose of Versailles Kids)*,
serialized in the *Asahi News* Saturday edition, is drawing the interest of fans new and old.

Official webpage: http://www.ikeda-riyoko-pro.com/

VERSAILLES NO BARA Volume 2
© 1972,1973 IKEDA RIYOKO PRODUCTION
All rights reserved.
Engish translation rights arranged with IKEDA RIYOKO PRODUCTION
through Tuttle-Mori Agency, Inc. Tokyo.

AGE: Young Adult (13+)
BISAC: CGN004050 CGN004140 CGN004130 CGN009000
LIBRARY SUBJECT: Manga, Graphic Novel, Historic Fiction, LGBTQ

www.udonentertainment.com

First Printing February 2020
Second Printing November 2021
ISBN: 978-1-927925-94-2
Printed in China

**HALF HOLLOW HILLS
COMMUNITY LIBRARY
55 Vanderbilt Parkway
Dix Hills, NY 11746**